Cafer’s Psychopharmacology:

Visualize to Memorize™
270 Medication Mascots

First Edition, 2020

Author: Jason Cafer, MD

Editor: Julianna Link, PA-C

Cafer's Psychopharmacology: Visualize to Memorize 270 Medication Mascots

First Edition

Author: Jason Cafer, MD

Editor: Julianna Link, PA-C

Illustrations: Coccus from 99Designs

Cover design: BengsWorks from 99Designs

Licensed images: Shutterstock and Wikimedia Commons

ISBN: 978-1-7350901-4-6

Contact: jason@cafermed.com

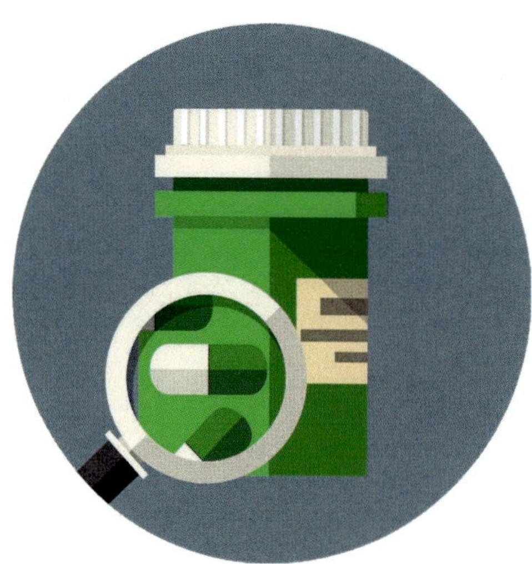

This book contains 270 medication monographs. Any prescription medication affecting the central nervous system or interacting with psychotropic medications was considered for inclusion. Not all medications are intended for prescription by psychiatrists.

The scope of drug-interaction information is limited to what can be digested and applied to routine clinical practice. There are countless unmentioned drug-drug interactions that could be relevant to some patients but are omitted because the amount of material would be overwhelming.

This book is focused on medications, not overarching psychiatric care. Although chemicals are necessary for treatment of mania or acute psychosis, pharmacologic treatment of depression/anxiety/insomnia/etc., is not always the best medicine. Always consider interventions including cognitive behavioral therapy, diet, exercise, mindfulness, sleep hygiene, etc.

Dosing recommendations are for healthy adults, and may differ from FDA prescribing guidelines. Refer to other sources for treatment of children, older adults, pregnancy/breastfeeding, and renal/hepatic insufficiency.

Every effort has been made to provide accurate and up-to-date information. Author/editors/publisher/reviewers disclaim all liability for direct or consequential damages resulting from the use of this material. Readers are encouraged to confirm information with other sources before incorporating it into your prescribing practice. Information should be compared with official instructions from the drug manufacturer.

Contents

Note that antidepressant chapters are color-coded with various shades of "**the blues**".

Antipsychotic chapters are green. A psychotic patient may see "**little green men**".

Anticholinergic effects are famously described as "Hot as a hare, dry as a bone, blind as a bat, **red as a beet**, and mad as a hatter"

The color code for Addiction Medicine chapter and Opioids chapter is purple, as in "**Purple Drank**" or opium poppies.

PHARMACODYNAMICS VS PHARMACOKINETICS

Drug-drug interactions fall into two main categories: **pharmacokinetic** and **pharmacodynamic**.

Pharmacodynamics is what a drug does to the body. Pharmacodynamic interactions are based on the drugs' mechanisms of action and do not involve alteration in blood levels of either interacting drug.

Pharmacokinetics is what the body does to a drug. Kinetic derives from the Greek verb *kinein*, "to move". In this case we're talking movement into and out of the body, for instance absorbing the chemical from the gut and processing it for excretion in urine or feces. Pharmacokinetic (PK) interactions are generally manifested by alteration of blood levels of one of the interacting drugs.

For simplicity's sake, let's drop the *pharmaco-* prefix and refer to these concepts as **kinetic** interactions and **dynamic** interactions.

PHARMACODYNAMIC INTERACTIONS

Dynamic interactions are intuitive if you understand how the interacting drugs work. Although dynamic interactions are understandable without silly pictures, here are a couple anyhow.

Dynamic interactions can be **additive/synergistic**, with enhanced effects brought about by combining medications with similar or complementary effects.

Like-minded "**dyn**os" ganging up to reduce blood pressure, which is an additive/synergistic effect.

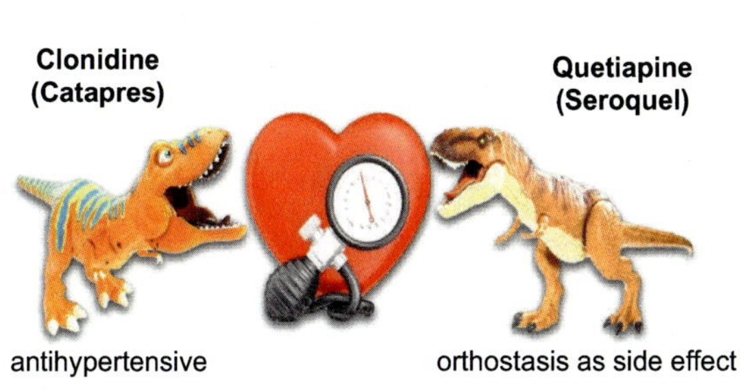

Other dynamic interactions are **antagonistic**, for instance combining a dopaminergic such as pramipexole (for restless legs) with an antidopaminergic like haloperidol (antipsychotic). Here's another example:

Fighting "**dyn**os" involved in an antagonistic interaction.

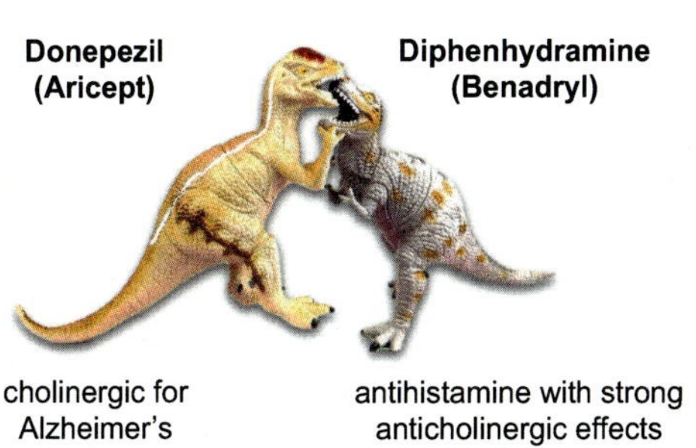

PHARMACOKINETIC INTERACTIONS

Kinetics involves the rate at which a drug gets into or out of the body or brain.

Drug-drug Interactions involving absorption are generally straightforward. For instance, anticholinergics slow gut motility and delay gastrointestinal absorption of other medications.

Kinetic interactions involving rate of elimination from the body are challenging to learn and daunting to memorize. It is important to consider these interactions to avoid underdosing or overdosing certain medications. This book tackles these tricky elimination interactions by illustrating:

- Phase I metabolism involving the six most important cytochrome P450 (CYP450) enzymes
- Phase II metabolism involving UGT enzymes, as applicable to lamotrigine (Lamictal)
- Renal clearance of lithium (page 26)

A mysterious type of kinetic interaction involves drugs getting across the blood-brain barrier, as is necessary for a psychiatric medication to take effect. If such an interaction is occurring, the effect will not be detectable in serum drug levels. This will be discussed in the context of P-glycoprotein (page 9).

CYTOCHROME P450 ENZYMES

In the liver, kinetic interactions predominantly involve **CYtochrome P450 enzymes**, **CYP** enzymes for short, which can be pronounced "sip". Instead of concerning yourself with the origin of P450 nomenclature, take a moment to contemplate this picture of Ken (kinetic) taking a "sip" (CYP).

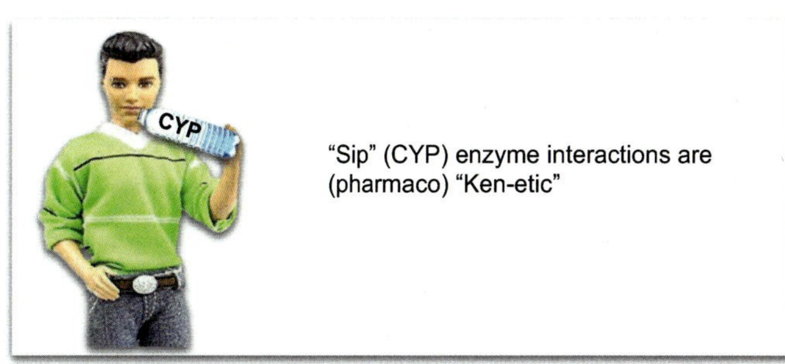

"Sip" (CYP) enzyme interactions are (pharmaco) "Ken-etic"

CYP enzymes, which reside primarily in the liver, make chemicals less lipid-soluble so they can be more easily excreted in urine or bile. Of over 50 CYP enzymes, six play a major role in the biotransformation of medications: 1A2, 2B6, 2C9, 2C19, 2D6 and 3A4. Our visual mnemonics will be built on the following phraseology:

The three most important CYPs are **1A2, 2D6** and **3A4**. For psychiatrists, 2C19 can be important, while 2B6 and 2C9 are rarely significant.

SUBSTRATES

A drug that is biotransformed by a particular enzyme is referred to as a **substrate** of that enzyme. When the substrate is biotransformed (metabolized) it is then referred to as a **metabolite**.

Each CYP enzyme can metabolize several substrates and most substrates can be metabolized by several CYP enzymes. Substrates are the "victims" of the interactions described in this chapter. Throughout this book we use the following visuals for CYP substrates:

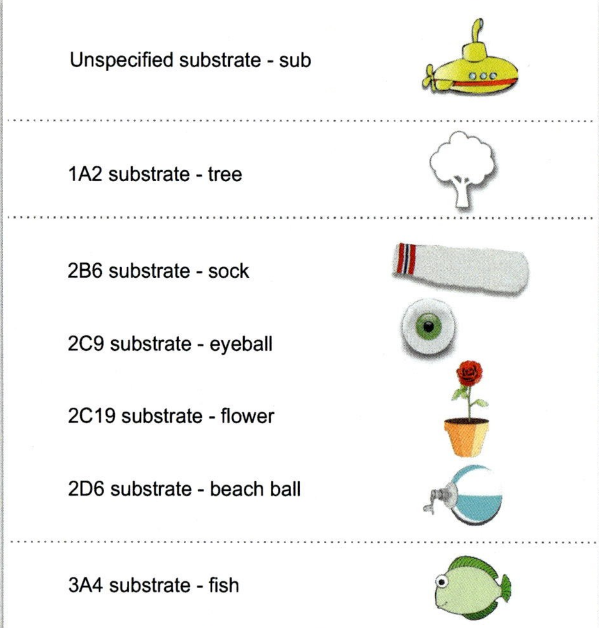

Unspecified substrate - sub
1A2 substrate - tree
2B6 substrate - sock
2C9 substrate - eyeball
2C19 substrate - flower
2D6 substrate - beach ball
3A4 substrate - fish

"Aggressor" medications affect how long victim substrates linger in the blood, and the relative serum concentration of parent drug (substrate) to metabolite. For a given enzyme, interfering medications (aggressors) are either inDucers or inHibitors. **InDucers** stimulate (inDuce) production of metabolic enzymes. **InHibitors** interfere with an enzyme's ability to metabolize other medications.

ENZYME INHIBITION

InHibition of an enzyme occurs when one drug (the inHibitor) binds more tightly to the enzyme than the victim substrate binds. The inHibitor itself may be metabolized by the enzyme, or act as a non-competitive inhibitor. When an inhibitor is bound to an enzyme, the victim substrate must find another enzyme to metabolize it, or hope that it can eventually be excreted unchanged. Strong inhibitors may cause the victim substrate to linger longer, prolonging the victim's half-life and elevating its concentration in the blood. For victim substrates that cross the blood brain barrier (as is necessary to be psychoactive), inhibition leads to increased drug concentration in the central nervous system.

Why is H being emphasized? Well, when an inHibitor is added to an individual's medication regimen, levels of victim drugs can escalate (H for High). InHibition takes effect quickly, within Hours (H for Hurried), although the effect may not be clinically evident for 2 to 4 days, until the victim substrate accumulates.

Some (but not all) substrates are also competitive inHibitors of the same CYP enzyme.

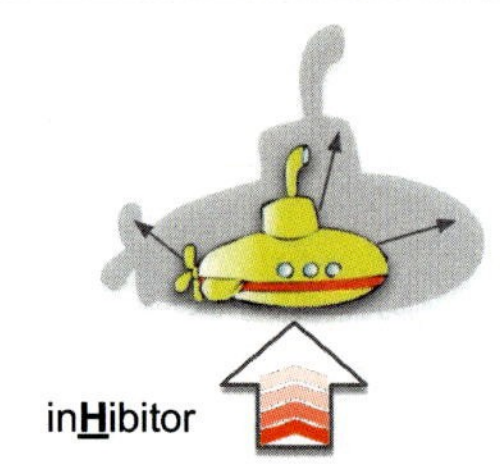

Increased concentration of substrate (and increased ratio of serum substrate:metabolite)

H for High and Hurried, within 2–4 hours, although the effect may not be clinically evident for 2–4 days

InHibitors of CYP enzymes will be represented by:

The magnitude to which an inHibitor increases the serum concentration of a specific substrate depends on the number of alternative pathways available to metabolize the substrate. If the drug is a substrate of, e.g., 1A2, 2D6 *and* 3A4, then inhibiting one of the three pathways should be of no consequence. Such substrates may be described as multi-CYP.

For a substrate metabolized by a single pathway, the effect of inhibition (and induction) will be dramatic. An example is lurasidone (Latuda), which is contraindicated with strong 3A4 inhibitors or inducers.

Some inhibitors are stronger than others. In general, expect blood levels of susceptible substrates to increase in the ballpark of:

- mild inhibitor ~ 25% - 50% increase
- moderate inhibitor ~ 50% - 100% increase
- strong inhibitor > 100% increase

Expect these numbers to vary widely between substrates and individuals, often unpredictably. Note that magnitude of inhibition tends to be dose-related over the dosage range of the inhibitor.

The "fluffers" – notorious strong inHibitors:

- **fluvoxamine** (Luvox) - SSRI
- **fluoxetine** (Prozac) - SSRI
- **fluconazole** (Diflucan) - antifungal
- **ketoconazole** (Nizoral) - antifungal

The last two are "cone"-azole antifungals.

ENZYME INDUCTION

The opposite of inHibition is **inDuction**. InDuction occurs when an inDucer stimulates the liver to produce extra enzymes, leading to enhanced metabolism and quicker clearance of victim drugs.

The D is for Down, i.e., Decreased serum concentrations of victim substrates. Unlike inHibition (H for Hurried), inDuction is Delayed, not taking full effect for 2 to 4 weeks while we…
wait for the liver to ramp up enzyme production.

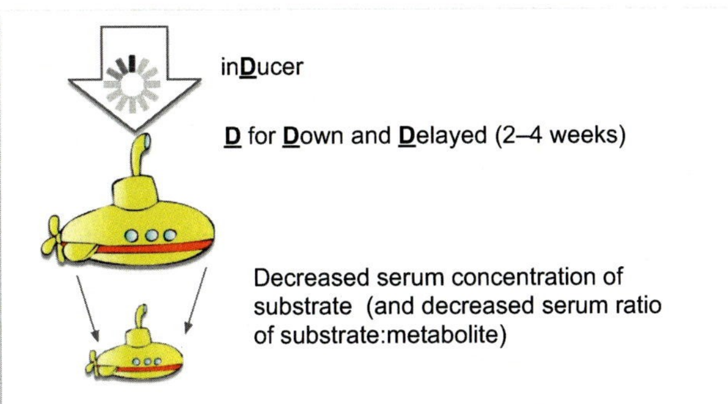

inDucer
D for Down and Delayed (2–4 weeks)
Decreased serum concentration of substrate (and decreased serum ratio of substrate:metabolite)

InDucers will be depicted by:

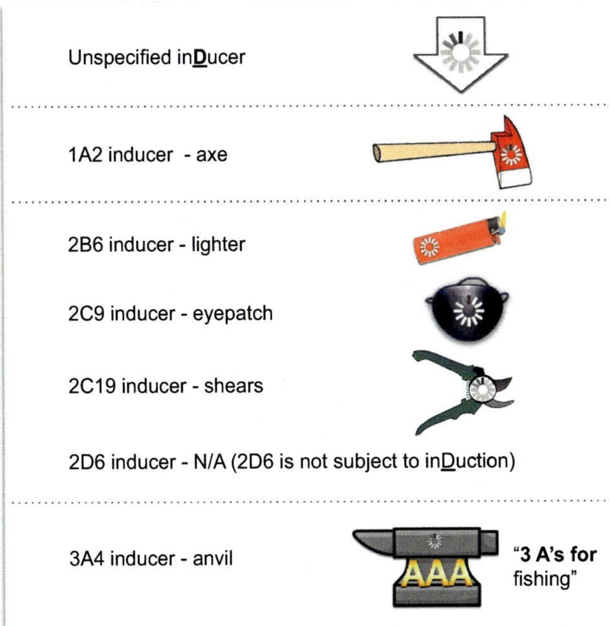

2B6 inducer - lighter
2C9 inducer - eyepatch
2C19 inducer - shears

3A4 inducer - anvil

More often than not, an inducer is itself a substrate of the enzyme. For example, carbamazepine (Tegretol) is represented as both an anvil and a fish on page 31.

THE SHREDDERS

The **"shredders"** are four **strong inDucers** of several CYPs, which cause countless chemicals to be quickly expelled from the body:

- **carbamazepine** (Tegretol) - antiepileptic
- **phenobarbital** (Luminal) - barbiturate
- **phenytoin** (Dilantin) - antiepileptic
- **rifampin** (Rifadin) - antimicrobial

Dr. Jonathan Heldt refers to the shredders as **"Carb & Barb"** in his book *Memorable Psychopharmacology*.

St John's Wort (herbal antidepressant) also inDuces several CYPs, but does so with less potency than the four shredders.

Can shredding be problematic even if the patient is not taking a victim medication? Consider this:

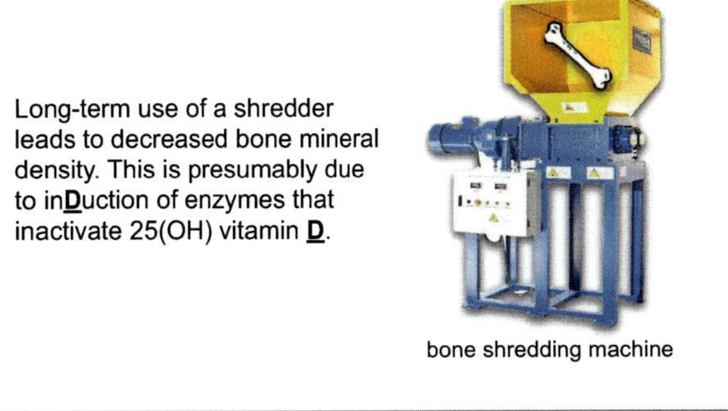

Long-term use of a shredder leads to decreased bone mineral density. This is presumably due to inDuction of enzymes that inactivate 25(OH) vitamin D.

bone shredding machine

REVERSAL OF INHIBITION/INDUCTION

All things being equal, it is best to avoid prescribing strong inducers or inhibitors. Even if there is no problematic interaction at the time, having a strong inhibitor or inducer on board may complicate future medication management.

Consider an individual on an established medication regimen who stops taking an inducer or inhibitor. The serum concentration of victim substrate(s) will change due to the **reversal** of induction/inhibition.

After an inDucer is withdrawn, the concentration of a victim substrate will increase gradually (D for Delayed) over a few weeks because the extra CYP enzymes are degraded without being replenished.

When an inHibitor is stopped, levels of a victim substrate will decrease as soon as the aggressor exits the body. "Hurriedly" does not mean immediately, because it takes about **five half-lives** for the inhibitor to be completely cleared.

For a patient on several psychotropic medications, reversal of inhibition or induction can really throw things out of whack.

While ePrescribe systems may warn the doctor when starting an interacting medication, there will be **no warning** when stopping a medication will lead to a reversal situation.

For an example of **reversal of inHibition**, consider a patient taking alprazolam (Xanax, 3A4 substrate) who suddenly stops fluvoxamine (Luvox, 3A4 inHibitor). In absence of the inhibitor, alprazolam levels drop (from double) to normal. Since fluvoxamine has a short elimination half-life of 15 hours, it should be out of the body at 75 hours (15 hr x 5). So, you would expect the patient on Xanax to become more anxious 3 days after stopping Luvox. It may be difficult to discern whether the patient's emerging distress is due to serotonin withdrawal or decreased alprazolam levels.

An example of **reversal of inDuction** involves tobacco, which is a 1A2 inDucer. A patient taking clozapine (1A2 substrate) stops smoking, reversing inDuction and causing clozapine levels to potentially double over the first week (which is faster than occurs with other inducers). The individual may become obtunded, hypotensive, or even have a seizure. To avoid this, the recommendation is to decrease clozapine dose by 10% daily over the first four days upon smoking cessation, and to check clozapine blood levels before and after the dose adjustment. Note that nicotine products (gum, patches, e-cigs) do not induce 1A2.

Although reversal of inHibition is typically faster than reversal of induction, this does not apply to inhibitors with extremely long half-lives. For instance, fluoxetine (Prozac) has a long elimination half-life of about 7 days, keeping itself around for about 35 days (7 days x 5). Consider a patient with schizophrenia on aripiprazole (Abilify, 2D6 substrate) who stops Prozac (2D6 inHibitor). The patient is doing well at one month, but becomes paranoid two months out. Unless the prescriber anticipated this possibility, no one will realize what happened.

PRODRUGS

Phase I metabolism typically involves biotransformation of an active drug to an inactive (or less active) chemical.

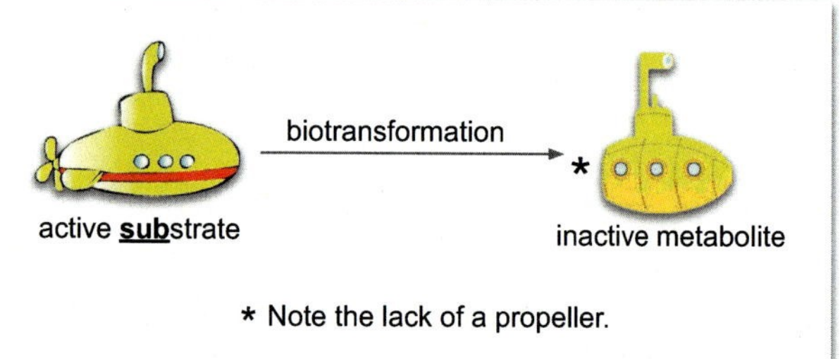

For a few medications, the parent drug has low therapeutic activity until it is biotransformed by a CYP enzyme. In such cases, the substrate is called a **prodrug**, and the biotransformation process can be referred to as **bioactivation**.

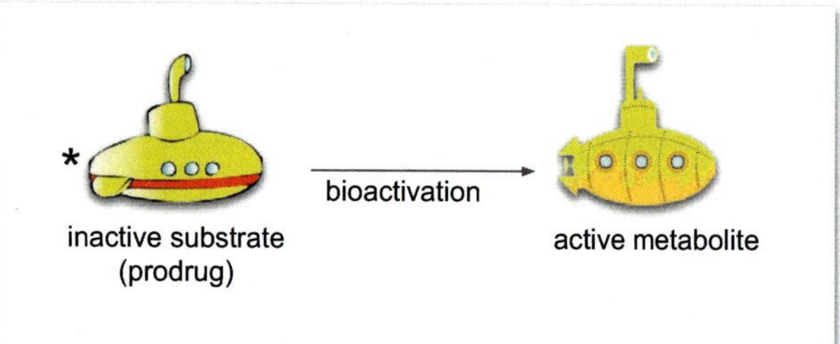

For most medications (active parent drug to inactive metabolite) in**D**uction decreases (**D** for **D**own) effect of the drug and in**H**ibition (**H** for **H**igh) amplifies the therapeutic effect and/or side effects.

With prodrugs, the opposite effect is observed clinically. Induction increases and inhibition decreases the medication's effect(s).

Don't let prodrugs confuse you. In**H**ibitors increase and In**D**ucers decrease the levels of substrate regardless of whether the parent drug is pharmacologically active.

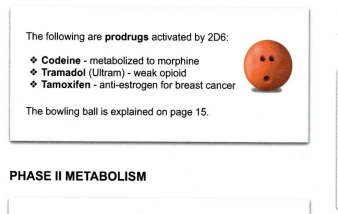

The following are **prodrugs** activated by 2D6:

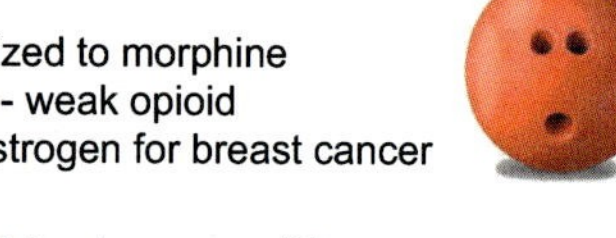

- **Codeine** - metabolized to morphine
- **Tramadol** (Ultram) - weak opioid
- **Tamoxifen** - anti-estrogen for breast cancer

The bowling ball is explained on page 15.

PHASE II METABOLISM

Phase II metabolism occurs in the liver and is subject to kinetic interactions. CYP enzymes are not involved.

Two Kens without a bottle to "CYP" (sip)

Phase II reactions typically involve **conjugation** of a substrate with **glucuronic acid**. This makes the drug water-soluble and prepped for renal excretion.

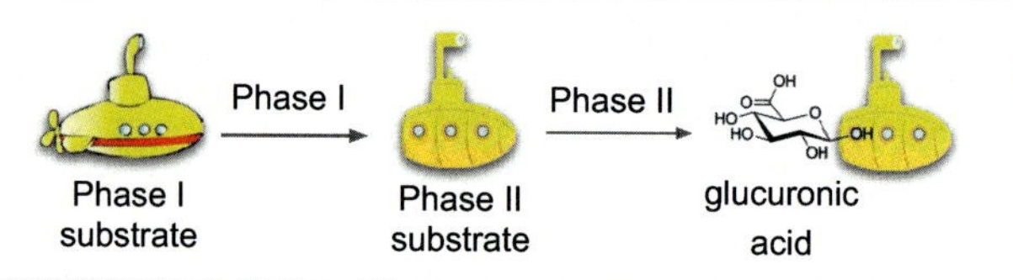

The responsible enzyme is UDP-glucuronosyltransferase, abbreviated **UGT**, as in "U Got Tagged" with glucuronic acid.

Medications metabolized primarily by Phase II are relatively immune to drug interactions. Examples of clinically relevant Phase II interactions are those involving lamotrigine (Lamictal) as a substrate, as featured on page 17.

RENAL CLEARANCE

A few medications are excreted in urine without being metabolised. Such drugs are not subject to Phase I or II interactions, but may be victims of kinetic interactions. Renal "aggressors" act by slowing or hastening the rate of excretion of the victim drug in urine.

Interactions affecting renal clearance of victim drugs are also considered (pharmaco)"Ken"etic.

The aggressor in a renal interaction is not referred to as an inducer or inhibitor, because no enzyme is involved. Nor is the victim called a substrate, because it is not being biotransformed.

Lithium, excreted unchanged in urine, is subject to victimization as illustrated on page 26.

CYP GENETIC PROFILES

Genetic polymorphisms can influence an individual's medication kinetics, which is most relevant for 2D6 and 2C19. Let's talk about 2D6, arguably the most consequential example.

Most individuals are genetically equipped with 2D6 genes that produce normal 2D6 enzymes that metabolize 2D6 substrates at the usual rate. These normal individuals are said to have a 2D6 **extensive metabolizer** (EM) genotype, resulting in a 2D6 EM phenotype.

Here is a cute representation of how a normal individual, i.e., 2D6 **extensive metabolizer** (EM), processes 2D6 substrates. The air inside the beach ball represents the substrate, which is being expelled from the ball as metabolite at the usual rate. 2D6 substrates will have typical elimination half-lives.

About 5% of the population have extra copies of 2D6 genes, resulting in an **ultrarapid metabolizer** (UM) phenotype. These individuals clear 2D6 substrates quickly.

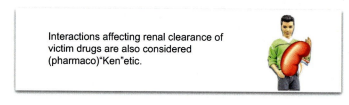

For 2D6 **ultrarapid metabolizers** (UM), the air (2D6 substrate) flows out of the ball quickly as metabolite. 2D6 substrates could be ineffective for these individuals (with the exception of 2D6 prodrugs, which could be be too strong).

About 10% of individuals have defective 2D6 enzymes resulting in a 2D6 **poor metabolizer** (PM) phenotype. This condition may be found on a diagnosis list as "Cytochrome P450 2D6 enzyme deficiency".

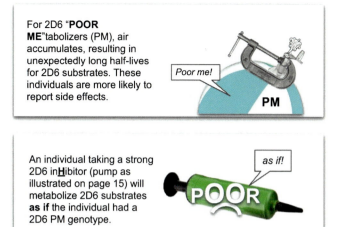

For 2D6 "**POOR ME**"tabolizers (PM), air accumulates, resulting in unexpectedly long half-lives for 2D6 substrates. These individuals are more likely to report side effects.

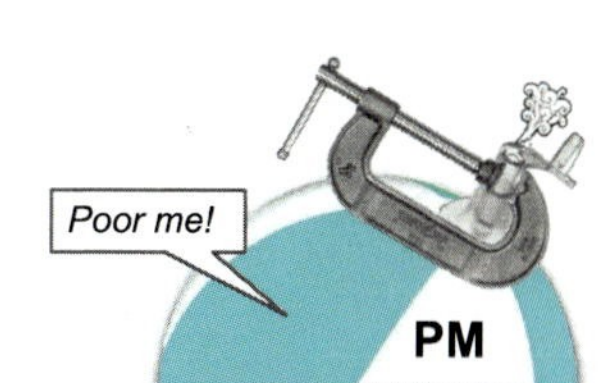

An individual taking a strong 2D6 in**H**ibitor (pump as illustrated on page 15) will metabolize 2D6 substrates **as if** the individual had a 2D6 PM genotype.

In summary, genetic testing of CYP polymorphisms will interpret the individual's metabolizer profile for a given enzyme as either:

- Extensive metabolizer (EM) - normal
- Ultrarapid metabolizer (UM) - fast clearance of substrates
- Poor metabolizer (PM) - slow clearance of substrates

A genetic test result of **intermediate metabolizer** (IM) means that enzyme activity is likely to be a bit lower than that of an EM, i.e., an intermediate between EM and PM. Generally, IM individuals can be clinically managed normally, like an EM individual.

Standalone 2D6 genotyping costs at least $200. GeneSight or Genecept panels cost about $4,000 and report the six relevant CYPs and two UGT enzymes (UGT1A4 and UGT2B15). 23andMe ($199) reports 1A2, 2C9, and 2C19, among 100s of other genes. 23andMe does not report the most relevant CYP genotype, 2D6, because the genetics of 2D6 metabolism is more complicated.

Genotyping may be useful when choosing which medication to prescribe an individual patient. With GeneSight, about 1 in 5 patients have a genetic variation relevant to their treatment. For an individual already established on a medication, serum drug levels may be more useful than genotyping. There are situations when knowing the actual blood levels of clozapine, risperidone, olanzapine, aripiprazole, haloperidol, lamotrigine, etc. are clinically relevant. Unfortunately, these tests usually must be sent to an outside lab, and it may take a week to see the results. Levels of lithium, carbamazepine, phenytoin, and valproic acid are usually reported the same day.

P-GLYCOPROTEIN

P-glycoprotein (P-gp) is a gatekeeper at the gut lumen and the blood-brain barrier. P-gp pumps P-gp substrates out of the brain—"Pumpers gonna pump".

"Pumpers gonna pump" P-gp substrates out of the brain

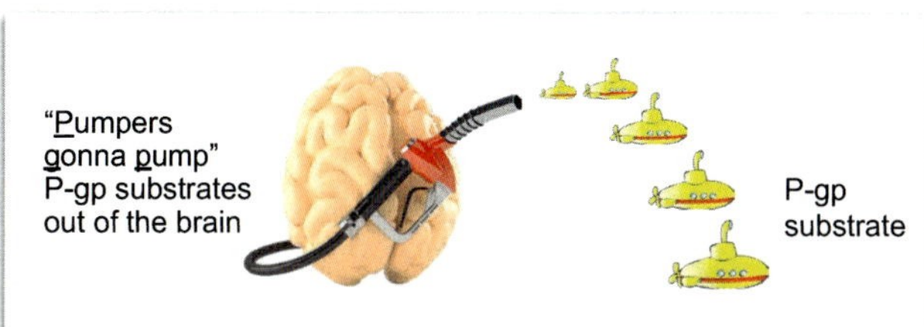

An example of a relevant P-gp interaction involves the OTC opioid antidiarrheal loperamide (Imodium). Loperamide does not cause central opioid effects under normal circumstances. If the individual takes a potent P-gp inhibitor, megadose loperamide can stay in the brain long enough to cause euphoria. The P-gp inhibitor typically used the achieve this recreational effect is omeprazole (Prilosec).

THE NATURE OF THIS INFORMATION

The information presented in the remainder of this chapter is a synthesis of sources including the OpeRational ClassificAtion (ORCA) system (as presented in *The Top 100 Drug Interactions* by Hansten & Horn, 2019), Lexicomp, DrugBank, Flockhart Table, ePocrates, Carlat Medication Fact Book, Stahl's Essential Psychopharmacology, The Medical Letter, Current Psychiatry, GeneSight, Genecept, various research papers and FDA prescribing information for the individual drugs.

Reputable sources are often at odds with each other regarding the strength of specific inducers/inhibitors, the vulnerability of specific substrates to induction/inhibition, or even which CYPs are relevant to a specific medication. CYP interactions are continuously being discovered and clarified. Even with the freshest information and full knowledge of a patient's genotype, the magnitude of a specific CYP interaction is difficult to predict.

HOW TO APPLY THIS INFORMATION

Refer to the tables on pages 20 and 21. Highlight the medications that you prescribe. First acquaint yourself with the in**D**ucers because the list is short. Memorize the bolded inducers (shredders) and those that you highlighted. After you know the inducers, move to the in**H**ibitor column. Memorize the bolded inhibitors (fluffers) and your highlighted medications.

When it comes to substrates, memorization is less important. Substrates are only relevant when an inducer or inhibitor is on board, or if the patient has a special metabolizer genotype. Of the medications you prescribe, be aware of the more susceptible substrates.

Consider running an interaction check whenever a patient is taking a shredder, fluffer, systemic antifungal, HIV medication, or cancer medication. ePocrates.com and the ePocrates app are adequate, and free.

Keep things simple. When choosing new medications, avoid major inducers and inhibitors if suitable alternatives are available. For the complicated psychiatric patient on several medications, try to avoid carbamazepine (shredder inducer) and the **flu**ffer SSRIs (**flu**oxetine and **flu**voxamine). Among SSRIs, escitalopram (Lexapro) and sertraline (Zoloft) are good choices—they are 2C19 substrates but do not affect the metabolism of other medications.

Also think about choosing less vulnerable substrates. Each drug mascot on pages 18 and 19 is depicted in box/bubble because it is generally not involved in clinically significant kinetic interactions (although dynamic interactions almost always apply). You don't have to worry much about benzodiazepine interactions if you stick to the "LOT" benzos—lorazepam, oxazepam and temazepam. Most antipsychotics are susceptible substrates, but not so much for ziprasidone, loxapine and paliperidone.

This book uses picture association as a memorization technique. Pages 10 through 17 establish a visual mnemonic framework for various kinetic interactions that will be reinforced by a mascot for each of 270 medications. The mascots serve a double purpose of helping you remember US trade name/generic name pairings.

Since you probably won't be mentioning CYP nomenclature in casual conversation, you might want to bypass the technical naming system altogether. Instead of keeping a list of "3A4 substrates" in your memory bank, you could just learn the school of "fish".

I hope this book empowers you to understand and memorize topics that are otherwise daunting, so you can use your knowledge to improve patient care. Without further ado, let's start our journey to becoming a superhero of psychotropic medication management.

1A2 accounts for 10–15% of CYP activity in the liver

Cytochrome P450 1A2 (CYP1A2)

"One Axe to Grind; One Axe to Grow"

52% of individuals are 1A2 ultrarapid metabolizers; < 1% are poor metabolizers

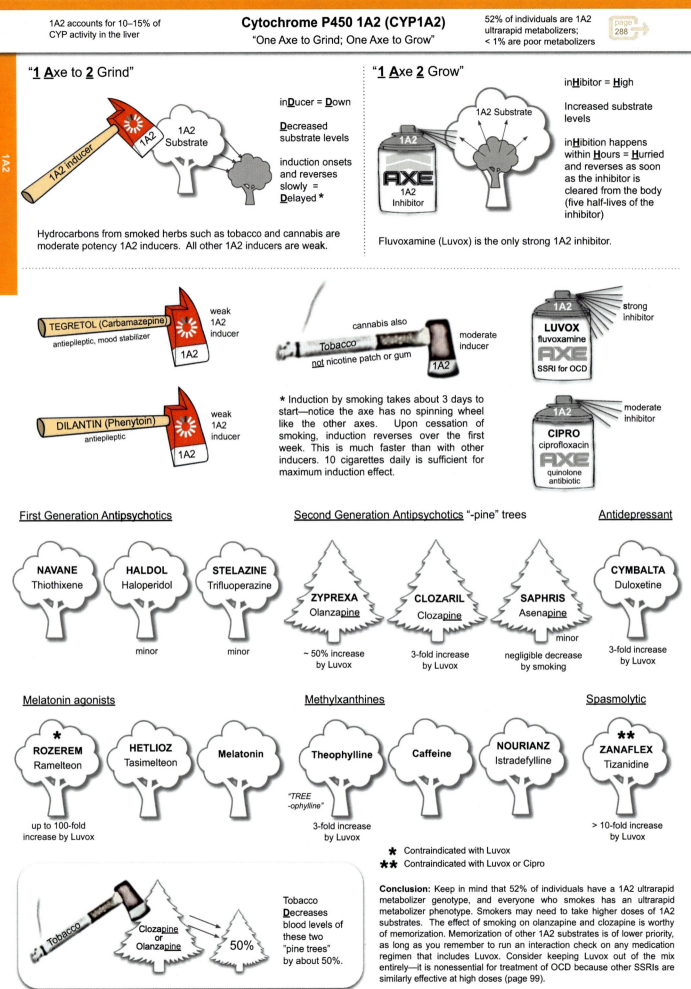

"1 Axe to 2 Grind"

inDucer = Down

Decreased substrate levels

induction onsets and reverses slowly = Delayed *

Hydrocarbons from smoked herbs such as tobacco and cannabis are moderate potency 1A2 inducers. All other 1A2 inducers are weak.

"1 Axe 2 Grow"

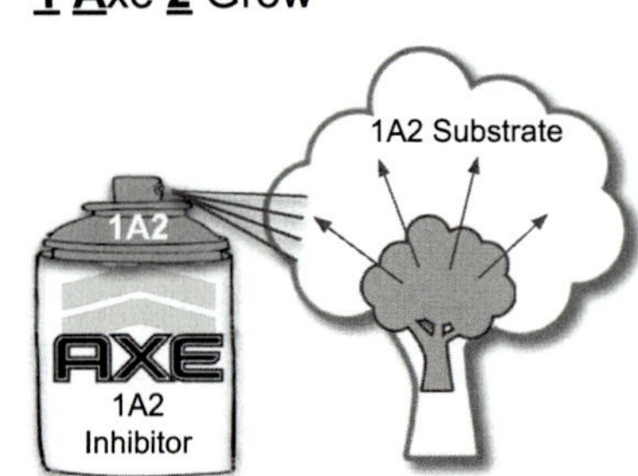

inHibitor = High

Increased substrate levels

inHibition happens within Hours = Hurried and reverses as soon as the inhibitor is cleared from the body (five half-lives of the inhibitor)

Fluvoxamine (Luvox) is the only strong 1A2 inhibitor.

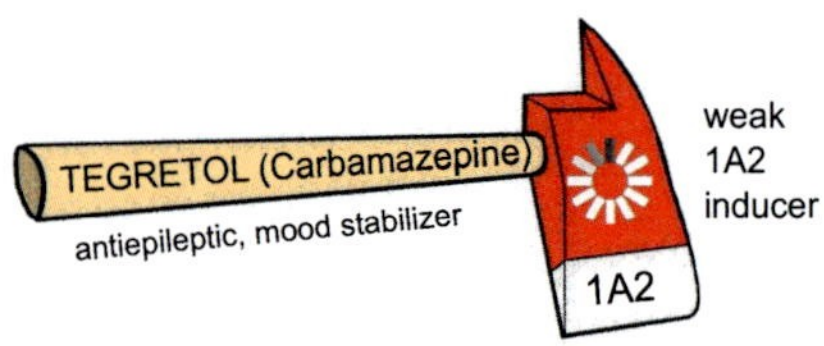

weak 1A2 inducer

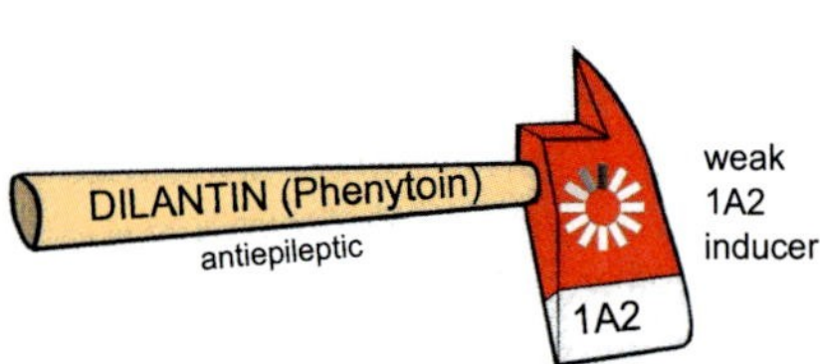

weak 1A2 inducer

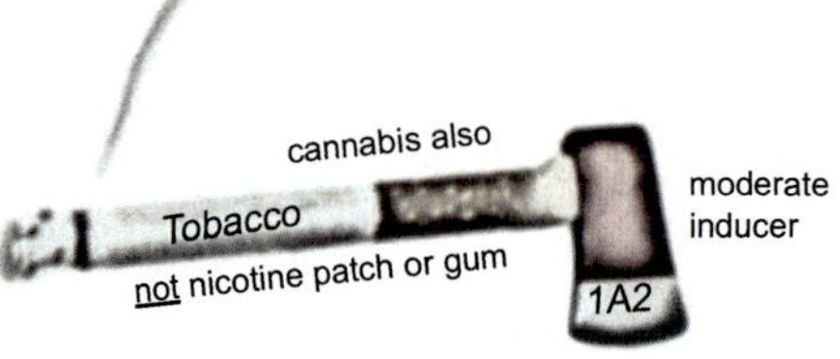

moderate inducer

* Induction by smoking takes about 3 days to start—notice the axe has no spinning wheel like the other axes. Upon cessation of smoking, induction reverses over the first week. This is much faster than with other inducers. 10 cigarettes daily is sufficient for maximum induction effect.

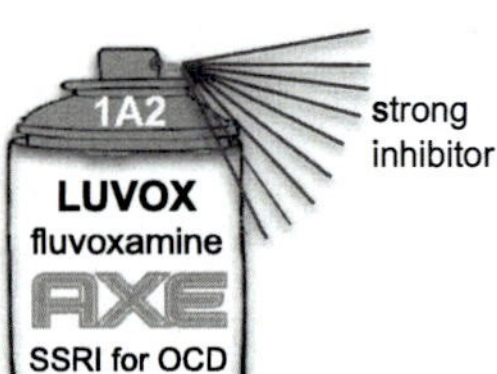

strong inhibitor

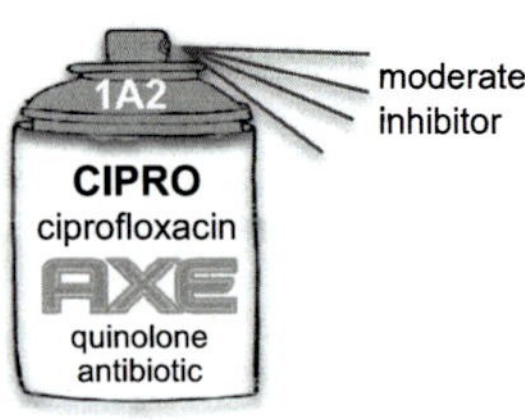

moderate inhibitor

First Generation Antipsychotics | Second Generation Antipsychotics "-pine" trees | Antidepressant

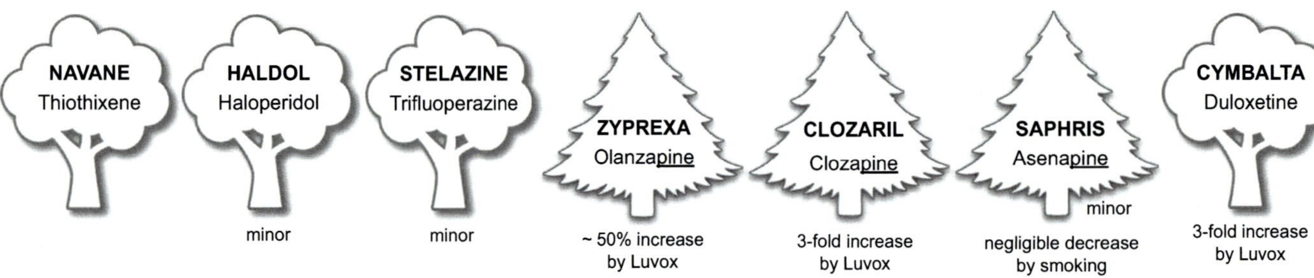

Melatonin agonists | Methylxanthines | Spasmolytic

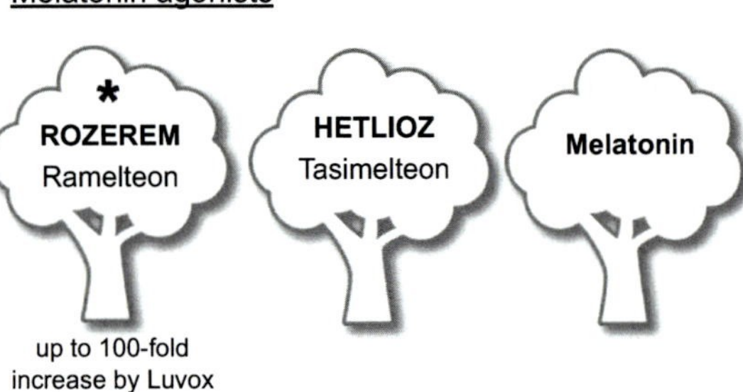

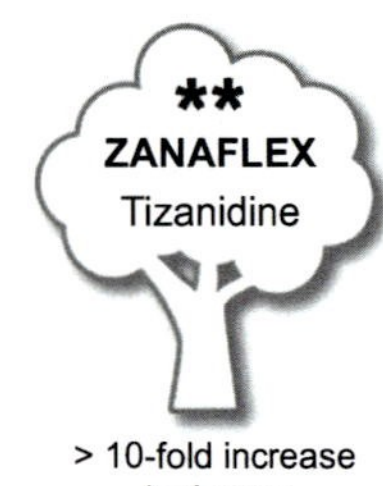

* Contraindicated with Luvox

** Contraindicated with Luvox or Cipro

Tobacco Decreases blood levels of these two "pine trees" by about 50%.

Conclusion: Keep in mind that 52% of individuals have a 1A2 ultrarapid metabolizer genotype, and everyone who smokes has an ultrarapid metabolizer phenotype. Smokers may need to take higher doses of 1A2 substrates. The effect of smoking on olanzapine and clozapine is worthy of memorization. Memorization of other 1A2 substrates is of lower priority, as long as you remember to run an interaction check on any medication regimen that includes Luvox. Consider keeping Luvox out of the mix entirely—it is nonessential for treatment of OCD because other SSRIs are similarly effective at high doses (page 99).

Ciprofloxacin, a moderate 1A2 in**H**ibitor, increases clozapine levels about 2-fold.

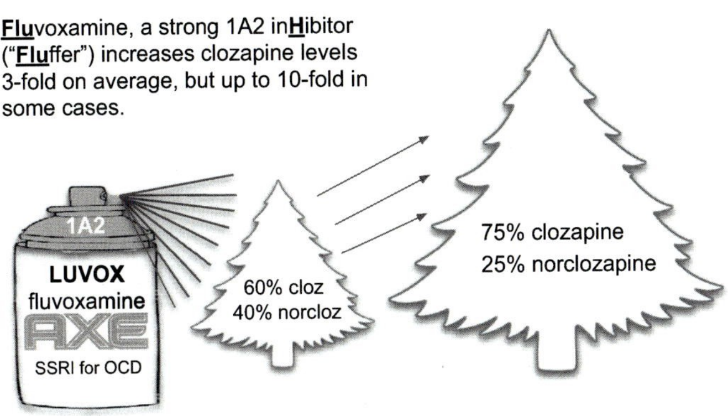

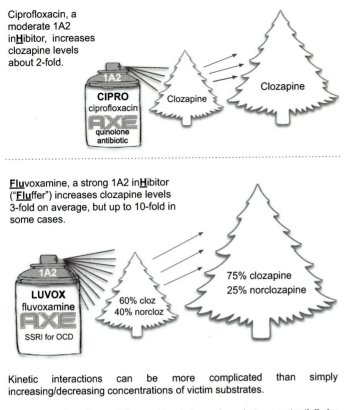

Fluvoxamine, a strong 1A2 in**H**ibitor ("**Flu**ffer") increases clozapine levels 3-fold on average, but up to 10-fold in some cases.

Kinetic interactions can be more complicated than simply increasing/decreasing concentrations of victim substrates.

Combining clozapine and fluvoxamine is hazardous, but can potentially be used for therapeutic advantage. Close monitoring of serum **clozapine levels** would be required.

Norclozapine is the main metabolite of clozapine, formed by 1A2 metabolism. When clozapine blood levels are reported, clozapine and metabolite (norclozapine) levels are provided separately. Through 1A2 in**H**ibition, Luvox increases the **clozapine:norclozapine ratio**. A **H**igher serum clozapine:norclozapine ratio of at least 2:1 is generally considered desirable for maximum efficacy*. Norclozapine provides little antipsychotic benefit and causes weight gain, diabetes, seizures, and neutropenia.

Patients given clozapine 100 mg + Luvox 50 mg daily (compared to clozapine 300 mg monotherapy) demonstrated more improvement with less weight gain and less drooling. Clozapine levels were similar for both groups with, as expected, lower norclozapine levels for those taking Luvox.
(Lu ML et al, 2018; randomized controlled trial, N=85).

*The negative aspect of a **H**igher clozapine:norclozapine is greater anticholinergic burden (pages 161–162). Clozapine is anticholinergic, whereas norclozapine is cholinergic. Consequently, clozapine causes constipation, while norclozapine does not. The anticholinergic properties of clozapine may impair cognition, whereas norclozapine may provide cognitive benefits such as enhanced working memory (page 177).

Certain physiologic states may increase levels of olanzapine and clozapine up to 2-fold.

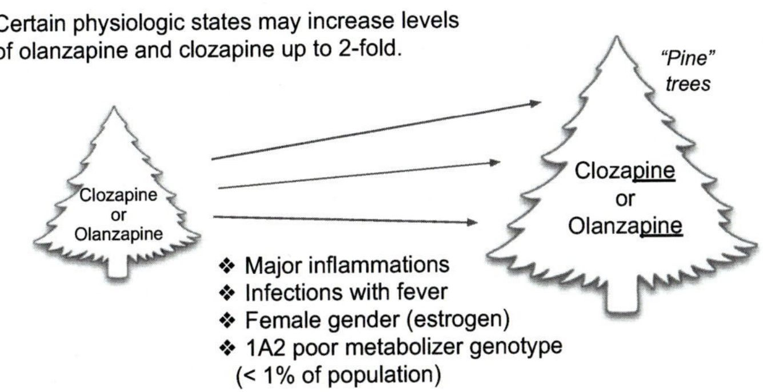

- Major inflammations
- Infections with fever
- Female gender (estrogen)
- 1A2 poor metabolizer genotype (< 1% of population)

For a patient with efficacy or tolerability issues, consider monitoring serum levels of the antipsychotic. The author checks clozapine levels routinely, and olanzapine levels in some cases.

Fluvoxamine and ramelteon should not be prescribed concomitantly because ramelteon levels will be increased up to 100-fold!

Cytochrome P450 2B6 (CYP2B6)

"Tube Socks"

3% of individuals are 2B6 ultrarapid metabolizers; 7% are poor metabolizers

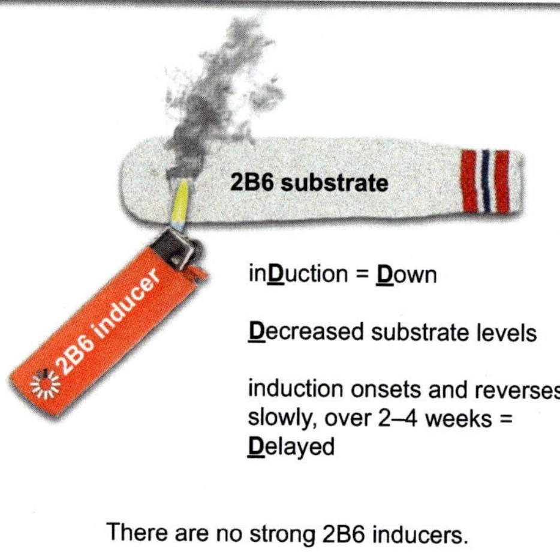

in**D**uction = **D**own

Decreased substrate levels

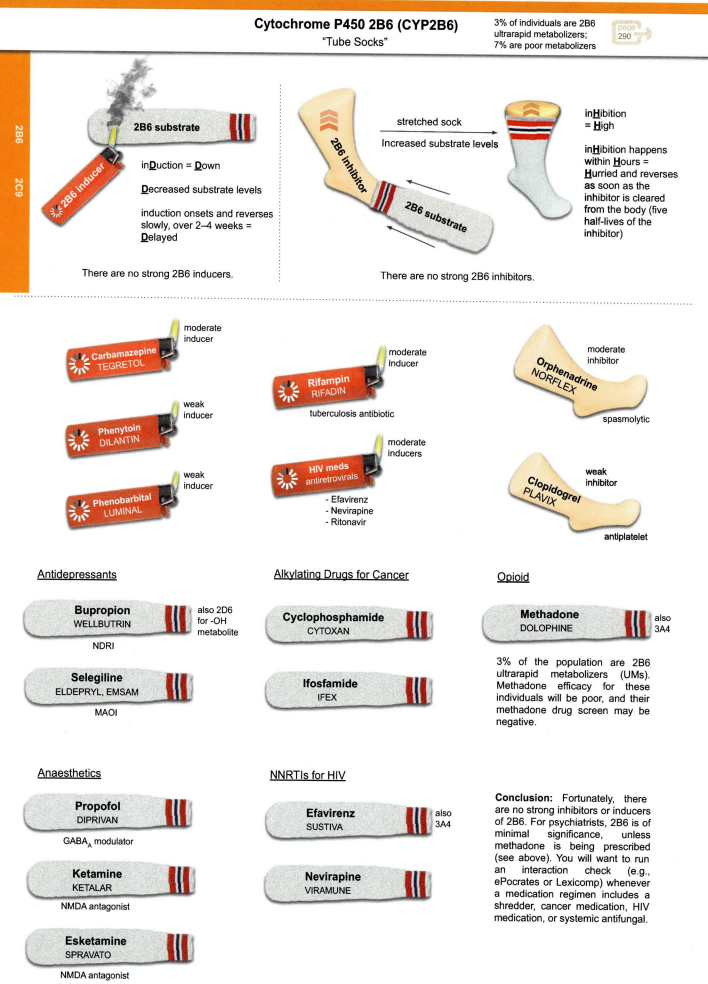

induction onsets and reverses slowly, over 2–4 weeks = **D**elayed

There are no strong 2B6 inducers.

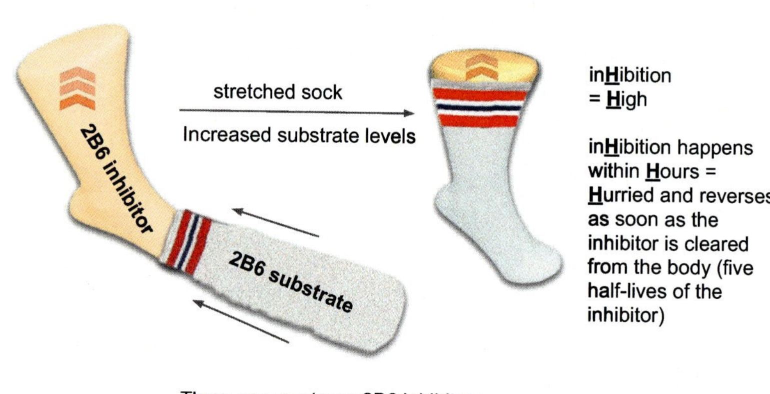

in**H**ibition = **H**igh

in**H**ibition happens within **H**ours = **H**urried and reverses as soon as the inhibitor is cleared from the body (five half-lives of the inhibitor)

There are no strong 2B6 inhibitors.

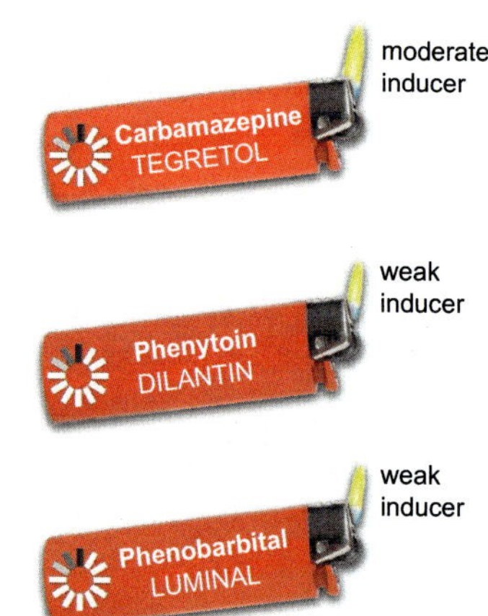

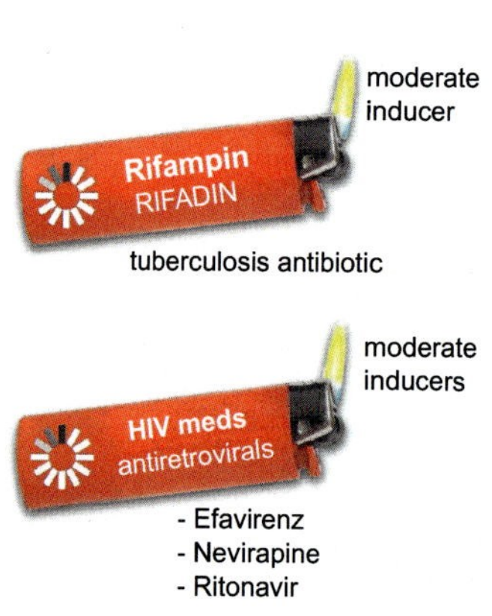

- Efavirenz
- Nevirapine
- Ritonavir

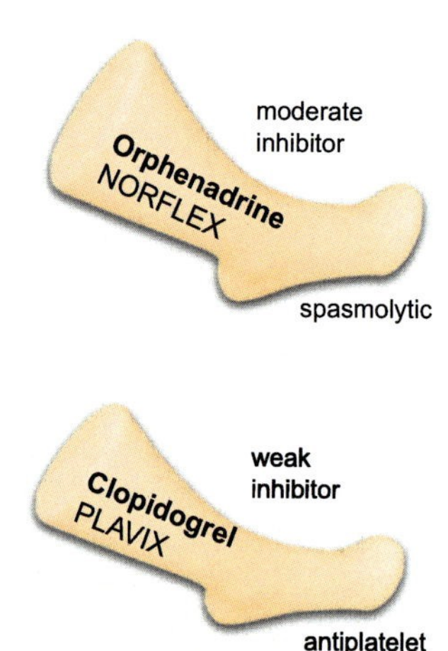

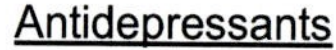

Antidepressants

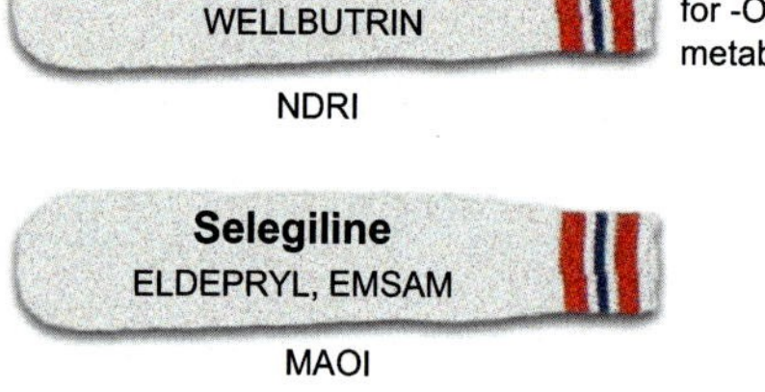

Alkylating Drugs for Cancer

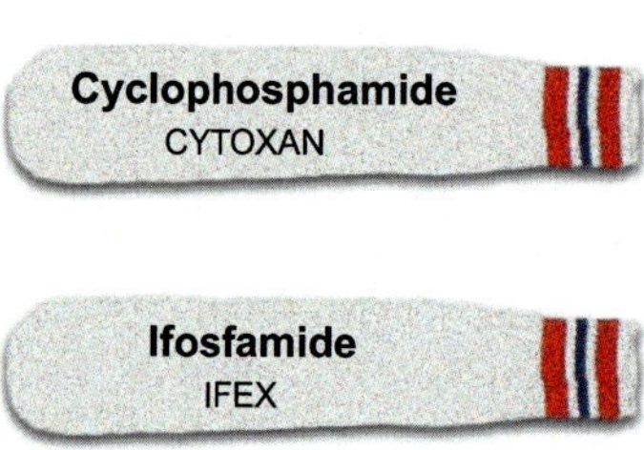

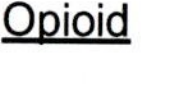

Opioid

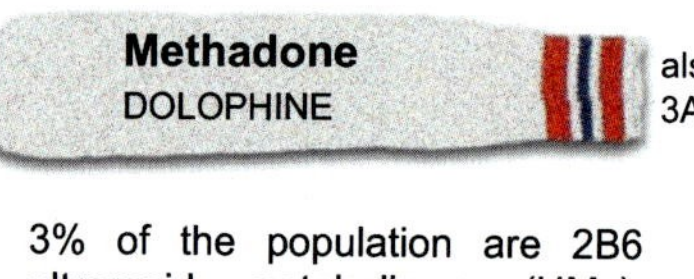

3% of the population are 2B6 ultrarapid metabolizers (UMs). Methadone efficacy for these individuals will be poor, and their methadone drug screen may be negative.

Anaesthetics

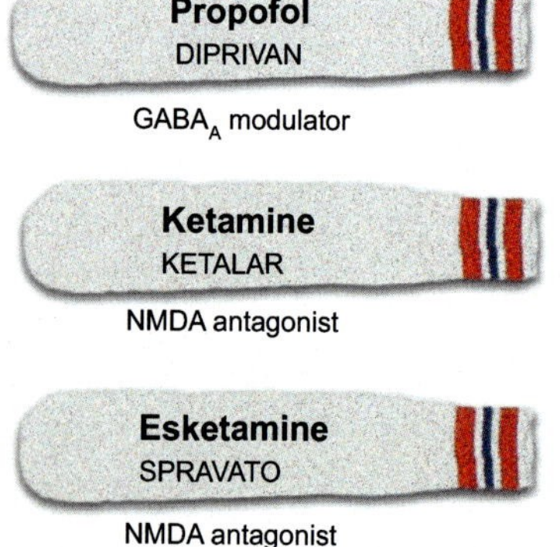

NNRTIs for HIV

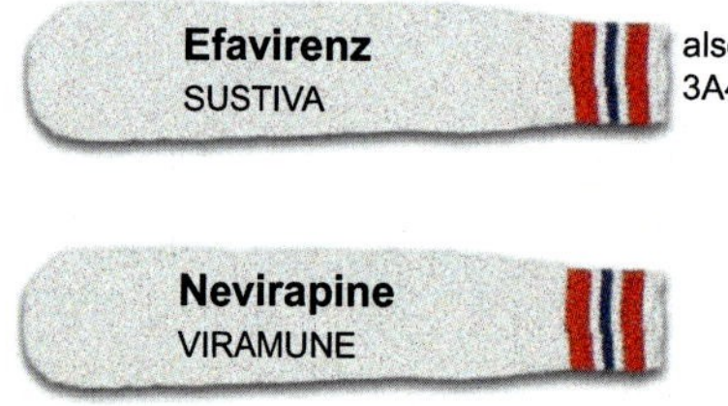

Conclusion: Fortunately, there are no strong inhibitors or inducers of 2B6. For psychiatrists, 2B6 is of minimal significance, unless methadone is being prescribed (see above). You will want to run an interaction check (e.g., ePocrates or Lexicomp) whenever a medication regimen includes a shredder, cancer medication, HIV medication, or systemic antifungal.

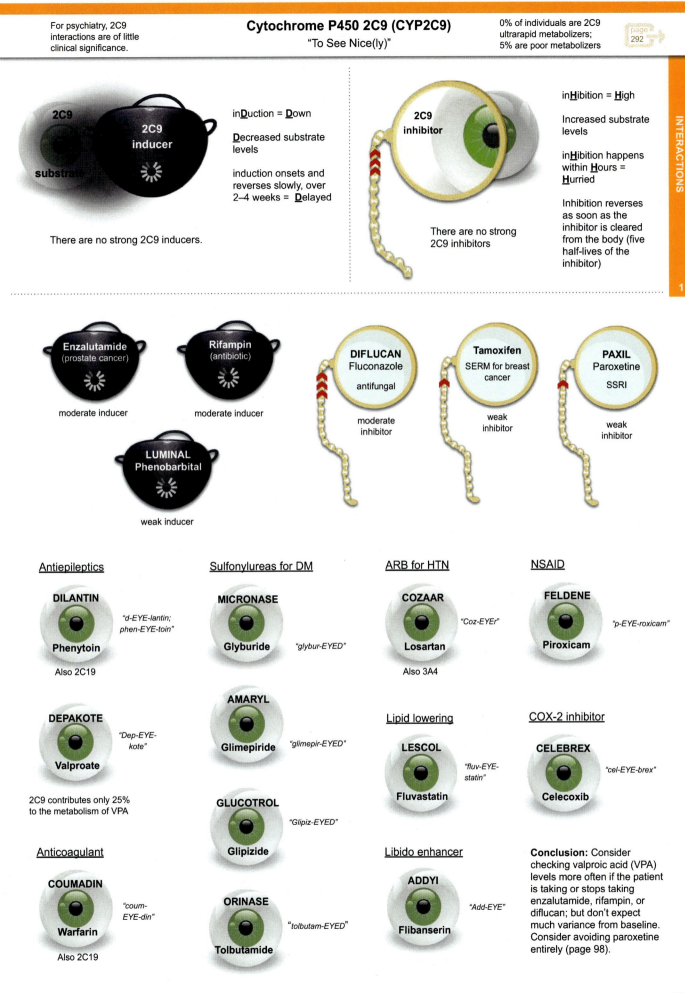

For psychiatry, 2C9 interactions are of little clinical significance.

Cytochrome P450 2C9 (CYP2C9)

"To See Nice(ly)"

0% of individuals are 2C9 ultrarapid metabolizers; 5% are poor metabolizers

page 292

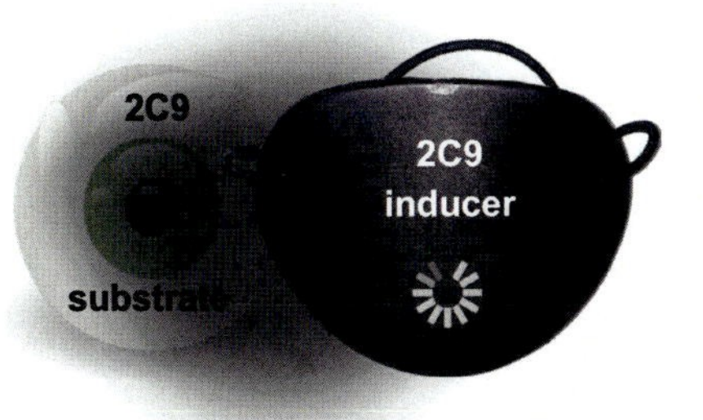

in**D**uction = **D**own

Decreased substrate levels

induction onsets and reverses slowly, over 2–4 weeks = **D**elayed

There are no strong 2C9 inducers.

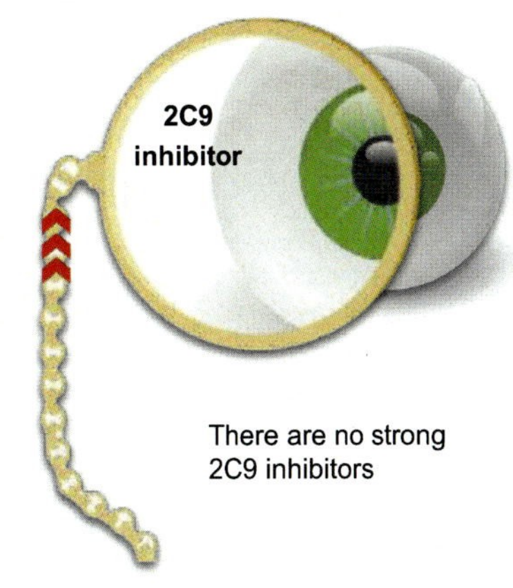

There are no strong 2C9 inhibitors

in**H**ibition = **H**igh

Increased substrate levels

in**H**ibition happens within **H**ours = **H**urried

Inhibition reverses as soon as the inhibitor is cleared from the body (five half-lives of the inhibitor)

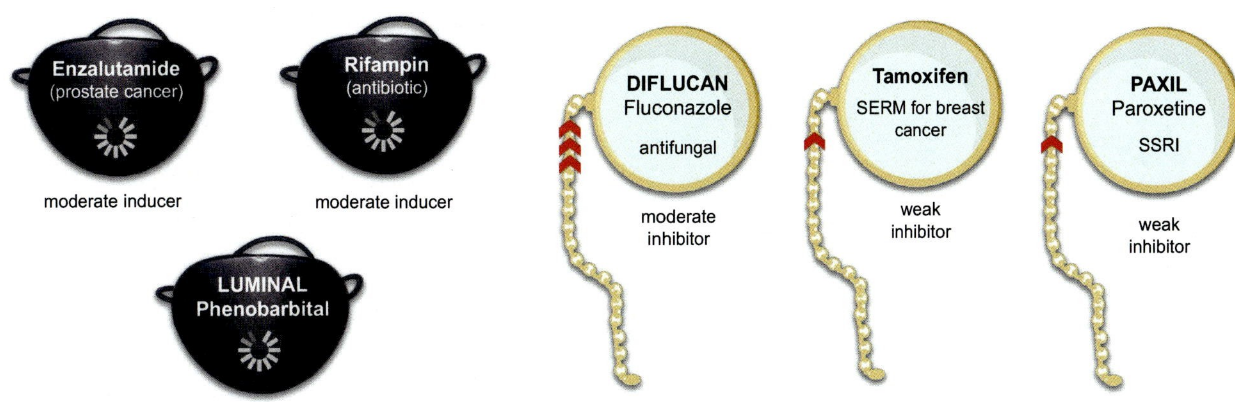

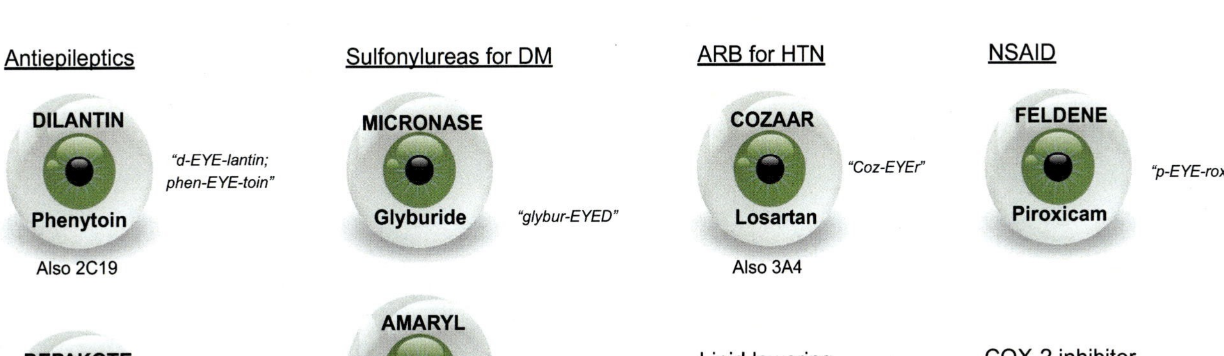

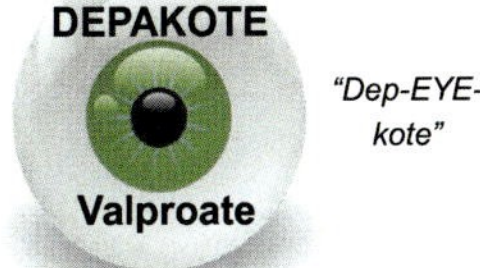

2C9 contributes only 25% to the metabolism of VPA

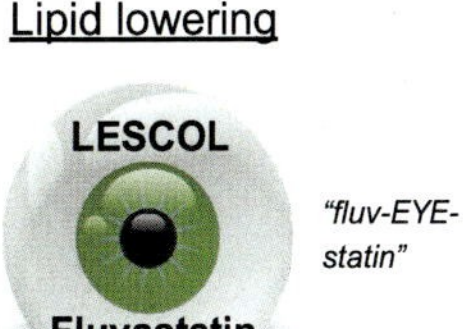

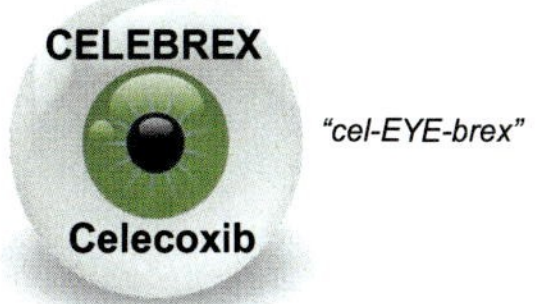

Anticoagulant

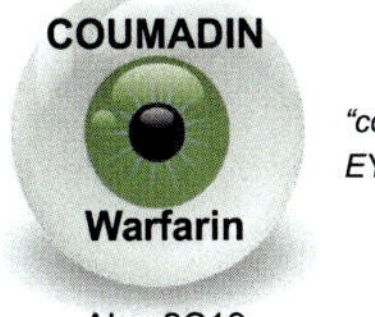

Also 2C19

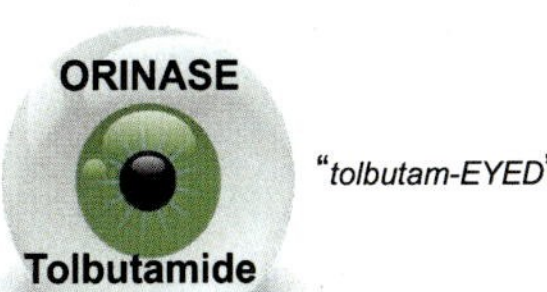

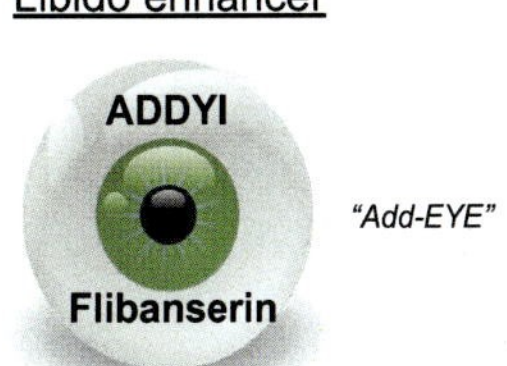

Conclusion: Consider checking valproic acid (VPA) levels more often if the patient is taking or stops taking enzalutamide, rifampin, or diflucan; but don't expect much variance from baseline. Consider avoiding paroxetine entirely (page 98).

Cytochrome P450 2C19 (CYP2C19)

"To See Nice Things (grow)"

10% of individuals are 2C19 ultrarapid metabolizers; 5% are poor metabolizers

page 294

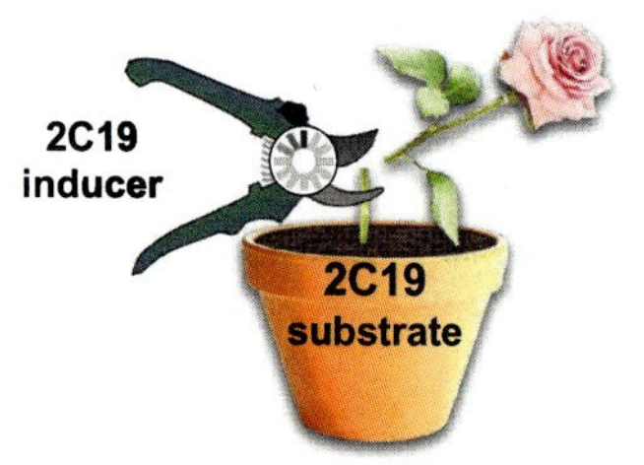

inDuction = Down

Decreased substrate levels

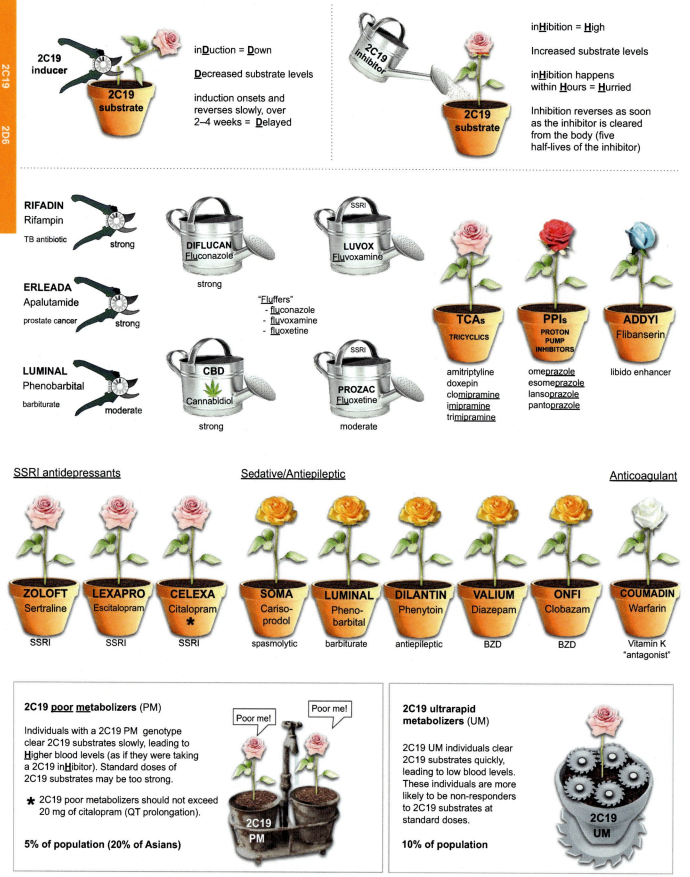

induction onsets and reverses slowly, over 2–4 weeks = Delayed

inHibition = High

Increased substrate levels

inHibition happens within Hours = Hurried

Inhibition reverses as soon as the inhibitor is cleared from the body (five half-lives of the inhibitor)

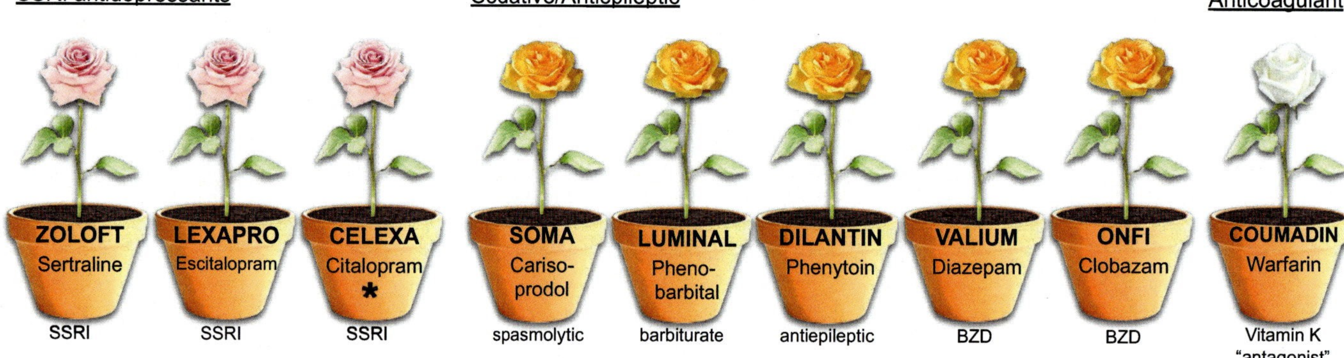

2C19 poor metabolizers (PM)

Individuals with a 2C19 PM genotype clear 2C19 substrates slowly, leading to Higher blood levels (as if they were taking a 2C19 inHibitor). Standard doses of 2C19 substrates may be too strong.

* 2C19 poor metabolizers should not exceed 20 mg of citalopram (QT prolongation).

5% of population (20% of Asians)

2C19 ultrarapid metabolizers (UM)

2C19 UM individuals clear 2C19 substrates quickly, leading to low blood levels. These individuals are more likely to be non-responders to 2C19 substrates at standard doses.

10% of population

Conclusion: 2C19 genotyping is not typically ordered as a standalone test, but if 2C19 metabolizer genotype is known (e.g., from GeneSight or Genecept), the information can be put to good use when dosing (es)citalopram and sertraline. Knowledge of metabolizer status is not essential because these SSRIs can be titrated the old-fashioned way, according to response and side effects. In any event, avoid prescribing Soma, Valium, or phenobarbital for anxiety due to their particularly high risk of abuse and dependence. Avoid St. John's Wort due to interactions, and because it only works for mild depression.

2D6 metabolizes ~ 12% of prescription drugs. Notice how all of the -oxetine's are 2D6 inhibitors and/or substrates.

Cytochrome P450 2D6 (CYP2D6)

"Too Darn Sexy"

5% of individuals are 2D6 ultrarapid metabolizers (UM). 10% are poor metabolizers (PM).

page 296

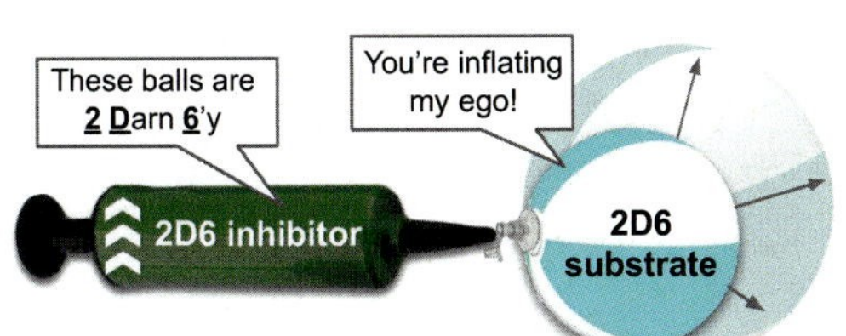

2D6 enzymes cannot be induced.

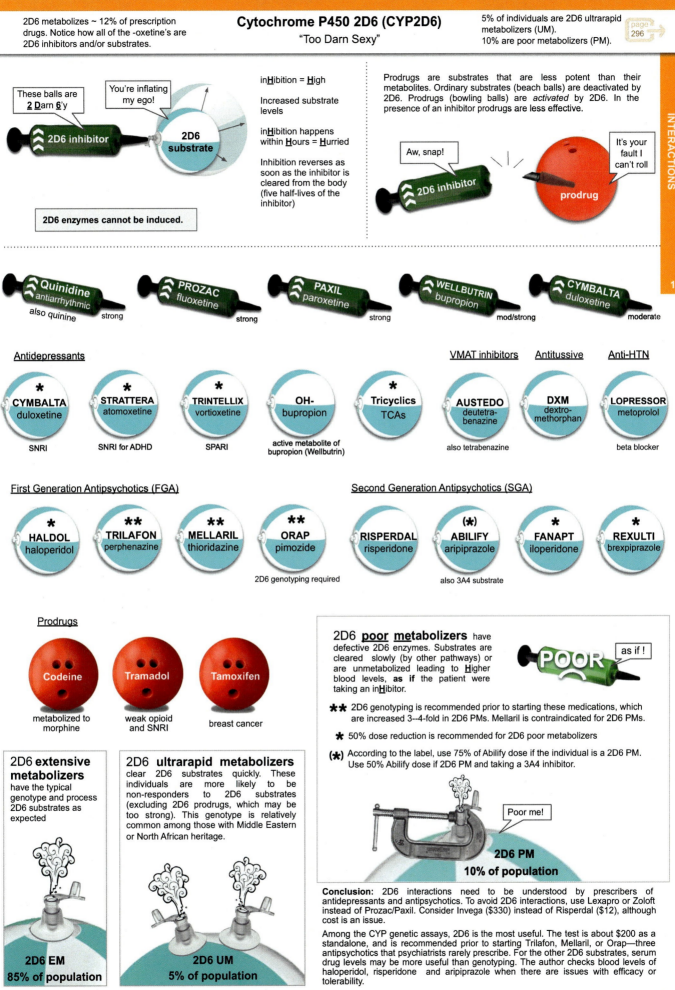

inHibition = High

Increased substrate levels

inHibition happens within Hours = Hurried

Inhibition reverses as soon as the inhibitor is cleared from the body (five half-lives of the inhibitor)

Prodrugs are substrates that are less potent than their metabolites. Ordinary substrates (beach balls) are deactivated by 2D6. Prodrugs (bowling balls) are *activated* by 2D6. In the presence of an inhibitor prodrugs are less effective.

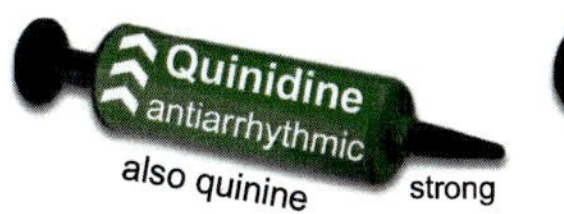

strong

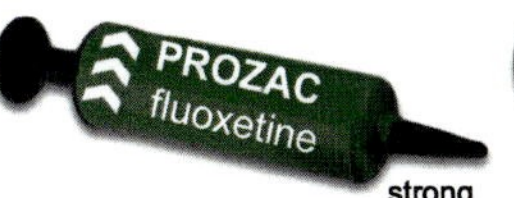

strong

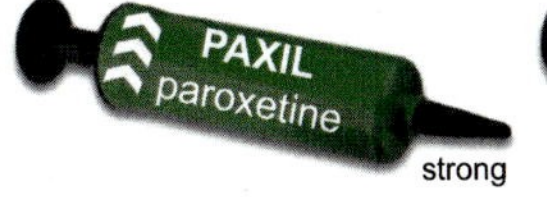

strong

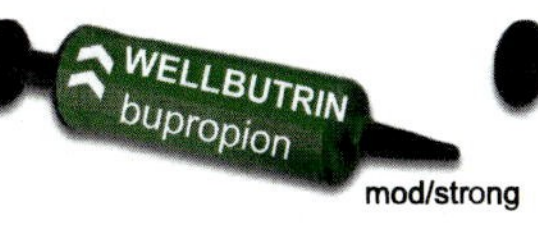

mod/strong

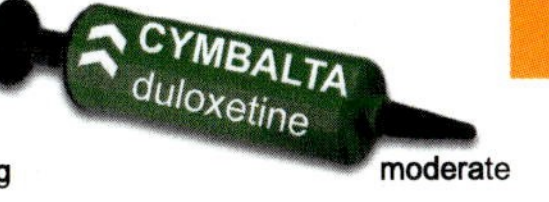

moderate

Antidepressants

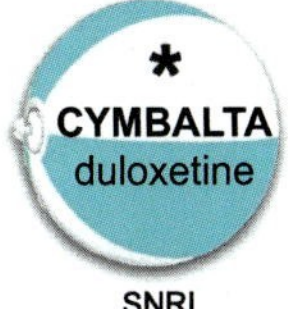

SNRI

SNRI for ADHD

* TRINTELLIX vortioxetine

SPARI

active metabolite of bupropion (Wellbutrin)

VMAT inhibitors

AUSTEDO deutetrabenazine

also tetrabenazine

Antitussive

DXM dextromethorphan

Anti-HTN

beta blocker

First Generation Antipsychotics (FGA)

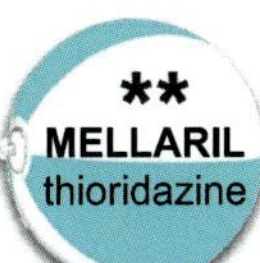

2D6 genotyping required

Second Generation Antipsychotics (SGA)

also 3A4 substrate

Prodrugs

metabolized to morphine

weak opioid and SNRI

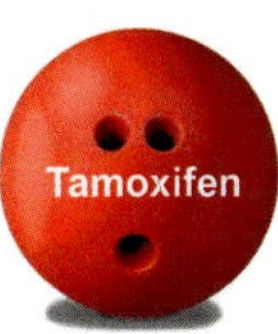

breast cancer

2D6 poor metabolizers have defective 2D6 enzymes. Substrates are cleared slowly (by other pathways) or are unmetabolized leading to Higher blood levels, **as if** the patient were taking an inHibitor.

** 2D6 genotyping is recommended prior to starting these medications, which are increased 3--4-fold in 2D6 PMs. Mellaril is contraindicated for 2D6 PMs.

* 50% dose reduction is recommended for 2D6 poor metabolizers

(*) According to the label, use 75% of Abilify dose if the individual is a 2D6 PM. Use 50% Abilify dose if 2D6 PM and taking a 3A4 inhibitor.

2D6 extensive metabolizers have the typical genotype and process 2D6 substrates as expected

2D6 ultrarapid metabolizers clear 2D6 substrates quickly. These individuals are more likely to be non-responders to 2D6 substrates (excluding 2D6 prodrugs, which may be too strong). This genotype is relatively common among those with Middle Eastern or North African heritage.

Conclusion: 2D6 interactions need to be understood by prescribers of antidepressants and antipsychotics. To avoid 2D6 interactions, use Lexapro or Zoloft instead of Prozac/Paxil. Consider Invega ($330) instead of Risperdal ($12), although cost is an issue.

Among the CYP genetic assays, 2D6 is the most useful. The test is about $200 as a standalone, and is recommended prior to starting Trilafon, Mellaril, or Orap—three antipsychotics that psychiatrists rarely prescribe. For the other 2D6 substrates, serum drug levels may be more useful than genotyping. The author checks blood levels of haloperidol, risperidone and aripiprazole when there are issues with efficacy or tolerability.

> 50% of prescription drugs are 3A4 substrates—plenty of fish!

Cytochrome P450 3A4 (CYP3A4)

"3 A's For (fishing)"

0% of individuals are 3A4 ultrarapid metabolizers; < 1% are poor metabolizers

page 298

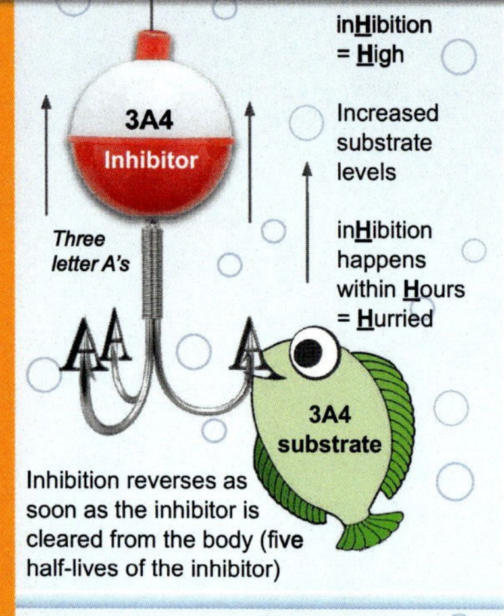

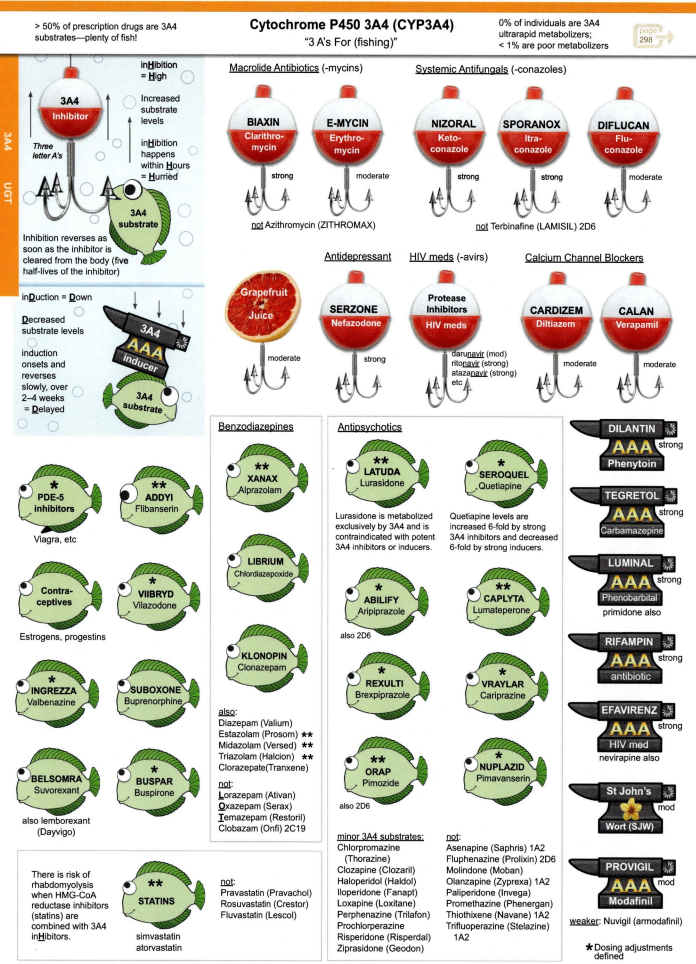

inHibition = High

Increased substrate levels

inHibition happens within Hours = Hurried

Inhibition reverses as soon as the inhibitor is cleared from the body (five half-lives of the inhibitor)

inDuction = Down

Decreased substrate levels

induction onsets and reverses slowly, over 2–4 weeks = Delayed

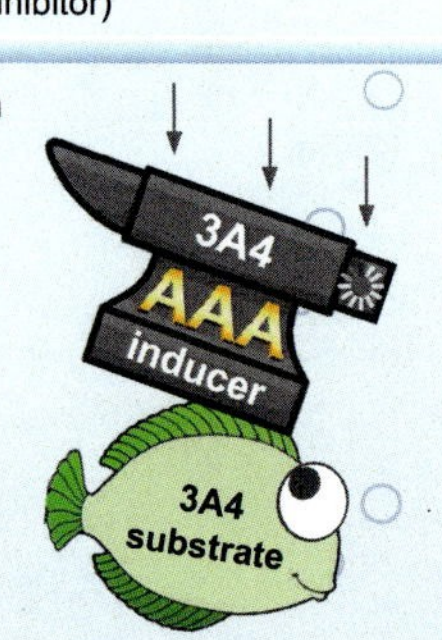
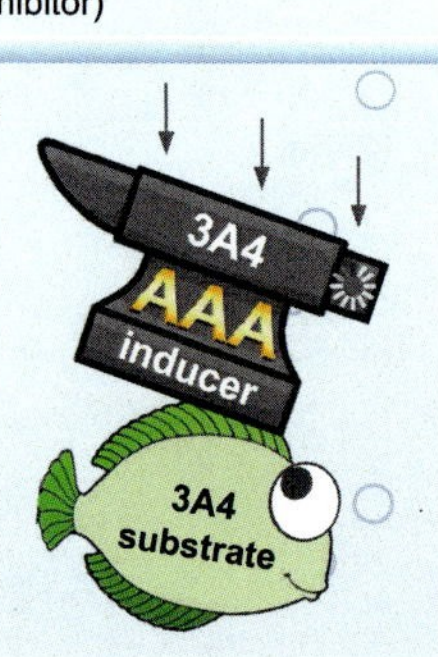
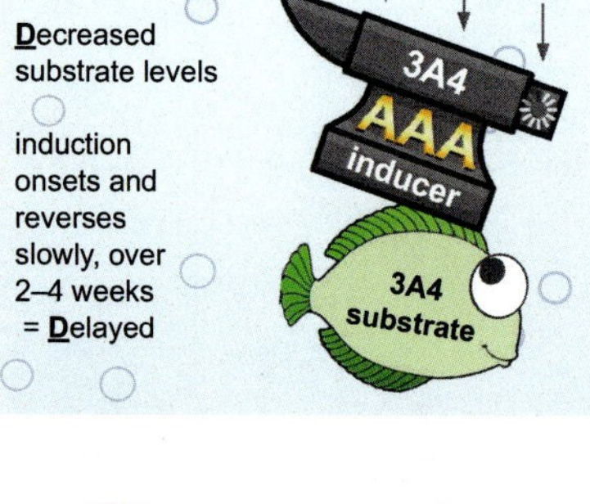

Macrolide Antibiotics (-mycins)

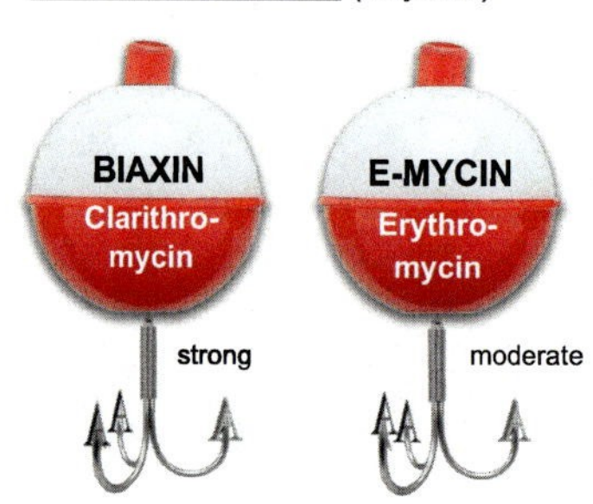

not Azithromycin (ZITHROMAX)

Systemic Antifungals (-conazoles)

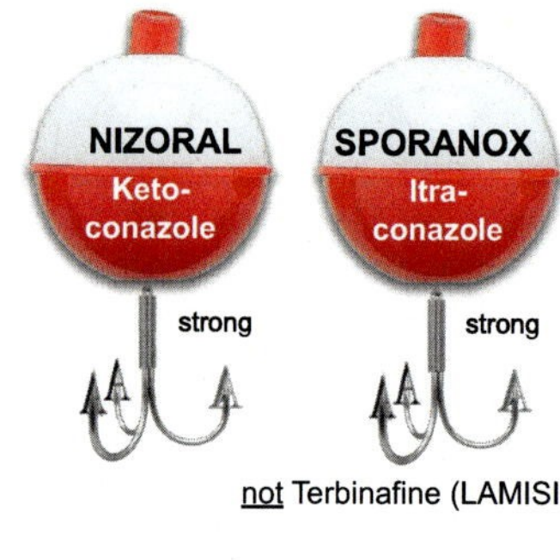

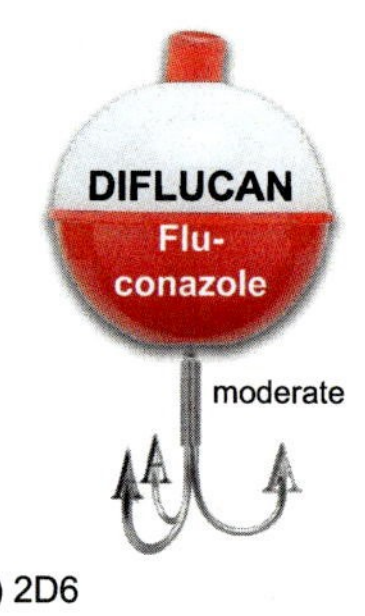

not Terbinafine (LAMISIL) 2D6

Antidepressant

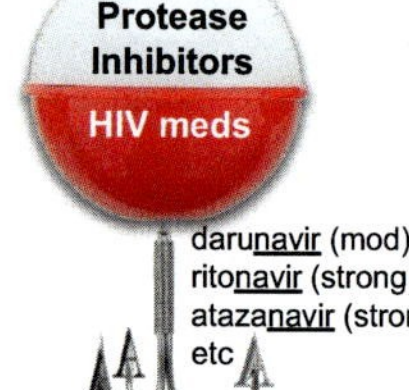

HIV meds (-avirs)

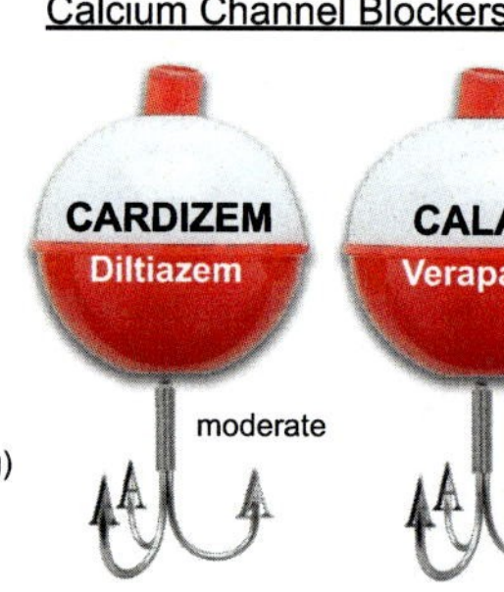

darunavir (mod)
ritonavir (strong)
atazanavir (strong)
etc

Calcium Channel Blockers

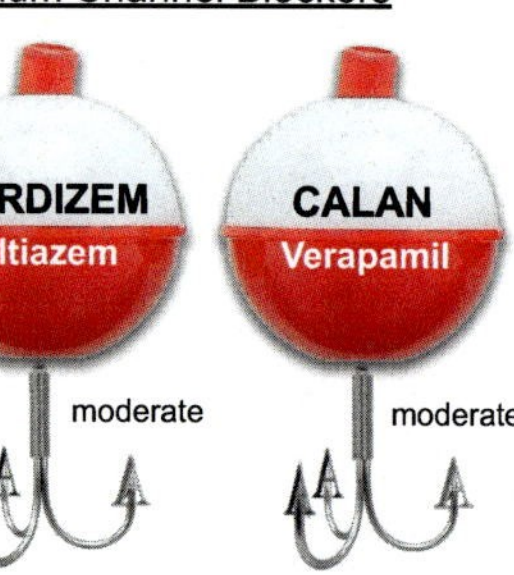

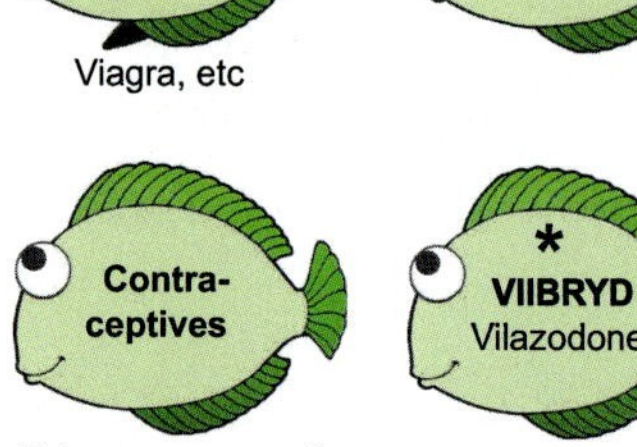

Viagra, etc

Estrogens, progestins

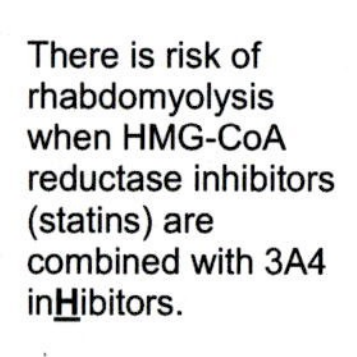

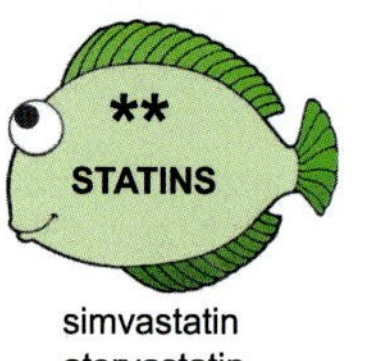

also lemborexant (Dayvigo)

Benzodiazepines

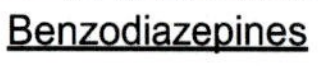

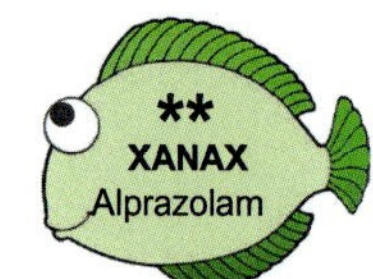

also:
Diazepam (Valium)
Estazolam (Prosom) **
Midazolam (Versed) **
Triazolam (Halcion) **
Clorazepate(Tranxene)

not:
Lorazepam (Ativan)
Oxazepam (Serax)
Temazepam (Restoril)
Clobazam (Onfi) 2C19

Antipsychotics

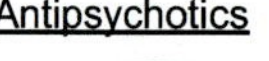

Lurasidone is metabolized exclusively by 3A4 and is contraindicated with potent 3A4 inhibitors or inducers.

Quetiapine levels are increased 6-fold by strong 3A4 inhibitors and decreased 6-fold by strong inducers.

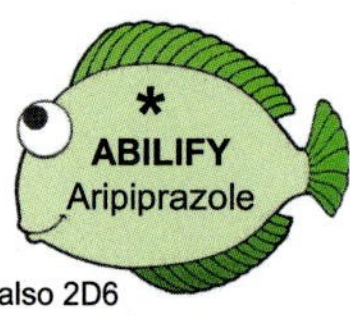

also 2D6

also 2D6

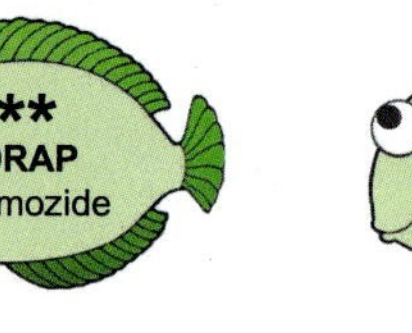

minor 3A4 substrates:
Chlorpromazine (Thorazine)
Clozapine (Clozaril)
Haloperidol (Haldol)
Iloperidone (Fanapt)
Loxapine (Loxitane)
Perphenazine (Trilafon)
Prochlorperazine
Risperidone (Risperdal)
Ziprasidone (Geodon)

not:
Asenapine (Saphris) 1A2
Fluphenazine (Prolixin) 2D6
Molindone (Moban)
Olanzapine (Zyprexa) 1A2
Paliperidone (Invega)
Promethazine (Phenergan)
Thiothixene (Navane) 1A2
Trifluoperazine (Stelazine) 1A2

There is risk of rhabdomyolysis when HMG-CoA reductase inhibitors (statins) are combined with 3A4 inHibitors.

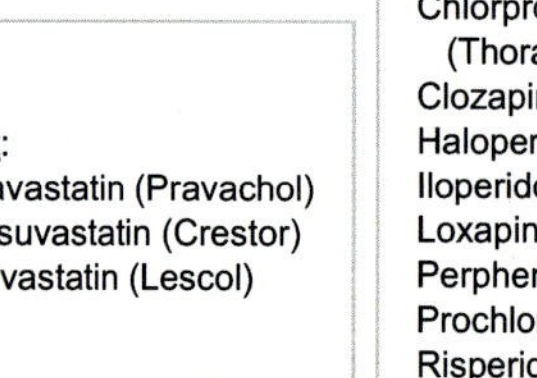

simvastatin
atorvastatin

not:
Pravastatin (Pravachol)
Rosuvastatin (Crestor)
Fluvastatin (Lescol)

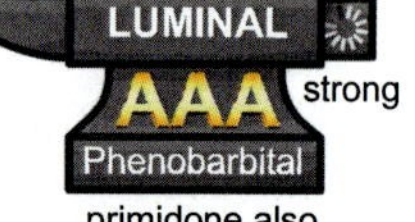

primidone also

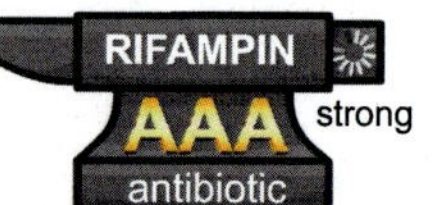

nevirapine also

weaker: Nuvigil (armodafinil)

* Dosing adjustments defined

** Has contraindications related to kinetic interactions

Conclusion: 3A4 is the workhorse of CYP metabolism, accounting for 30% of hepatic CYP activity and 70% of CYP activity in the gut. Since > 50% of drugs are 3A4 substrates, think twice before prescribing strong 3A4 inhibitors or inducers.

18% of individuals are UGT1A4 ultrarapid metabolizers; 0% are poor metabolizers

There are two phases of drug metabolism. CYP enzymes are responsible for most phase I reactions, which make chemicals less fat-soluble (i.e., more water-soluble), usually by oxidation. Phase II reactions are usually by conjugation with glucuronic acid to render the chemical even more water-soluble. Chemicals conjugated with glucuronic acid are ready to be excreted in the urine or feces. The main phase II enzyme is UDP-glucuronosyltransferase (UGT), as in "U Got Tagged!" with glucuronic acid. The most relevant specific UGT enzyme for lamotrigine metabolism is UGT1A4.

Mood stabilizers metabolized by Phase II conjugation include valproic acid (VPA) and lamotrigine (Lamictal). UGT enzymes attach more strongly to VPA than to lamotrigine.

The presence of VPA slows the rate of Phase II metabolism of lamotrigine, causing lamotrigine blood levels to double.

There are several glucuronidation pathways involving several specific UGT enzymes. In this book, UGT activity and phase II metabolism are only visualized in the context of lamotrigine and the antipsychotic lumateperone (Caplyta)—both substrates of UGT1A4. Other UGT1A4 substrates (that could be depicted as sheep) include amitriptyline, doxepin, valproate, haloperidol, clozapine, olanzapine, and asenapine. GeneSight reports UGT**1A**4 and UGT**2B**15 (easy-to-recall sequence) metabolizer genotypes.

UGT2B15 is not visualized in this book. UGT2**B**15 substrates include the "LOT" **B**enzos—lorazepam, oxazepam and temazepam. The major UGT2B15 inHibitor is VPA. Nobody is a UGT2B15 ultrarapid or poor metabolizer, although some individuals are intermediate metabolizers.

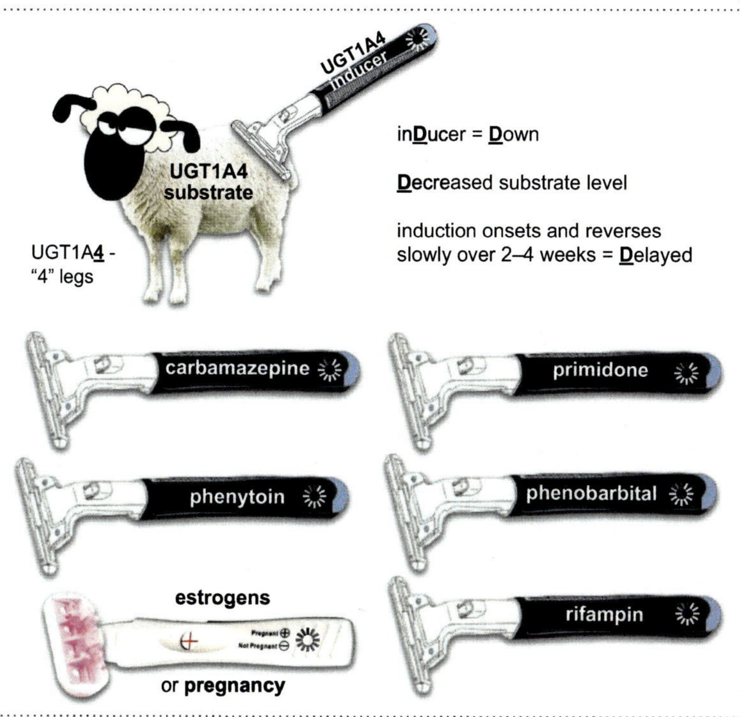

in**D**ucer = **D**own

Decreased substrate level

induction onsets and reverses slowly over 2–4 weeks = **D**elayed

in**H**ibitor = **H**igh

Increased substrate level

in**H**ibition happens within **H**ours = **H**urried

Inhibition reverses as soon as the inhibitor is cleared from the body (five half-lives of the inhibitor). In the case of VPA, 5 x 14 hours = about 3 days.

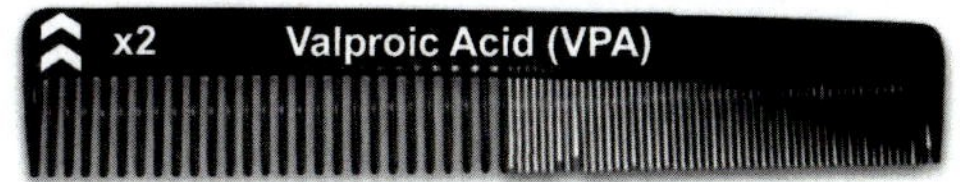

VPA doubles lamotrigine levels.

UGT1A4 substrates

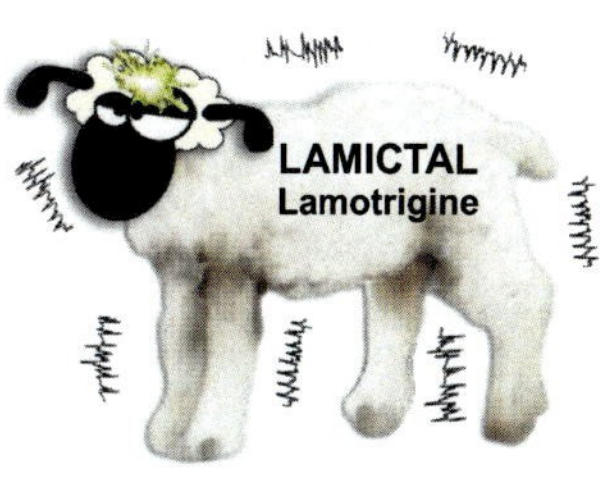

Mood stabilizer / Antiepileptic

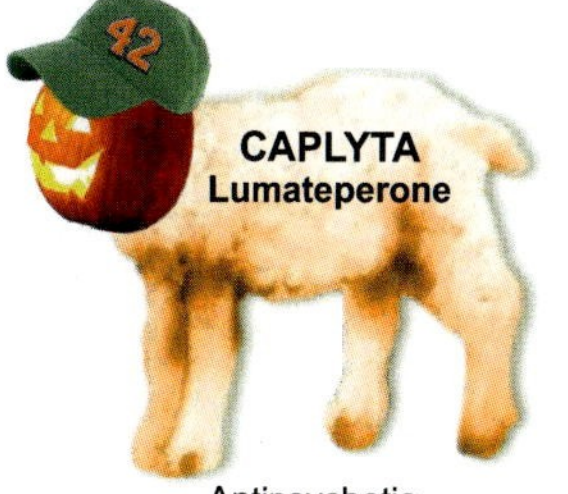

Antipsychotic

UGT1A4 ultrarapid metabolizers (UM)

Represented by a fast-shedding sheep, individuals who have a UGT1A4 ultrarapid metabolizer genotype clear UGT1A4 substrates quickly. These individuals are more likely to be non-responders to lamotrigine and lumateperone.

18% of population

Before lamotrigine became generically available, three Lamictal starter packs were available to address these interactions:

Starter pack	For those taking	Lamotrigine dose
Orange	No interacting medications	25 mg x 2 weeks, then 50 mg x 2 weeks, then 100 mg x 1 week. The usual maintenance dose starting on week 6 is 200 mg.
Blue	Valproate (Depakote)	Half strength. Maintenance dose is 100 mg QD.
Green	Carbamazepine (Tegretol) Phenytoin (Dilantin) Phenobarbital (Luminal) Primidone (Mysoline)	Double strength. Maintenance dose is 200 mg BID.

Lamotrigine and pregnancy: Lamotrigine is considered the safest anticonvulsant for pregnancy. It is non-teratogenic, other than a small risk of cleft palate.

Since **pregnancy can reduce lamotrigine levels by 50%**, it may be necessary to dose it higher during pregnancy and lower it upon childbirth. Compared with the early third trimester, postpartum lamotrigine serum levels increased an average of 172% (range 24–428%) within 5 weeks of giving birth (Clark et al, 2013).

At delivery, the mean umbilical cord lamotrigine level is ⅔ of the maternal level. In breastfed infants, the mean lamotrigine level in the child's blood is ⅓ of the maternal level. This is higher than expected with most drugs.

Conclusion: In management of bipolar disorder, lamotrigine can be combined with any mood stabilizer or antipsychotic. Lamictal plus lithium is a favorable pairing, as long as renal function is normal. The combination of lamotrigine and VPA may increase the risk of Stevens-Johnson syndrome. For patients on lamotrigine plus VPA or carbamazepine (CMZ), consider checking lamotrigine blood levels before discontinuation of VPA/CMZ and after lamotrigine dose is adjusted to account for reversal of inhibition/induction (page 7).

Non-participants

Medications that do not become significantly involved in kinetic interactions are depicted **"in a bubble"**.

Some of these medications are **"in a box"** (with a hole in it) to indicate that kinetic interactions exist, but usually do not need be taken into consideration when prescribing the medication.

Dynamic interactions still apply to bubbled/boxed medications.

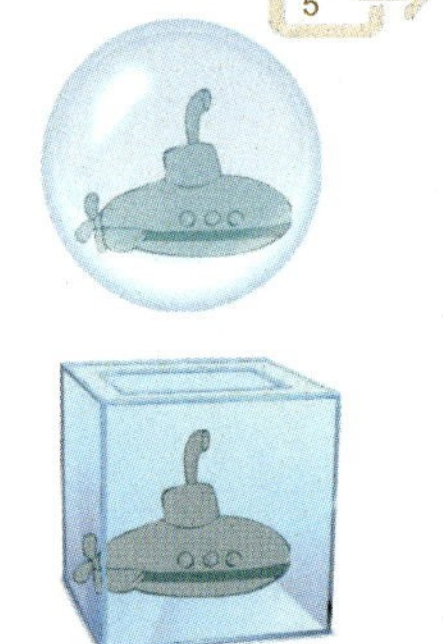

We will display medications "in a bubble" or "in a box" if they are not expected to serve as *clinically significant* substrates, inducers or inhibitors. There is a hole at the top of the boxes to suggest some degree of vulnerability to relevant kinetic interactions, but not to an extent prescribers need to routinely worry about. In general, medications that are renally cleared have relatively few drug–drug interactions because their metabolism does not rely on CYP enzymes.

For a substrate metabolized through multiple pathways, serum levels are not significantly affected by in**H**ibition of a single CYP. For instance, over half of prescription drugs are 3A4 substrates, but will not be depicted as fish (page 16) if they are multi-CYP substrates. Multi-CYP substrates are depicted in a box (not a bubble) because interactions do occur but are unlikely to matter much.

A multi-CYP substrate is more likely to be victimized by an in**D**ucer than by an in**H**ibitor. It is worthwhile to run an interaction check on a patient's medication list if they are taking a "shredder" in**D**ucer (page 7), even for the boxed medications.

A bubble/box certifies the medication is:

- ❖ No more than a weak CYP inducer or inducer, and...
- ❖ Either a multi-CYP substrate or a substrate not metabolized by any CYP

A bubble does **not** imply that a medication does not participate in dynamic interactions, because almost all drugs do. Acamprosate (Campral) and N-acetylcysteine (NAC) are rare exceptions, depicted in a double bubble.

This book contains over 270 monographs of medications with mascots designed to help you pair trade names with generic names, and to remember kinetic interactions. The mascots inside the bubbles/boxes will be introduced in subsequent chapters.

Dynamic interactions:
Not applicable to every drug in class

"Bubbled" or "boxed" medications are unlikely to be involved in clinically significant kinetic interactions:

Antipsychotics

- ❖ EPS (page 127)
- ❖ Sedation
- ❖ Weight gain
- ❖ Hyperglycemia
- ❖ QT prolongation (page 82)
- ❖ Myelosuppression
- ❖ Anticholinergic
- ❖ Lowers seizure threshold

HAPPENS
INVEGA
Paliperidone

GEODON
Ziprasidone

Loxapine

Molindone

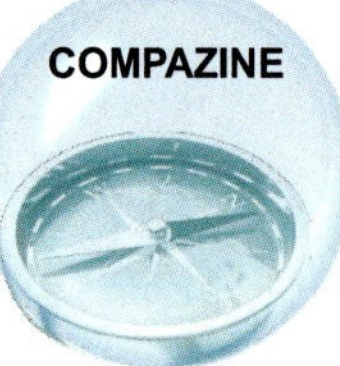

Prochlorperazine

Antidepressants

- ❖ Serotonergic (most)
- ❖ QT prolongation (page 82)
- ❖ Sedation (some)
- ❖ Weight gain
- ❖ Hyponatremia
- ❖ Antiplatelet
- ❖ Hypo/hypertension
- ❖ Anticholinergic

Trazodone

Mirtazapine

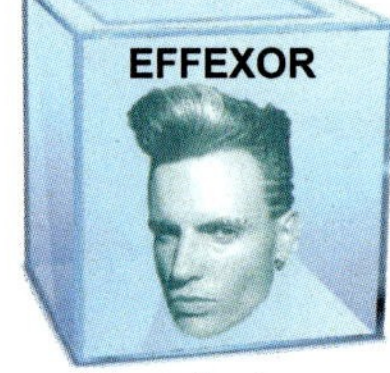

Venlafaxine

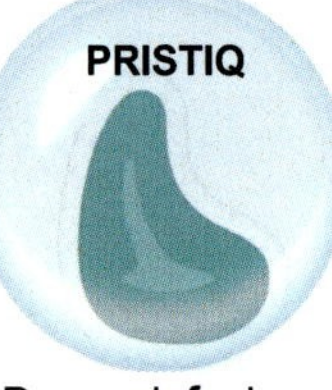

Desvenlafaxine

Milnacipran

Antiepileptics

- ❖ Sedation
- ❖ Stevens-Johnson Syndrome (page 28)
- ❖ Hyponatremia (page 33)
- ❖ Acidosis
- ❖ Myelosuppression

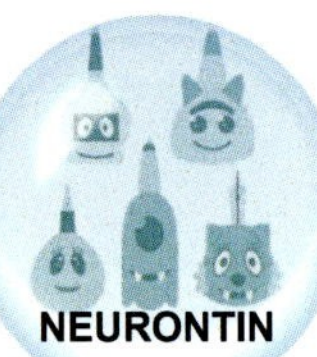

Gabapentin

Levetiracetam

Pregabalin

Lacosamide

Vigabatrin

Sedatives

- ❖ Sedation
- ❖ Respiratory depression

Lorazepam

Oxazepam

Temazepam

Brexanolone

Sodium Oxybate

The 3 "LOT" benzos—No CYP interactions but levels may double with VPA (Depakote) due to UGT2B15 inHibition

Dynamic interactions:
Not applicable to every drug in class

"Bubbled" or "boxed" medications are unlikely to be involved in clinically significant kinetic interactions:

Antihistamines
- ❖ Anticholinergic
  - constipation
  - urinary retention
  - cognitive impairment
- ❖ Sedation

Diphenhydramine

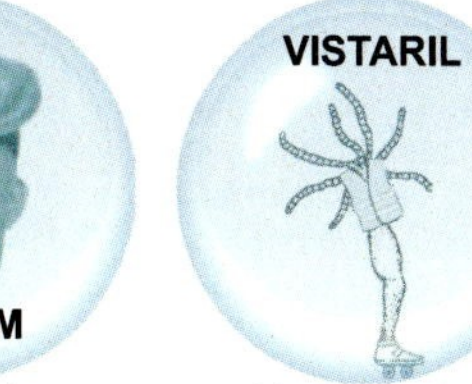

Doxylamine

Hydroxyzine

ANTIVERT
Meclizine

Cyproheptadine

Anticholinergics
- ❖ Anticholinergic
  - constipation
  - urinary retention
  - cognitive impairment
- ❖ Sedation

Benztropine

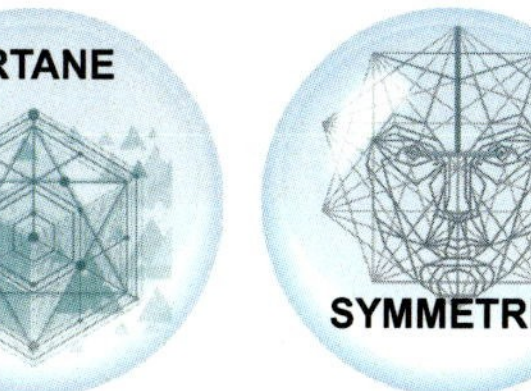

Trihexyphenidyl

Amantadine

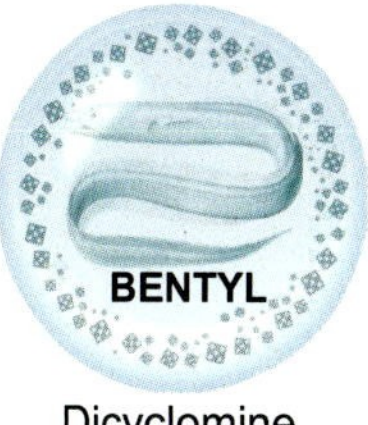

Dicyclomine

Glycopyrrolate

Cognitive Enhancers
- ❖ Cholinergic
- ❖ Lowers seizure threshold

EXELON
Rivastigmine

RAZADYNE
Galantamine

NAMENDA
Memantine

NICORETTE
Nicotine

The hydrocarbons in smoked tobacco in**D**uce 1A2. Nicotine itself does not.

Addiction Medicine

For some, dynamic interactions are part of their mechanism of action, e.g., opioid antagonism by naltrexone and naloxone.

Varenicline

Naltrexone

Naloxone

Acamprosate

Double bubble: acamprosate has no known kinetic or dynamic interactions.

Sympatholytics
- ❖ Hypotension
- ❖ Bradycardia
- ❖ Sedation / fatigue

Clonidine

Prazosin

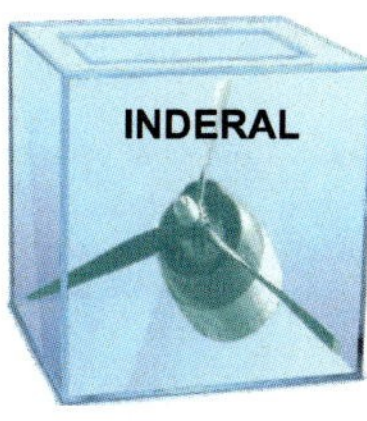

Propranolol

Dexmedetomidine

Spasmolytics
- ❖ Sedation
- ❖ Hypotension
- ❖ Anticholinergics
- ❖ Lowers seizure threshold

Methocarbamol

Baclofen

Metaxalone

Stimulants
- ❖ Hypertensive
- ❖ Dopaminergic
- ❖ Noradrenergic
- ❖ Lowers seizure threshold

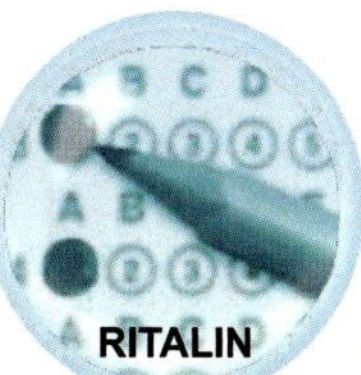

Methylphenidate

Solriamfetol

Supplements

Double bubble: NAC has no known kinetic or dynamic interactions.

N-acetylcysteine

L-Methylfolate

RELEVANT PHARMACOKINETIC INTERACTIONS, general overview

INDUCERS	INHIBITORS	SUBSTRATES
InDuction Decreases substrates slowly, over 2 to 4 weeks (Delayed). With smoked tobacco, induction (1A2) starts in 3 days and reverses in about 1 week.	InHibition increases substrate levels (High), happening within Hours (Hurried). Inhibition reverses as soon as the inhibitor is cleared from the body (five half-lives of the inhibitor).	"Victims" of inducers and inhibitors 
1A2 inducers Ψ **Tobacco/Cannabis** (faster on/off) Ψ Carbamazepine Ψ Phenytoin 	1A2 inhibitors Ψ **Fluvoxamine** Ciprofloxacin 	1A2 substrates Ψ Asenapine Ψ **Clozapine** Ψ Duloxetine Ψ Olanzapine Ψ **Ramelteon** Ψ Thiothixene 
2B6 inducers Ψ Carbamazepine Rifampin HIV MEDS 	2B6 inhibitors Ψ Orphenadrine (Norflex) 	2B6 substrates HIV MEDS CANCER MEDS Ψ Bupropion Ψ Ketamine Ψ Methadone Ψ Selegiline 
2C9 inducers **Rifampin** Ψ St John's Wort 	2C9 inhibitors **Fluconazole** 	2C9 substrates Ψ Valproate (VPA) 
2C19 inducers Ψ Phenobarbital Rifampin Apalutamide  **Ultrarapid metabolizer (UM)** genotype (10% of population) 	2C19 inhibitors Ψ **Cannabidiol** (CBD) **Fluconazole** Ψ Fluoxetine Ψ Fluvoxamine  **Poor metabolizer (PM)** genotype (10% of population) 	2C19 substrates Ψ Citalopram Ψ Diazepam Ψ Escitalopram Ψ Phenobarbital Ψ Phenytoin Ψ Sertraline Ψ Methadone Warfarin 
2D6 inducers None **Ultrarapid Metabolizer (UM)** genotype (5% of population)	2D6 inhibitors Ψ **Bupropion** Ψ Duloxetine Ψ **Fluoxetine** Ψ **Paroxetine** **Quinidine** **Poor metabolizer (PM)** genotype (10% of population)	2D6 substrates Ψ Tricyclics (TCAs) Ψ Aripiprazole Ψ Atomoxetine Ψ Brexpiprazole Ψ Bupropion-OH Ψ Codeine *PRODRUG* Ψ Deutetrabenazine Ψ Dextromethorphan Ψ Duloxetine Ψ Haloperidol Ψ Iloperidone Ψ **Perphenazine** Ψ **Pimozide** Ψ Risperidone Tamoxifen *PRODRUG* Ψ Tetrabenazine Ψ **Thioridazine** Ψ Tramadol *PRODRUG* Ψ Vortioxetine
3A4 inducers Ψ **Carbamazepine** Ψ Modafinil Ψ **Phenobarbital** Ψ **Phenytoin** **Rifampin** Ψ St John's Wort 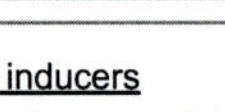 	3A4 inhibitors Protease Inhibitors (HIV) Clarithromycin Diltiazem Grapefruit juice **Ketoconazole** **Itraconazole** Ψ **Nefazodone** Verapamil 	3A4 substrates Immunosuppressants Progestins Ψ Alprazolam Ψ Aripiprazole Ψ Brexpiprazole Ψ Buprenorphine Ψ **Buspirone** Ψ Carbamazepine Ψ Cariprazine Ψ Chlordiazepoxide Ψ Clonazepam Ψ **Fentanyl** Ψ **Flibanserin** Ψ **Lemborexant** Ψ **Lumateperone** Ψ **Lurasidone** Ψ Pimavanserin Ψ Pimozide Ψ **Quetiapine** Sildenafil **Simvastatin** Ψ Suvorexant Tadalafil Ψ Valbenazine Ψ **Vilazodone**
UGT inducers Ψ Carbamazepine Estrogens Ψ Phenobarbital Ψ Phenytoin Rifampin 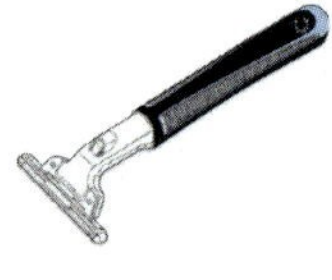	UGT inhibitors Ψ **Valproate (VPA)** 	UGT substrates Ψ **Lamotrigine** Ψ **Lumateperone** 

Lithium levels	Decreased by:	Increased by:		
	Acetazolamide Ψ Caffeine Mannitol Theophylline Ψ Topiramate Ψ Zonisamide 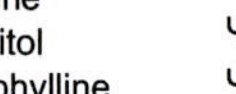 	**Thiazides:** - HCTZ - Chlorthalidone	**NSAIDS:** - Celebrex - Ibuprofen - Indomethacin - Naproxen - Diclofenac	ACE Inhibitors "-prils" ARBs "-sartans" Antimicrobials: - Tetracyclines - Metronidazole 

Ψ = CNS meds (psychoactive)

Pharmacokinetic Drug-Drug Interactions

INDUCERS

InDuction decreases (Down) substrates slowly, over 2 to 4 weeks* (Delayed).

Inducer	CYP
Ψ Armodafinil	(3A4) weak
Apalutamide (prostate cancer)	2C19, 3A4 & (2C9)
Ψ Cannabis	1A2 fast
Chargrilled meat	1A2
Ψ Carbamazepine (Tegretol)	3A4, 2B6 & (1A2)
Efavirenz (HIV)	3A4, 2B6
Enzalutamide (prostate cancer)	3A4, 2C9 & 2C19
Estradiol	UGT
Ψ Modafinil	3A4
Nevirapine	2B6 (3A4)
Ψ Phenobarbital (Luminal)	3A4 (1A2), (2B6, 2C9) & UGT
Ψ Phenytoin (Dilantin)	3A4 (1A2), (2B6), UGT
Ψ Primidone (Mysoline) metab to phenobarb	3A4 (1A2), (2B6, 2C9) & UGT
Rifampin (Rifadin)	2C19, 3A4, 2B6, 2C9 (1A2) & UGT
Ritonavir (HIV)	2B6 (2C19) (1A2, 2C9)
Ψ St John's Wort	1A2, 2C9 & 3A4
Ψ Tobacco	1A2 fast
Ψ Topiramate ≥200 mg	(3A4)

inDuction reverses gradually over a few weeks* after the inducer is discontinued.

*With smoking (tobacco or cannabis), induction is faster (a few days).

INHIBITORS

InHibition increases substrate levels (High). Inhibition happens within Hours (Hurried).

Inhibitor	CYP
Amiodarone	(2C9, 2D6, 3A4)
Ψ Asenapine	(2D6) weak
Ψ Bupropion	2D6
Ψ Cannabidiol	2C19, UGT
Cimetidine	(multi) weak
Ciprofloxacin	1A2, (3A4)
Clarithromycin	3A4
Clopidogrel	(2B6)
Darunavir (HIV)	3A4, (2D6)
Diltiazem	3A4, (2D6)
Ψ Duloxetine	2D6
Efavirenz (HIV)	2C9, 2C19
Erythromycin	3A4
Esomeprazole	(2C19) weak
Fluconazole	2C9, 2C19, 3A4
Ψ Fluoxetine	2D6, 2C19
Ψ Fluvoxamine (Luvox)	1A2, 2C19, & (3A4, 2C9)
Grapefruit juice	3A4
Isoniazid	(3A4) weak
Indinavir	3A4
Itraconazole	3A4
Ketoconazole	3A4, (2C19)
Ψ Methadone	(2D6) weak
Ψ Modafinil	(2C19) weak
Nelfinavir	3A4
Omeprazole	2C19
Ψ Nefazodone	3A4
Ψ Orphenadrine	2B6
Ψ Paroxetine	2D6
Quinidine	2D6, (3A4)
Ritonavir	3A4 Black Box
Ψ Sertraline ≥150mg	(2D6)
Terbinafine	2D6
Ψ Thioridazine	2D6
Ψ Valproate (VPA)	UGT-1A & -2B
Voriconazole	3A4,2C19,(2C9)
Verapamil	3A4, (1A2)

InHibition is reversed as soon as the inhibitor is cleared, which will be about 5 half-lives after it is discontinued.

UGT & UGT-1A refer to UGT1A4. UGT-2B refers to UGT2B15.

( ) = weak inducer/inhibitor; less susceptible substrate

Ψ = CNS medication (psychoactive)

SUBSTRATES

"Victims" of inducers and inhibitors

In general, substrates that are metabolized through only one pathway are more vulnerable to drug interactions. For drugs metabolized by multiple CYPs, strong inDuction of a single CYP is likely to reduce substrate levels, but inHibition of one CYP is unlikely to significantly increase substrate levels.

Substrate	CYP
Apixaban	3A4
Atazanavir (HIV)	3A4
Ψ Alprazolam	3A4
Ψ Amitriptyline	2D6, 2C19
Amlodipine	3A4
Ψ Amoxapine	2D6
Ψ Amphetamine salts	(2D6)
Ψ Aripiprazole	2D6, 3A4
Ψ Armodafinil	3A4
Ψ Asenapine	(1A2)
Ψ Atomoxetine	2D6, (2C19)
Atorvastatin	3A4
Avanafil	3A4
Ψ Brexpiprazole	2D6, 3A4
Ψ Buprenorphine	3A4
Ψ Bupropion	2B6; 2D6 (OH-)
Ψ Buspirone	3A4, (2D6)
Ψ Caffeine	1A2 (etc)
Ψ Carbamazepine	3A4
Ψ Cariprazine	3A4, (2D6)
Ψ Carisoprodol	2C19
Carvedilol	2D6 (etc)
Celecoxib	2C9, (3A4)
Ψ Chlordiazepoxide	3A4
Ψ Chlorpromazine	2D6, (1A2, 3A4)
Ψ Citalopram	2C19, (3A4,2D6)
Clarithromycin	3A4
Ψ Clomipramine	2D6, 2C19, 1A2
Ψ Clonazepam	3A4
Clopidogrel	2C19, (3A4)
Ψ Clozapine	1A2 (2D6, etc)
Ψ Codeine *2D6 prodrug	*2D6, (3A4)
Ψ Cyclobenzaprine	1A2, (2D6, 3A4)
Cyclophosphamide	2B6, 2C19
Cyclosporine	3A4 (etc)
Ψ Desipramine	2D6, (1A2)
Ψ Deutetrabenazine	2D6
Ψ Dextromethorphan	2D6 (etc)
Ψ Diazepam	2C19, 3A4
Diclofenac	multi
Diltiazem	3A4 (2C19,3A4)
Ψ Doxepin	2D6, 2C19 (etc)
Ψ Donepezil	(2D6, 3A4)
Ψ Duloxetine	2D6, 1A2
Efavirenz (HIV)	2B6, 3A4
Ψ Escitalopram	2C19,(3A4,2D6)
Esomeprazole	2C19, (3A4)
Estradiol	1A2, 2C9, 3A4
Ψ Eszopiclone	3A4
Ψ Fentanyl 3A4 Black Box	3A4 (etc)
Flecainide	2D6, 1A2
Ψ Flibanserin 3A4 Black Box	3A4, 2C9, 2C19
Ψ Fluoxetine	2D6, 2C9 (etc)
Ψ Fluphenazine	2D6
Ψ Flurazepam	3A4
Fluvastatin	2C9 (2B6, 3A4)
Ψ Fluvoxamine	2D6, 1A2
Ψ Galantamine	(2D6, 3A4)
Glimepiride	2C9
Glipizide	2C9
Glyburide	2C9
Ψ Guanfacine	3A4
Ψ Haloperidol	2D6, 3A4, (1A2)
Ψ Hydrocodone Black Box	3A4
Ifosfamide	2B6 (& others)
Ψ Iloperidone	2D6, (3A4)
Ψ Imipramine	2D6, 2C19 (etc)
Ψ Ketamine	2B6, 2C9, 3A4
Ψ Lamotrigine	UGT
Lansoprazole	2C19, 3A4
Ψ Lemborexant	3A4
Ψ Levomilnacipran	3A4, (2D6)
Ψ Lorazepam	UGT-2B (VPA)
Losartan	2C9, 3A4
Ψ Loxapine	(1A2, 2D6,3A4)
Ψ Lumateperone	3A4, UGT-1A
Ψ Lurasidone *contraind*	3A4
Medroxyprogesterone	3A4
Meloxicam	2C9, (3A4)
Ψ Meperidine Black Box	3A4
Ψ Methadone	3A4, 2B6, (etc)
Ψ Methamphetamine	2D6
Metoprolol	2D6, (2C19)
Mexiletine	1A2, 2D6
Ψ Midazolam	3A4, (2B6)
Ψ Mirtazapine	2D6, 3A4, 1A2
Ψ Modafinil	3A4 (2D6)
Nevirapine	3A4 (2B6, 2D6)
Ψ Nefazodone	3A4; 2D6 mCPP
Nifedipine	3A4, (2D6)
Norethindrone	3A4
Ψ Nortriptyline	2D6 (etc)
Ψ Olanzapine	1A2; (2D6)
Omeprazole	2C19 (etc)
Ψ Oxazepam	UGT-2B (VPA)
Ψ Oxycodone	3A4, (2D6)
Pantoprazole	2C19,(2D6, 3A4)
Ψ Paroxetine	2D6
Ψ Perphenazine	2D6 (etc)
Ψ Phenobarbital	2C19,(2C9)
Ψ Phenytoin	2C9, 2C19,(3A4)
Ψ Pimavanserin	3A4
Ψ Pimozide	2D6, 3A4 (1A2)
Piroxicam	2C9
Ψ Promethazine	(2B6, 2D6)
Propafenone	2D6, (1A2, 3A4)
Ψ Propofol	2B6 (etc)
Ψ Propranolol	2D6, 1A2,(2C19)
Ψ Protriptyline	2D6
Ψ Quetiapine	3A4, (2D6)
Ψ Ramelteon	1A2 (3A4,2C19)
Ψ Risperidone	2D6, (3A4)
Rivaroxaban	3A4
Ψ Selegiline	2B6 (etc)
Ψ Sertraline	2C19 (2B6,2D6)
Sildenafil	3A4, (etc)
Simvastatin	3A4
Ψ Suvorexant	3A4
Tacrolimus	3A4
Tadalafil	3A4
Tamoxifen *2D6 prodrug	*2D6, 3A4, 2C9
Ψ Tasimelteon	1A2, 3A4
Ψ Temazepam	UGT-2B (VPA)
Ψ Tetrabenazine	2D6
Theophylline	1A2, (3A4)
Ψ Thioridazine	2D6, (2C19)
Ψ Thiothixene	1A2
Ψ Tiagabine	3A4
Ψ Tizanidine	1A2
Tolbutamide	2C9, (2C19)
Ψ Tramadol *2D6 prodrug*	3A4,(2D6*; 2B6)
Ψ Trazodone	3A4 (2D6 mCPP)
Ψ Triazolam	3A4
Ψ Trifluoperazine	1A2
Ψ Trimipramine	2D6, 2C19, 3A4
Ψ Valproate (VPA)	(multi); Aspirin*
Ψ Valbenazine	3A4 (2D6)
Vardenafil	3A4
Ψ Venlafaxine	2D6, 3A4,(2C19)
Ψ Vilazodone	3A4,(2C19,2D6)
Vincristine	3A4
Voriconazole	2C9, 2C19, 3A4
Ψ Vortioxetine	2D6, 3A4, etc
Warfarin	2C9, 2C19,(3A4)
Ψ Zaleplon	(3A4)
Ψ Zolpidem	3A4 (etc)

Lithium levels

LITHIUM

Decreased by:

Acetazolamide
Ψ Caffeine
Mannitol
Theophylline
Ψ Topiramate
Ψ Zonisamide (weak)

Increased by:

Benazepril
Celecoxib
Chlorthalidone
Diclofenac
Doxycycline
Enalapril
Etodolac
HCTZ
Ibuprofen
Indomethacin
Irbesartan Lisinopril
Tetracycline
Losartan
Metronidazole
Minocycline
Naproxen
Olmesartan
Ramipril
Valsartan

With high-dose aspirin, Depakote (VPA) will be stronger than suggested by total VPA level because aspirin (highly protein-bound) bumps VPA off of albumin (page 29).

#40 most prescribed US
1993
$4–$250

Chemical structure

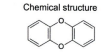

Generic Name (TRADE NAME)

[pronunciation]

mnemonic phrase

❖ Class of medication
❖ Mechanism of action

100
<u>200</u>
400
mg

Year the drug was introduced to the U.S. market

Monographs focus on the unique aspects of the individual drug, to be considered in context of the medication class. Most of the medications in this book are psychotropic, i.e., capable of affecting the mind, emotions and behavior.

Price range for a month's supply of the generic (if available) version of the drug. The price is generally applicable to the most common prescription, which would be #30 for drugs usually dosed QD, #60 for those dosed BID, and #90 for those usually dosed TID. The applicable milligram strength is the number underlined in the upper righthand corner. The bottom dollar value is the lowest GoodRx price, available with a coupon at select pharmacies. The high dollar value is the average retail price circa 2019–2020. The wide price range from pharmacy to pharmacy shows the importance of checking a source like GoodRx before filling a script for cash.

Each monograph features a mascot designed to pair the drug's generic name with the most common U.S. trade name.

A representative pill of the underlined strength, either a branded or generic version. The main purpose is to show whether we're talking capsules or tablets. For tablets, we try to show the side with score lines. If no score lines are shown, assume that the pill is not intended to be split. For any splittable psychotropic medication, giving a half dose for the first two days may be a good idea, depending on acuity of symptoms.

Dosing: When provided, dosing recommendations are applicable to healthy adults. Refer to other sources for pediatric recommendations. Older adults should generally be given lower doses. Doses may need to be modified when considering kinetic/dynamic interactions, pharmacogenetics, body weight, and renal/hepatic insufficiency.

Boxes like this contain contextual information about the drug.

A link to a page with relevant content looks like this:

3A4 substrate

The box with rounded corners contains a visual hybrid of the mascot and CYP interaction mnemonic(s). Over half of prescription drugs are metabolized by 3A4, so there are plenty of fish.

Recurring Visuals

Dopaminergic medication for Restless Legs Syndrome (RLS)

Medication for Parkinsonian tremor

Antiepileptic drug (AED)

Medication that may cause agitation (various angry faces)

Barbiturate

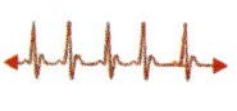

QT interval prolonging medication

Tricyclic antidepressant (TCA)

Antipsychotic (various spooky characters)

Benzodiazepine

Non-benzodiazepine (Z-drug)

Antidepressant (rain cloud)

MAOI Inhibitor (Chairman MAO)

Anticholinergic with CNS effects (Mad as a hatter)

Antihistamine (push pin) - "anti-hiss-tamine"

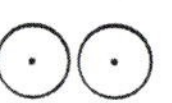

Opioid (pinpoint pupils)

Opioid antagonist (dilated pupils)

Medication with stimulant properties/ wakefulness promoting agent

Antihypertensive/sympatholytic - high pressure spray representing blood pressure

Amphetamine (Adderall, etc)

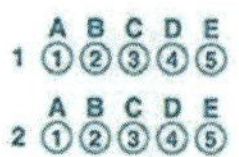

Methylphenidates (Ritalin, etc) - Scantron sheet on "Math final date"

Cholinergic medication - "SLUDGE buckets"

Calcium channel blocker

Mood Stabilizers

Mood stabilizers are used to treat bipolar disorder (type I and II). They can also be used off-label for mood swings characteristic of borderline personality disorder, preferably as an adjunct to Dialectical Behavior Therapy (DBT). With the exception of lithium, all mood stabilizers are antiepileptic drugs (AEDs). When stopping any AED, it is important to taper gradually. Abrupt discontinuation of an AED may cause a seizure, even with individuals without epilepsy.

Mood Stabilizer/monthly cost		Blood levels	Recommended lab work	Comments
Lithium Lithium IR (ESKALITH) Lithium ER (LITHOBID) Lithium Citrate Syrup	 $5 $20 $100	0.6–1.0 for maintenance 1.0–1.4 for acute mania	Lithium level TSH (hypothyroidism) CMP (renal insufficiency) EKG if cardiac disease Pregnancy test (Ebstein's anomaly)	Most effective medication for prevention of mania recurrence and lowering risk of suicide; Narrow therapeutic index; Risk of renal damage; Neuroprotective
Valproate Divalproex DR (DEPAKOTE) Divalproex ER (DEPAKOTE ER) Valproic Acid (DEPAKENE) syrup	 $15 $40 $25	50–100 for maintenance 80–120 for acute mania	Valproic acid (VPA) level CMP (liver) CBC (thrombocytopenia) Ammonia if suspicion of encephalopathy Pregnancy test (low IQ, neural tube)	Risk of hepatotoxicity; Significant tremor is possible (reversible)
Lamotrigine (LAMICTAL) Lamotrigine ER (LAMICTAL XR)	$10 $50	Not required (2–20)	None	Few side effects or health risks; Must titrate slowly to avoid SJS, making it useless for acute mania.
Carbamazepine (TEGRETOL) Carbamazepine XR (CARBATROL)	$40 $50	4–12 for seizure disorder undefined for bipolar disorder	Carbamazepine level (optional) CBC (anemia, neutropenia) CMP (sodium, liver) HLA-B*1502 for Asians (SJS) Pregnancy test (neural tube defects)	"Shredder" in**D**ucer of several CYP enzymes, **D**ecreasing levels of numerous medications; Blood levels required for treatment of epilepsy but not for bipolar maintenance.
Oxcarbazepine (TRILEPTAL)	$25	Not required (15–35)	Metabolic panel (low sodium) HLA-B*1502 for Asians (SJS)	Off-label for bipolar; Risk of hyponatremia

SJS = Stevens-Johnson Syndrome

Antiepileptics with (possible) weak mood stabilizing properties

Clinical guidelines generally consider these two medications to be non-mood stabilizing antiepileptics. However, some psychiatrists regard them as adjunctive stabilizers for bipolar disorder. At worst they are unlikely to destabilize mood, which is something that cannot be said of all antiepileptics. These can prescribed at low dose for anxiety, off-label.

Antiepileptic/monthly cost		Levels needed	Recommended lab work	Comments
Gabapentin (NEURONTIN)	$10	No	None	Off-label for anxiety, neuropathic pain, borderline personality, alcoholism, PTSD nightmares
Topiramate (TOPAMAX)	$10	No	CMP looking for low bicarbonate (CO_2) which indicates acidosis; Pregnancy test (hypospadias, oral clefts)	Causes cognitive impairment ≥ 200 mg; Off-label for weight loss

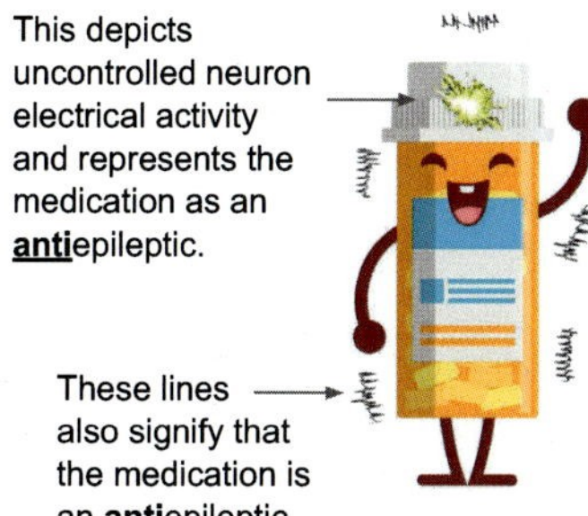

This depicts uncontrolled neuron electrical activity and represents the medication as an **anti**epileptic.
These lines also signify that the medication is an **anti**epileptic.

Antipsychotics are not considered mood stabilizers, but are used for similar purposes, often in combination with a stabilizer. Antipsychotics work faster than stabilizers to relieve acute mania. For acute mania, it is best to hospitalize the patient and use a stabilizer + antipsychotic + benzodiazepine. To minimize sedatives while treating mania, consider blue-light blocking glasses (as described on page 48) for experimental "virtual darkness therapy".

The benzo can be tapered off (or made PRN) while mania is resolving, and it may be possible to taper the antipsychotic within a few months. Keep the stabilizer on board to prevent recurrence of mania or replace it with lamotrigine (Lamictal) for maintenance. Lamotrigine is safer, has fewer side effects, and is effective for prevention of manic and depressive episodes. Antidepressants may be useful for bipolar depression in the short term but may destabilize mood when used long term for individuals with bipolar disorder.

Other than lithium, all mood stabilizers are AEDs, but not all AEDs are stabilizers. Bipolar patients on a non-stabilizing antiepileptic should, if possible, be switched to valproate, lamotrigine, carbamazepine, or oxcarbazepine (in collaboration with the neurologist).

The following medication monographs include a mechanism of action in the upper right-hand corner. Realize, however, the usual AED has several mechanisms of unclear significance. In general, AEDs enhance GABA activity and/or decrease glutamate activity. GABA is the brain's principal inhibitory neurotransmitter, while glutamate is the principal excitatory neurotransmitter. Several AEDs block voltage-gated sodium and/or voltage-gated calcium channels of presynaptic neurons.

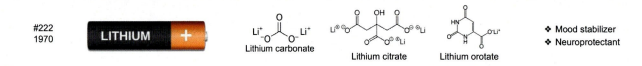

#222
1970

LITHIUM

Li⁺ Lithium carbonate

Lithium citrate

Lithium orotate

❖ Mood stabilizer
❖ Neuroprotectant

FDA-approved for:

- ❖ Acute mania
- ❖ Bipolar disorder (maintenance)

Used off-label for:

- ❖ Depression
- ❖ Suicidal ideation
- ❖ Dementia
- ❖ Alcoholism
- ❖ Agitation
- ❖ Headaches
- ❖ Neutropenia
- ❖ SIADH
- ❖ Longevity

Lithium is the gold standard treatment for bipolar disorder. It is superior to all medications at preventing suicide, reducing risk 5-fold for individuals with recurrent unipolar depression and 6-fold for those with bipolar disorder (Tondo et al, 2016). It works by several mechanisms that are not entirely understood.

Lithium is an element on the periodic table, classified as an alkali metal. Its atomic number is 3, making it the 3rd lightest element. Lithium was one of the first three elements in existence with the big bang (along with helium and hydrogen) over 13 billion years ago.

Lithium citrate was added to 7-Up (originally known as Bib-Label Lithiated Lemon-Lime Soda) from 1929–1950. The "7" refers to Lithium's atomic mass. Prescription lithium is available as lithium citrate syrup but is usually dispensed as lithium carbonate tablets or capsules.

FDA-approved in 1970, lithium is the only mood stabilizer that is not an antiepileptic. Antiepileptics raise seizure threshold. Lithium modestly decreases seizure threshold, making seizures slightly more likely to occur.

Lithium is neuroprotective, i.e., keeps neurons from dying. It is arguably an essential trace nutrient for mental wellbeing. Small amounts of lithium are present in vegetables and drinking water. Higher amounts of naturally occurring lithium in drinking water have been associated with decreased rates of suicide and violent crime (GN Schrauzer et al, 1990). Lithium has been shown to extend healthy lifespan of *Drosophila* fruit flies by about 8% (Castillo-Quan et al, 2016). Long-term exposure to low dose lithium appears to promote longevity in humans (Zarse et al, 2011). Lithium is an effective treatment for Alzheimer's disease (Mauer et al, 2014) and might prevent pre-dementia from progressing to Alzheimer's disease (Forlenza et al, 2011). The mechanism of neuroprotection and mood stabilization appears to involve brain-derived neurotrophic factor (BDNF).

Lithium is a first-line add-on for treatment-resistant unipolar depression, usually at a low to moderate dose. 68% of depressed patients over age 65 responded to lithium augmentation, improving faster than younger individuals. 47% of those < 65 responded (Buspavanich et al, 2019). Lithium is used off-label for prevention of migraine, cluster, and vascular headaches. Lithium increases white blood cell (WBC) count, making it a treatment option for neutropenia, including clozapine-induced neutropenia. Lithium inhibits antidiuretic hormone (ADH) and can be used to counter syndrome of inappropriate ADH secretion (SIADH).

7-up contained lithium until 1950

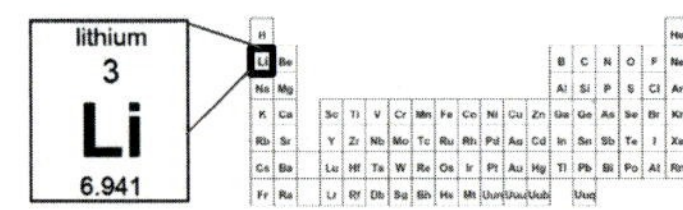

Lithium is renally cleared, unmetabolized. As an element, there is nothing it could be metabolized to. Therefore it is not involved in CYP enzyme interactions. Lithium is subject to kinetic interactions when other drugs affect the rate of lithium clearance by the kidneys. Lithium has a narrow therapeutic index, i.e., the toxic range is not far from the therapeutic range. A **black box warning** advises to start lithium only if a facility is available for prompt serum level testing. Signs of lithium toxicity include tremor, diarrhea, vomiting, abdominal pain, weakness, and sedation. Consequences of lithium toxicity may include renal damage, seizure, and coma.

Although toxic lithium levels can result in cardiac conduction delays, at therapeutic doses lithium is cardioprotective and lowers the risk of myocardial infarction. Lithium does not increase risk of stroke, which cannot be said of carbamazepine (Chen et al, 2019).

To avoid lithium toxicity, patients should be advised to avoid NSAIDS (ibuprofen, naproxen) and instead use aspirin or acetaminophen for pain. Patients should also remind their other doctors that they are on lithium, especially when diuretics or blood pressure medications are discussed. The most significant contributors to lithium toxicity are NSAIDS and thiazide diuretics, including hydrochlorothiazide (HCTZ) and chlorthalidone. See page 26 for the full list of "battery chargers" that increase lithium levels (ACE inhibitors, ARBs, metronidazole, etc).

Lithium side effects are dose-dependent, including weight gain, fine tremor, acne, excessive thirst, and frequent urination. If thirst and polyuria are extreme, the cause may be lithium-induced nephrogenic diabetes insipidus (deficient response by kidneys to ADH). If nausea is a problem, reduce dose or switch to Lithium ER (Lithobid). Otherwise, immediate-release lithium is preferable for maintenance treatment. Taking the entire daily dose of immediate-release lithium at bedtime reduces polyuria and decreases the risk of renal problems (Gitlin et al, 2016) by giving the kidneys a break during daytime.

Lithium increases the incidence of hypothyroidism 6-fold. Since about 15% of lithium-treated patients will become hypothyroid, TSH should be monitored routinely so levothyroxine (Synthroid) can be added if TSH gets high. Renal function needs to be monitored with a metabolic panel (BMP or CMP). When lithium is combined with a 1st generation antipsychotic, extrapyramidal symptoms (EPS) and neuroleptic malignant syndrome (NMS) may be more likely, which is considered a neurotoxic effect of unknown mechanism. Rarely, lithium may contribute to serotonin syndrome. For individuals over age 50, it is recommended to get an EKG prior to starting (standard dose) lithium because arrhythmias are possible. Very rarely lithium is associated with intracranial hypertension (pseudotumor cerebri), which presents as headache and ringing in the ears with heartbeats. If untreated, intracranial hypertension can lead to loss of vision.

When taken during the first trimester of pregnancy, lithium poses a low risk (1 in 1,500) of Ebstein's anomaly, a cardiac condition involving the tricuspid valve. Lithium is certainly less teratogenic than valproic acid (Depakote, Depakene) or carbamazepine (Tegretol). Lithium is considered safe for fetal development after the first trimester, but maintaining steady lithium levels during pregnancy and after delivery is challenging. Lithium concentration of fetal blood is equal to that of maternal blood with levels continually decreasing in the first and second trimesters, risking subtherapeutic concentration. Lithium concentration gradually increases in the third trimester and in the postpartum, risking toxicity. If lithium is continued during pregnancy, levels should be checked weekly.

In 2019 the FDA lowered the approved minimum age for lithium from 12 to 7 years.

Lithium works well in combination with valproic acid (Depakote, Depakene), lamotrigine (Lamictal), and second generation antipsychotics (SGAs).

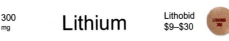

Eskalith $4–$13 — 150, 300, 600 mg

Lithotabs $11–$32  300 mg

Lithium

Lithobid $9–$30 — 300 ER, 450 ER mg

Liquid $67–$196 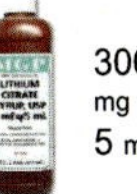 300 mg per 5 mL

With lithium treatment (at standard doses), it is necessary to monitor blood levels. As for any drug, blood levels should be checked at "trough", which is about 12 hours after the last dose. For treatment of acute mania, a relatively high level of 1.0 to 1.4 mmol/L is desired. Once mood has stabilized, the maintenance dose should be decreased to achieve a level of 0.6 to 1.0 mmol/L.. For augmentation of treatment-resistant depression (TRD), the recommended target serum level is 0.5–0.8 mmol/L. A level of 2.0 mmol/L is considered toxic. Discontinuation of lithium is ideally accomplished by slow taper over about 6–12 weeks.

It could be argued that there is no such thing as a subtherapeutic lithium level. Some naturopathic doctors recommend tiny dose 5–20 mg (equivalent) lithium orotate capsules as a nutritional supplement. These capsules are available over-the-counter (OTC) at health food stores and on Amazon.com.

Tremor is a telltale sign that lithium level may be too high. If tremor occurs at therapeutic blood level, consider adding low dose propranolol (about 20 mg TID), which is effective treatment for many types of tremor.

Heavy sweating (for a healthy and adequately hydrated individual) may decrease lithium levels, because sweat-to-serum ratio for lithium exceeds that for sodium by a factor of 4 (Jefferson et al, 1982). Dehydration, however, can contribute to lithium toxicity and renal insufficiency.

Of 38,487 single-drug exposures to lithium reported to Poison Control, there were 1,994 major serious outcomes and 61 deaths (Nelson & Spyker, 2017). This equates to a mortality risk of 1 in 630.

Five strengths of lithium

Strength	Purpose	Blood level (mmol/L)	Approximate total daily dose	Status	Comments
	Acute mania	0.8–1.4	1,200–1,800 mg	FDA-approved	For acute mania, start at least 300 mg TID of extended-release Lithium ER (Lithobid). Adjust dose every 3 days based on response and blood level. Consider using the ER formulation initially to minimize side effects. Transition to a lower dose of immediate-release lithium (caps or tabs) preferably dosed entirely at night, which is easier on the kidneys.
	Maintenance of bipolar disorder	0.6–0.8*	900–1,200 mg	FDA-approved	For an outpatient who is not acutely manic, one strategy is to start Lithium ER or IR 300 mg HS x 5 days, then 600 mg HS x 5 days, then 900 mg HS. Adjust dose based on blood level, and transition to immediate-release lithium (Eskalith) dosed entirely at night. *For bipolar maintenance, the usual target is 0.6–0.8. Decrease target to 0.4–0.6 if good response but poor tolerance. Target 0.8–1.0 if insufficient response and good tolerance.
	Treatment resistant depression	0.5–0.8	600 mg	Off-label	Lithium is one of the most effective adjuncts to an antidepressant for refractory depression. Consider starting Lithium ER (Lithobid) 300 mg BID and transitioning to 600 mg Lithium IR (Eskalith) at bedtime.
	Neuroprotection; Dementia; Suicide prevention; Headaches	0.1–0.4	150–300 mg	Off-label	The author is a big fan of low-dose lithium 150–300 mg HS for anyone at risk of committing suicide. The rationale is that lithium has been proven to prevent suicide and prevent dementia, so why not prescribe a neuroprotective dose that is safe and has no expected side effects? Monitoring of lithium level is entirely unnecessary at the 150 mg dose, and probably unnecessary at the 300 mg dose unless the patient has side effects or is taking a battery charger (see next page). TSH and renal function should be monitored for all patients.
	Nutritional supplement	< 0.1	5–60 mg	Off-label/ Over-the-counter	Since trace lithium in drinking water has been shown to prevent suicide, some naturopaths recommend tiny dose over-the-counter lithium as an "essential trace nutrient" for mental wellbeing. See below for dosing options.

Microdose lithium pills are available on Amazon as 5, 10, and 20 mg (equivalent) capsules of lithium orotate, costing about $4–$10 monthly. 130 mg of lithium orotate is equivalent to 5 mg of elemental lithium. Lithium orotate is not available by prescription. 60 mg of daily lithium can be accomplished with prescription lithium citrate liquid, which is 300 mg (equivalent) per 5 mL. So, 1 mg of liquid would be 60 mg daily. If you prescribe a 500 mL bottle, it will last for over a year. Less precise tiny doses could be accomplished by chopping 300 mg lithium carbonate tablets into tiny pieces.

Dynamic interactions:

- CNS depression
- Decreased seizure threshold
- Serotonergic (mild)
- Decreased ability of antidiuretic hormone (ADH), vasopressin (AVP), and desmopressin (DDAVP) to concentrate urine
- Nephrotoxicity

Idiosyncratic interactions (unknown mechanism, rare):

- Increased risk of extrapyramidal effects (EPS) with first generation antipsychotics (FGAs)
- Neurotoxicity when combined with verapamil (calcium channel blocker)
- Neurotoxicity when combined with carbamazepine (Tegretol)

Kinetic interactions (illustrated on the next page)

- Enhanced renal excretion of lithium in alkaline urine, as caused by carbonic anhydrase inhibitors such as acetazolamide (Diamox), topiramate (Topamax), and zonisamide (Zonegran)
- Enhanced renal excretion of lithium by osmotic diuretics such as mannitol
- Enhanced renal excretion of lithium by methylxanthines such as caffeine and theophylline, which are mild diuretics
- Decreased renal excretion by the "battery chargers" (shown on the next page) may result in lithium toxicity; most often with NSAIDS and thiazide diuretics
- Interferes with production of thyroid hormone

Lithium kinetic interactions
involving renal clearance

Lithium is removed from the body almost exclusively by the kidneys. Several medications affect the rate of lithium clearance. Since lithium has a narrow therapeutic index, blood levels need to be closely followed.

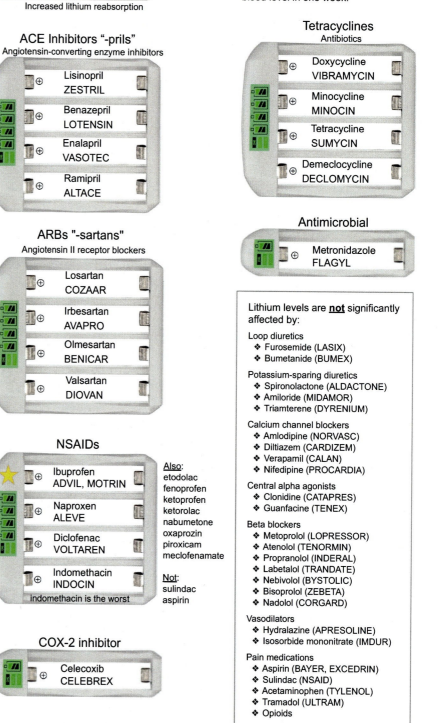

Serum lithium levels are mildly **decreased** by:

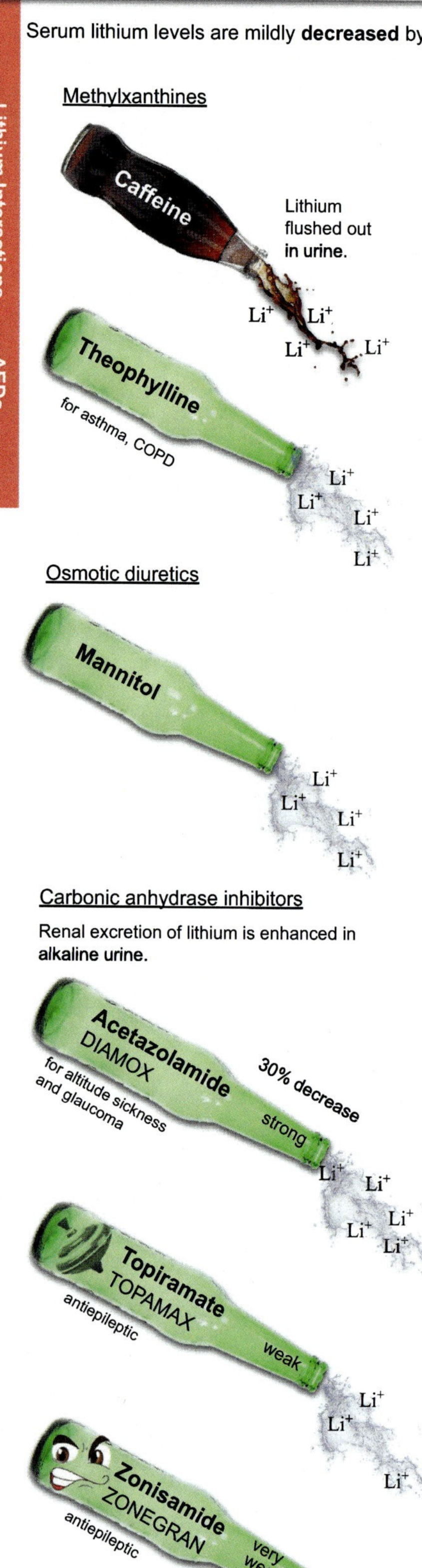

Methylxanthines

Lithium flushed out **in urine.**

Osmotic diuretics

Carbonic anhydrase inhibitors

Renal excretion of lithium is enhanced in **alkaline urine.**

Lithium levels are **increased** by:

Thiazide Diuretics

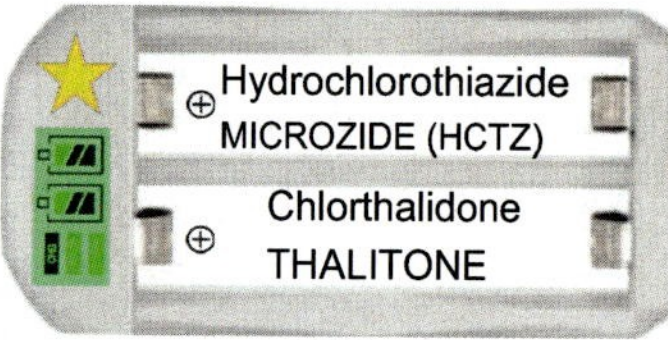

Increased lithium reabsorption

ACE Inhibitors "-prils"

Angiotensin-converting enzyme inhibitors

Lisinopril
ZESTRIL

Benazepril
LOTENSIN

Enalapril
VASOTEC

Ramipril
ALTACE

ARBs "-sartans"

Angiotensin II receptor blockers

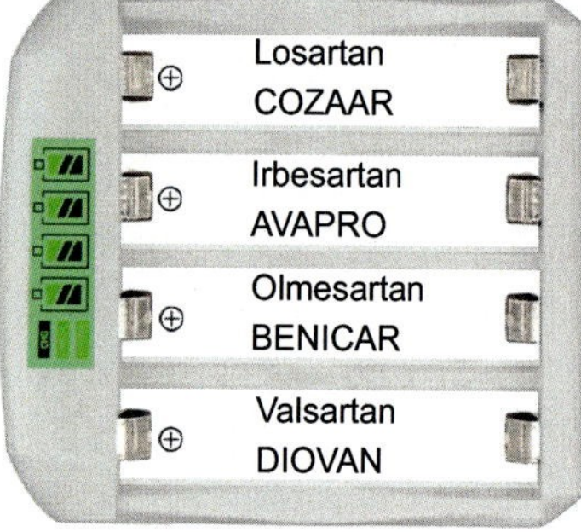

NSAIDs

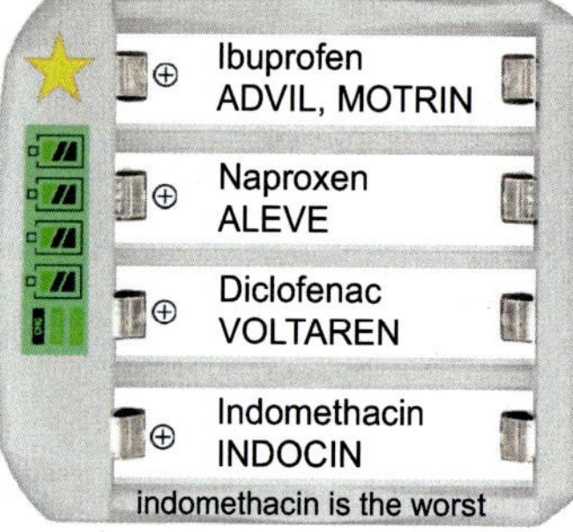

indomethacin is the worst

Also:
etodolac
fenoprofen
ketoprofen
ketorolac
nabumetone
oxaprozin
piroxicam
meclofenamate

Not:
sulindac
aspirin

COX-2 inhibitor

Celecoxib
CELEBREX

★ Thiazide diuretics and NSAIDS have the greatest potential to increase lithium concentrations, usually 25% to 40%. Rarely the increase may be much greater, leading to lithium toxicity. If another prescriber insists on adding a thiazide or NSAID, a reasonable approach is to decrease lithium dose by about 30% and recheck blood level in one week.

Tetracyclines

Antibiotics

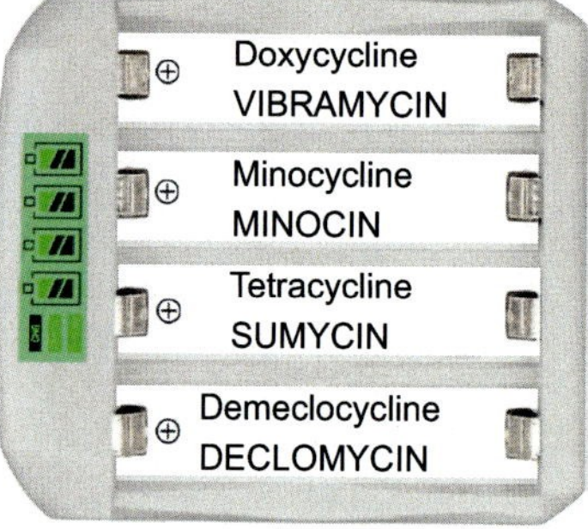

Antimicrobial

Lithium levels are **not** significantly affected by:

Loop diuretics
- Furosemide (LASIX)
- Bumetanide (BUMEX)

Potassium-sparing diuretics
- Spironolactone (ALDACTONE)
- Amiloride (MIDAMOR)
- Triamterene (DYRENIUM)

Calcium channel blockers
- Amlodipine (NORVASC)
- Diltiazem (CARDIZEM)
- Verapamil (CALAN)
- Nifedipine (PROCARDIA)

Central alpha agonists
- Clonidine (CATAPRES)
- Guanfacine (TENEX)

Beta blockers
- Metoprolol (LOPRESSOR)
- Atenolol (TENORMIN)
- Propranolol (INDERAL)
- Labetalol (TRANDATE)
- Nebivolol (BYSTOLIC)
- Bisoprolol (ZEBETA)
- Nadolol (CORGARD)

Vasodilators
- Hydralazine (APRESOLINE)
- Isosorbide mononitrate (IMDUR)

Pain medications
- Aspirin (BAYER, EXCEDRIN)
- Sulindac (NSAID)
- Acetaminophen (TYLENOL)
- Tramadol (ULTRAM)
- Opioids

Conclusion: Educate patients that NSAIDS, blood pressure meds, and diuretics can cause lithium toxicity. For OTC pain medications, they should choose Tylenol or aspirin. Advise them to inform the prescriber if they are planning to change their caffeine intake. Excedrin is OK (combo of aspirin, acetaminophen, and caffeine). Check lithium levels frequently for patients on interacting medications. Teach the signs of lithium toxicity including tremor, nausea, diarrhea, fatigue, and drowsiness.

Antiepileptic drugs (AEDs)

New AEDs are often initially approved as adjuncts for focal seizures (formerly called partial seizures) but are prescribed off-label for adjunctive treatment of bilateral tonic-clonic seizures (formerly primary generalized seizures) and/or as monotherapy. GABA is the brain's principal inhibitory neurotransmitter. AEDs with "gab" in their name are either structurally related to GABA and/or lead to GABA(A) receptor activation. Several benzodiazepines (Chapter 4) are approved for epilepsy but are excluded from this list. Phenobarbital and primidone are barbiturates, featured in Chapter 3.

The monographs in this chapter are presented in order of mood stabilizers followed by the non-mood stabilizing AEDs in descending order of popularity in terms of number of prescriptions issued (Rx #).

Rx #	AED	~ Cost	Psychiatric uses	Comments
#1	Gabapentin (NEURONTIN)	$10	Pain, Anxiety, Alcoholism	#13 prescribed drug overall, usually for indications other than seizure disorder including neuropathic pain, fibromyalgia, and restless legs syndrome (RLS)
#2	Lamotrigine (LAMICTAL)	$10	1st line mood stabilizer	#70 overall. First-line for bipolar maintenance and seizure disorders because of relative safety and benign side effect profile; Dose must be titrated over 5 weeks to avoid Stevens-Johnson Syndrome (SJS). Broad spectrum AED
#3	Pregabalin (LYRICA)	$100	Anxiety	#83 overall; FDA-approved for focal seizures (adjunct), neuropathic pain, fibromyalgia, and post-herpetic neuralgia; Schedule V controlled substance (least restrictive); Similar to gabapentin; Approved for generalized anxiety in the UK
#4	Topiramate (TOPAMAX)	$10	Bipolar adjunct, weight loss, alcoholism, PTSD	#85 overall; Commonly causes (reversible) cognitive impairment at doses ≥ 200 mg; 15% risk of renal stones and possible metabolic acidosis, both attributable to alkalinization of urine
#5	Levetiracetam (KEPPRA)	$15	No!	#89 overall; Broad spectrum AED, often first-line for epilepsy; High incidence of irritability and mood disturbance, with potential for suicidal ideation, psychosis, and aggression
#6	Divalproex DR (DEPAKOTE)	$15	1st line mood stabilizer	#129 overall; The active drug is valproic acid (VPA). Potential for hepatotoxicity, hyperammonemic encephalopathy, tremor, and polycystic ovary syndrome (PCOS)
#7	Carbamazepine (TEGRETOL)	$40	2nd line mood stabilizer	#197 overall; Shredder CYP inDucer (Page 7); Several serious health risks; Narrow spectrum AED
#8	Phenytoin (DILANTIN)	$25	No	#201 overall; Shredder CYP inDucer that decreases blood levels of countless co-administered drugs; May cause gingival hypertrophy, coarse facial features, nystagmus, and cognitive impairment; Blood level monitoring is required; Narrow spectrum AED
#9	Primidone (MYSOLINE)	$15	No	#237 overall; This barbiturate is metabolized to phenobarbital. Off-label treatment of tremor; Not a controlled substance
#10	Oxcarbazepine (TRILEPTAL)	$20	2nd line mood stabilizer	#244 overall; Similar to carbamazepine with fewer risks and fewer interactions, but with greater risk of hyponatremia
#11	Phenobarbital (LUMINAL)	$30	Alcohol detox	Schedule IV controlled barbiturate; The oldest AED still in use, discovered in 1912; For anxiety treatment, barbiturates have been replaced by the safer benzodiazepines
#12	Zonisamide (ZONEGRAN)	$20	Alcoholism, Nightmares	May cause irritability and cognitive impairment; Rare incidence of psychosis; May cause weight loss; Broad spectrum AED
#13	Lacosamide (VIMPAT)	$900	No	Schedule V controlled substance (least restrictive) due to possible euphoria; Low incidence of mood problems; Narrow spectrum AED; Off patent in 2022
#14	Ethosuximide (ZARONTIN)	$100	No	Used only for petit mal (absence) seizures; Rarely associated with psychotic behavior; Risk of Stevens-Johnson syndrome (SJS)
#15	Eslicarbazepine (APTIOM)	$1000	No (due to cost)	Prodrug of an active metabolite of oxcarbazepine; Risk of hyponatremia and Stevens-Johnson syndrome; Off patent in 2021; Potential mood stabilizer
#16	Rufinamide (BANZEL)	$1000	Experimental for bipolar	Approved in 2008 as an adjunct for Lennox-Gastaut syndrome, but has potential as a broad spectrum AED; Can shorten QT interval
#17	Felbamate (FELBATOL)	$200	No	Considered relatively benign in terms of psychiatric adverse effects. Broad spectrum AED; Small risk of aplastic anemia and hepatic failure
#18	Brivaracetam (BRIVIACT)	$1000	No!	Analog of levetiracetam; Less likely to cause disturbance of mood/behavior than levetiracetam; Schedule V controlled (least restrictive)
#19	Tiagabine (GABITRIL)	$100	Mood stabilization and anxiety	GABA reuptake inhibitor; increases percentage of slow wave sleep; Can interfere with color perception; May *induce* seizures in patients without epilepsy
#20	Perampanel (FYCOMPA)	$500	No!	AMPA receptor antagonist; Schedule III controlled; **Black box warnings** for severe psychiatric and behavioral reactions including hostility, aggression, and homicidal ideation—*"Fight-compa"*
#21	Vigabatrin (SABRIL)	$4000	No!	Blocks breakdown of GABA; Restricted distribution due to risk of vision loss; May cause irritability, depression, and confusion; Narrow spectrum AED
NEW 2020	Cenobamate (XCOPRI)	$1000	No	Slow titration over 11 weeks is necessary to avoid Drug Reaction with Eosinophilia and Systemic Symptoms (DRESS).

An angry face means that a medication may cause significant irritability and potentially aggression, to the extent it should not be used as a mood stabilizer. Be aware almost any psychotropic drug has a potential for irritability with certain individuals.

#70
1994
$3–$67

Lamotrigine (LAMICTAL)

lah MO tre jeen / lah MIK tal

"Lamb ictal"

- Antiepileptic
- Voltage-gated sodium and calcium channel blocker
- Glutamate ⇩

25
100
150
200
mg

Lamotrigine

VPA

FDA-approved for:
- Bipolar I maintenance
- Focal seizures
- Lennox-Gastaut syndrome
- Bilateral tonic-clonic seizures

Used off-label for:
- Bipolar II maintenance
- Major depressive disorder
- Borderline personality disorder
- Neuropathic pain
- Fibromyalgia
- PTSD
- Other seizure disorders

Lamotrigine is the mood stabilizer of choice for maintenance of bipolar disorder. Lamotrigine has few health risks and few side effects. The most commonly reported side effects at high doses are dizziness and blurred vision. Lamotrigine does not cause weight gain and is generally non-sedating. No lab monitoring is required. It is the most effective stabilizer for preventing bipolar depressive episodes and has been demonstrated to be effective for unipolar depression.

Lamictal is of no use for an acute manic episode because the dose must be slowly titrated over 5 weeks to avoid life-threatening skin reactions including Stevens-Johnson syndrome (SJS) and toxic epidermal necrolysis (TEN). Lamotrigine should be stopped immediately in the event of a serious dermatologic reaction. Notwithstanding the risk of SJS, lamotrigine is one of the safest psychotropic medications. It is relatively benign in overdose. Dose is determined by clinical response rather than serum levels. If a lamotrigine level is ordered, results may take a week because local laboratories must send the blood sample to an outside lab.

Lamotrigine has some unique aspects. Among several mechanisms of actions, it blocks the release of glutamate, excitatory neurotransmitter.

"Ictal" refers to a neurologic event such as a seizure.

Lamotrigine is a broad-spectrum AED, effective for several types of seizures.

High dose lamotrigine can shorten QT interval, which does not pose a clinical risk, except in the case of familial short QT syndrome or in combination with other QT-shortening drugs such as rufinamide (Banzel), digoxin or magnesium. Contrast this with the many psychotropic medications that prolong QT interval.

Stevens-Johnson syndrome (SJS)	Benign rash
Usually occurs between 1–12 weeks	Peaks at 10–14 days
Purpuric (non-blanching), may be tender	Non-tender
Rapidly confluent and wide-spread	Spotty (non-confluent)
Usually involves neck and above	Below the neck
Can involve conjunctiva, mucous membranes	No involvement of mucous membranes
With fever, malaise or lymphadenopathy	No fever, malaise or lymphadenopathy
Leukocytosis	Normal CBC and CMP

Before lamotrigine became generically available, three Lamictal starter packs were available to address these interactions:

Starter pack	For those taking	Pack contains	Standard titration	Max Dose
Orange pack	No interacting medications	5 week supply = 25 mg tabs #42, 100 mg tabs #7	25 mg QD x 2 wks, then 50 mg x 2 wk, then 100 mg x 1 wk. The usual maintenance dose starting on week six is **200 mg** dosed AM, HS or divided 100 mg BID.	400 mg total (200 mg BID)
Blue (half strength)	Valproate (Depakote) Valproic acid (Depakene)	5 wk supply = 25 mg tabs #35	25 mg every other day x 2 wk, then 25 mg QD x 2 wk, then 50 mg QD x 1 wk. Usual maintenance dose starting week six is **100 mg QD**.	200 mg total (100 mg BID)
Green (double strength)	Carbamazepine (Tegretol), Phenytoin (Dilantin), Phenobarbital (Luminal) or Primidone (Mysoline)	5 wk supply = 25 mg tabs #84 100 mg tabs #14	50 mg QD x 2 wk, then 50 mg BID x 2 wk, then 100 mg BID x 1 wk,then 150 mg BID x 1 wk. Usual maintenance dose is **200 mg BID** starting week 6.	700 mg total (350 mg BID)

Lamotrigine is principally metabolized by UDP-glucuronosyltransferase (UGT) in the liver, as in "U Got Tagged!" (conjugated) with glucuronic acid. Specifically, UGT1A4 is the most relevant UGT enzyme. CYP450 enzymes are not involved. Lamotrigine is not an inducer or inhibitor of other drugs, and is only a victim (vulnerable substrate) in a small number of kinetic interactions.

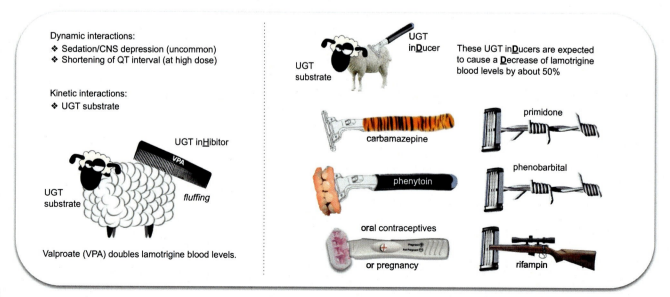

Dynamic interactions:
- Sedation/CNS depression (uncommon)
- Shortening of QT interval (at high dose)

Kinetic interactions:
- UGT substrate

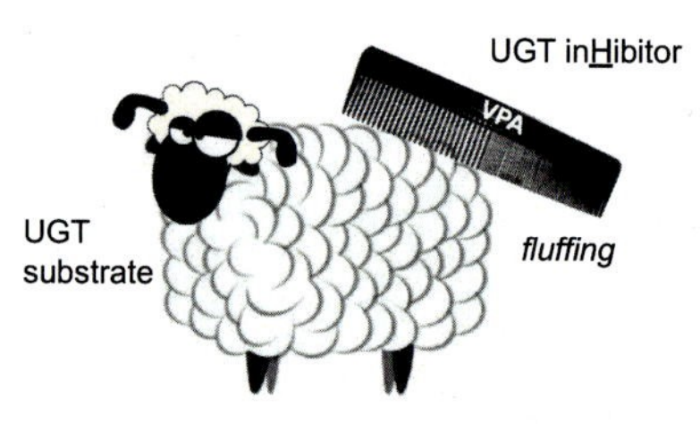

Valproate (VPA) doubles lamotrigine blood levels.

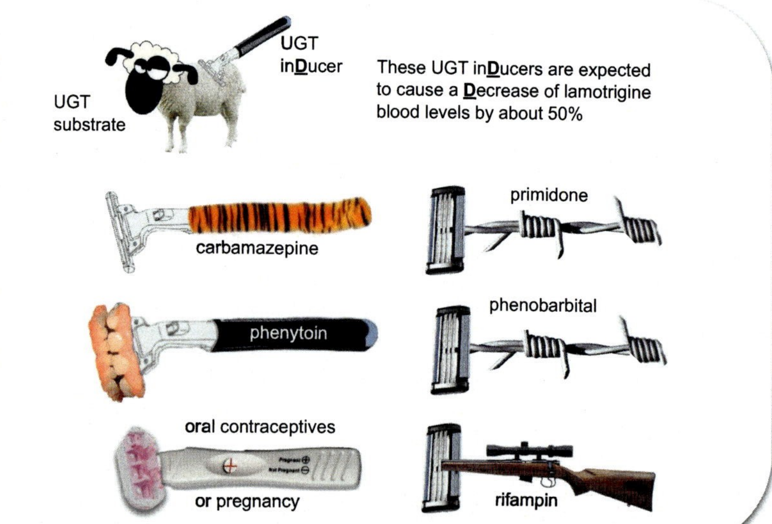

These UGT inDucers are expected to cause a Decrease of lamotrigine blood levels by about 50%

1962
$26–$83 caps
$21–$68 liquid

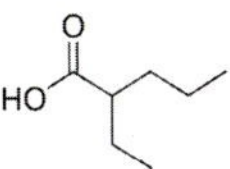

Valproic Acid (DEPAKENE)

val PROE ik / DEP a keen

"Dip a Keno (ball in) acid"

- ❖ Antiepileptic
- ❖ Voltage-gated sodium channel blocker
- ❖ Glutamate ⇩

250 mg liquid-filled caps

FDA-approved for:

- ❖ Bipolar disorder, acute mania
- ❖ Focal impaired awareness seizure
- ❖ Absence seizures
- ❖ Migraine prophylaxis

Used off-label for:

- ❖ Bipolar maintenance
- ❖ Aggression (drug of choice)
- ❖ Lennox-Gastaut syndrome (1st line)

Valproate (available as valproic acid and **divalproex)** is the drug of choice for acute mania. Depakene is the pure form of VPA, available as liquid filled capsules and oral solution. Depakene caps are uncommonly prescribed, because Depakene causes more gastrointestinal upset than divalproex (Depakote). Depakene oral solution is used for patients prone to cheeking pills to collect or surreptitiously dispose of them. The most common complaint patients have about VPA is feeling sedated.

Depakene may be more effective than Depakote for mania. Wassef et al (2005) found that hospital stays were 32.7% longer for those started on Depakote (over Depakene). For those patients started on Depakene, only 6.4% had to be switched to Depakote due to GI distress.

VPA has several black box warnings including hepatotoxicity, pancreatitis (including fatal hemorrhagic pancreatitis), and teratogenicity (neural tube defects, autism, low IQ). The teratogenicity of VPA is partially due to depletion of folate. VPA is also less than ideal for women of childbearing age due to fetal risks and 10% risk of polycystic ovary syndrome (PCOS).

VPA may elevate ammonia levels, which may lead to hyperammonemic encephalopathy. Ammonia level should be checked if there are mental status changes. Since hyperammonemia is dose-related, it may resolve when Depakote dose is reduced. Hepatotoxicity is a rare idiosyncratic reaction that is not dose-related, with most cases occurring within 3 months. With VPA, asymptomatic increase of liver enzymes is not necessarily indicative of hepatic dysfunction. It is also possible to have hyperammonemia without elevated liver enzymes.

VPA is approved for acute manic episodes, not for bipolar maintenance. Although it is effective for preventing relapse of mood episodes and is effective for rapid cycling, VPA is less than ideal for bipolar maintenance due to side effects. 50% of patients gain > 10% body weight. Tremor

Forms of valproate:

page 30

Valproic acid (VPA) DEPAKENE	Divalproex DEPAKOTE
HO, O	O, HO, O⁻Na⁺, O
The active drug, of which serum levels are monitored	The most commonly prescribed form of valproate (see next page)

can be severe for some patients. Over 20% develop reversible thrombocytopenia at high-end doses. VPA may rarely cause edema.

VPA can cause hair loss, which can be remedied with supplementation of zinc 30 mg, selenium 200 mcg, and biotin 10 mg daily, taken at a different time than VPA (which interferes with their absorption). Chelated zinc is easier on the stomach. Hair loss stops when VPA is stopped.

VPA is metabolized in the liver with CYP450 enzymes only playing a minimal role, so it has relatively few drug-drug interactions. The lack of kinetic interactions is a major advantage of VPA over the "shredder" carbamazepine (Tegretol). VPA doubles lamotrigine (Lamictal) levels by inHibiting UGT (phase II metabolism). There is increased risk of encephalopathy if VPA is coadministered with topiramate (Topamax).

VPA is highly protein bound. Only unbound (free) VPA is active. When coadministered with high dose aspirin (which is also highly protein bound), the percentage of free VPA will increase and Depakene will be stronger than suggested by the standard VPA level (total VPA). If the patient has low albumin, the percentage of free VPA will be predictably higher.

Of 36,800 single-drug exposures to valproate reported to Poison Control, there were 924 major serious outcomes and 37 deaths (Nelson & Spyker, 2017).

Dosing: Initial dosing is the same as Depakote (see next page). Maintenance dose is guided by VPA blood levels. The active medication that is monitored through the standard blood test is total valproic acid (VPA). Therapeutic range for bipolar disorder is defined as 50 to 125 µg/mL. For acute mania, aim for VPA level of 80–120 µg/mL. For bipolar maintenance, shoot for 50–100 µg/mL. Over 150 µg/mL is considered toxic. For migraine prophylaxis start 500 mg x 1 week, then 1,000 mg. See above for situations where ordering a free VPA level may be indicated. If used long-term, add folic acid (folate) 0.4 mg daily, which is depleted by VPA.

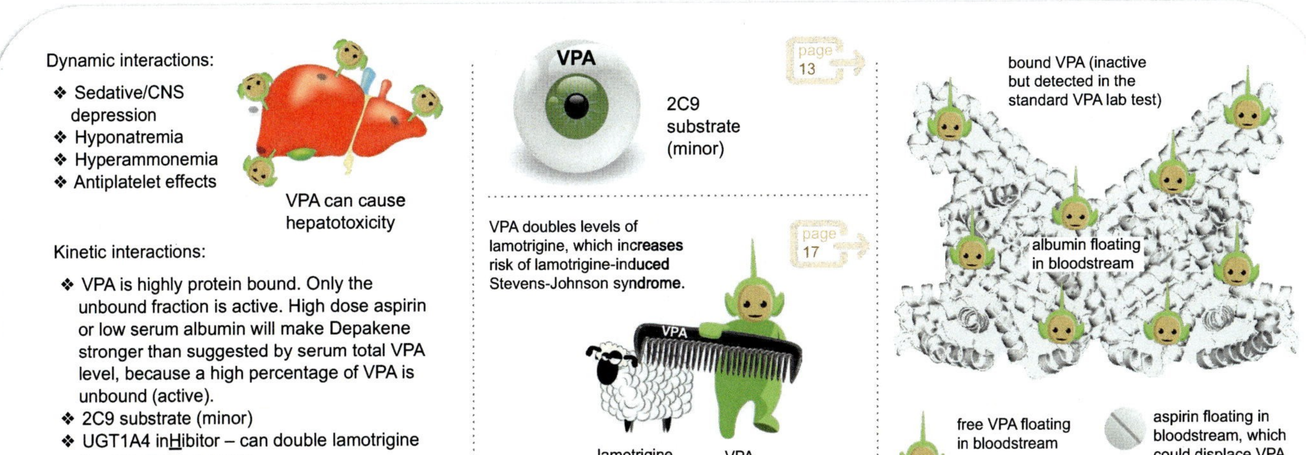

Dynamic interactions:
❖ Sedative/CNS depression
❖ Hyponatremia
❖ Hyperammonemia
❖ Antiplatelet effects
VPA can cause hepatotoxicity
Kinetic interactions:
❖ VPA is highly protein bound. Only the unbound fraction is active. High dose aspirin or low serum albumin will make Depakene stronger than suggested by serum total VPA level, because a high percentage of VPA is unbound (active).
❖ 2C9 substrate (minor)
❖ UGT1A4 inHibitor – can double lamotrigine (Lamictal) blood levels
❖ UGT2B16 inHibitor – can double blood levels of "LOT" benzos (lorazepam, oxazepam, temazepam)
VPA
page 13
2C9 substrate (minor)
VPA doubles levels of lamotrigine, which increases risk of lamotrigine-induced Stevens-Johnson syndrome.
page 17
VPA
lamotrigine (UGT substrate)
VPA (UGT inHibitor)
bound VPA (inactive but detected in the standard VPA lab test)
albumin floating in bloodstream
free VPA floating in bloodstream
aspirin floating in bloodstream, which could displace VPA from albumin

#129
1996
$14–$128

Divalproex (DEPAKOTE)

dye val PRO ex / DEP a kote

"Dip-a-Coat"

- Antiepileptic
- Voltage-gated sodium channel blocker
- Glutamate ⇩

125
250
<u>500</u>
mg

Indications:

- See Depakene monograph on preceding page.

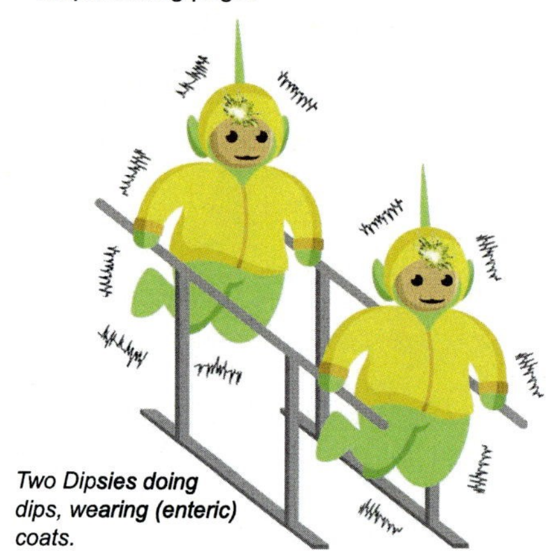

Two Dipsies doing dips, wearing (enteric) coats.

Divalproex is a compound formed by adding sodium hydroxide to two valproic acid (VPA) molecules, yielding a molecule that is double the size of Depakene. In the small intestine divalproex is broken down to the two molecules of VPA.

Depa<u>kote</u> is the enteric "<u>kot</u>ed" form of VPA that causes less gastrointestinal upset. Depakote and Depakene are bioequivalent per mg dose. The VPA of Depakote is absorbed more slowly than Depakene. Because of this, Depakote is described as a "delayed-release" (DR) version of VPA.

<u>"Regular" Depakote</u> is listed in ePrescribe systems as <u>Depakote DR</u> (delayed-release), intended for BID dosing. There is no "Depakote IR" (immediate-release) because that would be Depakene (straight valproic acid). When the doctor orders Depakote, "Depakote <u>DR</u> is what the doctor ordered".

Dosing: A reasonable starting dose for <u>bipolar mania</u> is a minimum of 10 mg/pound split BID. Although Depakote DR it is intended for BID dosing, some doctors prescribe the entire daily dose of Depakote DR at bedtime to enhance compliance and minimize side effects. <u>For migraine prophylaxis</u> start 500 mg x 1 week, then 1,000 mg. If used long-term, add folic acid (folate) 0.4 mg daily, which is depleted by VPA. Refer to the Depakene monograph on the preceding page for the basic information about this drug, target blood levels, and situations where ordering a <u>free</u> VPA level may be indicated.

Dynamic interactions:

- Sedative/CNS depression
- Hyponatremia
- Hyperammonemia
- Antiplatelet effects

Kinetic interactions:

- VPA is highly protein bound. Only the unbound fraction is active. High dose aspirin or low serum albumin will make Depakote stronger than suggested by serum total VPA level, because a high percentage of VPA is unbound (active).
- 2C9 substrate (minor)
- UGT in<u>H</u>ibitor (refer to Depakene monograph on page 29) – can double blood levels of "LOT" benzos and lamotrigine

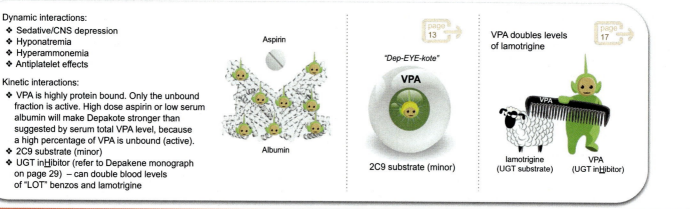

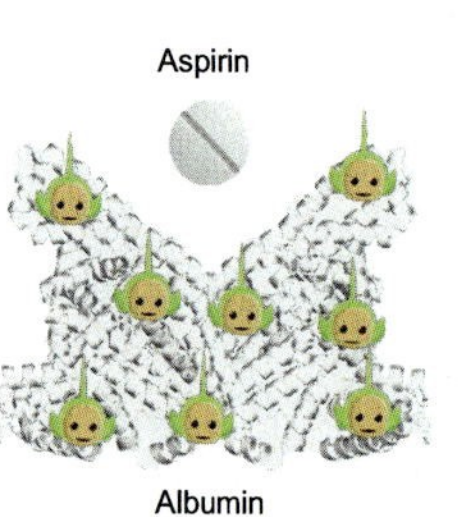

page 13

2C9 substrate (minor)

page 17

VPA doubles levels of lamotrigine

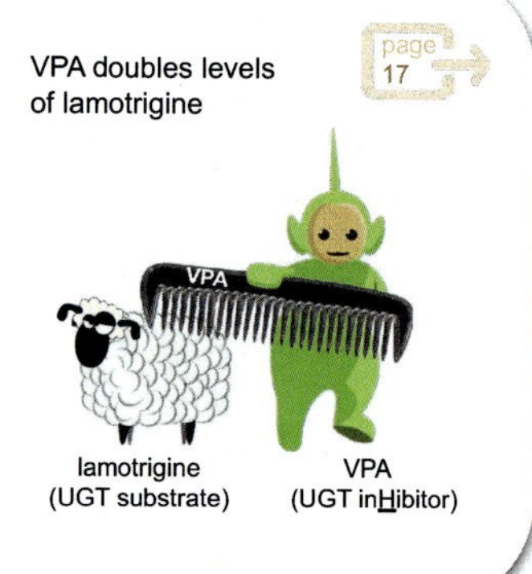

2000
$28–$229

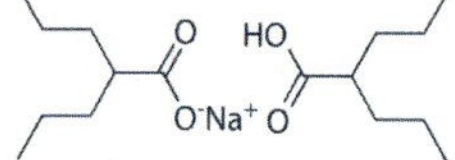

Divalproex (DEPAKOTE ER)

di val pro ex / DEP a kote

"Dip-a-coat ER"

- Antiepileptic
- Voltage-gated sodium channel blocker
- Glutamate ⇩

250
<u>500</u>
mg

Indications:

- See Depakene monograph on preceding page.

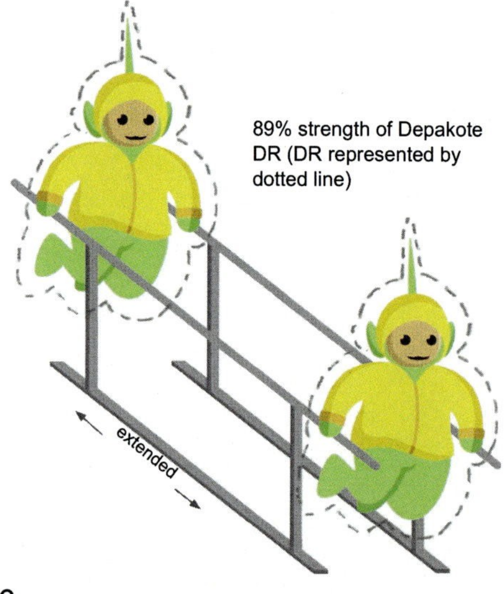

89% strength of Depakote DR (DR represented by dotted line)

The once-daily formulation of divalproex is Depakote ER (extended-release). The label instructs to give it with food.

Regular Depakote (Depakote DR) and Depakote ER are not bioequivalent. Depakote ER delivers only about 89% of the VPA available by other formulations. It is baffling that Depakote DR is available in 125, 250, and 500 mg tabs and Depakote ER also comes in 250 and 500 mg tabs.

The ER formulation, intended for once daily dosing, costs twice as much as regular Depakote (DR). Many doctors prescribe regular Depakote (DR) once daily at bedtime anyhow. Think "Depakote <u>E</u>rro<u>R</u>"—the doctor may have ordered Depakote ER in error. If so, giving the ER formulation will lead to underdosing because <u>Depakote ER has 89% bioavailability of the more commonly prescribed Depakote DR</u>.

Depakote ER may have utility in certain situations, for instance when tapering off Depakote. There may be circumstances when it makes sense to change from DR to ER at the same dose to effect a slight reduction in strength.

Dosing: 89% bioequivalent to Depakote DR. The label instructs to "<u>increase total daily dose by 8–20% if switching from DR to ER</u>". For bipolar disorder, dose as you would with Depakote DR, but give the entire daily dose with the evening meal. The therapeutic range for bipolar disorder is officially defined as 50 to 125 μg/mL. For acute mania, aim for VPA level of 80–120 μg/mL. For bipolar maintenance, shoot for 50–100 μg/mL. Over 150 μg/mL is considered toxic. For <u>migraine prophylaxis</u> start 500 mg QD with food x 1 week, then 1,000 mg.

#197
1962
$23–$65

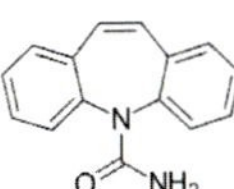

Carbamazepine (TEGRETOL)

kahr buh MAZ uh peen / TEG ra tal

"Tiger tail (in the) Car Maze"

- Antiepileptic
- Voltage-gated sodium channel blocker
- Glutamate ⇩

FDA-approved for:
- Seizure disorder
- Trigeminal neuralgia
- Acute manic/mixed episode of bipolar I disorder (ER formulation)

Used off-label for:
- Bipolar maintenance
- Neuropathic pain
- Restless legs syndrome
- Migraine prophylaxis

eating its own tail = in**D**ucing its own metabolism by CYP3A4 (auto-in**D**uction)

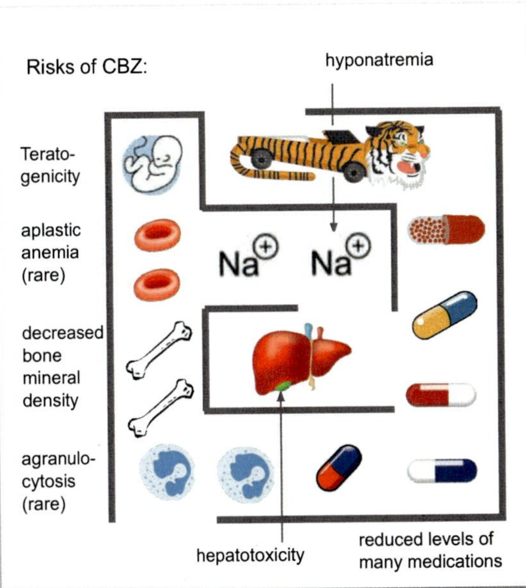

Carbamazepine (CBZ), released in 1962, is effective for bipolar mania but is considered second-line behind lithium and valproate. CBZ's usefulness is limited by drug-drug interactions. CBZ is a "shredder" in**D**ucer of multiple CYP enzymes, resulting in significantly **D**ecreased blood levels of a long list of medications. Always run an interaction check if CBZ is in the mix.

Carbamazepine even in**D**uces its own metabolism (CYP3A4). The effect occurs within 2 to 3 weeks (**D**elayed), then stabilizes. CBZ has an elimination half-life of 24 hours initially, then 15 hours after auto-induction kicks in. Therefore we expect CBZ blood level to be lower at week 4 compared to week 1.

The formulation of CBZ that is FDA approved for bipolar mania is the ER capsule branded EQUETRO ($275) which may have slightly fewer side effects, e.g., less nausea. However, psychiatrists usually just prescribe generic IR carbamazepine ($30) and refer to the medication as Tegretol. If CBZ ER is desired, CARBATROL ER ($45) is exactly the same as Equetro, although FDA approved for seizures.

The advantage of CBZ over lithium and valproate is that CBZ does not cause weight gain or tremor. CBZ can be rather sedating, which can be desirable for acute mania.

CBZ may render birth control pills ineffective due to 3A4 induction. It is contraindicated during pregnancy. Teratogenic risks include "anticonvulsant face", neural tube defects, cleft palate, and malformations of the cardiovascular and urinary systems.

CBZ was recently found to be associated with stroke, whereas lithium and lamotrigine were not (Chen et al, 2019).

Of 23,806 single-drug exposures to carbamazepine reported to Poison Control, there were 950 major serious outcomes and 16 deaths (Nelson & Spyker, 2017).

Dosing: The recommended dose for a manic episode is 400–600 mg BID, starting at 200 mg BID, and increasing by 200 mg/day. Starting at 200 mg TID would be reasonable for a hospitalized patient. Bipolar dosing is guided by clinical response, although most psychiatrists do check blood levels. When used for seizure disorders, the therapeutic CBZ blood level is 4–12 mcg/mL. For bipolar disorder, monitoring of blood levels may be useful for verification of drug compliance and assessing safety, but a therapeutic range is undefined. Remember, due to 3A4 auto-induction, CBZ levels will be lower at week 4 compared to week 1.

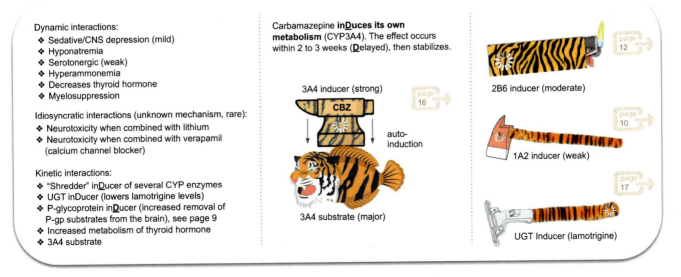

Dynamic interactions:
- Sedative/CNS depression (mild)
- Hyponatremia
- Serotonergic (weak)
- Hyperammonemia
- Decreases thyroid hormone
- Myelosuppression

Idiosyncratic interactions (unknown mechanism, rare):
- Neurotoxicity when combined with lithium
- Neurotoxicity when combined with verapamil (calcium channel blocker)

Kinetic interactions:
- "Shredder" in**D**ucer of several CYP enzymes
- UGT inDucer (lowers lamotrigine levels)
- P-glycoprotein in**D**ucer (increased removal of P-gp substrates from the brain), see page 9
- Increased metabolism of thyroid hormone
- 3A4 substrate

Carbamazepine **inDuces its own metabolism** (CYP3A4). The effect occurs within 2 to 3 weeks (**D**elayed), then stabilizes.

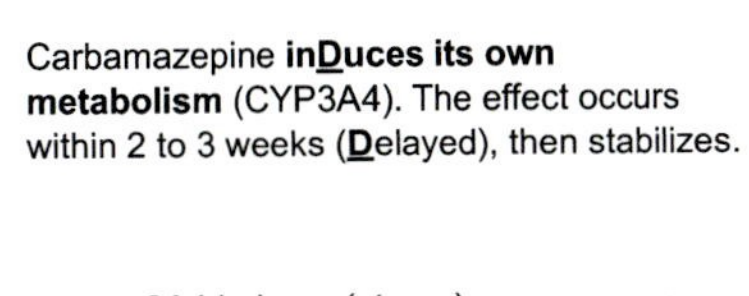

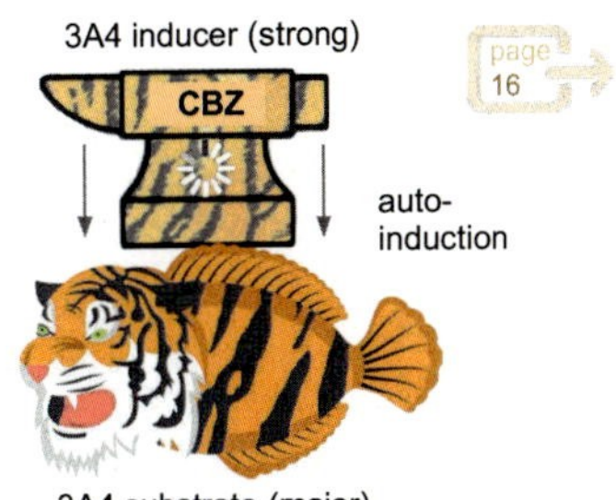

Continued...

The FDA recommends Asian patients, who have a 10-fold higher incidence of CBZ-induced Stevens-Johnson syndrome (SJS) and toxic epidermal necrolysis (TEN), be screened for the **HLA-B*1502** allele, which would be a contraindication for starting CBZ.

Mnemonic: "Hey Look, Asian Blood! 1502, no Tegretol for you!"

AEDs that are highly effective for **neuropathic pain**:

- ▶ Pregabalin (Lyrica)
- ▶ Gabapentin (Neurontin)
- ▶ Carbamazepine (Tegretol)

Pregabalin and gabapentin may cause weight gain, while carbamazepine does not.

Combinations with carbamazepine

Acute mania necessitates a combo of mood stabilizer + antipsychotic + benzodiazepine. Also, most individuals with bipolar I disorder are maintained on more than one medication. Since CBZ is a shredder inDucer, finding a suitable combination can be tricky.

"Good" Combos - serum levels not significantly decreased by CBZ

- **Lithium** - although there have been rare cases of neurotoxicity with this combo, lithium ameliorates hyponatremia and neutropenia caused by CBZ.
- **Gabapentin** (Neurontin)
- **Fluphenazine** (Prolixin), even **long-acting injectable (LAI) Prolixin Decanoate**
- **Olanzapine** (Zyprexa)
- **Asenapine** (Saphris)
- **Loxapine** (Loxitane)
- **Iloperidone** (Fanapt
- **Ziprasidone** (Geodon)
- **The "LOT" benzodiazepines** (page 55) - **Lorazepam** (Ativan), **Oxazepam** (Serax), and **Temazepam** (Restoril)

OK Combos - but higher doses will be needed

- **Lamotrigine** (Lamictal) - Use double dose; be vigilant for Stevens-Johnson syndrome (SJS).
- **Valproate** (Depakote) - Depakote is to be dosed based on VPA blood levels, as usual
- **Risperidone** (Risperdal) - **oral**—do not use long-acting injectable (LAI).
- **Haloperidol** (Haldol) - If using LAI Haldol Decanoate, consider supplementing with PO Haldol so that, if CBZ is stopped, the PO Haldol can be stopped also. Otherwise, serum haloperidol levels from the LAI will be too strong when induction is reversed.
- **Paliperidone** (Invega) - **oral**—do not use LAI
- **Aripiprazole** (Abilify) - **oral**—do not use LAI

"Bad" Combos

- **Lurasidone** (Latuda) - contraindicated because lurasidone levels are Decimated by CBZ
- **Quetiapine** (Seroquel) - blood levels Decreased 5 -fold by CBZ; may need to use a higher quetiapine dose, which will be hazardous if CBZ is ever stopped (reversal of induction). If started along with CBZ for acute mania, quetiapine will work for a couple of weeks but by week 4 it will be essentially useless. This might not be a problem if mania is resolved and the prescriber and patient are aware of the interaction.
- **Clozapine** (Clozaril) - CBZ Decreases clozapine levels and both medications can suppress bone marrow.
- **Long-acting injectable (LAI)** formulations of aripiprazole, risperidone, or paliperidone

#244
2000
$9–$115

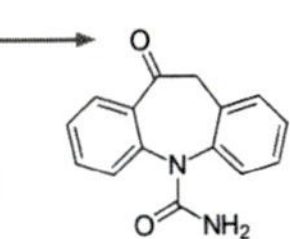

Oxcarbazepine (TRILEPTAL)

OX car baz a peen / tri LEP tal

"Oscar Leapt"

❖ Antiepileptic
❖ Voltage-gated sodium channel blocker
❖ Glutamate ⇩

150
300
400
mg

Structurally, oxcarbazepine is the same as carbamazepine, other than this ketone.

Trileptal trashes sodium

FDA-approved for:

❖ Focal seizures

Used off-label for:

❖ Bipolar disorder
❖ Trigeminal neuralgia

Oxcarbazepine (Trileptal) is FDA approved for seizure disorders and used off-label for bipolar disorder. Oxcarbazepine has several advantages over carbamazepine, but unfortunately there is less evidence for effectiveness of oxcarbazepine for bipolar disorder.

It commonly causes hyponatremia, so it is necessary to monitor serum sodium with a metabolic panel (BMP or CMP). Normal sodium range is around 136–148. Symptoms of hyponatremia may occur at ≤ 130. Critical low sodium of ≤ 120 may cause seizures, brain swelling and coma. If hyponatremia is corrected too quickly, the myelin sheaths of nerve cells in the pons may be damaged by osmotic demyelination (central pontine myelinolysis).

It is relatively benign in overdose. Of 2,329 single-drug exposures to oxcarbazepine reported to Poison Control, there were 35 major serious outcomes but no deaths (Nelson & Spyker, 2017).

Signs of hyponatremia (sodium ≤ 130)

❖ Irritability
❖ Confusion
❖ Headache
❖ Blurred vision
❖ Weakness/fatigue
❖ Muscle cramps
❖ Nausea/vomiting

Risks with sodium ≤ 120

❖ Seizures
❖ Brain swelling
❖ Coma

Risk factors for hyponatremia:

❖ Polydipsia
❖ Sweating with sports
❖ Oxcarbazepine
❖ SSRI antidepressants
❖ Desmopressin (DDAVP)
❖ Diuretics

To decrease risk of hyponatremia during sports, drink Gatorade instead of water.

	Carbamazepine (TEGRETOL)	Oxcarbazepine (TRILEPTAL)
Structure		
Entered U.S. market	1962	2000
Approx cost/30-day supply	$38	$20
FDA approved for	Seizure disorder Trigeminal neuralgia Bipolar I disorder (ER)	Focal seizures
Therapeutic drug monitoring	Required when used for seizure disorders. Traditionally checked when used for bipolar disorder.	May be useful, but not required.
Bipolar dosing	Start 200 mg BID. Target 400–600 mg BID or blood level 6–10 mcg/mL	Start 300 mg BID. Target 600–1200 mg BID
Risk of Stevens-Johnson syndrome (SJS)	Yes	Yes
HLA-B*1502 testing for Asians (SJS risk factor)	required	recommended
Risk of significant hyponatremia = Low sodium < 125 mmol/L	Yes, but less than with oxcarbazepine	This is So Dum! Yes
Risk of bone marrow toxicity (Aplastic anemia, agranulocytosis)	Yes	minimal
Risk of hepatotoxicity	Yes	minimal
Inducer of drug metabolism	3A4 (strong) 2B6 (moderate) 1A2 (weak) UGT (lamotrigine)	3A4 (weak)
Auto-induction of own metabolism	Yes	No
Bioequivalent dosing for ER formulations	Yes (BID, same mg)	No (ER is weaker than IR)

Dynamic interactions:
❖ Hyponatremia (major)
❖ Sedative (mild)
❖ Serotonergic (mild)

Kinetic interactions:
❖ Oxcarbazepine is a weak 3A4 inducer, unlikely to be of much clinical significance.

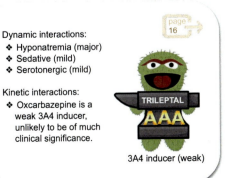

page 16

3A4 inducer (weak)

Dosing: For off-label treatment of bipolar disorder, the author usually starts 300 mg BID x 2 days, then 300 mg TID x 2 days, then to the target dose of 600 mg BID. Maximum total daily dose is 2,400 mg (1,200 mg BID). As for any antiepileptic drug, taper to discontinue. Extended- and immediate-release formulations are not interchangeable on a mg-for-mg basis. When converting from Trileptal IR to the ER formulation (Oxtellar XR), a higher dose may be required.

#11
1993
$11–$92

Gabapentin (NEURONTIN)

gab a PEN tin / nur RON tin

"Gabba pen tin" = "Neuron tin"

- ❖ Antiepileptic
- ❖ Voltage-gated calcium channel blocker
- ❖ Glutamate ⇩

100
300
400
mg

FDA-approved for:
- ❖ Focal seizures
- ❖ Post-herpetic neuralgia
- ❖ Restless legs syndrome (as Horizant ER)

Used off-label for:
- ❖ Neuropathic pain
- ❖ Fibromyalgia
- ❖ Migraine prophylaxis
- ❖ Anxiety
- ❖ Bipolar disorder (adjunct)
- ❖ Alcoholism (sobriety maintenance)
- ❖ Alcohol withdrawal
- ❖ Cannabis use disorder
- ❖ Nightmares
- ❖ Improved quality of sleep
- ❖ Vasomotor menopause symptoms (hot flashes)

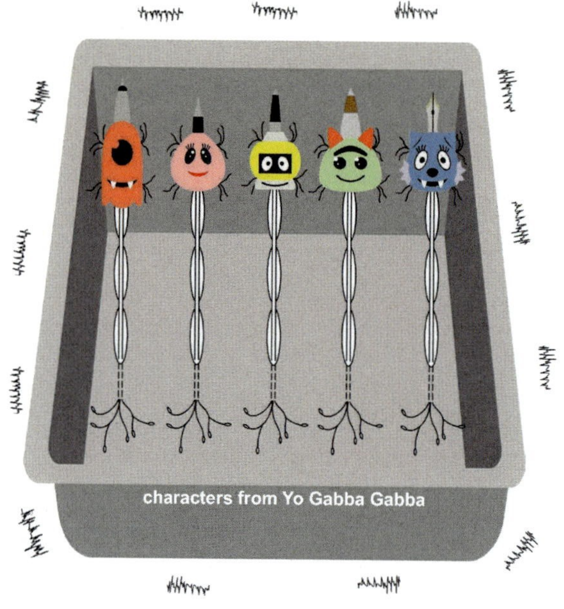
characters from Yo Gabba Gabba

Gabapentin (Neurontin) has the reputation of being a well-tolerated though not a particularly powerful antiepileptic drug (AED).

The name derives from its structural similarity to GABA, the brain's chief inhibitory neurotransmitter. Despite its name and structure, gabapentin does not affect GABA activity in any way. Gabapentin does not bind GABA receptors (as do benzodiazepines and barbiturates), inhibit GABA reuptake (like tiagabine), or block degradation of GABA (like vigabatrin). Gabapentin blocks voltage-gated calcium channels (as do lamotrigine, topiramate and pregabalin).

Gabapentin is the #1 prescribed medication of the AED class, and the #11 overall prescribed drug. Most commonly, gabapentin is prescribed for conditions other than seizure disorders, many of which are off-label. It is widely prescribed for neuropathic pain. Gabapentin is sometimes used adjunctively for bipolar disorder, but it has little, if any, mood stabilizing efficacy. It does have anxiolytic properties.

Gabapentin may cause modest weight gain. Some patients experience sedation, dizziness, ataxia, fatigue, and dyspepsia. There is a small risk of DRESS Syndrome (Drug Reaction with Eosinophilia and Systemic Symptoms), which is potentially fatal.

Neurontin is excreted unchanged in urine, making it immune from CYP interactions. There are no genetic polymorphisms that influence its metabolism. In other words, no one is a poor metabolizer or ultrarapid metabolizer of gabapentin.

As of 2020, gabapentin is not a DEA controlled substance. Some US states have begun regulating gabapentin, starting with Kentucky in 2017 as a result of gabapentin being detected in up to a third of the state's fatal overdoses. In 2020 the FDA required a label warning about the risk of life-threatening respiratory depression for patients with respiratory risk factors (COPD, the elderly, those taking opioids). Of 9,174 single-drug exposures to gabapentin reported to Poison Control, there were 109 major serious outcomes and 8 deaths (Nelson & Spyker, 2017).

Gabapentin was initially regarded as having no abuse potential, but issues have arisen. Prison physicians no longer commonly prescribe it due to high rates of diversion. About 20% of individuals who abuse opioids will also overuse gabapentin because it can potentiate the opioid high. Otherwise, only 1–2% of patients overuse gabapentin.

Gabapentin is similar in structure and mechanism to pregabalin (Lyrica). Gabapentin and pregabalin constitute the gabapentinoid class of medication. Side effects attributed to pregabalin on the next page, such as peripheral edema, may also apply to gabapentin.

A gabapentin withdrawal syndrome is possible. It can include disorientation, anxiety, palpitations, diaphoresis, and abdominal cramps. Sudden withdrawal of any antiepileptic can precipitate a seizure, even for an individual without a seizure disorder.

Dosing: The lowest-strength capsule is 100 mg. The minimum effective dose is generally 300 mg TID. For seizure disorder, start 300 mg TID. For other conditions, the label recommends starting 300 mg QD x 1 day, then 300 mg BID x 1 day, then 300 mg TID. The maximum total daily dose is 3,600 mg, which is probably too high for psychiatric conditions. The author's target dose is 300–600 mg TID and occasionally as high as 900 mg TID. For patients with opioid use disorder, it is recommended not to exceed 900 mg daily (300 mg TID) due to risk of overdose (Gomes et al, 2017). For nightmares or improvement of sleep quality, a reasonable dose is 300–600 mg HS. As for any antiepileptic drug, taper to discontinue.

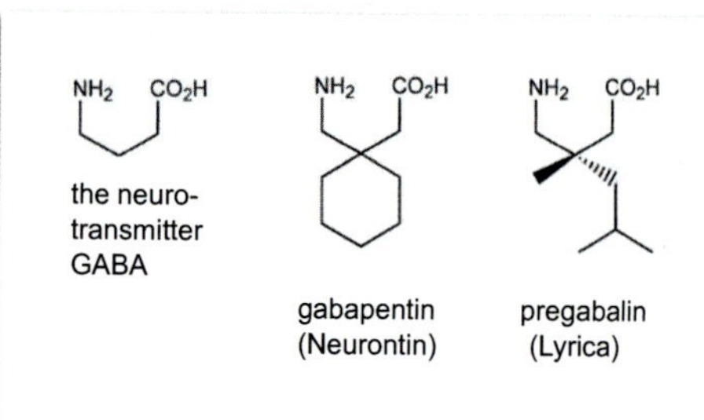

Dynamic interactions:
- ❖ Sedation/CNS depression (mild)
- ❖ Weight gain (modest)
- ❖ Respiratory depression

Kinetic interactions:
- ❖ None significant because it is excreted unmetabolized in urine - "in a bubble"

page 18

#83 (trending up) 2005 $18–$591		**Pregabalin (LYRICA)** pre GAB a lin / LEER ik uh "Preg gobblin' Lyrics"	❖ Antiepileptic ❖ Voltage-gated calcium channel blocker ❖ Glutamate ⇩ ❖ DEA Schedule V	25 50 75 100 150 200 225 mg

FDA-approved for:
- ❖ Focal seizures (adjunct)
- ❖ Neuropathic pain
- ❖ Fibromyalgia
- ❖ Post-herpetic neuralgia

Used off-label for:
- ❖ Generalized anxiety
- ❖ Social anxiety
- ❖ Alcohol dependence
- ❖ Alcohol or benzo withdrawal

Pregabalin, FDA-approved in 2005, is a voltage-gated calcium channel blocker, as is gabapentin (Neurontin). Gabapentin and pregabalin constitute the gabapentinoid class of medication. Their structure is similar to GABA, but neither bind GABA receptors.

Lyrica is not metabolized, but rather excreted unchanged in the urine. Half-life is 6 hours, similar to that of Neurontin. Lyrica is a Schedule V controlled substance (least restrictive) because euphoria is possible. Generic pregabalin has been available since 2019.

It is approved for generalized anxiety in the UK. Large randomized-controlled trials supports its use (off-label) for generalized and social anxiety disorders.

Monographs in this book do not routinely address use during pregnancy, but since "preg" is in this drug's name—consider avoiding use of pregabalin during pregnancy. Teratogenicity is not expected, but pregabalin was not good for fetuses of animals given double the recommended human dose.

Of 1,821 single-drug exposures to oxcarbazepine reported to Poison Control, there were 44 major serious outcomes but no deaths (Nelson & Spyker, 2017).

Side effects:
- ▶ Dizziness
- ▶ Sedation
- ▶ Headache
- ▶ Concentration problems
- ▶ Peripheral edema
- ▶ Weight gain (usually not)
- ▶ Angioedema (rare)
- ▶ Myoclonus (rare)
- ▶ Rhabdomyolysis (rare)

AEDs that are highly effective for **neuropathic pain**:
- ▶ Pregabalin (Lyrica)
- ▶ Gabapentin (Neurontin)
- ▶ Carbamazepine (Tegretol)

	Gabapentin (NEURONTIN)	Pregabalin (LYRICA)
Structure (similar to GABA)		
Entered U.S. market	1993	2005
Cost/30 days (January 2020)	$11/$92 (with/without GoodRx coupon)	$18/$591 (with/without GoodRx coupon)
FDA-approved for	Focal seizures; Restless legs syndrome; Post-herpetic neuralgia	Focal seizures (adjunct); Neuropathic pain; Fibromyalgia; Post-herpetic neuralgia
Mechanism	Voltage-gated calcium channel blocker	Voltage-gated calcium channel blocker
Metabolism	Excreted unchanged in urine	Excreted unchanged in urine
Usual dosing	TID	BID–TID
Controlled substance	Not federally, but is regulated in some states	Schedule V
Starting dose	300 mg QD x 1 day, 300 mg BID x 1 day, then 300 mg TID	50 mg TID, may incr. to 100 mg PO TID within 1 wk
Max dose	3,600 mg/day (1,200 mg TID) although this may be too much	600 mg/day (200 TID or 300 BID)

In 2020 the FDA issued a warning of respiratory depression in individuals with respiratory risk factors (COPD, obesity, those taking opioids). The warning applied to gabapentin also.

Dosing: For most indications, start 50 mg TID or 75 mg BID. May increase to total daily dose of 300 mg within one week; 300–600 mg/day in divided doses is an effective maintenance dose for generalized/social anxiety disorders; Maximum total daily dose is 600 mg.

Dynamic interactions:
- ❖ Sedation (mild)
- ❖ Respiratory depression

Kinetic interactions:
- ❖ None significant because it is excreted unmetabolized in urine - "in a bubble"

page 18

#85
1996
$4–$82

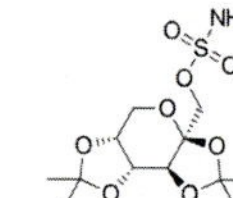

Topiramate (TOPAMAX)

toh PEER a mate / TOH pah max

"Top at max (speed on) Top (of) pyramid"

- ❖ Antiepileptic
- ❖ Voltage-gated sodium and calcium channel blocker
- ❖ Glutamate ⇩

25
50
100
200
mg

FDA-approved for:

- ❖ Focal seizures
- ❖ Bilateral tonic-clonic seizures
- ❖ Lennox-Gastaut syndrome
- ❖ Migraine prophylaxis
- ❖ Obesity, long-term treatment (in combination with phentermine)

Used off-label for:

- ❖ Alcoholism (relapse prevention)
- ❖ Bipolar disorder (adjunct)
- ❖ Weight loss (monotherapy)
- ❖ Anxiety
- ❖ Binge eating disorder
- ❖ PTSD
- ❖ Nightmares

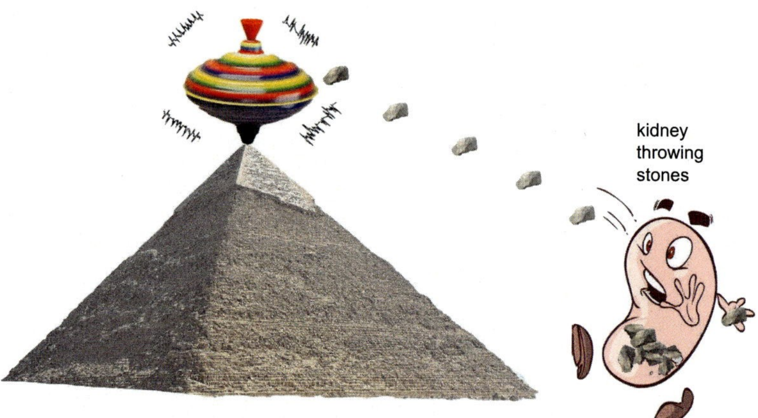

Topiramate is prescribed by psychiatrists for several off-label uses. The most compelling data is for preventing alcohol relapse. Although not FDA-approved for alcoholism, it is recommended in the 2015 US Veterans Affairs guidelines for moderate/severe alcohol use disorder.

Nicknamed "Dopamax" or "Stupamax", topiramate commonly causes cognitive problems including "brain fog", psychomotor slowing, difficulty concentrating and word-finding difficulty. Cognitive impairment due to topiramate is reversible, and usually only problematic at doses over 200 mg daily. A patient taking 200 mg BID told the author that, at a stoplight, she had trouble remembering if green meant stop or go. The recommended dose for epilepsy is 200–400 mg daily. It can be dosed lower for other purposes. The starting dose for any purpose, except nightmares, is 25 mg BID (25 mg HS for nightmares).

The two AEDs prescribed by psychiatrists that are highly effective for migraine prophylaxis are topiramate and valproate (Depakote, Depakene). The recommended topiramate dose to prevent migraines is 50 mg BID, which is not expected to impair cognition.

Paresthesia (tingling sensation) is common, and a favorable predictor of migraine prophylaxis. Dysgeusia (metallic taste) is possible.

Because topiramate is excreted unchanged in urine, there are few pharmacokinetic interactions. There are no genetic polymorphisms that affect its metabolism. In other words, no one is a poor metabolizer or ultrarapid metabolizer of topiramate.

Topiramate has undesirable carbonic anhydrase activity, hence alkalinizing urine and bringing a 15% risk of kidney stones with chronic use.

Another consequence of the carbonic anhydrase activity is lowered blood pH (acidification) due to raised urine pH (alkalization). Evidence of lowered blood pH is seen on a metabolic panel as low bicarbonate, which is listed as CO_2. Signs of metabolic acidosis (serum bicarbonate < 20 mmol/L) include tachycardia, headache, confusion, fatigue, nausea, and vomiting. Chronic acidosis can contribute to osteoporosis.

Topiramate is commonly prescribed off-label as an appetite suppressant. Topiramate ER is available in a fixed-dose combination with phentermine (appetite-suppressing stimulant) branded as Qsymia ($190) for long-term treatment of obesity. Qsymia is available only from certified pharmacies and certified prescribers to ensure female patients are counseled on the risk of birth defects. Topiramate itself increases the risk of oral clefts 4-fold.

It may be prescribed for anxiety at low dose. It may be useful for those who tend to overeat when they are nervous. Gabapentin (Neurontin) is more commonly used for anxiolytic purposes, but has the potential for weight gain.

Dosing: For nightmares, start 25 mg HS and go to 50 mg HS if necessary. For migraine prophylaxis or obesity, give 25 mg BID x 1 week then 50 mg BID. The maintenance dose for seizure disorders is 100–200 mg BID. Since topiramate impairs cognition when dosed 200 mg/day or higher, for other psychiatric uses try not to exceed 100 mg BID. For alcoholism titrate to 100 mg BID. Extended-release formulations of topiramate (Trokendi XR, Qudexy XR) can be dosed once daily. For anxiety (off-label) do not exceed 50 mg/day.

Dynamic interactions:

- ❖ Sedation/CNS depression
- ❖ Increased risk of hyperammonemia with valproic acid (Depakene, Depakote), that can present as encephalopathy
- ❖ Increased risk of hypokalemia with hydrochlorothiazide (HCTZ)
- ❖ Increased risk of acidosis with metformin, which also decreases bicarb (CO2). Keep this in mind when prescribing weight loss medications. Metformin or topiramate can be prescribed off-label for weight loss, but they should not be prescribed in combination.

Topiramate is a weak 3A4 inDucer, which is insignificant at lower doses. However, if dosed > 200 mg/day, topiramate's induction of 3A4 may be clinically significant, i.e., by Decreasing blood levels of 3A4 substrates

page 16

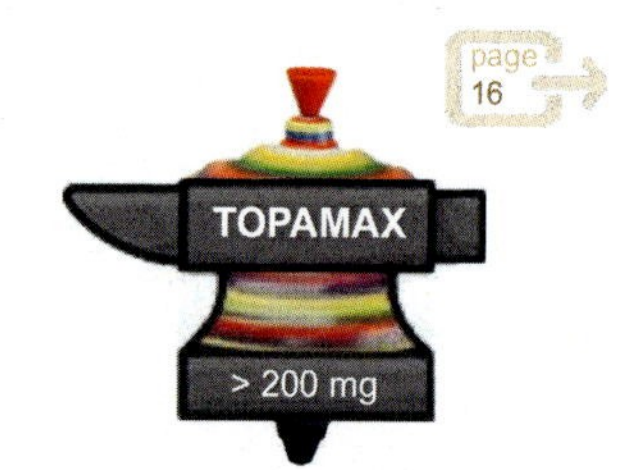

Topiramate can decrease lithium levels. As a carbonic anhydrase inhibitor, it raises urine pH, which increases excretion of lithium. The effect is expected to be mild and of little clinical significance. Topiramate can alter levels of other drugs whose excretion is affected by pH of urine.

page 26

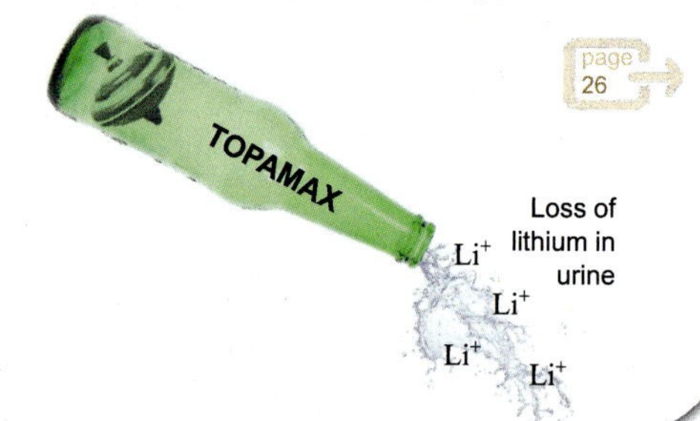

#89
2000
$6–$117

Levetiracetam (KEPPRA)

LEE ve tye RA se tam / KEP ruh

"Levitate Keeper"

- Antiepileptic
- Inhibitor of glutamate release

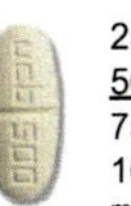

250
500
750
1000
mg

FDA-approved for:

- Focal seizures (adjunct)
- Juvenile myoclonic epilepsy (adjunct)
- Bilateral tonic-clonic seizures (adjunct)

Used off-label for:

- Other types of seizures

Keppra can cause hostility/aggression.

Levetiracetam entered the U.S. market in 2000 as an AED with a novel mechanism of action. It binds SV2A, a synaptic vesicle glycoprotein. This reduces the release of glutamate, the brain's principal excitatory neurotransmitter, thereby preventing hypersynchronization of epileptiform burst firing.

Levetiracetam has become one of the most prescribed medications for the treatment of epilepsy. It is not prescribed by psychiatrists. Advantages of levetiracetam as an AED include efficacy for a broad-spectrum of seizure types, lack of cognitive impairment, and lack of drug interactions. It can be started at an effective 500 mg BID dose on day one, which is also nice. Half-life is about 7 hours. 66% is excreted unchanged in the urine.

The most common side effects are dizziness, fatigue, and insomnia. The more troublesome problem with Keppra can be irritability and mood changes. This may occur to some degree in up to a third of patients taking the medicine (Dr. Robert Fisher, epilepsy.com). The array of psychiatric adverse effects may include depression, suicidal ideation, psychosis, hostility, and aggression. If a patient on Keppra experiences behavioral disturbance, they can be switched to brivaracetam (Briviact), a similar AED with a lower incidence of mood disruption.

Dosing: A typical adult dose for levetiracetam is 500–1500 mg twice a day. Dr. Fisher usually starts with 250 mg BID x 1 wk, then 500 mg BID x 1 wk, then 1000 mg AM + 500 mg PM x 1 wk, then 1000 mg BID. This is slower than the package insert suggests.

Alternate mascot with a phrase useful for pronunciation:

"Leave it to racist Kappers"

Dynamic interactions:

- Sedation (minimal)

Kinetic interactions:

- None significant
  - "in a bubble"

page 18

#201
1953
$21–$43

Phenytoin (DILANTIN)

fen i TOH in / di LAN tin

"Funny tunes Die laughin'"

❖ Antiepileptic
❖ Voltage-gated sodium channel blocker
❖ Glutamate ⇩

100 mg

FDA-approved for:
- ❖ Seizure disorder
- ❖ Status epilepticus
- ❖ Neurosurgery seizure prophylaxis

Used off-label for:
- ❖ Antiarrhythmic for suppression of ventricular tachycardia

Phenytoin was FDA-approved as an antiepileptic in 1953. Phenytoin is not a first-line antiepileptic due to risks and side effects, and is not prescribed for psychiatric purposes.

Phenytoin can literally make you ugly by increasing connective tissue growth factor (CTGF). Facial features may become coarse. About 50% of patients develop disfiguring gingival hypertrophy. Of all cases of drug-induced gingival overgrowth (DIGO), about 50% are attributed to phenytoin, 30% to cyclosporine (immunosuppressant for transplant recipients), and 10–20% to calcium channel blockers. Other possible consequences of increased CTGF are increased hair growth (arms, back, forehead) and Peyronie's disease (curved penis).

As with other antiepileptics, phenytoin can impair cognition and poses a risk of Stevens-Johnson syndrome (SJS).

Therapeutic index is narrow, so blood levels must be checked. Therapeutic serum range is 10 to 20 µg/mL, applicable to both antiepileptic and off-label antiarrhythmic uses. Nystagmus may be observed at levels greater than 20 µg/mL.

Dosing: For initial treatment of status epilepticus, give 15–20 mg/kg IV x 1. May give additional 10 mg/kg IV x 1 after 20 min if no response to initial dose. Begin maintenance dose 12 hours after the loading dose. For maintenance, aim for a trough blood level of 10–20 µg/mL, which may be achieved with 300–400 mg total daily dose divided BID or TID. Maximum per single dose is 400 mg. Note that phenytoin displays non-linear kinetics, i.e., doubling the dose will more than double the blood level.

The **"shredders"** are four **strong inDucers** of several CYPs, which cause countless chemicals to be quickly expelled from the body:

- **carbamazepine** (Tegretol) - antiepileptic
- **phenobarbital** (Luminal) - barbiturate
- **phenytoin** (Dilantin) - antiepileptic
- **rifampin** (Rifadin) - antimicrobial

Dr. Jonathan Heldt refers to the shredders as **"Carb & Barb"** in his book *Memorable Psychopharmacology*.

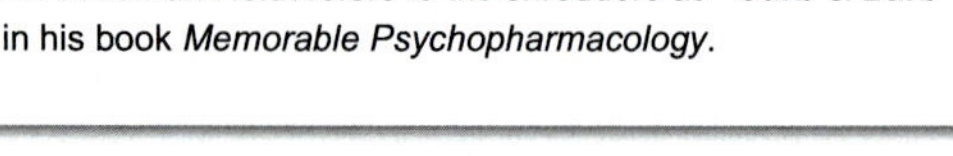

Dynamic interactions:
- ❖ Sedative

Kinetic interactions:
- ❖ "Shredder" inducer (see below)
- ❖ 2C9 substrate
- ❖ 2C19 substrate
- ❖ Increased metabolism of thyroid hormone

page 13

2C9 substrate

page 14

2C19 substrate

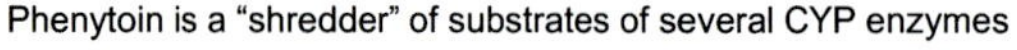

Phenytoin is a "shredder" of substrates of several CYP enzymes

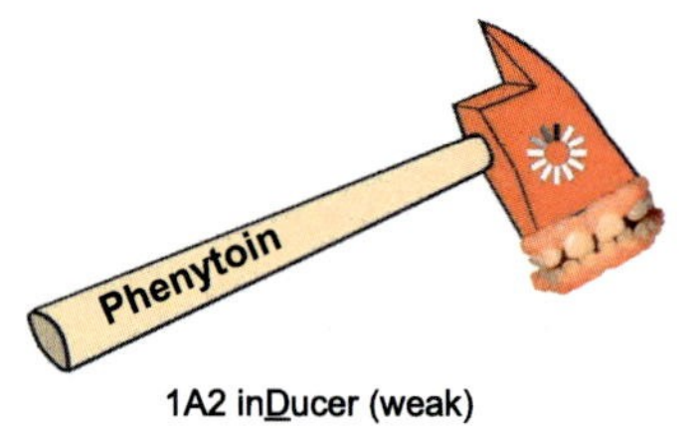

1A2 inDucer (weak)

page 10

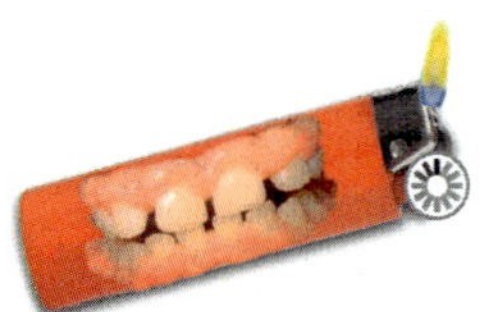

2B6 inDucer (weak)

page 12

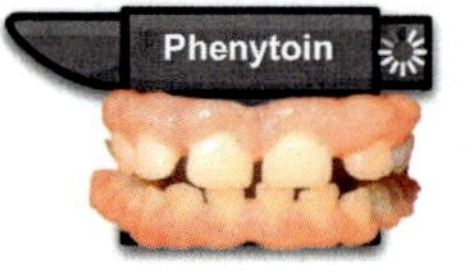

3A4 inDucer (strong)

page 16

inDucer of lamotrigine metabolism (50% decrease)

page 17

2000
$24–$188

Zonisamide (ZONEGRAN)

zoe NIS a mide / ZAHN uh gran

"Zone is mighty, Zone is grand"

- Antiepileptic
- Voltage-gated sodium channel blocker
- Glutamate ⇩

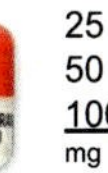

25
50
100
mg

FDA-approved for:
- Focal seizures

Used off-label for:
- Other types of seizures
- PTSD nightmares
- Sleep-related eating disorder
- Obesity
- Binge eating disorder
- Alcohol use disorder
- Migraine prophylaxis
- Parkinsonian symptoms associated with Lewy body dementia

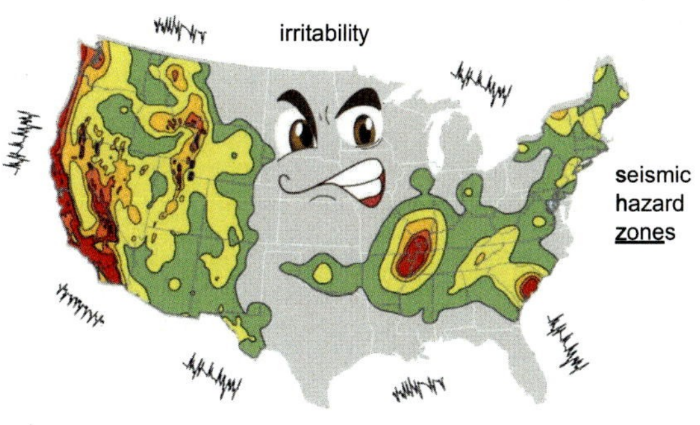

seismic hazard zones

Zonisamide (Zonegran) is a broad-spectrum antiepileptic drug (AED) that blocks sodium and calcium channels and increases dopaminergic and serotonergic transmission. It is unrelated to other antiseizure medications.

Zonisamide decreases appetite and has been shown to decrease binge-eating. Cognitive impairment including "brain fog", confusion, difficulty concentrating, and word-finding difficulty are relatively common. It is not used as a mood stabilizer because it may cause irritability. There have been rare cases of zonisamide-induced psychosis.

Due to carbonic anhydrase inhibitor activity (although weak) there is a chance of kidney stones (4%) and metabolic acidosis. Aplastic anemia and agranulocytosis have been reported. Stevens-Johnson syndrome (SJS) and toxic epidermal necrolysis (TEN) have been reported. Oligohidrosis (decreased ability to sweat) has occurred with children.

Half-life is over 60 hours. About 30% is excreted unchanged in the urine.

Zonisamide has a sulfonamide structure, so it is contraindicated in patients allergic to sulfa drugs. Other sulfonamides include the antibiotic sulfamethoxazole (Bactrim, Septra) and the disease-modifying antirheumatic drug (DMARD) sulfasalazine. Unlike the other two sulfonamides, zonisamide does not have "sulfa" in its name.

Dosing: Start 100 mg daily. May increase by 100 mg q 2 weeks for a maximum of 600 mg. However, doses above 400 mg are rarely more effective. As with any antiepileptic medication, taper dose gradually to discontinue.

Zonisamide can cause weight loss.

Dynamic interactions:
Sedative (mild)
Hypokalemia
Metabolic acidosis
Decreased renal perfusion
Kinetic interactions:
Urine alkalization (minor)
3A4 substrate (minor)
page 26
ZONEGRAN
Loss of lithium in urine (minor)
Li+
Li+
Zonegran can decrease lithium levels. As a carbonic anhydrase inhibitor, it alkalinizes urine, which increases excretion of lithium.
page 16
3A4 substrate (minor)

2014
$858–$1,094

Lacosamide (VIMPAT)

la KOE sa mide / VIM pat

"Lacrosse Vampire"

- ❖ Antiepileptic
- ❖ Voltage-gated sodium channel blocker
- ❖ Glutamate ⇩
- ❖ DEA Schedule V

50
100
150
200
mg

FDA-approved for:
- ❖ Focal seizures, adjunct (2009)
- ❖ Focal seizures, monotherapy (2014)

Used off-label for:
- ❖ Other types of seizures

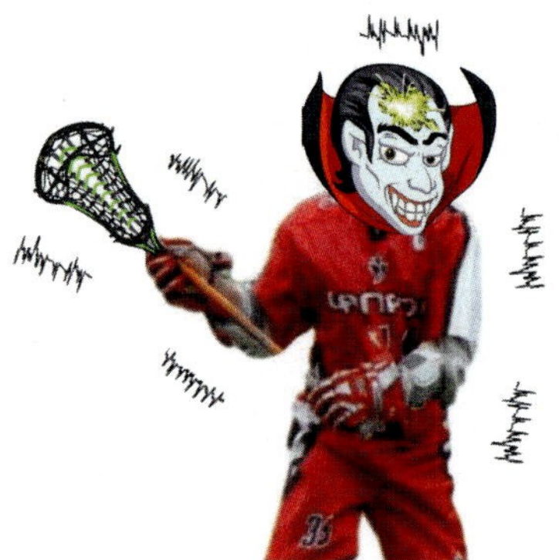

Lacosamide (Vimpat) is an antiepileptic synthesized from the amino acid serine. It blocks voltage-gated sodium channels, although in a different way than other antiepileptics.

Lacosamide is a Schedule V controlled substance (least restrictive) due to possible euphoria. It is not prescribed for psychiatric purposes although it has a low incidence of adverse psychiatric effects. As with any antiepileptic drug (AED), there is at least a slight risk of mood disruption. Labeling for all AEDs list suicidal thoughts as a possible risk.

Expect lacosamide to be an increasingly popular AED when it becomes available generically. The patent expires in 2022.

Side effects may include dizziness, headache, nausea, somnolence, fatigue, ataxia, diplopia, and tremor. Rarely, lacosamide causes first-degree AV block due to PR interval prolongation.

Dosing: For monotherapy of focal seizures, the maintenance dose is 150–200 BID; Start: 100 mg PO/IV BID, increase by 100 mg/day each week; FDA max is 400 mg/day; For conversion from AED monotherapy, give lacosamide maintenance dose for > 3 days before gradual withdrawal of previous AED over > 6 weeks; taper dose over > 1 week to stop.

page 18

Dynamic interactions:
- ❖ Use caution if combining with other PR interval prolonging drugs (e.g., beta blockers, calcium channel blockers).

Kinetic interactions:
- ❖ Substrate of 2C19 (and to a lesser extent, 3A4 & 2C9). Interactions with 2C19 inhibitors and inducers are not considered clinically significant— "in a box"

1960
$82–$253

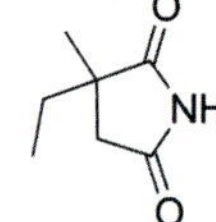

Ethosuximide (ZARONTIN)

ETH oh SUX i mide / zuh RON tin

"Zorro's Ethics suck!"

- ❖ Antiepileptic
- ❖ T-type calcium channel blocker

250
mg

FDA-approved for:
- ❖ Absence seizures

Used off-label for:
- ❖ N/A

sux

Child having petit mal seizure

Available since 1960, ethosuximide is the drug of choice for absence (petit mal) epilepsy. It is **ineffective for other seizure types**. It seems to work by inhibiting low voltage-activated (T-type) calcium channels.

It is not used for psychiatric purposes and may rarely cause behavioral changes or even psychosis.

Other possible side effects include nausea, lethargy, headache and hiccups. Rare risks include hematologic abnormalities, erythema multiforme, Stevens-Johnson syndrome (SJS), and systemic lupus erythematosus (SLE).

Dosing: Maintenance dose for absence epilepsy is 250–750 mg BID; Start 250 mg BID, may increase by 250 mg/day q 4–7 days; Max is 1.5 g/day; The therapeutic serum range for ethosuximide is 40 to 100 mcg/mL; As with any AED, taper dose gradually to discontinue.

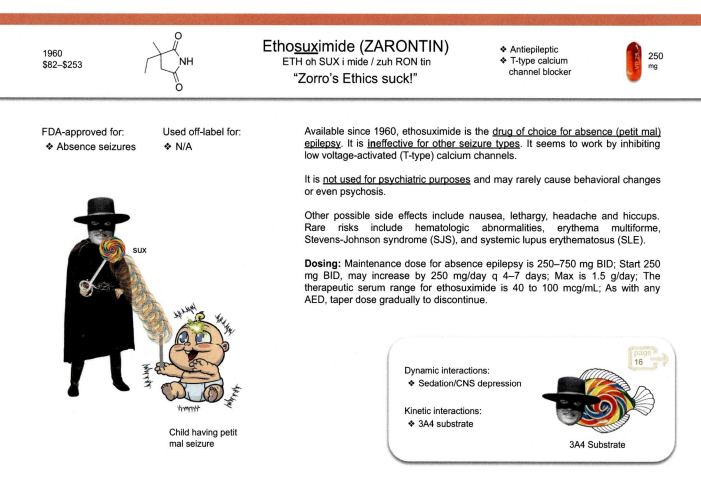

page 16

Dynamic interactions:
- ❖ Sedation/CNS depression

Kinetic interactions:
- ❖ 3A4 substrate

3A4 Substrate

2013
$960–$1,182

Eslicarbazepine (APTIOM)

ES li kar BAZ e peen / ap TEE om

"Slick car App time!"

- ❖ Antiepileptic
- ❖ Voltage-gated sodium channel blocker

200
400
600
800
mg

FDA-approved for:
- ❖ Focal seizures, adjunct (2013)
- ❖ Focal seizures, monotherapy (2015)

Used off-label for:
- ❖ Other types of seizures

Eslicarbazepine is FDA-approved for treatment of focal seizures. It is not currently used as a mood stabilizer. It costs about $1,000 monthly and will not be off patent until 2021.

Eslicarbazepine is similar in structure and mechanism to carbamazepine (Tegretol, CBZ) and oxcarbazepine (Trileptal, OCBZ). Specifically, it is a prodrug of an active metabolite of oxcarbazepine.

Aptiom may have potential as a mood stabilizer, which is unsurprising given its similarity to CBZ. Nath et al (2012) reported successful treatment of a patient with bipolar mania who could not tolerate other anti-manic drugs.

Side effects can include dizziness, sedation, nausea, headache, diplopia, and ataxia. About 10% of patients stop it due to side effects. It is safer than CBZ, with similar risk profile to OCBZ. It is subject to more kinetic interactions than OCBZ but far fewer interactions than the shredder CBZ.

Patients who have experienced a serious rash from taking CBZ or OCBZ should avoid eslicarbazepine.

Dosing: Maintenance dose is 800–1600 mg QD; Start 400–800 mg QD, increase by 400–600 mg/day q week; Max is 1600 mg/day; As with any AED taper dose gradually to stop. Eslicarbazepine is 66% renally excreted, so the dose should be adjusted for those with renal impairment.

page 16

Dynamic interactions:
- ❖ Sedation/CNS depression
- ❖ Hyponatremia

Kinetic interactions:
- ❖ UGT substrate
- ❖ 3A4 inducer (minor)

3A4 inducer (minor)

2009
$2,846–$3,494

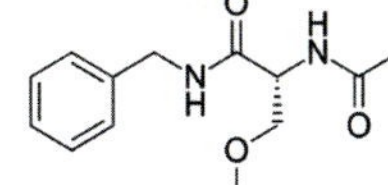

Rufinamide (BANZEL)

rue FIN a mide / BAN zel

"Ruffin' Ban"

- ❖ Antiepileptic
- ❖ Voltage-gated sodium channel blocker

200
400
mg

FDA-approved for:
- ❖ Lennox-Gastaut syndrome (LGS)

Used off-label for:
- ❖ N/A

Lennox-Gastaut syndrome (LGS), pronounced *gas-TOE*, is a rare and severe form of childhood-onset epilepsy. LGS is characterized by multiple and concurrent seizure types, cognitive dysfunction, and slow spike waves on EEG. In 75% of cases there is an identifiable cause such as tuberous sclerosis, perinatal hypoxia or meningitis.

Rufinamide was released in 2009. It is FDA-approved for LGS in children ≥ 4 years old. Rufinamide works by prolonging the inactive state of voltage-gated sodium channels, thus stabilizing the neuronal membranes. It costs about $3,000 monthly, but a generic form may be available sometime after 2022.

Rufinamide shortens QT interval, which does not pose a clinical risk, unless patients have familial short QT syndrome or in combination with other QT shortening meds such as lamotrigine (Lamictal), digoxin, or magnesium. Contrast this with the many psychiatric medications that prolong QT.

Dosing: Start: 200–400 mg BID, increase by 400–800 mg/day every 2 days to 1600 mg BID which is both the recommended maintenance dose and FDA max; It should be given with food to promote absorption. If not taken with food, serum levels will be decreased up to 50%; Taper dose by 25% every other day to stop.

page 16

Dynamic interactions:
- ❖ Sedation/CNS depression

Kinetic interactions:
- ❖ UGT substrate
- ❖ Rufinamide is a minor CYP3A4 inDucer, unlikely to be of any clinical significance other than in combination with triazolam (Halcion), which rufinamide decreases by 35%.

3A4 inducer (minor)

1993
$138–$438

Felbamate (FELBATOL)

FEL ba mate / FEL bah tol

"Fell bat / Fell bam!"

❖ Antiepileptic
⇧ GABA activity
⇩ Glutamate activity

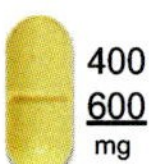

400
600
mg

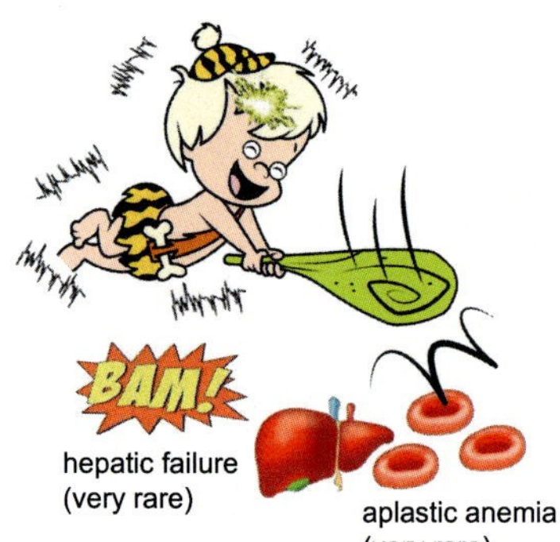

FDA-approved for:

❖ Seizure disorders refractory to other antiepileptics

Felbamate (Felbatol), approved in 1993, is the first antiepileptic with dual actions on excitatory (NMDA) and inhibitory (GABA) activity in the brain. Specifically, felbamate inhibits NMDA responses and strengthens GABA responses. This unique combination of effects could account for its broad spectrum of antiepileptic activity (Rho JM et al, 1994). Although structurally similar to the anxiolytic meprobamate (Miltown, Schedule IV), felbamate is not a controlled substance.

In 1994, one year after its release, the FDA placed a warning on the label about risk of aplastic anemia and hepatic failure. A registry was created, but was discontinued after more than 1,000 patients had been entered and no adverse events were reported (Sofia et al, 2000). It is not to be used as a first-line medication, and the patient must sign an informed consent form acknowledging the risks. Felbamate is not available in Canada, the UK, or Australia.

Compared to other antiepileptics, felbamate is less likely to cause psychiatric adverse events or impair cognitive functioning. However, it is not prescribed by psychiatrists.

Felbamate is structurally similar to meprobamate (Miltown), the "minor tranquilizer" which became the first blockbuster psychotropic drug in the 1950s as an (abusable) anxiolytic.

page 194

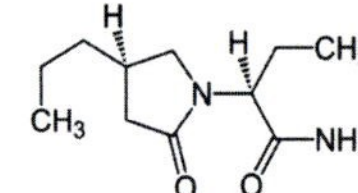

meprobamate

Dynamic interactions:

❖ Sedation/CNS depression
❖ Antiplatelet effects

Kinetic interactions:

❖ Felbamate decreases plasma concentrations of carbamazepine (Tegretol) by about 30% but increases concentrations of the active metabolite carbamazepine-10,11-epoxide by about 60% (Howard JR et al, 1992).
❖ Felbamate increases levels of phenytoin (Dilantin) and valproate (Depakote).

page 14

2C19 inHibitor (moderate)

page 16

3A4 Substrate (major)

2016
$1,134–$1,390

Brivaracetam (BRIVIACT)

BRIV a RA se tam / BRIV ee act

"Brave act (in a) Brave race"

❖ Antiepileptic
❖ Inhibitor of glutamate release
❖ DEA Schedule V

10
25
50
75
100
mg

FDA-approved for:

❖ Focal seizures

Used off-label for:

❖ Temporal lobe epilepsy
❖ Focal impaired awareness seizures
❖ Focal aware seizures
❖ Secondarily generalized seizures

Brivaracetam (Briviact) was approved in 2016 for adjunctive treatment of focal seizures in patients ≥ 16 years old. New drugs for epilepsy are often approved only as adjunctive treatment for focal seizures, because researchers aren't going to do placebo-controlled trials as monotherapy for individuals with generalized seizures. Once approved, new antiepileptic are typically used for several types of refractory seizures off-label. As expected for a new drug, it costs over $1,000 monthly.

Brivaracetam is an analog of levetiracetam (Keppra). As with levetiracetam, brivaracetam may cause anxiety and depression, and can be associated with aggression and psychosis. Psychiatric adverse reactions were reported in 13% of patients receiving brivaracetam (compared to 8% for placebo). Disturbance of mood and behavior is less severe than with levetiracetam. The main side effects of brivaracetam are somnolence and sedation (16%). It is a Schedule V (five) controlled substance (least restrictive schedule).

Brivaracetam has no off-label uses beyond seizure control. Psychiatrists do not prescribe it.

Unlike some antiepileptics, brivaracetam has a clearly defined mechanism of action. It binds selectively to synaptic vesicle protein 2A (SV2A) in the brain. Brivaracetam has a more rapid onset of action than levetiracetam and about a 20-fold higher affinity for SV2A than levetiracetam. Brivaracetam is also a partial antagonist on neuronal voltage-gated sodium channels.

Brivaracetam may cause aggression (but less so than levetiracetam)

Dynamic interactions:

❖ Sedation/CNS depression

Kinetic interactions:

❖ Rifampin (moderate 2C19 inDucer) Decreases brivaracetam levels by almost half.
❖ 2C19 poor metabolizers have about 40% higher brivaracetam levels.

page 14

2C19 Substrate (major)

1998
$66–$226

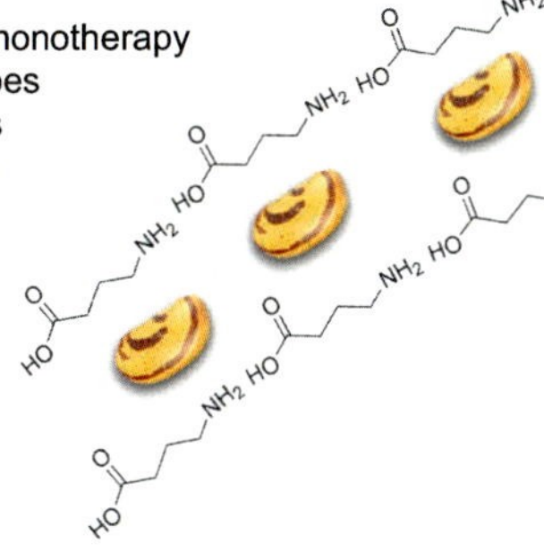

Tiagabine (GABITRIL)

ti AG a bean / GAB ih tril

"Tiger beans (on the) GABA trail"

- ❖ Antiepileptic
- ❖ GABA reuptake inhibitor

2, 4, 12, 16 mg

FDA-approved for:

- ❖ Focal seizures, adjunct

Used off-label for:

- ❖ Focal seizures, monotherapy
- ❖ Other seizure types
- ❖ Anxiety disorders
- ❖ Neuropathic pain
- ❖ Sleep quality

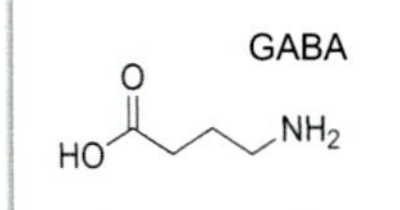

Tiagabine (Gabitril), released in 1998, is a specific GABA reuptake inhibitor, doing so by blocking GABA Transporter 1 (GAT-1). Currently, it is the only available medication with this mechanism of action.

It has been used off-label to increase deep sleep (stage 3 and 4, slow wave) to make a person feel more rested in the morning.

The main side effect is dizziness, followed by somnolence. Less common side effects include syncope, tremor, paresthesia and memory difficulties. Tiagabine can interfere with color perception, which was demonstrated in 41% of patients (Sorri et al, 2005).

GABA

The evidence supporting tiagabine for psychiatric purposes is very weak, and its use for mood or anxiety is discouraged. Tiagabine may *induce* seizures in those without epilepsy, particularly if combined with medications that lower seizure threshold. It can cause status epilepticus in overdose situations.

Dosing: For focal seizures, the maintenance dose is 32–56 mg/day divided BID–QID; Start 4 mg QD x 1 week, then 4 mg BID x 1 week, then may increase by 4–8 mg/day q week; Max is 56 mg/day; Take with food; As with any AED taper dose gradually to stop.

Dynamic interactions:

- ❖ Sedation/CNS depression

Kinetic interactions:

- ❖ 3A4 substrate (major) - When combined with a 3A4 inducer, the half-life of tiagabine is reduced (from 8 hours) to about 5 hours.

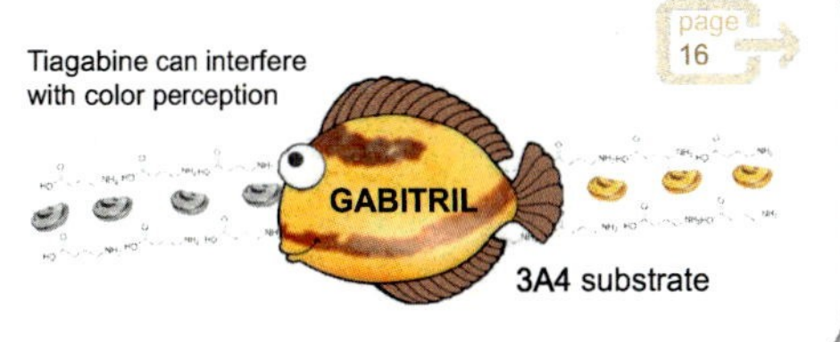

page 16

2014
$485–$1,161

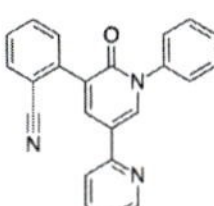

Perampanel (FYCOMPA)

per AM pa nel / fye COM puh

"FICO Perm panel"

- ❖ Antiepileptic
  - ⇧GABA activity
  - ⇩ Glutamate activity
- ❖ DEA Schedule III

2, 4, 6, 8, 10, 12 mg

FDA-approved for:

- ❖ Adjunctive treatment of focal seizures and tonic-clonic seizures in patients ≥ 12 years

Used for:

- ❖ Temporal lobe epilepsy
- ❖ Focal impaired awareness seizures
- ❖ Focal aware seizures
- ❖ Secondarily generalized seizures
- ❖ Tonic-clonic seizures

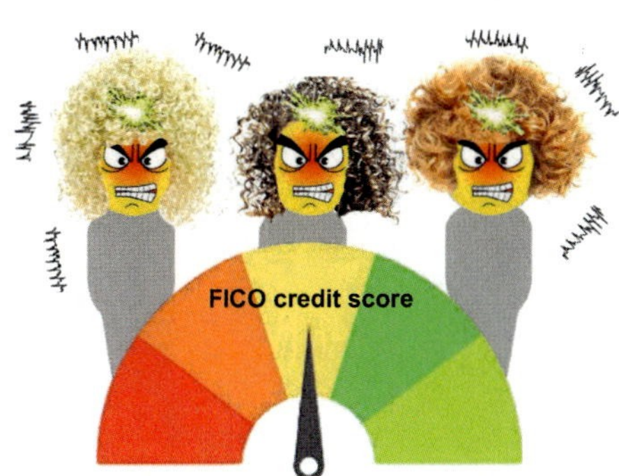

Perampanel (Fycompa) was approved in 2014 as a first-in-class noncompetitive AMPA receptor antagonist. AMPA receptors are a subtype of glutamate receptors involved in excitatory neuronal activity.

Perampanel carries a black box warning for severe psychiatric and behavioral reactions that can be serious or life-threatening, particularly hostility and aggression. Alternate mnemonics include "Fight-compa" and "Fight complicator".

Fycompa is a Schedule III controlled substance due to potential to induce euphoria. Very high doses produce dissociation similar to ketamine, although less pleasant.

Dose-dependent side effects include dizziness, somnolence, and blurred vision. Perampanel is not recommended for those with severe hepatic or renal impairment.

Dynamic interactions:

- ❖ Sedation/CNS depression

Kinetic interactions:

- ❖ 3A4 substrate (major) - Blood levels of perampanel are decreased 67% by carbamazepine (Tegretol) and 50% by phenytoin (Dilantin).

3A4 Substrate (major)

page 16

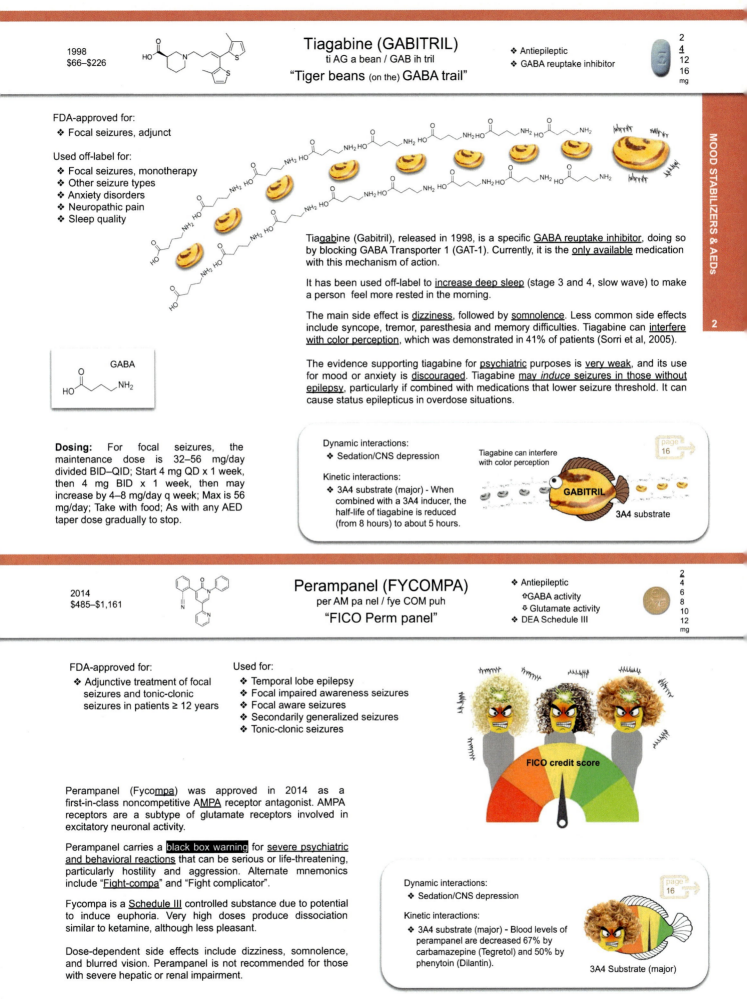

2020
$975–$1,010

Cenobamate (XCOPRI)

sen oh BAM ate / EX cop ree

"Cinnabon Ex-couple"

- ❖ Antiepileptic
- ❖ $GABA_A$ modulator
- ❖ DEA Schedule V

SK 12.5, 25, 50, 100, 150, 200 mg

FDA-approved for:

- ❖ Partial-onset seizures (adults)

Cenobamate (Xcopri) is the newest antiepileptic drug (AED), released in 2020. There are some serious risks, side effects and kinetic drug-drug interactions.

Dosing is similar to lamotrigine (Lamictal), with a slow titration to a recommended dose of 200 mg over 11 weeks. As with lamotrigine, maximum dose is 400 mg—but titration of lamotrigine only takes 5 weeks. The slow titration of cenobamate is necessary to avoid Drug Reaction with Eosinophilia and Systemic Symptoms (DRESS), also known as multiorgan hypersensitivity. There were no cases of DRESS among over 1,000 patients with adherence to the slow titration schedule.

Cenobamate shortens QT interval and is contraindicated with Familial Short QT Syndrome. QTc interval under 300 is dangerous.

Dose-dependent side effects are common (36% at 200 mg; 57% at 400 mg) including somnolence/fatigue, dizziness, diplopia/blurred vision, cognitive impairment, and headaches. Dropout rates were 11%, 9%, and 21% respectively for patients randomized to receive Cenobamate 100 mg/day, 200 mg/day, and 400 mg/day (versus 4% for placebo).

Cenobamate is a Schedule V (five) controlled substance (least restrictive) due to the possibility of euphoric feelings at high doses. The risk of psychiatric adverse effects appears to be about 1 in 333. All antiepileptics have a risk of suicidal ideation. In the clinical trial there were 4 suicides among over 25,000 patients, versus none for 16,000 patients on placebo. Causation was not established. A withdrawal syndrome was observed with sudden discontinuation, including tremor, mood disturbance, and insomnia.

At 400 mg (maximum dose), liver enzymes were elevated with ALT greater than 3x upper limit of normal in almost 3% of patients. Cenobamate may also elevate serum potassium.

Dosing: The initial dose is 12.5 mg QD, to be titrated over 11 weeks to the recommended maintenance dose of 200 mg QD; May take with or without food, at any (consistent) time of day; The recommended titration schedule should not be exceeded to avoid DRESS; Maximum dose is 400 mg QD (200 if mild/moderate hepatic impairment); To discontinue, taper over at least 2 weeks.

Dynamic interactions:

- ❖ Sedation/CNS depression
- ❖ QT shortening
- ❖ Hypokalemia
- ❖ Liver enzyme elevation

Kinetic interactions:

- ❖ 2C19 in**H**ibitor
  - Increases levels of phenytoin (Dilantin) by 75%, requiring dose adjustment
  - Increases levels of phenobarbital (Luminal) and active metabolite of clobazam (Onfi)
- ❖ 3A4 in**D**ucer
  - Decreases levels of hormonal contraceptives and carbamazepine (Tegretol)
- ❖ UGT in**D**ucer
  - Decreases levels of lamotrigine (Lamictal)

page 14
page 16

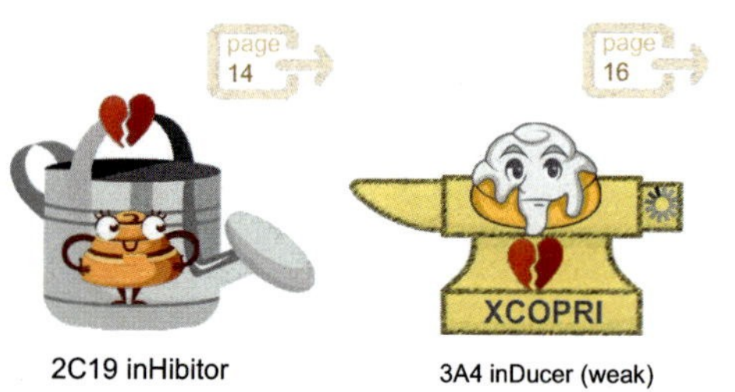

2C19 inHibitor

3A4 inDucer (weak)

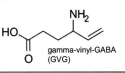

2009
$3,772–$10,670

HO(C=O)–CH2–CH2–CH(NH2)–CH=CH2 gamma-vinyl-GABA (GVG)

Vigabatrin (SABRIL)

vi GAB a trin / SAB reel

"Violent GABA Sabre!"

❖ Antiepileptic
❖ GABA transaminase inhibitor

500 mg

FDA-approved for:

❖ Focal impaired awareness seizures in adults who are refractory to several antiepileptic drugs
❖ Monotherapy for infantile spasms

"Vision Gone" - concentric peripheral visual field deficits

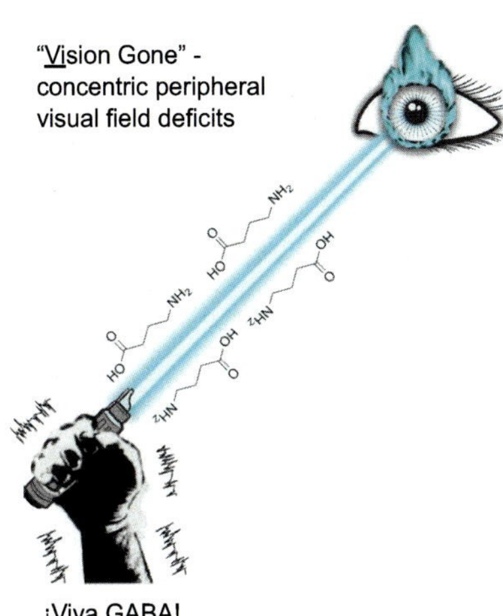

¡Viva GABA!

Vigabatrin, also known as GVG (gamma-vinyl-GABA), was approved in 2009. It is a first-line treatment for infantile spasms (West syndrome) particularly when associated with tuberous sclerosis.

The "Vi" stands for vinyl, but it could be for "vision gone" due to risk of irreversible retinal damage. GVG is available through a restricted distribution program which includes exams for peripheral visual field deficits. Concentric peripheral visual field deficits are common with vigabatrin. For patients over age 12, 40% have visual loss at > 6 months of treatment. Visual loss is less common for younger patients. Affected individuals may not notice the peripheral visual loss until they are left with tunnel vision.

GVG has been available in other countries for many years. It is incredibly expensive in the US.

Vigabatrin increases concentration of GABA in the CNS by inhibiting GABA transaminase, an enzyme that degrades GABA. An alternate mnemonic is ¡Viva GABA!

About 20% of children < 3 years old treated with vigabatrin will have MRI evidence of white matter edema in the brain. This is reversible and may not "matter" clinically. It does not appear to occur in individuals ≥ 3 years old.

Other adverse effects may include weight gain, balance problems, somnolence, violent behavior, depression, suicidal ideation and expressive language disorder.

Dosing: Maintenance dose is 1,500 mg BID; Start 500 mg BID; May increase by 500 mg/day in weekly intervals; As with any AED, taper to stop.

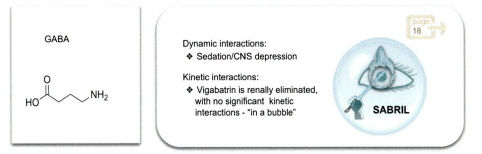

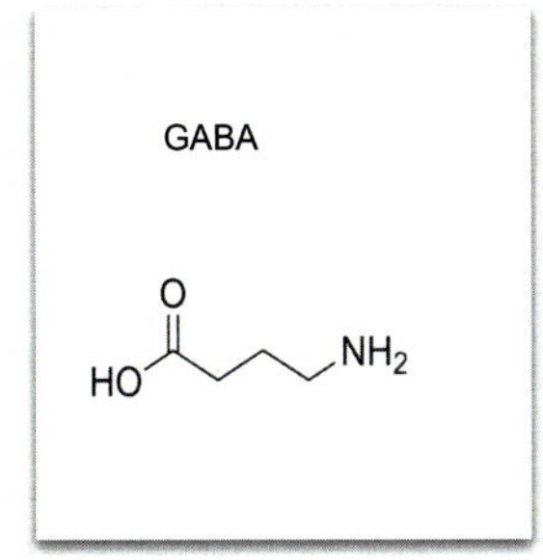

Dynamic interactions:

❖ Sedation/CNS depression

Kinetic interactions:

❖ Vigabatrin is renally eliminated, with no significant kinetic interactions - "in a bubble"

This Venn Diagram serves as an introduction to our next medication, cannabidiol (CBD).

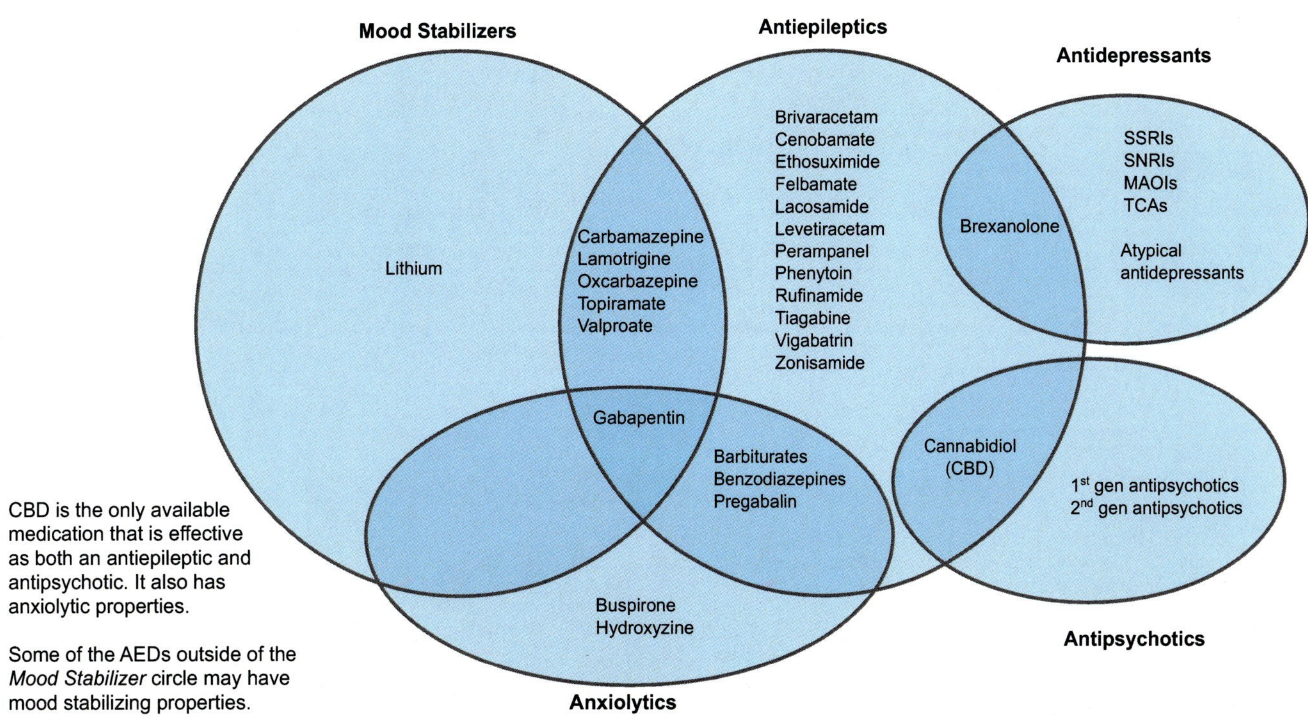

CBD is the only available medication that is effective as both an antiepileptic and antipsychotic. It also has anxiolytic properties.

Some of the AEDs outside of the *Mood Stabilizer* circle may have mood stabilizing properties.

2018
$1,290–$3,041

Cannabidiol (CBD; EPIDIOLEX)

can na bi DI ol / e pid e oh LEX

"Cannabis B.I.D. oil"

- ❖ Cannabinoid
- ❖ Antiepileptic
- ❖ Antipsychotic
- ❖ Neuroprotectant
- ❖ Non-controlled

100 mg/mL

FDA-approved for:
- ❖ Lennox-Gastaut syndrome
- ❖ Dravet syndrome

Used off-label for:
- ❖ Schizophrenia
- ❖ Anxiety

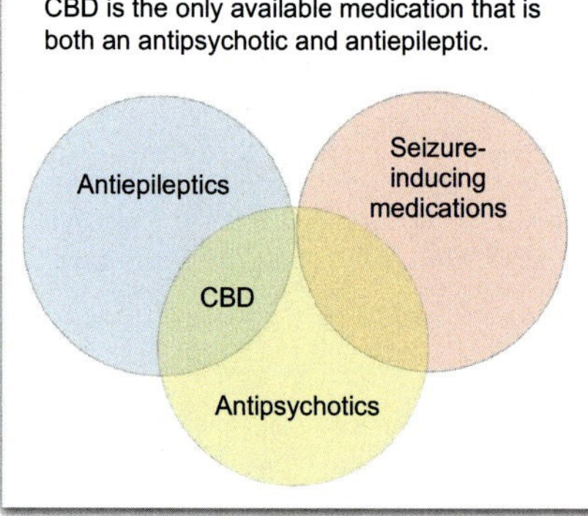

Epidiolex, pharmaceutical grade cannabidiol (CBD), was FDA-approved in 2018 for treatment of seizures associated with Lennox-Gastaut syndrome (LGS) and Dravet syndrome in children (age 2 and older). Lennox-Gastaut syndrome (LGS) is a type of childhood-onset epilepsy starting between 2–6 years of age. LGS is characterized by a triad of multiple seizure types, intellectual impairment, and characteristic EEG findings.

CBD is one of over 100 cannabinoids contained in marijuana. It should not be confused with "medical marijuana". In 2018 the DEA labeled Epidiolex as having low potential for abuse, classifying it as a Schedule V (five) controlled substance (lowest level of restriction). In 2020 the DEA dropped the restriction, so Epidiolex is no longer a controlled substance.

In clinical trials for schizophrenia, the subjects themselves were unable to tell whether they were in the treatment or placebo group.

CBD is an indirect antagonist of CB1 and CB2 cannabinoid receptors. CBD is an antipsychotic, neuroprotectant, and appetite suppressant which does not get the consumer "high". In many ways it is the opposite of tetrahydrocannabinol (THC), the main psychoactive component of cannabis. THC is a CB1 and CB2 agonist which makes it "The High Causer" in marijuana. Pure CBD is **not likely to cause a false positive drug screen** for marijuana (THC).

Epidiolex is an oral solution that (thankfully for the purpose of this mnemonic) is dosed BID. Somnolence is the main side effect of CBD. It has a good safety profile, but hepatotoxicity is possible.

CBD appears to work as an antiepileptic by inactivating voltage-gated sodium channels of the neuronal cell membrane.

CBD has demonstrated efficacy for schizophrenia at high dose. It is postulated to work as an antipsychotic through the endocannabinoid system. It is not FDA-approved for schizophrenia, but the future is promising. CBD may also be effective for social anxiety (Blessing EM et al, 2015).

Over-the-counter CBD oil is legal in all 50 states as long as it is extracted from the hemp plant, a variety of cannabis containing minimal THC. Of 84 online products tested, only 30% contained the advertised amount of CBD, and 21% contained THC (Boon-MIller et al, 2017).

Dosing: The dose for schizophrenia is 800–1,200 mg daily, which is at least $1,000 of the OTC product monthly. For anxiety, 25–200 mg daily is a reasonable dose. Reputable CBD products include Elixinol, Encore Life and Bluebird Botanicals.

	Tetrahydrocannabinol (THC)	Cannabidiol (CBD)
Pure Rx form	Dronabinol (Marinol), nabilone (Cesamet) - Schedule III	Epidiolex
Psychoactive?	The High Causer in marijuana; cognitive impairment	No "high" feelings, but may reduce anxiety
Psychosis	Cannabis use in adolescence triples the risk of psychotic disorders (Jones HJ et al, 2018)	Antipsychotic properties
Seizure	Epileptogenic (lowers seizure threshold)	Anticonvulsive (raises seizure threshold)
Neurotoxicity	Likely neurotoxic	Likely neuroprotective (antioxidant and cholinergic)
Munchies?	Yes. The Hunger Causer.	No; May cause weight loss.
FDA approval	Dronabinol (Marinol) to stimulate appetite (1985)	Epidiolex for pediatric seizures (2018)
Mechanism	CB1 and CB2 agonist	Indirect antagonist of CB1 and CB2 receptors
Drug interactions	Pure THC has few clinically significant interactions	Substrate of 3A4 and 2C19. InHibitor of 2C9, 2C19, UGT enzymes and others.

Dynamic interactions:
- ❖ Sedation/CNS depression

Kinetic interactions:
- ❖ 2C19 inHibitor (strong) - CBD may increase levels of 2C19 substrates such as diazepam (Valium) and clobazam (Onfi). Clobazam, a benzodiazepine approved for Lennox-Gastaut syndrome, is increased 3-fold by CBD.
- ❖ 3A4 substrate (minor)
- ❖ 2C19 substrate (minor)
- ❖ UGT inhibitor

page 14

2C19 inHibitor (strong)

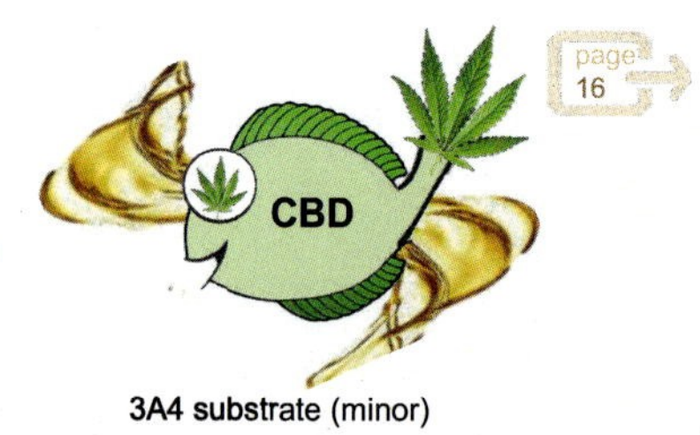

page 16

3A4 substrate (minor)

Epileptogenic Drugs

Medications that lower seizure threshold

Seizure threshold is the minimum electrical shock necessary to induce a seizure, as could be measured with electroconvulsive therapy (ECT). Antiepileptic drugs (AEDs) raise seizure threshold. Epileptogenic drugs decrease seizure threshold, thereby increasing the likelihood of a spontaneous seizure. Seizures due to epileptogenic medications tend to occur early in treatment or when dose is increased. Be careful when combining seizure-threshold-lowering medications due to aggregate risk of convulsions. "Convulsants" (see below) are agents that were given for the purpose of causing seizures, historically.

Class	Epileptogenic medications	Medications with minimal to no risk of seizures
Antipsychotics	#1 Clozapine (Clozaril) 10x risk at high dose #2 Olanzapine (Zyprexa) 3x #3 Quetiapine (Seroquel) 2x #4 Chlorpromazine (Thorazine) 2x	Risk is minimal for other antipsychotics. The following appear to be especially safe: risperidone, haloperidol, fluphenazine, thiothixene and some rarely used FGAs (molindone, pimozide, thioridazine). The only antipsychotic with antiepileptic activity is cannabidiol.
Antidepressants	#1 Maprotiline (Ludiomil) TCA, very high risk #2 Amoxapine (Asendin) TCA, high risk #3 Clomipramine (Anafranil) TCA 1–3% risk #4 Bupropion IR* (Wellbutrin) 1–2% risk—minimal with SR or XL None of these are commonly prescribed. *Most Wellbutrin prescriptions are SR or XL formulations.	For a long time, there has been a misconception that all antidepressant drugs have proconvulsant effects (Kanner, 2016). Many antidepressants do cause seizures with overdose, but excluding tricyclics and bupropion IR, the risk of seizure with antidepressants at a therapeutic dose is less than placebo, actually cutting risk of seizure in half (Alper et al, 2007). Note that depression itself lowers seizure threshold. MAOIs have the lowest seizure risk. Bupropion extended-release formulations (Wellbutrin SR and XL) at standard doses have minimal seizure risk.
Mood stabilizers	Lithium	All other mood stabilizers are antiepileptic drugs.
Anxiolytics	Buspirone (Buspar)	Benzodiazepines are antiepileptics. Beware of withdrawal seizures from any seizure-threshold-lowering medication. Alprazolam (Xanax) has a particularly high risk of withdrawal seizures due to short half-life.
Flumazenil	Flumazenil (Romazicon), the antidote for BZD overdose, is an antagonist at the BZD binding site on the GABA(A) receptor. For a brain accustomed to benzos, the addition of flumazenil is very likely to precipitate a seizure.	Since the body does not produce endogenous BZDs, flumazenil has no effect when administered in the absence of a BZD.
ADHD medications	Atomoxetine (Strattera) Methylphenidate (Ritalin, Concerta, etc) Amphetamine (Dexedrine, Adderall, Vyvanse, etc)	The antihypertensives used for ADHD: - Clonidine (Catapres) - Guanfacine (Tenex, Intuniv)
Antihistamines/ Anticholinergics	Trihexyphenidyl (Artane) Diphenhydramine (Benadryl) - in overdose or withdrawal Hydroxyzine (Vistaril) - in overdose or withdrawal	N/A
Cognitive enhancers	Donepezil (Aricept) Rivastigmine (Exelon) Memantine (Namenda)	N/A
Narcolepsy meds	Sodium oxybate (Xyrem) - sedative Modafinil (Provigil) - stimulant	N/A
Muscle relaxants (antispasmodics)	Baclofen (Lioresal) - GABA(B) agonist - in overdose Cyclobenzaprine (Flexeril) - tricyclic Methocarbamol (Robaxin)	Tizanidine (Zanaflex) - alpha-2 agonist Orphenadrine (Norflex) Carisoprodol (Soma)
Pain medications	Tramadol (Ultram) Tapentadol (Nucynta) Opioids (most)	Acetaminophen (Tylenol) NSAIDs
Other	Caffeine Cocaine Ginkgo biloba (herbal) Ondansetron (Zofran) - antiemetic PDE inhibitors (Viagra, etc)	Acetazolamide (Diamox) is a diuretic with many uses including glaucoma, intracranial hypertension, and altitude sickness. It is FDA-approved for seizure disorders but tolerance to the antiepileptic effect develops within weeks. It has value in treatment of epilepsy when taken for 14 day periods with one week's stop in between (Hoddevik, 2000).

Withdrawal seizures may be produced by abrupt discontinuation of any medication that raises seizure threshold, especially those with short half-lives. Withdrawal-induced seizures are seen with antiepileptic drugs, benzodiazepines (especially alprazolam), barbiturates, alcohol, anaesthetics, baclofen, carisoprodol (Soma), 1st gen antihistamines (diphenhydramine, hydroxyzine), and doxepin (TCA).

Historical convulsant	Trivia
Pentetrazol	GABA(A) receptor blocker, initially used as a circulatory and respiratory stimulant. Starting in 1934 it was used in high doses for shock therapy, i.e., intentionally producing convulsions in the treatment of depression. Because of uncontrollable seizures, it was replaced by electroconvulsive therapy (ECT), which debuted in 1938. The FDA revoked approval for pentetrazol in 1982.
Flurothyl	GABA(A) antagonist, used experimentally (by inhalation) for shock therapy in 1953 as an alternative to ECT. Flurothyl induced seizures were deemed clinically equal to electrical seizures with lesser effects on cognition and memory. Nonetheless, flurothyl is no longer used for shock therapy.

100% blue-light-blocking glasses (orange-tinted) were found highly effective for treatment of acute mania, adjunctively to standard antimanic medications (Henriksen et al, 2016). Patients hospitalized for mania were instructed to wear their glasses from 6pm to 8am, other than when lights were out.

The control group wore gray-tinted lenses. All subjects were managed with medications as usual. Results were dramatic, with improvement seen within 3 days. The blue blocking glasses group ended up requiring substantially fewer sedating medications (hypnotics, anxiolytics, antipsychotics) than those randomized to the control group. The mechanism likely involves the suprachiasmatic nucleus of the hypothalamus, where melatonin also acts. The glasses used in the study are available from Lowbluelights.com.

The original approach started in the 1990s as (actual, not virtual) darkness therapy. This involved keeping the manic patient in pitch darkness from 6pm to 8am.

Blue is the shortest wavelength of light on the visible spectrum. The retina contains melanopsin photoreceptors that only detect blue light, projecting to the suprachiasmatic nucleus (SCN), which is the brain's "master clock" in the hypothalamus. When these receptors are not exposed to blue light, the master clock thinks it is immersed in total darkness. Melatonin also signals to the SCN that it is dark, by binding MT1 and MT2 melatonin receptors.

For individuals with bipolar disorder, a strategy to prevent mania would involve wearing the glasses for 1–2 hours before bedtime (The Carlat Psychiatry Report, February 2019). Note the incidence of mania peaks in the spring when the amount of sunlight rapidly increases (Parker et al, 2018), typically in April.

Glasses from LowBlueLights.com block 100% of blue light, $25–$60. Glasses that block 98% of blue light are available from Uvex for as low as $10.

Another way to trick to brain into thinking it's dark out is to use blue light-blocking amber light bulbs (in an otherwise pitch-black room). Smart phones or tablets can be used in an otherwise dark room if set to filter blue light, which is call Night Mode (Android) or Night Shift (iOS), although this setting does not filter as much light as the glasses.

Blue-light-blocking glasses are also useful for insomnia in non-bipolar individuals when worn 1 to 2 hours prior to bedtime. No one should wear the glasses prior to 6 pm because this will mess with circadian rhythms and potentially disrupt mood. Wearing them in the morning could lead to depression. For depression, phototherapy with a light box would be the proper morning time treatment.

Henriksen et al. Blue-blocking glasses as additive treatment for mania: a randomized placebo-controlled trial. Bipolar Disord. 2016 May;18[3]:221–32

1912 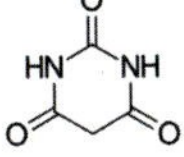 barbituric acid

Barbiturates

bahr BICH er it

"Barb wire"

Barbiturates are all derived from barbituric acid, which was discovered on the day of the Feast of Saint Barbara in 1864. Barbiturates, although dangerous, are effective for sleep, anxiety, and seizures. The first medicinal use of a barbiturate was in 1903 when it was discovered barbital would induce sleep in dogs. Shortly thereafter, barbital was marketed as a hypnotic, displacing chloral hydrate for this indication. Barbital is no longer available.

Phenobarbital was discovered in 1911 and hit the market almost immediately as a hypnotic in 1912. In the early 1920s, use of phenobarbital for epilepsy became widespread, eventually displacing potassium bromide for seizure prophylaxis (Yasiry & Shorvon, 2012). Due to safety concerns in the 1960s, benzodiazepines (BZDs/benzos) replaced barbiturates for anxiolytic and hypnotic purposes. However, the average barbiturate is less addictive than the average benzodiazepine because barbiturates have slower onset and longer duration of action.

Compared to BZDs (Chapter 4) barbiturates have a higher risk of death with overdose due to respiratory arrest. While BZDs have an antidote (flumazenil), there is no antidote for a barbiturate overdose. BZDs depress respiration but do not cause death unless combined with alcohol or other sedatives.

Barbiturates are shredders—strong inDucers of CYP450 enzymes. BZDs neither induce nor inhibit. BZDs are only CYP victims, mostly as 3A4 substrates.

Like BZDs, barbiturates bind to GABA(A) receptors at a distinct binding site. While benzodiazepines increase the frequency of chloride channel opening, barbiturates increase the duration of chloride channel opening—think barbiDURate (mnemonic from *Dirty USMLE*). Barbiturates also block glutamate receptors.

All BZDs are regulated as DEA Schedule IV controlled substances. As shown in the table below, some barbiturates are more restricted than others, ranging from Schedule II to non-controlled.

GABA(A) receptor

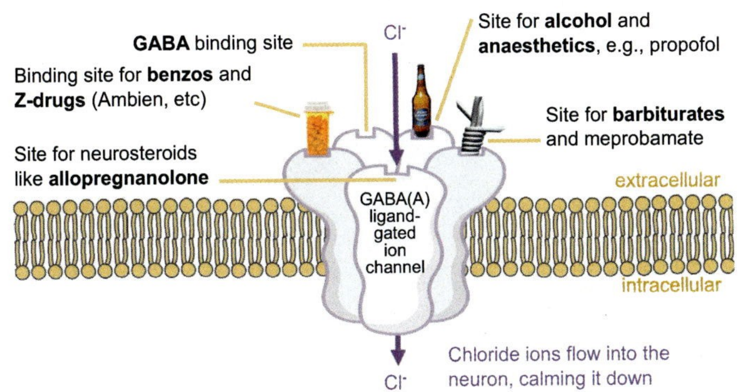

GABA receptor ligands

GABA(A) agonists

- ❖ Alcohol
- ❖ Ativan, alprazolam, etc (benzos)
- ❖ Amytal, etc (barbiturates)
- ❖ Ambien, etc (Z-drugs)
- ❖ Anesthetics
- ❖ Allopregnanolone (brexanolone)

GABA(A) antagonist

- ❖ Flumazenil (Romazicon) at the benzodiazepine site

GABA(B) agonists

- ❖ Baclofen (antispasmodic)
- ❖ GHB (Xyrem)

Note that gabapentin (Neurontin) and pregabalin (Lyrica) have chemical structures similar to GABA but they do **not** bind GABA receptors.

Barbiturate	cost / month	DEA Schedule	Duration of effect	Comments
Phenobarbital (LUMINAL) ← Metabolized to	$40	IV	10–12 hr	Phenobarbital, available since 1912, is the oldest antiepileptic still in use. It is the #10 most prescribed antiepileptic drug. It has a long half-life and can be used to treat withdrawal from alcohol.
Primidone (MYSOLINE)	$15	non-controlled	~ 6 hr	Off-label treatment of tremor; One active metabolite of primidone is phenobarbital.
Butabarbital (BUTISOL)	$140	IV	~ 6 hr	FDA-approved for preoperative sedation and short-term treatment of insomnia; very rarely prescribed
Mephobarbital (MEBARAL)	N/A	II	10–12 hr	Anxiety pill available from 1935, discontinued in 2012
FIORICET butalbital + acetaminophen + caffeine	$20	non-controlled	~ 4 hr	Butalbital is found in combination pills for tension headaches. These combos are not recommended. Butalbital in Fioricet is a common cause of positive drug screens for barbiturates.
FIORICET with codeine	$100	III	~ 4 hr	Will cause positive drug screen for barbiturates (butalbital) and opioids (codeine)
Secobarbital (SECONAL)		II	~ 6 hr	A drug of choice for physician-assisted suicide and the death penalty; The most potent p450 enzyme inDucer of the barbiturate family.
Pentobarbital (NEMBUTAL)		II	~ 6 hr	Used for animal euthanasia and physician-assisted suicide; The pills were known as "yellow jackets".
Amobarbital (AMYTAL)		II	~ 6 hr	Intravenous amobarbital has been called a truth serum. The "Amytal interview" has been used by ER physicians to differentiate between psychiatric and physiologic catatonia-like states.
Thiopental (SODIUM PENTOTHAL)		III	ultra-short 20–30 min	Used for induction of general anesthesia, largely replaced by propofol; Unavailable since 2011, when the European Union banned selling it to countries using it for executions

1912
$16–$42

Phenobarbital (LUMINAL)

fee no BAR bi tal / LUM i nal

"Fear no barbed 'Luminati"

- Barbiturate
- DEA Schedule IV

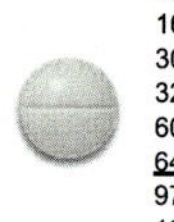

15 mg
16.2
30
32.4
60
<u>64.8</u>
97.2
100

Dosing: For 14-day <u>outpatient benzo detox</u> the initial dose is 30 mg QID, tapered down to 15 mg QID by day 6, then and down to 15 mg QOD by day 10. Do not use for anyone at risk of overdosing.

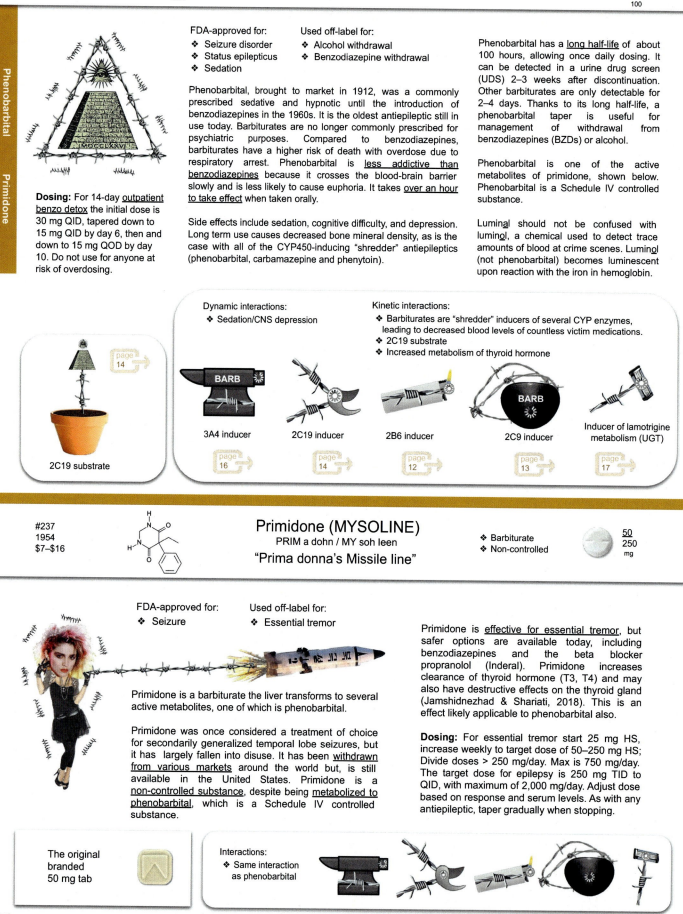

FDA-approved for:
- Seizure disorder
- Status epilepticus
- Sedation

Used off-label for:
- Alcohol withdrawal
- Benzodiazepine withdrawal

Phenobarbital, brought to market in 1912, was a commonly prescribed sedative and hypnotic until the introduction of benzodiazepines in the 1960s. It is the oldest antiepileptic still in use today. Barbiturates are no longer commonly prescribed for psychiatric purposes. Compared to benzodiazepines, barbiturates have a higher risk of death with overdose due to respiratory arrest. Phenobarbital is <u>less addictive than benzodiazepines</u> because it crosses the blood-brain barrier slowly and is less likely to cause euphoria. It takes <u>over an hour to take effect</u> when taken orally.

Side effects include sedation, cognitive difficulty, and depression. Long term use causes decreased bone mineral density, as is the case with all of the CYP450-inducing "shredder" antiepileptics (phenobarbital, carbamazepine and phenytoin).

Phenobarbital has a <u>long half-life</u> of about 100 hours, allowing once daily dosing. It can be detected in a urine drug screen (UDS) 2–3 weeks after discontinuation. Other barbiturates are only detectable for 2–4 days. Thanks to its long half-life, a phenobarbital taper is useful for management of withdrawal from benzodiazepines (BZDs) or alcohol.

Phenobarbital is one of the active metabolites of primidone, shown below. Phenobarbital is a Schedule IV controlled substance.

Lumin<u>a</u>l should not be confused with lumin<u>o</u>l, a chemical used to detect trace amounts of blood at crime scenes. Lumin<u>o</u>l (not phenobarbital) becomes luminescent upon reaction with the iron in hemoglobin.

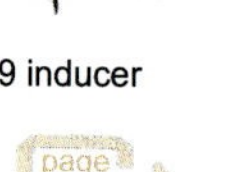

page 14

2C19 substrate

Dynamic interactions:
- Sedation/CNS depression

Kinetic interactions:
- Barbiturates are "shredder" inducers of several CYP enzymes, leading to decreased blood levels of countless victim medications.
- 2C19 substrate
- Increased metabolism of thyroid hormone

3A4 inducer page 16

2C19 inducer page 14

2B6 inducer page 12

2C9 inducer page 13

Inducer of lamotrigine metabolism (UGT) page 17

#237
1954
$7–$16

Primidone (MYSOLINE)

PRIM a dohn / MY soh leen

"Prima donna's Missile line"

- Barbiturate
- Non-controlled

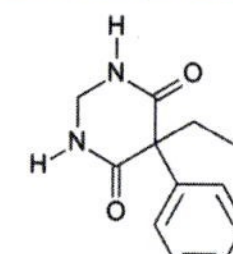

<u>50</u>
250
mg

FDA-approved for:
- Seizure

Used off-label for:
- Essential tremor

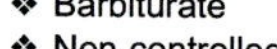

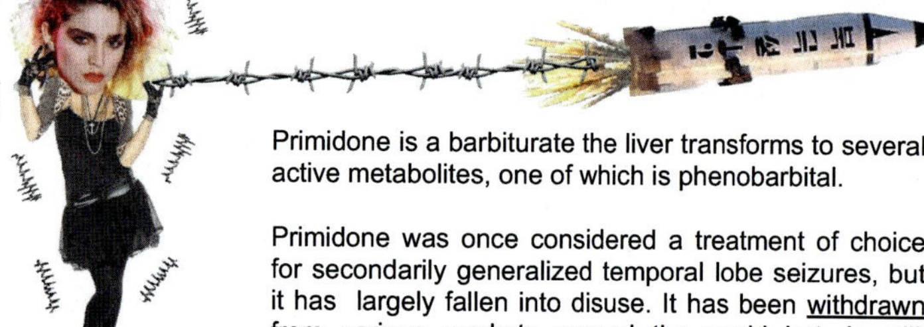

Primidone is a barbiturate the liver transforms to several active metabolites, one of which is phenobarbital.

Primidone was once considered a treatment of choice for secondarily generalized temporal lobe seizures, but it has largely fallen into disuse. It has been <u>withdrawn from various markets</u> around the world but, is still available in the United States. Primidone is a <u>non-controlled substance</u>, despite being <u>metabolized to phenobarbital</u>, which is a Schedule IV controlled substance.

Primidone is <u>effective for essential tremor</u>, but safer options are available today, including benzodiazepines and the beta blocker propranolol (Inderal). Primidone increases clearance of thyroid hormone (T3, T4) and may also have destructive effects on the thyroid gland (Jamshidnezhad & Shariati, 2018). This is an effect likely applicable to phenobarbital also.

Dosing: For essential tremor start 25 mg HS, increase weekly to target dose of 50–250 mg HS; Divide doses > 250 mg/day. Max is 750 mg/day. The target dose for epilepsy is 250 mg TID to QID, with maximum of 2,000 mg/day. Adjust dose based on response and serum levels. As with any antiepileptic, taper gradually when stopping.

The original branded 50 mg tab

Interactions:
- Same interaction as phenobarbital

1958
$131–$142

Butabarbital (BUTISOL)

bue ta BAR bi tal / BUE ti sol

"Butter barb"

❖ Barbiturate
❖ DEA Schedule III

30 mg

Butabarbital is an intermediate-acting barbiturate FDA-approved for preoperative sedation and short-term treatment of insomnia. It is still available but rarely prescribed. It is a Schedule III controlled substance, which is more restricted than phenobarbital (Schedule IV) but less restricted than the others. In the 1950s and 1960s marketing focused on treatment of female neurosis, although not exclusively—there was a "now he can cope" ad also.

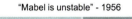

"Mabel is unstable" - 1956

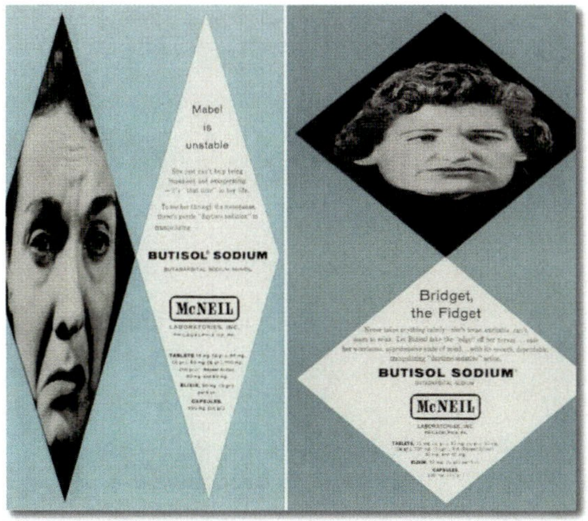

1964

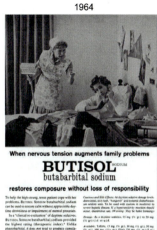

When nervous tension augments family problems

BUTISOL SODIUM

butabarbital sodium

restores composure without loss of responsibility

McNEIL

1969

now she can cope...

thanks to

Butisol SODIUM

(SODIUM BUTABARBITAL)

"daytime sedative" for everyday situational stress

1935
N/A since 2012

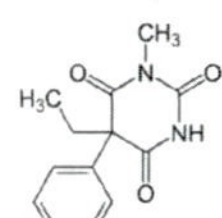

Mephobarbital (MEBARAL)

meph o BAR bi tal / MEB a ral

"Mephisto barbed My barrel"

❖ Barbiturate
❖ Off market

Unavailable

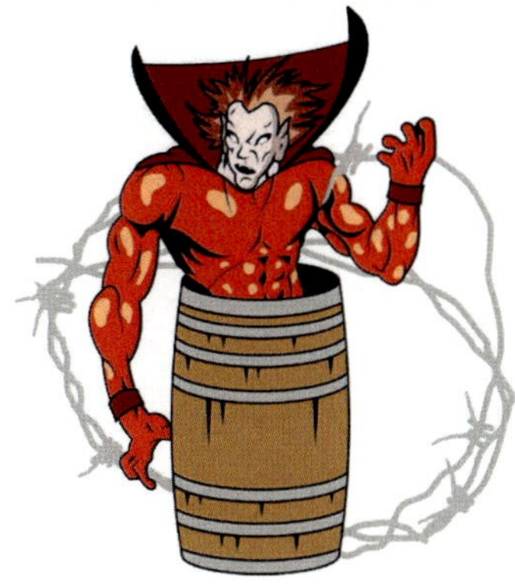

Mephisto is a Marvel comics supervillain

Mephobarbital, also known as methylphenobarbital, was discontinued in 2012 under the Unapproved Drugs Initiative. The FDA was no longer willing to allow the drug to be grandfathered, and the company declined to re-apply for approval. By 2012, its use as an anxiolytic had been mostly abandoned, but a few patients were still taking it as an anticonvulsant.

Decades ago, it was marketed to physicians as a treatment for the patient who "overreacts to any situation". It was a Schedule II controlled substance.

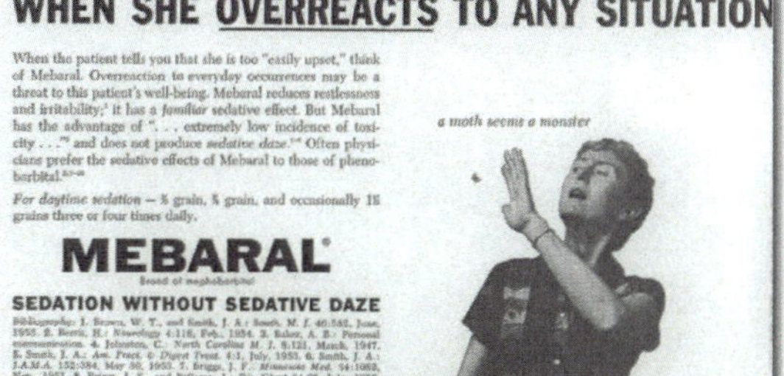

WHEN SHE OVERREACTS TO ANY SITUATION
a moth seems a monster
MEBARAL
SEDATION WITHOUT SEDATIVE DAZE

1959

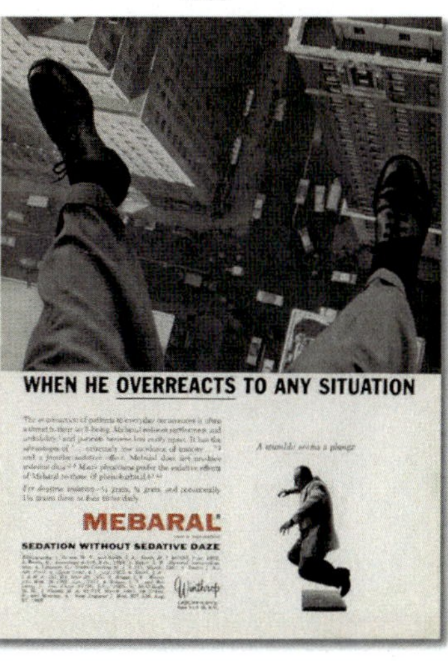

WHEN HE OVERREACTS TO ANY SITUATION
MEBARAL
SEDATION WITHOUT SEDATIVE DAZE

1970
$17–$43

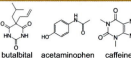

butalbital acetaminophen caffeine

Butalbital combo (FIORICET)

bue TAL bi tal / fee OR a set

"Butane Fire setter"

❖ Headache combo:
- Barbiturate
- Acetaminophen
- Caffeine

50/325/40 mg

FDA-approved for:
❖ Tension headaches

Butalbital is available in combination headache pills, but is not available individually. The butalbital component is included as a sedative. It does not directly help headaches, and may lead to overuse headache. These combos are not recommended. Fioricet is the most common cause of positive drug screens for barbiturates.

The various butalbital combos are FDA-approved for tension headaches, the most common headache type. There is a black box warning, but just regarding risk of hepatotoxicity with > 4,000 mg/day of acetaminophen.

Fioricet = butalbital, acetaminophen, and caffeine—non-controlled substance

Fiorinal = butalbital, aspirin, and caffeine

Fioricet #3 = butalbital, acetaminophen, caffeine, and codeine. It is a Schedule III controlled substance because it contains codeine.

Butalbital is a weaker CYP450 in**D**ucer than phenobarbital.

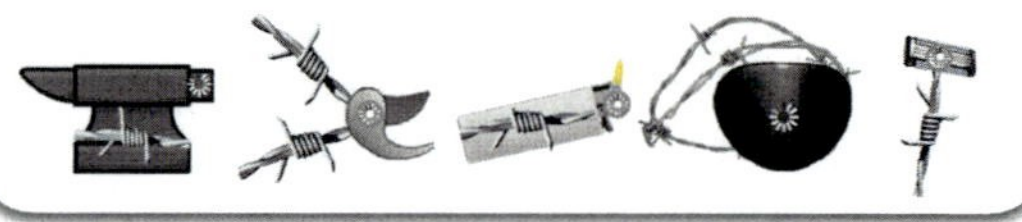

1934
$2,314–$4,317

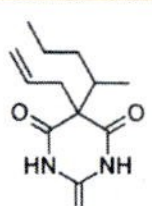

Secobarbital (SECONAL)

SEE ko BAR bi tal / sec on ALL

"Second barb"

❖ Barbiturate
❖ DEA Schedule II

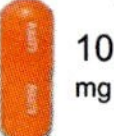

100 mg

Secobarbital is used for physician-assisted suicide. A lethal dose of secobarbital prescribed under Death with Dignity laws recently cost about $4,000.

For death penalty executions, secobarbital (which induces sleep) is given before pancuronium bromide (to paralyze the diaphragm), and potassium chloride (to stop the heart).

Countdown to death—notice the "barb" is the second hand

The capsules were once widely abused, nicknamed "red devils" or "reds".

Secobarbital is a Schedule II controlled substance, meaning it is more tightly restricted than some other barbiturates.

Among barbiturates, secobarbital is the most potent in**D**ucer of CYP450 enzymes.

Seconal is the most potent CYP inducer of the barbiturates.

1930
$1,000/gram

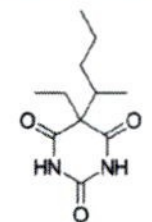

Pentobarbital (NEMBUTAL)

pen toe BAR bi tal / nem bu TAL

"Nimble Pinto"

❖ Barbiturate
❖ DEA Schedule II

FDA-approved for:
❖ Insomnia (short term use)
—no longer prescribed for sleep
❖ Preoperative sedation

Pentobarbital is a high potency, short acting barbiturate used for physician-assisted suicide, the death penalty, and animal euthanasia (Euthasol brand for dogs). It was originally developed for narcolepsy. Pentobarbital is a Schedule II controlled substance.

Pentobarbital has been used for physician-assisted suicide in California, Colorado, Hawaii, Montana, Oregon, Vermont, and Washington. It has been used for the death penalty in Missouri.

Liquid pentobarbital cost about $500 for a lethal dose (10 grams) until around 2012, when the price rose to about $20,000 due to the European Union's ban on exports to the US for capital punishment. The powder form is still available for only $270 for a lethal dose.

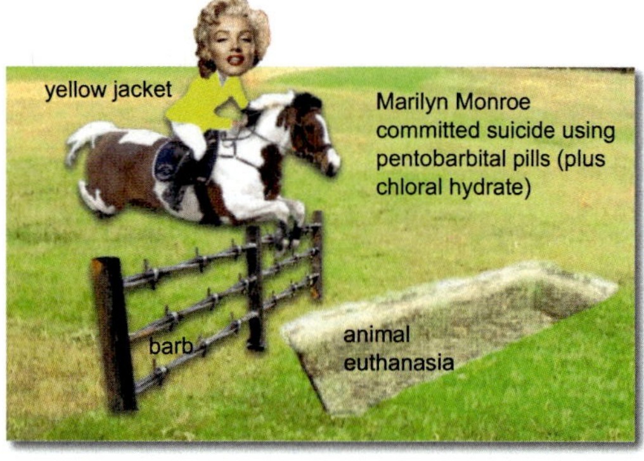
yellow jacket
Marilyn Monroe committed suicide using pentobarbital pills (plus chloral hydrate)
barb
animal euthanasia

The capsules, no longer available, were widely abused. They were referred to as "yellow jackets".

Amobarbital (AMYTAL)

1930
$117 (500 mg vial)

am oh BAR bi tal / AM a tal

"Am I tall?"

- Barbiturate
- DEA Schedule II

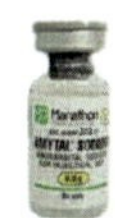

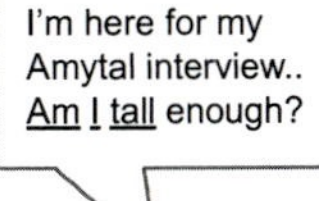
I'm here for my
Amytal interview..
Am I tall enough?

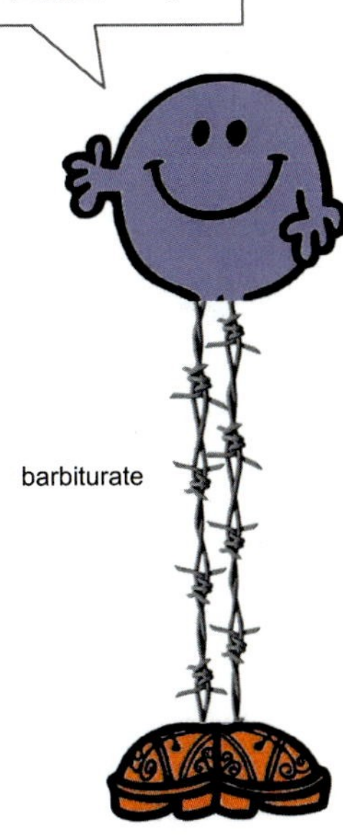

barbiturate

Amobarbital (Amytal) is a Schedule II controlled barbiturate that has been administered intravenously as a "truth serum".

The Amytal interview was introduced in 1930 as a specific technique for administration of IV amobarbital to patients with psychosis. Over the next 20 years, indications for the Amytal Interview multiplied, and the technique became known as "narcosynthesis". The Amytal interview has been used to recover memory in psychogenic amnesia and fugue states, and to treat conversion disorder.

In the emergency department setting, the Amytal interview can be used to evaluate mute, catatonic or stuporous patients in order to differentiate organic from psychogenic causes.

The Amytal interview involves telling the patient the medication is to help him relax and feel like talking. Amobarbital is infused no faster than 50 mg/min to prevent sleep or respiratory depression. The infusion continues until either rapid lateral nystagmus is present or drowsiness is noted, which usually requires 150–130 mg. The infusion continues at 5–10 mg/min until the interview is concluded (Perry & Jacobs, 1982). The expected total amount of amobarbital needed is in the ballpark of 500–750 mg.

For surgical patients about to undergo a temporal lobectomy (for refractory epilepsy), amobarbital is used to determine which side of the brain controls language and memory. This technique is called the intracarotid sodium amobarbital procedure (ISAP) or Wada test (WAH-duh), named for the surgeon who invented it. The procedure is done by injecting amobarbital into the right or left internal carotid artery to put that hemisphere of the brain to sleep. If the epileptic focus is in the dominant hemisphere, the patient is a poor surgical candidate.

The pills, nicknamed Blue 88s were given to battle fatigued US soldiers in World War II. It allowed the soldier to relax for a couple of days before returning to front-line duties. The capsules are no longer available.

Thiopental (Sodium Pentothal)

1934
Unavailable
since 2011

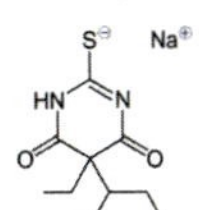

thi oh PENT al / PENT o thal

"Tire Penthouse"

- Barbiturate
- DEA Schedule III

Unavailable

Sorry WE'RE
CLOSED

Sodium thiopental is ultra-short-acting barbiturate and a Schedule III controlled substance. It was used in the induction phase of general anesthesia, although it has been largely replaced by propofol. With an IV infusion, consciousness is lost in 30 to 45 seconds and returns in 5 to 10 minutes.

Thiopental is used intravenously for physician-assisted suicide to induce coma. It is typically followed by pancuronium bromide which paralyzes the diaphragm thus stopping respiration. In 2009 Ohio became the first state to use a one-drug method for the death penalty, that drug being thiopental.

In 2011 sodium thiopental was removed from the US market due to a European Union ban. The ban was in response to America's use of the drug for death penalty executions. This prompted the American Society of Anesthesiologists to release a statement about being "extremely troubled", characterizing the ban on this "critical drug" as an important patient safety issue. Until 2011, sodium thiopental was still considered a first-line anesthetic in many cases.

Thiopental is a Schedule III controlled substance.

Dynamic interactions:
- Sedation/CNS depression

Kinetic interactions:
- Barbiturates are "shredder" inducers of several CYP enzymes, leading to decreased blood levels of countless victim medications.
- Increased metabolism of thyroid hormone

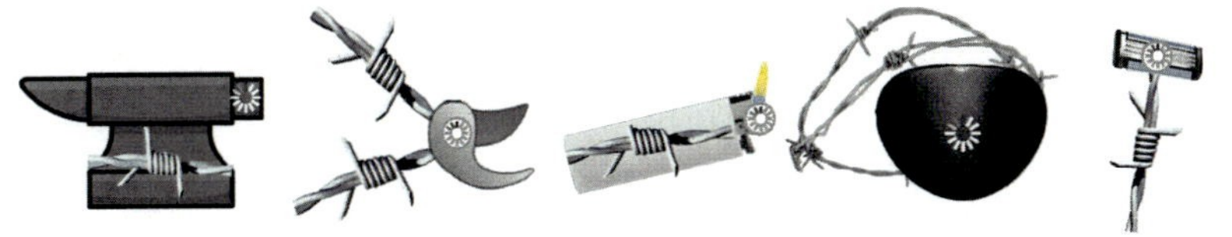

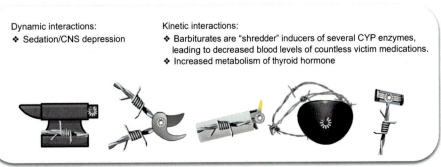

This edition of *Cafer's Psychopharmacology* was released in November 2020. Subscribe to cafermed.com for the updated PDF edition with over 1,000 internal links and bookmarks for ultrarapid navigation. The PDF edition is updated frequently with new mascots. Visit cafermed.com/update for more information.

Discount code for cafermed.com subscription: **ULTRARAPID**

Never "been so" calm. Benzodiazepines (BZDs/benzos) comprise the main class of sedatives used for short-term relief of generalized anxiety disorder (GAD), panic disorder, and social anxiety disorder. About 10% of adults have taken a benzodiazepine over the course of a year. They are the second-most abused class of prescription drugs, behind opioids. The core structure of a BZD is a <u>benz</u>ene ring fused to a seven-membered <u>diazepine</u> ring. Members of the BZD class are similar, varying in duration of action, speed of onset, and tendency to accumulate in the body.

BZDs are indirect GABA(A) receptor agonists that alter the configuration of the receptor, increasing the receptor's affinity for GABA. GABA is the main neurotransmitter involved in inhibiting neuronal activity in the brain.

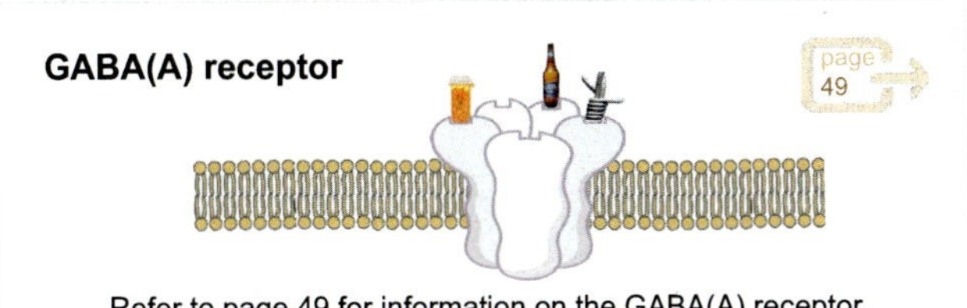

Refer to page 49 for information on the GABA(A) receptor.

<u>All BZDs are Schedule IV</u> controlled substances (less strictly restricted than opioids or ADHD stimulants, which are Schedule II). Due to their addictive nature, BZDs are <u>intended for short-term use</u>. If used for long-term treatment, BZDs are ideally taken PRN on non-consecutive days. Otherwise, efficacy is diminished as <u>tolerance</u> develops. For long term treatment of anxiety, SSRI or SNRI antidepressants are preferable. Stopping (or even decreasing the dose of) a chronically used BZD is difficult due to withdrawal symptoms and <u>rebound anxiety</u>. Individuals continuing a BZD for 3 years were more anxious and depressed than those whose BZD was stopped (Rickels et al, 1991). BZDs are ineffective and potentially harmful for the treatment of PTSD and phobias. BZD treatment increases the incidence of psychiatric hospitalization.

The main side effects of BZDs are <u>sedation</u>, fatigue, and forgetfulness. There are few side effects otherwise. BZDs do not affect metabolic parameters (weight, glucose tolerance, etc), are not anticholinergic, and do not require laboratory monitoring. Benzodiazepines are significantly <u>safer than barbiturates</u>, which were the predominant anxiolytics prior to the 1960s. BZD overdose is usually not fatal. However, they can lead to respiratory arrest in combination with alcohol and opioids. BZDs <u>should not be co-prescribed with opioids</u>. They are particularly dangerous in combination with methadone.

BZDs should be used only with extreme caution by patients with sleep apnea. From 2006–2008 BZDs were not covered by Medicare Part D due to risk of hip fracture from falls. BZDs can cause behavioral disinhibition, similar to how alcohol can lead to bar fights. Rarely, BZDs have caused acute rage reactions.

Benzos are akin to "alcohol in pill" in that ethanol also binds to the GABA(A) receptor, although at a different distinct site. BZD and alcohol dependence is a result of a conformational change to the GABA(A) receptor that decreases its affinity for GABA. Medically, <u>alcohol withdrawal and BZD withdrawal are essentially the same condition</u>. Withdrawal symptoms can include tremor, sweating, nausea/vomiting, and perceptual disturbances (tactile, auditor, and/or visual). Management of either type of withdrawal includes substituting a long-acting BZD or barbiturate dosed according to symptoms.

Withdrawal symptoms from stopping a BZD can occur after 4 weeks of continuous use. BZD withdrawal onset is within 12–48 hours, depending on the half-life of the BZD being stopped. Intensity of withdraw peaks in intensity around days 1–5. Duration of withdrawal can extend 7–21 days.

A **black box warning** advises concomitant use of BZDs and opioids triples the risk of opioid-related fatalities. Long-term BZD use is associated with a 2-fold increase in development of dementia, although the absence of a dose-response association argues against causality (Gray et al, 2016).

For patients established on high dose BZD treatment, discontinuation should be by slow taper over 4 to 8 weeks. Since BZDs are antiepileptics, abrupt <u>discontinuation can precipitate a seizure</u>. <u>Withdrawal</u> from BZDs, barbiturates, or alcohol <u>can be fatal</u>. This is not the case with withdrawal from other classes of addictive drugs.

BZDs are necessary for treatment of alcohol-withdrawal delirium (in combination with an antipsychotic). <u>BZDs may worsen other types of delirium</u>. Delirium from any etiology can be managed with an antipsychotic with minimal anticholinergic properties such as haloperidol, aripiprazole, quetiapine, risperidone, or ziprasidone.

BZDs are <u>useful for acute mania</u>, in combination with a mood stabilizer and an antipsychotic. Some experts regard BZDs as the first-line option for <u>treatment of tardive dyskinesia</u>. BZDs are the first-line <u>treatment for catatonia</u>, a stuporous condition with odd mannerisms and little response to external stimuli. The "lorazepam challenge" test (page 58) can help elucidate whether catatonia is due to psychological or organic factors.

There are three available BZDs that do not need to be metabolized by CYP enzymes—<u>L</u>orazepam, <u>O</u>xazepam and <u>T</u>emazepam = "**LOT**". These three BZDs are preferable for the elderly and those with hepatic insufficiency.

Metabolism of the non-LOT BZDs is through oxidation, catalyzed by CYP enzymes. Since the liver's ability to oxidize (Phase I metabolism) declines with age, the <u>elderly are especially sensitive to the accumulation of non-LOT BZDs</u>.

The three "LOT" BZDs are metabolized by conjugation with glucuronide (Phase II metabolism). The liver's Phase II metabolic capability does not significantly decline with age. LOT benzos are substrates of UGT2B15, which is inhibited of valproate (Depakote). Valproate can double blood levels of lorazepam.

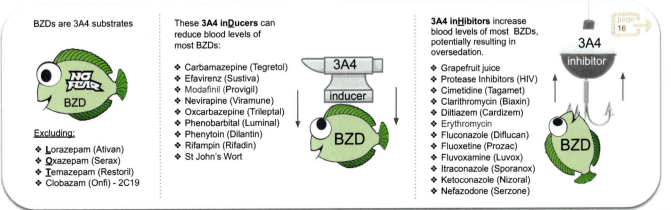

BZDs are 3A4 substrates

<u>Excluding:</u>

- <u>L</u>orazepam (Ativan)
- <u>O</u>xazepam (Serax)
- <u>T</u>emazepam (Restoril)
- Clobazam (Onfi) - 2C19

These **3A4 in<u>D</u>ucers** can reduce blood levels of most BZDs:

- Carbamazepine (Tegretol)
- Efavirenz (Sustiva)
- Modafinil (Provigil)
- Nevirapine (Viramune)
- Oxcarbazepine (Trileptal)
- Phenobarbital (Luminal)
- Phenytoin (Dilantin)
- Rifampin (Rifadin)
- St John's Wort

3A4
inducer
BZD

3A4 in<u>H</u>ibitors increase blood levels of most BZDs, potentially resulting in oversedation.

- Grapefruit juice
- Protease Inhibitors (HIV)
- Cimetidine (Tagamet)
- Clarithromycin (Biaxin)
- Diltiazem (Cardizem)
- Erythromycin
- Fluconazole (Diflucan)
- Fluoxetine (Prozac)
- Fluvoxamine (Luvox)
- Itraconazole (Sporanox)
- Ketoconazole (Nizoral)
- Nefazodone (Serzone)

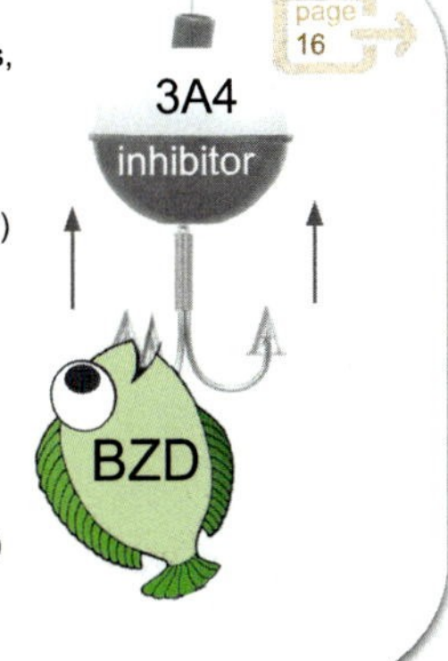

Benzodiazepines used for anxiety (anxiolytics) and/or insomnia (hypnotics)

#Rx	Benzodiazepine (approx cost/month)	Onset*	Duration	mg equiv	Details
#1	Alprazolam (XANAX) $10 Xanax XR $15 Alprazolam ODT $10	rapid	short	0.5	The most prescribed, least sedating, and most addictive BZD; High risk of seizures if suddenly discontinued due to short half-life XR = extended-release; ODT = orally disintegrating table
#2	Clonazepam (KLONOPIN) $10	med	med/long	0.25–0.5	Similar effect to lorazepam but with longer half-life and vulnerability to CYP interactions as a 3A4 substrate
#3	Lorazepam (ATIVAN) $10 Lorazepam IM (per dose) $10	med	short/med	1	The first-line BZD for anxiety, especially in the elderly and individuals with liver disease; No CYP interactions
#4	Diazepam (VALIUM) $10	rapid	long	5	Addictive due to rapid onset; used for alcohol withdrawal due to long half-life
#5	Temazepam (RESTORIL) $10	slow	med	15	The original branded capsules have "for sleep" printed on them.
#6	Chlordiazepoxide (LIBRIUM) $15	med	long	25	The first benzo (1960); useful for alcohol withdrawal due to long half-life
#7	Triazolam (HALCION) $50	med	short	0.25–0.5	#1 prescribed sleep medication until 1990s when shown to be more dangerous than other BZDs
#8	Clorazepate (TRANXENE) $100	med	long	7.5	Marketed as an anxiolytic with less sedation
#9	Oxazepam (SERAX) $100	slow	short	15	Lowest potential for abuse and lowest fatality index due to slow onset
#10	Flurazepam (DALMANE) $25	med	long	15	For insomnia but half-life is too long, tends to accumulate
#11	Estazolam (PROSOM) $50	med	med	1	For insomnia, rarely prescribed
#12	Quazepam (DORAL) $500	med	long	7.5	For insomnia, rarely prescribed

*Rapid onset—within 15 minutes. Slow onset 30–60 minutes. Duration of action is generally shorter than plasma half-life. Note that onset of action can be expedited by taking the BZD sublinguilly, which allows directly entry into blood, bypassing first-pass metabolism through the liver.

Other benzodiazepines

Benzo	Onset	Half-life	Details
Clobazam (ONFI) $750	rapid	long	Approved in 2011 for seizures due to Lennox-Gastaut syndrome; used for anxiety in other countries; It is the only available BZD with a 1,5 diazepine ring (rather than 1,4).
Midazolam (VERSED) $15	rapid	short	IV route for general anesthesia and sedation while on mechanical ventilation; the only water-soluble BZD, making it suitable for intranasal treatment of seizures; not available PO
Flunitrazepam (ROHYPNOL)	rapid	long	Similar to diazepam; infamous "Roofie" date rape drug; not sold in the US but available for prescription in Mexico for anxiety and insomnia. Travelers to the US can bring a 30-day supply if declared to customs.

Other GABA(A) ligands (not benzos)

Flumazenil	The antidote for BZD overdose; GABA(A) receptor antagonist at the BZD binding site
Barbiturates	Phenobarbital, primidone, butalbital and other "-barbitals"; In addition to binding GABA(A) receptors, barbiturates block glutamate receptors
Chloral hydrate (NOCTEC)	Discovered in the 1830s, this was the first true hypnotic drug. Chloral hydrate was a popular sleep medication until superseded by the barbiturates in the early 1900s. It is dangerous due to respiratory depression. Chloral hydrate has been unavailable since 2013 when the manufacturer voluntarily withdrew it from market. Prior to 2013 it was available in liquid-filled capsules as a Schedule IV controlled substance, although it was not FDA-approved for any indication. An alcoholic beverage laced with chloral hydrate was known as a "Mickey Finn". To "slip a Mickey" is to give someone these "knockout drops" without their knowledge to incapacitate them. Mr. Finn was a bartender accused of slipping Mickeys to rob customers, circa 1903. Chloral hydrate does not disrupt sleep architecture and does not cause withdrawal.
Methaqualone (Quāālud)	A multifaceted GABA(A) receptor modulator, Quāālude [KWAY - lude] was a popular prescription sedative in the 1970s. Its trade name derived from "quiet interlude" and stylized after Maalox, a widely-used antacid from the same manufacturer. It was discontinued in 1984 after becoming infamous for addictiveness and recreational abuse. Bill Cosby allegedly put 'ludes in womens' drinks for date-rape purposes.
Propofol (DIPRIVAN)	Milky white IV anesthetic, nicknamed "milk of amnesia". Michael Jackson's personal physician administered propofol to Jackson on a regular basis for sleep. Authorities believe the doctor fell asleep while the drug was being administered and may have awakened to find Jackson dead.
Meprobamate (MILTOWN)	Released in 1955, meprobamate was the first blockbuster psychotropic drug. It was referred to as a "minor tranquilizer" (anxiolytic) to distinguish it from the major tranquilizers (antipsychotics). Meprobamate is rarely prescribed today. The muscle relaxant carisoprodol (Soma).

GABA(B) ligands

Baclofen (LIORESAL)	Baclofen is a muscle relaxant that activates GABA(B) receptors *("B" for baclofen)*, relieving spasticity without producing euphoria or pleasant effects. Baclofen is associated with a withdrawal syndrome similar to benzodiazepines or alcohol. It is an effective off-label maintenance treatment of alcohol use disorder.
Xyrem (GHB; sodium oxybate)	Sodium salt of the club drug gamma-hydroxybutyric acid (GHB), approved for narcolepsy/cataplexy. It is an agonist at GHB receptors and GABA(B) receptors. GHB is present in the body naturally in small amounts, and can be obtained illegally for recreational and date rape purposes.

#19
1981
$9–$36
$17–$70 ER

Alprazolam (XANAX)

al PRAY zuh LAM / ZAN ax

"Lil Xan, the Alp-raised Lamb"

- ❖ Benzodiazepine
- ❖ Rapid onset
- ❖ Short duration
- ❖ DEA Schedule IV

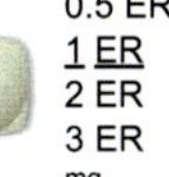

0.5 ER
1 ER
2 ER
3 ER
mg

0.25
0.5
1
2
mg

FDA-approved for:
- ❖ Anxiety 0.5 mg TID–1 mg QID
- ❖ Panic disorder 0.5 mg TID–3 mg TID

Used off-label for:
- ❖ Insomnia

The 2 mg Xanax "bar" is the strongest anxiety pill available. On the street a 2 mg bar is referred to as a "Xanny bar" or, if yellow, a "school bus", sold for about $4 each.

The stage name of Lil Xan, a rapper with face tattoos rising to fame in 2017, originated from his addiction to this benzo.

Released in 1981 for panic disorder, alprazolam remains the most prescribed benzodiazepine (BZD), particularly among primary care physicians. Psychiatrists are more likely to choose less addictive BZDs such as clonazepam (Klonopin) or lorazepam (Ativan). Xanax has the advantage of causing the least sedation among BZDs. It can be effective for panic attacks unresponsive to other BZDs. To spell the trade name correctly, think *"X for anXiety"*.

Xanax should not be used first-line because it is more habit forming than other benzos. It relieves anxiety "too well", which reinforces dependence on a quick fix and potentially interferes with development of healthy coping skills. Prescribed in small quantity, Xanax is a suitable PRN for infrequent panic attacks or specific phobias such as fear of flying.

Xanax fits the profile of an addictive substance, i.e., quick onset and short duration of action—the same reasons intravenous drugs and cigarettes are so addictive. The rapid rise of alprazolam levels in the CNS can induce euphoric feelings. Although the elimination half-life of alprazolam is 12 hours, the duration of action is much shorter, requiring TID dosing if taken on a scheduled basis. Xanax's short duration of action may lead to patients "watching the clock" in anticipation of the next available dose.

For context: Presuming oral route of administration, Xanax tends to be more addictive than PO amphetamine (Adderall) but less addictive than opioids (hydrocodone, oxycodone, etc).

It is not recommended to prescribe Xanax to individuals with a significant history of abusing alcohol or recreational drugs. Patients who doctor shop for Xanax are also likely to seek opioids. Benzodiazepines in general increase the risk of opioid-related fatalities 3-fold. Such patients may request Xanax bars by name, often persistently, claiming nothing else works. They may claim to be "allergic" to other weaker benzos and non-addictive anxiolytics such as hydroxyzine (Vistaril) and buspirone (Buspar). A clinic in Louisville KY stopped writing scripts for Xanax altogether because doctors tired of "funneling a great deal of your energy into pacifying, educating, bumping heads with people over Xanax". *"All of my patients ask for alprazolam"* —Madalyn Hoke, PA-S

Although Xanax reduces seizure risk when taken regularly, it should not be prescribed to patients with seizure disorder. Overall, Xanax is associated with a higher risk of seizures than most psychotropic medications. Seizures occur during the withdrawal phase, owing to Xanax's short half-life. Xanax XR is less likely to cause withdrawal seizures.

An individual established on ≥ 4 mg/day of alprazolam is likely physically and psychologically dependent on the medication, and an interruption in supply may be catastrophic from rebound anxiety.

The extended-release (ER) formulation, Xanax XR, is less addictive because the onset is slower, and the therapeutic effect wears off more gradually. Xanax XR is a long-acting BZD, with a duration of action longer than clonazepam (Klonopin). For a patient needing scheduled daily Xanax, the XR formulation may be the way to go.

Alprazolam appears to have antidepressant properties, which cannot be said about other benzos.

Due to short half-life, Xanax may be undetectable by a urine drug screen at 24 hours. Contrast this with long-acting BZDs like chlordiazepoxide (Librium) and diazepam (Valium), which can potentially be detected at one week.

When alprazolam tablets are taken sublingually, peak plasma concentration is higher (17.3 vs 14.9 ng/ml) and achieved faster (1.17 vs 1.73 hours) than when swallowed (Scavone & Shader, 1987; N=13).

Dosing: Approved range for panic disorder is 0.5–3 mg TID, which allows a very high max of 9 mg/day. The max for anxiety disorder (without panic) is 4 mg/day. You may divide dose to QID if interdose symptoms occur with TID dosing. Taper dose by no more than 0.5 mg/day q 3 days to discontinue. Doing the math, a patient on the maximum of 9 mg/day needs to be tapered off over 2 months. Consider treating alprazolam discontinuation like an alcohol detox using chlordiazepoxide (Librium). With Xanax XR, start at 1 mg QD for max of 6 mg QD.

Dynamic interactions applicable to all benzodiazepines:
- ❖ Sedation/CNS depression
  - Black box warning combing benzos and opioids may result in respiratory depression, coma, and death
  - Do not combine with alcohol

Kinetic interactions:
- ❖ 3A4 substrate (major)
  - Alprazolam levels may be doubled by fluvoxamine (Luvox), which a strong 3A4 inHibitor
  - Alprazolam levels are modestly elevated by grapefruit juice (weak 3A4 inHibitor)
  - Alprazolam levels are significantly decreased by potent 3A4 inDucers such as carbamazepine (Tegretol)

page 16

3A4 substrate (major)

#42
1975
$9–$38

Clonazepam (KLONOPIN)

kloh NEY zuh pam / KLON o pin

"Cloned pin"

- ❖ Benzodiazepine
- ❖ Intermediate onset
- ❖ Intermediate/Long duration
- ❖ DEA Schedule IV

0.5
1
2
mg

FDA approved for:

- ❖ Seizure disorder
- ❖ Panic disorder

Used off-label for:

- ❖ Generalized anxiety disorder
- ❖ Anxious distress of depression
- ❖ Mania (adjunct)
- ❖ Akathisia
- ❖ Insomnia
- ❖ Tardive dyskinesia
- ❖ Catatonia
- ❖ Restless legs syndrome
- ❖ Night terrors
- ❖ REM sleep behavior disorder
- ❖ Tourette's disorder

Dosing: For anxiety disorders, start 0.25 mg BID, increase by 0.25 mg/day every 1–2 days for FDA max of 4 mg/day. It is best not to exceed 2 mg/day. Consider PRN dosing, e.g. 4x/week. For acute mania (adjunct) start at least 0.5 mg BID and increase by 0.5 mg/day every 1–2 days, taper prior to discharge. As for any anticonvulsant, taper to discontinue.

Clonazepam (Klonopin) is less addictive than alprazolam (Xanax) because its onset is less rapid, and the effect wears off more gradually. Clonazepam is less sedating than the average benzo.

Clonazepam may have anti-manic properties distinct from sedation, making it useful as an adjunct for bipolar mania. For the hospitalized manic patient, a useful trio is clonazepam, plus an antipsychotic and a mood stabilizer. Ideally, clonazepam is tapered off prior to discharge from the hospital.

For benzodiazepines in general, duration of effect is much shorter than half-life. For clonazepam, half-life is 30–40 hours but duration of action is only 6–12. Clonazepam can be detected in blood for over 6 days (half-life x5). Nonetheless, standard drug screens may produce false negative results with clonazepam.

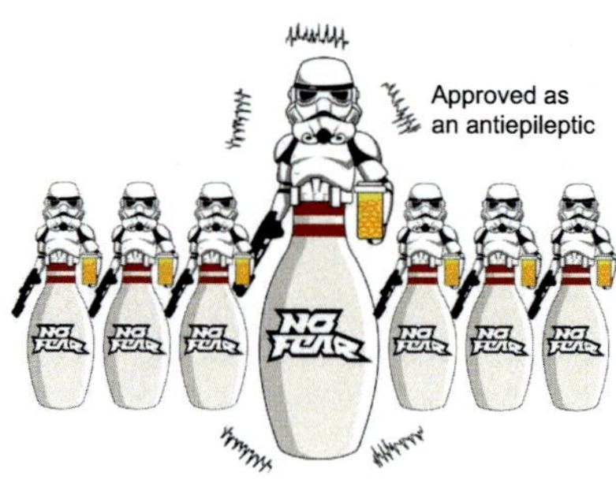

Klonopin wafers are a special formulation designed for sublingual administration. They take effect in 10–20 minutes. Standard PO clonazepam kicks in within 30– 60 minutes when swallowed.

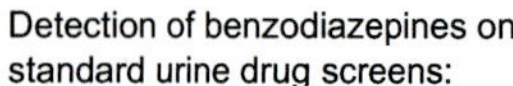

Detection of benzodiazepines on standard urine drug screens:

Usually detected:
Diazepam (Valium)
Alprazolam (Xanax)
- although short half-life

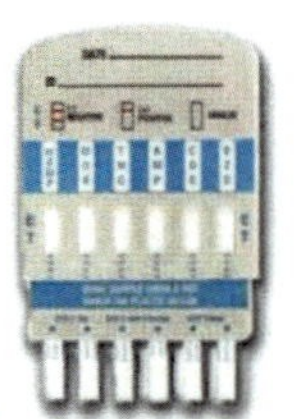

Sometimes missed:
Lorazepam (Ativan)

Commonly missed:
Clonazepam (Klonopin)

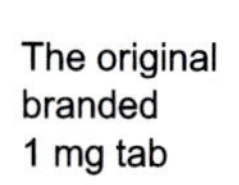

The original branded 1 mg tab

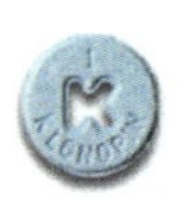

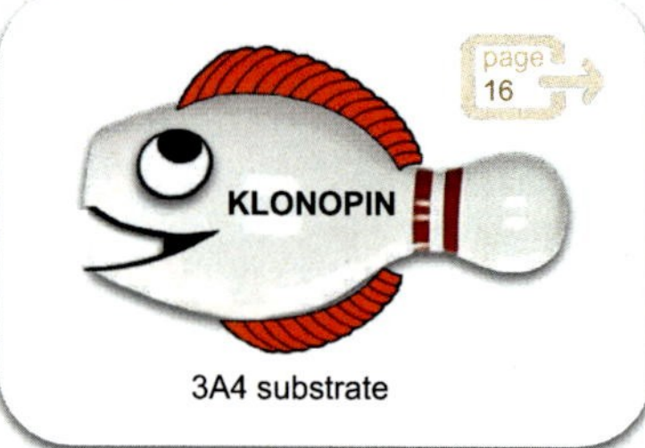

page 16

3A4 substrate

#57
1977
$9–$44

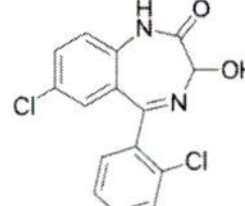

Lorazepam (ATIVAN)

lor az e pam / AT uh van

"Lorax's ATV"

- ❖ Benzodiazepine
- ❖ Intermediate onset
- ❖ Intermediate/Short duration
- ❖ DEA Schedule IV

0.5
1
2
mg

FDA-approved for:

- ❖ Anxiety
- ❖ Insomnia (short term treatment)
- ❖ Status epilepticus (IM, IV)

Used off-label for:

- ❖ Same as with clonazepam

If a benzo is necessary, lorazepam is a good choice. Lorazepam does not have an overly long half-life and there are no active metabolites to accumulate.

Ativan is a BZD of choice for those with liver disease and older adults because it metabolized by phase II conjugation only (as opposed by being oxidized by CYP enzymes).

Lorazepam is the only BZD commonly used for IM injection. For intravenous infusion, three benzos are available: lorazepam, diazepam (Valium), and midazolam (Versed).

For acute agitation in an aggressive patient, Ativan 2 mg IM can be coadministered with haloperidol (Haldol) 5 mg IM, a combo health care professionals refer to as a "five and two".

In treatment of epilepsy, lorazepam can be prescribed as a rescue medication for patients who have clusters of seizures It works reasonably quickly when taken orally and the anti-seizure effect lasts for 2 to 6 hours. A lorazepam concentrate of 2 mg (1 ml of liquid) can be taken sublingually in urgent situations (Dr. Robert Fisher, epilepsy.com).

Benzodiazepines are the mainstay of treatment for catatonia, a stuporous condition with odd mannerisms and little response to external stimuli. The "lorazepam challenge" test can help elucidate whether catatonia is due to psychological or organic factors. Upon intravenous administration of 1–2 mg of lorazepam, there may be a marked improvement of catatonia within 10 minutes. A mute patient may be able to speak. A positive lorazepam challenge confirms the diagnosis of catatonia of psychiatric etiology (McEvoy JP, 1986).

Dosing: For anxiety, start 1 mg PO BID or TID. FDA max is 10 mg/day, try not to exceed 4–6 mg/day. For insomnia, start 2 mg ½ to 1 tab HS PRN. For acute mania, start 2 mg TID and taper off as mania improves; For status epilepticus, give 4 mg IV or IM x 1. The standard IM dose for acute agitation is 2 mg. It may be coadministered with Haldol 5 mg IM.

Ativan is the only BZD commonly available for IM injection. It is the preferred IM to abort a seizure.

Dynamic interactions:

- ❖ Sedation
- ❖ Respiratory depression
- ❖ Do not combine with alcohol or opioids

Kinetic interactions:

- ❖ UGT2B15 substrate
  - Lorazepam blood levels can be doubled by valproate (Depakote)

page 18

#112
1963
$6–$12

Diazepam (VALIUM)

die AZ uh pam / VAL ee um

"Daisy & Pam (are) Valley (girls)"

- ❖ Benzodiazepine
- ❖ Rapid onset
- ❖ Long duration
- ❖ DEA Schedule IV

2
5
10
mg

FDA-approved for:

- ❖ Anxiety (PO)
- ❖ Preoperative sedation (IM)
- ❖ Sedation for cardioversion (IV)
- ❖ Sedation for endoscopy (IV)
- ❖ Alcohol withdrawal (PO, IV)
- ❖ Muscle spasm (PO)
- ❖ Seizure disorder (PO)
- ❖ Status epilepticus (IV)
- ❖ Seizure clusters (rectal gel)
- ❖ Seizure clusters (nasal)

Approved as an antiepileptic

Diazepam was introduced in 1963 and was widely prescribed for "anxiety neurosis" (DSM-II). Valium is credited as the "little yellow pill" in the Rolling Stones' 1966 hit *Mother's Little Helper*, although meprobamate (Miltown) had the same reputation preceding Valium.

For anxiety, it is dosed BID to QID. Due to its rapid onset of action, diazepam is one of the more addictive benzodiazepines, but has less potential for addiction than alprazolam (Xanax).

Due to diazepam's very long half-life, abrupt discontinuation is less likely to result in withdrawal seizures compared to alprazolam. Active metabolites of diazepam include desmethyldiazepam (100-hour half-life), oxazepam (available as Serax), and temazepam (available as Restoril).

Diazepam is more effective for muscle spasms than other BZDs. It may be given rectally for emergency seizure control.

Diazepam is FDA-approved for alcohol withdrawal, IV or PO. An oral benzo would be used for uncomplicated withdrawal, either chlordiazepoxide (Librium) or Valium. Intravenous diazepam is the drug of choice for complicated alcohol withdrawal (delirium tremens).

Dosing: 5 mg is the standard full-strength oral dose. For anxiety, start 2 mg or 2.5 mg PO BID PRN. FDA max is 40 mg/day divided BID–QID. High doses are needed for treatment of alcohol withdrawal, e.g., 20 mg q 2 hr based on Clinical Institute Withdrawal Assessment (CIWA) score, to call physician if 5 doses given (100 mg).

The original branded 5 mg tab

VALTOCO, approved in 2020, is an intranasal formulation of diazepam for intermittent episodes of frequent seizure activity (seizure clusters), as an alternative to diazepam rectal gel (DIASTAT). The other benzo approproved for cluster seizures is midazolam (page 64).

page 14

page 16

2C19 substrate

3A4 substrate

#185
1981
$1–$23

Temazepam (RESTORIL)

te MAZ e pam / REST or il

"The 'mazing Rest troll"

- ❖ Benzodiazepine
- ❖ Slow onset
- ❖ Intermediate duration
- ❖ DEA Schedule IV

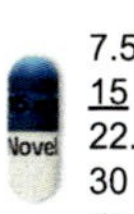

7.5
15
22.5
30
mg

FDA-approved for:

- ❖ Insomnia, short-term use

Temazepam is an intermediate duration BZD taken at bedtime for insomnia. It is never intended to be taken during the day.

Temazepam is a suitable BZD for the elderly or for those with liver disease because it metabolized by phase II conjugation as opposed to being oxidized by CYP enzymes. This applies to Lorazepam, Oxazepam and Temazepam, the "LOT" benzos.

The American Academy of Sleep Medicine (AASM) guideline (2017) states "We suggest that clinicians use temazepam as a treatment for sleep onset and sleep maintenance (vs no treatment)" based on trials of 15 mg. The direction and strength of the recommendation was "weak" and quality of the evidence was "moderate". The only other medications suggested for both onset and maintenance were the Z-drugs zolpidem (Ambien) and eszopiclone (Lunesta).

Dosing: Start 15 mg HS PRN, may increase to FDA max of 30 mg HS. Start 7.5 mg for elderly patients.

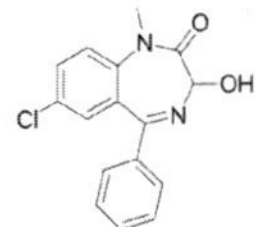

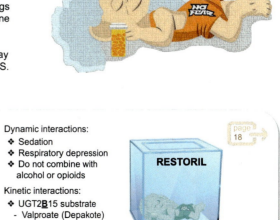

The original branded 15 mg capsule says "for sleep"

Dynamic interactions:

- ❖ Sedation
- ❖ Respiratory depression
- ❖ Do not combine with alcohol or opioids

Kinetic interactions:

- ❖ UGT2**B**15 substrate
  - Valproate (Depakote) Increases levels of "LOT" **b**enzos

page 18

1960
$8–$14

Chlordiazepoxide (LIBRIUM)

klor die as uh POK side / LIB ree um

"Lord, Liberate (me from alcohol withdrawal)"

- Benzodiazepine
- Intermediate onset
- Long duration
- DEA Schedule IV

5
10
25
mg

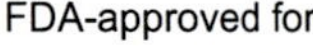

FDA-approved for:

- Anxiety (mild to moderate) 5–10 mg TID–QID
- Severe anxiety 20–25 mg TID–QID
- Preoperative anxiety 5–10 mg TID–QID
- Alcohol withdrawal 50–100 mg PRN (max 30 days)

Chlordiazepoxide (Librium) was the first benzodiazepine, available since 1960. Oral chlordiazepoxide is useful for managing uncomplicated withdrawal from alcohol or from other benzos, thanks to its long half-life. Due to Librium's tendency to accumulate, it is not very useful for any other indication. It is only available PO, so it is necessary to have IM lorazepam (Ativan) or IV diazepam (Valium) handy in the event of an alcohol-withdrawal seizure.

With regular use, chlordiazepoxide can be detected in urine a week after discontinuation. The same applies to diazepam. Contrast this to alprazolam (Xanax), which may be undetectable at 24 hours.

Dosing: See above; Taper to discontinue

Management of alcohol withdrawal

Alternatives include

- Chlordiazepoxide (Librium) - PO
- Lorazepam (Ativan) - PO, IM
- Diazepam (Valium) - PO, IV
- Midazolam (Versed) - IV
- Phenobarbital (Luminal) - PO, IV

Hospital protocols may prefer one agent over another. They are usually dosed according to a severity assessment scale such as Clinical Institute Withdrawal Assessment (CIWA). For ICU patients who are in severe withdrawal and cannot respond to questions, the Minnesota Detoxification Scale (MINDS) is used.

Consider adding haloperidol (Haldol) for a patient experiencing hallucinations or psychosis, known as delirium tremens—aka the "DT's".

Alternate mnemonic: *Cooler dies of pox (in the) Library*

Dynamic interactions:

- Sedation
- Respiratory depression
- Do not combine with alcohol or opioids

Kinetic interactions:

- 3A4 substrate

3A4 substrate

page 16

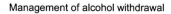

1982
$36–$102

Triazolam (HALCION)

tri A zo lam / HAL see on

"HAL Tries lamenting"

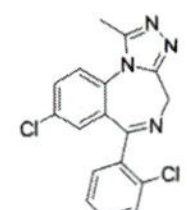

- Benzodiazepine
- Intermediate onset
- Short duration
- DEA Schedule IV

0.125
0.25
mg

FDA-approved for:

- Insomnia (short term treatment)

Short tripod, short half-life of 1.5 to 5.5 hours. This is the shortest half-life of any **oral** benzodiazepine (parenteral midazolam has a half-life of 1 to 4 hours).

Triazolam was released to the US market in 1982. It became the #1 prescribed sleep medication until the early 1990s when it was found to be more dangerous than other BZDs. Risks include anterograde amnesia and sleep activities, like those seen with the Z-drugs (Ambien, etc). Triazolam has been blamed for murders and suicides.

It is now rarely prescribed by psychiatrists. However, the American Academy of Sleep Medicine (AASM) 2017 guidelines state "We suggest that clinicians use triazolam as a treatment for sleep onset insomnia (versus no treatment)". Strength of the suggestion was "weak" with "high" quality evidence and "benefits approximately equal to risks".

Due to its short half-life, triazolam is not effective for patients who experience frequent night or early morning awakening. For those with initial insomnia, the short half-life is desirable, with no morning grogginess expected.

Sublingual administration of triazolam increases bioavailability by 28% by bypassing first-pass metabolism by the liver (Scavone et al, 1986).

I wish I were sorry

HAL 9000 from *2001: A Space Odyssey*

Dosing: Start 0.125 or 0.25 mg HS PRN. FDA max is 0.5 mg HS. Take immediately before bedtime. Use lower dose with elderly patients. Taper to discontinue.

Dynamic interactions:

- Sedation
- Respiratory depression
- Do not combine with alcohol or opioids

Kinetic interactions:

- 3A4 substrate (major)
  - Grapefruit juice, a weak 3A4 inHibitor, increases exposure to triazolam by 50%

HALCION

3A4 substrate (major)

page 16

1972
$62–$208

Clorazepate (TRANXENE)

klor AZ e pate / TRAN zeen

"(Cloraze)**peyt**on Trancing"

- Benzodiazepine
- Intermediate onset
- Long duration
- DEA Schedule IV

3.75
7.5
15
mg

FDA-approved for:

- Anxiety
- Alcohol withdrawal
- Focal seizures (adjunct)

Approved as an antiepileptic

Long trance, long half-life

This benzo has a unique name, ending in -pate, rather than -pam. Clorazepate (Tranxene) is water-soluble, which is unusual among benzodiazepines. Clorazepate is a prodrug with a lipid-soluble active metabolite. Clorazepate, which cannot be absorbed from the GI tract, is hydrolyzed in the stomach to its active form, desmethyldiazepam. Desmethyldiazepam is long-lasting, and a small amount of it is further metabolised into oxazepam (Serax, shown below).

Clorazepate is rarely prescribed, so most pharmacies will not keep it in stock. The marketing slogan for Tranxene was "Awake on the job, yet anxiety controlled". It is purportedly less sedating than the average benzo. This mnemonic might have been *Transit-ing* rather than *Trance-ing* if the marketing hype was believable.

Dosing: For anxiety, start 7.5 mg QD, with target dose of 15–60 mg/day divided BID–TID; Alternatively, 15–30 mg HS; As with any antiepileptic, taper to discontinue.

The original branded 15 mg tablet

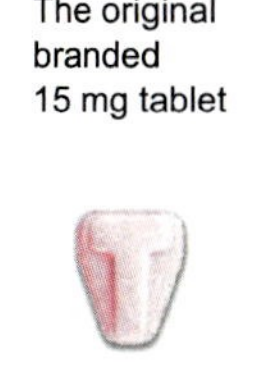

3A4 substrate

1965
$41–$126

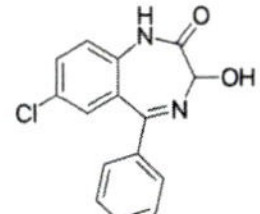

Oxazepam (SERAX)

ox A ze pam / SER ax

"Sara axed Ox"

- Benzodiazepine
- Slow onset
- Short duration
- DEA Schedule IV

10
15
30
mg

FDA-approved for:

- Anxiety
- Alcohol withdrawal (not ideal due to short half-life)

Shortened life, short half-life.

"Sera cut the ox's life short"

Among BZDs, oxazepam has the lowest fatality index and the lowest abuse potential, likely due to its slow onset of action. It is slowly absorbed and enters the brain gradually. The therapeutic effect builds over 3 hours, which is much more delayed than other BZDs (30–90 minutes). Slow onset is also the reason for the relative underutilization of oxazepam, as anxious patients may not want to wait 3 hours for relief.

Oxazepam is not involved in CYP kinetic interactions, as it is metabolized by phase II conjugation. This applies to Lorazepam, Oxazepam, and Temazepam—the "LOT" benzos. These three BZDs have no active metabolites and do not accumulate with long term use.

As expected for a rarely-prescribed old drug, oxazepam is relatively expensive, and most pharmacies do not stock it.

Dosing: The FDA approved range for anxiety is 10–30 mg TID to QID. Do not exceed 15 mg/dose for elderly patients. Taper to discontinue. Be advised smaller pharmacies will not have it in stock.

You can't set her free. But you can help her feel less anxious.

To help you relieve anxiety and tension

Serax (oxazepam)

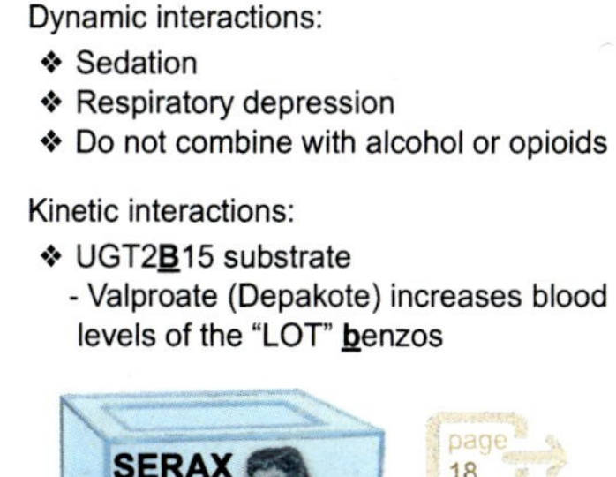

Dynamic interactions:

- Sedation
- Respiratory depression
- Do not combine with alcohol or opioids

Kinetic interactions:

- UGT2**B**15 substrate
  - Valproate (Depakote) increases blood levels of the "LOT" **b**enzos

1970
$16–$31

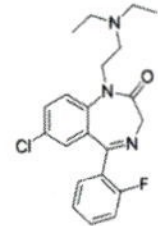

Flurazepam (DALMANE)

flure AZ e pam / DAHL mane

"Dalmatian on Floor"

- ❖ Benzodiazepine
- ❖ Intermediate onset
- ❖ Long duration
- ❖ DEA Schedule IV

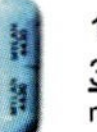

15
30
mg

FDA-approved for
- ❖ Insomnia, short-term use

Long dog, long half-life. Flurazepam has been available in the US since 1970. We're getting into rare territory, so pharmacies are unlikely to have it in stock.

When used as a hypnotic, flurazepam's 80-hour half-life may lead to daytime grogginess and accumulation of the drug. *This dog is too long.* Prescribe temazepam (Restoril) instead.

Dosing: The FDA-approved range for insomnia is 15–30 mg HS. Do not exceed 15 mg with elderly patients. Taper to discontinue.

One less concern
for your patient
with insomnia
because patient safety
is of equal concern
Dalmane
(flurazepam HCl)

Dynamic interactions:
- ❖ Sedation
- ❖ Respiratory depression
- ❖ Do not combine with alcohol or opioids

page 16

Kinetic interactions:
- ❖ 3A4 substrate

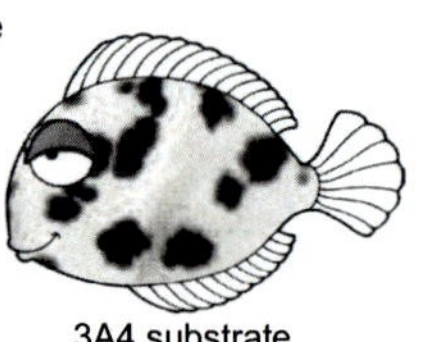

3A4 substrate

1979
$19–$56

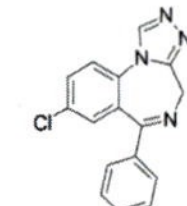

Estazolam (PROSOM)

es TAE zo lam / PRO som

"Stay Prostrate & som(nolent)"

- ❖ Benzodiazepine
- ❖ Intermediate onset
- ❖ Intermediate duration
- ❖ DEA Schedule IV

1
2
mg

FDA-approved for:
- ❖ Insomnia, short-term use

Estazolam is a rarely prescribed benzodiazepine not stocked by many pharmacies. As the trade name suggests, Prosom was marketed for insomnia. Its intermediate half-life is well suited for this indication.

Dosing: Start: 1 mg HS PRN. Max dose is 2 mg. For elderly patients, start 0.5 mg HS. Taper to discontinue.

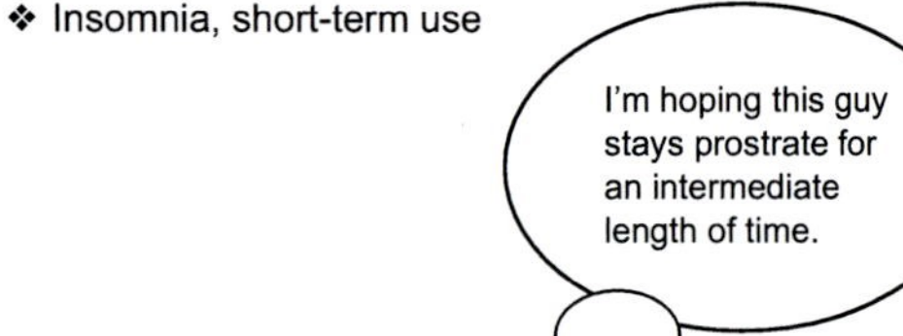

I'm hoping this guy stays prostrate for an intermediate length of time.

The sleep of their dreams
NEW
ProSom
estazolam

1977
$701–$746

Quazepam (DORAL)

qua ze pam / DOR al

"Quasimodo & Dora"

- ❖ Benzodiazepine
- ❖ Intermediate onset
- ❖ Long duration
- ❖ DEA Schedule IV

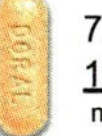

7.5
15
mg

FDA-approved for:

- ❖ Insomnia, short-term use

Long bed, long half-life of about 36 hours.

Structurally, quazepam is a benzodiazepine, but its mechanism is closer to a nonbenzodiazepine Z-drug such as zolpidem (Ambien). You might say its a "quasi-Z-drug". Compared to other benzos, quazepam has less potential to induce tolerance or respiratory depression.

Quazepam has a longer duration of action than Z-drugs, which may be longer than desired for a night's sleep. There may be marked next day impairment due to accumulation of quazepam and its long-acting metabolites. It is not recommended.

Of the older benzodiazepines, quazepam is the most expensive and the least prescribed. Health insurance plans won't cover it and the pharmacy would have to special-order it.

Doral is better known as a brand of cigarettes that debuted in 1969, preceding the pharmaceutical (1977).

Dosing: The FDA-approved dose range is 7.5–15 mg HS.

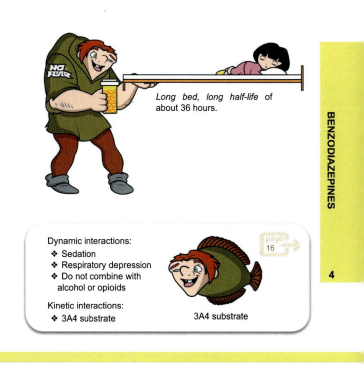

Dynamic interactions:

- ❖ Sedation
- ❖ Respiratory depression
- ❖ Do not combine with alcohol or opioids

Kinetic interactions:

- ❖ 3A4 substrate

page 16

3A4 substrate

BENZODIAZEPINES 4

2011
$36–$904

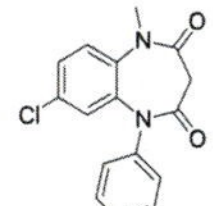

Clobazam (ONFI)

KLOE ba zam / ON fee

"Clobber On wi-fi"

- ❖ 1,5 benzodiazepine
- ❖ Rapid onset
- ❖ Long duration
- ❖ DEA Schedule IV

10
20
mg

FDA-approved for:

- ❖ Seizures of Lennox-Gastaut syndrome (LGS)

When recalling this mnemonic, pronounce WiFi as *WIFE-ee*, not *WHY-fye*.

Clobazam, long available in other countries, was finally FDA-approved in the US in 2011 for adjunctive treatment of seizures associated with Lennox-Gastaut Syndrome (ages 2 years or older). Outside of the US it was marketed as an anxiolytic since 1975 and an anticonvulsant since 1984.

Lennox-Gastaut syndrome (LGS), pronounced *gas-TOE*, is a type of childhood-onset epilepsy characterized by the triad of multiple seizure types, intellectual impairment, and characteristic EEG findings.

Clobazam is a Schedule IV controlled substance like all of the other benzos. While most benzos are 3A4 substrates, clobazam is a 2C19 substrate. Cannabidiol (CBD oil), also approved for Lennox-Gastaut syndrome, is a 2C19 inHibitor that increases exposure to clobazam 3-fold. Ingestion of alcohol increases the blood concentration of clobazam by about 50%.

So, what is so special about clobazam? Probably not much. It does have a unique structure. Clobazam is the only available 1,5 BZD. Unlike the 1,4 BZDs, clobazam is thought to be advantageous due to a rapid onset of action, broad spectrum of activity, and long half-life. However, the other benzos were not directly compared to clobazam for treatment of LGS.

The clinical advantage of clobazam is it appears to be less sedating than other benzos.

Dosing: For those >30 kg start 5 mg BID x 1 week, then 10 mg BID x 1 week, then to target dose of 20 mg BID. Maximum is 40 mg/day. Use a half-strength dose for 2C19 poor metabolizers. Also, as with any antiepileptic, taper to discontinue.

Dynamic interactions:

- ❖ Sedation
- ❖ Respiratory depression
- ❖ Do not combine with alcohol or opioids

Kinetic interactions:

- ❖ While most benzos are 3A4 substrates, clobazam is a 2C19 substrate (major)
- ❖ Cannabidiol (CBD), also approved for Lennox-Gastaut syndrome, is a 2C19 inHibitor that increases exposure to clobazam 3-fold.

page 14

2C19 substrate (major)

1975
$15

Midazolam (VERSED)

mye DAZ oh lam / ver SED

"Midas' Versus..."

- ❖ Parenteral benzodiazepine
- ❖ DEA Schedule IV

5 mg/mL

FDA-approved for:

- ❖ Procedural sedation
- ❖ Preoperative sedation (IM, PO syrup)
- ❖ General anesthesia induction and maintenance
- ❖ Mechanical ventilation sedation
- ❖ Seizure clusters (nasal spray)

Midazolam (Versed) is a benzodiazepine primarily administered intravenously. It is not used in psychiatry. Midazolam has the shortest half-life of any benzodiazepine, of 1 to 4 hours.

Midazolam is not available as a pill, (in the US) but a cherry syrup is available for preoperative sedation, for instance in dentist offices. Prior to availability of the syrup, some doctors mixed the parenteral midazolam solution into acetaminophen syrup for pediatric preoperative sedation (Shrestha et al, 2007).

A few US states use midazolam to induce sleep for death penalty executions, in combination with pancuronium bromide (to paralyze the diaphragm), and potassium chloride (to stop the heart).

Midazolam is one of the few water-soluble BZDs. Its unique chemical structure makes it water soluble at pH < 4, and lipid-soluble at physiologic pH so that it can cross the blood-brain barrier. Water soluble medications are less painful upon injection.

Water-solubility makes midazolam the only BZD that can be administered intranasally. It is given by paramedics when transporting highly agitated patients. The injectable liquid can be put in a mucosal atomization device and used for acute seizure management, as an alternative to diazepam rectal solution (De Hann et al, 2010). If the nasal spray is used, first give lidocaine nasal spray because the low-pH midazolam spray is going to sting. The nasal spray formulation (NAYZILAM) was finally FDA-approved in 2019 for cluster seizures.

As a side note, you won't see drug users crushing and snorting BZD pills (e.g., Xanax) because they are not water soluble and therefore cannot be absorbed through the nasal mucosa.

Alternate mnemonic: *"the Verse said by Midas".*

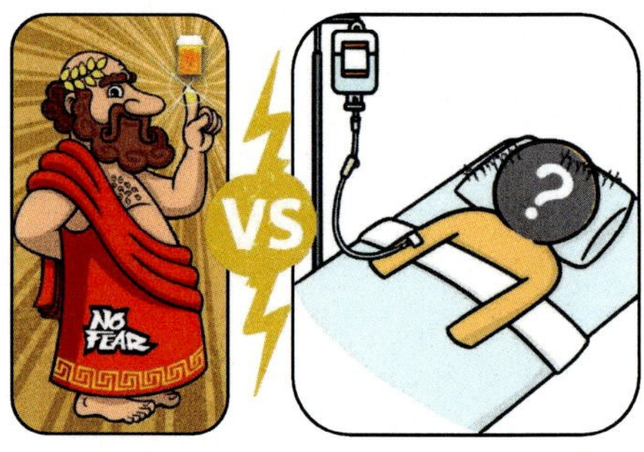

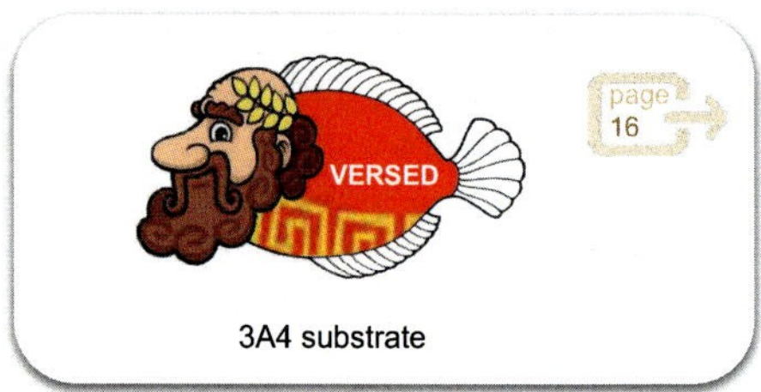

1987
$61

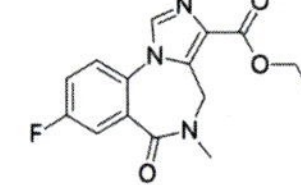

Flumazenil (ROMAZICON)

floo MAZ e nil / ro MAZ e con

"Flume a 'zepine"

- ❖ GABA(A) receptor antagonist
- ❖ Antidote for BZD overdose

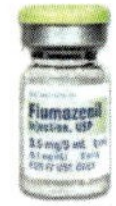

0.1 mg/mL

FDA-approved for:

- ❖ Benzodiazepine overdose
- ❖ Benzodiazepine sedation reversal

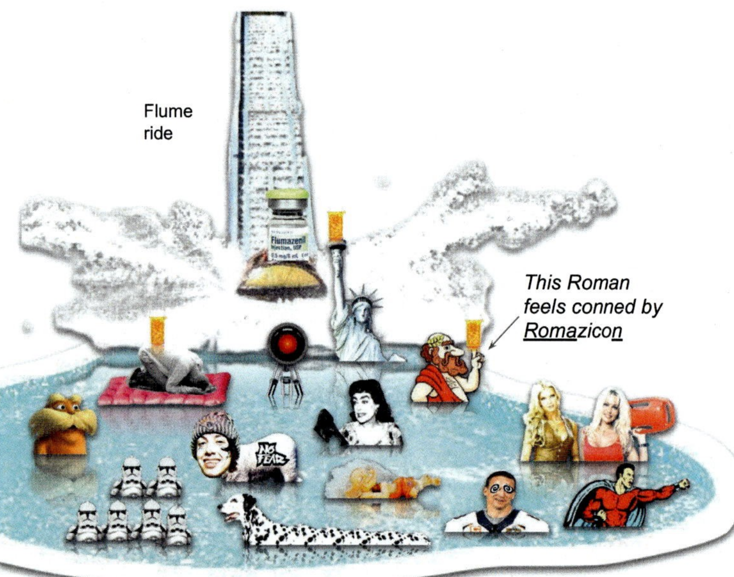

Dosing: 0.2 mg IV x 1, wait 30 seconds and give 0.3 mg IV x 1 PRN, then wait 30 seconds and give 0.5 mg IV PRN up to six doses for maximum of 5 mg total; If re-sedation occurs, repeat 0.5 mg IV (2 doses 30 seconds apart) q 20 minutes for a maximum of 3 mg/hour.

Flumazenil, the antidote for BZD overdose, is an antagonist at the BZD binding site on the GABA(A) receptor complex. Flumazenil also blocks nonbenzodiazepine Z-drugs. It does not block barbiturates. It is available for IV and intranasal delivery. Duration of action is only 30–60 minutes, necessitating multiple doses.

Since the body does not produce endogenous BZDs, flumazenil has no effect when administered in the absence of a BZD.

Flumazenil has a black box warning to prepare for the possibility of the patient having a seizure. If the person is physically dependent on BZDs, seizure is highly likely. Flumazenil is unlikely to cause a seizure for a person who overdosed on a bottle of someone else's benzo.

The usual consequences of a large BZD overdose are profound sedation and possible coma. A standalone BZD overdose does not typically cause respiratory arrest but can be life threatening due to aspiration.

Due to risk of seizure, flumazenil nasal spray is not dispensed to family members for home use (as is done with naloxone for opioids).

Another medication that blocks benzodiazepine binding in the brain is physostigmine, a cholinesterase inhibitor that is more commonly used to reverse anticholinergic toxicity.

In the 1950s, physicians referred to psychotropic medications as "major" and "minor" tranquilizers. Major tranquilizers are now known as antipsychotics. Minor tranquilizers are now called anxiolytics and/or hypnotics.

For chronic insomnia, medications are recommended as a temporary adjunct to cognitive behavioral therapy for insomnia (CBT-i), which was found equally effective to benzodiazepines for sleep (Pottie K et al, 2018). To use CBT-i, simply download the free smartphone app "CBT-i Coach", which was created by the US Dept of Veterans Affairs.

Be sure to rule out caffeine as a cause of insomnia. Drinking alcohol to fall asleep is not recommended because it disrupts sleep architecture and people tend to wake up around 3 am.

Medications for Insomnia

Class	Class representatives (monthly cost)		Comments
Benzodiazepines	Temazepam (RESTORIL) Lorazepam (ATIVAN)	$8 $8	Benzos are not first-line due to potential for addiction and rebound insomnia when stopped. They are fine for short term or PRN use. Temazepam works well for sleep onset and sleep maintenance.
Z-drugs	Zolpidem (AMBIEN)	$7	Also called nonbenzodiazepines, Z-drugs impair next-day driving and may rarely cause anterograde amnesia, where the individual does things without remembering.
Antihistamines OTC	Diphenhydramine (BENADRYL) Doxylamine (UNISOM)	$4 $8	First generation antihistamines may cause next-day sedation, which may impair driving. All are highly anticholinergic (dry mouth, constipation, urinary retention, confusion, increased risk of dementia).
Melatonin receptor agonists	Melatonin Ramelteon (ROZEREM)	$7 $390	Melatonin (OTC) is an agonist at MT1 and MT2 receptors in the hypothalamus. Ramelteon (Rx) is a strong agonist at MT1, effective for sleep onset but not sleep maintenance.
Orexin receptor antagonist	Suvorexant (BELSOMRA) Lemborexant (DAYVIGO)	$350 $300	They quiet the wake pathway by blocking orexin. Rarely cause reactions resembling narcolepsy. Safer than Z-drugs for the elderly and less likely to impair morning driving. No tolerance or withdrawal expected. They're expensive.
Tricyclic antidepressants	Doxepin (SILENOR) 3 mg, 6 mg Doxepin (generic) 10 mg	$440 $14	Tiny dose doxepin does not cause anticholinergic effects. When dosed as an antidepressant (150–300 mg), it is highly anticholinergic.
Atypical antidepressants	Trazodone (DESYREL) Mirtazapine (REMERON)	$4 $11	Trazodone 50 mg is a reasonable first-line option for insomnia but does not work as an antidepressant at this dose. Remeron is effective for insomnia associated with major depression but would rarely be used only for insomnia due to potential for weight gain.
Antipsychotics	Quetiapine (SEROQUEL)	$12	Weak antipsychotic used for sleep and anxiety. Not first-line due to potential for weight gain and diabetes. Tolerance to sedative effect may develop quickly. EPS uncommon but possible.

Medications for Anxiety

Fast onset, suitable for PRN use:

Class	Drugs	Comments All are inexpensive generics.
Benzodiazepines	Clonazepam (KLONOPIN) Lorazepam (ATIVAN) Alprazolam (XANAX)	Schedule IV controlled substances. Not first-line due to potential for dependence, tolerance and withdrawal. Klonopin and Ativan are preferred, because Xanax is more addictive. Minimal potential for interactions with Ativan.
Antihistamine	Hydroxyzine (VISTARIL)	Weaker than benzos. Not a controlled substance. Usual dose 25 mg or 50 mg PRN. Highly anticholinergic.
Beta blocker (HTN med)	Propranolol (INDERAL)	Off-label for performance anxiety. Improves standardized test scores. Good for public speaking but not for sports because it decreases heart rate. May be the best anxiolytic for those with tachycardia.

Slow and steady, should be taken every day:

SSRIs	See SSRI table (page 93)	Escitalopram (Lexapro) and paroxetine (Paxil) are FDA-approved for generalized anxiety disorder (GAD), but any SSRI should work. Escitalopram and sertraline (Zoloft) are preferred. Four weeks until full effect. Sexual dysfunction
SNRI antidepressants	Venlafaxine (EFFEXOR XR) Duloxetine (CYMBALTA)	Both are FDA-approved for generalized anxiety disorder (GAD). Venlafaxine is also approved for panic disorder and social anxiety disorder. Among antidepressants, duloxetine stands out as being particularly effective for GAD.
Serotonin receptor agonist (SRA)	Buspirone (BUSPAR)	FDA-approved for anxiety only (not for depression, fibromyalgia, or anything else). Despite its serotonergic effects, buspirone is not considered an antidepressant and is unlikely to contribute to serotonin syndrome.

Also used for anxiety:

Antiepileptic	Gabapentin (NEURONTIN) Topiramate (TOPAMAX)	Both off-label. Gabapentin is usually prescribed on a scheduled basis, starting 200–300 mg TID. Topiramate is less commonly used for anxiety, but can be useful for those who tend to overeat when nervous, up to 25 mg BID.
Alpha-1 blocker (HTN med)	Prazosin (MINIPRESS)	Used for PTSD-related nightmares, dosed at bedtime. Less commonly, it is given BID for daytime PTSD hyperarousal symptoms.
Antipsychotic	Quetiapine (SEROQUEL)	Off-label, low dose 12.5–25 mg, PRN and/or scheduled. XR formulation of quetiapine is one of the more effective medications for generalized anxiety disorder but has a high discontinuation rate due to weight gain/sedation.
Dietary supplement	Lavender oil (CalmAid)	SILEXAN brand lavender oil PO caps 160 mg QD outperformed Paxil 20 mg for general anxiety disorder (GAD) in a randomized double-blind trial (N = 539). Silexan is a prescription drug in other countries. It is available OTC in the US from the same manufacturer as CalmAid (Nature's Way) for less than $30/month. Recommend 80 mg PO HS and increase to 160 mg HS after 1 week. Effective for GAD by 2 weeks, with full effect at 3 months. Upon discontinuation, the therapeutic effect wears off gradually over 2–3 months. The only side effect was eructation (belching). Not recommended for children/adolescents due to weak estrogenic effects, which could cause gynecomastia. Among other mechanisms, it is a serotonin receptor agonist (like buspirone) and modulator of voltage-dependent calcium channels (similarly to an antiepileptic). Lavender oil aromatherapy also appears effective for GAD, possibly with faster onset than PO, with mechanism unrelated to its aroma. Potential for kinetic drug-drug interactions is unknown. See *Carlat Psychiatry Report*, August 2020.

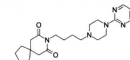

#90
1986
$7–$62

Buspirone (BUSPAR)

BU spi rone / BU spar

"Bus spear"

- ❖ Anxiolytic
- ❖ 5-HT_{1A} serotonin receptor partial agonist
- ❖ Non-addictive

5 mg
7.5
10
15
30

Some of the generic multi-scored tablets look like yellow school buses. However, most generics buspirone tabs are white, and "school bus" is slang for a multi-scored yellow 2 mg alprazolam (Xanax) tablet.

FDA-approved for:

- ❖ Anxiety

Used off-label for:

- ❖ Augmentation of SSRI for depression
- ❖ Antidepressant-associated sexual dysfunction
- ❖ SSRI-induced bruxism (tooth grinding)
- ❖ Movement disorders (high dose)
  - Tardive dyskinesia
  - Chorea
  - Levodopa induced dyskinesias
- ❖ Hostility in patients with cardiac impairment

Buspirone (BuSpar) is a serotonin 5-HT_{1A} receptor partial agonist (SRA) FDA-approved for generalized anxiety disorder (GAD). It is unrelated to other anxiolytics. Buspirone is non-addictive and generally non-sedating. Unlike other medications in this chapter, buspirone works in a slow and steady fashion, like an antidepressant. Contrast this with benzodiazepines, which work immediately but are addictive. Unlike benzodiazepines, buspirone is generally not useful as a PRN anxiolytic because optimum efficacy usually requires 2 to 4 weeks of regular administration. Some patients regard buspirone as an effective PRN, likely due to placebo effect.

"Buspar is benign." Buspirone is one of the safest psychotropic medications, with no need for laboratory monitoring. There are no absolute contraindications (other than allergy to buspirone). No deaths have been reported with single-drug overdose. It is generally well tolerated, but potential side effects include nausea, headache and jitters. It does not cause weight gain. Withdrawal is not an issue if buspirone is stopped without tapering.

"Buspirone doesn't have to be used alone!" (Madalyn Hoke, PA-S). Buspirone can be combined with practically any other psychotropic medication, with a couple of exceptions.

Buspirone is avoided with MAOIs, although there is evidence that buspirone does not cause serotonin syndrome (The scoop on serotonin syndrome; Foong et al; Canadian Pharmacists Journal, 2018)

It is redundant to combine buspirone with vilazodone (Viibryd) because vilazodone has intrinsic 5-HT_{1A} receptor partial agonist activity. Pharmacologically, *"Viibryd is like a hybrid"* of an SSRI and buspirone (page 111).

Buspirone is commonly prescribed along with an antidepressant, although caution is advised due to a small possibility of serotonin syndrome. An SSRI plus buspirone is good for anxiety, but there is better evidence for other augmenting agents for treatment-resistant depression (TRD). More effective adjuncts for TRD include lithium, aripiprazole (Abilify), quetiapine (Seroquel), risperidone (Risperdal), and liothyronine (Cytomel—T3 thyroid hormone). However, buspirone is safer and better tolerated than these more proven adjuncts.

Unlike most serotonergics, buspirone may enhance sexual functioning. Buspirone shares some properties with flibanserin (Addyi), a 5-HT_{1A} receptor agonist approved for hypoactive sexual desire disorder (page 267).

Buspirone can serve as an antidote for SSRI-induced bruxism (tooth grinding). Buspirone is used off-label at high dose for treatment of movement disorders including chorea, tardive dyskinesia and levodopa induced dyskinesias. It may improve cognitive functioning in schizophrenia and Alzheimer's disease. When used for anxiety with alcohol use disorder, it decreases drinking days (Kranzler et al, 1994).

"This school bus ain't for kids"—Although there are no safety issues, buspirone does not appear to be effective for treatment of GAD in individuals under age 18.

Buspirone has a short half-life of 2–3 hours, so it requires BID or TID dosing (usually TID). Although inconvenient, some patients prefer multiple daily dosing for better perceived control of symptoms. However, it is not expected to be immediately effective. Benefit is achieved gradually over 2–4 weeks, but placebo effect can be a powerful thing.

Dosing: Buspirone is typically started 7.5–10 mg BID or TID and titrated quickly to a target dose of 15 mg TID or 20 mg BID, with FDA maximum dose of 60 mg/day. Starting at 15 mg BID is ok. It is recommended to take buspirone consistently with food or consistently without food, because it is better absorbed when taken with meals. For off-label treatment of movement disorders, it may be necessary to titrate buspirone as high as 180 mg/day. A higher dose of buspirone will be needed if it is combined with a strong 3A4 inDucer such as carbamazepine (Tegretol). Unless the dose is very high, buspirone may be discontinued without tapering.

BuSpar was found to be ineffective for panic disorder.

Comparison with other medications that can improve sexual functioning via serotonin receptors:

Serotonergic medication	Indication	5-HT_{1A}	5-HT_{2A}
Flibanserin (ADDYI)	Hypoactive sexual desire	Agonist	(Antagonist)
Trazodone (DESYREL)	Depression/insomnia	(Agonist)	Antagonist
Nefazodone (SERZONE)	Depression	(Agonist)	Antagonist
Buspirone (BUSPAR)	Anxiety	Partial agonist	-
Pimavanserin (NUPLAZID)	Hallucinations and delusions associated with Parkinson's disease	-	Inverse agonist

page 16

Dynamic interactions:

- ❖ Serotonergic
- ❖ Sedative (weak)

Kinetic interactions:

- ❖ 3A4 substrate

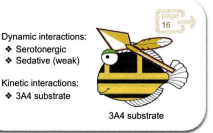

3A4 substrate

Nonbenzodiazepines, "Z-drugs", or "Z-hypnotics"

#Rx	Z-drug (cost/mo)	Month	Onset	Duration	Half-life	Driving impairment	Comments
#1	Zolpidem (AMBIEN) AMBIEN CR INTERMEZZO sublingual ZOLPIMIST oral spray	$7 $35 $7 $84	< 30 min < 30 min 20 min 20 min	short intermediate ultra-short short	2.5 hr (IR)	Yes	Ambien is the #1 prescription sleep medication.
#2	Eszopiclone (LUNESTA)	$20	< 30 min	intermediate	6 hr	Yes!	May have an unpleasant aftertaste – "Lunasty".
#3	Zaleplon (SONATA)	$14	< 30 min	ultra-short	1 hr	Unlikely	Thanks to its short half-life, Sonata can be used for middle of night awakening (off-label).

Z-drugs are hypnotics that attach to benzodiazepine (BZD) binding sites on GABA(A) receptors. They are more selective for a certain subtype of GABA(A) receptor. Z-drugs are also referred to as nonbenzodiazepines due to structural differences, i.e., they do not have a fused benzene and diazepine ring. Conceptually, Z-drugs would be better understood as a BZD subtype. Apply the general principles of prescribing BZDs to the Z-drugs. Within the Z-drug class, the main difference is duration of action.

Purportedly, Z-drugs do not disrupt stages of sleep, unlike BZDs, which inhibit REM sleep. Z-drugs have less of a muscle relaxant effect than BZDs and are regarded as safer than BZDs for obstructive sleep apnea (OSA) patients. They can help OSA patients adhere to CPAP machine usage.

Z-drugs are all Schedule IV controlled substances, which is the same schedule as benzodiazepines as shown in the table below. Abuse, withdrawal, and dependence can occur, but less commonly than with BZDs. Z-drugs are less likely to produce dependence partially because they are only taken at bedtime, so the brain is not exposed to the drug around the clock. Although tolerance may develop, Z-drugs are effective for at least six months. Ideally, they should be used PRN rather than every night, so that tolerance does not develop. Z-drugs are associated with behaviors that may occur without conscious awareness or without being remembered, such as sleepwalking or sleep eating. Complex sleep behaviors occur in at least 3% of individuals taking Z-drugs (as many as 15%). These events may be due to anterograde amnesia—the inability to remember what happened after the medication is taken. Z-drugs do not cause retrograde amnesia, so you won't lose memory of events occurring prior to taking the pill. To avoid these problems, do not exceed recommended doses, do not combine with other sedatives, and go to bed immediately after taking the medication. BZDs can also have these effects, most infamously with triazolam (Halcion). In 2019, a black box warning was added to all Z-drugs concerning the risk of complex sleep behaviors where patients engage in activities while not fully awake. There were 20 fatalities related to complex sleep behaviors on Z-drugs related to falls, motor vehicle accidents, drownings, homicides, and apparent completed suicides. Z-drugs are now contraindicated in patients who report an episode of complex sleep behavior on these medications.

It is advisable to avoid prescribing Z-drugs to older adults due to fall risk. If prescribed for the geriatric population, stick to low doses.

Controlled substances (for context)

The DEA classification system is a matter of legal restriction that does not align very well with actual addiction risk. LSD is Schedule I (illegal) but is essentially non-addictive and appears to be effective for PTSD and depression at low dose. Sustained release formulations of Schedule II stimulants (Vyvanse, Concerta) have relatively potential for abuse or addiction. The benzodiazepine alprazolam (Xanax) is highly addictive but is only a Schedule IV substance.

Schedule I - High potential for abuse, no accepted medical use (illegal)
Schedule II - High potential for abuse, with accepted medical use; refills not allowed
Schedule III - Potential for severe mental addiction or moderate physical addiction
Schedule IV - Abusing the drug may lead to mild addiction
Schedule V - Abusing the drug may lead to mild addiction, but lowest potential for abuse
Non-scheduled - Some of the examples shown may have abuse potential, but are not restricted by the DEA.

DEA	Opioids	Sedatives	AEDs	Stimulants	Cannabinoids	Other
Schedule I (illegal)	Heroin	Methaqualone (Quāālude) GHB (street)	n/a	Cathinone (from "Khat" plant)	Marijuana	DMT, LSD, MDMA (ecstasy), Mescaline, Psilocybin
Schedule II CII	Codeine (pure), Fentanyl, Hydrocodone (e.g., Vicodin), Hydromorphone (Dilaudid), Meperidine (Demerol), Methadone, Morphine, Opium tincture (antidiarrheal), Oxycodone (e.g., Percocet), Tapentadol (Nucynta)	Pentobarbital (barb) Secobarbital (barb)	n/a	Amphetamine (Adderall, etc) Cocaine (for surgery) Lisdexamfetamine (Vyvanse) Methamphetamine (Desoxyn) Methylphenidate (Ritalin)	Nabilone (Cesamet) - synthetic THC analogue	Phencyclidine (PCP)
Schedule III CIII	Buprenorphine (Subutex, Suboxone) Codeine high mg combos (e.g., Tylenol #3) Opium with camphor (Paregoric)	Butabarbital (barb) Ketamine, Esketamine **Sodium oxybate** (Xyrem) - prescription GHB Sodium thiopental (barb)	Perampanel (Fycompa)	Benzphetamine (diet pill) Phendimetrazine (diet pill)	Dronabinol (Marinol) - synthetic THC	Anabolic steroids: - Androstenedione - Testosterone Lysergic acid (Ergine)
Schedule IV CIV	Butorphanol (Stadol nasal spray) Pentazocine (Talwin) Tramadol (Ultram)	**Benzodiazepines & Z-Drugs** Carisoprodol (Soma) Flunitrazepam (Rohypnol) Lemborexant (Dayvigo) Meprobamate (Miltown) Suvorexant (Belsomra) Chloral hydrate	Phenobarbital (barb) Clobazam (Onfi) BZD	Armodafinil (Nuvigil) Cathine (from "Khat" plant) Diethylpropion (diet pill) Modafinil (Provigil) Phentermine (diet pill) Solfiramfetol (Sunosi)	n/a	Lorcaserin (Belviq)
Schedule V CV	Codeine low dose combos (cough syrup) Diphenoxylate with atropine* (Lomotil) Difenoxin with atropine*	n/a	Brivaracetam (Briviact) Cenobamate (Xcopri) Lacosamide (Vimpat) Pregabalin (Lyrica)	Pyrovalerone	n/a	Dextromethorphan (e.g., Robitussin)
Non-scheduled (2020)	Nalbuphine (Nubain) Kratom - illegal in 6 states Salvia divinorum - illegal in 29 states (κ-opioid agonist hallucinogen)	Alcohol Butalbital (barb) low dose combos (e.g., Fioricet) Propofol (Diprivan) **All antipsychotics**	Gabapentin (Neurontin) Primidone (barb)	Atomoxetine (Strattera) Bupropion (Wellbutrin) Caffeine Istradefylline (Nourianz) Nicotine Pitolisant (Wakix)	Cannabidiol (CBD)	Nitrous oxide (whippets)

*Difenoxin and Diphenoxylate (Lomotil) are Schedule V (for diarrhea) when mixed with atropine to cause unpleasantness if injected intravenously. Otherwise they are Schedule I and II, respectively.

#40
1992
IR $7–$69
ER $18–$157
SL $91–$283

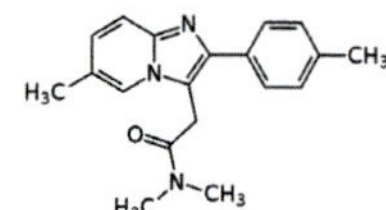

Zolpidem (AMBIEN)

ZOHL pi dem / AM be in

"Soul pie with Amnesia beans"

- ❖ Z-drug
- ❖ Schedule IV

1.75 SL
3.5 SL
mg

6.25 ER
12.5 ER
mg

5
10
mg

FDA-approved for:

- ❖ Insomnia, short-term treatment

Zolpidem (Ambien) is the #1 prescribed hypnotic in the US and the #40 prescribed drug overall. It is effective for sleep onset and sleep maintenance. It is well known in popular culture for causing people to do things in their sleep or doing things and not remembering to have done so, due to anterograde amnesia. Zolpidem was FDA-approved in 1992, and has been available generically since 2007. Although the half-life is 2.5 hours, the effects may last up to 8 hours. Onset of action is < 30 minutes, but food delays the effect of zolpidem by 1 hour.

The half-life is longer for the elderly, those with liver impairment, and women. Never exceed the recommended maximum dose (10 mg IR, 12.5 mg CR) with zolpidem.

In 2013 the FDA required the recommended starting dose be decreased for women (from 10 mg to 5 mg) because women have higher blood levels at 8 hours which could lead to driving impairment. As of 2018, Ambien is the only psychotropic with gender specific dosing recommendations. This warning is arguably unnecessary because the gender related difference in duration for Ambien is modest and probably insignificant. The reason for (modestly) lower zolpidem levels for men is testosterone can stimulate the activity of 3A4 in metabolizing certain (but not most) 3A4 substrates.

In 2019 the FDA placed a black box warning on the Z-drugs concerning the risk of injury from complex sleep behaviors. The warning was based on 66 cases of patients involved in activities while not fully awake. 20 of these cases resulted in fatalities. Of the 66 cases, 61 were using zolpidem. This is considered to reflect the high volume of prescriptions dispensed for zolpidem vs the other two Z-drugs, rather than zolpidem being uniquely dangerous.

Complex sleep behaviors occur in at least 3% of individuals taking Ambien (and possibly up to 15%). Food delays onset of action by about 1 hour, and delayed onset of sleep medications is a risk factor for complex sleep behaviors. Therefore, patients should not eat within 30 minutes of taking Ambien. Z-drugs should be discontinued if complex sleep behaviors occur.

The extended-release formulation Ambien CR (6.25–12.5 mg) should be used with caution (if used at all) because blood levels may remain high the next day and impair driving or cause falls. Ambien CR is good for about one additional hour of sleep compared to the IR formulation. Part of Ambien CR's extended duration relates to dose strength (6.25–12.5 mg for IR as opposed to 5–10 mg for ER).

Intermezzo is a low dose sublingual formulation of zolpidem. Intermezzo is the only hypnotic approved for middle-of-night awakening. A cheaper Z-drug with a short half-life, zaleplon (Sonata), can be used off-label for this purpose.

Dosing: Preferably dosed PRN rather than routinely; The patient should go to bed immediately after taking Ambien; Be cautious with dose for females and elderly patients; Ambien IR: The recommended dose for men is 5–10 mg PRN, but just 5 mg for women. The max dose for either gender is 10 mg. Ambien CR: 6.25–12.5 mg for men, 6.25 mg for women; Intermezzo for middle-of-night awakenings is dosed 3.5 mg for men (1.75 mg for women) once per night PRN if > 4 hours before planned waking time. Discontinue zolpidem immediately if the patient experiences complex sleep behavior.

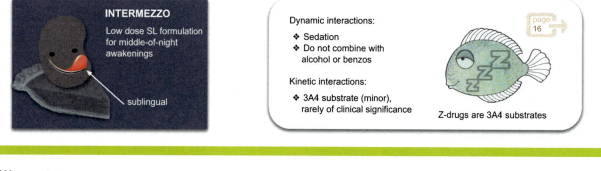

INTERMEZZO

Low dose SL formulation for middle-of-night awakenings

sublingual

Dynamic interactions:

- ❖ Sedation
- ❖ Do not combine with alcohol or benzos

Kinetic interactions:

- ❖ 3A4 substrate (minor), rarely of clinical significance

page 16

Z-drugs are 3A4 substrates

GABA(A) receptor

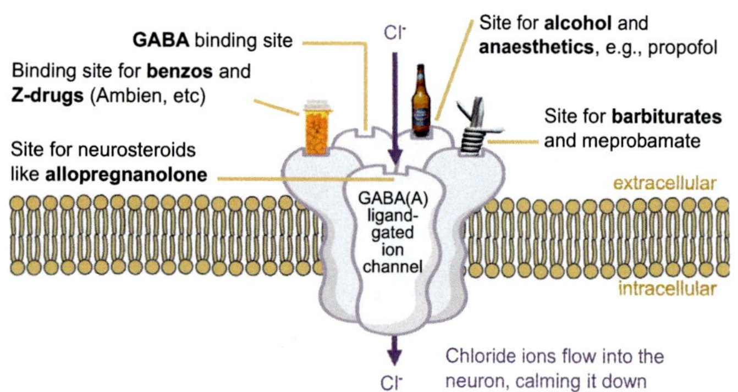

GABA receptor ligands

GABA(A) agonists

- ❖ Alcohol
- ❖ Ativan, alprazolam, etc (benzos)
- ❖ Amytal, etc (barbiturates)
- ❖ Ambien, etc (Z-drugs)
- ❖ Anesthetics
- ❖ Allopregnanolone (brexanolone)

GABA(A) antagonist

- ❖ Flumazenil (Romazicon) at the benzodiazepine site

GABA(B) agonists

- ❖ Baclofen (antispasmodic)
- ❖ GHB (Xyrem)

Note that gabapentin (Neurontin) and pregabalin (Lyrica) have chemical structures similar to GABA but they do **not** bind GABA receptors.

2004
$16–$246

Eszopiclone (LUNESTA)

ES zo pic lone / lu NES ta

"Lunar Easy pic"

- ❖ Z-drug
- ❖ GABA(A) receptor modulator
- ❖ DEA Schedule IV

1
2
3
mg

Easy to take a Polaroid pic

FDA-approved for:
- ❖ Insomnia

Eszopiclone (Lunesta) has the longest half-life of the Z-drugs, about 6 hours. For geriatric patients, the half-life is about 9 hours. Like Ambien, it is effective for sleep onset and sleep maintenance.

In 2014 the FDA recommended the starting dose of eszopiclone be reduced to 1 mg after it was shown that 3 mg could impair driving for more than 11 hours. The best policy is not to prescribe it to those who drive.

Lunesta has been nicknamed "Lu-nasty" because it may have a bitter/metallic aftertaste. Some individuals experience the bad taste, while others do not.

Food delays onset of action by about 1 hour, and delayed onset of sleep medications is a risk factor for complex sleep behaviors. Therefore, patients should not eat within 30 minutes of taking eszopiclone. Z-drugs should be discontinued if complex sleep behaviors occur.

Dosing: Start 1 mg HS. Max is 3 mg HS for healthy adults. Max is 2 mg HS for elderly patients. Avoid taking with high fat meal because it delays absorption.

Alternate mnemonic: "E-Z pic to clone"

"blue moon"

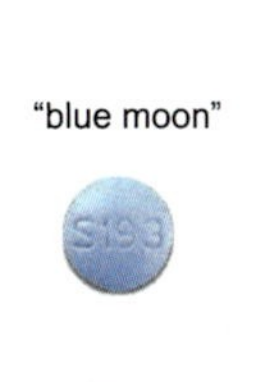

Dynamic interactions:
- ❖ Sedation

Kinetic interactions:
- ❖ 3A4 Substrate

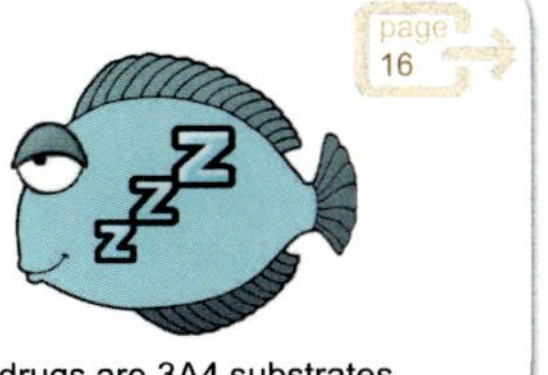
page 16

Z-drugs are 3A4 substrates

1999
$16–$89

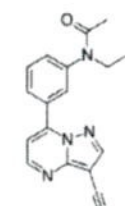

Zaleplon (SONATA)

zal e plon / so NAH tah

"Sonar Zale-plunger"

- ❖ Z-drug
- ❖ GABA(A) receptor modulator
- ❖ DEA Schedule IV

5
10
mg

FDA-approved for:
- ❖ Insomnia (sleep onset)

Zaleplon (Ambien) was approved in 1999 and has been available generically since 2008.

It is effective for sleep onset but not sleep maintenance. Sonata's ultra short half-life of 1 hour makes it suitable for middle-of-night awakenings. It is effect within 10 to 20 minutes of ingestion.

The FDA-approved medication for middle-of-night insomnia is Intermezzo, a low-dose sublingual formulation of zolpidem.

In Spanish, soñar means "to dream". Soñada means "dreamt". The name Sonata is more commonly associated with the Hyundai midsize car which debuted in 1985, and is still being manufactured.

Food delays the effect of zaleplon by about 2 hours!

Dosing: Start 5 mg HS. Target 5–10 mg HS. Max is 20 mg HS for healthy adults. Max is 10 mg HS for elderly patients. Take without food.

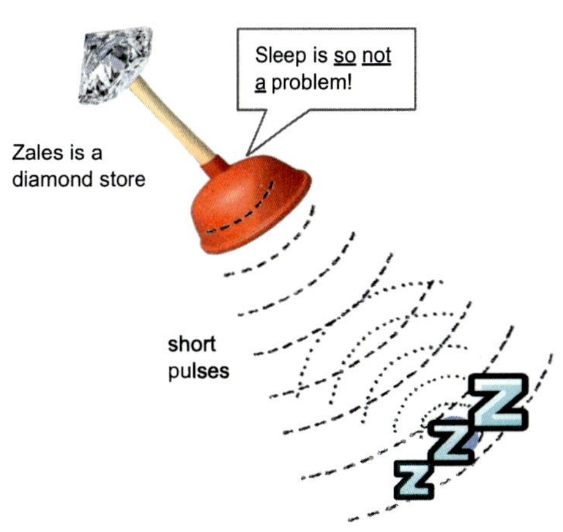

Dynamic interactions:
- ❖ Sedation

Kinetic interactions:
- ❖ 3A4 Substrate (minor)

page 16

Z-drugs are 3A4 substrates

$4–$11

Melatonin

mel la TOE nin

"The hormone of darkness"

- ❖ Sleep-promoting hormone
- ❖ Over-the-counter

3
5
10
mg

FDA-approved for:
- ❖ N/A

Likely effective for:
- ❖ Delayed sleep phase syndrome
- ❖ Non-24h sleep-wake disorder (blind patients)

Possibly effective for:
- ❖ Insomnia
- ❖ Jet lag
- ❖ Neuroprotection
- ❖ Stimulation of immune system
- ❖ Headaches
- ❖ Pre-operative anxiety
- ❖ Protection from radiation/sunburn
- ❖ GERD/heartburn
- ❖ Hypertension
- ❖ Chemotherapy-related thrombocytopenia

No clear evidence for:
- ❖ Sundowning/delirium
- ❖ Manic episodes

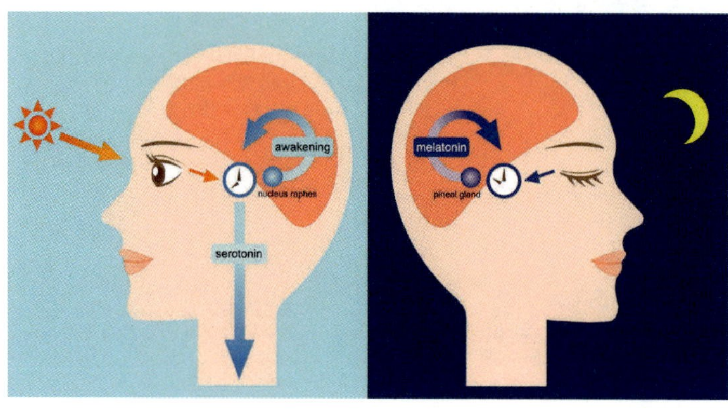

Melatonin, discovered in 1958, is a hormone synthesized from serotonin in the pineal gland. Melatonin binds to MT1 and MT2 receptors in the hypothalamus, which is the location of the brain's master circadian clock (suprachiasmatic nucleus). Melatonin is believed to act as a physiologic signal of darkness. In sighted persons, secretion of melatonin is suppressed by light. "Melano-" refers to darkness (think melanoma, a dark-colored skin cancer). The MT1 receptor appears to be more important for promoting sleep, and the MT2 receptor for setting the circadian rhythm.

Endogenous melatonin production decreases with aging. As children become teenagers, the nightly schedule of melatonin release is delayed, leading to later sleeping and waking times.

Synthetic melatonin has been available since the mid 1990s. It has not been approved by the FDA but is widely used as an over-the-counter dietary supplement. In Europe it is available only by prescription, classified as a neurohormone approved for insomnia in individuals over the age of 54.

Melatonin is a neuroprotectant that prevents brain cells from dying. Melatonin 10 mg has been found effective for treatment of tardive dyskinesia. Melatonin prevents migraines at 3 mg. It appears to be helpful for tinnitus and GERD.

On average, melatonin reduces sleep latency by about 10 minutes compared to placebo and provides a small improvement in quality of sleep.

Side effects may include sleepiness, headaches, nausea, and vivid dreams. Melatonin appears to be benign in overdose. It is not recommended for use during pregnancy or breastfeeding due to lack of safety evidence. Interestingly, the placenta and ovaries produce melatonin that increases at 24 weeks of pregnancy, and even more after 32 weeks. This might explain why women are more likely to go into labor at night or in the early morning.

Two prescription drugs are available which bind melatonin receptors. Ramelteon (Rozerem) binds preferentially to MT1 receptors, and is FDA-approved for initial insomnia. It has not been proven to be more effective than generic melatonin. Tasimelteon (Hetlioz), which costs over $500 per capsule (over $15,000 monthly), preferentially binds MT2 receptors. Tasimelteon is approved for non-24-hour sleep-wake disorder—common in totally blind individuals.

Dosing: Melatonin supplements work better for sleep when given 3 to 5 hours before desired bedtime. It may take 2 weeks to work. Commonly available pills contain 3 mg, 5 mg, and 10 mg strengths. The author considers 3 mg as the starting dose, with 12 mg as the maximum dose. Timed-release preparations are preferable. Source Naturals is a reputable brand.

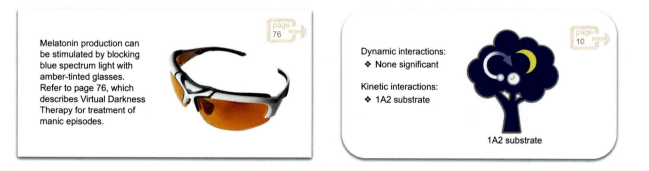

Melatonin production can be stimulated by blocking blue spectrum light with amber-tinted glasses. Refer to page 76, which describes Virtual Darkness Therapy for treatment of manic episodes.

page 76

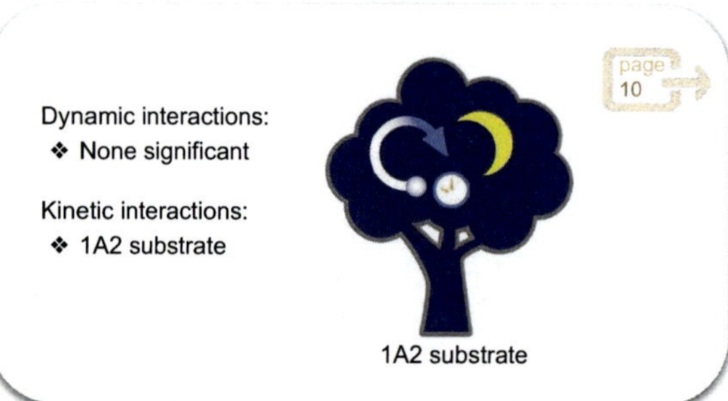

Dynamic interactions:
- ❖ None significant

Kinetic interactions:
- ❖ 1A2 substrate

1A2 substrate

page 10

2005
$391–$510

Ramelteon (ROZEREM)

ra MEL tee on / roe ZER um

"Ram melty on Rose"

- Melatonin receptor agonist
- MT1 > MT2
- Non-controlled

8 mg

FDA-approved for:

- Initial insomnia

Ramelteon (Rozerem) is a sleep agent that binds to the MT1 and MT2 receptors in the hypothalamus, with a stronger affinity for MT1. It is approved for initial insomnia, i.e., difficulty falling asleep. On average, patients fell asleep 8 to 15 minutes faster. It is not effective for sleep maintenance. Ramelteon's effect on awakenings during the night is no better than placebo. It has not been proven as more effective than synthetic melatonin, an inexpensive OTC drug.

The only available dose is 8 mg, typically taken 30 minutes before bedtime. Ramelteon should not be taken with a high fat meal because the maximum concentration of the drug will be decreased.

Common side effects include dizziness, headache, and change in taste. Ramelteon has no risk of addiction and does not cause withdrawal or rebound insomnia. Like melatonin, it appears to be safe at even 20 times the recommended dose (Griffiths et al, 2005). It elevates prolactin levels in 32% of patients but is not likely to cause gynecomastia.

As of 2019, most insurance companies cover Rozerem for a co-pay of around $70/month.

Alternate mnemonics: *"Doze in R.E.M."* or *"Rose o' R.E.M."*

Dosing: The starting, target, and max dose is 8 mg HS. Do not give with high fat meal because absorption of ramelteon will be decreased.

Dynamic interactions:

- None significant

Kinetic interactions:

- 1A2 substrate (major)
- The only medication with which ramelteon is absolutely contraindicated is fluvoxamine (Luvox), a strong 1A2 inHibitor which increases ramelteon levels by about 100-fold!

page 10

1A2 Substrate

ANXIOLYTICS & HYPNOTICS 5

2014
$15,500–$18,500

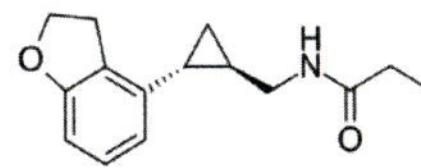

Tasimelteon (HETLIOZ)

TAS i MEL tee on / HET lee os

"Tassel melty on Heater"

- Melatonin receptor agonist
- MT2 > MT1
- Non-controlled

20 mg

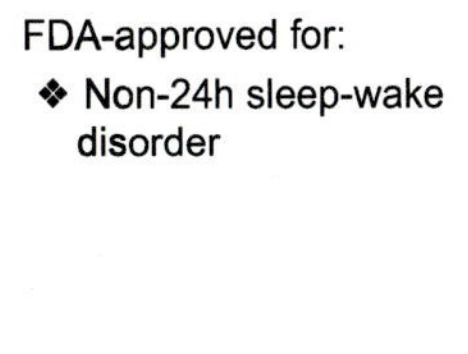

FDA-approved for:

- Non-24h sleep-wake disorder

Tasimelteon (Hetlioz) was approved in 2014 for treatment of non-24-hour sleep-wake disorder (non-24)—common in totally blind individuals. Tasimelteon has stronger affinity for MT2 (whereas ramelteon has a strong affinity for MT1). The MT2 receptor is necessary for phase shifting of the internal circadian clock.

In sighted persons, the light-dark cycle is the main signal that resets the circadian rhythm. In totally blind persons, the absence of light permits the circadian cycle to run longer than 24 hours, causing disruption of nighttime sleep and increased daytime sleepiness.

Tasimelteon is to be administered one hour before bedtime at the same time each night. It can take weeks to month(s) of daily use to see improvement. The expected benefit for the non-24 patient is to sleep about 30 minutes more at night, and 30 minutes less during the day. Side effects may include headache (17%), elevated liver enzymes (10%), and nightmares or strange dreams (10%). Use of tasimelteon is contraindicated with liver insufficiency.

Tasimelteon is expensive. Cheap over-the-counter melatonin has also been used with some success for non-24.

Dosing: The starting, target, and max dose is 20 mg HS.

Dynamic interactions:

- None significant

Kinetic interactions:

- 1A2 substrate
- Unlike ramelteon, tasimelteon is **not** absolutely contraindicated with fluvoxamine (Luvox)

page 10

1A2 Substrate

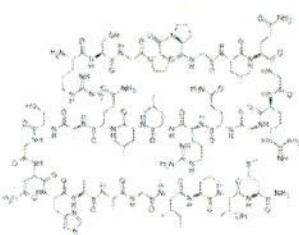

Orexin (hypocretin)

o REX in / hi poe KREE tin

"Hypocritical Oreo (from the hypothalamus)"

❖ Endogenous neuropeptide

Not an antidepressant

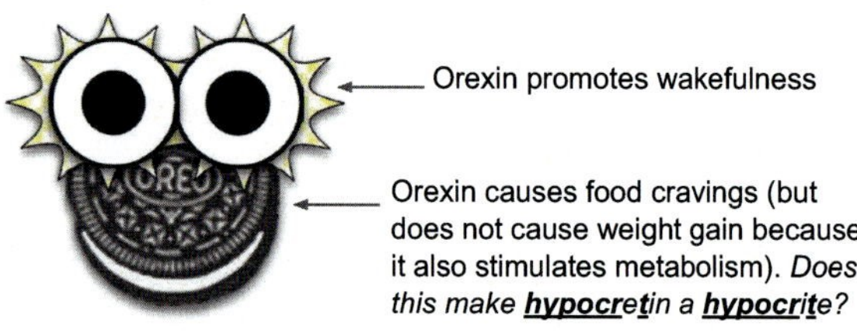

Orexin promotes wakefulness

Orexin causes food cravings (but does not cause weight gain because it also stimulates metabolism). *Does this make* ***hypocretin*** *a* ***hypocrite****?*

This monograph on the endogenous neuropeptide **orexin** (hypocretin) serves as an introduction to sleep medications that block orexin receptors—suvorexant (Belsomra) and lemborexant (Dayvigo). The information on narcolepsy is a preface to Xyrem (sodium oxybate), which is used to treat cataplexy and excessive daytime somnolence due to narcolepsy.

Orexin was discovered in 1998 almost simultaneously by two independent groups of researchers, one group naming it orexin and the other hypocretin. The name orexin derives from the Greek word *orexis*, meaning "appetite" (also part of the word anorexia). Orexin stimulates appetite (anorexia involves lack of appetite). Orexin also promotes wakefulness. The *hypo-* in hypocretin refers to the hypothalamus, where orexin-producing neurons reside.

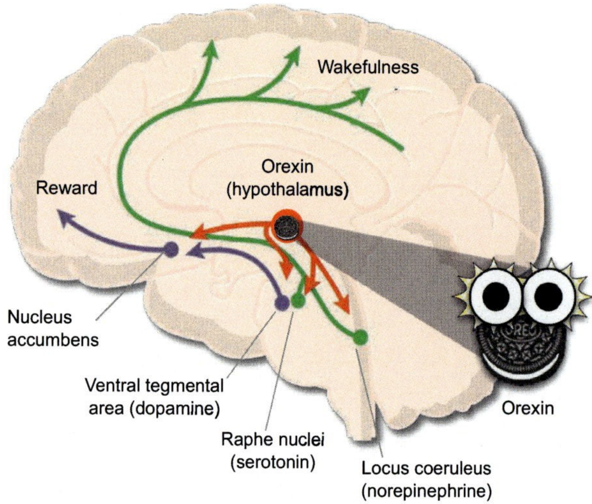

The sleep-wake cycle is maintained in several brain locations with about a dozen different neurotransmitters/hormones. Orexin is involved in coordinating the activity of several of these neurotransmitters/hormones to stabilize both sleep and wakefulness. This figure demonstrates the influence of orexin on dopamine, norepinephrine, and serotonin pathways. Orexin also influences the histamine and acetylcholine systems.

Orexin Receptor Antagonists

These medications are approved for insomnia. They may cause narcolepsy-like effects and are contraindicated for individuals with narcolepsy.

- ► Suvorexant (BELSOMRA) - 2015
- ► Lemborexant (DAYVIGO) - 2020

Narcolepsy

Narcolepsy (with cataplexy) is a condition of orexin deficiency. Narcolepsy is caused by autoimmune destruction of orexin-producing cells in the hypothalamus. The Greek derivative of the word narcolepsy means "to be seized by sleep". The disorder is characterized by recurrent periods of an irrepressible need to sleep. The disorder typically includes episodes of cataplexy, not to be confused with catalepsy (muscular rigidity and fixity of posture), which is not a feature of narcolepsy.

Cataplexy is a brief (seconds to minutes) episode of sudden loss of muscle tone, often precipitated by strong emotions. A patient may report "my knees sometimes buckle when I laugh". A person experiencing cataplexy stays awake and aware of what is happening, but cannot move for about a minute. They may fall asleep afterward.

The mechanism of cataplexy relates to the natural loss of muscle tone associated with rapid eye movement (REM) sleep. This natural paralysis is necessary to keep you from acting out your dreams and falling out of bed. With cataplexy, the paralysis of REM sleep occurs while the individual is awake.

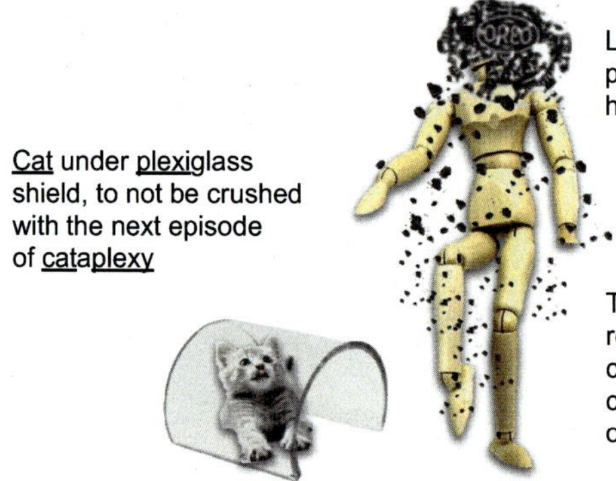

Lack of orexin production by the hypothalamus.

Cat under plexiglass shield, to not be crushed with the next episode of cataplexy

This mnemonic will remind you that cataplexy (not catalepsy) is a feature of narcolepsy.

When sleeping, individuals with narcolepsy/cataplexy may enter REM sleep quickly, for instance within 15 minutes rather than 90 minutes. Narcoleptic/cataplexic individuals may also experience sleep paralysis while falling asleep or awakening, remaining conscious but unable to move or speak. Sleep paralysis may be accompanied by hypnagogic or hypnopompic hallucinations. Hypnagogic refers to "going to sleep". Hypnopompic refers to the period of "pomping up" from sleep before being fully awake. These hallucinations may be auditory, visual, or tactile. Before being understood, sleep paralysis was called the "sleep hag" or "old hag" phenomenon, during which a person feels a presence of a supernatural malevolent being immobilizing them, e.g., by sitting on their chest.

Cataplexy, sleep paralysis and hypnogogic/hypnopompic hallucinations all involve going into a REM-like state too easily, caused by orexin deficiency.

Individuals with typical narcolepsy/cataplexy tend to eat less. This is as expected, since orexin is known to stimulate appetite. Despite eating less, these individuals tend to be overweight. This is because orexin is needed for development of brown fat, which (unlike white fat) burns calories.

Medications approved for Narcolepsy

The first five are stimulants with similar mechanism involving dopamine (DA) and norepinephrine (NE). Pitolisant has a novel stimulating mechanism. Sodium oxybate is a strong sedative.

- ► Methylphenidate (RITALIN) - DA > NE reuptake inhibitor (DNRI); Schedule II
- ► Amphetamine (ADDERALL) - DNRI plus DA > NE releaser; Schedule II
- ► Modafinil (PROVIGIL) - DA reuptake inhibitor (DRI); Schedule IV
- ► Armodafinil (NUVIGIL) - DRI; Schedule IV
- ► Solriamfetol (SUNOSI) - DNRI; Schedule IV
- ► Pitolisant (WAKIX) - Histamine-3 (H_3) antagonist (stimulating); Non-controlled
- ► Sodium oxybate (XYREM) - GHB, CNS Depressant, GABA analogue; Sched III

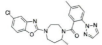

2015
$350–$483

Suvorexant (BELSOMRA)

sue voe REX ant / bel SOM ra

"Bell is som(nolent) / S.U.V. wrecks it"

- Orexin receptor antagonist
- DEA Schedule IV

5
10
15
20
mg

FDA-approved for:

- Insomnia

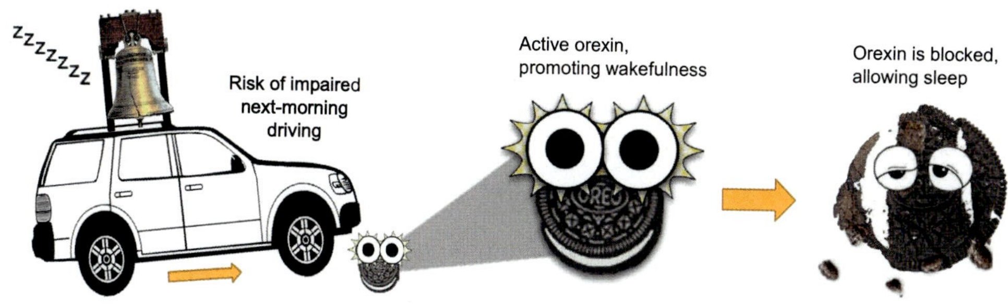

Suvorexant (Belsomra) was introduced in 2015 as the first orexin blocker approved for insomnia. It has been described as a DORA—dual orexin (OX1 & OX2) receptor antagonist. It was followed in 2020 by the second DORA, lemborexant (Dayvigo). DORAs are Schedule IV controlled substances.

As described in the preceding monograph, orexin (hypocretin) is a neuropeptide that regulates wakefulness and appetite. Orexin is represented by the wide-awake Oreo cookie. Orexin neurons sustain wakefulness. Suvorexant blocks orexin, quieting the wake pathway.

Suvorexant is recommended for sleep maintenance insomnia, but not for sleep onset insomnia. In other wards, it helps you stay asleep but is not very useful to help you fall asleep. At one year, patients on suvorexant (versus placebo) fell asleep an average of 10 minutes faster and stayed asleep 30 minutes longer. When stopped, withdrawal or rebound insomnia is not expected.

Narcolepsy-like side effects:
Adverse reactions characteristic of narcolepsy are possible, and can include cataplexy (sudden loss of muscle tone). Rarely, Belsomra can cause abnormal experiences during the transition to/from sleep, including sleep paralysis (inability to speak or move for up to a few minutes) and hypnagogic/hypnapompic hallucinations (perceptual disturbances when going to sleep/while waking).

The maximum approved dose is 20 mg, though 30–40 mg were shown to be more effective. Unfortunately, even the 20 mg dose impairs AM driving. The 10 mg dose is safe, but less effective.

Many psychiatrists consider suvorexant a third- or fourth-line insomnia treatment. However, the American Academy of Sleep Medicine (AASM) lists suvorexant as 1 of 5 medications recommended for sleep maintenance insomnia (2017), along with doxepin (Silenor 3–6 mg), zolpidem (Ambien), eszopiclone (Lunesta), and temazepam (Restoril). The AASM did not recommend suvorexant for sleep onset insomnia.

Obviously, suvorexant is contraindicated with narcolepsy, the disorder caused by orexin deficiency. It should not be taking within 7 hours of driving.

Dosing: 10 mg is the starting and target dose, taken within 30 minutes of going to bed with at least 7 hours remaining before planned awakening; Max is 20 mg HS; Onset of effect may be delayed by 1.5 hours if taken with or soon after a meal; No adjustment needed for mild/moderate hepatic impairment; Caution with morning driving when using the 20 mg dose.

Cataplexy

Blocking orexin can cause sudden loss of muscle tone. Cataplexy is a rare side effect of suvorexant.

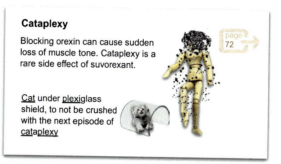

page 72

Cat under plexiglass shield, to not be crushed with the next episode of cataplexy

Controlled substances (for context):

DEA	Drug
Schedule I (illegal)	Ecstasy, Marijuana, Heroin, Psilocybin, Peyote, GHB (street)
Schedule II	Opioids (hydrocodone, etc), Ritalin, Adderall
Schedule III	Suboxone, Ketamine, Soma, Anabolic steroids, Xyrem (prescription GHB)
Schedule IV	Benzos, Z-Drugs, **suvorexant**, lemborexant, tramadol
Schedule V	Lyrica, Robitussin, Lomotil

The Belsomra TV ad employed fuzzy word-pets. A woman is cuddling her white "sleep cat", which runs away. She searches the house for the sleep cat, finding it cornered by her black "wake dog" (orexin, the wakefulness neurotransmitter). The sleep cat gets back into bed thanks to Belsomra, by blocking the effect of the orexin dog.

page 16

Dynamic interactions:

- Sedation/CNS depression

Kinetic interactions:

- 3A4 substrate
  - Not recommended with strong 3A4 inHibitors
  - Decreased levels by strong 3A4 inducers

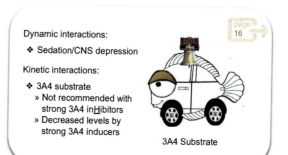

3A4 Substrate

Lemborexant (DAYVIGO)

lem boe REX ant / day VEE go

"Davy goes Limbo, wrecks it"

- ❖ Orexin receptor antagonist
- ❖ DEA Schedule IV

5
10
mg

FDA-approved for:

- ❖ Insomnia

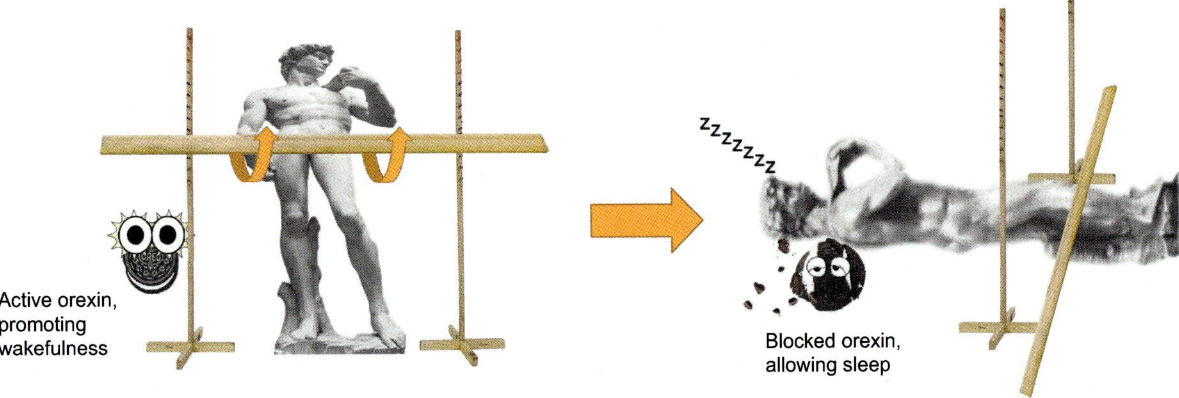

Active orexin, promoting wakefulness

Blocked orexin, allowing sleep

Lemborexant (Dayvigo) is the second orexin blocker, following suvorexant (Belsomra) by five years. Like suvorexant, lemborexant is a DORA - dual orexin (OX1 & OX2) receptor antagonist. It is a Schedule IV controlled substance. Lemborexant is approved for sleep onset and/or sleep maintenance insomnia. It appears safe and effective in older patients. Withdrawal symptoms are not expected with discontinuation.

Warnings include:

- ▶ Caution with next-day driving with the 10 mg (maximum) dose
- ▶ Contraindicated with narcolepsy, which is caused by orexin deficiency
- ▶ Possibility of narcolepsy-like symptoms
  - » Cataplexy (1 in 300)
  - » Hypnagogic/hypnopompic hallucinations (1 in 200)
  - » Sleep paralysis (1 in 66)
- ▶ Discontinue immediately if complex sleep behavior occurs
- ▶ Potential for worsening of depression/suicidal ideation (theoretical)
- ▶ It has not been studied with patients with sleep apnea or COPD
- ▶ If ineffective by 7–10 days, consider psychiatric or medical cause

6-month dropout rate was only 8% at 10 mg and 4% at 5 mg. Narcolepsy-like effects are rare. Daytime somnolence appears to be the only common issue with lemborexant. It should not be taken within 7 hours of driving.

Half-life is about 20 hours, which is longer than suvorexant (12 hours). The maximum dose of lemborexant (10 mg) is half that of suvorexant (20 mg). The label for lemborexant recommends dose adjustment for moderate hepatic impairment, whereas the label for suvorexant does not. Both medications are 3A4 substrates, but lemborexant is more susceptible to drug-drug interactions. Lemborexant is contraindicated with moderate/strong 3A4 inhibitors/inducers.

Dosing: 5 mg taken immediately before going to bed, with at least 7 hours remaining before planned awakening; Max is 10 mg HS (Max of 5 mg if moderated hepatic impairment or if taking a weak 3A4 inHibitor); Onset of effect may be delayed by 2 hours if taken with or soon after a meal; Do not use with severe hepatic impairment; Use is not recommended with moderate/strong 3A4 inHibitors or inDucers.

Dynamic interactions:

- ❖ Sedation/CNS depression

Kinetic interactions:

- ❖ 3A4 substrate, major
  - » Not recommended with moderate/strong 3A4 inHibitors (which may increase exposure to lemborexant up to 4-fold
  - » Not recommended with moderate/strong 3A4 inDucers
  - » Maximum dose of is 5 mg with weak 3A4 inHibitors
- ❖ 2B6 inDucer, weak
  - » Decreases bupropion, methadone

page 16

3A4 Substrate (major)

Note that 3A4 metabolizes lemborexant to an active metabolite. Therefore, 3A4 inDucers will not render lemborexant ineffective, but may decrease duration of action.

page 12

2B6 inDucer (weak)

2002
$10,900

Sodium Oxybate (XYREM)

SO dee um OX i bate / ZY rem

"Skyrim's Good Hard Beverage (GHB)"

- CNS Depressant
- GABA Analogue
- DEA Schedule III

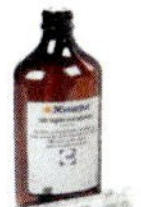

0.5 g/mL

FDA-approved for:
- Narcolepsy

Used off-label for:
- Sleep quality

Dragon from video game *The Elder Scrolls V: Skyrim*

GHB = Good Hard Beverage

Cataplexy sufferer

Note that GHB mechanism does not involve orexin

Sodium oxybate (Xyrem) is a central nervous system (CNS) depressant approved in 2002 as a Schedule III controlled substance for narcolepsy with cataplexy. It is present endogenously in small amounts, and acts upon GABA(B) receptors and GHB receptors. **Xyrem "X's out REM"** sleep, so that a greater percentage of the night is spent in deep sleep.

Sodium oxybate is the isolated sodium salt of gamma-hydroxybutyrate (GHB). Only two years earlier (2000) street GHB was outlawed as a Schedule I (illegal) drug by the Date-Rape Prevention Act. Clinical trials of sodium oxybate were already underway when GHB became widely recognized as something that can be slipped into a victim's drink. In combination with alcohol, GHB can knock a victim unconscious, for about an hour, to awaken with no memory of what transpired.

Xyrem is only available as a liquid. Street GHB is also a liquid, but can be available in powder, liquid, or pill forms. Street GHB is used as a club drug, known as "liquid ecstasy", Georgia Home Boy, or just "G". The club drug can produce an intoxicating euphoria, described as a combination of ecstasy and strong alcohol—a Good Hard Beverage indeed. Euphoria kicks in quickly and lasts about an hour. Unlike other club drugs, there is no significant hangover (that's Good). GHB is not considered physically addictive, but there may be psychological withdrawal described as a "feeling of doom".

Sodium oxybate is the same thing as sodium gamma-hydr**oxyb**utyr**ate** (GHB)

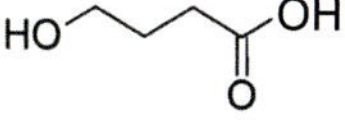

GH**B** is present endogenously in small amounts. It is an agonist at GHB receptors and GABA(**B**) receptors.

The body converts GHB to GABA, and vice versa. Unlike GABA, GHB can cross the blood-brain barrier.

For context, this is GABA:

Using "G" as a club drug is dangerous because a few extra drops and the user is knocked out (Hard). Recreational users should be warned to never mix it with alcohol, and never consume it in a party situation without someone to keep close watch. Partiers have written "G'" on their hands to alert others what happened in the event they lose consciousness. Abuse of GHB (or prescription Xyrem) may lead to respiratory depression, seizures, and coma. Mixing GHB with alcohol may be fatal, but most individuals who overdose on GHB recover completely.

Illegal GHB can be manufactured in the kitchen from a type of paint stripper (GBL). There is no need for a lab setup like what is required for cooking methamphetamine.

OK, back to the legal prescription form of GHB, sodium oxybate. It "repairs" and consolidates sleep, so less time is spent in REM and more time in deep sleep. Xyrem "X's out REM" sleep is a useful mnemonic, which also functions as a spelling cue—it starts with X, not Z. A patient reported "When I wake up, I feel completely refreshed; in comparison to the other drugs that are supposed to be 'clean,' G really is clean", which is very Good.

Xyrem reduces the frequency of cataplexy attacks by about 50%, and the improvement is immediate (that's very Good). Improvement in excessive daytime somnolence may take a couple of months. Side effects may include nausea (19%), headache (18%), and dizziness (18%). There are no kinetic interactions, as its main route of elimination is by conversion to carbon dioxide. Xyrem has black box warnings for CNS depression and abuse/misuse. To reiterate, do not combine with alcohol or other sedatives.

The patient is instructed to take the 1st dose while in bed and set an alarm to take the 2nd dose 2.5 to 4 hours later. Half-life is only 30–60 minutes. The label recommends not to drive within 6 hours of taking Xyrem. It is primarily excreted by the lungs as CO_2 and in the urine.

Xyrem is taken as an oral solution diluted by the patient with water using a syringe (Beverage).

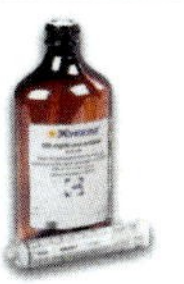

Xyrem has been found to be as effective as modafinil (Provigil, wakefulness promoting agent) for the excessive daytime sleepiness of narcolepsy. The combination of Xyrem and modafinil is better for narcolepsy than either medication taken alone. Sodium oxybate is very expensive, but the patent is set to expire in 2020.

Now back to illegal GHB. It has been used by bodybuilders because it increases secretion of growth hormone during sleep. It has a short half-life, and by 24 hours it will not be detectable by a urine drug test. In case you wondered, GHB is not the "Roofie" date rape drug—that would be the benzo Rohypnol (flunitrazepam).

Dynamic interactions:
- Do not combine with other sedatives

Kinetic interactions:
- None known
  - "in a bubble"

page 18

Dosing: Give at least 2 hours after food. Start 2.25 grams in bed at HS, repeat 2.25 grams when the alarm sounds 2.5 to 4 hours later (total starting dose 4.5 grams, divided). Increase by 1.5 grams/day (divided 0.75 grams/dose) q week to target of 6–9 grams (divided 3–4.5 grams/dose). Max is 9 grams (divided 4.5 grams/dose).

2002
$26

Propofol (DIPRIVAN)

PRO po fol / DIP ri van

"Deprivin' of Proper foil"

❖ Anesthetic
❖ $GABA_A$ modulator
❖ Other mechanisms
❖ Non-scheduled

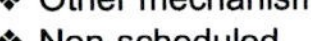

FDA-approved for:

❖ Anesthesia induction
❖ Anesthesia maintenance
❖ ICU sedation

Used off-label for:

❖ Refractory status epilepticus
❖ Pruritus related to epidural morphine
❖ Michael Jackson used it for sleep, not recommended!

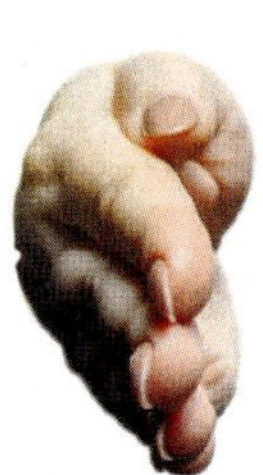

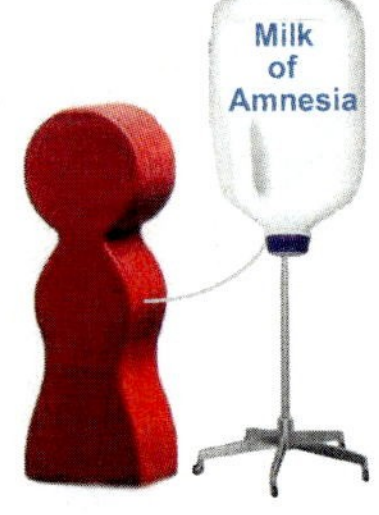

Propofol (Diprivan) is an intravenous anesthetic agent used to induce unconsciousness. Its white color led to the nickname "milk of amnesia". Propofol has several mechanisms of action, including binging $GABA_A$ receptors. It is not a controlled substance.

Recovery from propofol-induced anesthesia is rapid and without much residual drowsiness. Michael Jackson's personal physician administered propofol on a regular basis for sleep. This contributed to the performer's death.

The most common side effects with propofol are hypotension (20%) and stinging/pain near the infusion site (15%). Hypertension is also possible (8% of pediatric patients). Propofol can cause a constellation of metabolic derangements and organ system failure referred to as Propofol Infusion Syndrome.

page 12

Dynamic interactions:
❖ Sedation
❖ Hypotension

Kinetic interactions:
❖ 2B6 substrate

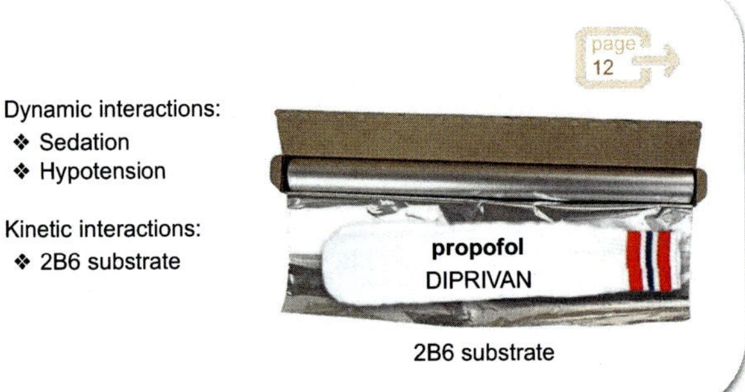

2B6 substrate

This edition of *Cafer's Psychopharmacology* was released in November 2020. Subscribe to cafermed.com for the updated PDF edition with over 1,000 internal links and bookmarks for ultrarapid navigation. The PDF edition is updated frequently with new mascots. Visit cafermed.com/update for more information.

Discount code for cafermed.com subscription:
ULTRARAPID

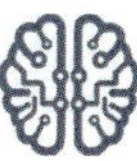

Neurotransmitters

Here is a simplified overview of neurotransmitters in the brain that are relevant to antidepressants. Serotonin, norepinephrine, dopamine, and histamine are referred to as monoamine neurotransmitters because they contain a single amine group ($-NH_2$). The monoamine neurotransmitters serotonin and dopamine are implicated in most psychiatric disorders.

The medications encountered in previous chapters (anticonvulsants, barbiturates, benzodiazepines, and hypnotics) predominantly enhance GABA-ergic activity. Antidepressants predominantly enhance serotonergic activity. Some antidepressants also have stimulating properties by enhancing the effects of norepinephrine and/or dopamine.

Neurotransmitter	Abbrev	Normal activity	Low activity	High activity	Comments
Serotonin (5-hydroxytryptamine)	5-HT	"Serenity" Calmness Satisfaction Euthymic mood Normal sleep	Depression Anxiety OCD	Sexual dysfunction, muscle twitching, hyperreflexia, dilated pupils, restlessness, gastrointestinal distress/nausea, serotonin syndrome, hallucinations (LSD)	Most antidepressants are serotonergic, i.e., enhance 5-HT neurotransmission.
Norepinephrine	NE	Energy, motivation, ability to focus and respond to stress	Fatigue Inattention Sexual dysfunction Hypotension	Insomnia, anxiety, nausea, loss of appetite, hypertension, seizure, dilated pupils	NE is also known as noradrenaline. Stimulants increase noradrenergic (NE) activity. Some antidepressants are noradrenergic.
Dopamine	DA	Motivation, ability to experience pleasure and strong emotions	Anhedonia, inattention, sexual dysfunction, parkinsonism, akathisia, dystonia, neuroleptic malignant syndrome (NMS), restless legs syndrome, antiemetic	Mania, euphoria, agitation, anger, aggression, chemical "high", paranoia, auditory hallucinations, compulsive behaviors, hypersexuality, insomnia, nausea, dilated pupils	Think pleasure, passion, paranoia. Drugs of abuse, colloquially known as "dope", cause euphoria by spiking DA in the nucleus accumbens. Many stimulants and Parkinson's disease medications are dopaminergic.Only a few antidepressants are dopaminergic.
Acetylcholine	ACh	"Rest and digest" parasympathetic activity, normal cognitive function	"Dry as a bone" - Constipation, urinary retention, dry mouth; "Mad as a hatter" - confusion, delirium with visual hallucinations; dilated pupils, tachycardia	"SLUDGE" - salivation, lacrimation, urination, diaphoresis, GI upset (including diarrhea), emesis; constricted pupils	Acetylcholine acts on muscarinic and nicotinic receptors. What are commonly described as "anticholinergic" effects would be more accurately termed "antimuscarinic".
Histamine	H	Alertness	Sedation Weight gain	Allergic reaction, pruritus, excessive gastric acid secretion	H_1 antihistamines are used for sleep and allergies; H_2 antihistamines (ranitidine, etc) reduce stomach acid; The H_3 antihistamine pitolisant (Wakix) promotes wakefulness.

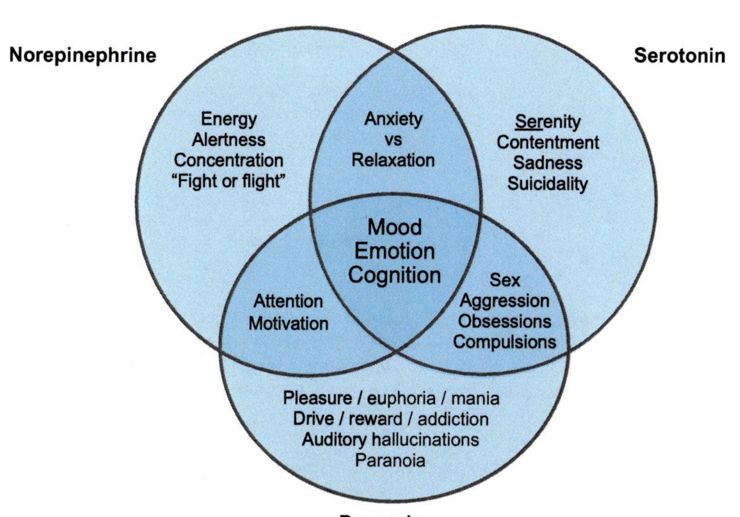

Selective serotonin reuptake inhibitors (SSRIs) block 5-HT transporters without significantly blocking DA or NE transporters. Serotonin-norepinephrine reuptake inhibitors (SNRIs) block 5-HT and NE transporters. The monoamine oxidase inhibitors (MAOIs) block the breakdown of all monoamine neurotransmitters, which is why MAOIs are more powerful antidepressants.

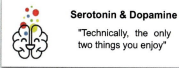

Serotonin & Dopamine

"Technically, the only two things you enjoy"

Most tricyclic antidepressants (TCAs) contribute anticholinergic (antimuscarinic) and antihistaminic side effects.

Class		Abbrev	Antidepressant	$/mo	Comments
Tricyclic Antidepressant		TCA	Amitriptyline (ELAVIL) → metabolized to Nortriptyline (PAMELOR) Imipramine (TOFRANIL) → Desipramine (NORPRAMIN) Clomipramine (ANAFRANIL) for OCD Doxepin 10 mg (generic) for sleep Doxepin 3 mg, 6 mg (SILENOR) for sleep Protriptyline (VIVACTIL) Maprotiline (LUDIOMIL) Amoxapine (ASENDIN) Trimipramine (SURMONTIL)	$10 $10 $10 $20 $200 $10 $400 $75 $50 $25 $100	TCAs are older antidepressants, rarely used for depression today. They are prescribed at low dose for insomnia and migraine prevention. TCAs are famous for anticholinergic side effects (constipation, dry mouth, urinary retention, confusion), orthostatic hypertension, weight gain, sedation, and sexual dysfunction. Not good for the elderly. Fatal in overdose due to disruption of cardiac conduction. There are significant differences between members of the TCA class—some are sedating, while others are energizing. Weight gain may be large.
Selective Serotonin Reuptake Inhibitor		SSRI	Sertraline (ZOLOFT) Escitalopram (LEXAPRO) Citalopram (CELEXA) Fluoxetine (PROZAC) Paroxetine (PAXIL) Fluvoxamine (LUVOX) for OCD	$5 $5 $5 $5 $5 $25	SSRIs are considered first-line treatment for depression and anxiety disorders. Side effects include sexual dysfunction, GI distress (nausea, diarrhea), headache, and fatigue. Possibility of modest weight gain with long term use. Risk of hyponatremia and impaired platelet functioning
Serotonin (5-HT) & Norepinephrine (NE) Reuptake Inhibitor		SNRI	Duloxetine (CYMBALTA) Venlafaxine ER (EFFEXOR XR) → Desvenlafaxine (PRISTIQ) Levomilnacipran (FETZIMA) Milnacipran (SAVELLA) for fibromyalgia	$20 $10 $40 $350 $350	SNRIs are better for pain than are SSRIs. SNRIs may cause a dose-dependent increase in blood pressure due to noradrenergic (NE) activity. Compared to SSRIs, SNRIs are less likely to cause weight gain with long-term.
Norepinephrine Reuptake Inhibitor		NRI	Atomoxetine (STRATTERA) for ADHD	$300	For ADHD; Not considered an antidepressant. Rare risk of serious hepatic injury
"Atypical Antidepressants"	Norepinephrine & Dopamine (DA) Reuptake Inhibitor	NDRI	Bupropion (WELLBUTRIN) TID Bupropion SR (WELLBUTRIN SR) Bupropion XL (WELLBUTRIN XL) Solriamfetol (SUNOSI) for somnolence	$30 $20 $20 $700	Stimulating. Modest weight loss and decreased urge to smoke. Improved sexual functioning. Risk of seizures at high dose.
	Noradrenergic & Specific Serotonergic Antidepressant	NaSSA	Mirtazapine (REMERON)	$10	Great for sleep and stimulation of appetite. At higher dose, noradrenergic (NE) activity is more prominent (stimulating). Weight gain is common, but less prominent than with amitriptyline.
	Serotonin Antagonist & Reuptake Inhibitor	SARI	Trazodone (DESYREL) Nefazodone (SERZONE)	$5 $75	Trazodone is widely prescribed at low dose as a sleep medication. Nefazodone, rarely prescribed, is less sedating.
	Serotonin Modulator & Stimulator	SMS	Vilazodone (VIIBRYD) Vortioxetine (TRINTELLIX)	$200 $300	Less likely to cause weight gain or sexual dysfunction than SSRIs. Both off-patent in 2022
Monoamine Oxidase Inhibitor (non-selective)		MAOI	Phenelzine (NARDIL) Tranylcypromine (PARNATE) Isocarboxazid (MARPLAN)	$50 $250 $750	Potentially fatal if combined with tyramine rich foods (hypertensive crisis) or other serotonergic medications (serotonin syndrome). Effective for treatment-resistant depression
Selective MAO-B Inhibitor (transdermal)		MAOI patch	Selegiline transdermal (EMSAM) for depression	$1600	OK to combine with tyramine-rich foods with the lowest dose (6 mg) patch.
NMDA Receptor Antagonist			Ketamine (KETALAR) - intravenous Esketamine (SPRAVATO) - nasal	$10 $5000	Schedule III controlled anesthetic, rapidly effective for treatment-resistant depression
Neurosteroid			Brexanolone (ZULRESSO)	$34000	Approved for postpartum depression. Given as an IV infusion over 60 hours. Excessive sedation is possible.
Medical food			L-Methylfolate (DEPLIN)	$200	Active form of folate, add-on to an antidepressant
Herbal		SJW	St John's Wort	$25	For mild depression only. Inducer of several CYP enzymes

This rain cloud indicates the medication is an antidepressant.

The asterisk means the medication is considered (or can be properly referred to as) an antidepressant, but is not typically prescribed for depression. Examples include clomipramine for OCD, fluvoxamine (Luvox) for OCD, trazodone (Desyrel) for insomnia, and milnacipran (Savella) for fibromyalgia.

Not an antidepressant

Some medications have mechanisms resembling depression medication but are not properly referred to as "antidepressants". Examples include the NRI atomoxetine (Strattera) and the NDRI solriamfetol (Sunosi).

With an antidepressant, improvement of mood can occur within the first two weeks, but it will take 4 to 6 weeks to achieve maximal benefit. About 60% of individuals experiencing a major depressive episode will respond to their first antidepressant. If no benefit is seen by 2 weeks, stay the course (if no side effects) because there is no advantage in switching to another antidepressant (Bschor et al, 2018). There is no disadvantage to switching antidepressants at 2 weeks either, so if the patient insists, go for it. Following resolution of a single depressive episode, the antidepressant should generally be continued for a year to consolidate recovery. For recurrent depressive episodes, long-term maintenance treatment may be indicated.

For adults, reasonable **first-line antidepressants** include:

First-line antidepressant	Class	Choose when	Sexual dysfunction	~ Cost/ month	Comments
Escitalopram (LEXAPRO)	SSRI	Depression with anxious distress	Yes	$5	Start 10 mg once daily (AM or PM). Usual maintenance dose is 10 to 20 mg. FDA max is 20 mg, but can go up to 60 mg for OCD (Stahl 2016). Always superior to citalopram (Celexa)
Sertraline (ZOLOFT)	SSRI	Depression with anxious distress	Yes	$5	Start 50 mg once daily (AM or PM). FDA max is 200 mg, but can go up to 400 mg for OCD (Stahl, 2016). More likely to cause nausea and diarrhea than Lexapro.
Bupropion (WELLBUTRIN)	NDRI	Depression with fatigue and oversleeping; comorbid ADHD or tobacco use disorder	No	$20	For XL formulation, start 150 mg AM; Max is 450 mg. For SR formulation, start 100 mg BID; Max 200 mg BID. The IR formulation (TID) is not recommended due to risk of seizure.
Mirtazapine (REMERON)	NaSSA	Depression with insomnia and loss of appetite	No	$10	Start 15 mg HS. FDA max is 45 mg, although 60 mg is safe. Higher doses are *less* sedating.

For first-episode depression, it is customary to start with an SSRI. For adults, no SSRI is clearly more effective than others, although escitalopram (Lexapro) has a slight advantage over the others for tolerability, and possibly for efficacy. For children, fluoxetine (Prozac) has the best evidence. For adults, escitalopram and sertraline (Zoloft) are preferred because they have fewer drug-drug interactions compared to fluoxetine or paroxetine (Paxil). Although quite safe, citalopram (Celexa) is a bit riskier than the other SSRIs due to mild QT prolongation, for which FDA lowered the recommended maximum from 60 mg to 40 mg. There is no reason to choose citalopram over escitalopram.

If the patient is not eating or sleeping, consider starting with mirtazapine (Remeron). If insomnia is prominent but weight gain is not desired, consider choosing an SSRI plus trazodone (Desyrel) 50 mg at bedtime, PRN or scheduled ($4). The FDA max for trazodone is 400 mg, but prescribed doses rarely exceed 200 mg.

For depressed patients with fibromyalgia or other types of chronic pain, an SNRI like venlafaxine (Effexor) or duloxetine (Cymbalta) would be a reasonable first-line choice. Effexor XR is dosed 75–225 mg QD. Cymbalta is 30–60 mg QD (FDA max 120 mg).

Treatment-resistant depression (TRD) is defined as failure of two 6-week antidepressant trials. For TRD, trying a third antidepressant is no more effective than placebo. Augmenting the antidepressant is twice as effective as placebo (Zhou et al, 2015). Lithium (0.5–0.8 mmol/L) and aripiprazole (Abilify) 5–15 mg are the top choices for augmentation. Other proven options include quetiapine (Seroquel) 100–300 mg HS, risperidone (Risperdal) 0.5–3 mg HS and liothyronine (Cytomel, T3 thyroid hormone) 50 mcg. There is moderate evidence for adding olanzapine (Zyprexa) 5–15 mg or buspirone (Buspar) 5–15 mg BID–TID. About 50% of TRD cases are actually bipolar disorder (Francesca et al, 2014), for which lithium or lamotrigine (Lamictal) are superior to antidepressants in preventing the next depressive episode.

Intravenous ketamine or intranasal esketamine are quickly effective for TRD. Electroconvulsive therapy (ECT) has the highest rate of response and remission of any form of antidepressant treatment.

All antidepressants have a black box warning of increased suicidal thoughts and behavior in children, adolescents and young adults. Increased risk of completed suicide has not been established. For adults beyond age 24, incidence of suicidal thoughts does not exceed placebo. For those age 65 and older, antidepressants decrease suicidal thoughts. In reduction of suicide risk, lithium is superior to antidepressants.

For children and adolescents, antidepressants (SSRIs, SNRIs) show more prominent benefit for anxiety than for depression (Locher et al, 2017).

All antidepressants have the potential to induce a "switch" to mania, usually in the context of undiagnosed bipolar disorder. Patients with known bipolar disorder suffering a depressive episode may be treated with an antidepressant combined with a mood stabilizer or an antipsychotic. Upon successful treatment of a bipolar depressive episode, consider tapering off the antidepressant after a few months to avoid destabilization of mood over the long term.

Following a Mediterranean diet can improve acute depression and prevent future depressive episodes (Jacka et al 2017; Parletta et al, 2017). 30–60 minutes of light therapy every morning can produce benefits comparable to medication for seasonal and non-seasonal depression (Penders et al, 2016). All depressed patients should be screened for hypothyroidism—ordering serum TSH level is sufficient.

Almost all antidepressants are metabolized, at least in part, by CYP2D6. For patients with a 2D6 ultrarapid metabolizer (UM) genotype (3%), non-response to a wide range of antidepressants (at standard doses) is possible.

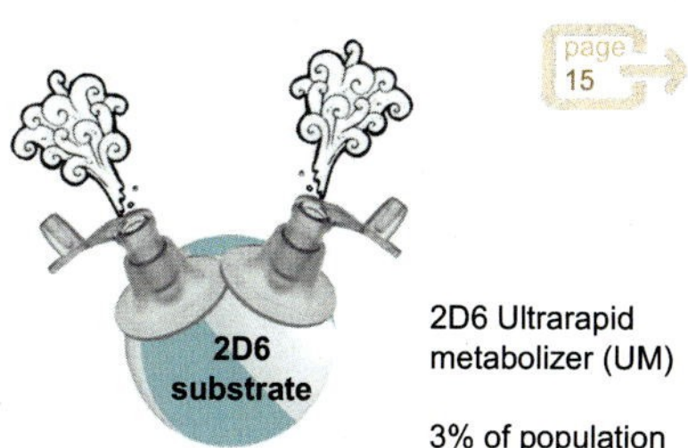

page 15

2D6 Ultrarapid metabolizer (UM)

3% of population

2D6 Poor metabolizer (PM)

10% of population

page 15

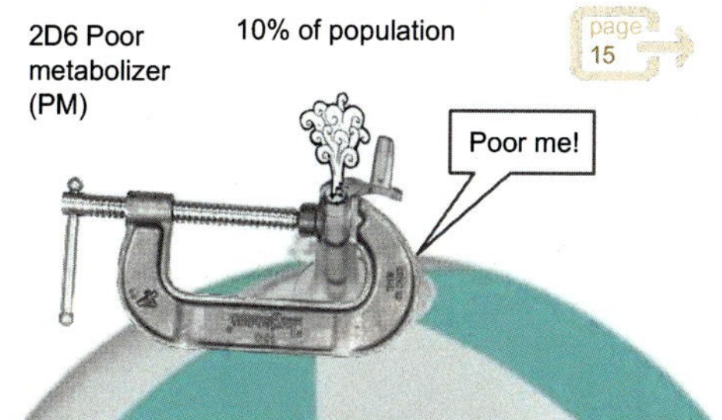

For the 10% of individuals who are 2D6 poor metabolizers (PM), antidepressant levels may be higher than expected, possibly leading to side effects. For a known 2D6 PM, it is recommended to dose the following at half-strength: tricyclics (TCAs), vortioxetine (Trintellix), and atomoxetine (Strattera).

The antidepressants not metabolized by 2D6:

- Desvenlafaxine (Pristiq)
- Selegiline (EMSAM patch)

Other antidepressants unlikely to be significantly affected by 2D6 interactions include citalopram (Celexa), escitalopram (Lexapro), sertraline (Zoloft), levomilnacipran (Fetzima), and vilazodone (Viibryd).

Toxicity of antidepressants in overdose

Listed from highest to lowest risk of fatality in single-drug overdose:

Class	Medication	Mortality Index
TCA	Amoxapine, desipramine	~ 130
TCA	Amitriptyline, doxepin, imipramine	~ 40
MAOI	Phenelzine, tranylcypromine	~ 35
TCA	Nortriptyline (Pamelor)	~ 30
SNRI	Venlafaxine (Effexor)	~ 10
NDRI	Bupropion (Wellbutrin)	~ 8
SNRI	Desvenlafaxine (Pristiq)	~ 5
SSRI	Citalopram (Celexa), fluvoxamine (Luvox)	~ 4
NaSSA	Mirtazapine (Remeron)	~ 3
SARI	Nefazodone (Serzone)	~ 3
SNRI	Duloxetine (Cymbalta)	~ 2
SSRI	Paroxetine (Paxil)	1.4
TCA	Clomipramine (Anafranil)	0–1
SNRI	Levomilnacipran (Fetzima)*, milnacipran (Savella)	0–1
SARI	Trazodone (Desyrel)	0–1
SMS	Vilazodone (Viibryd), vortioxetine (Trintellix)*	0–1
SSRI	Escitalopram (Lexapro), fluoxetine (Prozac), sertraline (Zoloft)	0–1

Mortality index = deaths per 10,000 single-drug exposures reported to Poison Control (about half of which were suicide attempts). *Small sample size. Main source is Nelson & Spyker, 2017.

Tricyclics: A relatively high percentage of single-drug TCA overdoses are fatal, but of those who reach the hospital, only 2–3% die (Tsai et al, 2017). Over 40% of antidepressant fatalities are due to amitriptyline, because it is the most prescribed TCA. Causes of death by TCA overdose include cardiac conduction disturbance, hypotension, seizure and coma. Clomipramine appears to be much safer than other tricyclics, with no reported deaths from 1,745 exposures. Risk of death from any medication is dose-dependent. Taking a thirty tabs of low-dose doxepin 10 mg will not be fatal.

SSRIs: Overdosing on a 30-day supply of an SSRI may cause minimal symptoms, with drowsiness as the primary manifestation. Pupils may become dilated. 15% have symptoms of serotonin toxicity as described on the next page. Taking > 75 times the common daily dose may cause seizures, EKG changes and decreased consciousness. A single drug overdose on Lexapro, Zoloft or Prozac is usually benign. An overdose on Celexa is 4x more dangerous than Lexapro due to cardiac conduction disturbance (QT prolongation), but the absolute risk is low.

Anticholinergic burden of antidepressants

Anticholinergic burden is strongly linked to adverse outcomes among older adults, potentially causing the individual to be:

"Dry as a bone"

- Constipation (risk of ileus, bowel rupture)
- Urinary retention (risk of urinary tract obstruction)
- Decreased sweating; flushing—"Red as a beet"
- Dry mouth (risk of sublingual adenitis)
- Dry nasal mucosa

"Blind as a bat"

- Cycloplegia (loss of accommodation); Lens cannot focus on near objects
- Photophobia due to mydriasis (dilated pupils)
- Increased intraocular pressure, glaucoma

"Mad as a hatter"

- Confusion, memory problems
- Increased risk of developing dementia
- Delirium with visual hallucinations

"Fast as flash"

- Tachycardia

Anticholinergic burden scale:

3 points (worst)	TCA: Amitriptyline, Imipramine, Clomipramine, Protriptyline, Maprotiline, Trimipramine, Doxepin 50 mg+ page 162
2 points (moderate)	TCA: Nortriptyline, Desipramine, Doxepin 25 mg
1 point (mild)	TCA: Amoxapine, Doxepin 10 mg SSRI: Paxil (paroxetine)—"Paxil packs it in" (constipation) Atypical antidepressants: Remeron (mirtazapine)
0 points (negligible)	TCA: Doxepin 3 mg to 6 mg (Silenor) SSRI: Prozac, Zoloft, Celexa, Lexapro, Luvox (all but Paxil) SNRI: Effexor, Cymbalta, Pristiq, Fetzima (all SNRIs) Atypical antidepressants: Trazodone, Wellbutrin, Viibryd, Trintellix MAOI: Selegiline, Phenelzine, Tranylcypromine, Isocarboxazid (all)

Anticholinergic load of a given medication is dose dependent. This table takes dose strength into account when describing doxepin. The same concept would apply to the other medications, i.e., a strong anticholinergic taken at low dose may not contribute significantly to anticholinergic burden.

Sexual Dysfunction

Serotonergic medications commonly decrease sexual desire, disrupt the sexual pleasure response, and increase latency to orgasm. Here are some drugs ranked (approximately) from worst to best in regard to sexual dysfunction:

- Paroxetine (Paxil) - the worst, > 70% of patients
- Sertraline (Zoloft) > 60% - *"so soft"*
- Escitalopram (Lexapro) and citalopram (Celexa) ~ 60%
- Fluoxetine (Prozac) ~ 60%
- Venlafaxine (Effexor) ~ 60%
- Fluvoxamine (Luvox) - least among the SSRIs but still > 50%
- Duloxetine (Cymbalta) - least among the SNRIs
- Vortioxetine (Trintellix) - minimal at 10 mg (44% at > 10 mg)
- Vilazodone (Viibryd) - slightly more than placebo
- Placebo - up to 30% sexual dysfunction
- Trazodone - possible enhancement (and risk of priapism)
- Nortriptyline and Desipramine (TCAs without serotonergic effects)
- Nefazodone (Serzone) - possible enhancement
- Mirtazapine (Remeron) - possible enhancement
- Bupropion (Wellbutrin) - enhances sexual functioning (female > male)
- Buspirone (BuSpar) - enhances sexual functioning (female > male)

About half of individuals taking antipsychotics also experience sexual dysfunction, particularly with antipsychotics that elevate prolactin like haloperidol (Haldol), risperidone (Risperdal), and paliperidone (Invega). Among antipsychotics, aripiprazole (Abilify) is the least likely to cause sexual dysfunction, followed by ziprasidone (Geodon), and quetiapine (Seroquel). Mood stabilizers are generally unlikely to cause sexual dysfunction. Lamotrigine (Lamictal) does not have sexual side effects.

Dapoxetine is a short acting SSRI available in over 50 countries (but not the US) for PRN treatment of premature ejaculation. Paxil could be used PRN for this purpose, off-label. Also, the OTC cough suppressant dextromethorphan (DXM) can be used to delay orgasms via serotonergic mechanism.

Serotonin syndrome, better understood as serotonin toxicity, is a rare condition that can occur when serotonergic drugs are combined, especially with monoamine oxidase inhibitors (MAOIs). The mechanism involves serotonin overload in the brain stem. 50% of cases onset within 2 hours of adding the offending serotonergic. Only 25% of cases persist longer than 24 hours. 70% of cases resolve within 24 hours.

15% of SSRI overdoses lead to serotonin toxicity. Overdoses of a combination of a SSRI plus a MAOI have a 50% likelihood of causing serotonin syndrome.

Although it may rarely progress to multi-organ failure and death, serotonin syndrome is not as dangerous as the Neuroleptic Malignant Syndrome (NMS) caused by antipsychotic medications. Refer to pages 128–129 for a head to head comparison of 5-HT toxicity and NMS.

The diagnosis of 5-HT Syndrome is defined by the Hunter Serotonin Toxicity Criteria with 84% sensitivity and 97% specificity. The criteria focus on clonus, ocular clonus, and hyperreflexia.

On physical exam, the sufferer of 5-HT toxicity may appear uncomfortable and twitchy. Deep tendon reflexes may be very brisk. Try to elicit clonus by flexing the patient's foot and watching for rhythmic contractions of the ankle. Assess for ataxia through observation of gait, Romberg testing, and point-to-point testing.

Be careful if combining antidepressants with other medications that have serotonergic properties:

- ❖ dextromethorphan (DXM) – cough suppressant
- ❖ tramadol (Ultram) – pain medication (SNRI + weak opioid)
- ❖ methadone – opioid
- ❖ fentanyl – opioid
- ❖ meperidine (Demerol) – opioid
- ❖ metaxalone (Skelaxin) – muscle relaxant, MAOI activity
- ❖ cyclobenzaprine (Flexeril) – a tricyclic muscle relaxant
- ❖ St. John's wort – herbal antidepressant
- ❖ LSD ("acid") – hallucinogen
- ❖ MDMA (ecstasy) – a common cause of serotonin toxicity
- ❖ linezolid (Zyvox) – an antimicrobial with MAOI activity
- ❖ methylene blue (Urelle) – urinary tract antiseptic

Mascots of ❖ red medications are featured in other chapters.

Despite an FDA warning, the risk of serotonin syndrome with a triptan migraine medication (Imitrex, Maxalt, etc) is miniscule, if not nonexistent. Orlova et al (2018) estimated the risk at about 1 in 10,000 person-years of exposure to a triptan plus an SSRI/SNRI. Serotonin syndrome is hypothesized to involve 5-HT_{2A} and 5-HT_{1A} receptors, while triptans are agonists at 5-HT_{1B} and 5-HT_{1D} receptors.

Combining SSRIs, combining SNRIs, or combining an SSRI with an SNRI makes no sense therapeutically, but is unlikely to cause serotonin toxicity at standard doses. Switching between SSRIs and SNRIs can generally be done without much of a washout period. A couple of days should suffice, other than when changing from fluoxetine (Prozac). Due to fluoxetine's long half-life, 1 to 2 weeks washout is prudent before starting a different SSRI or SNRI.

Treatment of 5-HT toxicity involves stopping the offending agent and aggressive cooling of high fever. In some cases, medications with anti-serotonergic activity may be helpful, such as the antihistamine cyproheptadine (Periactin) or the antipsychotic chlorpromazine (Thorazine).

"Twitchy frog"

Hyperreflexia

Antidepressant Combinations

Reasonable combos (although not necessarily effective):

- ▶ Antidepressant + lithium
- ▶ Antidepressant (excluding nefazodone) + quetiapine (Seroquel)
- ▶ Escitalopram or sertraline + aripiprazole (Abilify) or risperidone (Risperdal)
- ▶ SSRI + buspirone (Buspar)
- ▶ Trazodone + other antidepressant (excluding nefazodone)
- ▶ Trazodone + doxepin for sleep
- ▶ Fluoxetine + olanzapine (Zyprexa)
- ▶ SSRI + bupropion (Wellbutrin)
- ▶ Nortriptyline + escitalopram or sertraline
- ▶ SNRI + mirtazapine (Remeron) - "California Rocket Fuel" (page 55)
- ▶ MAOI + TCA without serotonergic activity—nortriptyline, desipramine, maprotiline, trimipramine = "Non-Disparaged MAOI Tagalongs"

"Bad" combinations

- ▶ 2 SSRIs
- ▶ 2 SNRIs
- ▶ SSRI + SNRI
- ▶ 2 TCAs
- ▶ SNRI + TCA
- ▶ Fluoxetine or paroxetine (strong 2D6 inhibitors) with 2D6 substrates (including all TCAs)
- ▶ Bupropion + noradrenergic TCA or SNRI
- ▶ Antidepressant + St John's wort
- ▶ SSRI or SNRI + tramadol (Ultram)
- ▶ Mirtazapine + clonidine or guanfacine
- ▶ Atomoxetine + SNRI, bupropion, fluoxetine or paroxetine

Dangerous combinations

- ▶ MAOI + other antidepressants, excluding those without serotonergic effects (trazodone, bupropion, nortriptyline, desipramine, maprotiline, trimipramine)

History lesson: A high-profile case of serotonin syndrome occurred in 1984. Libby Zion, an 18-year-old college freshman taking the MAOI phenelzine presented to the ER and was treated with meperidine (Demerol) to control "strange jerking movements" (think twitchy frog). She was hospitalized, developed a fever of 107°F, and died of a heart attack within hours.

Her father, an attorney, believed her death was the result of overworked resident physicians. In 1989 New York state adopted the "Libby Zion Law" which limited medical residents to 80 hours per week. In 2003 all accredited medical training institutions adopted a similar regulation, limiting residents to 80 hours per week and 24 consecutive hours.

QT prolongation

"Cutie heart"

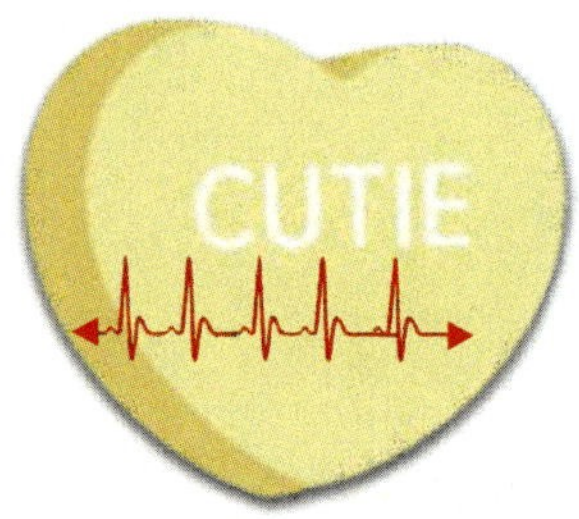

In this book, an ECG tracing like the one on this candy heart means that the medication prolongs QT interval.

On electrocardiogram (ECG), the QT interval, measured from the beginning of the QRS complex to the end of the T-wave, reflects the rate of electrical conduction through the ventricles as they contract and relax. The useful number for our purposes is the QT**c** interval, which is QT **c**orrected for heart rate, which takes into account that QT interval is naturally longer at slower heart rate.

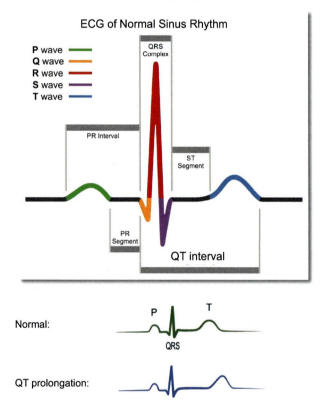

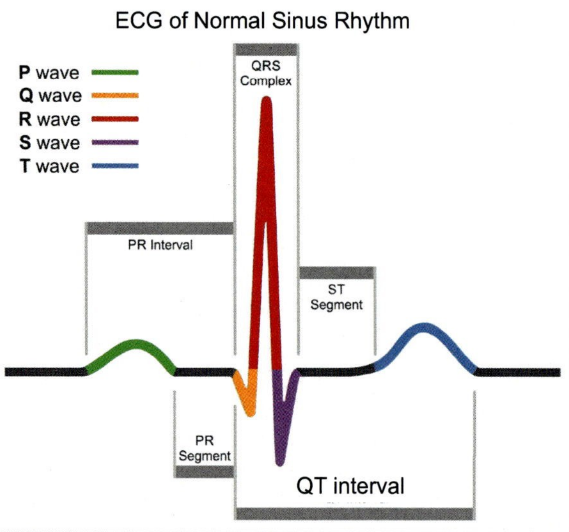

Normal: P T QRS

QT prolongation:

QT prolongation is a delay in cardiac conduction that can trigger ***Torsades de pointes*** (French "twisting of points"). This may precede sudden death.

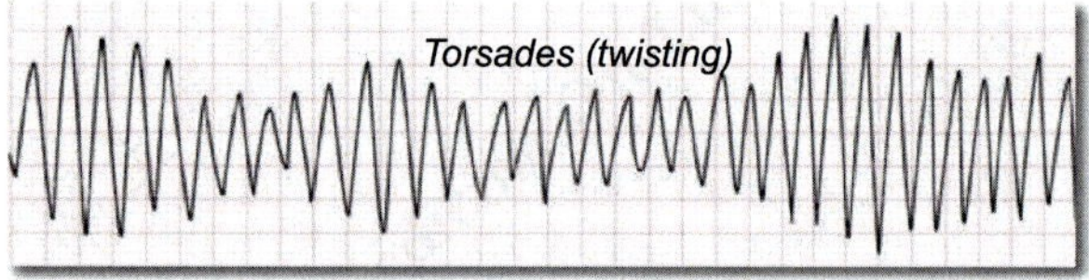

Many psychotropic medications prolong QT interval, including most antidepressants and antipsychotics. In overdose scenarios involving antidepressants or antipsychotics, QT interval is usually long, necessitating a trip to the ICU. As you will see in the next chapter, tricyclic antidepressants (TCAs) are particularly deadly in overdose due to disruption of cardiac conduction manifested by, among other measures, prolonged QT.

Roughly speaking, QTc > 460 milliseconds is long and QTc > 500 msec can be dangerous. An increase in QTc > 60 msec caused by a medication would be of concern.

The risk of torsades is the highest within the first few days of initiating treatment with a QT prolonger. For most drugs that prolong QT, the risk of torsades is so low that routine ECG screening is unnecessary. Although combining QT prolonging medications does prolong QT interval, the magnitude of the effect is likely to be tiny, with a very low probability of clinical consequences (Carlat Report, March 2018). However, it is prudent to check an ECG for patients taking high doses of multiple QT prolonging medications, or individuals with these risk factors:

Risk factors for QT prolongation

- Hypokalemia (low K+)
- Hypomagnesemia (low Mg+)
- Bradycardia
- Left ventricular hypertrophy

Patients with congenital long QT syndrome should not be given QT prolonging medications. Do not add a QT prolonging medication when QTc is near 500 msec.

QT prolongation by psychotropic medications:

Risk	Medication	Class
Highest	Thioridazine (Mellaril)	Antipsychotic
High	Pimozide (Orap) Ziprasidone (Geodon)	Antipsychotic Antipsychotic
Moderate	Iloperidone (Fanapt) Chlorpromazine (Thorazine) Haloperidol (Haldol)* Amitriptyline (Elavil) Desipramine (Norpramin) Imipramine (Tofranil) Maprotiline (Ludiomil) Citalopram (Celexa) Methadone (Dolophine) Pitolisant (Wakix)	Antipsychotic Antipsychotic Antipsychotic TCA TCA TCA TCA SSRI Opioid H3 antihistamine
Low risk except in combination or overdose	Most antidepressants Most antipsychotics	

*Intravenous haloperidol poses high risk of QT prolongation.

Due to the extent of QT prolongation caused by thioridazine (Mellaril), most psychiatrists avoid prescribing it. For healthy patients taking ziprasidone (Geodon), the author checks an ECG before exceeding the FDA maximum dose of ziprasidone (80 mg BID) or when combining 3 or more medications known to prolong QT interval. Check an ECG if a patient taking QT prolonging medications experiences palpitations or syncope/presyncope.

Other medications that prolong QT interval:

Class	Medication
Antiarrhythmic	Amiodarone (Cordarone) Flecainide (Tambocor) Quinidine (Cardioquin) Sotalol (Betapace)
Antimicrobial	Azithromycin (Zithromax) Ciprofloxacin (Cipro) Clarithromycin (Biaxin) Erythromycin (Erythrocin) Fluconazole (Diflucan) Hydroxychloroquine (Plaquenil) Levofloxacin (Levaquin)
Other	Cocaine Opioids (most) - generally mild except methadone Ondansetron (Zofran) - antiemetic (IV route) Propofol (Diprivan) - anesthetic

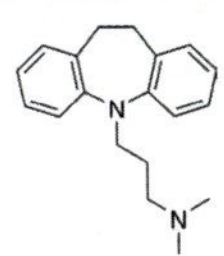
N
N

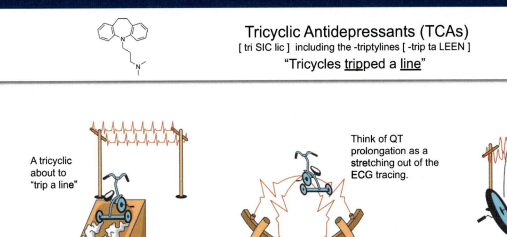

Tricyclic Antidepressants (TCAs)

[tri SIC lic] including the -triptylines [-trip ta LEEN]

"Tricycles tripped a line"

page 82

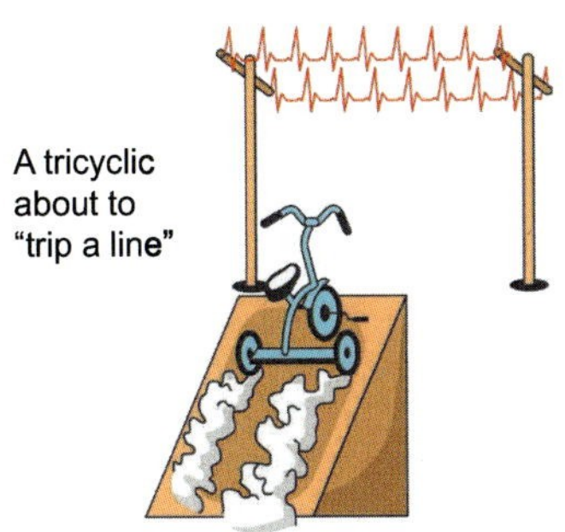
A tricyclic
about to
"trip a line"

Think of QT
prolongation as a
stretching out of the
ECG tracing.

If QT interval
is too long,
Torsades de
pointes may
result.

The TCAs are older antidepressants, derived from the three-ringed chemical (imipramine) shown above. They work by inhibiting reuptake of serotonin (5-HT) and/or norepinephrine (NE). TCAs differ from newer SSRIs and SNRIs in that TCAs are "dirty drugs", non-selectively affecting several other neurotransmitter systems. Most TCAs are antihistaminic (sedation and weight gain) and anticholinergic (dry mouth, constipation, urinary retention, and confusion). They also block alpha-1 adrenergic (NE) receptors, which may lead to orthostatic hypotension.

Mechanistically, the prototypical TCA is like a combination of venlafaxine (SNRI), diphenhydramine (antihistamine and anticholinergic) and prazosin (alpha-1 blocker). This does not apply to all TCAs, which are a diverse bunch. Amitriptyline and imipramine are prototypical TCAs.

TCAs were largely replaced by SSRIs, which are cleaner (selective), without the antihistaminic and anticholinergic baggage. Unlike the diverse TCAs, SSRIs are pretty much homogenous, with similar efficacy and side effects. The main difference between members of the SSRI class are half-life and potential for kinetic interactions.

This chapter highlights the differences between members of the TCA class. Some TCAs are anxiety-reducing (amitriptyline, doxepin), while others can be energizing (nortriptyline, desipramine).

Clomipramine is highly serotonergic, whereas four TCAs have so little serotonergic activity that they *could* be safely coadministered with an MAOI— nortriptyline, desipramine, maprotiline, trimipramine = "Non-Disparaged MAOI Tagalongs".

TCAs are deadly in overdose, some more dangerous than others. Overdose on a ten-day supply of a TCA can be life-threatening owing to disturbance of cardiac conduction. This is seen on EKG as prolongation of the QT interval and other forms of conduction delay. The exception is clomipramine, which is relatively benign in overdose.

Compared to SSRIs, TCAs are less likely to contribute to serotonin syndrome, with clomipramine as an exception.

Although TCAs are not addictive or abusable, they are reported on the basic urine drug screen (UDS). False positive tricyclic screens can be caused by carbamazepine (Tegretol), oxcarbazepine (Trileptal), cyclobenzaprine (Flexeril), quetiapine (Seroquel), chlorpromazine (Thorazine), thioridazine (Mellaril), and at toxic doses, diphenhydramine (Benadryl).

The muscle relaxant cyclobenzaprine (Flexeril) is a tricyclic by structure. Single-drug overdose on cyclobenzaprine is less dangerous than overdose on a prototypical TCA.

Rx	TCA	Cost	Sed	Wt	ACh	NE	5-HT	Comments
#1	Amitriptyline (ELAVIL) metabolized to	$10	+++	+++	+++	++	+++	Calming (as opposed to drive-enhancing). The most weight gain among TCAs. Highly anticholinergic so not good for the elderly.
#2	Nortriptyline (PAMELOR)	$10	+	+	+	++++	-	Drive-enhancing. The least orthostatic hypotension of TCAs. Active metabolite of amitriptyline.
#3	Doxepin (SILENOR)	$10 ($450)	+++	++	+++	++	+++	Highly antihistaminic. Effective for sleep at very low dose. 3 mg and 6 mg tablets are expensive. 10 mg capsules are cheap.
#4	Imipramine (TOFRANIL)	$15	++	++	++	++	+++	1st antidepressant approved in US. Metabolized to desipramine.
#5	Clomipramine (ANAFRANIL)	$380	+++	++	+++	-	++++	Highly serotonergic, for OCD only. The safest TCA in overdose.
#6	Desipramine (NORPRAMIN)	$15	+/-	+/-	+	++++	-	Energizing with minimal side effects. Exceptionally fatal in overdose. The only TCA likely to cause hypertension.
#7	Protriptyline (VIVACTIL)	$81	-	+/-	+++	++++	+/-	Energizing / drive-enhancing
#8	Maprotiline (LUDIOMIL)	$68	++	++	+	++++	-	Tetracyclic structure. Risk of inducing seizures.
#9	Amoxapine (ASENDIN)	$25	+	++	+/-	+++	++	Tetracyclic. Weak antipsychotic with potential to cause EPS.
#10	Trimipramine (SURMONTIL)	$88	+++	++	++	-	-	Highly sedating. Not a significant 5-HT or NE reuptake inhibitor. Antihistamine and 5-HT_{2A} antagonist.

Rx – sales rank; Cost – month's supply (see GoodRx.com); Sed – sedation; Wt – weight gain; ACh – anticholinergic; NE – noradrenergic (norepinephrine); 5-HT – serotonergic

#88
1961
$4–$16

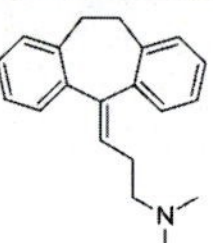

Amitriptyline (ELAVIL)

am i TRIP ta leen / EL a vil

"Am I trippin' (off the) Elevator?"

- Tricyclic Antidepressant (TCA)
- Serotonin and norepinephrine reuptake inhibitor (SNRI)
- 5-HT_2 receptor antagonist
- 5-HT > NE

10 mg
25
50
75
100
150

FDA-approved for:
- Depression

Used off-label for:
- Neuropathic pain
- Migraine prevention
- Fibromyalgia
- Postherpetic neuralgia
- Insomnia

Risk of falls for the elderly

"Elavil elevates your mood". Introduced in 1961, amitriptyline (Elavil) was heavily prescribed prior to the arrival of SSRIs. Amitriptyline remains the most prescribed TCA, and is the #88 most prescribed drug in the US. It appears to be more effective than newer antidepressants (Cipriani et al, 2018). Off-label uses include headache prevention, fibromyalgia, and insomnia.

Amitriptyline is anxiety-reducing (as opposed to drive-enhancing). Amitriptyline is not recommended for the elderly because it is more anticholinergic and antihistaminic than the average TCA. This can lead to falls. Of the tricyclics, it is the most likely to cause weight gain, averaging about 15 pounds over 6 months—*"Am I fat now?"*

Amitriptyline is highly anticholinergic. Dry mouth (an anticholinergic effect) occurs in almost everyone who takes 50 mg or more nightly.

Although amitriptyline is not the deadliest TCA, it is the most prescribed. As a result, over 40% of all antidepressant fatalities are caused by amitriptyline. It should not be prescribed to patients with a history of overdosing on pills. Of 33,219 single-drug exposures to amitriptyline reported to Poison Control, there were 145 deaths (Nelson & Spyker, 2017). This equates to a mortality risk of 1 in 229. Multi-drug overdoses including amitriptyline are much more dangerous.

Amitriptyline is metabolized to nortriptyline, which has fewer side effects and fewer interactions. So, why are more scripts written for amitriptyline than for nortriptyline? Possibly because the side effect of sedation is not a bug, it's a feature—amitriptyline is often intended to double as a sleep medication.

Dosing: For depression start 10 or 25 mg HS and titrate slowly due to sedative effects. The usual maintenance dose for depression is 50–150 mg HS. Maximum is 300 mg HS for depression and 150 mg for other uses. The target dose range for migraine prophylaxis is 10–100 mg HS. For neuropathic pain, consider dispensing a bottle of 10 mg tabs and instruct the patient to take 10 mg HS for one week and increase the dose by 10 mg weekly until pain is improved, up to 50 mg HS while they wait for their follow-up visit. Taper gradually to discontinue. Consider dispensing less than a 30-day supply if the patient is at risk of overdosing.

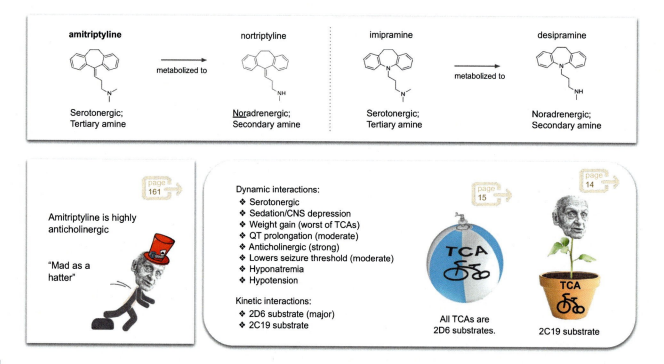

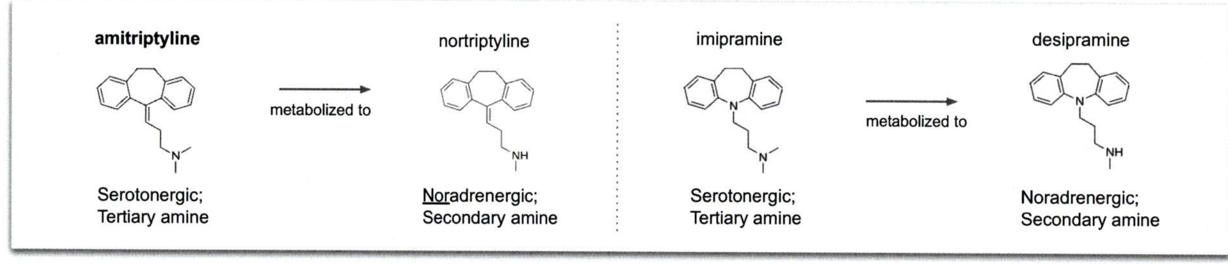

page 161
Amitriptyline is highly anticholinergic
"Mad as a hatter"

Dynamic interactions:
- Serotonergic
- Sedation/CNS depression
- Weight gain (worst of TCAs)
- QT prolongation (moderate)
- Anticholinergic (strong)
- Lowers seizure threshold (moderate)
- Hyponatremia
- Hypotension

Kinetic interactions:
- 2D6 substrate (major)
- 2C19 substrate

page 15

All TCAs are 2D6 substrates.

page 14

2C19 substrate

#192
1963
$4–$15

Nortriptyline (PAMELOR)

nor TRIP ta leen / PAM e lor

"North-tripping Pam"

❖ Tricyclic Antidepressant (TCA)
❖ Norepinephrine reuptake inhibitor (NRI)

10
25
50
75
mg

FDA-approved for:
❖ Depression

Used off-label for:
❖ Migraine prevention
❖ Smoking cessation
❖ ADHD
❖ Fibromyalgia
❖ Postherpetic neuralgia

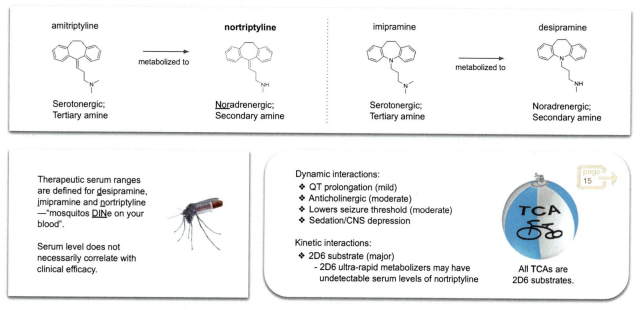

Nortriptyline (Pamelor) is the major active metabolite of amitriptyline. Sometimes nortriptyline is referred to as a second generation TCA (amitriptyline being the first generation). Nortriptyline is a **nor**epinephrine reuptake inhibitor (NRI) with no significant serotonergic activity. It is similar to bupropion (Wellbutrin), although with more side effects and greater toxicity in overdose. Because it is not serotonergic, nortriptyline *could* be safely combined with an MAOI for refractory depression (Thomas & Shin et al, 2015).

Nortriptyline is arguably underutilized because it is superior to other TCAs in terms of safety and tolerability (Gillman, 2007). It has a relatively wide margin between therapeutic effects and side effects/toxicity. Nortriptyline causes the least orthostatic hypotension among the TCAs, so the individual is less likely to become lightheaded and fall—Pamelor *"keeps Pam's head pointed North"*. It can be effective for SSRI non-responders. It is one of two antidepressants (citalopram) with demonstrated benefit for post-stroke depression.

Not all TCAs combine well with SSRIs, but nortriptyline plus sertraline (Zoloft) or escitalopram (Lexapro) is considered a favorable pairing. Nortriptyline has been shown more effective than escitalopram for depression in individuals with high C-reactive protein, which is a general marker of inflammation (Uher et al, 2014).

Sedation from nortriptyline is by antihistamine effect. The label instructs to give nortriptyline at bedtime. Considering its stimulating properties, AM dosing may be more appropriate for some patients.

Nortriptyline has been used off-label for smoking cessation and ADHD, which is reasonable because its mechanism of action resembles that of atomoxetine (approved for ADHD) and bupropion (approved for smoking, used off-label for ADHD).

Think twice before prescribing nortriptyline to anyone at risk of overdosing on pills. Risk of mortality in single-drug overdose is only slightly less than with amitriptyline.

Initial milligram dose for nortriptyline is the same as amitriptyline and imipramine, although the FDA max for nortriptyline (150 mg) is lower than for amitriptyline/imipramine (300 mg).

Dosing: According to the label, the target dose for depression is 50–150 mg HS; Start: 25–50 mg HS and increase by 25–50 mg/day q 2–3 days; Max dose is 150 mg/day; May give in divided doses, or in AM; Use lower dose for elderly patients. Taper dose gradually to stop. Therapeutic serum range is about 50–150 ng/mL, which is easy to remember since the recommended dose range is 50–150 mg. Serum level does not necessarily correlate with clinical efficacy.

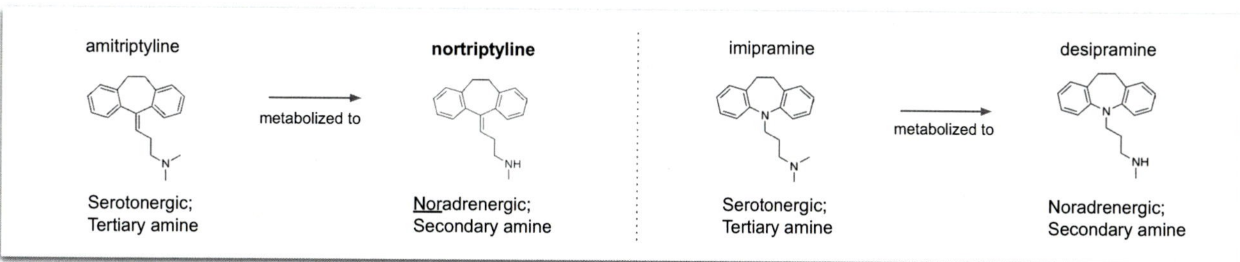

Therapeutic serum ranges are defined for desipramine, imipramine and nortriptyline —"mosquitos DINe on your blood".

Serum level does not necessarily correlate with clinical efficacy.

Dynamic interactions:
❖ QT prolongation (mild)
❖ Anticholinergic (moderate)
❖ Lowers seizure threshold (moderate)
❖ Sedation/CNS depression

Kinetic interactions:
❖ 2D6 substrate (major)
- 2D6 ultra-rapid metabolizers may have undetectable serum levels of nortriptyline

page 15

All TCAs are 2D6 substrates.

#239
1969
$10–$21 caps
$450–$550 tabs

Doxepin (SILENOR)

DOX e pin / SIGH len or

"Box pins (for a) Silent night"

- Tricyclic Antidepressant (TCA)
- NE & 5-HT reuptake inhibitor
- 5-HT_2 receptor antagonist
- Antihistamine (sedating)

Cheap: 10, 25, 50, 75, 100, 150

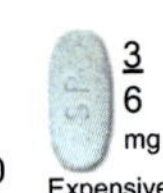

Expensive: 3, 6 mg

FDA-approved for:

- Depression (150–300 mg HS)
- Anxiety (150–300 mg HS)
- Insomnia (3–6 mg, branded Silenor)
- Pruritus (topical cream)

Used off-label for:

- Insomnia (10–25 mg generic Sinequan)

Doxepin (Sinequan) was released in 1969 as a tricyclic antidepressant (TCA). It is an incredibly strong antihistamine. It is available as a topical cream for pruritus.

Doxepin is rarely prescribed at antidepressant strength (150–300 mg capsules) but is commonly used at 10 mg for insomnia. The advantage of doxepin over other antihistamines for sleep is doxepin has minimal anticholinergic activity at a low dose. Traditional antihistamines such as diphenhydramine (Benadryl) and doxylamine (Unisom) are highly anticholinergic, as are the other sedating TCAs such as amitriptyline (Elavil) and clomipramine (Anafranil). In most circumstances, anticholinergic effects are undesirable (pages 161–162). Anticholinergics constipate, cause xerostomia, impair cognition ("mad as a hatter") and increase risk of dementia with long-term use. Doxepin's advantage is lost at a high dose where it becomes highly anticholinergic.

Overdosing on a bottle of any full-strength TCA can be fatal, However, low dose Doxepin is safe to prescribe, even for patients at risk for suicidal overdose for whom you would never prescribe most TCAs. A 30-day supply of Doxepin 10 mg is only 300 mg, which would not kill a patient downing the full bottle (although 300 mg could theoretically be contributory to a fatal multidrug overdose).

The original trade name of the (now generic) doxepin capsule is Sinequan. A tiny dose doxepin tablet was released in 2017, branded as Silenor, available in 3 mg and 6 mg strengths. Generic 3 mg or 6 mg pills do not exist. Branded Silenor costs about $15 per tablet, which is about $450 monthly. Compare this to 10 mg generic doxepin capsules, which are only $0.33 per capsule (about $10 monthly).

Generic doxepin (Sinequan) carries the same **black box warning** as all other antidepressants regarding suicidal thoughts and behaviors in children and young adults. Silenor (3 mg, 6 mg) does not have the boxed warning

Dosing: For depression or anxiety the target dose is 150–300 mg HS, starting at 25–75 mg HS; Max is 300 mg; May divide doses; Taper gradually to stop; For insomnia use 10 mg capsule HS; Max for insomnia is 50 mg, although if you stick with 10–20 mg then overdose on a 30-day supply will not be fatal; Avoid the 3 mg and 6 mg tabs (Silenor brand) due to cost.

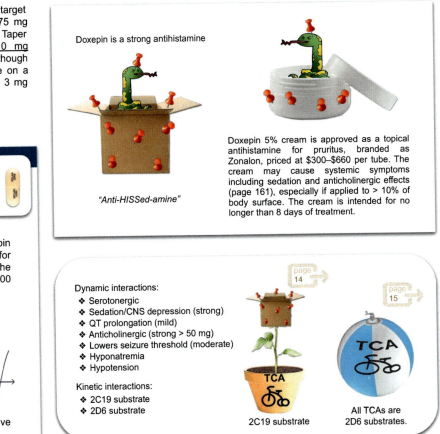

$11–$21 caps

Doxepin (SINEQUAN)

DOX e pin / SIN e qwan

"Box pin Sine wave"

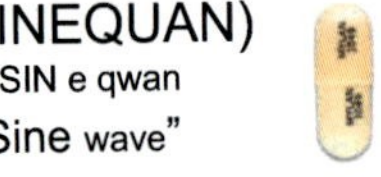

The original brand name of doxepin capsule was Sinequan, approved for depression and anxiety in the maintenance dose range of 150–300 mg HS.

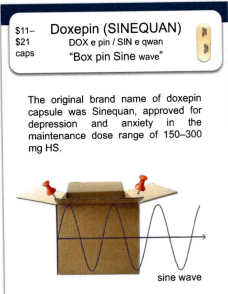

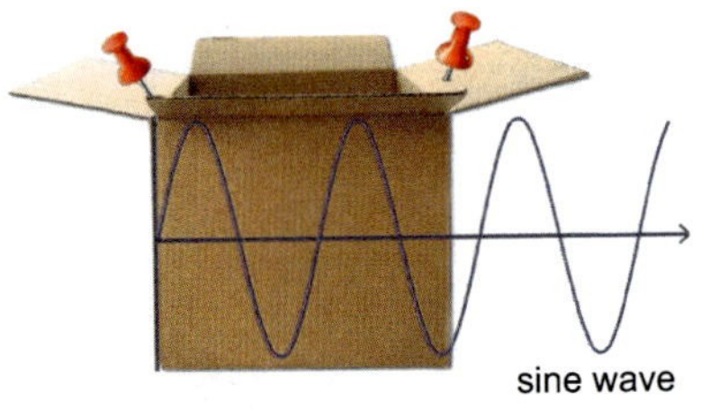

sine wave

Doxepin is a strong antihistamine

"Anti-HISSed-amine"

Doxepin 5% cream is approved as a topical antihistamine for pruritus, branded as Zonalon, priced at $300–$660 per tube. The cream may cause systemic symptoms including sedation and anticholinergic effects (page 161), especially if applied to > 10% of body surface. The cream is intended for no longer than 8 days of treatment.

Dynamic interactions:

- Serotonergic
- Sedation/CNS depression (strong)
- QT prolongation (mild)
- Anticholinergic (strong > 50 mg)
- Lowers seizure threshold (moderate)
- Hyponatremia
- Hypotension

Kinetic interactions:

- 2C19 substrate
- 2D6 substrate

page 14

2C19 substrate

page 15

All TCAs are 2D6 substrates.

1957
$21–$78

Imipramine (TOFRANIL)

im IP ra meen / TOE fra nil

"I'm stopping it! (with) toffee"

- Tricyclic Antidepressant (TCA)
- 5-HT > NE reuptake inhibitor (SNRI)
- Antihistamine

10
25
50
mg

FDA-approved for:

- Depression
- Enuresis (bedwetting)

Used off-label for:

- Generalized anxiety disorder
- Panic disorder
- Chronic pain
- Sleepwalking
- Sleep terrors
- Confusional arousals

the oldest bicycle, representing he oldest antidepressant

"I'm stopping it" due to side effects.

In 1957 imipramine (Tofranil) was released to the US market as the first antidepressant. It was widely prescribed prior to the arrival of better tolerated antidepressants. It is still prescribed for refractory depression.

Imipramine was originally synthesized in 1951 by tweaking the molecule of the antipsychotic chlorpromazine (Thorazine). At the time, these chemicals were classified as antihistamines. The antipsychotic effect of Thorazine was discovered in 1952. Imipramine was then tested as an antipsychotic but was ineffective for psychosis. Serendipitously, imipramine was found to relieve severe depression.

Imipramine is an example of a "dirty" chemical, i.e., it affects many neurotransmitter systems indiscriminately. It highly anticholinergic. Many patients report lightheadedness related to antagonism of alpha-1 adrenergic receptors, which causes orthostatic hypotension. Imipramine is a very poor choice for elderly patients who are at risk for falls.

Imipramine is considered a powerful antidepressant, more likely than others to lead to "switching" to mania when used for bipolar depression. Navarro et al (2019) found that 72% of nonresponders to venlafaxine (Effexor) showed remission of depression when changed to imipramine. By comparison, remission rate was only 39% when mirtazapine (Remeron) was added to venlafaxine. In other words, imipramine was shown to outperform "California Rocket Fuel" (page 109).

Imipramine and clomipramine are the TCAs established as effective for panic disorder.

Imipramine was used to treat nocturnal enuresis because it shortens the duration of deep sleep, when bedwetting occurs. Other TCAs can be effective for enuresis, but imipramine is the only psychotropic medication FDA-approved for this indication. The other medication approved for enuresis is desmopressin (DDAVP), an antidiuretic derived from vasopressin.

The liver converts imipramine into desipramine (desmethyl-imipramine) as a metabolite. Desipramine (Norpramin) is a "cleaner" drug, affecting fewer neurotransmitter systems and causing fewer side effects. In terms of tolerability, *"desipramine is more desirable than imipramine".*

Dosing: Dosing for imipramine is the same as for amitriptyline. For depression start at 10 or 25 mg HS and titrate slowly due to sedative effects. The usual maintenance dose for depression is 50–150 mg HS. Maximum is 300 mg HS (100 mg max for elderly patients); Taper gradually to stop. Therapeutic serum level is 150–300 ng/mL of combined imipramine plus desipramine.

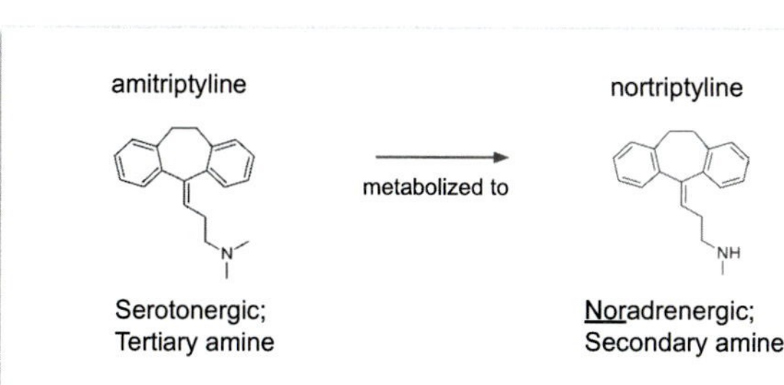

Serotonergic; Tertiary amine

Noradrenergic; Secondary amine

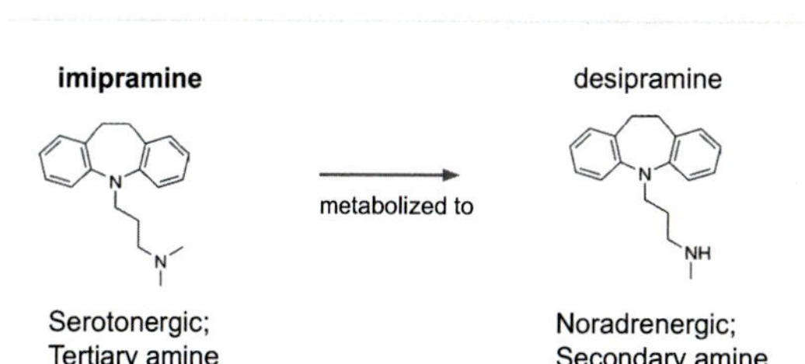

Serotonergic; Tertiary amine

Noradrenergic; Secondary amine

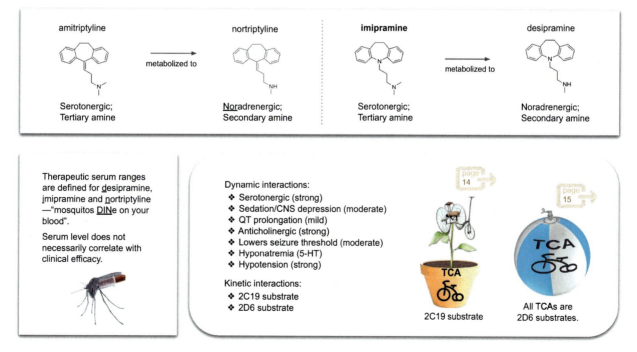

Therapeutic serum ranges are defined for desipramine, imipramine and nortriptyline —"mosquitos DINe on your blood".

Serum level does not necessarily correlate with clinical efficacy.

Dynamic interactions:

- Serotonergic (strong)
- Sedation/CNS depression (moderate)
- QT prolongation (mild)
- Anticholinergic (strong)
- Lowers seizure threshold (moderate)
- Hyponatremia (5-HT)
- Hypotension (strong)

Kinetic interactions:

- 2C19 substrate
- 2D6 substrate

page 14

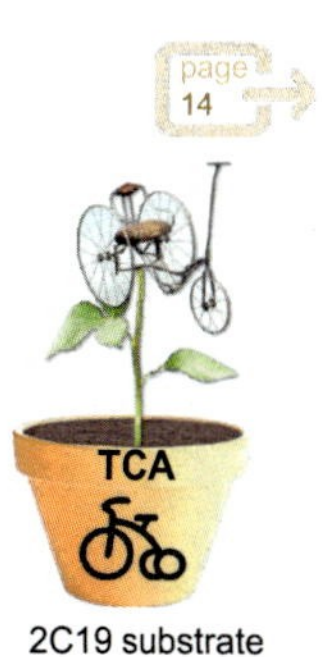

2C19 substrate

page 15

All TCAs are 2D6 substrates.

1990
$84–$239

Clomipramine (ANAFRANIL)

kloe MIP ra meen / an AF ra nil

"Anne Frank's Clompulsion"

- ❖ Tricyclic Antidepressant (TCA)
- ❖ 5-HT > NE reuptake inhibitor (SNRI)
- ❖ Antihistamine

25
50
75
mg

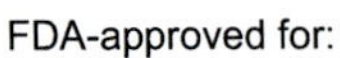

FDA-approved for:
- ❖ Obsessive-compulsive disorder (OCD)

Used off-label for:
- ❖ Cataplexy (in narcolepsy)
- ❖ Confusional arousals
- ❖ Sleep terrors
- ❖ Sleepwalking

Obsessive-"Clompulsive" behavior of aligning tricycles

Clomipramine is one of four antidepressants (maprotiline, amoxapine, and bupropion IR) known to significantly lower seizure threshold, i.e., may predispose the individual to having a seizure. The risk is dose-dependent.

Clomipramine (Anafranil) was engineered from imipramine in the early 1960s. It was approved for treatment of depression in Europe in 1970, but not available in the US until 1990. This delay was because the FDA considered it just a "me too" drug of imipramine. Eventually, the FDA approved it for obsessive-compulsive disorder (OCD).

∗ Clomipramine is the only available TCA not approved for depression. It has been established as effective for panic disorder, off-label.

Clomipramine was considered the gold standard for treatment of OCD due to potent serotonergic activity. The other medication approved for OCD but not for depression is the SSRI fluvoxamine (Luvox), which is also highly serotonergic.

Due to side effects, clomipramine is considered a third-line OCD treatment after two trials of high-dose SSRIs have failed (Robert Hudak, MD). It may be somewhat more effective than SSRIs for OCD.

Clomipramine may be the safest TCA. Of 680 single-drug exposures to clomipramine reported to Poison Control, there were no deaths and only 44 major serious outcomes (Nelson & Spyker, 2017). Protriptyline (Vivactil) may be safer, but the sample size was small (77 exposures).

Dosing: For OCD start 25 mg QD, increase by 25 mg QD every 4–7 days for maximum of 200 mg in the first 2 weeks, then to FDA maximum maintenance dose of 250 mg. Give in divided doses with food during initial titration. Taper gradually to discontinue.

Dynamic interactions:
- ❖ Serotonergic (very strong)
- ❖ Sedation/CNS depression
- ❖ Weight gain (moderate)
- ❖ QT prolongation (mild)
- ❖ Anticholinergic (strong)
- ❖ Lowers seizure threshold (strong)
- ❖ Hyponatremia (5-HT)
- ❖ Antiplatelet effects (5-HT)

page 81

Clomipramine poses a particularly high risk of **serotonin toxicity** if combined with another serotonergic drug.

Kinetic interactions:

Multi-CYP
- ❖ 2C19 substrate
- ❖ 2D6 substrate
- ❖ 1A2 substrate
- ❖ 3A4 substrate

Multi-CYP substrates are less likely to be involved in clinically significant interactions.

page 14

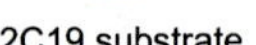

2C19 substrate

page 15

All TCAs are 2D6 substrates.

Serotonergic medications need to be dosed high to effectively treat obsessive-compulsive disorder. Citalopram (Celexa) is not a suitable SSRI for OCD due to QT prolongation at high dose.

Serotonergic medication	Class	FDA Maximum	Maximum for OCD (Stahl, 2016)
Clomipramine (Anafranil)	TCA	250 mg	250 mg
Fluvoxamine (Luvox)	SSRI	300 mg	450 mg
Escitalopram (Lexapro)*	SSRI	20 mg	60 mg
Fluoxetine (Prozac)	SSRI	80 mg	120 mg
Paroxetine (Paxil)	SSRI	60 mg	100 mg
Sertraline (Zoloft)	SSRI	200 mg	400 mg

*Off-label

1963
$17– $50

Desipramine (NORPRAMIN)

des IP ra meen / NOR pra min

"Deceased (No prayin', man)"

- Tricyclic Antidepressant (TCA)
- Norepinephrine reuptake inhibitor (NRI)

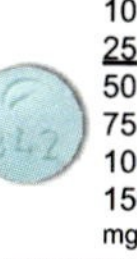

10
25
50
75
100
150
mg

FDA-approved for:
- Depression

Used off-label for:
- REM sleep behavior disorder
- ADHD

Released in 1963, desipramine (Norpramin) was once commonly prescribed, but is rarely used today. It is exceptionally fatal in overdose. Desipramine is an active metabolite of imipramine. In regard to side effects, *"desipramine is more desirable than imipramine".*

Desipramine (and nortriptyline) have been referred to as second generation TCAs, making imipramine (and amitriptyline) first generations.

Desipramine is "drive enhancing" (stimulating), as opposed to "anxiety reducing". It can be described as a relatively selective norepinephrinereuptake inhibitor (NRI). The trade name Norpramin is fitting because it is the most potent noradrenergic TCA. Don't confuse Norpramin with nortriptyline, which is also noradrenergic.

Desipramine has the weakest antihistamine activity of all TCAs, making it non-sedating. While other TCAs are useful for treating insomnia, desipramine can cause insomnia. Recommended dosing is once daily in the morning. Unlike most other TCAs, desipramine causes no weight gain, sexual dysfunction, or orthostatic hypotension. It is the only TCA that can cause hypertension.

The observation that desipramine helped ADHD was the basis for development of the NRI atomoxetine (Strattera).

The main disadvantage of desipramine is risk of mortality in single-dose overdose, which appears to be higher than any other antidepressant. Out of 680 single-drug overdoses, there were 11 deaths, and 52 had major serious outcomes (Nelson & Spyker, 2017).

Therapeutic serum ranges are defined for desipramine, imipramine and nortriptyline—"mosquitos DINe on your blood". On drug screens, desipramine can cause a false positive for amphetamine or LSD.

Dosing: Start 25–50 mg q AM and increase by 25–50 mg intervals every 2–3 days to target of 150–200 mg QD; Max is 300 mg; Taper gradually to stop. Therapeutic serum level is 150–300 ng/mL.

amitriptyline → metabolized to → nortriptyline

Serotonergic; Tertiary amine → Noradrenergic; Secondary amine

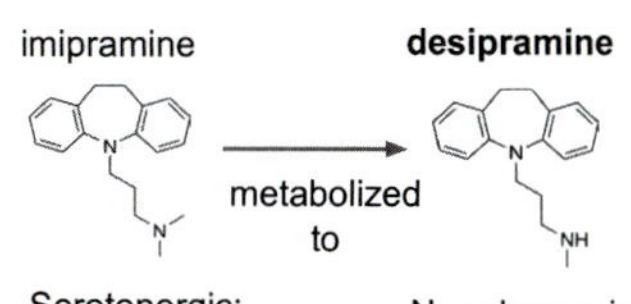

imipramine → metabolized to → **desipramine**

Serotonergic; Tertiary amine → Noradrenergic; Secondary amine

Dynamic interactions:
- QT prolongation (moderate)
- Anticholinergic (moderate)
- Lowers seizure threshold (moderate)
- Hypertensive (unlike other TCAs)

Kinetic interactions:
- 2D6 substrate

All TCAs are 2D6 substrates.

page 15

1966
$68–$181

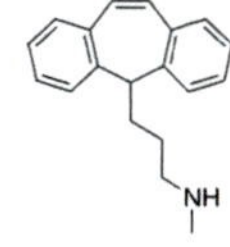

Protriptyline (VIVACTIL)

pro TRIP ta leen / viv ACT il

"Vivactil the pterodactyl's Pro tip (to lean)"

- Tricyclic Antidepressant (TCA)
- Norepinephrine reuptake inhibitor (NRI)

5
10
mg

FDA-approved for:
- Depression

Used off-label for:
- ADHD
- Narcolepsy (wakefulness promoter)
- Migraine prophylaxis
- Chronic pain
- Smoking cessation

I'm Vivactil the Pterodactyl. My pro tip is to lean like this.

As the trade name suggests, protriptyline (Vivactil) is a stimulating TCA. It is so energizing that it has been used to treat ADHD and to promote daytime wakefulness with narcolepsy. Protriptyline is safe to use with sleep apnea because it is a respiratory stimulant (the same can be said for fluoxetine, a relatively stimulating SSRI). Potential for weight gain is minimal. It appears to be less toxic in overdose than other TCAs, although sample size is small. Of 77 single-drug overdoses, there were no deaths and only 2 major serious outcomes.

Available since 1966, protriptyline is rarely prescribed, ranked #7 of 10 in TCA sales. Since 2000 it has been unavailable in several countries including the UK and Australia. Protriptyline is the only TCA given in TID–QID divided doses, but it could be dosed less frequently given its long half-life of about 80 hours.

Dosing: Protriptyline has uniquely low dosing among TCAs due to its long half-life of about 80 hours. Protriptyline's dose range is 15 to 40 mg/day (divided TID–QID) compared to the usual TCA range of 25–300 mg/day. Therapeutic serum range for protriptyline is about 70–250 ng/mL is similar to other TCAs.

Dynamic interactions:
- QT prolongation (moderate)
- Anticholinergic (strong)
- Lowers seizure threshold (moderate)
- Hypotensive (moderate)

Kinetic interactions:
- 2D6 substrate

All TCAs are 2D6 substrates.

page 15

1992
$19– $28

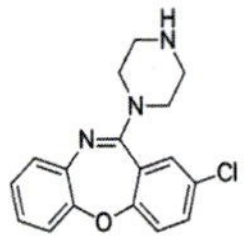

Amoxapine (ASENDIN)

a MOX a peen / a SEND in

"Ammo to Ascend"

- ❖ Tricyclic Antidepressant (TCA)
- ❖ Norepinephrine & Serotonin Reuptake inhibitor
- ❖ NE > 5-HT
- ❖ D2 antagonist (weak)

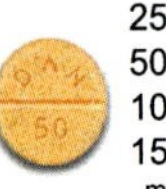

25
50
100
150
mg

FDA-approved for:
- ❖ Depression

100 CRTG .50 CAL LINK M9 4 - BALL M33 1 - TRACER M17 AC-13A454-191

Tricycle 1880s 6 USA

"I'm-a-sendin' ammo"

Amoxapine Maprotiline Trimipramine

Although grouped with the tricyclic antidepressants (TCAs), amoxapine (Asendin) is actually a <u>tetracyclic antidepressant</u> (TeCA) by structure with four hydrocarbon rings. Amoxapine is rarely prescribed. It is <u>the least anticholinergic</u> of all TCAs.

Amoxapine is one of two antidepressants (trimipramine) that <u>block D2 dopamine receptors</u>. Dopamine antagonism gives amoxapine <u>weak antipsychotic</u> properties as well as risk of <u>extrapyramidal symptoms</u> (EPS) and prolactin elevation. The first generation antipsychotic (FGA) loxapine (Loxitane) is metabolized to amoxapine. Note that other drugs with the <u>-pine suffix</u> are antipsychotics (olanzapine, quetiapine, clozapine, asenapine, etc).

Out of 71 single-drug exposures reported to Poison Control, there 7 major serious outcomes including 1 death (Nelson & Spyker, 2017). This is a high mortality index, but due to small sample size it is undetermined whether amoxapine is actually more dangerous than the average TCA. Regardless, a bottle of amoxapine may provide the suicidal patient *"<u>ammo to ascend</u>"* to heaven.

Dosing: Target dose for depression is 200–300 mg HS or in divided doses; The label recommends starting at 50 mg BID–TID; Max is 400 mg/day if outpatient (600 mg/day if inpatient); Divide doses > 300 mg daily; Taper gradually to stop.

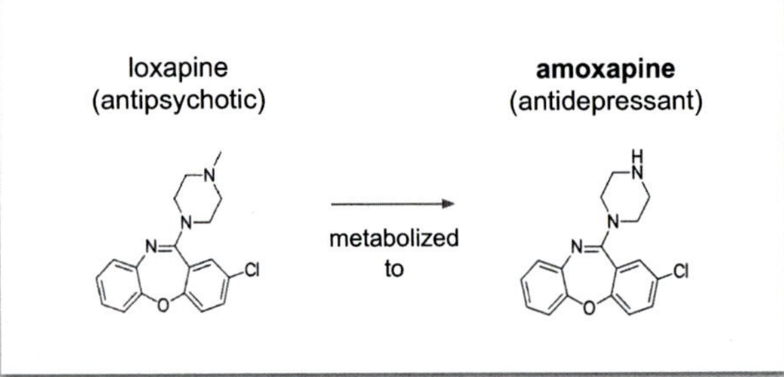

Amoxapine has a high risk of inducing seizures.

Risk of seizures:
#1 Maprotiline (LUDIOMIL) highest risk
#2 **Amoxapine** (ASENDIN) high risk
#3 Clomipramine (ANAFRANIL) 1–3% risk
#4 Bupropion (WELLBUTRIN) IR 1–2% risk

In general, antidepressants (other than TCAs) have a slight <u>anti</u>epileptic effect at therapeutic dose.

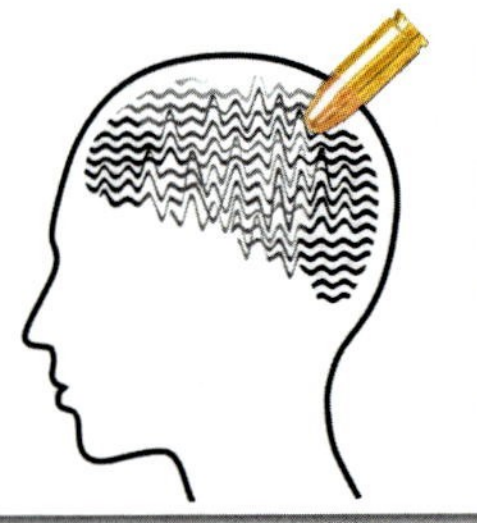

Dynamic interactions:
- ❖ Serotonergic
- ❖ Lowers seizure threshold (high risk)
- ❖ Extrapyramidal effects (D2 blocker)
- ❖ QT prolongation (mild)
- ❖ Anticholinergic (mild)
- ❖ Hypotensive (moderate)
- ❖ Hyponatremia (5-HT)

Kinetic interactions:
- ❖ 2D6 substrate

page 15

All TCAs are 2D6 substrates.

1976
$45–$84

Maprotiline (LUDIOMIL)

ma PRO ti leen / LU dee o mil

"Map telling Lude milf"

- ❖ Tricyclic Antidepressant (TCA)
- ❖ Norepinephrine reuptake inhibitor (NRI)

<u>25</u>
50
75
mg

FDA-approved for:

- ❖ Depression

I'm the Map telling this Lude milf she could have a seizure!

Maprotiline (Ludiomil) is a <u>tetracyclic</u> antidepressant commonly classified as a TCA. It is a <u>drive-enhancing</u> norepinephrine reuptake inhibitor (NRI) without serotonergic effects.

Of all available antidepressants, maprotiline is the most likely to cause a <u>seizure</u>, although risk is less than 1 in 1,000 at standard dose assuming no other risk factors. Seizure risk can be minimized by slow titration. Since there is also a risk of bone marrow suppression, nortriptyline or desipramine is a better choice if you are looking for NRI tricyclic.

Dosing: Target dose for depression is 75–150 mg HS or in divided doses; Start 75 mg HS, may increase by 25 mg daily in 2-week intervals; Max is 150 mg for outpatient use (225 mg max for inpatient); Max for elderly is 75 mg; The label instructs a faster inpatient titration, though seizure risk will be higher; Taper gradually to stop.

TCAs

7

Noradrenergic (NE) activity among TCAs:

<u>Most</u>:	<u>Least</u>:
Desipramine (NORPRAMIN)	Clomipramine (ANAFRANIL)
Protriptyline (VIVACTIL)	Trimipramine (SURMONTIL)
Maprotiline (LUDIOMIL)	

Antidepressants that lower seizure threshold:

#1 **Maprotiline** (LUDIOMIL) - highest <u>risk of seizure</u>
#2 Amoxapine (ASENDIN) - TCA
#3 Clomipramine (ANAFRANIL) - TCA
#4 Bupropion IR (immediate-release WELLBUTRIN)

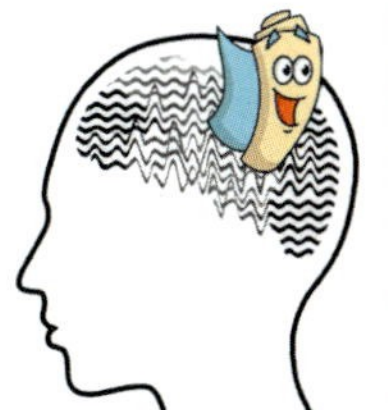

Dynamic interactions:

- ❖ Lowers seizure threshold (worst among antidepressants)
- ❖ QT prolongation (moderate)
- ❖ Anticholinergic (moderate)

Kinetic interactions:

- ❖ 2D6 substrate

page 15

TCA

All TCAs are 2D6 substrates.

1979
$42 - $128

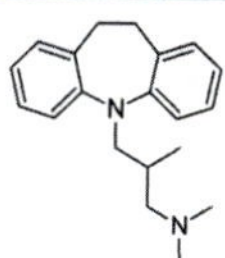

Trimipramine (SURMONTIL)

try MIP ra meen / SUR mon til

"Sermon 'til trimming"

- ❖ Tricyclic Antidepressant (TCA)
- ❖ 5-HT_{2A} antagonist
- ❖ Antihistamine (sedating)
- ❖ D2 antagonist (antipsychotic)

25
<u>50</u>
100
mg

Sermon 'til trimming!

FDA-approved for:

- ❖ Depression

Trimipramine (Surmontil) is the least prescribed of the TCAs available in the US. You'll probably never see it in the wild.

Trimipramine's <u>mechanism differs from other TCAs</u>. It is not a significant 5-HT or NE reuptake inhibitor. It is mainly an antihistamine and 5-HT_{2A} receptor antagonist. It is also one of two antidepressants (amoxapine) that <u>block D2</u> dopamine receptors This gives it <u>antipsychotic</u> properties and the potential to cause extrapyramidal symptoms (EPS) and elevate prolactin. Trimipramine has a receptor binding profile similar to the antipsychotic <u>clozapine</u> (Clozaril).

Trimipramine can be highly sedating, which is an H_1 antihistaminic effect.

Dosing: Target dose for depression is 50–150 mg HS or in divided doses; Max is 200 mg/day for outpatients (300 mg/day for inpatients); Max for elderly patients is 100 mg; Taper gradually to stop.

Dynamic interactions:

- ❖ Sedation/CNS depression
- ❖ Extrapyramidal effects (D2 blocker)
- ❖ Hypotension
- ❖ Anticholinergic (strong)

Kinetic interactions:

- ❖ 2C19 substrate
- ❖ 2D6 substrate

page 14

TCA

2C19 substrate

page 15

TCA

All TCAs are 2D6 substrates.

Listed from highest to lowest risk (approximate) of fatality in single-drug overdose:

Class		Medication	Mortality Index
TCA	Antidepressant	Desipramine (Norpramin) — *11 deaths from 680 overdoses*	141
TCA	Antidepressant	Amoxapine (Asendin)* — *1 death from 71 overdoses*	124
Combo		Perphenazine + amitriptyline (Triavil)	74
TCA	Antidepressant	Amitriptyline (Elavil), doxepin (Sinequan), imipramine (Tofranil)	~ 40
MAOI	Antidepressant	Phenelzine (Nardil), tranylcypromine (Parnate)	~ 35
Other		Aspirin	~35
TCA	Antidepressant	Nortriptyline (Pamelor)	~ 30
Other		Acetaminophen (Tylenol)	~25
Combo		Olanzapine + fluoxetine (Symbyax)	~25
SNRI	Antidepressant	Venlafaxine (Effexor)	9.7
AED	Mood stabilizer	Valproate (Depakote, Depakene)	8.1
NDRI	Antidepressant	Bupropion (Wellbutrin)	7.5
SGA	Antipsychotic	Olanzapine (Zyprexa), quetiapine (Seroquel), ziprasidone (Geodon)	~ 6–7
AED	Antiepileptic	Gabapentin (Neurontin)	5.8
AED	Mood stabilizer	Carbamazepine (Tegretol)	~ 5
SNRI	Antidepressant	Desvenlafaxine (Pristiq)	~ 5
OTC	Antihistamine	Diphenhydramine (Benadryl)	~ 5
SSRI	Antidepressant	Citalopram (Celexa), fluvoxamine (Luvox)	~ 4
Benzo	Anxiolytic	Benzodiazepines (alprazolam, clonazepam, lorazepam, etc)	3.4
NaSSA	Antidepressant	Mirtazapine (Remeron)	~ 3
SARI	Antidepressant	Nefazodone (Serzone)	~ 3
SGA	Antipsychotic	Risperidone (Risperdal)	2.5
AED	Mood stabilizer	Lamotrigine (Lamictal)	2.2
SNRI	Antidepressant	Duloxetine (Cymbalta)	2
SSRI	Antidepressant	Paroxetine (Paxil)	1.4
TCA	Antidepressant	Clomipramine (Anafranil), protriptyline (Vivactil)*	0–1
SNRI	Antidepressant	Levomilnacipran (Fetzima)*, milnacipran (Savella)	0–1
SARI	Antidepressant	Trazodone (Desyrel)	0–1
SMS	Antidepressant	Vilazodone (Viibryd), vortioxetine (Trintellix)*	0–1
SSRI	Antidepressant	Escitalopram (Lexapro), fluoxetine (Prozac), sertraline (Zoloft)	0–1
SGA	Antipsychotic	Aripiprazole (Abilify), lurasidone (Latuda)	0–1
AED	Antiepileptic	Oxcarbazepine (Trileptal), pregabalin (Lyrica)	0–1
SRA	Anxiolytic	Buspirone (Buspar) — *No deaths from 9,081 overdoses*	0–1

Mortality index = deaths per 10,000 single-drug exposures reported to Poison Control (about half of which were suicide attempts).

*Small sample size. Mortality index numbers are from Nelson & Spyker, 2017.

It is important for prescribers to have a general awareness of relative risk among medications and select drugs accordingly. Multi-drug overdoses are more serious. Certain drugs that are relatively benign in single-drug overdoses (e.g., benzodiazepines, quetiapine, gabapentin) are more dangerous when combined with or drugs or alcohol.

Patients presenting to the emergency department with a single-drug overdose on a drug with mortality index < 3 could probably be admitted directly to the behavioral health unit if there are no major mental status changes and ECG shows no cardiac conduction delay. Otherwise, most overdose patients should be admitted to the intensive care unit (ICU).

Toxicity

SSRIs

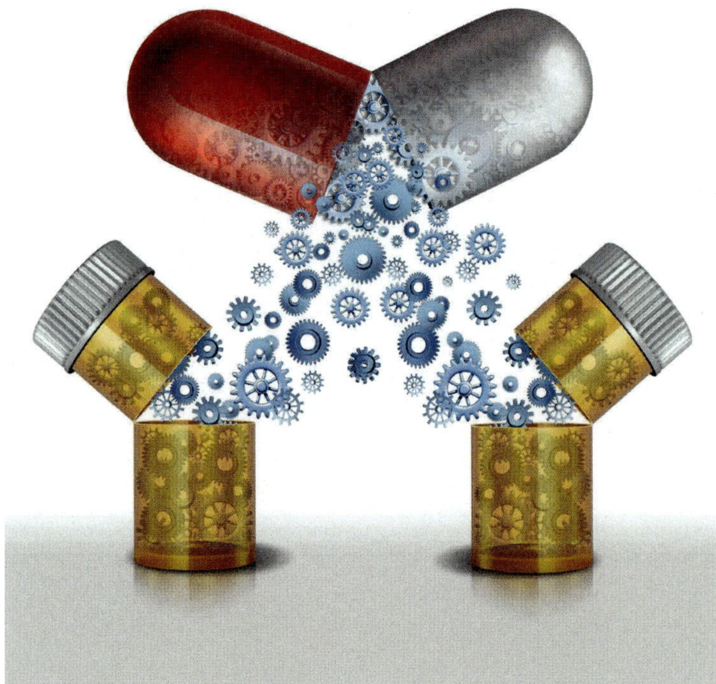

This edition of *Cafer's Psychopharmacology* was released in November 2020. Subscribe to cafermed.com for the updated PDF edition with over 1,000 internal links and bookmarks for ultrarapid navigation. The PDF edition is updated frequently with new mascots. Visit cafermed.com/update for more information.

Discount code for cafermed.com subscription:
ULTRARAPID

Selective Serotonin Reuptake Inhibitors (SSRIs)

SSRIs are the mainstay of treatment for depression, generalized anxiety disorder, panic disorder, and obsessive-compulsive disorder (OCD). By blocking serotonin transporters (SERT), SSRIs keep serotonin in the extracellular space where it can continue to bind serotonin receptors. Although an SSRI blocks SERT immediately, antidepressant effects are generally not seen until 2 to 4 weeks of continuous treatment. Over time, increased extracellular availability of serotonin (5-HT) causes $5HT_{1A}$ receptors to become desensitized to serotonin. $5HT_{1A}$ receptors are located on the far end of the presynaptic neuron (not shown, a mile above this page). As desensitization occurs, serotonin stops inhibiting its own release, so serotonin flows more freely from the end of the presynaptic neuron shown below. <u>$5HT_{1A}$ receptor desensitization</u> takes a few weeks, which correlates with onset of therapeutic effect. Anti-inflammatory effects of SSRIs may also contribute. Refer to *Stahl's Essential Psychopharmacology* book for a full visual explanation.

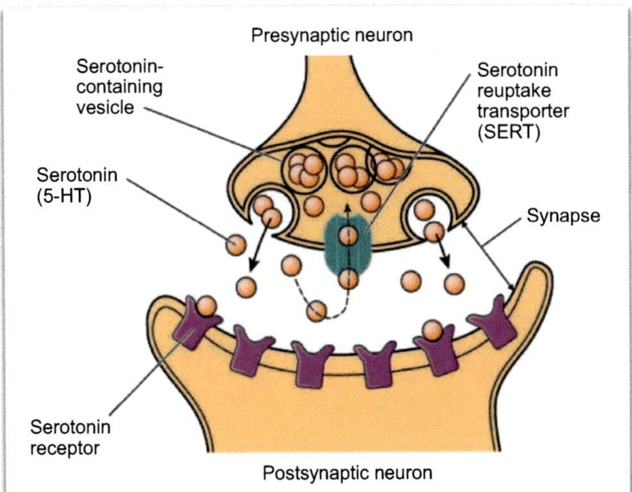

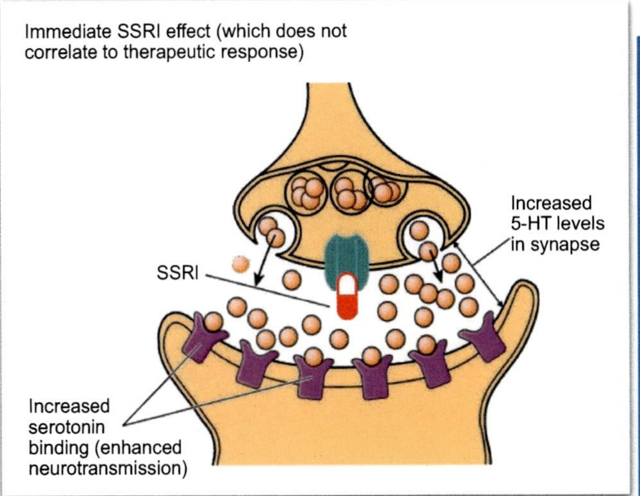

The main side effect leading to patients quitting their SSRI is <u>sexual dysfunction</u>. Unlike TCAs, SSRIs do not cause hypotension or major anticholinergic effects. Other than citalopram (Celexa), SSRIs do not cause significant cardiac conduction delays. SSRIs are initially associated with modest weight loss, which may be followed by modest weight gain with long-term use. SSRIs can cause hyponatremia (low serum sodium) secondary to inappropriate antidiuretic hormone secretion (SIADH) from the pituitary gland.

Rx	SSRI Antidepressant	Interactions	Half–life	Comments
#1	Sertraline (ZOLOFT)	Minimal	26 hr	More likely to cause nausea and diarrhea. OK for first-line
#2	Escitalopram (LEXAPRO)	The fewest interactions of the SSRIs	30 hr	Recommended as first-line SSRI. Fewer side effects and slightly more effective than the other SSRIs.
#3	Citalopram (CELEXA)	Minimal (substrate)	35 hr	QT prolongation if 40 mg dose is exceeded. Choose escitalopram instead.
#4	Fluoxetine (PROZAC)	Strong CYP inhibitor	7 <u>days</u>	More activating. Possible insomnia and appetite suppression. 5-HT discontinuation symptoms less likely thanks to long half-life.
#5	Paroxetine (PAXIL)	Strong CYP inhibitor	20 hr	"More calming". The most sexual side effects, weight gain, sedation, and anticholinergic constipation.
#6	Fluvoxamine (LUVOX)	Very strong CYP inhibitor	16 hr	For OCD only; Lots of kinetic interactions. Short half-life, dosed BID (other SSRIs are QD); Other SSRIs at high doses are similarly effective for OCD.

Uses of SSRIs

- ❖ Depression
- ❖ Anxiety
- ❖ Panic disorder (start low dose)
- ❖ OCD (titrate to high dose)
- ❖ Menopausal hot flashes
- ❖ Somatoform disorders
- ❖ Premature ejaculation
- ❖ Premenstrual dysphoric disorder (PMS)

SSRI risks

- ❖ GI bleed (inhibition of serotonin uptake by platelets)
- ❖ Hyponatremia (low serum sodium)
- ❖ Serotonin syndrome
- ❖ Suicidality (under age 24)
- ❖ Mania, destabilization of bipolar disorder

SSRI side effects

- ❖ Sexual dysfunction (all, especially paroxetine)
- ❖ Modest weight gain with long term use (especially paroxetine)
- ❖ Insomnia (especially fluoxetine)
- ❖ Nausea (short-lived)
- ❖ Diarrhea (sertraline) or constipation (paroxetine)
- ❖ Restlessness / dizziness (short-lived)
- ❖ Bruxism (teeth grinding) which can improve with addition of buspirone (Buspar)

FYI—Medications with the -<u>oxetine</u> suffix:

- ❖ Fluoxetine (Prozac) – SSRI
- ❖ Paroxetine (Paxil) – SSRI
- ❖ Duloxetine (Cymbalta) – SNRI
- ❖ Vortioxetine (Trintellix) – Serotonin modulator & stimulator (SMS)
- ❖ Atomoxetine (Strattera) – Norepinephrine reuptake inhibitor for ADHD

#14
1991
$3–$49

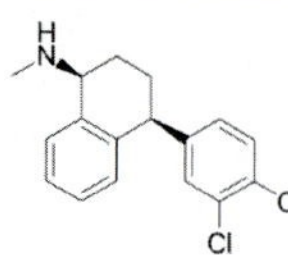

Sertraline (ZOLOFT)

SER tra leen / ZOE loft

"So Soft (on the) Shirt Line"

- Antidepressant
- Selective serotonin reuptake inhibitor (SSRI)

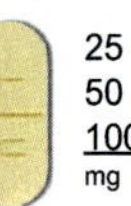

25
50
100
mg

FDA-approved for:

- Major depressive disorder
- Obsessive-compulsive disorder
- Panic disorder
- Post-traumatic stress disorder
- Premenstrual dysphoric disorder
- Social anxiety disorder

Used off-label for:

- Generalized anxiety disorder
- Bulimia nervosa
- Premature ejaculation

Sertraline is the preferred antidepressant for pregnancy and breastfeeding. Medication exposure to the fetus/baby is minimal.

Ideally, all psychotropic drugs should be avoided from weeks 3 - 10 post-conception, the period of organogenesis. However, untreated depression may be worse for mother and fetus than risk of exposure to most antidepressants..

Sertraline Escitalopram

"Sertraline blocks the serotonin transporter (SERT)" as do all SSRIs. Sertraline (Zoloft) is the #1 prescribed antidepressant and the #14 overall prescribed medication in the United States. It is a reasonable first-line treatment for any of its FDA-approved conditions. Sertraline has no real advantage over escitalopram (Lexapro), which has a slight advantage over sertraline in terms of side effects.

Among SSRIs, sertraline is the most likely to cause diarrhea—*"Zoloft makes your stools So Soft".* "So soft" also refers to sertraline's potential to cause erectile dysfunction, which is a side effect of all SSRIs. In terms of antidepressant-associated sexual dysfunction, sertraline is slightly better than paroxetine (Paxil) and slightly worse than escitalopram.

For any SSRI, treatment of obsessive-compulsive disorder (OCD) may require significantly higher doses than used for depression. Although the FDA max for Zoloft is 200 mg, it may be necessary to go as high as 400 mg for treatment of OCD (titrated gradually).

On drug screens, Zoloft can cause a false positive result for benzodiazepines.

Risk of mortality with single-drug overdose on sertraline is about 1 in 10,000 (Nelson & Spyker, 2017), which is similar to mortality risk of escitalopram.

Zoloft combines well with bupropion (Wellbutrin) for depression with prominent fatigue *("Well-off")*. Trazodone (Desyrel) is a common add-on for insomnia. For anxiety, sertraline combines well with buspirone (Buspar) or any benzodiazepine. For bipolar depression or refractory unipolar depression, sertraline can be combined with any mood stabilizer or antipsychotic. Buspirone can counter SSRI-induced sexual dysfunction and bruxism.

Dosing: 50 mg is the starting dose for most indications; FDA max is 200 mg; For treatment of OCD the dose may need to go as high as 400 mg (Stahl, 2016). Taper gradually to avoid unpleasant serotonin discontinuation symptoms.

Information applicable to all SSRIs:

SSRIs block the serotonin reuptake pump. Onset of therapeutic effect is delayed 2–4 weeks. They start working when serotonin $5HT_{1A}$ receptors become desensitized. Some patients experience immediate increased energy or unpleasant restlessness, which is more common with bipolar disorder. Side effects occur sooner than therapeutic effects and often improve over time—nausea, sweating, headache, and bruxism (teeth grinding). Sexual dysfunction is often problematic, and less likely than other side effects to improve with time. SSRIs may increase suicidal thoughts in individuals under age 24.

Following resolution of a single depressive episode, the antidepressant should generally be continued for a year to consolidate recovery. For recurrent episodes, treatment may need to be continued indefinitely. SSRIs are safe and effective for long-term use but some patients complain of feeling emotionally flat or "blah", experiencing what has been described as SSRI-Induced Apathy Syndrome. SSRIs may cause a modest weight loss initially, and a modest weight gain with long-term use.

With bipolar individuals, SSRIs may cause "switching" to mania or destabilize mood over time.

When abruptly discontinued, SSRIs may cause serotonin withdrawal symptoms including lightheadedness, "brain zaps", paresthesias, nausea, fatigue and irritability.

SSRIs may decrease serum sodium levels and impair platelet functioning, but risk of significant hyponatremia or bleeding is minimal.

The Zoloft Sad Blob debuted as an advertising mascot in 2001.

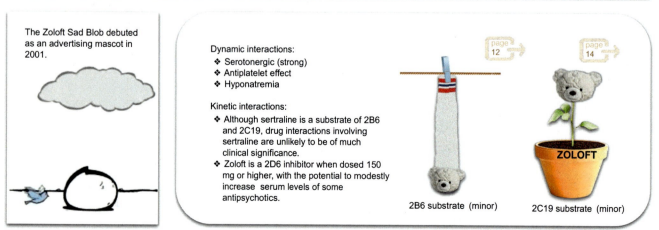

Dynamic interactions:

- Serotonergic (strong)
- Antiplatelet effect
- Hyponatremia

Kinetic interactions:

- Although sertraline is a substrate of 2B6 and 2C19, drug interactions involving sertraline are unlikely to be of much clinical significance.
- Zoloft is a 2D6 inhibitor when dosed 150 mg or higher, with the potential to modestly increase serum levels of some antipsychotics.

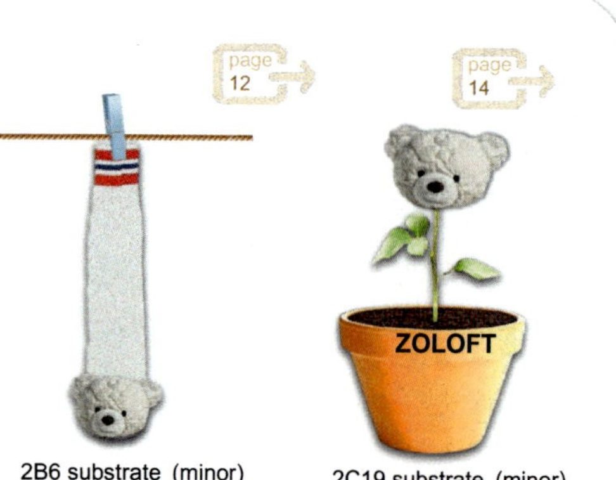

2B6 substrate (minor)

2C19 substrate (minor)

#26
2002
$3–$98

Escitalopram (LEXAPRO)

ess sit AL o pram / LEX a pro
"Lexus Pram"

❖ Antidepressant
❖ Selective serotonin reuptake inhibitor (SSRI)

5
10
20
mg

FDA-approved for:

❖ Major depressive disorder
❖ Generalized anxiety disorder

Used off-label for

❖ Obsessive-compulsive disorder
❖ Post-traumatic stress disorder
❖ Premature ejaculation
❖ Premenstrual dysphoric disorder
❖ Social anxiety disorder
❖ Autism spectrum disorder
❖ Bulimia nervosa

"Pram" is the British word for baby carriage.

E**s**citalopram (**L**exapro) is the "pure" form of Celexa (citalopram). E**s**citalopram is the **S**-enantiomer of the molecule, as explained in the citalopram monograph on the following page. Compared to Celexa, Lexapro is safer, often better tolerated, and possibly more effective. There is no reason to choose citalopram over escitalopram—*"S-citalopram is Superior to racemic citalopram"*.

S for "Sinister" = L for Left-handed enantiomer

Escitalopram is the best choice for a first-line antidepressant. It is the most selective inhibitor of the serotonin pump among all SSRIs. Several clinical trials and meta-analyses indicate escitalopram may be slightly more effective than other SSRIs. Escitalopram has an allosteric effect at the serotonin transporter that distinguishes it from other SSRIs. 10 mg of escitalopram is predictably more effective than 20 mg of citalopram (which contains 10 mg escitalopram and 10 mg R-citalopram).

Lexapro has the fewest side effects of all the SSRIs. At the starting dose of 10 mg, side effects are comparable to placebo. It is unlikely to cause weight gain or sedation. It has minimal drug-drug interactions. Lexapro is safe. Risk of mortality with single-drug overdose on escitalopram is about 1 in 9,000 (Nelson & Spyker, 2017).

For depression, escitalopram is at least as effective as SNRI antidepressants. Although venlafaxine (Effexor) and duloxetine (Cymbalta) have the additional mechanism of blocking the norepinephrine transporter, do not expect either of them to outperform Lexapro.

Although escitalopram may be the overall winner among SSRIs, with all psychotropic drugs there is marked inter-individual variability in tolerability and therapeutic response. If an individual is doing wonderfully on another antidepressant, there is usually no reason to change to escitalopram.

Escitalopram is regarded as safe for pregnancy and breastfeeding, but sertraline (Zoloft) is safer.

Serum levels of escitalopram peak about 5 hours after ingestion. Half-life is around 30 hours, so steady-state concentration should be achieved within 7 days. Upon discontinuation, escitalopram should be cleared from the body within 7 days.

Dosing: Start escitalopram 10 mg QD (AM or PM), after meals for the first few days, then with or without food. May increase to 20 mg in one week, but generally you would wait about 4 weeks to see if it is necessary to advance the dose. Although the FDA max for Lexapro is 20 mg, it is not unusual to see it prescribed up to 30 mg for major depression. It can be safely dosed up to 60 mg daily for OCD (Stahl, 2016). When converting from citalopram (Celexa), use half the milligram dose of escitalopram. 20 mg of Lexapro is predictable more effective than 40 mg of Celexa. Use a lower dose for elderly individuals because serum levels will be about 50% higher. If the patient is taking omeprazole (Prilosec) or esomeprazole (Nexium), consider starting escitalopram at 5 mg. Renal impairment: no adjustment needed. Hepatic impairment: consider lower dose. Taper to discontinue to avoid unpleasant serotonin withdrawal symptoms.

Dynamic interactions:

❖ Serotonergic (strong)
❖ QT prolongation (minimal)
❖ Antiplatelet effect
❖ Hyponatremia

Kinetic interactions:

❖ Fewer interactions than most SSRIs
❖ As a 2C19 substrate, escitalopram levels are increased by **proton pump inhibitors** (PPIs). Avoid omeprazole (Prilosec) and and esomeprazole (Nexium), which increase escitalopram levels by 80–90%. Instead, choose pantoprazole (Protonix) or lansoprazole (Prevacid), which only increase escitalopram by about 20%. Although more expensive, rabeprazole (Aciphex) does not affect escitalopram levels.

page 14

2C19 substrate

#21
1998
$2–$35

Citalopram (CELEXA)

si TAL o pram / SEL ex a

"Sell Lexus Pram"

❖ Antidepressant
❖ Selective serotonin reuptake inhibitor (SSRI)

10
20
40
mg

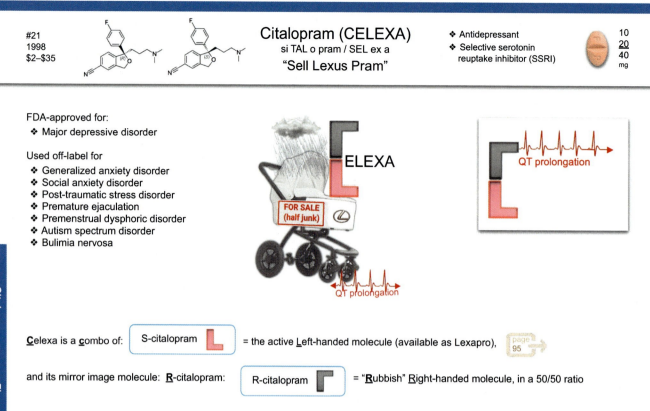

FDA-approved for:
❖ Major depressive disorder

Used off-label for
❖ Generalized anxiety disorder
❖ Social anxiety disorder
❖ Post-traumatic stress disorder
❖ Premature ejaculation
❖ Premenstrual dysphoric disorder
❖ Autism spectrum disorder
❖ Bulimia nervosa

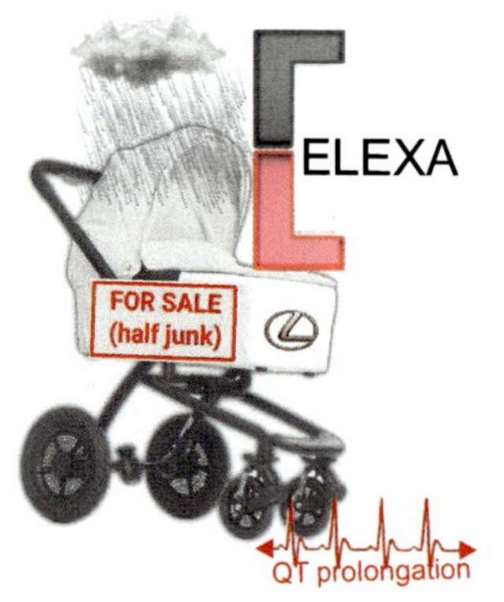

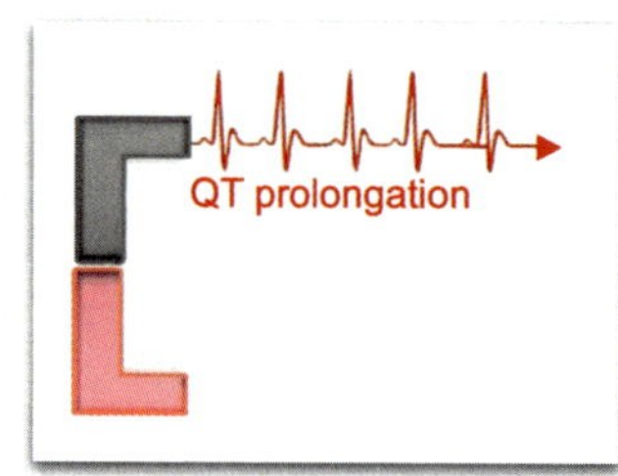

Celexa is a **c**ombo of: S-citalopram = the active **L**eft-handed molecule (available as Lexapro), 
page 95

and its mirror image molecule: **R**-citalopram: R-citalopram = "**R**ubbish" **R**ight-handed molecule, in a 50/50 ratio

Citalopram (Celexa) is the old 50% pure version of escitalopram (Lexapro). 50% of Celexa is the right-handed enantiomer R-citalopram. S-citalopram is the most selective (for serotonin reuptake inhibition) of all SSRIs. R-citalopram is ineffective and causes QT interval prolongation.

The plasma concentration of S-citalopram (escitalopram) is usually one third of the total citalopram concentration, with the implication that the other two thirds of the total citalopram concentration is inactive as an antidepressant (Burke & Kratochvil, 2002).

In 2012 the FDA released a warning for QT prolongation with Celexa and reduced the maximum approved dose from 60 mg to 40 mg. Lexapro does not have this warning. The warning may have been unwarranted, because rates of sudden unexpected death with high-dose citalopram is no higher than with other high-dose SSRIs (Ray et al, 2017). When VA patients were taken off citalopram because of the FDA warning, rates of depression increased and incidents of arrhythmias were not affected (Rector et al, 2016).

Although rarely clinically significant, QT prolongation by R-citalopram poses some risk in overdose situations. Although the risk of single-drug overdose death with Celexa is only about 1 in 1,850, mortality risk is over 4x higher than with Lexapro. QT prolongation by Celexa could potentially be risky when it is prescribed along with other QT-prolonging medications.

Celexa 20 mg is roughly equivalent to Lexapro 10 mg, as would be expected, given that half of Celexa is junk. Even at double the milligram dose, Celexa is predictably less effective than Lexapro. L-citalopram has an allosteric effect at the serotonin transporter that R-citalopram interferes with.

For initiation of antidepressant treatment, there is no reason to choose Celexa over Lexapro. So, why is anyone on citalopram? Many patients are on Celexa because, when their medication was started, Lexapro was more expensive. Celexa has been available generically since 2004. Lexapro went generic in 2012. When a drug goes off patent, it generally takes several years for enough manufacturers to enter the market for the drug to become dirt cheap.

Of the other SSRIs, paroxetine (Paxil) and sertraline (Zoloft) have always been pure enantiomers. Fluvoxamine (Luvox) lacks a chiral center, so a mirror image molecule does not exist. Fluoxetine (Prozac) is a racemic mixture, but R-fluoxetine and L-fluoxetine inhibit serotonin reuptake equally.

Bottom line: If starting an SSRI, choose escitalopram rather than citalopram. If a patient already established on citalopram is doing wonderfully, "don't try to fix what ain't broken".

Dosing: Celexa is started at 20 mg QD, dosed in AM or PM. In about 4 weeks may increase to FDA maximum of 40 mg. If higher strength is needed, change to Lexapro 20 mg, which is predictable more effective than Celexa 40 mg.

Dynamic interactions:
❖ Serotonergic (strong)
❖ QT prolongation (moderate)
❖ Antiplatelet effect
❖ Hyponatremia

Kinetic interactions:
❖ 2C19 substrate
❖ 2C19 poor metabolizers should not exceed 20 mg of citalopram
❖ See escitalopram monograph for preferred proton pump inhibitors (2C19 in**H**ibitors)

2C19 substrate

page 14

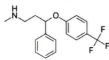

#29
1987
$2–$36

Fluoxetine (PROZAC)

flu OX e teen / PRO zak

"Prolonged sack of the Flustered ox"

- Antidepressant
- Selective serotonin reuptake inhibitor (SSRI)

10
20
40
mg

FDA-approved for:
- Major depressive disorder
- Obsessive-compulsive disorder
- Bulimia nervosa
- Panic disorder
- Premenstrual dysphoric disorder (Sarafem brand)

Used off-label for:
- Other anxiety disorders
- Premature ejaculation (to Prolong intercouse)
- Binge eating disorder

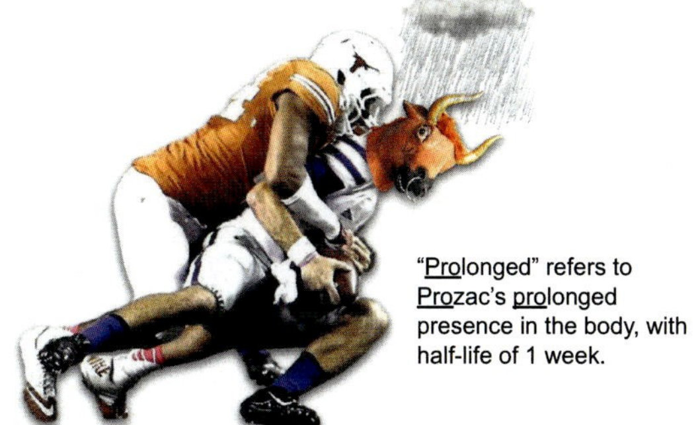

"Prolonged" refers to Prozac's prolonged presence in the body, with half-life of 1 week.

Fluoxetine (Prozac) was the first available SSRI, released to the US market in 1987. Among antidepressants, Prozac has the best evidence for treatment of depression among children and adolescents. It is the only FDA-approved medication for treatment of depression in children (age 8 and older).

For adults, Lexapro and Zoloft are generally preferred because Prozac interacts with numerous medications. Specifically, Prozac is an inHibitor of several CYP enzymes. If Prozac were a newly introduced drug, it would be unlikely to receive FDA approval due to the magnitude of these interactions.

Among SSRIs, Prozac is considered the most activating/energizing (as opposed to calming). As a result it is more likely to cause anxiety and insomnia than other SSRIs. It is safe for those with sleep apnea because it is a respiratory stimulant. It is not expected to cause weight gain and may result in modest weight loss. As with other SSRIs, the most troublesome side effect is sexual dysfunction.

Prozac has a very long elimination half-life of about 7 days. In other words, *Prozac has a Prolonged presence* in your body. A mnemonic from Dr. Jonathan Heldt's book *Memorable Psychopharmacology* compares the half-life of fluoxetine to the 7 days its takes to recover from the flu (influenza).

With chronic use, fluoxetine is detectable in the body up to five weeks after discontinuation (elimination half-life x 5). Since Prozac "tapers itself" off over weeks when stopped abruptly, there should be no serotonin withdrawal symptoms. Thanks to long half-life, missed doses are of less consequence (compared to antidepressants with shorter half-lives). If the patient forgets to take a dose on Monday, it is OK to take a double dose on Tuesday. This would not be advisable with most other psychotropics.

Fluoxetine is safe. Risk of death with single-drug overdose is no more than 1 in 10,000.

SYMBYAX is a fixed dose combination of fluoxetine with the antipsychotic olanzapine (Zyprexa), approved for acute depressive episodes of bipolar I disorder and for treatment-resistant major depression. Released in 2003, Symbyax (mnemonic *Symbiotic Ox*) was marketed heavily to primary care physicians, who likely underestimated olanzapine's potential for causing significant weight gain and diabetes. The fixed doses of olanzapine/fluoxetine in Symbyax are 3/25mg, 6/25 mg, 6/50 mg, and 12/50 mg taken in the evening.

For the sake of trivia, there exists a 90 mg fluoxetine ER capsule intended for once weekly dosing called PROZAC WEEKLY. It runs $50 per capsule. That's $200 monthly, compared to $4–$10 for a month of generic QD fluoxetine.

When discontinuing fluoxetine 40 mg or less, it may be ok just to stop without tapering, thanks to is long half-life. However, some patients may need a hyperbolic taper as described on page 112. To come off of higher doses, you will want to taper over several months. Switching from fluoxetine to another antidepressant can be tricky due to fluoxetine's long half-life. When switching to another modern serotonergic antidepressant, consider a washout period before starting the new antidepressant. The risk of serotonin syndrome is minimal with some overlap of two SSRIs (or an SSRI and an SNRI), so you do not have to wait for fluoxetine to be entirely cleared by the body. However, when switching from fluoxetine to an MAOI, there can be no overlap, because serotonin syndrome is a major risk. You need to wait at least five weeks after stopping fluoxetine to start the MAOI. For the other SSRIs, you only have to wait 2 weeks to start the MAOI.

Dosing:

Fluoxetine, available in 10 mg, 20 mg, and 40 mg capsules, is typically started (for adults) at 20 mg QD. It can be titrated in 20 mg increments to the FDA max dose of 80 mg QD. As a rule of thumb, you would want to wait about 4 weeks between dose increases. If there is a prior effective dose (for a particular patient) you are targeting, you can titrate faster. See above for discontinuation strategies.

For obsessive-compulsive disorder (OCD), you can go as high as 120 mg daily (Stahl, 2016). OCD often requires heroically high doses of SSRIs, and fluoxetine is a safe option.

For premenstrual dysphoric disorder (PMDD), you can take 20 mg QD starting 14 days prior to the anticipated onset of menses through the first full day of menstruation and repeating with each cycle. The brand SARAFEM (10 mg, 20 mg) is FDA-approved for this indication, but you will want to prescribe generic fluoxetine. For PMDD there is no proven benefit in exceeding 20 mg/day.

The "fluffers" - infamous inHibitors of CYP enzymes:
- Fluvoxamine (Luvox)
- Fluoxetine (Prozac)
- Fluconazole (Diflucan)

Fluoxetine is a less potent enzyme inhibitor than the other two.

Dynamic interactions:
- Serotonergic (strong)
- Antiplatelet effect
- Hyponatremia

Kinetic interactions:
- Fluoxetine is an inHibitor of 2D6 and 2C19. This results in numerous interactions that markedly increase blood levels of various victim drugs (substrates).
- Although fluoxetine itself is a 2D6 and 2C9 substrate,clinically significant victimization is not expected.

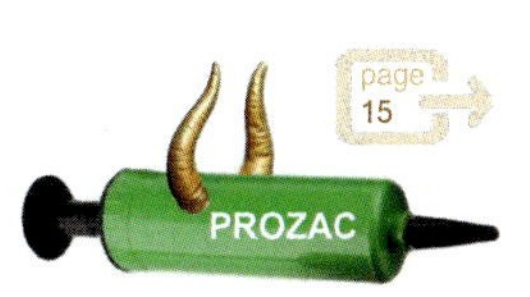

page 15

2D6 inHibitor (strong)

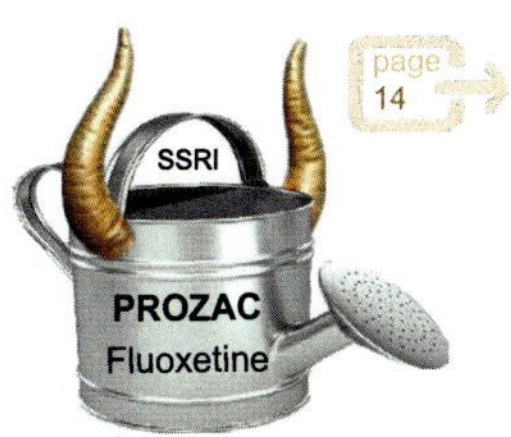

page 14

2C19 inHibitor (moderate)

MODERN ANTIDEPRESSANTS 8

#64
1992
IR $3–$37
ER $55–$140

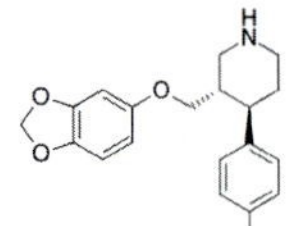

Paroxetine (PAXIL)

par OX e tine / PAX il

"Pear rocks a teen (Paxil Rose)"

❖ Antidepressant
❖ Selective serotonin reuptake inhibitor (SSRI)

ER
12.5
25
37.5
mg

10
20
30
40
mg

FDA-approved for:

❖ Major depressive disorder
❖ Obsessive-compulsive disorder
❖ Generalized anxiety disorder
❖ Panic disorder
❖ Social anxiety
❖ Post-traumatic stress disorder
❖ Menopausal vasomotor symptoms (hot flashes) at low 7.5 mg strength branded as BRISDELLE

Used off-label for:

❖ Premenstrual dysphoric disorder
❖ Premature ejaculation

Axl Rose
(Guns N' Roses)

Paroxetine (Paxil) has the reputation as a calming (as opposed to energizing) antidepressant. However, there are several reasons to choose a different SSRI. Although paroxetine is FDA-approved for more anxious conditions than other SSRIs, it has performed no better for anxiety in head-to-head trials (Sanchez et al, 2014).

Disadvantages of paroxetine compared to other SSRIs:

► More fatigue
► More weight gain
► More sexual dysfunction
► More likely to cause withdrawal symptoms with missed doses
► More CYP interactions (excluding fluvoxamine)
► More anticholinergic effects
► Risk of dementia (anticholinergic), unlike other SSRIs
► Risk of birth defects
► Less effective than escitalopram, even for anxiety disorders

Axl Rose has short stature. Among antidepressants, Paxil has a relatively short elimination half-life of 21 hours. A missed dose may result in unpleasant serotonin withdrawal symptoms.

Paroxetine is the only SSRI with significant anticholinergic effects, making it a bad SSRI choice for elderly individuals. As a result of this anticholinergic activity, Paxil is the most constipating SSRI—"Paxil packs it in". Paroxetine is the most likely SSRI to cause tachycardia, which is an anticholinergic effect. Prolonged exposure to anticholinergic medications is a risk factor for cognitive decline. Paxil is the only SSRI associated with increased risk (2-fold) of developing dementia (Heath et al, 2018).

Among SSRIs, Paxil has a relatively short half-life of 21 hours.

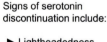

short

Paroxetine has more potential to cause fatigue and weight gain than other modern antidepressants, but less so than some TCAs.

All SSRIs commonly decrease sexual desire, disrupt the sexual pleasure response, and increase latency to orgasm. Among SSRIs, Paxil is the most likely to cause sexual dysfunction. Since Paxil is the "best" at interfering with orgasms, it is the SSRI of choice for off-label treatment of premature ejaculation. Its short half-life makes it handy as a PRN for this purpose.

There may be a possibility of birth defects if Paxil is taken in early pregnancy. Under pre-2015 FDA pregnancy risk categories, paroxetine was pregnancy Category D, while other SSRIs were Category C.

As a strong 2D6 inhibitor, paroxetine is more likely to cause problematic drug-drug interactions than the other commonly used SSRIs. Fluvoxamine (Luvox), a stronger inhibitor of CYP enzymes, is worse than Paxil in terms of interactions.

Signs of serotonin discontinuation include: page 112

► Lightheadedness
► Paresthesias
► Nausea
► Fatigue
► Irritability

The enteric coated controlled-release formulation of paroxetine, Paxil CR, is less likely to cause nausea. Nausea is a short-lived side effect, and after the first week the CR formulation offers little advantage over immediate-release paroxetine.

Dosing: Start 20 mg AM. Depending on the indication, FDA max is 50–60 mg. For OCD start 20 mg AM, increase by 10 mg weekly to target of at least 40 mg. FDA max for OCD is 60 mg, but can go as high as 100 mg (Stahl, 2016). The target dose for panic disorder is 40 mg. Consider twice daily dosing ≥ 40 mg. For menopausal hot flashes, rather than using expensive 7.5 mg paroxetine (Brisdelle), prescribe 10 mg generic paroxetine HS. Taper gradually to discontinue to avoid serotonin withdrawal symptoms.

Dynamic interactions:

❖ Serotonergic (strong)
❖ Antiplatelet effect
❖ Hyponatremia

Kinetic interactions:

❖ 2C9 inHibitor (moderate)
❖ 2D6 inHibitor (strong)
❖ 2D6 substrate

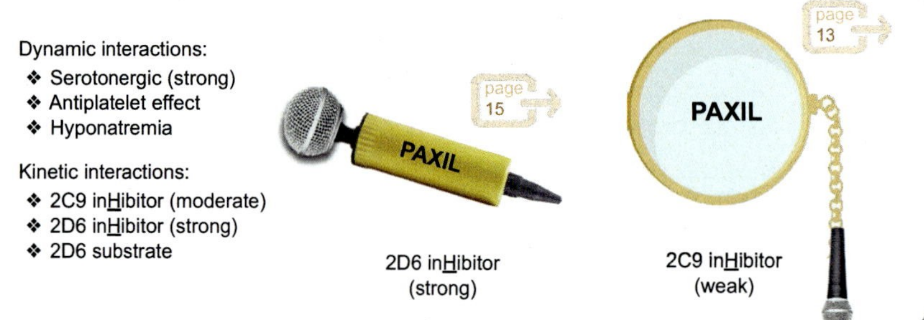

2D6 inHibitor (strong)

2C9 inHibitor (weak)

1996
$20–$120

Fluvoxamine (LUVOX)

flu VOX a meen / LU vox

"Glove-ox"

- ❖ Selective serotonin reuptake inhibitor (SSRI)
- ❖ OCD medication
- ❖ Potent CYP inHibitor

25
50
<u>100</u>
mg

FDA-approved for:

- ❖ Obsessive-compulsive disorder (OCD)

Used off-label for:

- ❖ Social anxiety disorder (rarely)
- ❖ Strategic inHibition of CYP1A2 with clozapine as described on page 11
- ❖ Premature ejaculation

Fluvoxamine (Luvox) is an SSRI approved <u>exclusively for OCD</u>, a disorder characterized by obsessions (recurrent intrusive thoughts) that the individual may attempt to neutralize with a compulsive repetitive behavior or ritual, e.g., flicking a light switch <u>50</u> times.

Three other SSRIs are FDA-approved for OCD—fluoxetine (Prozac), paroxetine (Paxil), and sertraline (Zoloft). Off-label, escitalopram (Lexapro) at high dose may be a better choice than fluvoxamine for OCD because it highly selective for blocking serotonin transporters and has fewer side effects.

✱ Although not used for depression, fluvoxamine is properly referred to as an antidepressant.

Luvox is a potent inHibitor of multiple CYP enzymes, causing <u>increased</u> serum levels of many co-administered medications. CYP1A2 inhibition by fluvoxamine can be used for strategic advantage in combination with clozapine (Clozaril) as explained on page 11.

<u>50</u> mg HS is the starting fluvoxamine dose for the first week, then <u>50</u> mg BID. Envision the mascot flicking a light switch 50 times. Additional dose increases will likely be necessary for fluvoxamine to be effective for OCD. With any SSRI, effective treatment of OCD demands a high dose, often exceeding the FDA max.

Fluvoxamine should be dosed <u>BID</u> for maintenance because it has the <u>shortest half-life</u> of all available SSRIs (15 hours). Other SSRIs are generally dosed once daily.

Among SSRIs, fluvoxamine is the least likely to cause sexual dysfunction (La Torre et al, 2013), although > 50% of patients are still affected. Owing to short half-life, fluvoxamine is a reasonable PRN treatment for premature ejaculation.

Dosing: For OCD <u>start 50 mg HS</u>, then increase to <u>50 mg BID</u> in 4–7 days. May increase by 50 mg/day every 4–7 days. FDA maximum is 300 mg/day but may go as high as 450 mg (Stahl, 2016) in divided doses. Dosing is similar for social anxiety disorder. Taper gradually to discontinue.

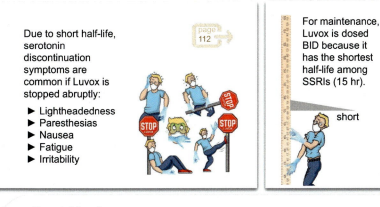

Serotonergic medications need to be prescribed at high dose to effectively treat obsessive-compulsive disorder.

*Escitalopram is used off-label for OCD.

Serotonergic med	Class	FDA max	Max for OCD (Stahl, 2016)
Clomipramine (Anafranil)	TCA	250 mg	250 mg
Fluvoxamine (Luvox)	SSRI	300 mg	450 mg
Escitalopram (Lexapro)*	SSRI	20 mg	60 mg
Fluoxetine (Prozac)	SSRI	80 mg	120 mg
Paroxetine (Paxil)	SSRI	60 mg	100 mg
Sertraline (Zoloft)	SSRI	200 mg	400 mg

Due to short half-life, serotonin discontinuation symptoms are common if Luvox is stopped abruptly:

- ► Lightheadedness
- ► Paresthesias
- ► Nausea
- ► Fatigue
- ► Irritability

page 112

For maintenance, Luvox is dosed BID because it has the shortest half-life among SSRIs (15 hr).

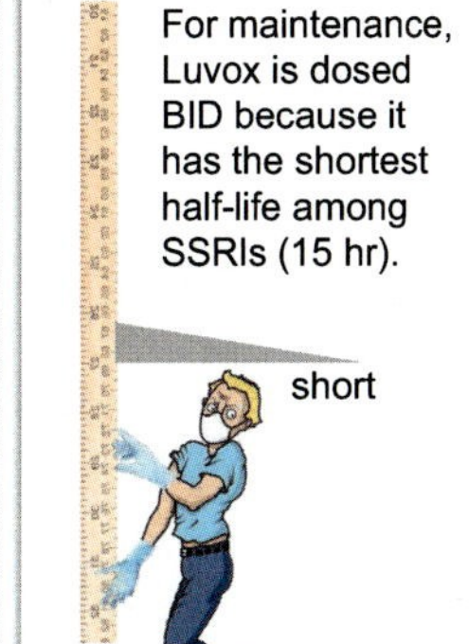
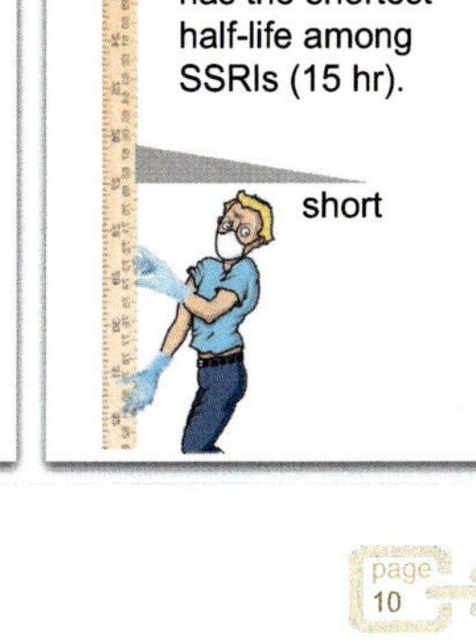

Dynamic interactions:

- ❖ Serotonergic (strong)
- ❖ Antiplatelet effect
- ❖ Hyponatremia

Kinetic interactions:

- ❖ Luvox is a "fluffer", i.e., inHibitor of several CYP enzymes. This results in numerous drug-drug interactions causing the serum level of the victim drug (substrate) to increase markedly
- ❖ Ramelteon (Rozerem) is contraindicated because ramelteon levels increase 100-fold! (1A2)
- ❖ Tizanidine (Zanaflex) is contraindicated because tizanidine levels increase 10-fold (1A2)
- ❖ Pimozide (Orap) is contraindicated (3A4)
- ❖ Although fluvoxamine Itself is a 2D6 and 1A2 substrate, clinically significant victimization is not expected

page 10
page 14
page 16

1A2 inHibitor (strong)

2C19 inHibitor (strong)

3A4 inHibitor (moderate)

Serotonin-norepinephrine reuptake inhibitors (SNRIs)

SNRIs increase the extracellular availability of neurotransmitters serotonin (5-HT) and norepinephrine (NE).
Think of serotonin as calming ("serene") and norepinephrine (NE), also known as noradrenalin, as eNErgizing.

SNRI Antidepressant	U.S. Market	Uses	Comments
Duloxetine (CYMBALTA)	2004	Depression, Fibromyalgia, Neuropathic pain, Anxiety	Duloxetine is involved in more CYP interactions, than the other SNRIs.
Venlafaxine (EFFEXOR)	1994	Depression, Anxiety, Chronic pain	More dangerous in overdose than other SNRIs
Desvenlafaxine (PRISTIQ)	2007	Depression	Less effective and more side effects than Effexor XR.
Milnacipran (SAVELLA)	2009	Fibromyalgia	Titration pack 12.5 mg (#5), 25 mg (#8), 50 mg (#42)
Levomilnacipran (FETZIMA)	2013	Depression	L-enantiomer of milnacipran (Savella)

Some tricyclic antidepressants (TCAs) are SNRIs by mechanism, although TCAs also block off-target receptors (acetylcholine, histamine, alpha-1).

TCA Antidepressant	U.S. Market	Uses	Comments
Amitriptyline (ELAVIL)	1961	Depression, Neuropathic pain, Migraine prophylaxis, Fibromyalgia, Postherpetic neuralgia, Insomnia	5-HT > NE More sedating than newer SNRIs; Also 5-HT$_2$ receptor antagonist
Doxepin (SINEQUAN, SILENOR)	1969	Depression, Insomnia	Sedating at low dose due antihistamine properties; NE > 5-HT at higher doses; Also 5-HT$_2$ receptor antagonist
Clomipramine (ANAFRANIL)	1990	Obsessive-compulsive disorder (OCD)	5-HT > > NE
Imipramine (TOFRANIL)	1957	Depression	5-HT > NE
Amoxapine (ASENDIN)	1992	Depression	NE > 5-HT, Antipsychotic properties due to D2 antagonism

SNRIs that are not classified as antidepressants:

Other SNRIs	U.S. Market	Uses	Comments
Tramadol (ULTRAM)	1995	Pain	Weak opioid also; Schedule IV controlled substance
Sibutramine (MERIDIA)	1997–2010	Obesity	Removed from market in 2010 due to risk heart attack and stroke

"Atypical Antidepressants"

Newer antidepressants not classified as TCAs, MAOIs, SSRIs, or SNRIs

Atypical antidepressant	Class	Abbrev	Cost/mo	
Nefazodone (SERZONE)	Serotonin Antagonist & Reuptake Inhibitor	SARI	$68	Developed as a non-sedating variant of trazodone. Rarely prescribed. Rare occurrence of severe liver damage.
Trazodone (DESYREL)		SARI	$4	Widely prescribed at low dose, solely as a sleep medication
Mirtazapine (REMERON)	Noradrenergic & Specific Serotonergic Antidepressant	NaSSA	$11	Great for sleep and appetite stimulation, more so at lower dose. At higher dose, noradrenergic (NE) activity is more prominent.
Bupropion (WELLBUTRIN)	Norepinephrine & Dopamine Reuptake Inhibitor	NDRI	$25	Like a mild stimulant—helpful for ADHD, appetite suppression and smoking cessation. Improves sexual functioning. Seizures at high dose.
Vilazodone (VIIBRYD)	Serotonin Modulator & Stimulator	SMS	$200	"Hybrid" of SSRI & 5-HT$_{1A}$ partial agonist. Mechanism of action is like a combo of an SSRI and the anxiolytic buspirone (Buspar).
Vortioxetine (TRINTELLIX)		SMS	$300	Serotonin reuptake inhibitor, 5-HT$_{1A}$ agonist, 5-HT$_{1B}$ partial agonist, 5-HT$_3$ antagonist & 5-HT$_7$ antagonist.

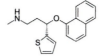

#48
2004
$6–$166

Duloxetine (CYMBALTA)

du LOX e tine / cym BAL ta

"Dueling Cymbals"

- ❖ Antidepressant
- ❖ Serotonin-norepinephrine reuptake inhibitor (SNRI)
- ❖ 5-HT > NE

20
30
40
60
mg

FDA-approved for:

- ❖ Major depressive disorder
- ❖ Generalized anxiety disorder
- ❖ Diabetic neuropathy
- ❖ Fibromyalgia
- ❖ Chronic musculoskeletal pain

Used off-label for:

- ❖ Stress urinary incontinence
- ❖ ADHD

The SNRI duloxetine (Cymbalta) is reasonable first-line choice for depressed patients with comorbid pain syndromes. Among antidepressants, it stands out as being particularly effective for generalized anxiety disorder (GAD).

Side effects may include nausea (22%), dry mouth (16%), fatigue (11%), dizziness (11%), somnolence, constipation, diarrhea, insomnia, agitation, sweating, headaches, and sexual dysfunction. Duloxetine is not expected to cause appreciable weight gain. Hypertension (1%) due to duloxetine does not appear to be dose-dependent. The discontinuation rate of duloxetine due to side effects was 15% (versus 5% for placebo).

Compared to the SNRI venlafaxine (Effexor), duloxetine is more likely to cause nausea but less likely to elevate blood pressure. Duloxetine is less likely than venlafaxine to cause serotonin withdrawal symptoms upon discontinuation.

Duloxetine is more likely to be involved in clinically significant CYP interactions than venlafaxine.

Serious liver damage is possible with duloxetine, although rare. It is not considered necessary to closely monitor liver enzymes (beyond routine screening labs for all patients).

Avoid prescribing duloxetine to alcoholics or those with known liver problems.

Risk of death from a single-drug overdose with duloxetine is about 1 in 3,500, making it safer than venlafaxine (1 in 800).

Peak plasma levels are achieved at 3 hours. Half-life is 12 hours, so steady-state concentrations are achieved within 3 days of oral dosing (5 x 12 hours). Upon discontinuation, duloxetine is cleared from the body within 3 days (also 5 x 12 hours) and there are no active metabolites.

For depression, the FDA maximum of 120 mg was found no more effective than 60 mg. For pain, the 120 mg dose (divided 60 mg BID) can be more effective.

Dosing: Duloxetine can be dosed BID or QD, either AM or HS. Consider starting 30 mg QD x 1 wk, then increase to target dose of 60 mg QD or 30 mg BID. For depression, the FDA maximum of 120 mg is rarely more effective than 60 mg. Doses over 60 mg may be more effective for pain. 120 mg dose is usually divided to 60 mg BID. Taper gradually to discontinue to avoid serotonin withdrawal symptoms.

Dynamic interactions:

- ❖ Serotonergic
- ❖ Antiplatelet effect
- ❖ Hyponatremia
- ❖ Hypertension

Kinetic interactions:

- ❖ 2D6 inHibitor (moderate)
- ❖ 1A2 substrate
  - – decreased 30% by smoking
  - – increased 3-fold by fluvoxamine (Luvox)
- ❖ 2D6 substrate

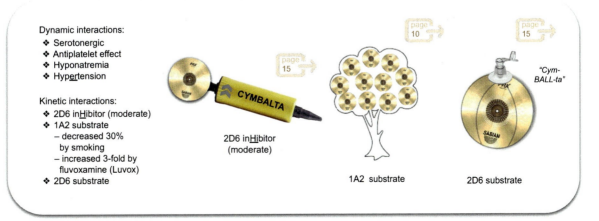

2D6 inHibitor (moderate)

1A2 substrate

2D6 substrate

#51
1995
$6–$105

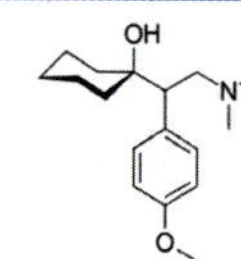

Venlafaxine (EFFEXOR)

ven la FAX ine / e FEX er

"Vanilla faxing (eFax'er)"

- Antidepressant
- Serotonin-norepinephrine reuptake inhibitor (SNRI)
- 5-HT > NE

XR

37.5
75
150
mg

FDA-approved for:

- Major depressive disorder
- Generalized anxiety disorder
- Social anxiety disorder
- Panic disorder

Used off-label for:

- ADHD
- Migraine prophylaxis
- Post-traumatic stress disorder
- Fibromyalgia
- Cataplexy
- Vasomotor symptoms of menopause
- Premenstrual dysphoric disorder

I'm depressed.
Must fax for help.
possible BP elevation

The SNRI venlafaxine (Effexor) is a reasonable second-line antidepressant, potentially first-line for depressed individuals suffering from chronic pain. Effexor XR and duloxetine (Cymbalta) are equally popular SNRIs, #51 and #48 most prescribed medications in the US, respectively.

When Effexor was introduced in 1995 prescribers nicknamed it "Side-Effexor" due to nausea and fatigue. Effexor XR (extended-release) was introduced in 1998 and became widely prescribed because it is much better tolerated. Choose the XR formulation, which is also less expensive than the rarely prescribed immediate-release venlafaxine. The only scenario when immediate-release Effexor is preferred is with bariatric surgery patients. For either formulation of Effexor, it is recommended to take it with food to minimize nausea.

Peak plasma concentrations are achieved within 2 to 3 hours for the IR formulation and within 5.5 hours for the XR formulation.

Effexor acts as an SSRI at low doses (37.5 mg, 75 mg) and an SNRI at higher doses (150 mg plus). 75 mg/day is the minimum effective dose for treatment of depression

Venlafaxine has a short half-life of 5 hours, and the half-life of the active metabolite O-desmethylvenlafaxine (ODV) is 11 hours. ODV is available as the antidepressant desvenlafaxine (Pristiq), which appears to be less effective than Effexor for depression.

Incidence of blood pressure elevation with the XR formulation is 1%. With the IR formulation, incidence of hypertension is about 5%, and as high as 13% at doses exceeding 300 mg.

In addition to raising blood pressure, venlafaxine may induce seizures in overdose, making it the most dangerous modern antidepressant (non-TCA, non-MAOI). Risk of single-drug overdose death with venlafaxine is about 1 in 839.

For depression, venlafaxine is no more effective than the SSRI escitalopram (Lexapro), which has fewer side effects. For generalized anxiety disorder, venlafaxine is more effective than buspirone (Buspar).

Venlafaxine can cause false positives for PCP on drug tests.

FDA max is 225 mg, but for severe depression 300 mg may be more effective. Take caution because blood pressure elevation is dose dependent. Taper off Effexor slowly to avoid symptoms of serotonin withdrawal syndrome.

XR Dosing: Specify the extended-release formulation Effexor XR, (venlafaxine ER) except for in bariatric surgery patients. Start Effexor XR 37.5 or 75 mg QD with food (to ameliorate nausea), with target of 150–225 mg QD. FDA max is 225 mg, but 300 mg may be more effective for depression. For treatment of pain the dose can go as high as high as 450 mg/day if blood pressure is monitored closely. May increase in 75 mg increments every 4–7 days.

IR dosing: For bariatric surgery patients, prescribe venlafaxine IR which is available in 25, 37.5, 50, 75, and 100 mg tablets, given in divided doses BID or TID. The FDA maximum for IR venlafaxine is 375 mg/day in divided doses (125 mg TID).

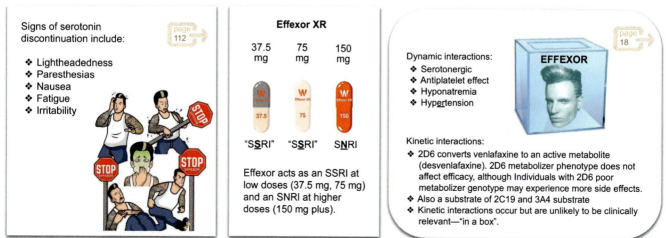

Signs of serotonin discontinuation include:

page 112

- Lightheadedness
- Paresthesias
- Nausea
- Fatigue
- Irritability

Effexor XR

37.5 mg	75 mg	150 mg
"S**S**RI"	"S**S**RI"	S**N**RI

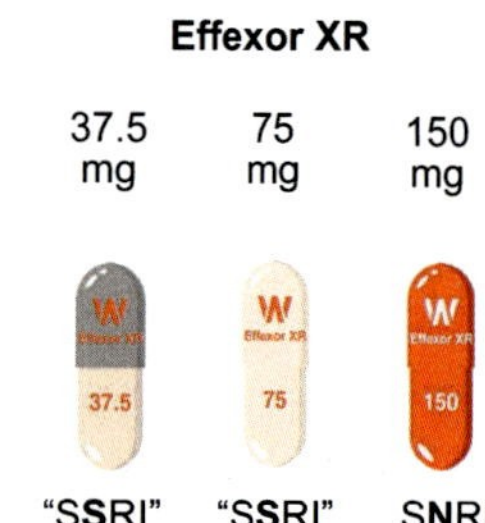

Effexor acts as an SSRI at low doses (37.5 mg, 75 mg) and an SNRI at higher doses (150 mg plus).

page 18

Dynamic interactions:

- Serotonergic
- Antiplatelet effect
- Hyponatremia
- Hyp**er**tension

EFFEXOR

Kinetic interactions:

- 2D6 converts venlafaxine to an active metabolite (desvenlafaxine). 2D6 metabolizer phenotype does not affect efficacy, although Individuals with 2D6 poor metabolizer genotype may experience more side effects.
- Also a substrate of 2C19 and 3A4 substrate
- Kinetic interactions occur but are unlikely to be clinically relevant—"in a box".

#272
2007
$33–$274

Desvenlafaxine (PRISTIQ)

des ven la FAX ine / Pris TIQ

"Desk faxing Pressed steak"

- Antidepressant
- Serotonin-norepinephrine reuptake inhibitor (SNRI)
- 5-HT > NE

25
50
100
mg

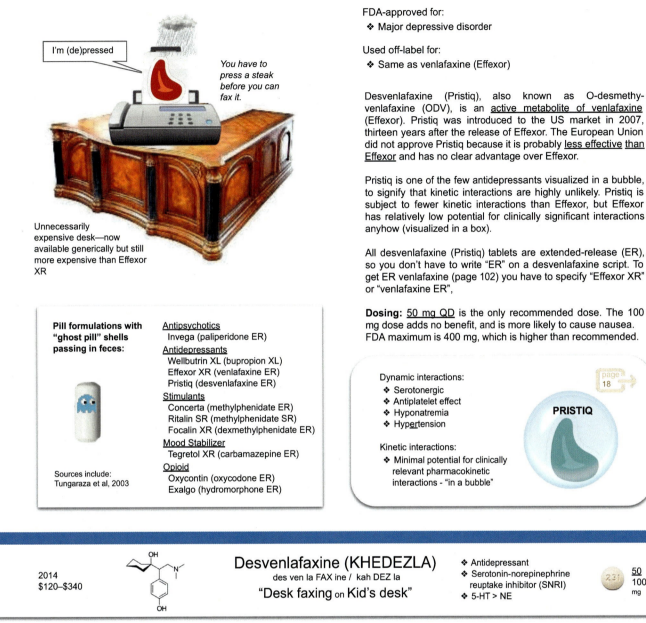

I'm (de)pressed

You have to press a steak before you can fax it.

Unnecessarily expensive desk—now available generically but still more expensive than Effexor XR

FDA-approved for:
- Major depressive disorder

Used off-label for:
- Same as venlafaxine (Effexor)

Desvenlafaxine (Pristiq), also known as O-desmethy-venlafaxine (ODV), is an active metabolite of venlafaxine (Effexor). Pristiq was introduced to the US market in 2007, thirteen years after the release of Effexor. The European Union did not approve Pristiq because it is probably less effective than Effexor and has no clear advantage over Effexor.

Pristiq is one of the few antidepressants visualized in a bubble, to signify that kinetic interactions are highly unlikely. Pristiq is subject to fewer kinetic interactions than Effexor, but Effexor has relatively low potential for clinically significant interactions anyhow (visualized in a box).

All desvenlafaxine (Pristiq) tablets are extended-release (ER), so you don't have to write "ER" on a desvenlafaxine script. To get ER venlafaxine (page 102) you have to specify "Effexor XR" or "venlafaxine ER",

Dosing: 50 mg QD is the only recommended dose. The 100 mg dose adds no benefit, and is more likely to cause nausea. FDA maximum is 400 mg, which is higher than recommended.

Pill formulations with "ghost pill" shells passing in feces:

Sources include:
Tungaraza et al, 2003

Antipsychotics
- Invega (paliperidone ER)

Antidepressants
- Wellbutrin XL (bupropion XL)
- Effexor XR (venlafaxine ER)
- Pristiq (desvenlafaxine ER)

Stimulants
- Concerta (methylphenidate ER)
- Ritalin SR (methylphenidate SR)
- Focalin XR (dexmethylphenidate ER)

Mood Stabilizer
- Tegretol XR (carbamazepine ER)

Opioid
- Oxycontin (oxycodone ER)
- Exalgo (hydromorphone ER)

Dynamic interactions:
- Serotonergic
- Antiplatelet effect
- Hyponatremia
- Hypertension

Kinetic interactions:
- Minimal potential for clinically relevant pharmacokinetic interactions - "in a bubble"

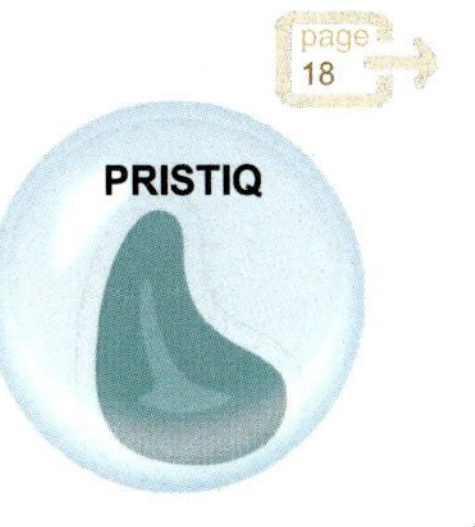

2014
$120–$340

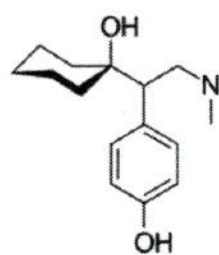

Desvenlafaxine (KHEDEZLA)

des ven la FAX ine / kah DEZ la

"Desk faxing on Kid's desk"

- Antidepressant
- Serotonin-norepinephrine reuptake inhibitor (SNRI)
- 5-HT > NE

50
100
mg

FDA-approved for:
- Major depressive disorder (adults)

Desvenlafaxine is also available as the brand name Khedezla (released 2014) which is equivalent to Pristiq (2007). Both Pristiq and Khedezla are extended-release (ER) formulations of desvenlafaxine, both indicated for major depressive disorder, both dosed once daily. Pristiq is a succinate salt with a half-life of 10.4 hours, while Khedezla is a base with a half-life of 10.6 hours.

The approval of Khedezla was based on the original Pristiq efficacy studies.

Studies have found desvenlafaxine to be ineffective for children with depression (Weihs et al, 2017). *"Kid's desk ain't for kids."*

Desvenlafaxine has been available generically since 2017.

Dosing: Same as Pristiq

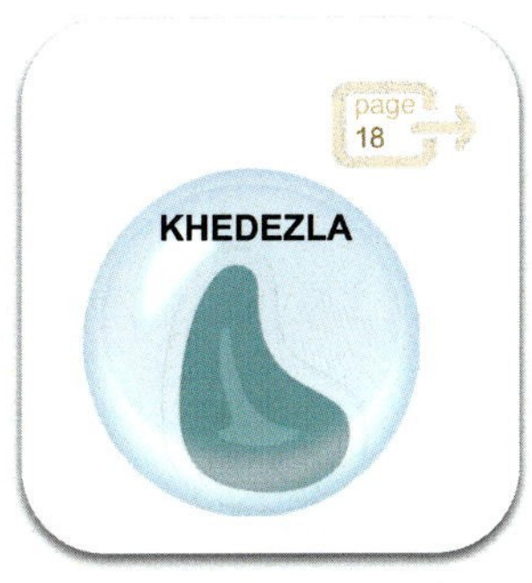

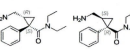

2009
$384–$476

Milnacipran (SAVELLA)

mil NA si pran / sa VEL la

"Milhouse ran to Save Ella"

- ❖ Serotonin-norepinephrine reuptake inhibitor (SNRI)
- ❖ Fibromyalgia medication
- ❖ 5-HT = NE

12.5
25
<u>50</u>
100
mg

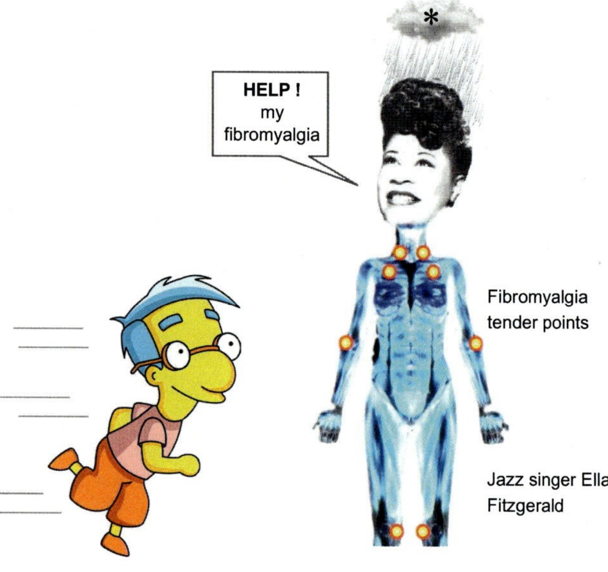

Not approved for depression

FDA-approved for:
- ❖ Fibromyalgia

* Milnacipran (Savella) is the SNRI <u>approved for fibromyalgia only</u>, not for depression. It is properly referred to as an antidepressant and is approved for depression in some other countries. It has not shown robust antidepressant efficacy.

At the usual maintenance dose milnacipran is a "<u>balanced</u>" SNRI that enhances <u>serotonin and norepinephrine activity by similar magnitude</u>. At lower doses, e.g., 25 mg BID, noradrenergic effects are more pronounced than serotonergic effects.

Milnacipran is fairly well tolerated, with fewer gastrointestinal issues than SSRIs. Side effects that are more prominent with milnacipran (compared to SSRIs) include dizziness, sweating, and urinary hesitancy.

Levomilnacipran (Fetzima), the pure L-enantiomer of milnacipran, is FDA-approved for depression.

Of 236 single-drug exposures to milnacipran reported to Poison Control, there were 5 major serious outcomes but <u>no deaths</u> (Nelson & Spyker, 2017).

Dosing: Titrate to <u>50 mg BID</u> using the starter pack shown below. Maximum dose is 200 mg (100 mg BID). Taper to discontinue to avoid unpleasant serotonin withdrawal symptoms.

SAVELLA (fibromyalgia)

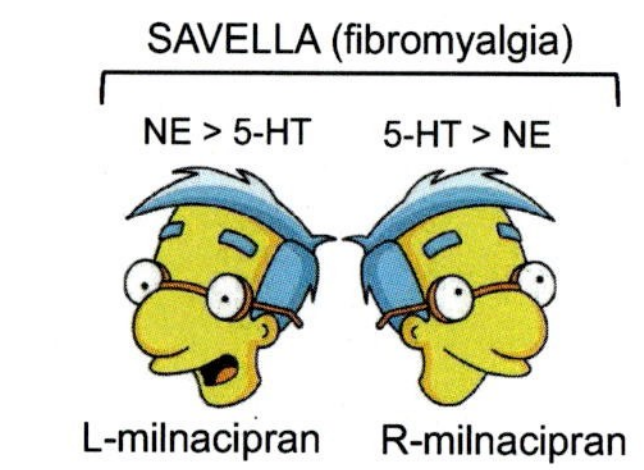

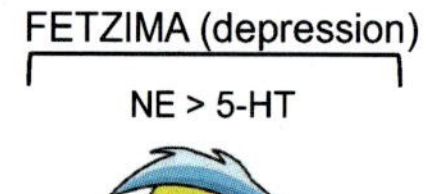

L-milnacipran

Savella is initiated by a titration that would be quite inconvenient without the "4 week convenience pack".

- ► 12.5 mg QD x 1 day,
- ► 12.5 mg BID x 2 days,
- ► 25 mg BID x 4 days,
- ► then 50 mg BID

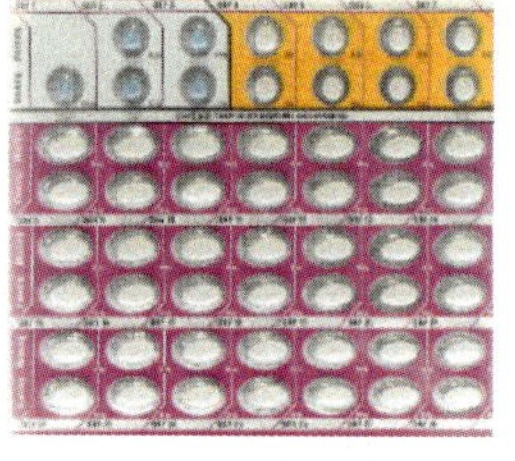

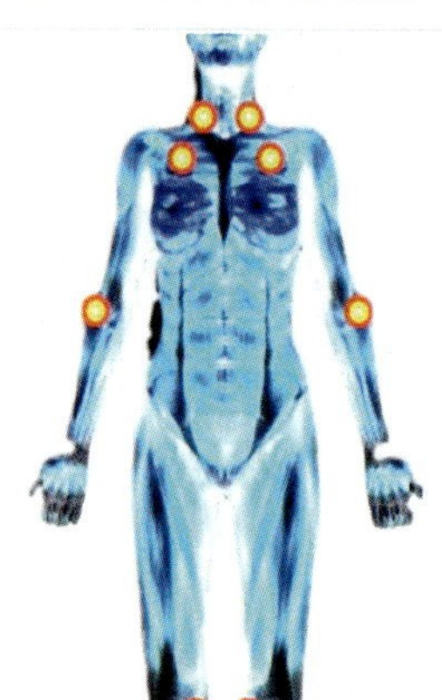

Medications for fibromyalgia

FDA-approved:
- ❖ Duloxetine (Cymbalta) – SNRI
- ❖ Milnacipran (Savella) – SNRI
- ❖ Pregabalin (Lyrica) – AED

Off-label:
- ❖ Venlafaxine (Effexor) – SNRI
- ❖ Gabapentin (Neurontin) – AED
- ❖ Amitriptyline (Elavil) – TCA
- ❖ Tramadol (Ultram) – weak opioid & SNRI

Dynamic interactions:
- ❖ Serotonergic
- ❖ Antiplatelet effect
- ❖ Hyponatremia
- ❖ Hyp<u>er</u>tension

page 18

Kinetic interactions:
- ❖ Milnacipran undergoes minimal CYP-related metabolism, with 55% of the dose excreted unchanged in urine. Kinetic interactions occur but are unlikely to be clinically relevant—"in a box".

2013
$394–$484

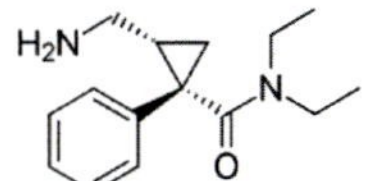

Levomilnacipran (FETZIMA)

LEE voe mil NA si pran / fet ZEE ma

"Leave Milhouse with a Zima Fetish"

- Antidepressant
- Serotonin-norepinephrine reuptake inhibitor (SNRI)
- NE >> 5-HT

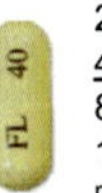

20
40
80
120
mg

FDA-approved for:

- Major depressive disorder

Used off-label for:

- Fibromyalgia
- Diabetic peripheral neuropathy
- Chronic musculoskeletal pain
- Vasomotor symptoms of menopause

Zima was a clear malt beverage available 1993–2008.

Levomilnacipran (Fetzima), released in 2013, is the pure L-enantiomer of milnacipran (Savella). Fetzima will be expensive until the patent expires in 2031.

Compared to other SNRIs, levomilnacipran enhances norepinephrine >> serotonin, making it more stimulating. By contrast, milnacipran is a "balanced" SNRI that enhances serotonin and norepinephrine activity by similar magnitude at the usual maintenance dose.

Levomilnacipran causes no weight gain. The most relevant side effect is nausea, especially as treatment is initiated. This why the dose should be titrated. Dose dependent urinary retention (5%) and tachycardia and may occur. It increases heart rate by an average of 7 beats/minute, which is a noradrenergic effect.

Levomilnacipran was found effective in patients over age 60, a population that is generally resistant to antidepressants.

It reaches peak serum concentration about 7 hours after ingestion. Half-life is about 12 hours. Kinetic interactions are unlikely to be clinically significant.

Of 56 single-drug exposures to milnacipran reported to Poison Control, there were no deaths or major serious outcomes, although this is a small sample size (Nelson & Spyker, 2017).

Dosing: Start 20 mg QD x 2 days, then increase to 40 mg QD. This can be accomplished with the 28-day starter pack that contains #2 of 20 mg caps and #26 of 40 mg caps. FDA maximum is 120 mg QD if renal function is normal. Do not use if severe renal impairment. Do not exceed 80 mg/day in the presence of a strong 3A4 inHibitor (e.g., ketoconazole, clarithromycin, ritonavir). Taper gradually to discontinue.

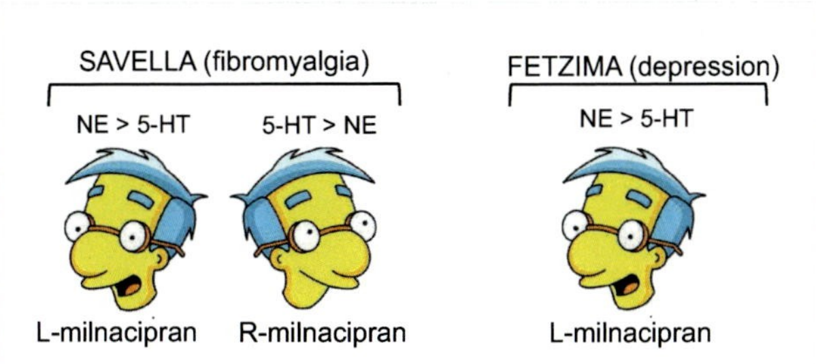

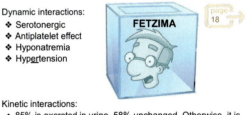

Dynamic interactions:

- Serotonergic
- Antiplatelet effect
- Hyponatremia
- Hypertension

page 18

Kinetic interactions:

- 85% is excreted in urine, 58% unchanged. Otherwise, it is primarily metabolized through 3A4/
- The package insert says not to exceed 80 mg/day in the presence of a strong 3A4 inHibitor (e.g., ketoconazole, clarithromycin, ritonavir). Otherwise, the max is 120 mg. The label for milnacipran (Savella) does not describe this interaction. As with Savella, we're putting Fetzima "in a box" to signify that kinetic interactions occur but are unlikely to be clinically significant.

#24
1981
$3–$18

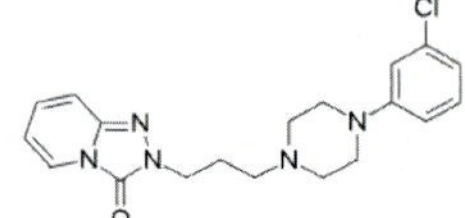

Trazodone (DESYREL)

TRA zo dohn / DES zi rel

"Trays o' bone / Dizzy reel"

- ❖ Antidepressant/sleep medication
- ❖ Serotonin antagonist and reuptake inhibitor (SARI)
  - – 5-HT_2 antagonist
  - – 5-HT_{1A} agonist

50
100
150
300
mg

FDA-approved for:

- ❖ Major Depressive Disorder (MDD) —rarely used for this indication

Used off-label for:

- ❖ Insomnia (first-line)
- ❖ PTSD nightmares

"Trays of bone" make you sleepy

Trazodone (Desyrel) was the first non-tricyclic / non-MAOI antidepressant approved in the US, predating the SSRIs. Many psychiatrists consider trazodone their first-line sleep medication. It is the author's #1 most prescribed drug. It can be combined with any other medication. Low-dose Trazodone 50–75 mg can even be combined with an MAOI (Jacobsen, 1990). The author regards significantly prolonged QTc interval (over 490 msec or so) as the only contraindication.

Although it is approved as an antidepressant, trazodone is usually prescribed at low dose for insomnia, with no antidepressant benefit expected. It is seldom used as a stand-alone treatment for depression due to sedation and orthostatic hypotension if dosed at antidepressant strength. Trazodone is often prescribed as an adjunct to SSRIs. It may be helpful for reducing PTSD nightmares (Warner MD et al, 2001).

Trazodone induces and maintains sleep without causing tolerance. Its half-life of 3–6 hours is ideal for sleep without causing daytime drowsiness. The most common side effect is xerostomia—a mouth that's "dry as a bone". Most medications causing dry mouth do so as an anticholinergic effect. This is not the case with trazodone, which lacks anticholinergic effects.

It is a preferred sleep medication for those with obstructive sleep apnea (OSA) because it does not depress respiration. It does not cause weight gain or sexual side effects.

Many sedatives work by blocking H_1 histamine receptors. Trazodone is sedating due to a combination of moderate H_1 antihistamine effect plus antagonism of 5-HT_{2A} and alpha-1 adrenergic receptors.

Priapism (painful prolonged erection) is a rare risk of Trazodone, and a medical emergency. Priapism is not considered a significant risk with any other psychotropic medication. Although the risk is low (1 in 6,000), think twice before prescribing trazodone to a man being discharged to jail, where prompt medical treatment for priapism might not be provided. Trazodone-induced priapism is likely attributable to antagonism of alpha-1 adrenoceptors, which interferes with the sympathetic control of penile detumescence.

Animal studies suggested trazodone could reduce the risk of dementia, but this does not appear to apply to humans (Brauer et al, 2019). At worst, trazodone does not contribute to dementia risk. Anticholinergic sleep medications like diphenhydramine (Benadryl) and doxylamine (Unisom) do increase risk of dementia.

The original trade name of trazodone was DESYREL, but no one calls it that because the generic name has such a nice ring to it. An extended-release version of trazodone branded as OLEPTRO (150, 300 mg) was available, but virtually no one prescribed it.

It is commonly misspelled as *trazadone*.

Dosing: Titrate slowly. The dose for insomnia is 25–200 mg, usually started at 50 mg, for routine or PRN use. For healthy adults, the author often prescribes 150 mg tablets with instructions to take ⅓ to 1 tab PRN which allows doses of 50, 75, 100, or 150 mg. QT prolongation may occur if the FDA max of 400 mg is exceeded. Antidepressant dosing is 300–600 mg, divided BID (as the label instructs) or taken all at HS which is better tolerated. 150 mg may be useful for depression for some patients.

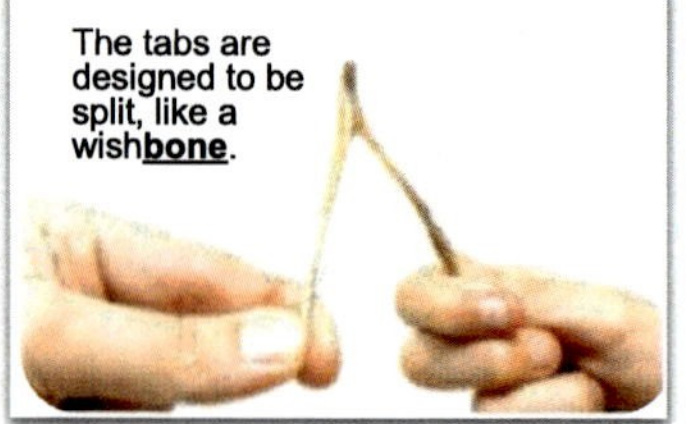

The tabs are designed to be split, like a wish**bone**.

All generic trazodone tabs are scored. The 150 mg and 300 mg generics are usually multi-scored:

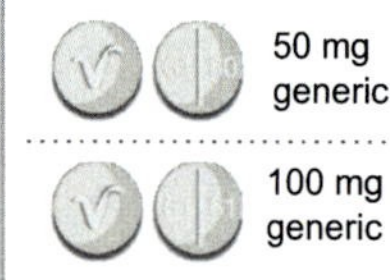

50 mg generic

100 mg generic

Some 150 mg generics

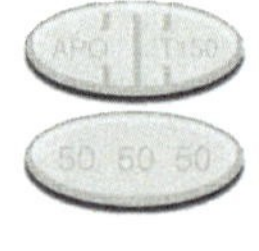

300 mg generic

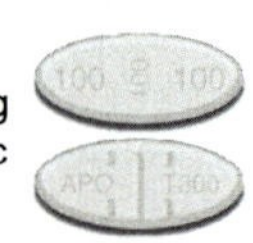

Dynamic interactions:

- ❖ Sedation/CNS depression
- ❖ QT prolongation (mild)

Kinetic interactions:

- ❖ We're depicting trazodone in a box because clinically significant kinetic interactions are unlikely, or at least not clearly defined. Trazodone is metabolized to m-chlorophenylpiperazine (mCPP) by 3A4. mCPP is then disposed of by 2D6. mCPP is a 5-HT agonist that can be associated with dysphoria, anxiety, and (rarely) hallucinations. mCPP only causes these effect when levels escalate quickly. Adding trazodone to a 2D6 inhibitor will rarely be an issue, especially if trazodone is started at a low dose for sleep. Adding a 2D6 inhibitor (e.g., fluoxetine, duloxetine, bupropion) to trazodone could cause transient anxiety/dysphoria by increasing mCPP abruptly. Note mCPP is also a metabolite of nefazodone, the other SARI antidepressant.
- ❖ Trazodone is an inducer of P-glycoprotein (P-gp), which pumps P-gp substrates out of the brain—"pumpers gonna pump"

page 18

Kinetic interactions are rarely an issue

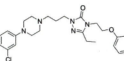

Nefazodone (SERZONE)

1994
\$79–\$173

nef FAH zoe dohn / SARE zone

"Nefarious Sear zone"

- ❖ Antidepressant/sleep medication
- ❖ Serotonin antagonist and reuptake inhibitor (SARI)
  - – 5-HT_2 antagonist
  - – 5-HT_{1A} agonist

50
100
150
200
250
mg

FDA-approved for:

- ❖ Major Depressive Disorder (MDD)

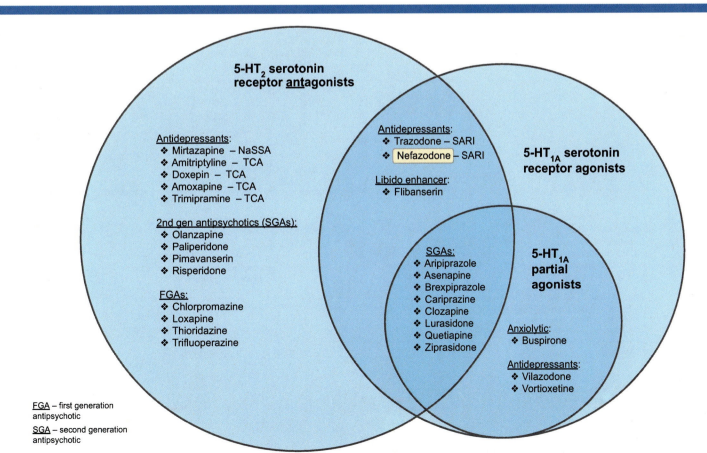

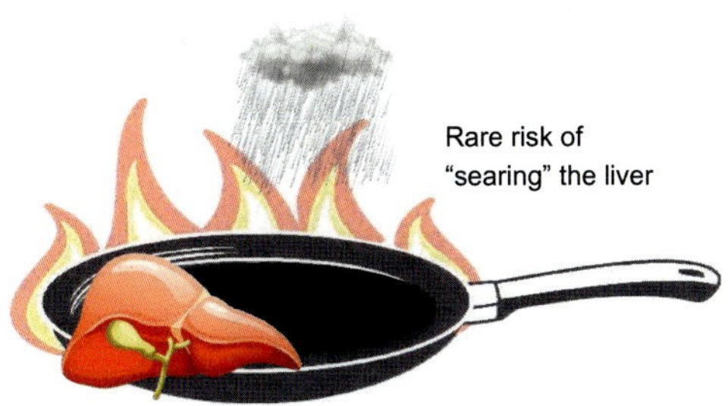

"The nefarious Trazodone"

Nefazodone (Serzone) is the second serotonin antagonist and reuptake inhibitor (SARI), developed as a less sedating derivative of trazodone. Nefazodone was released in 1994, and voluntarily withdrawn from market in 2004 by the original manufacturer due to decreasing sales related to **rare** occurrences of severe liver damage. The risk of severe liver damage is only 1 in every 250,000 to 300,000 patient-years.

Nefazodone is currently available, but rarely prescribed. It has a relatively mild side effect profile. Nefazodone has no anticholinergic activity, and only mildly antihistaminic. It does not cause priapism, which is a possible adverse event with trazodone. Nefazodone does not impair sexual functioning and may actually enhance it.

There are case reports of nefazodone causing visual trailing, which is a disturbance of motion perception where moving objects appear as a series of stroboscopic images. The illusion of trailing is common with LSD (via serotonergic mechanism), but is not associated with prescription psychotropic medications other than nefazodone.

Dosing: The target dose for depression is 200–300 mg divided BID, with max of 600 mg/day (300 mg BID); Start 100 mg BID; May increase by increments of 100–200 mg/day every week; Taper gradually to stop.

Dynamic interactions:

- ❖ Serotonergic

Kinetic interactions:

- ❖ Nefazodone is a potent 3A4 inhibitor, raising levels of some 3A4 substrates 5-fold. Trazodone does not do this.
- ❖ Nefazodone is a competitive inhibitor of 3A4, i.e., nefazodone is itself a 3A4 substrate.
- ❖ Nefazodone is metabolized to m-chlorophenylpiperazine (mCPP). Refer to the trazodone monograph for the possible significance of mCPP.

page 16

MODERN ANTIDEPRESSANTS 8

5-HT_2 serotonin receptor antagonists

Antidepressants:
- ❖ Mirtazapine – NaSSA
- ❖ Amitriptyline – TCA
- ❖ Doxepin – TCA
- ❖ Amoxapine – TCA
- ❖ Trimipramine – TCA

2nd gen antipsychotics (SGAs):
- ❖ Olanzapine
- ❖ Paliperidone
- ❖ Pimavanserin
- ❖ Risperidone

FGAs:
- ❖ Chlorpromazine
- ❖ Loxapine
- ❖ Thioridazine
- ❖ Trifluoperazine

Antidepressants:
- ❖ Trazodone – SARI
- ❖ Nefazodone – SARI

Libido enhancer:
- ❖ Flibanserin

5-HT_{1A} serotonin receptor agonists

SGAs:
- ❖ Aripiprazole
- ❖ Asenapine
- ❖ Brexpiprazole
- ❖ Cariprazine
- ❖ Clozapine
- ❖ Lurasidone
- ❖ Quetiapine
- ❖ Ziprasidone

5-HT_{1A} partial agonists

Anxiolytic:
- ❖ Buspirone

Antidepressants:
- ❖ Vilazodone
- ❖ Vortioxetine

FGA – first generation antipsychotic

SGA – second generation antipsychotic

#128
1996
$9–$52

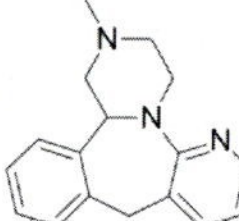

Mirtazapine (REMERON)

mir TAZ ah peen / rim er ON

"Mr Taz zapping (R.E.M.-a'roni)"

❖ Noradrenergic and Specific Serotonergic Antidepressant (NaSSA)
– Alpha-2 antagonist
– $5\text{-}HT_2$ antagonist
– $5\text{-}HT_3$ antagonist

7.5
15
30
45
mg

FDA-approved for:

❖ Major depressive disorder

Used off-label for:

❖ SSRI-induced sexual dysfunction
❖ Appetite stimulation
❖ Akathisia

Taz is too depressed to sleep or eat

Eating and sleeping well on Remeron

Mirtazapine (Remeron) is a noradrenergic and specific serotonergic (5-HT) antidepressant (NaSSA) with a relatively high response rate and low dropout rate (Cipriani et al, 2018). It is an antagonist at norepinephrine (alpha-2), $5\text{-}HT_2$, and $5\text{-}HT_3$ receptors. Mirtazapine is a suitable first-line antidepressant option for an underweight patient who can't sleep. Mirtazapine has antiemetic properties thanks to $5\text{-}HT_3$ antagonism, which is the principal mechanism of action of ondansetron (Zofran).

Remeron is a potent antihistamine, leading to sedation and appetite stimulation. About half of patients gain significant weight. However, at higher doses, its noradrenergic characteristics outshine its antihistamine effects. Hence, at high doses mirtazepine can be *less* sedating and cause *less* appetite stimulation. This is an unusual property among psychotropics, also noted with the TCA doxepin (Sinequan).

Mirtazapine may work a bit faster than other antidepressants. The patient will "remember" the prescriber fondly for making them feel better quickly with Remeron, then not so fondly for making them fat. Consider using Remeron for an acute depressive episode, then changing to another antidepressant (or increasing the dose of mirtazapine) if the patient starts gaining weight.

"California Rocket Fuel" is a combination of mirtazapine with the SNRI venlafaxine (Effexor). This combo was previously felt to be exceptionally effective for depression due to complementary mechanisms of action. Unfortunately, mirtazapine augmentation was recently found to be no better than placebo for individuals who had failed antidepressant monotherapy (Navarro et al, 2019).

Mirtazapine is a third-line treatment for akathisia (behind propranolol and clonazepam) at 15 mg. At higher doses mirtazapine may exacerbate akathisia. Other side effects of mirtazapine include dry mouth and constipation. There is a risk of neutropenia, although rare.

Remeron does not inhibit sexual functioning, and can actually be used as an adjunct to reverse SSRI-induced sexual dysfunction.

Dosing: Start 15 mg HS; FDA maximum is 45 mg, but 60 mg is safe and may be more effective for depression. Note that mirtazapine causes less somnolence and less weight gain at higher doses. For treatment of akathisia, do not exceed 15 mg.

Refer to the next page to see mirtazapine's mechanism of action in context of other medications. page 109

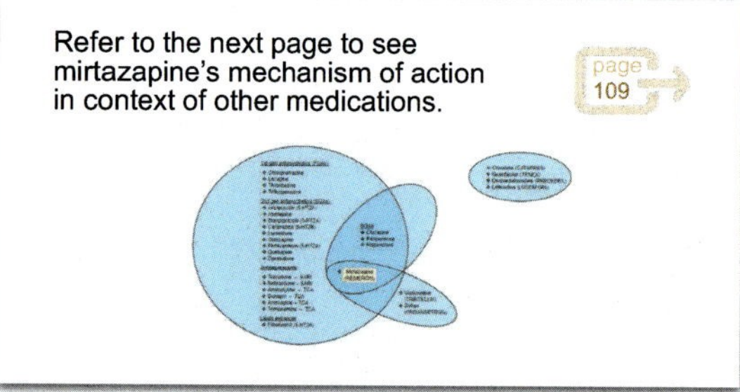

Dynamic interactions:

❖ Sedation/CNS depression (strong)
❖ QT prolongation (mild)
❖ Serotonergic effects (weak)
❖ Alpha-2 adrenoceptor antagonist
  – Do not add **mirtazapine** to alpha-2 agonists such **clonidine** (Catapres) or **guanfacine** (Tenex) because mirtazapine will block the effect of the alpha-2 agonist, potentially leading to hypertensive rebound. Do not add an alpha-2 agonist to Remeron, because the alpha-2 agonist may be ineffective.

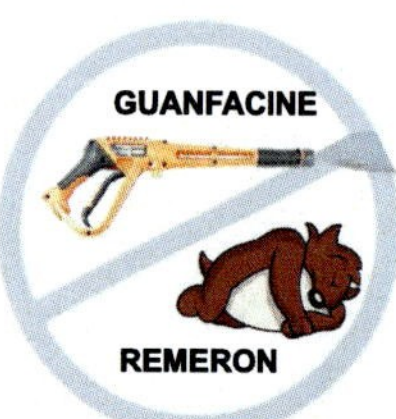

Kinetic interactions:

❖ Mirtazapine is metabolized by several CYP enzymes (1A2,2D6, 3A4). Kinetic interactions occur but are unlikely to be clinically significant.

Multi-CYP

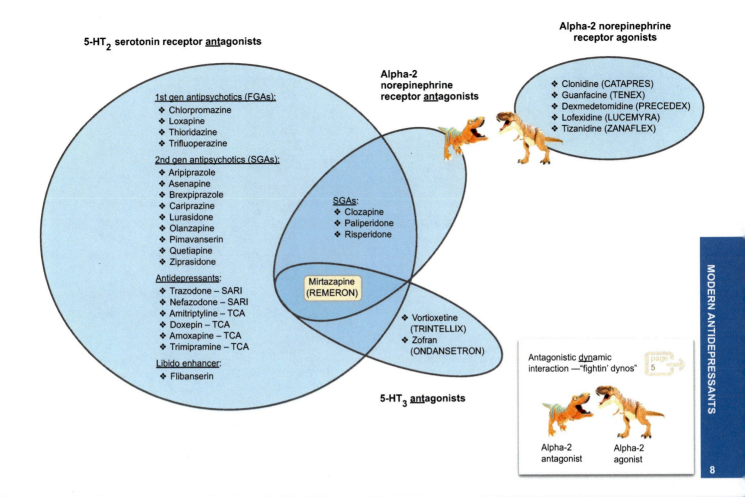

$5\text{-}HT_2$ serotonin receptor antagonists

1st gen antipsychotics (FGAs):
- Chlorpromazine
- Loxapine
- Thioridazine
- Trifluoperazine

2nd gen antipsychotics (SGAs):
- Aripiprazole
- Asenapine
- Brexpiprazole
- Cariprazine
- Lurasidone
- Olanzapine
- Pimavanserin
- Quetiapine
- Ziprasidone

Antidepressants:
- Trazodone – SARI
- Nefazodone – SARI
- Amitriptyline – TCA
- Doxepin – TCA
- Amoxapine – TCA
- Trimipramine – TCA

Libido enhancer:
- Flibanserin

Alpha-2 norepinephrine receptor antagonists

SGAs:
- Clozapine
- Paliperidone
- Risperidone

Mirtazapine (REMERON)

$5\text{-}HT_3$ antagonists
- Vortioxetine (TRINTELLIX)
- Zofran (ONDANSETRON)

Alpha-2 norepinephrine receptor agonists
- Clonidine (CATAPRES)
- Guanfacine (TENEX)
- Dexmedetomidine (PRECEDEX)
- Lofexidine (LUCEMYRA)
- Tizanidine (ZANAFLEX)

Antagonistic dynamic interaction —"fightin' dynos" page 5

Alpha-2 antagonist

Alpha-2 agonist

+

California Rocket Fuel

Venlafaxine (EFFEXOR) + Mirtazapine (REMERON)

- Antidepressant combination

"California Rocket Fuel", popularized by psychiatrist Stephen Stahl, is a combination of venlafaxine (SNRI) and mirtazapine (noradrenergic and specific serotonergic antidepressant, NaSSA). This combination boosts serotonin and norepinephrine neurotransmission in multiple ways. The STAR-D study found this combination to be at least as effective as the MAOI tranylcypromine (Parnate). In a series of 32 patients with refractory depression, 44% responded at four weeks and 50% at eight weeks (Hannan et al, 2007). The combination was generally well tolerated, although 12% of patients reported moderate to severe weight gain and, 12% reported at least moderate sedation.

Unfortunately, larger studies were disappointing. For 112 patients who failed to respond to venlafaxine, remission rate was 39% when mirtazapine was added, compared to 72% when venlafaxine was changed to the TCA imipramine (Navarro et al, 2019).

Strategic dynamic interaction

page 108

REMERON
Mirtazapine
NaSSA

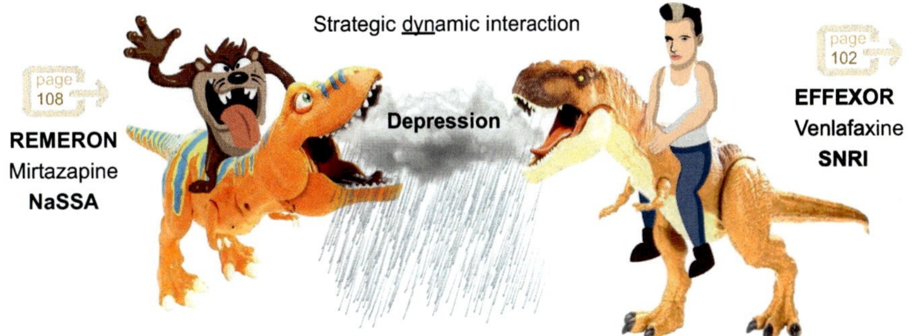

page 102

EFFEXOR
Venlafaxine
SNRI

This "heroic" treatment should be prescribed with caution due to risk of serotonin syndrome. California Rocket Fuel should be reserved for treatment of refractory unipolar depression. The combo should not be given to patients with a personal or family history of bipolar disorder due to risk of precipitating mania.

A similar combination of the SNRI duloxetine (Cymbalta) with mirtazapine has been referred to as "Limerick Rocket Fuel".

Dosing: In a case series, most patients who responded were titrated to relatively high doses of both medications —venlafaxine ER at least 225 mg/day and mirtazapine 30–45 mg HS.

Bottom line: There appears to be nothing magical about this combination. This combination is an example of two antidepressants with mechanisms that are synergistic on paper but disappointing in practice. See page 79 for proven options for treatment-resistant depression.

#260
2013
$357–$462

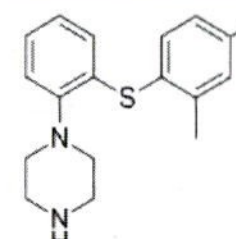

Vortioxetine (TRINTELLIX)

vor tye OX e teen / trin TELL ix

"Trent's Vortex"

- ❖ Multimodal antidepressant
- ❖ Serotonin modulator and stimulator (SMS)
  - 5-HT reuptake inhibitor
  - $5\text{-}HT_{1A}$ partial agonist
  - $5\text{-}HT_3$ antagonist

5
10
20
mg

FDA-approved for:
❖ Major depressive disorder

Used off-label for:
❖ OCD

"Serotonergic vortex"—Vortioxetine (Trintellix) is a "serotonin modulator and stimulator" (SMS) approved in 2013 for treatment of depression. The original trade name was BRINTELLIX, suggestive of "Bring Intelligence". In 2016 the trade name was changed to Trintellix to avoid confusion with antiplatelet drug BRILINTA (ticagrelor).

Although expensive, Trintellix is a reasonable first-line option for depression if cognitive deficits are prominent. Cognitive dysfunction characteristic of profound depression can be referred to as pseudodementia. Trintellix's marketing slogan is "fight the fog of depression", which refers to its ability to improve pseudodementia. This is useful because, on average, depression impairs cognition similarly to 24 hours of sleep deprivation (Mahableshwarkar et al, 2016). Vortioxetine improves cognition, although the effect is modest, roughly equivalent to 50 mg of caffeine (Jaeger et al, 2018).

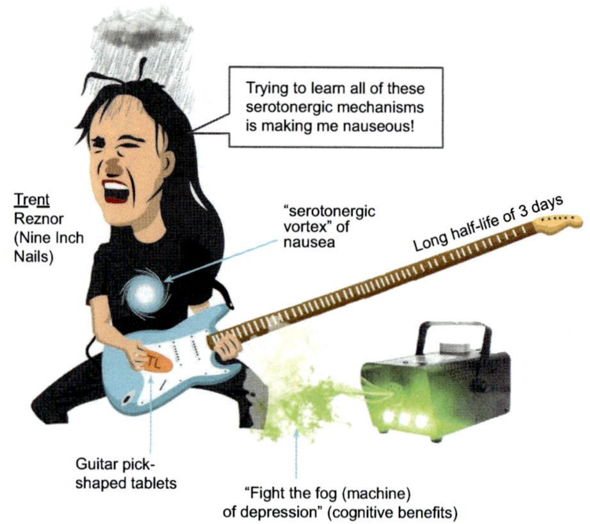

Side effects: Vortioxetine is relatively well-tolerated. At the suggested maintenance dose of 20 mg, incidence of sexual dysfunction is 44%. At 10 mg vortioxetine has fewer sexual side effects than SSRIs. Vortioxetine is more likely to cause constipation than diarrhea. Headache and dizziness have been reported. It does not cause weight gain or prolong QT interval. Vortioxetine appears to be among the safest psychotropic medications in overdose, with no known deaths, although sample size is small. Due to long half-life of 3 days, it does not cause discontinuation symptoms with missed doses.

About 30% of patients experience nausea, as could be expected from a "vortex" of serotonergic mechanisms. Nausea due to antidepressants (including vortioxetine) typically resolves after a couple of weeks. Nausea with vortioxetine is tempered by 5-HT3 antagonism. Other drugs that block 5-HT3 include the antiemetic ondansetron (Zofran) and the NaSSA antidepressant mirtazapine (Remeron). Ginger also relieves nausea via the same mechanism.

Dosing: The starting dose is 10 mg. The suggested maintenance dose for MDD is 20 mg, but staying at 10 mg may be adequate, with fewer side effects.

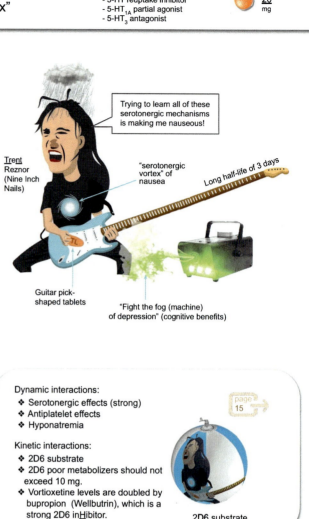

Dynamic interactions:
- ❖ Serotonergic effects (strong)
- ❖ Antiplatelet effects
- ❖ Hyponatremia

page 15

Kinetic interactions:
- ❖ 2D6 substrate
- ❖ 2D6 poor metabolizers should not exceed 10 mg.
- ❖ Vortioxetine levels are doubled by bupropion (Wellbutrin), which is a strong 2D6 inHibitor.

2D6 substrate

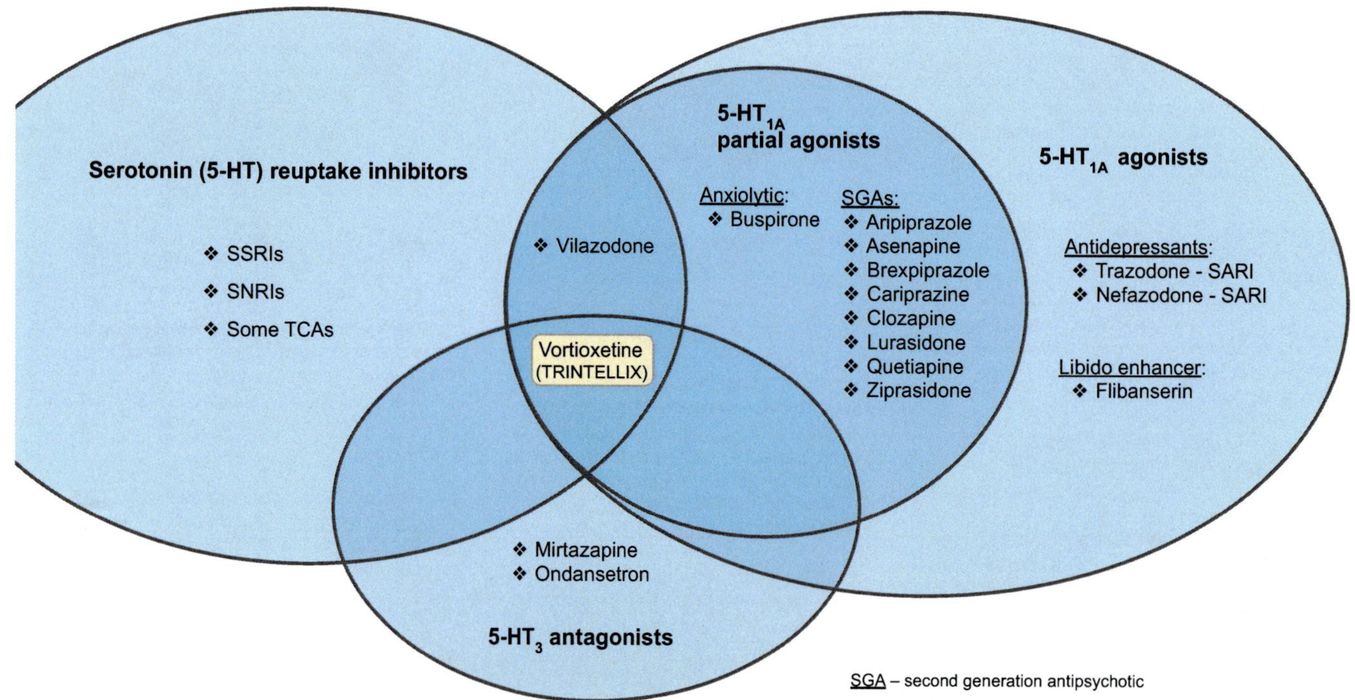

SGA – second generation antipsychotic

#278
2011
$276–$343

Vilazodone (VIIBRYD)

vil AZ o dohn / VY brid

"(what that) Vile lazer done (to that) Virile hybrid"

- ❖ Antidepressant
- ❖ Serotonin Modulator and Stimulator (SMS)
  - 5-HT reuptake inhibitor (SRI)
  - 5-HT_{1A} partial agonist

10
20
40
mg

FDA-approved for:

- ❖ Major depressive disorder

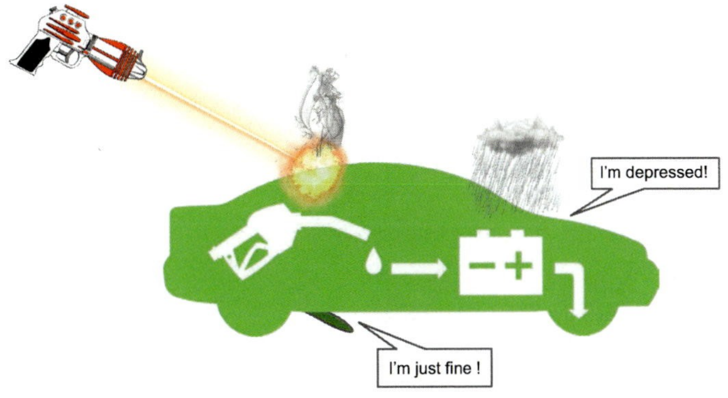

Vilazodone (Viibryd) is an atypical antidepressant released in 2011. It was described as the first serotonin partial agonist/reuptake inhibitor (SPARI). Alternately, it can be grouped with vortioxetine (Trintellix, 2013) as a serotonin modulator and stimulator (SMS). Vilazodone is less complicated than vortioxetine in terms of mechanism of action.

"Virile" Viibryd was marketed as having fewer sexual side effects than SSRIs, though it does cause slightly more sexual dysfunction than placebo.

Viibryd's mechanism is a "Hybrid" an SSRI and a 5-HT_{1A} partial agonist. In other words, vilazodone combines the pharmacologic actions of an SSRI and the anxiolytic buspirone (Buspar). SSRIs are famously detrimental to sexual functioning. Buspirone improves sexually functioning. To concoct a *"Poor Man's Viibryd"*, prescribe buspirone with the purest SSRI, escitalopram (Lexapro).

Until it goes generic, Viibryd is $300/month, and is unproven to be superior to an SSRI for treatment of depression.

Vilazodone needs to be taken with food for adequate absorption. Only 50% of the dose is absorbed on an empty stomach.

At 40 mg/day, the most common adverse effects are diarrhea (28% vs 9% placebo), nausea (23% vs 5% placebo), and insomnia (6% vs 2% placebo).

Dosing: Target dose is 20–40 mg QD with food. Must titrate with 10 mg QD for the first week, as shown below. The 30-day starter pack contains 10 mg tab x 7 and 20 mg tab x 23. To discontinue, taper off over about a week.

To avoid side effects, vilazodone needs to be titrated.

Tablet	Schedule
10	10 mg QD for days 1–7
20	20 mg QD day 8 onward
40	40 mg QD as early as day 15 onward (versus staying at 20 mg)

The 3 psychotropic medications that must be taken **with food** for adequate absorption—the *DONE-nuts.*

- ❖ Vilazodone (VIIBRYD) - antidepressant
- ❖ Ziprasidone (GEODON) - antipsychotic
- ❖ Lurasidone (LATUDA) - antipsychotic

Without food, absorption is only 50%.

"Poor Man's Viibryd"

An approximation of vilazodone's mechanism of action can be achieved by co-prescribing escitalopram and buspirone.

Escitalopram (Lexapro)
SSRI
$10
sexual dysfunction

Buspirone (Buspar)
5-HT_{1A} partial agonist
$10
sexual enhancement

"Bus spear"

Vilazodone (Viibryd)
SRI + 5-HT_{1A} partial agonist
$300
minimal sexual dysfunction

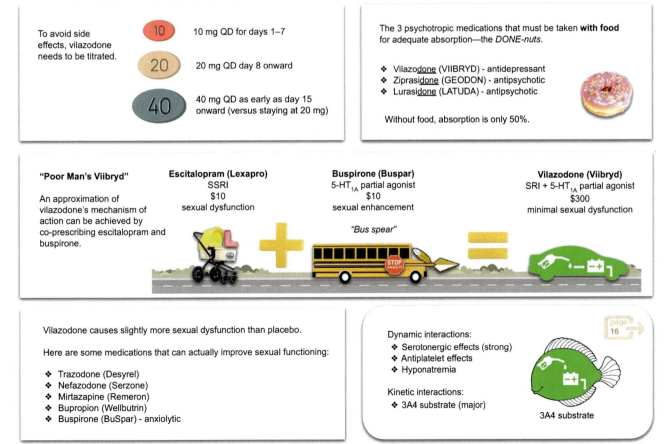

Vilazodone causes slightly more sexual dysfunction than placebo.

Here are some medications that can actually improve sexual functioning:

- ❖ Trazodone (Desyrel)
- ❖ Nefazodone (Serzone)
- ❖ Mirtazapine (Remeron)
- ❖ Bupropion (Wellbutrin)
- ❖ Buspirone (BuSpar) - anxiolytic

Dynamic interactions:

- ❖ Serotonergic effects (strong)
- ❖ Antiplatelet effects
- ❖ Hyponatremia

Kinetic interactions:

- ❖ 3A4 substrate (major)

page 16

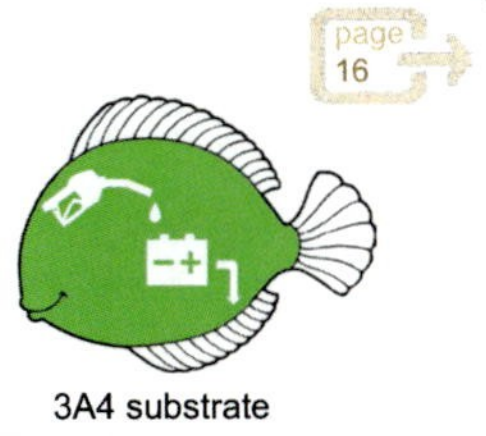

3A4 substrate

Serotonin Discontinuation Syndrome

"withdrawal" if an antidepressant is stopped abruptly

Serotonergic antidepressants are nonaddictive, but "withdrawal" symptoms may occur upon discontinuation, especially if the course of treatment has been > 2 months. Serotonin discontinuation syndrome includes flu-like symptoms, irritability, and unusual sensations described as "brain zaps". Serotonin withdrawal is unpleasant but not physically dangerous. It is more likely with serotonergics of short half-life, such as paroxetine (Paxil), venlafaxine (Effexor), and fluvoxamine (Luvox). Discontinuation syndrome is problematic even with extended-release Effexor XR. These unpleasant side effects can be avoided if the antidepressant is tapered to discontinue. Some patients may require a long-tail taper over several months to avoid serotonin withdrawal symptoms.

Venlafaxine (Effexor)

Paroxetine (Paxil)

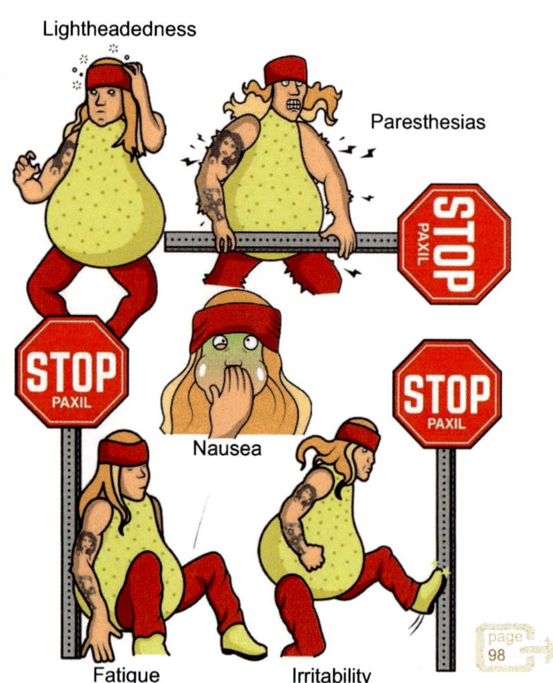

Fluvoxamine (Luvox)

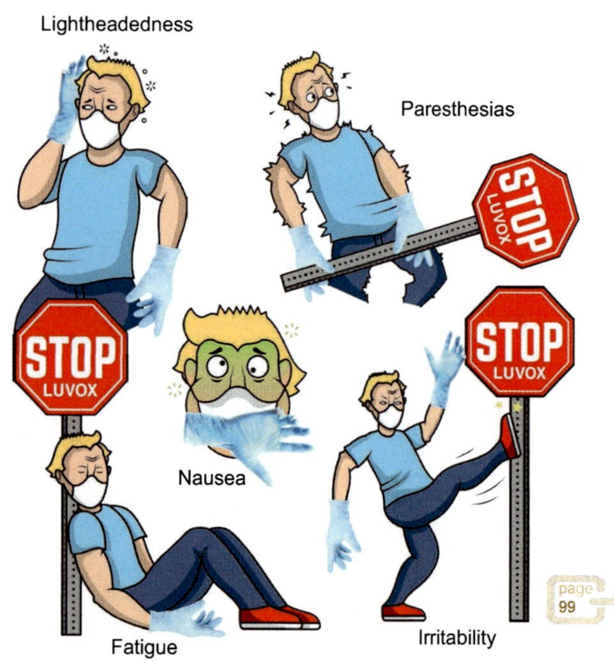

Linear tapering

Psychiatrists have traditionally tapered off antidepressants linearly, for instance decreasing from 40 mg to 30 mg x 1 week, then 20 mg x 1 week, then 10 mg x 1 week. Linear tapers are not ideal, often providing minimal benefit over abrupt discontinuation for avoiding serotonin withdrawal symptoms.

Hyperbolic tapering

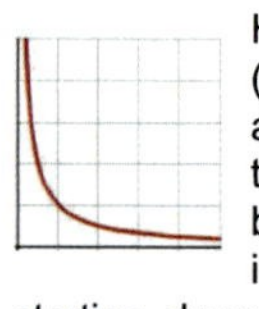

Horowitz & Taylor in *The Lancet Psychiatry* (June 2019) explain a more effective approach, referred to as the hyperbolic taper (as traditionally used to get off of benzodiazepines). Hyperbolic tapering involves a quick decrease to the usual starting dose, then a long-tail taper over a period of months, getting down to tiny doses well below the therapeutic range.

To get low-enough doses you need to use a compounding pharmacy, liquid formulations, or chop tablets into tiny fragments. Capsules are not ideal, but a patient who understands the concept could open them, discard an inexact fraction of the medication and reassemble.

Among SSRIs, liquid formulations are available for citalopram, escitalopram, fluoxetine, and sertraline (but not for fluvoxamine or paroxetine).

For the nitty gritty on parabolic tapering, Refer to my favorite newsletter, *The Carlat Psychiatry Report* (Drs Sazima & Aiken, Jun/Jul 2019).

Catecholamines

Neurotransmitter	Abbrev	Normal activity	Low activity	High activity	Comments
Norepinephrine	NE	Energy, Motivation, Ability to focus and respond to stress	Fatigue Inattention Sexual dysfunction	Insomnia Anxiety Loss of appetite Hypertension Seizure	NE is also known as noradrenaline. Stimulants increase noradrenergic (NE) activity.
Dopamine	DA	Ability to experience pleasure and strong emotions	Anhedonia, Inattention, Sexual dysfunction, Parkinsonism, Akathisia, Dystonia, Neuroleptic malignant syndrome (NMS), Restless legs syndrome	Mania, Euphoria, Agitation, Anger, Aggression, Chemical "high", Paranoia, Auditory hallucinations, Hypersexuality, Insomnia, Compulsive behaviors	Think pleasure, passion, paranoia. Drugs of abuse, colloquially known as "dope", cause euphoria by spiking DA in the nucleus accumbens.

Norepinephrine reuptake inhibitors (NRIs)

NRIs increase the availability of norepinephrine (NE) in the extracellular space. NE is energizing and may contribute to hypertension.

NRI	Main use	Comments
Atomoxetine (STRATTERA)	ADHD	Non-controlled substance; Less effective for ADHD than Schedule II stimulants; Rare hepatotoxicity

Some tricyclic antidepressants (TCAs) are NRIs by mechanism. While other TCAs are anxiety-reducing, these are drive-enhancing. Since TCAs are non-selective, their stimulating effects are tempered by antihistaminic effects. These noradrenergic TCAs *could* be co-prescribed with a monoamine oxidase inhibitor (MAOI) without causing serotonin syndrome, but expect the pharmacist to flip out. Taking serotonergic TCAs (amitriptyline, imipramine, clomipramine) with an MAOI could be catastrophic.

Tricyclic (TCA)	Main use	Comments
Nortriptyline (PAMELOR)	Depression Migraine prevention	The major active metabolite of amitriptyline. While amitriptyline is sedating, nortriptyline (like all medications on this page) is stimulating. It is safer and better tolerated than most TCAs.
Desipramine (NORPRAMIN)	Depression	Exceptionally fatal in overdose.
Maprotiline (LUDIOMIL)	Depression	Rarely prescribed. Tetracyclic structure. Most likely to induce seizures among available antidepressants.

Dopamine (or dopamine/norepinephrine) reuptake inhibitors

Norepinephrine-dopamine reuptake inhibitors (NDRIs) block reuptake of NE > DA

NDRI	Main use	Comments
Bupropion (WELLBUTRIN)	Depression Smoking cessation	Non-controlled; In addition to inhibiting reuptake of NE and DA, bupropion is a NE and DA releaser (NE > DA); Used off-label for ADHD and for SSRI associated sexual dysfunction.
Solriamfetol (SUNOSI)	Daytime sleepiness	Schedule IV controlled

Dopamine-norepinephrine reuptake inhibitors (DNRIs) block reuptake of DA > NE

DNRI	Main use	Comments
Methylphenidate (RITALIN)	ADHD	Schedule II controlled
Amphetamine (ADDERALL)	ADHD	Schedule II controlled; Also DA and NE release (DA > NE)
Lisdexamfetamine (VYVANSE)	ADHD Binge-eating disorder	Schedule II controlled; Also DA and NE release (DA > NE); Long-acting amphetamine less likely to be abused because of delayed onset of action. It is a prodrug converted to dextroamphetamine in red blood cells.
Dasotraline (trade name to be announced)	Binge-eating disorder	FDA-accepted 2019 for binge-eating disorder; It failed approval for ADHD

Dopamine reuptake inhibitors (DRIs) block reuptake of DA but not NE

DRI	Main use	Comments
Modafinil (PROVIGIL)	Daytime sleepiness	Schedule IV controlled; Binds dopamine transporter weakly
Armodafinil (NUVIGIL)	Daytime sleepiness	Schedule IV controlled; R-enantiomer of modafinil

#245
2002
$90–$352

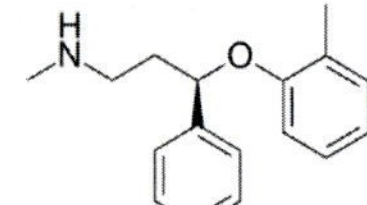

Atomoxetine (STRATTERA)

at om OX e tine / stra TARE uh

"Atomic Stratosphere"

❖ ADHD medication
❖ Norepinephrine reuptake inhibitor (NRI)
❖ Non-controlled

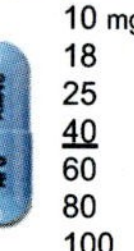

10 mg
18
25
40
60
80
100

Not an antidepressant

FDA-approved for:

❖ Attention-deficit/ hyperactivity disorder (ADHD) ≥ 6 years old

Used off-label for:

❖ Cataplexy
❖ Dyslexia

The consequence of Homer's inattention at the nuclear plant

Strattera straightens out your attention. Atomoxetine (Strattera) is a norepinephrine reuptake inhibitor (NRI) with the sole FDA-approved indication of ADHD. Although atomoxetine is not properly referred to as an antidepressant, it resides in the antidepressant chapter because its mechanism is similar to some antidepressants used off-label for ADHD including bupropion (Wellbutrin) and TCAs such as desipramine, nortriptyline, and protriptyline.

Although it has stimulating properties, atomoxetine is referred to as a "non-stimulant" to contrast it with the Schedule II ADHD stimulants (amphetamine, methylphenidate). Atomoxetine is not a controlled substance.

By inhibiting the norepinephrine transporter (NET), atomoxetine indirectly increases dopamine (DA) transmission in the prefrontal cortex (which is underactive with ADHD) without increasing DA in the nucleus accumbens (reward center). Therefore atomoxetine has no abuse potential because it does not increase DA in the nucleus accumbens.

When used to augment an SSRI, atomoxetine has the potential to improve anxiety and depression. Atomoxetine appears to improve reading skills in children with dyslexia (Shaywitz et al, 2017).

Atomoxetine poses a risk of suicidality in children/adolescents with ADHD, especially during the first months of treatment. Average risk of suicidal thoughts was 0.4% with atomoxetine vs 0% with placebo, but no suicides were reported. All antidepressants have a similar warning about suicide, which is another reason atomoxetine resides in this chapter. Other treatments for ADHD (Adderall, Ritalin, Tenex, Intuniv, etc) do not have this boxed warning.

Advantages of Strattera over Schedule II stimulants for treatment of ADHD:

- not a controlled substance
- no abuse potential
- does not worsen tics
- less likely to cause insomnia

Disadvantages:

- Less effective than stimulants—40% of patients are left with residual ADHD symptoms.
- Initial therapeutic effects are not seen until 2–4 weeks (whereas Schedule II stimulants work immediately).
- Rare risk of serious hepatic injury

Side effects of atomoxetine include headache, abdominal pain, and nausea. It may increase BP and heart rate.

If atomoxetine is stopped abruptly, withdrawal or other issues are not expected.

A similar "non-stimulant" option for off-label treatment of ADHD is the stimulating antidepressant bupropion (Wellbutrin), which has fewer risks and side effects than Strattera.

Adult dosing: For ADHD the target dose is 80 mg/day, either q AM or divided BID; Start 40 mg AM for at least 3 days, then may increase to maximum dose of 100 mg/day after 2–4 weeks; Use a lower dose with individuals who are known CYP2D6 poor metabolizers. When stopping, a gradual taper is considered unnecessary.

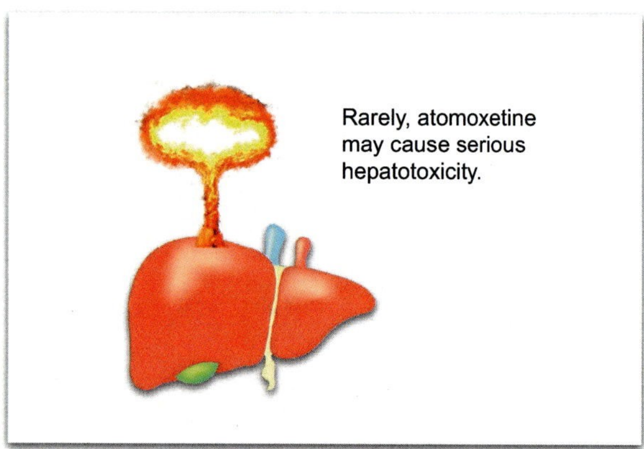

Rarely, atomoxetine may cause serious hepatotoxicity.

Dynamic interactions:

❖ Hypertensive effects

Kinetic interactions:

❖ 2D6 substrate
❖ For individuals with 2D6 poor metabolizers genotype (PM), blood levels may be increased two-fold

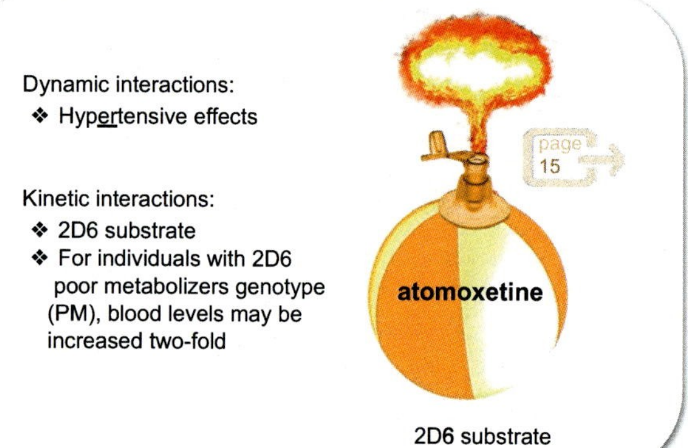

page 15

2D6 substrate

#28
1985
XL $12–$109 (#30)
SR $9–$76 (#60)

Bupropion (WELLBUTRIN)

bu PRO pi on / wel BYU trin

"Boop ropin' Well booty"

- Antidepressant
- Norepinephrine-dopamine reuptake inhibitor (NDRI)
- Non-controlled

SR: 100 150 200 mg

XL: 150 300 mg

FDA-approved for:
- Major depressive disorder
- Seasonal affective disorder
- Smoking cessation (Zyban brand)

Used off-label for:
- ADHD
- Appetite suppression/ weight loss
- SSRI-associated sexual dysfunction

Betty Boop is slender, and bupropion may cause weight loss.

"Wellbutrin helps your mood get well". Bupropion (Wellbutrin), the #28 most prescribed overall medication, is a stimulating antidepressant that enhances norepinephrine and dopamine activity. Unlike most other modern antidepressants, it does not enhance serotonin activity. It is used for smoking cessation because it is stimulating like nicotine. These stimulating properties also make it useful for ADHD. Bupropion has demonstrated cognitive benefits. Clinicians tend to avoid prescribing it to individuals with anxiety disorders, but despite its stimulating properties, bupropion does not appear to exacerbate anxiety (Wiseman, 2012).

The serotonergic antidepressants cause sexual dysfunction. Bupropion is not serotonergic and actually improves sexual functioning. It is used as an add-on to SSRIs to ameliorate sexual problems (off-label).

Bupropion is contraindicated in patients with a current or prior diagnosis of bulimia or anorexia because of a higher reported incidence of seizures in such patients taking Wellbutrin.

Wellbutrin suppresses appetite and may cause modest weight loss. As with other stimulant-type medications, bupropion decreases appetite via adrenergic and dopaminergic receptors in the hypothalamus. The incidence of weight loss greater than 5 pounds is about 28%. CONTRAVE is a fixed-dose combination of bupropion with the opioid antagonist naltrexone, approved for long term treatment of obesity (page 259).

If taken by individuals with bipolar disorder, bupropion appears less likely to induce mania compared to serotonergic antidepressants.

Bupropion's chemical structure is similar to synthetic "bath salt" drugs. Wellbutrin is not a controlled substance and is not generally considered a drug of abuse. It increases dopamine levels in the prefrontal cortex (underactive in ADHD) but not in the nucleus accumbens (reward center), at least not at standard doses. However, bupropion is avoided by many prescribers in correctional facilities because inmates have collected tabs to crush and snort as "poor man's cocaine".

Bupropion, an NDRI, is a much weaker inhibitor of DA and NE reuptake than the Schedule II controlled stimulants approved for ADHD like methylphenidate (Ritalin) and amphetamine (Adderall). Ritalin and Adderall are referred to as DNRIs because their dopaminergic effect is stronger than their noradrenergic effect. Solriamfetol (Sunosi), approved for excessive daytime sleepiness (due to narcolepsy or sleep apnea) is a Schedule IV NDRI.

Bupropion has anti-inflammatory properties as a tumor necrosis factor (TNF) inhibitor. For treatment-resistant depression, adding bupropion to an SSRI is effective for patients who are overweight or have high C-reactive protein (CRP), a marker of inflammation (Jha MK, 2017). Otherwise, adding bupropion to an SSRI appears to be of no benefit for treatment-resistant depressant.

Risk of overdose mortality with bupropion is higher than with most other modern antidepressants. Of 51,118 single-drug exposures to bupropion reported to Poison Control, there were 3,239 major serious outcomes and 47 deaths (Nelson & Spyker, 2017).

Dosing:

Formulation	Dosing	Starting dose	Usual target dose	Max	To minimize seizure risk:
Wellbutrin XL (bupropion ER)	QD	150 mg AM	300 mg AM	450 mg AM	XL (ER) is the preferred formulation because seizure risk is minimal.
Wellbutrin SR	BID	100 mg BID	150 mg BID	400 mg/day = 200 mg BID	Separate doses by at least 8 hours.
Wellbutrin IR	TID	75 mg TID	100 mg TID	450 mg/day = 150 mg TID	Not recommended due to seizure risk, except for gastric bypass patients. Separate doses by at least 6 hours.

Bupropion may cause **seizures** at high doses or with the immediate-release formulation. Convulsant effect of standard doses of extended-release bupropion is minimal (Alper et al, 2007).

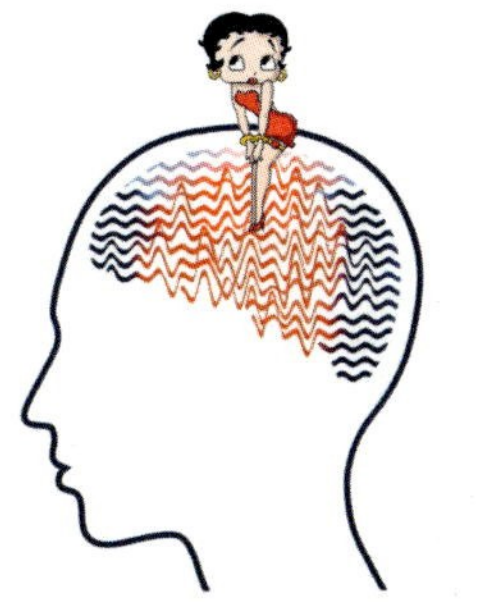

The maximum dose of Wellbutrin XL is 450 mg, taken once daily in the morning. This is typically accomplished with a 300 mg plus 150 mg tablet, or by three 150's. An expensive 450 mg tablet branded as FORFIVO exists. It is only mentioned for the cute name (4-5-0), and to aid in remembering the maximum dose of Wellbutrin XL.

2B6 substrate

2D6 inHibitor

continued...

Bupropion (Wellbutrin)

Dynamic interactions:

- ❖ CNS stimulation
- ❖ Hypertensive effects
- ❖ Lowers seizure threshold

Kinetic interactions:

- ❖ 2D6 inHibitor (strong)
- ❖ 2B6 substrate
- ❖ Active metabolite hydroxy-bupropion is a 2D6 substrate (see below)

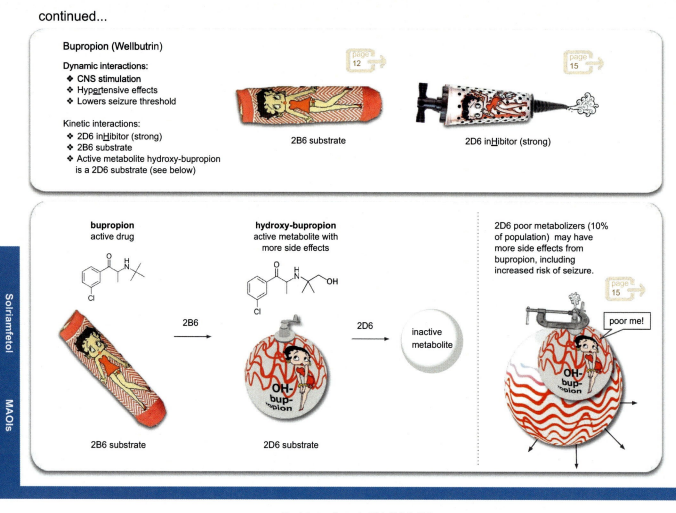

page 12

2B6 substrate

page 15

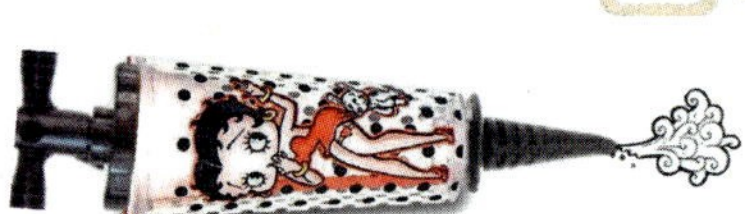

2D6 inHibitor (strong)

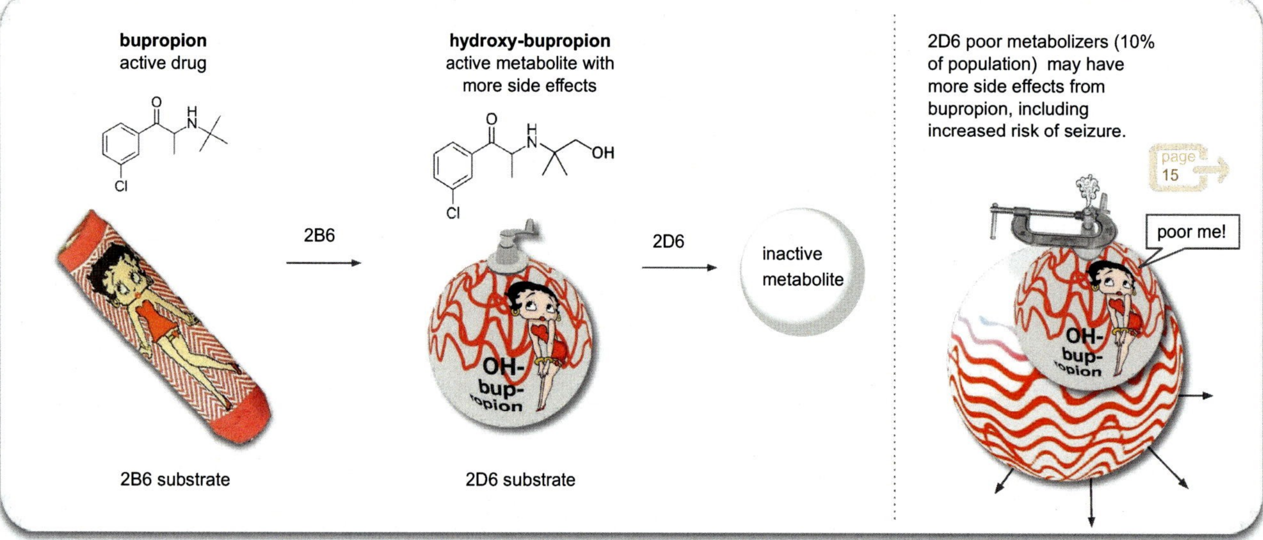

2019
$657–$714

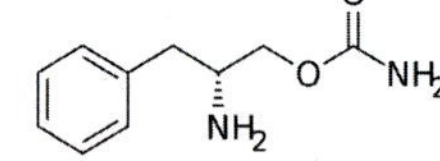

Solriamfetol (SUNOSI)

SOL ri AM fe tol / su NO see

"Sun nosey with Solar feet"

- ❖ Norepinephrine-dopamine reuptake inhibitor (NDRI)
- ❖ Schedule IV

75
150
mg

Not an antidepressant

FDA-approved for:

- ❖ Excessive daytime sleepiness due to:
  - Narcolepsy
  - Obstructive sleep apnea (OSA)

Solriamfetol (Sunosi) is a new wakefulness promoting medication that lasts for 9 hours. It is stimulating but not considered a "stimulant". It is a norepinephrine and weak dopamine reuptake inhibitor. Sunosi could be conceptualized as an atypical antidepressant with a mechanism similar bupropion (Wellbutrin). However, solriamfetol is not approved for depression, and clinical trials did not include psychiatric patients. About 1 in 25 subjects treated for narcolepsy/sleep apnea had psychiatric side effects such as irritability and anxiety.

Solriamfetol is a Schedule IV controlled substance. By comparison, bupropion is non-controlled but does have potential for abuse at high doses.

Subjects who abused drugs reported "drug liking" similar to the appetite-suppressing stimulant phentermine (Adipex) when solriamfetol was taken at supratherapeutic dose. Phentermine is also Schedule IV.

Other effects include nausea and appetite suppression. It may increase blood pressure and heart rate.

An advantage over bupropion is that solriamfetol is free from significant kinetic drug/drug interactions.

The two other wakefulness promoters approved for narcolepsy/sleep apnea are modafinil (Provigil) and armodafinil (Nuvigil), which are also Schedule IV. For context, methylphenidate (Ritalin) and amphetamine (Adderall) are more strictly regulated as Schedule II controlled substances, and are referred to as stimulants.

This is the only monograph in this book that resides in two chapters—*Modern Antidepressants* and *Stimulants*. The drug isn't that special, but space was available.

Dosing: Start 75 mg q AM. Dose may be increased to 150 mg after 3 days based on efficacy and tolerability. Maximum dose is 150 mg/day.

Dynamic interactions:

- ❖ Dopaminergic
- ❖ Hypertensive

Kinetic interactions:

- ❖ None significant
  - "in a bubble"

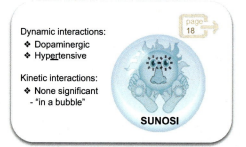

page 18

SUNOSI

Monoamine Oxidase Inhibitors (MAOIs)
"Chairman Mao"

Monoamine Oxidase (MAO) is the enzyme that breaks down the **monoamine neurotransmitters**:

Serotonin (5-HT) — Norepinephrine (NE) — Dopamine (DA)

MAOI	Use	Year	Cost/mo	5-HT	NE	DA	MAO select-ivity*	Dietary tyramine risk	Wt gain	Sed-ation	Anti-cholin ergic	Rever-sible?
Tranylcypromine (PARNATE)	MDD	1961	$240	+++	+++	+++	A & B	++++	-	low	no	no
Isocarboxazid (MARPLAN)	MDD	1959	$780	+++	+++	+++	A & B	++++	-	low	no	no
Phenelzine (NARDIL)	MDD	1961	$43	+++	+++	+++	A & B	++++	++	low	no	no
Selegiline transdermal (EMSAM)	MDD	2006	$1650	++	++	+++	(A) & B	++	loss	low	no	no
Selegiline PO (ELDEPRYL)	Parkinson's	1989	$26	++	++	+++	B	+	loss	low	no	no
Rasagiline (AZILECT)	Parkinson's	2006	$270	++	++	+++	B	+	loss	low	no	no
Safinamide (XADAGO)	Parkinson's	2017	$780	+	+	+++	B	+/-	-	low	no	yes

MDD – Major Depressive Disorder; 5-HT – serotonergic; NE – noradrenergic; DA – dopaminergic

*Selectivity is dose dependent. Above recommended doses, selective MAO-B inhibitors can also inhibit MAO-A.

Monoamine Oxidase Inhibitors (MAOIs) are among the oldest antidepressants, available since 1959. The first MAOI (isocarboxazid) entered the market two years after the oldest TCA (imipramine, 1957). MAOIs are highly effective for treatment of depression, including cases resistant to modern antidepressants. MAOIs are particularly effective for "atypical depression", characterized by increased appetite, excessive sleep, fatigue, sensitivity to rejection, and moods that are highly reactive to circumstances.

"TIPS" – the MAOIs approved for depression:

- **T**ranylcypromine (PARNATE)
- **I**socarboxazid (MARPLAN)
- **P**henelzine (NARDIL)
- **S**elegiline transdermal (EMSAM)

The three oral MAOIs approved for treatment of depression in the U.S. are *irreversible* inhibitors of both MAO-A and MAO-B. Strict dietary restrictions are necessary to avoid the "cheese effect" of hypertensive crisis described in the isocarboxazid monograph, which is also applicable to phenelzine and tranylcypromine. Half-life for these MAOIs is irrelevant because inhibition of MAO is irreversible, with effect continuing for up to two weeks after the medication is discontinued.

In a simplified sense, MAO-A is more responsible for breaking down 5-HT and NE, while MAO-B is more specific for DA. For treatment of Parkinson's disease, MAO-B needs to be blocked. For treatment of depression, MAO-A needs to be blocked (to enhance 5-HT and NE), and blocking MAO-B may also be helpful (to enhance DA). In some countries, safer reversible inhibitors of monoamine oxidase A (RIMAs) are available for treatment of depression. Selective MAOIs available in the US block MAO-B for treatment of Parkinson's disease, and only one of these is reversible—safinamide (Xadago).

Due to risk of serotonin syndrome, all serotonergic medications are contraindicated with MAOIs. A washout period is necessary when switching to an MAOI, dependent on the half-life of the serotonergic agent (SSRI, SNRI, etc). As a rule of thumb, a drug clears the body after 5 half-lives. Wait at least 5 weeks after stopping fluoxetine (Prozac), which has a long half-life of 1 week. For the other SSRIs, wait two weeks after stopping the SSRI to start the MAOI.

A few antidepressants are safe to pair with MAOIs, including bupropion, trazodone, and those TCAs with minimal serotonergic activity such as nortriptyline, desipramine, maprotiline and trimipramine (Thomas and Shin, 2015)—"Non-Disparaged MOAI Tagalongs".

It is recommended that MAOIs be discontinued at least 10 days prior to elective surgery to avoid potentially fatal interactions with anesthetic agents.

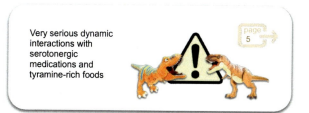

Very serious dynamic interactions with serotonergic medications and tyramine-rich foods

1959
$262–$286

Isocarboxazid (MARPLAN)

eye so kar BOX a zid / MAR plan

"Ice box Mars plan"

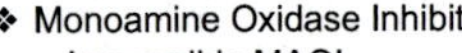

- Monoamine Oxidase Inhibitor
  - – Irreversible MAOI
  - – MAO-A & MAO-B
  - – 5-HT > NE > DA

FDA-approved for:

- Depression

The following information applies to all of the non-selective MAO inhibitors used for treatment of depression —"TIP"

- ▶ **T**ranylcypromine (PARNATE)
- ▶ **I**socarboxazid (MARPLAN)
- ▶ **P**henelzine (NARDIL)

Patients taking MAOIs (with the exception of the low strength EMSAM patch) must avoid tyramine-rich foods. The list of forbidden foods is long. Failure to adhere to a low tyramine diet may lead to what was originally called the "cheese effect", a potentially fatal hypertensive crisis.

Tyramine = "Tire Rim"

Tyramine is broken down by monoamine oxidase (MAO), which by definition MAOIs block. Without functioning MAO enzymes, tyramine accumulates and raises blood pressure.

The "tire rim" mnemonic can keep you from confusing tyramine with the amino acid tyrosine.

Note that if a patient is taking an oral MAOI for depression, phenelzine (Nardil) is the most likely prescription. Isocarboxazid (Marplan) scripts are exceedingly rare—it is the least prescribed of all antidepressants.

Dosing: Target dose is 20–60 mg/day divided BID–QID: Start 10 mg BID; May increase by 10 mg/day every 2–4 days; Max is 60 mg/day (20 mg TID or 30 mg BID); Taper gradually to stop.

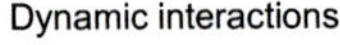

Tyramine accumulates, causing hypertensive crisis.

Dynamic interactions

- Serotonergic (strong) - contraindicated with other serotonergics
- Blocks tyramine breakdown (food interaction)
- Anticholinergic (mild)
- Hypertensive effects

Kinetic interactions

- None significant– "in a bubble"

page 18

1961
$25–$86

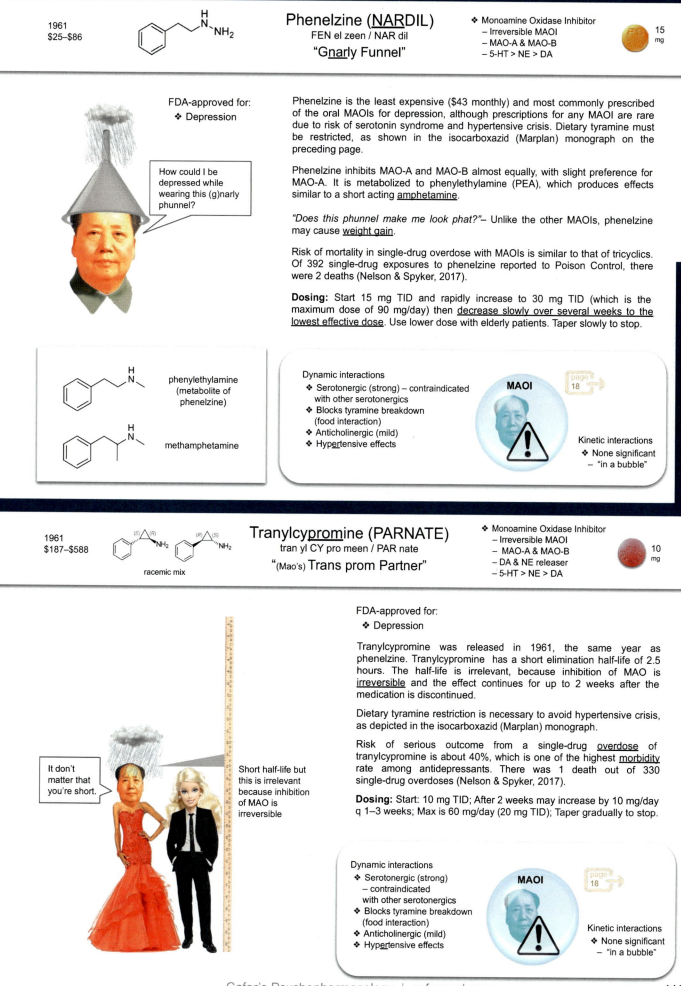

Phenelzine (NARDIL)

FEN el zeen / NAR dil

"Gnarly Funnel"

❖ Monoamine Oxidase Inhibitor
- Irreversible MAOI
- MAO-A & MAO-B
- 5-HT > NE > DA

15 mg

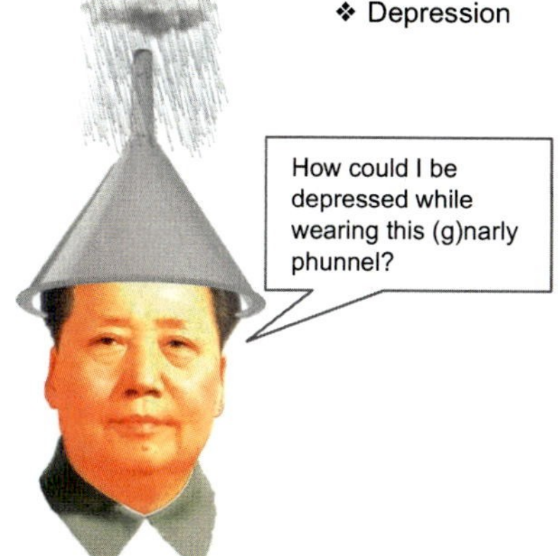

How could I be depressed while wearing this (g)narly phunnel?

FDA-approved for:
❖ Depression

Phenelzine is the least expensive ($43 monthly) and most commonly prescribed of the oral MAOIs for depression, although prescriptions for any MAOI are rare due to risk of serotonin syndrome and hypertensive crisis. Dietary tyramine must be restricted, as shown in the isocarboxazid (Marplan) monograph on the preceding page.

Phenelzine inhibits MAO-A and MAO-B almost equally, with slight preference for MAO-A. It is metabolized to phenylethylamine (PEA), which produces effects similar to a short acting amphetamine.

"Does this phunnel make me look phat?"– Unlike the other MAOIs, phenelzine may cause weight gain.

Risk of mortality in single-drug overdose with MAOIs is similar to that of tricyclics. Of 392 single-drug exposures to phenelzine reported to Poison Control, there were 2 deaths (Nelson & Spyker, 2017).

Dosing: Start 15 mg TID and rapidly increase to 30 mg TID (which is the maximum dose of 90 mg/day) then decrease slowly over several weeks to the lowest effective dose. Use lower dose with elderly patients. Taper slowly to stop.

phenylethylamine (metabolite of phenelzine)

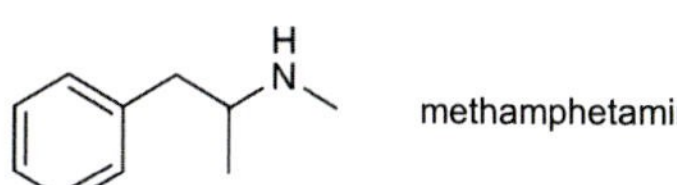

methamphetamine

Dynamic interactions
❖ Serotonergic (strong) – contraindicated with other serotonergics
❖ Blocks tyramine breakdown (food interaction)
❖ Anticholinergic (mild)
❖ Hypertensive effects

page 18

Kinetic interactions
❖ None significant
– "in a bubble"

1961
$187–$588

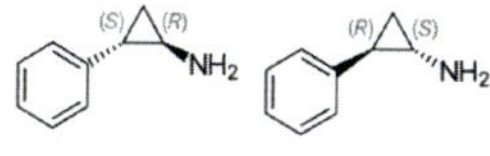

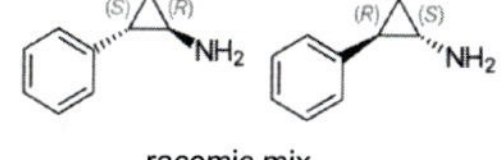

racemic mix

Tranylcypromine (PARNATE)

tran yl CY pro meen / PAR nate

"(Mao's) Trans prom Partner"

❖ Monoamine Oxidase Inhibitor
- Irreversible MAOI
- MAO-A & MAO-B
- DA & NE releaser
- 5-HT > NE > DA

10 mg

FDA-approved for:
❖ Depression

Tranylcypromine was released in 1961, the same year as phenelzine. Tranylcypromine has a short elimination half-life of 2.5 hours. The half-life is irrelevant, because inhibition of MAO is irreversible and the effect continues for up to 2 weeks after the medication is discontinued.

Dietary tyramine restriction is necessary to avoid hypertensive crisis, as depicted in the isocarboxazid (Marplan) monograph.

Risk of serious outcome from a single-drug overdose of tranylcypromine is about 40%, which is one of the highest morbidity rate among antidepressants. There was 1 death out of 330 single-drug overdoses (Nelson & Spyker, 2017).

Dosing: Start: 10 mg TID; After 2 weeks may increase by 10 mg/day q 1–3 weeks; Max is 60 mg/day (20 mg TID); Taper gradually to stop.

It don't matter that you're short.

Short half-life but this is irrelevant because inhibition of MAO is irreversible

Dynamic interactions
❖ Serotonergic (strong) – contraindicated with other serotonergics
❖ Blocks tyramine breakdown (food interaction)
❖ Anticholinergic (mild)
❖ Hypertensive effects

Kinetic interactions
❖ None significant
– "in a bubble"

2006
$1,631–$1,925

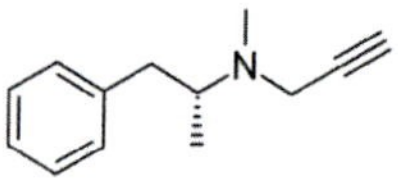

Selegiline transdermal (EMSAM)

se LE ji leen / EM sam

"YosEmite Sam Seals gills"

❖ Monoamine Oxidase Inhibitor
– MAO-B > MAO-A
– DA > NE > 5-HT

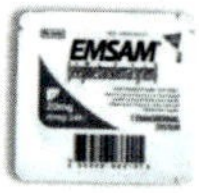

6
9
12
mg

FDA-approved for:
❖ Depression

Oral selegiline, at doses used for treatment of Parkinson's disease, is a selective inhibitor of MAO-B, which breaks down dopamine (DA). Oral selegiline at recommended doses does not inhibit MAO-A, making it ineffective for depression. It is necessary to block MAO-A to keep norepinephrine and serotonin from being broken down (oxidized).

The transdermal formulation of selegiline (EMSAM) allows the drug to achieve higher levels in the brain (where MAO-A breaks down serotonin) than in the gut (where MAO-A breaks down dietary tyramine).

Transdermal selegiline is the only MAOI available in the US for the treatment of depression that does not require dietary tyramine restriction at the clinically effective daily dose of 6 mg However, at higher doses, dietary restriction of tyramine is recommended.

Metabolism of selegiline produces a tiny amount of methamphetamine, which blocks dopamine reuptake and may contribute to the antidepressant benefit. The methamphetamine metabolite may produce a false positive on drug screens. Selegiline is not a controlled substance.

Selegiline is associated with a slight weight loss, which would be expected for something that is metabolized to methamphetamine.

Chairman Mao patch being used to seal his gills

Dosing: Start with 6 mg patch QD; may increase strength by 3 mg QD in 2-week intervals; Max is 12 mg patch/24 hours. Dietary tyramine restriction is recommended above 6 mg. Taper to discontinue.

$41–
$150

Selegiline (ELDEPRYL)

se LE ji leen / ELD e pril

"Elderly Seal's gills"

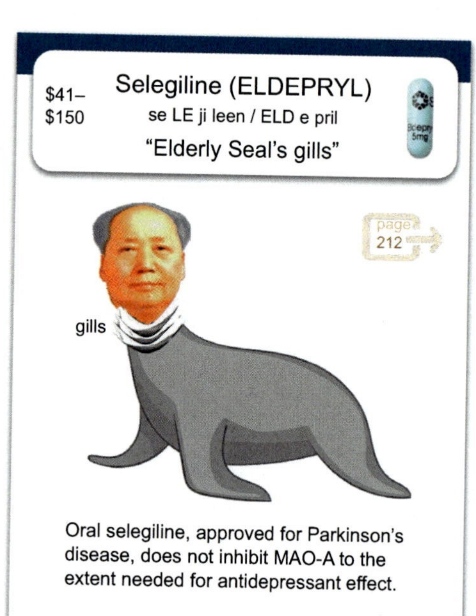

page 212

Oral selegiline, approved for Parkinson's disease, does not inhibit MAO-A to the extent needed for antidepressant effect.

selegiline

methamphetamine

Dynamic interactions
❖ Serotonergic (strong) – contraindicated with other serotonergics
❖ Blocks tyramine breakdown (food interaction)
❖ Anticholinergic (mild)
❖ Hypertensive effects

Kinetic interactions
❖ 2B6 substrate

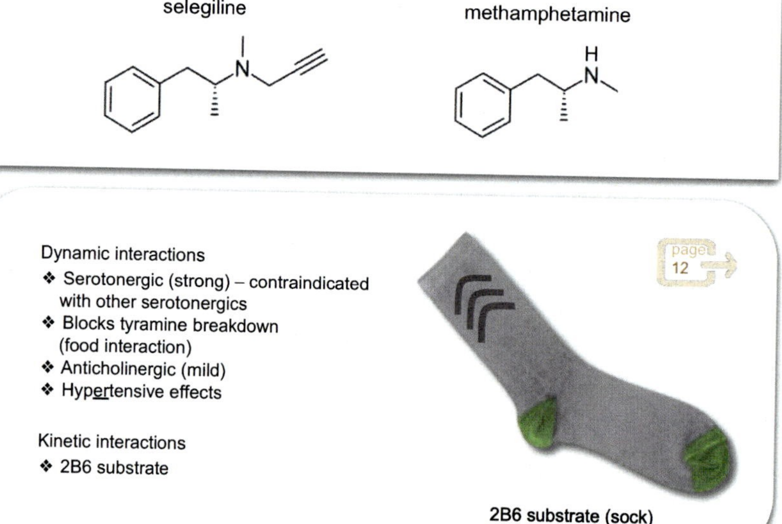

page 12

2B6 substrate (sock)

2010
$172–$225 Deplin
$30–$45 MethylPro
$18–$25 other generics
$2–$12 folic acid

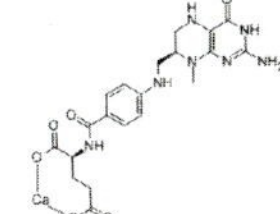

L-Methylfolate (DEPLIN)

meth il FO late / DEP lin

"Deep in My foliage"

- ❖ "Medical food" for depression
- ❖ Biologically active form of folate

7.5
15
mg

FDA-approved for:
- ❖ Augmentation of an antidepressant

Used off-label for:
- ❖ MTHFR deficiency

Folate (Vitamin B9), also known as folic acid, is necessary for synthesis of neurotransmitters including dopamine, norepinephrine, and serotonin. L-methylfolate is the active form of folate that crosses the blood-brain barrier with no need for enzymatic conversion.

About 1 in 3 individuals have difficulty converting folate to methylfolate due to a deficiency of the MTHFR enzyme (methylene tetrahydrofolate reductase). Among individuals with depression, about 60% have MTHFR mutations (Mischoulon et al, 2012). The 10% of individuals with 2 copies of the C677T MTHFR allele—*"poor M*TH**F***Rs"*—should be taking L-methylfolate.

Deplin is the brand of L-methylfolate marketed to physicians as a prescription-only "medical food" for depression. Other brands of L-methylfolate are now available without a prescription, though they are not FDA-regulated. There is no reason to believe Deplin is of higher quality than **MethylPro**, a reputable OTC version of L-methylfolate. Insurance rarely covers either brand, so the expense is borne out-of-pocket. Deplin costs 5x more than MethylPro and 50x more than generic folic acid.

L-methylfolate is intended to be an augmenting agent (add-on) to an antidepressant) in individuals who are not necessarily folate deficient. Refer to the "steps" advertisement below. As an augmenting agent, the number needed to treat with L-methylfolate was 6 (Papakostas et al, 2012).

Now that affordable brands are available, L-methylfolate is recommended over folic acid because it is more likely to be effective. There are no head-to-head trials of L-methylfolate vs folic acid, but results of L-methylfolate trials were more impressive.

Obese patients are more likely to respond to L-methylfolate, possibly because obesity causes inflammation, which impedes serotonin production (Shelton et al, 2015; *The Carlat Psychiatry Report*, Aug 2019). Generic folic acid may be adequate for non-obese individuals with normal MTHFR genes.

Supplementation of an antidepressant (fluoxetine specifically) with **generic folic acid** 0.5 mg/day demonstrated modest benefit at 10 weeks of treatment (Coppen & Bailey, 2000). The effect size was small, and some studies have not shown benefit from folate augmentation of antidepressants. Regardless, adding folate (vitamin B9) is a *benign* intervention—*folate is "Vitamin Be-nign"*.

Some studies combined folate (vitamin B9) with vitamins B6 and B12, Count by 3's—B6, B9, B12 = pyridoxine, folate, and cobalamin, respectively. Folic acid (B9) supplements can mask megaloblastic anemia that would otherwise lead to a diagnosis of vitamin B12 (cobalamin) deficiency. If untreated, B12 deficiency leads to peripheral neuropathy.

EnLyte is another prescription-only medical food containing 7 mg of L-methylfolate 7 mg and other "brain-ready, pre-metabolized coenzymes and cofactors". It costs about $170 monthly.

Folate is present in fresh green vegetables and other sources listed below. Garbanzo beans (chickpeas) contains an abundance of folate. Cooking reduces folate content by as much as 90%.

This "L" is for you, poor M*TH**F***R!
Garbanzo beans (chickpeas)

Now let's talk about actual folate deficiency. About 20% of depressed patients have low folate levels. Individuals with low folate do not respond as well to antidepressants. Patients with normal serum folic acid levels may still respond to treatment with folate because levels in the CNS may be low.

Folate deficiency leads to an elevation of homocysteine, a nonessential amino acid. Homocysteine is an NMDA receptor agonist and oxidant, i.e., something damaging to human cells An elevated homocysteine level is associated with cardiovascular disease.

No homo!

Folic acid deficiency during pregnancy leads to neural tube defects.

Dosing: For Deplin (expensive, prescription) or MethylPro (affordable, OTC) start 7.5 mg QD and increase to 15 mg, which is the target and maximum dose. MethylPro is available in 2.5, 5, 7.5, 10, 15 mg capsules. For generic folic acid (cheap) to augment an antidepressant you would give 0.5–5 mg QD. To treat folic acid deficiency, use 1 mg daily of generic folic acid plus a multivitamin. For a patient who responds to L-methylfolate for depression, consider changing to folic acid 3 mg (cheaper) at 6 months and see if recovery is maintained (Chris Aiken, MD, *The Carlat Psychiatry Report*, Aug 2019).

FOLINIC acid is a similar supplement, which may be better (than L-methylfolate) for individuals who do not have MTHFR mutations. Folinic acid has advantages over the other forms of folate for those with folate receptor-alpha autoantibodies.

From a Deplin advertisement:

Deplin®
Partial Response
Antidepressant
Depression

Top sources of folate in food:
#1 Garbanzo beans (chickpeas)
#2 Liver
#3 Pinto beans
#4 Lentils
#5 Spinach
#6 Asparagus
#7 Avocado
#8 Beets
#9 Black eyed peas
#10 Broccoli

page 18

Dynamic interactions:
- ❖ None significant

Kinetic interactions:
- ❖ Valproic acid and other anticonvulsants can deplete folate levels. This is unlikely to be relevant for medication management involving Deplin.

OTHERS FOR DEPRESSION 10

1970
$5–$20

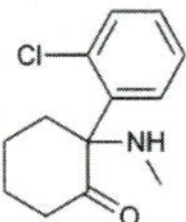

Ketamine (KETALAR)

KET a meen / KET a lar

"Cat (is) taller (than) Cat tamer"

- ❖ NMDA receptor antagonist
- ❖ Dissociative anaesthetic
- ❖ DEA Schedule III

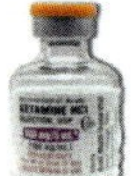

FDA-approved for:

- ❖ General anesthesia

Used off-label for:

- ❖ Treatment-resistant depression
- ❖ Agitation in emergency department or ambulance
- ❖ Refractory chronic pain

Ketamine (Ketalar) is a dissociative anaesthetic that has shown rapid efficacy in relieving refractory depression following intravenous infusion. It is not FDA-approved for this indication but is increasingly utilized as an alternative to electroconvulsive therapy (ECT).

Ketamine's rapid antidepressant effect has been demonstrated by over 20 controlled trials. The effects of ketamine on depression are apparent as early as 40 minutes after infusion and are maintained for at least 2–3 days. Within two hours of ketamine treatment, patients are generally lucid and not sedated. By four hours, there appears to be continued improvement in positive thinking and hopefulness. By one week after a single infusion, depressive symptoms are likely to recur to some extent.

Side effects of ketamine include dissociation, visual hallucinations, sialorrhea (hypersalivation), nausea, vertigo, tachycardia, and elevated blood pressure. Serious risks include increased intracranial and intraocular pressure. Unlike other general anesthetics, ketamine does not suppress respiratory drive, which makes it great for anesthesia in third world countries. However, there is a possibility of laryngospasm [luh RING go spaz um], sudden involuntary contraction of vocal cords that can be fatal via suffocation. Catastrophic outcomes are rare when ketamine is used at subanesthetic antidepressant doses, but the patient needs to be monitored with emergency services available.

Ketamine has a **black box warning** of a 12% risk of emergence reactions (as in emerging from general anesthesia) varying in severity from pleasant dream-like states to hallucinations, or delirium. This may manifest as confusion, excitement, or irrational behavior. The duration of an emergence reaction is usually a few hours, with recurrences up to 24 hours post-op in some cases, but with no residual psychological effects.

The presumed antidepressant mechanism of ketamine is NMDA receptor antagonism, which reduces the activity of glutamate, the brain's most important excitatory neurotransmitter. The mechanism appears to somehow involve the endogenous opioid system (endorphins). Ketamine is not an opioid, but when naltrexone (opioid antagonist) was administered prior to a ketamine infusion, ketamine was ineffective for depression (Williams NR et al, 2018). Naltrexone does not block the dissociative effect of ketamine. Benzodiazepines and Z-drugs (zolpidem, etc) can attenuate the antidepressant effect of ketamine, so they should be washed out prior to treatment.

Originally synthesized from phencyclidine (PCP, "angel dust"), ketamine is a Schedule III controlled substance with potential for abuse and psychological dependence. Ketamine has a half-life of 10–15 minutes, which is shorter than other dissociatives such as PCP and dextromethorphan. The total dissociative experience should last no longer than 1–2 hours.

Recreational users of "special K" can snort, inject, or take it orally. The desired recreational effects include euphoria, derealization, visual hallucinations, and increasing awareness of sound and color. A bad experience from too much ketamine is referred to as falling into a "K-hole", where the user feels trapped in a frozen state, as if stuck in a hole peering out, detached from their physical presence. While stuck in a "K-hole", the user can, for instance, think about moving their arm and then see an arm moving in front of them, but the association between the thought and the movement does not register.

Risks with long-term maintenance treatment of depression with ketamine are unknown. Studies in mice suggest the potential for irreversible cognitive decline with chronic use (Ding et al, 2016).

Dosing: For treatment-resistant depression, the optimal ketamine protocol has not been clearly established. The most common frequency is twice weekly infusions for up to 4 weeks using a relatively low dose of 0.5 mg/kg administered over 40 minutes. Compare this to the anesthetic dose of 1–4.5 mg/kg—also the IV/IM dose used for agitation in the ambulance or emergency department.

Ketamine is an alternative to:

- ▶ Electroconvulsive therapy (ECT)
- ▶ Transcranial magnetic stimulation (TMS)
- ▶ Deep brain stimulation (DBS)

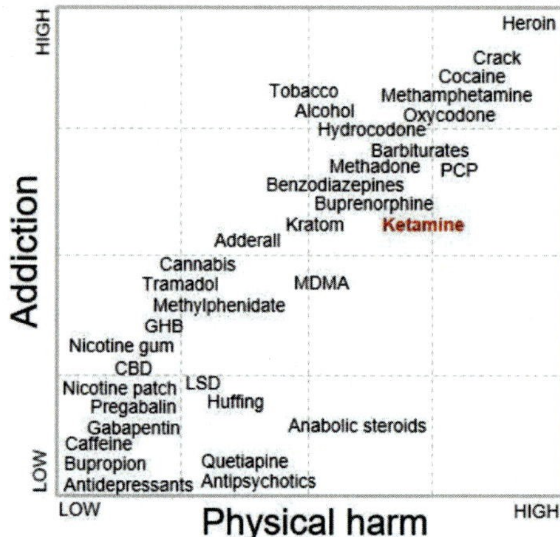

Physical harm is subjectively applied, as we are not comparing apples to apples. Since tobacco is responsible for 20% of deaths in the US, one could reasonably argue its relative harm is understated.

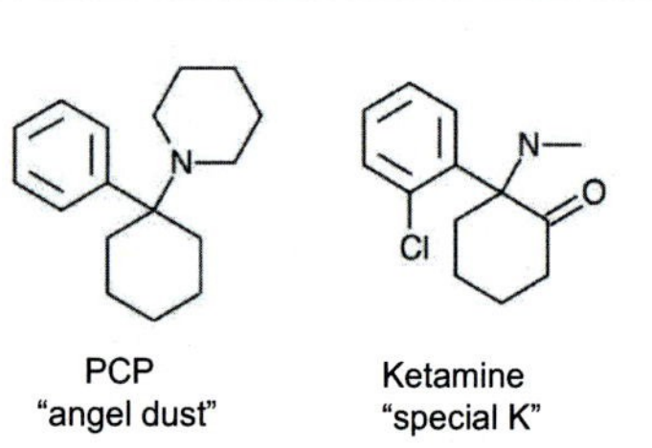

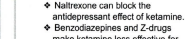

Dynamic interactions:

- ❖ Naltrexone can block the antidepressant effect of ketamine.
- ❖ Benzodiazepines and Z-drugs make ketamine less effective for depression.
- ❖ Hypertension
- ❖ Sedation

Kinetic interaction:

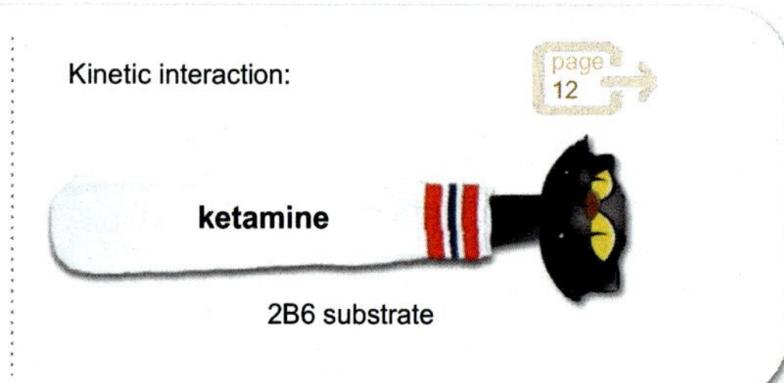

Esketamine (SPRAVATO)

es KET a meen / sprah VAH toe

"Scat tamer – Spray gato"

- ❖ NMDA receptor antagonist
- ❖ Dissociative drug
- ❖ DEA Schedule III

56
84
mg

FDA-approved for:

- ❖ Treatment-resistant depression
- ❖ Major depression with acute suicidal ideation or behavior

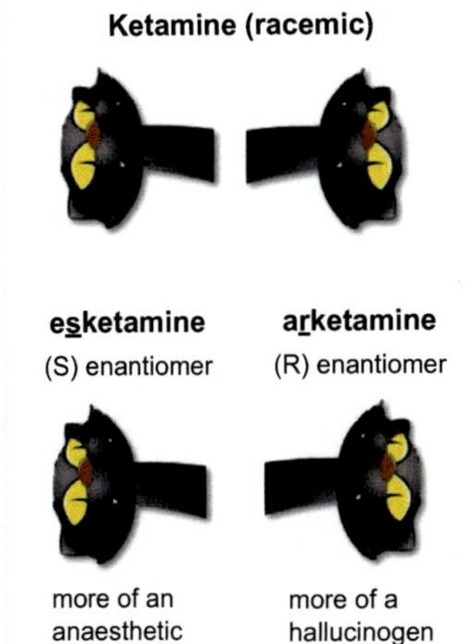

Esketamine nasal spray (Spravato) is the first novel antidepressant approved (2019) in over three decades. Esketamine is indicated for treatment-resistant depression (TRD) in conjunction with an oral antidepressant. It was developed for commercial purposes because the patent for ketamine was long expired.

As the name would suggest, esketamine is the S-enantiomer of ketamine, which has been increasingly used off-label for TRD. Like racemic ketamine, esketamine is a Schedule III controlled substance.

It is unknown whether the antidepressant action of the S-enantiomer is superior, inferior, or equal to racemic ketamine. The opposite enantiomer, R-ketamine (arketamine) is also under investigation. S-ketamine is more responsible for the anesthetic effect, while R-ketamine is more responsible for hallucinations because it is 3–4 times more potent at blocking NMDA receptors than R-ketamine. S-ketamine appears to be less effective than R-ketamine at reducing depressive symptoms (Stahl, 2015) but may be less likely to cause psychoactive side effects.

The induction phase for Spravato is twice weekly over 4 weeks, then weekly x 4, then every 1–2 weeks for maintenance treatment. It costs about $625 per dose.

Spravato is less convenient than would be expected for a nasal spray. It must be given in the presence of a health care provider and should never be dispensed to the patient for home use. The patient must be observed for 2 hours and cannot drive for the rest of the day. Due to the risk of vomiting, the patient must fast for 2 hours (no fluid for 30 minutes) prior to treatment.

Most of the therapeutic effect of esketamine is apparent by 24 hours after the first dose. Up to 75% of patients experience dissociation with Spravato. None of the clinical trials were controlled for the dramatic "high" esketamine produces. It was well-tolerated, with only 5% of subjects dropping out within one year due to side effects.

8 to 17% of patients have elevated blood pressure > 40 mmHg or diastolic BP elevation > 20 mmHg. 3% of patients will have systolic blood pressure elevation to about 180 mmHg. Blood pressure elevation peaks 40 minutes after administration and lasts about 4 hours. Due to this risk, esketamine is contraindicated with arteriovenous malformation or aneurysmal vascular disease (including aortic, intracranial, and peripheral arterial vessels). Stimulants such as Adderall or Ritalin could increase the risk of BP elevation.

With an 18% drug-placebo separation in relapse rates, esketamine's long-term benefits appear comparable to those seen with augmentation of an antidepressant with an atypical antipsychotic (Borges et al, 2014; The Carlat Psychiatry Report, Jun/Jul 2019). Long term use past one year has not been tested for the potential of cognitive impairment.

Esketamine prescribers must register through a Risk Evaluation and Mitigation Strategy (REMS) program, and the DEA will do an in-person inspection of the provider's office.

For cost savings, generic ketamine can be put into an atomizer for intranasal delivery as off-label option for 1% of the cost of esketamine.

The two available strengths of esketamine are 56 mg and 84 mg. The 56 mg dose is supplied in two 28 mg vials, and the 84 mg dose in three 28 mg vials. Each vial is delivered by 2 sprays, one in each nostril. Therefore 56 mg is delivered by 4 total sprays, and 84 mg by 6 total sprays. Wait 5 minutes between each 28 mg vial. Check BP before each dose and 40 minutes afterwards. Weigh risk/benefit if pre-treatment BP is > 140/90.

Dosing: The first dose should be 56 mg. Subsequent doses can be either 56 mg or 84 mg, depending on response and tolerability. Treatment is 2x/wk for first 4 weeks (8 treatments), then once weekly for the next 4 weeks (4 treatments), then every 1–2 weeks thereafter.

NMDA receptor

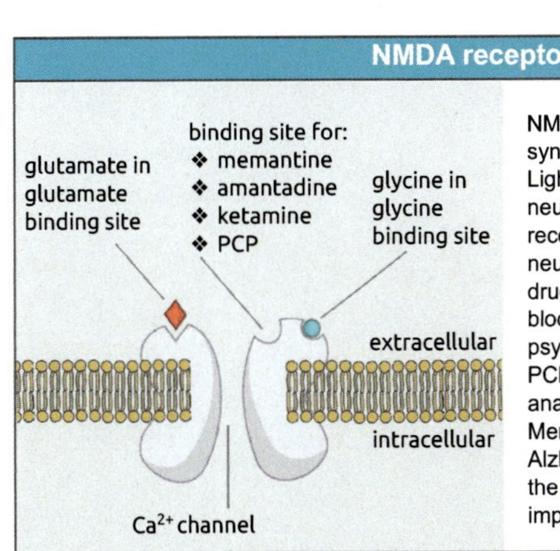

NMDA receptors are involved in synaptic plasticity and memory. Lightly blocking the receptor is neuroprotective. However, if the receptor is blocked completely, neurons cannot function. The street drug PCP, aka "angel dust", strongly blocks NMDA receptors, causing psychosis. Ketamine is weaker than PCP, but strong enough to cause anaesthesia and dissociation. Memantine (Namenda) is an Alzheimer's medication that blocks the NMDA receptor just enough to improve memory.

Dynamic interactions:

- ❖ Naltrexone can block the antidepressant effect of ketamine.
- ❖ Benzodiazepines and Z-drugs make ketamine less effective.
- ❖ Hypertension
- ❖ Sedation

Kinetic interaction:

page 12

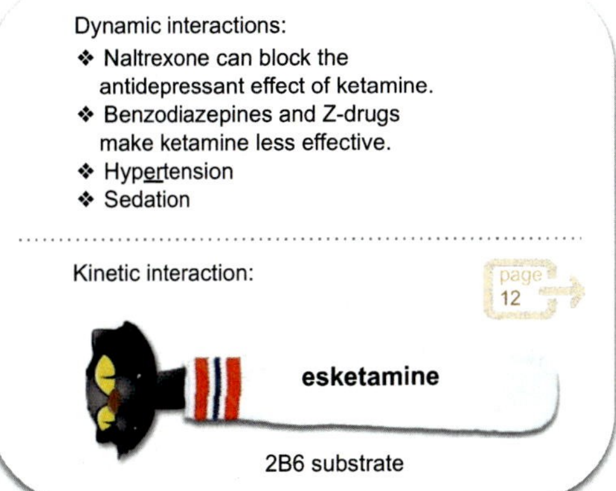

2019
$34,000

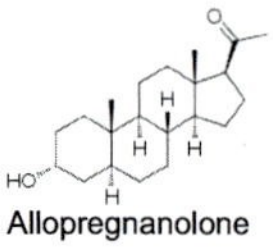

Allopregnanolone

Brexanolone (ZULRESSO)

brex AN oh lone / zul RESS o

"Zulu resigns (to) Brex (feed) alone"

❖ Neurosteroid for postpartum depression

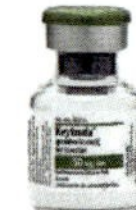

FDA-approved for:

❖ Postpartum depression

In 2019, the first two novel antidepressants in over three decades were approved—esketamine (Spravato) and brexanolone (Zulresso). Brexanolone is the first medication FDA-approved for postpartum depression. Brexanolone is a synthetic version of allopregnanolone (*"all pregnant and alone"*), an endogenous neurosteroid made from progesterone that is increased during pregnancy.

It is theorized that withdrawal from allopregnanolone after childbirth can lead to postpartum depression and anxiety. Conventional antidepressants are known to raise levels of endogenous allopregnanolone.

Brexanolone acts at the GABA-A receptor complex, as do several classes of drugs that calm down the central nervous system, including benzodiazepines and barbiturates (see below). Unsurprisingly for something that works through the GABA-A receptor, brexanolone has anxiolytic, sedative, and anticonvulsant properties.

Brexanolone is insultingly expensive and must be given as an IV infusion over 60 hours! The cost of the drug is $34,000 not including the cost of hospitalization.

The advantage of brexanolone is speed of symptom improvement. Roughly 75% of patients reported at least a 50% reduction in depressive symptoms. Remission of depression may occur within a couple of days. 94% of patients who responded maintained their response at one month. Not bad!

It appears to be safe with breastfeeding—*"Brex (feed) alone"*. The infant receives only 1–2% of maternal weight-adjusted dose. Excessive sedation is possible, so another adult should be present during treatment when mom has the baby. So you're technically not supposed to brexfeed *alone* on brexanolone.

Oral brexanolone is in development.

Allopregnanolone balance may play a role in other psychiatric disorders. Low levels are associated with depression and PTSD. High levels are also associated with depression, as well as anxiety and irritability (Bäckström et al, 2014).

Dosing: Given intravenously over 60 hours; Start 30 mcg/kg/hr for 4 hours, then 60 mcg/kg/hr for 20 hours then 90 mcg/kg/hr for 28 hours, then 60 mcg/kg/hr for 4 hours, then 30 mcg/kg/hr for 4 hours = 60 hours total

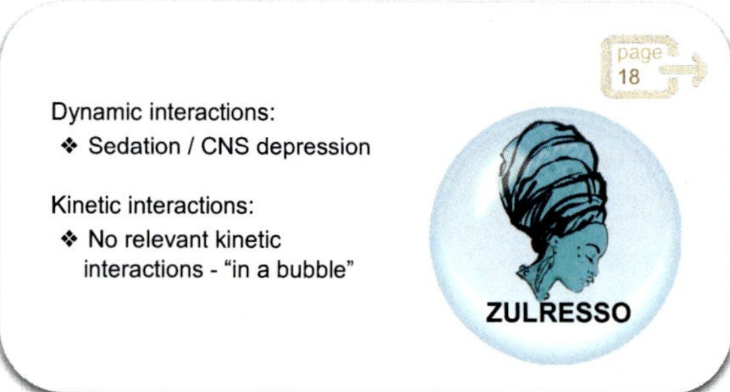

Dynamic interactions:

❖ Sedation / CNS depression

Kinetic interactions:

❖ No relevant kinetic interactions - "in a bubble"

GABA(A) receptor

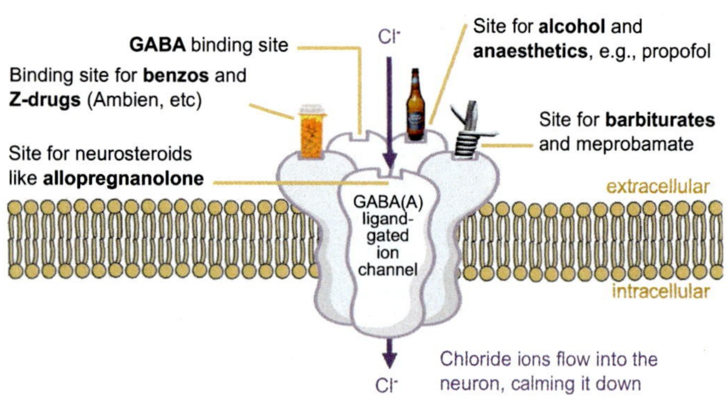

GABA receptor ligands

GABA(A) agonists

❖ Alcohol
❖ Ativan, alprazolam, etc (benzos)
❖ Amytal, etc (barbiturates)
❖ Ambien, etc (Z-drugs)
❖ Anesthetics
❖ Allopregnanolone (brexanolone)

GABA(A) antagonist

❖ Flumazenil (Romazicon) at the benzodiazepine site

GABA(B) agonists

❖ Baclofen (antispasmodic)
❖ GHB (Xyrem)

Note that gabapentin (Neurontin) and pregabalin (Lyrica) have chemical structures similar to GABA but they do **not** bind GABA receptors.

SJW
$7–$35

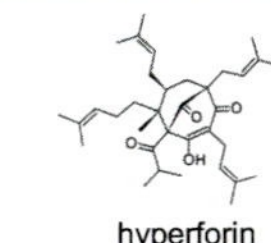

St John's Wort (SJW)

Hypericum perforatum

St John's "wart"

❖ Herbal antidepressant

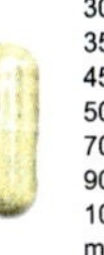

FDA-approved for:
- ❖ N/A

Effective for:
- ❖ Mild depression

Possibly effective for:
- ❖ Menopausal symptoms
- ❖ Social anxiety
- ❖ Somatoform disorders

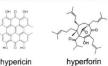

St John's wort (SJW) is an OTC herbal antidepressant. SJW has demonstrated superiority to placebo for treatment of mild depression. It is considered ineffective for moderate to severe depression. Most psychiatrists do not recommend it, although psychiatrists are rarely consulted for mild depression.

The only advantage of SJW is obtainability without a doctor's order. The main drawback is potential for drug-drug interactions.

As with any herbal supplement, St John's wort contains many chemicals. It is not entirely clear which are responsible for the antidepressant effect, but hypericin (about 0.3% of the extract) is likely involved. The primary phytochemical constituent of St John's wort is hyperforin (about 3%). The composition of various chemicals may vary greatly between brands.

The likely mechanism of SJW is serotonin reuptake inhibition, like many prescription antidepressants. It also inhibits reuptake of norepinephrine and dopamine. It also has potent affinity for the adenosine, serotonin 5HT1, benzodiazepine and γ-aminobutyric acid (GABA) receptors. Plus, it may weakly inhibit monoamine oxidase. Lots of chemicals, lots of pharmacologic effects.

There is no FDA-approved indication for SJW. In 2000, the FDA issued a warning that SJW can reduce the serum levels of many drugs through inDuction of CYP450 enzymes.

Side effects of SJW are generally mild and may include insomnia, vivid dreams, irritability and GI discomfort. At high doses it may cause phototoxic skin reactions. It is not recommended to combine SJW with antidepressants due to risk of serotonin syndrome.

Hypericin is metabolized through the liver with half-life of about 25 hours.

St. John's wort is so named because it blooms near June 24th, the birthday of John the Baptist. "Wort" is an old English word for plant.

Dosing: 250 mg BID to 600 mg TID (Typically 300 mg TID). Products are generally standardized to contain 0.1–0.3% hypericin and/or 3–6% hyperforin

Hypericin - *"Hyper rice"*

Hypericin may be the main chemical in St John's wort responsible for the antidepressant effect.

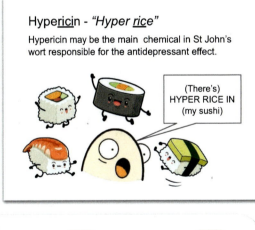

Dynamic interactions:
- ❖ Serotonergic
- ❖ Photosensitivity

Kinetic interactions:
- ❖ 1A2 inducer (major)
- ❖ 2C9 inducer (minor)
- ❖ 3A4 inducer (major)
- ❖ P-glycoprotein inducer (increased removal of P-gp substrates from the brain)

page 10

1A2 inDucer

page 13

2C9 inDucer (weak)

page 16

3A4 inDucer

This edition of *Cafer's Psychopharmacology* was released in November 2020. Subscribe to cafermed.com for the updated PDF edition with over 1,000 internal links and bookmarks for ultrarapid navigation. The PDF edition is updated frequently with new mascots. Visit cafermed.com/update for more information.

Discount code for cafermed.com subscription: **ULTRARAPID**

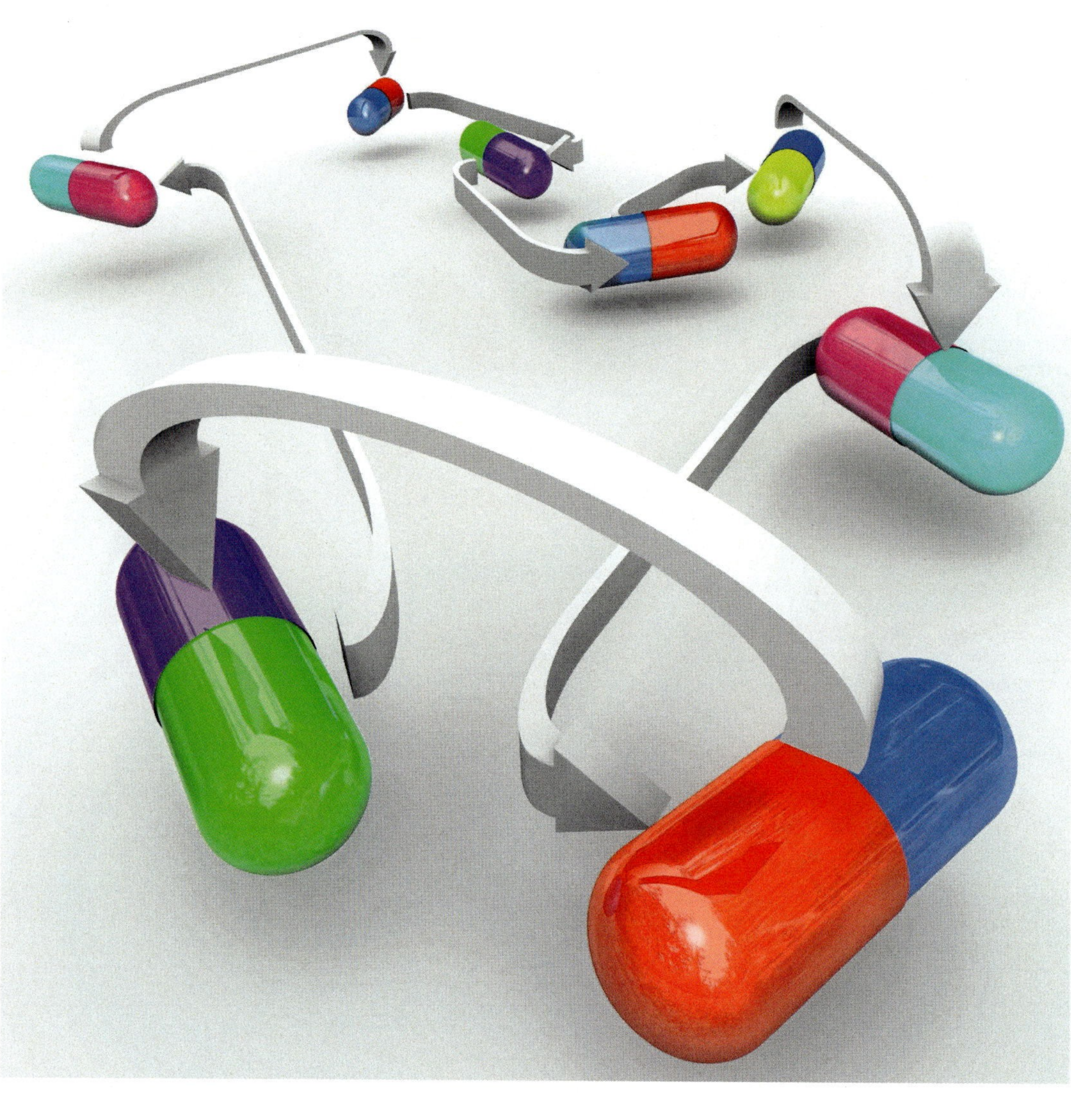

Antipsychotics work by blocking D2 dopamine receptors. Think Star Wars droid R2**D2**.

In the book *Memorable Psychopharmacology*, Dr. Heldt provides the mnemonic for antipsychotics as D2 receptor (D_2R) blockers for psychotic patients taking a "D_2R (detour) from reality".

Antipsychotics slow down thoughts. This effect is useful for treatment of mania, but can be detrimental for schizophrenia patients—manifested by worsening of negative symptoms (amotivation, anhedonia, blunting of affect).

When it comes to treatment of schizophrenia, the patient is generally started on the minimum effective dose for a given antipsychotic and considered for dose increase at two weeks. For aggressive patients, or for those hospitalized with acute psychosis, the dose can be titrated much faster. For first episode psychosis, it is a good idea to decrease dose of the antipsychotic after 6 months of remission. When the antipsychotic dose is reduced by 50% at 6 months, patients had better overall functioning 7 years later (Wunderlink et al, 2013).

It is considered best practice to stick with a single antipsychotic rather than combining two antipsychotics. For a psychiatric hospital to maintain accreditation, the psychiatrist must document the justification for multiple antipsychotics. The Joint Commission has identified three appropriate reasons for discharging a patient from the hospital on more than one antipsychotic:

- three failed trials of monotherapy
- cross-taper to monotherapy
- augmentation of clozapine (Clozaril)

In other words, the concurrent use of two or more antipsychotic medications should generally be avoided except in cases of three failed trials of monotherapy, preferably including clozapine—the most effective medication for refractory psychosis.

Antipsychotics commonly cause extrapyramidal symptoms (EPS). The extrapyramidal system ("outside of the pyramids") is an imprecise anatomic term referring to motor tracts other than those projecting through the pyramids of the medulla oblongata. The pyramidal system allows voluntary movements, while the extrapyramidal system coordinates motor activity without directly innervating motor neurons. Dysfunction of the extrapyramidal system leads to involuntary movements. Short term exposure to antipsychotic drugs may cause EPS resembling Parkinson's disease, while long term exposure can cause tardive dyskinesia, which resembles the choreiform movements of Huntington's disease.

The likelihood that an antipsychotic will cause EPS is proportional to its efficacy in blocking D2 receptors. Haloperidol (Haldol) is a high potency D2 blocker that commonly causes EPS. Since the likelihood of EPS is dose-related, haloperidol should be dosed at low strength. EPS is caused by a relative deficiency of dopamine and an excess of acetylcholine in the nigrostriatal pathway. This explains why anticholinergic medications such as benztropine (Cogentin) can quickly alleviate dystonia. Some of the newer antipsychotics are likely to cause akathisia (restlessness) but are relatively unlikely to cause the other kinds of EPS shown below. Note that "tardive" refers to delayed onset. Management would include dose reduction or discontinuation of the offending medication, or switching to a medication with minimal EPS such as quetiapine (Seroquel), clozapine (Clozaril), or pimavanserin (Nuplazid).

All antipsychotics now have a black box warning: "Not approved for dementia-related psychosis; increased mortality risk in elderly dementia patients."

Antipsychotics may cause an elevation in core body temperature that can be exacerbated by strenuous exercise and anticholinergic medications ("hot as a hare").

To maintain effectiveness, multiple daily dosing may not be needed. A continuous dopamine D2 receptor blockade is generally not necessary to sustain antipsychotic response. For instance, perphenazine (Trilafon) has a 10-hour half-life and, although the label instructs BID–TID dosing, once-daily dosing was found to be equally effective for maintenance treatment (Takeuchi et al, 2014).

Types of Extrapyramidal Symptoms (EPS)

Type of EPS	Usual onset	Description	Reversible?	Treatment
Dystonia	Quickly	Muscle contraction in the face, neck, trunk or extremities, and even the larynx. "Oculogyric crisis" is a dystonic reaction with prolonged upward deviation of the eyes.	Yes	Anticholinergics: - Benztropine (Cogentin) - Diphenhydramine (Benadryl)
Akathisia	Acute akathisia - quickly; Tardive akathisia - after several months	*Akathemi* is Greek for "never sit down". Akathisia is an uncomfortable feeling of internal motor restlessness with difficulty sitting still. The patient may fidget, pace, or rock back and forth.	Yes	Propranolol (Inderal) Benzodiazepines Anticholinergics (less effective)
Pseudo-parkinsonism	Months–years	Pill-rolling Parkinsonian tremor; Bradykinesia (e.g., "Thorazine shuffle" gait); Does not progress to Parkinson's disease	Usually	Amantadine (Symmetrel) Benzodiazepines
Tardive Dyskinesia	6 months–year(s)	Movement disorder that is often irreversible, characterized by tongue movements, lip smacking, excessive blinking, grimacing or raising of eyebrows; irregular finger movements as if playing an invisible piano or air guitar; chorea of extremities in severe cases. Often the patient is unaware of the movements. Older adults are at higher risk.	Usually not	Valbenazine (Ingrezza) Deutetrabenazine (Austedo) Benzodiazepines Amantadine (Symmetrel)

Antipsychotics are not always to blame for the involuntary movements presumed to be tardive dyskinesia. In the pre-antipsychotic era, there was a 4% incidence of dyskinesia with the first psychotic episode. 40% of those over age 60 with chronic schizophrenia demonstrated dyskinesia despite never taking an antipsychotic (Fenton, 2013). Spontaneous dyskinesia (unrelated to antipsychotic use) is also more prevalent in nonpsychotic first-degree relatives of schizophrenic individuals, likely due to genetically based dopamine dysfunction (Koning et al, 2010).

All antipsychotics are labeled with a black box warning of increased mortality in elderly patients with dementia-related psychosis. However, antipsychotics are commonly prescribed for this population, not only for psychosis but also for aggression and agitation associated with dementia. These symptoms are referred to as "behavioral and psychological symptoms of dementia" (BPSD). After BPSD symptoms are controlled with an antipsychotic for at least 3 months, it is recommended to gradually taper off of the medication (Bjerre et al, 2018).

Serotonin Syndrome -vs- Neuroleptic Malignant Syndrome (NMS)

Serotonin (5-HT) Syndrome and Neuroleptic Malignant Syndrome are rare psychiatric emergencies. These syndromes should be considered when an individual taking several psychotropic medications becomes acutely ill. Since some symptoms overlap, here is a head-to-head comparison.

5-HT "twitchy frog" syndrome

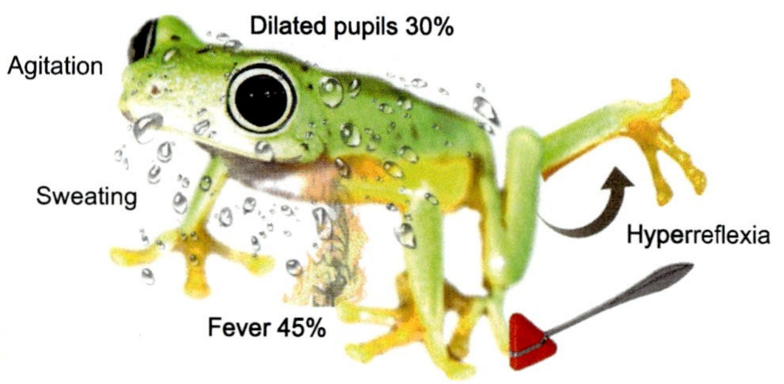

NMS - "can't Bend(er)"

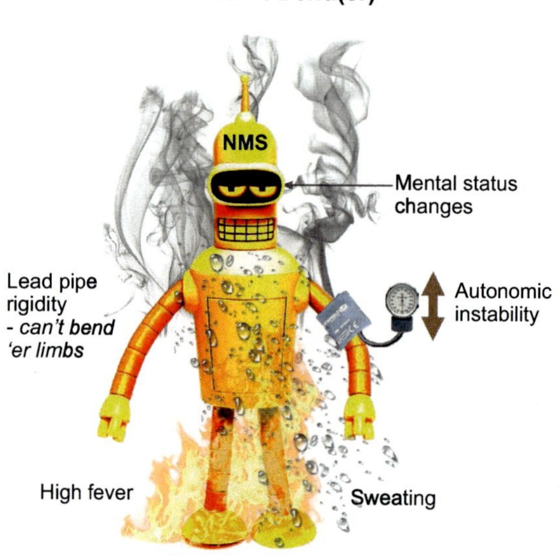

Bender from Futurama

	Serotonin Syndrome	Neuroleptic Malignant Syndrome (NMS)
Mechanism	Serotonin (5-HT) overload in the brain stem	Dopamine blockade in the hypothalamus (fever) and nigrostriatal pathway (rigidity)
Usual onset	Within 24 hours of combining antidepressants (or other serotonergics)	Within 30 days of starting or increasing an antipsychotic (anti-dopaminergic) or stopping a dopaminergic drug
Cardinal features	Myoclonic jerks > 50% Hyperreflexia > 50% Mental status changes > 50% Shivering > 50%	High fever 100% by definition Rigidity 100% by definition Mental status changes 99% Elevated or labile BP most
Fever	45%	Yes; Temp > 40°C (104°F) in 40% of cases
Autonomic instability	35% tachycardia 35% HTN 15% hypotension	99% overall 88% tachycardia 70% labile BP
Mental status change	51% confusion 50% restlessness/hyperactivity/agitation 29% unresponsiveness (may evolve to coma)	Confusion is the first symptom to present in 82% of cases, and may evolve to mutism, profound encephalopathy and coma.
Muscle rigidity	51% and less severe than with NMS	100% by definition; "lead pipe rigidity"
Motor activity	Hyperkinesia (restlessness/hyperactivity)	Bradykinesia (slowness of movement)
Hyperreflexia	52%	No
Clonus	23% - Examine for repetitive dorsiflexion of the ankle in response to one forcible dorsiflexion. Go to *cafermed.com/clonus* to see how its done.	No
Tremor	43%	Less prominent
Ataxia	40%	Uncommon
Shivering	> 50%	Uncommon
...with chattering teeth or bruxism	15%	No
Sweating (diaphoresis)	Common	Common
Sialorrhea (hypersalivation)	Often prominent	< 15%
Eyes	30% dilated pupils; 20% unreactive pupils; Ocular clonus is possible as seen on *cafermed.com/clonus*.	Usually not affected; Go to *cafermed.com/crisis* to see oculogyric crisis, a manifestation of dystonia which may co-occur with NMS.

You could *clone us* (clonus)

continued...

	Serotonin Syndrome	Neuroleptic Malignant Syndrome (NMS)
Nature of syndrome	Can be referred to as serotonin toxicity because it is a true toxidrome, caused by excess serotonin in a concentration-dependent way; Some cases are mild.	An idiosyncratic reaction, not a toxidrome; All cases of NMS are serious. Partial, early, or aborted presentations of NMS cases were described as *forme fruste*, especially with low potency antipsychotics. Rigidity may be absent or milder with clozapine.
Typical evolution	Rapid onset; May have prodrome of nausea and diarrhea; Serotonin toxicity may be mild to severe.	First: Mental status changes (confusion, mutism, catatonia); Second: Rigidity; Third: Fever and BP lability; Peak severity in as little as 3 days
Mortality	1% mortality if treated; When fatal, it is usually due to extreme fever, leading to the same complications as seen with NMS.	Fatal if untreated; 10% mortality when treated; Renal failure from rhabdomyolysis, heart attack, respiratory failure (from chest wall rigidity), DVT/pulmonary embolism, dehydration, electrolyte imbalance, disseminated intravascular coagulation (DIC), liver failure, seizures
Resolution	70% of cases completely resolve within 24 hours.	If not fatal, NMS typically resolves slowly over 1 to 2 weeks.
Most likely culprits	15% of SSRI overdoses lead to 5-HT toxicity; 50% incidence when overdosing on combo SSRI + MAOI; Clomipramine, imipramine are most likely among TCAs.	High potency 1st gen antipsychotics (FGAs); Haldol is responsible for 44% of cases. Long-acting injectable FGAs—haloperidol decanoate (Haldol D) and fluphenazine decanoate (Prolixin D)—pose an even higher risk.
Non-antidepressant/ antipsychotic culprits	LSD ("Acid") MDMA (Ecstasy) Dextromethorphan (DXM) L-Tryptophan Metaxalone (Skelaxin) Linezolid (Zyvox) Methylene blue (Urelle) St. John's Wort Tramadol (Ultram) Meperidine (Demerol) Fentanyl (Duragesic) Methadone (Dolophine) Buspirone (Buspar) - unlikely Triptans (Imitrex, Maxalt, etc) - highly unlikely	Antiemetics that are D2 blockers: - Metoclopramide (Reglan) - Prochlorperazine (Compazine) - Promethazine (Phenergan) - Trimethobenzamide (Tigan) TCA that blocks D2 receptors: - Amoxapine (Asendin) Dopamine depleting agents - Reserpine (Serpasil) - Tetrabenazine (Xenazine) - Deutetrabenazine (Austedo) - Valbenazine (Ingrezza)
Lithium?	Lithium may contribute to 5-HT syndrome, although unlikely	Lithium may contribute to NMS.
Caused by stopping...	N/A	Stopping a dopaminergic antiparkinson medication (e.g., levodopa) can induce NMS. This variety of NMS is referred to as parkinsonism-hyperpyrexia syndrome or "withdrawal-emergent hyperpyrexia and confusion".
Relatively low risk medications	Rarely caused by a lone antidepressant. Not caused by buspirone or triptans. Highly unlikely to be caused by mirtazapine, trazodone, cyclobenzaprine or lithium.	Low potency 1st gen antipsychotics—chlorpromazine (Thorazine) and thioridazine (Mellaril); 2nd gen antipsychotics—clozapine (Clozaril), quetiapine (Seroquel), olanzapine (Zyprexa)
Leukocytosis	Less prominent	> 75% of cases have WBC > 12,000
Creatinine kinase (CK) elevation	Less prominent	90% show creatine kinase (CK) over 3x upper limit of normal (ULN). CK of over 5x ULM is diagnostic of rhabdomyolysis (skeletal muscle breakdown), which can lead to renal failure and disseminated intravascular coagulation (DIC). The normal range of CK is 22 to 198 units/Liter. CK is also called creatine phosphokinase (CPK).
Management	Discontinue the contributing medication(s). Aim to normalize vital signs.	ICU admission, rapid cooling and hydration. Stop the antipsychotic or restart the dopaminergic med.
Potentially helpful meds	Benzodiazepines for agitation Cyproheptadine (anti-serotonergic antihistamine) Methysergide (anti-serotonergic migraine medication)	Bromocriptine (DA agonist) Amantadine (DA agonist, NMDA antagonist) Dantrolene (direct acting muscle relaxant)
Risk factors	Combinations of serotonergics, use of street drugs	Iron deficiency, dehydration, catatonia, Lewy body dementia, genetically reduced function of D2 receptors, rapid dose escalation, males under age 40
Incidence	Severe 5-HT toxicity is rare. Mild toxicity is more common.	Quite rare - About 1 in 5,000 on antipsychotics
Sequelae	None, although delirium may persist for a few days	Memory problems (although usually temporary)
Differential diagnosis	Serotonin discontinuation syndrome (withdrawal) in the context of cross-tapering/titrating antidepressants. Anticholinergic toxicity, which manifests as dry, flushed skin ("dry as a bone, red as a beet") rather than diaphoresis.	Alcohol withdrawal, thyrotoxicosis, sepsis, heat stroke, tetanus, acute hydrocephalus, status epilepticus
Formal diagnosis	Google *Hunter criteria*, which focuses on clonus (spontaneous or inducible), ocular clonus, and hyperreflexia	Defined by DSM 5; Severe rigidity and high fever are both necessary to make the diagnosis.
Notes	Some experts prefer the term serotonin toxicity to more accurately reflect the condition as a dose-dependent form of 5-HT poisoning.	Neuroleptic, a synonym of antipsychotic, refers to something that "grabs ahold of nerves". Idiopathic NMS (with no identifiable culprit drug) is called malignant catatonia.

Thanks to Ahmed Eid Elaghoury MD for contributing to this content.

1st and 2nd Generation Antipsychotics

The older antipsychotics came to be known as "typicals" (FGAs) upon the arrival of clozapine (Clozaril), the first "atypical" antipsychotic, in 1990. The atypicals (SGAs) purportedly caused fewer extrapyramidal symptoms (EPS) than the FGAs. Clozapine does not cause EPS, but most of the subsequent atypicals do cause EPS to some extent, which was disappointing. Despite side effects, all available antipsychotic drugs (FGAs and SGAs) are statistically significantly better than placebo for all-cause discontinuation (Leucht et al, 2013). In other words, any antipsychotic is less likely to be stopped than placebo when used to treat schizophrenia.

Class	First Generations Antipsychotics (FGAs)	Second Generation Antipsychotics (SGAs)
Also known as	Typical antipsychotics	Atypical antipsychotics
Mnemonic	The <u>F</u>ug<u>GA</u>s, as in "Old fuggers"	The <u>S</u>u<u>GA</u>s, as in "<u>S</u>u<u>GA</u>r diabetes"
Best known for	Extrapyramidal symptoms (EPS) ▶ Dystonia (muscle rigidity) ▶ Akathisia (restlessness) ▶ Pseudo-Parkinsonism - Google *parkinsonism gif* ▶ Tardive dyskinesia - Google *tardive gif*	Metabolic syndrome ▶ Weight gain ▶ Diabetes ▶ Dyslipidemia
Usual mechanism	D2 dopamine receptor blockade	D2 dopamine receptor blockade and $5\text{-}HT_{2A}$ serotonin receptor blockade; Mnemonic: 2A = **2**nd generation **A**ntipsychotic
Release date	1954 Chlorpromazine (Thorazine) 1956 Prochlorperazine (Compazine) 1957 Perphenazine (Trilafon) 1958 Trifluoperazine (Stelazine) 1960 Fluphenazine (Prolixin) 1967 Haloperidol (Haldol) 1967 Thiothixene (Navane) 1975 Loxitane (Loxapine) 1975 Molindone (Moban) 1978 Thioridazine (Mellaril) 1985 Pimozide (Orap)	1990 Clozapine (Clozaril) 1993 Risperidone (Risperdal) (metabolized to Paliperidone) 1996 Olanzapine (Zyprexa) 1997 Quetiapine (Seroquel) 2001 Ziprasidone (Geodon) 2002 Aripiprazole (Abilify)* 2006 Paliperidone (Invega) 2009 Asenapine (Saphris) 2009 Iloperidone (Fanapt) 2010 Lurasidone (Latuda) 2015 Brexpiprazole (Rexulti)* 2016 Cariprazine (Vraylar)* 2017 Pimavanserin (Nuplazid) - does not block DA 2020 Lumateperone (Caplyta) *D2 dopamine receptor partial agonists
Prolactin elevation ▶ gynecomastia ▶ galactorrhea ▶ sexual dysfunction ▶ osteopenia	Dopamine is also known as "prolactin-inhibiting factor" because it suppresses release of prolactin from the pituitary. All of the FGAs may elevate prolactin, which may result in growth of breast tissue. Hyperprolactinemia is caused by all FGAs because they have a high affinity for the D2 receptor and, once bound, are slow to dissociate from the D2 receptor.	About half of the SGAs increase prolactin, most prominently risperidone and paliperidone. Those SGAs that do not elevate prolactin are those that dissociate quickly from the D2 receptor and easily cross the blood-brain barrier (BBB). The prolactin-elevating effect of antipsychotics occurs outside of the BBB. Risperidone does not cross the BBB easily, so relatively high serum concentrations are necessary to achieve a therapeutic drug level in the central nervous system.
Noteworthy class members	Intermediate potency FGAs have relatively low potential to cause EPS: loxapine (Loxitane), perphenazine (Trilafon), and molindone (Moban)	Lurasidone (Latuda) and ziprasidone (Geodon) do not cause weight gain and may also lower lipids and blood sugar. Aripiprazole (Abilify) suppresses prolactin release.

D2 Receptor Partial Agonists – "Dopamine Stabilizers"

Mnemonic: "ABC"

D2 partial agonist	~ cost	Weight gain	Akathisia	Somnolence	Advantages
<u>A</u>ripiprazole ABILIFY	$20	+	++	+	Inexpensive as PO. Available in long-acting injectable formulations, which are about $2,000/mo (100x the cost of PO)
<u>B</u>rexpiprazole REXULTI	$1,200	++	+	+/-	Better tolerability and probably anxiolytic properties
<u>C</u>ariprazine VRAYLAR	$1,200	+/-	+++	-	Also a D3 partial agonist, which may contribute cognitive benefits and improvement of negative symptoms

An agonist is a chemical that binds to a receptor and activates it to produce a biological response. Partial agonists can act either as a functional agonist or a functional antagonist, depending on the surrounding levels of naturally occurring neurotransmitters (the full agonist being dopamine, in this case). Partial D2 agonists can serve as "dopamine stabilizers", providing functional antagonism in hyper-DA states and functional agonism in hypo-DA states.

Dopamine Neural Pathways

Dopamine Pathway	Effect of D2 antagonist	Effect of D2 partial agonist
Mesolimbic	↓ DA activity - reduction of positive symptoms of schizophrenia (hallucinations, delusions)	↓ DA activity
Mesocortical	↓ DA - potential worsening of negative symptoms (amotivation, anhedonia, blunting of affect)	↑ DA - potential improvement of negative symptoms; Possibility of hypersexuality or pathologic gambling
Nigrostriatal	↓ DA - EPS, risk of tardive dyskinesia	Akathisia is common, but low risk of tardive dyskinesia
Tuberoinfundibular	↓ DA - increased prolactin, risk of breast growth (gynecomastia)	↑ DA - decreased prolactin, no risk of gynecomastia

#Rx	Generic/TRADE	Cost	Potency	mg	Minimal effective	FDA 24 hr max	Dose range	Comments
#1	Haloperidol HALDOL	$11	High	0.5 1 2 5 10 20	4 mg total daily dose	100 mg too high	2–10 mg PO BID; 5–10 mg IM q 4 hr PRN; Decanoate 100–300 mg IM q month	Effective and inexpensive. Available as q 4 wk long-acting injectable (LAI), Haldol Decanoate. Short-acting intramuscular Haldol is commonly administered ($2) for acute agitation. Tardive dyskinesia is a major risk at high doses. FDA-approved for Tourette's syndrome. No weight gain. Drug of choice for delirium because it lacks significant anticholinergic effects.
#2	Chlorpromazine THORAZINE	$135	Low	10 25 50 100 200	200 mg total daily dose	1,000 mg too high	25–100 mg PO TID 25–50 IM q 4 hr PRN	Causes sedation, orthostatic hypotension, and photosensitivity. At high doses it can cause blue/grey pigmentation of skin and eyes. Relatively unlikely to cause TD. FDA-approved for intractable hiccups; Available IM.
#3	Perphenazine TRILAFON	$33	Med	2 4 8 16	20 mg total daily dose	64 mg	8–16 mg BID–QID	Perphenazine was the FGA used in the CATIE trial against SGAs. It has low EPS similar to an SGA. It is a vulnerable 2D6 substrate, subject to more interactions than other medium potency FGAs.
#4	Fluphenazine PROLIXIN	$50	High	1 2.5 5 10	4 mg total daily dose	40 mg too high	2.5–5 mg TID; Decanoate 25–50 mg IM q 3–6 wk	Similar to haloperidol. Available as fluphenazine decanoate (Prolixin-D) q 3 to 6 wk long-acting injectable (LAI).
#5	Thiothixene NAVANE	$34	High	1 2 5 10 20	8 mg total daily dose	60 mg too high	2–5 mg BID–TID	Smokers need higher dose because thiothixene is a 1A2 substrate. Antidepressant properties; Minimal anticholinergic effects, as expected for a high potency FGA; Slow onset of tranquilizing effect, 90 minutes.
#6	Loxapine LOXITANE	$16	Med	5 10 25 50	20 mg total daily dose	250 mg	10–50 mg PO TID Adasuve 10 mg inhaled q 24 hr PRN	In addition to blocking D2 receptors, loxapine is the only FGA that blocks serotonin 5-HT_{2A} receptors with sufficient affinity to behave like an SGA. Metabolized to the tetracyclic antidepressant amoxapine. No weight gain and minimal relevant kinetic interactions. Risk of cardiotoxicity and seizures with overdose. Available as ADASUVE inhalation powder since 2014.
#7	Trifluoperazine STELAZINE	$34	High	1 2 5 10	10 mg total daily dose	40 mg too high	2–5 mg BID	Stelazine's marketing slogan was "Calm, but still alert." FDA-approved for schizophrenia and non-psychotic anxiety. Rarely used because, while other high potency FGAs have multiple routes of delivery, Stelazine is only is available PO.
#8	Thioridazine MELLARIL	$19	Low	10 25 50 100	200 mg total daily dose	800 mg too high	50–100 mg TID	Rarely prescribed because it causes the most QT prolongation of all psychotropics. Also, it can cause irreversible retinal pigmentation and degenerative retinopathy > 800 mg. Risk of seizures. It is effective for anxiety, and safe if the dose is kept low.
#9	Pimozide ORAP	$60	High	1 2	4 mg total daily dose	10 mg too high	1–2 mg QD–BID	Approved for Tourette's syndrome only. Risky due to QT prolongation and susceptibility to interactions as a 2D6 and 3A4 substrate.
#10	Molindone MOBAN	$75	Med	5 10 25	20 mg total daily dose	225 mg	10–25 mg TID	Approved for schizophrenia only; Causes weight loss; short half-life of 1.5 hours; Of available antipsychotics, molindone is the least prescribed.

FGAs

12

Antiemetics that block D2 receptors

D2 blocking antiemetic	Cost	Potency	mg	Usual dose	Comments
Promethazine PHENERGAN	$8	Low	12.5 25 50	25 mg TID PRN	Much to weak of a D2 blocker to be used as an antipsychotic. Effectiveness as an antiemetic is mostly due to antihistamine activity. Approved for allergic conditions, motion sickness, nausea/vomiting, sedation, and urticaria.
Prochlorperazine COMPAZINE	$8	High	5 10	5–10 mg TID PRN	GoodRx lists Compazine as the #1 prescribed FGA, but today it is almost exclusively prescribed as an antiemetic. High risk of EPS, similar to haloperidol. It has old FDA approvals for schizophrenia and non-psychotic anxiety (12 wk max). Rectal formulation available.
Metoclopramide REGLAN	$6	High	5 10	10 mg QID PRN	High potency D2 blocker but not approved for psychosis. Black box warning for tardive dyskinesia. FDA-approved for GERD, diabetic gastroparesis, nausea/vomiting, small bowel intubation, and radiologic exam.

Side effect profile according to potency (of D2 blockade)

Potency	Trade (BRAND)	ACh	QT	↓ BP	↑ PRL	↑ Wt	EPS	NMS	Comments
Low	Chlorpromazine (THORAZINE) Thioridazine (MELLARIL) Promethazine (PHENERGAN)	+++	++	+++	++	++	++	+	Antihistamine properties
Medium	Loxapine (LOXITANE) Molindone (MOBAN) Perphenazine (TRILAFON)	++	-	++	++	-	+	+	EPS risk is similar to 2nd generation antipsychotics (SGAs).
High	Haloperidol (HALDOL) Fluphenazine (PROLIXIN) Pimozide (ORAP) Thiothixene (NAVANE) Trifluoperazine (STELAZINE) Prochlorperazine (COMPAZINE)	+	-	+	++	-	++++	+++	Pimozide causes less EPS than the other high potency FGAs.

Minimal effective = dose per 24 hours considered necessary to adequately treat first-episode schizophrenia; Potency = D2 blockade; LAI = long-acting injectable; ACh = anticholinergic (constipation, urinary retention, dry mouth); QT = QT interval prolongation; ↓ BP = orthostatic hypotension; ↑ PRL = prolactin elevation (gynecomastia, sexual side effects); ↑ Wt = weight gain; NMS = neuroleptic malignant syndrome

#243
1967
$12–$32

Haloperidol (HALDOL)

hal oh PER i dawl / HAL dawl

"Halo doll"

- ❖ Antipsychotic
- ❖ High potency FGA
- ❖ D2 antagonist

0.5
1
2
5
10
20
mg

FDA-approved for:
- ❖ Psychosis
- ❖ Tourette's disorder

Used off-label for:
- ❖ Agitation/aggression
- ❖ Delirium
- ❖ Mania
- ❖ Gastroparesis

This book uses spooky pictures for antipsychotic medications, because they are used to treat paranoid delusions and hallucinations.

Haloperidol (Haldol) is a High potency 1st generation antipsychotic (FGA), approved in 1967. It remains the most prescribed FGA, mainly used for chronic schizophrenia and acute aggression. Haloperidol is cheap and effective, but it commonly causes extrapyramidal symptoms (EPS). Due to high risk of tardive dyskinesia (TD), it is not a first-line maintenance antipsychotic. It is a reasonable third-line option when two SGAs have failed. Haldol does not cause weight gain. It can be used to augment a 2nd generation antipsychotic (SGA) at low dose.

Intramuscular haloperidol was once essential for treating acute agitation and aggression. IM Haldol is still regarded as a first-line option as a PRN for this purpose. Haloperidol immediate-release injections are inexpensive ($2) and are commonly used in combination with IM lorazepam (Ativan) and/or IM diphenhydramine (Benadryl). Health care professionals widely refer to an injection consisting of Haldol 5 mg and Ativan 2 mg as a "five and two".

A combination of a "five and two" (mixed in one syringe) plus a separate syringe containing Benadryl 50 mg is known as a "B-52". The B-52 is reserved for highly agitated patients who have high tolerance for sedative medication. In addition to sedation, the benzodiazepine (lorazepam) and antihistamine (diphenhydramine) serve to prevent haloperidol-induced akathisia and dystonia. Short-term use of haloperidol does not cause Parkinsonism or TD. Haldol is a drug of choice for acute delirium due to lack of anticholinergic activity.

Prolongation of QT interval with haloperidol can be prominent when administered intravenously. QT prolongation from oral haloperidol is generally insignificant, except in overdose.

The FDA max is 100 mg, which today is considered much too high, and very likely to cause TD with prolonged use. Anyone needing that much haloperidol would be better served by clozapine (Clozaril), which does not cause TD.

To prevent dystonia, the author usually adds the anticholinergic benztropine (Cogentin) 0.5 mg BID (for the short term) if the haloperidol dose is increased to 5 mg BID. EPS is caused by a relative deficiency of dopamine and an excess of acetylcholine in the nigrostriatal pathway. Benztropine may be needed to prevent dystonia because haloperidol has no intrinsic anticholinergic activity. After a month or so, try to taper benztropine or change it to PRN. Long-term use of anticholinergics can increase risk of TD and contribute to negative symptoms (amotivation, anhedonia, blunting of affect).

Dosing:

Haldol 2 mg PO is considered the "minimal effective" daily dose for first-episode psychosis. For multi-episode psychosis, the minimal effective dose is 4 mg. For PO haloperidol for maintenance treatment, the author usually starts 2.5 mg BID, which is half of a 5 mg tab. 10 mg BID is a reasonable maximum dose.

Haloperidol decanoate (Haldol D) is a long-acting injectable (LAI) given every 4 weeks. 100 mg every 4 weeks is equivalent to about 7–10 mg daily oral dose. Don't exceed 100 mg with the first injection and extend the PO dose for a 2-week overlap. FDA max is 450 mg/mo, which is equivalent to about 30–45 mg of a daily PO dose, although it is recommended not to exceed 200 mg monthly. The drug is in a oil suspension, which makes it more painful than other LAIs. It may leave a bump under the skin that can take weeks to resolve. Haloperidol decanoate costs about $50 monthly, much cheaper than the available 2nd generation LAI antipsychotics. See also page 160 for all LAIs.

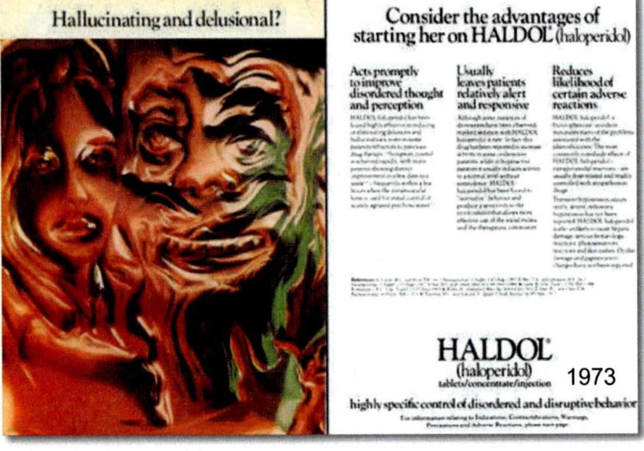

Dynamic interactions:
- ❖ Dopamine antagonist (strong)
- ❖ Extrapyramidal effects (high)
- ❖ Sedation/CNS depression
- ❖ QT prolongation (moderate)
- ❖ Hypotensive
- ❖ Lowers seizure threshold (mild)
- ❖ Prolactin elevating (strong)
- ❖ Hyponatremia
- ❖ Hyperammonemia

Kinetic interactions:
- ❖ 3A4 substrate
- ❖ 2D6 substrate
- ❖ 1A2 substrate (minor)

page 16

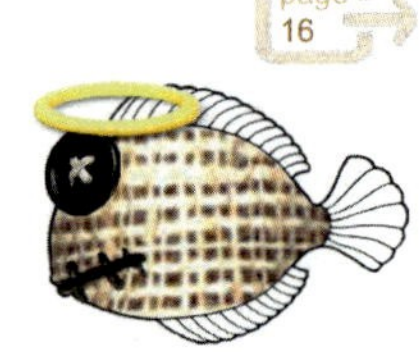

3A4 substrate

page 15

2D6 substrate

page 10

HALDOL

1A2 substrate (minor)

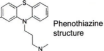

1954
$62–$157

Phenothiazine structure

Chlorpromazine (THORAZINE)

klawr PRO muh zeen / THOR a zeen

"Thor's Color promising" (to change)

- Antipsychotic
- Low potency FGA
- D2 antagonist
- 5-HT_2 antagonist
- Phenothiazine

10
25
50
100
200
mg

FDA-approved for:
- Psychosis
- Nausea/Vomiting
- Intractable hiccups
- Adjunct treatment of tetanus (IM)
- Acute intermittent porphyria (IM)

Used off-label for:
- Behavioral disturbance (IM or PO)
- Impulse control disorders
- Serotonin Syndrome, adjunct (IM)
- Anxiety (low dose)
- Insomnia (low dose)

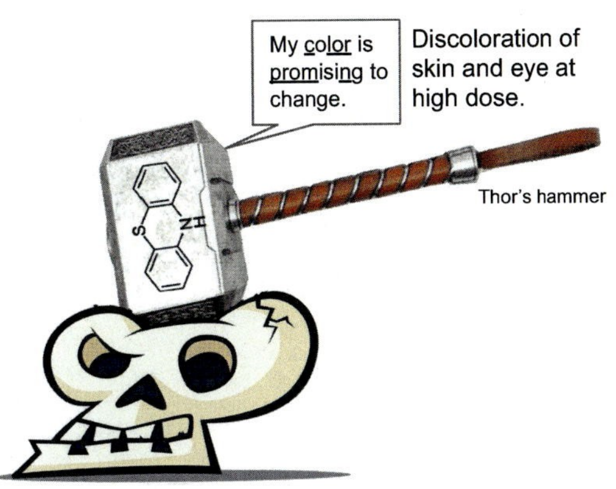
My color is promising to change.
Discoloration of skin and eye at high dose.
Thor's hammer

Antipsychotics are represented with spooky mascots.

Specific risks:
- ▶ Photosensitivity (common, phenothiazine class)
- ▶ Pigmentation of skin
- ▶ Pigmentation of eye (benign, unless the retina is involved)
- ▶ Corneal epithelial keratopathy (benign deposits in cornea)
- ▶ Corneal edema (with possible irreversible vision loss)

Phenothiazine structure
page 138

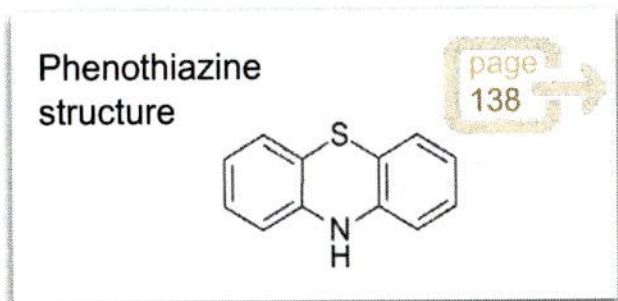

Chlorpromazine (Thorazine) is a low potency FGA—think *ch-lower-promazine*. In 1954, Thorazine revolutionized psychiatry. It largely replaced electroconvulsive therapy, hydrotherapy, psychosurgery (prefrontal lobotomy), and insulin shock therapy. In the 1950s it was used for almost every psychiatric condition, including anxiety and emotional distress associated with almost any medical condition.

Chlorpromazine is an example of a "dirty drug", one that antagonizes several types of receptors (dopaminergic, histaminergic, muscarinic, serotonergic). Thorazine's antihistamine activity contributes prominently to its sedative effect and made it useful in the 1950s for treatment of pruritus and peptic ulcers. Chlorpromazine has been described as possible therapy for serotonin syndrome, based on its antiserotonergic effect.

Although blamed for the "Thorazine Shuffle", chlorpromazine is much less likely to cause Parkinsonism than high potency neuroleptics like haloperidol (Haldol) or fluphenazine (Prolixin). Run a Google image search for *parkinson gait gif* to see what the shuffle looks like.

Currently chlorpromazine is more expensive than the other FGAs. This may be the result of price fixing by the pharmaceutical industry. In 2019, 44 states filed a lawsuit alleging major drug manufacturers conspired to artificially inflate the prices of more than 100 generic drugs. Goodrx.com is a great resource for keeping up with current prices at individual pharmacies.

Dosing: These days, Thorazine is rarely used as monotherapy for schizophrenia. More commonly it is used for anxiety or agitation at low doses (25–100 mg). It is dosed similarly to the SGA quetiapine (Seroquel), which is also a weak antipsychotic that works well for insomnia or anxiety. The FDA max dose is 1,000 mg/day (divided TID–QID), although doses exceeding 400 mg/day may lead to eye problems and skin discoloration.

Chlorpromazine is the only FGA that significantly lowers seizure threshold. There are three SGAs with a higher risk of seizures than chlorpromazine.

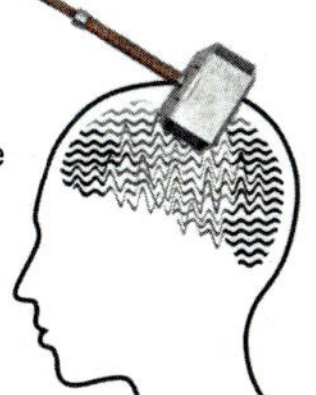

Seizure risk among Antipsychotics (dose-dependent):

#1 Clozapine (Clozaril) up to 10x risk
#2 Olanzapine (Zyprexa) 3x
#3 Quetiapine (Seroquel) 2x
#4 Chlorpromazine (Thorazine) 2x

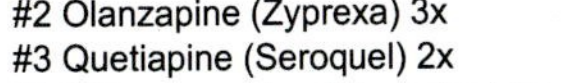

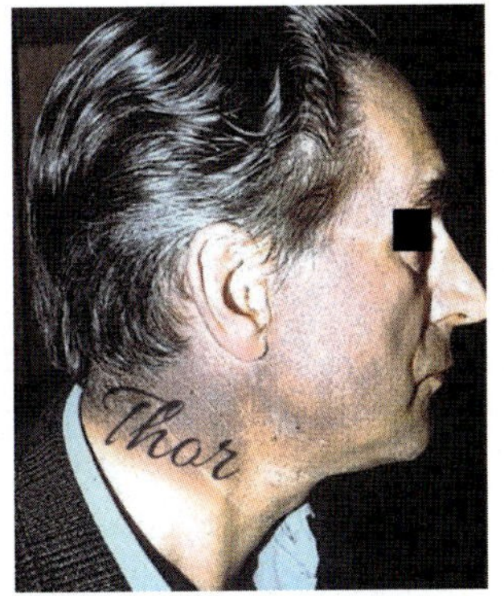
Thor

Some patients taking high-dose Thorazine develop a progressive blue-gray or purple discoloration in sun-exposed areas of the skin, with sparing of facial wrinkles. Pigmentation may involve sun-exposed portions of the eye. Thankfully, this condition is reversible.

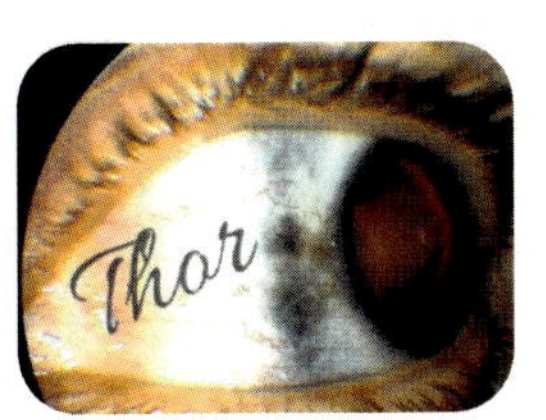
Thor

Corneal epithelial keratopathy caused by high dose thorazine. *Cornea verticillata* is the term for the whorl-like deposition of material in the corneal epithelium. The phenomenon is benign and reversible.

Dynamic interactions:
- Dopamine antagonist
- Extrapyramidal effects
- Sedation/CNS depression (strong)
- QT prolongation (moderate)
- Hypotensive (strong)
- Anticholinergic (strong)
- Lowers seizure threshold (significant)
- Prolactin elevating
- Hyponatremia
- Hyperglycemia
- Photosensitivity (phenothiazine)

Kinetic interactions:
- 2D6 substrate, like most phenothiazines
- 1A2 substrate (minor)
- 3A4 substrate (minor)

page 15

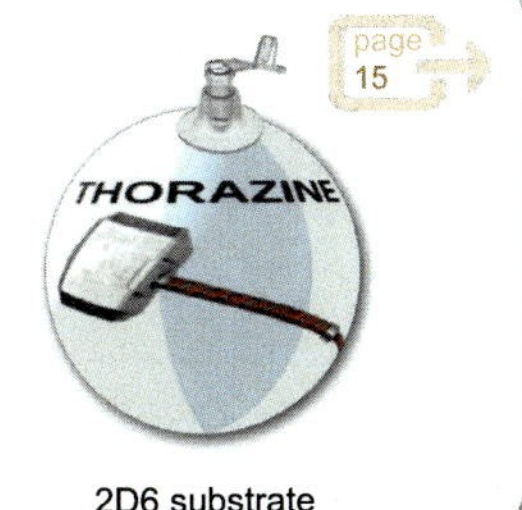
THORAZINE

2D6 substrate

Logo resembling phenothiazine structure

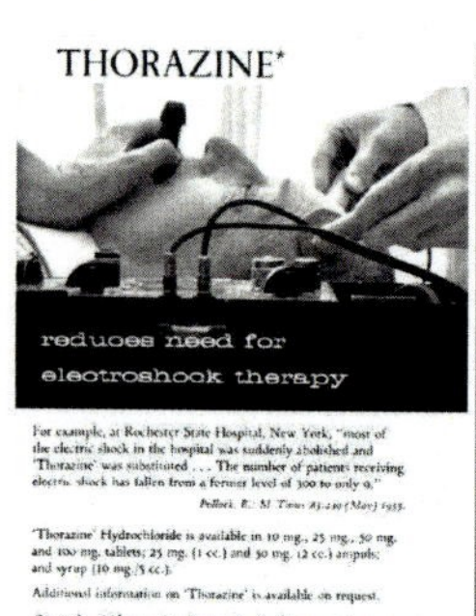

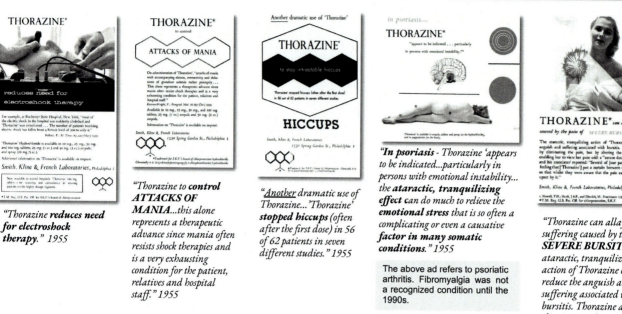

"Thorazine ***reduces need for electroshock therapy.****" 1955*

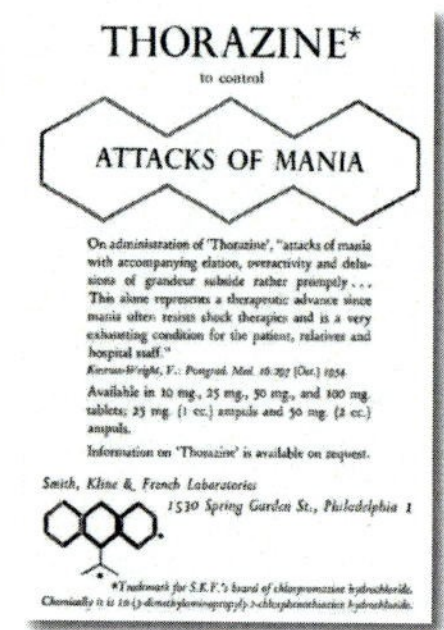

"Thorazine to ***control ATTACKS OF MANIA****...this alone represents a therapeutic advance since mania often resists shock therapies and is a very exhausting condition for the patient, relatives and hospital staff." 1955*

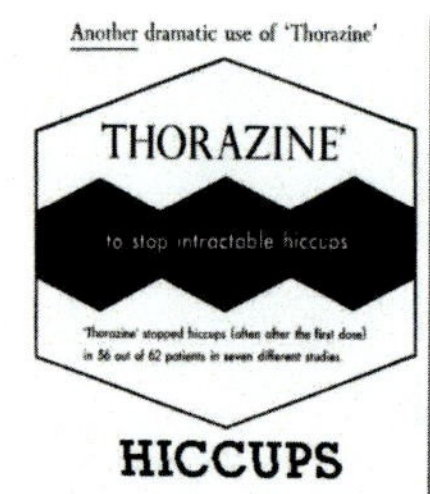

"Another dramatic use of Thorazine...'Thorazine' ***stopped hiccups*** *(often after the first dose) in 56 of 62 patients in seven different studies." 1955*

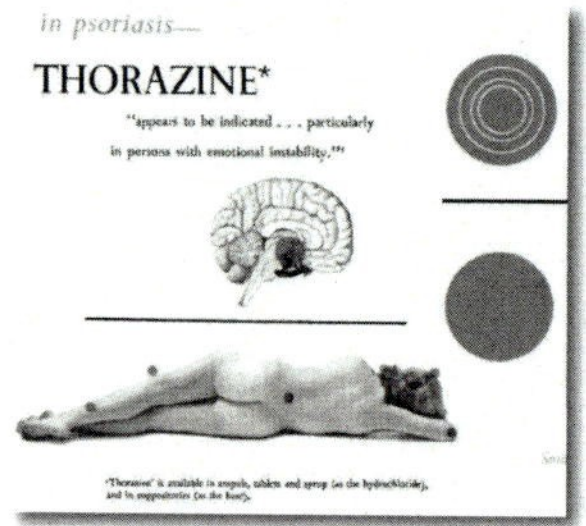

"In psoriasis *- Thorazine 'appears to be indicated...particularly in persons with emotional instability... the* ***ataractic, tranquilizing effect*** *can do much to relieve the* ***emotional stress*** *that is so often a complicating or even a causative* ***factor in many somatic conditions.****" 1955*

The above ad refers to psoriatic arthritis. Fibromyalgia was not a recognized condition until the 1990s.

"Thorazine can allay the suffering caused by the pain of ***SEVERE BURSITIS.*** *The ataractic, tranquilizing action of Thorazine can reduce the anguish and suffering associated with bursitis. Thorazine acts not by eliminating the pain, but by altering the patient's reaction -* ***enabling her to view her pain with a 'serene detachment'...*** *'Several of [our patients] expressed the feeling that ['Thorazine'] put a curtain between them and their pain, so that whilst they were aware that the pain existed, they were not upset by it.'" 1956*

"In the ***child with a behavior disorder*** *Thorazine reduces hyperactivity and aggressiveness; decreases anxiety and hostility; improves mood, behavior and sleeping habits;* ***establishes*** *accessibility to guidance or psychotherapy;* ***increases amenability to supervision****...bear in mind– 'Thorazine' may give the impression of a cure, simultaneous supportive counseling and guidance are necessary... 'Thorazine' should be administered discriminantly." 1956*

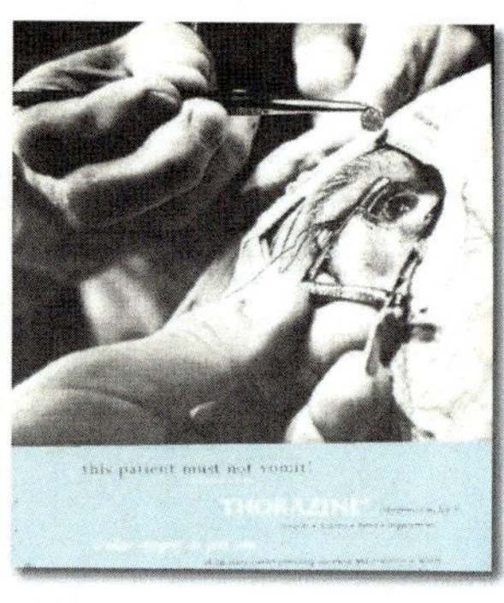

"This patient must not vomit! *Ocular surgery is just one of the many emesis-provoking situations and conditions...drugs, radiation, disease, pregnancy..." 1956*

"Thorazine helps ***keep more patients out of mental hospitals****...more patients can be treated in the community, at clinics or in the psychiatrist's office without being hospitalized at all." 1956*

THORAZINE*
can help your patients to endure the suffering caused by
severe pain
for example: in burns

"Thorazine's ***tranquilizing action*** *can reduce the suffering caused by the pain of severe burns... Thorazine produced 'a* ***quiet, phlegmatic acceptance of pain.****'" 1956*

"Severe asthma *is usually aggravated and prolonged by a strong emotional overlay... Thorazine promptly alleviates the emotional stress which may precipitate, aggravate or prolong an asthmatic attack. It enables the patient to sleep, yet does not depress respiration". 1958*

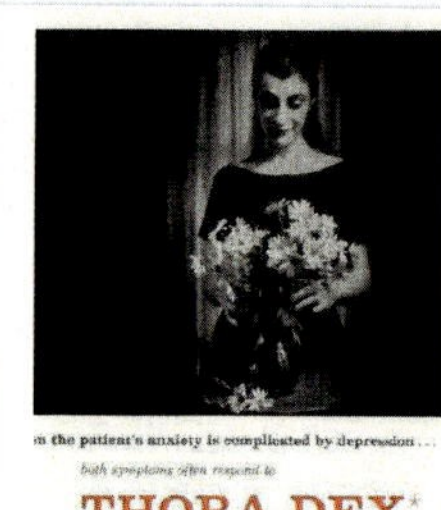

The combination of Thorazine & Dexedrine (dextroamphetamine) is no longer available. Anxious depression is no longer treated with an antipsychotic plus a Schedule II stimulant. Such combinations (as separate pills) are still used for hyperactive ADHD. The most prescribed antipsychotic for behaviorally disordered children is now risperidone (Risperdal). Dexedrine is similar to Adderall (mixed amphetamine salts).

"When the patient's anxiety is complicated by depression... both symptoms often respond to THORA-DEX, a combination of a specific ***anti-anxiety agent, 'Thorazine'****, and* ***a standard antidepressant, 'Dexedrine'****. The preparation is of unusual value in mental and emotional disturbances and in somatic conditions complicated by emotional stress - especially when depression occurs together with anxiety, agitation or apprehension. The patient treated with 'Thora-Dex' is generally both calm and alert...with normal interest, activity and capacity for work...Thora-Dex should be administered discriminantly." 1957*

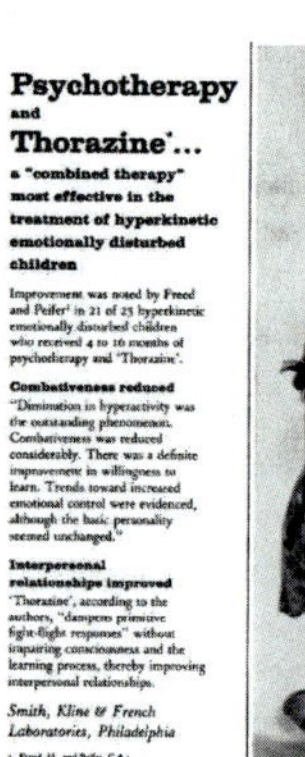

"Psychotherapy and Thorazine...a 'combined therapy' most effective in the treatment of ***hyperkinetic emotionally disturbed children****...Diminution in hyperactivity was the outstanding phenomenon." 1957*

"Doctor, what can you do for Pop?" 1957

Vintage Thorazine ads from physicians' journals

'One of the fundamental drugs in medicine' - Smith, Kline & French laboratories

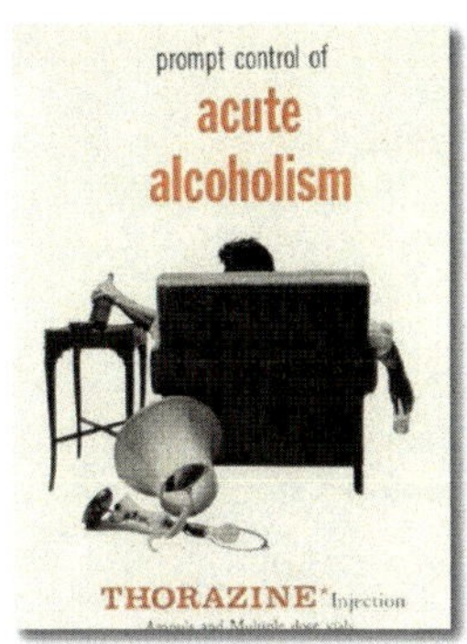

"Prompt control of acute alcoholism. Thorazine injection." 1959

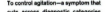

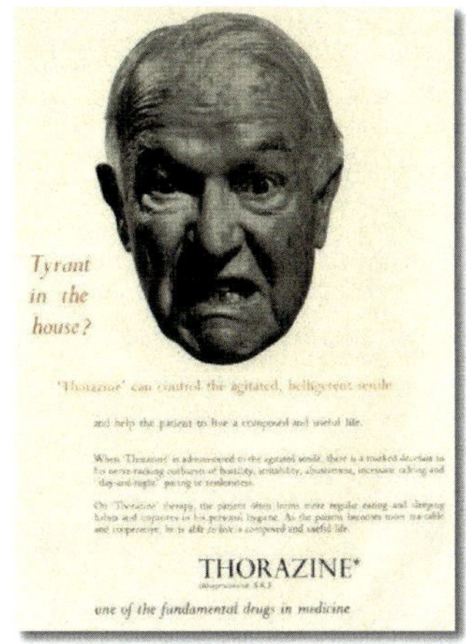

*"**Tyrant in the house?** Thorazine can control **the agitated, belligerent senile** and help the patient to **live a composed and useful life.** Thorazine, one of the fundamental drugs in medicine". 1959*

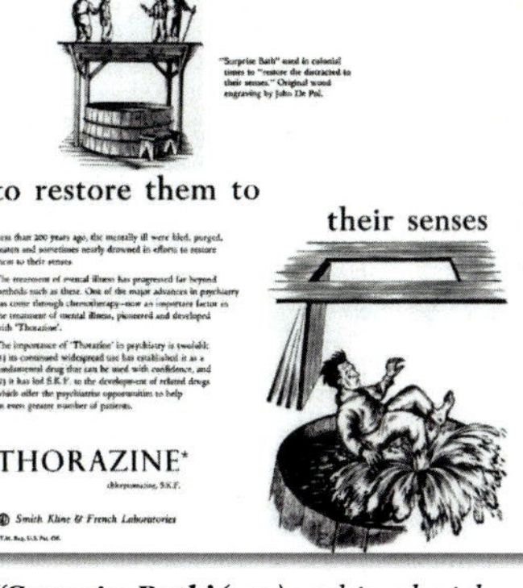

*"'**Surprise Bath'** (was) used in colonial times to **'restore the distracted to their senses.'** Less than 200 years ago, the mentally ill were bled, purged, beaten and sometimes nearly drowned...the treatment of mental illness has progressed far beyond...with chemotherapy... pioneered and developed with Thorazine." 1959*

*"**To free the mind from madness** - in nineteenth century psychiatry, **the 'rotator'** was a major therapeutic device. Today, psychopharmacologic therapy, pioneered and developed with Thorazine, is one of the most important methods used in the treatment of mental illness." 1959*

*"To control **agitation**—a symptom that cuts across diagnostic categories...Thorazine, a fundamental drug in psychiatry...Because of its **sedative** effect, Thorazine is especially useful in controlling hyperactivity, irritability and hostility." 1960*

All antipsychotics now have a black box warning: "Not approved for dementia-related psychosis; **increased mortality risk in elderly dementia patients.**"

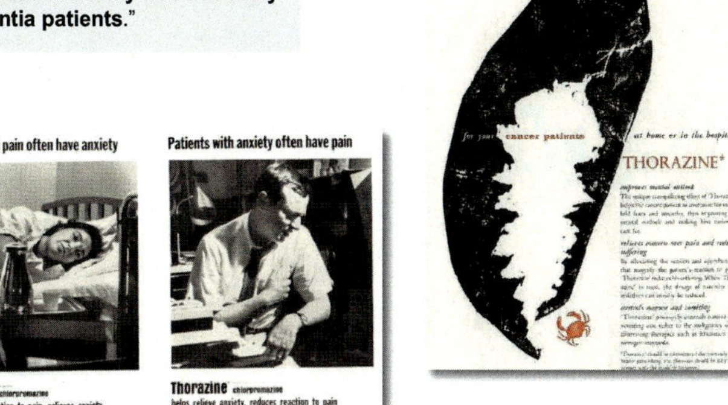

*"Patients with pain often have anxiety. Patients with anxiety often have pain. Thorazine helps **reduce reaction to pain, relieves anxiety.**" 1960*

Today, the antiepileptic drug gabapentin (Neurontin) is used for various co-presentations of pain and anxiety.

*"For your **cancer patients**, at home or in the hospital. Thorazine **improves mental outlook**. The **unique tranquilizing effect** of Thorazine helps the cancer patient to overcome his manifold fears and anxieties, thus improving his mental outlook and making him easier to care for...Thorazine reduces his suffering." 1961*

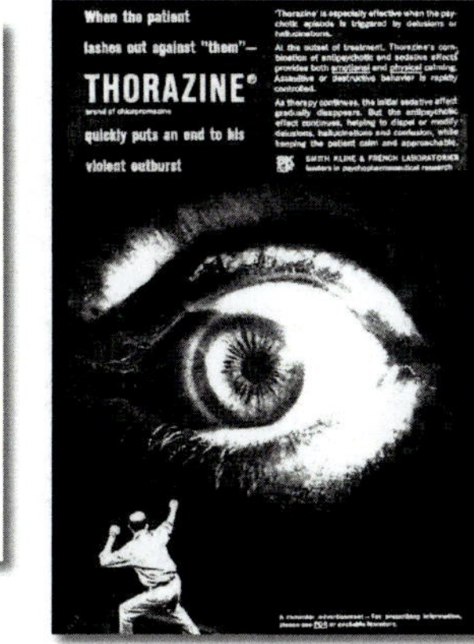

*"**When the patient lashes out against 'them'**— Thorazine quickly puts an end to his violent outburst." 1962*

*"**Restraint Closet - remember these?** About 13 years ago, Thorazine helped make them obsolete. In psychiatry, Thorazine remains **today's most widely prescribed ataractic...** Contraindication: Comatose states or the presence of large amounts of C.N.S. depressant; Precaution: Antiemetic effect may mask signs of overdosage of toxic drugs or obscure diagnosis of other conditions; Side Effect: **Parkinsonism-like symptoms on high dosages (in rare instances, may persist).**" 1967*

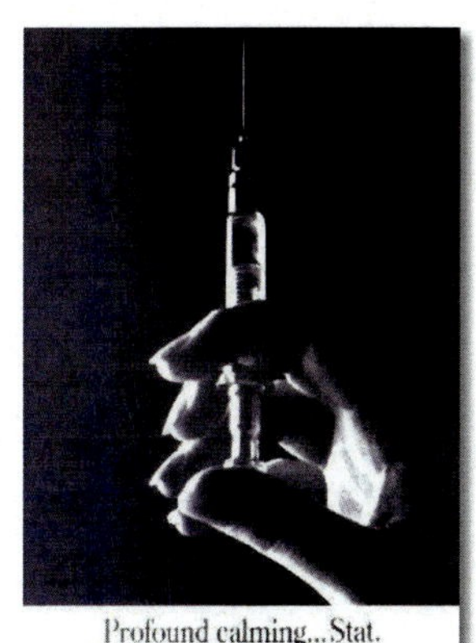

*"**Profound calming**...Stat." 1968*

HELPS KEEP THE REAL IN REALITY
THORAZINE
CHLORPROMAZINE

"Helps keep the real in reality." 1973

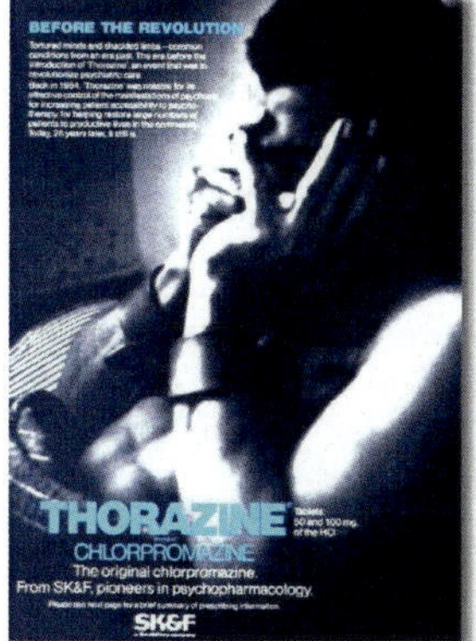

*"**Before the revolution...** Tortured minds and shackled limbs—common conditions from an era past. The era before the introduction of Thorazine, an event that was to revolutionize psychiatric care." 1982*

1957
$31–$115

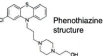

Phenothiazine structure

Perphenazine (TRILAFON)

per FEN uh zeen / TRIL uh fon

"Perple Trial phone"

- ❖ Antipsychotic
- ❖ Medium potency FGA
- ❖ D2 antagonist
- ❖ Phenothiazine

2
4
8
16
mg

FDA-approved for:
- ❖ Schizophrenia
- ❖ Nausea/vomiting

Antipsychotics are represented with spooky mascots.

Perphenazine (Trilafon) was the first generation antipsychotic (FGA) included in the CATIE schizophrenia trial (Lieberman et al, 2005), which compared it to several second generation antipsychotics (SGAs)—olanzapine (Zyprexa), risperidone (Risperdal), quetiapine (Seroquel), and ziprasidone (Geodon). Perphenazine showed comparable effectiveness and caused no more EPS than these SGAs. Perphenazine was no less effective in improving cognitive performance than the SGAs. Although these four SGAs are now affordable, they were much more expensive when the CATIE trial was conducted. Olanzapine, risperidone, and quetiapine are now cheaper than perphenazine.

When choosing a medium potency FGA, the author prefers loxapine (Loxitane) over perphenazine because loxapine has fewer relevant kinetic interactions. Perphenazine is such a susceptible 2D6 substrate that the FDA recommends 2D6 genotype testing before it is started, because levels will be increased 3-fold for 2D6 poor metabolizers.

Even though perphenazine's half-life is about 10 hours, maintenance dosing can be once daily. For antipsychotics in general, continuous dopamine D2 receptor blockade is not necessary to sustain antipsychotic response (Takeuchi et al, 2014).

Dosing: Suggested starting dose is 4 mg BID or TID. For maintenance treatment, once daily dosing is equally effective to BID–TID dosing. In the CATIE trial, patients received between 8–32 mg/day. FDA max is 24 mg/day for non-hospitalized patients. For hospitalized patients, the FDA max is 64 mg/day. Smokers and African Americans may need higher doses due to increased rate of clearance (Jin et al, 2010).

Perphenazine is available in a fixed-dose combo with the antidepressant amitriptyline (Elavil), branded as TRIAVIL. The combo is FDA-approved for (1) depression with anxiety and (2) psychosis with depression. Available since 1963, it is rarely used today.

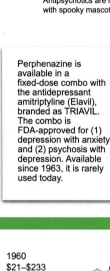

Dynamic interactions:
- ❖ Dopamine antagonist
- ❖ Extrapyramidal effects
- ❖ Sedation/CNS depression
- ❖ Hypotensive
- ❖ Anticholinergic (moderate)
- ❖ Lowers seizure threshold (mild)
- ❖ Prolactin elevating
- ❖ Hyponatremia
- ❖ Hyperglycemia
- ❖ Photosensitivity (phenothiazine)

Kinetic interactions:
- ❖ 2D6 substrate, like most phenothiazines
- ❖ FDA recommends 2D6 genotyping prior to starting perphenazine, levels of which are increased 3-fold for 2D6 poor metabolizers

page 15

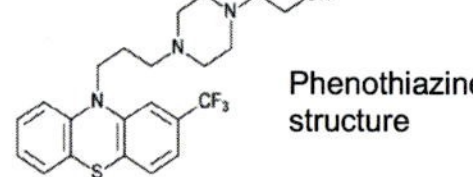

2D6 substrate (major)

1960
$21–$233

Phenothiazine structure

Fluphenazine (PROLIXIN)

flu FEN uh zeen / pro LIK sin

"Prolix Floppy hen"

- ❖ Antipsychotic
- ❖ High potency FGA
- ❖ D2 antagonist
- ❖ Phenothiazine

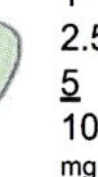

1
2.5
5
10
mg

FDA-approved for:
- ❖ Psychosis.

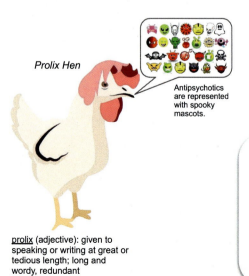

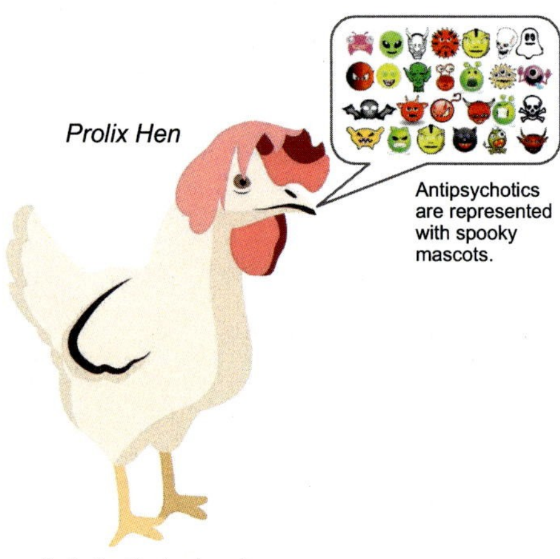

Antipsychotics are represented with spooky mascots.

prolix (adjective): given to speaking or writing at great or tedious length; long and wordy, redundant

"Prolix hen"—Prolixin (fluphenazine) is a high potency FGA. Prolixin's only FDA-approved indication is psychosis. It is very similar to haloperidol (Haldol). As a high potency D2 blocker, fluphenazine causes significant EPS including risk of tardive dyskinesia.

As with haloperidol, fluphenazine is available as a decanoate long-acting injectable (LAI). Fluconazole decanoate (Prolixin D) is given IM q 3 to 6 wk. It is also available as an oral liquid and immediate-release injectable.

Dosing: Start 1 mg TID. FDA max is 40 mg total daily dose, which is too high in most circumstances due to risk of tardive dyskinesia. A reasonable maintenance dose is 2.5 mg TID—5 mg TID. Stop if absolute neutrophil count (ANC) drops below 1,000. See page 160 for dosing of the long-acting injectable.

Dynamic interactions:
- ❖ Dopamine antagonist (strong)
- ❖ Extrapyramidal effects (high)
- ❖ Sedation/CNS depression
- ❖ Hypotensive
- ❖ Anticholinergic (moderate)
- ❖ Lowers seizure threshold (mild)
- ❖ Prolactin elevating (strong)
- ❖ Hyponatremia
- ❖ Hyperglycemia
- ❖ Photosensitivity (phenothiazine)

Kinetics interactions:
- ❖ 2D6 substrate, like most phenothiazines
- ❖ Relatively few relevant kinetic interactions

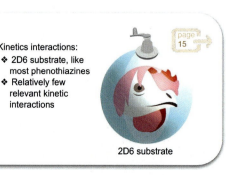

page 15

2D6 substrate

1967
$57 - $147

Thiothixene (NAVANE)

thye oh THIX een / NAH vane

"Thighs thick to Navel"

- ❖ Antipsychotic
- ❖ High potency FGA
- ❖ D2 antagonist

1
2
5
10
mg

FDA-approved for:

- ❖ Schizophrenia

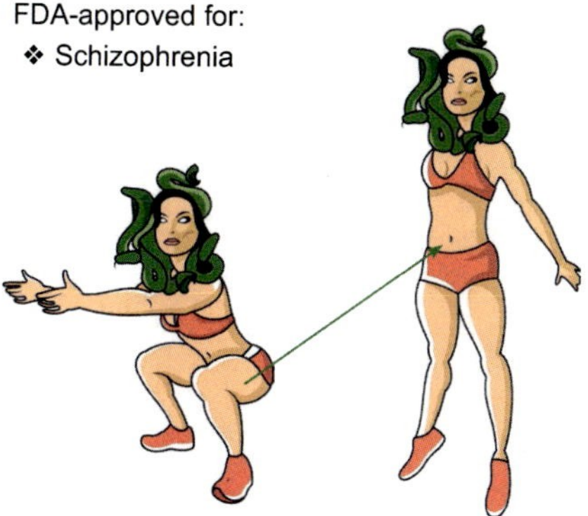

Antipsychotics are represented with spooky mascots.

Thiothixene (Navane) is a seldom prescribed first generation antipsychotic (FGA). It is <u>only available orally</u>, as a capsule. <u>High potency</u> FGA alternatives Haloperidol (Haldol) and fluphenazine (Prolixin) are each available in several formulations, including long-acting injectables. Thiothixene is not ideal for acute agitation because it takes 90 minutes to produce tranquilizing effect, which is slower than haloperidol or loxapine. When developed in the 1960s, thiothixene was also found to work as an antidepressant, but it is not used for that purpose. The only FDA-approved indication is for schizophrenia.

Dosing: According to the label, target dose is 2–5 mg BID–TID; The "minimal effective" dose to adequately treat first-episode schizophrenia is 8 mg/day; The label instructs to start 2 mg TID if mild/moderate psychosis; If severe psychosis, start 5 mg BID; FDA max is 60 mg/day, which is too high due to risk of tardive dyskinesia); It is best not to exceed 20 mg/day; Discontinue if absolute neutrophil count (ANC) drops below 1,000.

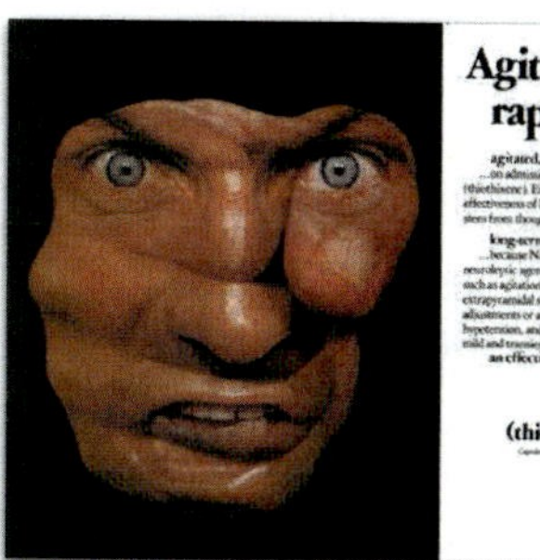

Agitation and hostility rapidly controlled
Navane
(thiothixene)(thiothixene HCl)

Dynamic interactions:

- ❖ Dopamine antagonist (strong)
- ❖ Extrapyramidal effects (high)
- ❖ Sedation/CNS depression
- ❖ Hypotensive
- ❖ Anticholinergic (mild)
- ❖ Lowers seizure threshold (mild)
- ❖ Prolactin elevating (strong)
- ❖ Hyponatremia

Kinetic interactions:

- ❖ 1A2 substrate
- ❖ Tobacco (1A2 in<u>D</u>ucer) lowers levels of thiothixene

page 10

1A2 substrate

1975
$21–$48

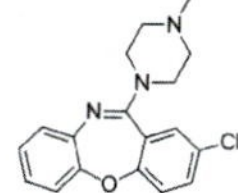

Loxapine (LOXITANE)

LOX a peen / LOX i tane

"Lots a' ping, Lots o' Tang"

- ❖ Antipsychotic
- ❖ Medium potency FGA
- ❖ D2 antagonist - ⇩ DA
- ❖ 5-HT$_{2A}$ antagonist - ⇧ DA

5
10
25
50
mg

FDA-approved for:

- ❖ Psychosis

Used off-label for:

- ❖ Bipolar mania

Loxapine (Loxitane) is a typical (1st generation) antipsychotic with atypical characteristics. In addition to blocking D2 receptors, loxapine <u>blocks serotonin 5-HT$_{2A}$ receptors as if it were a second generation</u> antipsychotic (SGA). Loxapine binds with higher affinity to <u>D4 receptors</u> than other dopaminergic receptors, similarly to clozapine. At high doses, loxapine has an adverse effects profile comparable to other FGAs. Loxapine <u>does not cause weight gain</u>. It is involved in fewer *clinically significant* interactions than most FGAs. Loxapine is metabolized to the tetracyclic antidepressant amoxapine (Asendin), which makes it more cardiotoxic in overdose than the average antipsychotic. In overdose, loxapine is likely to induce a seizure.

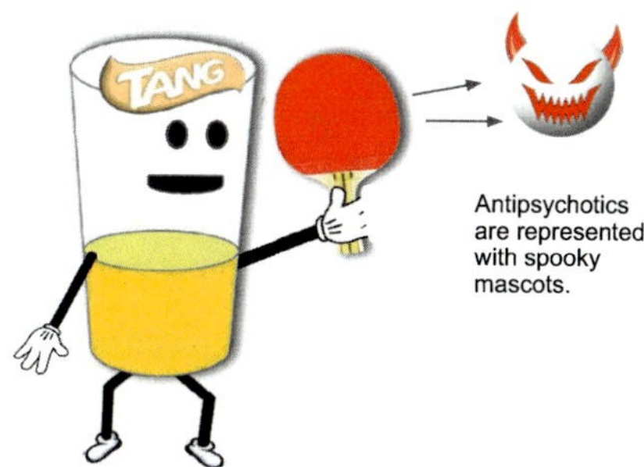

Antipsychotics are represented with spooky mascots.

Loxapine is the only psychotropic medication available <u>by inhalation</u>. ADASUVE, released in 2014, is a single-use disposable inhaler containing 10 mg of loxapine powder <u>approved for agitation</u> related to schizophrenia or bipolar I disorder. Adasuve has a black box warning of bronchospasm leading to respiratory distress and respiratory arrest. The inhaled product is rarely prescribed.

Dosing: The label instructs starting at 10 mg PO BID and titrating over 7-10 days; Severely disturbed patients may require starting dose of 25 mg BID; The "minimal effective dose" to adequately treat first-episode schizophrenia is 20 mg/day. FDA maximum total daily dose is 250 mg.

loxapine (antipsychotic) — metabolized to → amoxapine (antidepressant)

Dynamic interactions:

- ❖ Sedative
- ❖ Anticholinergic (moderate)
- ❖ Antidopaminergic (moderate)
- ❖ Extrapyramidal effects
- ❖ Hypotensive
- ❖ Prolactin elevating

Kinetic interactions:

- ❖ Substrate of 1A2, 2D6 and 3A4 (multi-CYP)
- ❖ Significant kinetic interactions are unlikely

page 18

in a box - relevant kinetic interactions are possible, but unlikely

1958 $64–$180	Phenothiazine structure	

Trifluoperazine (STELAZINE)

try floo uh PER uh zeen / STEL a zine

"Tri-flowered Stellation"

- ❖ Antipsychotic
- ❖ High potency FGA
- ❖ D2 antagonist
- ❖ 5-HT_2 antagonist
- ❖ Phenothiazine

1
<u>2</u>
5
10
mg

FDA-approved for:

- ❖ Schizophrenia
- ❖ Anxiety

Antipsychotics are represented with spooky mascots.

Trifluoperazine (Stelazine) is a <u>high potency antipsychotic like haloperidol</u>. Stelazine never gained much of a market share. It is only available as an oral tablet—no liquid or injectable formulations.

Stelazine was marketed to physicians in the 1970's as treatment for "<u>chronic neurotic anxiety</u>", a phrase which is out of use. The ads shown below imply doctors can prescribe Stelazine to "needy" patients in order to stop being bothered.

It was also marketed as "activating" and relatively non-sedating.

Due to risk of tardive dyskinesia, trifluoperazine is no longer prescribed for anxiety. Half-life is 18 hours.

Dosing: For any indication, start 1–2 mg BID; The "minimal effective dose" to adequately treat first-episode schizophrenia is 10 mg/day. For psychosis, the FDA maximum dose is 40 mg/day (which is too strong given the risk of tardive dyskinesia); For non-psychotic anxiety the max is 6 mg/day for 12 weeks; Discontinue if absolute neutrophil count (ANC) drops < 1,000.

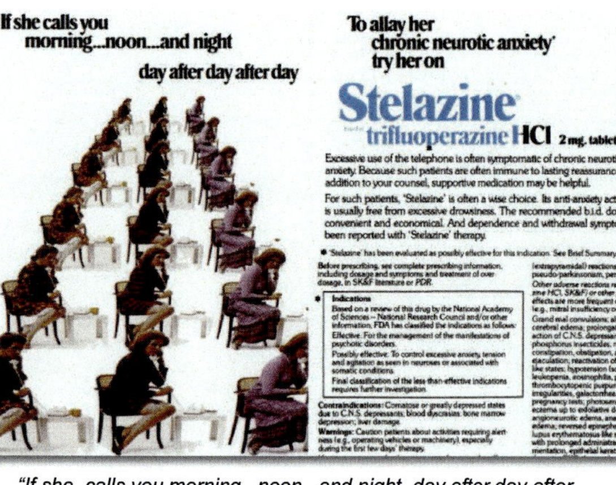

*"If she calls you morning...noon...and night, day after day after day. To **allay her chronic neurotic anxiety**, try her on Stelazine". 1973*

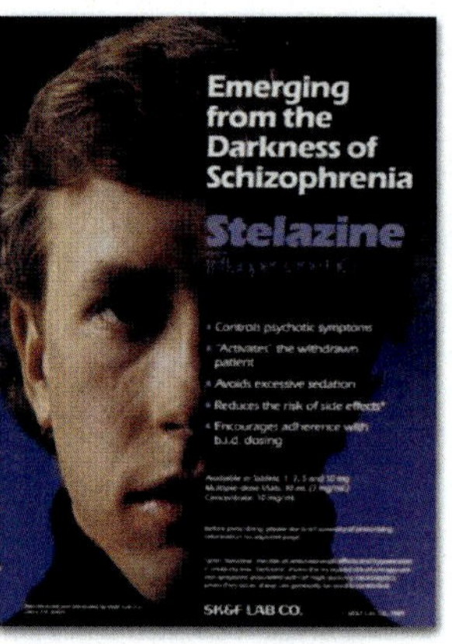

*"Emerging from the Darkness of Schizophrenia...Controls psychotic symptoms, **'Activates' the withdrawn patient**, Avoids excessive sedation." 1989*

*"You've talked...you've listened, **but here he is again**. To allay his chronic neurotic anxiety, try him on Stelazine." 1973*

The phenothiazines: drugs derived from phenothiazine

- ❖ Chlorpromazine (Thorazine)
- ❖ Flu<u>ph</u>enazine (Prolixin)
- ❖ Per<u>ph</u>enazine (Trilafon)
- ❖ Prochlorperazine (Compazine)
- ❖ Promethazine (<u>Ph</u>energan)
- ❖ Thioridazine (Mellaril)
- ❖ Trifluoperazine (Stelazine)

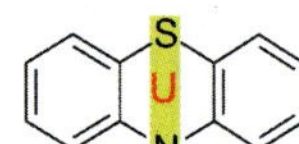

⇒ <u>Ph</u>enothiazines cause <u>ph</u>otosensitivity. <u>Ph</u>enothiazines cause <u>ph</u>otosensitivity. We added *U* to the to phenothiazine chemical structure to spell *SUN*.
⇒ Most are 2D6 substrates (not trifluoperazine)
⇒ Most are antipsychotics (not promethazine)

Dynamic interactions:

- ❖ Dopamine antagonist (strong)
- ❖ Extrapyramidal effects
- ❖ Sedation/CNS depression
- ❖ Hypotensive
- ❖ Anticholinergic (strong)
- ❖ Lowers seizure threshold (mild)
- ❖ Prolactin elevating (strong)
- ❖ Hyponatremia
- ❖ Hyperglycemia
- ❖ <u>Ph</u>otosensitivity (<u>ph</u>enothiazine)

Kinetic interactions:

- ❖ 1A2 substrate (minor)

page 10

1A2 substrate (minor)

1978
$13–$16

Phenothiazine structure

Thioridazine (MELLARIL)

thi uh RID uh zeen / MEL uh ril

"Mellow & Tired daze"

- ❖ Antipsychotic
- ❖ Low potency FGA
- ❖ D2 antagonist
- ❖ Phenothiazine

10
25
50
100
mg

FDA-approved for:

- ❖ Refractory schizophrenia

Used off-label for:

- ❖ Anxiety (low dose)

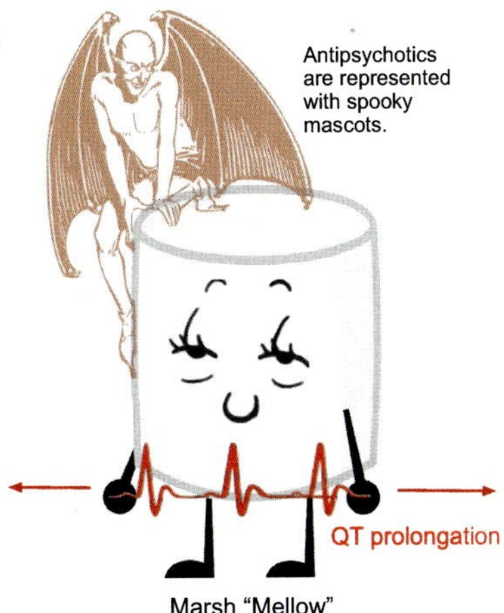
Antipsychotics are represented with spooky mascots.
QT prolongation
Marsh "Mellow"

Thioridazine (Mellaril) is approved for refractory schizophrenia only. Thioridazine is rarely prescribed due to the risk of cardiac arrhythmias. It has the highest risk of QT prolongation among all psychotropic medications.

Mellaril is also the antipsychotic known for irreversible retinal pigmentation/degenerative retinopathy, a risk at high doses. Contrast this with chlorpromazine (Thorazine) which causes corneal deposits but rarely affects the retina.

Mellaril works well for anxiety and can be prescribed safely at low doses.

The other medication FDA-approved for refractory schizophrenia is clozapine (Clozaril), which is more effective than thioridazine.

CYP2D6 genotyping is recommended prior to starting Mellaril, as explained below.

Dosing: For refractory schizophrenia, the target dose range is 200–800 mg divided BID–QID; Start 50–100 mg TID; Max is 800 mg/day; Check electrocardiogram (EKG) for QT prolongation before and during treatment; Stop if absolute neutrophil count (ANC) < 1000.

"Why take the risk of dystonic reactions…"

In the 1980s thioridazine was marketed as an atypical antipsychotic, despite having a conventional phenothiazine structure.

Low potency D2 blockers are less likely to cause EPS, as touted in this 1983 ad.

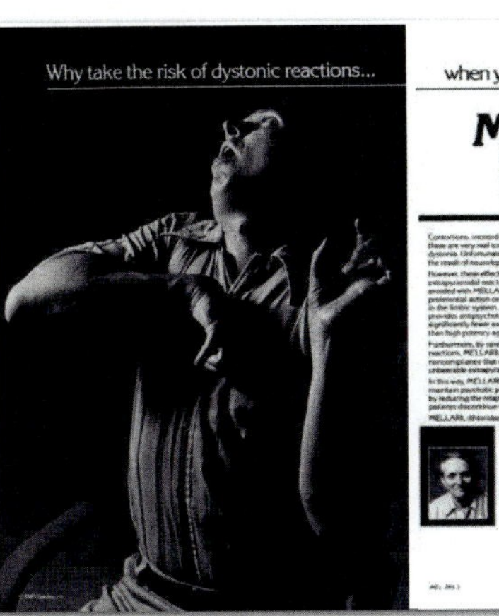
Why take the risk of dystonic reactions...

when you can often avoid them with

MELLARIL (thioridazine)

MELLARIL (thioridazine)
Keeps the risk of extrapyramidal side effects to a minimum

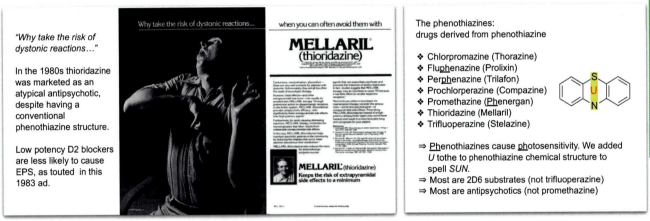

The phenothiazines:
drugs derived from phenothiazine

- ❖ Chlorpromazine (Thorazine)
- ❖ Fluphenazine (Prolixin)
- ❖ Perphenazine (Trilafon)
- ❖ Prochlorperazine (Compazine)
- ❖ Promethazine (Phenergan)
- ❖ Thioridazine (Mellaril)
- ❖ Trifluoperazine (Stelazine)

S U N

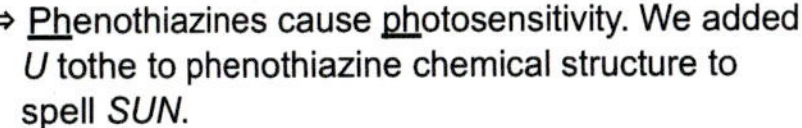

⇒ Phenothiazines cause photosensitivity. We added *U* tothe to phenothiazine chemical structure to spell *SUN*.
⇒ Most are 2D6 substrates (not trifluoperazine)
⇒ Most are antipsychotics (not promethazine)

Dynamic interactions:

- ❖ Dopamine antagonist
- ❖ Extrapyramidal effects
- ❖ Sedation/CNS depression (strong)
- ❖ QT prolongation (high risk)
- ❖ Hypotensive
- ❖ Anticholinergic (strong)
- ❖ Lowers seizure threshold (mild)
- ❖ Prolactin elevating
- ❖ Hyponatremia
- ❖ Hyperglycemia
- ❖ Photosensitivity (phenothiazine)

Kinetic interactions:

- ❖ 2D6 substrate (major)

page 15

2D6 genotyping is recommended prior to starting Mellaril, a susceptible 2D6 substrate. 2D6 poor metabolizers (PM) have 4-fold increased levels of this medication (10% of the population). Mellaril is contraindicated for 2D6 PMs. For this same reason, Mellaril is also contraindicated in combination with strong 2D6 inhibitors.

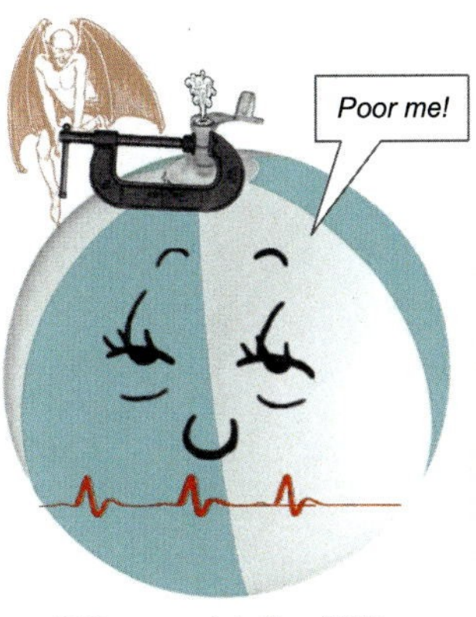
Poor me!
2D6 poor metabolizer (PM)

2D6 ultra-rapid metabolizers (UM) are likely to be nonresponders to Mellaril (3% of population).

2D6 ultrarapid metabolizer (UM)

FGAs
12

1985
$34–$72

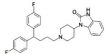

Pimozide (ORAP)

PIM o zide / OH rap

"Ol' rappin' Pimp"

❖ Antipsychotic
❖ High potency FGA
❖ D2 antagonist

1
2
mg

FDA-approved for:
❖ Tourette syndrome, severe

Used off-label for:
❖ Schizophrenia

Pimozide (Orap) is a 1st generation antipsychotic that was FDA-approved in 1985 as an orphan drug for the treatment of Tourette's syndrome. It is only to be used for tics that severely compromise daily life function and do not respond to standard treatment. The standard medications include alpha-2 agonists (clonidine, guanfacine) and antipsychotics less likely to prolong QT interval (haloperidol, risperidone, ziprasidone).

DSM-5 defines Tourette's Disorder as a neurodevelopmental motor disorder characterized by both (1) multiple motor tics and (2) one or more vocal tics, without onset prior to age 18. These tics characteristically wax and wane, can be suppressed temporarily, and are typically preceded by an unwanted urge or sensation in the affected muscles. Some common tics are eye blinking, coughing, throat clearing, sniffing, and facial movements. An example of a vocal tic is coprolalia. This is the production of obscenities as an abrupt, sharp bark or grunt utterance which lacks the prosody of similar inappropriate speech observed in human interactions.

Adult dosing: Check CYP2D6 genotype if planning to exceed 4 mg/day; Target dose is 2–10 mg either QD or divided BID; Start at 1 mg QD or 1 mg BID; May increase dose every 2 days (every 2 weeks for a 2D6 poor metabolizer; Max is 0.2 mg/kg/day up to 10 mg/day (max of 4 mg/day for 2D6 poor metabolizer); Check EKG for QT prolongation; Taper gradually to discontinue; Stop if absolute neutrophil count (ANC) drops below 1,000.

Dynamic interactions:
❖ Dopamine antagonist
❖ Extrapyramidal effects
❖ Sedation/CNS depression
❖ QT prolongation (high risk)
❖ Anticholinergic (moderate)
❖ Lowers seizure threshold (mild)

Kinetic interactions:
❖ 2D6 substrate
❖ 3A4 substrate

2D6 genotyping is recommended for doses over 4 mg/day to check for 2D6 poor metabolizer (PM) genotype.

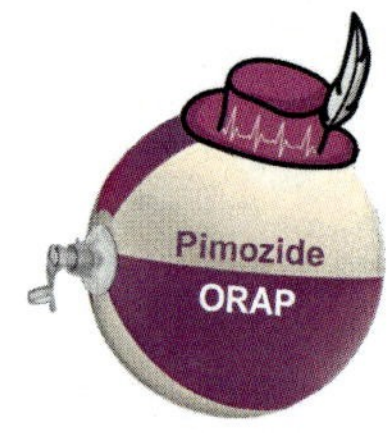

2D6 substrate

Pimozide is contraindicated in combination with many medications, including QT prolongers and 3A4 inhibitors. Sudden death has occured when the antibiotic clarithromycin (Biaxin) was added to ongoing pimozide therapy.

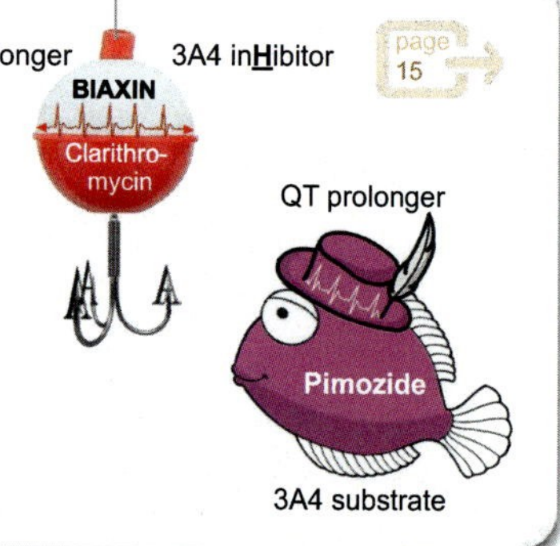

page 15

3A4 substrate

Pimozide Molindone Prochlorperazine

1975
$24–$42

Molindone (MOBAN)

mol in dohn / MO ban

"Mole Dome Mole ban"

❖ Antipsychotic
❖ Medium potency FGA
❖ D2 antagonist

5
10
25
mg

FDA-approved for:
❖ Schizophrenia

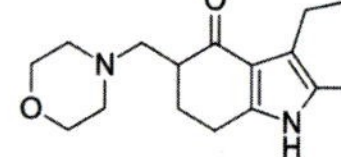

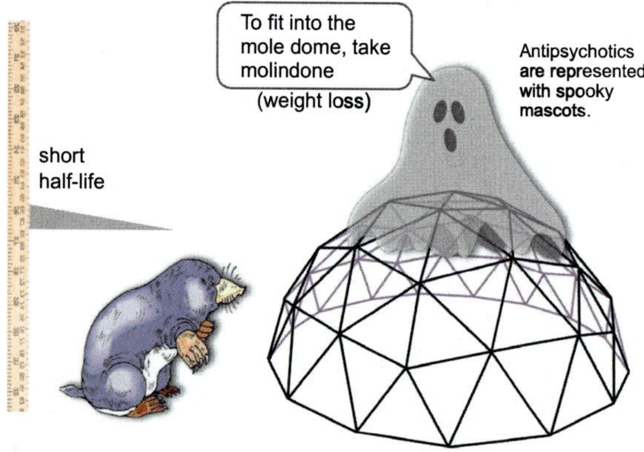

Dosing: Target dose for schizophrenia is 5–50 mg divided TID–QID; Start 50–75 mg/day divided TID–QID; May increase to 100 mg/day (25 mg QID) after 3–4 days; Max is 225 mg/day; Stop if absolute neutrophil count (ANC) drops below 1,000.

Molindone (Moban) is a rarely prescribed intermediate potency FGA, discontinued by the original manufacturer in 2010. It is still available, but you're unlikely to see it in the wild.

Molindone has a short half-life 1.5 hours but pharmacological effect from a single dose persists for 24–36 hours due to several active metabolites.

Molindone is associated with weight loss, averaging 7.6 kg after 3 months, with most of the loss occurred during the first month (among 9 schizophrenic patients, Gardos & Cole, 1977). Envision the mole being able to squeeze through the triangles of the dome as he loses weight.

Dynamic interactions:
❖ Dopamine antagonist
❖ Extrapyramidal effects
❖ Sedation/CNS depression
❖ Anticholinergic (moderate)
❖ Lowers seizure threshold (mild)
❖ Prolactin elevation (moderate)

Kinetic interactions:
❖ None significant

page 18

"in a bubble" - minimal clinically significant kinetic interactions

For context: Antiemetics

An antiemetic is a drug effective against nausea and vomiting (emesis). Some antiemetics work by blocking dopamine D2 receptors, which is the same mechanism employed by antipsychotics. The antiemetic effect is mediated by D2 blockade in the vomiting center of the brainstem, whereas the antipsychotic effect is mediated by D2 blockade in the mesolimbic pathway.

Other dopamine antagonists that work as off-label antiemetics include olanzapine (Zyprexa), haloperidol (Haldol), and chlorpromazine (Thorazine). Not all antipsychotics decrease nausea. In fact, the D2 partial agonists such as aripiprazole (Abilify) are likely to induce nausea.

In addition to being triggered by dopamine, the vomiting center in the brainstem is triggered by serotonin, histamine, and acetylcholine. Anti-serotonergics, antihistamines and anticholinergics work as antiemetics. Serotonergic antidepressants and cholinergic Alzheimer's medications have the opposite effect of inducing nausea. Unsurprisingly, dopaminergic medications for Parkinson's disease such as ropinirole (Requip) are likely to cause nausea.

Antiemetics that do not block dopamine receptors include:

- **Ondansetron (Zofran)** - blocks serotonin 5-HT_3 receptors in the brainstem's vomiting center and in the GI tract
- **Scopolamine (Transderm Scōp)** - anticholinergic effect in the brainstem and GI tract
- **Diphenhydramine (Benadryl)** - blocks H_1 histamine receptors in the brain, plus anticholinergic effects
- **Aprepitant (Emend)** - substance P antagonist (SPA) that mediates its effect by blocking the neurokinin 1 (NK1) receptor in the brain

As a side note, nausea is one of the most common reasons patients stop medications prematurely. Nausea tends to be a transient side effect that usually resolves spontaneously. Nausea can often be avoided altogether with slow titration. Another tip for medication-induced nausea is to take the pill after food—not with food, immediately after a meal. Also effective for nausea is ginger extract (one 550 mg capsule) taken 1 hour before a meal, for a maximum of 3 caps/day (Bodagh et al, 2019; Rajnish Mago, MD; The Carlat Psychiatry Report, Jun/Jul 2019). Ginger ale does not suffice.

D2 blocking antiemetic	Potency of D2 blockade	Antipsychotic?
Prochlorperazine (Compazine)	High	Yes
Metoclopramide (Reglan)	High	No
Promethazine (Phenergan)	Low	No
Trimethobenzamide (Tigan)	Low	No

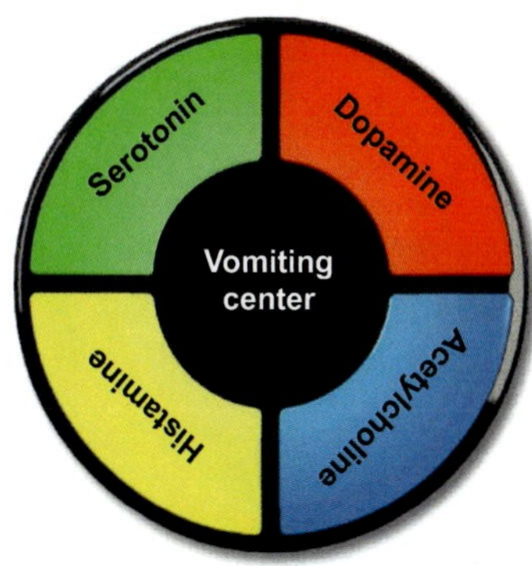

When the brainstem is overloaded by any of these 4 neurotransmitters, the vomiting center thinks the body is being poisoned. Blocking any of these neurotransmitters relieves nausea.

FGAs

#288
1956
$9–$23

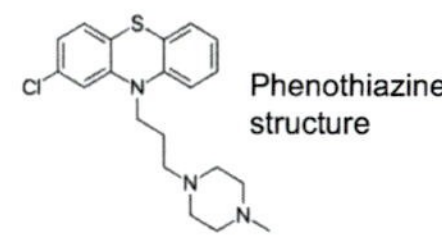

Phenothiazine structure

Prochlorperazine (COMPAZINE)

pro klor PEAR a zeen / COM pa zeen

"Procure, pear! (a Compass)"

- Antiemetic/Antipsychotic
- High potency FGA
- D2 antagonist
- Antihistamine
- Phenothiazine

5
10
mg

FDA-approved for:
- Nausea/vomiting, severe
- Schizophrenia
- Non-psychotic anxiety

Used off-label for:
- Migraines
- Status migrainosus (IV)

Procure that compass, pear!
It's our compass now!

Antipsychotics are represented with spooky mascots (witch hat)

Recommendation: Rather than prescribing a D2 blocking antiemetic, choose **ondansetron (Zofran)**. It works by blocking serotonin 5-HT_3 receptors, does not cause EPS, and carries no risk of tardive dyskinesia.

page 283

Although FDA-approved for schizophrenia, prochlorperazine (Compazine) is now almost exclusively used as an antiemetic. Psychiatrists rarely prescribe it.

The antiemetic effect of prochlorperazine is brought about by blocking D2 receptors in the vomiting center of the brainstem. Its antipsychotic effect is through blocking D2 receptors in the mesolimbic pathway.

Since Compazine is a high potency FGA, it can cause EPS including akathisia and dystonia with short-term use, and tardive dyskinesia with long-term use. It has the potential to cause neutropenia and should be stopped if there is an unexplained decrease in white blood cell count.

Dosing: For severe nausea/vomiting, use 5–10 mg q 6–8 hr; For anxiety, use 5 mg q 6–8 hr for a maximum of 12 weeks; For schizophrenia, start 5 mg TID; FDA max for schizophrenia is 150 mg/day, but this is too high due to risk of tardive dyskinesia.

Dynamic interactions:
- Dopamine antagonist (strong)
- Extrapyramidal effects (high)
- Sedation/CNS depression
- QT prolongation (mild)
- Hypotensive
- Anticholinergic (moderate)
- Lowers seizure threshold (mild)
- Prolactin elevating
- Hyponatremia
- Hyperglycemia
- Photosensitivity (phenothiazine)

Kinetic interactions:
- Minimal clinically significant kinetic interactions (in a bubble)

page 18

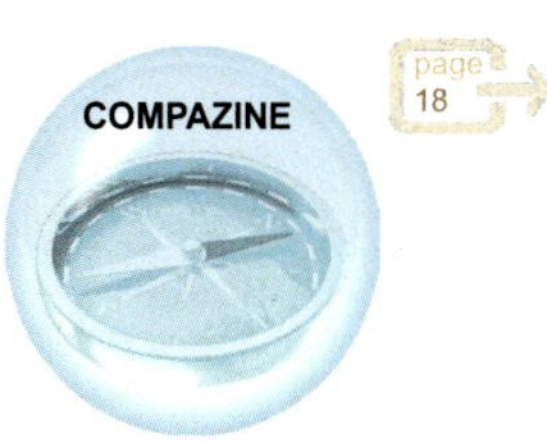

#160
1951
$3–$19

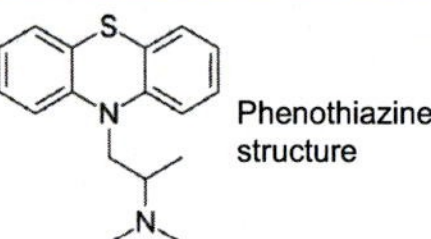

Promethazine (PHENERGAN)

proh METH uh zeen / FIN er gan

"Finnegan's Prom hazing"

- Weak D2 antagonist
- Antihistamine
- Antiemetic
- Phenothiazine

12.5
25
50
mg

Not an antipsychotic

FDA-approved for:

- Allergic conditions
- Urticaria
- Motion sickness
- Nausea/vomiting
- Sedation

They put too
much sizzurp in
my purple drank.

The hazing of Finnegan at prom

Phenergan is a phenothiazine. Promethazine (Phenergan) was the original antihistamine that revolutionized the treatment of allergies in the 1950s. This monograph would likely reside in the antihistamine/anticholinergic chapter if not for the phenothiazine structure.

Promethazine is the only available medication with a phenothiazine structure that is not useful as an antipsychotic. Today it is commonly prescribed as an antiemetic, but not for allergies. As with all first generation antihistamines, promethazine is highly sedating and strongly anticholinergic.

Like other phenothiazines, promethazine antagonizes D2 receptors, although weakly. Promethazine blocks D2 receptors at 10% potency of the antipsychotic chlorpromazine (Thorazine), which itself is low potency. Extrapyramidal effects are highly unlikely with such a weak D2 blocker, in contrast to the antiemetics metoclopramide (Reglan) and prochlorperazine (Compazine) which are high potency D2 blockers.

Promethazine is available IM, IV, and as a rectal suppository for occasions when vomiting would make the PO route ineffective. It is one of the few drugs that can turn urine green, apropos to this mnemonic.

Promethazine has two black box warnings, for respiratory depression and risk of severe tissue injury/gangrene—*"gang-green"*—with parenteral administration. Avoid co-administering with other respiratory depressants. Promethazine injection can cause severe chemical irritation and tissue damage including burning, thrombophlebitis, tissue necrosis, and gangrene when given IM or IV, but more likely with the IV route due to potential perivascular extravasation (unintentional leaking into the surrounding tissue). It should be injected into a large muscle to avoid unintentional intra-arterial insertion.

Promethazine is a component of prescription cough syrup with the opioid codeine. Promethazine is the antihistamine—as an alternative to diphenhydramine (Benadryl)—for sneezing, rhinorrhea, and watery eyes. The codeine component serves antitussive and analgesic purposes. The promethazine/codeine combo is not recommended and has nine (!!) black box warnings.

Promethazine is commonly misused by recovering opioid addicts to potentiate the high caused by methadone.

A concoction of promethazine/codeine syrup mixed with Sprite (and sometimes grape Jolly Ranchers candy) is known as "purple drank", sizzurp or "lean". The euphoria from sizzurp is derived from codeine, which is metabolized by 2D6 to morphine. The sedative "lean" (as in leaning against a wall) is from promethazine.

Dosing: For nausea, the recommended dose is 12.5–25 mg PO or IM q 4–6 hr PRN; Max is 50 mg/dose PO/IM (25 mg IV) and 100 mg/day; Product labeling states that promethazine may be given by slow IV push, but IM administration into a large muscle is preferred over IV due to risk of serious tissue injury with the IV route.

The phenothiazines:
drugs derived from phenothiazine

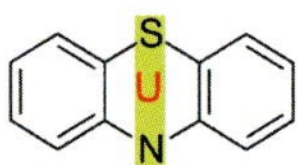

- Chlorpromazine (Thorazine)
- Fluphenazine (Prolixin)
- Perphenazine (Trilafon)
- Prochlorperazine (Compazine)
- Promethazine (Phenergan)
- Thioridazine (Mellaril)
- Trifluoperazine (Stelazine)

⇒ Phenothiazines cause photosensitivity. We added *U* to the chemical structure to spell *SUN*.
⇒ Most are 2D6 substrates (not trifluoperazine)
⇒ Most are antipsychotics (not promethazine)

Green urine can be caused by:

- Promethazine (Phenergan)
- Metoclopramide (Reglan)
- Amitriptyline (Elavil)
- Cimetidine (Tagamet)
- Propofol (Diprivan)
- Methylene blue

Dynamic interactions:

- Dopamine antagonist (weak)
- Extrapyramidal effects (mild)
- Sedation/CNS depression (strong)
- Respiratory depression
- QT prolongation (mild)
- Hypotensive
- Anticholinergic (strong)
- Lowers seizure threshold (mild)
- Prolactin elevating
- Hyponatremia
- Hyperglycemia
- Photosensitivity (phenothiazine)

page 15

Kinetic interactions:

- 2D6 substrate

2D6 substrate

1979
$4–$11

Metoclopramide (REGLAN)

met o KLOH pra mide / REG lan

"Ronald Reglan Met a clopper"

- ❖ Antiemetic
- ❖ High potency D2 antagonist

5
10
mg

Not an antipsychotic

FDA-approved for:
- ❖ GERD
- ❖ Diabetic gastroparesis
- ❖ Nausea/vomiting prevention (chemotherapy; postoperative)
- ❖ Small bowel intubation
- ❖ Radiologic exam

Howdy Clopper, I'm Ronald Reglan.
Nice to have met you.

Metoclopramide, introduced in 1979, is the only FDA-approved treatment for gastroparesis. It is useful after gastric surgery and for treatment of hyperemesis gravidarum (severe nausea and vomiting of pregnancy).

Metoclopramide is a dopamine D2 receptor antagonist. It exerts its effect in the vomiting center of the brain stem. It also antagonizes dopamine on gastrointestinal smooth muscle, which causes an indirect cholinergic effect, and can lead to the SLUDGE symptom diarrhea. The drug enhances gastric emptying, which is believed to minimize stasis that precedes vomiting.

Despite being a D2 blocker, you won't see metoclopramide in the antipsychotic section of most textbooks. Metoclopramide lacks antipsychotic efficacy except at a high dose, so it is not used for psychiatric purposes. Unsurprisingly, metoclopramide can cause sedation.

Metoclopramide can cause adverse effects like the antipsychotic class, including akathisia, hyperprolactinemia, neuroleptic malignant syndrome (NMS), and tardive dyskinesia (TD). It may be the most common cause of drug-induced movement disorders. It carries a black box warning not to exceed 12 weeks of treatment due to risk of TD. There are still thousands of active tardive dyskinesia lawsuits against the manufacturers of metoclopramide.

An off-label alternative treatment for gastroparesis is the cholinergic medication bethanechol (Urecholine), shown on page 180. Bethanechol does not cause tardive dyskinesia.

Dosing: 10–15 mg PO, IM, or IV 4x daily PRN; Use 5 mg for elderly patients; Maximum is 60 mg/day (30 mg/day for 2D6 poor metabolizers).

Dynamic interactions:
- ❖ Dopamine antagonist (strong)
- ❖ Extrapyramidal effects (high)
- ❖ Sedation/CNS depression
- ❖ Anticholinergic (moderate)
- ❖ Prolactin elevation

Kinetic interactions:
- ❖ 2D6 substrate

page 15

2D6 substrate

FGAs

1974
$39–$174

Trimethobenzamide (TIGAN)

try METH oh BENZ a mide / TEE gan

"Trim bendy Tigger"

- ❖ Antiemetic
- ❖ Low potency D2 antagonist

300
mg

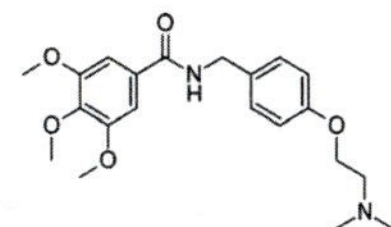

Not an antipsychotic

FDA-approved for:
- ❖ Nausea/vomiting

Used off-label for:
- ❖ Suppression of gag reflex in surgery

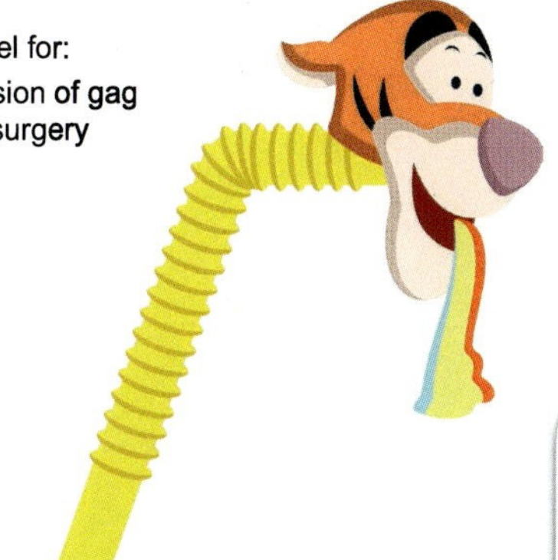

Trimethobenzamide (Tigan) has been shown to block the emetic reflex without causing sedation, hypotension or other undesirable side effects produced by other D2-blocking antiemetics. Tigan has weak antidopaminergic activity. When used parenterally for surgery, it has the added benefit of gag reflex suppression.

Tigan has a niche for the treatment and prevention of nausea caused by apomorphine (Apokyn) in rescue treatment of Parkinson's disease "off" episodes. Ondansetron (Zofran) is contraindicated with apomorphine because the combination can cause severe hypotension.

Tigan is also a suitable antiemetic for patient's with QT prolongation. Olanzapine (Zyprexa) used off-label is also suitable for this purpose.

Dosing: For nausea/vomiting (PO route) give 300 mg TID–QID; For IM route give 200 mg TID–QID.

Dynamic interactions:
- ❖ Dopamine antagonist (weak)
- ❖ Extrapyramidal effects (mild)
- ❖ Sedation/CNS depression
- ❖ Hypotension (IM use)
- ❖ Lowers seizure threshold (mild)

Kinetic interactions:
- ❖ Minimal clinically significant kinetic interactions (in a bubble)

This edition of *Cafer's Psychopharmacology* was released in November 2020. Subscribe to cafermed.com for the PDF edition with over 1,000 internal links and bookmarks for ultrarapid navigation. The PDF edition is updated frequently with new mascots. Visit cafermed.com/update for more information.

Discount code for cafermed.com subscription:
ULTRARAPID

All antipsychotics introduced after 1990 are classified as second generation antipsychotics (SGAs), also known as atypical antipsychotics. As a class, SGAs have a lower risk of EPS and a higher risk of weight gain and diabetes compared to first generation antipsychotics (FGAs). The FGA/SGA distinction is based more on convention than science. The best approach is to consider the properties of each antipsychotic individually.

What really distinguishes SGAs from FGAs is, with SGAs, therapeutic effects can usually be achieved at a dose lower than would cause EPS. If FGAs are dosed carefully as to avoid EPS, evidence suggests there is no overall advantage of SGAs over FGAs. In general, SGAs have more potential for metabolic disturbance (obesity, hyperlipidemia and diabetes), though there are exceptions (lurasidone, ziprasidone).

Patients taking SGAs need routine monitoring of weight, lipids and hemoglobin A1c.

Unopposed blockade of D2 dopamine receptors in the nigrostriatal pathway is what causes EPS. The prototypical FGA is just a D2 blocker. Most SGAs block D2 receptors and 5-HT**2A** serotonin receptors. Mnemonic: ***2**nd generation **A**ntipsychotic.* 5-HT_{2A} blockade indirectly increases dopamine in the basal ganglia, making EPS less likely.

It has become apparent that SGAs are safe during pregnancy, except risperidone and paliperidone—these two are associated with a small increase in congenital malformations (Huybrechts et al, 2016). Risperidone and paliperidone are also the two SGAs that prominently elevate prolactin levels.

Here are the SGAs available in the US, ranked by number of prescriptions:

Rx	Generic TRADE	$	Weight gain	Sedation	Akathisia	Involuntary movement risk*	Prolactin elevation	Constipation	Comments
#1	Quetiapine SEROQUEL	$10	+++	++++	-	-	-	+	A weak antipsychotic, more often prescribed for mood disorders than for schizophrenia. Orthostatic hypotension is common with the first few doses. Slight potential for recreational abuse.
#2	Aripiprazole ABILIFY	$20	+/-	+/-	++	-	-	-	D2 partial agonist. First-line for schizophrenia and bipolar. Few side effects other than akathisia. Long half-life of 3 to 6 days. Risk of compulsive behaviors (gamling, etc). Two long-acting injectable brands: ARISTADA and Abilify MAINTENA.
#3	Risperidone RISPERDAL	$10	++	+	++	++	+++	-	Second-line for men due to risk of gynecomastia. First-line option for women (although galactorrea possible). Titration needed. EPS at doses > 6 mg. Several pediatric indications including autism-associated irritability for ages 5+. LAI Risperdal CONSTA q 2 wk IM, PERSERIS q 4 wk sub-Q
#4	Olanzapine ZYPREXA	$20	++++	++	+/-	+/-	+	++	#2 most effective for schizophrenia. #1 weight gain and DM risk. The least likely antipsychotic to be stopped (all-cause) because it is effective with minimal side effects, other than weight gain and blood glucose elevation.
#5	Lurasidone LATUDA	$1200	-	++	++	++	-	-	Approved for schizophrenia and bipolar depression. Poorly absorbed unless taken with food, at least 350 calories. Dosed once daily, usually with the evening meal. Weight loss is more likely than weight gain. Improves Hgb A1c. Highly susceptible 3A4 substrate, contraindicated with Tegretol
#6	Ziprasidone GEODON	$30	-	+++	+	+	+	-	Less effective than Risperdal. Take BID with meals for adequate absorption. Shortest half-life of SGAs, 2.5 hours. Most QT prolongation among the SGAs, although not extreme. IM available for acute agitation. Risk of DRESS syndrome (Drug Reaction with Eosinophilia and Systemic Symptoms) which is rare but serious. Similar to lurasidone.
#7	Clozapine CLOZARIL	$100 + labs	++++	++++	-	-	-	++++	#1 most effective for schizophrenia. Risks of severe neutropenia, myocarditis, seizures. Weekly CBC for the first 6 months (neutropenia). No EPS. Constipation and hypersalivation can be severe. Titrate slowly (hypotension).
#8	Brexpiprazole REXULTI	$1200	+	+/-	+	+	-	-	D2 partial agonist similar to aripiprazole and cariprazine. Approved for schizophrenia and as an adjunct to antidepressant for major depressive disorder.
#9	Cariprazine VRAYLAR	$1200	-	+/-	+++	+	-	-	D2 partial agonist. Approved for schizophrenia and bipolar maintenance. Activating rather than sedating. Possible benefit for cognitive difficulties and negative symptoms of schizophrenia. Akathisia is common. Longest half-life of antipsychotics at 14 days.
#10	Paliperidone INVEGA	$300	++	+/-	+	++	+++	-	Active metabolite of risperidone. Cleared renally, suitable for those with liver problems. Long-acting injectable (LAI) Invega SUSTENNA q 4 wk and Invega TRINZA q 3 mo.
#11	Asenapine SAPHRIS	$600	++	+++	++	+	+	+	The only sublingual antipsychotic. FDA-approved for schizophrenia, bipolar. Rare serious allergic reactions.
#12	Iloperidone FANAPT	$500	+++	+/-	-	-	+	-	Titrate dose to avoid orthostatic hypotension. "No EPS", marketed for those sensitive to akathisia. #3 among antipsychotics for weight gain.
#13	Pimavanserin NUPLAZID	$2000	-	+/-	-	-	-	+/-	For hallucinations and delusions of Parkinson's disease. 5-HT_{2A} serotonin receptor inverse agonist. The only available antipsychotic that does not act at dopamine receptors. May cause edema. Caution with heart conditions.
NEW	Lumateperone CAPLYTA	$1300	+/-	+++	-	-	-	-	Modulates glutamate in addition to the usual SGA mechanisms, with low D2 receptor occupancy. 42 mg is the only recommended dose. Causes modest weight loss but modest elevation of hemoglobin A1c and lipids.

* There may be small risk of tardive dyskinesia from antipsychotics designated (-). Antipsychotics are not always to blame for involuntary movements presumed to be tardive dyskinesia. In the pre-antipsychotic era, 4% of individuals developed spontaneous dyskinesia with the first psychotic episode (Fenton, 2013).

#86
1997
$3–$124

Quetiapine (SEROQUEL)

kwe TYE a peen / SER o kwel

"Sera, Quit typing!"

- Antipsychotic (SGA)
- D2 antagonist (weak) - ⇩ DA
- 5-HT_{2A} antagonist - ⇧ DA
- NE reuptake inhibitor (metabolite)

25 mg
50
100
200
300
400

FDA-approved for:
- Schizophrenia
- Bipolar, manic episode
- Bipolar, depressive episode
  - XR formulation
- Adjunct (to antidepressant) for major depressive disorder

Used off-label for
- "Racing thoughts"
- Anxiety
- Insomnia
- Behavioral disturbance
- Coming down from meth binge

Sera! Quit typing (and get some sleep)!
mania

Antipsychotics are represented with spooky mascots.

The augmenting agents with best evidence for treatment-resistant unipolar depression (added to an antidepressant):

- ► Lithium
- ► **Quetiapine (Seroquel)**
- ► Aripiprazole (Abilify)
- ► Risperidone (Risperdal)

Antipsychotics approved for bipolar depression (2019):

Second generation antipsychotic (SGA)	Number needed to treat (for one patient to respond)
Olanzapine/fluoxetine combo (Symbyax)	4
Lurasidone (Latuda)	5
Quetiapine XR (Seroquel XR)	6
Cariprazine (Vraylar)	7

Sedation among SGAs, ranked:

1. Clozapine (Clozaril) - by far the most sedating
2. **Quetiapine (Seroquel)**
3. Ziprasidone (Geodon)
4. Olanzapine (Zyprexa)
5. Asenapine (Saphris)
6. Risperidone (Risperdal)
7. Lurasidone (Latuda)
8. Aripiprazole (Abilify) - minimal sedation
9. Iloperidone (Fanapt) - minimal sedation
10. Paliperidone (Invega) - the least sedating

Seizure risk among SGAs

1. Clozapine (Clozaril) - 10-fold
2. Olanzapine (Zyprexa) - 3-fold
3. **Quetiapine (Seroquel) - 2-fold**
4. Minimal risk with all others

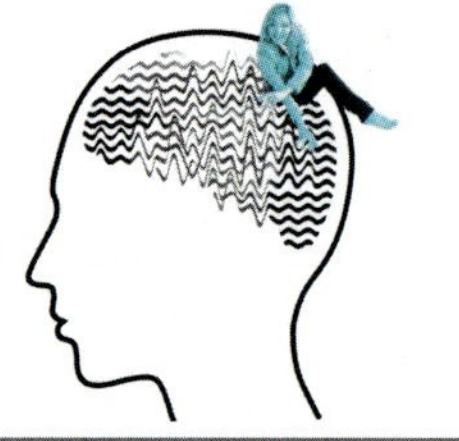

"Quetiapine quiets the voices of schizophrenia". Quetiapine (Seroquel), FDA-approved in 1997, is arguably the weakest antipsychotic, often not very effective for schizophrenia. It is widely used for bipolar disorder, and is the #1 most prescribed antipsychotic (#86 prescribed drug overall) in the US. Quetiapine is calming and great for coming down from a manic episode or methamphetamine binge. Although not a controlled substance, quetiapine has some potential for abuse and has modest street value, nicknamed "Susie Q".

Quetiapine can contribute to fatality if taken at high doses in combination with other sedatives, likely due to respiratory depression. In single-drug overdose, it is more dangerous than other SGAs, although absolute risk of death is only about 1 in 1,000 (Nelson & Spyker, 2017).

Quetiapine can cause weight gain and diabetes, but the risk is substantially less than with olanzapine (Zyprexa). Quetiapine can be highly sedating, especially with first few doses.

Quetiapine has minimal risk of causing EPS because it is a weak D2 receptor blocker with a high 5-HT_{2A}/D_2 blockade ratio. It was the drug of choice for treatment of delusions and hallucinations associated with Parkinson's disease until the arrival of pimavanserin (Nuplazid). Among SGAs, quetiapine and clozapine have the lowest incidence of akathisia. Anticholinergic effects with quetiapine are minimal. At low dose, quetiapine is a common choice for elderly patients who need an antipsychotic due to low anticholinergic effects and low incidence of EPS.

Quetiapine has a relatively short half-life of 6 hours. The package insert recommends twice daily dosing. However, for antipsychotics in general, there is no compelling efficacy argument for maintaining consistent blood levels throughout the day. Seroquel is commonly dosed once daily at bedtime. The Seroquel XR formulation is intended for once daily dosing and may be a bit less sedating than immediate-release quetiapine dosed twice daily.

The author usually prescribes the immediate-release (IR) formulation which is cheaper than XR. Maintenance dosing at HS is better tolerated than BID. The minimal effective dose for first-episode psychosis is 150 mg. For multi-episode psychosis, 300 mg is the minimal effective dose.

Dosing: Start 25–50 mg BID or HS and titrate to target dose over 4 days to avoid orthostatic hypotension; For schizophrenia, the target dose 150–750 mg/day divided BID–TID; For bipolar mania, start 50 mg BID, then increase by 100 mg/day to achieve 200 mg BID by day four; For bipolar depression, the target is 300 mg HS, although lower doses are often used; The maximum daily dose is 800 mg. It may cause respiratory depression at higher doses.

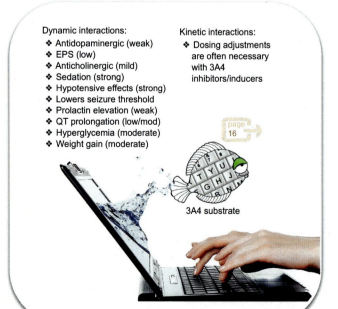

Dynamic interactions:
- Antidopaminergic (weak)
- EPS (low)
- Anticholinergic (mild)
- Sedation (strong)
- Hypotensive effects (strong)
- Lowers seizure threshold
- Prolactin elevation (weak)
- QT prolongation (low/mod)
- Hyperglycemia (moderate)
- Weight gain (moderate)

Kinetic interactions:
- Dosing adjustments are often necessary with 3A4 inhibitors/inducers

page 16

3A4 substrate

#131
2002
$21–$755

Aripiprazole (ABILIFY)

ar i PIP ra zole / a BIL e fy

"A ripped peep (is) Able to fly"

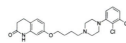

- Antipsychotic (SGA)
- D2 partial agonist - ⇔ DA
- $5\text{-}HT_{1A}$ partial agonist - ⇔ DA
- $5\text{-}HT_{2A}$ antagonist - ⇧ DA

2, 5, 10, 15, 20, 30 mg

FDA-approved for:
- Schizophrenia
- Bipolar mania
- Depression (adjunct)
- Irritability in autism
- Tourette's disorder

Used off-label for:
- Bipolar depression
- Adjunct to olanzapine (Zyprexa) to minimize weight gain
- Adjunct to risperidone or paliperidone to normalize prolactin levels

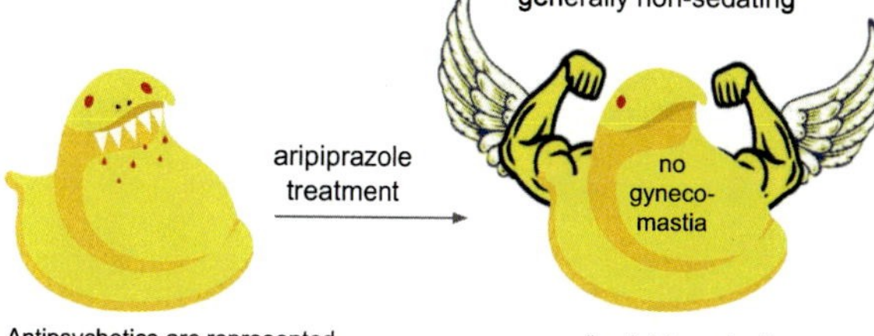

Advantages of aripiprazole over other antipsychotics:
- Generally non-sedating (usually taken in morning)
- "Weight neutral" (although some gain weight; others lose weight)
- Relatively low risk of diabetes
- No risk of gynecomastia (decreases prolactin levels)
- Low risk of irreversible movement disorders
- Fewer sexual side effects than other antipsychotics
- Insignificant QT prolongation
- Several long-acting injectable (LAI) options

Aripiprazole (Abilify) was released in 2002 as the first dopamine receptor partial agonist, known colloquially as a "dopamine stabilizer". It is available in several formulations for many FDA-approved indications, including pediatric. Abilify is a good first-line antipsychotic due to a favorable side effect profile. However, an individual's response to aripiprazole is less predictable than with other antipsychotics. Agitation, insomnia, and compulsive behavior may occur due to increased dopamine activity. Serum levels are less predictable due to the possibility of the individual being a 2D6 ultra-rapid (3%) or poor metabolizer (10%). Several kinetic interactions must be considered. High doses are no more effective than moderate doses.

Contrast aripiprazole with olanzapine (Zyprexa) which is predictably effective and more so at higher doses, though at the expense of weight gain and elevated blood sugar. Consider olanzapine for short-term use and aripiprazole for long-term use.

The main troublesome side effect of Abilify is akathisia, which is a feeling of inner restlessness and inability to keep still. Akathisia is usually short-lived, and more common for those treated for mood disorders compared to those treated for schizophrenia. Akathisia is easily addressed with addition of propranolol or a low dose benzodiazepine. Some patients experience nausea, headache, or insomnia.

Aripiprazole has been associated with new onset of impulse-control problems such as pathological gambling, compulsive eating, compulsive shopping, and hypersexual behavior. These problems may be related to increased dopamine activity in patients with low baseline dopamine tone.

There is no risk of gynecomastia with aripiprazole because it decreases prolactin levels, which is the opposite of many antipsychotics. Aripiprazole has a long half-life of 3 to 6 days.

Of 11,817 single-drug exposures to aripiprazole reported to Poison Control, there were no deaths (Nelson & Spyker, 2017).

There are two competing aripiprazole long-acting injectable (LAI) products—ARISTADA and ABILIFY MAINTENA. The Aristada injection, administered every 4 to 8 weeks, is more painful than Abilify Maintena, which is given every 4 weeks. After the first injection, oral aripiprazole needs to be continued for 2 weeks (Maintena) to 3 weeks (Aristada). With Aristada, as an alternative to the 3-week PO overlap, a single injection of ARISTADA INITIO can be be administered (deltoid) simultaneously with the first Aristada injection (gluteal), along with a one time 30 mg PO dose.

Dosing: For schizophrenia and bipolar the recommended starting dose of 10 mg is the same as the recommended maintenance dose. The FDA maximum is 30 mg, but exceeding 15 mg is rarely more effective. Adjunctively for depression, start 2 mg or 5 mg QD, with maintenance dose 5–10 mg QD. If sedation is an issue with AM dosing, change to HS. Since akathisia is common with initiation of treatment, consider splitting the starting dose in half for the first couple days. Adjust dose for the kinetic interactions described below. See page 160 for dosing of long-acting injectable (LAI) formulations.

Dynamic interactions:
- Antidopaminergic (balanced)
- EPS (low, other than akathisia)
- CNS depression (minimal)
- Hypotensive effects (mild)
- Hyperglycemia (possible)
- Weight gain (possible)

Kinetic interactions:
- 2D6 substrate (major)
- 3A4 substrate (major)

As a substrate of 2D6 and 3A4, Abilify is subject to victimization by many kinetic interactions.

Consider dosing aripiprazole at 50% strength if the patient is taking a 2D6 inHibitor such as:
- Fluoxetine (Prozac)
- Paroxetine (Paxil)
- Bupropion (Wellbutrin)
- Duloxetine (Cymbalta)

It is recommended to use a double strength dose of Abilify in the presence of a strong 3A4 inDucer such as:
- Carbamazepine (Tegretol)
- Phenytoin (Dilantin)
- Phenobarbital (Luminal)

If the patient is taking a 2D6 inHibitor (or is 2D6 PM) and taking a 3A4 inHibitor, prescribing ¼ of the usual dose is recommended, and it is worthwhile to check a serum aripiprazole level.

Known 2D6 poor metabolizers (PM) should be given aripiprazole at 50% strength. 2D6 genotyping can be ordered for about $200, but testing is generally not needed to prescribe Abilify. Consider starting at a low dose of 5 mg to account for the possibility of the patient being a 2D6 PM.

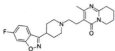

#159
1993
$4–$66

Risperidone (RISPERDAL)

ris PER i dohn / RIS per dal

"Breast-perdal"

❖ Antipsychotic (SGA)
❖ D2 antagonist - ⇩ DA
❖ $5\text{-}HT_{2A}$ antagonist - ⇧ DA
❖ Alpha-adrenergic antagonist

0.25
0.5
1
2
3
4 mg

FDA-approved for:

- Schizophrenia > 13 years old
- Bipolar > 10 years old
- Irritability of autism > 5 years old

Used off-label for:

- Treatment-resistant depression
- Tourette's disorder
- Aggression
- Agitation of dementia
- PTSD

Risperidone (Risperdal) was the second of the second generation antipsychotics (SGAs) to be released (1993), following clozapine (1990). It is one of the few antipsychotics approved for use in children. In *Memorizing Pharmacology,* Dr. Tony Guerra nicknamed the medication "whisper-dal" because it *quiets the whispers* of auditory hallucinations. Risperidone is relatively non-sedating because it has low affinity for blocking D4 receptors.

Risperidone causes increased release of prolactin from the pituitary, potentially leading to galactorrhea in women and gynecomastia in men. In the book *Memorable Psychopharmacology*, Dr. Jonathan Heldt offers a mnemonic about *rise-pair-idone* giving *"rise to a pair"* of breasts. The prolactin-elevating effect of antipsychotics occurs outside of the blood-brain barrier (BBB). Risperidone does not cross the BBB easily because it is pumped out by the P-glycoprotein (P-gp)—*"Pumpers gonna pump"*. Hence, relatively high serum concentrations of risperidone are necessary to achieve therapeutic levels in the brain. Those SGAs that cross the BBB easily are much less likely to elevate prolactin at therapeutic doses. Prolactin elevation may also cause sexual side effects. Retrograde ejaculation (into the bladder) is possible, although this is due to alpha-1 adrenergic receptor antagonism.

As an antipsychotic, risperidone has been found to be less effective than olanzapine, but more effective than ziprasidone and quetiapine. Risperidone can be regarded as a first-line antipsychotic for women, but second- or third-line for men. Risperidone commonly elevates prolactin levels, making gynecomastia common.

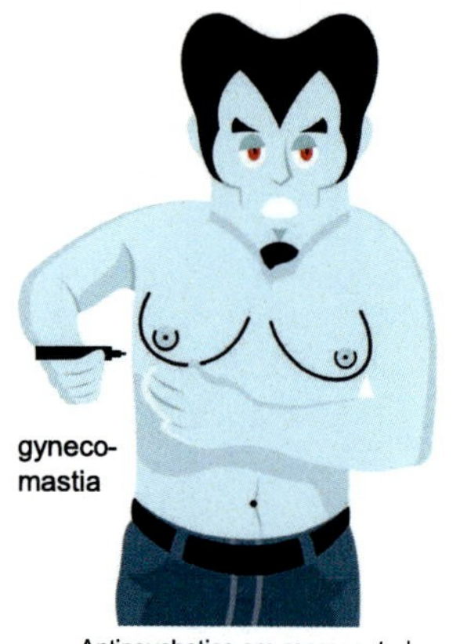

Antipsychotics are represented with spooky mascots.

If a man is doing well on risperidone (or paliperidone) but is concerned about the risk of gynecomastia, check a fasting prolactin level in early morning. If the prolactin level is substantially elevated, offer to stop or switch the medication. If prolactin level is below 20 ng/mL, reassure the patient that there is no risk of risperidone-induced gynecomastia.

Risperidone is available as a q 2 week long-acting injectable (LAI) called RISPERDAL CONSTA. Two weeks between injections is more frequent than the other antipsychotic LAIs—*you're getting shots CONSTAntly*. In 2019 a subcutaneous LAI was announced, called PERSERIS for q 4 week administration. Perseris is the only available subcutaneous LAI antipsychotic.

An active metabolite of risperidone, hydroxy-risperidone (OH-risp) is available as paliperidone (Invega), as featured on page 155. If the patient has liver problems, it is best to prescribe paliperidone. Otherwise, choose risperidone over paliperidone because risperidone is much less expensive. The liver converts risperidone to paliperidone (OH-risp) anyhow, mostly by CYP2D6.

Serum risperidone level can be checked, but results may take several days to arrive from an outside laboratory. The lab will report the level of risperidone and, separately, OH-risperidone.

Both risperidone and the OH-metabolite are biologically active, and therapeutic range is defined by the sum of the two chemicals. The relevant result is "risperidone and metabolite". 2 mg/day is expected to produce a combined level of 14 ng/mL. 16 mg/day produces a mean of 110 ng/mL. Risperdal/OH-risp serum ratio is usually < 1. An inverted ratio (> 1) means the patient is likely a CYP2D6 ultrarapid metabolizer (UM).

Adult dosing: For an acute manic episode, start 2 mg QD then titrate by 1 mg q 24 hr, to a max of 6 mg. For schizophrenia, start either 0.5 mg BID or 1 mg HS and increase in about a week to 1 mg BID or 2 mg HS. The "minimal effective dose" of risperidone for first episode psychosis is 2 mg. For multi-episode psychosis, the minimal effective dose is 4 mg. Doses > 4 mg/day are rarely more effective for schizophrenia. At doses above 6 mg risperidone behaves more like a first generation antipsychotic, i.e., carries a significant risk of EPS, including the possibility of tardive dyskinesia with long-term use. At risperidone's FDA maximum dose of 16 mg, it has no advantage over the FGAs in terms of EPS. The 0.25 mg tab is for pediatric use. See page 160 for dosing of the risperidone long-acting injectables (LAIs)—Risperdal Consta (q 2 wk IM) and Perseris (q 4 wk SQ).

PERSERIS
[per SAHR iss]
"Purse heiress"

Risperidone subcutaneous long-acting injectable (LAI), q 4 wk

Prolactin elevation among SGAs, most to least (approximate):

- Paliperidone (Invega) - high, equal to risperidone
- Risperidone (Risperdal) - high, equal to paliperidone
- Lurasidone (Latuda) - mild, ⅕ the extent of risperidone
- Ziprasidone (Geodon) - mild
- Iloperidone (Fanapt) - mild
- Olanzapine (Zyprexa) - minimal
- Asenapine (Saphris) - minimal
- Clozapine (Clozaril) - does not increase prolactin
- Quetiapine (Seroquel) - does not increase prolactin
- Aripiprazole (Abilify) - decreases prolactin

Note that all first generation antipsychotics (FGAs) elevate prolactin.

Dynamic interactions:

- Antidopaminergic (moderate)
- EPS (dose dependent)
- Sedation (mild)
- Hypotensive effects
- Prolactin elevation (strong)
- Hyperglycemia (moderate)
- Weight gain (moderate)
- QT prolongation (low/mod)

Kinetic interactions:

- 2D6 substrate
- 3A4 substrate

#225
1996
$5–$400 tab
$20–$500 ODT

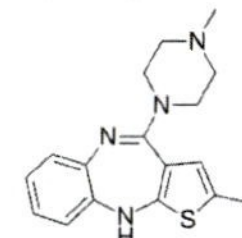

Olanzapine (ZYPREXA)

o lan za peen / zy PREX a

"Owl lands upon (cra)Zy pretzel"

❖ Antipsychotic (SGA)
❖ D2 antagonist - ⇩ DA
❖ 5-HT_{2A} antagonist - ⇧ DA

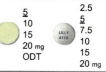

5, 10, 15, 20 mg ODT

2.5, 5, 7.5, 10, 15, 20 mg

FDA-approved for:

- Schizophrenia
- Bipolar mania
- Bipolar maintenance
- Bipolar depression (with fluoxetine)
- Treatment-resistant depression (with fluoxetine)
- Acute agitation of mania (IM route)

Used off-label for:

- Behavioral disturbance
- Nausea/vomiting
- Anorexia nervosa

Antipsychotics are represented with spooky mascots.

The first thing to know about the SGA olanzapine (Zyprexa) is its potential to cause type II diabetes and substantial weight gain. It is #1 among all psychotropic medications for causing these problems. This is unfortunate because olanzapine is highly effective and has minimal side effects otherwise. Among antipsychotics, olanzapine is the #2 most effective treatment for schizophrenia (after clozapine) available in the US. Amisulpride, an antipsychotic available in other countries, was ranked #2, with olanzapine #3 (Leucht, 2013). Olanzapine is the antipsychotic most similar to clozapine in terms of molecular structure, efficacy, weight gain, and low EPS. Risk of seizures with olanzapine is greater than other antipsychotics, but much less than with clozapine. Single-drug overdoses of olanzapine are rarely lethal.

Olanzapine is a reasonable first-line antipsychotic for schizophrenia and acute mania. The dose can be titrated quickly. Although olanzapine is FDA-approved for bipolar maintenance, there are other effective options with less potential for weight gain.

Beyond diet and exercise, there are several options for ameliorating olanzapine-induced weight gain. Metformin is a great add-on to minimize weight gain and elevation of blood glucose. Aripiprazole (Abilify) ameliorates weight gain as an adjunct to olanzapine (Henderson et al, 2009). Melatonin and the antiepileptic drug topiramate (Topamax) have also been used.

Olanzapine is an effective antiemetic comparable to promethazine (Phenergan). It is modestly effective for promoting weight gain with anorexia nervosa, but also half of anorexic patients discontinue it.

Half-life is 21 to 54 hours. IM olanzapine generally reaches maximum concentration in 15 to 45 minutes, compared with 4 hours after an oral dose.

Zyprexa ZYDIS is the orally disintegrating tablet (ODT) version of olanzapine, useful for patients liable to cheek and discard pills. The name is a contraction of "disintegrating Zyprexa".

IM Zyprexa, FDA-approved for acute agitation in schizophrenia or bipolar, is contraindicated in combination with IM lorazepam (Ativan) due to risk of respiratory depression. However, Evidence of risk with the IM olanzapine/benzodiazepine combination is lacking (Williams et al, 2018).

Zyprexa RELPREVV is the long-acting injectable (LAI) formulation. It is rarely prescribed because the patient must be monitored for at least three hours post-injection due to risk of post-injection delirium/sedation syndrome.

SYMBYAX is a branded fixed-dose combination of olanzapine (6–12 mg) and fluoxetine (Prozac), FDA-approved for acute depression in bipolar I disorder and treatment-resistant unipolar depression.

The FDA maximum is 20 mg/day, but higher doses are well-tolerated and associated with better efficacy. This is not the case with most other antipsychotics. High-dose olanzapine may be a safer alternative to clozapine for refractory psychosis. The main side effects at high dose are anticholinergic (page 161).

Therapeutic blood level monitoring for olanzapine may be useful, more so than with most antipsychotics. The therapeutic serum range is about 20–80 ng/mL, but higher concentrations may be necessary. There is no need to check olanzapine levels if the patient is doing well at modest doses (≤ 20 mg). Olanzapine level > 700 ng/mL is considered toxic and associated with QT prolongation.

PO Dosing: For schizophrenia, starting dose is usually 5–10 mg HS. FDA max is 20 mg/day, but for treatment-resistant cases, 30 mg or 40 mg total daily dose (typically divided BID) is commonly necessary. The author occasionally goes as high as 60 mg/day divided 30 mg BID. Stahl (2017) regards doses up to 90 mg/day as occasionally justifiable for short-term treatment. **For acute mania or psychosis** in the inpatient setting, the author generally starts 10 mg HS or BID, plus 5–10 mg PRN.

Oral dose does not need to be adjusted for renal impairment. Use a lower dose with moderate/severe hepatic impairment. As with most antipsychotics, treatment should be suspended if absolute neutrophil count (ANC) drops below 1,000 or if Drug Rash with Eosinophilia and Systemic Symptoms (DRESS syndrome) is suspected.

IM Dosing: The recommended initial injection for acute agitation is 10 mg. A second injection can be given after 2 hours, with no more than 3 injections within 24 hours.

Seizure risk among antipsychotics:

#1 Clozapine (Clozaril) 10x risk at high dose
#2 **Olanzapine (Zyprexa)** 3x
#3 Quetiapine (Seroquel) 2x
#4 Chlorpromazine (Thorazine) 2x

Risk is minimal for other antipsychotics. Risperidone (Risperdal), haloperidol (Haldol), fluphenazine (Prolixin), and thiothixene (Navane) are especially safe.

Weight gain among 2nd gen antipsychotics (SGAs), approximate rank:

1. **Olanzapine (Zyprexa)** - large weight gain, may be extreme
2. Clozapine (Clozaril) - nearly as much as olanzapine
3. Iloperidone (Fanapt) - higher than quetiapine
4. Quetiapine (Seroquel) - similar to risperidone
5. Risperidone (Risperdal)
6. Paliperidone (Invega) - equal to risperidone
7. Brexpiprazole (Rexulti)
8. Asenapine (Saphris) - low potential for weight gain
9. Aripiprazole (Abilify) - minimal
10. Cariprazine (Vraylar)
11. Ziprasidone (Geodon) - possible weight loss
12. Lurasidone (Latuda) - possible weight loss

Dynamic interactions:

- Antidopaminergic
- EPS (low)
- Anticholinergic (moderate)
- Sedation (moderate)
- Hypotensive effects (moderate)
- Lowers seizure threshold
- Prolactin elevation (weak)
- Hyperglycemia (high)
- Weight gain (high)

Kinetic interactions:

- 1A2 substrate
- Smokers may need a higher dose of olanzapine due to 1A2 inDuction by tobacco. Nicotine replacement products (gum, patches) do not induce 1A2.
- Use lower doses of olanzapine if co-administered with a 1A2 inhibitor such as fluvoxamine (Luvox).

1A2 substrate

page 10

Most women are slow at metabolizing 1A2 substrates. Expect a woman's olanzapine blood level to be up to double that of a man taking the same dose.

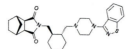

#227
2010
$1,212–$1,490

Lurasidone (LATUDA)

loo RAS i dohn / la TUDE a
"Lured (to the) Latitude"

- ❖ Antipsychotic (SGA)
- ❖ D2 antagonist - ⇩ DA
- ❖ 5-HT_{2A} antagonist - ⇧ DA

20
40
60
80
120
mg

FDA-approved for:

- ❖ Schizophrenia
- ❖ Bipolar I depressive episode - monotherapy
- ❖ Bipolar depression as adjunct to lithium or valproate (Depakote, Depakene)—but contraindicated with carbamazepine (Tegretol)

Used off-label for:

- ❖ Bipolar maintenance

Among antipsychotics, lurasidone (Latuda) is the most metabolically favorable. Weight loss is more likely than weight gain, and lurasidone actually *improves* Hgb A1c! The same can be said about ziprasidone (Geodon), which is the antipsychotic most similar to lurasidone.

Half-life of lurasidone is 18 to 40 hours. It is dosed once daily with at least 350 calories, usually with the evening meal. Food is necessary for absorption. Compare this to ziprasidone, which must be given with food for the same reason, but ziprasidone has a shorter half-life, necessitating twice daily dosing. Another advantage of lurasidone (over ziprasidone) is lack of QT prolongation. Most other antipsychotics prolong QT interval to some extent.

Despite these advantages, patients with schizophrenia in clinical trials were likely to discontinue treatment with Latuda, due to either lack of benefit and/or side effects. In the real world, Latuda is even more likely to be stopped due to cost.

Antipsychotics are represented with spooky mascots.

It is noteworthy that the SGAs that do not cause weight gain (Latuda and Geodon) are the most likely to be stopped, while those causing the most weight gain (Zyprexa and Clozapine) are the most likely to be continued.

Lurasidone is relatively more likely than other SGAs to cause extrapyramidal symptoms (EPS).

Lurasidone is almost exclusively metabolized by CYP3A4, making it highly vulnerable to kinetic interactions. With most substrate medications, interactions can be handled by adjusting the dose. With lurasidone, 3A4 interactions are of such high consequence that it is contraindicated with strong 3A4 inducers or inhibitors.

Although the patent for lurasidone has expired, it still costs over $1,200 monthly in the US. In 2019 the FDA granted five drugmakers permission to sell generic versions. These companies struck a deal with Latuda's manufacturer to keep generic lurasidone off the market until 2023. In Canada, the price of brand-name Latuda is less than $180 monthly, and generic lurasidone is available for less than $70.

Dosing: For schizophrenia, start 40 mg QD with evening meal, max 160 mg/day; For bipolar depression, start 20 mg QD with evening meal, max 120 mg/day. Decrease dose for hepatic insufficiency.

Antipsychotics approved for bipolar depression (2020), listed in order of apparent effectiveness:

Second generation antipsychotic	NNT*
Olanzapine/fluoxetine combo (Symbyax)	4
Lurasidone (Latuda)	5
Quetiapine XR (Seroquel XR)	6
Cariprazine (Vraylar)	7

*NNT = Number Needed to Treat, i.e., number of patients you need to treat for one patient to respond. The lower the NNT, the more effective the medication.

All-cause discontinuation of SGAs in clinical trials for schizophrenia, approximate rank from most to least likely to be stopped by doctor or patient:

- ❖ **Lurasidone (Latuda)** - most likely to be stopped
- ❖ Ziprasidone (Geodon) - slightly fewer discontinuations than lurasidone
- ❖ Iloperidone (Fanapt)
- ❖ Asenapine (Saphris)
- ❖ Quetiapine (Seroquel)
- ❖ Aripiprazole (Abilify)
- ❖ Risperidone (Risperdal)
- ❖ Paliperidone (Invega)
- ❖ Clozapine (Clozaril) - despite side effects and inconveniences, patients continue it because it is effective
- ❖ Olanzapine (Zyprexa) - effective and usually no issues other than weight gain and diabetes

The fish (our symbol for 3A4 substrate) is big because with lurasidone 3A4 interactions are a very big deal.

Lurasidone is **contraindicated** with strong 3A4 inDucers, because lurasidone will be useless due to rapid clearance, reducing lurasidone levels by about **6-fold:**

- ❖ Carbamazepine (Tegretol)
- ❖ Phenytoin (Dilantin)
- ❖ Phenobarbital (Luminal)
- ❖ St. John's wort
- ❖ Rifampin

Lurasidone is also **contraindicated** with strong 3A4 inHibitors due to radically increased lurasidone levels, up to **8-fold**:

- ❖ Fluconazole and other -azole antifungals
- ❖ Clarithromycin (antibacterial)
- ❖ Ritonavir (antiretroviral for HIV)

The minimal effective daily dose for schizophrenia is 40 mg. If coadministered with a **moderate** 3A4 inDucer, lurasidone may need to be titrated to a higher dose. If used with a moderate 3A4 inHibitor, give half of the usual dose.

Dynamic interactions:

- ❖ Antidopaminergic
- ❖ Extrapyramidal effects
- ❖ Sedation (moderate)
- ❖ Hypotensive effects
- ❖ Prolactin elevation (mild)

Kinetic interactions:

- ❖ 3A4 substrate (major)

page 16

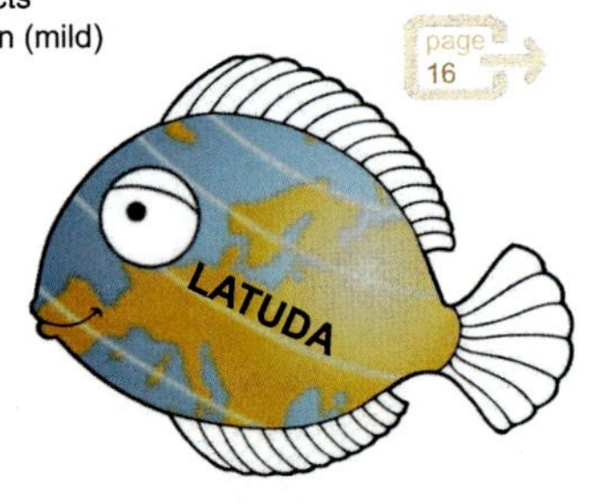

3A4 substrate (major)

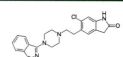

2001
$32–$292

Ziprasidone (GEODON)

zi PRAY si dohn / GEE o don

"Geode Don's Zipper"

- ❖ Antipsychotic (SGA)
- ❖ D2 antagonist - ⇩ DA
- ❖ 5-HT_{2A} antagonist - ⇧ DA

20
40
60
80
mg

FDA-approved for:

- ❖ Schizophrenia
- ❖ Bipolar mania
- ❖ Schizophrenia-associated agitation (IM)

Used off-label for:

- ❖ Bipolar maintenance
- ❖ Impulse control disorders
- ❖ Delirium
- ❖ Agitation of any type (IM)

For this antipsychotic, think *"Geo-down"*, as in bringing a psychotic or manic patient down to earth.

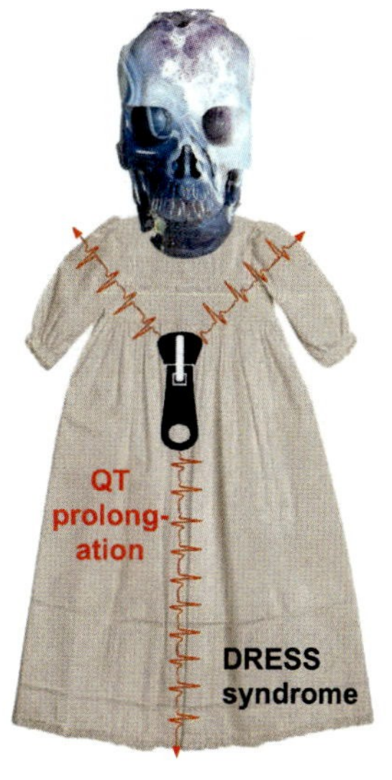

geode

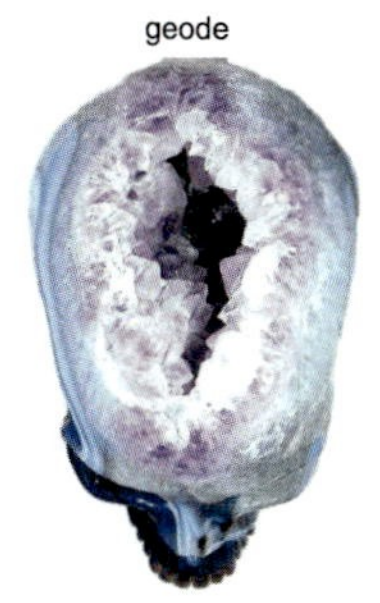

Antipsychotics are represented with spooky mascots.

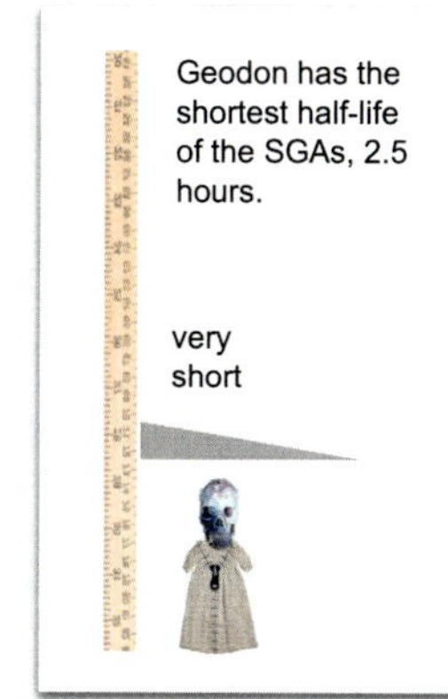

Geodon has the shortest half-life of the SGAs, 2.5 hours.
very short

Ziprasidone (Geodon) is recognized as <u>the SGA most likely to prolong QT interval</u>. At the maximum approved dose of 160 mg/day, ziprasidone is expected to prolong QTc by 10 msec. However, *clinically significant* QT prolongation (QTc > 500 msec) at 160 mg does not exceed placebo (Klein-Schwarz et al, 2007). QT prolongation with ziprasidone can be dangerous with overdose or polypharmacy. It is advisable to check an EKG before exceeding the FDA maximum dose or when combining ziprasidone with other QT prolonging drugs (page 82).

Ziprasidone has a <u>benign metabolic profile</u>, potentially having a positive impact on lipids and blood sugar. Patients may even have a <u>modest weight loss</u> with ziprasidone. Unfortunately, it is <u>not as effective</u> for schizophrenia as the more fattening SGAs like olanzapine (Zyprexa), risperidone (Risperdal), and clozapine (Clozaril). It is to be taken BID <u>with meals</u>, which is <u>necessary for adequate absorption</u>. The most similar antipsychotic to ziprasidone is lurasidone (Latuda), which may also improve metabolic parameters and must be taken with food for absorption. Ziprasidone is dosed BID, while lurasidone is QD.

Immediate-release IM ziprasidone is among first-line choices for acute psychotic agitation. IM ziprasidone is suitable for agitation associated with acute delirium because it <u>lacks significant anticholinergic effects</u>. IM ziprasidone can be prepared quickly, with a 30 second shake of the vial. There is no long-acting Injectable (LAI) formulation.

<u>DRESS syndrome</u> (Drug Reaction with Eosinophilia and Systemic Symptoms) is a rare but potentially fatal illness associated with ziprasidone. DRESS begins as a rash and progresses to swollen lymph nodes, fever, and inflammation of multiple organs. The heart, liver, kidneys, and pancreas may be damaged. Be especially vigilant for rash with ziprasidone and be quick to stop the medication if DRESS is suspected. Other medications that may rarely cause DRESS are the antipsychotic olanzapine (Zyprexa), modafinil (Provigil), several antibiotics, and several anticonvulsants including gabapentin (Neurontin).

Risk of death with single-drug overdose on ziprasidone is about 1 in 1,400, based on calls to Poison Control (Nelson & Spyker, 2017).

The 3 psychotropic medications that must be taken **with food** for adequate absorption - the *DONE-nuts*.

- ❖ Vilazo<u>done</u> (VIIBRYD) - antidepressant
- ❖ Zipras<u>idone</u> (GEODON) - antipsychotic
- ❖ Luras<u>idone</u> (LATUDA) - antipsychotic

Without food, absorption is decreased by 50%.

PO Dosing: <u>Titrate quickly for mania</u>, starting 40 mg BID with meals for one day (2 doses) then increase to the target dose of 60–80 mg BID. FDA maximum dose is 160 mg/day (80 BID), although safety data exists for up to 320 mg/day (160 mg BID); Check EKG before exceeding the FDA max; <u>Titrate slowly for schizophrenia</u>, starting at 20 mg BID. For schizophrenia "doses > 40 mg/day (20 mg BID) are rarely more effective". As with most antipsychotics, discontinue if absolute neutrophil count (ANC) drops below 1,000.

IM Dosing: For <u>schizophrenia-associated agitation</u> (or off-label for any kind of agitation) may give 10 mg IM q 2 hours PRN or 20 mg IM q 4 hours PRN; Max is 40 mg/day x 3 days. The author uses the 20 mg dose unless the patient is small, elderly or medically compromised.

QT prolongation among SGAs: 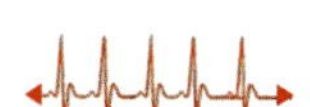 
page 82

Risk	Second Generation Antipsychotic
Mod/High	Ziprasidone (Geodon)
Moderate	Iloperidone (Fanapt)
Low/Mod	Asenapine (Saphris), Clozapine (Clozaril), Quetiapine (Seroquel), Risperidone (Risperdal)
Low	Paliperidone (Invega), Pimavanserin (Nuplazid)
Essentially none	Lumateperone (Caplyta), Lurasidone (Latuda), Olanzapine (Zyprexa); **All D2 partial agonists:** Aripiprazole (Abilify), Brexpiprazole (Rexulti), Cariprazine (Vraylar)

page 18

Dynamic interactions:

- ❖ Antidopaminergic
- ❖ EPS
- ❖ Sedation (strong)
- ❖ QT prolongation
- ❖ Hypotensive effects
- ❖ Prolactin elevation (mild)

Kinetic interactions:

- ❖ Metabolized in liver primarily by aldehyde oxidase, with small contribution from several CYP enzymes

in a bubble - minimal clinically significant kinetic interactions

1990
$42–$184 + labs

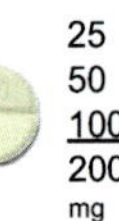

Clozapine (CLOZARIL)

KLOE za peen / KLOE za ril

"Clothes pin"

- Antipsychotic (SGA)
- D2 antagonist - ⇩ DA
- 5-HT_{2A} antagonist - ⇧ DA
- Alpha-adrenergic antagonist

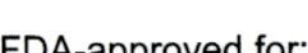

25
50
<u>100</u>
200
mg

FDA-approved for:

- <u>Treatment-resistant</u> schizophrenia
- Prevention of schizophrenia-associated <u>suicide</u>

Used off-label for:

- Treatment-resistant aggression
- Psychosis with tardive dyskinesia
- Psychosis with Parkinson's disease

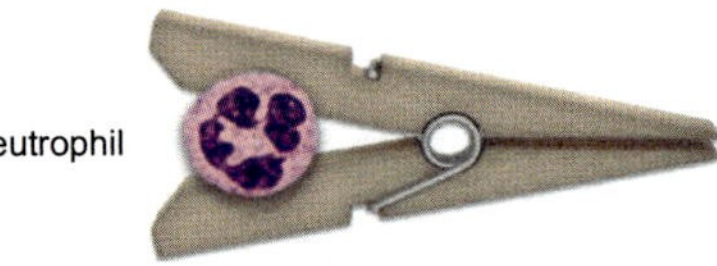

Clozapine, released in 1990 as <u>the first atypical</u> (2nd generation) antipsychotic, is clearly the <u>most effective treatment for schizophrenia</u>. Clozapine can be a <u>miracle drug</u> when nothing else works. It is the only antipsychotic approved specifically for treatment-resistant schizophrenia. Clozapine is the only antipsychotic shown to <u>reduce suicide</u> associated with schizophrenia. It is a truly atypical antipsychotic in that it does not cause EPS, which is a beautiful thing considering the population being treated with clozapine, i.e., individuals with severe psychosis who would otherwise be at high risk of tardive dyskinesia (TD) from high doses of other antipsychotics.

Although several SGAs do not cause EPS above placebo (olanzapine, quetiapine, iloperidone, pimavanserin, lumateperone), with clozapine the <u>risk of EPS is *less than* placebo</u> (Leucht et al, 2013). Clozapine <u>*improves* tardive dyskinesia</u>. Clozapine is an antipsychotic of choice for those with Parkinson's disease (along with quetiapine and pimavanserin).

Unfortunately, clozapine is plagued by <u>serious risks</u> and <u>severe side effects</u>. Of all available psychiatric medications, clozapine is <u>#2 for weight gain</u>, a close second to olanzapine. Clozapine is <u>#1 for constipation</u> and <u>#1 for sialorrhea</u> (salivation) due to <u>anticholinergic effect on the colon</u> and <u>cholinergic effect on salivary glands</u>, respectively. The S in the cholinergic SLUDGE mnemonic stands for salivation (page 161). Clozapine does not elevate prolactin levels.

Despite clozapine's superiority for treatment-resistant schizophrenia, only 5% of patients who would benefit from clozapine are prescribed it (Olfson et al, 2016). Many psychiatrists are understandably reluctant to prescribe clozapine, given the health risks and time/effort involved in the initial titration, which often includes <u>tapering off sedatives</u>, anticholinergics and other antipsychotics. All prescribers must certify in the Clozapine Risk Evaluation and Mitigation Strategy (REMS) program, which takes less than an hour. *The Clozapine Handbook* by Meyer & Stahl is recommended for prescribers of this complicated medication.

Clozapine increases the probability of <u>seizures</u> up to 10-fold. Clozapine is the only psychotropic drug with a **black box warning** for lowering seizure threshold. Since seizure risk is dose-dependent, consider adding a prophylactic antiepileptic (valproate or lamotrigine) when exceeding 600 mg/day. Other **black box warnings** concern severe <u>neutropenia</u>, orthostatic <u>hypotension</u> / bradycardia / syncope, <u>myocarditis</u> / cardiomyopathy / mitral valve incompetence and (applicable to all antipsychotics) mortality in dementia-related psychosis.

Risk of life-threatening neutropenia (agranulocytosis) necessitates frequent blood draws. <u>Absolute neutrophil count</u> (ANC) must be checked <u>weekly</u> for the first 6 months, twice monthly for the next 6 months, then monthly ad infinitum. Pharmacies will not dispense clozapine unless ANC values are current in the national clozapine REMS database, which trademarked the slogan "No Blood, No Drug" (apropos to our vampire mascot). Clozapine treatment should be interrupted if <u>ANC drops below 1,000</u> unless the patient had low baseline ANC as seen in some individuals of African descent, a condition known as Benign Ethnic Neutropenia (BEN).

A majority of patients on clozapine become <u>constipated</u>. Although agranulocytosis may be fatal, patients are more likely to die from clozapine-related <u>bowel obstruction</u>, which may progress to toxic megacolon and bowel rupture. It is wise to start docusate (Colace) 100 mg with senna 17.2 mg when starting clozapine. <u>Avoid anticholinergics</u>. Encourage hydration and physical activity to ameliorate constipation.

Half-life of clozapine is 12 hours. Clozapine must be <u>slowly titrated</u> to avoid orthostatic <u>hypotension</u> and <u>sedation</u>. If the patient becomes <u>febrile</u> within 6 weeks, <u>suspect myocarditis</u> and order EKG, C-reactive protein (CRP), and troponin. As clozapine is being titrated, it is often possible to taper off most of the patient's other psychotropic medications. Extreme caution should be used if combining clozapine with benzodiazepines, opioids, or other drugs that may depress respiration.

Dosing: BID dosing; AM and HS doses may be unequal with HS > AM dose. Consolidate to HS if sedation is problematic. <u>Tobacco</u> users may need double the dose due to 1A2 induction. Initial <u>outpatient titration</u> (non-smokers): 12.5 mg HS (days 1–2), 25 mg/day (days 3–5), 50 mg/day (days 6–8), 75 mg/day (9–11), 100 mg/day (days 12–14), 125 mg/day (days 15–17), 150 mg/day (days 18–20); 175 mg/day (days 21–23); 200 mg/day (days 24 onward). For initiation in <u>inpatient setting</u>, 200 mg/day can be achieved in 1–2 weeks; <u>Target dose</u> is 300–600 mg/day with max of 900 mg/day, guided by blood levels and clinical response. Check <u>clozapine blood level</u> 4 days after establishment of the full-strength dose. The target blood level for clozapine is <u>≥ 350</u> ng/ml, not including the norclozapine metabolite. It is less effective at blood level > 700 ng/ml; High seizure risk > 1200 ng/ml; Toxic > 1500 ng/ml.

In addition to neutropenia, major risks and side effects of clozapine include:

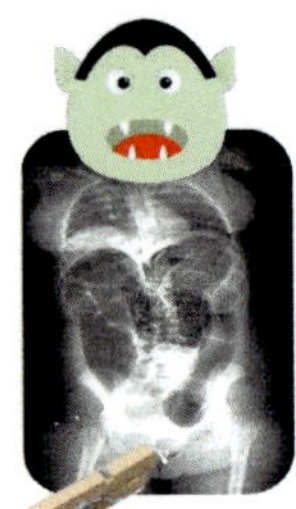

Severe constipation, which can lead to toxic megacolon and bowel rupture. Mechanism of constipation is anticholinergic and anti-serotonergic. See page 246 for constipation management.

Hypersalivation by cholinergic mechanism (the S in SLUDGE)

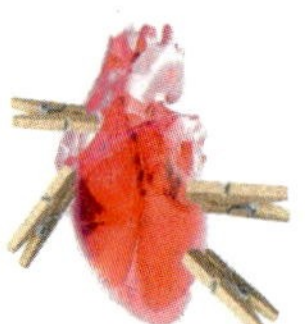

Potentially fatal myocarditis

Weight gain

Antipsychotics are represented with spooky mascots.

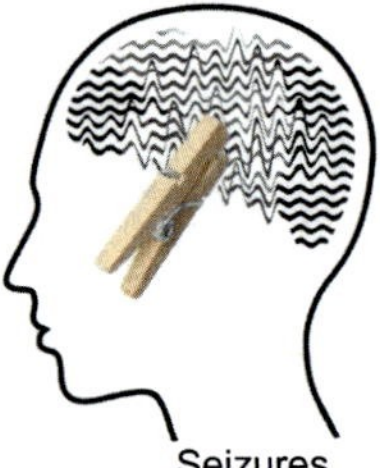

Seizures

By in<u>D</u>ucing 1A2, tobacco decreases serum clozapine levels by about 50%. Smokers require a double dose.

As a potent in<u>H</u>ibitor of 1A2, fluvoxamine (Luvox) increases clozapine levels 3-fold on average (but up to 10-fold in some cases). As a less potent 1A2 in<u>H</u>ibitor, ciprofloxacin increases clozapine exposure about 2-fold. See page 11 for important nuances of the fluvoxamine interaction.

Major inflammations, infections with fever or female gender (estrogen) may increase clozapine levels 2-fold (page 11).

Dynamic interactions:

- Antidopaminergic
- Anticholinergic (constipation)
- Sedation (strong)
- Hypotensive effects (strong)
- Lowers seizure threshold (high)
- Hyperglycemia (high)
- Weight gain (high)
- QT prolongation (low/moderate)
- Myelosuppression
- Respiratory suppression with benzos

Kinetic interactions:

- 1A2 substrate (major)
- 3A4 substrate (minor)

pages 10-11

1A2 substrate

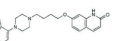

2015
$1,154–$1,351

Brexpiprazole (REXULTI)

brex PIP ra zole / rex UL tee

"Bee-Rex (Rex-salty)"

- Antipsychotic (SGA)
- D2 partial agonist - ⇔ DA
- $5\text{-}HT_{1A}$ partial agonist - ⇔ DA
- $5\text{-}HT_{2A}$ antagonist - ⇧ DA

0.25
0.5
1
2
3
4 mg

FDA-approved for:

- Schizophrenia
- Adjunct for major depression

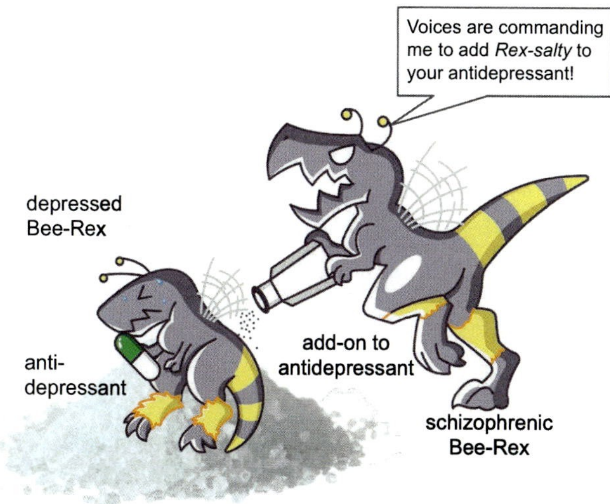

Brexpiprazole (Rexulti) was released in 2015 by the makers of aripiprazole (Abilify) as Abilify's patent was expiring. Rexulti has the same mechanism of action—dopamine D2 partial agonist, serotonin $5\text{-}HT_{1A}$ partial agonist and serotonin $5\text{-}HT_{2A}$ antagonist. It has been described as a Serotonin-Dopamine Activity Modulator.

Compared to Abilify, Rexulti has lower affinity for D2 receptors, thereby causing significantly less akathisia than Abilify. Rexulti has much higher affinity for $5\text{-}HT_{1A}$ and $5\text{-}HT_{2A}$ receptors, which may improve tolerability and contribute some anxiolytic effect.

Rexulti is FDA-approved for schizophrenia and as an adjunct to antidepressants for treatment of major depressive disorder (MDD).

Like Abilify, Rexulti is not expected to cause sedation.

Rexulti may be associated with more weight gain than Abilify. It does not lower prolactin (as does aripiprazole) but does not elevate prolactin to a clinically significant extent. Other side effects may include nausea, headaches, and dizziness.

Dosing: The recommended dose of Rexulti depends on the indication. For schizophrenia, the dose is higher, and the titration is faster than if augmenting an antidepressant. See below for details. It can be taken at morning or night, with or without food. As with most antipsychotics, discontinue if absolute neutrophil count (ANC) drops below 1,000.

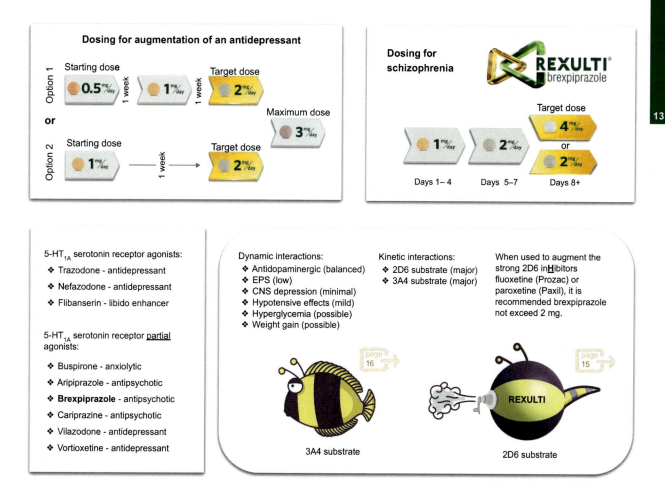

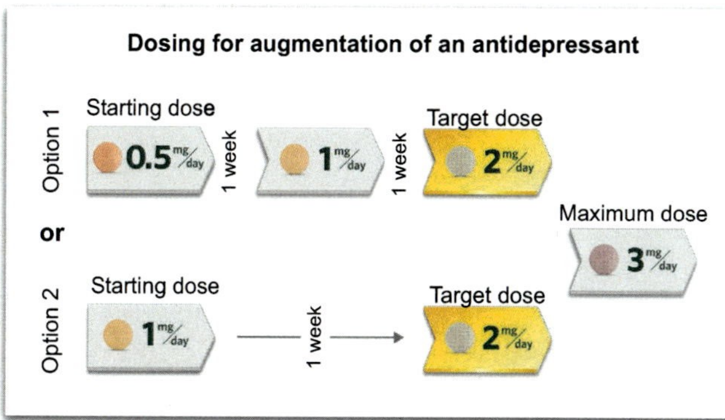

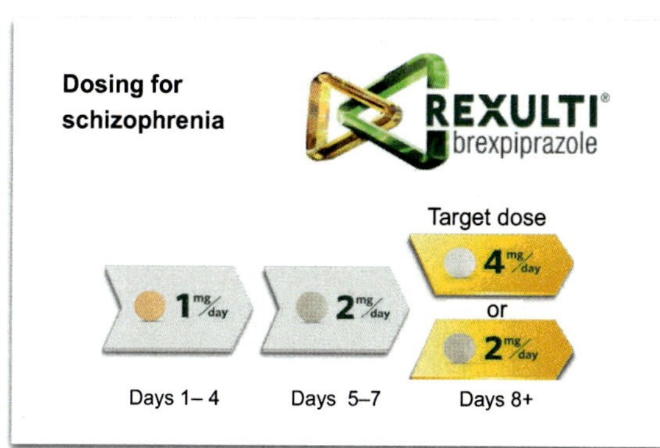

$5\text{-}HT_{1A}$ serotonin receptor agonists:

- Trazodone - antidepressant
- Nefazodone - antidepressant
- Flibanserin - libido enhancer

$5\text{-}HT_{1A}$ serotonin receptor partial agonists:

- Buspirone - anxiolytic
- Aripiprazole - antipsychotic
- **Brexpiprazole** - antipsychotic
- Cariprazine - antipsychotic
- Vilazodone - antidepressant
- Vortioxetine - antidepressant

Dynamic interactions:

- Antidopaminergic (balanced)
- EPS (low)
- CNS depression (minimal)
- Hypotensive effects (mild)
- Hyperglycemia (possible)
- Weight gain (possible)

Kinetic interactions:

- 2D6 substrate (major)
- 3A4 substrate (major)

When used to augment the strong 2D6 in**H**ibitors fluoxetine (Prozac) or paroxetine (Paxil), it is recommended brexpiprazole not exceed 2 mg.

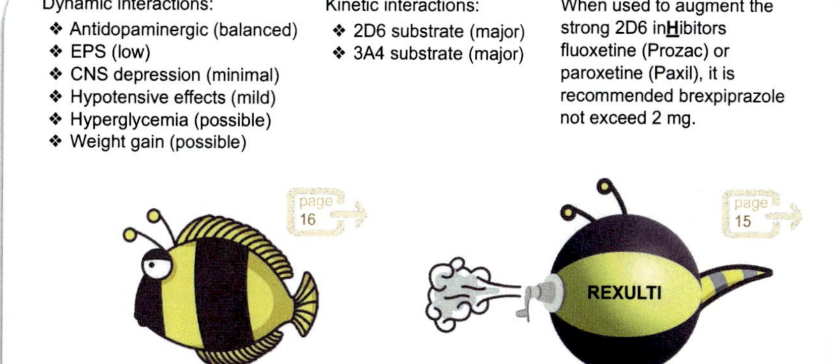

SGAs 13

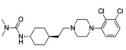

2016
$1,189–$1,452

Cariprazine (VRAYLAR)

kar IP ra zeen / va RAY lar

"Car ripper seen (going) Vroom!"

- Antipsychotic (SGA)
- D2 partial agonist - ⇔ DA
- D3 partial agonist - ⇔ DA
- 5-HT_{1A} partial agonist - ⇔ DA
- 5-HT_{2A} antagonist - ⇧ DA

1.5
3
4.5
6
mg

Take your pick of mnemonics: *"Car ripper seen (going) Vroom!", "Car's V-rays", "Car ripper praising V-rays".*

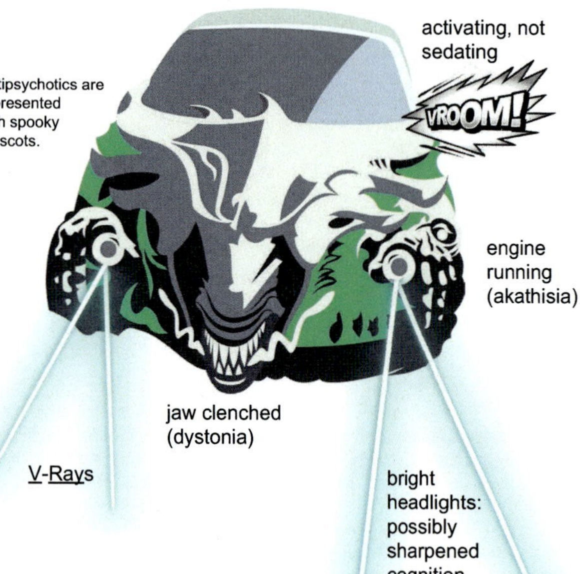

Antipsychotics are represented with spooky mascots.

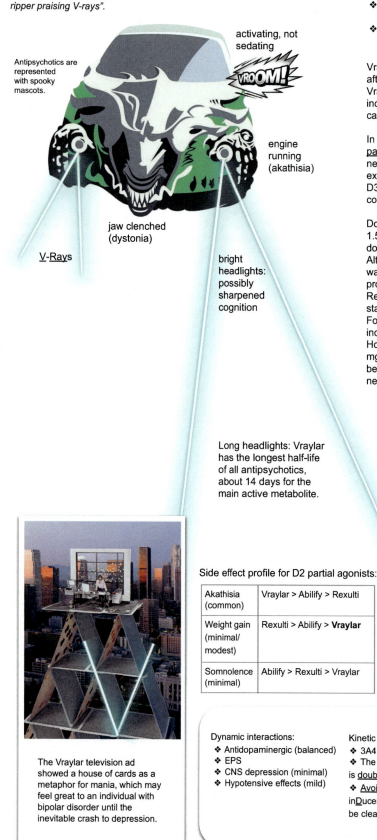

activating, not sedating

engine running (akathisia)

jaw clenched (dystonia)

V-Rays

bright headlights: possibly sharpened cognition

Long headlights: Vraylar has the longest half-life of all antipsychotics, about 14 days for the main active metabolite.

FDA-approved for
- Schizophrenia
- Bipolar I Disorder, manic/mixed episode
- Bipolar I Disorder, depressive episode

Used off-label for:
- Bipolar maintenance

Vraylar, released in 2016, is the third D2 partial agonist, after Abilify (aripiprazole) and Rexulti (brexpiprazole). Vraylar causes more EPS than Abilify and Rexulti, with 25% incidence of dystonia and 15% akathisia. It is more likely to cause nausea than other antipsychotics.

In addition to being a D2 partial agonist, Vraylar is D3 partial agonist, a unique property which may improve negative symptoms of schizophrenia (diminished emotional expression and avolition). Vraylar has a 5-fold selectivity for D3 over D2. Dopamine D3-preferring agents may provide cognitive benefits, although it may be too early to tell.

Dosing: For schizophrenia or mania, the label recommends 1.5 mg QD x 1 day, then 3 mg PO QD; May then adjust dose in 1.5 mg or 3 mg increments with max of 6 mg QD. Although higher doses were tested, no additional benefit was found at doses exceeding 6 mg; Because of the probability of akathisia, Dr. Tammas Kelly (Carlat Psychiatry Report, Aug 2019) recommends titrating more slowly, starting 1.5 mg QOD, increasing to 1.5 mg QD after a week. For bipolar depression the dose is 1.5 mg QD; At 14 days increase to the maximum dose for depression of 3 mg QD. However, the sweet spot for depression seems to be 1.5 mg, 3 mg causes more side effects without much additional benefit. As with most antipsychotics, discontinue if absolute neutrophil count (ANC) drops below 1,000.

Akathisia is an uncomfortable feeling of internal motor restlessness with difficulty sitting still. The patient may fidget, pace, or rock back and forth.

Akathisia among SGAs (most to least):

- Cariprazine (Vraylar) - high
- Lurasidone (Latuda) - high
- Risperidone (Risperdal)
- Aripiprazole (Abilify)
- Paliperidone (Invega)
- Asenapine (Saphris)
- Ziprasidone (Geodon)
- Olanzapine (Zyprexa)
- Brexpiprazole (Rexulti) - low
- Pimavanserin (Nuplazid) - low
- Iloperidone (Fanapt)
  - marketed for those with akathisia
- Clozapine (Clozaril) - very low
- Quetiapine (Seroquel) - least

The Vraylar television ad showed a house of cards as a metaphor for mania, which may feel great to an individual with bipolar disorder until the inevitable crash to depression.

Side effect profile for D2 partial agonists:

Akathisia (common)	Vraylar > Abilify > Rexulti
Weight gain (minimal/ modest)	Rexulti > Abilify > **Vraylar**
Somnolence (minimal)	Abilify > Rexulti > Vraylar

Dynamic interactions:
- Antidopaminergic (balanced)
- EPS
- CNS depression (minimal)
- Hypotensive effects (mild)

Kinetic interactions:
- 3A4 substrate (major)
- The concentration of Vraylar is doubled by 3A4 inHibitors
- Avoid prescribing with 3A4 inDucers because Vraylar will be cleared too quickly

page 16

3A4 substrate (major)

Cariprazine Paliperidone

2006
$224–$804

Paliperidone (INVEGA)

pal e PER i dohn / in VAY guh

"(Look what) Pale lips done In Vegas"

- Antipsychotic (SGA)
- D2 antagonist - ⇩ DA
- 5-HT_{2A} antagonist - ⇧ DA
- NE alpha-2 antagonist

1.5
3
<u>6</u>
9
mg

FDA-approved for:
- Schizophrenia
- Schizoaffective disorder

Used off-label for:
- Bipolar disorder
- Aggression

Antipsychotics are represented with spooky mascots.

Paliperidone (Invega) is <u>the active metabolite of risperidone</u> (Risperdal).

Paliperidone is cleared renally, so it is <u>prefered over risperidone for those with hepatic insufficiency</u>. Paliperidone has several other advantages to risperidone, including fewer interactions, slightly lower risk of EPS, and less sedation (although risperidone has relatively low sedation among antipsychotics). Paliperidone is <u>one of the least sedating</u> antipsychotics, allowing AM dosing. The only disadvantage of paliperidone is that, despite being available generically since 2015, it is > 10x more <u>expensive</u> than risperidone as of 2020. Refer to goodrx.com to see if this is still the case.

The tablet is extended-release, with a half-life of about 23 hours. The <u>long-acting injectable</u> (LAI) formulation (SUSTENNA) is given every 4 weeks. This is more convenient than the LAI version of risperidone (CONSTA), which is administered every 2 weeks. The monthly cost of Invega Sustenna and Risperdal Consta are equivalent, about $2,000 monthly.

Unfortunately <u>paliperidone elevates prolactin to the same extent as risperidone</u>. Either medication may cause gynecomastia, sexual dysfunction, and galactorrhea. With regard to prolactin elevation: risperidone = paliperidone >> all other second generation antipsychotics (SGAs).

Adult dosing: Start <u>6 mg</u> PO q AM, which may be an effective target dose. If needed, may increase by 3 mg/day in intervals of ≥ 5 days. Max is 12 mg/day. See page 160 for dosing of long-acting injectable (LAI) formulations of paliperidone.

Equivalent dosing

PO risperidone	PO paliperidone
1 mg	3 mg
2 mg	
3 mg	6 mg 9 mg 12 mg
4 mg	
6 mg	

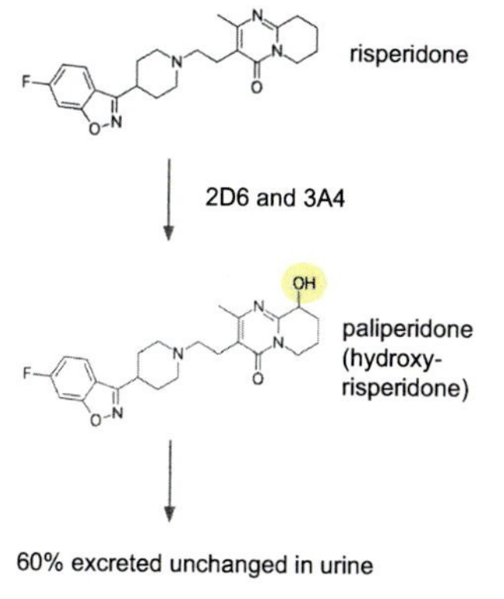

SGAs

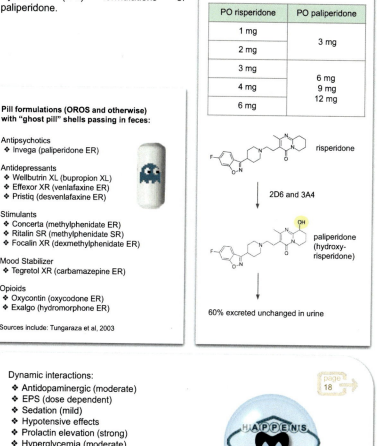

13

Long-acting injectable (LAI) options with paliperidone palmitate:

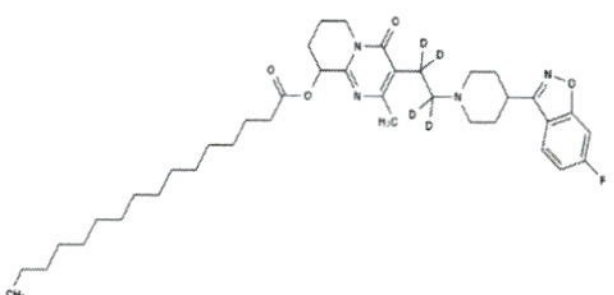

Invega SUSTENNA is q 4 weeks. <u>No PO overlap is needed</u>. This is a major advantage over the risperidone LAI (Risperdal Consta), which is q 2 weeks and requires a 3 week PO overlap.

Invega TRINZA, the q 3 month LAI, is available after 4 months of stability on Invega SUSTENNA.

Refer to page 160 for dosing.

Pill formulations (OROS and otherwise) with "ghost pill" shells passing in feces:

Antipsychotics
- Invega (paliperidone ER)

Antidepressants
- Wellbutrin XL (bupropion XL)
- Effexor XR (venlafaxine ER)
- Pristiq (desvenlafaxine ER)

Stimulants
- Concerta (methylphenidate ER)
- Ritalin SR (methylphenidate SR)
- Focalin XR (dexmethylphenidate ER)

Mood Stabilizer
- Tegretol XR (carbamazepine ER)

Opioids
- Oxycontin (oxycodone ER)
- Exalgo (hydromorphone ER)

Sources include: Tungaraza et al, 2003

The paliperidone tablet is an <u>O</u>smotic controlled <u>R</u>elease <u>O</u>ral delivery <u>S</u>ystem (OROS). The drug is expelled through tiny holes in the coating, and empty "ghost capsules" are passed in feces.

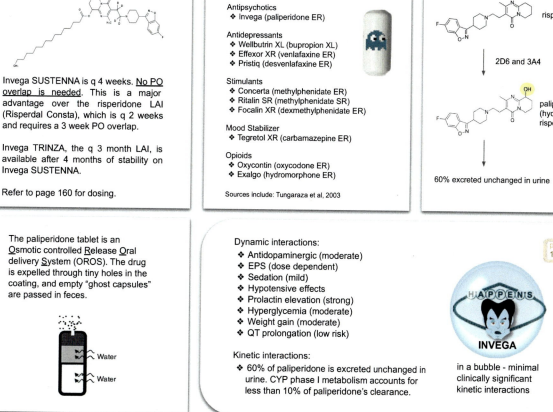

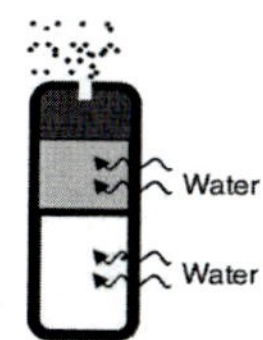

Dynamic interactions:
- Antidopaminergic (moderate)
- EPS (dose dependent)
- Sedation (mild)
- Hypotensive effects
- Prolactin elevation (strong)
- Hyperglycemia (moderate)
- Weight gain (moderate)
- QT prolongation (low risk)

Kinetic interactions:
- 60% of paliperidone is excreted unchanged in urine. CYP phase I metabolism accounts for less than 10% of paliperidone's clearance.

page 18

in a bubble - minimal clinically significant kinetic interactions

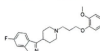

2009
$1,027–$1,116

Iloperidone (FANAPT)

eye loe PER i dohn / fan APT

"Fan Napped (with) Eye Opener"

- Antipsychotic (SGA)
- D2 antagonist - ⇩ DA
- 5-HT_{2A} antagonist - ⇧ DA

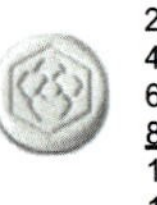

1
2
4
6
8
10
12 mg

FDA-approved for:
- Schizophrenia

Used off-label for:
- Bipolar disorder

"(Look what that) Eye Opener done (while that) Fan Napped."

Iloperidone (Fanapt), released in 2009, is marketed for patients taking antipsychotic medication who can't sit still, because it has low incidence of akathisia. Fanapt's only FDA-approved indication is schizophrenia.

The starting dose must be titrated to avoid orthostatic hypotension. Among antipsychotics, Fanapt has relatively high potential for weight gain, a distant #3 behind olanzapine and clozapine—*Fanapt gives you a fat fanny*.

Among available SGAs, Fanapt has a relatively high tendency to prolong QT interval, #2 behind ziprasidone (Geodon) among SGAs. Although the risk of clinically significant QT prolongation is minimal, advertisements for Fanapt caution "in choosing among treatments, prescribers should consider the ability of Fanapt to prolong the QT interval and the use of other drugs first".

Half-life is about 18 hours. It should be discontinued if absolute neutrophil count (ANC) drops below 1000 or if there is an unexplained drop in WBC.

As a point of trivia, iloperidone shares a mechanism of action with the rarely prescribed tricyclic antidepressant (TCA) trimipramine (Surmontil).

Iloperidone failed the approval process in Europe for treatment of schizophrenia, because risks of the drugs were deemed to outweigh potential benefits.

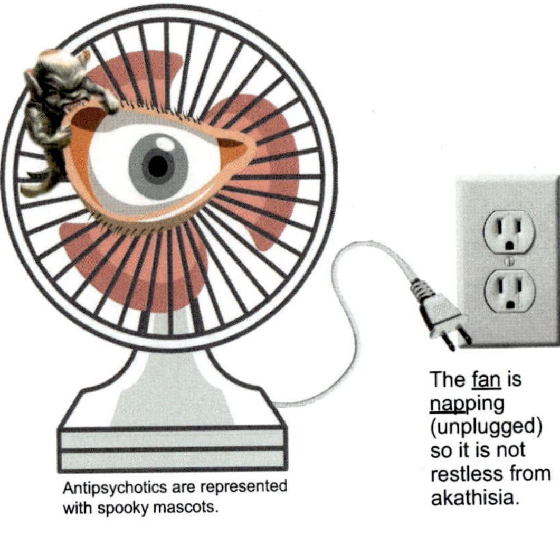

Antipsychotics are represented with spooky mascots.

The fan is napping (unplugged) so it is not restless from akathisia.

Dosing: See below for titration schedule. The titration pack contains #2 of 1 mg, #2 of 2 mg, #2 of 4 mg, and #2 of 6 mg tabs. The target dose for schizophrenia is 6–12 mg BID. Maximum 24 mg total daily dose. Adjust dose for kinetic interactions described below.

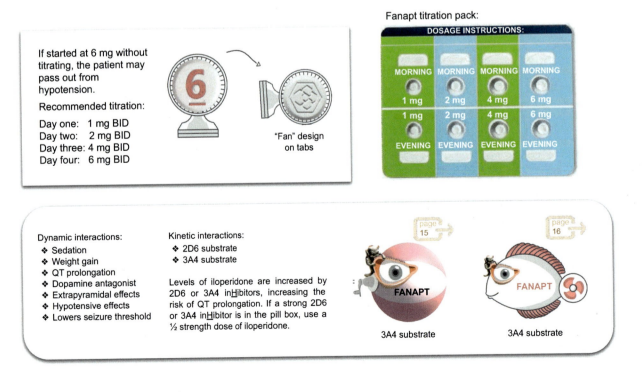

If started at 6 mg without titrating, the patient may pass out from hypotension.

Recommended titration:

Day one: 1 mg BID
Day two: 2 mg BID
Day three: 4 mg BID
Day four: 6 mg BID

"Fan" design on tabs

Fanapt titration pack:

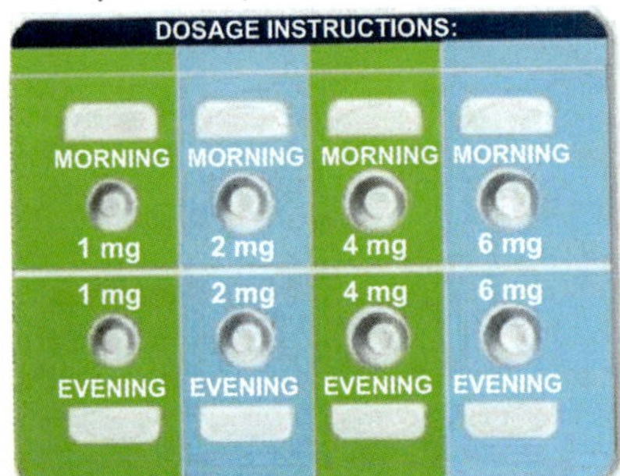

Dynamic interactions:
- Sedation
- Weight gain
- QT prolongation
- Dopamine antagonist
- Extrapyramidal effects
- Hypotensive effects
- Lowers seizure threshold

Kinetic interactions:
- 2D6 substrate
- 3A4 substrate

Levels of iloperidone are increased by 2D6 or 3A4 inHibitors, increasing the risk of QT prolongation. If a strong 2D6 or 3A4 inHibitor is in the pill box, use a ½ strength dose of iloperidone.

page 15

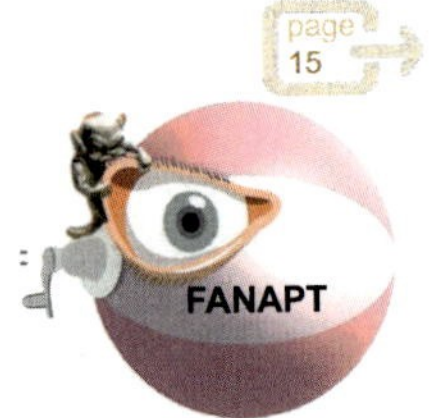

3A4 substrate

page 16

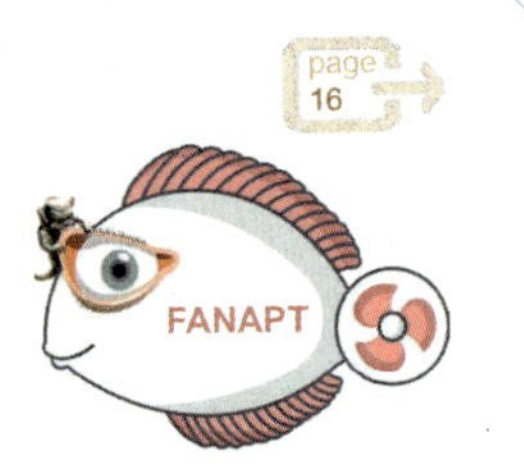

3A4 substrate

2009
$599–$728

Asenapine (SAPHRIS)

a SEN a peen / SAFF ris
"Sapphire (for an) Ass in a pine"

❖ Antipsychotic (SGA)
❖ D2 antagonist - ⇩ DA
❖ 5-HT_{2A} antagonist - ⇧ DA
❖ Alpha-adrenergic antagonist

2.5
5
10
mg

FDA-approved for:
❖ Schizophrenia
❖ Bipolar disorder (ages 10+)
- acute manic/mixed episode
- maintenance

Used off-label for:
❖ Acute agitation

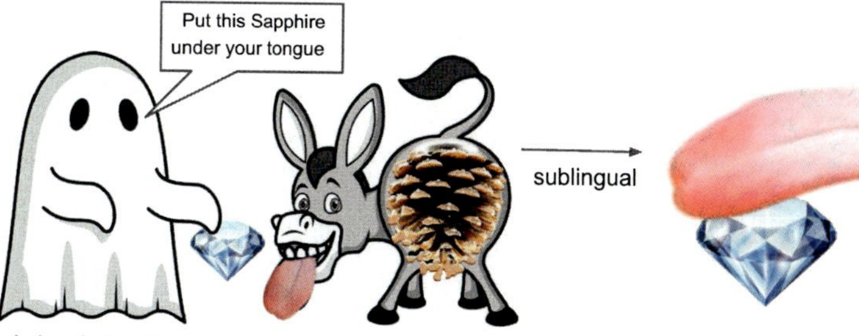
Put this Sapphire under your tongue
sublingual
Antipsychotics are represented with spooky mascots.

Asenapine (Saphris), approved in 2009, is the only sublingual antipsychotic. The patient should not eat or drink for 10 minutes after taking it because serum levels will be decreased by about 15%. The swallowed portion of the medication is subject to first-pass metabolism in the liver before entering the general circulation. Some patients report lingering bad taste or numbing of the tongue. Patients complained about the original taste, so it now has a black cherry flavor. The patent for Saphris expires in 2021.

Asenapine can be used as a rapid-acting PRN for acute agitation. With sublingual administration it is absorbed directly into the bloodstream. Peak serum concentration is reached within 1 hour. The label recommends BID dosing, but half-life is 24 hours, so dosing it once daily at HS is a viable treatment option.

Asenapine is approved for schizophrenia and bipolar disorder. It is not a first-line choice for either condition due to cost, and rare idiopathic hypersensitivity reactions including anaphylaxis. Reactions may occur with the first dose.

Other side effects may include sedation, hypotension, and dose-related akathisia. Asenapine has little potential for causing weight gain. Oral ulcers are possible. Anticholinergic effects are minimal. It is contraindicated with severe hepatic insufficiency, because levels may increase 7-fold.

Dosing: The "minimal effective" daily dose for psychosis is 10 mg. The label recommends starting 5 mg BID, but to minimize sedation it is best given at night only (half-life is 24 hours). 10 mg HS is also a reasonable starting dose and target dose. Maximum dose is 20 mg/day. The 2.5 mg dose is for ages 10–17. Avoid rapid discontinuation. Taper over 2–4 weeks.

Saphris is a fluffy, white tablet that is too delicate for bottling, so it comes in a special case containing 10 tabs.

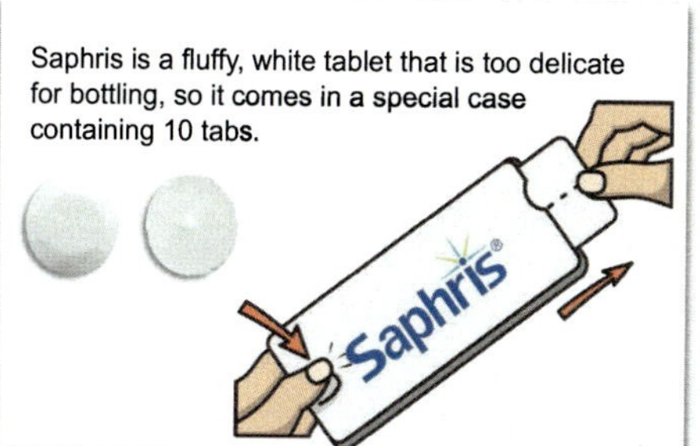
Saphris

Dynamic interactions:
❖ Antidopaminergic (moderate)
❖ EPS (dose dependent)
❖ Sedation (mild)
❖ Hypotensive effects
❖ Prolactin elevation (strong)
❖ Hyperglycemia (moderate)
❖ Weight gain (moderate)
❖ QT prolongation (low/moderate)

Kinetic interactions:
❖ 1A2 substrate (major)
- Smoking inDuces 1A2 and may lower levels of asenapine
- 1A2 inHibitors increase levels of asenapine, and dose adjustment is recommended.

1A2 substrate (minor)

page 10

SGAs

13

2019
$1,192

Asenapine transdermal (SECUADO)

a SEN a peen / seh kue AH doe
"See (the) caudal (end of an) Ass"

❖ Antipsychotic (SGA)
❖ D2 antagonist - ⇩ DA
❖ 5-HT_{2A} antagonist - ⇧ DA
❖ Alpha-adrenergic antagonist

3.8
5.7
7.6
/24 hr

FDA-approved for:
❖ Schizophrenia

Secuado (asenapine) is a once daily "transdermal drug delivery system" approved in 2019 for schizophrenia. This is the only transdermal antipsychotic. The transdermal route bypasses "first-pass" metabolism through the liver that oral medications are subject to. Asenapine tablets are not subject to "first-pass" metabolism either, because they are administered sublingually.

Onset of effect is much more gradual than with sublingual asenapine. It takes 12–24 hours for serum levels to peak (versus 1 hour sublingually).

Side effects include skin irritation (15%) and those associated with sublingual asenapine. Avoid exposing the patch to external heat sources during wear because drug absorption will be increased.

There have been no head-to-head comparisons between sublingual Saphris and transdermal Secuado.

Dosing: Start with the 3.8 mg/24 hours patch; The dosage may be increased to 5.7 mg/24 hours or 7.6 mg/24 hours, if needed, after one week; In short-term trials, there were more side effects and no added benefit with the maximum dose of 7.6 mg/24 hours

Dose equivalents: 3.8 mg/24 hours patch = 5 mg BID of sublingual asenapine; 7.6 mg/24 hours = 10 mg twice daily.

3.8 mg/24 hours
transdermal patch

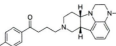

2020
$1300

Lumateperone (CAPLYTA)

LOO ma TE per one / kah PLY tah

"'Luminated Cap lighter"

- Antipsychotic (SGA)
- D2 antagonist - ⇩ DA
- 5-HT_{2A} antagonist - ⇧ DA
- Glutamate modulator

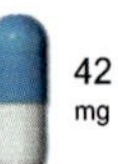

42 mg

FDA-approved for:

- Schizophrenia

Antipsychotics are represented with spooky mascots.

42 On Jackie Robinson Day (April 15), all players in Major League Baseball wear Robinson's uniform number, 42. For lumateperone, 42 mg is the only recommended dose.

Lumateperone is typically administered at night, which is also the time of day to illuminate a Jack-o'-lantern.

To improve tolerability, "take lumateperone with a bag of candy" (food) to delay peak blood levels.

Lumateperone (Caplyta) is a new antipsychotic that purportedly modulates glutamate in addition to the usual SGA mechanism of blocking D2 and 5-HT_{2A} receptors. However, the official prescribing information does not mention glutamate, suggesting the FDA saw insufficient evidence for lumateperone being a first-in-class novel antipsychotic. It appears to be equally effective as risperidone (Risperdal) with fewer side effects other than sedation (Citrome, 2016). Caplyta's effectiveness head-to-head with other antipsychotics is to be determined.

Lumateperone's D2 receptor occupancy is lower than most other antipsychotics. This means extrapyramidal side effects are unlikely. The other antipsychotics with low D2 occupancy are quetiapine (Seroquel) and clozapine (Clozaril).

Lumateperone is also a weak D2 receptor partial agonist. The stronger D2 partial agonists are aripiprazole (Abilify), brexpiprazole (Rexulti), and cariprazine (Vraylar).

Lumateperone has a favorable side effect profile. In clinical trials no single adverse effect led to > 2% discontinuation. The main side effects are somnolence/sedation (24% vs 10% placebo) and dry mouth (6% vs 2% placebo). At one year, lumateperone caused a modest weight loss of 3.2 kg (7 pounds) but a modest elevation in A1c and lipids. It does not appear to cause hypotension, prolactin elevation, or QT prolongation.

Lumateperone is extensively metabolized, resulting in more than twenty metabolites. Half-life is about 18 hours. It is a highly susceptible 3A4 substrate, making it contraindicated in combination with the medications listed below.

Because lumateperone can be highly sedating, it is typically administered at night. Taking lumateperone with food improves tolerability by delaying peak blood levels. This is more relevant if dosed during the day. Unlike ziprasidone (Geodon) and lurasidone (Latuda), taking lumateperone with food is not required for GI absorption.

Dosing: 42 mg is the only recommended dose, typically given at bedtime; Titration is not necessary (nor possible); No dose adjustment is required for renal impairment; Avoid with moderate/severe hepatic impairment.

Lumateperone is associated with a loss of 3.2 kg (7 pounds) at one year.

Dynamic interactions:

- Antidopaminergic
- Extrapyramidal effects (mild)
- Sedation (high/moderate)
- Hypotensive effects (minimal)
- Prolactin elevation (minimal)

Kinetic Interactions:

- 3A4 substrate
- UGT substrate

The fish (our symbol for a 3A4 substrate) is big because with lumateperone 3A4 interactions are a very big deal.

Lumateperone is contraindicated with 3A4 inDucers due to rapid clearance. Levels will be decreased up to 20-fold, rendering lumateperone useless when given concomitantly with:

- Carbamazepine (Tegretol)
- Modafinil (Provigil)
- Phenytoin (Dilantin)
- Phenobarbital (Luminal)
- Oxcarbazepine (Trileptal)
- St. John's wort
- Rifampin (20-fold decrease)

Lumateperone should also be avoided with moderate-to-strong 3A4 inHibitors which can dramatically increase blood levels. Strong 3A4 inhibitors include:

- Fluconazole and other -azole antifungals
- Clarithromycin (antibacterial)
- Ritonavir (antiretroviral, HIV treatment)

Lumateperone is a UGT substrate, which should not be combined with valproic acid (Depakote, Depakene)—a UGT inHibitor that dramatically increases lumateperone blood levels.

page 16

3A4 substrate (major)

page 17

UGT1A4 substrate

Lumateperone Pimavanserin

2017
$2,741–$3,097

Pimavanserin (NUPLAZID)

PIM a VAN ser in / Nu PLAHZ id

"Pima van (New plaster)"

- Novel antipsychotic
- Nondopaminergic
- 5-HT_{2A} inverse agonist

10 tab
17 tab
34 cap
mg

FDA-approved for:

- Psychosis associated with Parkinson's disease

Pimavanserin (Nuplazid), released in 2017, is FDA-approved for hallucinations and delusions associated with Parkinson's disease. Up to 50% of patients with Parkinson's disease develop these problems. Some sources refer to pimavanserin as a second generation antipsychotic (SGA), but its antipsychotic mechanism is entirely different from other medications in this class.

Antipsychotics are represented with spooky mascots.

Pimavanserin is the only available antipsychotic that does not act on dopamine receptors (unless you count cannabidiol). This makes pimavanserin ideal for Parkinson's disease, which is aggravated by dopamine blockade. Pimavanserin has a relatively unique mechanism as a selective serotonin inverse agonist that preferentially targets 5-HT_{2A} receptors. By definition, an inverse agonist binds to a receptor and produces effects opposite to those of an agonist. The effect of the inverse agonist can be blocked by an antagonist. A few other medications in this book are inverse agonists (among other mechanisms) but we refer to them as antagonists for simplicity.

Prior to pimavanserin the antipsychotic of choice for individuals with Parkinson's disease was quetiapine (Seroquel), which causes little to no extrapyramidal symptoms (EPS). Clozapine (Clozaril), which does not cause EPS, would be a good choice for this population if not for its numerous health risks and lab monitoring requirements.

Side effects of pimavanserin include peripheral edema (7%) and nausea (7%). It can cause angioedema, i.e., localized non-pitting edema of deep dermis and subcutaneous tissue. Pimavanserin may modestly prolong QT interval, but otherwise does not have side effects associated with other antipsychotics such as sedation, weight gain, constipation, gynecomastia or neutropenia.

All antipsychotics, pimavanserin included, carry a black box warning of increased mortality in elderly patients with dementia-related psychosis. For pimavanserin, the warning reads "not approved for dementia-related psychosis unrelated to the hallucinations and delusions associated with Parkinson's disease psychosis". Over the course of a 10-week controlled trial for the intended population, the rate of death was 4.5%, compared to a 2.6% in placebo-treated patients. Most of the deaths appeared to be either cardiovascular (e.g., heart failure, sudden death) or infectious (e.g., pneumonia). Exercise caution

in patients with uncorrected electrolyte abnormalities or any type of heart condition (recent heart attack, congestive heart failure, arrhythmia, bradycardia, etc.)

Nasrallah et al (2019) demonstrated successful treatment of clozapine-resistant psychosis with pimavanserin in individuals without Parkinson's disease. It appears to improve negative symptoms of schizophrenia (diminished emotional expression and avolition). Pimavanserin has potential for treatment-resistant depression as an adjunct to an SSRI or SNRI (Fava et al, 2019).

Oddly, the 10 mg and 17 mg pills are tablets while the 34 mg pill is a capsule.

Dosing: Start at 34 mg once daily, which is the target dose. Titration is unnecessary. In the presence of a strong 3A4 inhibitor, use a half strength dose of pimavanserin. With a strong 3A4 inducer, monitor for efficacy and exceed 34 mg if necessary.

Dynamic interactions:
- QT prolongation (low risk)

Kinetic interactions:
- 3A4 substrate (major)
  - dose adjustments apply (see above)

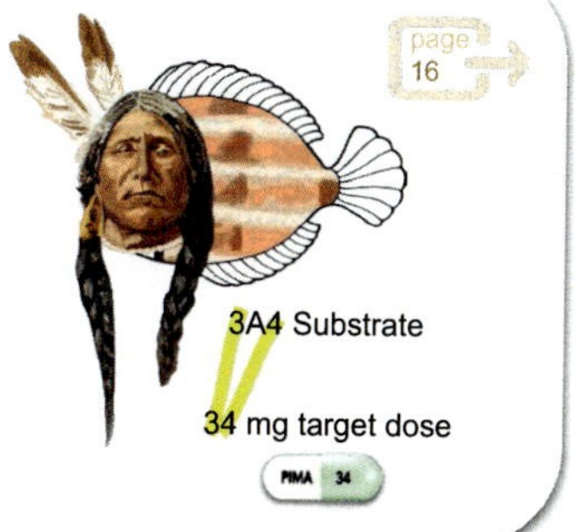

page 16

Long-Acting Injectable (LAI) antipsychotics

Although patients with schizophrenia are more likely to adhere to taking antipsychotics than placebo, compliance in the community is still less than 50%. To address this problem, several antipsychotics are available as long-acting injectables (LAIs). There are no LAI mood stabilizers, antidepressants, or stimulants. The older antipsychotics (haloperidol and fluphenazine) are "decanoate" formulations, which means the drug is in a sesame oil suspension. Decanoate injections are painful *(decan-OWW!-ate)* and can leave a tender bump under the skin that may take weeks to resolve. For decanoate shots, the Z-track injection technique is used. Confirm that the nurse will be injecting into the correct muscle (deltoid vs gluteal). With deltoid injections (smaller muscle), medication will be distributed more quickly and have a shorter half-life than with gluteal injections (larger muscle). The patient must first take the oral medication prior to receiving the LAI to establish tolerability, typically for at least 2 days. Tolerability to PO risperidone is sufficient to start LAI paliperidone, which is the active metabolite of risperidone. It is not advisable to give any LAI to someone with a history of neuroleptic malignant syndrome (NMS). Rather than being aggressive with the LAI dose, it may be a good strategy to go light on the LAI and supplement with a low PO dose that can be easily adjusted based on response and side effects. It is OK to give injections more frequently than the listed intervals if serum drug levels are monitored. Serum drug levels are worth following with LAIs in any event. Refer to official prescribing information for guidance on missed/late/early doses.

Medication	Strength	Given	PO overlap	Pain	Max	Info
HALDOL DECANOATE (haloperidol)	Usually 100 mg or 200 mg but can customize dose from vial	q 4 wk (q 3–4 wk) IM	1–3 wk	Yes	450 mg monthly (too high)	Traditionally given with 1–3 wk PO overlap, with a maximum of 100 mg for the first injection. If > 100 mg is needed, give the balance in 3–7 days if no EPS. According to Ereshefsky (1993) it can be given without a PO overlap if the loading dose of the LAI equals 20x the total daily PO dose. Subsequent monthly injections are typically 10–15 x the oral daily dose. 200 q 4 wk is equivalent to 14–20 PO QD, which is anticipated to produce a serum haloperidol level of 5–12 ng/mL. The FDA max of 450 mg/mo (equivalent to 30–45 mg PO daily) carries significant risk of tardive dyskinesia, so try not to exceed 200 mg of the LAI monthly (unless serum levels are lower than anticipated). Consider 25% dose decrease about every 3 months because it tends to accumulate. Gluteal is preferable, but deltoid is acceptable.
PROLIXIN DECANOATE (fluphenazine)	12.5 mg 25 mg 50 mg 100 mg	q 3–6 wk IM or SC	0–7 days	Yes	100 mg q 3 wk (too high)	Start 12.5 mg q 3 wk (roughly equivalent to 10 mg PO daily) or 25 mg q 3 wk. Onset of effect is within 24–72 hours. A realistic max dose is 50 mg q 3 wk or 100 mg q 6 wk, either of which is roughly equivalent to 40 mg PO daily. Since fluphenazine is a high potency typical antipsychotic (like haloperidol), there is significant risk of tardive dyskinesia. Gluteal is preferred, but deltoid is acceptable.
RISPERDAL CONSTA (risperidone)	12.5 mg 25 mg 37.5 mg 50 mg	q 2 wk IM	3 wk	No	50 mg q 2 wk	Rarely used because Risperdal Consta must be given every 2 weeks—*you're getting shots Constantly.* Also a 3-week PO overlap is required which is the time needed for microspheres to hydrolyze—so you are still taking pills past the 2nd injection. Must be refrigerated. Usual starting and maintenance dose is 25 mg q 2 wk. FDA max is 50 mg q 2 wk. May be given in gluteal or deltoid.
PERSERIS (risperidone)	90 mg 120 mg	q 4 wk SC	None needed	Yes	120 mg q 4 wk	Approved in 2018. Given subcutaneously (SC) in the abdomen via a thick 18-gauge needle. No loading dose or supplemental PO risperidone is recommended (after PO tolerability established). To be administered by a healthcare professional.
INVEGA SUSTENNA (paliperidone palmitate)	39 mg 78 mg 117 mg 156 mg 234 mg	q 4 wk IM	None needed	No	234 mg monthly	Onset within a few hours, no PO overlap required. Prefilled syringes, which do not need to be reconstituted or refrigerated. Standard dose is 234 mg once, then 156 mg on day 8 (with window of day 4 – day 12), then 117 mg monthly thereafter (equivalent to about 6 mg PO QD). Although not ideal, you can give the first dose (234 mg) on Monday and the second (156 mg) on Thursday to expedite a hospitalization. The q 4 wk injections can be +/- 7 days. PO risperidone is sufficient for establishing tolerability. First 2 injections in deltoid for faster distribution, with subsequent injections deltoid or gluteal.
INVEGA TRINZA (paliperidone palmitate)	273 mg 410 mg 546 mg 819 mg	q 3 mo IM	N/A—transition from Sustenna	No	819 mg q 3 mo	To use Trinza, the patient must first have received 4 monthly Sustenna injections, and the last two Sustenna doses must be the same strength. See dose conversion table below. The q 3 mo injections can +/- 14 days because medication release continues for up to 4.5 months. May be given gluteal or deltoid.
ABILIFY MAINTENA (aripiprazole)	300 mg 400 mg	q 4 wk IM	2 wk	No	400 mg monthly	The label recommends starting a maintenance dose of 400 mg/mo unless this patient is a 2D6 poor metabolizer (10% of population), then start 300 mg. It is recommended to back down to 300 mg if side effects occur. It is possible to give only 200 mg from the vial. Minimal pain with injection, certainly less painful than Aristada. Deltoid or gluteal.
ARISTADA (aripiprazole lauroxil)	441 mg 662 mg 882 mg 1064 mg	q 4–8 wk* IM	3 wk (unless started with Initio)	Yes	882 mg monthly	Prefilled syringes requiring no reconstitution. Must shake forcefully and inject immediately and rapidly so microcrystals do not clog the needle. *Given q 4 wk, other than the 882 mg strength which is q 4–6 wk, or the 1064 mg which is q 8 wk (equivalent to 882 mg q 6 wk). If changing from Maintena to Aristada, give the first Aristada injection 2 to 3 wk after the last Maintena injection. When transitioning from PO aripiprazole to Aristada, the 3 wk PO overlap can be replaced with a single 30 mg PO dose plus an Aristada Initio injection. The 441 mg strength may be given deltoid or gluteal. Higher strengths should be gluteal.
ARISTADA INITIO (aripiprazole)	675 mg	once	Single 30 mg PO dose	Yes	675 mg once	Aristada Initio is a one-time injection in the deltoid. It lets you start the q 4–8 wk Arista injections (see above) without a 3 wk PO overlap. On the same day, give aripiprazole 30 mg PO x 1, Initio injection x 1, and the first Aristada injection (or within 10 days). Tolerability to aripiprazole must first be established—in clinical trials this was done with aripiprazole 5 mg PO x 2 days, then on day three, 30 mg PO + Initio 675 mg in deltoid (preferably for quicker absorption) + Aristada 1064 mg in gluteal (to repeat Aristada 1064 mg q 2 mo). Initio must be given in deltoid.
ZYPREXA RELPREVV (olanzapine)	150 mg 210 mg 300 mg	q 2–4 wk IM	None needed	No	300 mg q 2 wk	Rarely prescribed due to **black box warning** of post-Injection delirium/sedation syndrome (PDSS) of olanzapine overdose which can lead to coma, likely due to intravascular injection. Restricted distribution program. Patients must be observed for at least 3 hours post-injection in a registered facility. Risk of PDSS is about 0.07% (about 1 in 1400 injections), with patients recovering within 72 hours. Deep intramuscular gluteal injection only. See package insert.

Dose conversions for risperidone/paliperidone products

PO risperidone	PO paliperidone	Risperdal Consta	Perseris	Invega Sustenna	Invega Trinza
1 mg	3 mg	12.5 mg q 2 wk	–	39 mg q 4 wk	–
2 mg		25 mg q 2 wk	–	78 mg q 4 wk	273 mg q 3 mo
3 mg	6 mg	37.5 mg q 2 wk	90 mg q 4 wk	117 mg q 4 wk	410 mg q 3 mo
4 mg	9 mg	50 mg q 2 wk	120 mg q 4 wk	156 mg q 4 wk	546 mg q 3 mo
6 mg	12 mg	–	–	234 mg q 4 wk	819 mg q 3 mo

Aripiprazole dose conversions

PO aripiprazole	Abilify Maintena	Aristada q 4 wk	Aristada q 6 wk	Aristada q 2 mo
10 mg	300 mg q 4 wk	441 mg q 4 wk	–	–
15 mg	400 mg q 4 wk	662 mg q 4 wk	882 mg q 6 wk	1064 mg q 2 mo
20 mg	–	882 mg q 4 wk**	–	–

**Note that Aristada 882 mg has been shown to be no more effective than lower doses (for q 4 week dosing).

Muscarinic (cholinergic) effects – everything wet

Before we discuss anticholinergic toxicity, let's discuss the opposite, for the sake of context. SLUDGE syndrome is a mnemonic for the result of overload of muscarinic acetylcholine receptors, as caused by poisoning with pesticide or nerve gas.

Signs of cholinergic overload:

S – Salivation
L – Lacrimation (also lactation)
U – Urination
D – Diaphoresis (also diarrhea)
G – Gastrointestinal upset (including diarrhea)
E – Emesis

Miosis (constricted pupils) and bradycardia would also be expected.

The treatment for SLUDGE poisoning is atropine, which is the strongest anticholinergic (antimuscarinic).

Anticholinergic toxicity, described below, is the opposite of SLUDGE. With cholinergic overload, everything is wet, filling the SLUDGE buckets. With anticholinergic toxicity, everything is "dry as a bone".

There could also be a bucket labeled Breast Milk, because cholinergic drugs can stimulate lactation for breastfeeding women.

Brady(cardia) Bunch SLUDGE buckets filled with fluids produced in excess with cholinergic toxicity

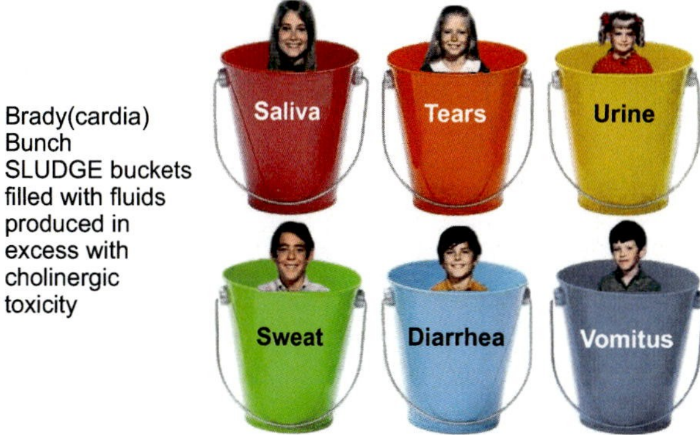

Cholinergic Alzheimer's medications such as donepezil (Aricept) can cause SLUDGE effects including nausea, vomiting, diarrhea, hypersalivation, miosis and bradycardia.

Sudden withdrawal of a high-dose anticholinergic medication such as benztropine (Cogentin) can cause SLUDGE symptoms by cholinergic rebound.

Anticholinergic (antimuscarinic) effects – everything dry

When we refer to "anticholinergic", we actually mean antimuscarinic. We're talking about blocking the action of the neurotransmitter acetylcholine at muscarinic receptors, not at nicotinic receptors. All five muscarinic receptor subtypes—M_1, M_2, M_3, M_4, and M_5—are present in various locations throughout the brain. Anticholinergic side effects are especially problematic for older adults. Ongoing use of strong anticholinergic medication can increase the risk of dementia by 50%.

Tacky (tachycardia) Auntie Choli is...

"Dry as a bone"

- Constipation (risk of ileus, bowel rupture)
- Urinary retention
- Decreased sweating; flushing—"Red as a beet" (this chapter's color)
- Dry mouth (risk of sublingual adenitis)
- Dry nasal mucus membranes
- Dry eyes
- Inhibition of lactation

"Mad as a hatter"

- Confusion, memory problems
- 50% increased risk of developing dementia
- Delirium with visual hallucinations

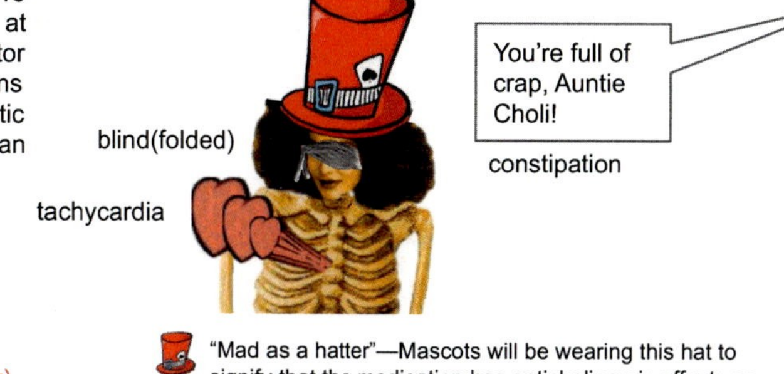

"Mad as a hatter"—Mascots will be wearing this hat to signify that the medication has anticholinergic effects on the central nervous system.

"Blind as a bat"

- Cycloplegia (loss of accommodation)—lens cannot focus on near objects
- Photophobia due to mydriasis (dilated pupils)
- Increased intraocular pressure; contraindicated in angle-closure glaucoma (unless already treated by laser iridotomy)

Anticholinergic Drugs

Anticholinergic (antimuscarinic) agents block muscarinic acetylcholine receptors. Atropine is the strongest anticholinergic. They are used to treat:

- **Parkinsonism, EPS** – benztropine (Cogentin), trihexyphenidyl (Artane), diphenhydramine (Benadryl) are given for dystonic reactions
- **Overactive bladder (OAB)** – oxybutynin (Ditropan), tolterodine (Detrol), etc decrease premature detrusor contractions
- **Irritable bowel syndrome (IBS)** – dicyclomine (Bentyl) and hyoscyamine (Levsin) slow GI transit time
- **To decrease secretions and spasms** of rhinorrhea, hypersalivation, hyperhidrosis, diarrhea, peptic ulcers, biliary colic, and renal colic
- **Vertigo and motion sickness** – meclizine (Antivert), scopolamine (Transderm Scōp)
- **Asthma and COPD** – inhaled ipratropium (Atrovent) works as a bronchodilator
- **Bradycardia** – injections of atropine increase heart rate; In cardiac arrest, atropine is given to reverse asystole and severe bradycardia.
- **Cycloplegia** – Atropine eye drops are used to paralyze the accommodation reflex and produce mydriasis (pupil dilation) for procedures
- **Nerve agent poisoning** – Atropine is used to counteract poisoning by agents that block the action of acetylcholinesterase, e.g., pesticides

Anticholinergics should not be routinely coadministered with high potency antipsychotics. Although some psychiatrists automatically add benztropine to haloperidol, this is not recommended, at least for long-term use. Anticholinergics do not prevent, but rather increase risk of tardive dyskinesia. Also, anticholinergics exacerbate the underlying cognitive impairment in patients with schizophrenia.

Anticholinergic Cognitive Effects

The elderly are especially susceptible to cognitive side effects of anticholinergic (antimuscarinic) medications. These "mad as a hatter" cognitive impairments may include:

- Memory problems
- Increased risk of developing dementia
- Delirium

Delirium is an acute confusional state that develops over a short period of time, typically hours to days. It tends to fluctuate from hour to hour. Classically, delirium is worse in the evening, a phenomenon colloquially referred to as "sundowning". Delirium involves impaired attention and disorientation. Visual hallucinations are common in the delirious state (as opposed to psychosis, which is more likely to manifest as auditory hallucinations). Medications that can contribute to delirium in elderly patients are listed below as 2 to 3 points on the anticholinergic burden scale. Most episodes of delirium are multifactorial, brought about by a combination of medications (anticholinergics, opioids, benzodiazepines, corticosteroids) and medical conditions. Delirium is very common among medically hospitalized elderly patients.

Treatment of acute delirium includes a short-term course of an antipsychotic, one with minimal anticholinergic properties. Antipsychotics scoring 0 or 1 points on the anticholinergic burden scale are suitable. For acute agitation associated with delirium, IM ziprasidone (Geodon) is a good choice. Benzodiazepine use should be minimized, unless the delirium is caused by withdrawal from benzodiazepines or alcohol (delirium tremens).

The anticholinergics that impair cognition:

- Block the M1 muscarinic receptor subtype
- Get past the blood brain barrier (BBB) by
  - being a small molecule
  - being lipid soluble (i.e., lipophilic, not hydrophilic)
  - having a neutral charge
  - not being a P-gp substrate

P-glycoprotein (P-gp) is an efflux transporter that pumps substances out of the CNS, back into systemic circulation. P-gp works as a component of the BBB, preventing the accumulation of certain drugs (P-gp substrates) in the brain.

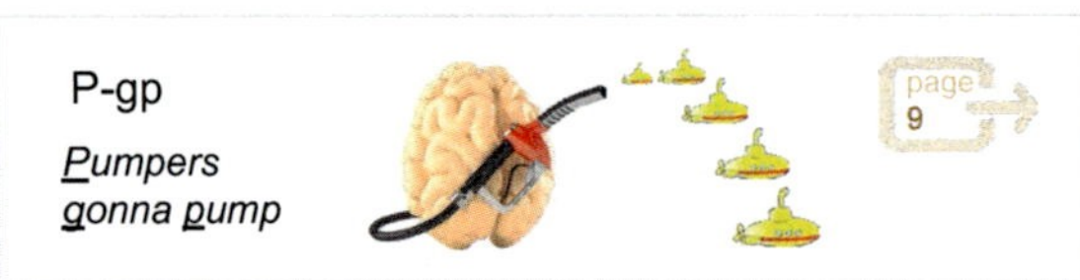

Anticholinergic Burden Scale (Risk of CNS impairment/dementia) – "mad as a hatter"

Anticholinergic load should be minimized with older adults. Dose should be taken into consideration when estimating risk.

	3 Points (worst)	2 points	1 point (mild)	0 points
TCA Antidepressants	Amitriptyline, Clomipramine, Doxepin ≥ 50 mg, Imipramine, Maprotiline, Protriptyline, Trimipramine	Desipramine (Norpramin) Doxepin ≤ 25 mg (Sinequan) Nortriptyline (Pamelor)	Amoxapine (Asendin) Doxepin ≤ 10 mg (Sinequan)	Doxepin ≤ 6 mg (Silenor)
Other Antidepressants	N/A	Paroxetine (Paxil) – *"Paxil packs it in"* (constipation as a peripheral anticholinergic effect)	Citalopram (Celexa) Fluoxetine (Prozac) MAOIs Mirtazapine (Remeron)	SNRIs, Other SSRIs, Bupropion (Wellbutrin), Trazodone, Nefazodone, Vilazodone (Viibryd), Vortioxetine (Trintellix)
Antipsychotics (and other D2 blockers)	Low potency FGAs: Chlorpromazine (Thorazine) Promethazine (Phenergan) Thioridazine (Mellaril)	Intermediate potency FGAs: Loxapine (Loxitane) Molindone (Moban) Perphenazine (Trilafon) SGAs: Clozapine (Clozaril) Olanzapine (Zyprexa)	High potency FGAs: Fluphenazine (Prolixin) Haloperidol (Haldol) Pimozide (Orap) Prochlorperazine (Compazine) Thiothixene (Navane) Trifluoperazine (Stelazine) SGAs: Pimavanserin (Nuplazid) Quetiapine (Seroquel)	SGAs: Aripiprazole (Abilify) Asenapine (Saphris) Brexpiprazole (Rexulti) Cariprazine (Vraylar) Iloperidone (Fanapt) Lurasidone (Latuda) Paliperidone (Invega) Risperidone (Risperdal) Ziprasidone (Geodon)
Antihistamines	Cyproheptadine (Periactin) Diphenhydramine (Benadryl) Doxylamine (Unisom) Meclizine (Antivert) Hydroxyzine (Vistaril)	Chlorpheniramine (Chlor-Trimeton),	Cetirizine (Zyrtec) Famotidine (Pepcid) Fexofenadine (Allegra) Loratadine (Claritin) Ranitidine (Zantac)	Levocetirizine (Xyzal)
Anticholinergics for OAB	Oxybutynin (Ditropan)	Tolterodine (Detrol)	Fesoterodine (Toviaz) Solifenacin (Vesicare)	Darifenacin (Enablex) Trospium (Sanctura)
Other Anticholinergics	Atropine (injected) Benztropine (Cogentin) Dicyclomine (Bentyl) Hyoscyamine (Levsin) Scopolamine (Transderm Scōp) Trihexyphenidyl (Artane)	Amantadine (Symmetrel) Atropine eye drops	Ipratropium inhaler (Atrovent) Note that ipratropium is like an inhaled form of atropine (the strongest anticholinergic)	Glycopyrrolate (Robinul)* *Strong anticholinergic but does not cross blood-brain barrier; Therefore it causes constipation but not cognitive problems.
Muscle relaxants	Carisoprodol (Soma) Orphenadrine (Norflex)	Cyclobenzaprine (Flexeril) Baclofen (Lioresal)	Methocarbamol (Robaxin)	Metaxalone (Skelaxin) Tizanidine (Zanaflex)
Sedatives	See antihistamines	See antihistamines	Diazepam (Valium) Temazepam (Restoril)	**Other benzodiazepines Z-drugs; barbiturates; melatonin
Mood stabilizers; Antiepileptics	N/A	Carbamazepine (Tegretol)	Lithium Oxcarbazepine (Trileptal)	Other anticonvulsants
Other	N/A	Cimetidine (Tagamet) Codeine Metoclopramide (Reglan) Pseudoephedrine (Sudafed)	Buspirone (Buspar) Pramipexole (Mirapex)	Antihypertensives, cognitive enhancers and ADHD stimulants; atomoxetine, ondansetron, tramadol, ropinirole

Compiled from many sources. There are at least 10 published anticholinergic risk/burden scales (including Beers criteria) which differ substantially in the estimation of anticholinergic load for certain medications.

**These sedatives may impair cognition, but not by anticholinergic effect.

1st generation H_1 antihistamines

All are sedating and highly anticholinergic

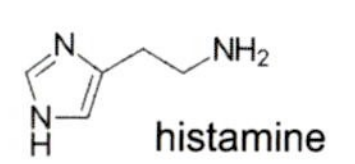

"Anti-HISSed-amine"

Antihistamine ~ monthly cost		Uses (*off-label)	Anti-cholinergic	Anti-serotonin	Comments
Diphenhydramine (BENADRYL)	$5	Allergy symptoms Urticaria/pruritus Allergic reactions (IM) Extrapyramidal symptoms (EPS) Insomnia (short-term) Sedation Motion sickness prevention	+++	no	PO Benadryl is available over-the-counter (OTC). IV or IM diphenhydramine is highly effective for the treatment of an acute dystonic reaction. In treatment of EPS, it is more effective for dystonia than for akathisia.
Doxylamine (UNISOM)	$10	Insomnia Allergy symptoms	+++	no	Available over-the-counter (OTC). Nearly identical to Benadryl.
Hydroxyzine (VISTARIL, ATARAX)	$15	Anxiety Urticaria/pruritus Sedation Nausea Insomnia	+++	no	Generally less sedating than Benadryl. Commonly used PRN as an anxiolytic. Those accustomed to benzodiazepines often report hydroxyzine is useless for anxiety. Hydroxyzine is metabolized to the 2nd generation antihistamine cetirizine (Zyrtec).
Cyproheptadine (PERIACTIN)	$20	Allergic rhinitis Urticaria *Appetite stimulation *Serotonin syndrome *Nightmares *Akathisia *Female anorgasmia (PRN) *SSRI-induced night sweats	+++	yes	May lead to large weight gain. A preferred agent for appetite stimulation. Due to anti-serotonergic properties, it can make antidepressants ineffective.
Meclizine (ANTIVERT, "DRAMAMINE LESS DROWSY")	$10	Motion sickness Vertigo *Nausea	+++	no	Similar to hydroxyzine with a shorter half-life. Less sedating than the others. Available Rx and OTC.
Dimenhydrinate (DRAMAMINE original)	$10	Motion sickness Nausea	+++	no	Available OTC, more sedating than meclizine
Orphenadrine (NORFLEX)	$20	Musculoskeletal pain	+++	no	Monograph is in muscle relaxants chapter, page 193
Promethazine (PHENERGAN)	$10	Nausea/vomiting Motion sickness Allergic conditions Urticaria Sedation	+++	no	Used mostly as an antiemetic. It has a phenothiazine structure like several first generation antipsychotics and is a weak D2 blocker. Monograph is in the first generation antipsychotic/antiemetic chapter, page 142.

Several antipsychotics and antidepressants are strong H_1 blockers. Such medications are sedating. The tricyclic antidepressant doxepin (page 86) is such a strong antihistamine that it is effective for insomnia at low doses and is available as a topical cream for pruritus.

2nd generation H_1 antihistamines

These are effective for allergies with relatively low anticholinergic or sedative effects. There is a theoretical slight risk of developing dementia with these with chronic use, other than with levocetirizine. In order of sales:

- #1 Cetirizine (ZYRTEC)
  - » crosses the blood-brain barrier slightly, may be sedating to some individuals
- #2 Loratadine (CLARITIN)
  - » less likely to cause sedation than cetirizine
- #3 <u>Levocetirizine (XYZAL)</u>
  - » technically an H_1 inverse agonist; <u>no potential for sedation</u>, recommended by "Wise Owl" on TV
  - » recommended because no apparent anticholinergic effects
  - » recommended by "Wise Owl" on TV, unlikely to pose risk of dementia with long-term use
- #4 Fexofenadine (ALLEGRA)
  - » less likely to cause sedation than cetirizine or loratadine

Stay wise – Levocetirizine (Xyzal) does not have sufficient anticholinergic effects to cause dementia, unlike older antihistamines.

H_2 antihistamines

In the stomach, histamine binds H_2 receptors to stimulate acid secretion. One point on the anticholinergic burden scale, therefore theoretical slight risk of dementia with long-term use. *"I take an H_2 blocker before <u>I</u> -<u>dine</u>* at a "table for (H) two"*. In order of sales:

- #1 Ranit<u>idine</u> (ZANTAC)
- #2 Famot<u>idine</u> (PEPCID)
- #3 Cimet<u>idine</u> (TAGAMET) – weak inhibitor of numerous metabolic enzymes
- #4 Nizat<u>idine</u> (AXID)

*All of the popular H_2 antihistamines end with *-(t)idine* as in "I dine", not to be confused with the three H_1 antihistamines that end in *-<u>a</u>dine* —namely cyprohept<u>a</u>dine, lorat<u>a</u>dine and fexofen<u>a</u>dine.

H_3 antihistamines

<u>Pitolisant (WAKIX)</u> was approved <u>for narcolepsy</u> in 2019. H_3 receptors are found mainly in the brain. <u>Blocking H_3 receptors has a stimulating effect</u>. This is the only medication approved for narcolepsy that is not a controlled substance (page 233).

#210
1946
$2–$8

Diphenhydramine (BENADRYL)

DYE fen HYE dra meen / BEN uh dril

"Dippin' hydra's Bean drill"

- 1st Generation antihistamine
- Anticholinergic
- Over-the-counter

25
50
mg

FDA-approved for:
- Allergy symptoms
- Urticaria/pruritus
- Allergic reactions (IM, IV)
- Extrapyramidal symptoms (EPS)
- Insomnia (short-term)
- Sedation
- Motion sickness prevention

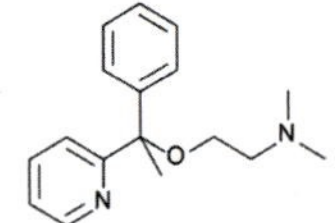

Anticholinergic with CNS effects—"mad as a hatter"

Diphenhydramine (Benadryl) is an effective OTC sleep aid with a half-life of 9 hours and duration of action of about 4–6 hours. It is a strong antihistamine and strong anticholinergic. Compared to other sleep medications, it may cause a bit more grogginess or "hangover" in the morning. Since anticholinergics are associated with an increased risk of dementia, Benadryl is not recommended for long-term daily use. For insomnia, trazodone (Desyrel) is a better choice.

Diphenhydramine is considered safe for children and during pregnancy and breastfeeding.

Intravenous or intramuscular diphenhydramine is classically used to treat severe allergic reactions as an antihistamine. IV or IM diphenhydramine is also a fast-acting and effective treatment for an acute dystonic reaction, due to anticholinergic effect. Another option for acute dystonia is benztropine (Cogentin).

Dosing: For most indications, a single dose is 25–50 mg, with a maximum of 100 mg/dose and 300 mg/day. For insomnia, take 30 minutes before bedtime PRN. For acute dystonia, use 25–50 mg IM or IV.

In the treatment of EPS, diphenhydramine is more effective for dystonia than for akathisia.

IM Benadryl is also useful for acute agitation. For extreme agitation with aggression (in a patient with high tolerance to sedatives) a "B-52" may be administered. This is slang for Benadryl 50 mg, haloperidol (Haldol) 5 mg, plus lorazepam (Ativan) 2 mg IM. The B-52 is two injections, the Haldol plus Ativan mixed in one syringe, and the Benadryl alone in the other.

If an antihistamine sleep medication is needed, a small dose of the TCA doxepin (Sinequan) is a better choice. At 10 mg doxepin is antihistaminic without much anticholinergic burden. At higher doses, doxepin is highly anticholinergic.

Tylenol PM is a combination of acetaminophen and diphenhydramine.

Dynamic interactions:
- Sedative
- Anticholinergic
  - constipation
  - confusion
  - urinary retention
  - dry mouth

Kinetic interactions:
- None significant

page 18

1956
$4–$9

Doxylamine (UNISOM)

dox IL a meen / YUN i som

"Un's som(nolent) Doxies"

- 1st Generation antihistamine
- Anticholinergic
- Over-the-counter

25
mg

FDA–approved for:
- Insomnia
- Allergy symptoms
- Nausea of pregnancy (Diclegis, see below)

Anticholinergic with CNS effects—"mad as a hatter"

Doxylamine (Unisom) is essentially the same as Benadryl. It is also available over-the-counter for insomnia. Doxylamine has a slightly longer duration of action of 6–8 hours, compared with 4–6 hours for diphenhydramine.

Doxylamine is a component of NyQuil, along with acetaminophen and dextromethorphan.

As with other strong anticholinergics, long-term use of doxylamine may increase risk of dementia. Anticholinergic effects can easily add up with polypharmacy. Refer to the anticholinergic burden scale on page 162.

Dosing: For insomnia, use 25–50 mg as needed given 30 min before bedtime; For allergies, use 12.5 mg q 4 hr PRN; Maximum dose is 75 mg/day.

DICLEGIS is a branded pill containing doxylamine with pyridoxine (Vitamin B6), FDA-approved for morning sickness in 2013. Both components relieve nausea. The original brand of this combo (BENDECTIN) was discontinued by the manufacturer in 1983 due to frivolous lawsuits from women blaming it for birth defects. Note that 1 in 33 babies have birth defects regardless of medication use during pregnancy.

Dynamic interactions:
- Sedative
- Anticholinergic
  - constipation
  - confusion
  - urinary retention

Kinetic interactions:
- None significant

#97
1957
$5–$15

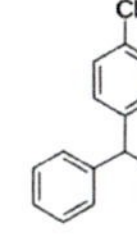
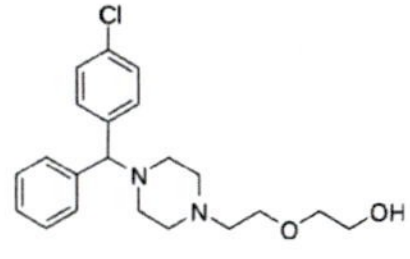

Hydroxyzine pamoate (VISTARIL)

hy DROX e zeen / VIS ta ril

"Hydra's Vest roll"

- ❖ 1st Generation antihistamine
- ❖ Anticholinergic
- ❖ Prescription

25
50
100
mg

Anticholinergic with CNS effects—"mad as a hatter"

FDA-approved for:
- ❖ Anxiety
- ❖ Urticaria/pruritus
- ❖ Insomnia
- ❖ Sedation (anesthesia adjunct) – IM

Used off-label for:
- ❖ Headaches

Vistaril (hydroxyzine pamoate capsule) is commonly used as a PRN for mild anxiety. Think of it as diphenhydramine (Benadryl) with a bit less sedation. The elimination half-life of hydroxyzine is around 20 hours, but the duration of anxiolytic effect is only 4–6 hours following administration of a single dose. Its onset of effect is about 15 minutes. The time to reach peak serum concentration (T_{max}) of hydroxyzine is about 2 hours.

The purpose of hydroxyzine is to the take the edge off of anxiety, not to obliterate it. Patients accustomed to benzodiazepines are likely to regard hydroxyzine as useless.

Hydroxyzine is metabolized to the 2nd generation H_1 antihistamine cetirizine (Zyrtec).

As with any strong anticholinergic, long-term use may increase risk of dementia.

Dosing: For anxiety, use 25–50 mg q 4–6 hours PRN. For insomnia, 50–100 mg given 30–60 minutes prior to bedtime PRN. Hydroxyzine is also available as an IM injection for sedation as an anesthesia adjunct, given 25–100 mg IM x 1.

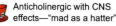

Dynamic interactions:
- ❖ Sedative
- ❖ Anticholinergic
  - – constipation
  - – confusion
  - – urinary retention
  - – dry mouth

Kinetic interactions:
- ❖ None significant

page 18

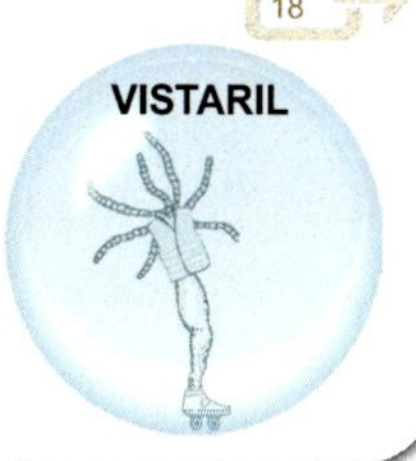

ANTICHOLINERGICS

#97
1956
$3–$23

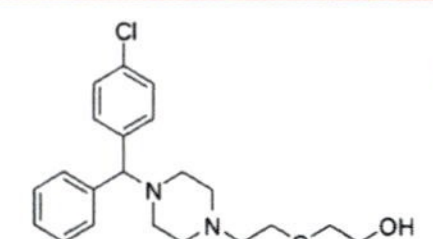

Hydroxyzine hydrochloride (ATARAX)

hy DROX e zeen / AT ar ax

"Hydra's Atari"

- ❖ 1st Generation antihistamine
- ❖ Anticholinergic
- ❖ Prescription

10
25
50
mg

FDA-approved for:
- ❖ Anxiety
- ❖ Urticaria/pruritus
- ❖ Insomnia
- ❖ Sedation

Used off-label for:
- ❖ Headaches

Anticholinergic with CNS effects—"mad as a hatter"

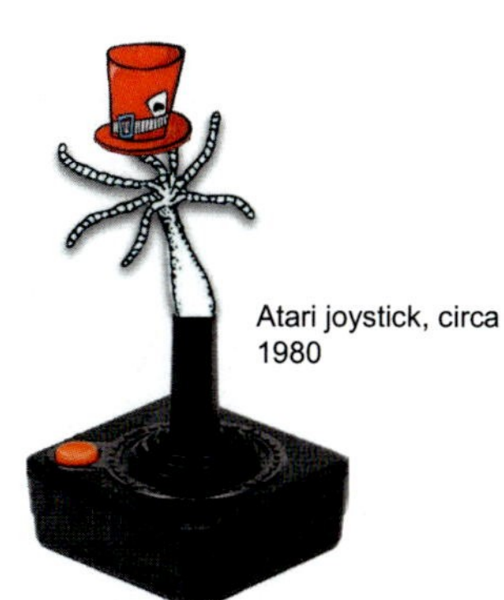

Atari joystick, circa 1980

Atarax (hydroxyzine hydrochloride) is equivalent to Vistaril (hydroxyzine pamoate). The only difference is that Atarax is a tablet, available in 10, 25, and 50 mg strengths. A 10 mg tab of Atarax is "a tiny" Vistaril.

Hydroxyzine hydrochloride is also available as an IM injection and PO syrup, whereas hydroxyzine pamoate is not.

As with any strong anticholinergic, Atarax should be avoided in the elderly due to risk of confusion and falls.

Dosing: The same as Vistaril, although a lower dose of 10 mg is available.

The button on an Atari joystick is the shape of a tablet (as opposed to a capsule).

Dynamic interactions:
- ❖ Sedative
- ❖ Anticholinergic
  - – constipation
  - – confusion
  - – urinary retention
  - – dry mouth

Kinetic interactions:
- ❖ None significant

page 18

#162
1953
$9–$18

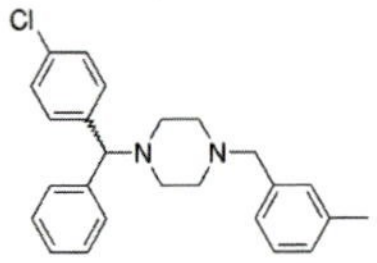

Meclizine (ANTIVERT)

MEK li zeen / ANT e vert

"McLizard is Anti-vertigo"

- 1st generation antihistamine
- Anticholinergic
- Over-the-counter

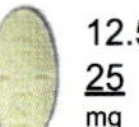

12.5
25
mg

FDA-approved for:
- Motion sickness
- Vertigo

Used off-label for:
- Nausea

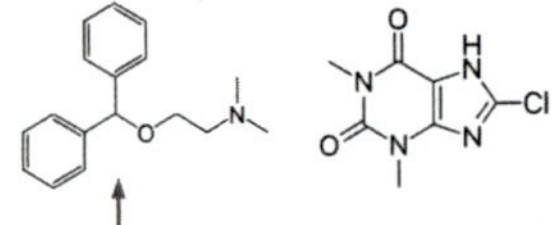

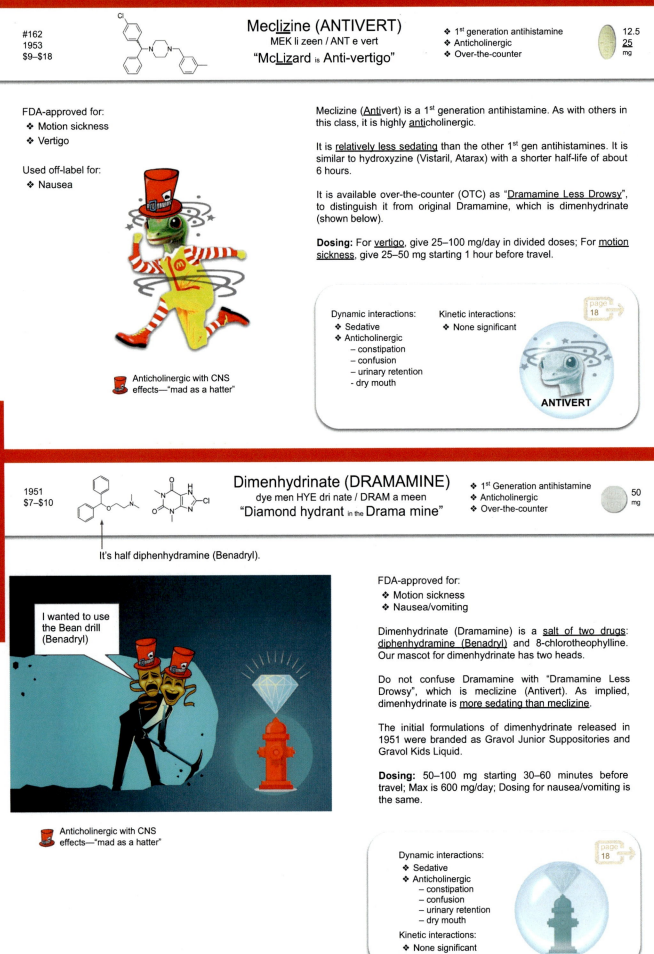

Anticholinergic with CNS effects—"mad as a hatter"

Meclizine (Antivert) is a 1st generation antihistamine. As with others in this class, it is highly anticholinergic.

It is relatively less sedating than the other 1st gen antihistamines. It is similar to hydroxyzine (Vistaril, Atarax) with a shorter half-life of about 6 hours.

It is available over-the-counter (OTC) as "Dramamine Less Drowsy", to distinguish it from original Dramamine, which is dimenhydrinate (shown below).

Dosing: For vertigo, give 25–100 mg/day in divided doses; For motion sickness, give 25–50 mg starting 1 hour before travel.

Dynamic interactions:
- Sedative
- Anticholinergic
  - constipation
  - confusion
  - urinary retention
  - dry mouth

Kinetic interactions:
- None significant

page 18

ANTIVERT

1951
$7–$10

Dimenhydrinate (DRAMAMINE)

dye men HYE dri nate / DRAM a meen

"Diamond hydrant in the Drama mine"

- 1st Generation antihistamine
- Anticholinergic
- Over-the-counter

50
mg

It's half diphenhydramine (Benadryl).

I wanted to use the Bean drill (Benadryl)

Anticholinergic with CNS effects—"mad as a hatter"

FDA-approved for:
- Motion sickness
- Nausea/vomiting

Dimenhydrinate (Dramamine) is a salt of two drugs: diphenhydramine (Benadryl) and 8-chlorotheophylline. Our mascot for dimenhydrinate has two heads.

Do not confuse Dramamine with "Dramamine Less Drowsy", which is meclizine (Antivert). As implied, dimenhydrinate is more sedating than meclizine.

The initial formulations of dimenhydrinate released in 1951 were branded as Gravol Junior Suppositories and Gravol Kids Liquid.

Dosing: 50–100 mg starting 30–60 minutes before travel; Max is 600 mg/day; Dosing for nausea/vomiting is the same.

Dynamic interactions:
- Sedative
- Anticholinergic
  - constipation
  - confusion
  - urinary retention
  - dry mouth

Kinetic interactions:
- None significant

page 18

1961
$14–$30

Cyproheptadine (PERIACTIN)

si pro HEP tuh deen / pear e ACT in

"Perry actin'…help to dine"

- 1st Generation antihistamine
- Anticholinergic
- 5-HT_2 serotonin receptor antagonist

4 mg

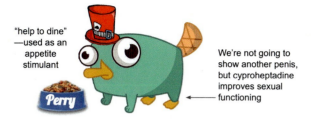

FDA-approved for:
- Allergic rhinitis
- Urticaria

Used off-label for:
- Appetite stimulation
- Serotonin syndrome
- Female anorgasmia
- Nightmares
- Akathisia
- SSRI-induced sweating

"help to dine" —used as an appetite stimulant
Perry
We're not going to show another penis, but cyproheptadine improves sexual functioning

Perry Actin'—In the cartoon *Phineas and Ferb*, Perry the Platypus is a crime-fighting spy, but is often undercover actin' like a docile pet. For Perry to act like a pet, it would help to dine on pet food.

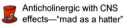

Anticholinergic with CNS effects—"mad as a hatter"

Cyproheptadine (Periactin), released in 1961, is a first generation antihistamine with antiserotonergic properties. As with all first generation antihistamines, cyproheptadine is highly anticholinergic.

Cyproheptadine is FDA-approved as an antihistamine for allergic rhinitis and urticaria but is not used for these conditions because it causes a lot of weight gain. Cyproheptadine is useful as an appetite stimulant off-label.

Cyproheptadine's antiserotonergic effects can oppose the action of antidepressants, potentially rendering them ineffective. Nonetheless, it has been used to counteract SSRI-induced night sweats. Cyproheptadine can be used as a treatment foror serotonin syndrome, though the main intervention is stopping the serotonergic culprit(s).

Cyproheptadine is used off-label to treat nightmares. Unless the patient needs to gain weight, prazosin (Minipress) and gabapentin (Neurontin) should be tried before resorting to cyproheptadine.

Cyproheptadine is also used off-label for treatment of female anorgasmia. Serotonergics (e.g., SSRIs) may cause anorgasmia, so it makes sense that an antiserotonergic could facilitate orgasm.

Dosing: To stimulate appetite start 2 mg QID and increase to target dose of 8 mg QID over 3 weeks. For serotonin syndrome give 12 mg x 1, then 2 mg q 2 hr until response (max 32 mg/day). To treat female anorgasmia, the dose is 4–12 mg PRN 1–2 hr prior to sex. For nightmares, start 4 mg HS but may need to go as high as 24 mg HS; Although cyproheptadine is no longer used for the FDA-approved indications of allergic rhinitis and urticaria, the dose would be 4 mg TID.

The structure of cyproheptadine is closely related to tricyclic antidepressants (TCAs), but cyproheptadine is antiserotonergic, not serotonergic like a TCA.

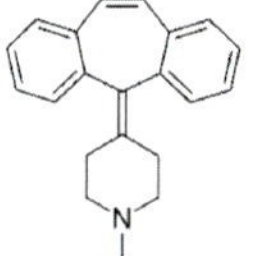
cyproheptadine (Periactin)

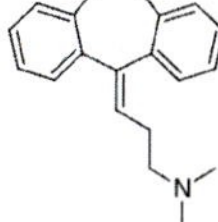
amitriptyline (Elavil) – TCA

Dynamic interactions:
- Antiserotonergic effects can oppose therapeutic effects of serotonergic antidepressants.
- Sedative
- Anticholinergic
  - constipation
  - confusion
  - urinary retention
  - dry mouth

Kinetic interactions:
- None significant

page 18

PERIACTIN

Medications classified as anticholinergics or 1st generation antihistamines (which are highly anticholinergic) are generally not involved in kinetic interactions. Therefore they are depicted in a bubble. There is no rhyme or reason to this. Most antipsychotics and antidepressants with strong anticholinergic properties are subject to kinetic interactions, mostly as CYP substrates.

K+
Anti-cholinergics

Solid forms of potassium are contraindicated with strong anticholinergics. Slowed GI transit may cause K+ exposure to a concentrated area, potentially leading to GI ulceration. This is not a problem with extended-release forms of potassium chloride.

Anticholinergics for Extrapyramidal Symptoms (EPS)

Antipsychotics lower dopamine (DA) activity by blocking D_2 receptors. Extrapyramidal symptoms are due to a relative deficiency of DA and an excess of acetylcholine in the nigrostriatal pathway. EPS can be relieved by blocking muscarinic acetylcholine receptors.

Anticholinergic cost/month		Uses (*off-label)	Comments
Benztropine (COGENTIN)	$12	Parkinsonism Extrapyramidal symptoms (EPS) Dystonic reactions *Hypersalivation *Hyperhidrosis (sweating)	Commonly used as an adjunct to Haldol to alleviate EPS, especially dystonia. May be slightly sedating, but less sedating than Benadryl. Usually dosed BID, with a half-life of about 16 hours. Available for IM injection.
Trihexyphenidyl (ARTANE)	$10	Parkinson's disease Extrapyramidal symptoms (EPS) *Hypersalivation *Hyperhidrosis	2nd line to benztropine, because the short half-life of 4 hours necessitates TID dosing. It has been used recreationally at high doses to cause hallucinations— "mad as a hatter".

Note that diphenhydramine (Benadryl) can be used for many of these purposes. Although diphenhydramine is classified as a 1st generation antihistamine, it is just as anticholinergic as medications classified as anticholinergics.

Anticholinergics for Clozapine-Induced Hypersalivation (Sialorrhea)

The antipsychotic clozapine has a cholinergic effect on salivary glands (causing salivation), but an anticholinergic effect on the colon (causing constipation).

Anticholinergic cost/month		Choice	Comments
Glycopyrrolate (ROBINUL)	$25	1st line	Glycopyrrolate does not cross the blood-brain barrier (BBB) so no "mad as a hatter" cognitive difficulties. May exacerbate clozapine-induced constipation. Start 1 mg PO HS, increase to 1–2 mg BID.
Ipratropium (ATROVENT) 0.03% nasal spray	$30	2nd line	1–3 sprays sublingual HS (not intranasal) up to 3x daily; Minimal systemic absorption
Atropine 1% ophthalmic drops	$45	3rd line	1 drop sublingual TID PRN; More systemic absorption than ipratropium nasal spray, with a possibility of cognitive impairment; May cause rebound hypersalivation.

Other antipsychotics that can cause hypersalivation include olanzapine, risperidone, and quetiapine. Other anticholinergics used to slow salivation include oxybutynin (Ditropan), benztropine (Cogentin), and trihexyphenidyl (Artane). The central alpha agonist clonidine (Catapres) can also work.

Anticholinergics for Overactive Bladder (OAB)

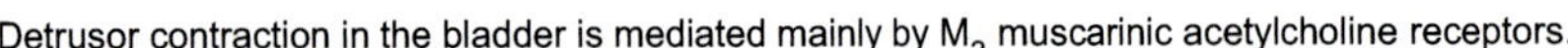

Detrusor contraction in the bladder is mediated mainly by M_3 muscarinic acetylcholine receptors.

Anticholinergic	Cost/ month	Release	Cognitive impairment	Comments
Oxybutynin (DITROPAN)	$24	1975	++++	Most likely to cause CNS impairment because it has a small molecular weight, is lipophilic with neutral charge, and is not a P-gp substrate (i.e., is not pumped out of CNS). It is also a moderate strength antihistamine.
Tolterodine (DETROL)	$64	1996	++	Less CNS impairment than oxybutynin because it is larger and has a neutral charge, therefore it does not cross the BBB as readily.
Fesoterodine (TOVIAZ)	$321	2009	++	Nonselective muscarinic receptor antagonist.
Solifenacin (VESICARE)	$368	2004	+	Moderately selective for the bladder.
Darifenacin (ENABLEX)	$385	2004	+/-	Highly selective for blocking muscarinic receptors in the bladder, not M1 receptors in the brain.
Trospium (SANCTURA)	$52	2004	-	"Brain is a Sanctuary"—Does not impair cognition. It does not cross the BBB because it is large, hydrophilic, positively charged, and a P-gp substrate (i.e., gets pumped out of CNS).

Beta3-adrenergic agonists are also used for OAB. They have no anticholinergic effects, but they can elevate blood pressure. An example is mirabegron (Myrbetriq) [mir a BEG ron / meer BEH trick] —"My rabbi trick is beggin'" is a mnemonic phrase to pair its trade name with generic name.

Anticholinergics for Irritable Bowel Syndrome (IBS)

Anticholinergic	Cost/ month	FDA-approved for	CNS side effects
Dicyclomine (BENTYL)	$13	IBS	Commonly causes somnolence, dizziness, and nervousness. Potential serious reactions include delirium, hallucinations, and psychosis. Selective for M1 and M3 muscarinic receptors, both of which are present in the GI tract.
Hyoscyamine (LEVSIN)	$35	IBS, GI tract spasms, bladder spasms, PUD, rhinitis, biliary colic, renal colic	Not selective for any of the subtypes of muscarinic receptors. Commonly causes drowsiness, ataxia, dizziness, nervousness, memory problems, and confusion. Serious reactions may include anticholinergic psychosis and hallucinations.

#211
1954
$12–$26

Benztropine (COGENTIN)

BENZ tro peen / co GENT in

"Benz Cog"

❖ Anticholinergic

0.5
1
2
mg

FDA-approved for:
- ❖ Parkinson's disease
- ❖ Extrapyramidal symptoms

Used off-label for:
- ❖ Sialorrhea (hypersalivation)
- ❖ Hyperhidrosis (sweating)

Benztropine (Cogentin) is an anticholinergic (antimuscarinic) frequently prescribed by psychiatrists as an add-on to high potency first generation antipsychotics to counter extrapyramidal symptoms (EPS), especially dystonia. Benztropine is not very effective for akathisia and can worsen tardive dyskinesia. Half-life is at least 12 hours.

Some prescribers, when starting haloperidol (Haldol), routinely start benztropine concurrently to prevent dystonia. However, benztropine does not prevent tardive dyskinesia (TD). If tardive dyskinesia develops, anticholinergics should be stopped because they may exacerbate TD.

Antipsychotics lower dopamine activity by blocking D2 receptors. Extrapyramidal symptoms are due to a relative deficiency of DA and an excess of acetylcholine in the nigrostriatal pathway. EPS can be relieved by increasing the availability of dopamine and/or blocking acetylcholine.

Intramuscular benztropine is available for treatment of an acute dystonic reaction such as oculogyric crisis or torticollis. IM diphenhydramine (Benadryl) is equally effective. Oculogyric crisis is a prolonged upward deviation of the eyes bilaterally. Torticollis is a dystonic reaction with the head persistently turned to one side, often associated with painful muscle spasms.

Laryngeal dystonia is also responsive to benztropine. This is a type of tardive dystonia occuring after prolonged antipsychotic use. The condition is caused by periodic spasms of the larynx (voice box) manifested by hoarseness or difficulty speaking.

Cognitive impairment ("mad as a hatter") from benztropine is a bigger problem than commonly appreciated (Lupu et al, 2017). As with any strong anticholinergic, long-term use may increase risk of dementia.

Dosing: A typical dosage of PO benztropine is 0.5–1 mg BID, with a maximum total daily dose of 4–6 mg. A reasonable PRN dosage is 1 mg q 8 hr. For acute dystonia, give 2 mg IM x 1. Discontinue by tapering to avoid cholinergic rebound (SLUDGE, page 161).

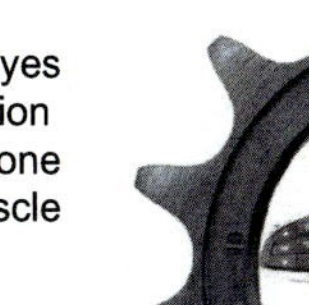

Mercedes Benz steering wheel inside a cogwheel

Anticholinergic with CNS effects—"mad as a hatter"

Cogwheeling – physical exam finding indicative of Parkinson's disease in which passive movement of an arm elicits ratchet-like start-and-stop movements.

Here are the high potency 1st generation antipsychotics (FGAs). They have the highest incidence of EPS and are therefore the most likely culprits to need an anticholinergic add-on:

- ❖ Haloperidol (Haldol)
- ❖ Fluphenazine (Prolixin)
- ❖ Pimozide (Orap)
- ❖ Thiothixene (Navane)
- ❖ Trifluoperazine (Stelazine)

Cogentin is rarely, if ever, needed in combination with these low EPS antipsychotics:

- ❖ Clozapine (Clozaril)
- ❖ Olanzapine (Zyprexa)
- ❖ Quetiapine (Seroquel)
- ❖ Aripiprazole (Abilify)
- ❖ Iloperidone (Fanapt)
- ❖ Pimavanserin (Nuplazid)

Cogentin is not needed if the patient is already taking a highly anticholinergic drug like diphenhydramine (Benadryl). Refer to the anticholinergic burden scale on page 162.

for the
triple threats
of extrapyramidal symptoms caused by phenothiazines
akathisia *
dystonia
akinesia **
TABLETS: 0.5 mg, 1 mg, and 2 mg
INJECTION: 1.0 mg per cc
COGENTIN MESYLATE
(BENZTROPINE MESYLATE | MSD)
when "pseudo-parkinsonism" follows full tranquilizer dosage... add
COGENTIN Mesylate
benztropine mesylate

* Anticholinergics are not first-line treatment for akathisia. More effective treatments for akathisia include the beta blocker propranolol (Inderal) or benzodiazepines.

** Akinesia is another term for pseudo-parkinsonism, including the "Thorazine shuffle".

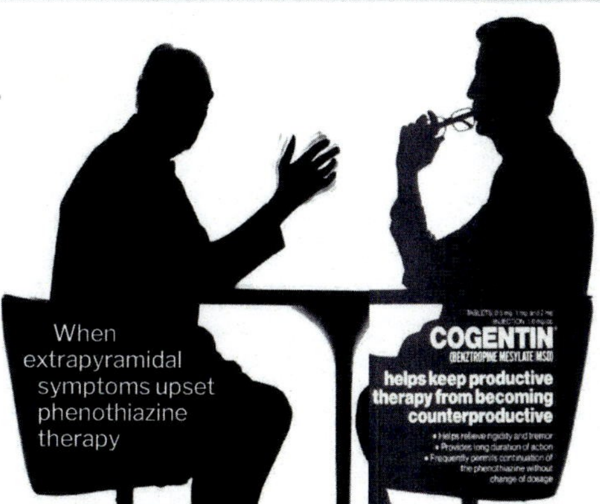

When extrapyramidal symptoms upset phenothiazine therapy
COGENTIN
(BENZTROPINE MESYLATE MSD)
helps keep productive therapy from becoming counterproductive

Dynamic interactions:
- ❖ Sedative (mild)
- ❖ Anticholinergic
  - – constipation
  - – confusion
  - – urinary retention
  - – dry mouth

Kinetic interactions:
- ❖ None significant

page 18

ANTICHOLINERGICS 14

1949
$4–$17

Trihexyphenidyl (ARTANE)

try hex e FEN id il / AR tane

"Triangle hexagon Art"

❖ Anticholinergic
❖ Possibly dopaminergic

2
5
mg

FDA–approved for:

❖ Parkinson's disease
❖ Extrapyramidal symptoms (EPS)

Used off-label for:

❖ Sialorrhea (hypersalivation)
❖ Hyperhidrosis (sweating)

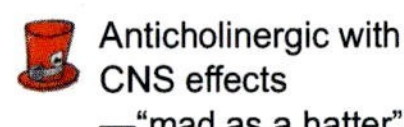

Anticholinergic with CNS effects —"mad as a hatter"

For treatment of EPS, Artane (trihexyphenidyl) is considered second-line to benztropine (Cogentin). Artane is dosed TID, while Cogentin is generally BID. Half-life is about 7 hours. It is only available orally.

Artane is not a controlled substance, but it is used recreationally as a hallucinogen, in large amounts. Artane is considered the most stimulating anticholinergic drug, possibly due to dopaminergic effect. It may produce euphoria. Although benztropine can also cause anticholinergic delirium at high dose, benztropine is not sought by recreational users.

As with any strong anticholinergic, long-term use may increase risk of dementia.

Dosing: Start 1 mg QD and increase to 2 mg TID over a few days. Standard maintenance dose is 2–5 mg TID, maximum of 15 mg/day. Discontinue by tapering to avoid cholinergic rebound (SLUDGE, page 161).

Dynamic interactions:

❖ Sedative (minimal)
❖ Anticholinergic
  – constipation
  – confusion
  – urinary retention
  – dry mouth

Kinetic interactions:

❖ None significant

page 18

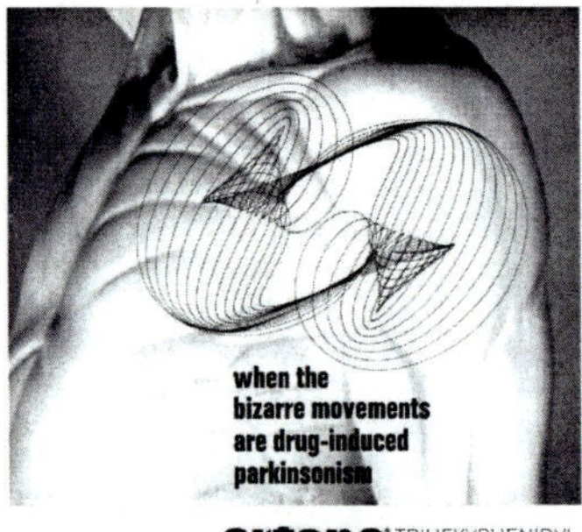

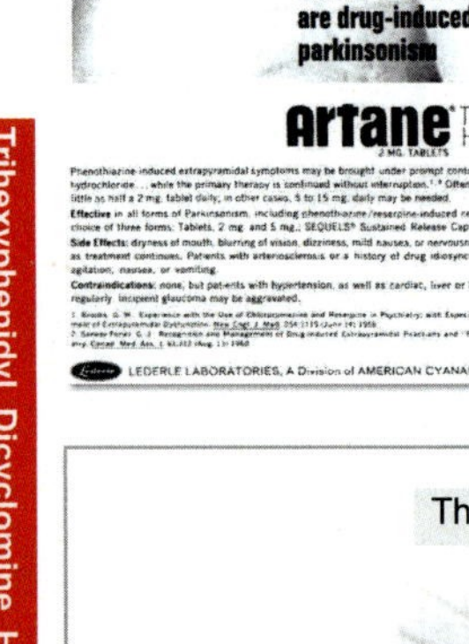

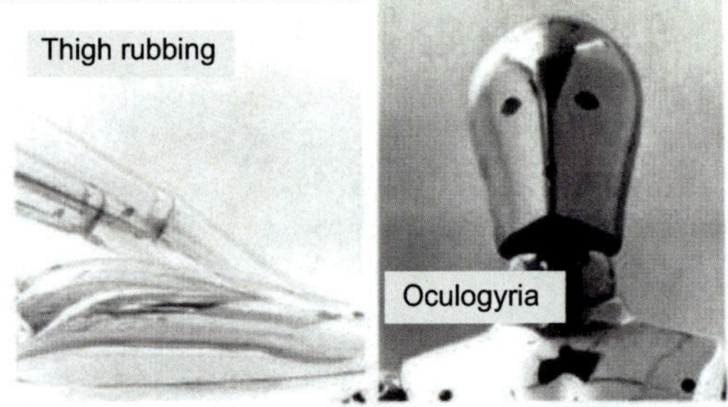

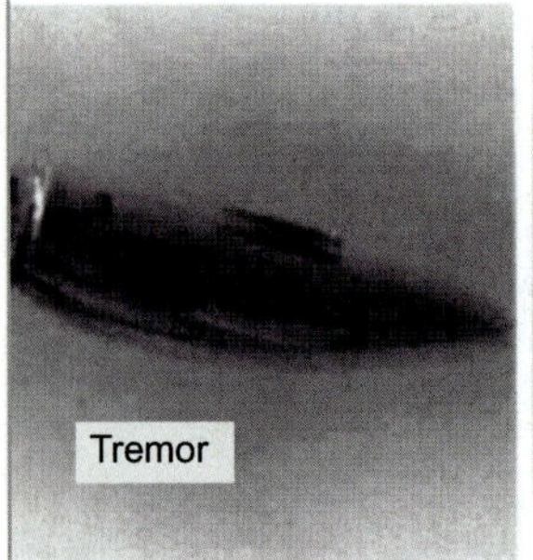

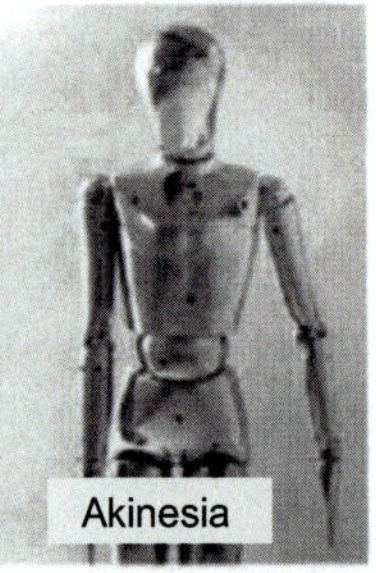

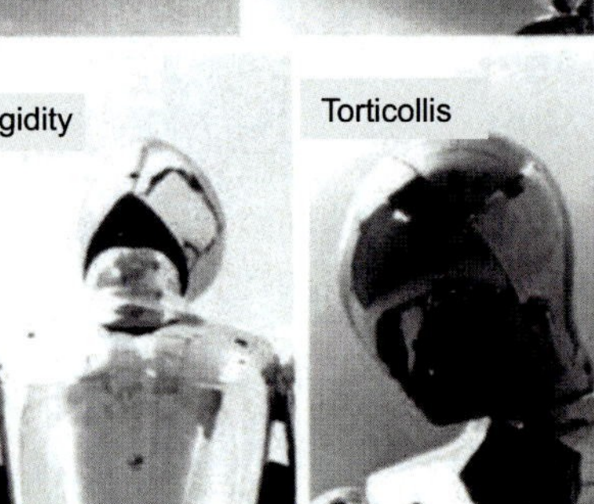

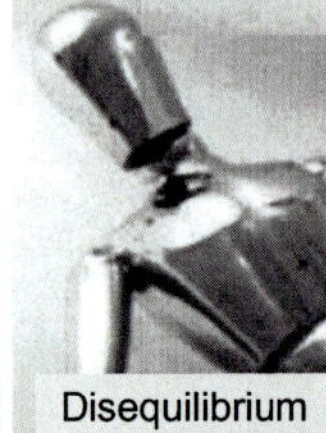

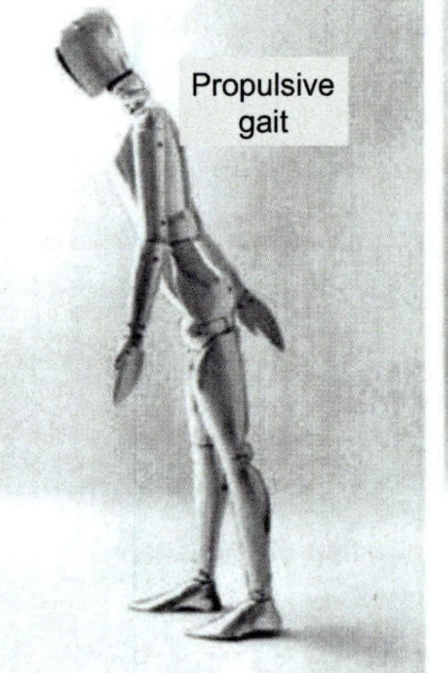

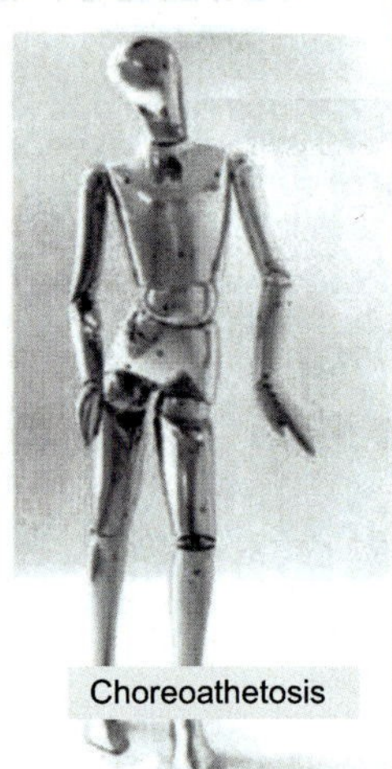

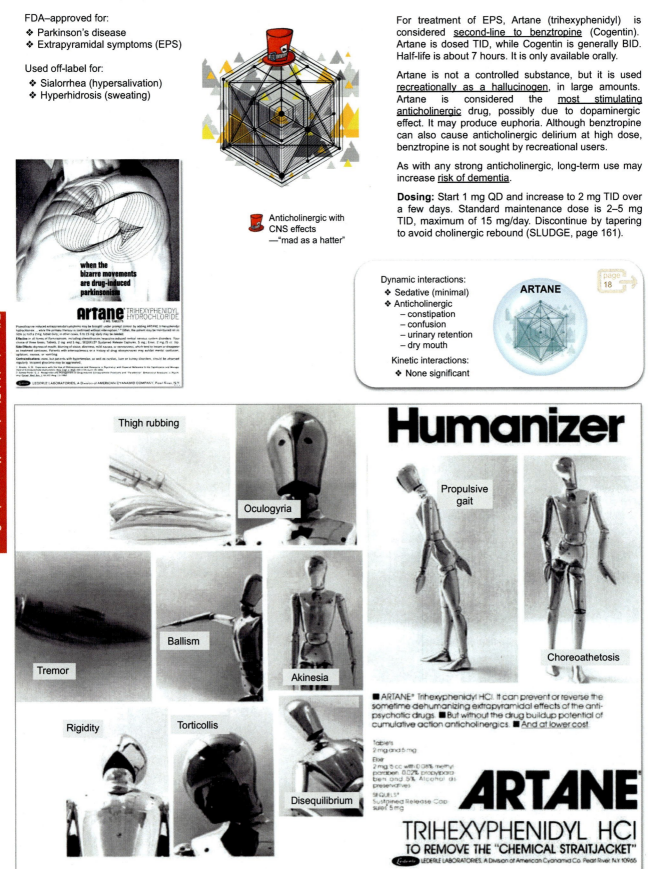

#178
1950
$17–$68

Dicyclomine (BENTYL)

dye SYE klo meen / BEN tyl

"Dice cycle ('round the) Bent eel"

❖ Anticholinergic for irritable bowel syndrome

10
<u>20</u>
mg

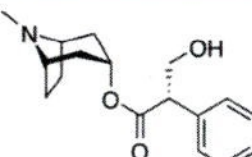

Anticholinergic with CNS effects—"mad as a hatter"

FDA-approved for:

❖ Irritable bowel syndrome (IBS)

Dicyclomine (Bentyl), also known as dicycloverine, is an <u>antispasmodic</u> used to treat irritable bowel syndrome (IBS). It is selective for M1 and M3 muscarinic acetylcholine receptors, both of which are present in the GI tract. It causes constipation and other anticholinergic side effects, including CNS effects such as confusion and risk of dementia. It is not absorbed well if taken at the same time as antacid medication.

Dosing: Start: 20 mg <u>QID</u>; May increase to 40 mg QID after 1 week, which is the max dose of 160 mg/day; Stop after 2 weeks if no improvement.

Dynamic interactions:
- ❖ Sedative
- ❖ Anticholinergic
  - – constipation
  - – confusion
  - – urinary retention

Kinetic interactions:
- ❖ None significant

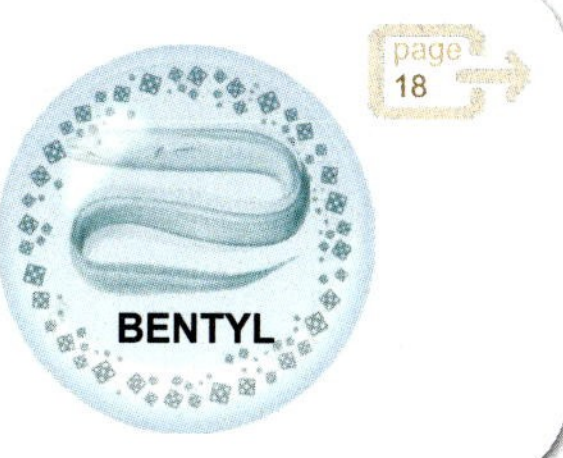

page 18

1955
$9–$26

Hyoscyamine (ANASPAZ, LEVSIN)

hye oh SYE a meen / LEV sin

"Hi yo, C ya! (Adios spaz…Leave soon!)"

❖ Multi-purpose anticholinergic

<u>0.125</u>
0.375
mg

FDA-approved for:
- ❖ Irritable bowel syndrome (IBS)
- ❖ Gastrointestinal tract spasms
- ❖ Bladder spasms
- ❖ Peptic ulcer disease (PUD)
- ❖ Rhinitis (runny nose)
- ❖ Biliary colic (gallstone pain)
- ❖ Renal colic (kidney stone pain)

Hyoscyamine occurs naturally in several plants including deadly nightshade, Jimson weed, and mandrake. These plants are powerful hallucinogens and deliriants due to anticholinergic chemicals including atropine, hyoscyamine, and scopolamine.

A dry goodbye

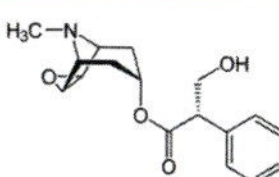

Anticholinergic with CNS effects—"mad as a hatter"

Hyoscyamine (Levsin) is a multi-purpose anticholinergic, <u>not selective</u> for any subtype of muscarinic acetylcholine receptors. It blocks the action of acetylcholine at parasympathetic sites in smooth muscle, secretory glands, and the CNS. It <u>reduces cardiac output</u>, <u>dries secretions</u>, and antagonizes histamine and serotonin.

The orally disintegrating tablet (ODT) formulation is branded as Anaspaz, referring to spasms of GI tract. In other words, hyoscyamine is an <u>antiperistaltic</u> agent, as are other anticholinergics.

Dosing: For all purposes, give 0.125–0.25 mg q 4 hours PRN; Max is 1.5 mg/day.

Dynamic interactions:
- ❖ Anticholinergic

Kinetic interactions:
- ❖ None significant

page 18

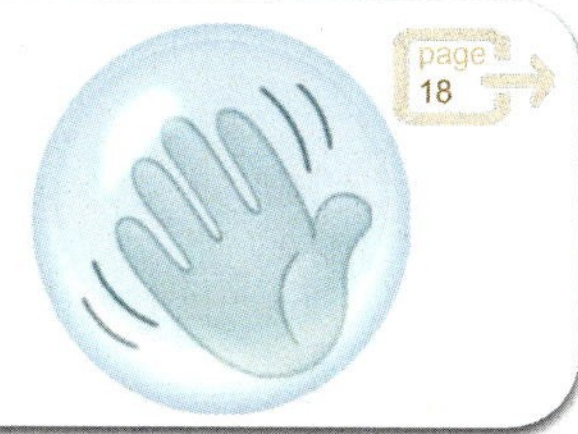

2007
$4–$20
/patch

Scopolamine (TRANSDERM SCŌP)

skoe PAL a meen / trans derm scope

"Scope o' lemon"

❖ Anticholinergic

1.5 mg patch

FDA-approved for:
- ❖ Postoperative nausea
- ❖ Motion sickness

Used off-label for:
- ❖ Sialorrhea (hypersalivation)

Scopolamine, also called hyoscine (similar in name and structure to hyoscyamine shown above) is an anticholinergic used clinically since around 1900. The TRANSDERM SCŌP patch has been available since 2007, to be worn <u>behind the ear for up to 3 days</u>. It may be used off-label for clozapine-induced hypersalivation.

Experiments have suggested intravenous scopolamine may have a rapid <u>antidepressant</u> effect.

Dosing: Apply 1.5 mg patch q 3 days PRN; Start > 4 hours prior to travel or the evening prior to surgery; Remove patch 24 hours after surgery.

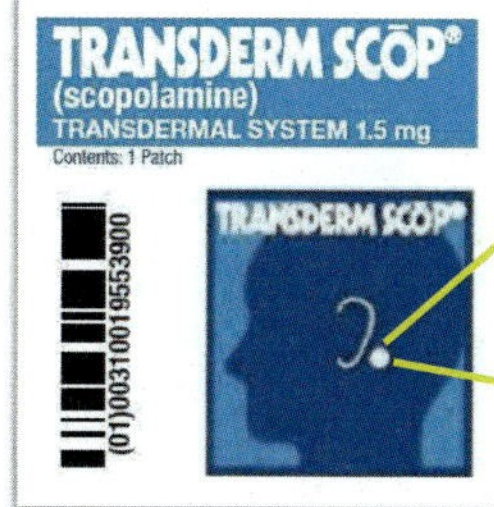

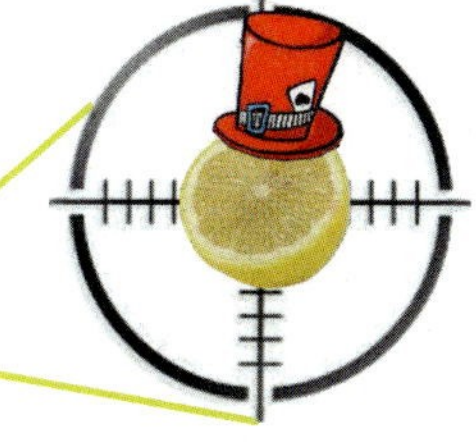

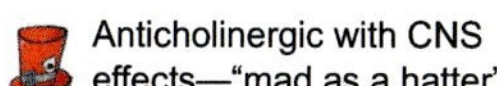

Anticholinergic with CNS effects—"mad as a hatter"

Dynamic interactions:
- ❖ Sedative
- ❖ Anticholinergic
  - – constipation
  - – confusion
  - – urinary retention
  - – dry mouth

Kinetic interactions:
- ❖ None significant

page 18

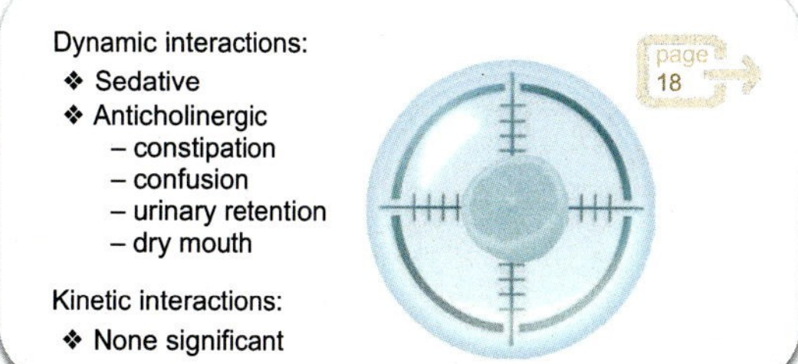

Glycopyrrolate (ROBINUL)

1961
$14–$63

GLY koe PIE roe late / ROB in ol

"Robbin' all Glad cops"

- ❖ Anticholinergic
- ❖ No CNS effects

1 mg

FDA-approved for:
- ❖ Peptic ulcer disease
- ❖ COPD (inhaler)
- ❖ Anesthesia adjunction (IV, IM)

Used off-label for
- ❖ Sialorrhea (hypersalivation) - 1st line PO
- ❖ Hyperhidrosis (sweating) - 1st line

✱ The Mad-Hatter hat is not depicted for glycopyrrolate because it does not cross the blood-brain barrier.

The anticholinergic medication glycopyrrolate (Robinul), also known as glycopyrronium, is the preferred (oral) antisialagogue for clozapine-induced hypersalivation (drooling). Glycopyrrolate dries the mouth without causing cognitive impairment because it does not cross the blood-brain barrier (BBB). "Mad as a hatter" does not apply. However, addition of an anticholinergic can exacerbate clozapine-induced constipation, which can be severe—potentially leading to bowel rupture. Inability to cross the BBB also makes glycopyrrolate useless for treatment of EPS. An alternative that can treat both sialorrhea and EPS is benztropine (Cogentin). To avoid constipation, a topical alternative for clozapine-induced hypersalivation is atropine ophthalmic (Atropisol) 1–3 drops sublingually at bedtime (shown on page 176).

Glycopyrrolate is the preferred treatment of hyperhidrosis (sweating). It works well as an add-on to address antidepressant-induced sweating (Mago, 2013). A topical form of glycopyrrolate called glycopyrronium (Qbrexza) is approved as an expensive underarm wipe for axillary hyperhidrosis (excessive underarm sweating). Glycopyrrolate and glycopyrronium are the same molecule.

As with most anticholinergics, there are no CYP interactions to worry about.

The inhaled formulation of glycopyrrolate is called Seebri Neohaler. For context, there are several more popular anticholinergic inhalers for COPD, including tiotropium (Spiriva), ipratropium (Atrovent), and umeclidinium (Incruse Ellipta).

Dosing: For drooling or sweating (off-label), give 1–2 mg PO q 6 hr PRN; Max is 8 mg/day; For peptic ulcer disease, give on a scheduled basis, 1–2 mg PO BID–TID Start: 1 mg PO tid; Max is 8 mg/day.

Dynamic interactions:
- ❖ Anticholinergic (peripheral effects)
  - constipation
  - urinary retention
  - dry mouth

Kinetic interactions:
- ❖ None significant

page 18

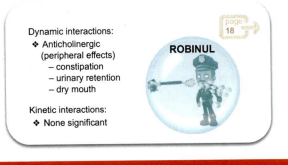

Glycopyrronium (QBREXZA)

2018
$549–$696

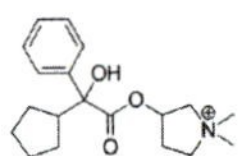

Same chemical as glycopyrrolate

GLYE koe PIR oh late / qu BREX zah

"Q-Bert's Gluey pepperoni"

- ❖ Topical anticholinergic

2.8 g
2.4%

FDA-approved for:
- ❖ Axillary hyperhidrosis (sweating)

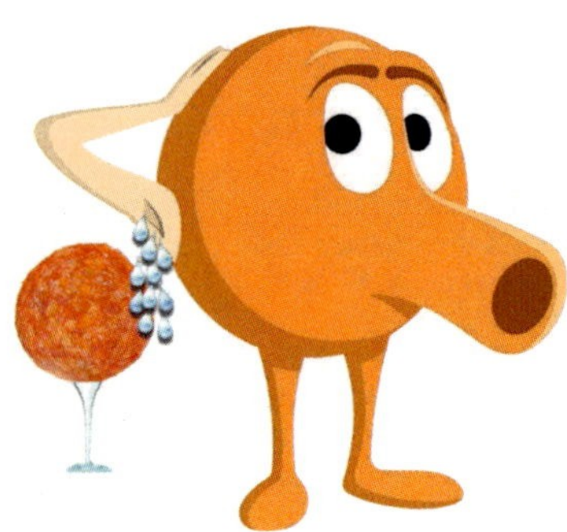

Qbrexza is a pre-moistened cloth containing glycopyrronium, a long-acting anticholinergic to be applied once daily under the arms for hyperhidrosis (sweating). Systemic absorption of topical glycopyrronium is minimal, but enough for almost 25% of patients to report dry mouth from applying Qbrexza.

Oral anticholinergics such as glycopyrrolate (Robinul) and oxybutynin (Ditropan) have been used off-label PO for hyperhidrosis. Those can cause systemic anticholinergic side effects. Another option for hyperhidrosis is Botox injection into the axillae, which costs about $1,200 and works for 6–9 months. If paying out of pocket, Botox is more cost effective than Qbrexza, which costs over $500 for a box of 30 wipes.

Qbrexza is included in this book to hammer home the point that anticholinergics decrease sweating —"dry as a bone", "hot as a hare".

Dosing: One pad to axillae daily; Use the same pad across both axillae; Max is 1 pad per day.

Glycopyrrolate & glycopyrronium are the same chemical

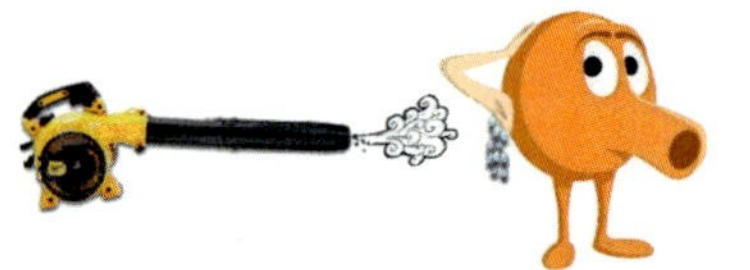

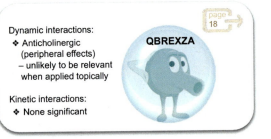

Dynamic interactions:
- ❖ Anticholinergic (peripheral effects)
  - unlikely to be relevant when applied topically

Kinetic interactions:
- ❖ None significant

page 18

Anticholinergics for Overactive Bladder (OAB)

Anticholinergic risk of cognitive impairment	3 Points (worst)	2 points	1 point (mild)	0 points
	Oxybutynin (Ditropan)	**Tolterodine (Detrol)**	Fesoterodine (Toviaz) Solifenacin (Vesicare)	Darifenacin (Enablex) Trospium (Sanctura)

#108
1975
IR $18–$43
ER $17–$91

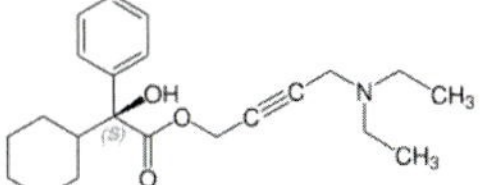

Oxybutynin (DITROPAN)

OX i BUE ti nin / DIT ro pan

"Ox's booty in a (ditro)pan"

❖ Anticholinergic for overactive bladder

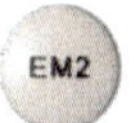

5 ER
10 ER
15 ER
mg

Anticholinergic with CNS effects—"mad as a hatter"

FDA-approved for:

❖ Overactive bladder

Used off-label for:

❖ Sialorrhea (hypersalivation)
❖ Vasomotor menopause symptoms (hot flashes)

Oxybutynin is a strong anticholinergic (3 points). It reduces episodes of urge incontinence by about 66%. It can cause somnolence, which can be problematic with the immediate release oral formulation. The oxybutynin transdermal patch is less likely to sedate. There is potential for serious psychiatric side effects. Psychotic behavior and hallucinations induced by oxybutynin have been reported.

Anticholinergic side effects of oxybutynin are not particularly common at lower doses. Oxybutynin 5 mg daily was not associated with a greater risk of side effects than placebo in cognitively impaired nursing home residents (Lackner et al, 2008).

Oxybutynin has been used for clozapine-induced hypersalivation, although the preferred anticholinergic for this purpose is glycopyrrolate (Robinul), which does not cross the blood brain barrier.

Dosing: With ER formulation, start 5–10 mg QD; May increase by 5 mg/day in weekly intervals; Max for ER is 30 mg/day; IR formulation is not recommended, but would be dosed BID–QID with a maximum of 5 mg QID (20 mg/day).

Anticholinergic side effect	Oxybutynin (Ditropan) IR	Oxybutynin ER	Oxybutynin transdermal	Tolterodine (Detrol)
Dry mouth	75%	30%	10%	25%
Constipation	30%	7%	1%	6%
Blurred vision	5%	2%	0%	1%
Dizziness	35%	5%	1%	2%
Drowsiness	40%	3%	2%	3%

Dynamic interactions:

❖ Anticholinergic
❖ Sedative

Kinetic interactions:

❖ Oxybutynin is a minor substrate of 3A4. Significant kinetic interaction are possible but unlikely, so it is depicted "in a box"

page 18

ANTICHOLINERGICS

#300
1996
IR $44–$197
ER $63–$236

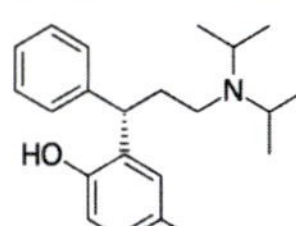

Tolterodine (DETROL)

tol TER oh deen / DET rol

"Total rodent Detrusor control"

❖ Anticholinergic for overactive bladder

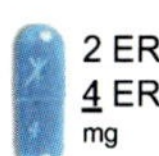

2 ER
4 ER
mg

1
2
mg

FDA-approved for:

❖ Overactive bladder

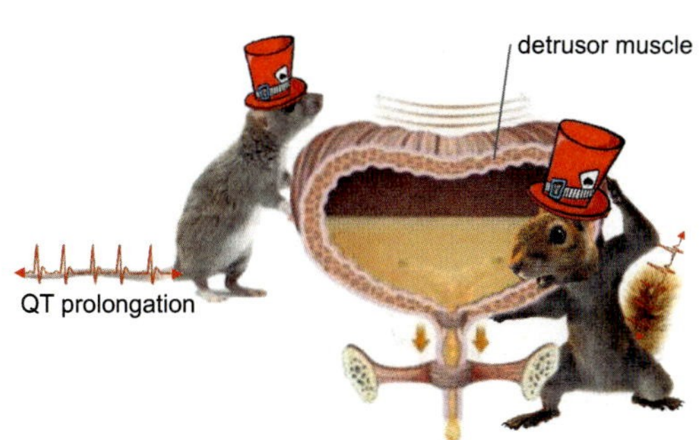

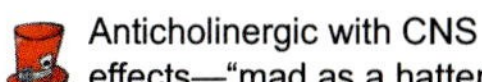

Anticholinergic with CNS effects—"mad as a hatter"

Overactive bladder (OAB) occurs because the detrusor muscle contracts inappropriately before the bladder is full. Anticholinergics suppress detrusor contractions.

Tolterodine (Detrol) is less anticholinergic than oxybutynin, making it better tolerated. There are some case reports of serious confusion and delusions related to tolterodine, but it rarely causes significant memory impairment, even for elderly patients.

Tolterodine has a maximum dose of 4 mg/day due to concerns of QT prolongation, particularly among CYP2D6 poor metabolizers.

Dosing: For IR formulation, start 2 mg BID (max dose), may decrease dose to 1 mg BID; For ER formulation, start 4 mg QD, may decrease to 2 mg QD.

Dynamic interactions:

❖ Anticholinergic
❖ QT prolongation

Kinetic interactions:

❖ 2D6 substrate
❖ 3A4 substrate

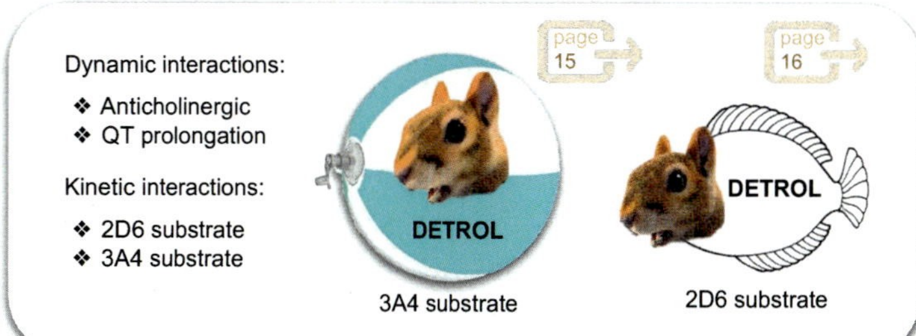

page 15
page 16

Anticholinergic risk of cognitive impairment	3 Points (worst)	2 points	1 point (mild)	0 points
	Oxybutynin (Ditropan)	Tolterodine (Detrol)	**Fesoterodine (Toviaz)** **Solifenacin (Vesicare)**	Darifenacin (Enablex) Trospium (Sanctura)

#170
2004
$387–$475

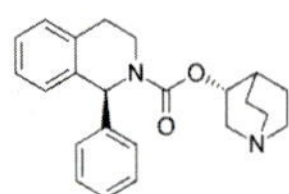

Solifenacin (VESICARE)

sol ee FEN a sin / VES i care

"Solar fencin' Vesica cares"

❖ Anticholinergic for overactive bladder

5
10
mg

FDA-approved for:

❖ Overactive bladder (OAB)

Used off-label for:

❖ Donepezil-induced GI distress

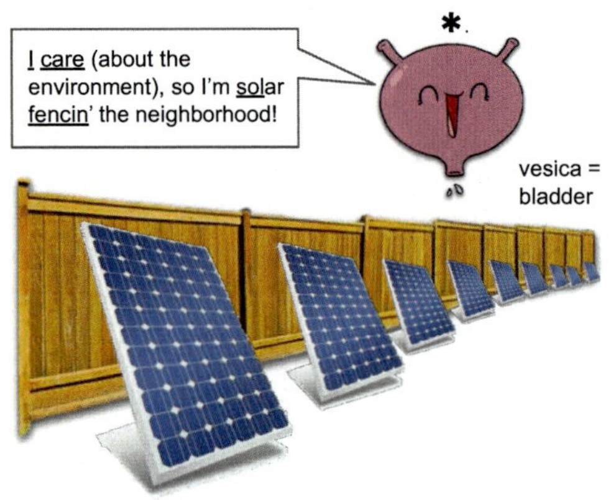

*
I care (about the environment), so I'm solar fencin' the neighborhood!
vesica = bladder

Solifenacin (Vesicare) is relatively selective antagonist of muscarinic acetylcholine receptors in the bladder. It scores 1 point on our anticholinergic burden scale for cognitive impairment, i.e., is unlikely to impair cognition.

Solifenacin has been used as an add-on to cholinergic Alzheimer's medications such as donepezil (Aricept). The dose-limiting side effect of cholinergics like donepezil is gastrointestinal distress. If a peripheral anticholinergic such as solifenacin is in place, higher doses of the cholinergic agent can be tolerated without nausea (Chase et al, 2017). This strategy only works with an anticholinergic without significant CNS effects—otherwise the cognitive benefit of the cholinergic agent is lost.

Dosing: For overactive bladder, start 5 mg QD; Max 10 mg QD; If used adjunctively (off-label) to ameliorate GI distress caused by donepezil (Aricept), start solifenacin 10 mg QD x 1 week, then 15 mg QD (Chase et al, 2017).

Dynamic interactions:
- ❖ Anticholinergic
- ❖ QT prolongation

Kinetic interactions:
- ❖ 3A4 substrate

page 16

3A4 substrate

2009
$288–$457

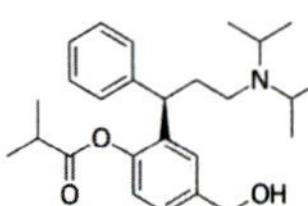

Fesoterodine (TOVIAZ)

fes oh TER oh deen / TOH vee az

"Two-vizor Fester"

❖ Anticholinergic for overactive bladder

4
8
mg

FDA-approved for:

❖ Overactive bladder

Uncle Fester from The Addams Family, needing to pee

✱ The Mad Hatter hat is not depicted for fesoterodine or solifenacin because the amount that crosses the blood-brain barrier (BBB) is negligible.

Fesoterodine (Toviaz) is a prodrug of the active metabolite of tolterodine (Detrol).

It has minimal potential for causing anticholinergic cognitive impairment. Like solifenacin, fesoterodine scores 1 point on the anticholinergic burden scale (page 162).

The football shaped tabs are inscribed with "FT" for FesoTerodine.

Dosing: Start 4 mg QD; the maximum dose of 8 mg QD is the usual maintenance dose for overactive bladder; tabs are ER and should not be split or crushed.

Dynamic interactions:
- ❖ Anticholinergic

Kinetic interactions:
- ❖ 3A4 substrate (major)
- ❖ 2D6 substrate (minor)

page 16

3A4 substrate (major)

page 15

2D6 substrate (minor)

Anticholinergics for Overactive Bladder (OAB)

Anticholinergic risk of cognitive impairment	3 Points (worst)	2 points	1 point (mild)	0 points
	Oxybutynin (Ditropan)	Tolterodine (Detrol)	Fesoterodine (Toviaz) Solifenacin (Vesicare)	**Darifenacin (Enablex)** **Trospium (Sanctura)**

Darifenacin (ENABLEX)

2004
$74–$356

dar e FEN a sin / en ABE lex

"Dairy fenced in / Dairy Enabler"

❖ Anticholinergic for overactive bladder

7.5
15
mg

FDA-approved for:

❖ Overactive bladder

Detrusor contraction is mediated mainly by M3 muscarinic acetylcholine receptors. Of the anticholinergics for overactive bladder (OAB), darifenacin (Enablex) has the greatest degree of M3 receptor selectivity. It has no effect on M1 receptors in the brain or M2 receptors in the heart. Since it does not cause cognitive impairment, darifenacin is suitable for older adults. It is well tolerated but can cause some unwanted peripheral anticholinergic effects such as dry mouth and constipation.

Dosing: Start 7.5 mg QD; The maximum dose of 15 mg is the usual maintenance dose for OAB. The tabs are ER, do not split or crush.

Dynamic interactions:
❖ Anticholinergic
❖ QT prolongation

Kinetic interactions:
❖ 3A4 substrate

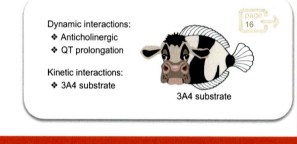

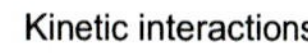

3A4 substrate

ANTICHOLINERGICS

Trospium (SANCTURA)

2004
IR tab $43–$136
ER cap $64–$178

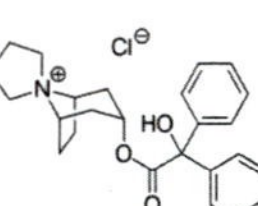

TROS pee um / sank TUR a

"Trusy pee'in Sanctuary"

❖ Anticholinergic for overactive bladder

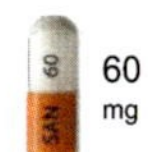

60 ER
mg

20
mg

FDA-approved for:

❖ Overactive bladder

"The brain is a Sanctuary"—This anticholinergic for OAB does not impair cognition. The chemical does not cross the blood brain barrier (BBB) because it is large, hydrophilic, positively charged, and a P-glycoprotein (P-gp) substrate. If it crosses the blood-brain barrier, P-gp pumps it out—*"pumpers gonna pump"*.

Dosing: IR tablets: 20 mg BID (20 mg HS if age > 75); ER capsules: 60 mg QD; With either formulation, give on an empty stomach > 1 hour before meal.

page
18

Dynamic interactions:
❖ Anticholinergic

Kinetic interactions:
❖ P-glycoprotein substrate
❖ Unlikely to be involved in kinetic interaction - "in a box"

#298
1960
$25–$67

Atropine

AT roe peen

"AT-AT dropping"

❖ Anticholinergic

1% eye drops

FDA-approved for:
- ❖ See below

Used off-label for:
- ❖ Clozapine-induced hypersalivation (eye drops applied sublingually)

AT-AT walker from Star Wars (All Terrain Armored Transport)
Anticholinergics dilate pupils.

"Atropine is anticholinergic". Atropine, first isolated in 1833, is the strongest anticholinergic. It occurs naturally in a number of plants including deadly nightshade, Jimson weed, and mandrake. These plants are powerful hallucinogens and deliriants due to anticholinergic chemicals including atropine, hyoscyamine, and scopolamine.

Uses of parenteral (SC, IM or IV) atropine:
- ❖ ATROPEN auto-injector for organophosphate poisoning (insecticides, nerve agents)
- ❖ ACLS protocol for bradycardia, to increase heart rate
- ❖ Anesthesia adjunct to decrease saliva

Uses of atropine ophthalmic drops (ATROPISOL):
- ❖ Dilation of pupils before eye exams to better visualize the retina
- ❖ To paralyze the ciliary muscle in order to determine the true refractive error of the eye (cycloplegic refraction)
- ❖ Treatment of amblyopia (lazy eye) by blurring the better-seeing eye as an alternative to wearing an eyepatch
- ❖ Treatment of uveitis (inflammation of iris, choroid, and ciliary body)
- ❖ Off-label treatment of clozapine-induced hypersalivation, given sublingually. Some systemic absorption is expected, and pupils may dilate to some extent. An alternative is ipratropium nasal spray given sublingually (Atrovent nasal, approved for rhinorrhea), which has less systemic absorption than atropine. For ipratropium, give 1–3 sprays SL at HS (not intranasal) up to 3x daily.

Oral atropine:
- ❖ In combination with the opioid diphenoxylate (LOMOTIL) for treatment of diarrhea. The atropine component contributes in small part to the antidiarrheal effect, included primarily as a determent to consuming large amounts of Lomotil to get high.

Dosing: For clozapine-induced hypersalivation**:** Atropine ophthalmic (Atropisol) 1–3 drops sublingually HS. Watch for possible daytime rebound salivation. May be used up to TID. See page 168 for other options for hypersalivation.

Dynamic interactions:
- ❖ Anticholinergic

Kinetic interactions:
- ❖ None significant

page 18

Atropine · Pupils

Causes of mydriasis and miosis

Mydriasis – dilated pupils "mad as a hatter" anti cholin-ergic	Sympathetic (fight or flight) With anticholinergic toxicity, also expect to see facial flushing. *Mydriasis – "Oh my... what big eyes you have"* Pronounced [mi DRAHY *uh* sis] or [mahy DRAHY *uh* sis]	❖ Anticholinergics – atropine eye drops are highly anticholinergic and given for the purpose of dilating pupils for ophthalmologic exam ❖ Antidepressants ❖ Serotonin syndrome ❖ Stimulants ❖ LSD, PCP, Hallucinogens ❖ Opioid withdrawal ❖ Meperidine (Demerol) – an opioid with anticholinergic and serotonergic properties
Miosis – constricted pupils opioid	Parasympathetic (rest and digest) *Miosis – "mini-pupils"*	❖ Opioids (other than meperidine) are the most potent pupillary constrictors ❖ Antipsychotics ❖ Trazodone (Desyrel) and mirtazapine (Remeron) – antidepressants with sedative properties ❖ Cholinergics, e.g., donepezil (Aricept)

In 2013, DSM-5 replaced the term *Dementia* with *Major Neurocognitive Disorder* because of stigma associated with a word derived from the Latin for "loss of mind". DSM-5 does not preclude the use of *Dementia* "where that term is standard", which is the case for pharmacology.

Medications currently available for dementia are not miracle drugs. They rarely bring about dramatic improvement, but can slow cognitive decline for about a year (best case scenario). After 3 years of use, they have little to no effect. For mild Alzheimer's, the standard practice is to start with donepezil (Aricept) and titrate to 10 mg HS. For moderate to severe Alzheimer's, donepezil and memantine (Namenda) are typically both used, titrated one at a time. It is reasonable to start with memantine off-label for mild Alzheimer's, as it is better tolerated than donepezil.

Do not use cholinesterase inhibitors or memantine for mild neurocognitive disorder (pre-dementia). These medications do **not** prevent progression of mild neurocognitive disorder (NCD) to major NCD (Sanford AM, 2017). Only 10–15% of mild NCD cases progress to dementia anyhow. The Mediterranean-DASH Intervention for Neurodegenerative Delay (MIND) diet can slow cognitive decline in older adults (Morris MC et al, 2015).

Cognitive enhancer	Cost	Mechanism	FDA-approved for	Details	
Donepezil (ARICEPT)	$13	Acetylcholinesterase (AChE) inhibitor = cholinergic agent	Alzheimer's dementia (mild, moderate, or severe)	The AChE inhibitors have a high incidence of gastrointestinal "SLUDGE" (cholinergic) side effects—nausea, vomiting, diarrhea, bradycardia. May cause agitation and vivid dreams.	Donepezil is by far the most prescribed AChE inhibitor.
Rivastigmine transdermal (EXELON PATCH)	$150		Alzheimer's dementia (mild–mod); Parkinson's dementia (mild–mod)		Patch is used because too many GI side effects with PO formulation.
Galantamine (RAZADYNE)	$50		Alzheimer's (mild–mod)		Rarely prescribed.
Memantine (NAMENDA)	$21	NMDA receptor antagonist	Alzheimer's (mod–severe)	Fewer side effects than the cholinergics. Appropriate for off-label use with mild Alzheimer's. Titrate over 4 weeks to target dose of 10 mg BID.	
Memantine ER + donepezil (NAMZARIC)	$460	NMDA antagonist + AChE inhibitor	Alzheimer's (mod–severe)	Namzaric is a combination pill for patients already stabilized on donepezil +/- memantine.	
Apoaequorin (PREVAGEN)	$60	Placebo that does not cross the blood-brain barrier	Nothing	OTC "from jellyfish" heavily marketed on TV for "mild memory loss related to aging" rather than to treat any specific disease. The Federal Trade Commission sued the company (unsuccessfully) for making false and unsubstantiated claims.	
Lithium	$10	Neuroprotectant; mechanism likely involves brain-derived neurotrophic factor (BDNF)	Bipolar I disorder	Lithium is effective treatment for Alzheimer's disease (Mauer et al, 2014) and might keep pre-dementia from progressing to Alzheimer's disease (Forlenza et al, 2011). The author prescribes lithium 150 mg HS for cognitive purposes. No need to monitor lithium blood levels at this dose. As with all patients, monitor renal function and TSH.	
N-acetylcysteine (NAC)	$10	Antioxidant active in CNS	Acetaminophen overdose, Mucolysis	Available OTC, 600–1,200 mg BID for general brain health. Very safe. Minimal side effects including gastrointestinal discomfort.	

Anticholinergic medications affecting the CNS will counteract the cholinergic activity of the AChE inhibitors, as a dynamic interaction. Anticholinergics should be avoided with the elderly in any case. Refer to the anticholinergic burden scale on page 162 for the "mad as a hatter" medications that can worsen dementia.

Acetylcholinesterase (AChE) Inhibitors – cholinergic medications for Alzheimer's

As you may recall, anticholinergic medications impair cognition. Cholinergic medications enhance cognition. Several Alzheimer's medications enhance cholinergic (muscarinic) activity by inhibiting acetylcholinesterase (AChE), the enzyme that breaks down acetylcholine.

AChE Inhibitors for Alzheimer's disease:

- ❖ Donepezil (Aricept)
- ❖ Rivastigmine (Exelon)
- ❖ Galantamine (Razadyne)

As previously presented, SLUDGE is a mnemonic for the results of muscarinic acetylcholine receptor overload: AChE inhibitors have the potential to produce any of the SLUDGE symptoms, as well as miosis (constricted pupils) and Brady(Bunch)-cardia (slow heart rate).

S – Salivation
L – Lacrimation (also lactation)
U – Urination
D – Diaphoresis (also diarrhea)
G – Gastrointestinal upset (including diarrhea)
E – Emesis

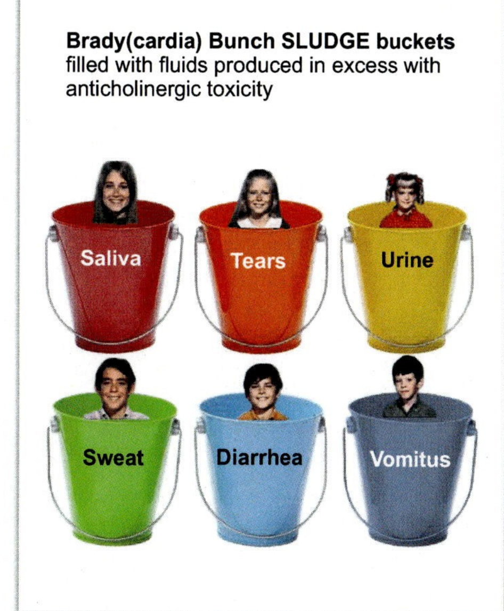

Once a patient is established on a cholinesterase inhibitor and is experiencing no side effects, the medication should probably be continued indefinitely. With discontinuation there is risk of a precipitous cognitive decline, and it may not be recoverable if the medication is restarted.

There is also an argument for "deprescribing", i.e., trying to get patients off these medications. Refer to *Evidence-based Clinical Practice Guideline for Deprescribing Cholinesterase Inhibitors and Memantine* from The University of Sydney (2018).

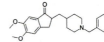

#98
1996
$7–$158

Donepezil (ARICEPT)

don ep e zil / AIR e cept

"Donnie Pez is Air except" (for an Alzheimer's brain)

- Cholinergic drug
- Cholinesterase inhibitor
- Cognitive enhancer

5
10
23
mg

FDA-approved for:

- Alzheimer's dementia, mild–moderate
- Alzheimer's dementia, moderate–severe

"Air" in Alzheimer's patient's brain

I have one of the great memories of all time.

Donepezil (Aricept) is the #1 prescribed medication for treatment of dementia. Aricept works as a cholinergic agent by inhibiting the acetylcholinesterase (AChE) enzyme. It is FDA-approved for Alzheimer's disease of any severity. It has better evidence for mild Alzheimer's than the other cholinesterase inhibitors.

Donepezil is generally well tolerated, but about 10% quit due to nausea, vomiting, or diarrhea. Think SLUDGE cholinergic effects. The gastrointestinal issues usually do not persist past a couple of weeks. It may slow heart rate. Bradycardia is a cholinergic effect. Other potential side effects are agitation and vivid dreams.

Aricept has a long half-life of about 3 days. It is dosed at bedtime but is non-sedating. It does not cause weight gain, and the 23 mg dose is associated with weight loss.

After the patient is established on donepezil, the NMDA receptor antagonist memantine (Namenda) is often added. Namzaric is a branded capsule containing both Namenda (memantine ER) and Aricept.

A strategic combination of donepezil with a peripherally acting anticholinergic such as solifenacin (Vesicare, approved for overactive bladder) can allow high doses of donepezil to be used. Solifenacin blocks donepezil's dose-limiting gastrointestinal side effects without impairing cognition. This strategy only works with anticholinergics without CNS effects—otherwise the cholinergic cognitive benefit of donepezil would be blocked.

Dosing: 5 mg HS x 4 weeks then 10 mg HS, which is the target dose for mild Alzheimer's dementia. Maximum dose is 23 mg HS (intended for moderate to severe dementia) which should not be used until the patient has tolerated 10 mg for 3 months. If given with solifenacin (Vesicare, page 174) at 15 mg, donepezil can be titrated to 40 mg HS without causing gastrointestinal distress (Chase et al, 2017). Solifenacin would be started at 10 mg QD x 1 week, then 15 mg QD, which is a high dose. Consider moving donepezil to AM dosing if it causes insomnia or disturbing dreams. Monitor for bradycardia. The usual next step is the addition of memantine (Namenda). Consider switching to the rivastigmine patch (Exelon transdermal) if cognitive decline continues past 6 to 9 months. If donepezil is stopped, it should be tapered over 4 weeks, but be advised that cognitive functioning may plummet, possibly irrecoverably.

Dynamic interactions:

- Avoid combining with anticholinergics (with CNS effects) due to opposing mechanism of action.
- Cholinergic toxicity (SLUDGE syndrome) is possible when combined with cholinergics such as bethanechol (Urecholine)
- Strategic combination with a peripheral anticholinergic (without CNS effects) can ameliorate GI distress.
- Caution with beta blockers (propranolol, metoprolol, etc) due to aggregate risk of bradycardia.
- Lowers seizure threshold

Kinetic interactions:

- 2D6 substrate
- 3A4 substrate (minor)

page 15

2D6 substrate

page 16

3A4 substrate (minor)

Donepezil Rivastigmine Galantamine

1993
N/A

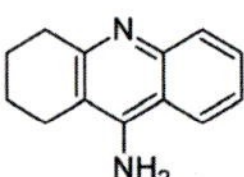

Tacrine (COGNEX)

TAC crin / COG nex

"Tacky cryin' (liver)"

- Cholinergic agent
- Cholinesterase inhibitor
- Cognitive enhancer
- Removed from market

Removed from market

Tacrine (Cognex) was the prototypical cholinesterase inhibitor, and the first medication for Alzheimer's disease. It was FDA-approved in 1993, but discontinued in 2013 due to the risk of acute hepatotoxicity. It was not considered very effective anyhow.

2000
$125–$454

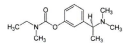

Rivastigmine (EXELON)

riv a stig meen / EX el on

"Excel on (the) River"

- ❖ Cholinergic drug
- ❖ Cholinesterase inhibitor
- ❖ Cognitive enhancer

4.6
13.3
mg patch

FDA-approved for:

- ❖ Alzheimer's dementia, mild–moderate
- ❖ Dementia of Parkinson's disease, mild–moderate

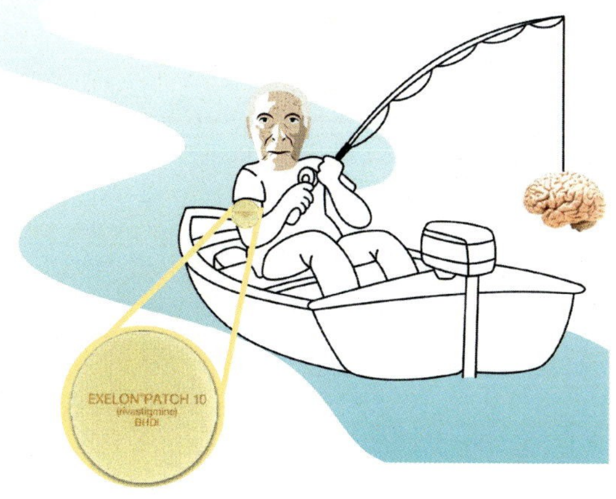

Rivastigmine (Exelon) is a second-line (to donepezil) cholinergic agent for the treatment of Alzheimer's disease. Rivastigmine is the only cognitive enhancer that is also FDA-approved for dementia associated with Parkinson's disease.

Rivastigmine inhibits butyrylcholinesterase and acetylcholinesterase, whereas donepezil (Aricept) and galantamine (Razadyne) only inhibit the latter. Some prescribers regard rivastigmine as more effective than Aricept. However, gastrointestinal side effects are worse with rivastigmine, at least with the PO formulation. Gastrointestinal distress from rivastigmine can be mitigated by using the transdermal patch formulation. Consider switching from donepezil to rivastigmine transdermal if there is continued cognitive decline after 6 to 9 months on donepezil.

Oral rivastigmine needs to be dosed twice daily due to its relatively short half-life of about 10 hours (compared to donepezil's 3-day half-life). Dosing should start low and be increased slowly so the patient doesn't vomit. There have been cases of cholinergic toxicity (SLUDGE) caused by applying new patches without removing old patches.

The patch goes off patent in 2019. Exelon also happens to be the name of the largest electric company in the US.

Dosing: Transdermal: Replace the patch q 24 hr. Start 4.6 mg patch x 4 weeks, the 9.5 mg patch x 4 weeks, then may increase to 13.3 mg patch/24 hr, which is the maximum dose. Re-titrate from 4.6 mg patch if treatment is interrupted by > 3 days; Oral rivastigmine is started 2.5 mg BID with food, increase by 1.5 mg/dose q 2 weeks as tolerated to a target dose of 3–6 mg BID. Max is 12 mg/day (6 mg BID). Monitor for bradycardia. Taper over 4 weeks to discontinue, but be advised that cognitive functioning may plummet, possibly irrecoverably.

page 18

Dynamic interactions:

- ❖ Cholinergic
- ❖ Bradycardia
- ❖ Lowers seizure threshold

Kinetic interactions:

- ❖ None significant

2001
$50–$170

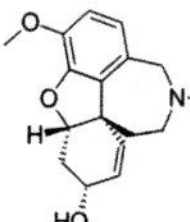

Galantamine (RAZADYNE)

gah LAN tah meen / RAZ a dine

"Go lantern! Raise a dyin' (brain)"

- ❖ Cholinergic drug
- ❖ Cholinesterase inhibitor
- ❖ Cognitive enhancer

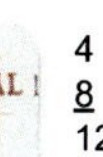

4
8
12
mg

FDA-approved for:

- ❖ Alzheimer's dementia, mild–moderate

In addition to inhibiting acetylcholinesterase, the cognitive enhancer galantamine (Razadyne) is also a nicotinic cholinergic receptor modulator. Despite this additional mechanism, galantamine is no better than donepezil. Galantamine is rarely prescribed due to SLUDGE cholinergic side effects. It is important to maintain adequate hydration during treatment because galantamine is excreted 95% renally and may cause diarrhea.

The original trade name was Reminyl. This was changed after dispensing mix-ups with the diabetes medication Amaryl (glimepiride). Natural galantamine extracted from the root of the red spider lily is available as an over-the-counter supplement.

Dosing: Start 4 mg BID (with food) and increase by 4 mg BID every 4 weeks to target dose of 8–12 mg BID; Maximum total daily dose is 24 mg; Re-titrate from 4 mg BID if treatment is interrupted by > 3 days; Reduce dose if renal or hepatic insufficiency. Taper over 4 weeks to discontinue, but be advised that cognitive functioning may plummet, possibly irrecoverably.

page 18

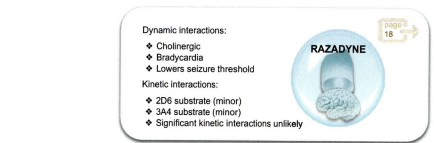

Dynamic interactions:

- ❖ Cholinergic
- ❖ Bradycardia
- ❖ Lowers seizure threshold

Kinetic interactions:

- ❖ 2D6 substrate (minor)
- ❖ 3A4 substrate (minor)
- ❖ Significant kinetic interactions unlikely

RAZADYNE

1976
$37–$173

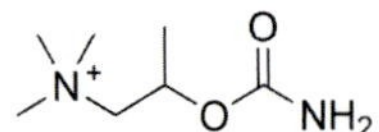

Bethanechol (URECHOLINE)

be THAN e call / yur e CO leen

"Bath of 'choline / Urine 'choline"

❖ Cholinergic (muscarinic) agonist

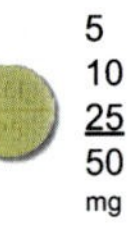

5
10
25
50
mg

Cholinergic "SLUDGE" buckets

FDA-approved for:
- ❖ Urinary retention
- ❖ Neurogenic bladder

Used off-label for:
- ❖ Urinary retention caused by psychiatric medications with anticholinergic properties
- ❖ Paralytic ileus following surgery

	Cholinesterase inhibitors	Muscarinic agonist
Class representatives	Donepezil (Aricept) Rivastigmine (Exelon) Galantamine (Razadyne)	Bethanechol (Urecholine)
Cholinergic mechanism	Inhibition of cholinesterase, the enzyme that breaks down acetylcholine.	Stimulation of muscarinic acetylcholine receptors. Unlike acetylcholine, bethanechol is not broken down by cholinesterase, prolonging bethanechol's duration of action.
Enters CNS	Yes	No
Cognitive enhancement	Yes	No, unless injected intrathecally (into the CNS)

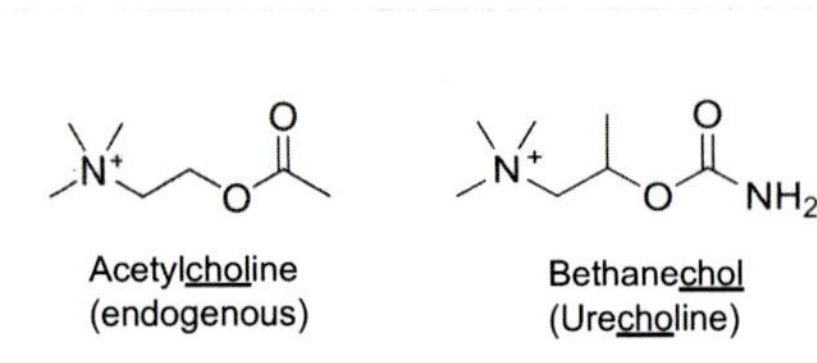

Acetylcholine (endogenous)

Bethanechol (Urecholine)

Mnemonic for signs of excessive cholinergic activity: *Brady(cardia) Bunch SLUDGE buckets*

Prior to the invention of the acetylcholinesterase inhibitors (donepezil, etc), bethanechol was experimentally injected intrathecally (into the CNS) for the treatment of Alzheimer's. Risks were found to outweigh benefits. Some psychiatrists prescribe bethanechol to counter urinary retention caused by anticholinergic psychotropics. Nausea is the main side effect. Onset of action is 30 minutes, with duration of action about 1 hour at standard doses.

Dosing: For urinary retention, start 5–10 mg hourly until response, up to 50 mg; Give on an empty stomach 1 hour before, or 2 hours after a meal to avoid vomiting. Maintenance dose is generally 10–50 mg TID–QID.

Dynamic interactions:
- ❖ Cholinergic toxicity (SLUDGE syndrome) is possible when combined with cholinergics such as donepezil (Aricept)

Kinetic interactions:
- ❖ None significant

page 18

Bethanechol Pilocarpine Xylitol

1951
$47–$140 tablets
$30–$104 eye drops

Pilocarpine (SALAGEN)

pye low KAR peen / SAL a gen

“Saliva-generating Pile o’ carp”

- ❖ Cholinergic (muscarinic) agonist
- ❖ Saliva production stimulator

ophth 1% 2% 4%

5 7.5 mg

FDA-approved for:

- ❖ Xerostomia (dry mouth) - PO
- ❖ Glaucoma - ophthalmic drops

Used off-label for:

- ❖ Xerostomia
  - ophthalmic drops swished in mouth

Pilocarpine is a muscarinic agonist available as PO tablets and eye drops. Oral pilocarpine (Salagen) is approved for treatment of xerostomia (dry mouth), often caused by Sjogren’s syndrome or damage to salivary glands from radiation treatment. Salagen is a sialogen, i.e., an agent that generates saliva. Response may take 6–12 weeks. Oral pilocarpine is rarely used for moderate xerostomia due to side effects. The effects expected from a non-selective muscarinic agonist (SLUDGE) include diarrhea, abdominal cramps, and hyperhidrosis (sweating).

Pilocarpine eye drops (Isopto Carpine) are used to treat glaucoma. As expected from a cholinergic agent, pilocarpine causes miosis (pupillary constriction, i.e., small pupils). This is the opposite of the mydriasis (pupillary dilation) that you get with ophthalmic atropine, which is anticholinergic and contraindicated in angle-closure glaucoma. Pilocarpine eye drops can be used to counter visual disturbance caused by anticholinergics. Headache is a potential side effect of pilocarpine ophthalmic.

Cholinergic “SLUDGE” buckets

To treat xerostomia caused by psychotropics (tricyclics, trazodone, stimulants, and anticholinergic antipsychotics), an off-label strategy is to use pilocarpine eye drops in the mouth. See below.

A similar PO anticholinergic approved for Sjogren’s-related dry mouth is cevimeline (Evoxac) which costs $46–$260. Cevimeline is not available as an ophthalmic solution.

Oral dosing: For PO formulation, start 5 mg TID, with maximum of 10 mg/dose and 30 mg/day; Off-label use of pilocarpine ophthalmic for dry mouth, prescribe pilocarpine ophthalmic 4%, place 3 drops into a half-teaspoon of water, swish, and spit; Do not swallow to avoid systemic effects (Rajnish Mago, MD; The Carlat Psychiatry Report, Jun/Jul 2019).

Sjogren’s syndrome [SHOW-grun] is an autoimmune disease that affects moisture-producing glands, resulting in dry eyes and dry mouth. “Joe grins if you have Sjogren’s (because Joe sells bottled water)”.

Mnemonic for signs of excessive cholinergic activity: *Brady(cardia) Bunch SLUDGE buckets*

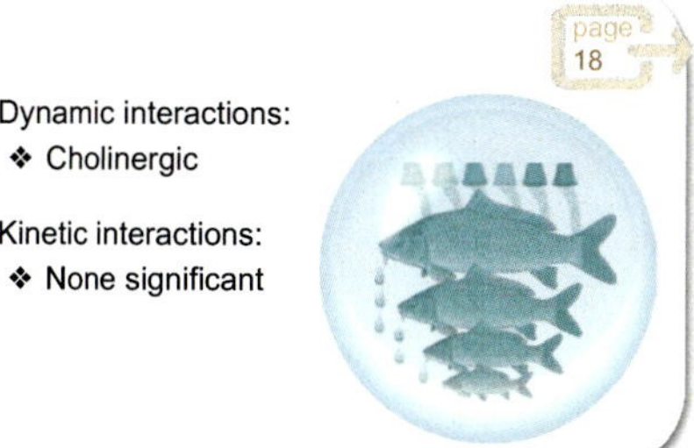

page 18

Dynamic interactions:

- ❖ Cholinergic

Kinetic interactions:

- ❖ None significant

1996
$0.25/each OTC

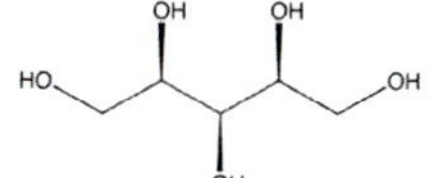

Xylitol (XyliMelts)

ZAI luh taal / ZAI luh melts

“tall Xylophone melting”

- ❖ Polyhydric alcohol
- ❖ Sugar substitute
- ❖ Over-the-counter

One more little sidetrack:

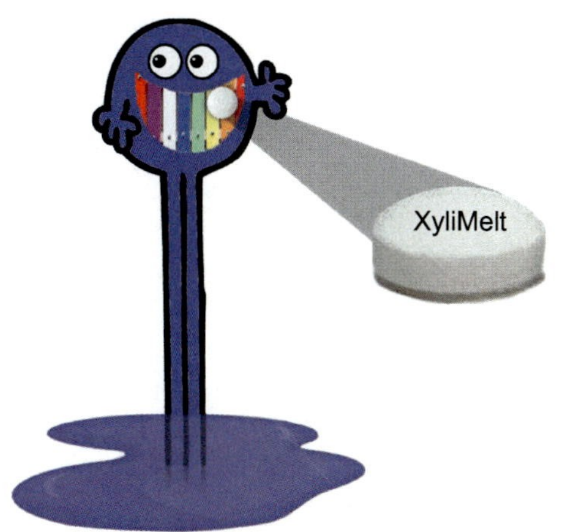

Used for:

- ❖ Xerostomia

Over-the-counter alternatives for individuals suffering from xerostomia include products containing the sugar xylitol (‘X’ for xerostomia) which stimulates salivation. Also known as birch sugar, bacteria cannot digest it. Using xylitol-containing products 4x daily can kill bacteria that cause bad breath and cavities, the latter being more prevalent with individuals taking mouth-drying psychotropics.

Rajnish Mago, MD; The Carlat Psychiatry Report, Jun/Jul 2019

XyliMelts are xylitol-containing discs that stick to gumline, and are good for overnight use to prevent gum disease and tooth decay. Xylitol-containing gum and mouthwash is also available. Xylitol is preferred over Biotene products, because they do not kill bacteria.

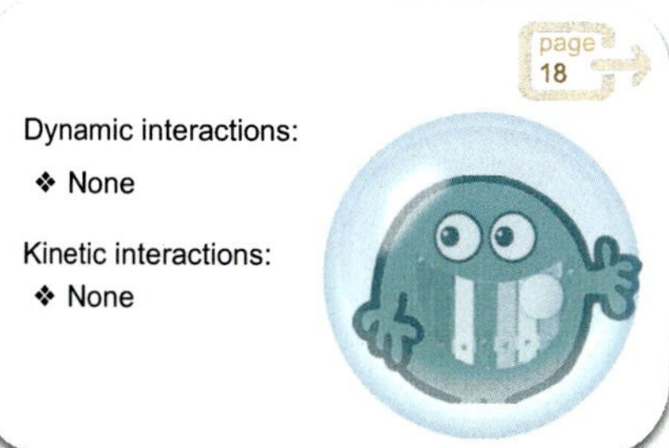

page 18

Dynamic interactions:

- ❖ None

Kinetic interactions:

- ❖ None

#147
2003
IR $15–$263
ER $108–$416

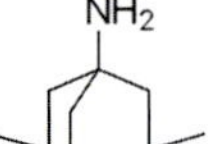

Memantine (NAMENDA)

mem an tine / na MEN da

"Memaw's Name reminder"

- ❖ NMDA receptor antagonist
- ❖ Cognitive enhancer

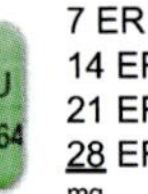

7 ER
14 ER
21 ER
28 ER
mg

5
10
mg

FDA-approved for:

- ❖ Alzheimer's dementia, moderate–severe

Used off-label for:

- ❖ Other types of dementia
- ❖ Neuroprotection
- ❖ Substance use disorders
- ❖ ADHD
- ❖ OCD
- ❖ Neuropathic pain
- ❖ Bipolar disorder
- ❖ Augmentation of clozapine for refractory psychosis

In a 2017 Saturday Night Live skit, Amazon partnered with AARP to present the Amazon Echo Silver, the only smart speaker device designed specifically to be used by the Greatest Generation. It's super loud and responds to any name even remotely close to Alexa.

"Memantine is for memory" and NaMenDA has NMDA in its name. This cognitive enhancer is an NMDA receptor antagonist approved for moderate to severe Alzheimer's dementia. It is used off-label for dementia of any type or severity. Don't confuse NMDA with MDMA (the club drug Ecstasy/Molly) which is unrelated.

The majority of patients treated for dementia patients end up on a combination of Namenda plus a cholinergic agent (usually Aricept).

Namenda has an outstanding tolerability profile (i.e., few side effects). The most prominent is headache, but this was only 5.7% (vs 2% for placebo). Agitation (1.6%) was less than placebo (4.6%). In other words, it reduces agitation. It does not cause weight gain or sedation. Nausea is highly unlikely with memantine, unlike with the cholinesterase inhibitors (donepezil, etc).

There may not be much evidence that Namenda works for conditions other than Alzheimer's, but some young go-getters in Silicon Valley consider it a nootropic [noh a TROP ik]—which is a brain enhancing pill for use by healthy individuals.

There are essentially no contraindications for memantine, other than allergy to amantadine (see similar structure on page 214) or serious renal insufficiency.

Dosing: Start 5 mg q AM x 1 week, then 5 mg BID x 1 week, then 10 mg q AM + 5 mg q PM x 1 week, then 10 mg BID which is the target dose (also max dose). 28 mg of the expensive ER formulation is equivalent to 10 mg BID of the IR generic. Use a lower dose if renal insufficiency.

NMDA receptor

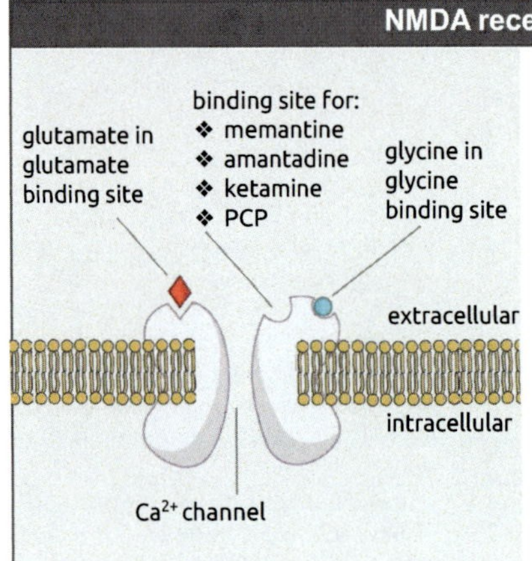

NMDA receptors are involved in synaptic plasticity and memory. Lightly blocking the receptor is neuroprotective. However, if the receptor is blocked completely, neurons cannot function. The street drug PCP, aka "angel dust", strongly blocks NMDA receptors, causing psychosis. Ketamine is weaker than PCP, but strong enough to cause anaesthesia and dissociation. Namenda blocks the receptor just enough to improve memory.

Dynamic interactions:

page 18

- ❖ None significant

Kinetic interactions:

- ❖ Inhibitor of organic cation transport (OCT) proteins (not discussed in this book) which makes memantine contraindicated with the antiarrhythmic dofetilide (Tikosyn). Elevated levels of dofetilide may lead to QT prolongation and cardiac arrhythmias.

2017
$463–$584

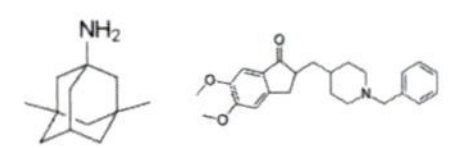

NAMZARIC (memantine ER + donepezil)

nam ZAIR ik

"Namenda + Aricept"

- ❖ Cognitive enhancer combo

7/10
14/10
21/10
28/10
mg

FDA-approved for:

- ❖ Alzheimer's dementia,moderate–severe

Namzaric is a combination pill for Alzheimer's dementia patients already stabilized on donepezil (or donepezil and memantine).

All capsules contain 10 mg of donepezil, with four different strengths of extended-release memantine. Each of the two components has a long half-life of about 3 days.

Dosing: The target maintenance dose is 28/10 mg QD, which is also the maximum dose. 28 mg of memantine ER is equivalent to 10 mg BID of IR memantine. The smaller pills exist only for titration when transitioning from donepezil monotherapy. There is a convenience pack for 7/10 mg QD x 1 week, then 14/10 mg QD x 1 week, then 21/10 mg QD x 1 week, then a week's worth of the target maintenance dose of 28/10 mg QD.

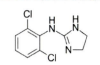

#76
1966
$2–$18

Clonidine (CATAPRES)

KLOE ni deen / CAT a press

"Clown dines (while) Cat oppresses"

❖ Central alpha-2 agonist
❖ Antihypertensive
❖ ADHD treatment

0.1
0.2
0.3
mg

FDA-approved for:
❖ Hypertension
❖ ADHD (extended-release KAPVAY)

Used off-label for:
❖ See below

Bottle caps - The ER formulation of clonidine approved for childhood ADHD (ages 6–17) is named KAPVAY.

Clonidine is a centrally acting alpha-2 adrenergic (norepinephrine) receptor agonist, FDA-approved for hypertension. "Central" refers to the central nervous system (CNS). Stimulation of alpha-2 autoreceptors reduces norepinephrine (NE) release as a negative feedback mechanism. Reduction of NE allows peripheral arteries to relax, which lowers blood pressure.

Alpha-1 receptors (postsynaptic) generally have opposing actions to alpha-2 receptors (presynaptic). Blood pressure is reduced by alpha-2 agonists like clonidine and also reduced by alpha-1 antagonists like prazosin (page 186). For psychiatrists, it is ok to conceptualize all of the medications in this chapter as "blood pressure meds" with CNS effects.

Clonidine is rarely used as a first-line medication for high blood pressure but would be a reasonable first-line antihypertensive for those with one of the following comorbid conditions, to kill two birds with one stone. Clonidine is a drug of choice for the treatment of hypertensive urgencies. Only stop clonidine by tapering. If clonidine is stopped abruptly, rebound hypertension may result, possibly leading to a hypertensive crisis.

Psychiatrists have found many off-label therapeutic uses of clonidine:

ADHD
Clonidine is considered safe and effective for childhood ADHD. It may be used as an alternative to, or in combination with, a stimulant. Clonidine is more effective for treatment of hyperactivity than for inattention. It is typically dosed BID for this indication. In 2018 an extended-release formulation of clonidine, branded KAPVAY, was released for treatment of ADHD. Guanfacine (Tenex), another central alpha-2 agonist for ADHD, is generally less sedating than clonidine.

Intermittent explosive disorder
Clonidine is useful in management of aggressive individuals who are highly irritable and impulsive. For violent children, consider trying clonidine before resorting to an antipsychotic.

Opioid withdrawal
Clonidine is a first-line treatment for opioid withdrawal. A clonidine transdermal patch can be applied with additional PO doses throughout the day as tolerated. There is a central alpha-2 agonist specifically approved for opioid withdrawal called lofexidine (Lucemyra), but it is expensive.

Tics/Tourette's disorder
Alpha-2 agonists are considered first-line for the treatment of tics. For Tourette's disorder, it is best to try clonidine prior to FDA-approved medications (antipsychotics).

Hot flashes
Clonidine can alleviate hot flashes/flushes, including those caused by SSRIs.

Sialorrhea (hypersalivation)
A side effect of clonidine is dry mouth, so it is suitable to counteract clozapine-induced hypersalivation. This should be done cautiously, because clozapine and clonidine both decrease blood pressure.

Anxiety
Clonidine is not considered an anxiolytic, but it can relieve physical symptoms associated with anxiety, such as tremor, sweating, and tachycardia.

Insomnia (rarely)
Some individuals are sensitive to the possible sedating effects of clonidine. For those individuals, clonidine may be useful as a sleep aid.

Akathisia (rarely)
Akathisia is sense of inner restlessness caused by antipsychotics. Clonidine may help alleviate akathisia, although it may be less effective than propranolol (Inderal) or benzodiazepines.

Smoking cessation (rarely)
Clonidine is possibly helpful for long-term maintenance of smoking cessation.

Dosing: For adults, the starting dose for most uses is 0.1 mg BID, to increase 0.1 mg/day in weekly intervals as tolerated. If baseline BP is in the low to normal range, start 0.05 mg BID instead. May be dosed more aggressively for inpatient management of opioid withdrawal. Max is 2.4 mg total daily dose. Taper slowly to stop to avoid rebound hypertension; For extended-release Kapvay (ADHD ages 6–17) the dose range is 0.1–0.4 mg/day divided QD–BID; Start Kapvay at 0.1 mg HS, may increase by 0.1 mg/day in weekly intervals; Divide doses > 0.2 mg/day; AM and HS doses may be unequal with HS > AM dose; Taper no faster than 0.1 mg/day in 3–7 day intervals, to avoid rebound hypertension.

Dynamic interactions:

❖ Hypotensive effects
❖ Sedation/CNS depression
❖ Do not add **mirtazapine (Remeron)** to clonidine because it will block the action of clonidine, potentially leading to a hypertensive crisis. Do not add clonidine to Remeron. Clonidine will be completely inactivated by Remeron because Remeron is a central alpha-2 blocker.

page 108

page 18

Kinetic interactions:
❖ None significant

SYMPATHOLYTICS 16

#156
1986
$6–$24

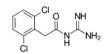

Guanfacine (TENEX)

GWAHN fa seen / TEN ex

"Gun facing Ten X's"

- ❖ Central alpha-2 agonist
- ❖ Antihypertensive
- ❖ ADHD treatment

1
2
mg

FDA-approved for:
- ❖ Hypertension
- ❖ Childhood ADHD (ER formulation)

Used off-label for:
- ❖ Opioid withdrawal
- ❖ Migraine prophylaxis
- ❖ Tourette's disorder
- ❖ Adult ADHD

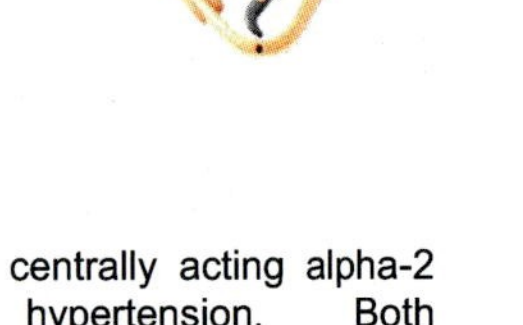

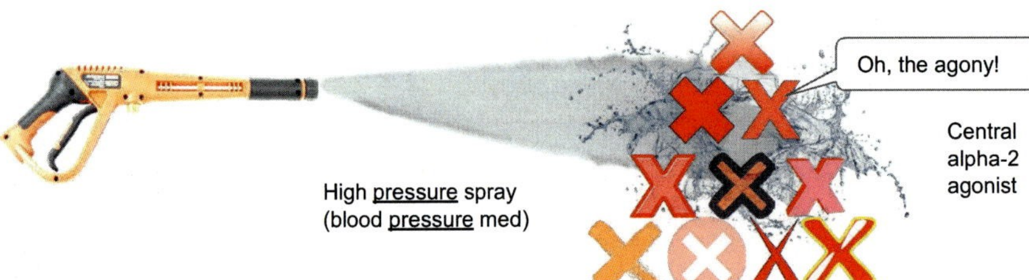

Guanfacine, like clonidine, is a centrally acting alpha-2 agonist, originally used for hypertension. Both antihypertensives are prescribed for ADHD. Most of the info from the clonidine monograph also applies to guanfacine.

Guanfacine is much more selective for alpha-2A receptors than clonidine, making it <u>less sedating than clonidine</u>. However, a touch of sedation may be desirable for the treatment of extreme hyperactivity or intermittent explosive disorder.

Dosing: <u>For ADHD</u>, start 1 mg q PM, increase to 1 mg BID at one week; maximum 4 mg total daily dose. <u>For hypertension</u>, it is dosed once daily at HS with maximum of 3 mg. Taper dose over 4–7 days to discontinue.

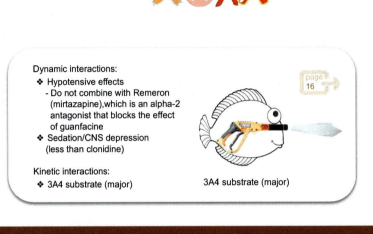

Dynamic interactions:
- ❖ Hypotensive effects
  - Do not combine with Remeron (mirtazapine),which is an alpha-2 antagonist that blocks the effect of guanfacine
- ❖ Sedation/CNS depression (less than clonidine)

Kinetic interactions:
- ❖ 3A4 substrate (major)

page 16

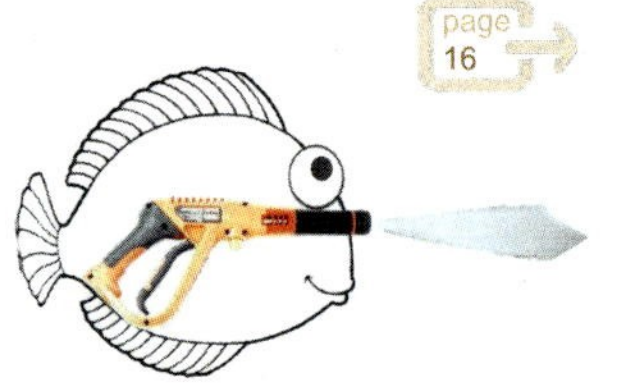

3A4 substrate (major)

2010
$21–$290

Guanfacine ER (INTUNIV)

GWAHN fa seen / in TUNE iv

"Gun facing (the) In-tune tuna"

- ❖ Central alpha-2 agonist
- ❖ Antihypertensive
- ❖ ADHD treatment

1
2
3
4
mg

FDA-approved for:
- ❖ ADHD (ages 6–17)

Used off-label for:
- ❖ Adult ADHD

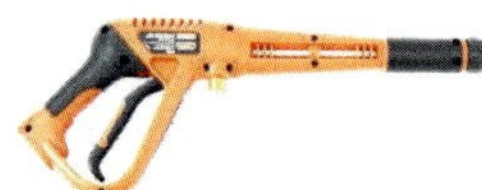

Intuniv is the extended-release (ER) formulation of guanfacine, approved for ADHD in 2010, for ages 6–17 as monotherapy or as an adjunct to a stimulant. Use of Intuniv for adult ADHD would be off-label.

The advantage of Intuniv over generic guanfacine (Tenex) is once-daily dosing. Generic guanfacine IR is given in divided doses, BID–TID. Contrast the QD dosing of guanfacine ER to that of the other extended-release alpha-2 agonist for childhood ADHD, clonidine ER (Kapvay), which is given BID above when dosed above 0.2 mg/day.

Dosing: Recommended dose is 1–4 mg once daily in the morning or evening, depending on the child's weight. <u>Start 1 mg once daily</u> and adjust in increments of no more than 1 mg/week. Do not administer with high-fat meals, because it will increase absorption. Do not substitute for immediate-release guanfacine tablets on a mg-per-mg basis, because of differing pharmacokinetic profiles. When discontinuing, taper the dose in intervals of no more than 1 mg every 3–7 days. Maximum dose of 7 mg/day for those over 58.5 kg (129 pounds), less for smaller kids.

page 16

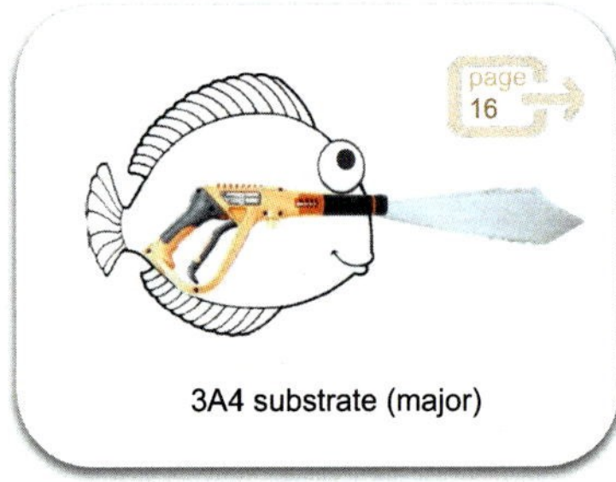

3A4 substrate (major)

2018
$1,960

Lofexidine (LUCEMYRA)

lo FEX i deen / LOO sem eer uh

"Lose my Loaf (on which) I dine"

❖ Central alpha-2 agonist
❖ Tx for opioid withdrawal

0.18 mg

FDA-approved for:

❖ Opioid withdrawal

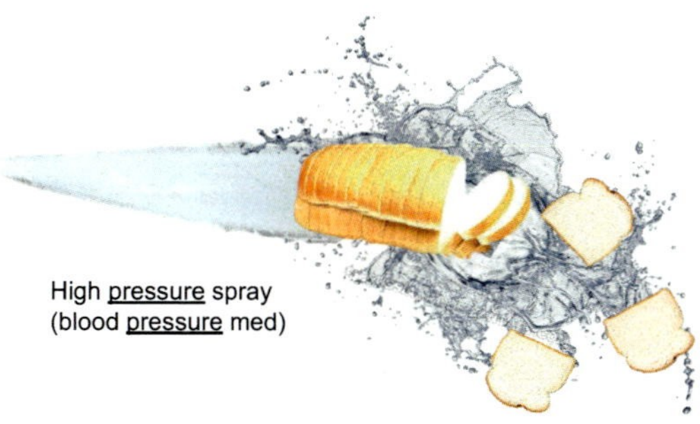
High pressure spray (blood pressure med)

Lofexidine (Lucemyra) was approved in 2018 for management of opioid withdrawal symptoms. It has been available in the UK since 1992.

Clonidine, a generic alpha-2 agonist, has long been used off-label in the US for this indication. Prescribers haven't been clamoring for another one of these sympatholytics, even one with an FDA indication for opioid withdrawal. Compared to clonidine, there is no suggestion that lofexidine is more effective. The advantage of lofexidine is it may cause less hypotension than clonidine.

Lucemyra prolongs QT interval whereas clonidine does not.

Lofexidine works by calming symptoms of noradrenergic overactivity such as sweating, anxiety, and irritability. Side effects may include syncope if blood pressure dips too low. It is dosed up to 4 times daily.

Note that buprenorphine (opioid partial agonist) is the drug of choice for opioid withdrawal. Buprenorphine may be continued as maintenance therapy, whereas lofexidine use is approved for up to 14 days.

Dosing: The only tablet strength is 0.18 mg. Start 3 tabs PO q 5–6 hours during peak withdrawal; Max: 4 tabs/dose up to 16 tabs/day. Consider lower doses for individuals 65 and older. Taper dose gradually over 2–4 days to stop.

Other medications for opioid withdrawal:

❖ Buprenorphine (Suboxone) - partial opioid agonist
❖ Methadone (long-acting full opioid agonist)
❖ Clonidine (central alpha-2 agonist)
❖ Actifed or Sudafed PRN for rhinorrhea
❖ Ibuprofen (Motrin) PRN for muscle aches
❖ Loperamide (Imodium) PRN for diarrhea
❖ Dicyclomine (Bentyl) PRN for abdominal cramps
❖ Ondansetron (Zofran) PRN for nausea/vomiting

Dynamic interactions:

❖ Hypotensive effects (less than clonidine)
❖ Sedation/CNS depression
❖ Bradycardia
❖ QT prolongation

Kinetic interactions:

❖ 2D6 substrate (minor)

page 15
2D6 substrate (minor)

1994
$40

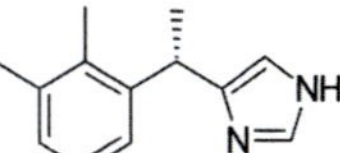

Dexmedetomidine (PRECEDEX)

DEX med e TOE mi deen / PRESS e dex

"Pre-sedate (for) Death metal toe meeting"

❖ Central alpha-2 agonist
❖ Intravenous sedative

100 mcg/mL

Nice to meet you

Let's get pre-sedated

High pressure spray (blood pressure med)

Spooky mascots are generally reserved for antipsychotics, with Precedex as an exception.

FDA-approved for:

❖ ICU sedation/procedural sedation

Dexmedetomidine (Precedex) is commonly used intravenously in the ICU to manage agitation and to facilitate mechanical ventilation. It is a centrally acting alpha-2 agonist like clonidine.

Dexmedetomidine is a good drug for ICU sedation, because it is less likely to cause delirium than alternatives such as propofol (Diprivan) or benzodiazepines.

It has sedative, anxiolytic, and analgesic properties. Onset of action is 15–30 minutes. This is delayed compared to alternatives such as midazolam or propofol. Effects persist for about 3 hours after the infusion is stopped.

Due to its effect on peripheral alpha receptors, cardiovascular adverse events are possible, including bradycardia and arrhythmias. Hypertension has occurred with the loading dose and hypotension with the maintenance infusion.

Dosing: The IV dose (mcg/kg/hr) for intubated ICU patients **>** non-intubated patients **>** those awake for fiberoptic intubation.

Precedex has been shown to cause significantly less delirium than other IV drugs for ICU sedation such as:

❖ Lorazepam (Ativan) - benzo
❖ Midazolam (Versed) - benzo
❖ Propofol (Diprivan) - $GABA_A$ modulator

Dynamic interactions:

❖ Sedation/CNS depression
❖ Hypotensive effects
❖ Bradycardia

Kinetic interactions:

❖ Minimal clinically significant kinetic interactions (in a bubble)

page 18

#220
1989
$12–$24

Prazosin (MINIPRESS)

PRA zoe sin / MIN e press

"Minnie press (Prays or sins)"

❖ Alpha-1 antagonist
❖ Antihypertensive
❖ Tx for PTSD

1
2
5
mg

FDA-approved for

❖ Hypertension

Used off-label for

❖ PTSD-associated nightmares (HS dosing)
❖ PTSD hyperarousal and flashbacks (BID dosing)
❖ Benign prostatic hypertrophy (BPH)
❖ Raynaud's phenomenon
❖ Alcohol use disorder

Alpha-1 receptors are mainly involved in smooth muscle contraction. α1 receptor blockers decrease blood pressure by decreasing peripheral vasoconstriction. They also relax smooth muscles within the prostate to ease urination. Their FDA-approved indications are hypertension and benign prostatic hyperplasia (BPH, enlarged prostate).

Prazosin, which crosses the blood brain barrier easily, is the α1 blocker commonly prescribed by psychiatrists. The only FDA-approved use of prazosin is hypertension, but it is used off-label for nightmares associated with PTSD. The beneficial effect for PTSD is by decreasing autonomic arousal, rather than suppressing dreams. In a controlled trial of military veterans with PTSD, prazosin did not alleviate distressing dreams or improve sleep quality. (Raskind et al, 2018). This was perplexing to many psychiatrists, who have seen a high success rate for prazosin in decreasing nightmares. In practice, most patients with PTSD want to continue it. Note that response to placebo in this trial was unusually high and there were other issues with this study (The Carlat Psychiatry Report, April 2019). Experts continue to recommend prazosin for PTSD.

Prazosin may cause a first-dose phenomenon with 1% of patients fainting after the initial dose if started at 2 mg or greater. Syncope from prazosin is due to orthostatic hypotension. The phenomenon is unlikely to reoccur and will not occur if the patient goes to bed immediately after taking the first dose. For this reason, prazosin is best started at 1 mg for a couple of days, then increased to the usual dose of 2 mg. The first-dose phenomenon may occur with other α1 blockers such as doxazosin (Cardura) and terazosin (Hytrin), but less commonly than with prazosin.

For treatment of nightmares, prazosin may be titrated up to 10 mg HS if necessary, in 1–2 mg increments. Be sure to advise patients to take it every night. If stopped and restarted, it should be titrated from 1 mg rather than starting with the previously established dose.

Some prescribers divide the dose BID to treat daytime PTSD-associated arousal symptoms, e.g., hypervigilance and heightened startle reaction. Alternative antihypertensives that can improve daytime arousal symptoms include propranolol and clonidine.

The ideal candidate for prazosin is someone with PTSD nightmares, high blood pressure and an enlarged prostate—to kill three birds with one stone.

About half of individuals with PTSD have obstructive sleep apnea. Prazosin is safe to use in patients with sleep apnea because it lacks muscle relaxant effects (as opposed to benzodiazepines and Z-drugs, which are not recommended with sleep apnea). Prazosin is not necessarily sedating, but individuals with PTSD report that it helps them fall asleep.

Prazosin is the most commonly prescribed nightmare medication. Other agents occasionally prescribed for nightmares include cyproheptadine (Periactin), gabapentin (Neurontin), and topiramate (Topamax). The α1 blocker doxazosin (Cardura) could also potentially work for nightmares.

The only two medications FDA-approved for PTSD are the SSRIs paroxetine (Paxil) and sertraline (Zoloft).

Patients with alcohol use disorder reported an average of 8 fewer drinks/week when taking 16 mg/day of prazosin, in divided doses (Simpson et al, 2018).

Prazosin can cause retrograde ejaculation (into the bladder) via alpha-1 blockade. Several antipsychotics are known to do this also, by the same mechanism (chlorpromazine, haloperidol, and risperidone). Kjærgaard, et al (1988) investigated prazosin as a possible male contraceptive pill, but found that it did not produce azoospermia following ejaculation at 10 mg.

Dosing: Off-label for PTSD nightmares, start 1–2 mg HS, increase by 1–2 mg/day q 3–4 days. Usual maintenance dose is 4–6 mg HS. Maximum bedtime dose is 10 mg. Advise patient to go immediately to bed after the first dose to avoid fainting (1% first-dose fainting if started at 2 mg or higher). Consider BID dosing to address PTSD flashbacks. For treatment of hypertension, the maximum dose is 20 mg divided BID or TID.

Top α1 blockers	FDA-approved for:
#1 Tamsulosin (Flomax)	BPH
#2 Terazosin (Hytrin)	BPH
#3 Prazosin (Minipress)	HTN
#4 Doxazosin (Cardura)	BPH + HTN
#5 Alfuzosin (Uroxatral)	BPH

Doxazosin, intended for once daily dosing, can also be effective for PTSD.

Dynamic interactions:
❖ Hypotensive effects

Kinetic interactions:
❖ None significant

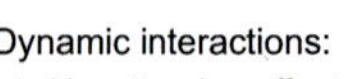

In a bubble - minimal kinetic interactions

Prazosin

Propranolol

#43
1965
IR $3–$44
ER $24–$61

Propranolol (INDERAL)

pro PRAN oh lol / IN de ral

"Prop ran, LOL (from) Ender"

❖ Beta Blocker (antihypertensive)

ER: 60, 80, 120, 160 mg

IR: 10, 20, 40, 80 mg

FDA-approved for:

- ❖ Hypertension
- ❖ Atrial fibrillation
- ❖ Angina
- ❖ Post-heart attack
- ❖ Migraine prevention
- ❖ Essential tremor

Used off-label for:

- ❖ Stage fright/performance anxiety/test taking
- ❖ Situational anxiety (e.g., social anxiety)
- ❖ Anxiety for individuals with tachycardia
- ❖ Akathisia
- ❖ Aggression
- ❖ Medication induced tremor (lithium, Depakote)
- ❖ Autism (to improve communication skills)
- ❖ PTSD prevention (investigational)
- ❖ Thyrotoxicosis (thyroid storm)
- ❖ Postural orthostatic tachycardia syndrome (POTS)
- ❖ Vasovagal syncope (prevention)

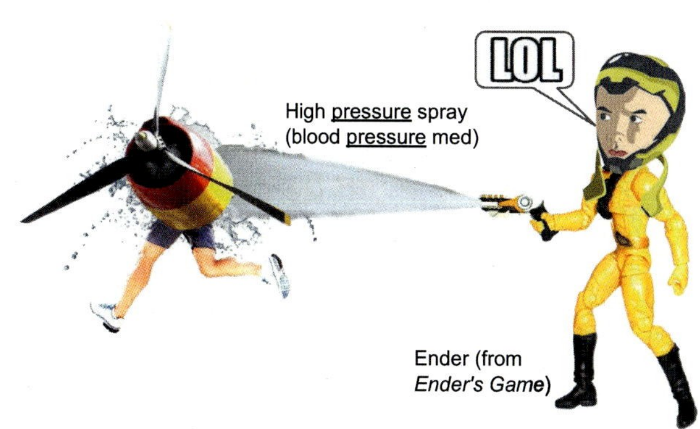

Propranolol (Inderal) is the beta blocker prescribed by psychiatrists to alleviate the physiologic symptoms of stress such as tachycardia, tremor and sweating. Propranolol is the most lipophilic (fat soluble) beta blocker, which helps it cross the blood brain barrier to exert psychotropic effects in addition to the peripheral physiologic effects. Half-life is 3–6 hours.

Side effects of propranolol are those related to bradycardia or hypotension, i.e., dizziness and fatigue. The heart rate-lowering effect is often more prominent than the blood pressure-lowering effect.

When taken daily at substantial doses, propranolol can cause glucose intolerance—potentially leading to diabetes and weight gain.

Propranolol is contraindicated with asthma, due to risk of bronchospasm related to blockade of beta-2 receptors. Metoprolol (Lopressor) and atenolol (Tenormin) are cardioselective (i.e., only block beta-1 receptors) and are safe for asthma. A mnemonic for the location of beta receptors is that you have 1 heart and 2 lungs. Propranolol crosses the blood brain barrier and appears to act directly on the brain.

Propranolol is one of eight antihypertensives potentially protective against depression, to modest extent. The others are enalapril, ramipril, amlodipine, verapamil, atenolol, bisoprolol, and carvedilol (Kessing et al, 2020). No antihypertensive medication is associated with increased risk of depression.

Performance Anxiety: Propranolol has been shown to improve scores on standardized tests, especially for students with test anxiety (Brewer, 1972; Drew et al, 1985). The dose prescribed for performance anxiety is typically 20 mg one hour prior to the event. Propranolol effectively relieves symptoms of physiologic arousal associated with stage fright such as tachycardia and sweaty palms (Brantigan et al, 1982). Propranolol 40 mg given to resident surgeons one hours prior to surgery decreased tremor and anxiety without untoward effects (Elman et al, 1998). Propranolol is not to be used for athletic performance because it decreases heart rate. Duration of action is about 6 hours.

Akathisia: Propranolol is the first-line treatment for akathisia, the restlessness caused by antipsychotic medication. Benzodiazepines are 2nd line for this indication. If akathisia is severe, consider starting clonazepam (Klonopin) and propranolol together, and stop clonazepam when propranolol is adequately titrated.

Autism: Propranolol may improve communication skills in those with autism (Sagar-Ouriaghli et al, 2018).

PTSD prevention (possibly): Propranolol is effective for reducing fear when given soon after trauma, theoretically preventing or dampening the later development of PTSD (Giustino et al, 2016).

Dosing: For performance anxiety give 20 mg (range 10–40 mg) about 60 minutes prior to performance. Take a dose to establish tolerability beforehand. For tremor or akathisia start 20 mg BID–TID (10 mg BID–TID if heart rate under 70 bpm); Hold dose if pulse is under 60 bpm; Titrate slowly depending on response and pulse rate. For akathisia high dose may be necessary, as high as 240 mg total daily dose, which is something that can not be achieved quickly. For hypertension, the total daily dose is usually 80–240 mg divided BID–TID, with maximum of 640 mg/day. Propranolol ER (Inderal LA) is available for once daily dosing. Taper gradually to discontinue.

Before prescribing propranolol, confirm that the patient does not have **bradycardia** or **asthma**.

Most-prescribed beta blockers:

1. #1 Metoprolol ER (Toprol XL)
2. #2 Metoprolol (Lopressor)
3. #3 Atenolol (Tenormin)
4. #4 Propranolol (Inderal)
5. #5 Timolol (glaucoma eye drops)
6. #6 Propranolol ER (Inderal LA)
7. #7 Labetalol (Trandate)
8. #8 Nebivolol (Bystolic)
9. #9 Bisoprolol (Zebeta)
10. #10 Nadolol (Corgard)

Dynamic interactions:

- ❖ Hypotensive effects
- ❖ Bradycardia
- ❖ Hyperglycemia
- ❖ Prolongs PR interval

Kinetic interactions:

- ❖ Multi-CYP substrate - Propranolol is metabolized by several CYP enzymes (1A2, 2D6, 2C19). Kinetic interactions will occur but are unlikely to be of any clinical significance, so we are depicting propranolol "in a bubble". We could have depicted it as a tree (1A2 substrate), beach ball (2D6 substrate), and flower (2C19 substrate).
- ❖ Propranolol(approved for migraine prevention) increases serum levels of migraine medications rizatriptan (Maxalt) and zolmitriptan (Zomig), possibly by competitive inhibition of monoamine oxidase A.

page 18

"in a box" - clinically significant kinetic interactions possible but unlikely

#5
1987
$4–$59

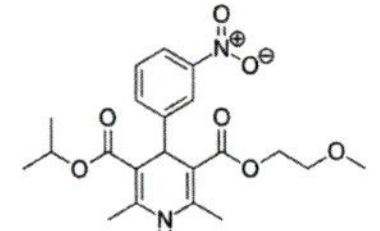

Amlodipine (NORVASC)

am LOE dih peen / NOR vask

"(I) Am loading Nora's vasc(ulature)"

❖ Calcium channel blocker

2.5
5
10
mg

FDA-approved for:

- ❖ Hypertension
- ❖ Coronary artery disease

Used off-label for:

- ❖ Raynaud's phenomenon (first-line)
- ❖ Bipolar maintenance, adjunct (rarely)
- ❖ Mania, adjunct (rarely)
- ❖ Vascular dementia (rarely)
- ❖ Involuntary movement disorders (rare)

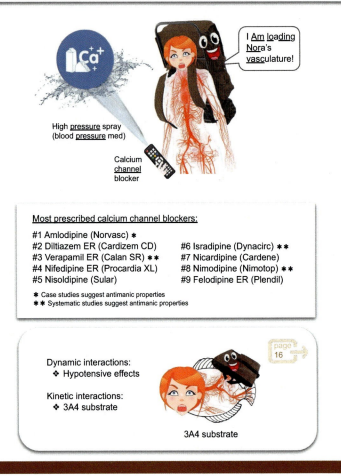

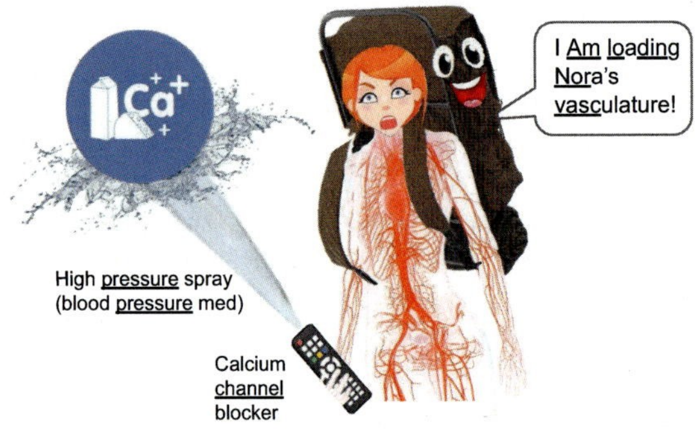

Calcium channel blockers (CCBs) are FDA-approved for hypertension, angina, atrial fibrillation, and migraines. They slow heart rate, slow cardiac conduction, diminish myocardial contractility, and dilate arteries. Amlodipine causes fewer side effects than other CCBs, making it the most prescribed CCB.

CCBs are fatal in overdose, accounting for 48% of deaths related to overdose of cardiovascular medication (Upreti et al, 2013). Amlodipine may be deadly in overdose, but is safer than other CCBs because it is more selective for arteries, having minimal effect on cardiac conduction and contractility. The main problem with amlodipine overdose is profound hypotension that can persist for several days.

Immediate-release formulations of CCBs typically have a short half-life and achieve peak plasma levels within 30 minutes. Amlodipine is the exception, reaching peak plasma level at about 6 hours, with a 40 hour half-life.

CCBs have been used experimentally for treatment of bipolar disorder. There are only case studies for amlodipine as an antimanic agent. Systematic studies have been conducted for mania using verapamil (Calan), isradipine (DynaCirc) and nimodipine (Nimotop). Amlodipine may be modestly protective against depression (Kessing et al, 2020).

Dosing: For hypertension, start 5 mg HS (2.5 mg for elderly patients or if used as a secondary agent); May adjust dose q 1–2 weeks; FDA max is 10 mg, although 15 mg may be appropriate.

Most prescribed calcium channel blockers:

- #1 Amlodipine (Norvasc) *
- #2 Diltiazem ER (Cardizem CD)
- #3 Verapamil ER (Calan SR) **
- #4 Nifedipine ER (Procardia XL)
- #5 Nisoldipine (Sular)
- #6 Isradipine (Dynacirc) **
- #7 Nicardipine (Cardene)
- #8 Nimodipine (Nimotop) **
- #9 Felodipine ER (Plendil)

* Case studies suggest antimanic properties
** Systematic studies suggest antimanic properties

Dynamic interactions:

- ❖ Hypotensive effects

Kinetic interactions:

- ❖ 3A4 substrate

3A4 substrate

page 16

Amlodipine

Nimodipine

1988
$280–$990

Nimodipine (NIMOTOP)

nih MO dih peen / NIM oh top

"Nemo"

❖ Calcium channel blocker

30
mg

FDA-approved for:

- ❖ Subarachnoid hemorrhage

Used off-label for:

- ❖ Migraine prophylaxis
- ❖ Ultra-rapid-cycling bipolar disorder (rarely)
- ❖ Mania, adjunct (rarely)

Nimodipine is relatively selective for cerebral vasculature, making it useful in prevention of cerebral vasospasm and resultant ischemia caused by cerebral vasospasm, a major complication of subarachnoid hemorrhage. The half-life of nimodipine is only 1–2 hours.

Nimodipine may be the preferred CCB for off-label treatment of mania and maintenance of ultra-rapid-cycling bipolar disorder, because it readily crosses the blood-brain barrier and acts on L-type (long-lasting) calcium channels. Unfortunately nimodipine is expensive. CCBs may be beneficial for Tourette's disorder, Huntington's disease, and tardive dyskinesia. CCBs are not effective for depression and possibly interfere with the therapeutic effects of antidepressants.

Side effects of nimodipine include a subjective sense of chest tightness and skin flushing.

Dosing: Give 1 hour before or 2 hours after meals; For subarachnoid hemorrhage, start within 96 hours of the bleed and take q 4 hours x 21 days; For ultra-rapid-cycling bipolar disorder, give 60 mg q 4 hours, up to 630 mg/day for brief use.

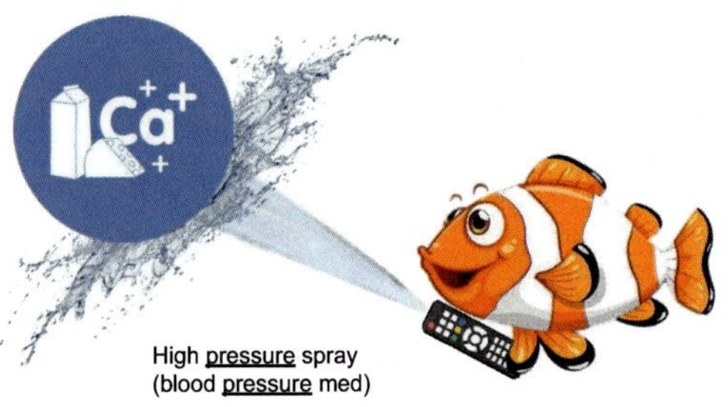

Dynamic interactions:

- ❖ Hypotensive effects

Kinetic interactions:

- ❖ 3A4 substrate

3A4 substrate

page 16

Centrally acting spasmolytics

Central muscle relaxants relieve muscle spasms through action in the central nervous system (CNS)—in the brainstem and spinal cord. They have no direct action on the contractile mechanism of muscles or the neuromuscular end plate.

Non-addictive spasmolytics

These centrally acting muscle relaxants are not controlled substances.

Muscle relaxant	cost/mo	Class	Details
Cyclobenzaprine (FLEXERIL)	$14	Tricyclic	#1 prescribed muscle relaxant. Structure is very similar to the TCA amitriptyline (Elavil). Cyclobenzaprine is a 5-HT_2 antagonist that works in the brainstem to reduce muscle tone by decreasing the activity of descending serotonergic neurons. Amitriptyline also does this.
Baclofen (LIORESAL)	$13	GABA(B) agonist	Baclofen is a derivative of the neurotransmitter GABA and works as a GABA(B) receptor agonist. Intrathecal administration through an implanted pump is typically reserved for spastic cerebral palsy.
Methocarbamol (ROBAXIN)	$18	Carbamate	Methocarbamol lacks the abuse potential of the Schedule IV carbamate carisoprodol (Soma). It is also much safer.
Tizanidine (ZANAFLEX)	$17	Central alpha agonist	Same mechanism as clonidine (Catapres) and guanfacine (Tenex) with less antihypertensive effect. Reduces spasticity by presynaptic inhibition of motor neurons. See blood pressure medication chapter.
Metaxalone (SKELAXIN)	$45	Oxazolidinone	Can contribute to serotonin syndrome; Most oxazolidinones are antibiotics, e.g., linezolid, which can also cause serotonin syndrome.
Orphenadrine (NORFLEX)	$42	Antihistamine/ anticholinergic	Structure very similar to diphenhydramine (Benadryl). Muscarinic antagonist and NMDA antagonist in CNS, interferes with neurotransmission from the spinal cord to the muscles. Has largely been superseded by newer drugs.

Schedule IV spasmolytics

These centrally acting muscle relaxants are DEA Schedule IV controlled substances with potential for abuse and addiction.

Muscle relaxant	cost/mo	Class	Details
Meprobamate (MILTOWN)	$110	Carbamate	The first blockbuster psychotropic medication, it was the most widely prescribed anxiolytic in the pre-benzodiazepine era. It is now rarely prescribed and is widely recognized as addictive and dangerous. Available in the US but removed from the market in the UK and Canada.
Carisoprodol (SOMA)	$12	Carbamate	The prodrug of meprobamate (Miltown). Soma is the #3 most prescribed muscle relaxant (behind Flexeril and Robaxin), despite being addictive and dangerous. Carisoprodol has been removed from the market in some countries.
Diazepam (VALIUM)	$9	Benzodiazepine	FDA-approved for anxiety, seizures, and muscle spasms. See Benzodiazepine chapter.

Direct acting muscle relaxant

Dantrolene (DANTRIUM)	Postsynaptic muscle relaxant that inhibits the release of Ca2+ ions from sarcoplasmic reticulum stores. It is the primary drug for the prevention and treatment of malignant hyperthermia—a condition triggered by general anesthesia. It is also used to treat antipsychotic induced neuroleptic malignant syndrome (NMS). PO dantrolene is approved for chronic spasticity, for instance with cerebral palsy. It carries a black box warning for hepatotoxicity.

Peripherally acting neuromuscular blockers

Neuromuscular blockers interfere with transmission at the neuromuscular end plate and have no CNS activity. They are used to cause paralysis.

Succinylcholine	Depolarizing neuromuscular blocking agent that causes short-term paralysis as part of general anesthesia. Similar to acetylcholine but more resistant to degradation by acetylcholinesterase, so it depolarizes muscle fibers longer. It is used during electroconvulsive therapy to keep muscles from contracting. Given IV, onset is within one minute and effects last for up to 10 minutes.
Botulinum toxin (BOTOX)	Botox prevents acetylcholine release at the neuromuscular junction. It is used cosmetically to paralyze upper facial muscles, alleviating wrinkles for 3 to 4 months. Botox injected between the eyebrows appears to have an antidepressant effect.

#46
1977
$2–$24

Cyclobenzaprine (FLEXERIL)

cy kloe BEN za preen / FLEX er il

"(tri) Cycle bends, Flexes 'n' rolls"

- ❖ Antispasmodic
- ❖ Tricyclic structure
- ❖ 5-HT_2 antagonist
- ❖ Non-controlled

5
7.5
<u>10</u>
mg

FDA-approved for:
- ❖ Muscle spasms

Used off-label for:
- ❖ Fibromyalgia
- ❖ Insomnia

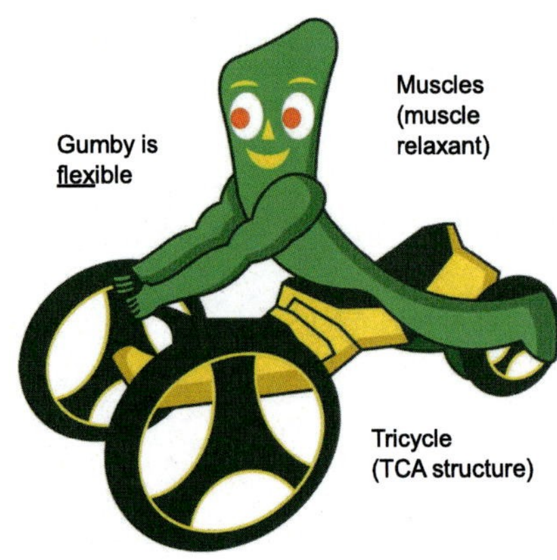

Released in 1977, cyclobenzaprine (Flexeril) remains the #1 most prescribed muscle relaxant. It is <u>not a controlled substance</u>. Half-life is 18 hours, and it is generally dosed TID. Flexeril is modestly effective for acute lower back pain with muscle spasm, although <u>efficacy begins to decrease after about 4 days</u>. It is not intended for long-term use because it is <u>not effective for muscle spasms beyond 2–3 weeks.</u> It is not useful for spasticity due to neurologic conditions such as cerebral palsy.

Flexeril is not used for the treatment of depression, but it has the structure of a <u>tricyclic</u> antidepressant (TCA) by structure. It differs from amitriptyline (Elavil) by just one double bond. Flexeril causes similar side effects as TCAs, but is much <u>less dangerous</u> in overdose. Of 209 cyclobenzaprine overdose cases, there were no deaths and the QT interval was not prolonged (Bebarta et al, 2011).

Flexeril reduces spasticity through central action, possibly at the brainstem level. It is a 5-HT_2 antagonist that reduces muscle tone by decreasing activity of descending serotonergic neurons. Amitriptyline (Elavil) and cyproheptadine (Periactin) have been shown to do this also (Honda et al, 2003).

Dynamic interactions are similar to those of TCAs.

Cyclobenzaprine can theoretically contribute to <u>serotonin syndrome</u> when combined with other serotonergics and is contraindicated with monoamine oxidase inhibitors (MAOIs). However, the risk is very low.

Kinetic interactions with cyclobenzaprine differ from interactions with TCAs. Cyclobenzaprine is a 1A2 substrate (tree) while all TCA antidepressants are 2D6 substrates (beach balls).

Incidence of <u>drowsiness</u> with cyclobenzaprine is 38%. As with some TCAs, cyclobenzaprine can be used as a sleep medication due to its effects on 5-HT_{2A}, alpha-1 adrenergic, and H_1 histamine receptors. Flexeril causes anticholinergic side effects, but less so than carisoprodol (Soma) or tizanidine (Zanaflex). None of these spasmolytics should be taken by elderly individuals.

When taken orally, first-pass metabolism in the liver converts much of the dose to norcyclobenzaprine, which is more responsible for the persistent grogginess of the drug. Tonix Pharmaceuticals was testing sublingual cyclobenzaprine for military-related PTSD at 2.8 mg and 5.6 mg strengths, but the trial was halted in Phase III (2018) due to inadequate separation from placebo.

Although it only works short-term as a muscle relaxant, some patients take cyclobenzaprine long-term for insomnia.

Dosing: For muscle spasms the recommended dose is 5–<u>10 mg</u> TID for up to 3 weeks. When used off-label for fibromyalgia, start 10 mg HS, with a maximum of 40 mg total daily dose divided BID–TID.

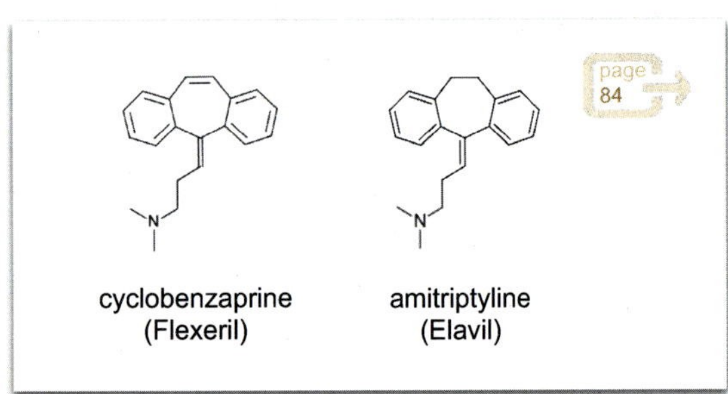

page 84

Dynamic interactions:
- ❖ Anticholinergic (moderate)
- ❖ Sedation/CNS depression
- ❖ Lowers seizure threshold

Kinetic interactions:
- ❖ 1A2 substrate

page 10

Cyclobenzaprine Baclofen

#124
1977
$14–$102

Cl—⟨benzene⟩—CH(CH2NH2)CH2COOH

Baclofen (LIORESAL)

BAK loe fen / li OR e sal

"Liar's re-saled Back fin"

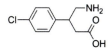

❖ Antispasmodic
❖ GABA(B) agonist
❖ Non-controlled

5
10
20
mg

FDA-approved for:

❖ Spasticity
❖ Cerebral palsy

Used off-label for:

❖ Alcohol use disorder
❖ Alcohol withdrawal
❖ Fibromyalgia
❖ Intractable hiccups
❖ Multiple sclerosis pain
❖ Intractable hiccups

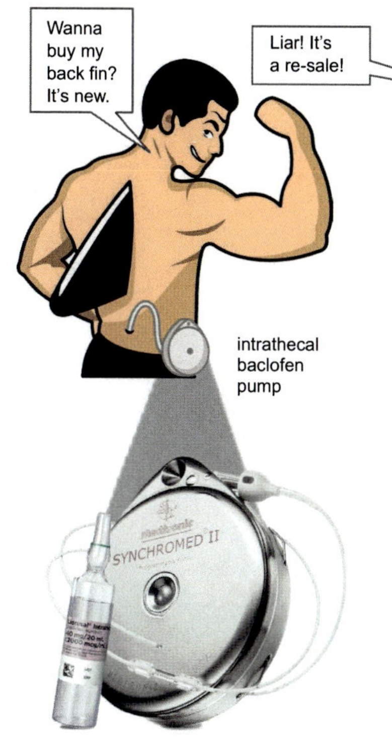

Wanna buy my back fin? It's new.
Liar! It's a re-sale!
intrathecal baclofen pump
SYNCHROMED II

The muscle relaxant baclofen is generally referred to by its generic name, which is cooler than the trade name (Lioresal). Baclofen activates GABA(B) receptors ("B" for baclofen), relieving spasticity without producing euphoria or pleasant effects. Although non-addictive, baclofen is associated with a withdrawal syndrome similar to GABA(A) receptor agonists (benzodiazepines, alcohol, etc).

For cerebral palsy, baclofen may be administered intrathecally (into cerebrospinal fluid) through an implanted pump. There are only two other drugs FDA-approved for intrathecal administration—morphine (opioid) and ziconotide (atypical analgesic that reduces release of Substance P).

There is a **black box warning** that abrupt discontinuation of intrathecal baclofen may result in high fever, altered mental status and exaggerated rebound spasticity, which in rare cases has advanced to rhabdomyolysis and multiple organ-system failure. Caregivers must understand the importance of keeping refill visits and heeding pump alarms.

Baclofen may elevate blood glucose, a side effect not seen with GABA(A) receptor agonists such as benzodiazepines.

Baclofen is used off-label for alcohol use disorder (AUD) to reduce anxiety and cravings. It may be more effective for AUD than the FDA-approved medications for this indication (acamprosate, naltrexone, disulfiram).

Lioresal
Intrathecal (baclofen injection)
"Personalized targeted treatment of severe spasticity"

Dosing: For spasticity, start 5 mg PO TID, may increase by 15 mg/day increments in 3-day intervals; Target dose is 20–80 mg divided TID–QID; Max is 80 mg/day; For alcohol use disorder there is no established dose, but most trials used fixed dosing of 30–80 mg/day in divided doses; Consider prescribing 5 mg TID x 3 days, then 10 mg TID, may increase dose to 20 mg TID; Taper gradually to stop.

MUSCLE RELAXANTS 17

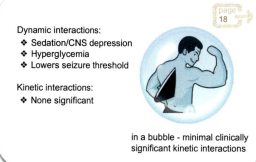

GABA receptor ligands

page 55

GABA(A) agonists

❖ Alcohol,
❖ Ativan, alprazolam (benzos)
❖ Amytal (barbiturates)
❖ Ambien
❖ Anesthetics
❖ Allopregnanolone (brexanolone)

GABA(A) antagonist

❖ Flumazenil (Romazicon) at the benzodiazepine site

GABA(B) agonists

❖ Baclofen (antispasmodic)
❖ GHB (Xyrem)

Note that neither gabapentin (Neurontin) nor pregabalin (Lyrica) bind to GABA receptors. Their chemical structures are similar to GABA.

page 18

Dynamic interactions:

❖ Sedation/CNS depression
❖ Hyperglycemia
❖ Lowers seizure threshold

Kinetic interactions:

❖ None significant

in a bubble - minimal clinically significant kinetic interactions

#187
1957
$5–$18

Methocarbamol (ROBAXIN)

meth uh CAR buh mawl / ro BAX in

"Row backs in (to) Metal car"

- ❖ Antispasmodic
- ❖ Unknown mechanism
- ❖ Non-controlled

500
750
mg

FDA-approved for:

- ❖ Muscle spasm
- ❖ Tetanus (adjunct)

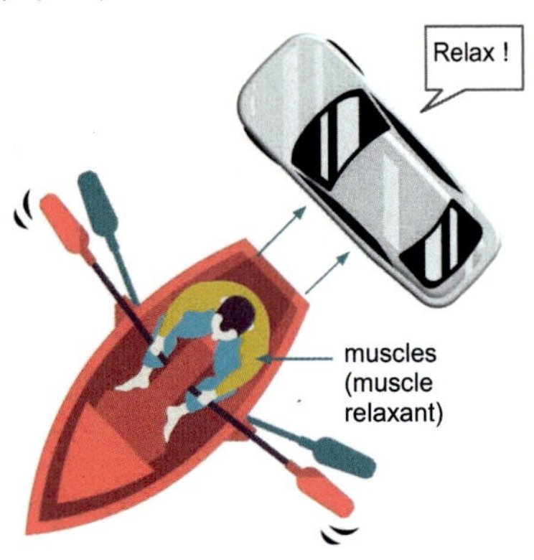

Methocarbamol (Robaxin) is a spasmolytic intended for short term use (2–3 days). It acts through the central nervous system by an unknown mechanism. It is a carbamate derivative of guaifenesin (Mucinex), but methocarbamol lacks the abuse potential of the Schedule IV carbamate carisoprodol (Soma) and is much safer. Methocarbamol has a high therapeutic index, i.e., has a wide range of safe and effective dosages.

Side effects include drowsiness and dizziness, similar to other centrally-acting muscle relaxants. Both tachycardia and bradycardia have been reported. Methocarbamol has the potential to cause mood disturbance, as is the case with most anything that affects the central nervous system. It may cause black/blue/green discoloration of urine.

Doing: For acute muscle spasm, 1,000–1,500 mg QID x 2–3 days. Maximum dose is 8,000 mg/day. Intended for short term use.

guaifenesin (Mucinex)

methocarbamol (Robaxin)

page 18

Dynamic interactions:

- ❖ Sedation/CNS depression
- ❖ Lowers seizure threshold

Kinetic interactions:

- ❖ None

#118
1996
$17–$96

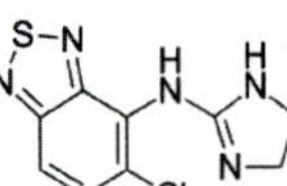

Tizanidine (ZANAFLEX)

tye ZAN i deen / ZAN a flex

"Zany flex (in a) Tizzy"

- ❖ Antispasmodic
- ❖ Central alpha-2 agonist
- ❖ Non-controlled

2
4
6
mg

FDA-approved for:

- ❖ Spasticity

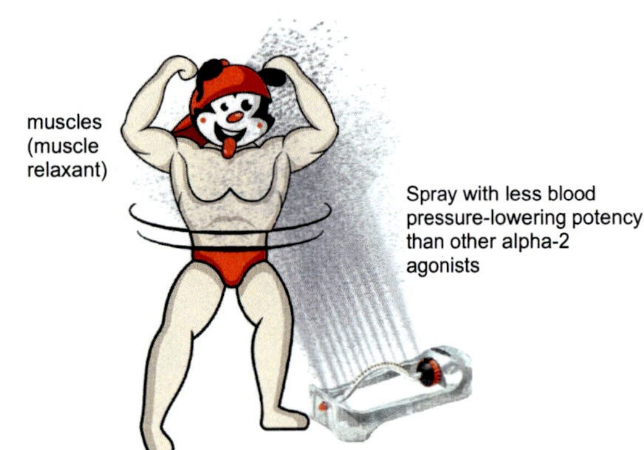

Tizanidine (Zanaflex) has the same mechanism as the antihypertensive clonidine (Catapres) but with about 10% of the antihypertensive potency of clonidine. Tizanidine reduces spasticity by presynaptic inhibition of motor neurons, although the relation between α2 receptor agonism and spasmolytic action is not fully understood. Tizanidine is intended for PRN dosing.

Dosing: Start: 2 mg q 6–8 hours PRN; Maximum 36 mg total daily dose; May increase 2–4 mg/dose every 1–4 days; Give consistently with food or on empty stomach; Taper dose by 2–4 mg/day to stop.

page 183

clonidine

tizanidine

page 10

Dynamic interactions:

- ❖ Hypotensive effects
- ❖ Sedation/CNS depression

Kinetic interactions:

- ❖ 1A2 substrate – contraindicated with 1A2 inHibitors fluvoxamine (Luvox) and ciprofloxacin (Cipro)

1A2 substrate (major)

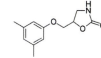

1962
$40–$144

Metaxalone (SKELAXIN)

me TAX a lone / ska LAX in

"Skeletor Relaxin' (with a) Meat ax, alone"

- ❖ Antispasmodic
- ❖ CNS depressant
- ❖ Serotonergic

400
800
mg

FDA-approved for:

- ❖ Acute musculoskeletal pain

Our spooky mascots are generally reserved for antipsychotics, with Skelaxin as an exception.

The spasmolytic mechanism of metaxalone (Skelaxin) is unknown, other than being a general CNS depressant. It may be weak monoamine oxidase inhibitor (MAOI). If taken in large doses metaxalone may be sufficiently potent to cause serotonin syndrome.

Metaxalone is an oxazolidinone by structure. Most oxazolidinones are antibiotics, e.g., linezolid, which is also a monoamine oxidase inhibitor that can contribute to serotonin toxicity.

Metaxalone is not commonly prescribed.

Dosing: For acute musculoskeletal pain, give 800 mg TID–QID on an empty stomach.

Dynamic interactions:

- ❖ Sedation/CNS depression
- ❖ Serotonergic (weak)

Kinetic interactions:

- ❖ Metabolized by seven different P450 enzymes (multi-CYP); Kinetic interactions occur but are unlikely to be clinically significant with so many metabolic pathways—"in a box".

page 18

Multi-CYP

1960
$11–$35

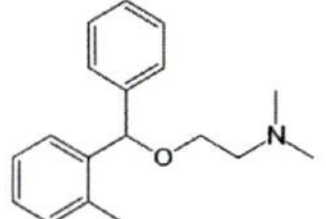

Orphenadrine (NORFLEX)

or FEN a drin / NOR flex

"No reflex Orphan drain"

- ❖ Antispasmodic
- ❖ Antihistaminergic
- ❖ Anticholinergic

100
mg

FDA-approved for:

- ❖ Musculoskeletal pain

Orphenadrine is an antispasmodic with an antihistaminergic mechanism of action. As with all old antihistamines, orphenadrine is highly anticholinergic. Orphenadrine is an analogue of diphenhydramine (Benadryl), which is also an antihistamine/anticholinergic. Orphenadrine distinguishes itself from diphenhydramine by inHibiting CYP2B6.

As with other anticholinergics, orphenadrine can improve motor function in Parkinson's disease. Prior to the development of amantadine (Symmetrel) in the late 1960s, anticholinergics like orphenadrine were the mainstay of Parkinson's treatment.

Orphengesic Forte is a fixed dose combination of orphenadrine with aspirin and caffeine.

Dosing: 100 mg HS or 100 mg BID

diphenhydramine
(Benadryl)

orphenadrine
(Norflex)

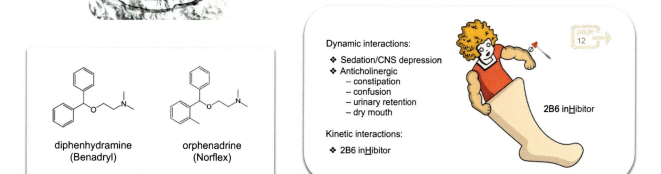

Dynamic interactions:

- ❖ Sedation/CNS depression
- ❖ Anticholinergic
  - – constipation
  - – confusion
  - – urinary retention
  - – dry mouth

Kinetic interactions:

- ❖ 2B6 inHibitor

page 12

2B6 inHibitor

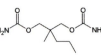

1955
$110–$156

Meprobamate (MILTOWN)

muh PROH buh mate / MIL town

“Mill Town (ain’t) m’ problem, mate”

- ❖ Anxiolytic
- ❖ Carbamate
- ❖ GABA(A) agonist
- ❖ DEA Schedule IV

200
400
mg

FDA-approved for:
- ❖ Anxiety

Meprobamate (Miltown) is included in this chapter as a preface to the muscle relaxant carisoprodol (Soma).

Released in 1955, this “minor tranquilizer” (anxiolytic) became the first blockbuster psychotropic drug. By 1957, over 36 million prescriptions had been filled for meprobamate in the US, accounting for a third of all prescriptions written. It was named after Milltown, New Jersey, population 7,000.

In 1965 its classification changed (from minor tranquilizer) to sedative. By the late 1960s, it was recognized as addictive. Although rarely prescribed today, it remains available in the US as a Schedule IV controlled substance (same schedule as benzodiazepines). The EU and Canada have removed meprobamate from the market, having determined risk outweighs benefit due to its narrow therapeutic index.

Meprobamate binds at the barbiturate binding site on GABA(A) receptors. While barbiturates are used for treatment of epilepsy, meprobamate can exacerbate grand mal seizures. Anxiety is the only approved indication for meprobamate.

The muscle relaxant carisoprodol (Soma) is metabolized in the liver to meprobamate. While meprobamate is rarely prescribed nowadays, Soma is the #3 most prescribed muscle relaxant (behind Flexeril and Robaxin) despite being addictive and dangerous. GoodRx categorizes meprobamate itself as a muscle relaxant, ranked #11.

page 18

Dynamic interactions:
- ❖ Sedation/CNS depression

Kinetic interactions:
- ❖ None significant

In overdose, meprobamate tablets can form a bezoar in the stomach. As the patient emerges from coma, gastric acidity will break up the bezoar and may re-induce coma if the bezoar is not removed by gastroscopy. Bezoar formation can also be a complication of overdose on extended-release tablets of various medications.

The anticonvulsant felbamate (Felbatol) is structurally similar to meprobamate.

Dosing: Meprobamate is no longer recommended for treatment of anxiety. The standard dose was 400 mg TID–QID. The maximum total daily dose is 2400 mg. Taper over at least 1–2 weeks to discontinue.

Syndromes of the 1960s

The computer-age compulsion

Predictions that man will soon be replaced by computers fail to reckon with his remarkable capacity to adopt and adapt. But in the process of competing with the machine, it seems man is in

Exaggeration? Not to the physician who is increasingly exposed to the byproducts of the new industrial revolution —peptic ulcer, mid-forty infarction and anxiety reaction—and to the victims of husband and father absenteeism: lonely, anxious, frustrated wives, and mother smothered "problem" children.

So when job demands engender anxiety and tension—in fact, whenever human emotions become folded, spindled and mutilated—'Miltown' can frequently be of help. It has been for more than a dozen years now.

MILTOWN
(MEPROBAMATE)

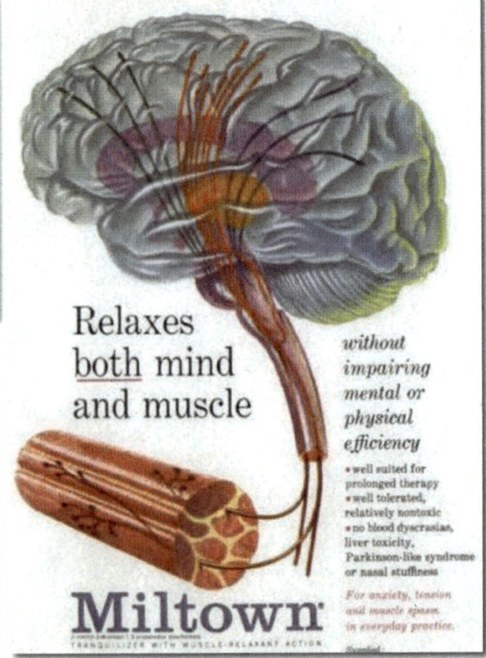

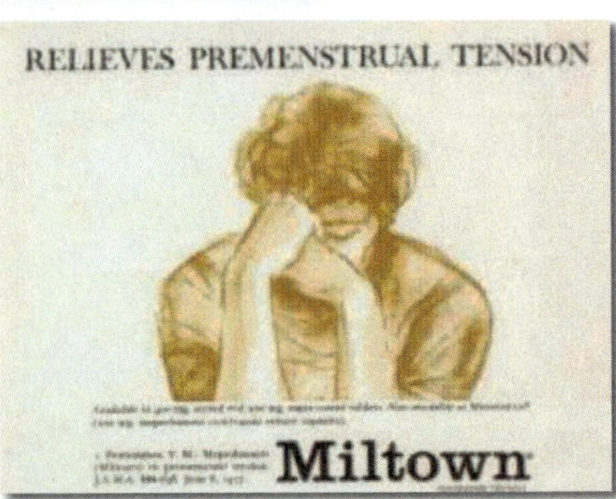

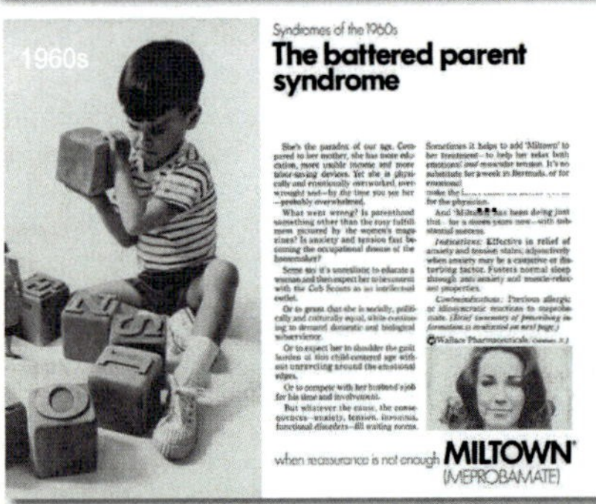

#181
1959
$12–$52

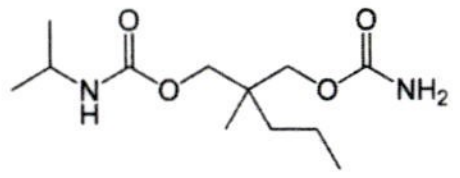

Carisoprodol (SOMA)

kar eye soe PROE dole / SO ma

"So-manly Car is so proud"

- ❖ Antispasmodic
- ❖ Carbamate
- ❖ GABA(A) agonist
- ❖ DEA Schedule IV

250
350
mg

FDA-approved for:
- ❖ Acute musculoskeletal pain

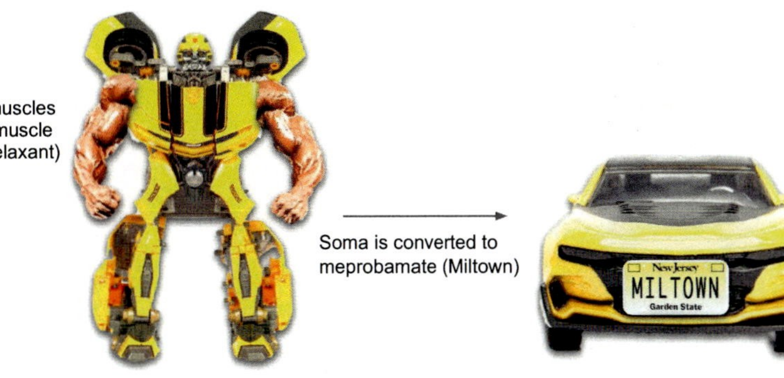
muscles
(muscle
relaxant)
Soma is converted to
meprobamate (Miltown)
New Jersey
MILTOWN
Garden State

In his 1932 novel *Brave New World*, Aldous Huxley described a purely fictional ideal pleasure drug called soma. In the book, soma was the happy pill the government used to enslave its citizens. Soma was described as having "all the advantages of Christianity and alcohol; none of their defects".

Fast forward to 1959, when carisoprodol was released, branded as Soma. The name likely derives from the word somatic rather than from Brave New World.

Soma went to market four years after meprobamate (Miltown), the blockbuster anxiolytic described on the preceding page.. Although carisoprodol is approved as a muscle relaxant, it is a prodrug of meprobamate, i.e., the body converts it into a chemical now recognized to be dangerous and addictive. However, Soma was not marketed as a psychoactive medication. Compare the ads shown here to those for Miltown, which are certainly Brave New Worldish.

If a person wants a muscle relaxer for recreational purposes, Soma is likely what they are seeking. The DEA eventually classified carisoprodol as a Schedule IV controlled substance in 2011. It has been removed from the market in some countries.

Soma remains the #3 most prescribed muscle relaxant, behind cyclobenzaprine (Flexeril) and methocarbamol (Robaxin), neither of which are controlled substances.

In the Netflix series "The Pharmacist", a doctor was prescribing a combination that drug abusers called "The Holy Trinity"—Oxycontin, Soma, and alprazolam (Xanax).

Dosing: For acute musculoskeletal pain, the recommended dose is 250–350 mg QID for a maximum of 2–3 weeks; Not recommended for long-term use, but if taken long term it should be tapered gradually when stopping.

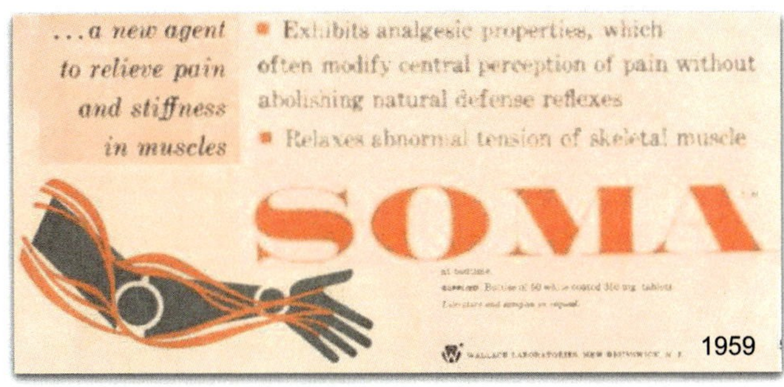
...a new agent
to relieve pain
and stiffness
in muscles
Exhibits analgesic properties, which often modify central perception of pain without abolishing natural defense reflexes
Relaxes abnormal tension of skeletal muscle
SOMA
1959

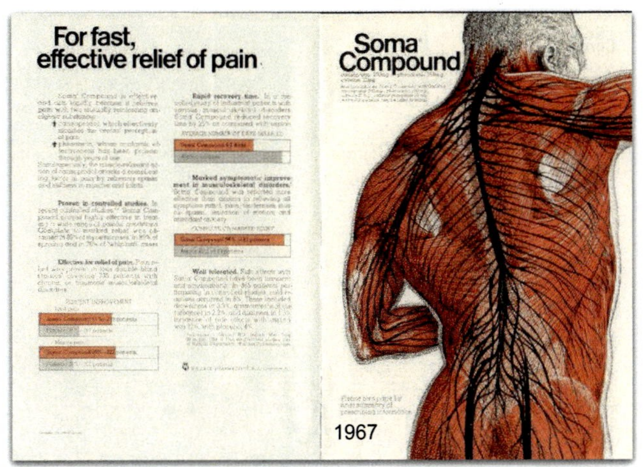
For fast, effective relief of pain
Soma Compound
1967

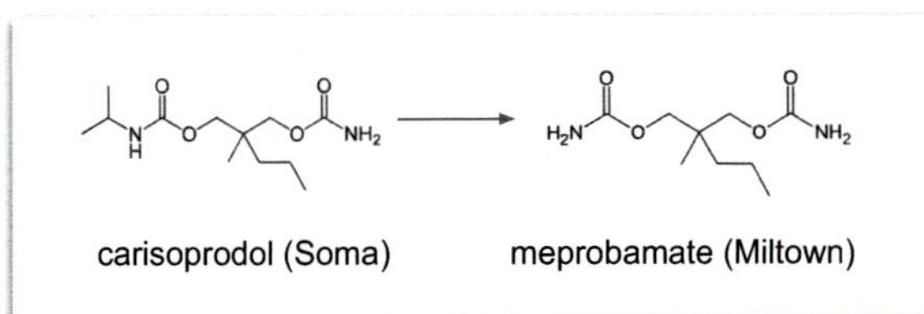

carisoprodol (Soma) meprobamate (Miltown)

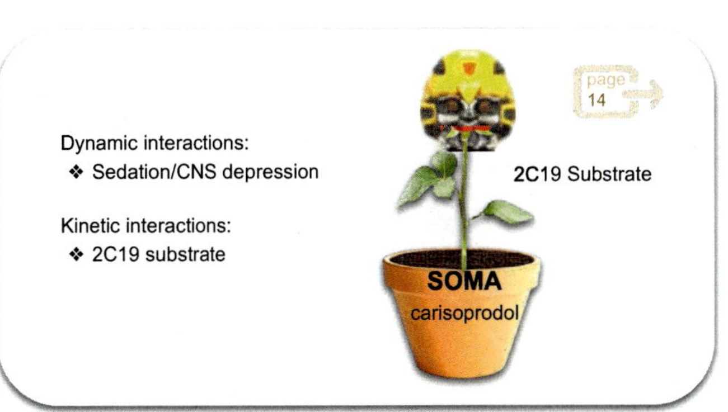
page 14
2C19 Substrate
SOMA
carisoprodol

Dynamic interactions:
- ❖ Sedation/CNS depression

Kinetic interactions:
- ❖ 2C19 substrate

1965
D/C 1982

Methaqualone (Quāālude)

meth aqua lone / KWAY lude

"QUiet InterIude (for) Metal aqua-lung"

❖ Illegal hypnotic

714's

Removed from market

Methaqualone is a CNS depressant of the quinazolinone class, outlawed since 1984. It was marketed as a "non-barbiturate". The origin of -aqualone is qu(in)a(zo)lone. Its trade name derived from "quiet interlude" and was stylized after Māālox, a successful medication from the same manufacturer. Unlike other specific medications, they are commonly referred to in the plural—You would say "a bottle of Quāāludes" but not, e.g., "a bottle of Prozacs".

The mechanism of Methaqualone is similar to barbiturates and BZDs, potentiating the effects of GABA at GABA(A) receptors. Its binding site is distinct from the binding sites of barbiturates and BZDs. This is apparently the sweet spot of the GABA(A) receptor complex because, if the user can stay awake, it quickly causes euphoria. Methaqualone induced sleep within 10–30 minutes and half-life was 20–60 hours.

There is a lot of nostalgia for these pills. They became increasingly popular in the 1970s as a recreational drug known as "ludes", "soaps" and "disco biscuits". Methaqualone use led to fatalities, especially when combined with alcohol. In the 1970s a popular college pastime was "luding out" on Quāāludes and wine.

Quāālude was manufactured by Rorer and Lemmon with the numbers 714 stamped on the tablet, so people often referred to Quāāludes as 714's or "Lemmons". The pills were white, not lemon-colored. The drug continues to be made in clandestine laboratories, stamped with 714.

Methaqualone was released in 1965 and its use peaked in the early 1970s as a sleep medication and muscle relaxant. In 1972, it was the #6 best selling sedative. In 1973 the DEA placed it on Schedule II. In the year 1980, 117 people died from methaqualone abuse. It was discontinued in 1982 by the manufacturer because "Quāālude accounted for less than 2% of our sales but created 98% of our headaches". The DEA made it an illegal drug (Schedule I) in 1984.

The comedian Bill Cosby admitted giving Quāāludes to women to facilitate sexual assault. *Playboy* publisher Hugh Hefner allegedly referred to Quāāludes as "thigh-openers".

In *The Wolf of Wall Street*, Leonardo DiCaprio's character became intoxicated on Quāāludes that had been stashed away for 15 years.

Tardive dyskinesia (TD) is a potentially irreversible movement disorder caused by dopamine D2 receptor-blocking medications taken for 6 months or longer. TD almost never occurs before 3 months on an antipsychotic. Haloperidol (Haldol) and metoclopramide (Reglan) are the most common culprits, because other medications with high risk of TD are rarely prescribed. The yearly incidence of developing TD is about the same throughout the course of treatment with a D2 blocker. In other words, the risk of developing TD during the first year on haloperidol is about the same as during the fifth year or the tenth year. Older adults are at higher risk.

First generation antipsychotics (FGAs) with strong affinity for D2 receptors (high potency FGAs) pose the highest risk of tardive dyskinesia. Second generation antipsychotics (SGAs) generally pose less of a risk because they block $5\text{-}HT_{2A}$ serotonin receptors with greater affinity than they block D2 receptors. Blocking $5\text{-}HT_{2A}$ receptors (on dopamine neurons) increases the release of dopamine in the basal ganglia, thereby preventing development of D2 receptor hypersensitivity, which leads to TD.

According to the maladaptive synaptic plasticity hypothesis, D2 receptor hypersensitivity and neuronal damage caused by oxidative stress can result in the formation of abnormal new connections between the basal ganglia and the cerebral cortex, leading to involuntary movements that persist even after the offending drug is removed. It stands to reason that general neuroprotectants (e.g., antioxidants) may improve or prevent TD (Deardorff et al, 2019).

Treatment of TD consists of tapering off the offending medication over a few weeks and, if necessary, replacing it with an antipsychotic with negligible D2 blocking potency such as clozapine (Clozaril), quetiapine (Seroquel), or pimavanserin (Nuplazid). Abruptly stopping the D2 blocker can worsen TD by suddenly exposing hypersensitive D2 receptors to more dopamine. TD caused by abruptly stopping a D2 blocker is called withdrawal-emergent dyskinesia.

If TD emerges, you should taper off of anticholinergics such as benztropine (Cogentin), diphenhydramine (Benadryl), and trihexyphenidyl (Artane). Although helpful for other types of extrapyramidal symptoms (EPS), anticholinergics worsen TD. It may take several months for TD movements to improve.

Medications proven to improve TD:

Medication	Class	Comments
Clonazepam (KLONOPIN)	Benzodiazepine	Consider for first-line treatment of TD
Amantadine (SYMMETREL)	NMDA antagonist and dopaminergic	FDA-approved for parkinsonism
Valbenazine (INGREZZA)	Dopamine depleting agent	The first FDA-approved TD treatment, 2017. Greater effect size than deutetrabenazine.
Deutetrabenazine (AUSTEDO)	Dopamine depleting agent	The second FDA-approved TD treatment, 2018. Also approved for Huntington's.
Tetrabenazine (XENAZINE)	Dopamine depleting agent	Approved as orphan drug for Huntington's in 2008, used off-label for TD.
Reserpine (SERPASIL)	Dopamine depleting agent	Reserpine depletes the reserves of dopamine in presynaptic neurons It was used for treatment of psychosis prior to modern antipsychotics. It is also used for HTN. Not recommended due to too many side effects, including hypotension
Ginkgo biloba extract	Antioxidant	"EGb-761" brand, 240 mg daily is well tolerated but risk of bleeding
Vitamin B6 (Pyridoxine)	Vitamin	400–1200 mg daily (high dose). 1200 mg may be effective even 8 weeks after cessation. Neuropathy (reversible) may occur at doses over 200 mg.
Botulinum toxin (BOTOX)	Neurotoxin that inhibits acetylcholine release from nerve endings	Botox is effective for localized tardive dystonia that may accompany tardive dyskinesia. The most common location is the neck (cervical dystonia). Not for injection into the tongue

Note that the dopamine depleting agents (VMAT2 inhibitors) may induce parkinsonism as an adverse effect.

Less proven TD treatments:

Medication	Class	Comments
Melatonin	Neuroprotectant	10 mg decreases symptoms 24–30% by 6 weeks. Benign,cheap, neuroprotective, and may help cognition; There is no reason not to try melatonin if tardive dyskinesia is a concern.
N-Acetylcysteine (NAC)	Neuroprotectant	Benign treatment with no expected risks, side effects, or interactions; Inexpensive; No reason not to try it
Vitamin E	Vitamin	The most studied agent in randomized controlled trials on the treatment of TD, although there was significant evidence of publication bias. Larger studies found only minor benefit, with smaller effect size than vitamin B6. May increase risk of prostate cancer.
Propranolol	Beta blocker	Also helps essential tremor and akathisia. Contraindicated with bradycardia or asthma
Buspirone (BUSPAR)	Anxiolytic	Very high doses have been used, up to 180 mg/day (60 mg TID). FDA max is 60 mg/day.
Mirtazapine (REMERON)	Antidepressant	20 of 22 cases of movement disorder (including TD) improved on mirtazapine 30 mg (Alarcón et al, 2003).

Other medications that may potentially improve TD include baclofen (Lioresal), valproate (Depakote), zolpidem (Ambien), donepezil (Aricept), zonisamide (Zonegran), and omega-3 fatty acids.

Principal sources:
Forgotten but not gone: new developments in the understanding and treatment of tardive dyskinesia; Jonathan Meyer; CNS Spectrums (2016).
An update on tardive dyskinesia: from phenomenology to treatment; Wain and Jankovic; Tremor and Other Hyperkinetic Movements (2013).
Pharmacologic treatment of tardive dyskinesia: a meta-analysis and system review; Bekir et al; Journal of Clinical Psychiatry (2020).

VMAT Inhibitors (dopamine depleting agents) for treatment of chorea

The involuntary movements of tardive dyskinesia (TD) and Huntington's disease (HD) are described as chorea (choreiform movements) derived from the Greek word for "dance". Chorea involves irregular movements (as opposed to repetitive movements) that appear to flow from one muscle to the next. Choreiform movements occur both at rest and with action. The patient may attempt to disguise chorea by incorporating involuntary movements into a purposeful activity such as adjusting clothes. A common example of chorea is "milkmaid's grip"—hand muscles squeezing and releasing as if milking a cow.

For context: Parkinson's disease (PD) does not manifest as chorea, but levodopa (PD treatment) can cause choreiform movements. For context, a parkinsonian tremor is a slow repetitive tremor. Characteristic of parkinsonism is the "pill rolling" tremor that looks like the individual is a rolling a pill between the thumb and other fingers. parkinsonian tremor is unique as a resting tremor that disappears with movement. With parkinsonism, the patient has no problem bringing a cup or soup spoon to their mouth but may spill the liquid while resting the cup/spoon on the lips.

Chorea of tardive dyskinesia: Only severe cases of tardive dyskinesia manifest as choreiform movements of the arms. TD is more likely to involve tongue movements, lip smacking, excessive blinking, grimacing or raising of eyebrows. Often the patient with TD will be unaware of orofacial movements. When TD affects the upper extremities, it starts as irregular finger movements—as if the patient is playing an invisible piano or air guitar (fretting hand, not strumming hand).

Vesicular monoamine transporter (VMAT) is a protein that transports monoamines (dopamine, serotonin, norepinephrine, epinephrine, and histamine) into synaptic vesicles of presynaptic neurons. By depleting dopamine from synaptic vesicles (and thereby depleting dopamine in the synapse), VMAT inhibitors have antipsychotic properties. The original VMAT inhibitor, reserpine, was used as an antipsychotic. In contrast to modern antipsychotics that block dopamine receptors, dopamine depleting drugs pose little to no risk of causing tardive dyskinesia. However, VMAT inhibitors can cause akathisia (restlessness) and parkinsonism.

Nowadays VMAT inhibitors are used to treat tardive dyskinesia (TD) and Huntington's disease. In both conditions, choreiform movements are caused by excessive dopamine activity in the areas of the brain that control movement. TD is caused by dopamine D2 receptor hypersensitivity on postsynaptic neurons, resulting from prolonged exposure to a D2 blocking medication such as haloperidol (Haldol) or metoclopramide (Reglan). Huntington's disease is an autosomal dominant disease that causes death of neurons. In the early stages of HD, chorea results from excessive activity of (presynaptic) dopaminergic neurons. Chorea diminishes at advanced stages of HD, at which time dystonia emerges.

Vesicular monoamine transporter inhibitors may cause depression and suicidal ideation by depleting serotonin, which is also a monoamine neurotransmitter.

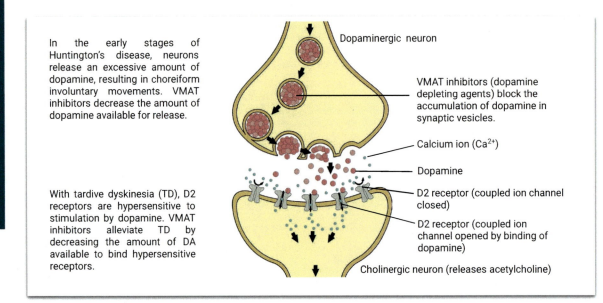

In the early stages of Huntington's disease, neurons release an excessive amount of dopamine, resulting in choreiform involuntary movements. VMAT inhibitors decrease the amount of dopamine available for release.

With tardive dyskinesia (TD), D2 receptors are hypersensitive to stimulation by dopamine. VMAT inhibitors alleviate TD by decreasing the amount of DA available to bind hypersensitive receptors.

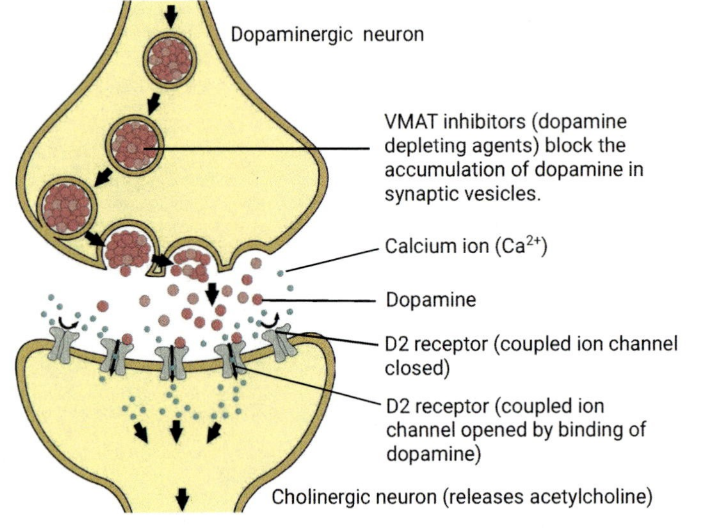

VMAT Inhibitors (dopamine depleting agents)

Drug	Year	Cost	Inhibitor of	Reversibility	FDA-approved for
Tetrabenazine (XENAZINE)	2008	$1,000	VMAT2	Reversible	Huntington's
Deutetrabenazine (AUSTEDO)	2017	$3,000	VMAT2	Reversible	Huntington's & TD
Valbenazine (INGREZZA)	2018	$10,000	VMAT2	Reversible	Tardive dyskinesia (TD)
Reserpine (SERPASIL)	1955	$30	VMAT2 > VMAT1	Irreversible	Hypertension

2008
$362–$2,300

Tetrabenazine (XENAZINE)

tet ra BEN uh zeen / ZEN uh zeen

"Xena's Tetris bin"

- ❖ VMAT2 Inhibitor
- ❖ Dopamine depleting agent
- ❖ Anti-chorea medication

12.5
25
mg

FDA-approved for:

- ❖ Huntington's disease

Used off-label for:

- ❖ Tardive dyskinesia
- ❖ Tic disorders including Tourette's
- ❖ Hemiballismus due to subthalamic nucleus damage
- ❖ Treatment-resistant schizophrenia

hunter =
Huntington's
chorea

Xena: Warrior Princess was a television series running from 1995 to 2001 as a spin-off from *Hercules: The Legendary Journeys*

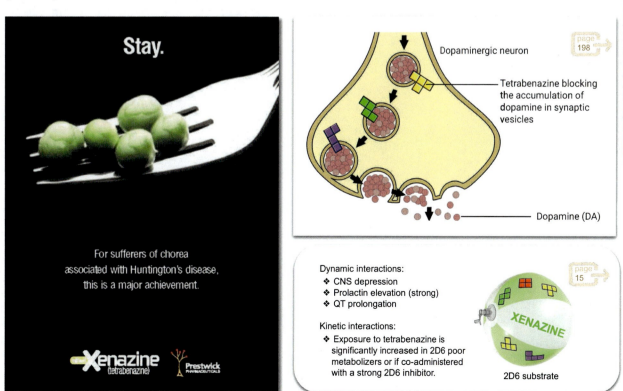

Tetrabenazine (Xenazine) is a presynaptic monoamine-depleting agent that can dampen abnormal dopamine release. Tetrabenazine was developed as a treatment for schizophrenia over 50 years ago.

Tetrabenazine was the first FDA-approved treatment for Huntington's chorea (2008), after it had been available in other countries for decades. Unlike subsequent VMAT inhibitors, tetrabenazine is not FDA-approved for tardive dyskinesia (TD), although it is effective for TD, off-label.

Psychiatric side effects of VMAT inhibitors are of major concern. Behavior change, depression, and suicide are possible with these medications. Per black box warning, VMAT inhibitors are contraindicated for Huntington's patients who are actively depressed. VMAT inhibitors may also cause cognitive deficits.

In addition to relieving tardive dyskinesia caused by antipsychotics, tetrabenazine has antipsychotic properties of its own. It has been used off-label for treatment-resistant schizophrenia, augmenting a modern antipsychotic.

Tetrabenazine can greatly increase prolactin levels by decreasing dopamine release. Dopamine, also known as "prolactin-inhibiting factor", inhibits release of prolactin from the pituitary gland.

In treatment of Huntington's disease it may be difficult to distinguish between adverse drugs reactions and progression of the underlying disease. There have been cases of neuroleptic malignant syndrome associated with tetrabenazine, caused by decreased dopamine transmission.

Dosing: Maintenance range is 25–100 mg/day in divided doses; Start at 12.5 mg q AM x 1 week, then 12.5 mg BID x 1 week; Then may increase by 12.5 mg/day in weekly intervals; Divide to TID if > 37.5 mg/day. Consider 2D6 genotyping if planning to exceed 50 mg/day, which is the maximum dose for patients who are 2D6 poor metabolizers or those taking a strong 2D6 inHibitor such quinidine, fluoxetine (Prozac), paroxetine (Paxil), or bupropion (Wellbutrin).

DA DEPLETING AGENTS 18

Stay.
For sufferers of chorea
associated with Huntington's disease,
this is a major achievement.
Xenazine
(tetrabenazine)
Prestwick

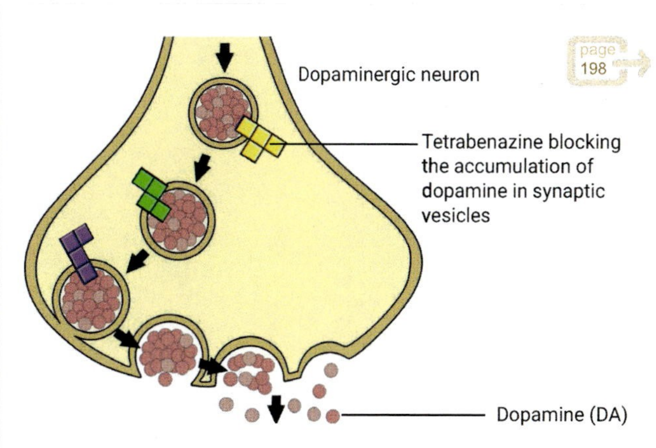
Dopaminergic neuron
Tetrabenazine blocking the accumulation of dopamine in synaptic vesicles
Dopamine (DA)

page 198

Dynamic interactions:

- ❖ CNS depression
- ❖ Prolactin elevation (strong)
- ❖ QT prolongation

Kinetic interactions:

- ❖ Exposure to tetrabenazine is significantly increased in 2D6 poor metabolizers or if co-administered with a strong 2D6 inhibitor.

XENAZINE

2D6 substrate

page 15

2017
$5,399–$5,725

Deutetrabenazine (AUSTEDO)

[du tet ra BEN uh zeen / ah STED oh
"Dueling tetris bins (to) Oust TD"

❖ VMAT2 Inhibitor
❖ Dopamine depleting agent

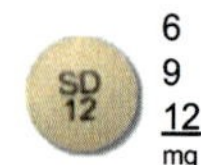

6
9
12
mg

FDA-approved for:
❖ Tardive dyskinesia
❖ Huntington's chorea

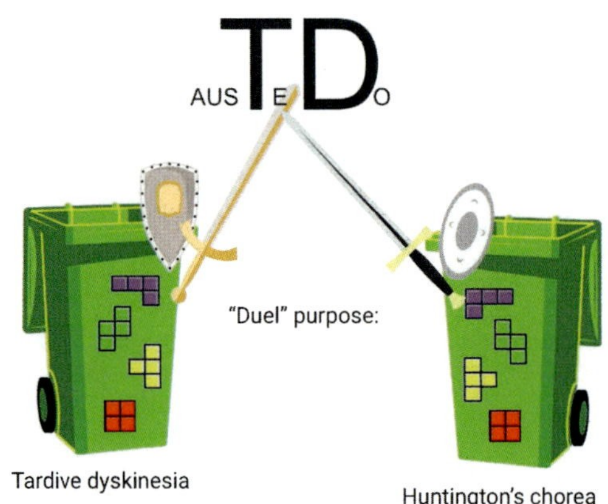

Deutetrabenazine (Austedo) is the VMAT inhibitor FDA-approved for both tardive dyskinesia (TD) and chorea of Huntington's disease. Compare this to tetrabenazine (Xenazine) which is only approved for Huntington's, and valbenazine (Ingrezza) which is only approved for TD.

Deutetrabenazine was the first drug containing deuterium, aka "heavy hydrogen" (an extra neutron), to receive FDA approval. Deuterated drugs take longer for the body to clear. Hence, deutetrabenazine has a longer duration of action than tetrabenazine, allowing for less frequent dosing.

Psychiatric side effects of VMAT inhibitors are a major concern when used for treating Huntington's chorea. Black box warnings state that VMAT inhibitors are contraindicated for Huntington's patients who are actively depressed due to risk of suicide.

TD patients tend to experience fewer psychiatric side effects than Huntington's patients, possibly because TD patients are also taking an antipsychotic. The incidence of somnolence was 11% (versus 4% placebo) for Huntington's patients. Somnolence was not an issue with TD patients. A few patients experienced insomnia.

Dosing: For TD, the initial dose is 12 mg/day, with recommended range of 12–48 mg/day. Divide doses to BID if total daily dose is above 12 mg. The recommended dose range for Huntington's chorea is slightly lower. Titrate at weekly intervals by 6 mg/day based on reduction of involuntary movements and tolerability. Consider checking an EKG for QT prolongation prior to exceeding 24 mg/day. Consider 2D6 genotyping prior to exceeding 36 mg/day (18 mg BID), which is the maximum dose for patients who are 2D6 poor metabolizers or those taking a strong 2D6 inHibitor.

Dynamic interactions:
❖ Prolactin elevation (strong)
❖ CNS depression
❖ QT prolongation

Kinetic interactions:
❖ Exposure to tetrabenazine is significantly increased in 2D6 poor metabolizers or if co-administered with a strong 2D6 inhibitor.

page 15

2D6 substrate

2018
$10,000

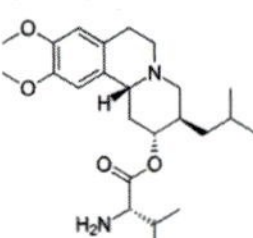

Valbenazine (INGREZZA)

val BEN uh zeen / in GREH zah
"Valved bin In grease"

❖ VMAT2 Inhibitor
❖ Dopamine depleting agent

40
80
mg

FDA-approved for:
❖ Tardive dyskinesia

Valbenazine (Ingrezza) is the VMAT inhibitor FDA-approved for tardive dyskinesia but not for Huntington's. The active metabolite of valbenazine is one of the four stereoisomers of tetrabenazine (Xenazine). Prolactin elevation is less pronounced with valbenazine compared to the other VMAT inhibitors. Ingrezza can be titrated more quickly than Austedo and has a longer half-life, allowing QD dosing rather than BID (as with Austedo) or TID (as with Xenazine). Effect size of valbenazine (0.72) is greater than with deutetrabenazine (0.40).

Valbenazine does not have the black box warning seen with other VMAT inhibitors (those approved for Huntington's) concerning risk of depression, behavioral change, and suicide. However, patients at risk for suicide or violent behavior were excluded from clinical trials.

The most common side effect is somnolence (11% vs 4% placebo). Otherwise, incidence of side effects is low, but some patients experience balance problems, dizziness, akathisia/restlessness, and arthralgia. As with other VMAT inhibitors, QT prolongation may occur at high doses.

Dosing: Start: 40 mg QD x 1 week, then increase to 80 mg QD (maintenance dose). Dose should not exceed 40 mg/day if taken with a strong 3A4 inHibitor. Concomitant use with a strong 3A4 inDucer is not recommended because valbenazine levels will be too low. Consider decreasing the dose for a 2D6 poor metabolizer, guided by tolerability.

2018 Advertisement:

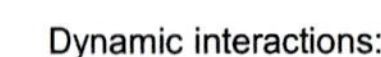

Dynamic interactions:
❖ Prolactin elevation
❖ CNS depression
❖ QT prolongation

Kinetic interactions:
❖ 3A4 substrate (major)
❖ 2D6 substrate

page 15
2D6 substrate
page 16
3A4 substrate (major)

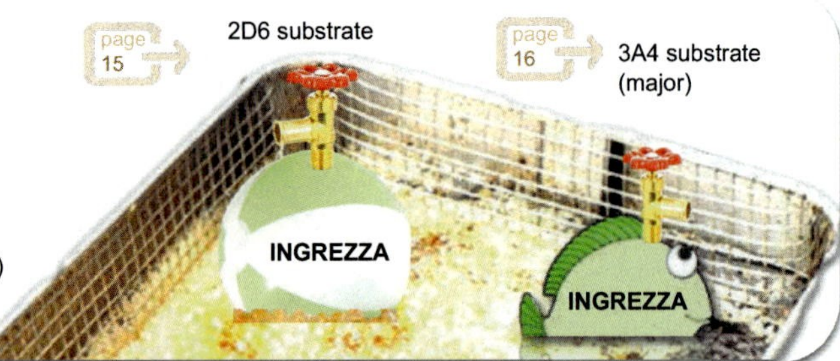

1955
$20–$37

Reserpine (SERPASIL)

re SER pine / SIR pa sil

"serpent re-slurping (dopamine)"

- ❖ Nonselective, irreversible VMAT Inhibitor
- ❖ Dopamine depleting agent
- ❖ Antihypertensive

0.1
0.25
mg

FDA-approved for:

- ❖ Hypertension

Used off-label for:

- ❖ Refractory schizophrenia (rarely)
- ❖ Huntington's chorea
- ❖ Thyrotoxicosis (thyroid storm)

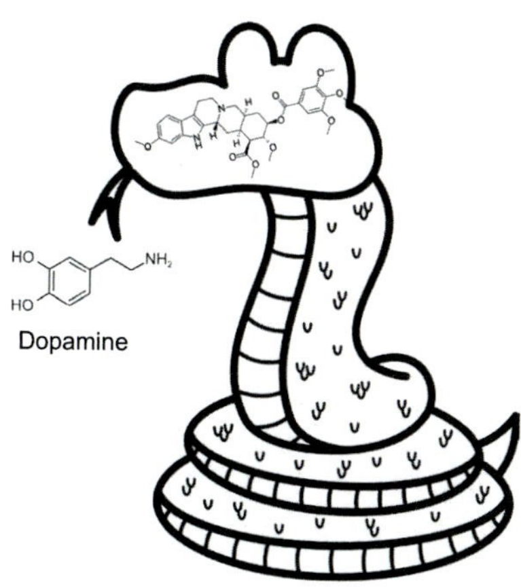

Reserpine depletes the reserves of dopamine in presynaptic neurons. Reserpine (Serpasil) is a nonselective vesicular monoamine transporter (VMAT) inhibitor, binding both VMAT1 and VMAT2. VMAT1 is mostly expressed in neuroendocrine cells. VMAT2 is mostly expressed in neurons. The newer VMAT inhibitors tetrabenazine (Xenazine), deutetrabenazine (Austedo), and valbenazine (Ingrezza) selectively block VMAT2.

Reserpine blocks VMAT irreversibly, so its effects are long lasting. It takes days to weeks for neurons to replenish the depleted transporters.

Reserpine was isolated in 1952 from Indian snakeroot (*Rauwolfia serpentina*) which had been used for centuries in India for the treatment of insanity. Reserpine is generally categorized as an antihypertensive, which is its only FDA-approved indication. A reserpine-hydrochlorothiazide combo pill is available for treatment of refractory high blood pressure. The reserpine-thiazide diuretic combination is one of the few hypertension treatments shown to reduce mortality in randomized controlled trials (JAMA, 1979).

Reserpine was used to treat schizophrenia prior to the arrival of chlorpromazine (Thorazine), which was more effective. The use of reserpine as an antipsychotic has largely been abandoned, but rarely psychiatrists will use it as an adjunct to a modern antipsychotic (dopamine D2 receptor blocker) for refractory cases.

Reserpine was the first compound shown to be an effective antidepressant in a randomized placebo-controlled trial, but it may be more likely to cause depression because it depletes serotonin. Reserpine's antihypertensive effect is mostly due to depletion of norepinephrine.

Reserpine was used to treat dyskinesia of Huntington's disease prior to arrival of the selective VMAT2 inhibitors, which are less likely to drop blood pressure and heart rate. Consider reserpine for treatment of tardive dyskinesia when comorbid with severe hypertension. Low dose reserpine is fairly well tolerated, with nasal congestion being the most common side effect.

Dosing: The usual dose for hypertension is 0.5 mg QD x 1–2 weeks, with maintenance dose of 0.1–0.25 mg QD. For schizophrenia it was dosed 0.1–1 mg QD, with the usual dose of 0.5 mg QD.

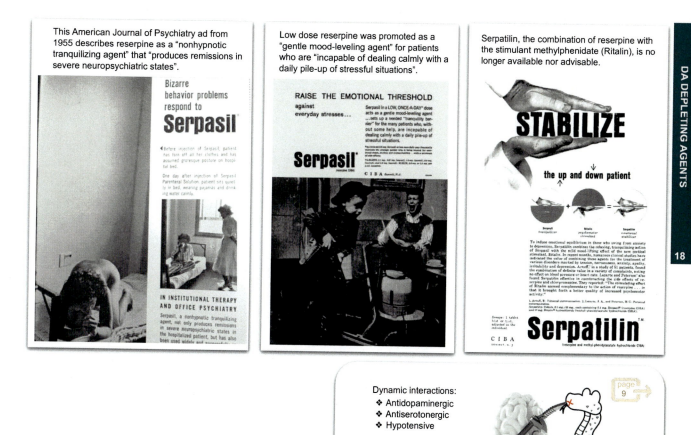

This American Journal of Psychiatry ad from 1955 describes reserpine as a "nonhypnotic tranquilizing agent" that "produces remissions in severe neuropsychiatric states".

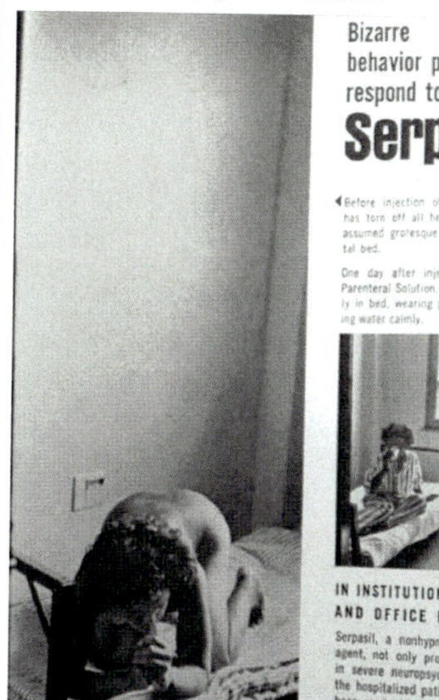

Low dose reserpine was promoted as a "gentle mood-leveling agent" for patients who are "incapable of dealing calmly with a daily pile-up of stressful situations".

Serpatilin, the combination of reserpine with the stimulant methylphenidate (Ritalin), is no longer available nor advisable.

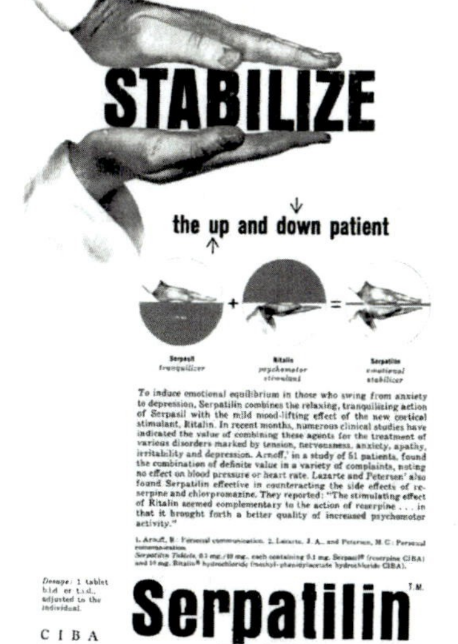

DA DEPLETING AGENTS

18

Dynamic interactions:

- ❖ Antidopaminergic
- ❖ Antiserotonergic
- ❖ Hypotensive

Kinetic interactions:

- ❖ P-gp inhibitor

page 9

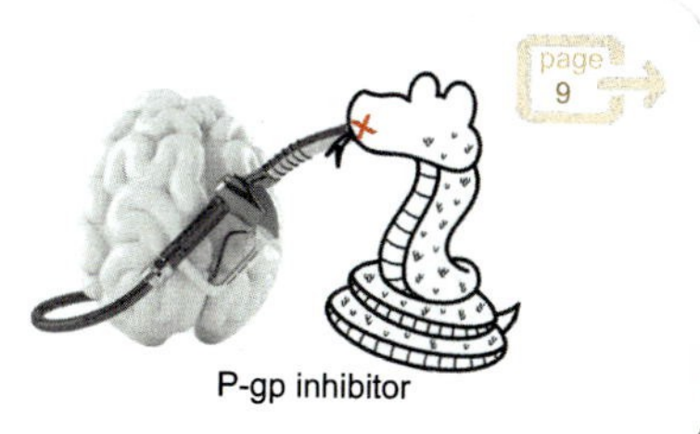

P-gp inhibitor

This edition of *Cafer's Psychopharmacology* was updated in November 2020. Subscribe to cafermed.com for an updated PDF with over 1,000 internal links and bookmarks for ultrarapid navigation. The PDF edition is updated frequently with new mascots. Visit cafermed.com/update for more information.

Discount code for cafermed.com subscription: **ULTRARAPID**

The motor symptoms of Parkinson's disease (PD) are caused by degeneration of dopaminergic (dopamine-producing) neurons in the substantia nigra ("black substance" in the midbrain). Lewy bodies can be seen within neurons on autopsy. The core motor symptoms are dystonia, bradykinesia (slow movement), pill-rolling resting tremor, shuffling gait, and postural (balance) instability. 25% of PD cases do not involve a significant tremor, but nearly all PD patients suffer from bradykinesia. Dyskinesias (choreiform arm movements, grimacing, and mouth/tongue movements) are not caused by PD, but are side effects of levodopa or dopamine agonists used to treat PD.

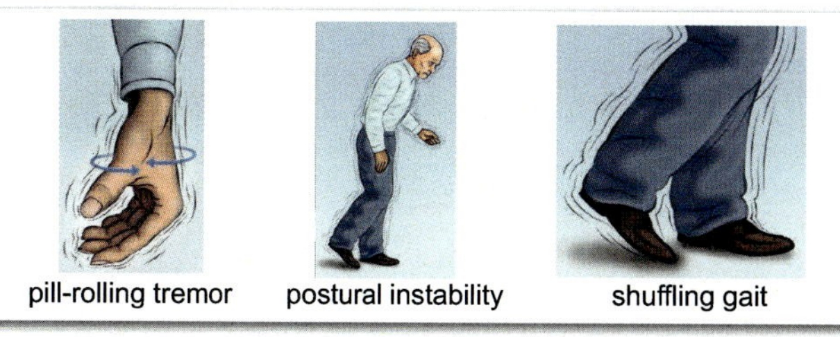

PD affects 1% of the population over age 60. There are some genetic risk factors, but the main risk appears to be unidentified neurotoxin(s) from rural areas. Diagnosis is made by neurologic exam. Inflammatory mechanisms contribute to degeneration of neurons in the substantia nigra. This usually begins over 10 years before onset of PD symptoms.

Neuroprotectants may prevent PD. Caffeine is associated with decreased risk of PD with relative risk of 0.76 per 300 mg/day increase in caffeine intake (Costa et al, 2010). Regular use of ibuprofen was associated with 57% reduced risk of Parkinson's disease with ≥ 10 years of regular use (Gao et al, 2011). Most of the neuroprotectants found to prevent PD also prevent Alzheimer's disease.

About 40% of patients with PD will exhibit hallucinations, delusions, and/or compulsive behaviors. These symptoms can be caused by PD and/or by medications used to treat PD, most of which augment dopamine activity.

About 50% of PD patients suffer from depression. Management includes the usual array of antidepressants, psychotherapy, and physical/mental exercise. The TCA nortriptyline is considered a good choice. If needed for refractory depression, electroconvulsive therapy (ECT) can transiently improve symptoms of PD.

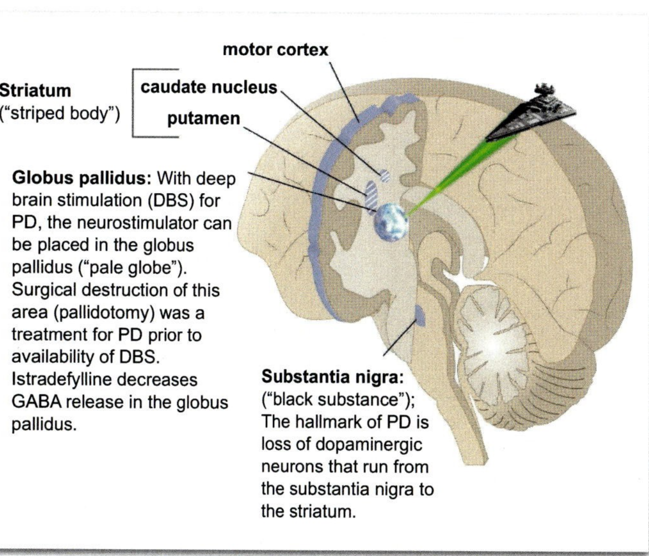

motor cortex
Striatum
("striped body")
caudate nucleus
putamen
Globus pallidus: With deep brain stimulation (DBS) for PD, the neurostimulator can be placed in the globus pallidus ("pale globe"). Surgical destruction of this area (pallidotomy) was a treatment for PD prior to availability of DBS. Istradefylline decreases GABA release in the globus pallidus.
Substantia nigra: ("black substance"); The hallmark of PD is loss of dopaminergic neurons that run from the substantia nigra to the striatum.

Parkinson's disease (PD) medications:

Since no available medication can change the course of the disease, the goal is to ameliorate symptoms with dopamine replenishment, extend "on time" (when the medication is working), and minimize "off time". Starting PD medication can be delayed until there is functional impairment. Carbidopa/levodopa monotherapy is usually the first step. Alternately, a dopamine agonist can be used for initial monotherapy for relatively young patients early in the course of PD. COMT inhibitors may be added to carbidopa/levodopa to help keep levodopa intact until it reaches the brain. Anticholinergics can be used in younger patients if tremor is prominent. MAO-B inhibitors can be added to reduce "off time" and extend "on time". Amantadine can be added if tremor is prominent or if levodopa-induced dyskinesia is problematic. Deep brain stimulation (DBS) surgery can be effective for younger patients, in combination with medication.

Dopamine precursor	
Carbidopa/ levodopa (SINEMET)	Levodopa (always combined with carbidopa) is the most effective treatment for motor symptoms of PD but gradual decline in responsiveness to levodopa is inevitable. It eventually stops working when most (dopamine-releasing) neurons in the substantia nigra have died. Although use of levodopa does **not** hasten the course of PD or make symptoms of PD worse, it does cause dyskinesias. When a PD patient displays tardive dyskinesia-like involuntary movements (e.g., choreiform arm movements, rocking, mouth/tongue movements, and grimacing), this is not a symptom of PD but rather a side effect of levodopa. Dopamine agonists (ropinirole, pramipexole, etc) are weaker than levodopa, making them less effective but also less likely to cause dyskinesias. The combination of levodopa with carbidopa (Sinemet) is a way to sneak dopamine into the brain. Dopamine (DA) itself cannot cross the blood brain barrier. Ingesting pure DA would produce no benefit, only nausea/vomiting and orthostatic hypotension. The body activates levodopa (L-dopa) to DA by decarboxylation. Carbidopa, which does not cross the blood-brain barrier, inhibits dopamine decarboxylase peripherally, allowing L-dopa to survive until it enters the brain to be decarboxylated (to dopamine). In addition to allowing enough L-dopa to reach the brain, carbidopa prevents unwanted peripheral effects of DA. Levodopa is effective for rigidity and bradykinesia (slowness), which are often the most debilitating symptoms of PD. It is not very effective for tremor. Levodopa initially works well for intervals of about 5–6 hours, which is referred to as "on time". After a few years, the duration of response to levodopa becomes progressively shorter, due to progressive neuronal death as is inevitable with PD. Episodes of immobility are referred to as "off time". Sudden decrease or discontinuation of levodopa can cause neuroleptic malignant syndrome.

Dopamine agonists	
Dopamine agonists bypass dysfunctional presynaptic DA neurons and directly activate DA receptors (mostly D2 receptors, the same receptors that antipsychotics block). DA agonists can be used as monotherapy before having to resort to levodopa, or adjunctively to levodopa later in the course of the disease. These "artificial dopamines" improve rigidity and bradykinesia, although less effectively than levodopa. Compared to levodopa, DA agonists are less likely to cause dyskinesia but more likely to cause hallucinations and delusions, especially in patients with dementia. DA agonists are well-known for causing compulsive behaviors such as gambling, spending, hypersexuality or excessive internet use. If compulsive behaviors arise, the DA agonist should be tapered, and the patient managed with levodopa. Yawning and sudden sleep attacks may occur with DA agonists. Withdrawal from DA agonists can include dysphoria, irritability and generalized pain. Antipsychotic medications counteract DA agonists, and vice versa. Like levodopa, DA agonists do not effectively alleviate tremors. Pergolide (Permax), a dopamine agonist used for many years, was withdrawn from the market in 2007 due to cardiac valve damage.	
Ropinirole (REQUIP) Pramipexole (MIRAPEX)	Widely used for PD and approved for restless legs syndrome (RLS). Reduces apathy in PD patients (especially pramipexole).
Rotigotine (NEUPRO)	Transdermal patch
Apomorphine (APOKYN)	Subcutaneous injection used as a rescue treatment for "off" episodes. Patients need to start a prophylactic antiemetic (trimethobenzamide, not ondansetron) at least 3 days before starting apomorphine due to the likelihood of vomiting. Apomorphine is also useful to treat neuroleptic malignant syndrome (NMS) that can result from abrupt withdrawal of levodopa.
Bromocriptine (PARLODEL)	Nonselective for D1 and D2 receptors; It can cause serious adverse effects and is no longer recommended for PD treatment. It can be used for treatment of hyperprolactinemia during pregnancy—otherwise cabergoline would be used for that indication.
Cabergoline (DOSTINEX)	Selective D2 agonist and 5-HT_{2B} receptor agonist. It is FDA-approved for hyperprolactinemia, not for PD. May damage heart valves.

MAO-B inhibitors	
Monoamine oxidase-B is one of the main enzymes responsible for metabolizing/deactivating DA in the nigrostriatal tract. The MAOIs used for Parkinson's disease are specific for blocking MAO-B, whereas those used for depression block bot MAO-A and MAO-B. Cannot be combined with L-DOPA due to risk of hypertensive crisis. Theoretically, MAO-B inhibitors can prevent further degeneration of DA by reducing free radical formation. At high doses they may inhibit MAO-A as well, which would predispose the patient to serotonin syndrome and hypertensive crisis from dietary tyramine.	
Selegiline (ELDEPRYL)	Irreversible MAO-B inhibitor. Its metabolism produces minute amounts of methamphetamine, which blocks dopamine reuptake and may provide antidepressant benefit. The oral formulation is approved for PD, while the transdermal patch is approved for depression.
Rasagiline (AZILECT)	Like selegiline, rasagiline is an irreversible MAO-B inhibitor that is metabolized to small amounts of methamphetamine.
Safinamide (XADAGO)	The only reversible MAOI available in the US. Much more selective for MAO-B (over MAO-A) than the other MAO-B inhibitors. It does not cause weight loss like selegiline and rasagiline.

COMT inhibitors	
Catechol-O-methyltransferase (COMT) degrades catecholamines (dopamine, epinephrine, and norepinephrine) and levodopa. When dopa decarboxylase (DDC) is blocked by carbidopa, COMT becomes the predominant metabolic pathway for L-dopa in the periphery (outside of the blood-brain barrier), thwarting L-dopa's journey into the brain. COMT inhibitors act peripherally (outside of the blood-brain barrier). They are added to levodopa/carbidopa in advanced disease.	
Entacapone (COMTAN)	The combination STALEVO combines levodopa with carbidopa and entacapone.
Tolcapone (TASMAR)	Risk of fatal hepatotoxicity

Anticholinergics	
Benztropine (COGENTIN) Trihexyphenidyl (ARTANE)	Both medications are approved for Parkinson's disease and extrapyramidal symptoms (EPS). Parkinsonian tremor is due to a relative deficiency of DA and an excess of acetylcholine in the nigrostriatal pathway. Although they can balance dopaminergic and cholinergic activity, anticholinergic medications are not geriatric-friendly. They may worsen cognitive functioning and cause delirium. They can help dry up excessive salivation associated with PD (due to decreased frequency of swallowing). Abrupt discontinuation can cause a severe exacerbation of symptoms.

Other medications for Parkinson's Disease	
Amantadine (SYMMETREL)	Amantadine increases dopaminergic activity, probably by increasing synthesis and release of DA. It also has anticholinergic effects and antagonizes NMDA receptors. Amantadine can be used as monotherapy early in the course of PD, providing a temporary modest improvement in tremor, rigidity, and bradykinesia. Later, it can ameliorate levodopa-induced dyskinesia.
Istradefylline (NOURIANZ)	Used in combination with levodopa/carbidopa for "off" episodes; similar to caffeine in structure (methylxanthine) and mechanism of action (adenosine receptor antagonist)
Rivastigmine (EXELON)	The only cholinesterase inhibitor approved for dementia of PD (mild/moderate). Donepezil (Aricept) and Galantamine (Razadyne) are approved for Alzheimer's but not PD. Rivastigmine inhibits both butyrylcholinesterase and acetylcholinesterase. Generally given as an Exelon transdermal patch.
Botulinum toxin (BOTOX)	Botox injection into salivary glands can be effective (off-label) for drooling related to decreased swallowing of saliva.

Deep brain stimulation (DBS)
DBS involves placement of a "brain pacemaker" (neurostimulator) in the bilateral subthalamic nucleus or globus pallidus. Motor function and dyskinesias improve, but not speech disturbance or cognitive problems. Not recommended for individuals over 70 or with cognitive impairment—can be worse after the procedure. Other indications for DBS include epilepsy, OCD, essential tremor, Tourette's disorder, tardive dystonia, and tardive dyskinesia.

Dopaminergics (PD meds) vs Antidopaminergics (antipsychotics)

Dopaminergic medications for Parkinson's disease (PD) are sort of the opposite of most antipsychotics, which are antidopaminergic. Potent dopamine-blocking antipsychotics such as haloperidol are essentially contraindicated in PD. Quetiapine (Seroquel) or clozapine (Clozaril) are OK but use low doses because patients with PD (and Lewy body dementia) are highly sensitive to antipsychotics.

The nigrostriatal tract, as its name suggests, is a dopaminergic pathway from the substantia nigra ("black substance") to the striatum ("stripe"). The nigrostriatal tract is the major component of the extrapyramidal motor system. For context, this is where extrapyramidal symptoms (EPS) arise when caused by antipsychotic medication.

As PD progresses, nearly all presynaptic neurons in the nigrostriatal tract degenerate, making levodopa ineffective. In contrast, the postsynaptic neurons remain intact and are able to respond to DA and DA agonists.

With several exceptions, the effectiveness of antipsychotics depends on the ability to block D2 receptors. Clozapine and quetiapine bind more strongly to D1 than D2 receptors.

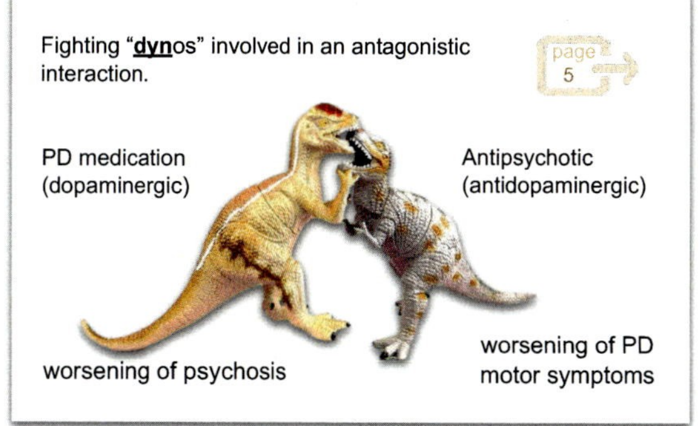

Giving levodopa at the same time as a D2 blocking antipsychotic will increase DA concentration, but the DA will not stimulate its receptors. The excess DA may over stimulate DA receptors elsewhere to produce/exacerbate psychosis.

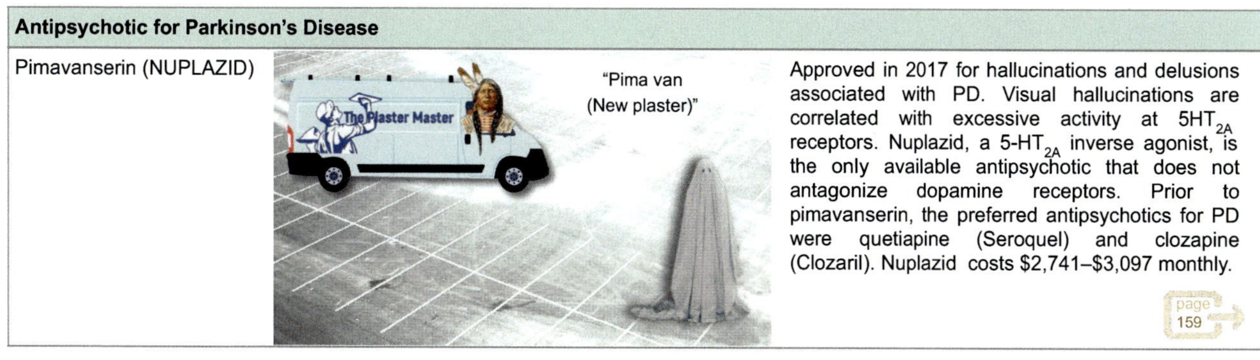

Antipsychotic for Parkinson's Disease		
Pimavanserin (NUPLAZID)	"Pima van (New plaster)"	Approved in 2017 for hallucinations and delusions associated with PD. Visual hallucinations are correlated with excessive activity at $5HT_{2A}$ receptors. Nuplazid, a $5\text{-}HT_{2A}$ inverse agonist, is the only available antipsychotic that does not antagonize dopamine receptors. Prior to pimavanserin, the preferred antipsychotics for PD were quetiapine (Seroquel) and clozapine (Clozaril). Nuplazid costs $2,741–$3,097 monthly. page 159

PD drug mechanisms in context of other psychotropics

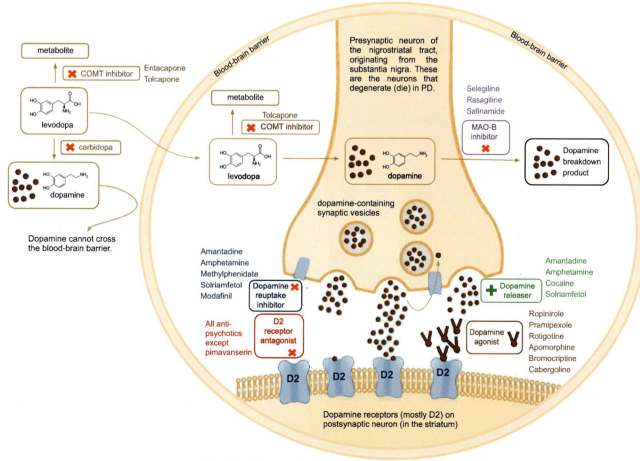

metabolite
COMT inhibitor — Entacapone, Tolcapone
levodopa
carbidopa
dopamine
Dopamine cannot cross the blood-brain barrier.

Blood-brain barrier

Presynaptic neuron of the nigrostriatal tract, originating from the substantia nigra. These are the neurons that degenerate (die) in PD.

metabolite
Tolcapone — COMT inhibitor
levodopa
dopamine
Selegiline, Rasagiline, Safinamide — MAO-B inhibitor
Dopamine breakdown product

dopamine-containing synaptic vesicles

Amantadine, Amphetamine, Methylphenidate, Solriamfetol, Modafinil — Dopamine reuptake inhibitor

All anti-psychotics except pimavanserin — D2 receptor antagonist

Amantadine, Amphetamine, Cocaine, Solriamfetol — Dopamine releaser

Ropinirole, Pramipexole, Rotigotine, Apomorphine, Bromocriptine, Cabergoline — Dopamine agonist

D2 D2 D2 D2

Dopamine receptors (mostly D2) on postsynaptic neuron (in the striatum)

#175
1971
$11–$56

Carbidopa – Levodopa (SINEMET)

KAR bi DOE pa - LEE voe DOE pa / SIN e met

"Dopey Cinema"

❖ Parkinson's Tx
❖ Dopaminergic

C/L
10/100
25/100
25/250
mg

FDA-approved for:
❖ Parkinsonism

Used off-label for:
❖ Dopamine-responsive dystonia
❖ Sleep-related eating disorder
❖ Restless legs syndrome
❖ Amblyopia

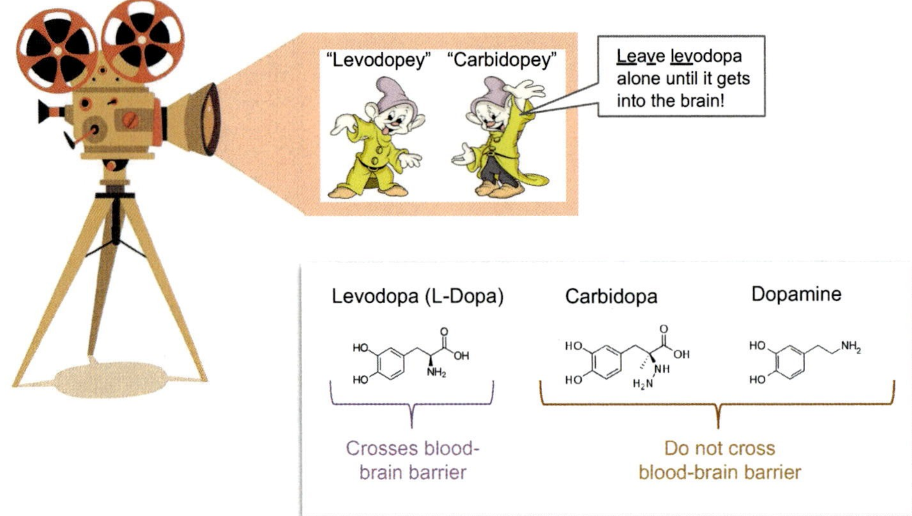

The involuntary movements of Parkinson's disease (PD) result from degeneration of dopaminergic neurons in the substantia nigra. Dopamine (DA) replacement can relieve parkinsonism, but DA cannot cross the blood-brain barrier (BBB). The medication levodopa (L-DOPA) crosses the BBB and is changed to DA by decarboxylase enzymes. Sinemet combines L-dopa with carbidopa, which inhibits decarboxylase in peripheral tissues, thus allowing L-DOPA to hang around long enough to pass the BBB. Without carbidopa, L-dopa would need to be dosed so high that peripheral side effects (nausea, orthostatic hypotension) would be problematic. The name Sinemet derives from "*sin emesis*" (without vomiting). Carbidopa prevents dopamine-induced emesis because the vomiting center in the brain stem is one of the few brain areas outside of the blood-brain barrier.

Levodopa is the most effective treatment for Parkinson's disease, and it continues to work until almost all nigrostriatal tract neurons degenerate and the remaining neurons can no longer synthesize/store/release dopamine. It works well for about 5 years, after which the duration of benefit becomes shorter and shorter, with patients eventually developing dyskinesias (involuntary choreiform movements) and unpredictable episodes of immobility. Some neurologists postpone treatment with Sinemet by using a different pro-DA medication first. Others use Sinemet first and for as long as possible before adding dopamine agonists.

Sinemet must not be discontinued abruptly due to risk of neuroleptic malignant syndrome (NMS), which can be fatal. This variation of NMS is sometimes referred to as "dopaminergic malignant syndrome" or "withdrawal-emergent hyperpyrexia and confusion", to distinguish it from NMS caused by actual neuroleptics (antipsychotics).

When starting treatment, side effects include nausea/vomiting, loss of appetite and orthostatic hypotension. Side effects arising later may late include agitation, hallucinations, psychosis, and hypersexual behavior—as would be expected with excess DA activity.

Supplemental carbidopa pills (without levodopa) are available as an adjunct for patients developing nausea on Sinemet, since the nausea is attributable to too much peripheral dopamine.

Carbidopa/levodopa is available as enteral suspension (DUOPA) for advanced PD. The medication is pumped into the jejunum through a percutaneous endoscopic gastrostomy with a jejunal tube (PEG-J) over a 16-hour infusion period daily, with extra doses available for "off" episodes.

Carbidopa/levodopa is approved for restless legs syndrome (RLS) in Europe. Dopaminergic drugs are beneficial for most patients with RLS. However, dopaminergics can cause drug-induced "augmentation" (worsening) of symptoms, including possible spreading restlessness to arms/trunk. If augmentation occurs, gradual tapering of the offending dopaminergic is better tolerated than sudden withdrawal (Rosenstein et al, 2015). "Rebound" recurrence of restlessness can also occur with dopaminergic treatment of RLS. Augmentation and rebound of RLS occurs more commonly with levodopa compared to dopamine agonists like ropinirole (Requip) and pramipexole (Mirapex).

Dosing: The usual range for Parkinson's disease is 300–1500 mg/day divided into 3 or 4 doses; More frequent dosing of up to 6 divided doses/day may be needed as the "wearing-off" phenomenon progresses; Maximum daily dose is 2,000 mg of levodopa; Regarding carbidopa, 70–100 mg/day is needed to saturate peripheral DA decarboxylase and minimize adverse effects; Some patients may require up to 200 mg of carbidopa daily. For conditions other than Parkinson's diseases, lower doses of levodopa/carbidopa are utilized.

Dynamic interactions:

❖ Antagonistic effects if combined with antipsychotic medications, which decrease DA activity
❖ Hypertensive crisis if combined with non-selective MAOI antidepressants (phenelzine, tranylcypromine, isocarboxazid)
❖ Additive hypotensive effects with blood pressure medications

page 18

Kinetic interactions:

❖ Carbidopa is added to L-dopa to produce a strategic kinetic interaction, allowing L-dopa to get into the CNS.
❖ Concomitant intake of large protein loads (amino acids) will compete with transport of L-dopa into the brain.
❖ Otherwise, Sinemet is not involved in kinetic interactions (in a bubble)

#111 1997 $5–$54 $25–$78 ER	**Ropinirole (REQUIP)** roe PIN uh roll / REE qwip "Rope in a roll (to) Re-equip"	❖ Dopamine agonist	2 ER, 4, 6, 8, 12 mg	0.25, 0.5, 1, 2, 3, 4, 5 mg

FDA-approved for:
- ❖ Parkinson's disease
- ❖ Restless legs syndrome

Used off-label for:
- ❖ Sleep-related eating disorder
- ❖ REM sleep behavior disorder
- ❖ Augmentation of antidepressants

Ropinirole (Requip) is approved for the treatment of both early (without levodopa) and advanced (with levodopa) Parkinson's disease (PD). It was the first drug approved for restless legs syndrome (2005).

Ropinirole is a D2 agonist, i.e., it stimulates the same receptors that antipsychotics block. It also binds D3 receptors. For context, the other mention of D3 receptors in this book was with cariprazine (Vraylar), the antipsychotic that works as a D3 receptor partial agonist. With cariprazine, D3 partial agonism may help negative symptoms of schizophrenia and provide possible procognitive benefits.

Side effects may include nausea (40%), vomiting (10%), postural hypotension (13%), dizziness (5%), and fatigue (5%). Excessive daytime sleepiness may occur with Parkinson's patients, but the risk with ropinirole is < 2%. Like other dopamine agonists, ropinirole can cause compulsive behaviors (pathologic gambling, hypersexuality), hallucinations, confusion, or psychosis. Psychiatric symptoms are less likely when used for treatment of RLS (evening dosing only) compared to treatment of PD (TID dosing).

Syncope, sometimes associated with bradycardia, has occurred in about 12% of patients with early disease, usually associated with an increase in dosage. In advanced disease being treated with levodopa, syncope has occurred in about 3% of patients taking ropinirole.

Ropinirole reaches peak concentration 1–2 hours after ingestion. Half-life is about 6 hours.

Dosing: For Parkinson's disease, start at 0.25 mg TID and titrated upward in 0.25 mg increments over 4 weeks to 1 mg TID; Maximum dose is 8 mg TID; For restless legs syndrome, start 0.25 mg q PM x 2 days, then may increase to 0.5 mg q PM x 5 days, then may increase by 0.5 mg/day in weekly intervals until 3 mg PO q PM is reached; After one week at 3 mg, may increase to 4 mg HS (maximum); For RLS, it should be taken 1–3 hours before bedtime; Taper gradually to stop.

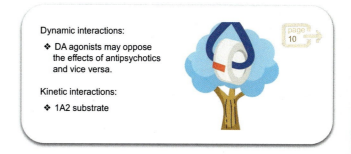

Dynamic interactions:
- ❖ DA agonists may oppose the effects of antipsychotics and vice versa.

Kinetic interactions:
- ❖ 1A2 substrate

page 10

Restless Legs Syndrome (RLS)

This single question has nearly 100% sensitivity and 97% specificity for diagnosis of RLS (Ferri et al, 2007): "When you try to relax in the evening or sleep at night, do you ever have unpleasant, restless feelings in your legs that can be relieved by walking movement?"

RLS has a circadian pattern with peak symptoms in the evening or night. There are many possible causes, including iron deficiency. Check ferritin level, and if < 50 ng/mL, supplement with ferrous sulfate 325 mg BID. Consider adding vitamin C (ascorbic acid) 500 mg BID to enhance iron absorption.

In patients with bipolar disorder or schizophrenia, dopamine agonists should probably be avoided due to risk of psychosis. Other medications used for RLS include benzodiazepines, gabapentin (Neurontin) and pregabalin (Lyrica).

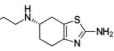

#204
1997
$5–$65

Pramipexole (MIRAPEX)

pram i PEX ole / MIR a pex

"Pray (to) my pecs Off / Mirror pecs"

❖ Dopamine agonist

0.125
0.25
0.5
0.75
1
1.5 mg

FDA-approved for:

❖ Parkinson's disease
❖ Restless legs syndrome

Used off-label for:

❖ Sleep-related eating disorder
❖ REM sleep behavior disorder
❖ Augmentation of antidepressants

Most of the info from the ropinirole monograph (preceding page) is applicable to pramipexole. Pramipexole (Mirapex) was approved for Parkinson's disease (PD) in 1997 and for restless legs syndrome (RLS) in 2006.

Serum concentrations peak in about two hours, and it has a half-life of about 10 hours.

Hallucinations are more common with pramipexole (than with ropinirole), occurring in about 10% of patients with early PD and 20% of those with advanced disease.

Symptomatic orthostatic hypotension is uncommon with pramipexole, an advantage over ropinirole. The most common side effects for pramipexole (at RLS dosing) are nausea (16%) and somnolence (6%).

Addition of pramipexole to an SSRI or SNRI can enhance antidepressant efficacy (Cusin et al, 2013).

PD patients taking levodopa and/or dopamine agonists show improvement of apathy. In a head-to-head comparison, improvement of apathy scores with pramipexole was significantly better than with ropinirole and levodopa (Perez-Perez, 2015).

In rats, pramipexole protects against brain damage caused by methamphetamine (Sethy et al, 1997). Bromocriptine, another dopamine agonist, demonstrated this neuroprotective effect also.

Dosing: For Parkinson's disease, start at 0.125 mg TID; May gradually increase to 0.5 mg TID over 3 weeks; FDA maximum dose is 4.5 mg/day but there is minimal additional benefit and more side effects above 1.5 mg/day; For restless legs syndrome, start: 0.125 mg q PM, may increase by 0.125 mg/day in 4–7 day intervals; Max 0.5 mg/day; Give 2–3 hours before bedtime; To augment an antidepressant, start pramipexole low (0.125–0.25 mg/day) and increase by 0.25 mg every week as needed; Taper dose gradually to discontinue.

Dynamic interactions:

❖ DA agonists may oppose the effects of antipsychotics and vice versa.

Kinetic interactions:

❖ Few because it is excreted in the urine unchanged - "in a box"
❖ Cimetidine (Tagamet) increases pramipexole levels by 50% by inhibiting renal secretion

page 18

2004
$1,048

Apomorphine (APOKYN)

a poe MOR feen / uh POE kyne

Ape 'mophin (into) A Poké

❖ Dopamine agonist

10 mg/mL

FDA-approved for:

❖ Acute intermittent hypomobility of Parkinson's disease
❖ Restless legs syndrome

Used off-label for:

❖ Reversal of neuroleptic malignant syndrome (NMS) precipitated by abrupt discontinuation of levodopa
❖ Erectile dysfunction

Apomorphine (Apokyn) is a potent dopamine agonist, administered <u>subcutaneously for rescue treatment of "off" episodes</u> of Parkinson's disease (PD). Since it is an injection, an alternate mnemonic is "<u>Ape went a' pokin'</u>". It activates D2 receptors, and to a much lesser extent, D1 receptors. It is also a 5-HT_2 serotonin receptor antagonist and α-adrenergic antagonist.

Contrary to its name, apomorphine does not contain morphine or its skeleton, nor does it bind to opioid receptors. Historically, apomorphine was made by boiling morphine in acid. The apo- prefix means "from".

Patients need to start a <u>prophylactic antiemetic</u> at least 3 days before starting apomorphine due to the likelihood of vomiting, though tolerance to this side effect can eventually develop. <u>Trimethobenzamide (Tigan)</u> has a niche for treatment/prevention of nausea caused by apomorphine. Trimethobenzamide has weaker antidopaminergic activity than prochlorperazine (Compazine) or metoclopramide (Reglan), so it is less likely to block the effect of apomorphine or worsen symptoms of PD. Ondansetron (Zofran), our usual go-to antiemetic, is contraindicated with apomorphine because the combination can cause severe hypotension.

Apomorphine can <u>rapidly reverse neuroleptic malignant syndrome (NMS) precipitated by abrupt withdrawal of levodopa</u>.

Like oral dopamine agonists, apomorphine can cause nausea, orthostatic hypotension, confusion, hallucinations, and psychosis. Yawning and drowsiness are common. Hypersexuality and frequent erections have happened.

Dynamic interactions:

❖ DA agonists may oppose the effects of antipsychotics and vice versa.
❖ Antiserotonergic - may cause profound hypotension in combination with ondansetron (Zofran)

Kinetic interactions:

❖ Unlikely to participate in clinically significant kinetic interactions - "in a bubble"

page 18

2007
$669–$818

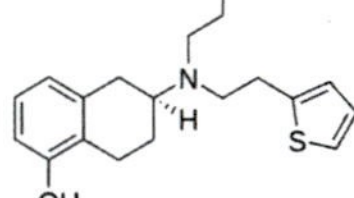

Rotigotine (NEUPRO)

roe TIG oh teen / NEW pro

"New pro Rotisserie - Rote' a goat"

❖ Dopamine agonist

1
2
3
4
6
8
mg

FDA-approved for:

❖ Parkinson's disease
❖ Restless legs syndrome

New Pro Rotisserie

Restless legs

Rotigotine (Neupro) is the transdermal dopamine agonist for the treatment of Parkinson's disease (PD) and restless legs syndrome (RLS).

It was originally released in 2007, withdrawn from the market in 2008 (faulty patches), and re-released in 2012.

Oral dopamine agonists are dosed several times a day, possibly causing pulsatile dopamine stimulation. Theoretically, a constant stream of medication release from the patch could decrease the "wearing-off" effect, or prevent development of dyskinesia.

In treatment of RLS, rotigotine was found equally effective as gabapentin ER (Neurontin) and pregabalin (Lyrica).

Dosing: <u>For early stage Parkinson's disease (PD)</u>, maintenance dose is 4–6 mg/24 hr patch (starting with 2 mg patch); <u>For advanced stage PD</u>, start with 4 mg patch, with maintenance dose of 4–8 mg; <u>For restless legs syndrome</u> (RLS), start with 1 mg/24 hr patch, with max of 3 mg/24 hr; Taper to discontinue (by 2 mg QOD for PD and by 1 mg QOD for RLS)

Dynamic interactions:

❖ DA agonists may oppose the effects of antipsychotics and vice versa.

Kinetic interactions:

❖ Unlikely to participate in clinically significant kinetic interactions - "in a bubble"

page 18

Bromocriptine (PARLODEL)

1975
$46–$135

BROE moe KRIP teen / PAR lo del
"Bromance Parlor"

❖ Dopamine agonist (D1, D2)

2.5 mg

FDA-approved for:

❖ Acromegaly
❖ Hyperprolactinemia
❖ Parkinson's disease

Bromocriptine (Parlodel) is an older dopamine agonist. It is a semi-synthetic derivative of a natural ergot alkaloid (from ergot fungus). The other two ergot dopamine agonists, cabergoline (Dostinex) and pergolide (Permax), may damage heart valves. Bromocriptine does not. Pergolide was removed from the market, and cabergoline is approved for hyperprolactinemia but not for Parkinson's disease (PD).

Due to serious risks and side effects, bromocriptine is no longer recommended for the treatment of PD. Bromocriptine is used during pregnancy for treating hyperprolactinemia —otherwise cabergoline (Dostinex) is the preferred hyperprolactinemia treatment because of its effectiveness and tolerability.

As with other dopamine agonists, bromocriptine may cause compulsive behaviors/impulse control disorders including pathological gambling, compulsive shopping, binge eating, kleptomania, and compulsive sexual behavior. Abrupt discontinuation of bromocriptine can precipitate neuroleptic malignant syndrome (NMS).

DA agonists:

- ▶ Ropinirole (REQUIP)
- ▶ Pramipexole (MIRAPEX)
- ▶ Bromocriptine (PARLODEL)
- ▶ Rotigotine (NEUPRO)
- ▶ Apomorphine (APOKYN)
- ▶ Cabergoline (DOSTINEX)

Dynamic interactions:
❖ May oppose the effects of antipsychotics and vice versa

Kinetic interactions:
❖ 3A4 substrate

page 16

Cabergoline (DOSTINEX)

2005
$45–$258

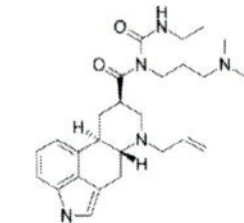

ca BER goe leen / DOS tin ex
"Cabbage goal line is Doused next'"

❖ Dopamine agonist (D2)
❖ $5\text{-}HT_{2B}$ receptor agonist

0.5 mg

Not for Parkinson's disease

FDA-approved for:

❖ Hyperprolactinemia

Hyperprolactinemia

Causes include:
- ▶ Pituitary prolactinoma
- ▶ Antipsychotics

Elevated prolactin levels can cause:
- ▶ Gynecomastia
- ▶ Galactorrhea
- ▶ Amenorrhea
- ▶ Decreased libido
- ▶ Inhibition of orgasm in women

Antipsychotics increase prolactin by D2 blockade. Common culprits include risperidone, paliperidone, and the FGAs. Antipsychotics that do *not* increase prolactin include aripiprazole, brexpiprazole, cariprazine, clozapine, lurasidone, and ziprasidone.

Cabergoline (Dostinex) is a long-acting dopamine agonist FDA-approved for treatment of hyperprolactinemia. Pituitary microadenoma (prolactinoma) can cause hyperprolactinemia, or it can be idiopathic. Cabergoline is preferred over bromocriptine (Parlodel) because it is more effective and better tolerated.

Cabergoline is a selective D2 dopamine agonist that inhibits prolactin secreting cells in the pituitary gland. Bromocriptine has more side effects because it also blocks D1 receptors.

Long-term use of cabergoline can cause cardiac valve abnormalities because it stimulates $5\text{-}HT_{2B}$ serotonin receptors. This is the same mechanism of heart valve damage for which the appetite suppressant fenfluramine was removed from the market.

Frequent side effects of cabergoline include gastrointestinal distress, headache, and dizziness. Bromocriptine has similar side effects, but to a greater extent.

Duration of treatment is indefinite, because hyperprolactinemia is expected to return upon discontinuation. Surgical removal of a pituitary prolactinoma has a high rate of recurrence and is generally not recommended.

Cabergoline is generally not recommended for treatment of antipsychotic-induced hyperprolactinemia due to health risks, side effects, and opposing mechanism of action that could render the antipsychotic (D2 blocker) ineffective. If elevated prolactin is problematic, the antipsychotic should be changed to aripiprazole, brexpiprazole, cariprazine, clozapine, lurasidone or ziprasidone.

Because cabergoline has a long half-life, it is dosed twice weekly.

Dynamic interactions:
❖ DA agonists may oppose the effects of antipsychotics and vice versa

Kinetic interactions:
❖ In a bubble - unlikely to participate in clinically significant kinetic interactions

1998
$90–$439

Entacapone (COMTAN)

en TAK a pone / COMT an

"Compton into Capone"

❖ COMT inhibitor

200 mg

FDA-approved for:

❖ Parkinson's disease, adjunct to carbidopa/levodopa

American gangster Al Capone, aka "Scarface" meets Straight Outta Compton by N.W.A. (Dr. Dre, et al)

3-O-methyl dopa

catechol-O-methyl transferase (COMT) — ✖ COMT inhibitor — Entacapone, Tolcapone

levodopa

Dopa decarboxylase — ✖ carbidopa

dopamine

COMT — ✖ COMT inhibitor — Entacapone, Tolcapone

3-methoxy tyramine

Entacapone (COMTan) is a COMT antagonist, i.e., an inhibitor of catechol-O-methyltransferase. Entacapone is used as an adjunct to carbidopa/levodopa to keep levodopa and dopamine around longer and reduce motor fluctuations ("wearing-off" phenomenon) of Parkinson's disease (PD). Entacapone's effect on COMT is in the periphery (outside of CNS).

Side effects may include dyskinesia, nausea, diarrhea (less so than tolcapone), somnolence, and discoloration of urine. Hypertension, tachycardia, and arrhythmias are possible. It does not cause liver toxicity. Duration of action is only 2 hours.

STALEVO is a fixed-dose combination of carbidopa/levodopa/entacapone.

Dosing: Give 200 mg with each dose of carbidopa/levodopa; Max is 1,600 mg/day.

Dynamic interactions:
- ❖ CNS depression
- ❖ Contraindicated with nonselective MAOIs

Kinetic interactions:
- ❖ In a bubble - unlikely to participate in clinically significant kinetic interactions

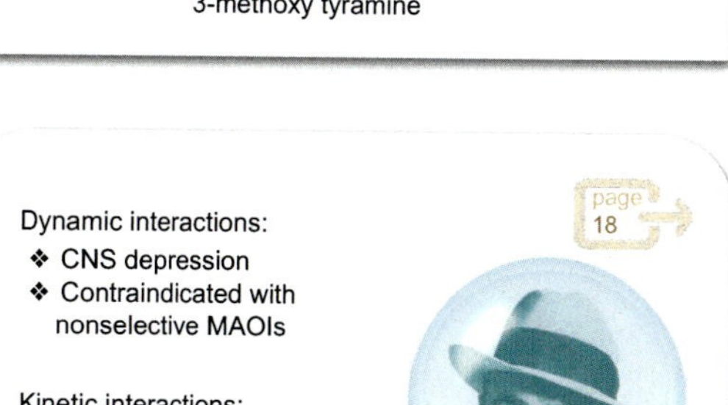
page 18

1998
$2,318–$4,469

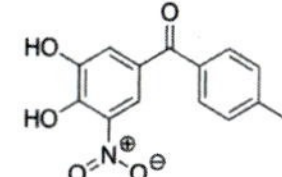

Tolcapone (TASMAR)

TOLE ka pone / TAS mar

"Total Capone Taskbar"

❖ COMT inhibitor

100 mg

FDA-approved for:

❖ Parkinson's disease, adjunct to carbidopa/levodopa

Tolcapone (Tasmar) is a second-line COMT inhibitor available for the treatment of PD as an adjunct to carbidopa/levodopa. Unlike entacapone, tolcapone crosses the blood-brain barrier to work in the CNS, making it more effective than entacapone. Tolcapone is reserved for patients with normal liver function, who have not responded to entacapone. Use of tolcapone requires written informed consent and monitoring of liver enzymes every 2–4 weeks for at least 6 months.

Tolcapone is more likely to cause diarrhea than entacapone, but otherwise has similar side effects. A major disadvantage of tolcapone is the risk of fatal hepatotoxicity.

Dosing: Start 100 mg TID; Max is 200 mg TID; Does not need to be taken at same time as levodopa/carbidopa; Discontinue within 3 weeks if no benefit.

COMT genetic polymorphisms

The gene encoding the COMT enzyme has common variants that affect an individual's risk of developing schizophrenia, performance on tests of working memory and executive functioning, subjective sensation of reward/well-being from a wide variety of daily events, novelty seeking, extroversion/introversion, and neurotic personality traits. COMT is one of the pharmacodynamic gene variations reported by the Genecept Assay as involved in response to stimulants.

Dynamic interactions:
- ❖ CNS depression
- ❖ Contraindicated with nonselective MAOIs

Kinetic interactions:
- ❖ In a bubble - unlikely to participate in clinically significant kinetic interactions

page 18

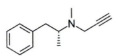

1989
$41–$150

Selegiline PO (ELDEPRYL)

se LE ji leen / ELD e pril

"Elderly Seal's gills"

- Monoamine Oxidase Inhibitor
- Irreversible
- MAO-B > MAO-A
- DA > NE > 5-HT

5 mg

FDA-approved for:

- Parkinson's disease, adjunctive treatment

Selegiline is an irreversible inhibitor of monoamine oxidase type B (MAO-B). The "Sel" is for selective, as in selective for MAO-B—"*B for bradykinesia*" versus "*A for affect, anhedonia or agony*".

As Parkinson's disease (PD) progresses, dopamine levels decrease, leading to an increase in motor dysfunction. Most monoamine oxidase in the brain is type B. By Inhibiting MAO-B in the striatum, dopamine levels increase and motor dysfunction decreases.

When added to levodopa in advanced PD, selegiline can allow levodopa to be used at lower doses. When used off-label as monotherapy in early PD, selegiline can delay the need to initiate levodopa/carbidopa.

The maximum daily dose is 10 mg, given as 5 mg BID. If taken above the maximum recommended dose, MAO-A of the gut is inhibited, and the patient is at risk of hypertensive crisis if tyramine rich foods are consumed.

Metabolism of selegiline produces minute amounts of methamphetamine, which blocks dopamine reuptake and may provide antidepressant benefits. The methamphetamine metabolite may produce a "false" positive on drug screens. Selegiline is not a controlled substance.

Selegiline is associated with weight loss, as would be expected for something metabolized to an amphetamine.

Selegiline is available as a transdermal patch (EMSAM), FDA-approved for treatment of depression.

Dosing: 5 mg BID is the target and max dose; Give with breakfast and lunch

selegiline   methamphetamine

Selegiline transdermal (EMSAM)

The transdermal formulation of selegiline, approved for depression, allows high enough levels of selegiline to inhibit MAO-A. This is necessary for antidepressant effects.

Dynamic interactions

- Dopaminergic
- Serotonergic (weak with PO route)
- Blocks dietary tyramine breakdown (mild)
- May intensify anticholinergic effects of other medications
- Hypertensive effects

Kinetic interactions

- 2B6 substrate

page 12

2B6 substrate (sock)

Monoamine Oxidase Inhibitor (MAOI)	Use	Year	Cost/ mo	5-HT	NE	DA	MAO selectivity*	Dietary tyramine risk	Wt gain	Sed-ation	Anti-cholin ergic	Rever sible?
Phenelzine (NARDIL)	MDD	1961	$43	+++	+++	+++	A & B	+++++	++	low	no	no
Tranylcypromine (PARNATE)	MDD	1961	$240	+++	+++	+++	A & B	+++++	no	low	no	no
Isocarboxazid (MARPLAN)	MDD	1959	$780	+++	+++	+++	A & B	+++++	-	low	no	no
Selegiline transdermal (EMSAM)	MDD	2006	$1650	++	++	+++	(A) & B	++	loss	low	no	no
Selegiline PO (ELDEPRYL)	Parkinson's	1989	$26	++	++	+++	B	+	loss	low	no	no
Rasagiline (AZILECT)	Parkinson's	2006	$270	++	++	+++	B	+	loss	low	no	no
Safinamide (XADAGO)	Parkinson's	2017	$780	+	+	+++	B	+/-	-	low	no	Yes

MDD - Major Depressive Disorder; 5-HT - serotonergic; NE - noradrenergic; DA - dopaminergic

* Selectivity is dose-dependent. At above recommended doses, selective MAO-B inhibitors can start inhibiting MAO-A also.

2012
$216–$564

Rasagiline (AZILECT)

ras AJ il een/ AZE i lect

"Raise a lean Aztec"

- ❖ MAOI for Parkinson's
- ❖ Monoamine Oxidase Inhibitor
- ❖ Selective for MAO-B
- ❖ Reversible

0.5
1
mg

FDA-approved for:

- ❖ Parkinson's disease

Rasagiline is used to treat symptoms of Parkinson's as monotherapy or in combination with other drugs. It is effective for both early and advanced Parkinson's disease (PD). It is selective for MAO-B over MAO-A by a factor of 14.

As PD progresses, dopamine (DA) levels decrease, causing an increase in motor dysfunction. The "on" state is when levodopa is working. "Off" episodes are when the effects of levodopa have worn off and bradykinesia/dystonia are acutely problematic. MAO-B inhibitors reduce the "off" motor fluctuations. Inhibiting MAO-B increases DA in the striatum.

Rasagiline is especially useful in dealing with Parkinson's related fatigue, because it is partly metabolized to methamphetamine. However, it is not a controlled substance. Weight loss is likely while on rasagiline (lean Aztec).

The label warns of a risk of serotonin syndrome if combined with antidepressants. This risk is extremely low (Stocchi et al, 2015).

Dietary restriction of tyramine is unnecessary at recommended doses. If the recommended dose is exceeded, hypertensive crisis from tyramine rich foods is possible.

Start 0.5 mg QD; Max dose is 1 mg QD; taper to stop

Dynamic interactions:

- ❖ Caution is advised when combining with serotonergics or dopaminergics, many of which are contraindicated

Kinetic interactions:

- ❖ 1A2 substrate

1A2 Substrate

page 10

2017
$776–$928

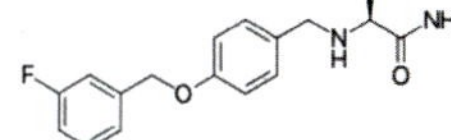

Safinamide (XADAGO)

sa FIN a mide / za DA go

"dopamine (DA) goes (in the) fin safe"

- ❖ MAOI for Parkinson's
- ❖ Monoamine Oxidase Inhibitor
- ❖ Selective for MAO-B
- ❖ Reversible

50
100
mg

FDA-approved for:

- ❖ Parkinson's disease, adjunctive treatment

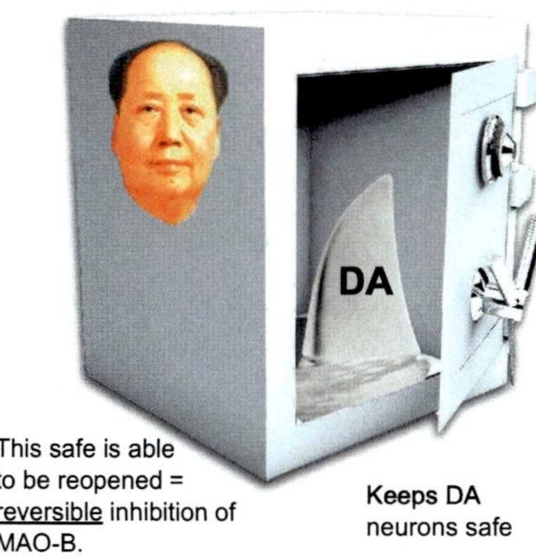

This safe is able to be reopened = reversible inhibition of MAO-B.

Keeps DA neurons safe

Released in 2017, Xadago is the first reversible MAOI available in the US. Xadago is FDA-approved as an adjunct to levodopa/carbidopa (Sinemet) for managing "off" episodes of Parkinson's disease (PD). Xadago is much more selective for MAO-B than selegiline (Eldepryl) or rasagiline (Azilect). Unlike the other MAO-B inhibitors (selegiline and rasagiline), Xadago is not approved as monotherapy.

Xadago is highly dopaminergic and mildly serotonergic. It also serves as a neuroprotectant by inhibiting glutamate release from neurons. This could theoretically prevent further degeneration of DA neurons. It causes neither weight loss nor weight gain.

Dyskinesia is the most common adverse effect of safinamide at about 20%. At higher than recommended doses, safinamide loses its selectivity for MAO-B and can put patients at risk for a hypertensive crisis if tyramine-rich food is consumed. Xadago can cause impulsive and hypersexual behavior, and can exacerbate psychosis if given to an individual with schizophrenia.

In overdose, safinamide may cause mydriasis (pupil dilatation) and blood pressure disturbance (either hypertension or hypotension).

Dosing: Start: 50 mg QD x 2 weeks, then may increase to the max dose of 100 mg QD; To stop, taper over 1 week.

Dynamic interactions:

- ❖ Caution is advised when combining with serotonergics or dopaminergics, many of which are contraindicated.

Kinetic interactions:

- ❖ Unlikely to participate in clinically significant kinetic interactions — "in a bubble"

page 18

1966
$11–$75

NH_2

A<u>man</u>tadine (SYMMETREL)

a MAN ta deen / SIM i trel

"Symmetrical man to dine"

- ❖ Anti-Parkinson agent
- ❖ NMDA antagonist
- ❖ Dopaminergic

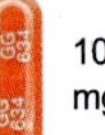

100 mg

FDA-approved for:

- ❖ Extrapyramidal symptoms (EPS)
- ❖ Parkinsonism
- ❖ Influenza A (not used because most strains are resistant)

Used off-label for:

- ❖ Fatigue of multiple sclerosis
- ❖ Cognitive problems post brain injury
- ❖ Neuroleptic malignant syndrome (NMS)
- ❖ Sexual dysfunction
- ❖ Antipsychotic-associated weight gain
- ❖ Antipsychotic-induced hyperprolactinemia
- ❖ Treatment-resistant depression
- ❖ ADHD
- ❖ OCD

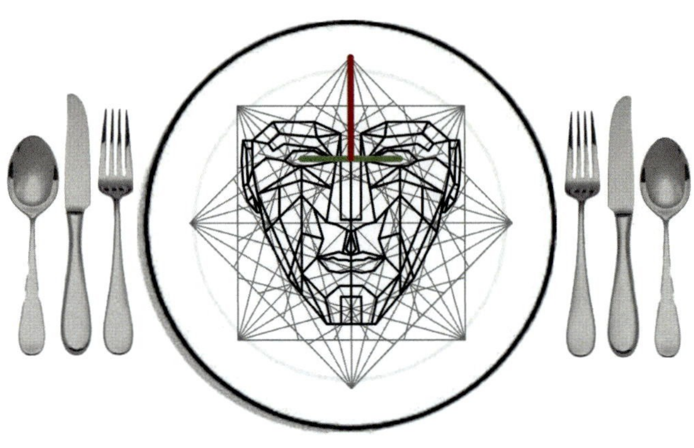

Antipsychotics lower dopamine (DA) activity. Extrapyramidal symptoms are caused by a relative deficiency of DA and an excess of acetylcholine in the nigrostriatal pathway. The anticholinergics diphenhydramine (Benadryl), benztropine (Cogentin), and trihexyphenidyl (Artane) relieve EPS by opposing acetylcholine activity. By contrast, amantadine (Symmetrel) primarily <u>relieves EPS by enhancing DA activity</u>. Although the mechanism is not well understood, amantadine probably increases synthesis and release of DA.

While anticholinergics worsen tardive dyskinesia (TD), amantadine has been shown to <u>improve TD</u>. Amantadine is useful for treatment of EPS when the anticholinergic side of effects of Benadryl, Cogentin, or Artane cannot be tolerated (e.g., due to dry mouth, constipation, confusion, or vision problems). Amantadine is only <u>moderately anticholinergic</u>. The other three choices for treatment of EPS are highly anticholinergic. Amantadine has the added benefit of <u>countering antipsychotic-induced weight gain and hyperprolactinemia</u>. Theoretically, amantadine could worsen psychosis by dopaminergic effects, but this problem is rarely encountered.

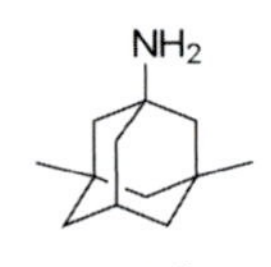

memantine

Note the structural similarity to memantine (Namenda), which is FDA-approved for moderate to severe Alzheimer's dementia.

Amantadine is used as monotherapy in early Parkinson's disease (PD) and as an adjunct in later stages, usually for patients with levodopa-induced dyskinesia. Amantadine may be effective in controlling PD tremor, which is often resistant to levodopa. Unfortunately, for some PD patients the benefit lasts only a few weeks.

Amantadine is structurally related to me<u>mant</u>ine (Namenda). Both may enhance cognition, but a<u>mant</u>adine has more potential risks and side effects. Amantadine may cause loss of appetite, nausea, dizziness, insomnia, confusion, hallucinations, <u>edema</u>, and livedo reticularis (purplish red, net-like, blotchy spots on skin). <u>Congestive heart failure</u> is possible with chronic therapy.

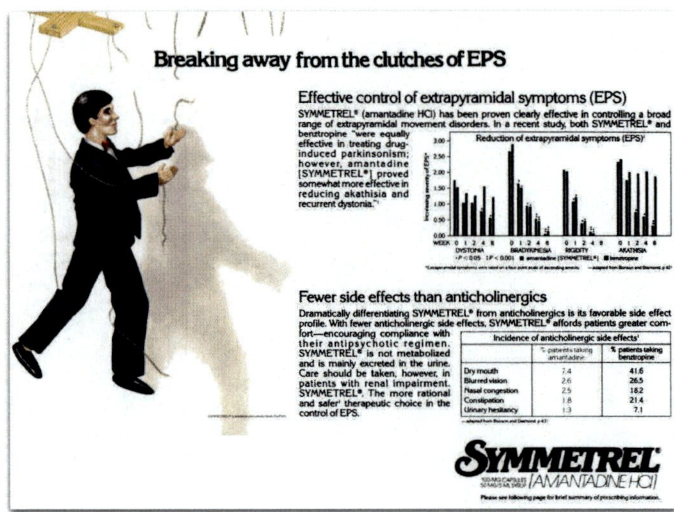

Like memantine, amantadine is a weak NMDA receptor antagonist. Additionally, amantadine increases dopamine (DA) release. It is the dopaminergic effect that makes amantadine useful for treatment of parkinsonism, EPS, and NMS (all of which are caused by DA deficiency or DA blockade). Dopaminergic side effects of amantadine can include hallucinations and <u>compulsive behaviors</u> such as gambling, spending sprees, or sexual indiscretions. Theoretically, amantadine could induce mania or psychosis. <u>Sudden withdrawal of amantadine may cause NMS</u>.

Dosing: To <u>treat EPS</u>, the recommended dose is 100 mg BID. The maximum dose for EPS is 300 mg total daily dose; It is dosed similarly for <u>Parkinson's disease</u>, with a maximum of 400 mg/day; <u>To counter prolactin elevation from antipsychotic medication</u>, 100 mg BID has been used; Taper gradually to discontinue to avoid NMS. Use lower dose if renal insufficiency.

Dynamic interactions:

- ❖ Dopaminergic
- ❖ Anticholinergic (moderate)

Kinetic interactions:

- ❖ Amantadine is not metabolized. It is excreted primarily through the kidneys. Hence, minimal drug-drug interactions.

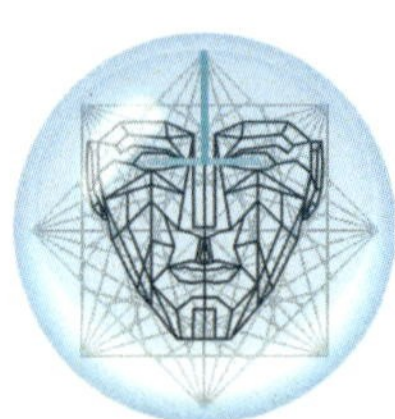

"in a bubble" - minimal clinically significant kinetic interactions

page 18

2019
$1,500

Istradefylline (NOURIANZ)

IS tra DEF i lin / NO ur ee anns

"Nori is tradin' felines"

❖ Adenosine A_{2A} receptor antagonist

20
40
mg

FDA-approved for:

❖ Parkinson's disease (adjunct)

Istradefylline is a selective adenosine A_{2A} receptor antagonist approved for use in combination with levodopa/carbidopa for "off" episodes of Parkinson's disease. An "off" episode is when levodopa is not working well. Istradefylline improves motor control. The result of blocking A_{2A} receptors is a decrease of GABA released in the globus pallidus.

Istradefylline is nondopaminergic. It is similar to caffeine in structure (methylxanthine) and mechanism of action (adenosine receptor antagonism). Caffeine blocks A_1 and A_2 adenosine receptors, while istradefylline is selective for the A_{2A} subtype.

Methylxanthines:

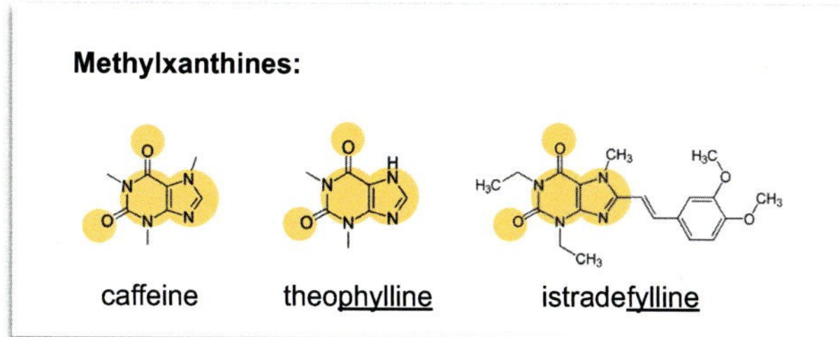

Adenosine A_{2A} receptors are on neurons that release GABA in the globus pallidus (GP). Loss of dopaminergic activity with PD results in hyperactivation of the GP, which istradefylline reverses. Note that the GP is one of several possible sites for electrode implant for deep brain stimulation (DBS), and was the area destroyed by pallidotomy, the surgical treatment for PD before DBS was available.

Istradefylline was shown to improve daytime sleepiness in PD patients (Suzuk et al, 2017). It also improves restless legs syndrome (RLS)—commonly comorbid with PD (Nuermaimaiti et al, 2018).

Side effects of istradefylline may include dyskinesia, constipation, hallucinations, dizziness, nausea and insomnia.

Caffeine, a nonspecific A_{2A} receptor antagonist, reduces the risk of developing PD. Istradefylline is expected to have a similar neuroprotective effect.

Because it is a new drug, experience with overdose on istradefylline is limited. In clinical trials, one patient took six 20 mg tabs with alcohol and developed hallucinations, agitation, and worsening dyskinesia.

Istradefylline is excreted 48% in feces and 39% in urine, none unchanged because it is a big molecule. Half-life is about 83 hours. By comparison, caffeine has a half-life of about 5 hours and is excreted almost entirely in urine.

Dosing: 20 mg QD is the standard dose, with max of 40 mg QD; Use the 40 mg dose if smoking > 20 cigarettes; Do not exceed 20 mg QD with concomitant 3A4 inhibitors; Do not use with strong 3A4 inducers, because levels will be too low.

Adenosine

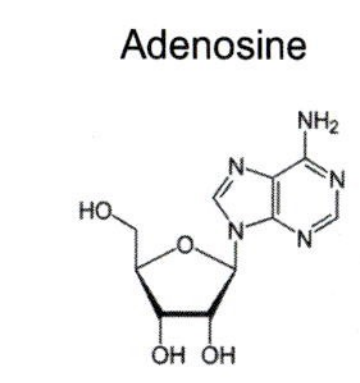

Adenosine is a purine nucleoside. Its derivatives include ATP, ADP, and cAMP. Adenosine itself is a **neuromodulator** involved in promoting sleep and suppressing arousal. Istradefylline is a selective adenosine receptor antagonist.

Dynamic interactions:

❖ None identified

Kinetic interactions:

❖ 3A4 substrate
❖ 1A1 (major) and 1A2 substrate (minor)
  - istradefylline levels are reduced by about 45% for individuals using tobacco products

page 10

page 16

1A2 substrate

3A4 substrate

PARKINSON'S 19

This edition of *Cafer's Psychopharmacology* was released in November 2020. Subscribe to cafermed.com for the updated PDF edition with over 1,000 internal links and bookmarks for ultrarapid navigation. The PDF edition is updated frequently with new mascots. Visit cafermed.com/update for more information.

Discount code for cafermed.com subscription: **ULTRARAPID**

Psychostimulants are "sympathomimetics" that mimic the action of norepinephrine (NE) and dopamine (DA) to activate the sympathetic (fight or flight) nervous system. NE and DA directly bind to NE and DA receptors. Stimulants act indirectly by inhibiting the release or slowing reuptake of NE and DA. In general, stimulants increase energy, improve focus/concentration, and suppress appetite. Dry mouth is a common side effect.

Medication	~ Retail cost	Class	DEA sched	Uses (*off-label)	Comments
RITALIN (methylphenidate)	$75	methylphenidate	II	ADHD, Narcolepsy	DA > NE reuptake inhibitor (DNRI)
CONCERTA (methylphenidate ER)	$250	methylphenidate	II	ADHD	DA > NE reuptake inhibitor (DNRI); Extended- release
FOCALIN (dexmethylphenidate)	$250	methylphenidate	II	ADHD	
ADDERALL (amphetamine salts)	$90	amphetamine	II	ADHD, Narcolepsy	DA > NE reuptake inhibitor (DNRI) and releaser
VYVANSE (lisdexamfetamine)	$325	amphetamine	II	ADHD, Binge eating disorder	Long-acting abuse-deterrent amphetamine
DEXEDRINE (dextroamphetamine)	$150	amphetamine	II	Narcolepsy *Obesity, short-term *ADHD	DA > NE reuptake inhibitor (DNRI) and releaser; 100% D-isomer of amphetamine; By comparison, Adderall is 75% D-amphetamine and 25% L-amphetamine.
DESOXYN (methamphetamine)	$700	amphetamine	II	ADHD Obesity, short-term	Desoxyn is legal meth! Rarely prescribed.
ADIPEX (phentermine)	$30	appetite suppressant	IV	Obesity, short-term	May induce mania due to long half-life of 24 hours, which interferes with sleep.
PROVIGIL (modafinil)	$700	dopamine reuptake inhibitor	IV	Narcolepsy Sleep apnea-related fatigue Shift work sleep disorder *Fatigue; *Depression *ADHD; *Jet lag	1:1 mixture of both R- and S-enantiomers
NUVIGIL (armodafinil)	$550	dopamine reuptake inhibitor	IV	Same as modafinil	R-enantiomer of modafinil
Caffeine (Vivarin, NoDoz)	$4	adenosine antagonist	N/A	Fatigue Apnea of prematurity (infant)	#1 most used psychoactive drug in the world. Can worsen anxiety.
SUDAFED (pseudoephedrine)	$6	α1-adrenergic receptor agonist	N/A**	Nasal congestion *Fatigue	[SU doe ee FED rin]; Non-addictive **but controlled by some states because it is used to manufacture meth; *"The Feds are interested in Sudafed"*
SUDAFED PE (phenylephrine)	$6	α1-adrenergic receptor agonist	N/A	Nasal congestion	[FEN il EFF rin]; Not useful for making meth. Less effective than regular Sudafed for congestion; *"Your efforts to make meth are Eff'd"*
SUNOSI (solriamfetol)	$650	norepinephrine and dopamine reuptake inhibitor (NDRI)	IV	Excessive daytime sleepiness	Not approved for depression, but could be conceptualized as an atypical antidepressant similar to bupropion (Wellbutrin)

Recreational Stimulants

Drug	Class/Mechanism	Comments
Methamphetamine (meth, ice)	amphetamine (DA and NE reuptake inhibitor and releaser)	Commonly abused street drug, smoked or injected. Common cause of manic or psychotic episodes that resolve in a few days. It is available as a prescription pill (Desoxyn) for ADHD.
MDMA (ecstasy, Molly)	amphetamine	3,4-Methylenedioxymethamphetamine. Highly serotonergic. Also a hallucinogen. Brings a sense of intimacy with others. FDA Schedule I, indicating no legal medical use. However, since research has found MDMA useful for PTSD exposure therapy, it is on track for possible FDA approval.
Cocaine	dopamine reuptake inhibitor (DRI)	Powder derived from the coca plant. Inhibits reuptake of 5-HT, NE, and DA. Illegal other than for anaesthesia of the nasal mucosa (Schedule II). Crack is cocaine cooked with baking soda so it can be smoked. Crack earned its name from the crackling sound it makes when heated to smoke. It would be useful for ADHD, but it cannot be absorbed by oral route because it constricts capillaries in the GI tract.
Catha edulis (khat)	cathinone	African plant chewed as stimulant; Schedule I (no legal medical use). Addictive, but the World Health Organization (WHO) does not consider khat addiction to be seriously problematic.
MDPV (bath salts)	synthetic cathinone	Norepinephrine-dopamine reuptake inhibitor (NDRI) with no serotonergic activity. MDPV is 10x more addictive than meth, according to rats pressing levers repeatedly to obtain it. Schedule I illegal drug.
Mephedrone (bath salts)	synthetic cathinone	Serotonin-norepinephrine-dopamine releasing agent. Schedule I illegal drug since 2011. Often snorted, described as similar to MDMA (Ecstasy).
Nicotine	nicotinic acetylcholine receptor agonist	Nicotine in gum or transdermal patches is not carcinogenic, and actually protects against glutamate excitotoxicity. It has a procognitive effect and is used off-label for Parkinson's disease.

Unfortunately, there is no established replacement therapy for stimulant use disorders. Opioid addicts can be effectively maintained on methadone or buprenorphine, but it is not recommended to treat cocaine or methamphetamine use disorder with a less abusable stimulant.

Treatment of ADHD with Schedule II Stimulants (amphetamine and methylphenidate) 

The principal target symptoms for treatment of attention deficit hyperactivity disorder (ADHD) are inattention and impulsivity. Patients with ADHD have difficulty activating areas of the prefrontal cortex due to weak dopaminergic and noradrenergic transmission. Stimulants "wake up" these sleepy pathways by blocking reuptake of dopamine (DA) and norepinephrine (NE).

Most children with predominantly hyperactive ADHD eventually "grow out of it" as these neural pathways strengthen with age. Predominantly inattentive ADHD usually does not tend to improve throughout adulthood. Although adults with ADHD may be impaired by inattentive symptoms, ADHD is often not the focus of pharmacotherapy because of comorbid conditions. If applicable to a given patient, drug/alcohol addiction should be top priority, followed by mood disorders, then anxiety disorders, then ADHD,(and then smoking cessation).

Note that there is no such thing as adult-onset ADHD. As defined by DSM-5, symptoms must be present prior to age 12. Unfortunately, ADHD medications across the board have been found to be less efficacious and less well tolerated in adults than in children/adolescents (Cortese et al, 2018).

The first-line treatment of ADHD is a stimulant of the amphetamine or methylphenidate class. Milligram per milligram, Adderall (amphetamine) is about twice as potent as Ritalin (methylphenidate). Adderall 10 mg is approximately equivalent to Ritalin 20 mg. These medications are dramatically effective for 75% of individuals with ADHD. Some of the stimulants are approved for children as young as age 3, but most are approved for ages 6 and above. Generally, stimulants start working within 0.5–2 hours and lose all effectiveness by evening—otherwise they would interfere with sleep. They are detectable in serum at subtherapeutic levels for about 48 hours.

Prescription amphetamines and methylphenidates are all Schedule II controlled substances, the same level of restriction as opioid pain medications. Prescriptions for Schedule II substances cannot be phoned into the pharmacy or include refills.

The Schedule II stimulants (amphetamines and methylphenidates) have a Black Box Warning for risk of abuse and dependence. However, risk of addiction with prescription stimulants taken as prescribed is very low. No other boxed warnings have been applied to Schedule II stimulants.

Amphetamine can be addictive when taken at high dose and is highly addictive if injected intravenously. PO opioids are much more addictive than PO amphetamines. While withdrawal from opioids is highly distressing, withdrawal from stimulants is less severe and mostly consists of fatigue, hypersomnia, irritability, and increased appetite.

Many psychiatrists believe prescription amphetamines are overly regulated, especially in the case of lisdexamfetamine (Vyvanse) which has gradual onset of action, even if snorted or injected.

Modafinil (Provigil) is a less restricted (Schedule IV) stimulant that may have comparable efficacy for ADHD when used off-label (Wang et al, 2016). Although less addictive than amphetamine, modafinil is not necessarily safer or better tolerated. The norepinephrine reuptake inhibitor atomoxetine (Strattera) is noncontrolled and approved for ADHD but is substantially less effective than stimulants.

At doses effective for ADHD, the difference between amphetamine and methylphenidate is minimal, like Coca-Cola vs Pepsi—both inhibit reuptake of dopamine (DA) by blocking the dopamine transporter (DAT). When abused, the potential for addiction is greater with amphetamine. At high dose, amphetamine has the additional mechanism of entering neurons and displacing DA from synaptic vesicles and causing DA to be released in the reward pathway, resulting in euphoria.

Slow-release stimulant formulations do not have pleasurable effects and can be more effective for ADHD than immediate-release formulations. Blocking the dopamine transporter (DAT) causes entirely differing responses depending on how quickly and completely DAT is blocked. If DAT occupancy is rapid (e.g., taken IV or snorted), intermittent and saturated, the result is a euphoric "high". ADHD symptoms are best relieved when DAT occupancy is gradual, non-saturated, constant and prolonged. This is best accomplished by a modestly dosed, slow-onset, long-duration stimulant formulation. For most individuals, the FDA maximum dose for a given stimulant is no more effective than a moderate dose.

On college campuses, prescription stimulants are commonly diverted for nonmedical uses such as all-night studying and countering sedation from binge drinking. Prescribers can minimize risk of diversion (i.e., patients sharing their pills) by limiting supply to one extended-release capsule daily. Vyvanse and Mydayis are suitable long-acting amphetamines. Suitable methylphenidate products include Concerta, Aptensio XR and Adhansia XR. These stimulants can also be more effective for ADHD by providing a slow-rising and constant steady-state level of stimulant.

If the dose is too high, stimulants can cause tremor, restlessness, and irritability. At even higher doses stimulants can produce paranoia, arrhythmias, and elevated body temperature. In overdose, stimulants can cause heart failure, seizure, and stroke.

Even at therapeutic doses, stimulants increase blood pressure (averaging 2 to 4 mmHg) and heart rate (averaging 3–6 bpm); some individuals have larger increases. Sudden death has been reported in association with stimulants at recommended doses in pediatric patients with structural cardiac abnormalities or other serious heart problems. Avoid prescribing stimulants to patients with known cardiac abnormalities, cardiomyopathy, serious heart arrhythmias, or coronary artery disease. Several large studies have found **no** evidence that stimulants increase the risk of serious cardiovascular events for individuals without known heart problems. A screening EKG is **not** necessary prior to starting a stimulant for an individual with no history of heart disease. Patients on stimulants who develop exertional chest pain or unexplained syncope need further evaluation.

Stimulants may worsen tic disorders in ⅓ of cases by increasing DA activation in brain areas involved in movement. For some individuals, stimulant-related tics improve when the dose is decreased. For a smaller group of individuals, stimulants may trigger tics that persist for several months after the stimulant is stopped, before eventually resolving spontaneously.

Stimulants may induce manic or psychotic episodes. Stimulants are to be avoided in patients with unstable bipolar disorder or schizophrenia. However, bipolar patients stabilized on an antipsychotic are often able to tolerate a stimulant for ADHD. While the stimulant increases DA activity in the prefrontal cortex (at D_1 receptors) the antipsychotic blocks DA activity in the limbic system (at D_2 receptors) sufficiently to prevent recurrence of mania or psychosis. Bipolar patients should be monitored closely for mood destabilization and the stimulant discontinued immediately if signs of mania arise.

Stimulants may increase anxiety in some individuals, but those with ADHD are more likely to experience stimulants as calming if dosed appropriately. Paradoxically, some patients with ADHD complain stimulants make them overly slowed or even "zombified".

Stimulants decrease appetite by increasing adrenergic and dopaminergic activity in the hypothalamus. Children ages 7–10 years old taking stimulants 7 days per week throughout the year demonstrate growth retardation, averaging 2 cm, without evidence of growth rebound upon discontinuation of the stimulant. Taking periodic "drug holidays" from the stimulant can minimize stunting of growth. For children with severe ADHD, drug holidays may not be advisable.

Rarely, stimulants can cause priapism in boys and men. It is possible to develop priapism upon stopping the stimulant, e.g., for a drug holiday. Stimulants rarely cause Raynaud's phenomenon, which is expected to resolve with dose reduction or discontinuation.

Several stimulants are approved for narcolepsy. One amphetamine product is approved for short-term treatment of obesity (Evekeo), and another for long-term treatment of binge eating disorder (Vyvanse). Stimulants are used off-label for short-term treatment of depression, particularly in elderly patients. Tolerance to the antidepressant effect is expected to develop in 2 to 4 weeks. Poststroke lethargy and apathy may respond to stimulants, with potential long-term effectiveness. 70–90% of individuals with multiple sclerosis experience fatigue, which may be responsive to stimulants.

For treatment of ADHD there is no intervention nearly as effective as medication. Adjunctive interventions that may be beneficial include omega-3 fatty acids, sleep hygiene interventions, and cognitive behavioral therapy (CBT). EEG neurofeedback is time consuming, expensive, and ineffective, at least for adults (Schönenberg et al, 2017).

FDA-approved Schedule II stimulants for ADHD

The main purpose of the mnemonics in this chapter is to help you differentiate the "Adderalls" (amphetamines) from the "Ritalins" (methylphenidates). Amphetamine pictures include an amplifier, while methylphenidates are depicted as scantron sheets.

Class	Generic/TRADE	Notes
Methylphenidates Dopamine and norepinephrine reuptake inhibitors	Methylphenidate (RITALIN)	Ritalin is 1:1 racemic mix of D- and L-methylphenidate. The L-isomer is practically inert. There are at least 14 branded methylphenidate products.
	Dexmethylphenidate (FOCALIN)	Focalin is the D-isomer of methylphenidate, which is the active isomer. 20 mg Focalin is equivalent to 40 mg of Ritalin.
Amphetamines DA and NE reuptake inhibitors that are transported into neurons via the dopamine transporter	Amphetamine (ADDERALL)	Amphetamine salts with a 75% dextro- and 25% levo-amphetamine isomers.
	Dextroamphetamine (DEXEDRINE)	100% D-amphetamine
	Methamphetamine (DESOXYN)	Rarely prescribed pure version of a commonly abused street drug (crystal meth)
	Lisdexamfetamine (VYVANSE)	Also approved for binge eating disorder; Activated by stomach enzymes, inactive if snorted or injected;

Other medications for ADHD

The less restricted sympathomimetics (atomoxetine, bupropion, modafinil) are generally less effective (have a smaller effect size) than the Schedule II stimulants for ADHD. The less restricted sympathomimetics are commonly lumped into a "nonstimulant" category but they may be better conceptualized as weak stimulants. "Nonstimulants" are recommended for treatment of ADHD in patients with comorbid bipolar or substance use disorders that could be destabilized by increased DA activity. It may take 8 weeks for the full benefit of a nonstimulant to be achieved. By contrast, Schedule II stimulants are effective for ADHD on day 1.

Paradoxically, certain sympatholytic medications (the opposite of sympathomimetic) can improve ADHD symptoms, although they are more beneficial for hyperactivity than for inattention. The sympatholytics useful for ADHD are central alpha-2 agonists traditionally used as antihypertensive. Specifically, the two sympatholytics approved for ADHD are extended-release (ER) formulations of clonidine (Kapvay) and guanfacine (Intuniv).

"Nonstimulants" Approved for ADHD

Generic/TRADE	Class	Notes
Atomoxetine (STRATTERA)	Norepinephrine reuptake inhibitor (NRI)	Not referred to as a "stimulant" or an antidepressant, but it can be conceptualized as an antidepressant-like stimulating medication, somewhat similar to bupropion (Wellbutrin).
Tenex (GUANFACINE)	Central alpha-2 agonist (HTN med)	Sympatholytic (opposite of stimulant); FDA-approved formulation is guanfacine ER (Intuniv); Less sedating than clonidine.
Clonidine (CATAPRES)	Central alpha-2 agonist (HTN med)	Like guanfacine but can be more sedating; FDA-approved formulation is clonidine XR (Kapvay).
Pemoline (CYLERT)	Dopaminergic (exact mechanism unknown)	Removed from the market in 2005 due to 21 cases of liver failure.

Off-label Medications for ADHD

Generic/TRADE	Class	Notes
Bupropion (WELLBUTRIN)	Norepinephrine-dopamine reuptake inhibitor (NDRI)	Antidepressant approved for depression and smoking cessation
Modafinil (PROVIGIL)	Dopamine reuptake inhibitor (DRI)	Schedule IV wakefulness promoting agent
Armodafinil (NUVIGIL)	Dopamine reuptake inhibitor (DRI)	R-enantiomer of modafinil
Venlafaxine (EFFEXOR)	Serotonin-norepinephrine reuptake inhibitor (SNRI)	Antidepressant approved for depression and several anxiety disorders
Duloxetine (CYMBALTA)	Serotonin-norepinephrine reuptake inhibitor (SNRI)	Antidepressant approved for depression, anxiety, and several pain disorders
Nortriptyline (PAMELOR)	Tricyclic antidepressant (TCA)	Highly noradrenergic with minimal serotonergic activity.
Desipramine (NORPRAMIN)	Tricyclic antidepressant (TCA)	Similar to nortriptyline; Exceptionally fatal in overdose.

#47
1955
$25–$91

50% D 50% L

Methylphenidate (RITALIN)

meth uhl FEN i deyt / RIT a lin

wRite a line on Math final date

- ❖ Methylphenidate stimulant
- ❖ DA > NE reuptake inhibitor
- ❖ DEA Schedule II

5
10
<u>20</u>
mg

FDA-approved for:

- ❖ ADHD
- ❖ Narcolepsy

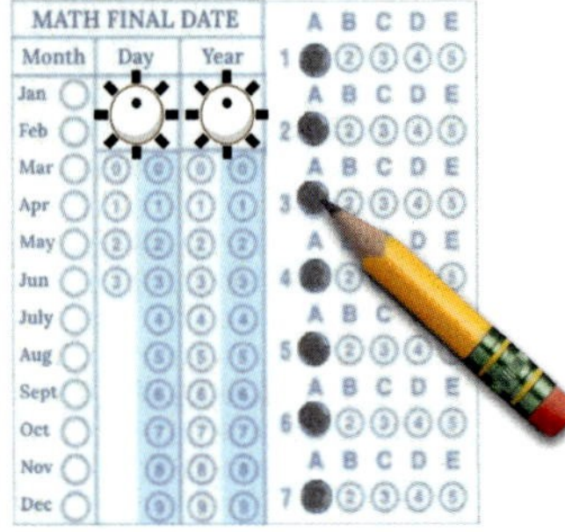

Scantron pictures signify that the medication is a methylphenidate (in contrast to the amphetamines, which are illustrated with amplifiers).

Methylphenidate (Ritalin) was introduced in 1955 and has been prescribed to hyperactive children since 1960. Prescription of methylphenidate skyrocketed in the early 1990s.

ADHD was not defined until 1980 with the publication of DSM-III, which called it ADD with or without hyperactivity. The closest DSM-II diagnosis was Hyperkinetic Reaction of Childhood. Before that, it was called 'minimal brain dysfunction' or 'minimal brain damage.'

<u>Children have fewer side effects</u> on methylphenidate compared to amphetamine, although <u>for adults it is the opposite</u> (Cortese et al, 2018).

Ritalin is 1:1 racemic mix dextro:levo methylphenidate. The <u>L-isomer is practically inert</u> and largely does not reach the systemic circulation due to first-pass metabolism by the liver and gut wall.

The chemist who discovered it named it after his wife Rita, who used it compensate for low blood pressure.

Immediate-release methylphenidate (Ritalin) <u>takes effect quickly, in 15–30 minutes</u> (compared to 1 hour for onset of Adderall). Ritalin's duration of action is about 4 hours (while Adderall works for 5–6 hours). There are a dozen extended-release formulations of methylphenidate, shown below. Focalin is purely D-methylphenidate without the inactive L-isomer.

Refer to pages 218–219 for general information about stimulants, with risks and warnings.

Adult dosing: Start 5–10 mg BID with doses separated by about 4 hours; may increase by 5–10 mg/day increments in 7-day intervals; Max is 60 mg/day, which would be 20 mg TID; It should not be given within 4–5 hours from bedtime; Ideally it is given 30–45 minutes before meals; Taper gradually to stop.

This ad from the 1960s touts Ritalin as treatment for "Minimal Brain Dysfunction" (MBD), the condition now known as ADHD. DSM-II (1968) called the condition "Hyperkinetic Reaction of Childhood". DSM-III (1980) renamed it "Attention-Deficit Disorder (ADD) with or without hyperactivity". DSM-III-R (1987) refined the name to Attention-Deficit Hyperactivity Disorder (ADHD).

page 18

Dynamic interactions:

- ❖ CNS stimulant
- ❖ Hypertensive effects
- ❖ Lowers seizure threshold

Kinetic interactions:

- ❖ Minimal clinically significant kinetic interactions (in a bubble)

Formulations of methylphenidate

Medication	~ Dose equiv	Ritalin conversion	Available strengths	Dose range	Approx Duration	Splittable	Notes
Ritalin	20 mg	x 1	5, 10, 20 mg	5 mg <u>BID</u>–20 mg <u>TID</u>	4 hr	Yes	See above; Divide doses 4 hours apart
Ritalin LA	20 mg	x 1	10, 20, 30, 40 ER	20–60 mg AM	8 hr	Can sprinkle	Beads: 50% IR, 50% delayed
Metadate ER	20 mg	x 1	20 mg	20–60 mg AM	8 hr	No	Wax matrix makes release less predictable
Metadate CD	20 mg	x 1	10, 20, 30, 40, 50, 60 mg	20–60 mg AM	8 hr	Can sprinkle	Beads: 30% IR, 70% ER
Methylin ER	20 mg	x 1	10, 20 mg	20–60 mg AM	6 hr	No	Sustained release formulation
Methylin liquid	20 mg	x 1	5 mg or 10 mg/5 ml	5 mg <u>BID</u>–20 mg <u>TID</u>	4 hr	Solution	Ritalin in liquid form, grape flavor
Focalin**	10 mg	x 0.5	2.5, 5, 10 mg	2.5–10 mg <u>BID</u>	4–5 hr	Yes	**Dexmethylphenidate, double the potency of Ritalin
Focalin XR**	10 mg	x 0.5	5, 10, 15, 20, 25, 30, 35, 40	20–40 mg AM	9–10 hr	Can sprinkle	Mimics Focalin IR split into two doses given 5 hours apart
Concerta	27 mg	x 1.2	18, 27, 36, 54 mg	18–72 mg AM	10–12 hr	No	22% IR, 78% delayed; 18 mg is equivalent to Ritalin 5 TID but smoother, without peaks and troughs
Adhansia XR	un-defined	undefined	25, 35, 45, 55, 70, 85 mg	25–85 mg AM	16 hr	Can sprinkle	Delivery is 20% IR and 80% ER
Aptensio XR	20 mg	x 1	10, 15, 20, 30, 40, 50, 60	10–60 mg AM	10–12 hr	Can sprinkle	[ap-TEN-see-oh] Beads - 40% IR, 60% delayed
Cotempla XR ODT	17.3 mg	x 0.86	8.6, 17.3, 25.9 mg	17.3–51.8 mg AM	10 hr	No	[koh TEM pluh] Orally disintegrating tab; 25% IR, 75% ER
Daytrana patch	un-defined	undefined	10, 15, 20, 30 per 9 hours	10–30 mg AM	10 hr	Patch	Effects may persist for 5 hours after removal
Jornay PM	27 mg	x 1.35	20, 40, 60, 80, 100 mg	20–100 <u>PM</u>	9 hr	Can sprinkle	[JOR-nay] Onset 8 hrs after taking it
QuilliChew ER	20 mg	x 1	20, 30, 40 mg	20–60 mg AM	8 hr	Yes	[QUIL-ih-choo]
Quillivant XR	20 mg	x 1	25 mg per 5 mL	20–60 mg AM	12 hr	Liquid	20% IR, 80% ER

2001
$29–$88

100% D

Dexmethylphenidate (FOCALIN)

D-enantiomer of Ritalin

"Focus in on D on Math final date"

- ❖ Methylphenidate stimulant
- ❖ DA > NE reuptake inhibitor
- ❖ DEA Schedule II

2.5
5
10
mg

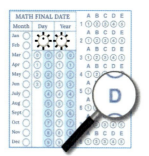

FDA-approved for:
- ❖ ADHD

Focalin is the D-isomer of methylphenidate, which is the active isomer. Ritalin is a racemic mix, of which the L-isomer is practically inert. Hence, Focalin is twice as potent as Ritalin and prescribed at about half of the mg dose. There is no 3:1 mixture of these isomers, as seen with some amphetamine formulations. There is little evidence Focalin is better than Ritalin, though Focalin may have a slightly longer duration of action. The cost of generic Focalin is comparable to generic Ritalin. Refer to pages 218–219 for general information about stimulants, with risks and warnings.

Adult dosing: 2.5–10 mg BID with doses separated by 4–5 hours; Start: 2.5 mg BID; May increase by 2.5–5 mg/day increments in 7-day intervals; Max is 20 mg/day, which would be 10 mg BID; If converting from methylphenidate (Ritalin), start at 50% of methylphenidate dose; Do not take within 5 hours of bedtime; Taper gradually to stop.

Formulations of dexmethylphenidate

Medication	Dose conversion	Strengths	Dose range	~Duration	Pills	Notes
Focalin	10 mg of Focalin is equivalent to 20 mg of Ritalin	2.5, 5, 10 mg	2.5–10 mg BID dosed 5 hours apart	4–5 hr	Splittable tablets	Peak plasma concentrations achieved within 60–90 minutes following oral administration in fasting patients. Peak plasma concentrations for extended-release capsules (Focalin XR) are attained at 1.5 hours and again at 6.5 hours after a dose.
Focalin XR		5, 10, 15, 20, 25, 30, 35, 40 mg	20–40 mg AM	9–10 hr	Capsules, can sprinkle	Mimics Focalin IR split into two doses given 5 hours apart

Bart Simpson was diagnosed with ADHD in 1999, and prescribed the fictional stimulant "FOCUSYN", which predated Focalin, approved 2001.

Dynamic interactions:
- ❖ CNS stimulant
- ❖ Hypertensive effects
- ❖ Lowers seizure threshold

Kinetic interactions:
- ❖ Minimal clinically significant kinetic interactions (in a bubble)

page 18

2000
$91–$276

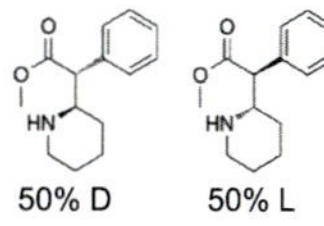

50% D 50% L

CONCERTA

Long-acting methylphenidate

"Concert on Math final date"

- ❖ Methylphenidate stimulant
- ❖ DA > NE reuptake inhibitor
- ❖ DEA Schedule II

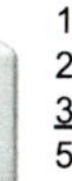

18
27
36
54
mg

FDA-approved for:
- ❖ ADHD

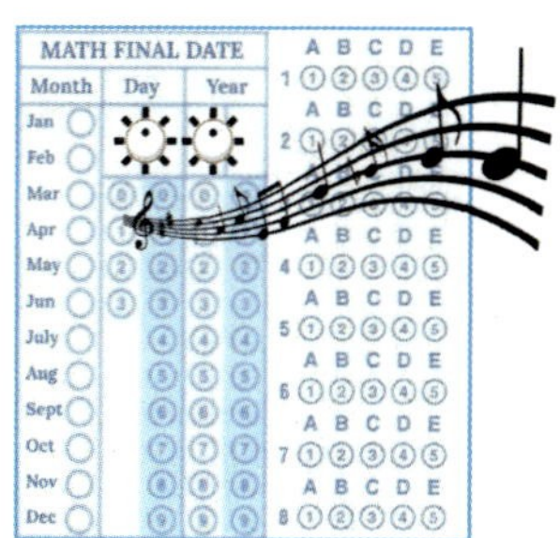

"Concerta helps you concentrate". Many prescribers use Concerta as their go-to methylphenidate formulation. It is the most prescribed methylphenidate, more widely used than immediate-release generic Ritalin. Because of Concerta's delivery system, only 83% of the medication is released. 18 mg of Concerta is roughly equivalent to 15 mg of Ritalin given in 3 divided doses spaced 4 hours apart. Coverage with Concerta is smoother, without the peaks and troughs of Ritalin TID, as shown below.

Duration of effect is 12 hours. Onset of effectiveness is within 60–90 minutes.

Dose conversion: If taking 20–30 mg of another form of methylphenidate, start Concerta at 36 mg; if on 35–45 mg of another methylphenidate, start Concerta at 54 mg; if on 50+ mg of another methylphenidate, start Concerta at 72 mg; Taper gradually to stop.

The tablet is an Osmotic controlled Release Oral delivery System (OROS). The drug is expelled through tiny holes in the coating, and the empty "ghost capsules" are passed in feces.

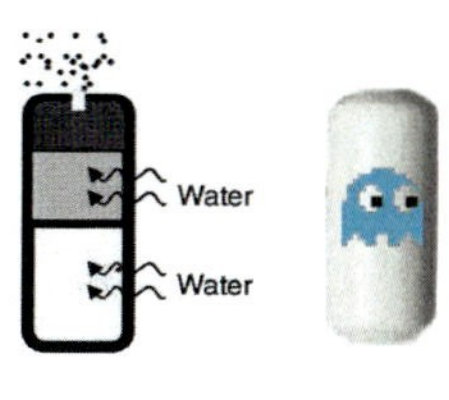

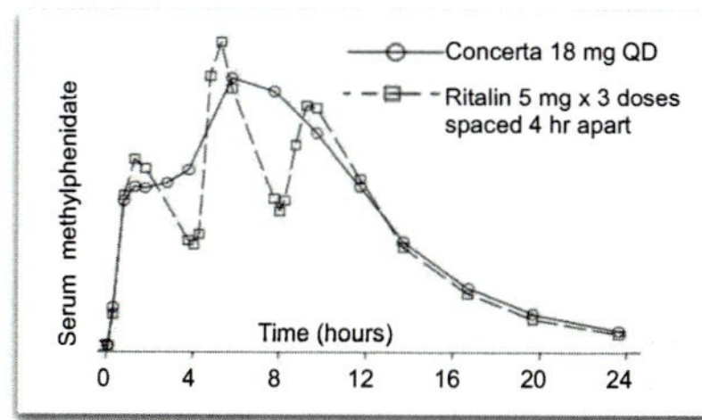

Adult dosing: 18–72 mg q AM; Start 18–36 mg; May increase by 18 mg/day increments in q 7-day intervals; Max is 72 mg (or up to 108 mg off-label); Do not cut, crush, or chew the tablet. See above for switching from other forms of methylphenidate.

Dynamic interactions:
- ❖ CNS stimulant
- ❖ Hypertensive effects
- ❖ Lowers seizure threshold

Kinetic interactions:
- ❖ Minimal clinically significant kinetic interactions (in a bubble)

page 18

2015
$240–$276

50% D 50% L

APTENSIO XR

Long-acting methylphenidate

"App tensioₙ"

- ❖ Methylphenidate stimulant
- ❖ DA > NE reuptake inhibitor
- ❖ DEA Schedule II

10
15
20
30
40
50
60
mg

FDA-approved for:

❖ ADHD

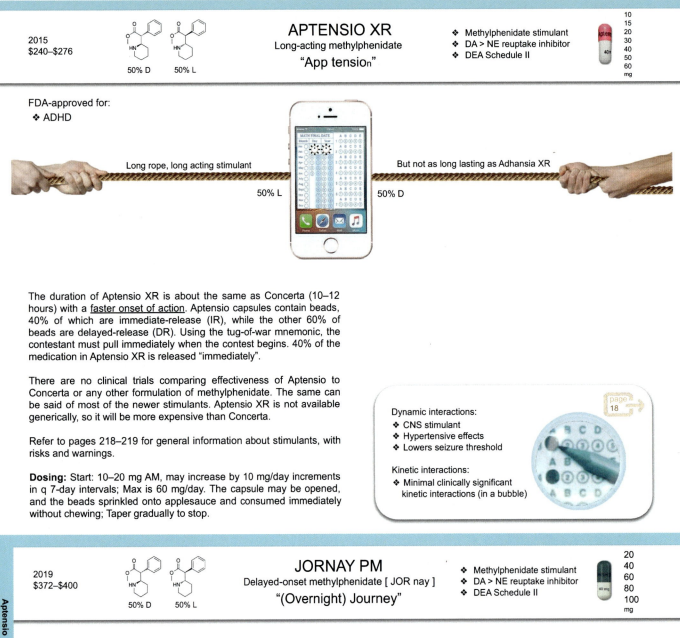

Long rope, long acting stimulant

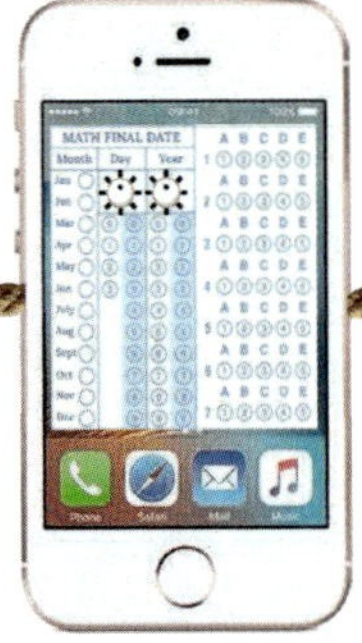

50% L

50% D

But not as long lasting as Adhansia XR

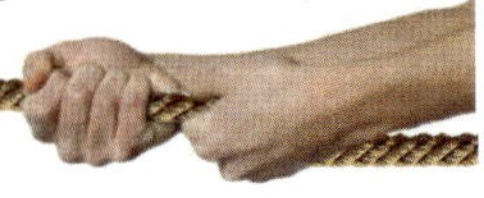

The duration of Aptensio XR is about the same as Concerta (10–12 hours) with a faster onset of action. Aptensio capsules contain beads, 40% of which are immediate-release (IR), while the other 60% of beads are delayed-release (DR). Using the tug-of-war mnemonic, the contestant must pull immediately when the contest begins. 40% of the medication in Aptensio XR is released "immediately".

There are no clinical trials comparing effectiveness of Aptensio to Concerta or any other formulation of methylphenidate. The same can be said of most of the newer stimulants. Aptensio XR is not available generically, so it will be more expensive than Concerta.

Refer to pages 218–219 for general information about stimulants, with risks and warnings.

Dosing: Start: 10–20 mg AM, may increase by 10 mg/day increments in q 7-day intervals; Max is 60 mg/day. The capsule may be opened, and the beads sprinkled onto applesauce and consumed immediately without chewing; Taper gradually to stop.

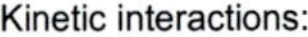

page 18

Dynamic interactions:
- ❖ CNS stimulant
- ❖ Hypertensive effects
- ❖ Lowers seizure threshold

Kinetic interactions:
- ❖ Minimal clinically significant kinetic interactions (in a bubble)

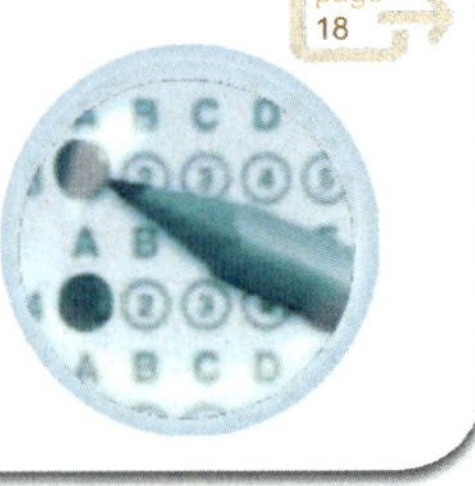

2019
$372–$400

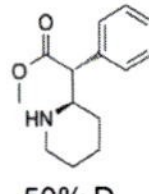

50% D 50% L

JORNAY PM

Delayed-onset methylphenidate [JOR nay]

"(Overnight) Journey"

- ❖ Methylphenidate stimulant
- ❖ DA > NE reuptake inhibitor
- ❖ DEA Schedule II

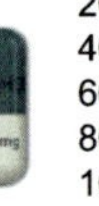

20
40
60
80
100
mg

FDA-approved for:

❖ ADHD

Jornay PM is a unique formulation of methylphenidate taken at night. It starts working 10 hours later. It should **not** be taken in the morning. Currently there is no amphetamine product formulated for nighttime dosing. You can think of the song *Lights* by Journey (1978) which starts out *"When the lights go down in the City…"*

With Jornay PM the initial absorption of methylphenidate into plasma is delayed such that no more than 5% of total drug is available within the first 10 hours. After the lag period, the absorption of methylphenidate occurs in a single peak with maximum serum concentration reached at 14 hours, followed by a gradual decline throughout the rest of the day.

In clinical trials of patients aged 6 to 12 years, the most common dosing time (> 70% of patients) was 8:00 pm, with an allowed range between 6:30 pm and 9:30 pm.

The capsules are inscribed with "IRONSHORE" but should probably say "Take at night!" It remains to be seen if there will be much demand for this niche product.

Dosing: Do not substitute Jornay PM for other methylphenidate products on a milligram-per-milligram basis.The recommended starting dose for patients 6+ years old is 20 mg once daily in the evening. The dose may be titrated weekly in increments of 20 mg. Max dose is 100 mg. It is recommended to initiate Jornay at 8:00 pm and then adjust timing between 6:30 pm and 9:30 pm to optimize efficacy. It should be taken consistently with food or without food. The capsule may be opened, the contents sprinkled onto applesauce, and consumed immediately without chewing.

page 18

Dynamic interactions:
- ❖ CNS stimulant
- ❖ Hypertensive effects
- ❖ Lowers seizure threshold

Kinetic interactions:
- ❖ Minimal clinically significant kinetic interactions (in a bubble)

2019
$302–$354

50% D 50% L

ADHANSIA XR

Extended-release methylphenidate

"ADH__ answer"

- ❖ Methylphenidate stimulant
- ❖ DA > NE reuptake inhibitor
- ❖ DEA Schedule II

25
35
45
55
70
85
mg

FDA-approved for:
- ❖ ADHD

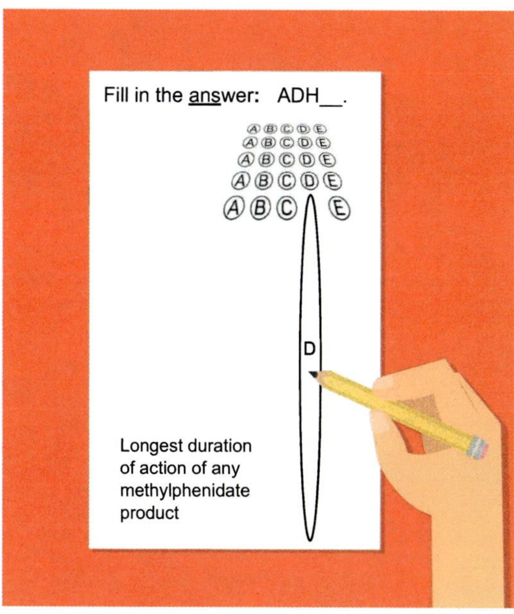

Fill in the answer: ADH__.
D
Longest duration of action of any methylphenidate product

Adhansia XR, released in 2019, has the longest duration of action of any methylphenidate formulation—16 hours. Do not substitute for other methylphenidate products on a milligram-per-milligram basis because of different methylphenidate base compositions and differing pharmacokinetic profiles. The 45 mg capsules contain FD&C Yellow No. 5 (tartrazine) which may cause allergic-type reactions in susceptible persons. This is frequently seen in patients who also have aspirin hypersensitivity.

Dosing: Start 25 mg AM; May increase in increments of 10–15 mg/day at intervals of at least 5 days; Dosages above 85 mg in adults (above 70 mg in children) are associated with disproportionate increases in the incidence of insomnia, dry mouth, and nausea. Take with or without food. Can sprinkle onto a tablespoon of applesauce or yogurt. If sprinkled, do not chew the beads. If the mixture is not consumed within 10 minutes of adding the beads, it should be discarded.

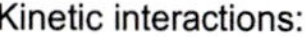

Dynamic interactions:
- ❖ CNS stimulant
- ❖ Hypertensive effects
- ❖ Lowers seizure threshold

Kinetic interactions:
- ❖ Minimal clinically significant kinetic interactions (in a bubble)

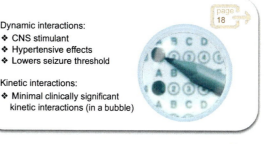

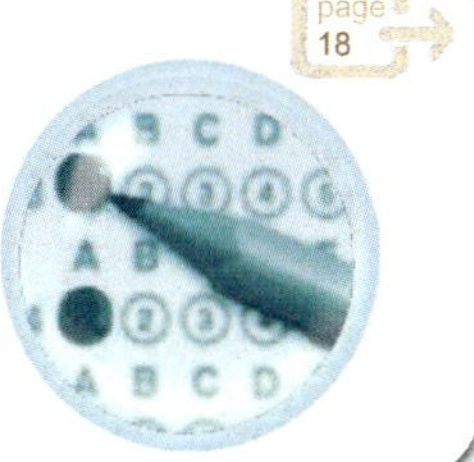
page 18

2016
$371–$444

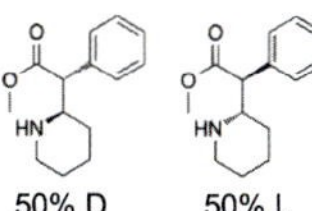

50% D 50% L

COTEMPLA XR-ODT

Extended-release methylphenidate ODT

"Coat template"

- ❖ Methylphenidate stimulant
- ❖ DA > NE reuptake inhibitor
- ❖ DEA Schedule II

8.6
17.3
25.9
mg

FDA-approved for:
- ❖ ADHD

Cotempla is the only methylphenidate formulation that is both extended-release (XR) and an orally disintegrating tablet (ODT). Onset of effect is about 1 hour and duration is 10–12 hours.

The tablet contains two different types of microparticles. 25% are immediate-release (IR) and 75% are XR. The XR microparticles are fancy, with two different polymer coats. The exterior coating of the XR microparticles is pH dependent, and the interior coating functions as a diffusion barrier.

Adult dosing: Start 17.3 mg AM and increase in increments of 8.6–17.3 mg/day at weekly intervals; Max is 51.8 mg/day. See table for Ritalin dose equivalents.

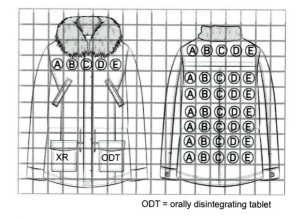

ODT = orally disintegrating tablet

Ritalin equivalent	Cotempla dose	Accomplished with
10 mg	8.6 mg	One tab
20 mg	17.3 mg	One tab
30 mg	25.9 mg	One tab
40 mg	34.6 mg	Two 17.3 mg tabs
50 mg	43.2 mg	17.3 mg tab + 25.9 mg tab
60 mg	51.8 mg	Two 25.9 mg tabs

Dynamic interactions:
- ❖ CNS stimulant
- ❖ Hypertensive effects
- ❖ Lowers seizure threshold

Kinetic interactions:
- ❖ Minimal clinically significant kinetic interactions (in a bubble)

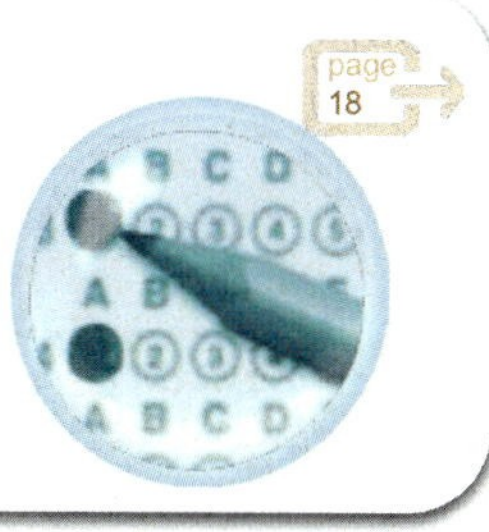
page 18

2006
$371–$396

50% D 50% L

DAYTRANA

methylphenidate transdermal
day TRA na
"Day trainer"

- ❖ Methylphenidate stimulant
- ❖ DA > NE reuptake inhibitor
- ❖ DEA Schedule II

10
15
20
30
mg

FDA-approved for:
- ❖ ADHD

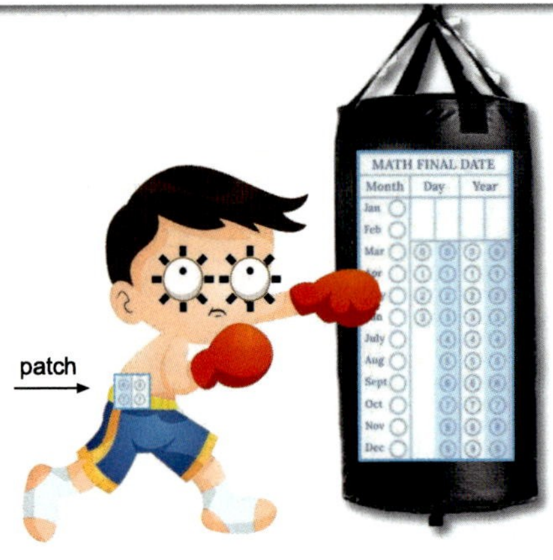

Daytrana is the transdermal formulation of methylphenidate, marketed giving parents more control with a "motherly touch" as "the care they wear." The patch is intended to allow control of the duration of effect. It is intended to be worn for 9 hours. The transdermal formulation may have less potential for abuse.

There are several reasons to avoid Daytrana. Onset of effect is slow (1–2 hours) and the effect continues for 2–5 hours after the patch is removed! This could be problematic if parents forget to remove the patch as bedtime approaches. With excessive heat, absorption of methylphenidate can be amplified, leading to a mild overdose. The patch may fall off or the child can remove it.

Daytrana has the potential to cause permanent loss of skin color around the application site, a condition known as chemical leukoderma.

Transdermal delivery of methylphenidate avoids the first-pass effect, which allows a lower dose of methylphenidate on a mg/kg basis compared to oral dosages. With oral administration of methylphenidate, the concentration of the drug is greatly reduced before it reaches systemic circulation by first-pass metabolism in the liver and gut wall. It is worth noting that first-pass metabolism of oral methylphenidate filters out most of the L-methylphenidate (which is practically inert). With transdermal administration of racemic methylphenidate, exposure to L-methylphenidate is nearly as high as to D-methylphenidate.

The labeled strength of each patch refers to the approximate mg of methylphenidate delivered if the patch is worn for 9 hours. The actual mg per patch is more than double the nominal dose, as shown in the table.

Dosing: Apply 1 patch QD x 9 hours; Start 10 mg; Increase to next patch size in weekly intervals; Max is 30 mg patch.

Nominal dose delivered over 9 hr	Rate of delivery	Total methylphenidate content per patch	Patch size
10 mg	1.1 mg/hr	27.5 mg	12.5 cm^2
15 mg	1.6 mg/hr	41.3 mg	18.75 cm^2
20 mg	2.2 mg/hr	55 mg	25 cm^2
30 mg	3.3 mg/hr	82.5 mg	37.5 cm^2

page 18

Dynamic interactions:
- ❖ CNS stimulant
- ❖ Hypertensive effects
- ❖ Lowers seizure threshold

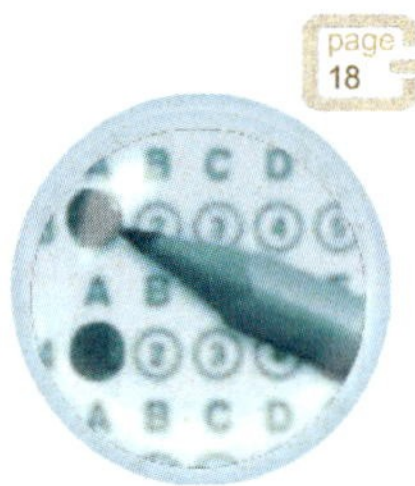

Kinetic interactions:
- ❖ Minimal clinically significant kinetic interactions (in a bubble)

#45
1995
IR $29–$92
XR $40–$206

75% D
25% L

Mixed amphetamine salts (ADDERALL)

am FET a meen / AD uh rawl

"Amp to Add it all "

- Amphetamine stimulant
- DA > NE reuptake inhibitor
- DA > NE releaser
- DEA Schedule II

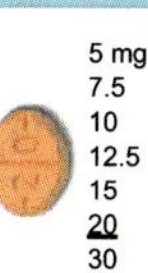

XR	5 mg
5	7.5
10	10
15	12.5
20	15
25	20
30	30

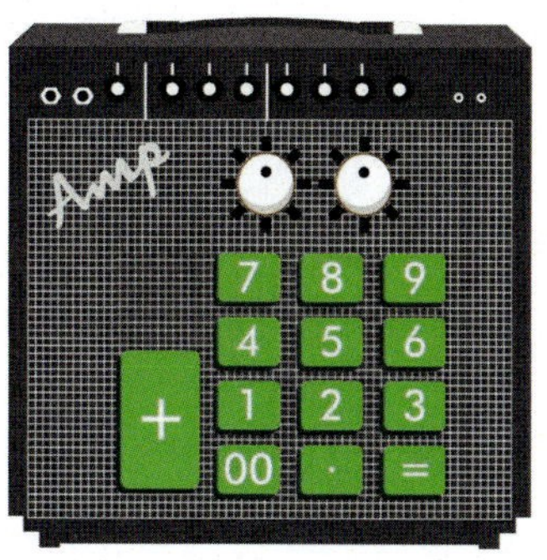

An amplifier signifies that the medication is an amphetamine (in contrast to the methylphenidates which are illustrated with a Scantron sheet).

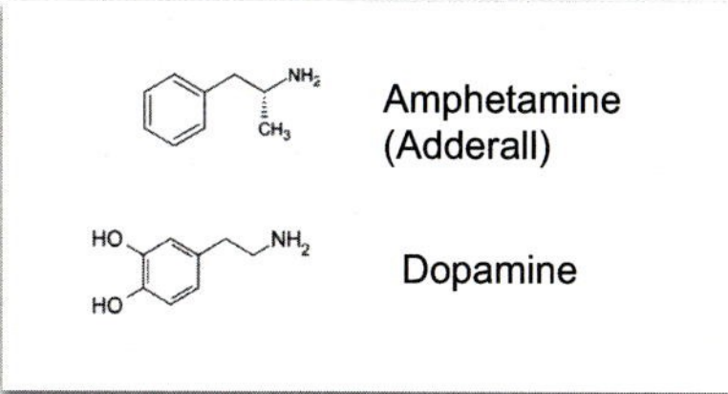

FDA-approved for:
- ADHD (age 3+)
- Narcolepsy

Used off-label for:
- Weight loss (short-term)
- Post-stroke fatigue
- Severe depression (short-term adjunct)

Amphetamine (Adderall) is a dopamine (DA) and norepinephrine (NE) reuptake inhibitor, as is methylphenidate (Ritalin). Amphetamine has the additional mechanism of causing DA release from presynaptic neurons. Compared to methylphenidate (Ritalin), Adderall tends to be more effective and better tolerated for adults (Cortese et al, 2018). For children, Adderall may be more effective but with more side effects than Ritalin. Adderall was shown to increase diastolic BP for children, but not for adults (Cortese et al, 2018).

Amphetamine is roughly twice as potent (per mg) as methylphenidate (Ritalin). Adderall has a slightly longer duration of action than Ritalin. Duration of action for immediate-release Adderall is 5–6 hours, for Ritalin it is about 4 hours.

Adderall is a 3:1 isomer mix of amphetamine salts with a 75% dextro- and 25% levo-amphetamine isomers. D-amphetamine is a stronger DA reuptake inhibitor, while the two isomers have similar strength of NE reuptake inhibition.

Individuals with substance use disorder generally should not be prescribed Adderall because it indirectly activates mu-opioid receptors. At high doses, this activation can cause euphoria.

When prescribed to college students, immediate-release Adderall is quite likely to be shared with classmates to boost academic performance. To minimize diversion, it is wise to prescribe a single daily pill of extended-release amphetamine. The longest-acting amphetamine formulation is Mydayis, which is expected to last 16 hours! Vyvanse (lisdexamfetamine) has a delayed and gradual onset (even if injected) which makes it unlikely to cause euphoria.

The extended-release formulation of mixed amphetamine salts (Adderall XR) is among the most commonly prescribed ADHD medications. Adderall XR 20 mg is comparable to two doses of Adderall IR 10 mg dosed 4 hours apart. This is accomplished by a capsule containing two types of beads designed to give a double-pulsed delivery of amphetamine.

The Adderall brand was launched in 1996. The same mixture of amphetamine had been previously available as Obetrol, used for weight loss. It is now the #45 most prescribed drug in U.S., just ahead of Ritalin (#47). Refer to pages 218–219 for general information, risks, and warnings about stimulants.

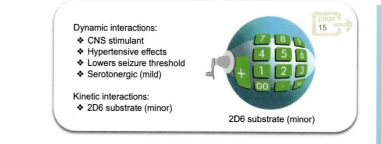

Adult dosing:

Adderall immediate-release
For ADHD, doses > 40 mg/day are rarely more effective; Divide BID–TID with doses separated by 4–6 hours; Start 5 mg BID; May increase by increments of 5 mg in weekly intervals; For narcolepsy, Start 10 mg q AM; may increase by increments of 10 mg in weekly intervals; divide BID–TID; Taper gradually to stop.

Adderall XR
For ADHD, may convert from IR Adderall to ER at same total daily mg dosed once daily in AM; Otherwise, start 20 mg q AM; May increase in increments of 10 mg in weekly intervals; Max is 60 mg/day; Doses > 20 mg/day are rarely more effective; May open capsule, but do not crush/chew beads; Taper gradually to stop.

Dynamic interactions:
- CNS stimulant
- Hypertensive effects
- Lowers seizure threshold
- Serotonergic (mild)

Kinetic interactions:
- 2D6 substrate (minor)

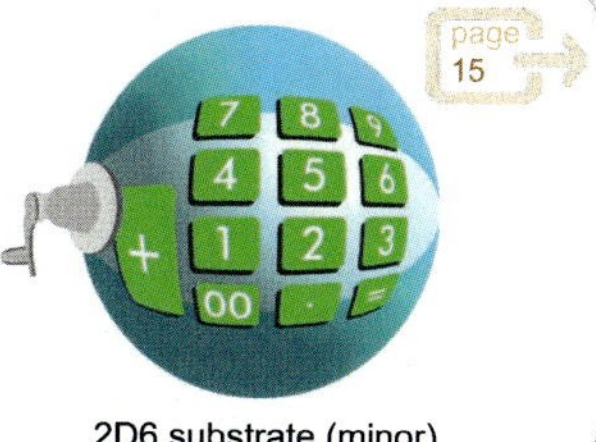

2D6 substrate (minor)

Formulations of amphetamine

Medication	Dose equiv	Adderall conversion	Available strengths (mg)	Approximate Duration	Splittable?	Notes
Adderall (mixed amphetamine salts)	20 mg	x 1	5, 7.5, 10, 12.5, 14, 20, 30	5 hr	No	75% D- and 25% L-amphetamine isomers
Adderall XR	20 mg	x 1	5, 10, 15, 20, 25, 30	10 hr	Can sprinkle	
Adzenys XR-ODT	12.5 mg	x 0.63	31, 6.3, 9.4, 12.5, 15.7, 18.8	10 hr	No	[add-ZEN-iss] Orally disintegrating tablet (ODT)
Mydayis			12.5, 25, 37.5, 50	16 hr	Can sprinkle	
Vyvanse (lisdexamfetamine)	50 mg	x 2.6	10, 20, 30, 40, 50, 60, 70	10–14 hr	Can dissolve	Prodrug converted to 100% D-amphetamine
Dexedrine	15 mg	x 0.83	5, 10	4 hr	Can sprinkle	
Evekeo (formerly Benzedrine)	20–30 mg	x 1.3	5, 10	4 hr	Yes	50% D- and 50% L-isomers; formerly Benzedrine
Desoxyn (methamphetamine)			5	4 hr	Yes	Methamphetamine

1976
IR $36–$220
XR $55–$212

100% D

Dextroamphetamine (DEXEDRINE)

DEX tro am FET a meen / DEK si dreen

"Decks o' amps / Decks drain'"

- ❖ Amphetamine stimulant
- ❖ DA > NE reuptake inhibitor
- ❖ DA > NE releaser
- ❖ DEA Schedule II

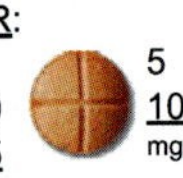

XR: 5, 10, 15 mg

5, 10 mg

FDA-approved for:
- ❖ ADHD (age 3+)
- ❖ Narcolepsy

Used off-label for:
- ❖ Weight loss (short-term)
- ❖ Treatment-resistant depression (short-term)
- ❖ Chronic fatigue

100% D
Amp

Dexedrine contains 100% of the more potent D-isomer of amphetamine. Compare this to Adderall, which is 75% D- and 25% L-amphetamine. Omission of the L-isomer makes Dexedrine slightly less likely to cause motor tics. It is approved for children as young as age 3. The only disadvantage to the more popular Adderall (5 hours) is Dexedrine's shorter duration of action (4 hours).

The extended-release version of dextroamphetamine is branded as Dexedrine Spansule, a capsule containing immediate-release and gradual-release beads. The first peak of serum amphetamine for the XR formulation is 1.6 hours, with a second peak at 6.5 hours, giving a duration of action of at least 8 hours.

Refer to pages 218–219 for general information about stimulants, with risks and warnings.

Adult dosing: For ADHD, Start 5 mg q AM; May increase in 5 mg increments in weekly intervals; Max is 60 mg/day, although doses ≥ 40 mg/day are rarely more effective. Divide IR dose BID–TID; Dexedrine XR is dosed once daily in AM; For narcolepsy, dose range is the same but start 10 mg/day; Taper gradually to stop.

THORA-DEX is a historical medication, no longer available or advisable. It was a combo of dextroamphetamine with the antipsychotic chlorpromazine (Thorazine).

when the patient's anxiety is complicated by depression . . .
both symptoms often respond to
THORA-DEX

*"When the patient's anxiety is complicated by depression...both symptoms often respond to THORA-DEX, a combination of a specific **anti-anxiety agent, 'Thorazine'**, and **a standard antidepressant, 'Dexedrine'**. The preparation is of unusual value in mental and emotional disturbances and in somatic conditions complicated by emotional stress—especially when depression occurs together with anxiety, agitation or apprehension. The patient treated with 'Thora-Dex" is generally both calm and alert...with normal interest, activity and capacity for work...'Thora-Dex should be administered discriminantly."*

Adderall : Dexedrine equivalent dosing

Adderall	Dexedrine	Accomplished with
10 mg	7.5 mg	1 and ½ of 5 mg Dexedrine tab
20 mg	15 mg	1 and ½ of 10 mg Dexedrine tab
30 mg	22.5 mg	2 and ¼ of 10 mg Dexedrine tab

Dynamic interactions:
- ❖ CNS stimulant
- ❖ Hypertensive effects
- ❖ Lowers seizure threshold
- ❖ Serotonergic (mild)

Kinetic interactions:
- ❖ 2D6 substrate (minor)

page 15

2D6 substrate (minor)

2016
$357–$434

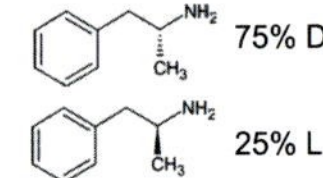

75% D
25% L

Adzenys XR-ODT (amphetamine)

add-ZEN-iss / am FET a meen

"Zen Amp'"

- ❖ Amphetamine stimulant
- ❖ DA > NE reuptake inhibitor
- ❖ DA > NE releaser
- ❖ DEA Schedule II

3.1 mg, 6.3, 9.4, 12.5, 15.7, 18.8

FDA-approved for:
- ❖ ADHD (age 6+)

Adzenys is an orally disintegrating tablet (ODT) version of Adderall XR formulated to dissolve on the tongue. Duration of effect is about 10 hours for either formulation. The only advantage of Adzenys is for patients unable to swallow pills. Adzenys has higher bioavailability than oral Adderall XR.

Dosing: According to the label, the maximum dose for ages 6–12 is higher (18.8 mg q AM) than for ages 13 and over (12.5 mg q AM); On a mg/kg body weight basis children clear amphetamine faster than adolescents and adults; For patients ages 6–17 the recommended starting dose is 6.3 mg q AM; For adults the recommended starting dose is 12.5 mg, which is also the target and maximum approved dose. See conversion table for those being switched from Adderall XR capsules to Adzenys.

Amp
XR
ODT

Not to be confused with Zenzedi, which is an off-brand of Dexedrine (dextroamphetamine)

Adderall XR dose equivalent	Adzenys dose	Inscription on tablet
5 mg	3.1 mg	A1
10 mg	6.3 mg	A2
15 mg	9.4 mg	A3
20 mg	12.5 mg	A4
25 mg	15.7 mg	A5
30 mg	18.8 mg	A6

Dynamic interactions:
- ❖ CNS stimulant
- ❖ Hypertensive effects
- ❖ Lowers seizure threshold
- ❖ Serotonergic (mild)

Kinetic interactions:
- ❖ 2D6 substrate (minor)

page 15

2D6 substrate (minor)

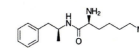

#99
2007
$306–$364

Lisdexamfetamine (VYVANSE)

lis dex am FET a meen / VY vance

"Long duration amp reVIVal"

- Amphetamine stimulant
- DA > NE reuptake inhibitor
- DA > NE releaser
- DEA Schedule II

10 mg, 20, 30, 40, 50, 60, 70

FDA-approved for:

- ADHD (Age 6+)
- Binge-eating disorder (moderate to severe)

Used off-label for:

- Weight loss (short-term)

Released in 2007, lisdexamfetamine (L-lysine-D-amphetamine) is a prodrug of dextroamphetamine (Dexedrine). Lisdexamfetamine becomes active upon cleavage of the lysine portion by enzymes in red blood cells, extending duration of action to 10–14 hours. Compared to Dexedrine, Vyvanse works in a smooth and steady fashion throughout the day. It does not have an afternoon "drop-off" effect including fatigue and irritability sometimes seen with immediate-release stimulants. Onset of therapeutic effect of Vyvanse is 1–2 hours.

Vyvanse is considered an abuse-deterrent form of Dexedrine by making the release of active drug more gradual. If the powder within the capsules is snorted or injected there will be no euphoric rush because active amphetamine is not immediately available. With taken orally, amphetamine abusers reported lower scores on a "drug-liking" scale with Vyvanse compared to other PO amphetamines. Regrettably, Vyvanse is a Schedule II controlled substance like all other prescription amphetamines. Refills are not allowed on Schedule II drugs, which is an inconvenience for patients and prescribers.

Vyvanse is the only stimulant approved for binge-eating disorder. This makes sense, because D-amphetamine has a greater appetite suppressive effect than the L-isomer. It may be used long-term for this indication. It is not approved for obesity without binge-eating, but it could be used short-term for that purpose, off-label.

Adult dosing: For ADHD, start 30 mg q AM; May increase by increments of 10–20 mg in 1-week intervals; Max is 70 mg/day; For binge eating disorder, the target dose is 50–70 mg q AM; start 30 mg q AM and increase to 50 mg after one week. The capsules contain powder that can be dissolved in water; Taper gradually to stop.

Lisdexam**feta**mine is spelled *-feta* (like the cheese) rather than *pheta* like the others.

Adderall XR equivalent	Vyvanse dose
5 mg	20 mg
10 mg	30 mg
15 mg	40 mg
20 mg	50 mg
25 mg	60 mg
30 mg	70 mg

Dynamic interactions:

- CNS stimulant
- Hypertensive effects
- Lowers seizure threshold
- Serotonergic (mild)

Kinetic interactions:

- 2D6 substrate (minor)

page 15

2D6 substrate (minor)

2017
$282–$330

75% D
25% L

MYDAYIS (amphetamine)

The longest acting amphetamine

"My (entire) day is amped"

- Amphetamine stimulant
- DA > NE reuptake inhibitor
- DA > NE releaser
- DEA Schedule II

12.5, 25, 37.5, 50 mg

FDA-approved for:

- ADHD (age 13+)

Mydayis has a 16 hour duration of therapeutic effect, making it the longest-acting amphetamine formulation.

The capsules contain two types of beads. IR beads release amphetamine at a pH of 5.5 (stomach pH) and delayed-release beads at a pH of 7.0 (distal portion of small intestine pH). Onset of therapeutic benefit is about 2 hours.

Mydayis is approved for treatment of ADHD for ages 13 and older. It should not be given to children under 13 because of higher plasma exposure and more frequent side effects, including insomnia and appetite suppression. Most other stimulants for ADHD are approved for ages 6 and older, with some stimulants approved for age 3 and older.

Mydayis is not an abuse-deterrent amphetamine like Vyvanse. Users could open a capsule of Mydayis, crush the beads with a mortar and pestle, and snort the powder for an immediate high comparable to cocaine. However, crushed Mydayis beads do not work for intravenous injection, according to an online forum for drug experimenters, erowid.org.

Adult dosing: Start 12.5 mg q AM; Increase in increments of 12.5 mg in weekly intervals; Max is 50 mg/day; Taper gradually to stop.

Dynamic interactions:

- CNS stimulant
- Hypertensive effects
- Lowers seizure threshold
- Serotonergic (mild)

Kinetic interactions:

- 2D6 substrate (minor)

page 15

2D6 substrate (minor)

2015
$113–$422

50% D
50% L

Evekeo (amphetamine)

e VEEK e oh

"Evil key hole"

- ❖ Amphetamine stimulant
- ❖ DA > NE reuptake inhibitor
- ❖ DA > NE releaser
- ❖ DEA Schedule II

5
10
mg

FDA-approved for:

- ❖ ADHD (age 3+)
- ❖ Narcolepsy
- ❖ Obesity (short-term)

Evekeo, released in 2018, is a new vesion of a previously available amphetamine known as Benzedrine. It is a 1:1 racemic mixture of L- and D-amphetamine, which is a higher L-amphetamine percentage than any other available prescription amphetamine. For most individuals with ADHD, this drug will be less effective than formulations with more D-amphetamine. Think "L" for loser. D-amphetamine is a stronger DA reuptake inhibitor, while the L- and D- isomers have similar strength when inhibiting NE reuptake.

Evekeo's potential for abuse is less than Dexedrine (pure D-amphetamine) but more than Ritalin (methylphenidate).

Benzedrine was the first available amphetamine, released in 1932 as an over-the-counter inhaler for nasal congestion and asthma. Consumers quickly discovered its energizing and euphoric effects. Benzedrine oral tablets were developed, and in 1936, they were marketed for narcolepsy, obesity, and low blood pressure. These pills became known as Bennies colloquially.

By the late 1930s, it became apparent that Benzedrine reduced hyperactivity in children. In 1959, the FDA made Benzedrine a prescription drug. It fell out of favor after a 1976 crossover study found it less effective for ADHD than Ritalin or Dexedrine. However, 15% of individuals in the study did better on Benzedrine.

Amphetamines have long been used for weight loss, but this is the only amphetamine approved by the FDA for obesity. Note that lisdexamfetamine (Vyvanse) is approved for binge-eating disorder, but not specifically for obesity.

Evekeo is an immediate-release formulation with duration of therapeutic effect of about 4 hours. 25 mg of Evekeo is approximately equivalent to 20 mg of Adderall.

Refer to pages 218–219 for general information about stimulants, with risks and warnings.

Adult dosing: For ADHD, start 5 mg BID (doses separated by 4–6 hours); May increase in 5 mg increments in weekly intervals; Max is 60 mg/day but doses > 40 mg/day are rarely more effective; For narcolepsy, start 10 mg AM; May increase by 10 mg increments in weekly intervals; For obesity (short-term treatment) the target dose is 15–30 mg/day divided TID, given 30–60 minutes before meals; Taper gradually to stop.

Dynamic interactions:

- ❖ CNS stimulant
- ❖ Hypertensive effects
- ❖ Lowers seizure threshold
- ❖ Serotonergic (mild)

Kinetic interactions:

- ❖ 2D6 substrate (minor)

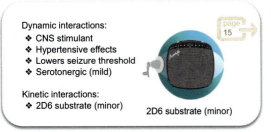

page 15

2D6 substrate (minor)

1943
$216–$875

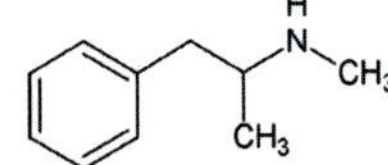

Methamphetamine (DESOXYN)

It's legal meth !

"I Desire oxy and Meth"

- ❖ Amphetamine stimulant
- ❖ DA > NE reuptake inhibitor
- ❖ DA > NE releaser
- ❖ DEA Schedule II

5
mg

Evekeo Meth Modafinil

FDA-approved for:

- ❖ ADHD (age 6+)
- ❖ Obesity (short-term)

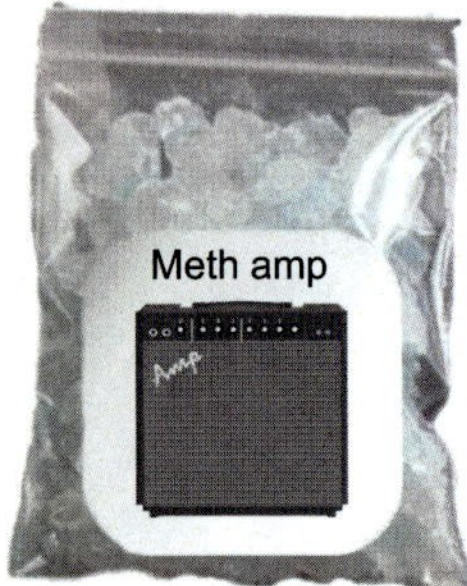

Prescription methamphetamine (Desoxyn) is rarely prescribed. Fewer than 20,000 scripts for Desoxyn are issued yearly. Desoxyn is unlikely to be abused due to cost. Crystal meth from the friendly neighborhood dealer is the same chemical.

Desoxyn is more potent than Adderall because the methyl group allows easier passage across the blood-brain barrier. Oral methamphetamine at recommended doses is not highly addictive, but it is abusable and addictive if injected intravenously. Street methamphetamine (meth, ice, crystal, speed, dope) is addictive due to method of delivery. If injected or smoked, it penetrates the blood-brain barrier in seconds.

Mechanism of action and effects of crystal meth are similar to crack cocaine. Meth has become more popular than cocaine due to lower cost and longer duration of high. Street meth is a common cause of drug-induced mania and psychosis, especially when consumed over multi-day binges. Medical complications of meth are a result of high dose amphetamine and impurities of the product. Meth abusers commonly develop rotting teeth ("meth mouth") due to the combination of vasocontraction and bruxism.

Methamphetamine Amphetamine (Adderall)

Adult dosing: For ADHD, Start 5 mg BID (AM and noon); May increase in 5 mg increments in weekly intervals; Usual target dose is 10 mg BID; Max is 25 mg total daily dose; For obesity, the dose is 5 mg TID.

Dynamic interactions:

- ❖ CNS stimulant
- ❖ Hypertensive effects
- ❖ Lowers seizure threshold
- ❖ Serotonergic (mild)

Kinetic interactions:

- ❖ 2D6 substrate (minor)

page 15

2D6 substrate (minor)

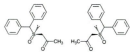

#284
1995
$33–$890

Modafinil (PROVIGIL)

mo daf i nil / pro VIJ il

"Moe daffodil is Pro-vigilant"

- ❖ Wakefulness promoter
- ❖ DA reuptake inhibitor
- ❖ Other possible mechanisms
- ❖ DEA Schedule IV

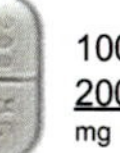

100
200
mg

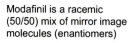

Modafinil is a racemic (50/50) mix of mirror image molecules (enantiomers)

S-modafinil R-modafinil

The pure R-enantiomer is available as armodafinil (NUVIGIL), described on the next page.

FDA-approved for:

- ❖ Narcolepsy
- ❖ Obstructive sleep apnea
- ❖ Shift work sleep disorder

Used off-label for:

- ❖ ADHD
- ❖ Jet lag
- ❖ Multiple sclerosis-related fatigue
- ❖ "Chronic fatigue syndrome"

Modafinil (Provigil) is a stimulant marketed as a "wakefulness promoting agent" approved for narcolepsy, shift work sleep disorder, and daytime fatigue caused by obstructive sleep apnea (OSA).

Modafinil's principal mechanism of action is a subject of controversy. It binds the dopamine transporter (DAT) like the Schedule II stimulants (amphetamine and methylphenidate). Modafinil binds DAT weakly, sufficiently to improve wakefulness, but insufficiently to induce euphoria. It is very selective for the dopamine transporter, with little to no effect on the norepinephrine or serotonin transporters.

Modafinil also causes the hypothalamus to release histamine and orexin. Both endogenous chemicals promote wakefulness. We know antihistamines (e.g., doxylamine, diphenhydramine) cause drowsiness by the opposite mechanism (blocking histamine). Suvorexant (Belsomra) also uses an opposite mechanism to oppose orexin and cause drowsiness (pages 72–73). We know promoting orexin is not modafinil's principal mechanism because modafinil is effective for narcoleptic individuals who lack orexin-porducing neurons.

In the United States, modafinil is a Schedule IV controlled substance, the same level of restriction as benzodiazepines. Modafinil is more tightly restricted in some countries, and in other countries, not regulated as a controlled substance at all.

Patients taking modafinil to combat daytime fatigue related to obstructive sleep apnea (OSA) are also expected to comply with their continuous positive airway pressure (CPAP) machine overnight.

Modafinil is used off-label for ADHD, particularly in patients with substance abuse issues. However, it appears to be ineffective in adults for ADHD (Cortese et al, 2018). For some children, the benefit of Modafinil for ADHD may be comparable to amphetamine or methylphenidate (Wang et al, 2016) although it is not necessarily safer or better tolerated than amphetamine/methylphenidate.

Modafinil improved sleep quality in individuals recovering from chronic cocaine use (Morgan et al, 2010).

Overdose of Provigil will cause agitation and insomnia, but there have been no overdose fatalities. The lethal dose is over #365 of 200 mg tabs, a year's supply.

The most common side effects are insomnia, headache, and nausea. It makes some patients irritable or nervous. Adverse effects become prominent at doses above 400 mg/day. Rare serious reactions are possible including Stevens-Johnson syndrome (SJS), Toxic epidermal necrolysis (TEN), Drug Reaction with Eosinophilia and Systemic Symptoms (DRESS syndrome), and Erythema Multiforme (consisting of raised edematous papules).

Dosing: The recommended dose for most indications is 200 mg q AM (100 mg if hepatic impairment). The max is 400 mg/day, but doses > 200 mg/day are rarely more effective for the FDA-approved indications. 400 mg may be more effective for ADHD. For shift work sleep disorder, take it 1 hour before work. If symptoms are not adequately controlled in the late afternoon, split the dose to BID given in AM and at noon.

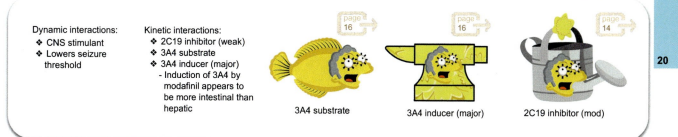

Dynamic interactions:

- ❖ CNS stimulant
- ❖ Lowers seizure threshold

Kinetic interactions:

- ❖ 2C19 inhibitor (weak)
- ❖ 3A4 substrate
- ❖ 3A4 inducer (major)
  - Induction of 3A4 by modafinil appears to be more intestinal than hepatic

page 16

3A4 substrate

page 16

3A4 inducer (major)

page 14

2C19 inhibitor (mod)

2007
$38–$564

Armodafinil (NUVIGIL)

ar mo daf i nil / nu VIJ il

"Armored Daffodil"

- ❖ Wakefulness promoter
- ❖ DA reuptake inhibitor
- ❖ Other possible mechanisms
- ❖ DEA Schedule IV

50
150
200
250
mg

FDA-approved for:
- ❖ Narcolepsy
- ❖ Obstructive sleep apnea

Used off-label for:
- ❖ Shift work sleep disorder
- ❖ ADHD
- ❖ Jet lag
- ❖ Multiple sclerosis-related fatigue
- ❖ "Chronic fatigue syndrome"

Nuvigil has a longer duration of action than Provigil. Think of the armor as protecting R-modafinil from being metabolized.

"The New Provigil". The wakefulness-promoting agent armodafinil (Nuvigil) was FDA-approved in 2007 and went generic in 2016 (following Provigil, which was approved in 1998 and went generic in 2012).

As the name suggests, **arm**odafinil is the **R**-enantiomer of modafinil (modafinil being a 50/50 mixture of R-modafinil and its mirror image S-modafinil). Nuvigil is FDA-approved for somnolence due to obstructive sleep apnea, narcolepsy, or shift-work sleep disorder. Despite some evidence of Nuvigil being effective for jet lag, the FDA declined to approve it for that indication in 2010.

Provigil (racemic modafinil) and Nuvigil (R-modafinil) have similar cost, clinical effects, and side effects. Nuvigil is preferred because it has a longer duration of effect (8 hours) and fewer kinetic interactions than Provigil (6 hours). Otherwise, the information from the modafinil (Provigil) monograph on the preceding page is applicable to Nuvigil.

Dosing: For most indications, maintenance dose is 150–250 mg q AM. For shift work sleep disorder, dose 1 hour before start of work shift.

Nuvigil inhibits/induces similar enzymes as Provigil, but to a weaker extent.

Dynamic interactions:
- ❖ CNS stimulant
- ❖ Lowers seizure threshold

Kinetic interactions:
- ❖ 2C19 inhibitor (weak)
- ❖ 3A4 substrate
- ❖ 3A4 inducer (major)

page 16
page 16

3A4 substrate

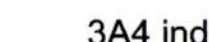
3A4 inducer (major)

page 14

2C19 inhibitor (mod)

2019
$657–$714

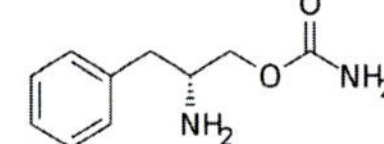

Solriamfetol (SUNOSI)

SOL ri AM fe tol / su NO see

"Sun nosey with Solar feet"

- ❖ Norepinephrine-dopamine reuptake inhibitor (NDRI)
- ❖ Schedule IV

75
150
mg

FDA-approved for:
- ❖ Excessive daytime sleepiness due to:
  - Narcolepsy
  - Obstructive sleep apnea (OSA)

Solriamfetol (Sunosi) is a new wakefulness promoting medication that lasts for 9 hours. It is not considered a stimulant. It is a norepinephrine and weak dopamine reuptake inhibitor. Sunosi could be conceptualized as an atypical antidepressant with a mechanism similar bupropion (Wellbutrin). However, solriamfetol is not approved for depression, and clinical trials did not include psychiatric patients. About 1 in 25 subjects treated for narcolepsy/sleep apnea had psychiatric side effects such as irritability and anxiety.

Solriamfetol is a Schedule IV controlled substance. By comparison, bupropion is non-controlled but does have potential for abuse at high doses.

Subjects who abused drugs reported "drug liking" similar to the appetite-suppressing stimulant phentermine (Adipex) when solriamfetol was taken at supratherapeutic dose. Phentermine is also Schedule IV.

Other effects include nausea and appetite suppression. It may increase blood pressure and heart rate.

An advantage over bupropion is that solriamfetol is free from kinetic drug/drug interactions.

The two other wakefulness promoters approved for narcolepsy/sleep apnea are modafinil (Provigil) and armodafinil (Nuvigil), which are also Schedule IV. For context, methylphenidate (Ritalin) and amphetamine (Adderall) are more strictly regulated as Schedule II controlled substances.

Dosing: Start 75 mg q AM. Dose may be increased to 150 mg after 3 days based on efficacy and tolerability. Maximum dose is 150 mg/day.

Dynamic interactions:
- ❖ Dopaminergic
- ❖ Hypertensive

Kinetic interactions:
- ❖ None significant
  - "in a bubble"

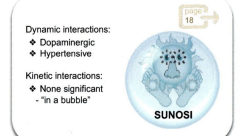

page 18

#226
1959
$10–$36

Phentermine (ADIPEX)

FEN ter meen / ADD i pex

"Fun termites (for) Adipose extraction"

- Appetite suppressant
- Stimulant (noradrenergic)
- DEA Schedule IV

8
15
30
37.5
mg

FDA-approved for:
- Obesity (short-term)

Phentermine is a sympathomimetic anorectic (appetite suppressing stimulant) ranked #226 of most prescribed medications. Most psychiatrists do not prescribe it due to its potential to induce mania. The problem with phentermine is sleep disruption due to a half-life of 24 hours. By comparison, amphetamine (Adderall) has a 12 hour half-life.

Phentermine has been referred to as an atypical amphetamine or substituted amphetamine. Since phentermine has slight potential for abuse and addiction,it is restricted on DEA Schedule IV (like a benzodiazepine) rather than Schedule II like dopaminergic stimulants (Adderall and Ritalin). Phentermine reduces hunger through the hypothalamus, mostly by norepinephrine release. It causes the release of dopamine and serotonin to a lesser extent.

Phentermine is approved for short-term (up to 12 weeks) weight reduction, along with exercise and behavioral modification. It is effective in suppressing appetite, but tolerance develops. Most of the loss occurs through the first few weeks but may continue at a slower rate if continued (off-label) through the ninth month.

Phentermine is contraindicated with any cardiac condition. It may increase blood pressure and heart rate and should be used with caution in patients with even mild hypertension. It should not be prescribed to individuals with bipolar or schizophrenia spectrum disorders.

Phentermine was introduced in 1959 with fenfluramine as a combination branded as Fen-Phen. The combination pill was discontinued in 1997 because fenfluramine was found to cause valvular heart disease due to its effect on 5-HT_{2B} receptors, which are plentiful in heart valves. About 15% of Fen-Phen users were affected. Fenfluramine was also associated with pulmonary hypertension and irreversible loss of cerebral serotonergic nerve fibers.

Dosing: 18.75–37.5 mg q AM before breakfast; When tolerance to the anorexiant effect develops, taper to discontinue; Do not exceed the recommended dose. If the patient insists on taking it long-term, consider alternating one month on and one month off.

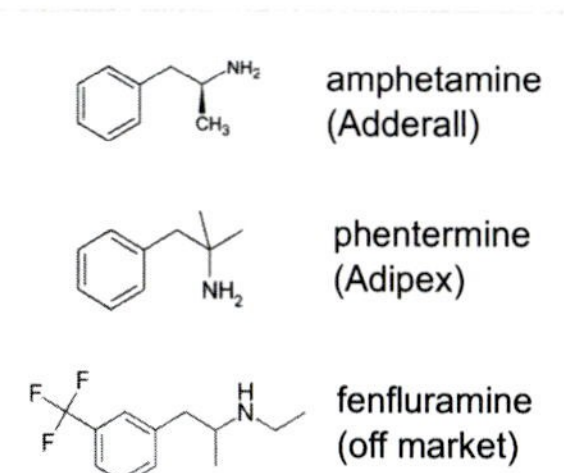

amphetamine (Adderall)

phentermine (Adipex)

fenfluramine (off market)

Recommendation: If a weight loss pill is needed, use metformin instead. Metformin is suitable for long-term use, may prevent diabetes, and possibly promote longevity.

Dynamic interactions:
- CNS stimulant (noradrenergic)
- Hypertensive
- Serotonergic (weak)
- Dopaminergic (weak)

Kinetic interactions:
- Kinetic interactions are unlikely because phentermine is excreted in urine, unchanged.

page 18

2013
$195–$231

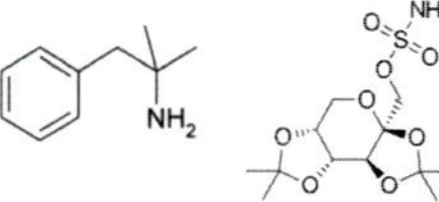

QSYMIA (phentermine + topiramate ER)

kyoo SIM e uh

"Quiz me!"

- Weight loss combo
- Atypical amphetamine
- Antiepileptic
- DEA Schedule IV

3.75/23
7.5/46
11.25/69
15/92
mg

FDA-approved for:
- Obesity (long-term)

Qsymia is a fixed-dose combination of phentermine and extended-release (ER) topiramate (Topamax). It is approved for those with body mass index (BMI) ≥ 30 kg/m², which is the definition of obesity. It is also approved for individuals who are merely overweight (BMI ≥ 27 kg/m²) with hypertension, dyslipidemia, or type 2 diabetes. It is associated with a weight loss of about 10% body weight, which is more than with either component drug alone. The effect of Qsymia on cardiovascular morbidity has not been established. It should be stopped if 5% of body weight is not lost while on the maximum dose for 3 months. The dose of each component medication is lower than if used for monotherapy. Topiramate alone is not FDA-approved for weight loss. Although unproven, topiramate may have mood stabilizing properties that could theoretically counteract phentermine's risk of inducing mania.

Qsymia is available only from certified pharmacies and certified prescribers to ensure female patients are counseled on the risk of birth defects caused by topiramate, which increases risk of oral clefts by about 4-fold. The topiramate component can also cause cognitive impairment, paresthesia (almost 20%), dysgeusia (metallic taste), renal stones, and metabolic acidosis. The phentermine component can elevate heart rate and cause insomnia, constipation, and dry mouth.

Dosing: Note that comparable (although not exact) doses can be achieved with generic phentermine and topiramate prescribed separately; Qsymia is dosed once daily in AM (with or without food); Start 3.75/23 mg (phentermine/topiramate ER) x 2 weeks, then 7.5/46 mg QD in AM. If 3% weight loss not achieved by 12 weeks, either stop or increase dose. Once the maximum dose of 15/92 mg is achieved, if 5% loss is not achieved at 12 weeks. As for any seizure medication (topiramate), taper to discontinue. Do not exceed 7.5/46 mg if renal (phentermine) or hepatic (topiramate) impairment.

Topiramate

Dynamic interactions:
- There are several, as detailed on page 36.

page 36

Kinetic interactions:
- Topiramate is a weak 3A4 in**D**ucer, which is insignificant at doses < 200 mg/day. Since the max dose of topiramate for treatment with Qsymia is 92 mg, kinetic interactions should not be an issue.

page 16

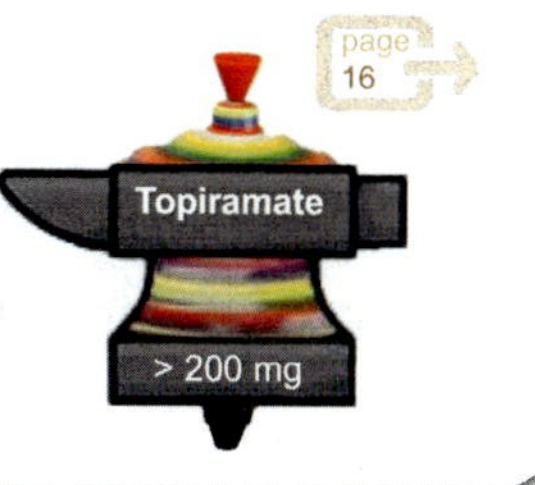

STIMULANTS 20

2012–2020
Removed from market

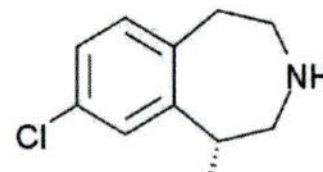

Lorcaserin (BELVIQ)

lor KAS er in / bell VEEK
"Lowercase Belly"

- ❖ Appetite suppressant
- ❖ 5-HT_{2C} receptor agonist
- ❖ DEA Schedule IV

ER: 20 mg

IR: 10 mg

Removed from market

FDA-approved for:
- ❖ Obesity (long-term)

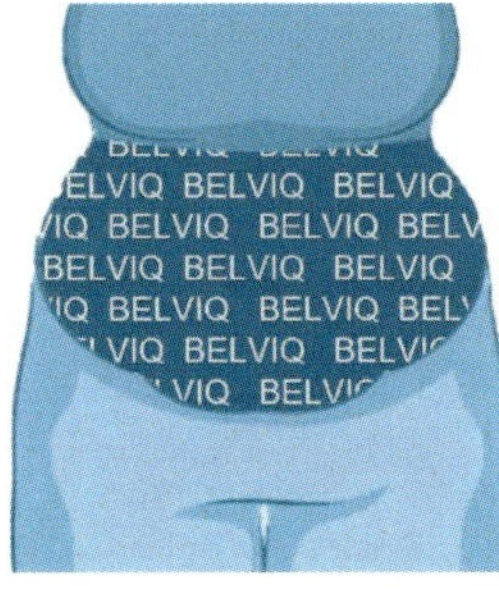

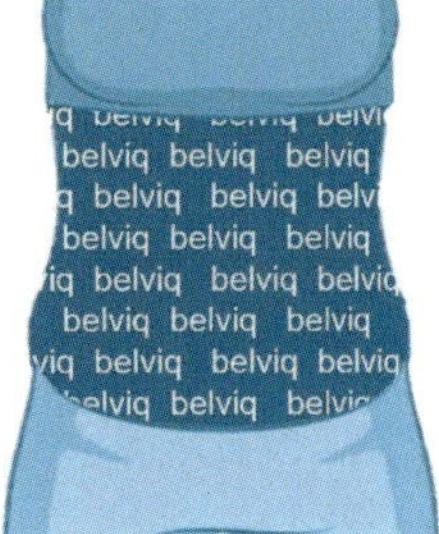

Lorcaserin (Belviq) was a weight loss medication removed from the market in 2020 after a large study showed increased risk of cancer, 7.7% versus 7.1% for placebo.

Lorcaserin (Belviq) is a selective 5-HT_{2C} serotonin receptor agonist. This receptor is thought to regulate satiety (feeling full). "I'd like '2C' my feet". In other words, lorcaserin suppresses appetite.

Like other weight loss medications, lorcaserin was approved for individuals who are obese (BMI ≥ 30) or overweight (BMI ≥ 27) with a weight-related comorbid condition (diabetes, hypertension, hyperlipidemia). Patients were instructed to stop taking after 12 weeks if < 5% of body weight was lost.

Lorcaserin was a Schedule IV controlled substance because dissociation and euphoria are possible at high doses.

It raises prolactin levels to a modest extent, which poses a risk of gynecomastia. Risk of serotonin syndrome if used with other serotonergics.
The label warned that damage to heart valves is theoretically possible based on experience with fenfluramine (see preceding page). However, fenfluramine was a 5-HT_{2B} agonist, whereas lorcaserin is mostly specific for 5-HT_{2C}, with some weak 5-HT_{2B} agonist activity.

Depression/suicide may be possible with serotonergic medications. All antidepressants have a black box warning to this effect, but lorcaserin did not.

Dynamic interactions:
- ❖ Serotonergic (strong)
- ❖ Prolactin elevation (mild)
- ❖ 5-HT2B receptor agonist (minor)
  - avoid with other 5-HT2B agonists like cabergoline due to risk of heart valve damage

Kinetic interactions:
- ❖ 2D6 inHibitor (weak)
  - » contraindicated with thioridazine (Mellaril) due to risk of QT prolongation from high thioridazine levels

page 15

2D6 inHibitor (weak)

Mechanism	Example	Effect	Mnemonic
5-HT_{2A} agonist	LSD	Hallucinations and serotonin syndrome	"I'd like 2 Acid trips"
5-HT_{2B} agonist	Fenfluramine - removed from market	Suppresses appetite but damages heart valves	"I'd like 2B thin but not dead"
5-HT_{2C} agonist	Lorcaserin - removed from market	Suppresses appetite without damaging heart	"I'd like 2C my feet"

Pills approved for weight loss

All of these are approved for long-term treatment except for phentermine (short-term). Plenity capsules are considered a medical device, not a medication. Off-label treatments include metformin, topiramate (monotherapy), and lisdexamfetamine (Vyvanse).

Medication	Approx weight loss	Comments/Side effects
Naltrexone/bupropion (CONTRAVE)	~ 6% body weight	Nausea, headache, constipation, dizziness, dry mouth; Bupropion is a strong 2D6 inHibitor.
Phentermine (ADIPEX)	~ 5% body weight	Schedule IV controlled; Insomnia, anxiety, elevated BP and HR, mania; Contraindicated with cardiovascular disease
Phentermine/topiramate ER (QSYMIA)	~ 10% body weight	Topiramate: paresthesias, dizziness, altered taste, renal stones, acidosis, confusion; Phentermine: see preceding page
Lorcaserin (BELVIQ)	3–10% body weight	Removed from market in 2020; Previously a Schedule IV controlled stimulant; Selective 5-HT2C receptor agonist that suppresses appetite; Labeling includes a warning of cardiac valvulopathy because fenfluramine damaged heart valves via 5-HT2B agonism.
Orlistat (ALLI)	~ 10% body weight	Over-the-counter; Inhibits gastric and pancreatic lipases, causing triglycerides to be excreted in feces. High rate of discontinuation due to GI distress, flatulence, and greasy orange fecal incontinence; Interferes with vitamin absorption.
Liraglutide (SAXENDA)	5–10% body weight	Subcutaneous medication branded as Victoza for diabetes; Black box warning of thyroid tumors; Also risk of nephrotoxicity and pancreatitis
Cellulose and Citric Acid (PLENITY)	10% on average	An FDA-cleared prescription "device" taken as pills before meals with 16 ounces of water; superabsorbent hydrogel particles expands 100-fold to fill the stomach, then pass undigested; Side effects similar to placebo

2019
$7,262–$8,869

Pitolisant (WAKIX)

pi TOL i sant / way kicks

"Wacky Pitstop"

❖ Histamine-3 antagonist
❖ Approved for narcolepsy
❖ Non-controlled

4.45
17.8
mg

FDA-approved for:

❖ Excessive daytime sleepiness (EDS) with narcolepsy

Used off-label for:

❖ Somnolence/fatigue due to other conditions

Penelope Pitstop's car (the Compact Pussycat) from the Hanna-Barbera animated series Wacky Races (1968)

Pitolisant (Wakix) debuted in 2019 as the first approved histamine-3 (H_3) antagonist. It is highly selective for H_3 receptors, with no appreciable binding H_1, H_2, or H_4 receptors. Unlike other narcolepsy medications it is not a controlled substance and has no apparent potential for abuse/misuse.

Blocking H_3 receptors in the brain has a stimulating effect, in contrast with blocking H_1 which causes sedation.

Compared to modafinil (Provigil), pitolisant had similar efficacy but better tolerability (Romigi et al, 2018). It may take up to 8 weeks for some patients to achieve a clinical response.

Side effects may include insomnia, nausea and anxiety. It possibly may suppress appetite.

Dosing: Start 8.9 mg QD x 1 week, then 17.8 mg QD which can be the target dose, or on week three may increase to the maximum dose of 35.6 mg QD; Do not exceed 17.8 QD if 2D6 poor metabolizer genotype, concomitant use of a strong 2D6 inHibitor, or moderate hepatic/renal insufficiency; May take with or without food.

Dynamic interactions:

❖ Central histamine effects
❖ QT prolongation

No interactions with:

❖ Sodium oxybate (Xyrem)
❖ Modafinil (Provigil)
❖ Armodafinil (Nuvigil)

Kinetic interactions:

❖ 2D6 substrate
- For individuals with a 2D6 poor metabolizer (PM) genotype (10% of population), do not exceed 17.8 mg
- Do not exceed 17.8 mg if taking a strong 2D6 inHibitor (fluoxetine, paroxetine, bupropion)
- Contraindicated with quinidine (strong 2D6 inHibitor that also prolongs QT interval)

❖ 3A4 inDucer (weak)
- May make hormonal contraception ineffective

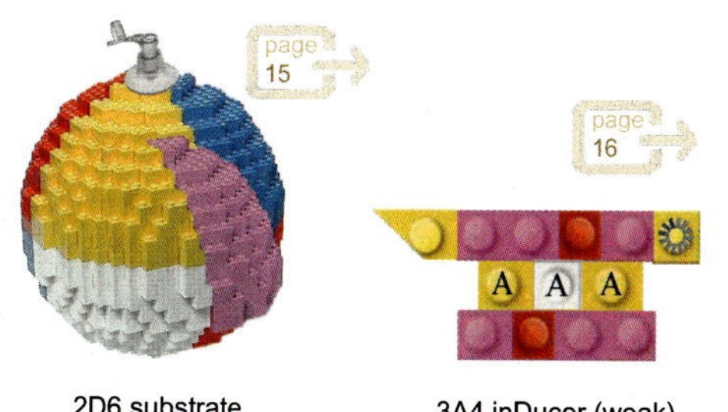

2D6 substrate

3A4 inDucer (weak)

Medications approved for narcolepsy:

Narcolepsy medications	GoodRx coupon/ Full retail price	DEA Schedule	Nature	Mechanism	
Pitolisant (WAKIX)	$7,262/$8,869	N/A	Stimulant	Histamine-3 (H_3) antagonist	Similar efficacy to modafinil with reportedly fewer side effects
Methylphenidate (RITALIN, etc)	$25/$91	II	Stimulant	DA > NE reuptake inhibitor (DNRI)	Expensive ER formulations also approved
Amphetamine (ADDERALL, etc)	$29/$92	II	Stimulant	DNRI plus DA > NE releaser	Expensive ER formulations also approved
Modafinil (PROVIGIL)	$38/$564	IV	Stimulant	DA reuptake inhibitor (DRI)	Also causes the hypothalamus to release histamine and orexin
Armodafinil (NUVIGIL)	$38/$564	IV	Stimulant	DRI	Longer-acting R-enantiomer of modafinil
Solriamfetol (SUNOSI)	$657/$714	IV	Stimulant	DNRI	Like bupropion, but not approved for depression
Sodium oxybate (XYREM)	$10,900 retail (coupon N/A)	III	Sedative	GABA analogue	Same as the club drug GHB; Improves sleep quality by suppressing REM sleep

$4–$8

Caffeine (Vivarin, NoDoz, Jet-Alert)

❖ Adenosine receptor antagonist

100
200
mg

Adenosine

Caffeine is considered a wakefulness promoting agent rather than a stimulant. Structurally, caffeine is a methylxanthine, as are theobromine (found in chocolate) and theophylline (prescription medication for asthma).

Caffeine works as an adenosine receptor antagonist. While awake, adenosine accumulates in the neuronal synapse and eventually induces drowsiness. Caffeine temporarily blocks the effect of adenosine.

Caffeine is the world's most consumed psychoactive drug, legal in all countries. It has not been banned anywhere since 1823 in Sweden.

Caffeine has moderate neuroprotective properties, preventing Parkinson's disease (PD) with a linear dose-response relation, higher caffeine intake is associated with a lower risk of PD (Costa et al, 2010). About 300 mg of daily caffeine reduced PD risk by about 25%, 500 mg reduced risk by about 50%.

"Caffeine Use Disorder" is **not** recognized as a DSM-5 diagnosis, although it is found in an addendum to DSM-5 as a "condition for further study" with proposed criteria not intended for clinical use. If a caffeine use-related disorder is to be included in DSM-6 there needs to be high diagnostic threshold because of the high rate of habitual nonproblematic daily caffeine use in the general population. DSM-5 does recognize Caffeine Intoxication and Caffeine Withdrawal.

Adenosine

Adenosine is a purine nucleoside. Its derivatives include ATP, ADP, and cAMP. Adenosine itself is a **neuromodulator** involved in promoting sleep and suppressing arousal. Caffeine is an adenosine receptor antagonist.

Product	Caffeine
Decaffeinated coffee (8 ounces)	~ 7 mg
Coca-Cola (12-ounce can)	34 mg
Pepsi (12-ounce can)	38 mg
Diet Coke (12-ounce can)	42 mg
Excedrin Migraine (with 250 mg acetaminophen and 250 mg aspirin)	65 mg
Espresso shot (1 ounce)	~ 70 mg
Mountain Dew (12-ounce can)	71 mg
Red Bull (8.46 ounces)	80 mg
White caffeine pills (Jet-Alert)	100 mg
Monster energy drink (16 ounces)	160 mg
Average daily consumption in US	164 mg
5 Hour Energy (2 ounces)	200 mg
Yellow caffeine pills (Vivarin)	200 mg
Coffee (12 ounces)	~ 200 mg
Redline Power Rush (8-ounce bottle)	316 mg
10 Hour time release energy shot (1.93 ounce)	422 mg

Symptoms of caffeine intoxication generally occur at greater than 1,000 mg/day including muscle twitching, rambling speech, tachycardia or cardiac arrhythmia, periods of inexhaustibility, and psychomotor agitation. An overdose of 2,000 mg may require hospitalization. Over 5,000 mg can be fatal due to arrhythmias, rhabdomyolysis, and renal failure. A bottle of caffeine pills generally contains over 10,000 mg.

Symptoms of caffeine withdrawal may include headaches, fatigue, dysphoria or irritability, difficulty concentrating, and flu-like symptoms (nausea, vomiting, or muscle pain/stiffness).

A short nap preceded by caffeine has been shown to outperform either independently for improving alertness (Reynor et al, 1997). Naps longer than 20 minutes can cause residual grogginess from waking in the middle of deeper sleep. Consider a taking a caffeine nap, or "nappuccino", consuming caffeine before lying down for a power nap.

Individuals who have difficulty waking in the morning can set an early alarm 30–60 minutes before the desired wake time as a prompt to take a caffeine pill at bedside. Jet-Alert 100 mg tablets are suitable because they are cheap and small enough to be swallowed without water.

Caffeine is readily reabsorbed by the renal tubules so only a small percentage is excreted unchanged in the urine.

Dosing: The author recommends Jet-Alert 100 mg tabs. They are small white tablets costing $0.04 each; For difficulty waking, keep 100–200 mg at bedside to take with an early alarm set 1 hour before desired waking time; Consider consuming caffeine before taking a 10–20 minute power nap.

Dynamic interactions:

- ❖ CNS stimulant
- ❖ Hypertensive effects (minor)
- ❖ Lowers seizure threshold (minor)

Kinetic interactions:

- ❖ 1A2 substrate
- ❖ Decreases lithium levels (minor)

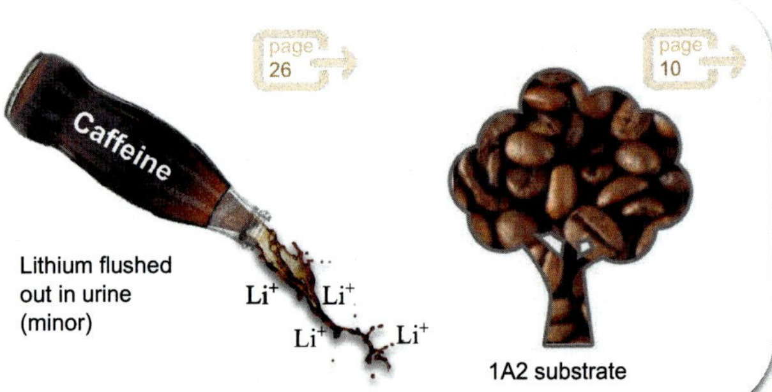

page 26

page 10

Lithium flushed out in urine (minor)

1A2 substrate

Medications for Tobacco Cessation

Medication	Cost/mo	Class	Details
Varenicline (CHANTIX)	$400–$500	Partial agonist/antagonist of nicotinic acetylcholine receptors	Twice as effective as bupropion and nicotine replacement. There was previously a black box warning of risk of suicidal thoughts, hostility, and depression. The warning was removed in 2016 when varenicline was found no worse than placebo in producing psychiatric adverse events.
Bupropion (ZYBAN)	$10–$100	NE & DA reuptake inhibitor (NDRI) antidepressant	FDA-approved for smoking cessation under the trade name ZYBAN, bupropion is better known as WELLBUTRIN, as described in the antidepressant chapter. Half as effective as varenicline.
Nicotine replacement (Gum, transdermal, etc.)	$30–$150	Agonist of nicotinic acetylcholine receptors	Although tobacco is carcinogenic, nicotine itself is neuroprotective. Most effective when two formulations are used together, e.g., gum plus patch.

Medications for Alcohol Use Disorder

Medication	FDA approved	Mechanism	Details
Disulfiram (ANTABUSE)	Yes	Acetaldehyde dehydrogenase inhibitor	Causes acute illness with vomiting if the patient drinks
Acamprosate (CAMPRAL)	Yes	Partial GABA(A) agonist and weak NMDA antagonist	Supports abstinence by decreasing the “stick" (discomfort) of alcohol abstinence—prevents “the first drink”
Naltrexone (ReVia)	Yes	Opioid antagonist	Prevents excessive drinking by decreases the “carrot” (reinforcing effects) of drinking—prevents “the second drink”
Naltrexone LAI (VIVITROL)	Yes	Opioid antagonist (long-acting injectable)	More effective than oral naltrexone
Topiramate (TOPAMAX)	No	Voltage-gated sodium and calcium channel blocker	Possibly decreases the “stick” and “carrot”
Gabapentin (NEURONTIN)	No	Voltage-gated calcium channel blocker	Decreases craving and the “stick" (discomfort) of abstinence
Baclofen (LIORESAL)	No	GABA(B) agonist	Suppresses anxiety and reduces cravings; May be more effective than the FDA-approved medications

Opioid antagonists for Opioid Overdose

Medication	Cost/dose	Details
Naloxone auto-injector (EVZIO)	$1,900	The device provides on the spot voice and visual instructions to guide a bystander to administer 2 mg IM into the thigh, through the clothing if necessary. May repeat every 2–3 minutes until the ambulance arrives.
Naloxone intranasal (NARCAN)	$70	The bystander sprays Narcan into one nostril. May repeat every 2–3 minutes in alternating nostrils.

Medications for Opioid Use Disorder

Medication	Formulation	cost/mo	Mechanism	Details
Naltrexone	ReVia - PO tab Vivitrol - IM q 4 wk	$33 $1300	opioid antagonist	Not a controlled substance. Also approved for alcohol dependence. Adherence is poor. Does not decrease overall mortality. Same mechanism as naloxone, but longer acting.
Buprenorphine	Subutex - SL tabs Probuphine - q 6 mo implant Sublocade - SC q month	$170 $820 $1580	partial opioid agonist	Schedule III. A wonderful drug because it has a ceiling effect and blocks full opioid agonists. Unless the patient is pregnant, buprenorphine is best combined with naloxone as an abuse deterrent.
Buprenorphine + Naloxone	Suboxone - SL tabs Bunavail - buccal film Cassipa - SL film Zubsolv - SL tabs	$85 $450 $470 $400	partial opioid agonist + opioid antagonist	Schedule III. The drug of choice for maintenance of opioid use disorder. Naloxone is included as an abuse deterrent to keep users from snorting or injecting buprenorphine.
Methadone	PO tabs PO solution	$13 $20	full opioid agonist	Schedule II. QT prolongation. It reduces mortality compared to no treatment, but is itself involved in overdose deaths.

Gum (1984)
$0.13–$0.50/piece

Patch (1991)
$0.90–$3/each

Nicotine

Nicorette gum
NicoDerm CQ patch

❖ Nicotinic cholinergic receptor agonist

7
14
21
mg

2
4
mg

Tobacco is the #2 most used psychoactive substance worldwide, second to caffeine. Tobacco accounts for 20% of deaths in the US. Cigarettes are highly addictive. Each year about half of smokers try to quit, although only about 6% will be successful in a given year, with 60% relapsing within the first week. Although nicotine is the component of tobacco that causes physical dependence, nicotine itself may be less addictive than commonly regarded. Animals studies have shown that nicotine is a weak reinforcer (Clemens et al., 2009). Denicotinized cigarettes provide greater satisfaction than intravenous nicotine in healthy smokers, which suggests that non-nicotine components in cigarettes, e.g., acetaldehyde, contribute to addictiveness of smoking (Rose et al., 2000).

Nicotine stimulates nicotinic cholinergic receptors (which normally are stimulated by acetylcholine) causing release of dopamine in the brain's reward center (nucleus accumbens). The faster a drug enters the brain, the more reinforcing it is. With smoking, nicotine enters the brain quickly, causing a rapid dopamine spike in the nucleus accumbens, resulting in pleasure. Nicotine replacement products are much less reinforcing because entry into the brain is gradual and delayed. The same principle applies to other addictive substances. For instance, amphetamine has low addictive potential when a delayed-release formulation is taking orally but is highly addictive when administered intravenously. Nicotinic cholinergic receptors adapt to intermittent pulsatile delivery of nicotine in a way that leads to addiction. The receptors become desensitized, meaning they do not respond to nicotine or acetylcholine. With chronic desensitization, the receptors are unregulated (i.e., more receptors are present) which strengthens cravings.

To maximum success with nicotine replacement products, use two products concurrently, e.g., gum and transdermal patch. Other nicotine formulations are available including lozenges, nasal spray, and the Nicotrol inhaler. No single form of nicotine replacement therapy has been shown to be more effective than another.

"Nicotine dependence" as defined by DSM-IV was revised for DSM-5 to "Tobacco use disorder" (not nicotine use disorder) because use of nicotine without the carcinogens is rarely problematic. Nicotine provides a neuroprotective benefit to the brain, potentially preventing Alzheimer's disease and Parkinson's disease. Nicotine improves cognitive functioning in Alzheimer's patients and in healthy individuals. Long-term use of nicotine medications does not appear to cause medical harm (Shields 2011, as cited in DSM-5), though there may be a modest increase of blood sugar and triglycerides.

Almost 90% of individuals with schizophrenia smoke, compared to 33% in the general population and 45–70% in patients with other psychiatric diagnoses (Lohr & Flynn, 1992), with ADHD and bipolar disorder at the upper end of this range. Nicotine appears to be used as self-medication for cognitive deficits and sensory disruption of schizophrenia. Alpha-7 nicotinic receptor agonists are under development as potential medications for schizophrenia and Alzheimer's disease.

DSM-5 defines Tobacco Withdrawal, but not tobacco/nicotine "intoxication". A potentially fatal dose of nicotine for an adult is at least 500–1000 mg, which is not feasible unless you are drink nicotine insecticide.

Nicotine is mostly metabolized by CYP2A6, an enzyme not visualized in this book. Individuals who are 2A6 poor metabolizers are less likely to become dependent smokers, and those who smoke consume fewer cigarettes than those smokers with normal nicotine metabolism (Pianezza et al, 1998). The main metabolite of nicotine is cotinine—"pickin' tobacco leaves and cotton".

Nicotine transdermal (NicoDerm CQ)
Nicotine patches are available in 7, 14, and 21 mg strengths. The CQ in the branded product stands for "Committed Quitters". The patch may be changed every 24 hours or removed at bedtime. Vivid dreams are very common for individuals who wear the patch overnight.

Nicotine gum (Nicorette)
Nicotine polacrilex [po LAC ri lex], available over-the-counter, is nicotine bound to a resin to maximize the amount of nicotine released and absorbed by the oral mucosa. 80 to 90% of the nicotine released from the gum is absorbed by the mouth. The remainder is swallowed and may cause nausea. Chew the gum briefly until tingling is felt, then park it between cheek and gumline until tingling stops, then repeat for about 30 minutes.

Gum Dosing: Use PRN, up to 24 pieces/day. Available in 2 mg and 4 mg strengths. Use 4 mg strength for those smoking > 1 pack/day. For lighter smokers use 2 mg or, for cost savings, half of 4 mg pieces. For weeks 1–6, chew every 1–2 hours and try to decrease frequency of use every 3 weeks. Gum is addictive if continued longer than 6 months. However, health risks are minimal if it is continued indefinitely.

Tobacco

Dynamic interactions:

❖ Hyperglycemia (nicotine)

Kinetic interactions:

❖ The hydrocarbons in smoked tobacco are potent inDucers of 1A2 that significantly reduce serum levels of several antipsychotics.

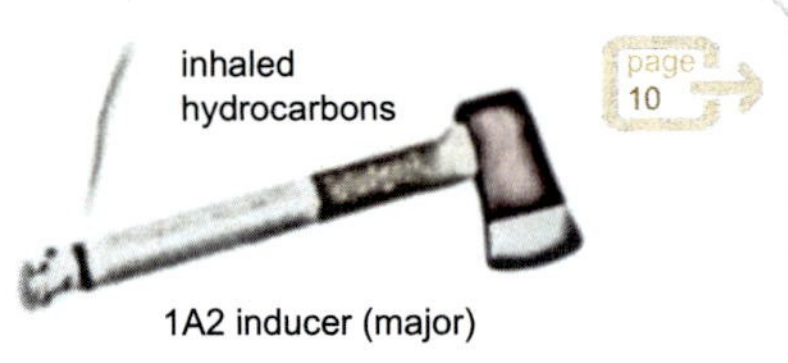

page 10

Nicotine

Dynamic interactions:

❖ Hyperglycemia (insulin resistance)

Kinetic interactions:

❖ CYP2A6 substrate; 2A6 is not discussed elsewhere in this book. Some medications induce or inhibit 2A6 and could thereby affect the amount of nicotine the individual self-administers. Individuals who are 2A6 poor metabolizers, if they smoke, are likely to smoke fewer cigarettes and hence are less likely to develop lung cancer. Nicotine is visualized in a box because kinetic interactions involving pure nicotine exist, but do not need to be taken into consideration when prescribing medication.

page 18

2006
$422–$522

Varenicline (CHANTIX)

var EN e kleen / CHANT ix

"Very inclined Chanting"

❖ Nicotinic receptor partial agonist

0.5
1
mg

FDA-approved for:

❖ Smoking cessation

Chant-ix!
Chant-ix!
Chant-ix!
Chant-ix!

nicotine

"Chantix helps you quit cancer sticks". Vare**nic**line, which has "nic" in the name, is a partial agonist/antagonist of **nic**otinic acetylcholine receptors. Varenicline stimulates these receptors but not to the extent they become desensitized (as is the case with nicotine) thereby reducing cravings. Varenicline also blocks nicotine from binding, thus decreasing the pleasurable effect of smoking. This is analogous to the mechanism of buprenorphine (Subutex, Suboxone) in the treatment of opioid addiction.

Chantix is the most effective smoking cessation medication. Compared to placebo, Chantix increases quit rates almost 4-fold. Since success rate with placebo is abysmal, this means "only" 10% are abstinent at one year. Chantix is twice as effective as bupropion (Wellbutrin, Zyban) or nicotine replacement products.

With varenicline, the patient may choose how to approach quitting from the fixed, flexible, and gradual quit options. With the "fixed quit approach", start Chantix and stop smoking in one week (44% success at 12 weeks). With the "flexible quit approach", start Chantix and quit on a specified date any time within the first month (54% success at 12 weeks). With the "gradual quit approach", start varenicline and cut smoking in half during the first 4 weeks, then continue reducing the number of cigarettes with the goal of quitting at 12 weeks (32% success at 24 weeks). If smoking cessation is successful (regardless of approach), the course of treatment should extend to a total of 6 months.

In 2009 the FDA added a black box warning of risk of suicidal thoughts, hostility and depression. The warning was removed in 2016 when varenicline was found to be no worse than placebo in producing psychiatric adverse events. Irritability, and even hostility, is possible with smoking cessation with or without varenicline.

Common side effects include nausea, insomnia and vivid dreams. Note that wearing nicotine patches overnight will also cause vivid dreams.

Nicotinic receptors are also involved in alcohol reward pathways. There is mixed evidence that varenicline may be helpful with alcohol use disorder.

The patent for varenicline is set to expire in 2020.

Dosing: "Flexible quit approach" Start Chantix and quit smoking on a specified date sometime between days 7 and 35 of treatment. Start 0.5 mg QD x 3 days, then 0.5 mg PO BID x 4 days, then 1 mg BID x 11 weeks, for a total of 12 weeks (1 starting pack + 2 continuing packs); Stop Chantix at 12 weeks if the patient was unable to stop smoking; If smoking cessation was successful, continue treatment for a total of 6 months; Maximum dose is 2 mg/day. Unsuccessful patients who are still motivated to quit should be encouraged to make another attempt with Chantix once factors contributing to the failed attempt have been addressed. Take the pill after eating with a full glass of water. See above for the "fixed quit approach" and "gradual quit approach" options.

ADDICTION

21

Medications for smoking cessation

- ❖ Nicotine gum
- ❖ Nicotine transdermal
- ❖ Nicotine lozenge
- ❖ Varenicline (Chantix)
- ❖ Bupropion (Wellbutrin) - Zyban brand
- ❖ Nortriptyline (Pamelor) - off-label
- ❖ Clonidine (Catapres) - off-label

The Chantix television commercial encourages you to quit smoking "slow turkey" rather than cold turkey.

CHANTIX
reduces the
urge to smoke

page 18

Dynamic interactions:

❖ Nicotine receptor partial agonist

Kinetic interactions:

❖ None significant
- "in a bubble"

CHANTIX

1994
$214–$566

Dronabinol (THC, MARINOL)

droe NAH bih nol / MARE I nol

"the Merry Drone"

❖ Cannabinoid receptor agonist

2.5
5
10
mg

FDA-approved for:

- ❖ AIDS wasting syndrome (appetite stimulant)
- ❖ Nausea and vomiting of chemotherapy

Used off-label for:

- ❖ Chronic pain
- ❖ Glaucoma
- ❖ Multiple sclerosis

THC = The High Causer

Dronabinol is synthetic tetrahydrocannabinol (THC), available since 1985. THC is the primary ingredient of marijuana responsible for the psychoactive high. Dronabinol is legal in all 50 States as a Schedule II controlled substance.

Marinol capsules are round and contain dronabinol as a light-yellow resinous oil. After oral administration, dronabinol has an onset of action of approximately 0.5–1 hour and peak effect at 2–4 hours. Duration of action for psychoactive effects is 4–6 hours, but the appetite stimulant effect of dronabinol may continue for 24 hours or longer after administration. Tolerance develops to the psychoactive effects, but does not appear to develop for the appetite stimulant effect. Dronabinol may cause dysphoric reactions in older patients.

The potential for abuse and addiction of oral THC is less than smoked marijuana, which has quicker onset and shorter duration of action. For smoked marijuana, 9% of individuals will become addicted. The risk of addiction rises to 17% for those who start in their teens.

Endogenous cannabinoids (endocannabinoids) such as anandamide ("ananda" meaning bliss in Sanskrit) act on CB1 and CB2 cannabinoid receptors. Endocannabinoids are involved in the normal process of neural pruning during adolescence. Regular cannabis use by age 18 is associated with 2–6x increase in developing schizophrenia, possibly due to interfering with this process. Exogenous cannabinoids including THC also act at CB1 and CB2 receptors.

Marijuana contains over 100 cannabinoids, including THC and cannabidiol (CBD). CBD (page 46) is a non-intoxicating compound in cannabis with antipsychotic properties that opposes the actions of THC. Marinol contains no CBD, and therefore lacks the favorable properties described below.

Some growers have succeeded in lowering the CBD-to-THC proportion in marijuana plants for a THC-dominant product with a more potent high. The average potency of THC in cannabis has risen from 4% to 12% from 1995–2014.

Synthetic cannabinoids (K2, spice, etc sprayed on inert plant material) have no CBD component and are stronger CB1 agonists than natural cannabis, making the synthetics more likely to induce psychosis.

Dosing: To stimulate appetite, start: 2.5 mg BID; May increase by 2.5 mg/day gradually; Max is 20 mg/day; Give 1 hour before lunch and dinner; Taper to discontinue if prolonged high dose use.

Smoked marijuana

page 10

Dynamic interactions:

- ❖ Sedation/CNS depression
- ❖ Weight gain

Kinetic interactions:

- ❖ As with tobacco, the hydrocarbons in smoked marijuana induce 1A2.

inhaled hydrocarbons

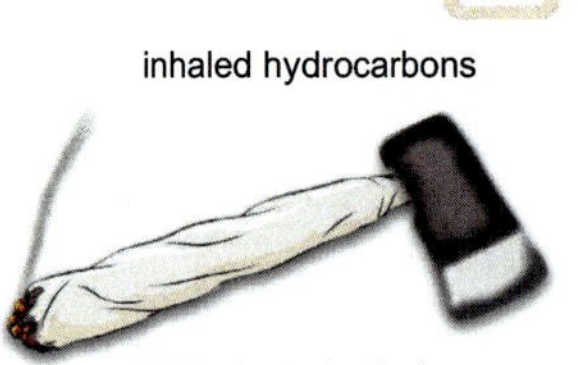

1A2 inducer (major)

Pure THC

page 16

Dynamic interactions:

- ❖ Sedation/CNS depression
- ❖ Weight gain

Kinetic interactions:

- ❖ 3A4 substrate (minor)
- ❖ 2C9 substrate (minor)

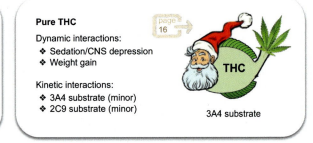

3A4 substrate

	Tetrahydrocannabinol (THC)	Cannabidiol (CBD)
Pure Rx form	Dronabinol (Marinol), nabilone (Cesamet) - Schedule III	Epidiolex - Schedule V
Psychoactive?	The High Causer in marijuana; cognitive impairment	No high, but may reduce anxiety
Psychosis	Cannabis use in adolescence triples the risk of psychotic disorders (Jones HJ et al, 2018)	Antipsychotic properties
Seizure	Epileptogenic (lowers seizure threshold)	Anticonvulsive (raises seizure threshold)
Neurotoxicity	Likely neurotoxic	Likely neuroprotective (antioxidant and cholinergic)
Munchies?	Yes. The Hunger Causer.	No; May cause weight loss.
FDA approval	Dronabinol (Marinol) to stimulate appetite (1985)	Epidiolex for pediatric seizures (2018)
Mechanism	CB1 and CB2 agonist	Indirect antagonist of CB1 and CB2 receptors
Drug interactions	Few clinically significant interactions	Substrate of 3A4 and 2C19. InHibitor of 2C9, 2C19, UGT enzymes and others.

page 46

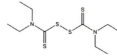

1951
$40–$105

Disulfiram (ANTABUSE)

di SUL fi ram / AN tuh byoos

"Ant abuse; Die sufferin'"

❖ Acetaldehyde dehydrogenase inhibitor

250
500
mg

FDA-approved for:

❖ Alcohol use disorder (mod/severe)

Used off-label for:

❖ Lyme disease

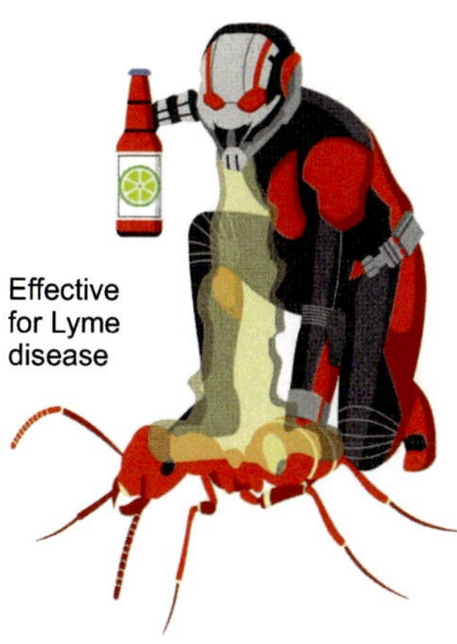

Effective for Lyme disease

At least 1 in 3 individuals of East Asian heritage (Chinese/Japanese/Korean) have facial flushing from alcohol. Due to aldehyde dehydrogenase deficiency, it is as if the individuals were taking disulfiram. As expected, alcohol use disorder is rare in these individuals.

After alcohol (ethanol) is consumed it is converted to acetaldehyde, which is detoxified by acetaldehyde dehydrogenase. Disulfiram blocks this enzyme, resulting in accumulation of acetaldehyde in the blood, and causing unpleasant (and potentially dangerous) effects. The patient should avoid alcohol from any source, including cough syrup and mouthwash. Topicals such as aftershave and hand sanitizer containing alcohol should be avoided.

The severity of the disulfiram-alcohol reaction depends on the amount of alcohol consumed. A mild reaction (e.g., from using alcohol-containing mouthwash) involves facial flushing, sweating and mild headache. A moderate reaction includes "instant hangover" symptoms, nausea/vomiting, palpitations, tachycardia, hyperventilation and lightheadedness. Consumption of large amounts of alcohol while taking disulfiram is potentially fatal due to respiratory depression, cardiovascular collapse, unconsciousness, and convulsions.

Wait at least 12 hours after alcohol consumption to begin disulfiram. Full effect is achieved by 12 hours from the first dose. If alcohol is consumed, the reaction occurs within 5–25 minutes and lasts about 30–60 minutes, although it can extend to several hours in severe cases. The reaction can occur 1–2 weeks after disulfiram is stopped. Tolerance to disulfiram does not develop. The longer a patient stays on disulfiram, the more exquisitely sensitive (s)he becomes to alcohol.

Disulfiram is recommended for select highly-motivated patients. Its effectiveness is limited because patients tend to stop taking it. Long-acting injectable disulfiram is not available in the US. Treatment is continued until the patient has developed skills to maintain sobriety without medication assistance, but is preferably limited to a few months due to risk of neurotoxicity.

Even if alcohol is avoided, side effects of disulfiram may include fatigue, acne, mild allergic dermatitis, and metallic taste. It may induce psychosis, although uncommonly. Hepatic failure rarely occurs, with peak incidence at 60 days. Hepatic damage is reversible if disulfiram is stopped. Wright et al (1988) recommend liver function test (LFTs) before treatment, q 2 weeks for 2 months, and q 3–6 months thereafter.

Even without alcohol, there is a risk of neurotoxicity that increases after 1 year. Disulfiram is the most neurotoxic medication psychiatrists prescribe (most other psychiatric medications are not neurotoxic). It has the potential to cause peripheral neuropathy, optic neuropathy, extrapyramidal symptoms (EPS), and basal ganglia lesions. No other medication prescribed by psychiatrists causes brain lesions. Potential benefit often outweighs risk, as heavy alcohol consumption is also neurotoxic.

Disulfiram is contraindicated with severe heart disease and is probably not a good idea with the elderly or anyone with a serious medical condition (renal insufficiency, liver insufficiency, epilepsy, etc).

Originally, it was thought that every patient should suffer a supervised alcohol-disulfiram reaction as aversion therapy. This is no longer recommended because of health risks. A detailed warning of the reaction should suffice. Patients are advised "If you drink on Antabuse you *probably* won't die but you'll wish you were dead". There is a black box warning to never administer without the patient's full knowledge or during alcohol intoxication. Relatives should be instructed accordingly.

Experimentally, disulfiram has shown efficacy in treatment of various infections and cancers. Recently, disulfiram has been identified as a potential breakthrough treatment for persistent Lyme disease (tick-borne illness caused by Borrelia burgdorferi bacteria).

Dosing: The dose range is 125–500 mg QD. Start 250 mg, which will usually suffice. However, some people can drink without a reaction at the 250 mg dose. Many patients are unable to tolerate side effects at the 500 mg dose. Although usually taken in the morning, it can be administered at bedtime if the patient experiences sedative effect.

Dynamic interactions:

❖ Toxicity when combined with ethanol
❖ Disulfiram is contraindicated with the antibiotic **metronidazole** (Flagyl) because the combo can result in acute confusion or even psychosis. Metronidazole alone is rumored to cause a "disulfiram-like" reaction when drinking, although by unknown mechanism. Metronidazole does not cause acetaldehyde to accumulate. When there was a national shortage of disulfiram in 2019 the author used metronidazole as a fill-in for a patient successfully established on disulfiram. The patient resumed drinking, and there was no adverse reaction. Unfortunately, the patient later tried drinking while taking disulfiram which resulted in a 3-day ICU hospitalization.

Kinetic interactions:

❖ Multi-CYP - Disulfiram is a substrate of 6 separate CYPs, so it is unlikely that induction/inhibition of one (or even two) of the pathways would significantly alter disulfiram levels. Depicted "in a box" (with a hole in it) because kinetic interactions exist, but probably do not need to be considered when prescribing this medication.
❖ Disulfiram is a weak 1A2 inhibitor and a strong 2E1 inhibitor. 2E1, not discussed elsewhere in this book, works alongside alcohol dehydrogenase and aldehyde dehydrogenase to detoxify alcohol.
❖ Disulfiram interferes with metabolism of phenytoin, so close monitoring is necessary to assure phenytoin level does not get too high. You probably will not encounter this interaction because phenytoin is only used for treatment of epilepsy, and it may be inadvisable to give disulfiram to individuals predisposed to seizures.

Multi-CYP

page 18

2004
$63–$276

Acamprosate (CAMPRAL)

a KAM proe sate / CAM pral

"A camp roast"

- ❖ Tx for alcoholism
- ❖ Partial GABA(A) agonist
- ❖ Weak NMDA antagonist

333 mg

FDA-approved for:

- ❖ Alcohol use disorder, maintenance treatment

Used off-label for:

- ❖ Fragile-X-syndrome associated autistic spectrum disorder
- ❖ Tinnitus

The approved dose is 666 mg TID

Acamprosate (Campral) is an analogue of the amino acid taurine with a structure that resembles GABA. Acamprosate (Campral) is safe and modestly effective in reducing alcohol consumption, craving, and relapse. It is not addictive or abusable. It has no sedative or anxiolytic properties.

Acamprosate appears to work about as well as oral naltrexone, which is also modestly effective. The combination of acamprosate plus naltrexone may be more effective than either drug alone according to some (but not all) studies. Acamprosate supports abstinence by decreasing the "stick" (discomfort) of not drinking, in contrast to naltrexone which decreases the "carrot" (pleasure) of drinking. Acamprosate is good for preventing "the first drink", while naltrexone is good for preventing "the second drink". In other words, *Acamprosate is for Abstinence while Naltrexone is for Not getting drunk.*

When an alcoholic sees liquor, glutamate is released. This stimulates NMDA receptors and excites neurons related to cravings. Acamprosate is thought to restore the imbalance between excitatory (glutamate) and inhibitory (GABA) neurotransmission that is otherwise disrupted when the patient refrains from drinking. Although acamprosate's precise mechanism has not been determined, it is believed to act as an NMDA receptor antagonist. Based on acamprosate's structure it was initially thought to act via GABA(A) receptors, but this appears to be untrue.

Half-life is around 26 hours. Acamprosate is renally cleared and should not be given to those with renal insufficiency. Acamprosate tablets are 333 mg, and the recommended dose is 666 mg TID. Using the Mark of the Beast for the recommended dose was an odd ad by the manufacturer, but easy to remember. There are no black box warnings.

Dosing: The approved dose is 666 mg TID with meals. If moderate renal insufficiency, use 333 mg TID. For patients weighing less than 60 kg (132 pounds), consider giving 5 tabs/day rather than 6 tabs/day.

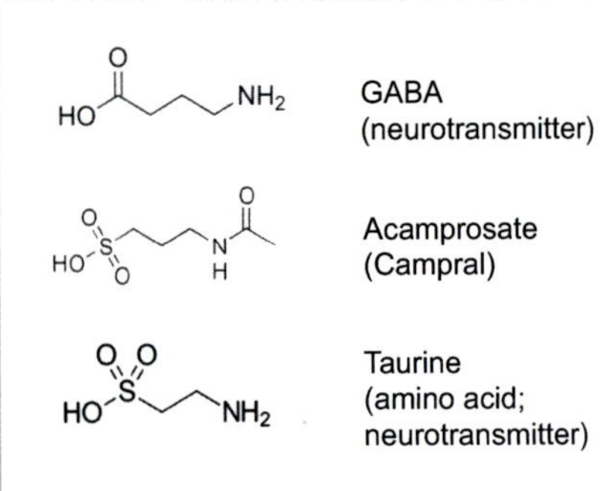

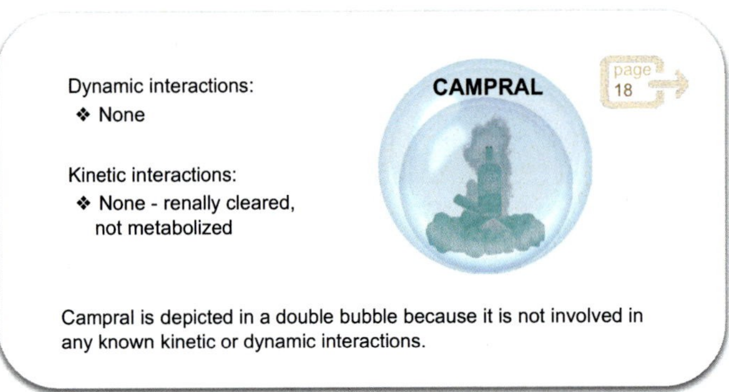

Dynamic interactions:
❖ None
Kinetic interactions:
❖ None - renally cleared, not metabolized
CAMPRAL
page 18
Campral is depicted in a double bubble because it is not involved in any known kinetic or dynamic interactions.

1953
$7–$11

Dextromethorphan (DXM)

dex troe meth OR fan

"Dexter the Thor fan"

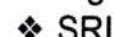

- ❖ Cough suppressant
- ❖ Dissociative
- ❖ NMDA antagonist
- ❖ Sigma-1 agonist
- ❖ SRI

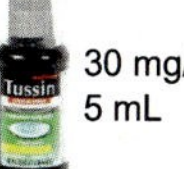

30 mg/ 5 mL

FDA-approved for:
- ❖ Cough suppression

Used off-label for:
- ❖ Neuropathic pain
- ❖ Opioid withdrawal
- ❖ Postoperative pain
- ❖ Premature ejaculation
- ❖ Agitation of dementia

Dextromethorphan (DXM) is an over-the-counter cough suppressant. It is kept behind the counter due to its dissociative properties, which lend to recreational use among young people. DXM is a component of Robitussin, NyQuil, Dimetapp, and Mucinex DM.

At high doses, DXM may produce euphoria and dissociative effects similar to ketamine. With prolonged use, psychological dependence is possible. It does not cause physical dependence, but can produce symptoms of antidepressant discontinuation syndrome owing to DXM's effects as a serotonin reuptake inhibitor (SRI).

In addition to being a SRI, DXM is an NMDA receptor antagonist and sigma-1 receptor agonist. Sigma-1 receptors in the limbic system of the brain may be involved in control of emotions, possibly explaining the benefit of DXM for treatment of pseudobulbar affect (in combination with quinidine, which serves to extend half-life of DXM). An endogenous ligand for the sigma-1 receptor is yet to be identified, but we know some androgenic steroids activate the receptor.

Experimentally, DXM is being used to treat depression and negative symptoms of schizophrenia.

Dextromethorphan cough syrup is not to be confused with the cough syrup used to make "purple drank" (aka sizzurp), would is prescription-strength codeine and promethazine syrup. Unlike DXM, codeine can cause physical dependence.

Thanks to Julianna Link PA-C for help with this mnemonic.

Dynamic interactions:
- ❖ Serotonergic

Kinetic interactions:
- ❖ 2D6 substrate (major)

Dextromethorphan is a 2D6 substrate. When combined with a strong 2D6 inhibitor, its half-life is extended. This interaction is used for therapeutic effect by NUEDEXTA—a combination of DXM and quinidine (a strong 2D6 inhibitor).

page 15

2D6 substrate

DXM with quinidine (NUEDEXTA)

new DEX ta / KWIH nih deen

"Nude Dexter"

❖ Tx for PBA
❖ DXM plus 2D6 inhibitor

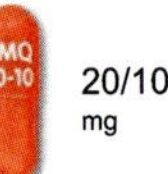

20/10 mg

FDA-approved for:
❖ Pseudobulbar affect

Used off-label for:
❖ Alzheimer's-related agitation

Nuedexta is the only FDA-approved medication for pseudobulbar affect (PBA), a condition characterized by sudden and uncontrollable laughing or crying, disproportionate to the emotion being experienced. PBA is a neurologic condition, not a psychiatric disorder. It occurs with a wide range of diseases including multiple sclerosis (MS) and amyotrophic lateral sclerosis (ALS, aka motor neuron disease, Lou Gehrig's disease, or Stephen Hawking's disease). Prevalence of PBA with ALS is about 50%. The emotional outbursts are believed to originate in the brain stem due to loss of regulatory control by the frontal lobe. PBA rarely occurs without an underlying neurologic condition.

Nuedexta provides a great example of strategic use of a kinetic drug-drug interaction. Dextromethorphan is traditionally a cough suppressant and quinidine an antiarrhythmic. In treatment of PBA, dextromethorphan (DXM) is the therapeutic agent, suppressing laughs as if they were coughs. Quinidine (strong 2D6 inHibitor) serves only to extend the half-life of DXM (2D6 substrate).

Quinidine, derived from the bark of the cinchona tree, is a class IA antiarrhythmic no longer produced as a standalone drug. Quinidine is included in Nuedexta at a tiny dose. Contraindications for quinidine include prolonged QT interval, complete AV block (without pacemaker), or heart failure. Use caution when combining quinidine with other QT prolonging medications, but keep in mind the dose of quinidine in Nuedexta is too small to realistically cause cardiac conduction problems.

Nuedexta has shown modest efficacy for Alzheimer's-related agitation, off-label (Cummings et al, 2015). The drug company incurred a $100 million fine for promoting Nuedexta to geriatric psychiatrists for this off-label use. Some physicians were accused of fraudulently diagnosing nursing home residents with PBA to obtain Medicare coverage for this expensive drug.

Agitation with dementia is challenging, considering black-box warnings for antipsychotics and risk of falls with other sedatives. So, Nuedexta is a reasonable option for this indication. The main risk is falls (~8% vs ~4% with placebo). Side effects are minimal, with dizziness of ~5%, which is about double that of placebo (~2.5%). It goes without saying that non-pharmacologic interventions for agitation (music therapy, activities, etc) should be used before resorting to medication.

Adverse effects of Nuedexta are infrequent, but may include dizziness, falls, and diarrhea. Quinidine can cause several kinds of toxicity but is not a factor at this dose.

Note that for the 10% of individuals with a 2D6 poor metabolizer genotype, the quinidine component is unnecessary.

Although Nuedexta is the only FDA-approved PBA medication, many clinicians consider Nuedexta as second-line to SSRIs and TCAs for treatment of PBA.

Generic DXM is available but generic quinidine is no longer produced. Is there another suitable 2D6 inhibitor we could combine with DXM to make a poor man's Nuedexta? Probably not, but here are some ideas: Fluoxetine (Prozac) is also a potent 2D6 inhibitor which could theoretically replace the quinidine component, although serotonin syndrome is possible because DXM inhibits serotonin reuptake. Tonic water contains quinine, which is the stereoisomer of quinidine. Tonic water plus generic DXM would not be a suitable replacement because quinine in dietary doses do not sufficiently inhibit 2D6. Quinine sulfate capsules (FDA-approved for malaria) are 324 mg, which is much higher than needed and may cause hematologic toxicity.

A feasible alternative is to use a compounding pharmacy. It is not allowable to compound a pill with 20 mg DXM and 10 mg quinidine because of patent law. You can order the combo as two separate drugs: quinidine compounded suspension (10 mg daily) plus dextromethorphan ER 20 mg/5 mL (5 mL daily). Alternately, you can compound a single capsule containing a different dose combo, such as 10 mg quinidine plus 30 mg DXM (instead of 20 mg DXM), which should cost between $45–$80 monthly (Chris Aiken, MD; The Carlat Psychiatry Report, February 2020).

Dosing: Nuedexta is a fixed-dose combination of 20 mg DXM and 10 mg quinidine sulfate. Give one capsule daily x 7 days, then one capsule BID. For perspective, a typical DXM dose for cough is 30 mg, and quinidine tablets for arrhythmia (when available) were 200–300 mg.

Dynamic interactions:
❖ QT prolongation (Quinidine)
❖ Serotonergic (DXM)

Kinetic interactions:
❖ 2D6 inHibitor (Quinidine)
❖ 2D6 substrate (DXM)

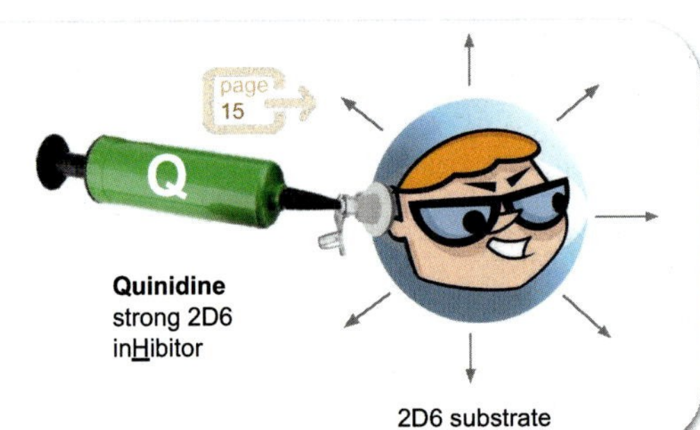

Hallucinogens

Hallucinogens, also known as psychedelics, cause perceptual changes in a state of full wakefulness and alertness (as opposed to a state of delirium or sedation). It may be more accurate to refer to these drugs as "illusionogens" because their prominent effect is distortion or enhancement of existing stimuli (Abigail Herron, DO). They do not predominantly cause the user to hallucinate (i.e., experience something that is not present) or cause auditory hallucinations as experienced by individuals with schizophrenia. Reality testing generally remains intact, but it is common for the user to think they have developed profound insight into the meaning of life or the nature of God, the soul, or the universe.

Psychedelics are distinguished from drugs classified as dissociatives such as ketamine, nitrous oxide (laughing gas), and dextromethorphan. There is some overlap between these two classes. Classic dissociatives work by antagonizing NMDA receptors.

"Classic hallucinogens" are those with a serotonergic mechanism such as LSD, DMT, mescaline (peyote), and psilocybin (mushrooms). They can contribute to serotonin syndrome. Cross-tolerance exists between the classic hallucinogens. They do not usually cause craving or dependence with recurrent use.

The effect of a hallucination can vary greatly depending on environment and initial state of mind. If a hallucinogen is taken while in a state of emotional distress, a "bad trip" is more likely. Bad trips can be terrifying, but the individual can sometimes be reasoned with or calmed by reassurance that the trip will not last forever and that, e.g., the universe is not collapsing.

Hallucinogens can cause "flashbacks", i.e., reexperience of perceptual disturbance after use has stopped. Occurrence of flashbacks is unrelated to the dose or number of exposures. They usually resolve within 1–2 years. If problematic, the condition is known as Hallucinogen Persisting Perception Disorder per DSM-5.

Hallucinogen	Mechanism	Comments
Lysergic acid diethylamide (LSD)	5-HT_{2A} serotonin receptor agonist	Synthesized in 1938, not naturally occurring; Consumed by piece of blotter paper on the tongue; More info on subsequent page
Dimethyltryptamine (DMT)	5-HT_{2A} serotonin receptor agonist	Nicknamed "Dimitri" and "Businessman's Trip" due to short duration of about 1 hour; May be smoked; Tiny amounts are present endogenously, produced by the pineal gland, considered to serve no purpose for modern humans, but possibly for our ancestors?
Mescaline (peyote)	5-HT_{2A} agonist with amphetamine-like properties	Ingested as buttons from the crown of the peyote cactus; Lasts 4–8 hours; DEA Schedule I (illegal) with an exception for Native American religious ceremonies.
Psilocybin (mushrooms)	5-HT_{2A} serotonin receptor agonist	"Magic mushrooms" or "shrooms"; Ingested for a trip lasting 4–6 hours; DEA Schedule I (illegal); May cause psychosis/detachment from reality; Reported mystical-like experiences or feelings of inner peace.
MDMA (Ecstasy, X, Molly)	Highly serotonergic, with stimulant effects and oxytocin-mediated effects	Described as a "psychedelic amphetamine" and "empathogen". Only 55% of users hallucinate; Extended duration; Altered perception of time (90%), euphoria (97%), increased awareness of emotions (50%), *decreased* impulsivity (25%), increased empathy and connection to others due to oxytocin release from the pituitary. It may cause desire to touch others, but not necessarily in a sexual way, described as something similar to a *post*-orgasmic state. Can cause bruxism—it's the reason pacifiers are seen at raves ; Risk of cognitive decline due to irreversible brain damage from massive release of serotonin; Risk of hyponatremia and toxidrome including rhabdomyolysis; The only hallucinogen with a defined withdrawal syndrome. "Molly" is powdered MDMA in a capsule; "Ecstasy" is a pressed pill; Both are commonly laced with other drugs.
Phencyclidine (PCP, Angel Dust)	NMDA antagonist with serotonergic properties;	Bad stuff! Perceptual distortions may last for week(s) and may precipitate a persistent psychotic episode resembling schizophrenia; Classically causes vertical nystagmus and decreased perception of pain; Extensive cardiovascular and neurological toxicity; DSM defines PCP Use Disorder separately, while everything else is lumped into the "Other Hallucinogen Use Disorder" diagnosis. Although DSM-5 defines it as a hallucinogen, other sources categorize it as a dissociative.
Salvia (*Salvia divinorum*)	Kappa opioid agonist, not serotonergic	Green leaf traditionally ingested by chewing or drinking juice; Very short duration; Not banned federally but illegal in 29 states; Intense with onset < 1 minute; Short duration of < 30 minutes; Feelings of detachment from external reality
Bufotenine	Serotonergic	Bufotenine has been consumed by licking toads of the genus *Bufo* or drinking their venom. Not everyone hallucinates and side effects such as nausea and headaches are common. It is reportedly only a worthwhile experience if smoked in freebase form. It is particularly unpleasant when injected.
Ayahuasca	Multiple	A brew containing DMT, MAOIs, and other hallucinogens; Legalized for religious use among Native Americans

1943

Lysergic acid diethylamide (LSD)

"Lucy's Serotonergic Drug"

- Hallucinogen
- DEA Schedule I (illegal)
- $5\text{-}HT_{2A}$ agonist

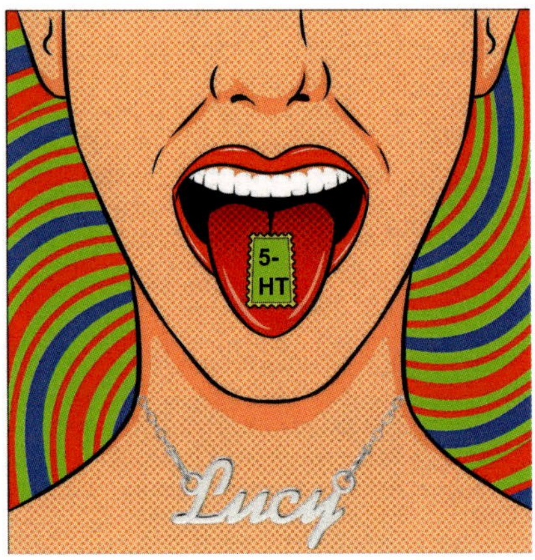

Although John Lennon denied that it is a drug song, the Beatles' '"Lucy in the Sky with Diamonds" is obviously about LSD.

Picture yourself in a boat on a river
With tangerine trees and marmalade skies
Somebody calls you, you answer quite slowly
A girl with kaleidoscope eyes…

Follow her down to a bridge by a fountain
Where rocking horse people eat marshmallow pies
Everyone smiles as you drift past the flowers
That grow so incredibly high

Lysergic acid diethylamide (LSD) is a semisynthetic product of lysergic acid, a natural substance from an ergot fungus. Referred to as "acid", LSD is a recreational hallucinogenic typically consumed in small doses on the tongue as blotter paper that was soaked in an LSD-containing solution and dried.

The hallucinogenic effect of LSD was discovered in 1943. It was a popular legal recreational drug in the early 1960s, but has been illegal since 1968.

LSD is gaining traction as a therapeutic drug. It has been found to treat and prevent cluster headaches and may work for treatment-resistant depression. Therapeutic effects may be achievable in micro doses that are sub-psychedelic (i.e., do not cause hallucinations). Even at psychedelic strength, LSD has minimal potential for addiction and may have potential as a treatment of addiction to other substances.

The effect of LSD is felt to be due entirely to prolonged stimulation of $5\text{-}HT_{2A}$ serotonin receptors, which is the same mechanism of other classic hallucinogens like DMT, psilocybin and mescaline. These are the receptors blocked by many second generation antipsychotics (SGAs). Endogenous serotonin binds these receptors briefly, while LSD is essentially locked onto the receptor for hours. LSD is mostly cleared from the bloodstream within 6 hours, but the hallucinogenic effect continues for an average of 12 hours because this is how long LSD is stuck to a $5\text{-}HT_{2A}$ receptor. Unsurprisingly, LSD can be a contributor to serotonin syndrome.

Overdose deaths on LSD alone are essentially non-existent, but are possible with 100–200x the usual dose. Terrifying "bad trips" are possible. Due to LSD's effects on the hypothalamus, it may elevate body temperature, raise blood pressure and make it virtually impossible to fall asleep while it is in effect.

Following cessation of LSD, the user may experience persisting perceptual disturbances as "LSD flashbacks", for instance seeing trails of moving objects, afterimages, or misperceptions of images as too large (macropsia) or too small (micropsia). Flashbacks may occur in individuals with minimal exposure to LSD. Flashbacks only constitute a disorder (Hallucinogen Persisting Perception Disorder, DSM-5) if they cause clinically significant distress or impairment.

LSD is regulated by the DEA as a Schedule I (illegal) controlled substance. Lysergic acid (without the 'D'), commonly known as ergine from morning glory seeds, has milder psychedelic properties and is Schedule III. Other lysergic acid derivatives include the dopaminergic agonist bromocriptine, and the headache medications ergotamine and methysergide.

For context, LSD's stimulation of $5\text{-}HT_{2A}$ receptors is the opposite of what second-generation antipsychotics (SGAs) do. Mnemonic: 2A for **2**nd Gen **A**ntipsychotics, which block $5\text{-}HT_{2A}$ receptors.

LSD has serotonin essentially embedded in its structure.

$N(CH_2CH_3)_2$ LSD

HO NH_2 Serotonin

Dilated pupils are seen with LSD use and with serotonin syndrome, which can be caused by LSD .

page 16

Dynamic interactions:
- Serotonergic (strong)

Kinetic interactions:
- LSD is metabolized by 3A4 and other CYP enzymes.

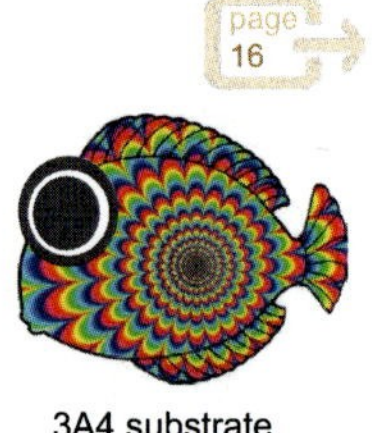

3A4 substrate

An **opiate** is a drug derived from the opium poppy plant – opium, morphine, codeine and heroin. Use the mnemonic "The rabbit ate the opium poppy". An **opioid** (rhymes with droid) is anything that acts on opioid receptors to produce morphine-like effects. Some synthetic drugs have a similar molecule structure to morphine (hydrocodone, oxycodone, etc) while others look completely different (methadone, fentanyl, etc). **Narcotic** is synonymous with opioid in medical parlance, but the legal definition relates to a broader range of controlled substances (including cocaine) with particularly severe criminal consequences. Eating poppy seeds (eg, from bagels) can result in a false positive drug screen for opioids.

The opium poppy

Opium dripping from *Papaver somniferum*

The two types of opioid receptors discussed in this chapter are μ (mu) and κ (kappa). Mu opioid receptors are involved in analgesia, miosis (constricted pupils), euphoria, physical dependence and respiratory depression. Kappa receptors are involved in analgesia and miosis, but not the other stuff. The first group of opioids we present are nonselective agonists for both receptor subtypes.

Opioids are the strongest pain medications, but they are highly addictive and cause respiratory depression via mu receptors. Tolerance to the effects of opioids develops over time. The maintenance dose for a tolerant user might kill an opioid-naïve individual. Most opioids are approved for "moderate to severe" pain, which is generally understood as ≥ 5 on 0–10 scale, with 10 defined as the worst pain imaginable. However, opioids should not be used first-line for moderate pain. For acute pain, a scheduled combination of acetaminophen and ibuprofen often works well.

There are 3 types of pain – nociceptive, neuropathic and migraine. Opioids should not be used for migraine headaches. Neuropathic pain is less responsive to opioids than nociceptive pain. Nociceptive pain is the result of sensory neurons performing their assigned duty. Causes of nociceptive pain include surgery, skin lesions, bone fracture, heart attack, and arthritis of joints. Neuropathic pain results from damaged or pinched nerves, manifesting as radiating pain along the nerve with a stabbing or burning "pins and needles" sensation. Examples of neuropathic pain include sciatica, cervical radiculopathy, diabetic neuropathy, shingles, multiple sclerosis, some strokes and chemotherapy-induced nerve damage. Neuropathic pain is better managed with non-opioids such as gabapentin (Neurontin), pregabalin (Lyrica), or SNRI antidepressants such as duloxetine (Cymbalta).

Equianalgesic (equivalent in controlling pain) dosing has been defined for available opioids. However, patients vary in their response to different opioids due to incomplete tolerance, CYP interactions and genetics. For individuals maintained on an opioid for long-term pain control, it is good practice to periodically "rotate" to a different opioid because cross-tolerance to analgesic effect may be incomplete. A patient tolerant to opioid #1 may have improved pain control with opioid #2 at a dose lower than equianalgesic dose table (see below). When rotating opioids, convert to a dose 35–50% lower than the listed equianalgesic dose and then titrated based on response.

Opioid	Equianalgesic dose / 24 hr		DEA Schedule	Comments
	Oral	Intravenous		
Morphine	30 mg	10 mg	II	The prototype mu opioid agonist to which others are compared for defining analgesic efficacy; Morphine is metabolized to hydromorphone.
Buprenorphine (SUBUTEX)	0.4 mg (SL)	0.3 mg	III	Partial mu opioid agonist for opioid use disorder; Suboxone is buprenorphine with naloxone.
Codeine	200 mg	100 mg	II (pure)	Codeine is mainly a cough suppressant but about 10% is converted by 2D6 to morphine
Fentanyl	N/A	0.1 mg	II	100x stronger than morphine; For opioid tolerant patients only
Hydrocodone	40 mg	N/A	II	Combo with acetaminophen is Vicodin, Norco, Lortab; Weaker and slower than oxycodone; Hydrocodone is metabolized to hydromorphone.
Hydromorphone (DILAUDID)	6 mg	1.5 mg	II	Stronger than morphine with less itching and nausea
Meperidine (DEMEROL)	300 mg	100 mg	II	Not recommended due to neurotoxic metabolite; Serotonergic effects
Methadone	Variable	1 mg**	II	For opioid tolerant patients only; Long half-life; Approved for opioid use disorder; typically to replace heroin addiction; **Do not initiate based on equianalgesic dose due to variability in patient response and delayed peak effects. 2% of opioid sales but 30% of prescription opioid deaths.
Oxycodone	20 mg	N/A	II	Combo with acetaminophen is Percocet; Stronger and faster acting than hydrocodone; Oxycodone is metabolized to oxymorphone.
Oxymorphone (NUMORPHAN, OPANA)	10 mg	1 mg	II	Reformulation of Opana ER to a crush-resistant tablet had the unintended consequence of opioid abusers switching from nasal route to injection
Tapentadol (NUCYNTA)	150	N/A	II	Moderate strength opioid + norepinephrine reuptake inhibitor (NRI)
Tramadol (ULTRAM)	300 mg	N/A	IV	Weak opioid + SNRI

Opioid-induced hyperalgesia (OIH) is when an opioid (usually at high dose) sensitives pain receptors, decreasing the individual's tolerance to pain. Under chronic opioid treatment, a patient's requirement for dose escalation may be due to tolerance to the drug, OIH, or a combination of both. If OIH is occurring, increasing the opioid dose will paradoxically cause the patient to experience more pain throughout the body. Although uncommon, OIH should be suspected when a patient complains of increasing pain after a dose increase.

Most prescription opioids have at least 8 black box warnings relating to addiction/abuse/misuse, respiratory depression, risks of combining with benzodiazepines/alcohol/sedatives, accidental ingestion killing children, neonatal opioid withdrawal syndrome, and Risk Evaluation and Mitigation Strategy (REMS) program. For prescribers, participation in a REMS-compliant education program is strongly encouraged but not required. Certification is required to prescribe buprenorphine for Opioid Use Disorder in clinic settings.

If an opioid is used for chronic pain, ideally it should be prescribed by a pain management specialist. Psychiatrists do not prescribe opioids for pain other than buprenorphine (Subutex, Suboxone) and methadone for treatment of opioid use disorder.

All opioids are Schedule II controlled substances other than tramadol (Schedule IV) because it is relatively weak, and buprenorphine because it is a partial opioid agonist. Tramadol has 8 boxed warnings just like the Schedule II opioids. Buprenorphine only has 4 boxed warnings. Codeine, a weak opioid, is Schedule III in combination pain pills, Schedule V in cough syrup, and Schedule II (like the other opioids) when in pure form.

Note that prescribing Schedule III substances tends to be more burdensome than schedule II. For example, providers of buprenorphine and esketamine must register and the DEA will come to the clinic for in-person audits.

DEA	Opioids	Other drugs (for context)
Schedule I (illegal)	Heroin	Marijuana LSD
Schedule II Ⓒ II	Codeine (pure) Fentanyl (Duragesic) Hydrocodone (e.g., Vicodin) Hydromorphone (Dilaudid) Levorphanol (Levo-Dromoran) Meperidine (Demerol) Methadone Morphine Opium tincture (antidiarrheal) Oxycodone (e.g., Percocet) Tapentadol (Nucynta)	Amphetamine (Adderall, etc) Cocaine (for surgery) Lisdexamfetamine (Vyvanse) Methamphetamine (Desoxyn) Methylphenidate (Ritalin) Pentobarbital (barbiturate) Phencyclidine (PCP)
Schedule III Ⓒ III	Buprenorphine (Subutex, Suboxone) Codeine high mg combos (e.g., Tylenol #3) Opium with camphor (Paregoric)	Anabolic steroids Butabarbital (barbiturate) Dronabinol (Marinol) – synthetic THC Ketamine, Esketamine Sodium oxybate (Xyrem) – Rx GHB Sodium thiopental (barbiturate)
Schedule IV Ⓒ IV	Butorphanol (Stadol nasal spray) Pentazocine (Talwin) Tramadol (Ultram)	Benzodiazepines Z-Drugs (Ambien, etc) Carisoprodol (Soma) Suvorexant (Belsomra)
Schedule V	Codeine low dose combos (cough syrup) Diphenoxylate with atropine* (Lomotil) Difenoxin with atropine*	Antiepileptics: – Brivaracetam (Briviact) – Cenobamate (Xcopri) – Lacosamide (Vimpat) – Pregabalin (Lyrica)
Non-scheduled (2019)	Nalbuphine (Nubain) Kratom – illegal in 6 states Salvia divinorum – illegal in 29 states (κ-opioid agonist hallucinogen)	Alcohol Butalbital (barb) low dose combos (e.g., Fioricet) Propofol (Diprivan) Antipsychotics (all)

*Difenoxin and Diphenoxylate (Lomotil) are Schedule V (for diarrhea) when mixed with atropine to cause unpleasantness if injected intravenously. Otherwise they are Schedule I and II, respectively.

Opioids delay gastric emptying and peristalsis, which may interfere with absorption of other medications, which is an example of a kinetic drug-drug interaction. For patients taking an opioid, serum levels of some psychiatric medications will be lower.

Opioids are highly constipating. Slowed peristalsis leads to more fluid being removed from GI tract, making stools hard. About 50% of patients will experience opioid-induced constipation (OIC) which is managed differently than constipation caused by psychiatric medications, which is usually anticholinergic. It is good practice to start a laxative when the opioid is started. Here is a cost-effective protocol for medication-induced constipation, contrasting opioid-induced vs idiopathic constipation. The mainstay of treatment for OUC is Senna, a natural laxative containing sennosides that irritate the lining of the bowel.

	Opioid-induced constipation (OIC)	**Idiopathic constipation**
Step 1	Senna/Docusate 1 tab BID	Hydration, exercise, dietary fiber
Step 2	Senna/Docusate 2 tabs BID + Lactulose or Sorbitol 15 mL BID	Fiber 2 scoops BID + Docusate 100 mg BID + Milk of magnesia (MOM) 30 mL QD PRN
Step 3	Senna/Docusate 3 tabs BID + Lactulose or Sorbitol 30 mL BID	Lactulose 15 mL BID + Docusate 100 mg BID + MOM 30 mL QD PRN
Step 4	Senna/Docusate 4 tabs BID + Lactulose or Sorbitol 30 mL BID	Lactulose 30 mL BID + Docusate 200 BID + MOM 30 mL QD PRN
Step 5	Senna/Docusate 4 tabs BID + Lactulose or Sorbitol 30 mL BID + Milk of magnesia (MOM) 30 mL after breakfast	Lactulose 45 mL BID + Docusate 200 BID + MOM 30 mL QD PRN
Step 6	Senna/Docusate 4 tabs BID + Lactulose or Sorbitol 30 mL QID + MOM 30 mL after breakfast + Bisacodyl Suppository 10 mg after breakfast	Lactulose 45 mL BID + Docusate 200 BID + Bisacodyl 10 mg BID + MOM 30 mL QD PRN
Step 7	Sodium phosphate enema or oil retention enema	Polyethylene Glycol (PEG) 17g PO BID + Docusate 200 BID + Bisacodyl 20 mg BID + MOM 30 QD
Step 8	Mu-opioid receptor antagonists – Methylnaltrexone (Relistor) – Naloxegol (Movantik) Chloride channel activator – Lubiprostone (Amitiza)	Magnesium Citrate 300 mL PO once + Fleet enema BID x 3 days

Awareness of how the body metabolizes opioids can be useful in interpreting drug screens. Both codeine and heroin are metabolized to morphine. Everything connected by orange arrows is metabolized to hydromorphone. Hydromorphone and oxymorphone are less susceptible to kinetic interactions.

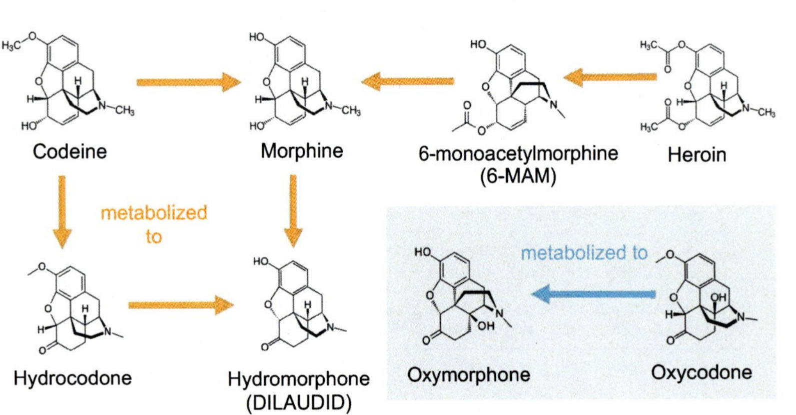

Opioid antagonists:

Centrally acting to block effect of opioids in CNS:

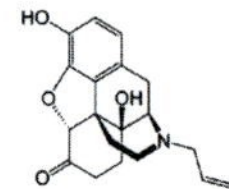

Naloxone (short-acting)

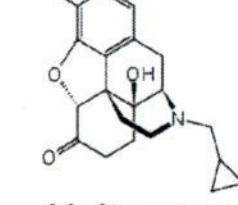

Naltrexone (long-acting)

For opioid-induced constipation, do not enter CNS:

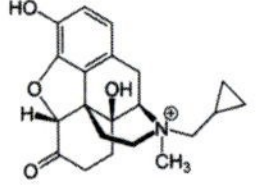

Methylnaltrexone (RELISTOR)

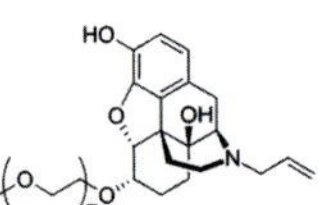

Naloxegol (MOVANTIK)

Opioids without the core structure of morphine. These will not be detected by a standard opioid drug screen.

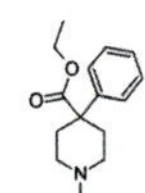

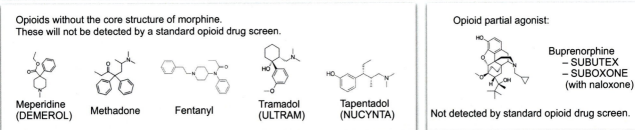

Meperidine (DEMEROL)

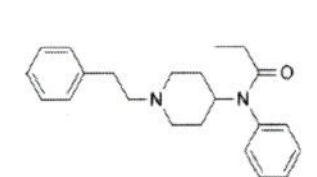

Methadone

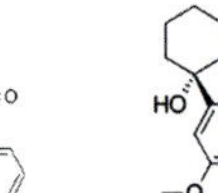

Fentanyl

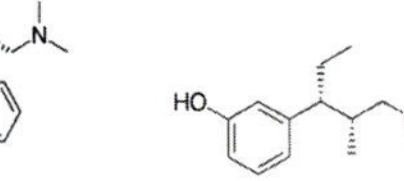

Tramadol (ULTRAM)

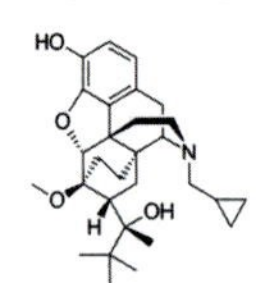

Tapentadol (NUCYNTA)

Opioid partial agonist:

Buprenorphine
– SUBUTEX
– SUBOXONE (with naloxone)

Not detected by standard opioid drug screen.

1971
IR $20–$60
ER $22–$141

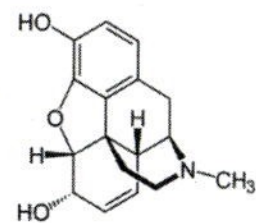

Morphine (MS CONTIN)

MOR feen / m s CON tin

"Ms. Cotton(tail) Morphing"

❖ Opioid
❖ Schedule II

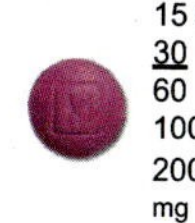

15 ER
30
60
100
200
mg

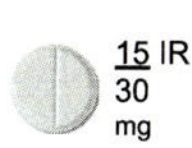

15 IR
30
mg

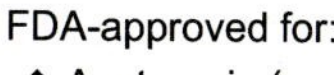

Opioids constrict pupils

FDA-approved for:

❖ Acute pain (mod–severe)
❖ Chronic pain (mod–severe)

Used for:

❖ Angina / myocardial infarction
❖ Acute pulmonary edema due to left ventricular dysfunction
❖ Dyspnea in palliative medicine

Morphine is the prototype μ (mu) opioid receptor agonist to which other opioids are compared for defining analgesic efficacy. Morphine can be referred to as an opi<u>ate</u>, meaning that it is present in the opium poppy.

When it was discovered that the pituitary gland makes natural opioids, they were named end<u>orphin</u>s as a contraction of "endogenous m<u>orphine</u>".

Morphine causes release of histamine, which can cause <u>severe pruritus</u>. <u>Urinary retention</u> is common with intrathecal administration because opioids suppress the micturition reflex at the brainstem level.

The most prescribed PO formulation is the extended-release <u>MS Contin</u>, which is short for <u>contin</u>uous <u>m</u>orphine <u>s</u>ulfate. MS Contin is for around-the-clock use and <u>should not be used PRN</u>. Other routes of administration include intravenous (IV), intramuscular (IM), subcutaneous (SQ), epidural, and rectal (PR). IV administration can be given by patient-controlled analgesia (PCA) pump. It is not available as a transdermal patch.

The body metabolizes codeine (weak) to morphine, which is an upgrade in terms of opioid potency. Heroin is also metabolized to morphine, which is a downgrade.

Dosing: Individualize based on opioid tolerance. For immediate–release morphine sulfate start 15–30 mg PO q4h prn; Morphine ER (MS Contin) is dosed q 8 – 12 hours scheduled (not PRN); The 100 mg and 200 mg MS Contin tablets are reserved for opioid-tolerant patients. If prolonged use, taper dose by 25–50% every 2 to 4 days to discontinue.

Dynamic interactions:

❖ Opioid agonist
  – Constipation
  – Sedation / CNS depression
  – Respiratory depression
  – Hyp<u>o</u>tension
❖ Lowers seizure threshold
❖ Serotonergic (weak)

Kinetic interactions:

❖ Delayed gastric emptying
❖ Otherwise, minimal clinically significant kinetic interactions
  – "in a box"

page 18

1926
$20–$74

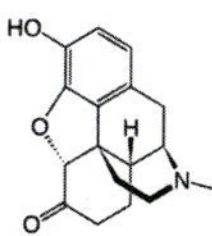

Hydromorphone (DILAUDID)

HYE droe MOR fone / di LAWD id

"Dial, you did (to say) Hi (on) more phones"

❖ Opioid
❖ Schedule II

2
4
8
mg

FDA-approved for:

❖ Pain (mod–severe)

Hydromorphone is 5x stronger than morphine per mg. Accidental substitution of hydromorphone for morphine has resulted in overdose. It causes <u>less itching and nausea than morphine</u>. Long-term use is only recommended for cancer pain in <u>opioid-tolerant patients</u>. There are nine **Black Box Warnings** including risk of overdose if the ER tablets are chewed.

Dosing: Individualize dose based on opioid tolerance. It is generally administered around the clock, not PRN. Use shorter-acting opioids for breakthrough pain. If more than 2 doses of rescue medication are needed within a 24-hour period for 2 consecutive days, hydromorphone may need to be increased. A typical regimen is 8 - 64 mg of the extended-release (ER) tablet, branded EXALGO, administered every 24 hours. The immediate-release (IR) tablet is dosed every 3 – 6 hours. Taper to discontinue.

Opioids constrict pupils

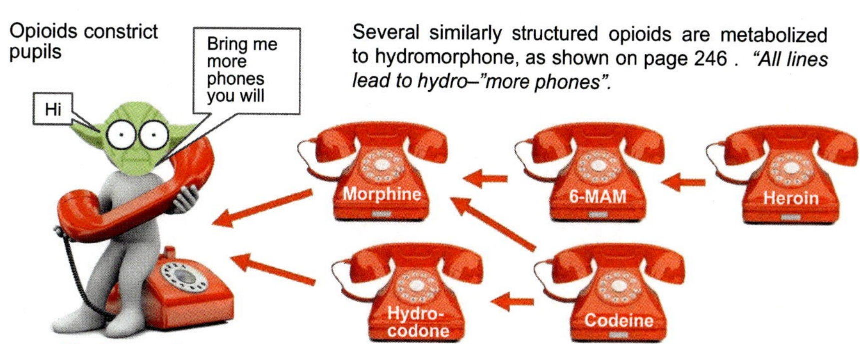

Several similarly structured opioids are metabolized to hydromorphone, as shown on page 246 . *"All lines lead to hydro–"more phones".*

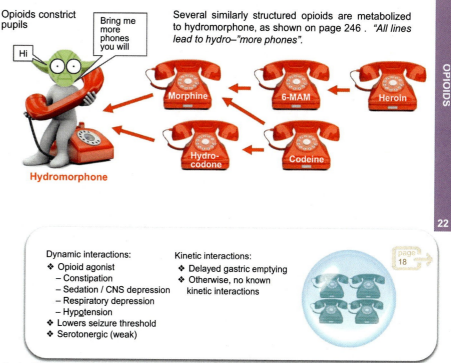

Dynamic interactions:

❖ Opioid agonist
  – Constipation
  – Sedation / CNS depression
  – Respiratory depression
  – Hyp<u>o</u>tension
❖ Lowers seizure threshold
❖ Serotonergic (weak)

Kinetic interactions:

❖ Delayed gastric emptying
❖ Otherwise, no known kinetic interactions

page 18

1959
$46–$316

Oxymorphone (NUMORPHAN)

OX ee MOR fone / nu MOR fan

"Ox sees more phones" (numerous phones)

- ❖ Opioid
- ❖ Schedule II

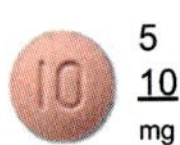

5
<u>10</u>
mg

FDA-approved for:

- ❖ Severe pain (acute or chronic)

Oxymorphone is about twice as strong as oxycodone per mg. As with the other "more phone" opioid (hydromorphone), oxymorphone is a metabolite of another opioid (oxycodone). Both of the "more phones" (hydro- and oxy-) are the "end of the line" metabolically, with no active metabolites of their own. Since hydro- and oxy-morphine are not subject to further CYP-mediated biotransformation, they are <u>not susceptible to kinetic interactions</u> and are therefore depicted "in a bubble".

After OxyContin (oxycodone ER) tablets were reformulated as abuse-deterrent, drug abusers switched to snorting Opana ER (oxymorphone ER) tablets. When those tablets were engineered to be un-snortable in 2011, abusers injected the product and developed thrombotic thrombocytopenic purpura (TTP). In 2017 that formulation of oxymorphone ER was removed from the market at the request of the FDA. Other formulations of oxymorphone are still available.

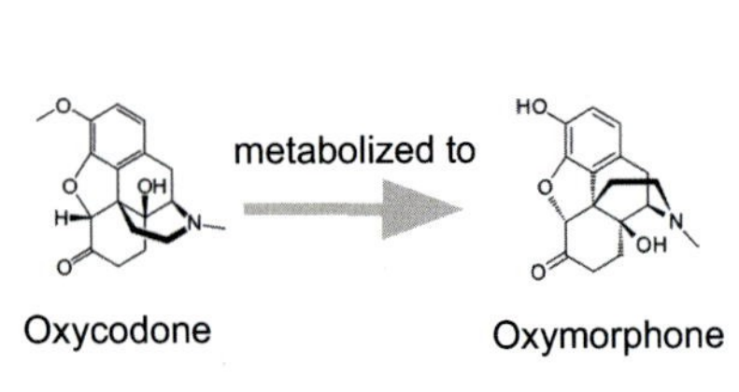

page 18

Dynamic interactions:

- ❖ Opioid agonist
  - – Constipation
  - – Sedation / CNS depression
  - – Respiratory depression
  - – Hyp<u>o</u>tension
- ❖ Lowers seizure threshold
- ❖ Serotonergic (weak)

Kinetic interactions:

- ❖ Delayed gastric emptying
- ❖ Otherwise, no known kinetic interactions

#13
1943
$27 – $115

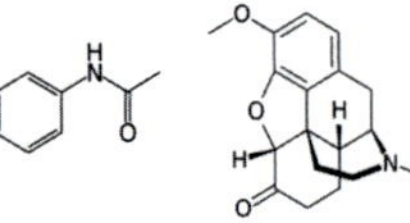

Hydro<u>cod</u>one/APAP (VI<u>COD</u>IN)

HYE droe KOE done / VIKE o din

"Viking's Hydrant code"

APAP = acetaminophen

- ❖ Opioid
- ❖ Schedule II

2.5 / 325
5 / 325
7.5 / 325
<u>10</u> / 325
mg

FDA-approved for:

- ❖ Moderate to severe pain

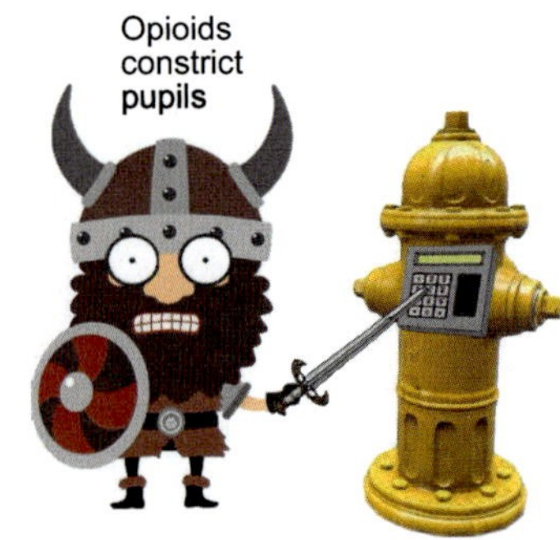

Hydrocodone with acetaminophen is the most prescribed fixed-dose opioid combo, intended for PRN use. Other brands of hydrocodone with acetaminophen include <u>Norco, Lortab and Lorcet</u>. Acetaminophen is also known as <u>Tylenol, paracetamol and APAP</u> (acetyl-para-aminophenol). Hydrocodone is also available in a fixed-dosed combination with ibuprofen (Vicoprofen). Hydrocodone is very rarely prescribed as a standalone pill, although a couple of expensive abuse-deterrent pills (Zohydro ER and Hysingla ER) have 1% market share.

In 2014 the DEA rescheduled hydrocodone combination products, increasing restriction from Schedule III to Schedule II. Vicodin was originally Schedule III based on the assumption that less hydrocodone would be needed to control pain with the adjuvant medication included, and that hydrocodone consumption would be limited by the maximum recommended dose of acetaminophen (1,000 mg/day and 4,000 mg/day). It turned out that Vicodin is highly addictive and abusable. Opioid abusers were not deterred by the <u>risk of hepatotoxicity from exceeding 4,000 mg/day of acetaminophen</u>, which is the subject of one of Vicodin's 9 black box warnings.

Hydrocodone is weaker and less likely to cause euphoria than oxycodone, the other opioid commonly combined with acetaminophen, branded as Percocet. <u>Oxycodone is twice as potent as hydrocodone</u>, which means <u>Percocet has the "perk" of being stronger than Vicodin</u>.

Dosing: See upper left for available strengths of hydrocodone / APAP tablets. The standard dose of hydrocodone is 5 mg; Dose range is 2.5 – 10 mg of hydrocodone q 4 – 6 hr PRN; With respect to acetaminophen (from all sources), do not exceed 1,000 mg q 4 hr or 4,000 mg/day; Use lowest effective dose and shortest effective treatment duration; taper dose by 25-50% q2-4 days to discontinue if long-term use.

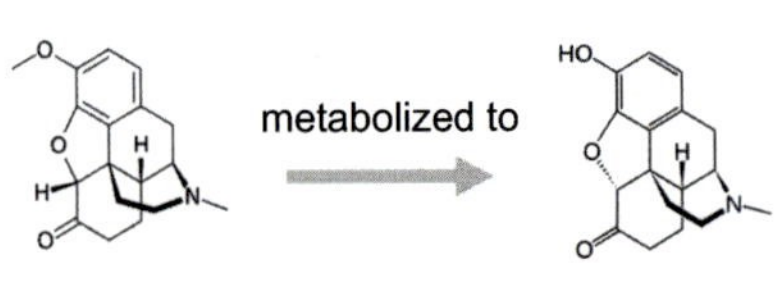

page 16

Dynamic interactions:

- ❖ Opioid agonist
  - – Constipation
  - – Sedation / CNS depression
  - – Respiratory depression
  - – Hyp<u>o</u>tension
- ❖ Lowers seizure threshold
- ❖ Serotonergic (weak)

Kinetic interactions:

- ❖ Delayed gastric emptying
- ❖ 3A4 substrate
- ❖ Black box warning: concomitant use with 3A4 inhibitors or discontinuation of 3A4 inducers may cause fatal hydrocodone concentration

3A4 substrate

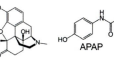

#54
1950
$9 - $34

APAP

Oxycodone/APAP (PERCOCET)

ox e COE dohn / PERC o cet

"Perky Ox codin'"

APAP = acetaminophen

❖ Opioid
❖ Schedule II

2.5 / 325
5 / 325
7.5 / 325
10 / 325
mg

FDA-approved for:
❖ Pain, moderate to severe (but should be reserved for severe pain

Compared to hydrocodone, oxycodone is twice as strong and scores higher on a "drug liking" scale among drug abusers. The street value of a bottle of #90 oxycodone 30 mg is about $2,700 when sold by the pill (filled at pharmacy for $20 - $100).

Although approved for moderate-to-severe pain, Oxycodone should be reserved for severe pain that cannot be adequately relieved by hydrocodone. Oxycodone works quickly, with serum levels peaking in 20 – 30 minutes. It take 60+ minutes for hydrocodone to peak.

Note that the available mg / mg combinations are the same for oxycodone/APAP (Percocet) and hydrocodone/APAP (Vicodin, Norco) but, again, Percocet has the "perk" of being stronger and faster acting than Vicodin.

Oxycontin (oxycodone ER) was reformulated with abuse-deterrent properties which resulted in decreased abuse and diversion of the product. Original Oxycontin tablets were easy to crush and inject, and an 80 mg tablet was worth up to $80 on the street. The unintended consequence of the abuse-deterrent formulation was increased heroin use.

Opioids constrict pupils

Dosing: For Percocet, 2.5 - 10 mg oxycodone q 6 hr PRN; q 4 hr dosing may be needed if severe pain or opioid-tolerance; For acetaminophen, do not exceed 1,000 mg per 4 hr or 4,000 mg/day to avoid liver damage (from all sources); Taper gradually to stop if long-term use.

Formulation of oxycodone	Release	FDA certified as an abuse-deterrent opioid?	
Oxycodone (ROXICODONE)	IR	No	Easy to snort or inject; High street value
OXYCONTIN	ER	Yes	Resists crushing; Extraction in solvent produces a viscous gel that is difficult to inject.
Oxycodone / Acetaminophen (PERCOCET, ROXICET, ENDOCET)	IR	No	Liver damage from acetaminophen if taken excessively
Oxycodone / Aspirin (PERCODAN, ENDODAN)	IR	No	Ototoxicity / tinnitus from aspirin if taken excessively
Oxycodone / Ibuprofen (COMBUNOX)	IR	No	Renal damage from ibuprofen if taken excessively
ROXYBOND	IR	Yes	Resists crushing; Extraction in solvent produces a viscous gel that is difficult to inject.
OXAYDO	IR	No*	*Not FDA certified as abuse-deterrent but uses "Aversion Technology"™ causing irritation to nasal mucosa; However, only 30% of recreational users said this would discourage them from snorting it again. The product gels if extracted.
XTAMPZA	ER	Yes	Microspheres resist crushing; difficult to inject if dissolved
Oxycodone ER / Naltrexone (TROXYCA)	ER	Yes	Pellets of oxycodone surrounding sequestered naltrexone (opioid antagonist), which remains sequestered unless crushed

Dynamic interactions:
❖ Opioid agonist
 – Constipation
 – Sedation / CNS depression
 – Respiratory depression
 – Hypotension
❖ Lowers seizure threshold
❖ Serotonergic (weak)

Kinetic interactions:
❖ Delayed gastric emptying
❖ 3A4 substrate
❖ 2D6 substrate (minor)
❖ Black box warning: concomitant use with 3A4 inhibitors or discontinuation of 3A4 inducers may cause fatal oxycodone concentration

page 16

3A4 substrate

page 15

2D6 substrate (minor)

1960
$9 - $33

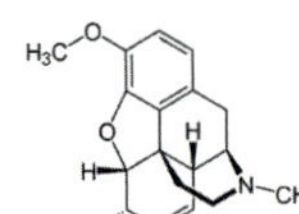

Codeine/APAP (TYLENOL #2, #3, #4)

KOE deen

"Coding"

APAP = acetaminophen

- ❖ Opioid prodrug
- ❖ Cough suppressant
- ❖ Schedule II

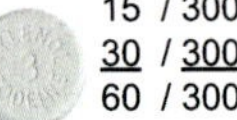

15 / 300 "#2"
30 / 300 "#3"
60 / 300 "#4"
mg

FDA-approved for:
- ❖ Mild-to-moderate pain

Used off label for:
- ❖ Cough
- ❖ Diarrhea

Codeine is a weak opioid, although about 10% is converted by CYP2D6 to morphine. Codeine is an opiate, meaning that it is found naturally in the opium poppy. Codeine is distinguished from other opioids by suppressing cough at low dose, much lower than needed for pain relief. The combination of antitussive and analgesic properties can be useful for patients with lung or tracheal cancer. Codeine may be the most constipating opioid, making it useful off-label for diarrhea.

The analgesic effect comes from codeine's metabolite, morphine. In addition to the boxed warnings applicable to all opioids, codeine has two black box warnings relating to its conversion to morphine. The 5% of Individuals who are 2D6 ultra-rapid metabolizers (UM) are exposed to more morphine, more quickly. Children with 2D6 UM genotypes have died of respiratory depression. Codeine is now contraindicated in children < 12. Furthermore, it is contraindicated for those < 18 post-tonsillectomy. The other warning relates to concomitant use (or discontinuation of) inhibitors / inducers of 2D6 and 3A4.

Numerous formulations containing this opiate are available. The pure form, codeine sulfate, is a Schedule II controlled substances The most popular combos are Tylenol #3, and Tylenol #4, which are Schedule III (as is the lower strength Tylenol #2). The combo of carisoprodol/aspirin/codeine for muscle pain (Soma Compound with Codeine) is schedule III also. In case you were wondering, there was a Tylenol #1 and #2, which also contained codeine.

Other combinations with low-dose codeine are Schedule V, the least restrictive classification. Codeine is combined with the expectorant guaifenesin (Robitussin AC), butalbital/acetaminophen/caffeine for headaches (Fioricet with Codeine), butalbital/aspirin/caffeine (Fiorinal with Codeine), the antihistamine chlorpheniramine for cold symptoms (Tuxarin ER), and with promethazine as cough syrup (used to make the famed concoction known as "purple drank".

"Coding morphine"

The active metabolite of codeine is morphine.

Dosing: The usual dose range for codeine is 15 – 60 mg q 4 hr PRN; Doses > 60 mg are rarely more effective or well-tolerated in opioid-naive patients

Dynamic interactions:
- ❖ Opioid agonist
  - – Constipation (strong)
  - – Sedation / CNS depression
  - – Respiratory depression
  - – Hypotension
- ❖ Lowers seizure threshold
- ❖ Serotonergic (weak)

Kinetic interactions:
- ❖ Delayed gastric emptying
- ❖ 2D6 substrate (with morphine as metabolite)
- ❖ 3A4 substrate
- ❖ Black box warning: concomitant use of (or discontinuation of) 2D6 inducers or 3A4 inhibitors / inducers are complex, requiring careful consideration of the effects on codeine and its active metabolite (morphine)

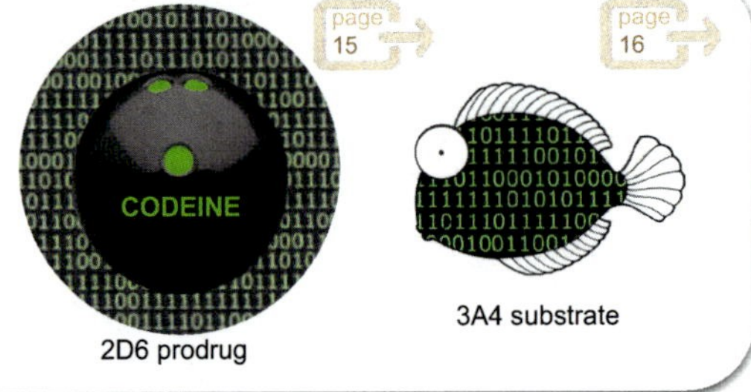

Cytochrome P450 2D6 (CYP2D6)

"Too Darn Sexy"

2D6 metabolizes ~ 12% of prescription drugs

5% of individuals are 2D6 ultrarapid metabolizers (UM).
10% are poor metabolizers (PM).

These balls are 2 Darn 6'y !

You're inflating my ego !

2D6 inhibitor

2D6 substrate

2D6 enzymes cannot be induced.

Increased substrate levels

inHibition = High

inHibition happens within Hours = Hurried

Inhibition reverses within 5 half-lives of the inhibitor.

Pro-drugs (like codeine) are substrates that are less potent than their metabolites (morphine). Codeine is responsible for antitussive effects and morphine is responsible for analgesia and respiratory depression. Ordinary substrates (beach balls) are deactivated by 2D6. Prodrugs (bowling balls) are *activated* by 2D6. In the presence of **an inhibitor prodrugs are less effective**.

2D6 UM

2D6 ultrarapid metabolizers (UM) clear 2D6 substrates quickly. These individuals are more likely to be non-responders to 2D6 substrates (excluding 2D6 prodrugs like codeine, which may be too strong). 5% of the population has a 2D6 UM genotype, which is relatively common among individuals with Middle Eastern or North African heritage.

2D6 poor metabolizers have defective 2D6 enzymes. Substrates are cleared slowly (by other pathways or unmetabolized) leading to Higher blood. levels, **as if** the patient were taking an inHibitor.

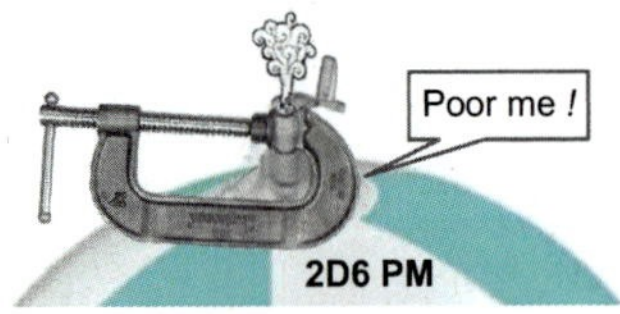

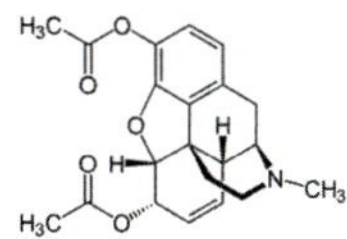

Heroin (diamorphine)

"Heroine"

❖ Opioid
❖ Schedule I (illegal)

Heroin (diamorphine) is one of the most dangerous and addictive substances known to man. It is typically injected intravenously but can also be smoked or snorted. 23% of individuals who try it become addicted. The onset of effect is immediate and lasts a few hours. Users report "falling in love with" heroin upon shooting up for the first time, reporting a pleasurable experience beyond imagination. It has been described as a feeling warm waves of total relaxation, bliss, peace and safety.

Tolerance to heroin's euphoric effects leads to escalation of use, and the addition is maintained by withdrawal symptoms occurring within 6 – 8 hours of the last dose. Ongoing heroin use is not solely to avoid withdrawal because, even with chronic use, individuals experience brief euphoria lasting 30 – 60 minutes.

Signs of opioid withdrawal according to the Clinical Opioid Withdrawal Scale (COWS) are tachycardia, sweating, dilated pupils, bone/joint aches, runny nose, lacrimation (tears), GI upset, tremor, yawning, gooseflesh skin ("cold turkey"), restlessness, anxiety and irritability (Wesson et al, 2003).

Heroin has stronger psychoactive effects than other opioids because it is highly lipophilic, allowing it to cross the blood-brain barrier quickly. It was first synthesized in 1874 from morphine. It was made available commercially in 1989 by the Bayer company, marketed as "the sedative for coughs". It was also used as a "non-addictive" remedy for addiction to morphine (which itself was originally touted as non-addictive remedy for opium addiction). Two-thirds of the world's illicit heroin now comes from Afghanistan.

Although heroin is illegal in the US, it is available for medical use in the UK, where it goes by the name diamorphine. In the UK diamorphine is sometimes used as a maintenance treatment for heroin addiction and routinely used for palliative care, myocardial infarction, post-operative pain and pulmonary edema (which they spell oedema).

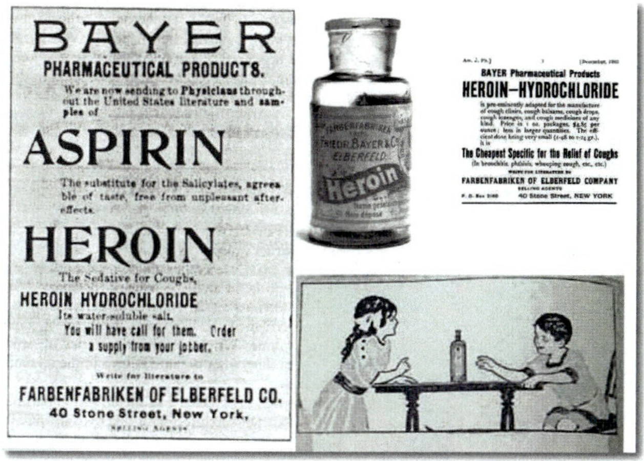

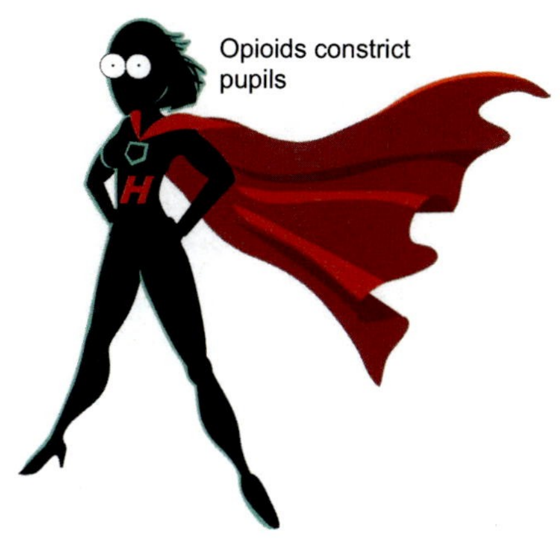

As with other opioids, heroin is a common cause of death by overdose. Heroin is often administered from shared needles, placing the user at risk for bacterial endocarditis, hepatitis B and C, and HIV infection. Hepatitis C is especially common among IV drug users.

A "speedball" is a mixture of cocaine and heroin injected from the same syringe. There is synergistic effect because cocaine and heroin share common metabolic pathways.

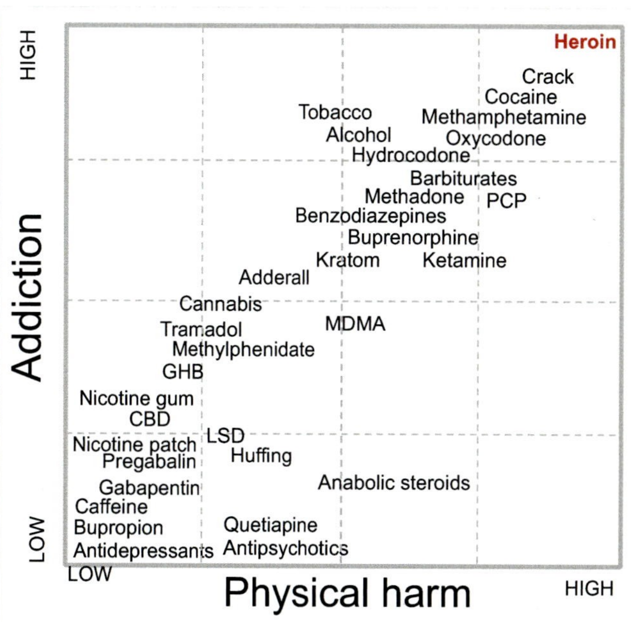

Physical harm is subjectively applied, as we are not comparing apples to apples. Since tobacco is responsible for 20% of deaths in the US, one could reasonably argue that its relative harm is understated.

Awareness of how the body metabolizes opioids can be useful in interpreting drug screens. Both codeine and heroin are metabolized to morphine.

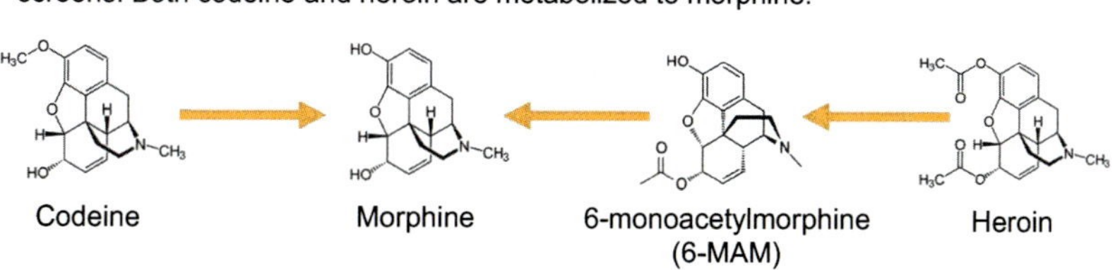

3A4 substrate

1942
$17 - $41

Meperidine (DEMEROL)

me PER i deen / DEM er ol

"Meeper Demoralized"

❖ Opioid
❖ Serotonergic
❖ Schedule II

50
100
mg

FDA-approved for:
❖ Moderate-to-severe pain

Meperidine (Demerol), also called pethidine, was the first synthetic opioid. Since it is synthetic, you would not refer to it as an opiate. Eduardo Fraifeld, MD opined that Demerol is "toxic and sedating" and "should not be used at all". Withdrawal symptoms are worse than with morphine. Meperidine should not be used for chronic pain. Its use for acute pain should be reserved for those allergic to first-line opioids. Oral administration is not advised due to extremely poor bioavailability. The usual route of administration is intramuscular (IM). It is not available for intravenous (IV) administration. Duration of action is very short, about 3 hours.

Although primarily a mu opioid receptor agonist, meperidine has more affinity for the kappa receptor than morphine, making meperidine more likely to cause dysphoria, hallucinations, and dissociation.

The metabolite of meperidine (normeperidine) is neurotoxic and may accumulate in cases of renal or hepatic impairment.

You are toxic and sedating. You should not be used at all.
MEEP!

Meperidine is distinguished from other opioids by its serotonergic properties, caused by 5-HT reuptake inhibition. Meperidine was involved in a high-profile death from serotonin syndrome in 1984, which killed an 18-year-old college student named Libby Zion. The reaction occurred when meperidine added to the MAOI phenelzine (Nardil).

Opioids, meperidine excluded, are potent pupillary constrictors. Due to meperidine's serotonergic and anticholinergic properties, it can cause dilation of pupils in some individuals. Withdrawal from meperidine manifests with dilated pupils like the other opioids. It is more likely than other opioids to cause seizures with overdose.

Dynamic interactions:
❖ Opioid agonist
 – Constipation
 – Sedation / CNS depression
 – Respiratory depression
 – Hypotension
❖ Lowers seizure threshold
❖ Prolongs QT interval
❖ Serotonergic (moderate)
❖ Anticholinergic
❖ Neurotoxicity

Kinetic interactions:
❖ Delayed gastric emptying
❖ 3A4 substrate
❖ Black box warning: concomitant use with 3A4 inhibitors or discontinuation of 3A4 inducers may cause fatal meperidine concentration

page 16

MEEP!
3A4 substrate (major)

1984
$41 - $151

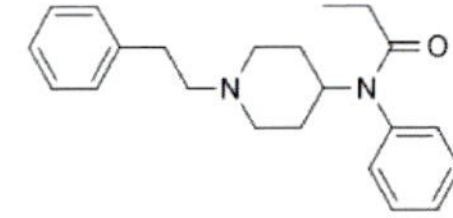

Fentanyl (DURAGESIC)

FEN ta nil / dur a GEES ik

"Fountain eel's Durable analgesic"

❖ Potent opioid
❖ Schedule II

FDA-approved for:
❖ Severe chronic pain

Fentanyl is a very high-potency opioid, dosed by mcg rather than mg. It is 100 times stronger than morphine. Recreational drugs (heroin, cocaine, etc.) may be laced with illegally-made fentanyl from China. Fentanyl is the most common cause of opioid overdose fatality, accounting for almost half of total opioid-related deaths (including similar strong synthetics). Fentanyl transdermal (Duragesic) is for opioid-tolerant patients only.

Fentanyl is not available as a pill but buccal soluble film and as a sucker (lozenge on a stick), although these formulations are not recommended. When injected epidurally it stays in the region it is injected into (segmental spread). There is an intranasal spray formulation.

Compared to morphine, fentanyl is less constipating and less likely to cause hypotension. It can cause muscle rigidity including "fentanyl chest wall rigidity syndrome", also known as "wooden chest". Fentanyl does not cause histamine release like morphine or oxycodone, so it does not cause pruritis or exacerbate asthma. It is less likely to cause hypotension. Fentanyl may cause muscle rigidity than is not dose-related, mostly commonly of chest wall.

Fentanyl has weak serotonergic properties, and there are case studies of it causing serotonin syndrome when combined with an antidepressant.

There is a black box warning that the patch releases the drug more rapidly at high temperatures which could potentially lead to overdose if exposed to a heating pad, hot tub or sauna.

Used fentanyl patches can still contain a large quantity of unabsorbed medication. The label specifically instructs flushing discarded patches down the toilet.

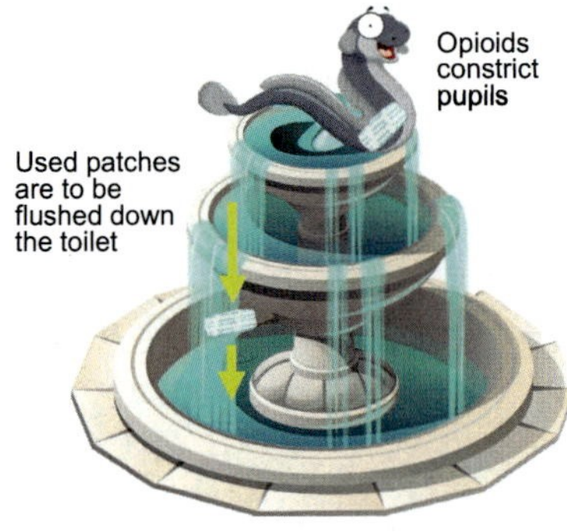
Opioids constrict pupils
Used patches are to be flushed down the toilet

Dosing: The patch is applied every 72 hours. For patients with high tolerance to opioids, two patches can be worn simultaneously. Do not convert mcg for mcg among fentanyl produced (patch, transmucosal, lozenge, buccal, nasal, sublingual).

Dynamic interactions:
❖ Opioid agonist
 – Constipation
 – Sedation / CNS depression
 – Respiratory depression
 – Hypotension
❖ Lowers seizure threshold
❖ Serotonergic (weak)

Kinetic interactions:
❖ Delayed gastric emptying
❖ 3A4 substrate
❖ Black box warning: concomitant use with 3A4 inhibitors or discontinuation of 3A4 inducers may cause fatal fentanyl concentration

page 16

3A4 substrate

1947
$12 - $41

Methadone (DOLOPHINE)

METH a dohn / DOLE o fene

"Dolphin's Method (to be) done" (using heroin)

- Long-acting opioid
- Schedule II

10 mg / ml

5 10 40 mg

FDA-approved for:

- Opioid dependence
- Chronic pain

Methadone (Dolophine), commonly used as maintenance treatment for heroin addiction, is a synthetic opioid with an exceptionally long half-life of 24 to 55 hours. Like other opioids, methadone is a Schedule II controlled substance. It has a 60 – 90% success rate for treating opioid use disorder (OUD), substantially more effective than abstinence-based treatment. This approach to addiction is considered "harm reduction" – the patient remains addicted to an opioid but avoids the social, health (overdose, dirty needles) and legal morbidity of using heroin. For short-acting opioids (heroin, morphine, oxycodone, etc) withdrawal symptoms may start within 6 – 8 hours from the last dose. The advantage of methadone is that withdrawal does not start until 24 hours.

Side effects are those typical of opioids. However, thanks to methadone's long half-life, tolerance to side effects develops quickly. So, with methadone there will be less persisting constipation, dizziness, sedation, nausea, and miosis compared other opioids (oxycodone, hydrocodone, morphine, hydromorphone, etc). The analgesic duration of action is shorter than half-life. Since methadone accumulates, the dose may need to be reduced after about 5 days to avoid toxicity.

Although less addictive, methadone is not safer than other opioids. It accounts for 2% of opioid sales but 30% of prescription opioid deaths.

Methadone is second line to buprenorphine (Subutex, Suboxone), which is the gold-standard medication for maintenance of opioid use disorder. Methadone is more abusable and more dangerous than buprenorphine. The main risk is death by overdose due to respiratory depression. Methadone prolongs QT interval and increases risk for torsades de pointes at high dose. Managing concomitant medications can be hazardous because methadone is a substrate of several CYP enzymes.

Methadone, when used for opioid addiction (21-day detox or long-term maintenance) must only be dispensed by certified opioid treatment programs, under strict regulation. Patients must show up every day to receive their dose. This may be preferable (to buprenorphine) for those needing daily monitoring. Eventually patients can earn take-home doses for weekends. Methadone programs are publicly funded and more affordable for those without health insurance. Many buprenorphine clinics do not accept Medicaid. Some patients feel more stable on methadone than with buprenorphine.

According to federal regulations, clinics had to dispense methadone in liquid form. Patients must take the medicine at the clinic daily, and eventually may earn take-home doses for weekends. Due to restrictions for dispensing methadone, travel is burdensome for patients, earning it the nickname "liquid handcuffs".

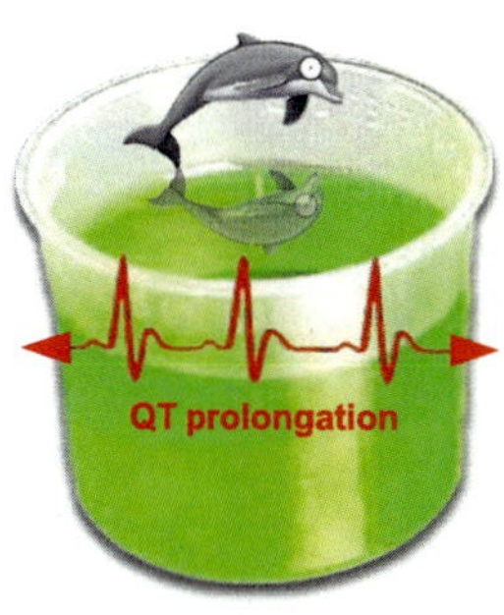

Methadone is the preferred treatment for opioid dependence during pregnancy, although buprenorphine without naloxone is a relatively safe alternative. The mother will need higher or more frequent methadone dose during pregnancy. Neonatal opioid withdrawal syndrome may occur.

Methadone has a unique ability among opiates to block NMDA receptors. It has weak serotonergic properties, making it a possible but unlikely contributor to serotonin syndrome when combined with antidepressants.

Benzodiazepines should not be prescribed to patients taking any opioid due to ~3x increase in death from opioid overdose, as both classes of medication depress respiration. The risk is even higher when benzodiazepines and methadone are combined, ~ 7x

There are 10 Black Box Warnings: 1. Appropriate use (pain management or addiction specialists, not for PRN use); 2. Addiction; 3. Required risk evaluation and mitigation strategy (REMS) program; 4. Respiratory depression; 5. Accidental injection can kill kids; 6. QT prolongation; 7. Neonatal opioid withdrawal syndrome; 8. CYP450 interactions; 9. Don't use with benzos; 10. Limitations on unsupervised administration.

Dosing: When rotating from another opioid to methadone, equianalgesic dose tables should not be used. Start low and go slow. Initial dose is 20 – 30 mg for heavy users of heroin (half this dose for patients without high tolerance currently) then smaller PRN doses for withdrawal symptoms, not exceeding 40 mg on day one. Special documentation is mandated if initial dose exceeds 30 mg or total first-day dose exceed 40 mg. Depending on reference source, the recommended maintenance dose is 40 - 100 mg/day versus 80 – 120 mg/day. Some sources list 60 mg/day as the recommended minimum maintenance dose, because patients on lower doses are much more likely to relapse on heroin. Take-home doses were previously not permitted for those taking > 100 mg. Doses above 120 mg previously required prior approval by regulatory agencies. The dose may need to be reduced after about 5 days to avoid toxicity. For management of chronic pain, the dose will be much lower.

Dynamic interactions:

- Opioid agonist
  - Constipation
  - Sedation / CNS depression
  - Respiratory depression
  - Hypotension
- Lowers seizure threshold
- Prolongs QT interval (moderate)
- Serotonergic (weak)

Kinetic interactions:

- Delays gastric emptying
- 2B6 substrate (major)
- 2C19 substrate
- 3A4 substrate

Black Box Warning: concomitant use with inhibitors of 3A4, 2B6, 2C19, 2C9, or 2D6 or discontinuation of concomitant inducers of these enzymes may cause potentially fatal respiratory depression.

3% of the population are 2B6 ultrarapid metabolizers (UMs). Methadone will be poorly effective for these individuals, and methadone may even be negative on standard drug screens.

page 12

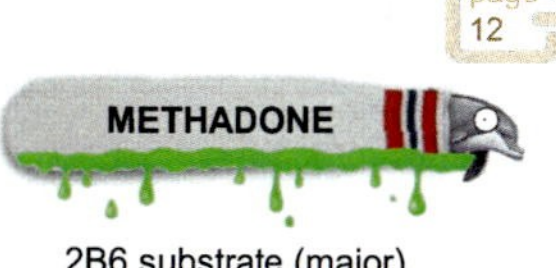

2B6 substrate (major)

page 14

page 16

2C19 substrate

3A4 substrate

OPIOIDS

22

#39
1995
IR: $7 - $41
ER: $32 - $123

Racemic mix

Tramadol (ULTRAM)

TRAM a dol / UL tram

"Ultra ram Trauma doll"

Pain medication
- Weak opioid
- SNRI
- DEA Schedule IV

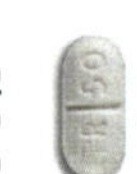

ER:
100
200
300
mg

50
mg

FDA-approved for:
- Acute pain (mod to severe)
- Chronic pain (mod to severe) – ER formulation

Used off-label for:
- Fibromyalgia
- Premature ejaculation

Tramadol is a partial (weak) agonist at the μ (mu) opioid receptor with onset of pain relief in about 1 hour, with duration of about 6 hours. Tramadol is also a serotonin–norepinephrine reuptake inhibitor (SNRI) like venlafaxine (Effexor) and duloxetine (Cymbalta). Tramadol is not considered an antidepressant but may have some antidepressant and anxiolytic properties. Tramadol is not typically prescribed by psychiatrists. Tramadol can be a contributor to serotonin syndrome if combined with serotonergic antidepressants.

Tramadol was released in the US in 1995 and became a Schedule IV controlled substance in 2015 due to potential for abuse as an opioid. Compared to other opioids, respiratory depression and constipation are less of a problem with tramadol. With overdose, tramadol is more likely (than traditional opioids) to cause seizures than traditional opioids.

Side effects are similar to other opioids. In order of frequency, adverse effects occurring within 90 days included constipation (46%), nausea (40%), dizziness (33%), headache (32%), somnolence (25%), vomiting (17%), pruritus (11%) and psychiatric effects (14%). Tramadol has 8 black box warnings, comparable to other opioid medications.

It is available in a fixed dose combination with acetaminophen (Tylenol) called Ultracet

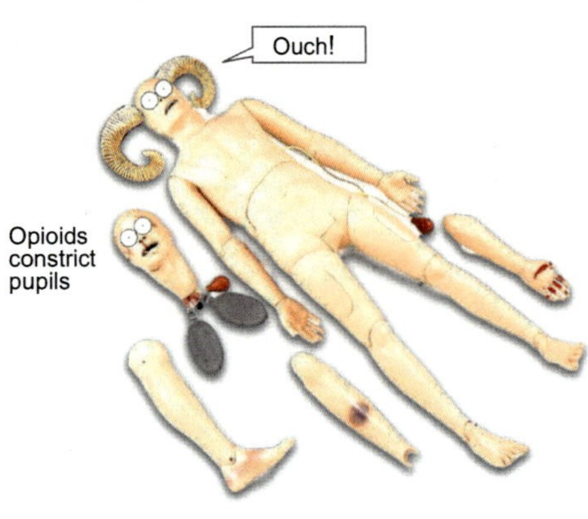
Ouch!
Opioids constrict pupils

Tapentadol, as described on the next page, is a much stronger opioid than tramadol.

Dosing: For IR formulation, the standard dose is 50 - 100 mg q4-6 hr PRN; Although it tends to be started at 50 mg, the label recommends to go slower "unless immediate onset is required" by starting 25 q AM; May increase by 25 mg/day in 3-day intervals to 25 mg q 6 hr PRN, then may increase by 50 mg in 3-day intervals to 50 mg q 6 hr PRN; Maximum is 400 mg /day (300 mg/day for > 75 years); use lowest effective dose and shortest effective treatment duration; To stop (if prolonged use), taper slowly, by no more than 10-25% in 2-4 week intervals; For ER formulation, which is for chronic pain, start 100 mg ER QD, may increase by increments of 100 mg in 5-day intervals (using the lowest effective dose) with a maximum of 300 mg ER daily; May convert from IR to ER at the same total daily dose, rounding down to the nearest 100 mg.

Dynamic interactions:
- Opioid agonist
  - Constipation
  - Sedation / CNS depression
  - Respiratory depression
  - Hypotension
- Lowers seizure threshold
- QT prolongation
- Serotonergic

Kinetic interactions:
- Delays gastric emptying
- 3A4 substrate
- Tramadol is transformed by 2D6 to an active metabolite (desmethyltramadol) which is responsible for most of the opioid effect.
- Tramadol may be less effective for individuals with 2D6 poor metabolizer (PM) genotype (10% of population) or for individuals taking 2D6 inHibitors such as fluoxetine, paroxetine or bupropion.
- Black box warning: Respiratory depression and death have occurred in children with 2D6 ultra-rapid metabolizer (UM) genotype (5% of population).
- Black box warning: "Concomitant use or discontinuation of concomitant 3A4 inDucers, 3A4 inHibitors, or 2D6 inHibitors are complex; Such interactions require careful consideration of the effects on tramadol and its active metabolite".

page 15

ULTRAM

2D6 prodrug

page 16

3A4 substrate

Tramadol Tapentadol

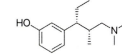

2009
IR: $197 - $235
ER: $755 - $912

Tapentadol (NUCYNTA)

ta PENT a dol / Nu SEN ta

"Tap into doll's New scent"

Pain medication
- ❖ Full-strength opioid
- ❖ NE reuptake inhibitor
- ❖ DEA Schedule II

ER: 50, 100, 150, 200, 250 mg

IR: 50, 75, 100 mg

FDA-approved for:
- ❖ Acute pain (mod to severe) – IR formulation
- ❖ Chronic pain (severe) – ER formulation
- ❖ Pain associated with diabetic peripheral neuropathy – ER formulation

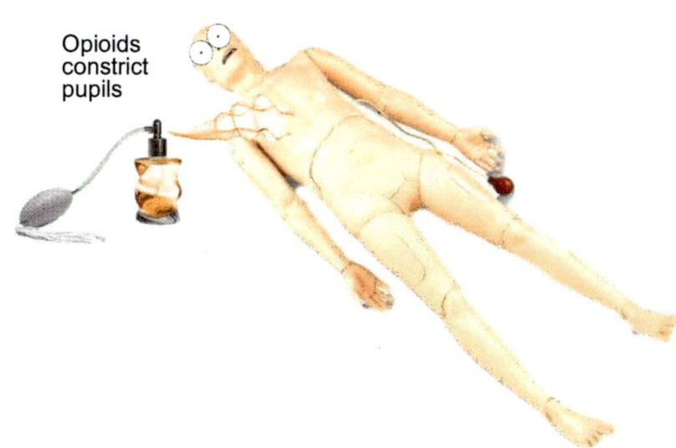
Opioids
constrict
pupils

8 black box warnings (comparable to other opioids):
- ► Potent opioid; ER formulation not for PRN use
- ► Addiction, Abuse, and Misuse
- ► Risk evaluation and mitigation strategy (REMS)
- ► Respiratory depression
- ► Accidental ingestion can kill children
- ► Neonatal opioid withdrawal syndrome
- ► Avoid alcohol
- ► Avoid benzodiazepines / other sedatives

"The 'Nu' Tramadol" - tapentadol (Nucynta) was approved in 2009 for acute pain (moderate to severe) such as post-surgical pain. Tapentadol works as a mu opioid agonist and norepinephrine reuptake inhibitor (NRI). Tapentadol does not significantly inhibit serotonin reuptake like Tramadol does.

Tapentadol is a Schedule II controlled substance like traditional opioids such as morphine, oxycodone, hydrocodone, etc. Its actual opioid strength is weaker than oxycodone, and about equal to hydrocodone. Its (total) analgesic efficacy is about equivalent to oxycodone, with fewer gastrointestinal side effects. Nausea occurred about 50% of the time with tapentadol, compared to 70% with oxycodone.

The label warns not to combine tapentadol with serotonergic antidepressants, but in clinical trials patients took it concurrently with SSRIs without adverse effects. Because of tapentadol's noradrenergic activity, pace of upward titration is more limited than with pure opioid agonists. Onset of analgesia is about 30 minutes with duration of 4 to 6 hours. Elimination half-life is about 4 hours. Like tramadol, it lowers seizure threshold.

For context: atomoxetine (Strattera) is a stand-alone NRI indicated for treatment of ADHD that does not have opioid effects. The tricyclic antidepressants (TCAs) that are essentially pure NRIs include nortriptyline (Pamelor), desipramine (Norpramin), maprotiline (Ludiomil) and trimipramine (Surmontil).

The extended release formulation of tapentadol (Nucynta ER) is FDA-approved for severe chronic diabetic neuropathic pain (and for unspecified severe chronic pain) for those needing an opioid around-the-clock opioid, not for PRN use.

Tapentadol has 8 black box warnings, as is standard for opioid medications.

Dosing: 50-100 mg q 4–6 hours PRN; Start: 50-100 mg x1, may repeat dose in 1 hour; Maximum is 700 mg on day one and 600 mg/day on subsequent days; Use the lowest effective dose and the shortest effective duration; To stop (if prolonged use), taper by no more than 25% q 2–4 weeks

	Tramadol	Tapentadol
Mechanism	Opioid + SNRI	Opioid + NRI
DEA Schedule	IV	II
FDA-approved for	Acute and chronic pain	Acute pain*
μ-opioid agonist	weak	moderate
Transformed by 2D6 to active metabolite	yes	no

Dynamic interactions:
- ❖ Opioid agonist
  - – Constipation
  - – Sedation / CNS depression
  - – Respiratory depression
  - – Hypotension
- ❖ Lowers seizure threshold
- ❖ Hypotensive effects

Kinetic interactions:
- ❖ Delayed gastric emptying
- ❖ None otherwise
  - – "in a bubble"

page 18

NUCYNTA

1953
$1,200 - $4,500

HO / N (chemical structure)

Levorphanol (LEVO-DROMORAN)

lee VOR fa nole / LEE voe DROH mor an

"Leveraged Dromedary"

❖ Opioid
❖ SNRI
❖ DEA Schedule II

1
2
3
mg

FDA-approved for:

❖ Moderate to severe pain

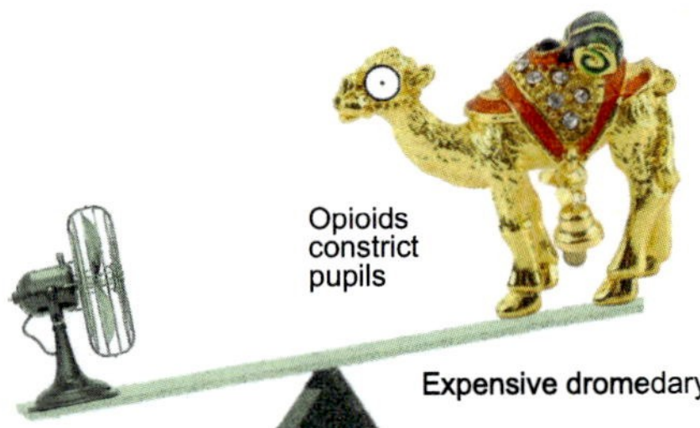

Levorphanol is a strong opioid pain medication that is very rarely used. Despite being old (1953) it costs over $1,000 / bottle. It was under $100 until the manufacturer discontinued it due to low demand. One small company makes it now.

Levorphanol has more side effects than other opioids. It is more likely to cause hallucinations or delirium. It has a long half-life of 16 hours which can lead to accumulation.

Levorphanol's niche was treatment of neuropathic pain. Its mechanism similar to tramadol and tapentadol in that it is an opioid plus SNRI.

Levorphanol also serves as a full agonist at κ (kappa), δ (delta) and nociceptin pain receptors. It is an NMDA receptor antagonist (like ketamine, dextromethorphan and methadone). At high concentrations it is also a glycine receptor antagonist and GABA receptor antagonist, which is great way to induce a seizure.

Dosing: Levorphanol is dosed q 6 - 8 hr PRN; Start 1 mg - 2 mg for opioid-naive patients; titrate with caution; Taper gradually to stop if prolonged use

Dynamic interactions:

- ❖ Opioid agonist
  - Constipation
  - Sedation / CNS depression
  - Respiratory depression
  - Hypotension
- ❖ Lowers seizure threshold
- ❖ Serotonergic
- ❖ Noradrenergic

Kinetic interactions:

- ❖ Slows gastric emptying
- ❖ 2D6 substrate
- ❖ 3A4 substrate

page 15

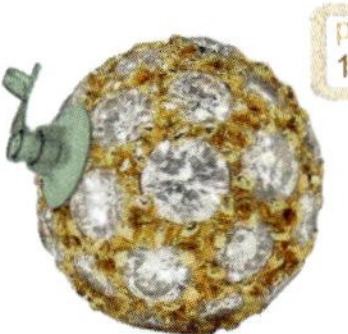

2D6 substrate

page 16

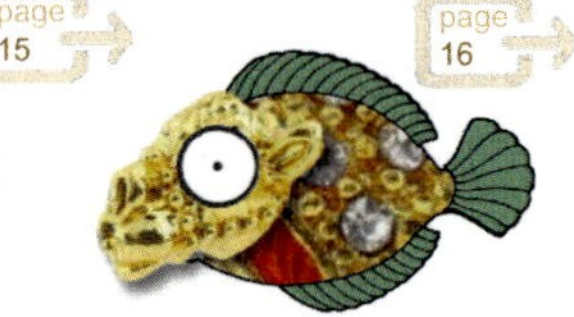

3A4 substrate

Opioid receptor binding

Opioid receptor agonists

The opioids we have presented thus were nonselective full agonists at opioid receptors. Some activate the receptors potently (fentanyl), others weakly (tramadol). The two subtypes of opioid receptors discussed in this chapter are μ (mu) and κ (kappa). μ (mu) opioid receptors are involved in analgesia, miosis (constricted pupils), euphoria, physical dependence and respiratory depression. κ (kappa) opioid receptors are involved in analgesia and miosis, but not the other stuff. A pure kappa agonist would have no abuse potential and, at high dose, would produce dysphoria rather than euphoria.

Opioid agonist	μ (mu)	κ (kappa)	Other	Opiate structure
Morphine (MS Contin)	Agonist			yes
Hydromorphone (Dilaudid)	Agonist			yes
Oxymorphone (Numorphan)	Agonist			yes
Hydrocodone (Vicodin, Norco)	Agonist			yes
Oxycodone (Percocet)	Agonist			yes
Codeine (Tylenol #3)	Agonist			yes
Diamorphine (Heroin)	Agonist			yes
Meperidine (Demerol)	Agonist		5-HT	no
Fentanyl (Duragesic patch)	Agonist			no
Methadone (Dolophine)	Agonist			no
Tramadol (Ultram)	Agonist (weak)		SNRI	no
Tapentadol (Nucynta)	Agonist		SNRI	no
Levorphanol (Levo-Dromoran)	Agonist		SNRI	some-what

Opioid receptor antagonists

Next, we will present the opioid antagonists - Naloxone (short-acting) and naltrexone (long-acting), which have identical mechanisms of action. They block opioid receptors tightly and nonselectively.

Naloxone (Narcan) is used to reverse opioid overdose and serve as an abuse-deterrent when combined with opioid agonists (whereby naloxone is not activated unless the product is crushed or injected). Naltrexone (ReVia, Vivitrol) is prescribed for opioid and alcohol use disorders. The principal mechanism of naltrexone for opioid dependence is by blocking μ (mu) receptors. Naltrexone's mechanism of action in alcohol dependence is via blocking an endogenous opioid (dynorphin, associated with negative emotional states) at κ (kappa) opioid receptors – think "alkohol".

Opioid antagonist	μ (mu)	κ (kappa)	Opiate structure
Naltrexone (ReVia, Vivitrol)	Antagonist		yes
Naloxone (Narcan)	Antagonist		yes

Partial agonists

The best-known opioid receptor partial agonist is buprenorphine (Subutex, Suboxone). Think of a full opioid agonist (heroin, methadone, etc) as a car key that, when put in the ignition, makes the car go 100 miles per hour. A full antagonist (naloxone, naltrexone) jams the ignition and the car stops. A partial agonist (buprenorphine) starts the car but only lets it go 40 mph (Petros Levounis, MD). Buprenorphine only allows opioid receptors to be 40% stimulated. Buprenorphine binds tightly to opioid receptors and will displace full opioid agonists. If a dependent individual has a full opioid agonist (e.g. heroin) in their system, buprenorphine will precipitate withdrawal symptoms. Giving buprenorphine to an opioid-naïve patient (to whom 40 mph would be really fast) will get them high and could even lead to overdose with respiratory depression. Pentazocine (Talwin) and butorphanol (Stadol nasal spray) and similar to buprenorphine in their ability to displace full opioid agonists and precipitate withdrawal. Nalbuphine (Nubain) binds mu receptors loosely and will not displace traditional opioids.

Opioid partial agonist	μ (mu)	κ (kappa)	Opiate structure
Buprenorphine (Subutex, Suboxone)	Partial agonist	Antagonist	yes
Butorphanol (Stadol nasal spray)	Partial agonist		somewhat
Pentazocine (Talwin)	Partial agonist	Agonist	somewhat
Nalbuphine (Nubain)	Partial agonist (weak)	Agonist	yes

Levorphanol Naltrexone

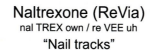

1998
$25 - $107

Naltrexone (ReVia)

nal TREX own / re VEE uh

"Nail tracks"

opioid antagonist

50 mg

FDA-approved for:

- Opioid use disorder
- Alcohol use disorder

Used off-label for:

- Self-mutilation / "cutting"
- Behavioral addictions (gambling, paraphilias)
- Weight loss (in combination with bupropion)
- Anorexia nervosa (leads to weight gain)
- Chronic pain (micro-dose)

Naltrexone is a high-affinity antagonist of the μ (mu) opioid receptor. It also antagonizes delta and kappa opioid receptors. Naltrexone blocks the effect of all opioids, including endogenous opioids (endorphins). It shares the same mechanism as naloxone. The NA in naltrexone (and naloxone) could stand for Narcotic Antagonist. In contrast to naloxone (quick-acting / short-acting opioid antagonist used as antidote to opioid overdose), naltrexone has a prolonged duration of action, intended "long treks". Half-life for naltrexone (including active metabolite) is about 14 hours (versus 1 hour for naloxone). Naltrexone's duration of effectiveness for opioid use disorder exceeds the half-life, because it takes 5x half-life for any drug to be eliminated. Contrast this with anxiolytic medications, whose duration of effectiveness is generally less their half-life.

Naltrexone prevents opioids from exerting their full euphoric effects, so if the individual relapses the reinforcing effect of the opioid is greatly diminished. Naltrexone can prevent a slip from becoming a full-blown relapse.

In treatment of opioid use disorder (OUD), naltrexone is an alternative (to buprenorphine or methadone) for highly motivated patients who do not want to take an opioid. Naltrexone is not a controlled substance. An opioid-dependent person should not receive naltrexone before detoxification, because opioid withdrawal will be precipitated within 30 minutes. Before starting naltrexone, the individual must abstain from opioids for 7 – 10 days (including buprenorphine) to avoid precipitating immediate opioid withdrawal. This makes naltrexone a hard sell, considering that buprenorphine can be started shortly after withdrawal has commenced and methadone can be started before onset of withdrawal symptoms. Due to poor adherence, oral naltrexone is rarely useful for opioid use disorder. Among those successfully inducted, naltrexone long-acting injectable (LAI) is similar to buprenorphine (Subutex, Suboxone) in terms of efficacy and safety.

Naltrexone's mechanism of action in alcohol dependence is via blocking an endogenous opioid (dynorphin, associated with negative emotional states) at κ (kappa) opioid receptors – think "al**k**ohol". Benefit of naltrexone for alcohol use disorder is modest. After a few weeks of treatment, cravings for alcohol decrease, although the mechanism is not clearly understood. With addiction, dopamine neurons stop responding to the primary reinforcer (alcohol) and instead respond to the conditioned stimulus (the sight or smell of alcohol), producing craving. Blockade of opioid receptors is thought to prevent the increased dopamine release responsible for cravings.

Form of Naltrexone	FDA-approved for	Comments
Naltrexone tablets (ReVia)	Opioid use d/o Alcohol use d/o	Low success rate due to nonadherence; Used off-label to reduce cutting.
Naltrexone long-acting injectable (VIVITROL)	Opioid use d/o Alcohol use d/o	q 4-week injection; as effective as buprenorphine for opioid use disorder but is a hard sell because patients must first abstain for opioids for 7 – 10 days.
Low-dose naltrexone	N/A	Used to stimulate release of endorphins without blocking their effects (see next page).
Naltrexone/ bupropion (CONTRAVE)	Obesity (long-term)	Bupropion (Wellbutrin) decreases appetite and naltrexone blocks the reward response of food.
Morphine sulfate / naltrexone (EMBEDA)	Chronic pain (mod to severe)	Abuse-deterrent morphine capsules. When taken PO the naltrexone has no effect. If crushed, sequestered naltrexone is released.
Methylnaltrexone (RELISTOR)	Opioid-induced constipation	Does not cross the blood-brain barrier so it does not cause withdrawal or interfere with central analgesic effects. It counters peripheral effects of opioids including constipation and itching. It does interfere with analgesia mediated by opioid receptors on peripheral sensory neurons.

Oral naltrexone appears to work about as well as acamprosate. The combination of acamprosate (666 mg TID) with naltrexone (50 mg per day) may be more effective than either drug alone, while not increasing the side effect profile.

The most common side effects reported with naltrexone are diarrhea and abdominal cramping, which are symptoms analogous to opioid withdrawal. Headaches, somnolence, fatigue, dysphoria and anxiety have been reported. Naltrexone blocks endogenous opioids (endorphins) which can block "natural highs" associated with exercise and food. If an opioid is needed for emergency pain control, the analgesic effect will be blocked. Naltrexone has a relatively small therapeutic index for causing hepatotoxicity, which can occur at less than 5x the therapeutic dose. Liver enzymes should be monitored.

Naltrexone is associated with modest weight loss because it may decrease the the pleasure / reward associated with food. Contrave is a fixed dose combination of naltrexone with the antidepressant bupropion (Wellbutrin), which acts as a modest appetite suppressant. Note the dose of naltrexone in Contrave is low but still higher than would be indicated for "low dose naltrexone" treatment as explained on the next page.

Naltrexone is commonly prescribed off-label to reduce non-suicidal self-injurious behavior by cutting. The endogenous opioid system is felt to playa central role in repetitive self-injury. Naltrexone blocks the reward experienced when cutting. Patients taking naltrexone for cutting tend to adhere to the pills and do not need naltrexone long-acting injectable (Vivitrol).

Dosing: For opioid use disorder, the individual must be opioid-free for 7 – 10 days; Check liver enzymes at baseline; Start 25 mg PO once and repeat in 1 hour if no withdrawal; The maintenance dose is 50 mg QD. Alternatively it can be taken 100 mg every other day or 150 mg every third day (e.g., q Mon, Wed and Fri); If any suspicion that the patient may not have abstained from opioids for 7 – 10 days, start with a test dose of naloxone (shorter-acting); For alcohol use disorder, the maintenance dose is also 50 mg QD (without the QOD or q 3-day dosing options); There is no requirement for a prolonged period of alcohol abstinence to start naltrexone (although the individual must be free of opioids for 7 – 10 days). Check liver enzymes periodically; For paraphilias, a higher dose of 100 – 150 mg QD may be necessary, with more frequent monitoring of liver enzymes.

Dynamic interactions:

- Blocks opioid agonists

Kinetic interactions:

- None significant – "in a bubble"

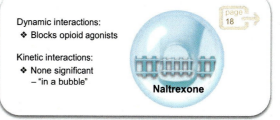

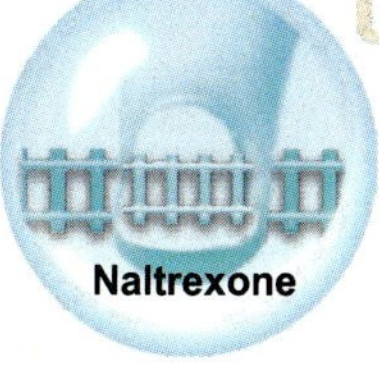

page 18

1998
$1,296 - $1,597

Naltrexone LAI (VIVITROL)

nal TREX own / VIV it rol

"Vivid trolley"

opioid antagonist

380 mg

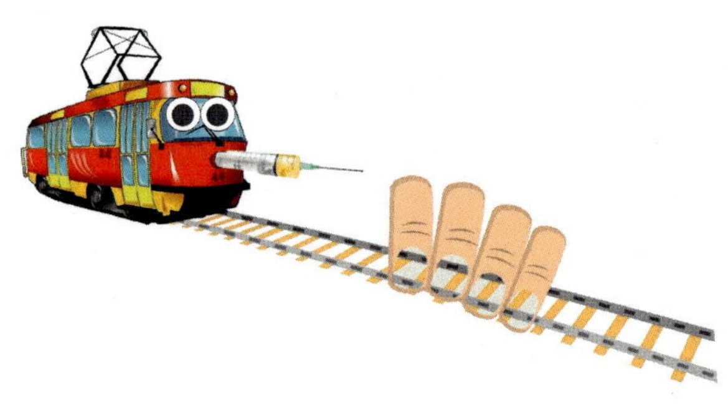

FDA-approved for:

- ❖ Opioid use disorder
- ❖ Alcohol use disorder

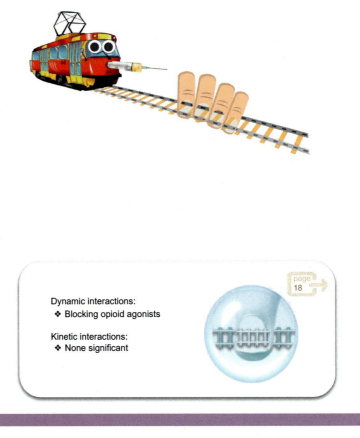

Vivitrol is an intramuscular injection given in the gluteal every 4 weeks. All the information about naltrexone from the preceding page is applicable. Vivitrol is more effective than PO naltrexone, which patients simply stop taking.

Once treatment is established for opioid use disorder, relapse rates with Vivitrol and buprenorphine are similar. Opioid detox with Vivitrol is less likely to succeed than with buprenorphine (partial opioid agonist) because buprenorphine induction begins when the patient is in early withdrawal. Naltrexone may not be started until 7 to 10 days after the last opioid dose.

For alcoholism, the best results were demonstrated when patients were sober for 1 week prior to starting the medication. Heavy-drinking days were reduced for 49% of patients (compared to 31% with placebo injection).

Vivitrol is more likely to cause sedation than oral naltrexone. Serious injection site reactions are possible, including necrosis requiring surgery.

Dosing: The same dose is used for alcohol or opioid use disorder, which is 380 mg IM (gluteal) q 4 wk; The individual must be opioid-free for 7 – 10 days; Establish tolerability with oral naltrexone first; Vivitrol is active immediately so PO overlap is not needed, nor recommended; Check liver enzymes at baseline and periodically thereafter

page 18

Dynamic interactions:

- ❖ Blocking opioid agonists

Kinetic interactions:

- ❖ None significant

From compounding pharmacies, ~$30/mo, not covered by insurance

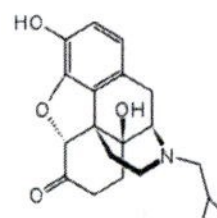

Low Dose Naltrexone (LDN)

opioid antagonist to stimulate endorphin production (off-label)

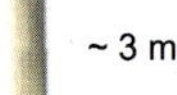

~ 3 mg

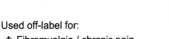

FDA-approved for:

- ❖ N/A

Used off-label for:

- ❖ Fibromyalgia / chronic pain
- ❖ Depression
- ❖ Immune stimulation
- ❖ Dissociative disorders

In response to pain, the pituitary gland makes natural opioids called endorphins, a contraction of "endogenous morphine". Endorphin release is increased with exercise and is responsible for the "runner's high". Endorphins are associated with states of pleasure such as laughter, love and eating tasty food.

At the FDA-approved dose of 50 mg, naltrexone blocks the effects of endorphins and may blunt these natural pleasures. Unlike higher doses of naltrexone, low-dose naltrexone (LDN) around 3 mg stimulates endorphin release, decreases inflammatory markers (eg, ESR, CRP) and enhances immune functioning. LDN appears to stimulate production of endorphins for weeks after LDN is no longer in the system (Gironi, 2008).

Adverse effects are not expected. The most common side effect is vivid dreams which seem to decrease after a few nights.

LDN is not FDA-approved and is only available from compounding pharmacies. In 2016 LDN was approved in Nigeria to increase immune functioning for individuals with HIV disease.

To provide context, naltrexone 8 mg is combined with 90 mg of bupropion to constitute Contrave, approved for obesity as described on the subsequent page. Although Contrave's 8 mg of naltrexone is a small dose, it is more than the 3 mg typically used for LDN treatment as described here.

Dosing: LDN can be ordered from compounding pharmacies. LDN is typically dosed 0.5 mg HS for several weeks, followed by 0.5 to 1.0 mg incremental increases over several weeks to 3 mg, with a typical maximum of 4.5 mg HS. Change to AM dosing if vivid dreams are problematic. If you are unconcerned about precise dosing, you could prescribe #30 of 50 mg naltrexone tabs to be chopped into 16 pieces (approx 3 mg each) which would be at least a 12-month supply (taking into account a lot of discarded crushed fragments and powder). A year of LDN from a compounding pharmacy would cost about $400.

Main source: Schwaiger, Timothy. The Uses of Low-Dose Naltrexone in Clinical Practice, Potential benefits for a wide range of conditions. *Natural Medical Journal.* April 2018.

2014
$272

CONTRAVE (naltrexone + bupropion)

CON trave (nal TREX own + bu PRO pi on)

"Count Rave"

Weight loss combo:
- ❖ Opioid antagonist
- ❖ Norepinephrine-dopamine reuptake inhibitor (NDRI)

8 / 90 mg

FDA-approved for:
- ❖ Obesity (long-term)

Contrave is a fixed dose combination of bupropion 90 mg with naltrexone 8 mg, approved for long term treatment of obesity as an adjunct to diet and increased physical activity in patients with a body mass index (BMI) ≥30 or BMI ≥27 with a weight-related comorbidity (hypertension, diabetes, or dyslipidemia). Neither component is a controlled substance.

Bupropion (Wellbutrin) is an NDRI antidepressant. Like other stimulant-type medications, bupropion decreases appetite by activating adrenergic and dopaminergic receptors in the hypothalamus. With bupropion alone, the incidence of weight loss greater than 5 pounds is about 28%.

Naltrexone is an opioid antagonist that may decrease the pleasure associated with food (as well as pleasure from alcohol and opioids, for which naltrexone is FDA-approved). However, naltrexone monotherapy has failed to produce clinically significant weight loss in controlled studies. Naltrexone has shown promise in ameliorating antipsychotic-associated weight gain.

These two drugs were combined strategically. Bupropion stimulates neurons in the hypothalamus to decrease appetite. These neurons also release beta-endorphin, which decreases the anorexigenic effect. Naltrexone blocks the effect of beta-endorphin. The combination was shown to produce more weight loss than bupropion alone.

About 50% of subjects lost at least 5% of body weight, with an average of 6% weight reduction at one year. Contrave was also associated with improvements in glycemic control and other cardiovascular risk factors. As is common in obesity trials, completion rate was only about 50%. Patients taking the active drug were twice as likely to discontinue than those taking placebo. The most common side effects was nausea (30%).

Bupropion is an antidepressant, and all antidepressants have a black box warning of increased suicidal thoughts and behavior in children, adolescents and young adults.

Dosing: Start with one 8/90 mg tab q AM x1 week, then 1 tab BID x1 week, then 2 tabs AM and 1 tab PM x 1 week, then to maintenance dose of two tabs BID, which is also the maximum dose; Stop if weight loss is less than 5% after 12 weeks on the max dose; Avoid administration with a high-fat meal.

Medications approved for weight loss

All of these are approved for long-term treatment except for phentermine (short-term).

Medication	Approx weight loss	Comments / Side effects
Naltrexone/bupropion (CONTRAVE)	~ 6% body weight	Nausea, headache, constipation, dizziness, dry mouth; Bupropion is a strong 2D6 inHibitor.
Phentermine (ADIPEX) page 231	~ 5% body weight	Schedule IV controlled; Insomnia, anxiety, elevated BP and HR, mania; Contraindicated with cardiovascular disease
Phentermine/topiramate ER (QSYMIA)	~ 10% body weight	Topiramate: paresthesias, dizziness, altered taste, renal stones, acidosis, confusion; Phentermine: see above
Lorcaserin (BELVIQ) page 232	3-10% body weight	Stimulant removed from market; Selective 5-HT2C receptor agonist that suppresses appetite; Labeling included a warning of cardiac valvulopathy because fenfluramine damaged heart valves via 5-HT2B agonism.
Orlistat (ALLI)	~ 10% body weight	Over-the-counter; Inhibits gastric and pancreatic lipases, causing triglycerides to be excreted in feces. High rate of discontinuation due to GI distress, flatulence, greasy orange fecal incontinence; Interferes with vitamin absorption.
Liraglutide (SAXENDA)	5 – 10% body weight	Subcutaneous medication branded as Victoza for diabetes; Black box warning of thyroid tumors; Also risk of nephrotoxicity and pancreatitis

Off-label treatments include metformin, topiramate (monotherapy), lisdexamfetamine (Vyvanse). The author recommends the 16/8 intermittent fasting diet and metformin.

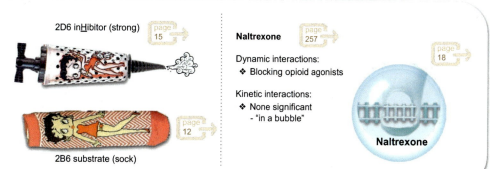

Bupropion 

Dynamic interactions:
- ❖ CNS stimulation
- ❖ Hypertensive effects
- ❖ Lowers seizure threshold

Kinetic interactions:
- ❖ 2D6 inHibitor (strong)
- ❖ 2B6 substrate
- ❖ Active metabolite hydroxy-bupropion is a 2D6 substrate (visualized on page 116)

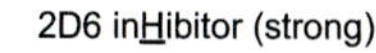

2D6 inHibitor (strong) page 15

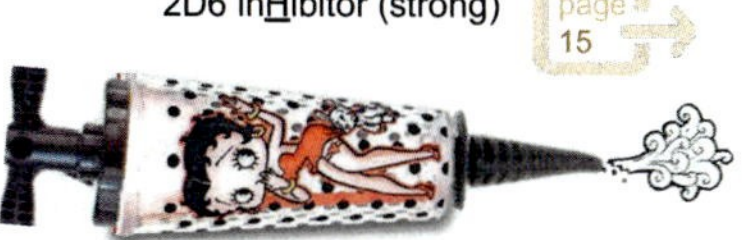

page 12

2B6 substrate (sock)

Naltrexone 

Dynamic interactions:
- ❖ Blocking opioid agonists

Kinetic interactions:
- ❖ None significant
  - "in a bubble"

page 18

OPIOIDS

22

1971
$130 - $145

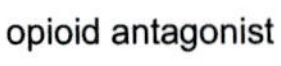

Na<u>lox</u>one (NARCAN)

nah LOX own / NAR can

Narwhal can (pick) Nail locks

opioid antagonist

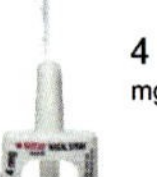

FDA-approved for:

- ❖ Known or suspected opioid overdose
- ❖ Opioid reversal (full or partial)

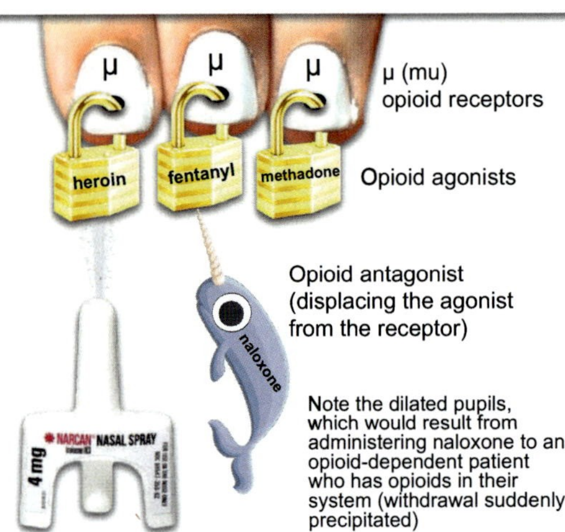

Na<u>lox</u>one is the quick-acting / short-lasting opioid antagonist used to reverse opioid overdose by "opening the <u>locks</u>" representing opioid agonists in this mnemonic. The most likely causes of opioid overdose are heroin, fentanyl and methadone. Contrast naloxone with nal<u>trex</u>one, which is for "long <u>treks</u>". Formulations of naltrexone are available to first responders and loved ones of those at risk for opioid overdose. In most states, pharmacists can prescribe and dispense naloxone products.

In the absence of opioids, naloxone has no effect (other than transiently blocking endorphins, which is of no consequence). Naloxone can serve as a diagnostic tool for the unconscious patient of unknown etiology. <u>If there are no opioids in the system, Narcan will constrict the pupils</u> (like an opioid). <u>If the patient has opioids in their system, Narcan will dilate pupils</u> (due to opioid withdrawal).

The recommended formulation for the opioid partial agonist buprenorphine includes naloxone as an abuse deterrent. Naloxone is <u>not bioavailable sublingually</u>, which is the route by which buprenorphine/suboxone (Suboxone) is administered. If Suboxone is crushed and injected, naloxone causes opioid withdrawal.

With overdose on a handful of extended-release tablets of prescription opioids, a bezoar (clumped up mass of pills stuck together) can form in the stomach. Naloxone will revive the patient, but coma will recur as the bezoar continuous to release the opioid, re-inducing coma if the bezoar is not removed by gastroscopy.

Naloxone's onset of action is within 1-2 minutes following intravenous administration and within 2-5 minutes when given subcutaneously or intramuscularly (IM). Duration of action is longer with the IM route. Naloxone (rather than naltrexone) is used in the treatment of overdose because it is a short-acting agent it can be dosed accurately without causing unnecessary prolonged withdrawal symptoms.

Dosing: For <u>opioid overdose (SC/IM/IV)</u> administer 0.4 - 2 mg q 2-3 minutes PRN; May repeat q 1-2 hours if symptoms recur; Check under clothes for a fentanyl patch to remove; Reassess treatment if no response after 10 mg; For <u>Evzio auto-injector</u>, administer 2 mg IM into the thigh, through the clothing if necessary; may repeat every 2-3 minutes until the ambulance arrives; For <u>Narcan nasal</u>, the bystander sprays into one nostril and may repeat every 2-3 minutes PRN in alternating nostrils until the ambulance arrives.

Form of Naloxone	FDA-approved	Details
Naloxone (NARCAN)	Opioid overdose	SC/IM/IV administration for opioid overdose
Naloxone auto-injector (EVZIO)	Opioid overdose	$1,900 /dose; The device provides on-the-spot voice and visual instructions to guide a bystander to administer IM to the thigh.
Naloxone nasal (NARCAN NASAL)	Opioid overdose	$70 /dose; The bystander sprays every 2-3 minutes PRN minutes in alternating nostrils.
Buprenorphine/naloxone (SUBOXONE) page 262	Opioid dependence	Buprenorphine is an opioid partial agonist for maintenance treatment of opioid use disorder; Schedule III controlled; Naloxone is an abuse-deterrent that is not bioavailable when taken sublingually but precipitates opioid withdrawal if the medication is injected.
Pentazocine/naloxone (TALWIN NX) page 264	Pain (mod-severe)	Pentazocine is an agonist at κ (kappa) opioid receptors and antagonist at μ (mu) opioid receptors; Available since 1964, Schedule IV controlled; May cause hallucinations; With oral administration naloxone has no effect, but if injected naloxone neutralizes the action of pentazocine.

page 18

Dynamic interactions:

- ❖ Blocks opioid agonists
- ❖ Renders buprenorphine ineffective if injected intravenously

Kinetic interactions:

- ❖ None significant – "in a bubble"

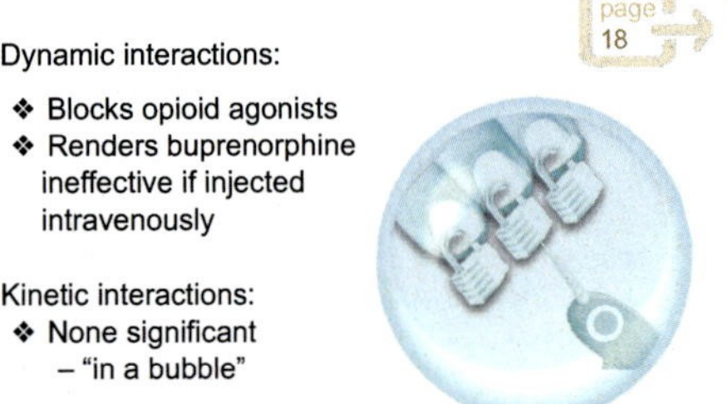

2011
$75 - $332

Buprenorphine (SUBUTEX)

BUE pre NOR feen / SUB u tex

"Bumper orphan Sub(marine)"

- Mu opioid partial agonist
- Kappa opioid antagonist
- DEA Schedule III

2 8 mg

FDA-approved for:
- Opioid dependence, induction
- Opioid dependence, maintenance
- Pain (moderate - severe)

Used off label for:
- Opioid detox

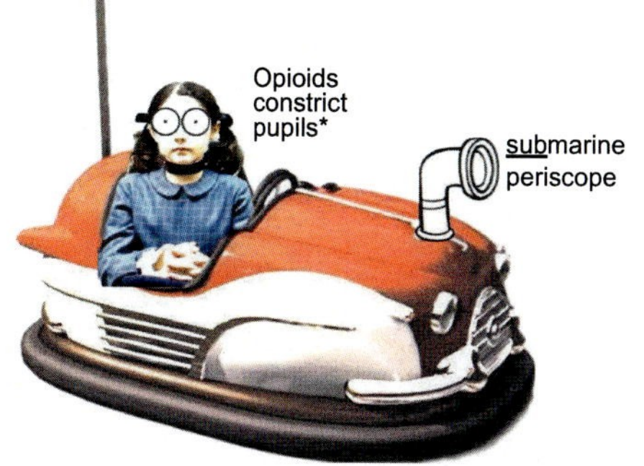
Opioids constrict pupils*
submarine periscope

*Although a buprenorphine-precipitated withdrawal from a full opioid agonist would cause dilated pupils

Buprenorphine is indicated for treatment of opioid dependence. It has lower potential for misuse than methadone, which is a full opioid agonist. As a partial agonist, buprenorphine only allows opioid receptors to be 40% stimulated. Buprenorphine binds tightly to opioid receptors and will displace full opioid agonists. If a dependent individual has a full opioid (e.g. heroin) in their system, buprenorphine will precipitate withdrawal symptoms. For an individual maintained on adequate dose of bupe, relapsing would be a waste of good heroin because the opioid effect is locked on a 40% ceiling.

Think of a full opioid agonist (heroin, methadone, etc) as a key that, when put in the ignition, makes the car go 100 miles per hour. A full antagonist (naloxone, naltrexone) jams the ignition and the car stops. A partial agonist (buprenorphine) starts the car but only lets it go 40 mph (Petros Levounis, MD). Giving buprenorphine to an opioid-naïve patient (to whom 40 mph would be really fast) will get them high and could even lead to overdose with respiratory depression. Overdoses on buprenorphine are not fatal, unless combined with sedatives like alcohol or benzodiazepines.

Buprenorphine has poor oral bioavailability and therefore it delivered as a sublingual tablet, sublingual film, buccal film, transdermal patch, IM, IV or subdermal implant. The transdermal patch (Butrans) and IM/IV version (Buprenex) are indicated for chronic pain only and illegal to use off-label for opioid use disorder.

The usual formulation is not pure buprenorphine (Subutex) but the buprenorphine/naloxone combo (Suboxone). Unlike Suboxone, Subutex can be ground up and injected. There are some situations where Subutex is useful, such as during pregnancy. Some individuals may be "allergic" to naloxone. Some clinics use buprenorphine without suboxone for induction before switching to bupe/suboxone, although this is likely unnecessary because sublingual absorption of naloxone is minimal.

To start buprenorphine the individual coming of heroin needs to be experiencing moderate opioid withdrawal, e.g., above 12 on the Clinical Opioid Withdrawal Scale (COWS), which occurs 12 to 24 hours since the last heroin injection. If enough time has elapsed, the first buprenorphine dose will ameliorate withdrawal symptoms. If the first dose of buprenorphine is given too early, withdrawal symptoms will be induced. Using our car key analogy, the car needs to be going no faster than 40 mph to avoid the discomfort of rapid deceleration.

A small 2 mg test dose is given initially (not more, because withdrawal symptoms may worsen). Over a few days the dose is titrated to 8 mg. Refer to the subsequent page (buprenorphine with naloxone) for further dosing information.

Buprenorphine has a long half-life (24 – 48 hours), so once-daily dosing is possible. Every-other-day dosing may even be effective. Nonetheless, the typical maintenance regimen for opioid use disorder is 8 mg BID of Suboxone. Maximum dose is 32 mg/day, but generally 16 mg/day is enough. Doses above 16 mg/day may be effective in patients with limited response to lower doses. For a heroin addict, a higher buprenorphine dose (within the therapeutic range) is not bad because of buprenorphine's 40% ceiling effect. Heroin will be more completely blocked in the event of relapse, making the experience less reinforcing. Patients should not be prescribed a higher-than-necessary dose because leftovers are liable to be diverted to other users.

If used for pain, at least daily dosing is needed because the analgesic duration is much shorter than the anti-craving duration.

To prescribe buprenorphine for opioid use disorder on an outpatient basis, a special DEA number is required. If the doctor's primary DEA number is FC1234567, the special DEA number will be XC1234567. To receive the DEA waiver, the physician must complete an 8-hour CME course. The waiver is good for 30 patients during the first year, and 100 patients thereafter. The waiver is not required to prescribe buprenorphine on an inpatient basis or for pain management.

Individuals dependent on exceptionally high amounts of heroin may require methadone instead of buprenorphine. For suppression of cravings, buprenorphine works about as well as 60 mg/day of methadone but less effective than 80-100 mg/day methadone.

Side effects of buprenorphine are the same as full opioid agonists - constipation, nausea, somnolence, dizziness, and possible liver enzyme elevation. Withdrawal symptoms are expected if buprenorphine is stopped abruptly, although the withdrawal will be less severe than from cessation of a full opioid agonist.

The impact of kinetic interactions with buprenorphine is generally less significant than with methadone; however, dose adjustments may be necessary with 3A4 inhibitors/inducers. Unlike methadone, buprenorphine does not significantly prolong QT interval.

For context, varenicline (Chantix) has an analogous partial agonist effect on nicotine receptors.

Buprenorphine has only 4 black box warnings. Full opioid agonists usually have 8.

- Addiction, abuse, misuse
- Respiratory depression
- Neonatal withdrawal syndrome
- Profound sedation with benzos

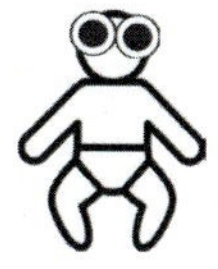

Opioid withdrawal manifests with dilated pupils

Items on Clinical Opioid Withdrawal Scale (COWS):

- GI distress (cramps, vomiting, diarrhea)
- dilated pupils
- yawning
- tachycardia
- sweating
- restlessness
- tremor
- gooseflesh skin
- runny nose / tearing
- bone or joint aches
- anxiety or irritability

Dynamic interactions:
- Blocks full opioid agonists
- Blocked by opioid antagonists (naloxone, naltrexone)
- Constipation
- Sedation
- Hypotension
- Decreased seizure threshold
- Serotonergic (mild)

page 16

Kinetic interactions:
- 3A4 substrate
- Delayed gastric emptying

3A4 substrate

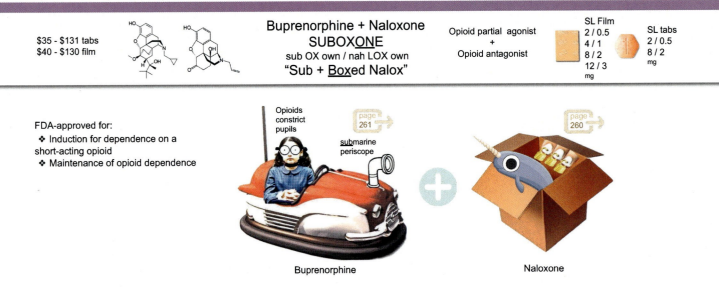

$35 - $131 tabs
$40 - $130 film

Buprenorphine + Naloxone
SUBOXONE
sub OX own / nah LOX own
"Sub + Boxed Nalox"

Opioid partial agonist
+
Opioid antagonist

SL Film
2 / 0.5
4 / 1
8 / 2
12 / 3
mg

SL tabs
2 / 0.5
8 / 2
mg

FDA-approved for:
- ❖ Induction for dependence on a short-acting opioid
- ❖ Maintenance of opioid dependence

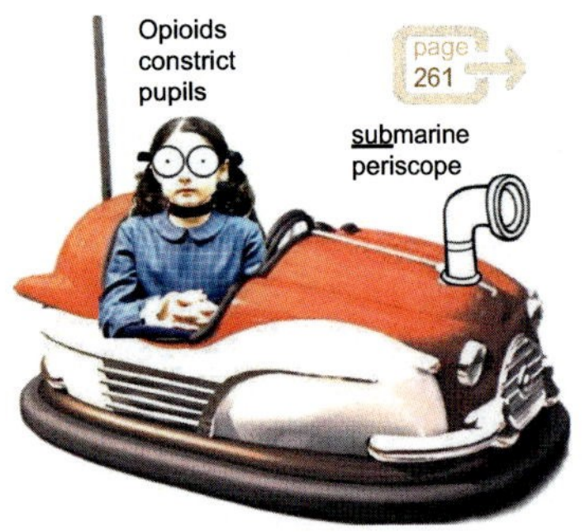

page 261

Buprenorphine

page 260
Naloxone

Suboxone is a combination of buprenorphine and naloxone in a 4:1 ratio. Buprenorphine is the therapeutic component, with naloxone serving as the abuse-deterrent. Naloxone has poor sublingual bioavailability and exerts minimal effect when Suboxone is taken under the tongue as instructed. If the medication is injected, naloxone blocks opioid receptors, thereby blocking the effect of buprenorphine and possibly precipitating opioid withdrawal.

Suboxone is the gold standard treatment for maintenance of opioid use disorder if a replacement opioid is needed. For heroin use disorder, long-term outcomes are generally better than attempts at stopping opioid use altogether.

Medication	Buprenorphine	Methadone	Oxycodone, Hydrocodone, etc
Mechanism	Partial opiate agonist	Full opioid agonist	Full opioid agonist
DEA Schedule	Schedule III	Schedule II	Schedule II
Tolerance develops	Minimal	Yes	Yes
Clinic visits	Frequent	Very frequent	Less frequent
Analgesic effect	Relatively weak	Strong	Strong
Danger in overdose	Low	High	High
# of patients per prescriber	100 first year, then 275	No limit	No limit
Withdrawal begins	36 – 72 hours	36 - 72 hours	6 - 12 hours
QT prolongation	Not at standard doses	Yes	Less than with methadone

Refer to the preceding two page for info on the individual components of Suboxone.

Naloxone stays "in the box" (not absorbed systemically) if Suboxone is taken sublingually as intended. If the medication is injected, naloxone blocks the effect of buprenorphine, and may precipitate opioid withdrawal

Methadone decrease heroin craving, but the user (although subject to frequent drug screens) can relapse on heroin with full reinforcing effects and significant risk of death by overdose. An individual on buprenorphine who relapses on heroin will experience reduced reinforcement with much lower risk of fatality.

Withdrawal from suboxone begins more slowly than full opioid agonists, generally no sooner than 36 hours. Physical withdrawals symptoms from buprenorphine are generally milder but can persist for a month.

The sublingual film formulation (as opposed to sublingual tablet) of Suboxone is preferred by some patients because absorption is faster, and they reportedly taste better. The films can be cut into small sizes. Diversion is easier because the films can be easily mailed.

Expensive options: CASSIPA is a more expensive 16 mg SL film. Buccal films (BUNAVAIL) stick to the cheek while dissolving and are dosed lower (2.1 mg – 12.6 mg) due to better bioavailability. ZUBSOLV SL tabs have a menthol flavor and are dosed lower (0.7 mg – 11.4 mg), also due to better bioavailability.

Dosing: Begin when moderate withdrawal symptoms have started; For induction (Day one) start 2 mg SL x1; May increase by 2-4 mg q 2 hr up to 8 mg/day on Day one; On day two, give up to 16 mg; Usual maintenance range is 12 – 16 mg/day, often 8 mg BID; Max is 24 mg/day; Taper gradually to stop.

Buprenorphine

page 16

Dynamic interactions:
- ❖ Blocks full opioid agonists
- ❖ Blocked by opioid antagonists (naloxone, naltrexone)
- ❖ Constipation
- ❖ Sedation
- ❖ Hypotension
- ❖ Decreased seizure threshold
- ❖ QT prolongation (at high dose)
- ❖ Serotonergic (mild)

Kinetic interactions:
- ❖ 3A4 substrate
- ❖ Delayed gastric emptying

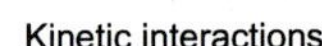
3A4 substrate

Naloxone

page 18

Dynamic interactions:
- ❖ Blocks opioid agonists
- ❖ Renders buprenorphine ineffective if injected intravenously

Kinetic interactions:
- ❖ None significant – "in a bubble"

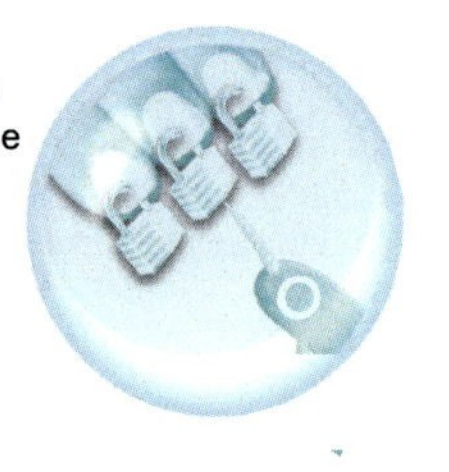

Buprenorphine

2018
$1,580

Buprenorphine LAI (SUBLOCADE)

BUE pre NOR feen / SUB lo cade

"(partial) Sub blockade"

- ❖ Mu opioid partial agonist
- ❖ Kappa opioid antagonist
- ❖ Monthly, subcutaneous
- ❖ DEA Schedule III

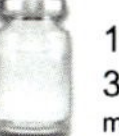

100
300
mg

FDA-approved for:
- ❖ Opioid dependence (moderate to severe)

Used off label for:
- ❖ Chronic pain

Sublocade is once-monthly subcutaneous (SC) long-acting injectable (LAI) buprenorphine, injected into the abdomen by a healthcare provider. If necessary, the Sublocade depot can be surgically excised within 14 days of injection. The advantage of Sublocade over SL buprenorphine is improved adherence and no risk of diversion. The only real disadvantage is cost.

With Sublocade 100 mg at steady state (achieved at about 5 months), average plasma buprenorphine concentrations are slightly higher than the maximum approved sublingual dose of 24 mg/day, which should suffice. 12 weeks into treatment with Sublocade, hydromorphone (Dilaudid) is no more likeable than placebo.

Sublocade is only available through a restricted program due to risk of thromboembolism if injected intravenously. Sublocade forms a solid mass within the vein, which could be life-threatening - "vein blockade".

Dosing: 2 monthly initial doses of 300 mg followed by 100 mg monthly maintenance doses; Prior to initiating Sublocade, tolerability needs to be established with 7 days of SL bupropion at 8-24 mg/day.

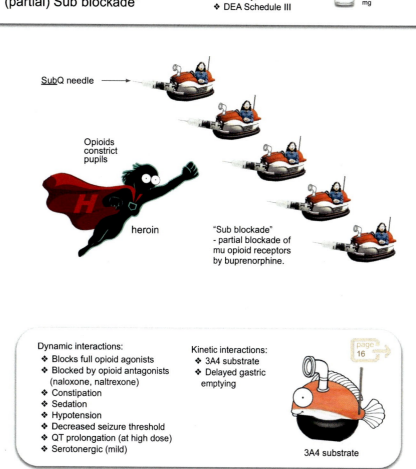

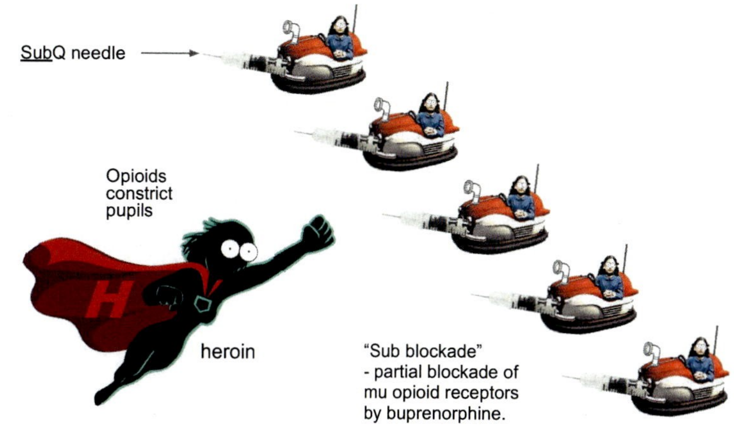

Dynamic interactions:
- ❖ Blocks full opioid agonists
- ❖ Blocked by opioid antagonists (naloxone, naltrexone)
- ❖ Constipation
- ❖ Sedation
- ❖ Hypotension
- ❖ Decreased seizure threshold
- ❖ QT prolongation (at high dose)
- ❖ Serotonergic (mild)

Kinetic interactions:
- ❖ 3A4 substrate
- ❖ Delayed gastric emptying

2016
$4,950 / 6 mo

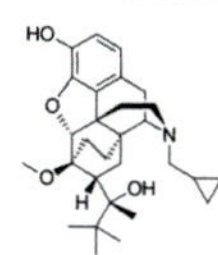

Buprenorphine Implants (Probuphine)

BUE pre NOR feen / pro BUE feen

"Probe o' buprenorphine"

- ❖ Mu opioid partial agonist
- ❖ Kappa opioid antagonist
- ❖ Subdermal rods
- ❖ DEA Schedule III

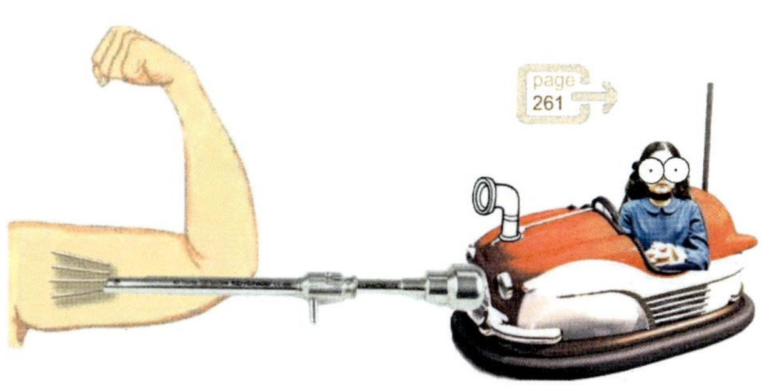

FDA-approved for:
- ❖ Opioid dependence

Used off label for:
- ❖ Chronic pain

Probuphine consists of 4 subdermal rods placed in the arm. The implants are removed every 6 months and replaced in the opposite arm.

A major shortcoming of this product is that 4 implants are only equivalent to about 8 mg/day of sublingual buprenorphine, which is a lower dose than many patients need. Much higher buprenorphine levels are achieved by Sublocade (see above). It may also cause scarring.

There is a **black box warning** of risks associated with insertion and removal of the implants, including embolism and death from improper implant insertions. Another boxed warning is that expelled implants should be kept away from others, especially children who could die from respiratory depression.

Some buprenorphine formulations approved for pain but not for opioid use disorder (OUD). Using these for OUD is illegal.

BUPRENEX	Parenteral (intravenous, intramuscular) 300 mcg IM/IV q 6-8h hr PRN
BUTRANS	7-day transdermal patch 5 mcg/hr, 7.5 mcg/hr, 10 mcg/hr, 15 mcg/hr, 20 mcg/hr
BELBUCA	Q 12 hr buccal strips available in low dose for opioid-naïve patients (75 – 900 mcg q 12 hr)

1979
$29 - $86

Butorphanol (STADOL)

byoo TOR fa nole / STAY doll

"Stay doll! says the Butter fan"

- ❖ Partial opioid agonist
- ❖ DEA Schedule IV

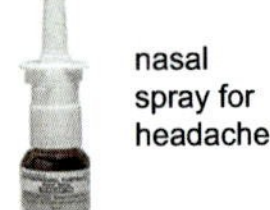

nasal spray for headaches

FDA-approved for:

- ❖ Moderate to severe pain

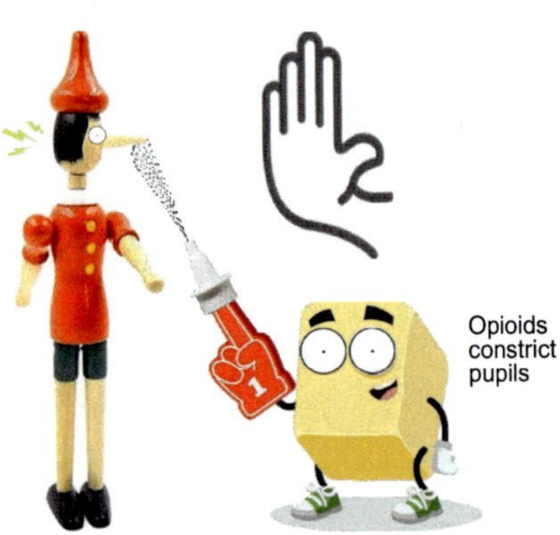

Opioids constrict pupils

Butorphanol (Stadol) is a μ (mu) opioid receptor partial agonist like buprenorphine. At κ (kappa) opioid receptors butorphanol is a partial agonist, whereas buprenorphine is a potent antagonist. As with buprenorphine, butorphanol can precipitate withdrawal in individuals accustomed to full opioid agonists.

Buprenorphine is available for humans as an intranasal spray for migraines. Duration of action is 3 – 4 hours. It is not available for oral administration in humans due to low bioavailability, but is available as a PO tablet for dogs, cats and horses.

In parenteral form, it is used for pain during labor. It is more effective analgesic for women than for men. As a kappa agonist, it is effective at reducing postoperative shivering.

Dosing: One spray equals 1 mg; The bottle contains 8 to 10 doses; The recommended dose is one spray q 3-4 hours for severe pain; An initial dose of 2 mg (one spray in both nostrils) if the pain is able to remain recumbent (in a position where they won't fall) in the event of drowsiness or dizziness; Use lowest effective dose and duration; Taper dose 25-50% q 2-4 days to stop if prolonged use.

Dynamic interactions:

- ❖ Blocks full opioid agonists
- ❖ Blocked by opioid antagonists (naloxone, naltrexone)
- ❖ Constipation
- ❖ Sedation
- ❖ Hypotension
- ❖ Decreased seizure threshold
- ❖ Serotonergic (mild)

Kinetic interactions:

- ❖ 3A4 substrate
- ❖ Delayed gastric emptying

page 16

3A4 substrate

1964
$62 - $243
(with naloxone)

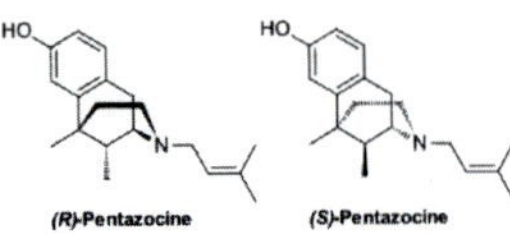

Pentazocine (TALWIN)

pen TAZ oh seen / TAL win

"Towel wins a Pentagram"

- ❖ Partial mu opioid agonist
- ❖ Full kappa opioid agonist
- ❖ DEA Schedule IV

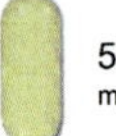

50 / 0.5 mg

FDA-approved for:

- ❖ Moderate to severe pain

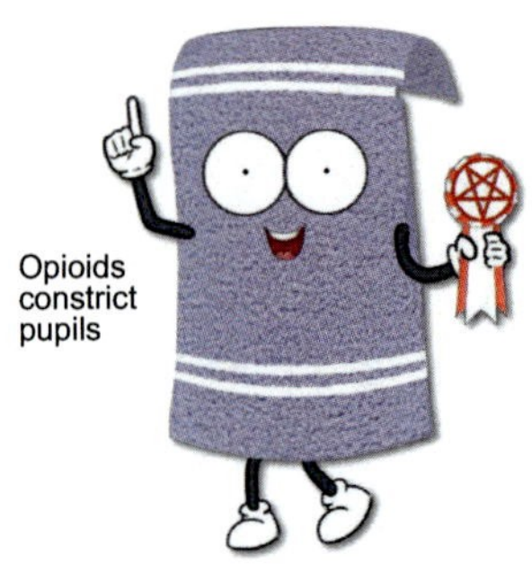

Opioids constrict pupils

Pentazocine (Talwin) exerts analgesia mostly through kappa opioid receptors.

Unlike most available opioids, pentazocine exists as two enantiomers (mirror-image molecules). Compared to other opioids it is more likely to cause hallucinations/psychosis.

Currently it is only available in an abuse-deterrent tablet combined with naloxone (Talwin NX). The naloxone component has poor bioavailability if ingested but is active if the tablets are dissolved and injected.

In the late 1970's, recreational drug users discovered that combining pentazocine (p-gp substrate) with an old antihistamine called tripelennamine (p-gp inhibitor) produced euphoria. Without inhibition of p-gp ("pumpers gonna pump"), pentazocine is pumped out of the brain too quickly for potent effect. The combination, referred to as "T's and Blues" (tripelennamine tabs were blue) was a major problem in St. Louis through the early 1980's. Intravenous T's and Blues was involved in 62 homicides, 7 fatal intoxications and 137 emergency room visits in 1980, and 64% of admissions to drug rehab programs (Poklis, 1982). The problem stopped when naloxone was added to the pentazocine tablets.

Pentazocine is only available in combination with Naloxone, which stays "in the box" (not absorbed systemically) if the tablet is swallowed as intended. If injected, naloxone blocks opioid effects and may precipitate withdrawal.

page 260

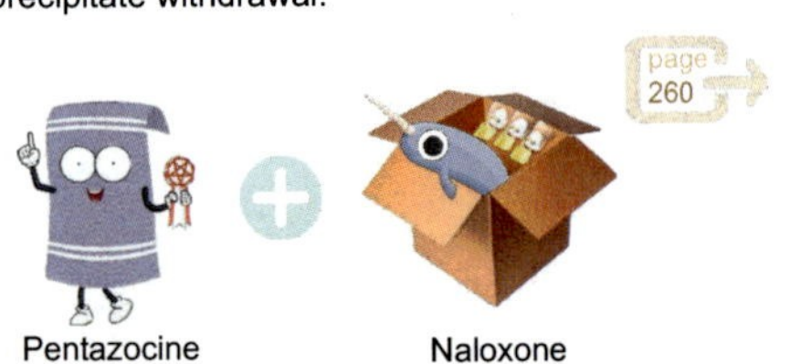

Pentazocine Naloxone

Dynamic interactions:

- ❖ Opioid agonist
  - – Constipation
  - – Sedation / CNS depression
  - – Respiratory depression
  - – Hypotension
- ❖ Lowers seizure threshold
- ❖ Serotonergic (mild)

Kinetic interactions:

- ❖ Delayed gastric emptying
- ❖ p-gp substrate

page 9

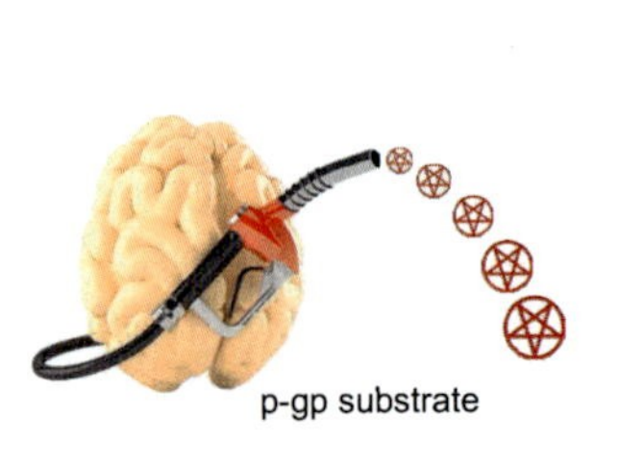

p-gp substrate

1979
$4

Nalbuphine (NUBAIN)

NAL bue feen / NEW bane

"Newbie's Nail booth"

- ❖ Kappa opioid agonist
- ❖ Mu opioid antagonist
- ❖ Non-controlled

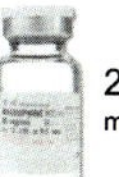

20 mg/mL

FDA-approved for:

- ❖ Moderate to severe pain

Nalbuphine (Nubain) is a parenteral opioid analgesic, generally administered intravenously (IV). Its analgesic mechanism is the same as pentazocine (Talwin), i.e., mostly through kappa opioid receptors.

Nalbuphine is a lightly bound partial agonist at mu opioid receptors, so it has little capacity for euphoria or respiratory depression. There is a "ceiling effect" on respiration (as a mu partial agonist) but no ceiling on the analgesic effect (as a strong kappa agonist). Nonetheless, it has 3 black box warnings (most opioids have about 8) for addiction/abuse/misuse, respiratory depression and risk in combination with benzodiazepines/alcohol. The first two are class warnings and are not applicable to nalbuphine.

Opioids constrict pupils, but nalbuphine is less likely to do so than mu agonists.

Nalbuphine was initially regulated as a Schedule II controlled substance like most other opioids. Now, it is not controlled at all. Nalbuphine is the only prescription opioid that is not a controlled substance. Included in this book chapter are two other non-controlled medications, naloxone and naltrexone, but these are purely opioid antagonists.

Although nalbuphine is partial mu opioid receptor agonist (like buprenorphine), it does so weakly and does not block traditional opioids if administered concurrently.

Nalbuphine is used for pre/post-operative and labor/delivery analgesia. It is helpful to counter morphine-induced pruritus (itching). Onset is within 3 minutes after intravenous administration (15 minutes IM or subcutaneously). Analgesic effect lasts about 4 hours.

It is well tolerated, with possible side effects including sweating/clamminess (9%), nausea (6%) and dizziness (5%). It does not cause dysphoria, hallucinations or dissociation at therapeutic doses. At high doses, kappa agonists would produce dysphoria rather than euphoria. Recall that kappa is where the endogenous opioid dynorphin (associated with negative emotional states) binds.

Opioid partial agonist	μ (mu)	κ (kappa)	Opiate structure
Buprenorphine (Subutex, Suboxone)	Partial agonist	Antagonist	yes
Butorphanol (Stadol nasal spray)	Partial agonist		somewhat
Pentazocine (Talwin)	Partial agonist	Agonist	somewhat
Nalbuphine (Nubain)	Partial agonist (weak)	Agonist	yes

Dynamic interactions:

- ❖ Weak mu opioid receptor antagonist but interferes minimally with other opioids
- ❖ Constipation
- ❖ Sedation
- ❖ Hypotension
- ❖ Decreased seizure threshold
- ❖ Serotonergic (mild)

Kinetic interactions:

- ❖ Delayed gastric emptying
- ❖ 3A4 substrate (minor)

page 16

3A4 substrate

#256
1991
$3 - $8

Loperamide (IMODIUM)

loe PER a mide / em ODE e um

"Loops Immobilize (to) Lower peristalsis"

- ❖ Anti-diarrheal
- ❖ Peripherally-acting opioid
- ❖ Schedule V controlled

2 mg

FDA-approved for:
- ❖ Diarrhea

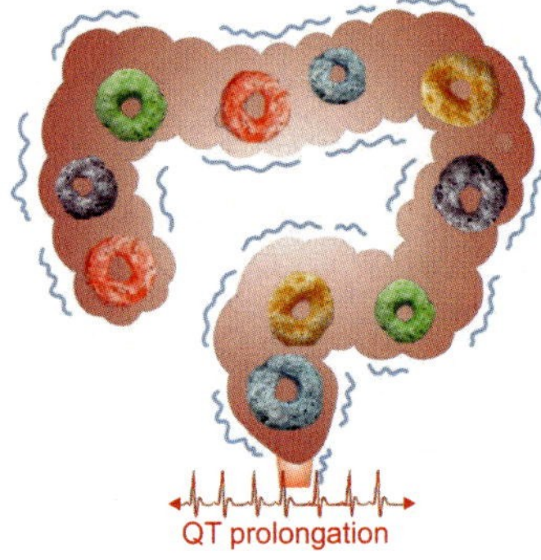

Loperamide (Imodium) is an anti-diarrheal that binds to opioid receptors in the gut wall, inhibiting peristalsis and increasing anal sphincter tone. It is great for diarrhea caused by opioid withdrawal.

Loperamide prolongs QT interval. Torsades de pointes and death have reported with high doses. It does not cause analgesia or euphoria under normal circumstances. It is a Schedule V (five) controlled substance, the lowest level of restriction.

Loperamide passively crosses the blood-brain barrier but is quickly pumped out of the brain by P-glycoprotein (P-gp, "pumpers gonna pump). If the individual takes a strong P-gp inhibitor, loperamide can stay in the brain long enough to cause euphoria. The P-gp inhibitor traditionally used for this purpose recreationally is omeprazole (Prilosec).

Dosing: For acute diarrhea, start 4 mg PO x 1, then 2 mg after each loose stool for a maximum of 16 mg/day; To "get high", doses well above 50 mg (25 pills) are required.

Dynamic interactions:
- ❖ Constipation
- ❖ QT prolongation

Kinetic interactions:
- ❖ 3A4 substrate
- ❖ p-gp substrate

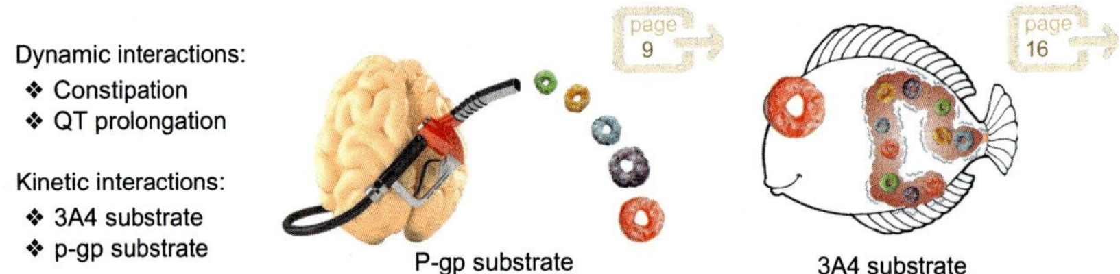

#298
1962
$13 - $30

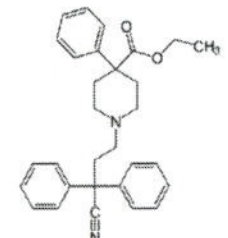

Diphenoxylate / Atropine (LOMOTIL)

DYE fen OX i late / A troe peen

"Dippin' (Dots to) Lower motility"

- ❖ Anti-diarrheal
- ❖ Centrally-acting opioid
- ❖ Anticholinergic (abuse deterrent)
- ❖ Schedule V controlled

2.5 / 0.025 mg

FDA-approved for:
- ❖ Diarrhea

Diphenoxylate is a centrally active opioid used in a combination with atropine (strong anticholinergic) for the treatment of diarrhea. Mechanism is the same as with loperamide. Diphenoxylate has no analgesic properties at standard doses, although higher doses can cause euphoria. The combination is regulated as a Schedule V (five) drug, like loperamide.

Atropine is included as an abuse deterrent to discourage consumption of enough diphenoxylate to cause analgesia/euphoria. Atropine contributes in small part to the antidiarrheal effect ("dry as a bone" anticholinergic). If dosed excessively, the unpleasant anticholinergic effects outweigh the euphoric opioid effects. Anticholinergic effects include flushing, tachycardia, nausea, restlessness and confusion.

Lomotil should not be used for *clostridium difficile* diarrhea because slowing peristalsis can interfere with clearing of bacteria and toxins. The same caution applies to loperamide.

Dosing: Start 2 tabs PO QID PRN; Maximum of 8 tablets/day; Reduce dose as symptoms are controlled; Stop after 10 days if no improvement.

Dynamic interactions:

Diphenoxylate:
- ❖ Constipation
- ❖ CNS depression / sedation

Atropine:
- ❖ Anticholinergic

Kinetic interactions:
- ❖ None significant – "in a bubble"

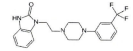

2015
$99–$427

Flibanserin (ADDYI)

fli BAN se rin / ADD ee

"Flibbin' Addicted (to love)"

- ❖ Norepinephrine-dopamine disinhibitor (NDDI)
- ❖ 5-HT_{1A} agonist
- ❖ 5-HT_{2A} antagonist

100 mg

FDA-approved for:

- ❖ Hypoactive Sexual Desire Disorder in premenopausal women

Flibanserin (Addyi), released in 2015, is FDA-approved for Hypoactive Sexual Desire Disorder in premenopausal women (it has not been tested in men or postmenopausal women). It was originally developed as an antidepressant.

Addyi has been colloquially referred to as the "female Viagra", but it has nothing in common with Viagra (sildenafil). Its mechanism involves dopamine, norepinephrine, and serotonin (5-HT).

	Viagra (sildenafil)	Addyi (flibanserin)
Mechanism	PDE inhibitor	5-HT_{1A} agonist and 5-HT_{2A} antagonist, which leads to increase of DA and NE activity
For use by	Men	Women
Purpose	Erection	Increased interest in sex
Response rate	80%	10% showed benefit over placebo
Effect size	Substantial improvement	Slight improvement
# scripts/year	> 2,000,000	About 5,000
Cost	$6 per tablet	$14 per tablet ($415/mo)
Instructions	PRN	Every day at HS
Contraindicated with	Nitroglycerine (hypotension)	Alcohol within 2 hours (hypotension); 3A4 inhibitors; Fluconazole (fluffer inHibitor of several relevant CYPs)
Other uses	Pulmonary arterial HTN	None

Physicians had to be certified to prescribe Addyi, but this restriction was lifted in 2019. Originally women taken Addyi were expected to abstain from alcohol because the combination can cause severe hypotension/syncope. In 2019 the contraindication with alcohol was softened. Addyi is contraindicated with liver impairment and with (strong to moderate) 3A4 inHibitors. These contraindications all relate to increased risk of hypotension/syncope and are all presented as black box warnings.

Women taking flibanserin reported an increase in "satisfying sexual events" from 2.8 to 4.5 events per month. Women taking placebo improved from 2.7 to 3.7 events per month.

Flibanserin has turned out to be a flop of a medication, with only about 5,000 annual prescriptions. Its lack of popularity is unsurprising given its disappointing efficacy, costs, and (previously) mandated alcohol abstinence pledge. In 2019 the label warning for alcohol use was softened to state "women should discontinue drinking alcohol at least two hours before taking Addyi at bedtime or skip the Addyi dose that evening. Women should not consume alcohol at least until the morning after taking Addyi at bedtime".

For context, blocking 5-HT_{2A} is the opposite of what hallucinogens do. LSD is a 5-HT_{2A} agonist. Second generation antipsychotics also block 5-HT_{2A}—*2A for 2nd gen Antipsychotic.*

Dosing: For Addyi, the starting and maintenance dose is 100 mg QD HS. It is not recommended to take it during the day due to the possibility of hypotension/syncope. It should be stopped after 8 weeks if no improvement.

Comparison with other medications that can improve sexual functioning via serotonin receptors:

	Indication	5-HT_{1A}	5-HT_{2A}
Flibanserin (ADDYI)	Hypoactive sexual desire disorder	Agonist	(Antagonist)
Trazodone (DESYREL)	Depression (off-label for insomnia)	(Agonist)	Antagonist
Nefazodone (SERZONE)	Depression	(Agonist)	Antagonist
Buspirone (BUSPAR)	Anxiety	Partial agonist	-
Pimavanserin (NUPLAZID)	Hallucinations and delusions associated with Parkinson's	-	Inverse agonist

Dynamic interactions:

- ❖ Sedation/CNS depression
- ❖ Hypotensive
  - contraindicated with alcohol

Kinetic interactions:

- ❖ 3A4 substrate
  - contraindicated with moderate to strong 3A4 inHibitors, which may increase flibanserin levels, leading to hypotension.
- ❖ 2C9 substrate
- ❖ 2C19 substrate
- ❖ Contraindicated with fluconazole (Diflucan) which is a "fluffer" inHibitor of the 3 CYPs that metabolize flibanserin, causing 7-fold increase in flibanserin levels, leading to hypotension

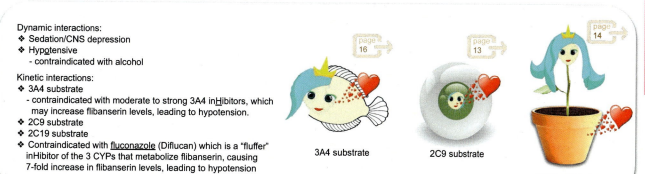

page 16

3A4 substrate

page 13

2C9 substrate

page 14

2C19 substrate

2019
$745–$894/injector

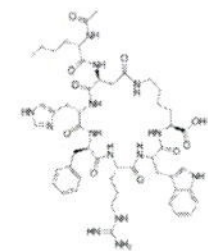

Bremelanotide (VYLEESI)

BRE me LAN oh tide / vie LEE see

"Vial of easy br(ings) Melanin tide"

- ❖ Melanocortin receptor agonist
- ❖ Female libido enhancer

1.75 mg/0.3 mL

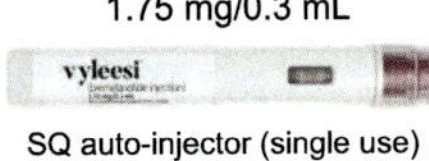

SQ auto-injector (single use)

FDA-approved for:

- ❖ Hypoactive Sexual Desire Disorder in premenopausal women

Bremelanotide (Vyleesi), approved in 2019, is a peptide for premenopausal women to inject subcutaneously for hypoactive sexual desire disorder (HSDD). The medication is a peptide that acts as an agonist of melanocortin receptors.

Bremelanotide is an analogue of α-melanocyte-stimulating hormone, which affects the skin and hypothalamus. Melanocytes make melanin, the pigment that colors skin. If bremelanotide were injected every day, it would bring a "tide of melanin" to the skin, causing discoloration. In fact, drugs similar to bremelanotide were studied as a potential sunless tanning agents. Use of bremelanotide is limited to once per 24 hours and 8 times per month, which keeps the risk of hyperpigmentation at 1%. The hyperpigmentation typically occurs on the gingivae or breasts and might not resolve upon stopping treatment.

Bremelanotide is not actually dispensed in vials but rather in single use auto-injection pens. It is injected subcutaneously in the in abdomen or thigh PRN at least 45 minutes before sex. The elimination half-life of bremelanotide is 2.7 hours. If it lasted longer, hypertension or skin discoloration could be problematic.

Bremelanotide, approved in 2019, is a peptide for premenopausal women to inject subcutaneously to increase libido, in treatment of hypoactive sexual desire disorder (HSDD). The medication is a peptide that acts as an agonist of melanocortin receptors.

The effectiveness of bremelanotide in stimulating libido is meager at best. 25% of women responded (vs 17% with placebo). The monthly number of "satisfying sexual events" did not exceed placebo. Nausea was reported in 40% of patients. In other words, it is more likely to make her nauseous than increase her sex drive. 8% of patients stopped the trial prematurely due to nausea, and 13% of patients needed an antiemetic. To be fair, nausea improved for most patients with the second dose.

Studies of a similar drug in the 1960s showed increased sexual arousal in rats. A researcher who injected himself with more than intended (of the similar drug) experienced an 8-hour erection with nausea and vomiting. Bremelanotide appears to be effective for erectile dysfunction, but there already are several highly effective PDE-5 inhibitors (Viagra, etc) that cause minimal side effects.

Bremelanotide causes a transient increase in blood pressure and decrease in heart rate, which occurs after each dose and usually resolves within 12 hours. Bremelanotide does not cause weight gain, and likely suppresses appetite.

Dosing: 1.75 mg SC x 1 given > 45 minutes before sexual activity; Maximum of 1 dose/day and 8 doses/month; Stop after 8 weeks if no improvement

Bremelanotide is not involved in CYP interactions, but it slows gastric emptying which results in lower levels of several medications, most prominently with **naltrexone (ReVia)** and furosemide (Lasix).

page 18

	Addyi (flibanserin)	Vyleesi (bremelanotide)
Indication	Hypoactive Sexual Desire Disorder in premenopausal women	The same
Mechanism	5-HT$_{1A}$ agonist; 5-HT$_{2A}$ antagonist	Melanocortin receptor agonist
Purpose	Increased interest in sex	The same
Administration	PO every day at bedtime	Subcutaneous injection PRN
Response rate	Low; 10% showed benefit over placebo	Low; 25% of women responded (vs 17% with placebo)
Side effects	Hypotension, somnolence, nausea, fatigue, insomnia, dry mouth	Nausea (40%), flushing, headache, hyperpigmentation
Blood pressure	Decreased BP	Increased BP
Contraindications	Alcohol (hypotension), 3A4 inhibitors	Uncontrolled hypertension or cardiovascular disease
Alcohol interaction	Hypotension when combined with alcohol	No issues
Interactions	Contraindicated with moderate to strong 3A4 inHibitors, which increase flibanserin levels, leading to hypotension	Slows gastric emptying and impacts absorption of concomitantly administered oral medications, see below

PDE-5 inhibitors

In most situations, the first-line treatment for erectile dysfunction (ED) is a PDE-5 inhibitor such as sildenafil (Viagra) or tadalafil (Cialis). These medications include the suffix "-afil", as in "fill" the penis. PDE-5 inhibitors are highly effective for ED. They do not increase sexual desire and do not cause erection in the absence of sexual stimulation. If taken by a man without erectile dysfunction, the erection will be more rigid. Women given Viagra reported improved sensation in the genital area, 57% versus 44% with placebo (Berman et al, 2003).

Phosphodiesterase type 5 (PDE-5) is an enzyme in cells lining blood vessels of various tissues and the corpora cavernosa (literally "cave-like bodies") of the penis. When PDE-5 is inhibited by an "-afil" medication, the spongy tissue of the penis dilates to fill with blood and cause a "Pubic Display of Erection". PDE-5 is also present in the lungs. PDE-5 inhibitors can alleviate pulmonary hypertension by dilating arterioles in the lungs.

The major risk of PDE-5 inhibitors is severe hypotension when combined with other vasodilators. PDE-5 inhibitors are contraindicated with nitrodilators. Contraindicated medications have "nitr-" in their name—nitroglycerine, isosorbide (mono/di)nitrate, nitric oxide, and nitroprusside. The hypotensive reaction can also occur if taken in combination with recreational inhalation of alkyl nitrite "poppers". PDE-5 inhibitors are safe for patients with stable coronary artery disease not taking nitrates. Use caution for patients with recent myocardial infarction, unstable angina, or congestive heart failure.

Other side effects of PDE-5 inhibitors may include headache, flushing and dyspepsia. Because PDE-5 is present in the retina, color discrimination can be impaired at high doses. A rarely reported side effect is sudden loss of hearing or tinnitus. Painful erection lasting > 6 hours (priapism) is rare, but is a medical emergency.

PDE-5 inhibitors increase clitoral blood flow and improve orgasmic function in women with SSRI-induced sexual dysfunction (Kyratsas et al, 2013).

When filling a PDE-5 inhibitor prescription, the best deal is usually to pay out of pocket with a GoodRx coupon. Getting a prescription through an online prescription service is expensive. Although the online doctor visit is free, Roman charges $34 per dose of generic Viagra. This is about 30 times more expensive than generic Viagra filled at Walmart with a GoodRx coupon.

Rx	PDE-5 inhibitor	Trade name	mg	FDA-approved for	Cost with GoodRx coupon (Walmart, Dec 2019)	Without coupon
#1	Sildenafil	VIAGRA	25, 50, 100	Erectile dysfunction	~ $33 for #30 of 50 mg or 100 mg tabs	~ $850
		REVATIO	20	Pulmonary HTN	$26 for #90 of 20 mg tabs	$256
#2	Tadalafil	CIALIS	2.5, 5, 10, 20	Erectile dysfunction Benign prostatic hyperplasia	~ $40 for #30 of 10 mg or 20 mg tabs = the best deal among the PDE-5 inhibitors	~ $1,900
		ADCIRCA	20	Pulmonary HTN	~ $40 for #90 of 2.5 or 5 mg tabs (BPH dosing)	~ $950
		ALYQ				
#3	Vardenafil	LEVITRA	5, 10, 20	Erectile dysfunction	~ $172 for #10 of any strength tab	~ $450
		STAXYN	10 ODT	Erectile dysfunction	$48 for #4 ODT tabs	$133
#4	Avanafil	STENDRA	50, 100, 100	Erectile dysfunction	$397 for #6 tabs	$427

#242
1998
$26–$1,994

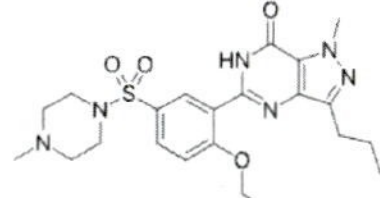

Sildenafil (VIAGRA)

sil DEN a fil / vi AG ra

"Slide to fill (Niagara)"

- PDE-5 inhibitor
- Erectile dysfunction Tx

20
25
50
100
mg

FDA-approved for:
- Erectile dysfunction (VIAGRA; 25, 50, 100 mg)
- Pulmonary arterial hypertension (REVATIO; 20 mg)

Bobby Leach, and his Barrel:—(Copyright, 1911, by Photo Specialty Co.)

Bobby Leach, who went over Niagara Falls in a barrel in 2011, was a *"Revel without a cause"*. REVATIO is the trade name for sildenafil approved for pulmonary hypertension—*"Revel's bravato"*.

Sildenafil (Viagra) was the first available PDE-5 inhibitor, released to much acclaim in 1998. It was approved for pulmonary hypertension in 2005, branded as REVATIO. Onset of effect is usually within 15–20 minutes, with usual duration of at least 2 hours. Absorption may be delayed by 60 minutes when taken with a high-fat meal. See above for general information on PDE-5 inhibitors.

Dosing: For erectile dysfunction, start 50 mg given a half-hour to 2 hours before sex PRN; Avoid taking with a high-fat meal because absorption will be delayed; Start at 25 mg if over ago 65 or taking CYP3A4 inhibitor; Max is 100 mg/dose and 1 dose/day. For pulmonary hypertension, the target dose is 20 mg TID, which is also the maximum dose;

page 16

Dynamic interactions:
- Vasodilation
- Ototoxicity

Kinetic interactions:
- 3A4 substrate (major)
- 2C9 substrate (minor)

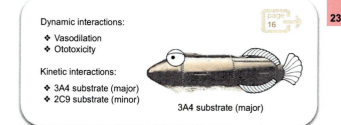

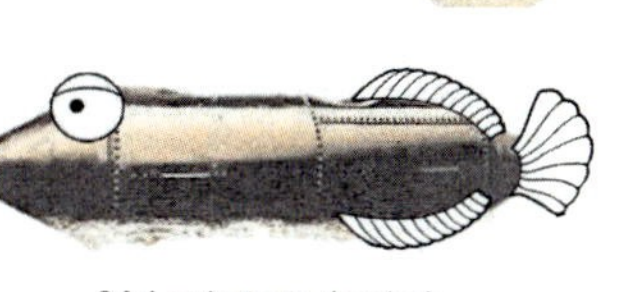
3A4 substrate (major)

#280
2002
$19–$313

Tadalafil (CIALIS)

tah DA la fil / see AHL is

"See Alice, the Tadophile"

❖ PDE-5 inhibitor
❖ Erectile dysfunction Tx

12.5
5
10
20
mg

FDA-approved for:

❖ Erectile dysfunction (CIALIS; 5, 10, 20 mg)
❖ Benign prostatic hyperplasia (CIALIS; 2.5 mg, 5 mg)
❖ Pulmonary arterial hypertension (ADCIRCA, ALYQ; 20 mg)

Alternate mnemonics include "Tad filler" or "See Alice, tah dah...filled!" T<u>a</u>d<u>a</u>l<u>a</u>fil is spelled with 3 consecutive A's.

Tadalafil (Cialis) is known as the "weekend pill" because <u>duration of action is about 36 hours</u>, which is 10 times longer than the other three PDE-5 inhibitors. Onset of action for Cialis (1 hour) is slower than for Viagra (15–30 minutes), unless Viagra is taken with food. Absorption of Cialis is not slowed when taken with food. Cialis is no more expensive than Viagra.

Cialis is approved for PRN dosing (10–20 mg) or every day dosing (5 mg). Cialis is the only PDE-5 inhibitor approved for benign prostatic hypertrophy. Cialis and Viagra are approved for pulmonary hypertension at high doses. Refer to the preceding page for general information about PDE-5 inhibitors.

Dosing: <u>PRN dosing regimen for erectile dysfunction</u>: Start 10 mg PRN taken 1 hour before sex, with or without food; Max of 20 mg/dose and 1 dose/day; <u>Daily dosing regimen for ED</u>: Start 2.5 mg QD with max of 5 mg/day; For <u>benign prostatic hyperplasia</u> (BPH), give a low dose of 5 mg daily; <u>Pulmonary hypertension</u> demands a high dose of 40 mg daily.

page 16

Dynamic interactions:

❖ Vasodilation
❖ Ototoxicity

Kinetic interactions:

❖ 3A4 substrate

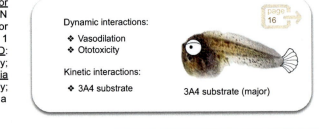

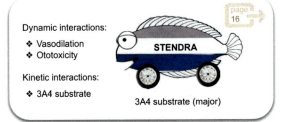

3A4 substrate (major)

2003
$142–$391

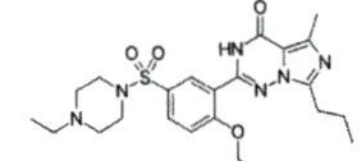

Vardenafil (LEVITRA)

var DEN a fil / le VEET ra

"Levi's Garden to fill"

❖ PDE-5 inhibitor
❖ Erectile dysfunction Tx

2
3
5
6
10 mg

FDA-approved for:

❖ Erectile dysfunction.

Vardenafil is a PDE-5 inhibitor with a relatively <u>slow onset of action, about 1 hour</u>. Duration of effect is about 2 hours. It offers no advantages over sildenafil (Viagra). Taking vardenafil with a <u>high-fat meal may decrease serum levels by 50%</u>. Refer to the preceding page for general information about PDE-5 inhibitors.

STAXYN is a peppermint orally disintegrating tablet (ODT) formulation of vardenafil.

Dosing: Start 10 mg <u>one hour before sex</u>; Max is 20 mg/dose, 1 dose/day; Consider starting 5 mg for patients ≥ 65 years old.

page 16

Dynamic interactions:

❖ Vasodilation
❖ Ototoxicity
❖ QT prolongation (mild)

Kinetic interactions:

❖ 3A4 substrate (major)
❖ 2C9 substrate (minor)

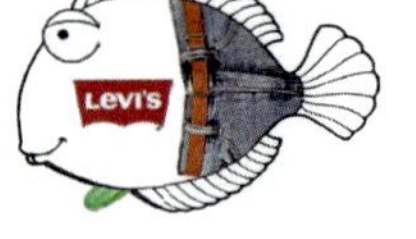

3A4 substrate (major)

2013
$305–$506

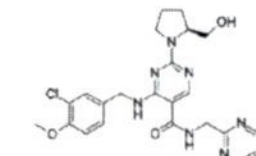

Avanafil (S<u>TEND</u>RA)

a VAN a fil / STEN dra

"A van to fill, ex<u>tend</u>ed"

❖ PDE-5 inhibitor
❖ Erectile dysfunction Tx

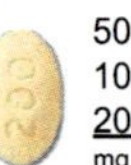

50
100
200
mg

FDA-approved for:

❖ Erectile dysfunction

Avanafil was marketed as <u>the fastest-acting PDE-5 inhibitor</u>. The label recommends taking avanafil 15 minutes before sex. About ⅔ of men will have therapeutic effect within 15 minutes, but some men will need to take it 30 minutes before sex. Absorption of avanafil is <u>not delayed by food</u>, an advantage over Viagra. Duration of effect is about 2 hours. Refer to the preceding page for general information about PDE-5 inhibitors.

Dosing: 100 mg taken <u>15–30 minutes before sex</u>; Max is 200 mg/dose, 1 dose/day.

page 16

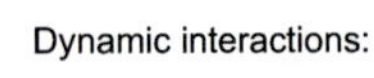

Dynamic interactions:

❖ Vasodilation
❖ Ototoxicity

Kinetic interactions:

❖ 3A4 substrate

STENDRA

3A4 substrate (major)

#173
1988
$6–$30

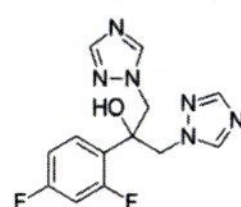

Fluconazole (DIFLUCAN)

floo KOE na zole / di FLU can

"Flunkin' a-holes Die flunkin'"

- Azole antifungal
- "Fluffer" CYP inhibitor

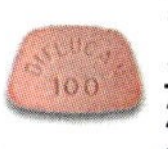

50
100
150
200
mg

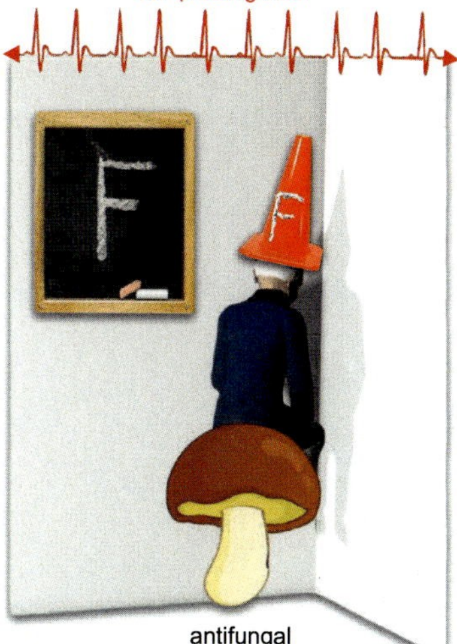

FDA-approved for:

- Vulvovaginal candidiasis (yeast infection)
- Oropharyngeal candidiasis (thrush)
- Esophageal candidiasis
- Cryptococcal meningitis
- Prophylaxis for bone marrow transplant

Used off-label for:

- Candidal cystitis/pyelonephritis
- Onychomycosis (tinea unguium)
- Sporotrichosis (rose gardener's disease)
- Coccidioidomycosis (Valley fever)
- Coccidioidal meningitis
- Tinea versicolor (pityriasis versicolor)

Fluconazole is in this book because it is a fluffer inHibitor of several CYPs, making it a major player in kinetic drug interactions involving psychotropics. Fluconazole's status as an inHibitor is expected, given that the therapeutic action of azole antifungals is to inhibit a fungal CYP. By inhibiting CYP51A1, Azoles interfere with the synthesis of ergosterol, a constituent of fungal cell membrane. Ergosterol is used by fungi and protozoa like cholesterol is used by humans, to make cell membranes sturdier. Azoles are not selective for CYP51A1, but rather hit several of the CYPs involved in psychotropic drug metabolism.

Fluconazole is the antifungal of choice for treating infections with *Candida albicans*, *Cryptococcus*, and *Coccidioides*. Common side effects include nausea, diarrhea, and elevated liver enzymes. It prolongs QT interval and lowers seizure threshold. Don't fixate on the "die" part of the mnemonic, it is kind of unfair to Diflucan because it is less likely to kill you than ketoconazole (also a fluffer). Ketoconazole (Nizoral) is rarely used because it has black box warnings regarding QT prolongation and hepatotoxicity. With fluconazole these risks are not drastic enough to earn any boxed warnings.

Topical fluconazole is not available. The topical antifungals include clotrimazole (Lotrimin), miconazole (Monistat), and tolnaftate (Tinactin).

The "**fluffers**" - strong CYP inHibitors of several CYP enzymes:

- fluvoxamine (Luvox) - SSRI
- fluoxetine (Prozac) - SSRI
- fluconazole (Diflucan) - antifungal
- ketoconazole (Nizoral) - antifungal

page 6

The last two are "cone"-azole antifungals.

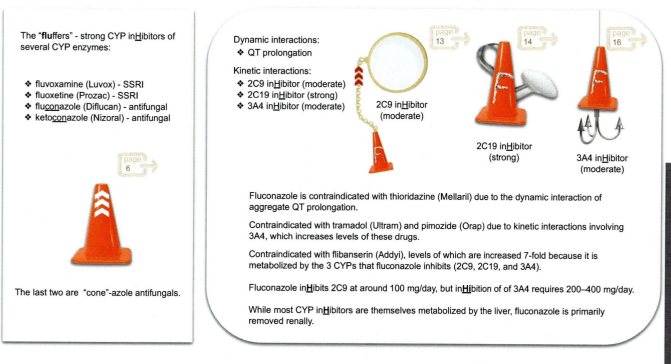

Dynamic interactions:

- QT prolongation

Kinetic interactions:

- 2C9 inHibitor (moderate)
- 2C19 inHibitor (strong)
- 3A4 inHibitor (moderate)

page 13
page 14
page 16

Fluconazole is contraindicated with thioridazine (Mellaril) due to the dynamic interaction of aggregate QT prolongation.

Contraindicated with tramadol (Ultram) and pimozide (Orap) due to kinetic interactions involving 3A4, which increases levels of these drugs.

Contraindicated with flibanserin (Addyi), levels of which are increased 7-fold because it is metabolized by the 3 CYPs that fluconazole inhibits (2C9, 2C19, and 3A4).

Fluconazole in**H**ibits 2C9 at around 100 mg/day, but in**H**ibition of of 3A4 requires 200–400 mg/day.

While most CYP inHibitors are themselves metabolized by the liver, fluconazole is primarily removed renally.

#229
1971
IR $34 - $114
ER $182–$674

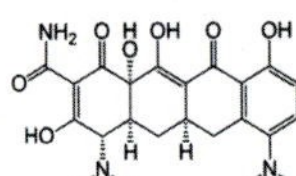

Minocycline (MINOCIN)

min o CY kleen / MIN o sin

"Mini Cyclone"

- Tetracycline antibiotic
- Neuroprotectant
- Off-label for schizophrenia

50
75
100
mg

FDA-approved for:
- Bacterial infections
- Acne
- Mycobacterium marinum infection

Used off-label for:
- Schizophrenia
- Huntington's disease (neuroprotective adjunct)
- MRSA skin infections
- Rheumatoid arthritis
- Lyme disease (preferred over doxycycline because minocycline crosses the blood-brain barrier)
- Leprosy

Minocycline is a second generation tetracycline with apparent neuroprotective effects. Several studies have found it useful as an adjunct for schizophrenia, especially for improving negative symptoms (Solmi et al, 2017). It has a safety and tolerability profile suitable for long-term use, although it may cause blue-grey staining of teeth.

Minocycline works as a neuroprotectant by several proposed mechanisms. It appears to increase BDNF (brain derived neurotrophic factor) and may reduce the hypothetical inflammatory component of schizophrenia. As a general neuroprotectant, minocycline has the potential to help a wide array of psychiatric and neurologic conditions. *"Minocycline is good for your mind"*. It dramatically reduced irritability with autism as an adjunct to risperidone (Ghaleiha et al, 2016).

With prolonged therapy, monitor CBC (hemolytic anemia) and metabolic panel (renal). Advise patients to remain hydrated (renal) and limit sun exposure (photosensitivity).

Dosing: For schizophrenia, start with IR formulation BID, switch to ER formulation QD if side effects. Most studies demonstrating psychiatric benefit utilized at least 100 mg BID (200 mg total). The maximum total daily dose is 400 mg.

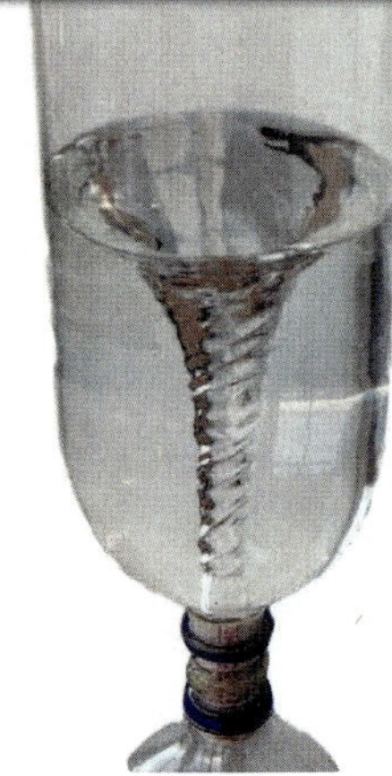

May cause dizziness

	Minocycline	Doxycycline
Treatment of acne	Less commonly used, but equally as effective for acne	Commonly used for acne
U.S. sales rank	#229	#110
Cost	$34–$114	$13–$113
Side effects	Nausea, diarrhea, dizziness, photosensitivity, allergic reactions, and kidney problems.	Fewer side effects than minocycline
Staining of teeth	Blue-grey with chronic use (all ages)	Brown (children)
Schizophrenia	Improvement of positive, negative and cognitive symptoms. May help acute catatonic schizophrenia.	No
Psychiatric uses	Schizophrenia, general neuroprotectant	N/A
Crosses blood-brain barrier	Yes	Not so much

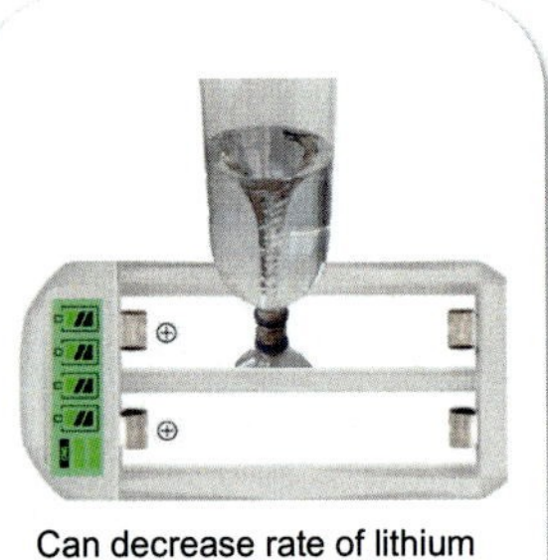

Can decrease rate of lithium clearance, leading to modestly increased lithium levels.

1991
$26–$119

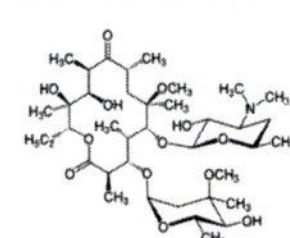

Clarithromycin (BIAXIN)

kla RITH roe MYE sin / bi AX in

"Clear mice in (there) By accident"

- Macrolide antibiotic
- Potent 3A4 inhibitor

250
500
mg

FDA-approved for:
- Bacterial infections
- Bacterial exacerbation of chronic bronchitis
- Community-acquired pneumonia
- Streptococcal pharyngitis/tonsillitis
- Mycobacterium avium complex
- Helicobacter pylori (part of triple or quadruple treatment)

There's mice in there!

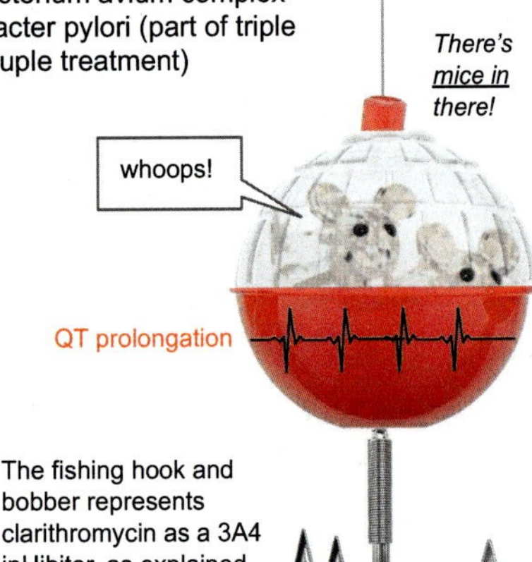

The fishing hook and bobber represents clarithromycin as a 3A4 inHibitor, as explained on page 16.

Clarithromycin (Biaxin) is a macrolide antibiotic. It is a potent CYP3A4 inHibitor. 3A4 metabolizes over 50% of prescription drugs so there are many potential drug-drug interactions. There is a long list of psychotropic medications whose blood levels will be increased if clarithromycin is added. Since inHibition happens Hurriedly, within Hours, results of 3A4 inhibition by clarithromycin can be dramatic.

There have been case reports of psychosis caused by clarithromycin (with or without interacting psychotropics) with usual onset at 5 days after starting treatment and resolving 1 to 3 days after clarithromycin is stopped (Bandettini di Poggio et al, 2011).

Clarithromycin has the potential to prolong QT interval. Adding clarithromycin to a 3A4 substrate that also prolongs QT can be dangerous, most notoriously with the antipsychotic pimozide (Orap) as shown on page 140.

Clarithromycin has no established psychiatric uses. Theoretically, it could be used to treat hypersomnolence because it is a negative allosteric modulator of GABA-A receptors (Trotti et al, 2015).

Clarithromycin is less commonly prescribed than clindamycin (Cleocin), another macrolide antibiotic that is not a CYP inhibitor.

page 16

Potent 3A4 inHibitor

#102 (Cipro)
1987
$4–$29

Cipro

(Fluoro)Quinolones

"-floxacins"

"Flocks of sinners Sin alone"

- ❖ Quinolone antibiotic
- ❖ 1A2 inhibitor
- ❖ Dangerous

Cipro
250
500
750
mg

In 2016 the FDA added a black box warning to all quinolone antibiotics of "disabling and potentially permanent serious side effects" that can involve the tendons, muscles, joints, nerves, and central nervous system. Use of quinolones may lead to Achilles tendon rupture. There have been over 60 cases of diabetic coma attributable to quinolones.

In 2018 the FDA added warnings to all systemic fluoroquinolones about delirium, agitation, nervousness, and disturbances in attention, memory, and orientation. These effects can occur after a single dose.

Other than delafloxacin (Baxdela), quinolones prolong QT interval.

FDA advises that fluoroquinolone use should be reserved for patients with no alternative treatment options for acute bacterial sinusitis, acute bacterial exacerbation of chronic bronchitis, or uncomplicated UTI. However, ciprofloxacin, the most prescribed quinolone, is still the #102 most prescribed drug in the US.

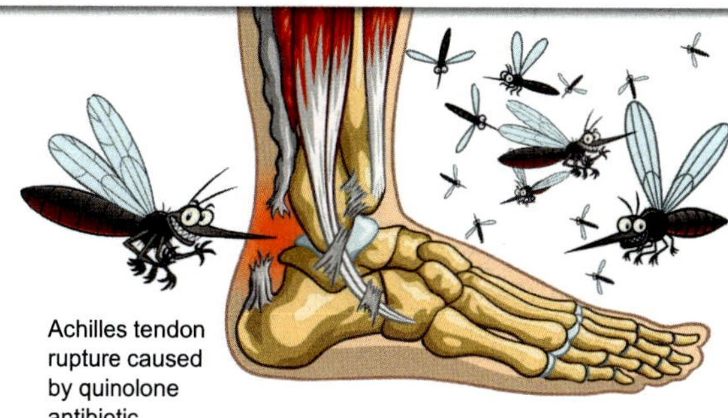

Achilles tendon rupture caused by quinolone antibiotic

Sales	Quinolone	Route	Comment
#1	Ciprofloxacin (Cipro)	PO, IV	FDA-approved for urinary tract infections, intra-abdominal infections, bone/joint infections, prostatitis, hospital-acquired pneumonia, anthrax, typhoid fever, plague
#2	Levofloxacin (Levaquin)	PO, IV, eye drops	Frequently prescribed for urinary tract infections, although Bactrim DS (trimethoprim/sulfamethoxazole) is a safer choice for uncomplicated UTI.
#3	Ofloxacin (Ocuflox)	PO, eye drops, ear drops	"O" for ophthalmic and otologic
#4	Moxifloxacin (Vigamox)	PO, IV, eye drops	Ophthalmic (Vigamox, Moxeza), PO tabs (Avelox)
#5	Gatifloxacin (Zymaxid)	Eye drops	$40–$111
#6	Besifloxacin (Besivance)	Eye drops	$174–$207
#7	Ozenoxacin (Xepi)	Topical	> $300
#8	Delafloxacin (Baxdela)	PO, IV	PO or IV FDA-approved for skin infections $1,470–$1,588

page 10

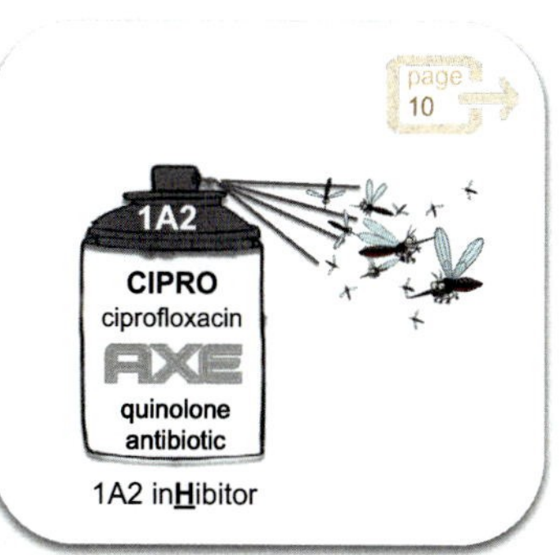

1A2 inHibitor

1971
$42–$131

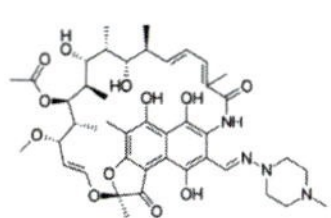

Rifampin (RIFADIN)

rif AM pin / rif AD in

"Rifle fade-in"

- ❖ Rifamycin antibiotic
- ❖ Tuberculosis treatment
- ❖ "Shredder" CYP inducer

150
300
mg

FDA-approved for:

- ❖ Tuberculosis (active, latent)
- ❖ Meningococcal prophylaxis (2 days)

Used off-label for:

- ❖ Endocarditis
- ❖ Leprosy
- ❖ Anthrax
- ❖ Brucellosis

Rifampin, aka rifampicin, is an antibiotic with broad spectrum activity against intracellular and extracellular organisms. Its main use is for treatment of tuberculosis, as part of a regimen that may also include isoniazid, pyrazinamide, ethambutol (or streptomycin), and pyridoxine (vitamin B6). Rifampin decreases levels of countless medications by CYP inDuction. It may turn urine, sweat, and tears orange. Contact lenses may become discolored.

"Rifampin revs up the liver"

► Risk of hepatotoxicity

► InDuces CYP enzymes in liver

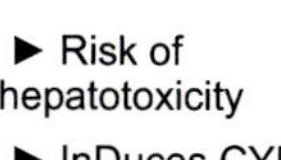

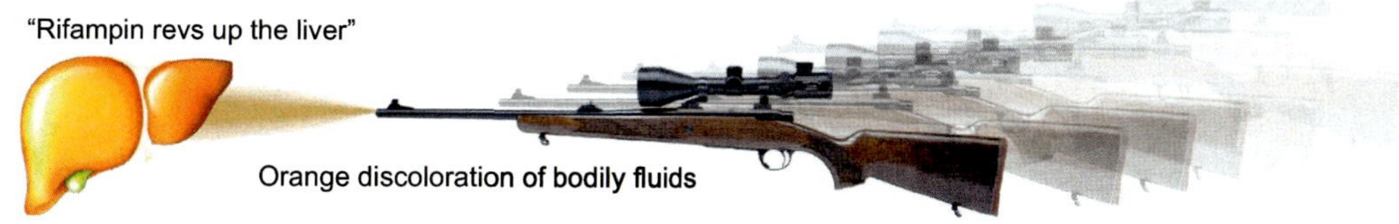

Orange discoloration of bodily fluids

Rifampin is a "shredder" inDucer of multiple CYPs—"D" for Down and Delayed

page 12

2B6 inducer

page 13

2C9 inducer

page 14

2C19 inducer

page 16

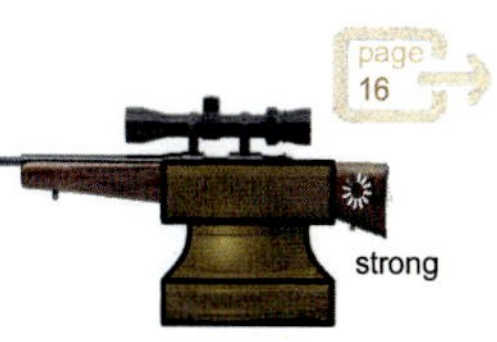

3A4 inducer

page 17

UGT inducer (lamotrigine)

This edition of *Cafer's Psychopharmacology* was released in November 2020. Subscribe to cafermed.com for the updated PDF edition with over 1,000 internal links and bookmarks for ultrarapid navigation. The PDF edition is updated frequently with new mascots. Visit cafermed.com/update for more information.

Discount code for cafermed.com subscription: **ULTRARAPID**

A hormone (derived from Greek "setting in motion") is a signaling molecule that affects tissues throughout the body. A neurotransmitter is a signaling molecule that only affects adjacent neurons. Some neurotransmitters can also function as hormones, including dopamine, epinephrine, and norepinephrine (but not serotonin, glutamate, glycine, or acetylcholine).

Hormones affected by psychotropics include prolactin (increased by some antipsychotics), orexin (blocked by suvorexant and lemborexant), antidiuretic hormone (interfered with by lithium), thyroid hormone (decreased by lithium and some anticonvulsants), and growth hormone (increased by sodium oxybate). Melatonin is the hormone of darkness. Bremelanotide (Vyleesi) is an analogue of melanocyte-stimulating hormone. Certain antipsychotics contribute to insulin resistance.

Psychiatrists monitor thyroid stimulating hormone (TSH) in all patients to screen for hypo/hyperthyroidism. T3 thyroid hormone is an effective adjunct for treatment-resistant depression. Some psychiatrists prescribe low dose testosterone for female sexual dysfunction; also they may prescribe desmopressin (DDAVP)—an analogue of antidiuretic hormone—for bedwetting.

Thyroid hormone

The name thyroid derives from the Greek word for "shield", based on its shape. Thyroid hormone exerts a profound influence on every organ system including the central nervous system. It acts on most of the body's cells, enhancing oxygen consumption and increasing the basal metabolic rate. It speeds the metabolism of carbohydrates, lipids, and proteins. The thyroid gland mostly secretes T4, the inactive form of thyroid hormone. T4 contains four iodine atoms. When T4 loses one of the iodine atoms it becomes T3, the active form of thyroid hormone.

Thyroid hormone is transported in the serum bound to protein (with the unbound fraction referred to as free T3 and free T4). Thyroid hormone is lipid-soluble. It passes through the cell membrane to bind intracellular receptors, resulting in activation/deactivation of gene transcription.

Hypothyroidism (underactive thyroid)

Common signs/symptoms of hypothyroidism include weight gain from "slow metabolism", fatigue/weakness/lethargy (> 95%), decreased body temperature, cold intolerance (89%), constipation (61%), generalized body aches, "brain fog" (> 50%), slow pulse, delayed (relaxation of) tendon reflexes, dry/coarse skin (> 90%), and hair loss, especially outer third of eyebrows—known as Queen Anne's sign. Severe hypothyroidism invariably leads to depression.

80% of hypothyroidism cases are caused by an autoimmune process called Hashimoto's thyroiditis. 5% of the population is affected by Hashimoto's during their life. Lithium is a common non-autoimmune cause. Iodine deficiency, formerly the #1 cause, is now rare thanks to iodized salt.

Psychiatric patients have a high incidence of hypothyroidism, which can cause depression and exacerbate bipolar disorder. Most psychiatric hospitals check thyroid stimulating hormone (TSH) for all patients upon admission (along with CMP, CBC, UA, pregnancy test, and drug/alcohol screen). TSH should be checked yearly for individuals with active psychiatric symptoms. For non-symptomatic patients, there is no consensus as to whether screening is necessary. Routine screening of TSH in asymptomatic patients often yields abnormal results that do not necessarily reflect thyroid dysfunction.

For patients being treated for hypothyroidism, following TSH is usually sufficient. Free T4 does not necessarily need to be tracked. "Free" means unbound to serum proteins. Following free T3 levels is not recommended, unless the patient is taking Cytomel (100% T3). The consensus for effective/safe treatment of hypothyroidism is synthetic T4 (levothyroxine) without T3.

TSH may be increased by antidopaminergics (antipsychotics) and decreased by dopaminergics (Parkinson's disease medications).

Subclinical hypothyroidism

"Subclinical hypothyroidism" is a mild elevation of TSH with normal free T4. This condition applies to about 5% of the general population and > 10% of depressed individuals. Elevated TSH is suggestive of a low thyroid state, but not necessarily indicative of thyroid gland dysfunction. The reference range for serum TSH is 0.45–4.5. Elevated TSH indicates that the pituitary gland considers itself hypothyroid. Overt symptoms of hypothyroidism are unlikely if TSH is < 10. Although subclinical hypothyroidism does not generally cause physical symptoms, it is associated with depression. Patients with subclinical hypothyroidism have a higher lifetime prevalence of depression and decreased response to antidepressants. Abnormal thyroid function with depression may reflect the impact of the depression on the thyroid, rather than vice versa.

Whether patients with TSH concentrations of 4.5–10 with normal FT4 concentrations should be treated is controversial. If a psychiatrically unstable patient has subclinical hypothyroidism, treatment is probably worthwhile, considering levothyroxine (Synthroid) is benign if dosed properly. Adverse reactions to thyroid supplementation are rare, other than symptoms of hyperthyroidism if the dose is too strong. However, patients started on levothyroxine tend to stay on it forever whether it is necessary or not.

If treated, an ideal TSH is about 1.0. Even a TSH in the upper 25th percentile of the reference range may be associated with depression. It is reasonable to treat any TSH above 2.5 if the patient is symptomatic, e.g., always feeling tired, cold, and unable to lose weight. It is also reasonable to not treat elevated TSH up to 10.0 if there are no symptoms. If TSH is > 10.0, it should always be treated.

Elderly patients with subclinical hypothyroidism are less likely to benefit from supplementation. Subclinical hypothyroidism should not be treated for older individuals with osteoporosis because thyroid supplementation can cause loss of bone mineral density.

Hyperthyroidism

Hyperthyroidism (thyrotoxicosis) is caused by excessive production of T3 and T4 by the thyroid gland. The condition can also be produced by taking excessive amounts of supplemental thyroid hormone or iodine. Signs/symptoms include chest pain, increased pulse rate, palpitations/arrhythmia/tachycardia, excessive sweating, heat intolerance, tremor, nervousness, insomnia, diarrhea/increased bowel motility, and menstrual irregularities. Due to a negative feedback loop, high T3 and T4 levels will result in a very low TSH level.

Thyroid storm is a life-threatening condition with severe tachycardia, hypertension, and elevation of body temperature. Suicidal overdose of exogenous thyroid hormone can result in thyroid storm.

50–80% of hyperthyroidism cases are the result of Graves' disease, an autoimmune condition caused by antibodies stimulating TSH receptors. Graves' is characterized by an enlarged thyroid gland (goiter), exophthalmos (bulging eyes), and nonpitting pretibial edema (myxedema). Eye protrusion is not caused by hyperthyroidism, but by autoimmune swelling of tissues in the eye socket.

Synthroid (T4)

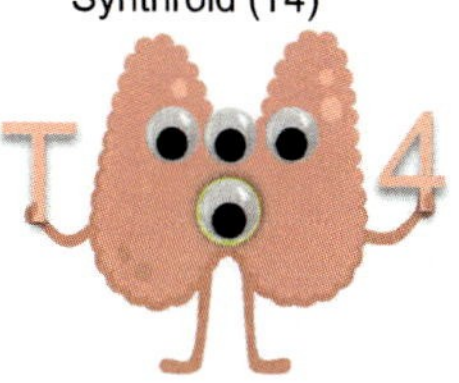

T4 is the "four I'd monster" (4 iodine atoms). Synthetic T4 is the most commonly prescribed thyroid hormone. It is not biologically active.

Cytomel (T3)

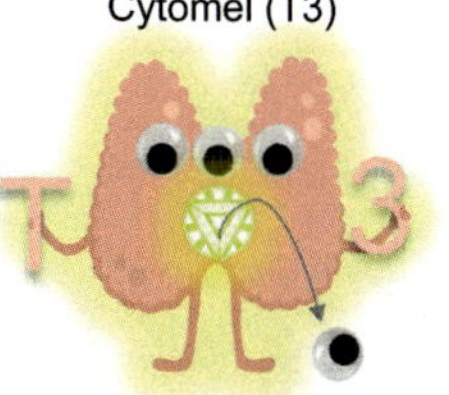

T4 is activated when one of its four "I's" (iodine atoms) is plucked out, to become T3.

Armour Thyroid

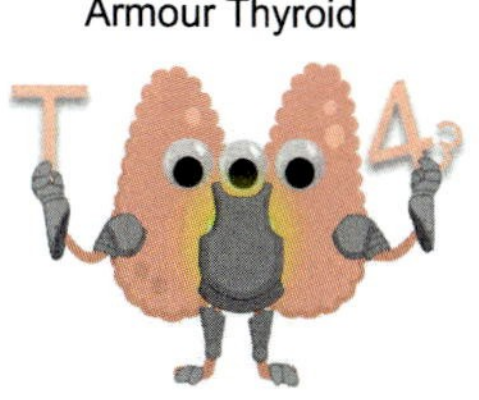

Armour Thyroid comes from desiccated (dried) thyroid gland from pigs. It contains T3:T4 in a 4:1 ratio.

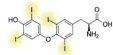

#1
1951
$10–$31

Levothyroxine (SYNTHROID)

LEE voe thye ROX een / SYN throid

"Four I'd monster"

❖ Thyroid hormone (T4)

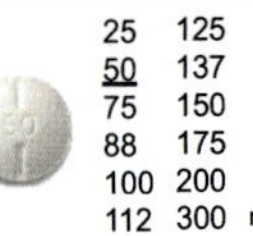

25	125
50	137
75	150
88	175
100	200
112	300 mcg

FDA-approved for:
- ❖ Hypothyroidism (1st line)
- ❖ TSH suppression with thyroid cancer

Used off-label for:
- ❖ Subclinical hypothyroidism
- ❖ Treatment-resistant depression (although T3 is more commonly used)

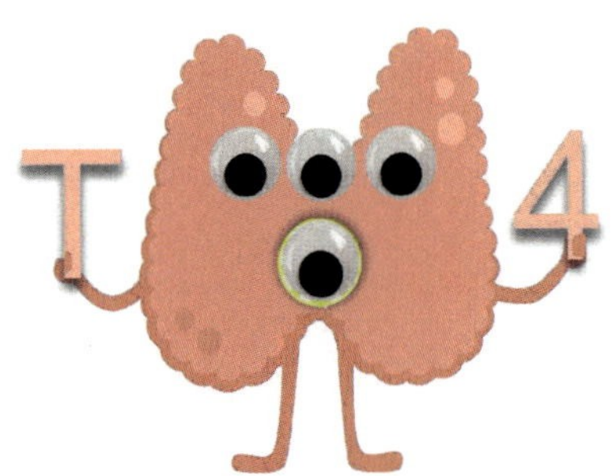

T4 is the "four I'd monster" (4 iodine atoms). Synthetic T4 is the most-commonly prescribed thyroid hormone. It is not biologically active.

Levothyroxine (LT4) is the #1 most prescribed drug in the US. It is a synthetic form of endogenous thyroxine (T4), the inactive form of thyroid hormone. T4 is inactive until one of the iodine atoms is plucked off. Levothyroxine (LT4) is the drug of choice for hypothyroidism. If treating depression, liothyronine (T3, the active form) is usually preferred.

As with other fat-soluble hormones, T3 works by modulating gene transcription. It affects most cells of the body.

Levothyroxine has a half-life of about 1 week. This allows a steady state despite occasional missed doses. Steady state is reached after about 5 weeks (5x half-life).

Levothyroxine should cause no side effects unless the dose is too high. Adverse effects would be symptoms of hyperthyroidism—anxiety/jitters, tremor, palpitations/tachycardia, elevated body temperature, weight loss, and increased bowel movement frequency.

Many people who receive levothyroxine do not need it, but also many people receiving levothyroxine are undertreated. For those being treated, the goal for TSH is around 1.0 (reference range is 0.45–4.5).

Generic levothyroxine formulations from different manufacturers are not always bioequivalent, so it is worthwhile to recheck TSH a couple of months after a brand change. This is not a big deal, but it occurs more often with levothyroxine than with other types of medications.

Dosing: The starting dose depends on the patient age, cardiac risk factors, and lab values; For subclinical hypothyroidism (high TSH but normal free T3 and free T4), it is usually started at 25–50 mcg. Ideally, levothyroxine should be taken on an empty stomach with a full glass of water 45 minutes before breakfast, without other medications. Food interferes with absorption, but levothyroxine can be taken any time of day (with or without other medications/food) as long as administration is consistent—the eventual dose will be established based on lab results anyhow. A full replacement dose for symptomatic hypothyroidism is about 75–100 mcg QD, unless the patient is elderly or has cardiac disease (start 25 mcg). Patients treated with full replacement doses will become euthyroid sooner, with little added risk. Doses are typically adjusted every 4–6 weeks based on lab results (TSH). Following free T4 is usually unnecessary and free T3 should not be ordered. After TSH is stable, recheck labs every 6–12 months. If the patient has secondary hypothyroidism (caused by low TSH), follow free T4 and maintain it in the mid-upper normal range.

Dynamic interactions:
- ❖ Amiodarone inhibits conversion of T4 (inactive) to T3 (active)
- ❖ Cardiac risks when combined with amphetamine
- ❖ Lithium decreases production of thyroid hormone

Kinetic interactions:

page 5

- ❖ Absorption of levothyroxine is decreased by antacids, calcium, iron, orlistat, sucralfate, raloxifene,
- ❖ Phenobarbital and carbamazepine increase hepatic metabolism of T3 and T4

Medication	Levothyroxine (SYNTHROID)	Liothyronine (CYTOMEL)	Desiccated thyroid (ARMOUR THYROID)	Liotrix (THYROLAR)
Thyroid hormone	T4 (inactive form)	T3 (active form)	T3:T4 in a 1:4 ratio	T3:T4 in a 1:4 ratio
Info	"Syn = Senescent" (actually "synthetic")	"Lio = Live"; synthetic	For dried thyroid glands of pigs	Synthetic
Sales rank (US)	#1	#257	#119	> #300
Uses	Most cases of hypothyroidism	Treatment-resistant depression (off-label)	Hypothyroidism, often by patient preference	Rarely used
Half-life	7 days	1 day	1 day (T3); 7 days (T4)	1 day (T3); 7 days (T4)
Dose adjustments*	4 to 6-week intervals	1 to 2-week intervals	4 to 6-week intervals	4 to 6-week intervals
Equivalencies	100 mcg	25 mcg	60 mg	1 grain (60 mg)

*Recommendations for frequency of checking TSH and Free T4 is based on half-life. It takes five half-lives for a drug to reach steady state. (Just as it takes five half-lives for a drug to be eliminated when it is stopped).

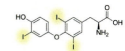

#257
1956
$25–$96

Liothyronine (CYTOMEL)

LYE oh THYE roe neen / CY toe mel

"Three I'd monster"

❖ Thyroid hormone (T3)

5
25
50
mcg

FDA-approved for:
- ❖ Hypothyroidism
- ❖ Myxedema
- ❖ Nontoxic goiter
- ❖ Thyroid suppression tes

Used off-label for:
- ❖ Treatment-resistant depression
- ❖ Weight loss (dangerous)

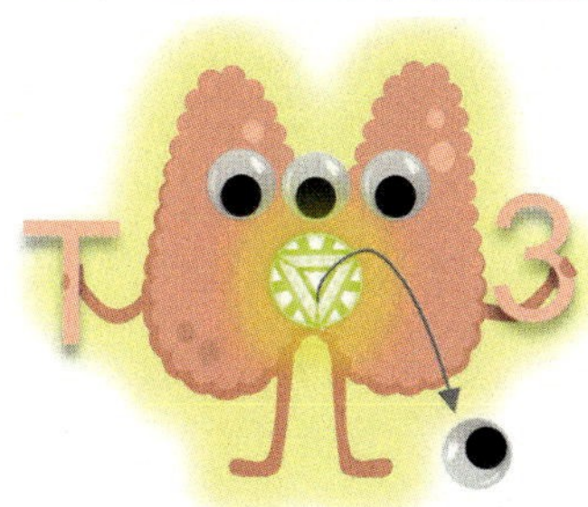

T4 becomes active when it loses 1 of its 4 "I's" (iodine atom) is plucked out.

Liothyronine (LT3) is a manufactured form of triiodothyronine (T3), the active form of thyroid hormone. Although LT3 can be given as monotherapy or in conjunction with LT4 (levothyroxine, synthetic T4), it should not be used to treat hypothyroidism. LT3 should be used only for adjunctive treatment of refractory depression. Problems with LT3 include cardiac concerns (atrial fibrillation), unstable T3 levels, increased risk of iatrogenic (treatment-induced) thyrotoxicosis, and the possibility of thyroid hormone resistance (a similar concept to insulin resistance).

The half-life of liothyronine (LT3) is about 1.5 days, which is much shorter than half-life of LT4 (7 days). Dose adjustments with LT3 are made in 1 to 2-week intervals, rather than 4 to 8-week intervals with FT4.

Liothyronine (T3) is not recommended for treatment of hypothyroidism in most cases. The American Association for Clinical Endocrinology (AACE) recommended against routinely prescribing T3 or checking serum total or free T3 levels. The American Thyroid Association (ATA) recommended against the routine addition of T3 due to insufficient evidence but did not does explicitly rule out use of T3 under certain circumstances (2014).

For obese patients with hypothyroidism, supplementation is expected to facilitate weight loss by thermogenesis (increased basal body temperature) from burning brown fat. There is a black box warning that thyroid hormones (especially T3) should not be used for weight loss in euthyroid patients due to risk of serious toxicity, especially when taken with amphetamines.

LT3 is the most studied hormone for the augmentation/acceleration of antidepressant (TCA or SSRI) effect. This augmentation strategy is intended for euthyroid patients. Patients given LT3 are twice as likely to respond (versus antidepressant plus placebo). Some experts suggest using LT4 instead for refractory depression, but LT3 likely works faster. The therapeutic mechanism may involve increasing brain derived neurotrophic factor (BDNF).

Guidelines for augmenting an antidepressant with LT3:
(Touma et al, 2017; Rosenthal 2011)

- ► Check TSH, free T3, and free T4 levels prior to initiating treatment.
- ► Recheck abnormal labs to rule out lab error or transient stressors.
- ► Start 25 mcg daily and titrate to 50 mcg after one week.
- ► Use 12.5 mcg to 25 mcg with older patients.
- ► Recheck labs at 3 months and then every 6–12 months.
- ► Goal for TSH can be below normal if no hyperthyroid signs.
- ► TSH can be below the lower limit of normal.
- ► Free T3 level can be maintained at the upper limit of normal range.
- ► Monitor bone density every 2 years in postmenopausal women.

Side effects are not expected with T3 unless the patients is over treated. The patient should be monitored for elevated heart rate (should not exceed 90) and increased body temperature (should not exceed 98.6 degrees). The dose should be decreased if the patient feels jittery or experiences palpitations. Even with ideal dosing, hair loss may temporarily worsen before it rebounds in 3–6 months.

Dosing: Typically given once daily, but doses may be split, given on an empty stomach 45 minutes prior to breakfast and lunch; For augmentation/acceleration of an antidepressant effect for euthyroid individuals, 25 mcg daily is a safe dose that is unlikely to cause signs of thyroid hormone excess. Dose-dependent response has not been clearly established, so it may be unnecessary to go higher. Refer to guidelines above; 50 mcg is equivalent to the amount of endogenous T3 production and could possibly cause signs of thyroid excess. The dose should probably not exceed 88 mcg, which would require close monitoring of vital signs; For addition to LT4 for treatment of hypothyroidism (not recommended), start low and go slow. 5 mcg/day would be a prudent starting dose; For monotherapy of hypothyroidism (not recommended), the label instructs starting at 25 mcg daily and increasing 12.5–25 mcg q 1–2 weeks (5 mcg/day q 1–2 weeks in elderly patients); Target dose is 25–75 mg QD; When switching a patient established on LT4 to LT3 (not recommended), discontinue LT4 and initiate LT3 at a low dosage, increase gradually according to the patient's response. When selecting a starting dosage, bear in mind that LT3 has a rapid onset of action, and residual effects of the LT4 preparation may persist for the first several weeks of therapy; For a thyroid suppression test, the dose of liothyronine is 75 to 100 mcg/day for 7 days. Radioactive iodine uptake is determined before and after administration of the hormone.

#119
1934
$27–$39

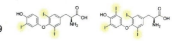

Desiccated thyroid (ARMOUR THYROID)

DES i kay ted THYE roid

"Armored thyroid"

❖ Thyroid Hormone (T3 and T4)

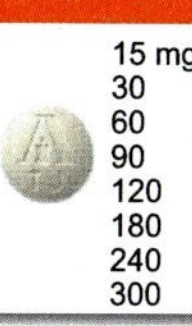

15 mg
30
60
90
120
180
240
300

Desiccated (dried) thyroid hormone, also called thyroid extract or porcine thyroid, consists of crushed pig thyroid glands containing T3:T4 in a 1:4 ratio. It is prescribed in milligrams, not micrograms like synthetic thyroid hormone pills. The ratio of pig T3:T4 is higher than in the human thyroid gland (1:10 ratio). The United States Pharmacopeia (USP) has standardized natural preparations to contain between 0.17–0.23% iodine, an indirect indicator of biologic activity.

The recommended treatment of hypothyroidism is levothyroxine (LT4 without LT3). In most situations, the risks of adding LT3 outweighs potential benefits. Refer to the Cytomel (LT3) monograph above. Nonetheless, many patients report feeling healthier when LT3 is added to LT4.

Patients who could theoretically benefit from the addition of LT3 to LT4 include those with high levels of inflammation (which can interfere with conversion of T4 to T3) or those with persisting symptoms of hypothyroidism despite normal TSH and free T4 levels.

Armour Thyroid pills have a bad taste/odor. The synthetic combination of T3:T4 is called liotrix (Thyrolar). It contains a 1:4 ratio like Armour Thyroid. Liotrix does not stink, but costs twice as much.

Dose equivalencies: 100 mcg levothyroxine = 25 mcg liothyronine = 60 mg desiccated thyroid = 1 grain liotrix

Dosing: The usual maintenance dose is 60–120 mg daily; Start 30 mg and increase in 15 mg increments in 6-week intervals based on TSH; May start full replacement dose for healthy patients under 65 without cardiac disease.

1980
$10

Oxytocin (PITOCIN)

oks i TOE sin / pit TOE sin

"Ox toes in (love)"

- ❖ Neuropeptide hormone
- ❖ Uterine contraction promotor
- ❖ Empathogen

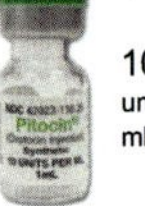

10 units/mL

FDA-approved for:
- ❖ Labor induction or augmentation
- ❖ Postpartum hemorrhage
- ❖ Abortion adjunct (elective, inevitable, or incomplete)

Used off-label for:
- ❖ Autism spectrum disorder
- ❖ Resistant depression
- ❖ Anorexia nervosa
- ❖ Substance use disorders
- ❖ Alcohol withdrawal

Oxytocin is a neuropeptide hormone produced in the hypothalamus, nicknamed the "love hormone", "cuddle chemical", and "moral molecule".

Oxytocin promotes mother-child bonding. Oxytocin is released by the pituitary gland in response to stretching of the cervix during labor and to nipple stimulation when breastfeeding. Estrogen increases secretion of oxytocin and expression of its receptor in the brain. Oxytocin appears to have a role in pair bonding and orgasm.

Postpartum reversal of oxytocin's effect may contribute to postpartum depression. Lactation has been associated with decreased postpartum depression, possibly related to ongoing increase of oxytocin (prolactin may also play a role).

Response to oxytocin varies among individuals. Polymorphisms in a single oxytocin receptor (OXTR) gene contribute to an individual's temperament. Individuals with a certain OXTR variation are more empathetic and have lower rates of autism. Another variation is associated with callous/unemotional traits and decreased stress tolerance.

Oxytocin has potential therapeutic value for a variety of psychiatric conditions, administered experimentally as a nasal spray or sublingual tablet. Autism spectrum disorder is an obvious area of interest. Intranasal oxytocin showed rapid benefit for treatment-resistant depression. It has been speculated that dysregulation of oxytocin function is associated with depressive symptoms including social isolation and reduced appetite.

Oxytocin may have utility in treatment of substance use disorders because it modulates dopamine concentrations in the limbic system. Oxytocin has anxiolytic activity. Patients with anorexia nervosa have reduced levels of oxytocin, and intranasal oxytocin has been studied as treatment for eating disorders.

The club drug MDMA ("X", "Ecstasy", "Molly") has been described as an "empathogen" that enhances feelings of connection to others and increased awareness of emotions. These effects result from MDMA causing a release of oxytocin from the pituitary. Phencyclidine (PCP, "Angel dust") lowers hypothalamic oxytocin and decreases social interaction with prolonged use.

Oxytocin has also been nicknamed the "amnestic neuropeptide" owing to its ability to reduce consolidation and retrieval of memories, especially memories of relationship conflicts. Circulating levels of oxytocin may be elevated in complicated grief.

The prefix -toco refers to childbirth. Atosiban (ANTOCIN) is an oxytocin antagonist used in Europe as a tocolytic agent, i.e., suppressor of uterine contractions in prevention of preterm labor. Atosiban is unavailable in the US, where we use tocolytics like terbutaline (β2 agonist) and nifedipine (calcium channel blocker). Antagonism of oxytocin prevents pair bonding in animals. Pitocin has a **black box warning** stating that it is not for elective labor induction, i.e., induction without medical indication.

page 18

Dynamic interactions:
- ❖ Hyponatremia

Kinetic interactions:
- ❖ None - "in a bubble"

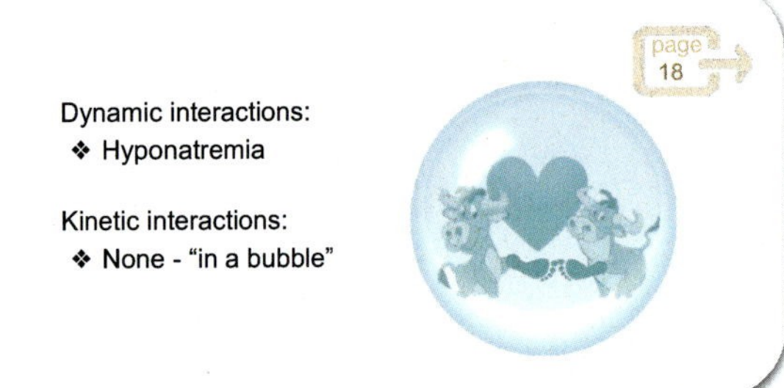

Oxytocin | Tamoxifen

#238
1990
$20–$80

Tamoxifen (NOLVADEX)

ta MOX i fen / NOLV a dex

"Tame ox defends (against breast cancer)"

❖ Selective estrogen receptor modulator (SERM)
❖ Protein kinase C (PKC) inhibitor

10
20
mg

FDA-approved for:
- ❖ Breast cancer (estrogen receptor-positive)
- ❖ Ductal carcinoma in situ
- ❖ Breast cancer prevention

Used off-label for:
- ❖ Acute mania (experimental)
- ❖ Mastalgia (breast pain
- ❖ Ovulation induction
- ❖ Precocious puberty
- ❖ Gynecomastia (prevention/treatment)

Tamoxifen (Nolvadex) is included because some antidepressants (2D6 inhibitors) cut its effectiveness in half, which serves as a good example of the prodrug concept.

Experimentally, tamoxifen appears to be highly effective for the treatment of acute mania.

Tamoxifen is a selective estrogen receptor modulator (SERM) with different effects on different tissues. It can also be referred to as an estrogen agonist/antagonist. It blocks estrogen in the breast but is a has estrogenic effects in uterus, liver, and bones. It causes endometrial cancer and blood clots but prevents osteoporosis.

For breast cancer, tamoxifen is typically taken for 5 years. For an acute manic episode it was taken for 3 weeks.

Tamoxifen has a black box warning for risk of uterine cancer and blood clots (stroke, pulmonary embolism). Side effects include irregular periods, cognitive impairment, loss of libido, and hepatotoxicity.

Tamoxifen is a prodrug with relatively low affinity for estrogen receptors itself. The therapeutic effects of tamoxifen are through active metabolites (afimoxifene and endoxifen, which are unavailable as standalone medications) with 30–100x stronger affinity for estrogen receptors as the parent compound.

Yildiz-Yesiloglu (2006) found tamoxifen effective for acute mania. Tamoxifen was chosen not for its antiestrogenic effect, but for its inhibition of protein kinase C (PKC) in the brain. PKC is believed to be overactive during manic episodes of bipolar disorder. In a 3-week study, 14 of 29 acutely manic patients showed at least 50% improvement, compared to 1 of 21 with placebo. Side effects were minimal—flushing of face and acne.

For context, lithium and valproic acid (Depakene, Depakote) indirectly inhibit PKC, which may be involved in their mechanism of mood stabilization. Tamoxifen is the only available direct PKC inhibitor.

Dosing: To prevent recurrence of breast cancer, it is given 20 mg QD for 5 years; For mastalgia, it is given 10 mg QD for 4 months; To induce ovulation, tamoxifen is given at days 3 through 7 of the menstrual cycle; For mania (experimental), the dose was 20 mg BID, increased to 40 mg BID for a 3-week course.

Dynamic interactions:
- ❖ Estrogen receptor agonist/antagonist (depending on location)
- ❖ Thrombogenic effects

Kinetic interactions:
- ❖ Tamoxifen is a 2D6 prodrug with relatively low affinity for estrogen receptors itself. The therapeutic effects of tamoxifen are through active metabolites. Concomitant use of 2D6-inhibiting antidepressants double the risk of recurrence of breast cancer, even sertraline whose 2D6 inHibition(weak) is a non-factor in other contexts. The main 2D6 inHibitors are fluoxetine (strong), paroxetine (strong), bupropion (moderate/strong), and duloxetine (moderate).
- ❖ Tamoxifen is less effective for individuals with 2D6 poor metabolizer (PM) genotype (5% of population)
- ❖ Contraindicated with warfarin (2C9 substrate) due to increased risk of bleeding

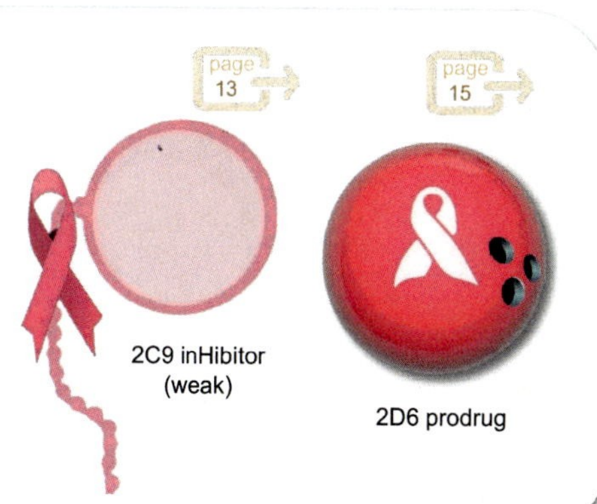

Prodrugs are substrates that are less potent than their metabolites. Ordinary substrates (beach balls) are deactivated by 2D6. Prodrugs (bowling balls) are *activated* by 2D6. In the presence of an inhibitor prodrugs are less effective.

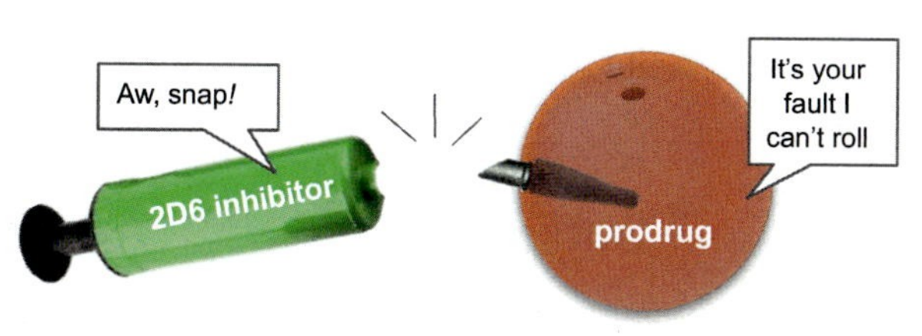

2D6 inhibitor antidepressants

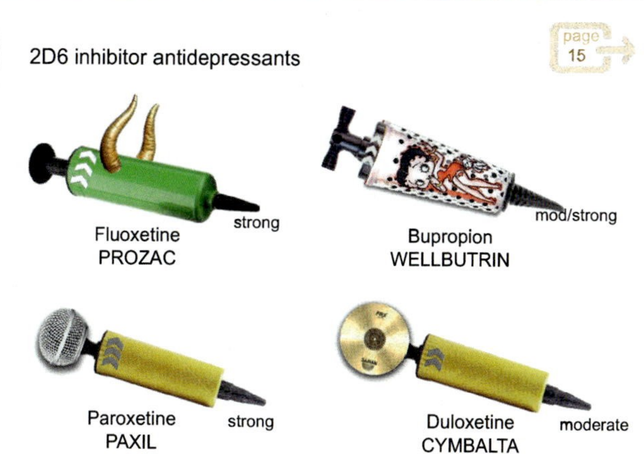

HORMONES 25

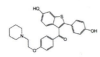

#294
1997
$54–$578

Raloxifene (EVISTA)

ra LOX i feen / e VIST a

"Evilest Rolex fiend"

❖ Selective estrogen receptor modulator (SERM)

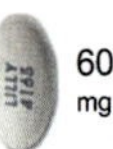

60 mg

FDA-approved for:

❖ Osteoporosis prevention (postmenopausal)
❖ Osteoporosis treatment (postmenopausal)
❖ Breast cancer prevention

Raloxifene (Evista) is an estrogen receptor agonist or antagonist, depending on location of body. It produces the beneficial effects of estrogen on bones without the negative effects (cancer) of estrogen on the breasts and uterus.

Experimentally, it was shown to improve cognition and memory in men and women with schizophrenia. The proposed mechanism of the effect is neurogenesis and reduction of inflammation in the brain. Other studies have found raloxifene to be ineffective or detrimental for women with schizophrenia.

Raloxifene has black box warnings for risk of venous thromboembolism and fatal stroke. Venous thromboembolism risk is considered a class effect with SERMs and risk appears intermediate between placebo and oral estrogen.

Dosing: The recommended dose for all purposes is 60 mg QD.

Rx	SERM	Breast cancer	Uterine cancer	Thrombo-embolism	Bone strength	Vaginal health	Year	Uses
#55	Estradiol (estrogen)	↑	↑	↑	↑	↑	1933	Approved for menopausal symptoms and advanced prostate cancer
#238	Tamoxifen (NOLVADEX)	↓	↑	↑	↑	-	1977	Approved for breast cancer prevention
#294	Raloxifene (EVISTA)	↓	↓	↑	↑	-	1997	Approved for breast cancer prevention and osteoporosis
> 300	Clomiphene (CLOMID)	-	↓	↑	↑	-	1967	Antagonist at hypothalamus; Approved for ovulation induction; Used off-label for spermatogenesis
> 300	Ospemifene (OSPHENA)	↓	↓	-	↑	↑	2013	Approved for vaginal dryness and dyspareunia

Dynamic interactions:

❖ Estrogenic/antiestrogenic
❖ Thrombogenic

Kinetic interactions:

❖ Raloxifene Interferes with GI absorption of thyroid hormone, but otherwise kinetic interactions are minimal - "in a box"

page 18

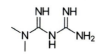

#4
1995
IR $4–$22
ER $4–$32

Metformin (GLUCOPHAGE)

met FORM in / GLU co faahj

"Mr. Met formin' Glucose fudge"

❖ Biguanide anti-hyperglycemic

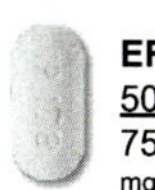

ER: 500 750 mg

500 850 1000 mg

FDA approved for:

❖ Diabetes mellitus, type 2

Used off-label for:

❖ Adjunct to 2nd gen antipsychotics
❖ Polycystic ovary syndrome (PCOS)
❖ Weight loss
❖ Longevity

Dosing: Starting dose for the IR formulation is 500 mg BID with meals. If treating diabetes, increase the dose in increments of 500 mg weekly. The maximum total daily dose is 2550 mg per day, which would be prescribed as 850 mg TID with meals. If gastrointestinal side effects with IR, change to ER. For the ER formulation start 1000 mg q PM with the evening meal, with maximum 2000 mg/day. Off-label treatment or prevention of antipsychotic-induced weight gain is dosed similarly to diabetes.

Hemoglobin A1c

Normal .... 4.0–5.6 %
Prediabetes .... 5.7–6.4 %
Diabetes .... ≥ 6.5 %

Average glucose of 100 .... 5.1 %
Average glucose of 200 .... 8.6 %
Average glucose of 300 .... 12.1 %

The diabetic patient needs more than just metformin if A1c ≥ 9.0%.

Metformin (Glucophage) is the first line medication for prevention and treatment of type II diabetes. It works by decreasing glucose production by the liver and increasing insulin sensitivity of body tissues. Metformin reduces hunger and promotes fat loss. Since metformin is renally excreted, unmetabolized, it is not involved in CYP interactions.

Metformin is the preferred medication to prevent or reverse weight gain caused by second generation antipsychotics (SGAs). If a patient on an SGA gains > 5 pounds in first month or > 10 pounds from baseline, consider adding metformin. Many psychiatrists use topiramate (Topamax) as their go-to weight loss medication, but metformin is probably a better choice (see table below). Obese patients (diabetic or otherwise) taking metformin typically lose about 7 kg (15 pounds). It could be argued that metformin should be given to most patients starting olanzapine (Zyprexa) or clozapine (Clozaril), the antipsychotics most likely to cause significant weight gain and diabetes. Refer to Maayan et al, *Neuropsychopharm*, 2010.

Metformin has been demonstrated to reduce inflammation and slow the aging process in several small lab animals. It is possible that metformin can prevent cancer and promote longevity in humans (Barzilai et al, 2016). A large study called Targeting Aging with Metformin (TAME) is in progress. Metformin appears to prevent cognitive decline with aging (Ng et al, 2014).

Metformin does not cause hypoglycemia. Fingerstick glucose monitoring at home is unnecessary when metformin is prescribed to non-diabetics. Even in overdose, only 10% of individuals develop hypoglycemia. Side effects are gastrointestinal including diarrhea (50%), nausea (25%), and flatulence (10%). GI side effects are less problematic with the ER formulation (10% diarrhea). There is a black box warning of the possibility of lactic acidosis, which is very rare at standard doses in healthy individuals. Do not prescribe metformin to patients with serious medical illness. Risk of acidosis with a large overdose is about 33%. A metabolic panel should be checked yearly. This would reveal acidosis as low bicarbonate (listed as CO_2). Signs of acidosis are nonspecific with subtle onset, including malaise, myalgias, abdominal pain, respiratory distress, or somnolence. Metformin has a 3% risk of contributing to Vitamin B12 deficiency due to malabsorption. Consider checking B12 levels at one year and then every 2 or 3 years.

Initiation of metformin is not recommended for patients with eGFR under 45 (renal insufficiency). Discontinue metformin if eGFR falls below 30. Temporarily discontinue metformin prior to iodinated contrast imaging procedures and restart in 48 hours if eGFR is normal.

Metformin blunts muscle growth from resistance exercise training in older adults (Walton et al, 2019).

Adjuncts to ameliorate antipsychotic-induced weight gain

Medication	Metformin (GLUCOPHAGE)	Topiramate (TOPAMAX)
Class	Diabetes medication	Antiepileptic
Site of action	Periphery	CNS
Benefits	Weight loss Prevention of diabetes Decreased lipids Possible anti-aging Possible cancer prevention	Weight loss Headache prevention
Risk of acidosis	Rare lactic acidosis	Relatively common metabolic acidosis
Other risks	Vitamin B12 deficiency (3%)	Kidney stones (15% with long-term use)
Most common side effects	Diarrhea and GI distress (tolerance usually develops)	Cognitive impairment, especially > 200 mg; Weight loss dose is 25 mg BID x 1 week then 50 mg BID which is unlikely to impair cognition.
Contraindications	Renal insufficiency	None
Cost	$4–$32	$4–$82

A 2010 meta-analysis of medication for antipsychotic-associated weight gain found metformin slightly more effective than topiramate (Maayan, et al, *Neuropsychopharmacology*).

Dynamic interactions:

❖ Black box warning for risk of lactic acidosis, which is increased by carbonic anhydrase inhibitors such as topiramate (Topamax), zonisamide (Zonegran), acetazolamide (Diamox), and dichlorphenamide (Keveyis)
❖ Heavy alcohol consumption increases the risk of acidosis with metformin

Kinetic interactions:

❖ Cimetidine (Tagamet) may compete with metformin for urinary excretion

"in a box" - clinically significant kinetic interactions are possible but unlikely

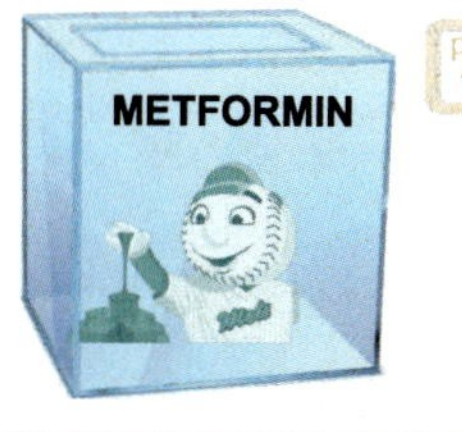

1968
$6–$40

Acetylcysteine (NAC)

a SEET il SIS teen

"Knack, (the) Ace of assisting"

❖ Antioxidant
❖ Neuroprotectant
❖ Mucus thinner
❖ Over-the-counter

500
600
1,000
mg

Acetylcysteine (NAC) is a derivative of the amino acid cysteine. NAC is a precursor of glutathione, the body's main natural antioxidant. NAC is a way to get glutathione into the brain where it is a neuroprotectant—it acts by reducing inflammation, normalizing glutamate transmission, and increasing brain growth factors.

The prescription product is called acetylcysteine (Acetadote, Mucomyst) and the over-the-counter product is called N-acetylcysteine (NAC). There is no difference between the two. Insurance plans are unlikely to cover acetylcysteine capsules for off-label psychiatric use.

NAC is inexpensive and ultra-safe. Most individuals have no side effects. Gastrointestinal side effects are possible including dyspepsia, nausea, diarrhea, cramping, and flatulence. Tolerance to GI side effects usually develops after a few weeks. The medication has a bad smell and taste. This is only an issue if the capsules are broken. Some brands smell worse than others.

NAC supplementation may slow the aging process. Fruit flies given NAC lived 25% longer.

NAC can improve liver function in patients with non-alcoholic fatty liver disease lowering liver enzymes and decreasing spleen enlargement (Khosbaten et al, 2010).

Knack character from a Playstation game

Used traditionally for:

- ❖ Acetaminophen (Tylenol) overdose, to protect liver (IV, PO)—Acetadote brand
- ❖ Breaking up mucus (mucolysis) for cystic fibrosis—Mucomyst brand (nebulized)
- ❖ Prophylaxis of radiocontrast-induced nephropathy

Used off-label for:

- ❖ Nail biting, hair pulling, skin picking
- ❖ Mood disorders
- ❖ Schizophrenia
- ❖ Obsessive compulsive disorder
- ❖ Memory loss associated with aging
- ❖ Drug abuse (marijuana, cocaine, cigarettes)
- ❖ Post-traumatic stress disorder (PTSD)
- ❖ Tardive dyskinesia
- ❖ Pneumonia (to decrease lung inflammation)
- ❖ Eye drops to thin mucus

Because NAC improves inflammatory response in patients with pneumonia (Zhange et al, 2018), it has been proposed for use in COVID-19 patients to prevent acute respiratory distress syndrome (ARDS).

Dosing: At least 600 mg BID. The author recommends 1,200 mg BID of the *NOW Supplements* or *Nutricost* brand, which run about $0.08 per 600 mg cap on Amazon. If gastrointestinal discomfort, back down to 600 mg BID or change to *Jarrow Formulas N-A-C Sustain* (extended release) tabs, which are $0.17 each. Ideally, NAC should be taken without food, i.e., outside of 30 minutes before or 2 hours after a meal. This prevents competition for absorption between NAC and dietary proteins.

Neuroprotection

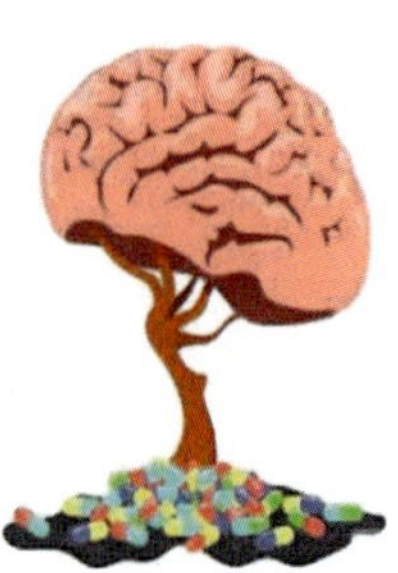

Neuroprotection is the prevention of cognitive decline by keeping neurons healthy. Neuroprotectants are chemicals that are good for the brain in a general sense, with the potential to ameliorate symptoms across a wide range of mental illnesses. Neuroprotectants should be considered for use adjunctively to standard psychotropics, or as monotherapy for anyone wanting to delay the onset of dementia and prevent neurodegenerative conditions such as Parkinson's disease (PD). Many anti-inflammatory drugs are neuroprotective and appear to be effective adjuncts for depression.

Probable neuroprotectants include:

- ❖ N-acetylcysteine (NAC)
- ❖ Lithium - low dose
- ❖ Melatonin
- ❖ Vitamin D
- ❖ Omega-3 fatty acids
- ❖ Minocycline (antibiotic)
- ❖ Caffeine (tea, coffee, pills) - caution that even diet soda doubles the risk of diabetes.
- ❖ Nicotine (gum, patches) - not tobacco, which is toxic
- ❖ Celecoxib (Celebrex) - effective in augmentation of antidepressants
- ❖ Ibuprofen - decreases inflammation, may prevent Parkinson's
- ❖ Resveratrol - extract from grape skins
- ❖ Cannabidiol (CBD)

The editorial *Are you neuroprotecting your patients?* is a worthwhile read (Henry Nasrallah MD, Current Psychiatry, Dec 2016).

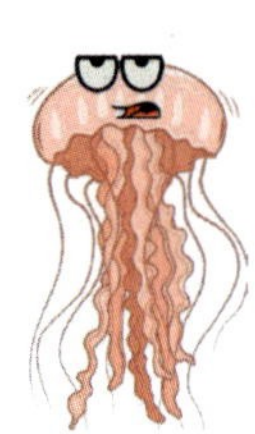

When patients enquire about Prevagen (apoaequorin) for memory improvement, the author recommends NAC or low dose lithium instead. Prevagen is heavily marketed for "mild memory loss related to aging". The "active" ingredient of Prevagen is apoaequorin, a protein found in jellyfish that is destroyed in the GI tract and does not enter the CNS. The Federal Trade Commission sued the company making Prevagen (although unsuccessfully) for making false and unsubstantiated claims.

Dynamic interactions:
- ❖ None

Kinetic interactions:
- ❖ None

Double bubble - no significant dynamic or kinetic interactions with other medications

page 18

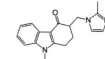

#91
1991
$3–$76 tab
$3–$76 ODT

Ondansetron (ZOFRAN)

on DAN se tron / ZO fran

"On Dancer Tron! (Go) so frantic!"

❖ Antiemetic
❖ Serotonin 5-HT_3 receptor antagonist

ODT 4 8 mg | tab 4 8 mg

FDA-approved for:
- Prevention of nausea/vomiting associated with:
  - Chemotherapy
  - Radiation therapy
  - Surgery

Used off-label for:
- Nausea/vomiting (other)
- Irritable bowel syndrome
- Tourette's syndrome
- Schizophrenia (adjunct)
- Tardive dyskinesia
- Obsessive-compulsive disorder (OCD)
- Alcoholism

Ondansetron (Zofran) is the first-line medication for nausea/vomiting. It blocks the 5-HT_3 serotonin receptor, which is involved in antidepressant-induced nausea. Ondansetron's receptor binding profile is "clean", i.e., it does not bind off-target receptors like other antiemetics. Ondansetron exerts its effect in the gastrointestinal tract and in the brain's chemoreceptor trigger zone.

Ondansetron is a more effective antiemetic than dopamine blockers such as metoclopramide (Reglan). Another advantage over metoclopramide is ondansetron's lack of extrapyramidal effects (EPS) and sedation. It does not work well for nausea due to motion sickness, which is better treated with an anticholinergic like diphenhydramine, promethazine, or scopolamine.

Ondansetron is very well-tolerated. It can be somewhat constipating. Otherwise, no side effects are expected.

In 2011 the FDA issued a warning about ondansetron causing QT prolongation, although this is not a black box warning. QT prolongation is not much of an issue with oral ondansetron. In 2012 the 32 mg IV dose was withdrawn due to QT prolongation. The maximum IV dose is now 16 mg. The maximum PO dose is 24 mg.

Ondansetron is available as an orally disintegrating tablet (ODT), branded as ONDISSOLVE, which costs no more than the swallowed tablet. The ODT formulation can be taken sublingually for faster onset of action.

An effective regimen for preventing vomiting from cancer chemotherapy is a combination of a "-setron" and the corticosteroid dexamethasone (Decadron). How corticosteroids prevent vomiting is unclear.

Antidepressant-induced nausea

Nausea is one of the most common reasons patients stop medications prematurely. Nausea tends to be a transient side effect that usually resolves spontaneously. Nausea can often be avoided altogether with slow titration. Other tips for medication-induced nausea is to take the pill after food—not with food, but immediately after a meal. Also effective for nausea is ginger extract (one 550 mg capsule) taken 1 hour before a meal, for a maximum of 3 caps/day (Bodagh et al, 2019; Rajnish Mago, MD; The Carlat Psychiatry Report, Jun/Jul 2019). Ginger ale does not suffice.

On Dancer Tron!
On Prancer Tron!
Go, so frantic!

QT prolongation (intravenous route)

Ondansetron may have value in the treatment of schizophrenia, as an adjunct to haloperidol (Zhang et al, 2006). Ondansetron has been proposed as a possible treatment for psychosis associated with Parkinson's disease (Zoldan et al, 1995). The mechanism of ondansetron's purported antipsychotic effect is unknown. It does not block dopamine receptors like traditional antipsychotics. It does not significantly block the 5-HT_{2A} receptor that is targeted by second generation antipsychotics and pimavanserin (Nuplazid). If ondansetron is proven to truly benefit schizophrenia, the etiology of psychosis may need to be reconsidered.

Ondansetron could possibly improve tardive dyskinesia (Zullino et al, 2001).

Similar serotonin receptor antagonist ("-setron") antiemetics include granisetron (Kytril), palonosetron (Aloxi), and dolasetron (Anzemet). Other chemicals that have antiemetic properties due to blocking 5-HT_3 receptors are ginger and mirtazapine (Remeron). The antidepressant vortioxetine (Trintellix) blocks 5-HT_3 receptors but may cause nausea by other serotonergic mechanisms.

Dosing: The orally disintegrating tablet (ODT) formulation is preferred. The standard dose for nausea/vomiting is around 4 mg q 4 hr PRN or 8 mg q 8 hr PRN. Scheduled dosing usually starts at 4 mg TID before meals. The maximum IV dose is 16 mg, limited due to QT prolongation. The maximum PO dose is 24 mg. For experimental psychiatric uses such as OCD and alcoholism, very low doses were used, for instance 0.25 mg BID for two weeks, then increased to 0.5 mg BID (Pallanti et al, 2013 for OCD).

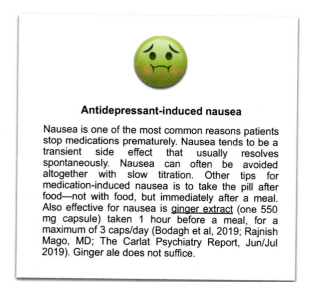

page 16

Dynamic interactions:
- QT prolongation
- Anti-serotonergic - potential for profound hypotension in combination with apomorphine (Apokyn)

Kinetic interactions:
- 3A4 substrate

3A4 substrate

Triptans for acute migraine headaches

Triptans are a family of tryptamine-based drugs used as abortive medication for migraines and cluster headaches. Triptans should be administered as quickly as possible upon headache onset. Early treatment decreases the likelihood of recurrence within 24 hours. The subcutaneous route is more effective but brings more side effects. Weakness or somnolence following triptan therapy may be part of the migraine attack, unmasked by the successful treatment of pain.

Longer-acting triptans such as naratriptan (Amerge) and frovatriptan (Frova) have a slower onset of action and lower initial response rate than other triptans, but they are better tolerated.

Triptans constrict blood vessels. They carry a small risk of heart attack, stroke, or seizure. All triptans are contraindicated with coronary artery disease, peripheral vascular disease, uncontrolled hypertension, history of stroke, or Wolff-Parkinson-White syndrome (extra electrical pathway in the heart with tachycardic episodes).

Triptans do not appear to cause serotonin syndrome.

About 25% of triptan users are also prescribed an SSRI or SNRI. In 2006 the FDA issued a warning that triptans could contribute to serotonin syndrome when combined with SSRIs or SNRIs. The warning did not change prescribing practices, and the risk appears miniscule to nonexistent. Orlova et al (2018) estimated the risk at about one case of serotonin syndrome per 10,000 person-years of exposure to a triptan plus an SSRI/SNRI.

Serotonin syndrome is hypothesized to involve 5-HT_{1A} and 5-HT_{2A} receptors, while triptans are agonists at 5-HT_{1B} and 5-HT_{1D} receptors.

In order of prescriptions written, available triptans include sumatriptan (Imitrex), rizatriptan (Maxalt), eletriptan (Relpax), zolmitriptan (Zomig), naratriptan (Amerge), frovatriptan (Frova), and almotriptan (Axert).

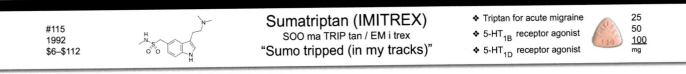

#115
1992
$6–$112

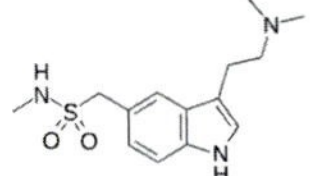

Sumatriptan (IMITREX)

SOO ma TRIP tan / EM i trex

"Sumo tripped (in my tracks)"

- Triptan for acute migraine
- 5-HT_{1B} receptor agonist
- 5-HT_{1D} receptor agonist

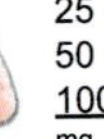

25
50
100
mg

FDA-approved for:

- Migraine headache (acute)
- Cluster headache (acute)
  - subcutaneous route

Sumatriptan (Imitrex) is a triptan available via several methods of delivery. Subcutaneous administration is the most effective but brings more side effects than the PO route. Onset of migraine relief is within 30–60 minutes with oral formulation, 10 minutes with subcutaneous, and 10–15 minutes with nasal powder. The efficacy of intranasal sumatriptan is partially dependent on GI absorption of the swallowed portion.

Elimination half-life is about 2 hours. Side effects may include paresthesia, chest tightness, warm/cold sensation, vertigo, and fatigue. TREXIMET is a fixed-dose oral combination of sumatriptan with the NSAID naproxen.

Dosing: Oral sumatriptan is dosed 50–100 mg, may be repeated after 2 hours of PO or after 1 hour of SC dose. PO maximum of 200 mg/day. Subcutaneous dosing is 1–6 mg SC x 1, may repeat after 1 hour for max of 12 mg/day. With mild to moderate hepatic impairment, the PO max is 50 mg/dose. With severe hepatic impairment both PO and SC sumatriptan is contraindicated.

page 18

Dynamic interactions:

- Serotonergic, but highly unlikely to contribute to serotonin syndrome
- Hypertensive effects

Kinetic interactions:

- None significant

#232
1998
$15–$186

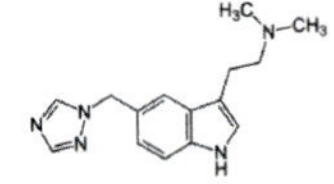

Rizatriptan (MAXALT)

RYE za TRIP tan / MAX alt

"RZA tripped (on) Max altitude"

- Triptan for acute migraine
- 5-HT_{1B} receptor agonist
- 5-HT_{1D} receptor agonist

5
10
mg

FDA-approved for:

- Migraine headache (acute)

Unlike sumatriptan, rizatriptan (Maxalt) is not approved for cluster headaches and is not available by subcutaneous route.

Rizatriptan is metabolized by monoamine oxidase-A, which is inhibited by propranolol. Concomitant use with propranolol increases blood levels of rizatriptan by 70%.

No dosage adjustment is needed with hepatic impairment, which is an advantage of rizatriptan over sumatriptan.

Dosing: 5 or 10 mg PO, may be repeated in 2 hours.

page 18

Dynamic interactions:

- Serotonergic, but highly unlikely to contribute to serotonin syndrome
- Hypertensive effects

Kinetic interactions:

- Minimal, but propranolol increases plasma concentrations of rizatriptan by 70% by inhibiting monoamine oxidase-A

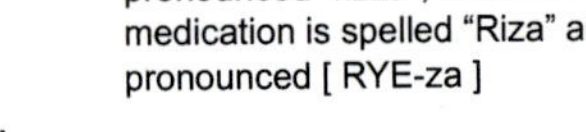

RZA of the Wu-Tang Clan, pronounced "rizza", while the medication is spelled "Riza" and pronounced [RYE-za]

Antibodies for migraine prevention

Calcitonin gene-related peptide (CGRP)—"Cerebrum Gets Really Painful"—has nothing to do with calcitonin functionally. CGRP is released from trigeminal ganglia cells and leads to inflammation and vasodilation. Serum levels of CGRP increase during migraine and cluster headaches. Injection of CGRP can induce a migraine.

Three monoclonal antibodies against CGRC (or CGRC receptors) debuted in 2018 for migraine prevention. They are effective within the first week, but the effect size is modest. Effectiveness is similar to Botox injections. They are usually used in combination with other migraine treatments. Because medications targeting CGRP are new, long term risks are unknown.

Since CGRP is a vasodilator, its suppression could theoretically contribute to an ischemic event. There are no official contraindications.

Note that no migraine prevention medication is a magic bullet. Migraine is not a homogeneous condition, defined by symptoms rather cause.

Antibody medications are proteins, not subject to kinetic interactions because they are not metabolized. Antibodies are too big to be excreted in urine, and very few of them are excreted in bile. Most are removed by phagocytic immune cells, that engulf the antibodies and degrade them to amino acids.

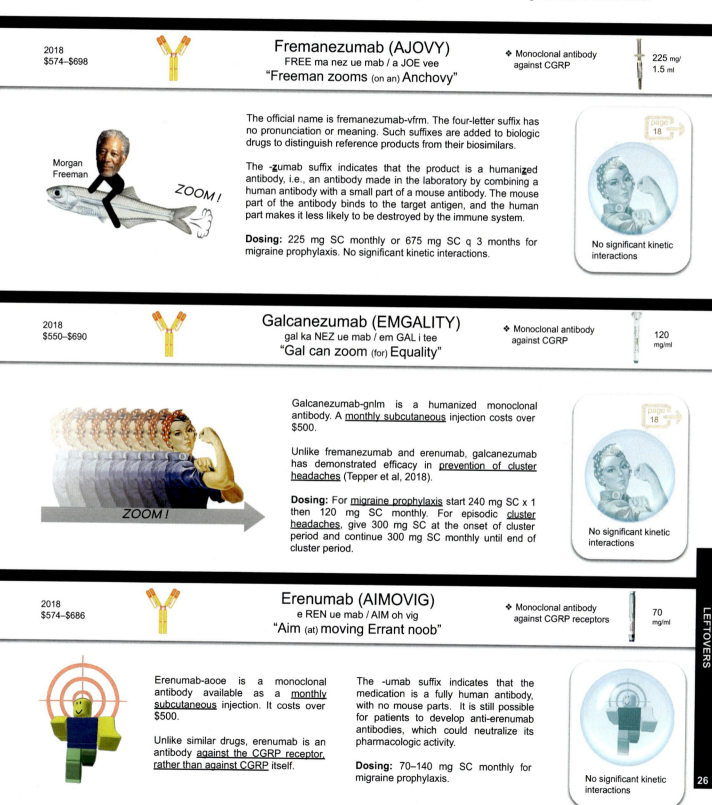

2018
$574–$698

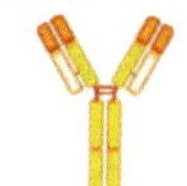

Fremanezumab (AJOVY)

FREE ma nez ue mab / a JOE vee

"Freeman zooms (on an) Anchovy"

❖ Monoclonal antibody against CGRP

225 mg/ 1.5 ml

The official name is fremanezumab-vfrm. The four-letter suffix has no pronunciation or meaning. Such suffixes are added to biologic drugs to distinguish reference products from their biosimilars.

The -zumab suffix indicates that the product is a humanized antibody, i.e., an antibody made in the laboratory by combining a human antibody with a small part of a mouse antibody. The mouse part of the antibody binds to the target antigen, and the human part makes it less likely to be destroyed by the immune system.

Dosing: 225 mg SC monthly or 675 mg SC q 3 months for migraine prophylaxis. No significant kinetic interactions.

page 18

No significant kinetic interactions

2018
$550–$690

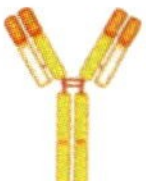

Galcanezumab (EMGALITY)

gal ka NEZ ue mab / em GAL i tee

"Gal can zoom (for) Equality"

❖ Monoclonal antibody against CGRP

120 mg/ml

Galcanezumab-gnlm is a humanized monoclonal antibody. A monthly subcutaneous injection costs over $500.

Unlike fremanezumab and erenumab, galcanezumab has demonstrated efficacy in prevention of cluster headaches (Tepper et al, 2018).

Dosing: For migraine prophylaxis start 240 mg SC x 1 then 120 mg SC monthly. For episodic cluster headaches, give 300 mg SC at the onset of cluster period and continue 300 mg SC monthly until end of cluster period.

page 18

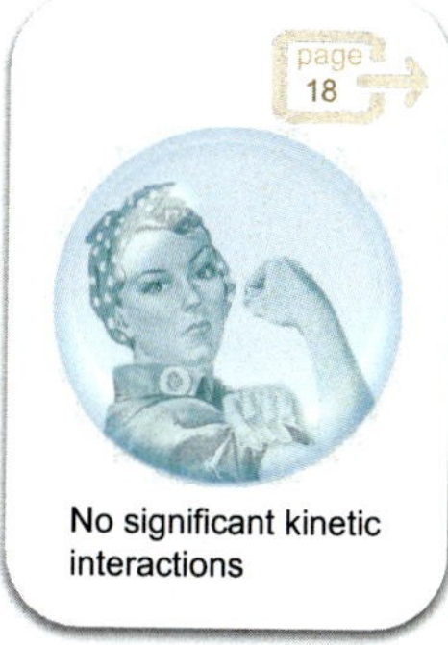

No significant kinetic interactions

2018
$574–$686

Erenumab (AIMOVIG)

e REN ue mab / AIM oh vig

"Aim (at) moving Errant noob"

❖ Monoclonal antibody against CGRP receptors

70 mg/ml

Erenumab-aooe is a monoclonal antibody available as a monthly subcutaneous injection. It costs over $500.

Unlike similar drugs, erenumab is an antibody against the CGRP receptor, rather than against CGRP itself.

The -umab suffix indicates that the medication is a fully human antibody, with no mouse parts. It is still possible for patients to develop anti-erenumab antibodies, which could neutralize its pharmacologic activity.

Dosing: 70–140 mg SC monthly for migraine prophylaxis.

No significant kinetic interactions

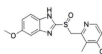

#7
1990
$8–$25

Omeprazole (PRILOSEC)

oh MEP ra zol

"Pry loose (Oh my!)"

❖ Proton pump inhibitor (PPI)

10
20
40
mg

FDA approved for:

- ❖ GERD
- ❖ Gastric ulcer
- ❖ Duodenal ulcer
- ❖ Hypersecretory conditions
- ❖ Helicobacter pylori infection

Used off-label for:

- ❖ Ulcer prophylaxis

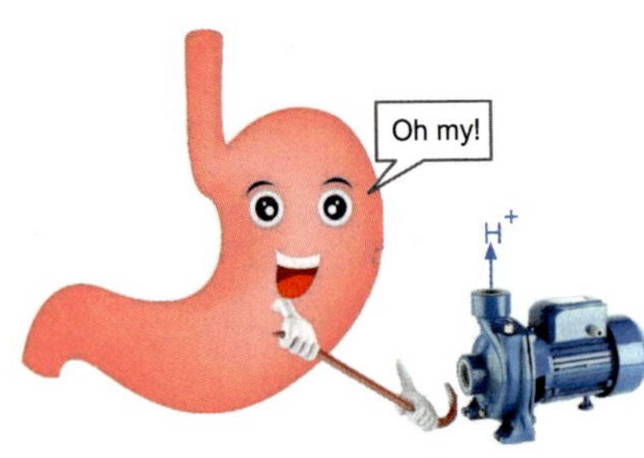

Omeprazole (Prilosec) is a proton pump inhibitor (PPI) available over-the-counter. It is included in this book due to its potential for kinetic drug-drug interactions. As a CYP2C19 inHibitor, it increases levels of certain SSRIs and benzodiazepines. As a P-glycoprotein inhibitor, it can allow certain drugs (e.g., loperamide) into the CNS that would otherwise be quickly pumped outside the blood-brain barrier.

PPIs are used for the treatment of heartburn. They stop secretion of H^+ ions (protons) into the gastric lumen by inhibiting the gastric parietal cell hydrogen-potassium ATPase, also known as the "proton pump". Although PPIs have a short serum half-life of about 1 hour, they inhibit gastric acid secretion for 24 hours by irreversibly inhibiting the proton pump through a permanent covalent bond.

PPIs decrease gastric acid secretion up to 99%, making them substantially more effective than H_2 receptor antagonists like ranitidine (Zantac) and famotidine (Pepcid).

PPIs are often taken longer than needed. If used for heartburn/GERD, they should be stopped after 4–8 weeks. The main long-term risk of PPIs is osteoporosis. Other risks include hypomagnesemia and vitamin B12 deficiency. PPI use has been associated with cognitive decline, but a causal relationship has not been established.

Omeprazole and esomeprazole are more likely to cause relevant kinetic drug-drug interactions than other than popular PPIs, as shown in the table below. *Esomeprazole is the 'Next omeprazole' (Nexium).*

There is no convincing evidence that any one PPI is more effective or better tolerated than the others. So, it is advisable to avoid omeprazole and esomeprazole to avoid interactions. For a prescription PPI, pantoprazole (Protonix) is preferred. For an OTC PPI, choose lansoprazole (Prevacid)—*I like Lance's Pants*.

Dosing: PPIs should be taken 30 minutes before a meal; For GERD, the dose is 20 mg QD x 4–8 weeks; For gastric ulcer, the dose is 40 mg QD x 8 weeks; For Zollinger-Ellison syndrome (hypersecretory condition), substantially higher doses are needed; For erosive esophagitis, long-term treatment is needed; For helicobacter pylori infection, it is given BID as part of a multi-drug combo including (for instance) bismuth (Pepto-Bismol), tetracycline, and metronidazole.

Rx	Proton pump inhibitor	OTC	Cost	Dose range	escitalopram level increase	
#4	Omeprazole (PRILOSEC)	Yes	$10–$30	20–40 mg	~90%	Increased levels of clonazepam (Klonopin) ~90%, diazepam (Valium) ~90%, sertraline (Zoloft) by ~40%, and citalopram (Celexa) by ~35%
#25	Pantoprazole (PROTONIX)	No	$8–$128	40 mg	~20%	Cost and fewer interactions makes pantoprazole the Rx PPI of choice. *I like Lance's Pants*
#69	Esomeprazole (NEXIUM)	Yes	$10–$30	20–40 mg	~80%	The (S)-(−)-isomer of omeprazole; Interactions are similar to those of omeprazole
#141	Lansoprazole (PREVACID)	Yes	$10–$30	15–30 mg	~20%	Fewer interactions makes lansoprazole the OTC PPI of choice. *I like Lance's Pants*
#190	Dexlansoprazole (DEXILANT)	No*	$209–$381	30–60 mg	?	(R)-(+)-isomer of lansoprazole; *Approved for OTC but not yet available OTC (2020)
#285	Rabeprazole (ACIPHEX)	No	$18–$292	20 mg	0%	All PPIs are 2C19 substrates, but rabeprazole does not inHibit 2C19

Dynamic interactions:

- ❖ Uncommonly, PPIs can cause hypomagnesemia. This increases the risk of torsades when combined with QT-prolonging medications

Kinetic interactions:

- ❖ Gastric alkalinizer
- ❖ P-gp inhibitor
- ❖ 2C19 inHibitor
- ❖ 2C19 substrate (all PPIs)
  - 2C19 ultrarapid metabolizers may need to take higher doses
  - 2C19 poor metabolizers can take lower doses

page 9

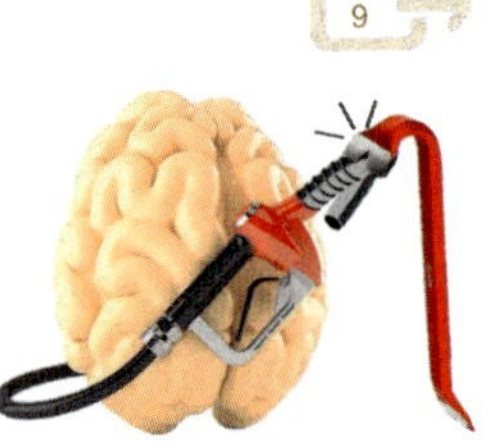

P-glycoprotein inhibitor

page 14

2C19 inHibitor (major)

also esomeprazole

page 14

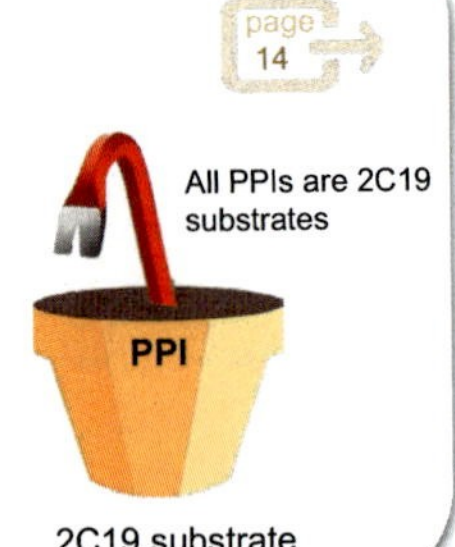

2C19 substrate

P-GLYCOPROTEIN

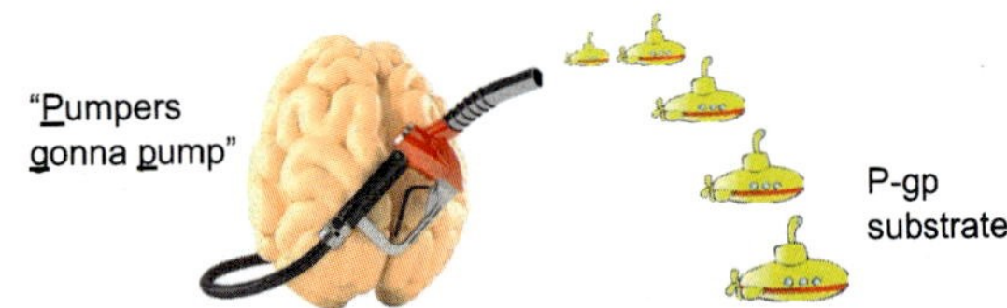

P-glycoprotein (P-gp) is a gatekeeper at the gut lumen and the blood-brain barrier. P-gp pumps P-gp substrates out of the brain—"Pumpers gonna pump".

An example of a relevant P-gp interaction involves the OTC opioid antidiarrheal loperamide (Imodium).

Loperamide does not cause central opioid effects under normal circumstances. If the individual takes a potent P-gp inhibitor, a megadose of loperamide can stay in the brain long enough to cause euphoria. The P-gp inhibitor typically used is omeprazole (Prilosec).

Lamotrigine interactions

Phase II metabolism, UGT1A4

18% of individuals are UGT1A4 ultrarapid metabolizers; 0% are poor metabolizers

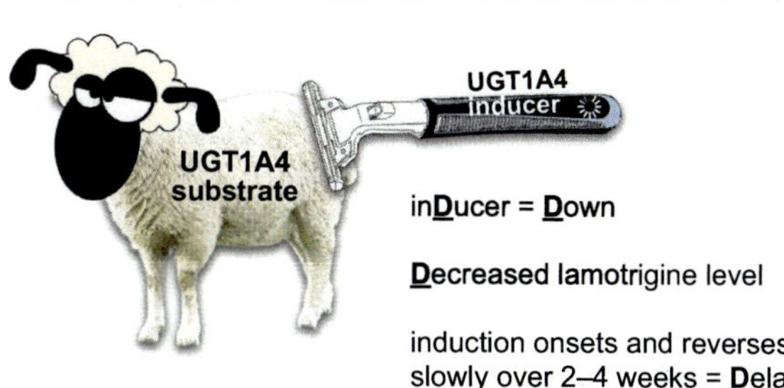

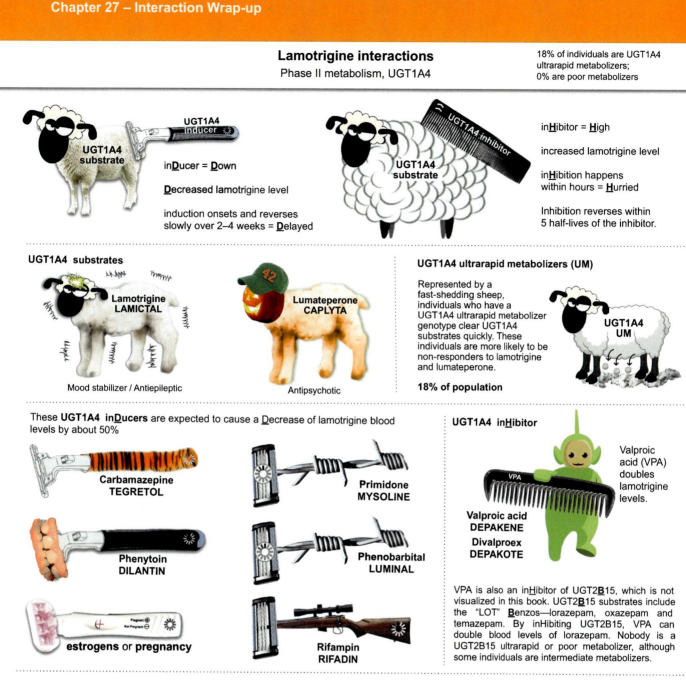

in**D**ucer = **D**own

Decreased lamotrigine level

induction onsets and reverses slowly over 2–4 weeks = **D**elayed

in**H**ibitor = **H**igh

increased lamotrigine level

in**H**ibition happens within hours = **H**urried

Inhibition reverses within 5 half-lives of the inhibitor.

UGT1A4 substrates

Mood stabilizer / Antiepileptic

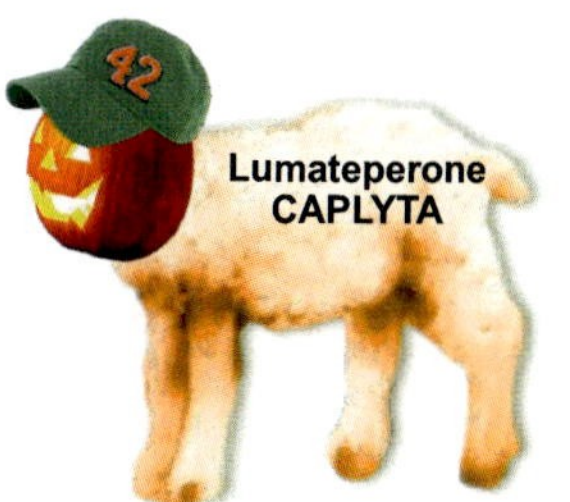

Antipsychotic

UGT1A4 ultrarapid metabolizers (UM)

Represented by a fast-shedding sheep, individuals who have a UGT1A4 ultrarapid metabolizer genotype clear UGT1A4 substrates quickly. These individuals are more likely to be non-responders to lamotrigine and lumateperone.

18% of population

These **UGT1A4 in<u>D</u>ucers** are expected to cause a <u>D</u>ecrease of lamotrigine blood levels by about 50%

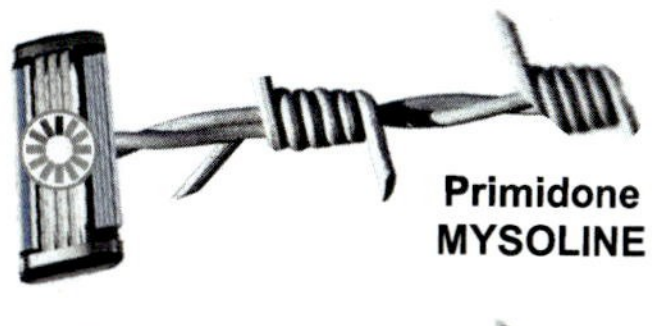

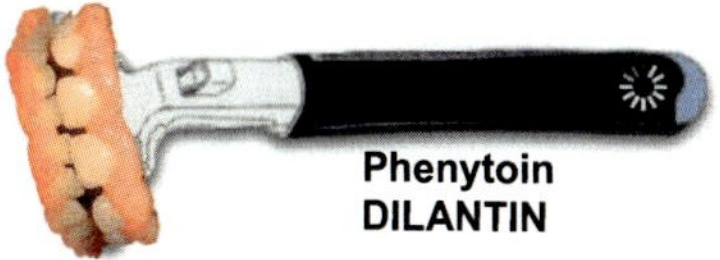

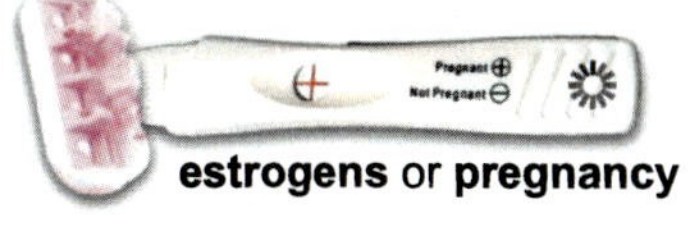

UGT1A4 in<u>H</u>ibitor

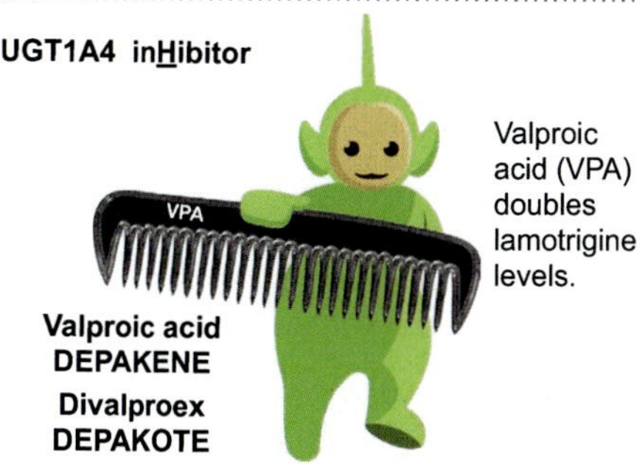

Valproic acid (VPA) doubles lamotrigine levels.

VPA is also an in<u>H</u>ibitor of UGT2<u>**B**</u>15, which is not visualized in this book. UGT2<u>**B**</u>15 substrates include the "LOT" <u>**B**</u>enzos—lorazepam, oxazepam and temazepam. By inHibiting UGT2B15, VPA can double blood levels of lorazepam. Nobody is a UGT2B15 ultrarapid or poor metabolizer, although some individuals are intermediate metabolizers.

Before lamotrigine became generically available, three Lamictal starter packs were available to address these interactions:

Starter pack	For those taking	Lamotrigine dose
Orange	No interacting medications	25 mg x 2 weeks, then 50 mg x 2 weeks, then 100 mg x 1 week. The usual maintenance dose starting on week 6 is 200 mg, which may be dosed in AM, HS, or divided to 100 mg BID.
Blue	Valproate (Depakote)	Half strength. Maintenance dose is 100 mg QD.
Green	Carbamazepine (Tegretol) Phenytoin (Dilantin) Phenobarbital (Luminal) Primidone (Mysoline)	Double strength. Maintenance dose is 200 mg BID.

Lamictal and pregnancy: Lamotrigine is considered the safest antiepileptic for pregnancy. It is non-teratogenic, other than a small risk of cleft palate.

Since **pregnancy can reduce lamotrigine levels by 50%**, it may be necessary to dose it higher during pregnancy and decrease the dose upon childbirth. Compared with the early third trimester, postpartum lamotrigine serum levels increased an average of 172% (range 24–428%) within 5 weeks of giving birth (Clark et al, 2013).

At delivery, the mean umbilical cord lamotrigine level is 2/3 of the maternal level. In breastfed infants, the mean lamotrigine level in the child's blood is 1/3 of the maternal level, which is higher than expected with most drugs.

Conclusion: In management of bipolar disorder, lamotrigine can be combined with any mood stabilizer or antipsychotic. Lamictal plus lithium is a favorable pairing, as long as renal functioning is normal. The combination of lamotrigine and VPA may increase the risk of Stevens-Johnson syndrome. For patients on lamotrigine plus VPA or carbamazepine (CMZ), consider checking lamotrigine blood levels before discontinuation of VPA/CMZ and after lamotrigine dose is adjusted to account for reversal of inhibition/induction.

1A2 accounts for 10–15% of CYP activity in the liver

Cytochrome P450 1A2 (CYP1A2)

"One Axe to Grind; One Axe to Grow"

52% of individuals are 1A2 ultrarapid metabolizers; < 1% are poor metabolizers

"1 Axe to 2 Grind"

inDucer = Down

Decreased substrate levels

induction onsets and reverses slowly = Delayed *

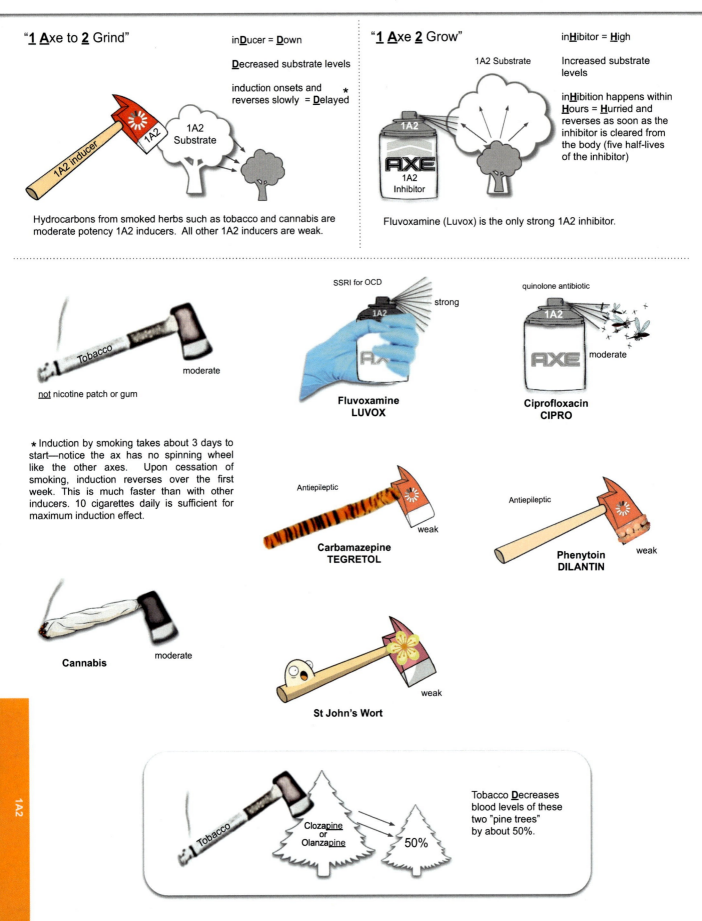

Hydrocarbons from smoked herbs such as tobacco and cannabis are moderate potency 1A2 inducers. All other 1A2 inducers are weak.

"1 Axe 2 Grow"

inHibitor = High

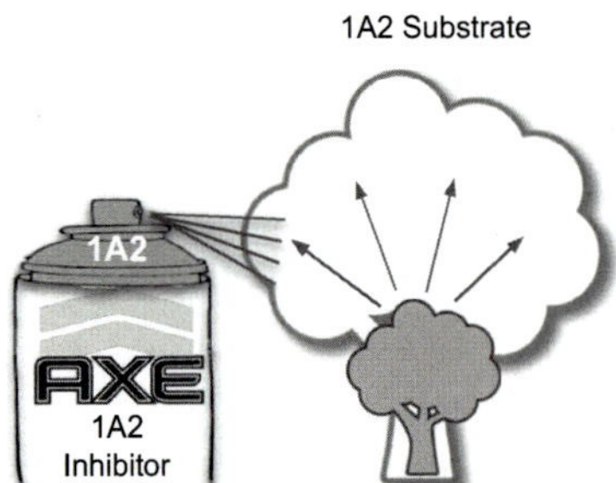

Increased substrate levels

inHibition happens within Hours = Hurried and reverses as soon as the inhibitor is cleared from the body (five half-lives of the inhibitor)

Fluvoxamine (Luvox) is the only strong 1A2 inhibitor.

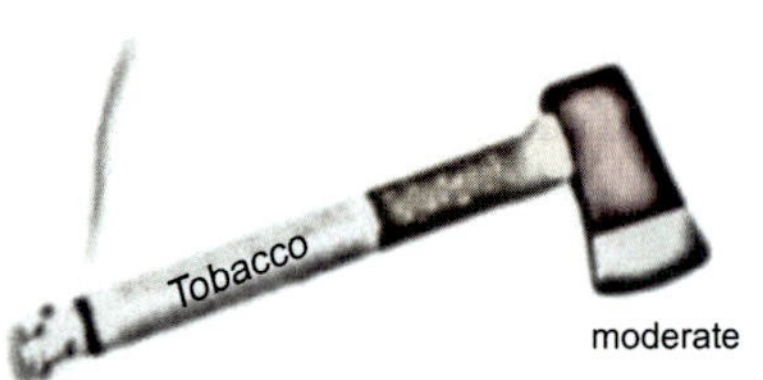

moderate

not nicotine patch or gum

SSRI for OCD

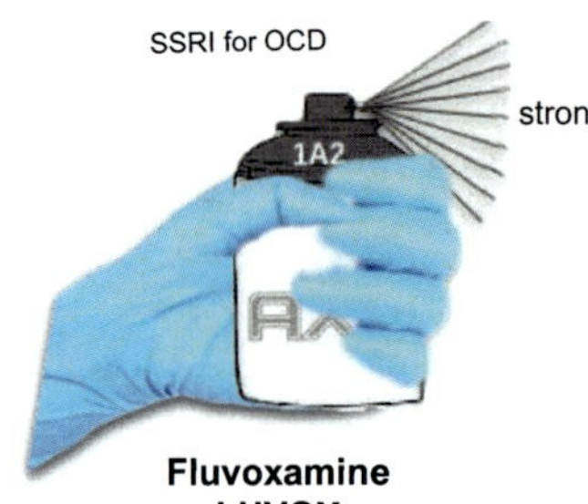

strong

Fluvoxamine
LUVOX

quinolone antibiotic

moderate

Ciprofloxacin
CIPRO

* Induction by smoking takes about 3 days to start—notice the ax has no spinning wheel like the other axes. Upon cessation of smoking, induction reverses over the first week. This is much faster than with other inducers. 10 cigarettes daily is sufficient for maximum induction effect.

Antiepileptic

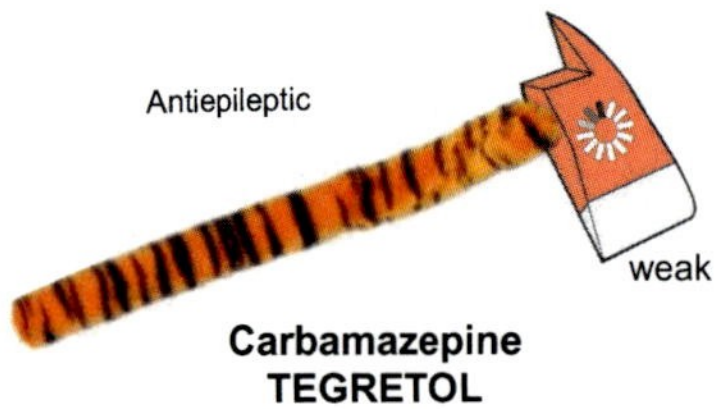

weak

Carbamazepine
TEGRETOL

Antiepileptic

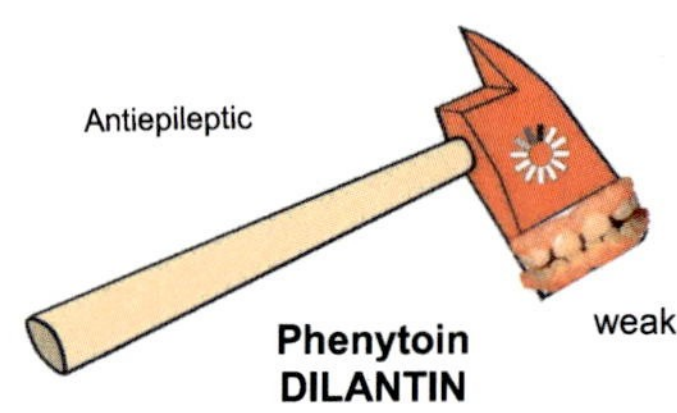

weak

Phenytoin
DILANTIN

Cannabis

moderate

weak

St John's Wort

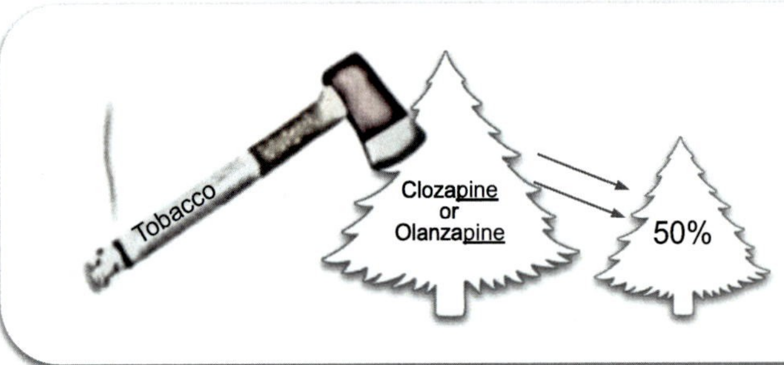

Tobacco Decreases blood levels of these two "pine trees" by about 50%.

1A2

1A2 substrates

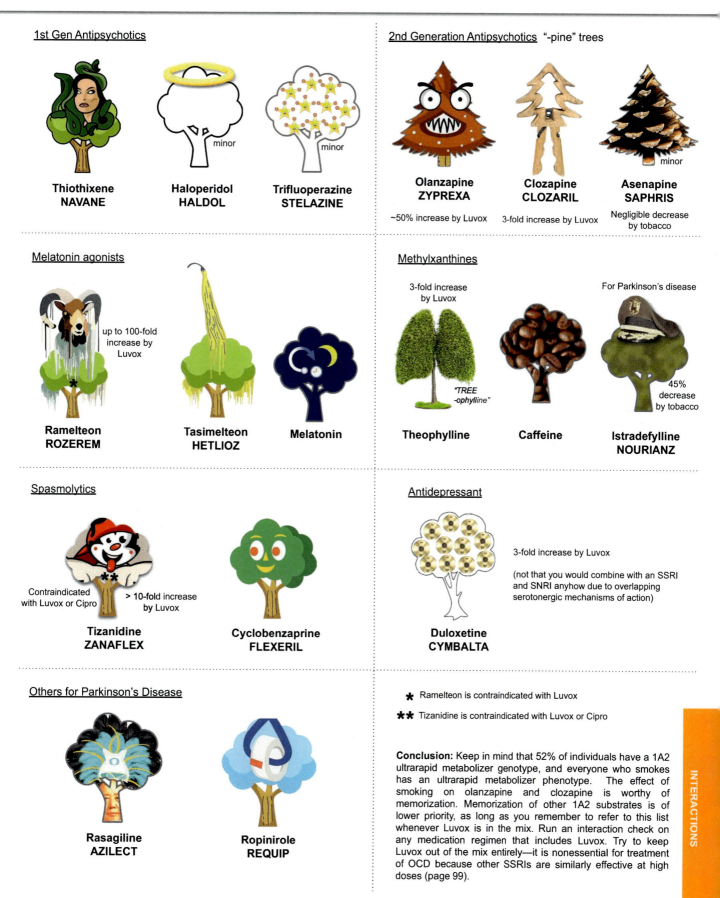

1st Gen Antipsychotics

Thiothixene
NAVANE

Haloperidol
HALDOL

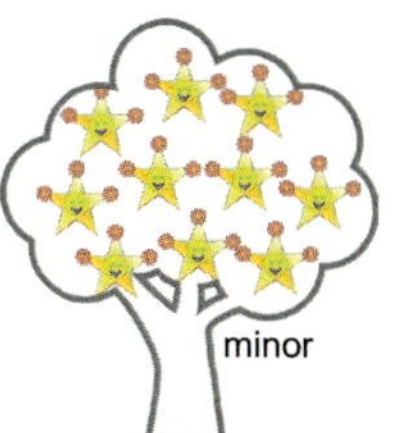

Trifluoperazine
STELAZINE

2nd Generation Antipsychotics "-pine" trees

Olanzapine
ZYPREXA

~50% increase by Luvox

Clozapine
CLOZARIL

3-fold increase by Luvox

Asenapine
SAPHRIS

Negligible decrease by tobacco

Melatonin agonists

up to 100-fold increase by Luvox

Ramelteon
ROZEREM

Tasimelteon
HETLIOZ

Melatonin

Methylxanthines

3-fold increase by Luvox

Theophylline

Caffeine

For Parkinson's disease

45% decrease by tobacco

Istradefylline
NOURIANZ

Spasmolytics

Contraindicated with Luvox or Cipro

> 10-fold increase by Luvox

Tizanidine
ZANAFLEX

Cyclobenzaprine
FLEXERIL

Antidepressant

3-fold increase by Luvox

(not that you would combine with an SSRI and SNRI anyhow due to overlapping serotonergic mechanisms of action)

Duloxetine
CYMBALTA

Others for Parkinson's Disease

Rasagiline
AZILECT

Ropinirole
REQUIP

* Ramelteon is contraindicated with Luvox

** Tizanidine is contraindicated with Luvox or Cipro

Conclusion: Keep in mind that 52% of individuals have a 1A2 ultrarapid metabolizer genotype, and everyone who smokes has an ultrarapid metabolizer phenotype. The effect of smoking on olanzapine and clozapine is worthy of memorization. Memorization of other 1A2 substrates is of lower priority, as long as you remember to refer to this list whenever Luvox is in the mix. Run an interaction check on any medication regimen that includes Luvox. Try to keep Luvox out of the mix entirely—it is nonessential for treatment of OCD because other SSRIs are similarly effective at high doses (page 99).

Cytochrome P450 2B6 (CYP2B6)

"Tube Socks"

3% of individuals are 2B6 ultrarapid metabolizers; 7% are poor metabolizers

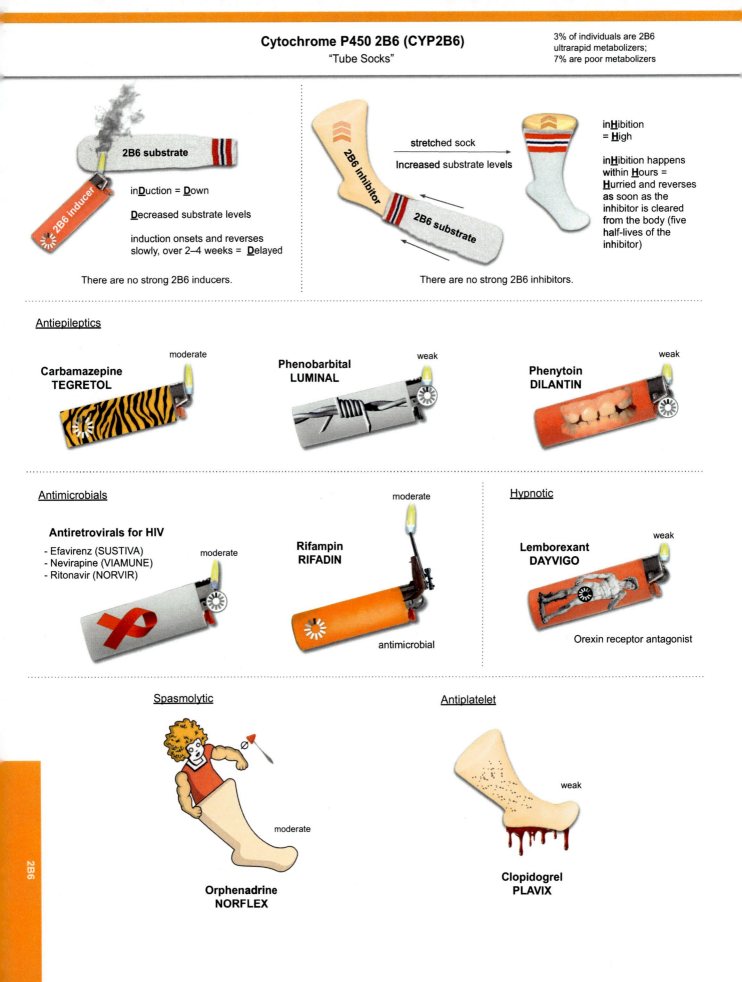

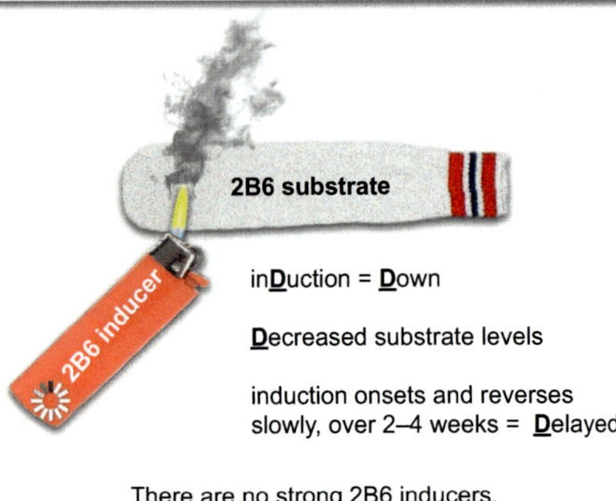

inDuction = Down

Decreased substrate levels

induction onsets and reverses slowly, over 2–4 weeks = Delayed

There are no strong 2B6 inducers.

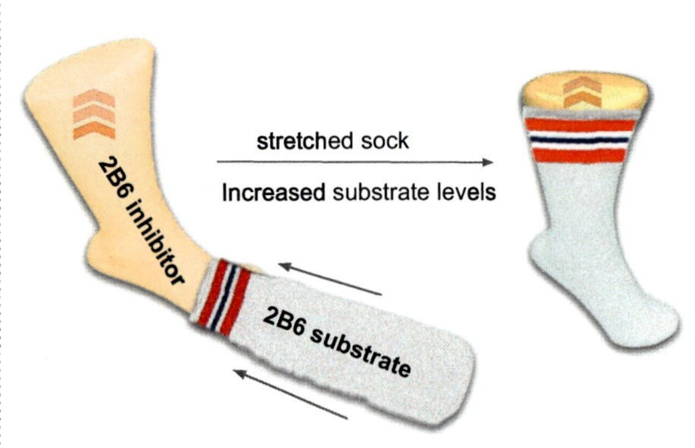

inHibition = High

inHibition happens within Hours = Hurried and reverses as soon as the inhibitor is cleared from the body (five half-lives of the inhibitor)

There are no strong 2B6 inhibitors.

Antiepileptics

Carbamazepine
TEGRETOL

moderate

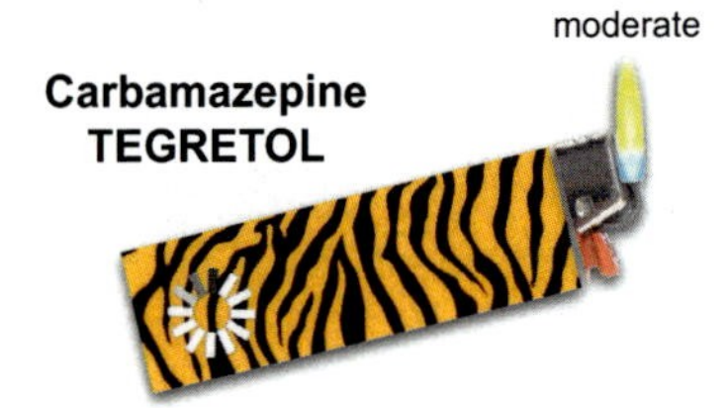

Phenobarbital
LUMINAL

weak

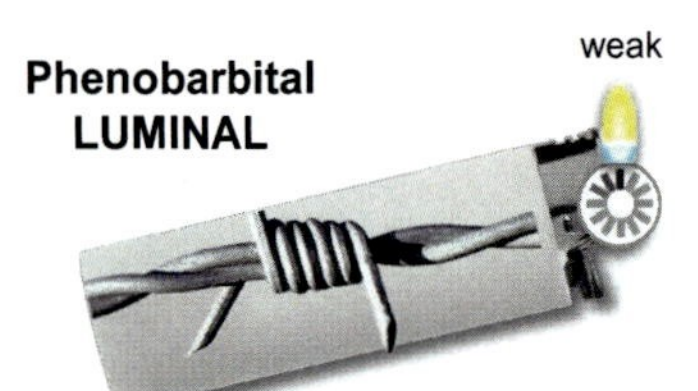

Phenytoin
DILANTIN

weak

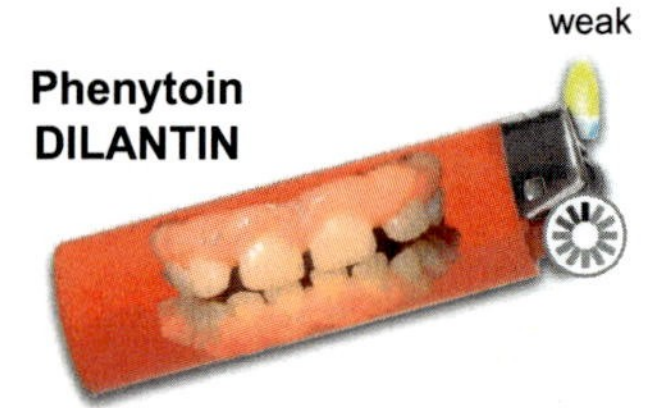

Antimicrobials

Antiretrovirals for HIV

- Efavirenz (SUSTIVA)
- Nevirapine (VIAMUNE)
- Ritonavir (NORVIR)

moderate

Rifampin
RIFADIN

moderate

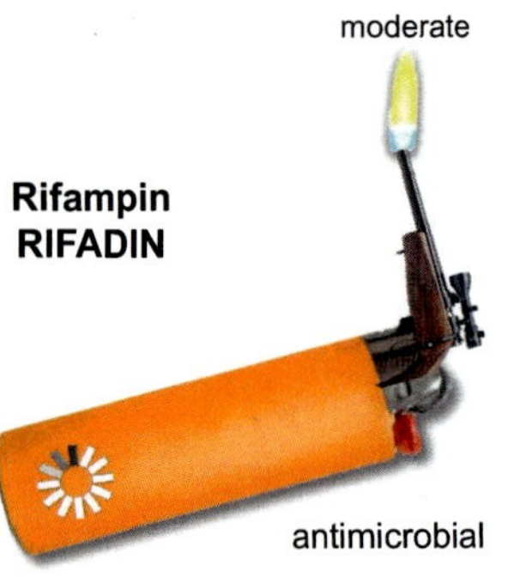

antimicrobial

Hypnotic

Lemborexant
DAYVIGO

weak

Orexin receptor antagonist

Spasmolytic

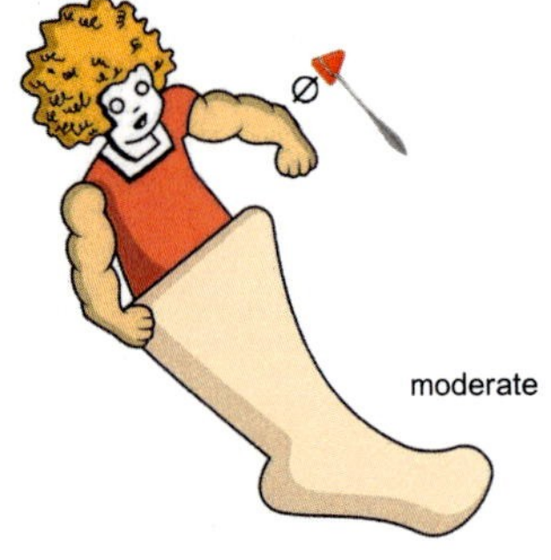

moderate

Orphenadrine
NORFLEX

Antiplatelet

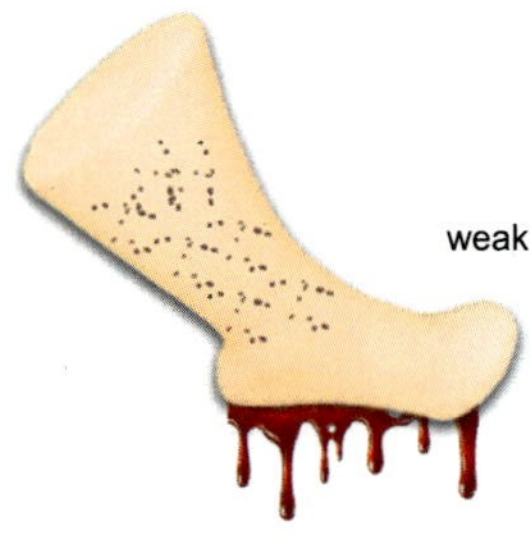

weak

Clopidogrel
PLAVIX

2B6

2B6 substrates

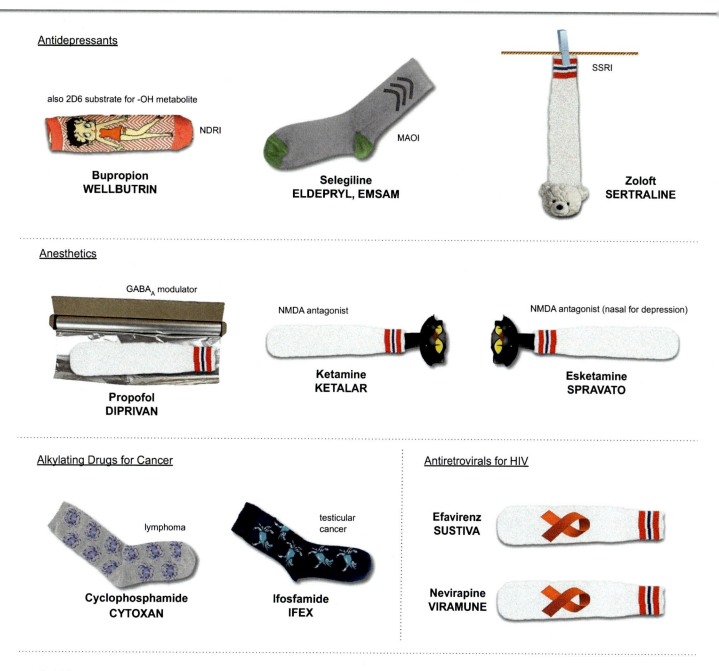

Antidepressants

also 2D6 substrate for -OH metabolite

NDRI

Bupropion
WELLBUTRIN

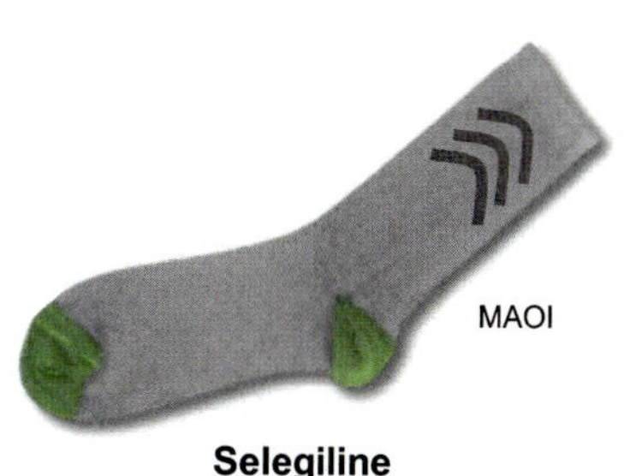

MAOI

Selegiline
ELDEPRYL, EMSAM

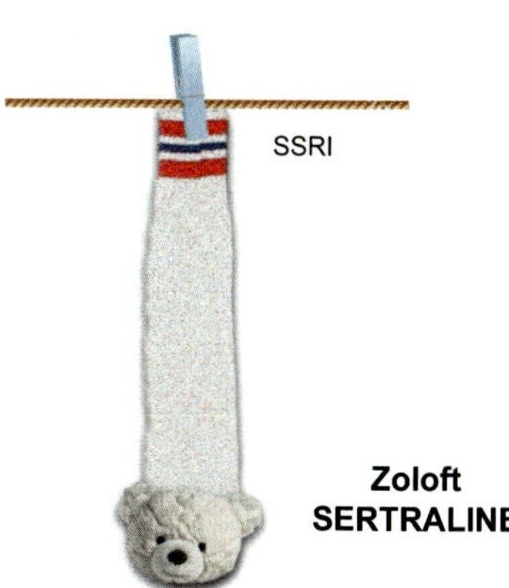

SSRI

Zoloft
SERTRALINE

Anesthetics

GABA$_A$ modulator

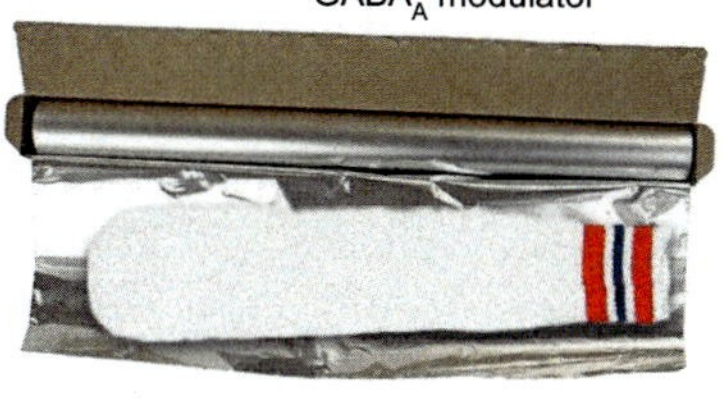

Propofol
DIPRIVAN

NMDA antagonist

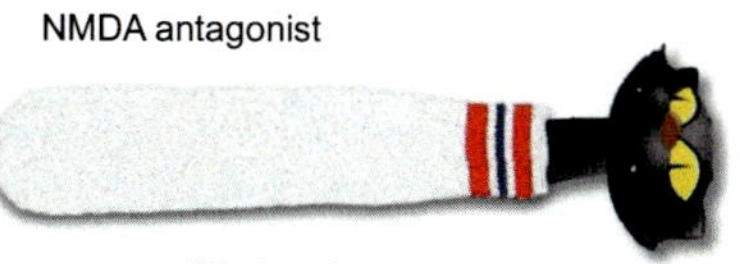

Ketamine
KETALAR

NMDA antagonist (nasal for depression)

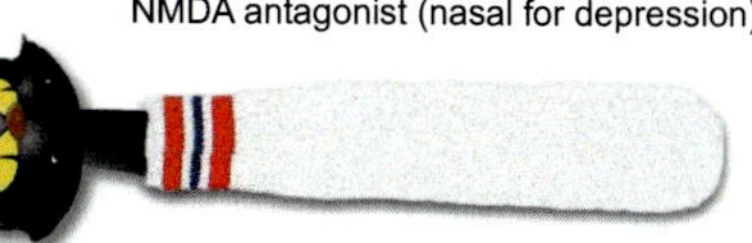

Esketamine
SPRAVATO

Alkylating Drugs for Cancer

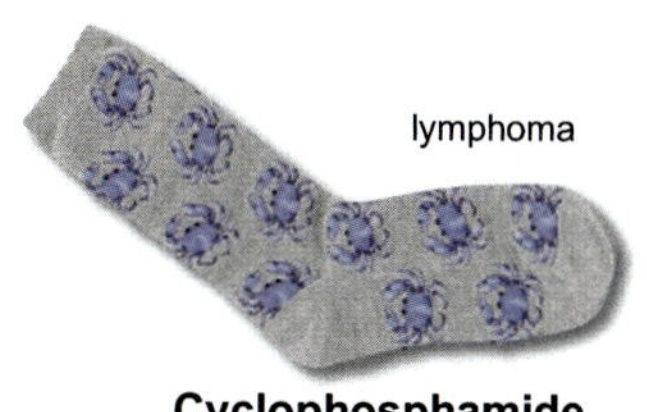

lymphoma

Cyclophosphamide
CYTOXAN

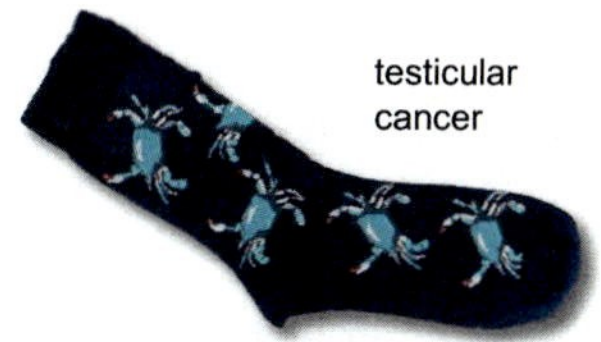

testicular cancer

Ifosfamide
IFEX

Antiretrovirals for HIV

Efavirenz
SUSTIVA

Nevirapine
VIRAMUNE

Opioid

Methadone
DOLOPHINE

3% of the population are 2B6 ultrarapid metabolizers (UMs). Methadone will be poorly effective for these individuals, and their methadone drug screen may be negative.

Conclusion: Fortunately, there are no strong inhibitors or inducers of 2B6. For psychiatrists, 2B6 is of minimal significance, unless methadone is being prescribed (see above). You will want to run an interaction check (e.g., ePocrates or Lexicomp) whenever a medication regimen includes a shredder, cancer medication, HIV medication, or systemic antifungal.

For psychiatry, 2C9 interactions are of little clinical significance.

Cytochrome P450 2C9 (CYP2C9)

"To See Nice(ly)"

0% of individuals are 2C9 ultrarapid metabolizers; 5% are poor metabolizers

2C9 substrate

2C9 inducer

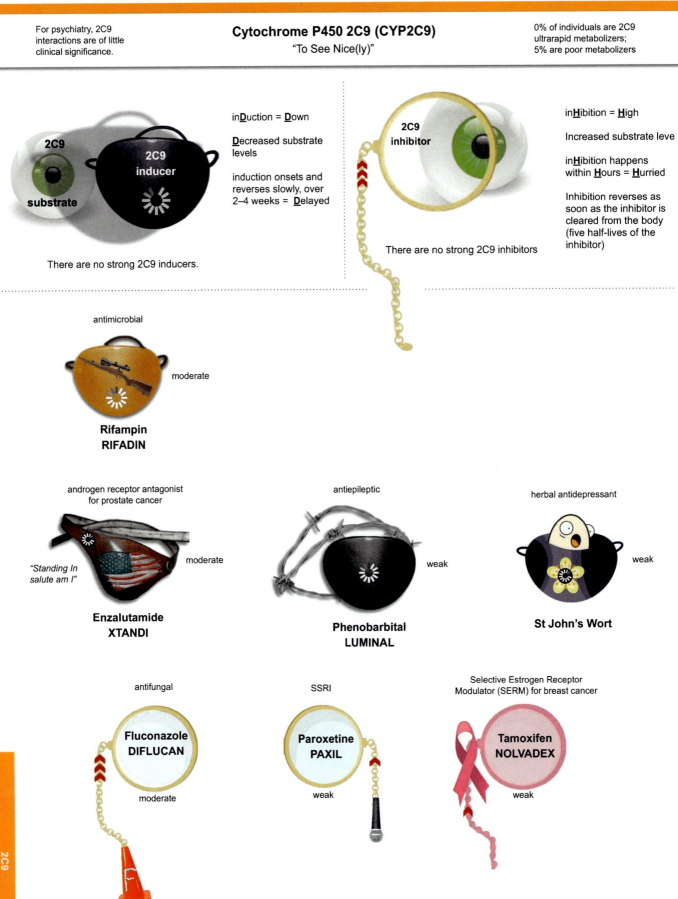

in**D**uction = **D**own

Decreased substrate levels

induction onsets and reverses slowly, over 2–4 weeks = **D**elayed

There are no strong 2C9 inducers.

2C9 inhibitor

in**H**ibition = **H**igh

Increased substrate leve

in**H**ibition happens within **H**ours = **H**urried

Inhibition reverses as soon as the inhibitor is cleared from the body (five half-lives of the inhibitor)

There are no strong 2C9 inhibitors

antimicrobial

moderate

Rifampin
RIFADIN

androgen receptor antagonist for prostate cancer

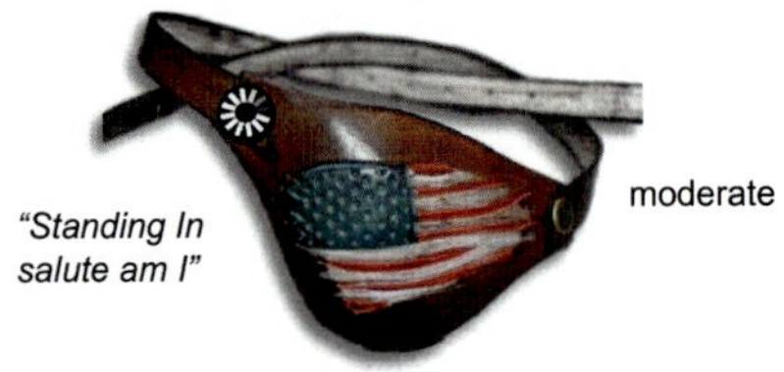

moderate

Enzalutamide
XTANDI

antiepileptic

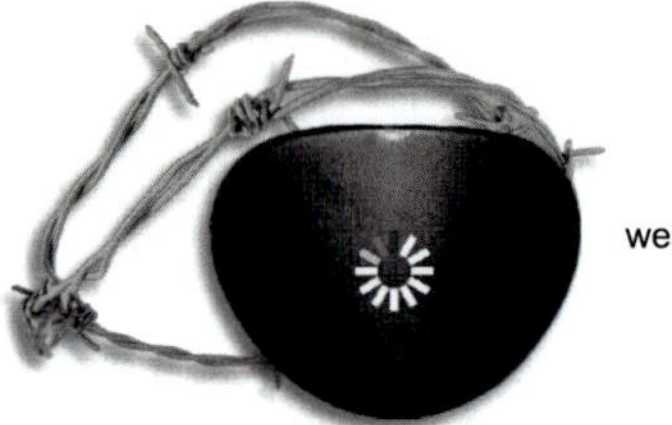

weak

Phenobarbital
LUMINAL

herbal antidepressant

weak

St John's Wort

antifungal

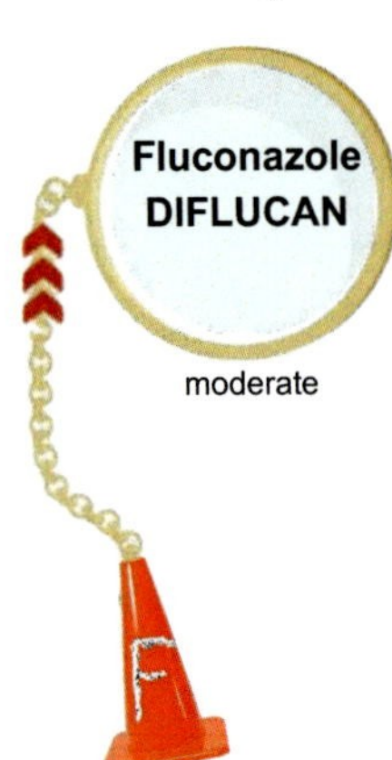

moderate

SSRI

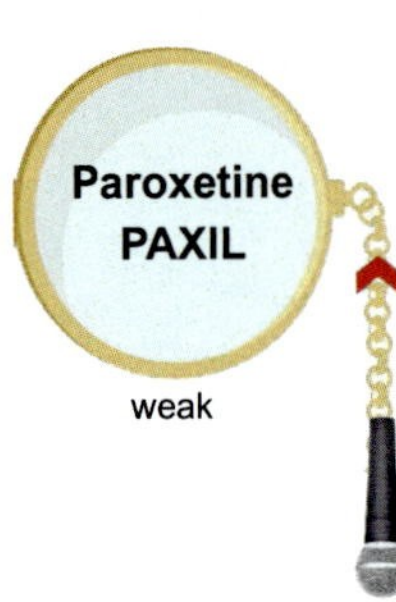

weak

Selective Estrogen Receptor Modulator (SERM) for breast cancer

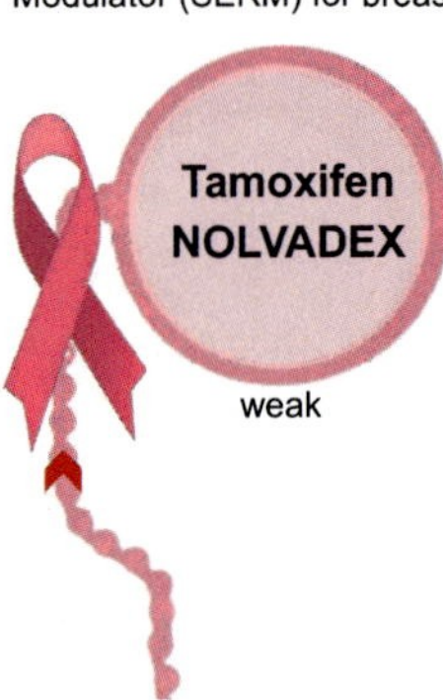

weak

2C9 substrates

0% of individuals are 2C9 ultrarapid metabolizers; 5% are poor metabolizers

Antiepileptics

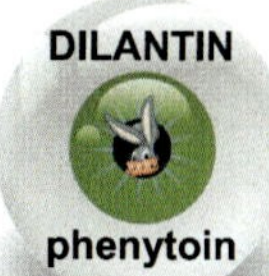

Also 2C19

"d-EYE-lantin; phen-EYE-toin"

minor
- 2C9 contributes only 25% to the metabolism of VPA

Libido enhancer

Also 2C19

Sulfonylureas for DM

"glybur-EYED"

"glimepir-EYED"

"Glipiz-EYED"

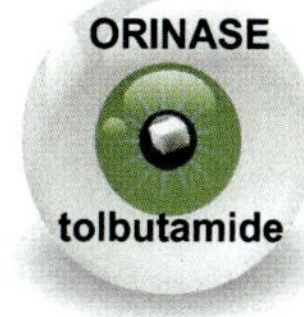

"tolbutam-EYED"

sugar cube

Anticoagulant

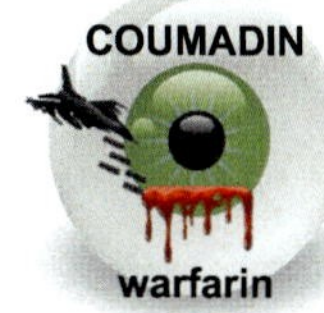

"Warfare Comin' down"

Also 2C19

"coum-EYE-din"

ARB for HTN

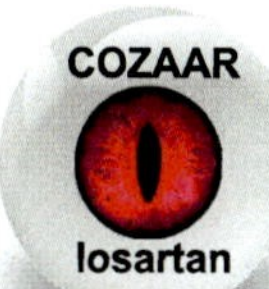

"Cozier (with) Lord Satan"

Also 3A4

"Coz-EYEr"

Lipid lowering

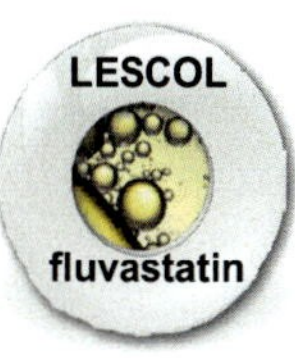

"fluv-EYE-statin"

NSAID

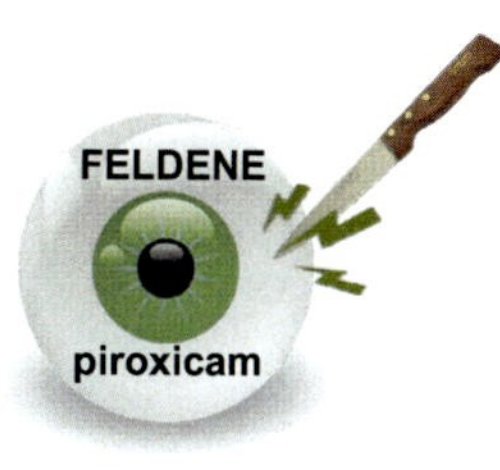

"p-EYE-roxicam"

COX-2 inhibitor

"2 Celebrating Cocks"

"cel-EYE-brex"

Conclusion: 2C9 interactions don't involve psychotropic medications, other than valproic acid. Check VPA levels more often if the patient is taking or stops taking enzalutamide, rifampin, or diflucan; but don't expect much variance from baseline.

Cytochrome P450 2C19 (CYP2C19)

"To See Nice Things (grow)"

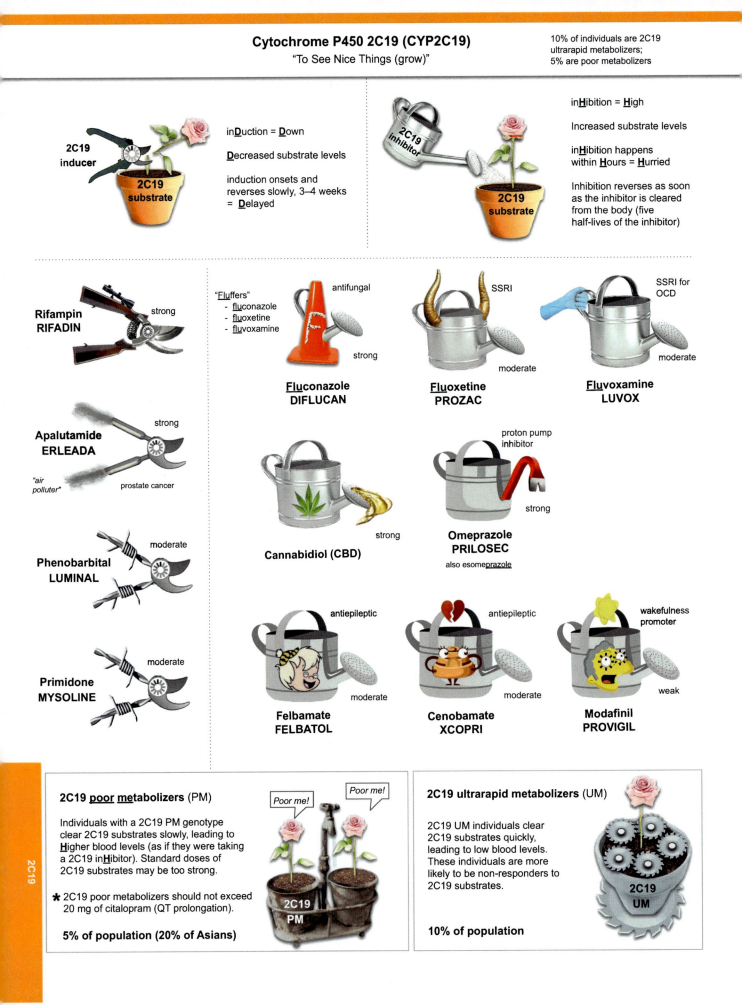

10% of individuals are 2C19 ultrarapid metabolizers; 5% are poor metabolizers

2C19 inducer

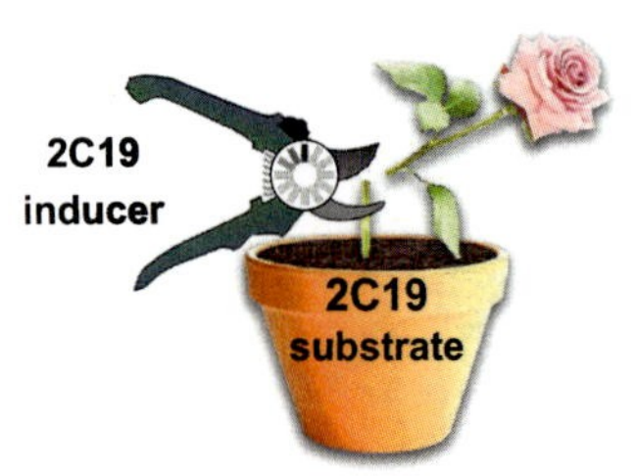

in**D**uction = **D**own

Decreased substrate levels

induction onsets and reverses slowly, 3–4 weeks = **D**elayed

in**H**ibition = **H**igh

Increased substrate levels

in**H**ibition happens within **H**ours = **H**urried

Inhibition reverses as soon as the inhibitor is cleared from the body (five half-lives of the inhibitor)

Rifampin
RIFADIN

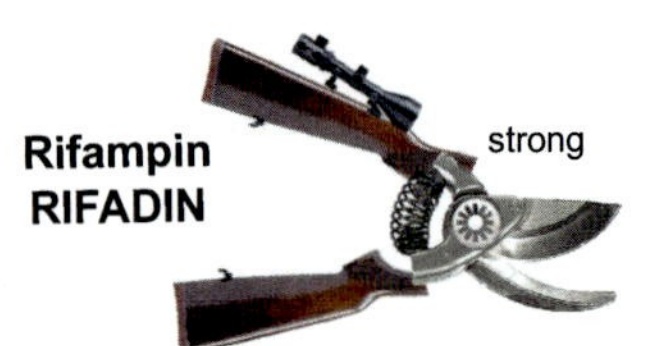

strong

Apalutamide
ERLEADA

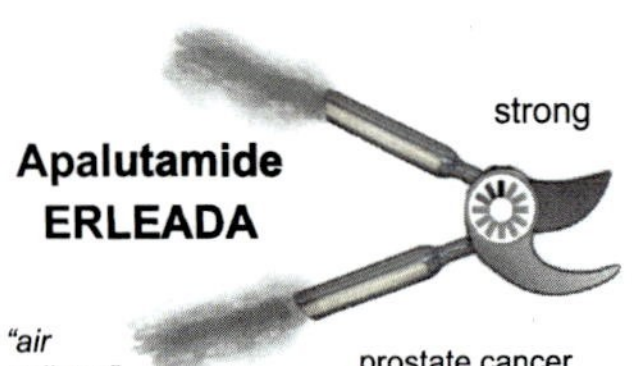

strong

"air polluter"

prostate cancer

Phenobarbital
LUMINAL

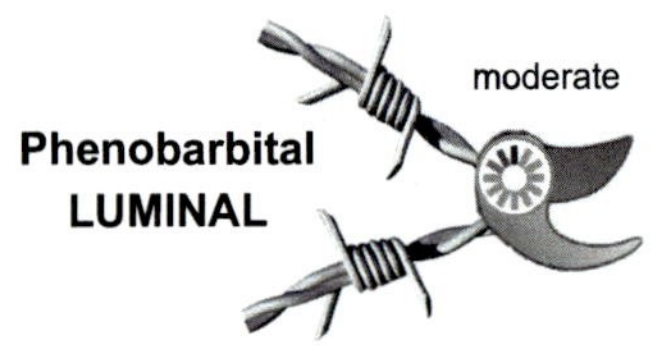

moderate

Primidone
MYSOLINE

moderate

"**Flu**ffers"
- **flu**conazole
- **flu**oxetine
- **flu**voxamine

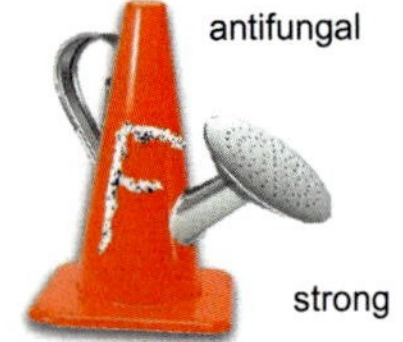

antifungal

strong

Fluconazole
DIFLUCAN

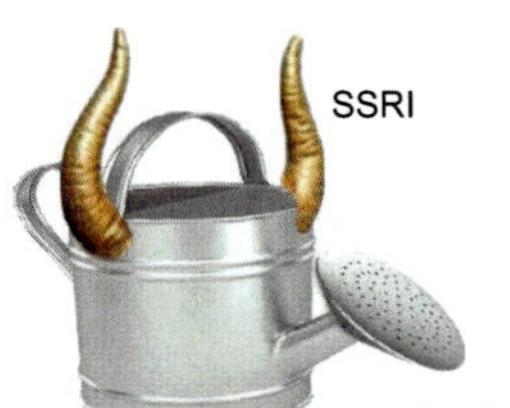

SSRI

moderate

Fluoxetine
PROZAC

SSRI for OCD

moderate

Fluvoxamine
LUVOX

strong

Cannabidiol (CBD)

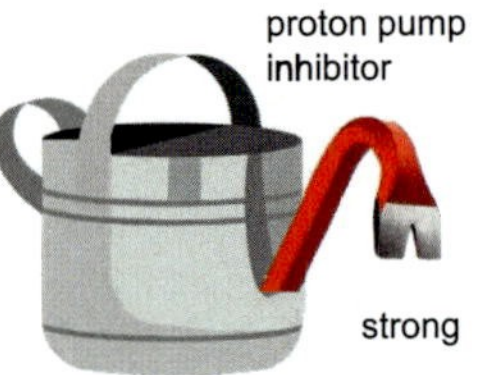

proton pump inhibitor

strong

Omeprazole
PRILOSEC

also esome**prazole**

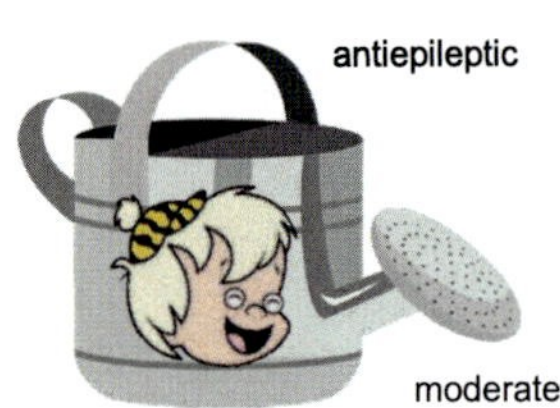

antiepileptic

moderate

Felbamate
FELBATOL

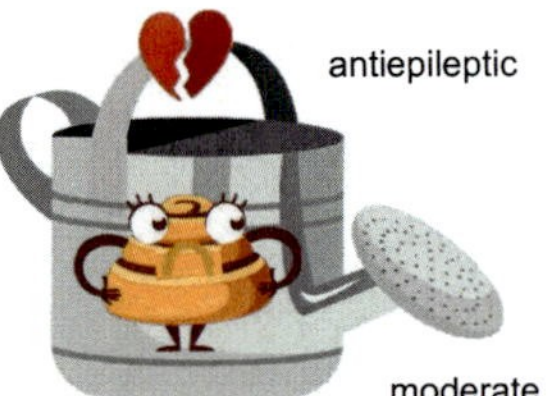

antiepileptic

moderate

Cenobamate
XCOPRI

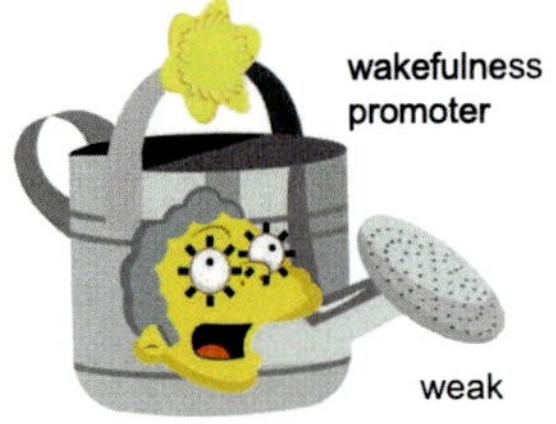

wakefulness promoter

weak

Modafinil
PROVIGIL

2C19 poor metabolizers (PM)

Individuals with a 2C19 PM genotype clear 2C19 substrates slowly, leading to **H**igher blood levels (as if they were taking a 2C19 in**H**ibitor). Standard doses of 2C19 substrates may be too strong.

* 2C19 poor metabolizers should not exceed 20 mg of citalopram (QT prolongation).

5% of population (20% of Asians)

2C19 ultrarapid metabolizers (UM)

2C19 UM individuals clear 2C19 substrates quickly, leading to low blood levels. These individuals are more likely to be non-responders to 2C19 substrates.

10% of population

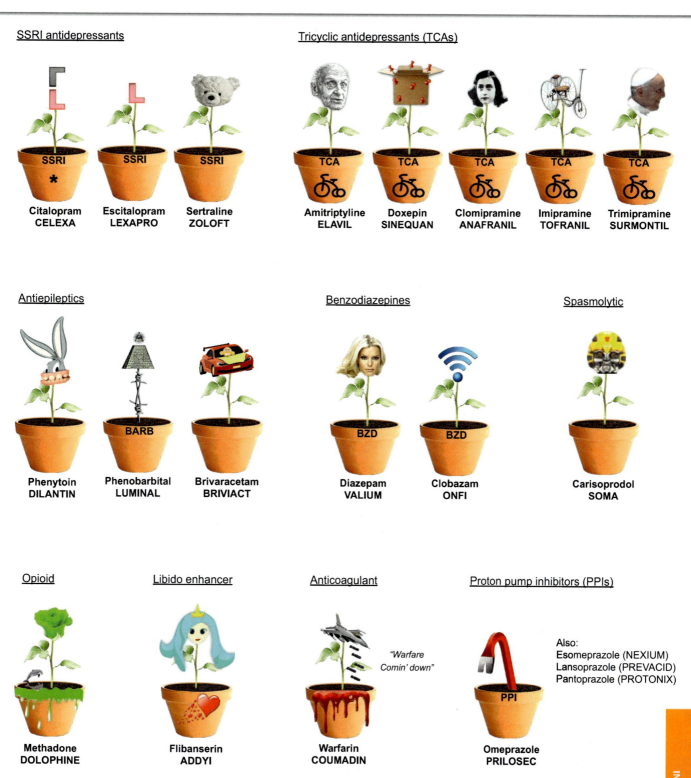

SSRI antidepressants

Citalopram CELEXA — **Escitalopram LEXAPRO** — **Sertraline ZOLOFT**

Tricyclic antidepressants (TCAs)

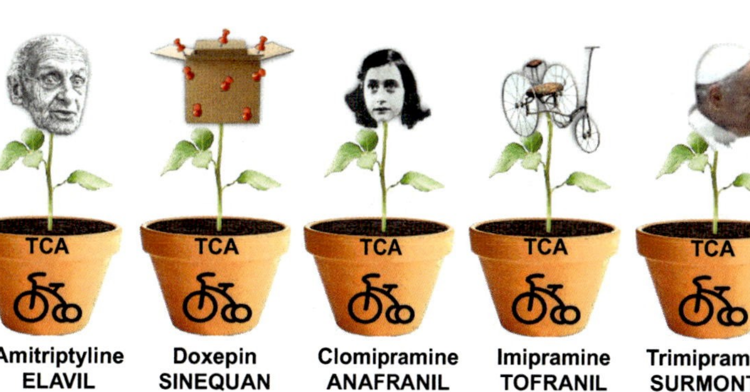

Amitriptyline ELAVIL — **Doxepin SINEQUAN** — **Clomipramine ANAFRANIL** — **Imipramine TOFRANIL** — **Trimipramine SURMONTIL**

Antiepileptics

Phenytoin DILANTIN

Phenobarbital LUMINAL

Brivaracetam BRIVIACT

Benzodiazepines

Diazepam VALIUM — **Clobazam ONFI**

Spasmolytic

Carisoprodol SOMA

Opioid

Methadone DOLOPHINE

Libido enhancer

Flibanserin ADDYI

Anticoagulant

"Warfare Comin' down"

Warfarin COUMADIN

Proton pump inhibitors (PPIs)

Omeprazole PRILOSEC

Also:
Esomeprazole (NEXIUM)
Lansoprazole (PREVACID)
Pantoprazole (PROTONIX)

Conclusion: 2C19 genotyping is not typically ordered as a standalone test, but if 2C19 metabolizer genotype is known (e.g., from GeneSight or Genecept), the information can be put to good use when dosing (es)citalopram and sertraline. Knowledge of metabolizer status is not essential because these SSRIs can be titrated the old-fashioned way, according to response and side effects. In any event, avoid prescribing Soma, Valium, or phenobarbital for anxiety due to their particularly high risk of abuse and dependence. Avoid St. John's Wort due to interactions and because it only works for mild depression.

2D6 metabolizes ~ 12% of prescription drugs. Notice how all of the –oxetine's are 2D6 inhibitors and/or substrates.

Cytochrome P450 2D6 (CYP2D6)

"Too Darn Sexy"

5% of individuals are 2D6 ultrarapid metabolizers (UM).
10% are poor metabolizers (PM).

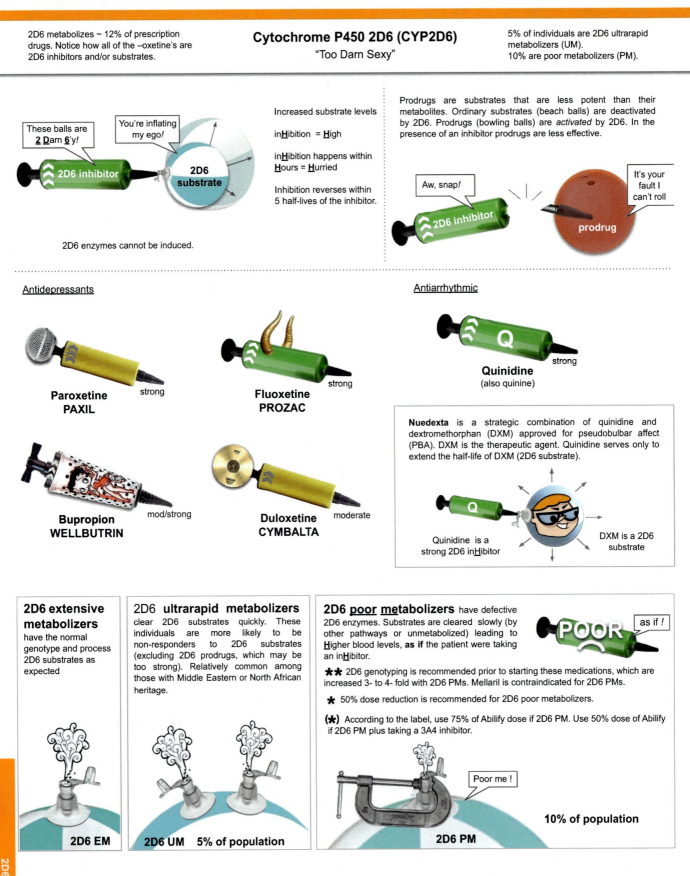

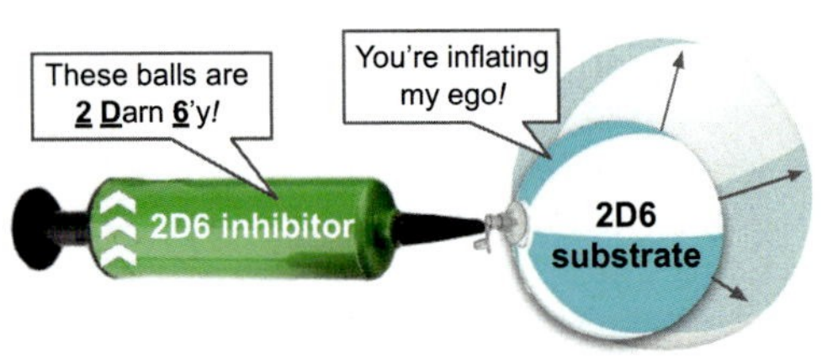
These balls are 2 Darn 6'y!
You're inflating my ego!
2D6 inhibitor
2D6 substrate

2D6 enzymes cannot be induced.

Increased substrate levels

inHibition = High

inHibition happens within Hours = Hurried

Inhibition reverses within 5 half-lives of the inhibitor.

Prodrugs are substrates that are less potent than their metabolites. Ordinary substrates (beach balls) are deactivated by 2D6. Prodrugs (bowling balls) are *activated* by 2D6. In the presence of an inhibitor prodrugs are less effective.

Aw, snap!
2D6 inhibitor
It's your fault I can't roll
prodrug

Antidepressants

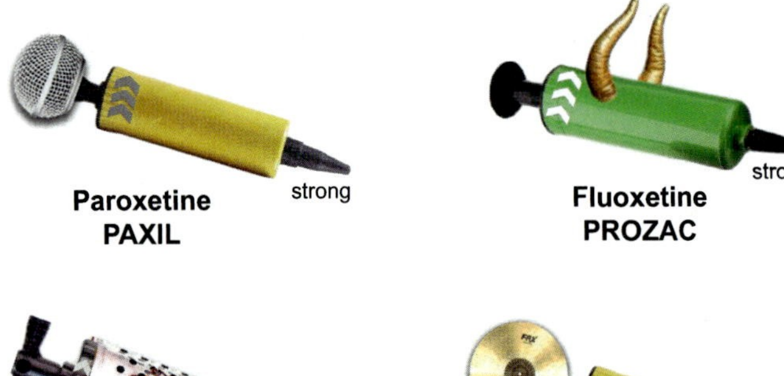

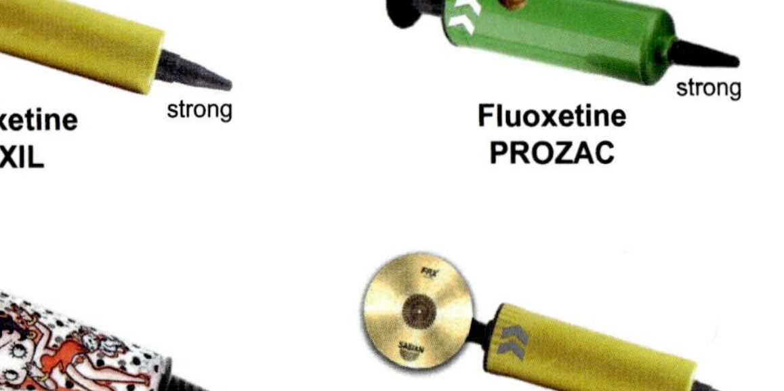

Paroxetine strong
PAXIL

Fluoxetine strong
PROZAC

Bupropion mod/strong
WELLBUTRIN

Duloxetine moderate
CYMBALTA

Antiarrhythmic

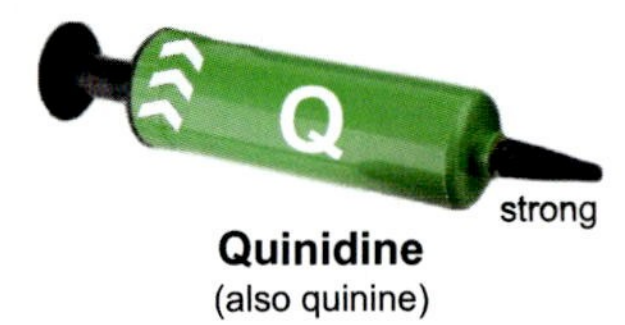
Q

Quinidine strong
(also quinine)

Nuedexta is a strategic combination of quinidine and dextromethorphan (DXM) approved for pseudobulbar affect (PBA). DXM is the therapeutic agent. Quinidine serves only to extend the half-life of DXM (2D6 substrate).

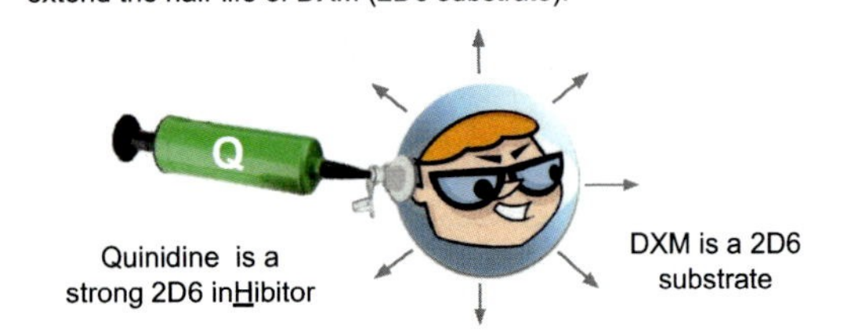
Q
Quinidine is a strong 2D6 inHibitor
DXM is a 2D6 substrate

2D6 extensive metabolizers have the normal genotype and process 2D6 substrates as expected

2D6 EM

2D6 **ultrarapid metabolizers** clear 2D6 substrates quickly. These individuals are more likely to be non-responders to 2D6 substrates (excluding 2D6 prodrugs, which may be too strong). Relatively common among those with Middle Eastern or North African heritage.

2D6 UM 5% of population

2D6 poor metabolizers have defective 2D6 enzymes. Substrates are cleared slowly (by other pathways or unmetabolized) leading to Higher blood levels, **as if** the patient were taking an inHibitor.

POOR
as if !

★★ 2D6 genotyping is recommended prior to starting these medications, which are increased 3- to 4- fold with 2D6 PMs. Mellaril is contraindicated for 2D6 PMs.

★ 50% dose reduction is recommended for 2D6 poor metabolizers.

(★) According to the label, use 75% of Abilify dose if 2D6 PM. Use 50% dose of Abilify if 2D6 PM plus taking a 3A4 inhibitor.

Poor me !
2D6 PM

10% of population

Conclusion: 2D6 interactions need to be understood by prescribers of antidepressants and antipsychotics. To avoid 2D6 interactions, use Lexapro or Zoloft instead of Prozac or Paxil.

Among the CYP genetic assays, 2D6 is the most useful. The test is about $200 as a standalone, and is recommended prior to starting Trilafon, Mellaril, or Pimozide. Psychiatrists rarely prescribe those three drugs anyhow. For the other 2D6 substrates, serum drug levels may be more useful than genotyping. The author commonly checks blood levels of haloperidol, risperidone, and aripiprazole if there are issues with efficacy or tolerability.

2D6 substrates

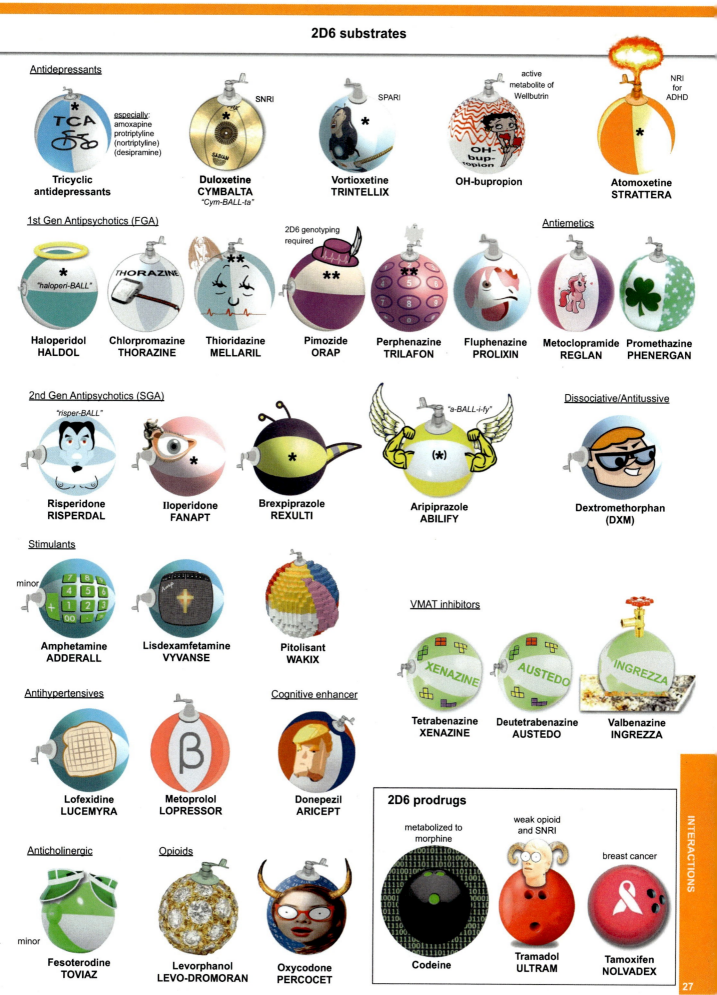

Antidepressants

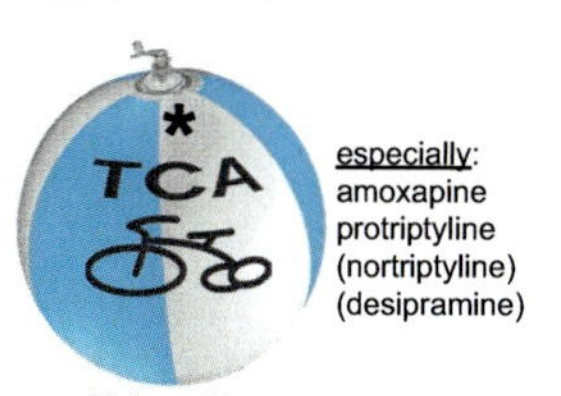

especially:
amoxapine
protriptyline
(nortriptyline)
(desipramine)

Tricyclic antidepressants

SNRI

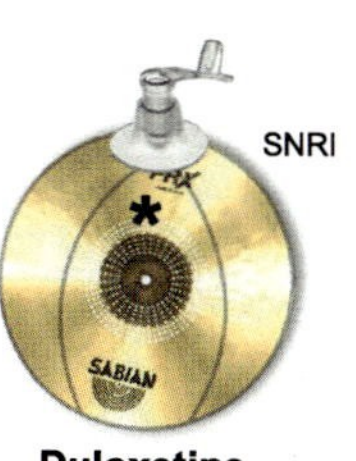

Duloxetine
CYMBALTA
"Cym-BALL-ta"

SPARI

Vortioxetine
TRINTELLIX

active metabolite of Wellbutrin

OH-bupropion

NRI for ADHD

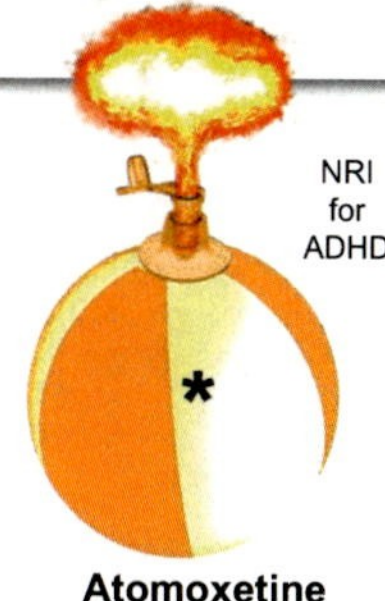

Atomoxetine
STRATTERA

1st Gen Antipsychotics (FGA)

Haloperidol
HALDOL

Chlorpromazine
THORAZINE

Thioridazine
MELLARIL

2D6 genotyping required

Pimozide
ORAP

Perphenazine
TRILAFON

Fluphenazine
PROLIXIN

Antiemetics

Metoclopramide
REGLAN

Promethazine
PHENERGAN

2nd Gen Antipsychotics (SGA)

"risper-BALL"

Risperidone
RISPERDAL

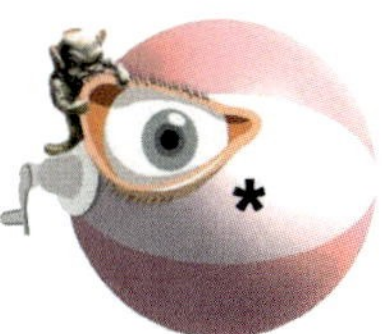

Iloperidone
FANAPT

Brexpiprazole
REXULTI

"a-BALL-i-fy"

Aripiprazole
ABILIFY

Dissociative/Antitussive

Dextromethorphan
(DXM)

Stimulants

minor

Amphetamine
ADDERALL

Lisdexamfetamine
VYVANSE

Pitolisant
WAKIX

VMAT inhibitors

Tetrabenazine
XENAZINE

Deutetrabenazine
AUSTEDO

Valbenazine
INGREZZA

Antihypertensives

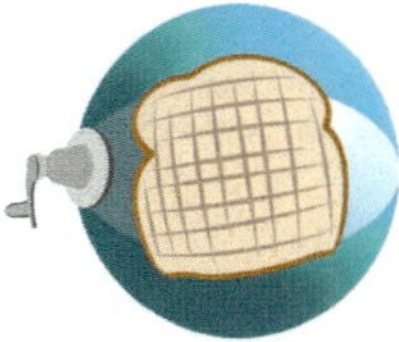

Lofexidine
LUCEMYRA

Metoprolol
LOPRESSOR

Cognitive enhancer

Donepezil
ARICEPT

Anticholinergic

minor

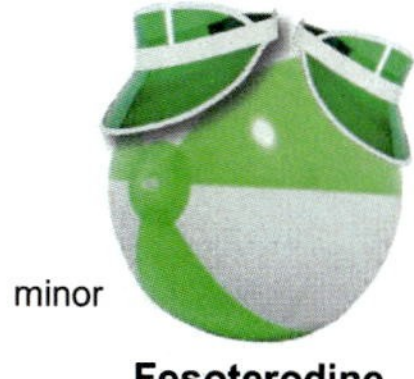

Fesoterodine
TOVIAZ

Opioids

Levorphanol
LEVO-DROMORAN

Oxycodone
PERCOCET

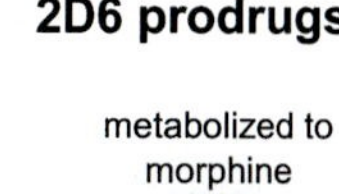

2D6 prodrugs

metabolized to morphine

Codeine

weak opioid and SNRI

Tramadol
ULTRAM

breast cancer

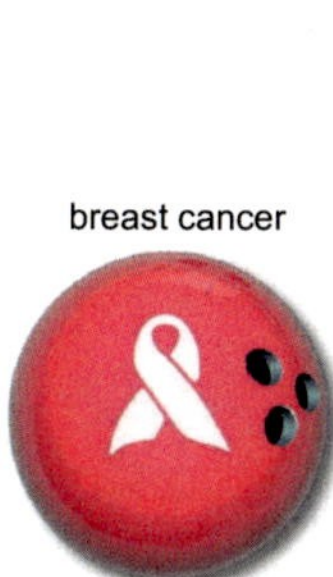

Tamoxifen
NOLVADEX

> 50% of prescription drugs are 3A4 substrates—plenty of fish!

Cytochrome P450 3A4 (CYP3A4)

"3 A's For (fishing)"

0% of individuals are 3A4 ultrarapid metabolizers; <1% are poor metabolizers

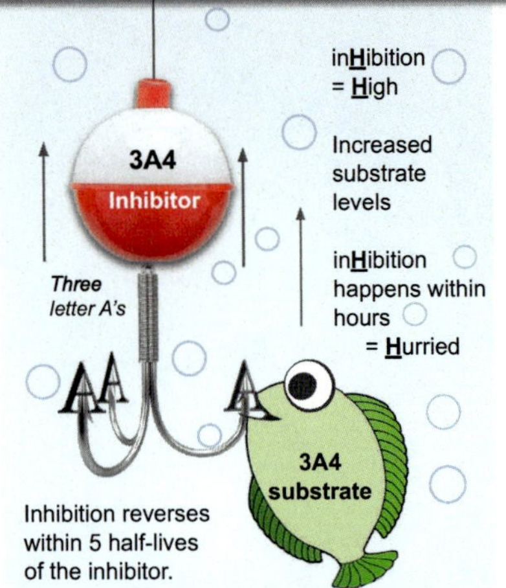

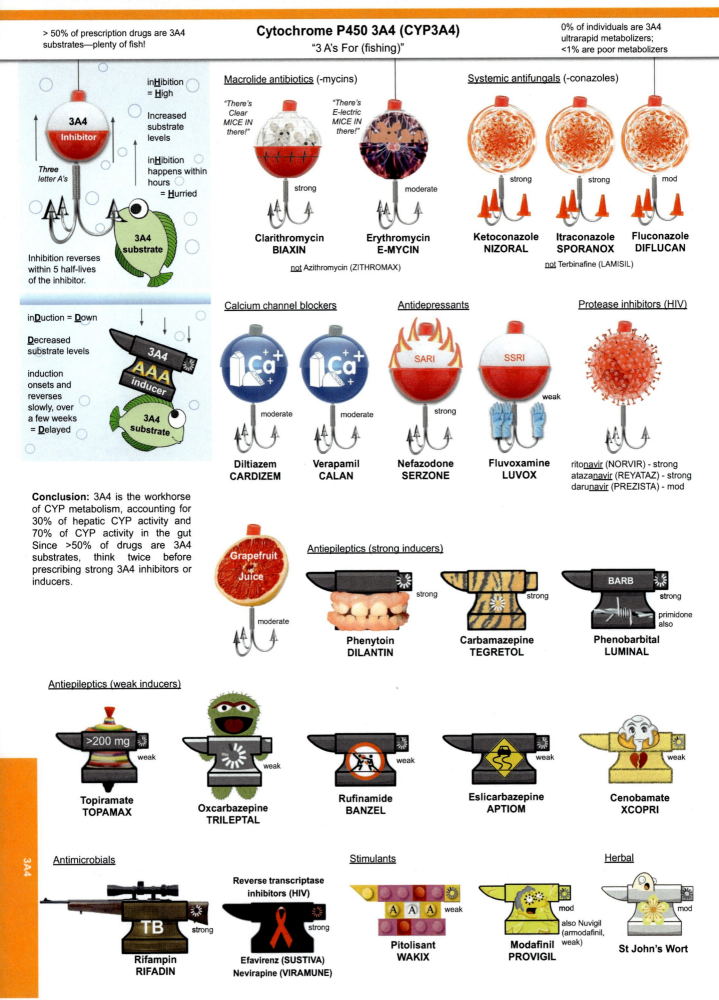

inHibition = High

Increased substrate levels

inHibition happens within hours = Hurried

Inhibition reverses within 5 half-lives of the inhibitor.

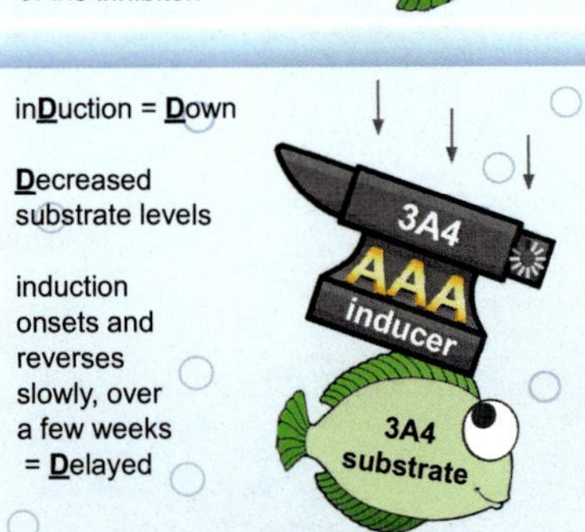

inDuction = Down

Decreased substrate levels

induction onsets and reverses slowly, over a few weeks = Delayed

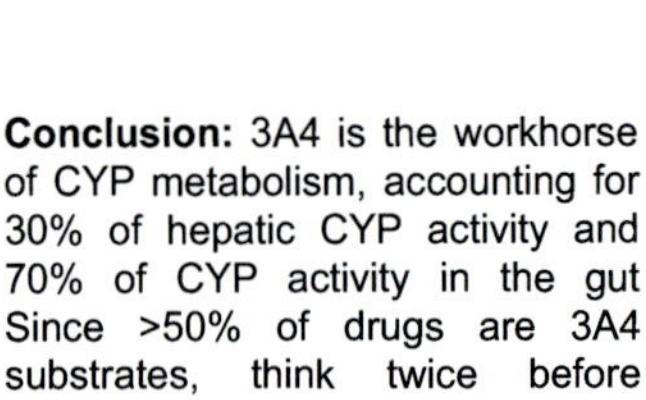

Conclusion: 3A4 is the workhorse of CYP metabolism, accounting for 30% of hepatic CYP activity and 70% of CYP activity in the gut Since >50% of drugs are 3A4 substrates, think twice before prescribing strong 3A4 inhibitors or inducers.

Macrolide antibiotics (-mycins)

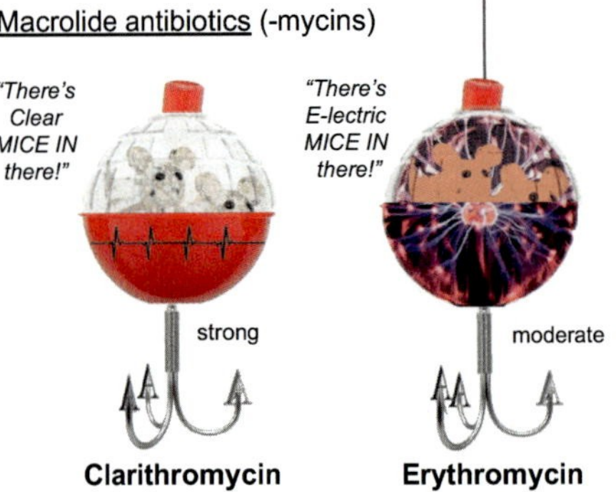

Clarithromycin BIAXIN

Erythromycin E-MYCIN

not Azithromycin (ZITHROMAX)

Systemic antifungals (-conazoles)

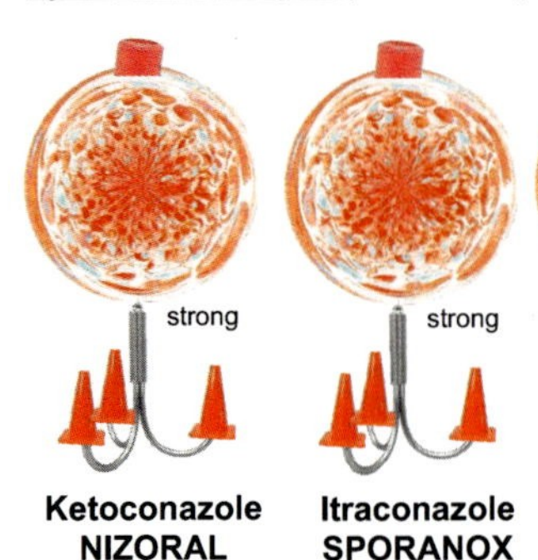
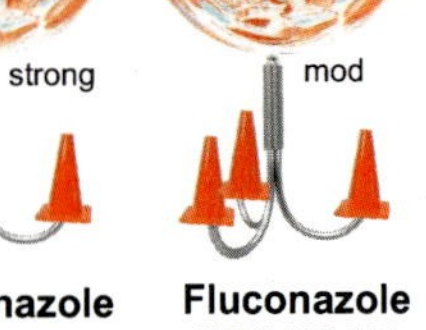

Ketoconazole NIZORAL

Itraconazole SPORANOX

Fluconazole DIFLUCAN

not Terbinafine (LAMISIL)

Calcium channel blockers

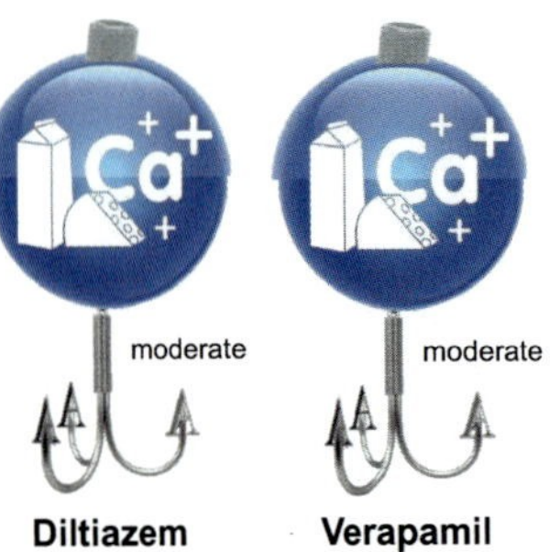

Diltiazem CARDIZEM

Verapamil CALAN

Antidepressants

Nefazodone SERZONE

Fluvoxamine LUVOX

Protease inhibitors (HIV)

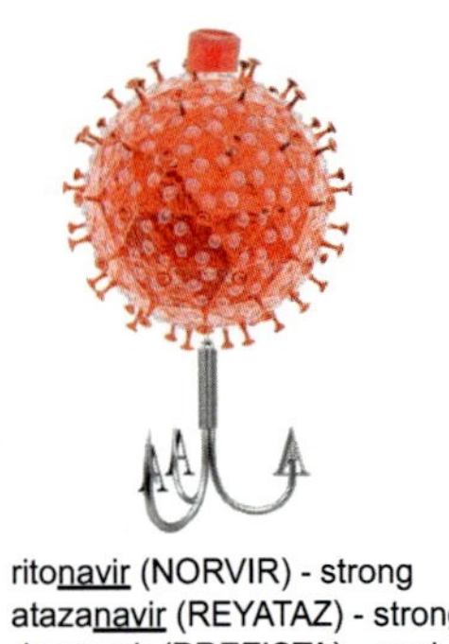

ritonavir (NORVIR) - strong
atazanavir (REYATAZ) - strong
darunavir (PREZISTA) - mod

Antiepileptics (strong inducers)

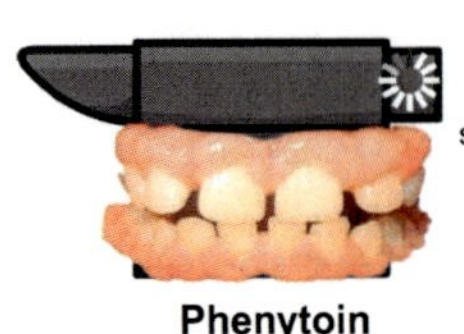

Phenytoin DILANTIN

Carbamazepine TEGRETOL

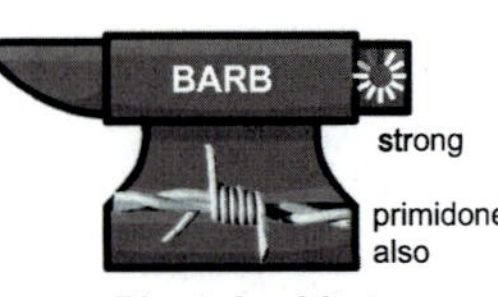

Phenobarbital LUMINAL

Antiepileptics (weak inducers)

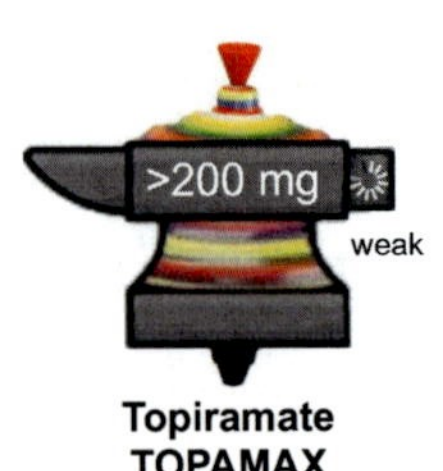

Topiramate TOPAMAX

Oxcarbazepine TRILEPTAL

Rufinamide BANZEL

Eslicarbazepine APTIOM

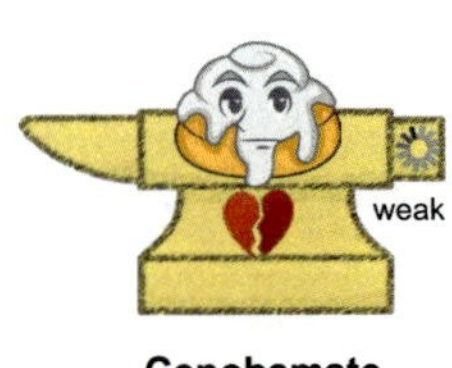

Cenobamate XCOPRI

Antimicrobials

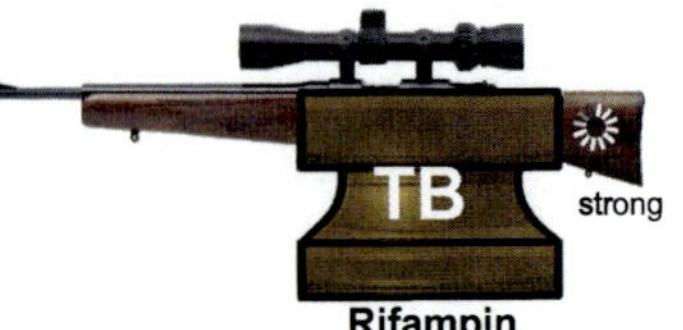

Rifampin RIFADIN

Reverse transcriptase inhibitors (HIV)

strong

Efavirenz (SUSTIVA)
Nevirapine (VIRAMUNE)

Stimulants

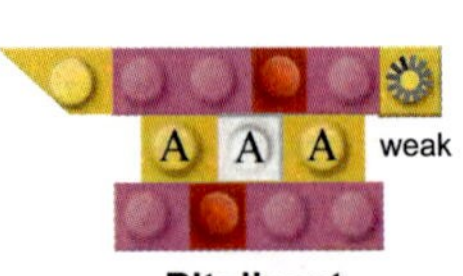

Pitolisant WAKIX

also Nuvigil (armodafinil, weak)

Modafinil PROVIGIL

Herbal

St John's Wort

3A4 substrates

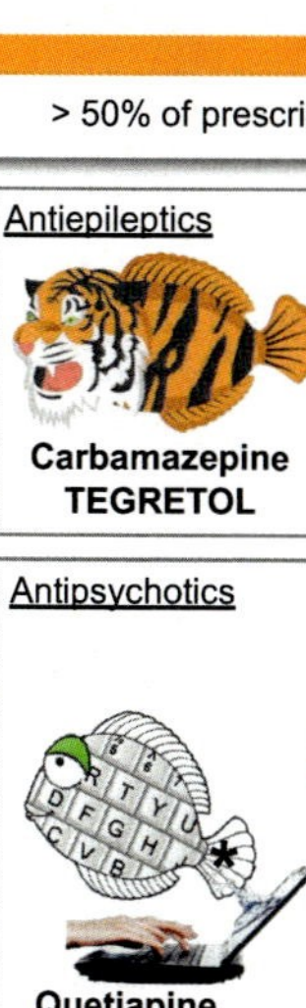

Antiepileptics

Carbamazepine TEGRETOL

Zonisamide ZONEGRAN

Tiagabine GABITRIL

Perampanel FYCOMPA

Felbamate FELBATOL

Ethosuximide ZARONTIN

Statins

Risk of rhabdomyolysis in combination with 3A4 inHibitors

Simvastatin (ZOCOR) **

Atorvastatin (LIPITOR)

Not:
Pravastatin (Pravachol)
Rosuvastatin (Crestor)
Fluvastatin (Lescol)

Antipsychotics

Quetiapine SEROQUEL *

Quetiapine is increased 6-fold by strong 3A4 inhibitors and decreased 6-fold by strong inducers.

Lurasidone LATUDA **

Lurasidone is contraindicated with potent 3A4 inhibitors or inducers.

Lumateperone CAPLYTA **

Aripiprazole ABILIFY *

Cariprazine VRAYLAR *

Brexpiprazole REXULTI *

Pimavanserin NUPLAZID *

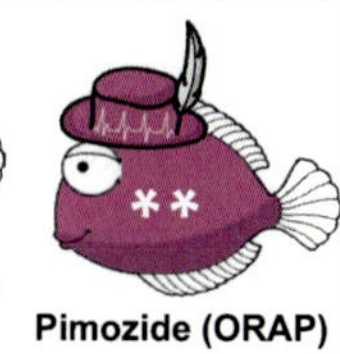

Pimozide (ORAP) **

Minor 3A4 substrates:

Haloperidol (HALDOL) * minor

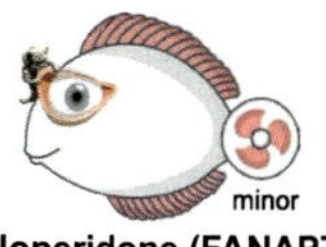

Risperidone RISPERDAL minor

Iloperidone (FANAPT) minor

Also (minor):
Chlorpromazine (Thorazine)
Clozapine (Clozaril)
Loxapine (Loxitane)
Perphenazine (Trilafon)
Ziprasidone (Geodon)

not:
Asenapine (Saphris) 1A2
Fluphenazine (Prolixin) 2D6
Molindone (Moban)
Olanzapine (Zyprexa) 1A2
Paliperidone (Invega)
Promethazine (Phenergan)
Thiothixene (Navane) 1A2
Trifluoperazine (Stelazine) 1A2

Benzodiazepines

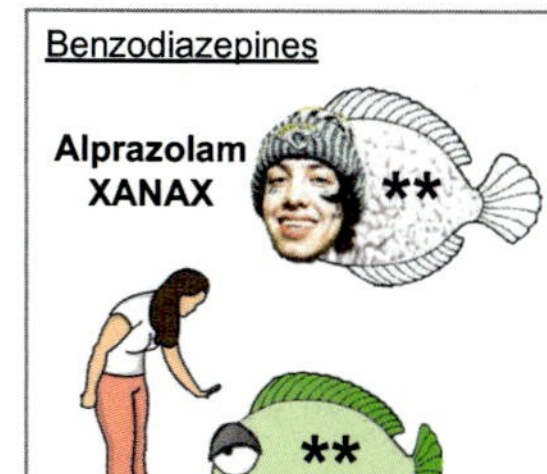

Alprazolam XANAX **

Estazolam (PROSOM) **

Diazepam VALIUM

Clonazepam KLONOPIN

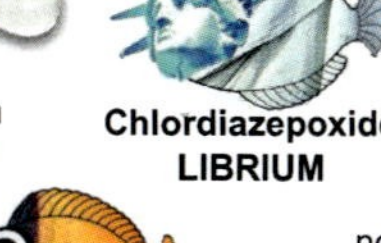

Chlordiazepoxide LIBRIUM

Quazepam DORAL

Midazolam VERSED **

Triazolam HALCION **

Clorazepate TRANXENE

not:
Lorazepam (Ativan)
Oxazepam (Serax))
Temazepam (Restoril)
Clobazam (Onfi) 2C19

Zolpidem (AMBIEN)

Eszopiclone LUNESTA

Suvorexant BELSOMRA

Lemborexant (DAYVIGO) **

Opioids

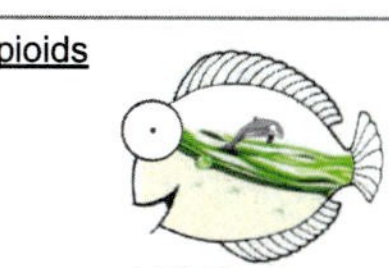

Methadone DOLOPHINE

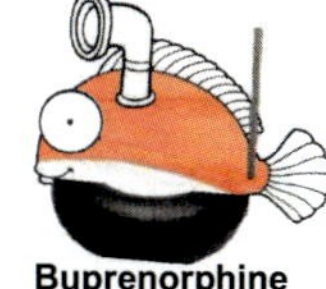

Buprenorphine SUBOXONE

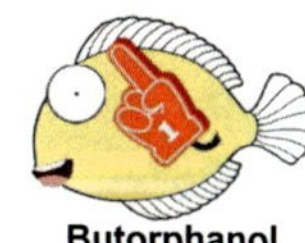

Butorphanol STADOL

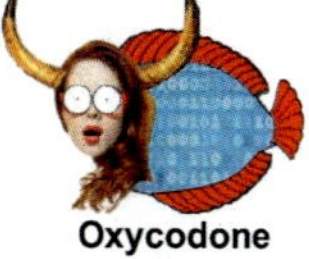

Oxycodone PERCOCET

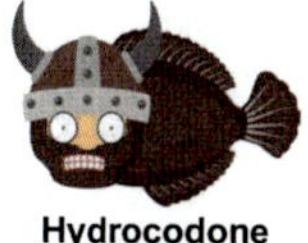

Hydrocodone VICODIN

Meperidine (DEMEROL)

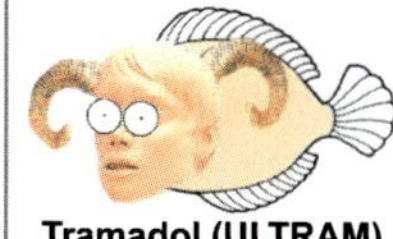

Tramadol (ULTRAM)

Nalbuphine (NUBAIN)

Levorphanol LEVO-DROMORAN

Fentanyl (DURAGESIC)

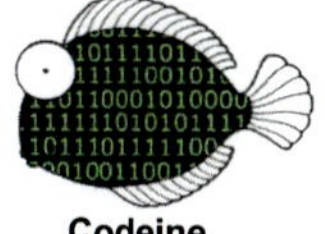

Codeine

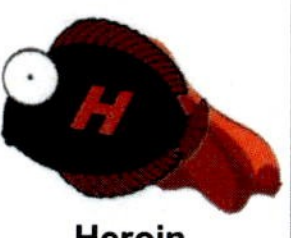

Heroin

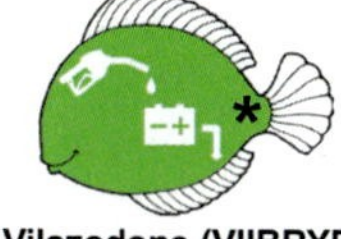

Vilazodone (VIIBRYD) *

Buspirone (BUSPAR) *

Anticholinergics

Tolterodine (DETROL

Darifenacin (ENABLEX)

Solifenacin (VESICARE)

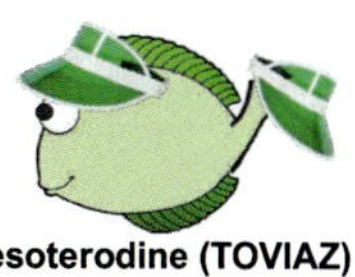

Fesoterodine (TOVIAZ)

PDE-5 inhibitors

"Pubic Displays of Erection"

Sildenafil (VIAGRA) *

Tadalafil (CIALIS) *

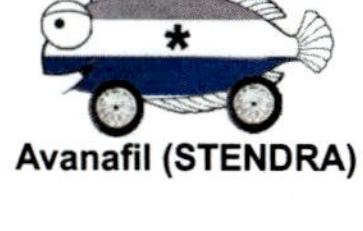

Avanafil (STENDRA) *

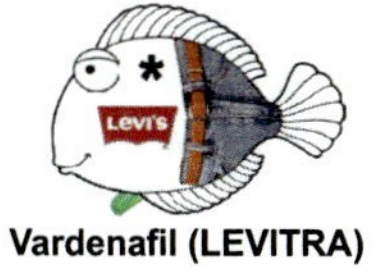

Vardenafil (LEVITRA) *

Antihypertensives

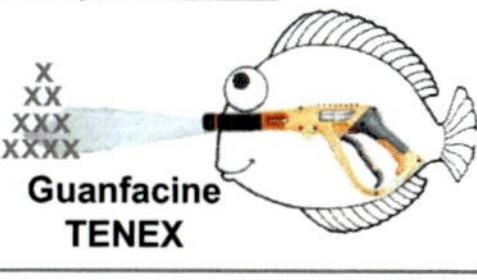

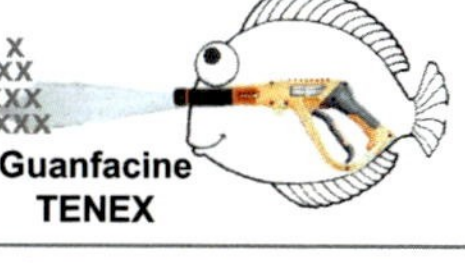

Guanfacine TENEX

Amlodipine (NORVASC)

Nimodipine NIMOTOP

Ondansetron (ZOFRAN)

Stimulants

Modafinil (PROVIGIL)

Armodafinil NUVIGIL

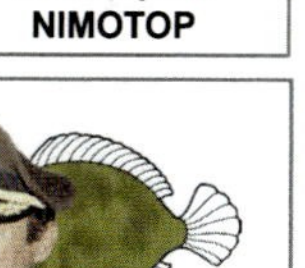

Istradefylline NOURIANZ

LSD

CBD

Flibanserin (ADDYI) **

Bromocriptine (PARLODEL)

Valbenazine INGREZZA *

THC

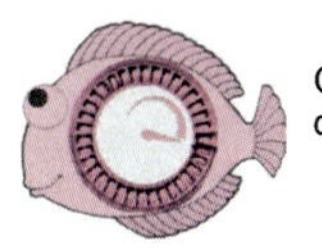

Contraceptives

Estrogens and progestins

Donepezil (ARICEPT)

* Dosing adjustments defined

** Has contraindications related to kinetic interactions

Lithium kinetic interactions
involving renal clearance

Lithium is removed from the body almost exclusively by the kidneys. Several medications affect the rate of lithium clearance. Since lithium has a narrow therapeutic index, blood levels need to be closely followed.

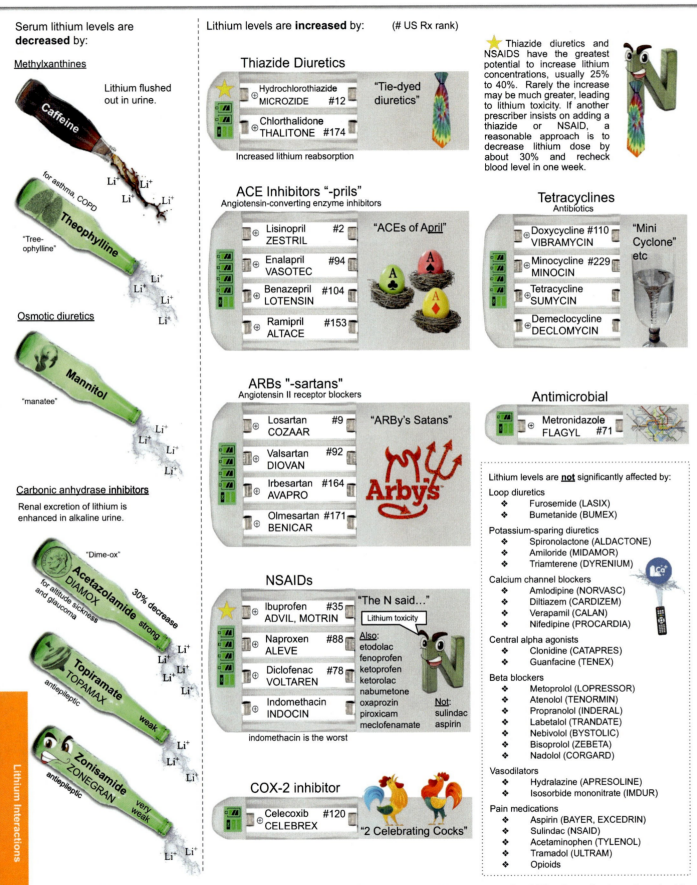

Serum lithium levels are **decreased** by:

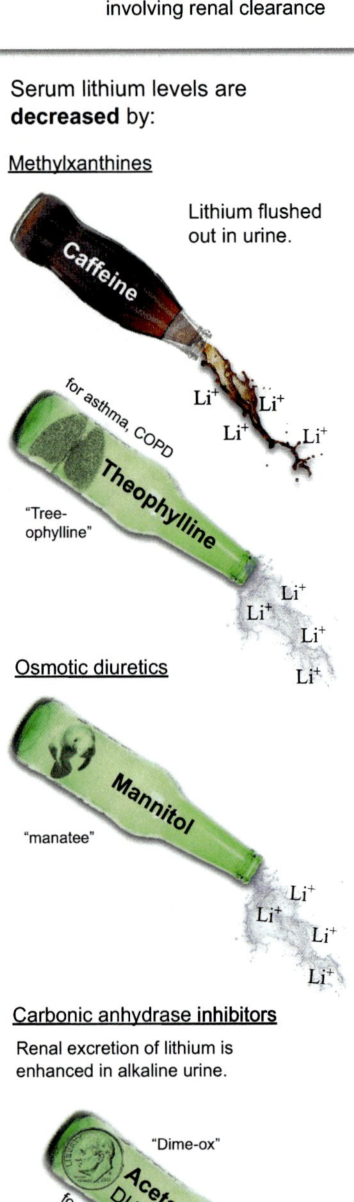

Methylxanthines

Lithium flushed out in urine.

Osmotic diuretics

Carbonic anhydrase inhibitors

Renal excretion of lithium is enhanced in alkaline urine.

"Dime-ox"

Acetazolamide DIAMOX — 30% decrease, strong — for altitude sickness and glaucoma

Topiramate TOPAMAX — weak — antiepileptic

Zonisamide ZONEGRAN — very weak — antiepileptic

Lithium levels are **increased** by: (# US Rx rank)

Thiazide Diuretics

- Hydrochlorothiazide MICROZIDE #12
- Chlorthalidone THALITONE #174

"Tie-dyed diuretics"

Increased lithium reabsorption

Thiazide diuretics and NSAIDS have the greatest potential to increase lithium concentrations, usually 25% to 40%. Rarely the increase may be much greater, leading to lithium toxicity. If another prescriber insists on adding a thiazide or NSAID, a reasonable approach is to decrease lithium dose by about 30% and recheck blood level in one week.

ACE Inhibitors "-prils"
Angiotensin-converting enzyme inhibitors

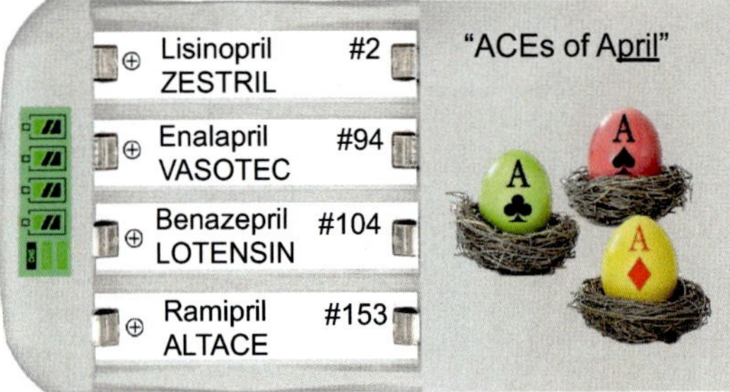

Tetracyclines
Antibiotics

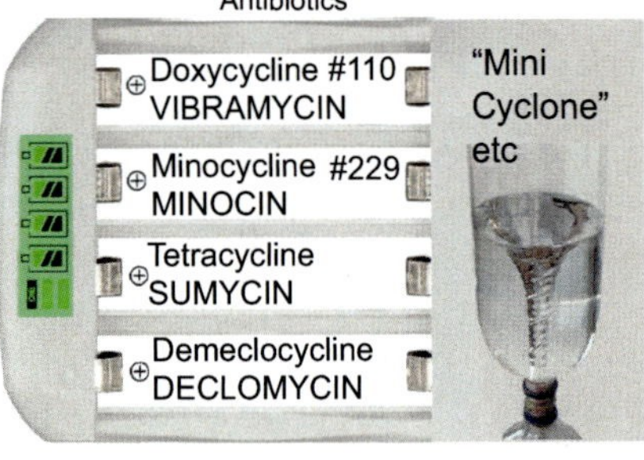

ARBs "-sartans"
Angiotensin II receptor blockers

Antimicrobial

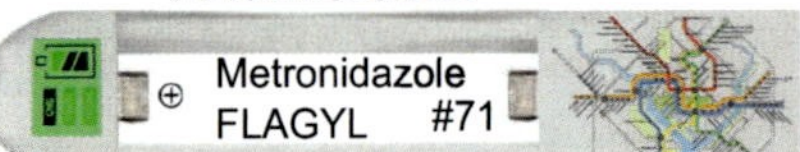

Lithium levels are **not** significantly affected by:

Loop diuretics
- Furosemide (LASIX)
- Bumetanide (BUMEX)

Potassium-sparing diuretics
- Spironolactone (ALDACTONE)
- Amiloride (MIDAMOR)
- Triamterene (DYRENIUM)

Calcium channel blockers
- Amlodipine (NORVASC)
- Diltiazem (CARDIZEM)
- Verapamil (CALAN)
- Nifedipine (PROCARDIA)

Central alpha agonists
- Clonidine (CATAPRES)
- Guanfacine (TENEX)

Beta blockers
- Metoprolol (LOPRESSOR)
- Atenolol (TENORMIN)
- Propranolol (INDERAL)
- Labetalol (TRANDATE)
- Nebivolol (BYSTOLIC)
- Bisoprolol (ZEBETA)
- Nadolol (CORGARD)

Vasodilators
- Hydralazine (APRESOLINE)
- Isosorbide mononitrate (IMDUR)

Pain medications
- Aspirin (BAYER, EXCEDRIN)
- Sulindac (NSAID)
- Acetaminophen (TYLENOL)
- Tramadol (ULTRAM)
- Opioids

NSAIDs

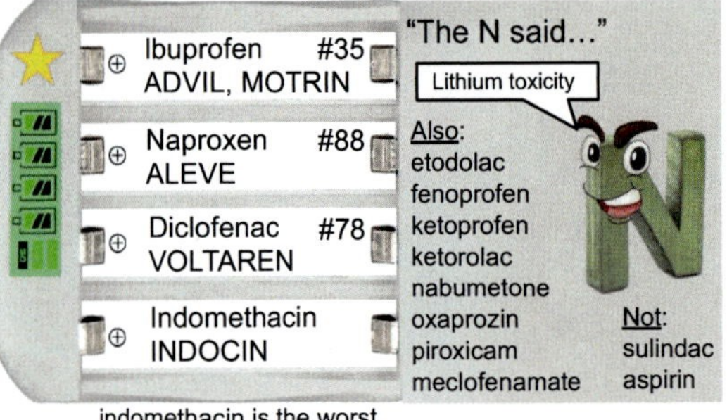

indomethacin is the worst

COX-2 inhibitor

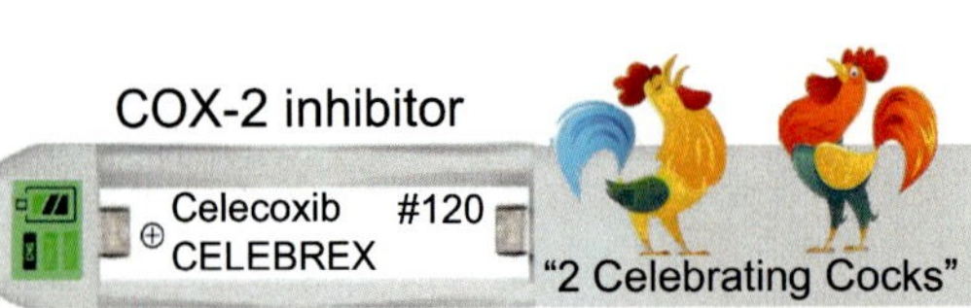

Conclusion: Educate patients that NSAIDS, blood pressure meds, and diuretics can cause lithium toxicity. For OTC pain medications, they should choose Tylenol or aspirin. Advise them to inform the prescriber if they are planning to change their caffeine intake. Excedrin is OK (combo of aspirin, acetaminophen, and caffeine). Check lithium levels frequently for patients on interacting medications. Teach the signs of lithium toxicity including tremor, nausea, diarrhea, fatigue, and drowsiness.

Glossary

About the author:

Dr Jason Cafer (pronounced KAY-fer) is Medical Director for Behavioral Health Services at SSM Health/St. Mary's Hospital in Jefferson City, Missouri where he serves as attending physician for a bustling 20-bed acute inpatient psychiatric ward. He graduated from University of Missouri-Columbia School of Medicine in 2003 and completed Psychiatric Residency at the same institution in 2007. He is a diplomate of the American Board of Psychiatry and Neurology and is also board-certified in Addiction Medicine by the American Board of Preventive Medicine. Prior to St. Mary's, he practiced inpatient psychiatry at Fulton State Hospital and outpatient at Comprehensive Health Systems. In 2007 he founded Iconic Health, a medical informatics startup that obtained angel round funding. He was Principal Investigator for Phase I and II Small Business Innovation Research (SBIR) grants for "Online Rural Telepsychiatry Platform" (2007–2009) funded by the United States Department of Agriculture. He is the inventor of United States Patent US8255241B2 which was the subject of an SBIR grant awarded by the Department of Health and Human Services for "Medication IconoGraphs: Visualization of Complex Medication Regimens". He completed *Cafer's Psychopharmacology* while serving as preceptor for Stephens College Master of Physician Assistant Studies program.

Also available:

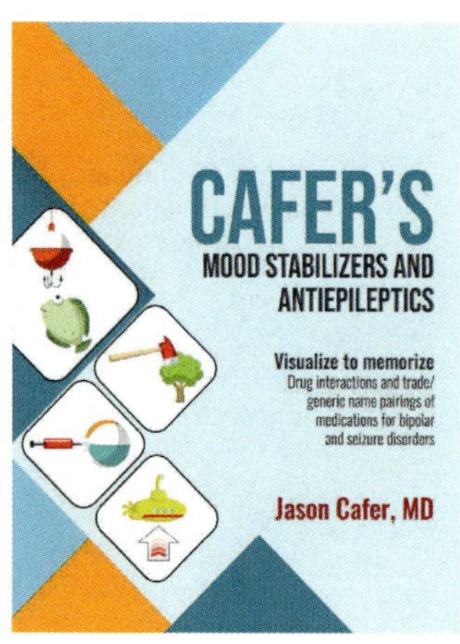

This edition of *Cafer's Psychopharmacology* was released in November 2020. Subscribe to cafermed.com for the updated PDF edition with over 1,000 internal links and bookmarks for ultrarapid navigation. The PDF edition is updated frequently with new mascots. Visit cafermed.com/update for more information.

Discount code for cafermed.com subscription:
ULTRARAPID

Made in the USA
Monee, IL
17 July 2021